447

The Essential Piaget

PHOTO: CHRISTIANE GILLIERON

THE
ESSENTIAL
PIAGET

EDITED BY

Howard E. Gruber

AND

J. Jacques Vonèche

Basic Books, Inc., Publishers   *New York*

Library of Congress Cataloging in Publication Data

Piaget, Jean, 1896–
    The essential Piaget.

    Bibliography: p. 447
    Includes index.
    1. Cognition (Child psychology)—Collected works.
2. Knowledge, Theory of—Collected works.   3.   Biology—
Collected works.   I.   Gruber, Howard E.   II.   Vonèche,
J. Jacques.   III.   Title.
BF723.C5P494   155.4'13'08   76–9337
ISBN: 0–465–02058–5

For our children:
Anne-Christine, Isabelle, Marina,
Sarah, and Simon.
And for the children of the world.

CONTENTS

PART I
Early Biology

PART II
Transitional Years: From Biology to Philosophy

* Translated especially for this volume by H. Gruber and J. Vonèche.

PART III

The Paris Period

PART IV

Egocentric Thought in the Child

PART V

The Mind of the Baby: From Action to Thought

PART VI

Logico-Mathematical Operations

* Translated by H. Gruber and J. Vonèche especially for this volume.

PART VII

The Representation of Reality: Action, Space, and Geometry, Time, Movement, and Speed

PART VIII

Figurative Aspects of Thought: Perception, Imagery, and Memory

PART IX

Piaget on Education

PART X

Piaget's Philosophy

PART XI

Factors of Development: Biology and Knowledge

FOREWORD

JEAN PIAGET

This fine volume, prepared by Howard E. Gruber and Jacques Vonèche, seems to me the best and the most complete of all the anthologies of my work.

It is, in addition, a model of its kind, because instead of limiting themselves to juxtaposing extracts of books or articles, leaving to the reader the task of disentangling their meaning and finding the relations among them, the collaborators have accompanied each selection with a very intelligent commentary that illuminates the general movement of thought as well as the particular meaning of a given selection. I could say that, in reading the explanatory texts, I came to understand better what I had wanted to do; especially in rediscovering the passages of my earlier works that Gruber and Vonèche have unearthed and interpreted in a manner most striking to me.

As for the selections they have chosen, I was extremely happy not to appear only as a child psychologist. The authors of this anthology have understood perfectly—and have succeeded in making it understandable to the reader—that my efforts directed toward the psychogenesis of knowledge were for me only a link between two dominant preoccupations: the search for the mechanisms of biological adaptation and the analysis of that higher form of adaptation which is scientific thought, the epistemological interpretation of which has always been my central aim.

Since one cannot do everything, I have unfortunately had to give up experimental research in biology, and I have had to content myself with a few minor works. But I have always insisted upon its importance as a source for epistemology, as my recent book, *Behavior, Motor of Evolution*,* once again confirms.

In epistemology, on the other hand, I am happy with what I have been able to glimpse, although always very conscious of the gaps remaining to be filled. This is what we are trying our utmost to do at our Centre International d'Epistémologie Génétique, which is now my chief source of satisfaction. To make of epistemology an experimental dis-

* Paris, Gallimard, "Idees," 1976.

cipline as well as a theoretical one has always been my goal, and I dare to hope that something durable will come of our efforts.

It is this whole context, of which the psychology of the child is only one aspect, that H. E. Gruber and J. Vonèche have understood so well, and I want to express my gratitude to them, as well as my admiration for their difficult achievement.

Pinchat, 22 November 1976

PREFACE

In this anthology we attempt to compress Jean Piaget's life work into one volume, a task formidable enough simply because of the magnitude of Piaget's *oeuvre*—over fifty books and monographs and hundreds of articles, published over a seventy-year period. This time scale compounds the problem of selection, since Piaget revisited certain problems several times. If, in the interest of brevity, we include only the latest statement as representing Piaget's final position on the subject, we commit two errors. First, we deprive the reader of the earlier works, which in some instances are less widely known and which are necessary for a picture of the growth of Piaget's ideas. Second, we may mislead the reader into thinking that there is a "final" position on any question, when there is only a man perpetually searching to deepen his grasp of an approach to the network of enterprises by which human beings obtain knowledge.

A further difficulty in selecting for this anthology stems from the multidisciplinary character of Piaget's life work, which is concerned with the nature of the growth of all knowledge—in all disciplines, and on the time scale of human intellectual history as well as the intellectual growth of one child. The scope of his intentions is exhibited in his *Introduction à l'Epistémologie Génétique*, volume 1 dealing with mathematical thought, volume 2 with physical thought, and volume 3 with biological, psychological, and sociological thought—on both of the time scales mentioned above. Piaget's more specialized studies range over the fields of biology, philosophy, psychology, and logic, with some forays into sociology, theology, and the history of science. In addition, his work on the growth of child thought leads him to consider some issues in physics and mathematics, at the very least insofar as this is necessary for understanding the thinking of children and adolescents about these matters. Since each one of the fields in which Piaget has labored has its special requirements, the most desirable course would be to present a combination of selections that give the reader both the necessary fundamentals and Piaget's own contribution.

In all scientific inquiries, a good strategy is to maximize the variable one is interested in. Piaget's strategic decision to approach epistemological problems by studying children's thinking may be viewed as such an attempt to study cognitive growth under conditions favorable for observing it. This leads to still another difficulty in composing our anthology. If we devote attention one-sidedly to children's thinking, we may lose sight of the more general epistemological aims. If we enlarge upon the latter we take up space that is necessary for concrete findings, experimental protocols, and other details that give substance to the argument.

We have tried, then, to organize this volume so that it shows the growth of Piaget's thought, its multidisciplinary nature, and the inter-relationships between empirical research and epistemological aims. Without oversimplifying, we have tried to present Piaget's work in a form that would be more readable for, and more accessible to, the general reader than has hitherto been the case.

To accomplish all these goals, we have used a variety of methods. The reader will find a number of new translations of works previously unavailable in English (and, for that matter, not easy to find in French). These fall mainly, but not exclusively, in the earlier part of Piaget's life. In selecting from previously translated material, which comprises the bulk of this volume, we have done our best to omit unduly opaque passages, while still preserving the continuity of Piaget's argument. Our own introductions, to the book as a whole and to the various sections, provide historical background, explain especially difficult passages, or fill gaps inevitable even in the most complete anthology.

As will be plain from the weight of this book, we have not assembled a collection of "nuggets" of Piaget's wisdom. With few exceptions, we try to present his work as a set of coherent wholes, primarily in his own words, but sometimes compensating for omissions by our summaries, either of whole books or of deleted passages. This approach has led to some repetition, of course, but try as we might we could not bring ourselves to use the editor's razor to eliminate all of it, and this for two quite different reasons. On the one hand, the repeated material is necessary for Piaget's argument. On the other hand, and more fundamentally, the ideas are never quite so repetitious as they may seem in a first reading. If Piaget's research has taught us one thing it is that one may profitably go over the child's thinking many times, for it is the working of an incredibly dense and complexly articulated structure. The same—no more, no less—is true of Piaget's own thinking. We believe, then, that the reader will profit from working through this book and encountering the same ideas in different theoretical contexts, as applied to different contents, or as expressed at different stages of Piaget's development.

No preface to an anthology is complete without a confessional, a list of works omitted for reasons of space. In the present instance, we draw the reader's attention to the underrepresentation of Piaget's theological writings,* and to the almost total absence of his sociological writings except as reflected in *The Moral Judgment of the Child*. Our decision not to translate any of *l'Introduction à l'Epistémologie Génétique* is perhaps less serious, since much of the ground covered there is represented in one form or another throughout this book. The absence of any selection from the 30 volumes (1957–1975) of the *Études* of the Centre International d'Epistémologie Génétique is explained in the same way; we note also that these volumes are often primarily a deepening by collaborators of an inquiry begun earlier by Piaget. Although the multidisciplinary nature of Piaget's work is certainly reflected in the

---

*Although we do give an almost complete translation of *La Mission de l'Idée*, other works are completely absent.

structure and contents of this anthology, we regret omitting Piaget's writings on the interrelationships among different branches of knowledge.

One of the characteristics of Piaget's method has led to the coining of the phrase, "the epistemic subject." Typically, Piaget uses one group of children for the investigation of one topic, such as children's ideas about chance, and another group for another topic, such as movement. Since his primary interest is not in the individual variations but in the typical, he must merge the results of different studies in order to get a comprehensive picture of the growth of knowledge. Now this composite does not apply to any real child, but only to a somewhat idealized growth process, hence "epistemic."

There is also an "epistemic Piaget," the one we refer to throughout this volume when we use his name to describe the work of the Geneva school. Piaget could not be, and indeed would not want to be, one person doing all these things. Many of his published works contain at the beginning a list of collaborators, the research assistants who worked with him on that study. In addition, many of his works have more than one author listed on the title page. By far the most frequent of his coauthors, often listed as the first author of important works, is his collaborator of some 40 years, Professor Bärbel Inhelder. It is hard to imagine the epistemic Piaget without the real Inhelder.

We ourselves owe much to Professor Inhelder for her encouragement, for valuable suggestions, and for practical help at every stage in the preparation of this anthology.

We are also indebted to Marie-Paule Michiels, Pierre Nicole, Laszlo Peczi, Sylvie Reichenbach, and Anne-Sylvie Vauclair—all at one time or another members of the staff of the Archives Piaget. Carol Doyle helped with some of the translations. When we were thoroughly lost in a thicket of our own making, Robert Cornman prepared an invaluable conceptual atlas to help us find our way again. Simon Gruber did a mammoth job of photocopying. Janet Demierre was a superb secretary, handling not only the typing of our manuscript but a complex correspondence regarding permissions to reprint material. In the background, there was Laura Vonèche-Cardia, tiding us over many difficult moments. We thank also Jakob Tschopp for bibliographic assistance and Gilbert Voyat for various suggestions.

We owe special thanks to Dr. Christiane Gillièron for many of the illustrations in this book, as well as for a critical reading of parts of the manuscript.

Herb Reich, our editor at Basic Books, did much to make this work possible, often going well beyond the customary duties of an editor. We thank him and his staff. One of us, H. Gruber, acknowledges help received from the John Simon Guggenheim Memorial Foundation and from the Research Council of Rutgers University, without which many trips to Geneva would have been impossible.

Both of us are grateful to our colleagues in the Institute for Cognitive Studies of Rutgers University and in the Faculté de Psychologie et des Sciences de l'Education of the University of Geneva for helping to create the atmosphere necessary to fruitful work; also the librarians of our respective institutions for innumerable services.

Finally, we thank Jean Piaget for encouraging us in our work, for giving us necessary permissions to publish materials, and for making available some unpublished material that would have otherwise been inaccessible. As we write these lines, his eighty-first birthday is approaching. We salute him for a wonderfully productive and illuminating career.

Bibliographic Note

When a book or article was coauthored by Piaget and someone else, we have indicated this in the table of contents by a parenthesis, e.g., "(with Inhelder)." The source note at the beginning of each selection and in the consolidated bibliography gives the sequence of authors' names as it appeared in the original publication. The names of other collaborators, such as students and research assistants, also appear in the source note and bibliography, but not in the table of contents.

The consolidated bibliography includes all works by Piaget or by Piaget and coauthors, cited in the volume, in the editors' comments, in the text of Piaget's works, and in the citations for the selections themselves. This is, however, not a complete bibliography of all of Piaget's writings; that would be a whole book in itself.*

---

*In the text, we have left Piaget's references to other authors in their original form, i.e., as footnotes, often incomplete. Our own references to other authors also appear only as footnotes, not in the consolidated bibliography.

With regard to personal pronouns, we have left previously translated works intact. In our own commentaries we have alternated between *she* and *he*, using one or the other (but not both) within a given context.

INTRODUCTION

"A man, therefore, who gets so far as making the supposed unity of the self twofold is already almost a genius, in any case a most exceptional and interesting person. In reality, however, every ego, so far from being a unity is in the highest degree a manifold world, a constellated heaven, a chaos of forms, of stages and stages, of inheritances and potentialities . . . not yet a finished creation but rather a challenge of the spirit"*

A tribute to the human need to know: the baby's delight in her first amazed discovery of her own hand, or that a parent comes when called, or that an object fallen from her grasp remains much the same when it is regained. Another tribute to the same need to know: scientific theories on all subjects repeatedly capture widespread public attention.

Psychological theories touch a special chord, our natural interest in ourselves and in each other. Different theories, although they may be seen as competing for the best way of integrating psychological knowledge, can also be viewed as reflecting different aspects of this complexity of self and social interest.

Only a few psychologists in our century have approached the status of household word: Freud and his lineal descendant Erikson, Pavlov and his lineal descendant Skinner, and Piaget. To understand Piaget's particular impact, it is useful to reflect a moment on the differences among these points of view. Psychoanalysis focuses its attention on the animal, irrational, unconscious aspects of human experience and conduct. It promises amelioration of human ills through new techniques for establishing healthier relations between the rational, which it does not deny, and the irrational, which it acclaims. Behaviorism challenges the simplistic rationalism of previous centuries from another quarter, denying scientific status to the very idea of consciousness, and promising control of behavior through the management of external stimuli and rewards. Whatever their raisons d'être, or their merits, neither psychoanalysis nor behaviorism dwells on certain essential human characteristics from which we derive our species name *homo sapiens*: we think, we know, we act knowingly, we strive for greater knowledge and understanding.

Piaget's whole scientific effort addresses itself to this human need to know. When he received the Distinguished Scientist Award from the American Psychological Association in 1969, the citation included this sentence: "He has approached questions up to now exclusively philo-

*H. Hesse, *Steppenwolf*.

sophical in a resolutely empirical manner, and has made epistemology into a science separate from philosophy, but related to all the human sciences." Piaget promises nothing direct in the way of practical application of his ideas, although others have drawn on his work for various purposes. He offers only a point of departure for that unquenchable curiosity that resides somewhere in each of us, to know more, to understand the sources of our own knowledge, to understand others by grasping how they have come to think as they do.

But he does not provide satisfaction in the form of a brief or easily summarized formula. One of his greatest merits, his scope, is also one of the sources of his readers' greatest despair. His ideas and discoveries are spread out in some fifty books and hundreds of articles. In his work as a psychologist, for which he is best known, he has tried to show the childhood origins of human knowledge in almost every sphere: logic, space, time, chance, morality, play, language, mathematics. He has dealt with a wide spectrum of psychological processes: reasoning, perception, imagery, memory, imitation, action. Beyond this, or rather interwoven with this vast effort, is his concern with elaborating a philosophical point of view, genetic epistemology, and with exploring in considerable depth its biological as well as its psychological implications.

In the present work we attempt to reduce Piaget's entire oeuvre to one volume. But a question remains: Can there be an *essential* Piaget? Is there a body of thought so fixed and stable that it can be captured and pinned down in any single volume without destroying its vitality? Piaget's incessant literary output can be understood to mean that his system or essence remains permanently under construction. He has said that he cannot think without pen in hand; for him thinking is writing. The products of his pen are not so much fixed ideas or "findings" or essences as they are the very flow of his thought.

In keeping with this view, our Introduction is not an attempt to provide a simplified summary of what is to follow. Rather, we try to give some sense of the restless interplay between a few major ideas, with special attention to the tensions produced, the unanswered questions. Our aim is to encourage the reader to join in thinking with Piaget about the next steps to be taken in the construction of knowledge. For us, that is the essence of Piaget's several essences.

Piaget's work, whether it be thought of as philosophy, biology, or psychology, is all directed at elaborating a theory of knowledge, of how the organism comes to know its world. Among possible theories, at one extreme is the Kantian view that the infant is born with a set of innate or a priori ideas which constitute the fundamental outlines of all knowledge. (Of Piaget's relation to apriorism we shall say more later.) At another extreme (and there are more than two extremes, since theories of knowledge do not comprise a simple linear array) is the empiricist view that the infant is born with no innate ideas, and that all knowledge results from the accumulation of experience, so that knowledge is a direct copy of the reality with which each person is incessantly confronted. Experience in this sense, then, is sensory or perceptual. But experience can be thought of in several ways: Do we mean the direct perception of external reality, which tells us what the world out there is like? Or do we mean our actions upon the world, or better, our interactions with it? And in either case—experience of world as perceived, or as acted in and upon—how is such experience affected by and incorporated into whatever knowledge has been previously acquired? These are the sorts of questions that Piaget's or indeed any theory of knowledge must confront.

We begin our discussion with a few observations made by Piaget at different points in time, all bearing on the relations among perception, action, and knowledge.

Reality and Perception: Action and Knowledge

Piaget questions children about the behavior of heavenly bodies:

Adult: Does the moon move or not?
Child (age 7): When we go, it goes.
Adult: What makes it move?
Child: We do.
Adult: How?
Child: When we walk. It goes by itself.*

Neither Piaget nor his young subjects, of course, were the first to notice that the moon seems to move when we do. Every child has seen it move, and adults can too, if they remember to look. Nor was Piaget the only psychologist to notice that children actually believe that their own actions cause the moon and clouds to move.†

What distinguishes Piaget's approach is his persistence in carrying the questions posed by such simple observations as far as possible. Piaget's work in the 1920s led him to describe a period of childhood egocentrism, characterized by a multitude of examples such as the observation above. Eventually, these efforts led him to search for the origins of egocentric thought in an infantile period of solipsism, in which the baby does not even distinguish himself from the world, and consequently cannot yet have an idea of distinct and permanent objects: there is nothing but a flux of appearances. After his studies of infancy, Piaget carried his questions forward into later childhood. With the emergence of the logic of concrete operations, the child acquires the tools necessary to separate appearances from reality, or to distinguish perception from other forms of knowledge.

Almost fifty years later, one of Piaget's collaborators investigated the child's handling of a contradiction produced by a conflict between a visual illusion and the child's knowledge of the real situation. In this study, for example, two sticks are first chosen by the child from a set of sticks as appearing to be the same size, which they are. Then the experimenter puts one of them in a horizontal position and the other

*J. Piaget, *The Child's Conception of the World*, pp. 146–147.
†Piaget cites another author, Rasmussen, to this effect. And Anne Roe describes a young child, later to become a distinguished scientist, who sent his little brother down to the bottom of the garden as an experiment to find out whether the moon's movement generated by the child at point A can be perceived by another child at point B. So this is serious business. See Anne Roe, *The Making of a Scientist* (New York: Dodd Mead and Co., 1952), p. 95.

vertical, forming an inverted T; this produces the well-known vertical-horizontal illusion, in which the vertical stick appears definitely longer than the horizontal one. It has been established that children and adults are quite uniformly susceptible to this illusion.

When the middle matchstick is seen as bisecting the lowest matchstick, it is seen as longer. When it is seen as bisected by the topmost stick, it is seen as shorter. (You can do this with three matchsticks in one plane, too.) Since we know that all three are the same size, this illustrates a contradiction between knowledge and perception.

Experimenter: (Puts sticks in inverted-T position.)
Child (6;6):* They are both the same size.
Experimenter: But when you look at them, they are the same?
Child: Yes.
Experimenter: You see them the same, or you only know it? When you look at them, isn't there a big one and a small one?
Child: I see them the same.
Experimenter: What did you do?
Child: I saw that they were both the same size.
Experimenter: When did you do that? When you chose them, or now while looking?
Child: Before and now.†

Another child gives a much less common reaction. When the sticks are presented in the illusion configuration, she sees the illusion, but changes her belief as to their length: if it looks longer it is longer.

Although the two children seem quite different, they have an important point in common, an insensitivity to contradiction, an inability to deal with it. One eliminates the problem by denying the illusion, the other by sacrificing his previous judgment that the sticks were equal. By the time they are about 8–10 years old both children will be able to accept the apparent contradiction and deal with it in a more stable logical framework. In this later research it is not so much the child's grasp of the distinction among perception, action, and knowledge that

*Ages are given in parenthesis throughout. E.g., (6;6) is 6 years, 6 months old.
†J. Piaget and C. Gillièron, "Conservation des longeurs et illusions perceptives," in Recherches sur la contradiction: II, Les Relations entre affirmations et négations, Etudes d'épistémologie génétique, vol. 32, p. 73–85, Presses Universitaires de France, 1974. Translated by H. E. G. and J. J. V.

interested Piaget; rather it is the growth of awareness of contradiction, the will to search for ways of thinking that can eliminate contradiction, in short the growth of logic.

From these observations, the "movement" of the moon and the changing size of objects in visual illusions, we might conclude that perception is not a reliable guide to knowledge, that if we permitted ourselves to be guided by our direct perception of the world we would often fall into serious error. This might seem adequate to refute the empiricist view that knowledge originates in our perception of the world. Not so. The empiricist can and does readily answer: of course, perception is unreliable, knowledge fallible, and only the accumulation of experience helps to reduce error.

Piaget's critique of empiricism runs somewhat deeper. Distinguishing perception from other forms of knowledge is not enough. In some sense, perception is of no direct use at all in informing us about the world. It is our previously elaborated understanding that enables us to make any sense of what we perceive. Consider the following example, Piaget's celebrated experiment on the conservation of matter:

> The child is given two containers A and L of equal height, A being wide and L narrow. A is filled to a certain height (one-quarter or one-fifth) and the child is asked to pour the same quantity of liquid into L. The dimensions are such that the level will be four times as high in L as in A for the same amount of liquid. In spite of this striking difference in the proportions, the child at this stage proves incapable of grasping that the smaller diameter of L will require a higher level of liquid. Those children who are clearly still at this stage are satisfied that there is "the same amount to drink" in L when they have filled it to the same level as A.*

Now the child can very well "see" that nothing has been added or taken away. But he cannot see it in a way that leads to the conclusion that matter has been conserved until he can carry out a certain group of mental operations on the events before him. Thus it is not through direct observation, but through the actions we carry out upon our perceptions, not so much the actions of the body but those of the mind, mental operations, that we come to know the world. It is not only our knowledge of the world, but even more important, mastery of these operations, that must be constructed in the course of cognitive growth.

Even after long study and reflection and immersion in the subject, it is astonishingly easy to slip into taking for granted that something obvious at one level of development is obvious at other levels. To get the full flavor of how tenacious and puzzling such problems can be, consider another example.

Piaget writes, "in a closed system of physical transformations nothing is created and nothing destroyed. . . ." Is this a statement of the principle of the conservation of matter? We put this question to a number of Piaget's advanced students and collaborators, all of whom answered in the affirmative. Yet the full quotation reads as follows, "Clearly, it is one thing to observe that in a closed system of physical transformations nothing is created and nothing destroyed, and quite another to infer from this a principle of conservation."† Piaget's mean-

*J. Piaget and A. Szeminska, *The Child's Conception of Number*, pp. 11–12.

†J. Piaget, "Piaget's Theory," in *Carmichael's Manual of Child Psychology*, 3rd ed. p. 715.

ing is plain enough in its context. The identity operation (nothing added, nothing taken away) is not enough to establish the full idea of conservation of matter, because changing the shape of something (e.g., flattening a clay ball into a "pancake") might conceivably change its amount. Moreover, the inversion operation (changing the shape back again and noting that the original amount is regained) does not entirely solve the problem, because the amount might still have been different while the shape was changed. Only when these two operations are combined with the compensation operation (in changing shape, a decrease in height is compensated for by an increase in diameter, etc.) can a stable solution to conservation problems be found.*

Thus, observation alone does not open the way to correct inferences, or for that matter to any inferences at all. Mental operations must be carried out on observations, and these operations themselves develop in the life history.

An Ontological Question

In all this, does Piaget mean to say that there is a reality external to the behaving and experiencing person, to which the individual gradually and imperfectly attains, and that it is the steady presence of this reality that regulates and corrects the course of adaptive cognitive growth? This is a plausible interpretation of Piaget's position and seems to be strongly implied by much of his activity as a scientist. It is certainly part of the interpretation of Piaget that has led dialectical materialists to claim him as one of their own kind. But when asked questions to this effect, he is likely to reply, "Je m'en fous de la réalité." (I don't give a damn about reality.) Seemingly a strange response from a man who has written a book entitled *The Construction of Reality in the Child*.

What can he mean? One possible alternative is the following. The individual and the social group are constantly in the process of constructing and reconstructing their views of the world. At a given moment, the most advanced (complex, flexible, adaptive) achievements in the pursuit of knowledge may play a regulatory role with regard to other achievements still to be made. But this does not give either the most advanced, or for that matter, as some would have it, the most primitive, kinds of knowledge the status of an ultimate "reality." The main fruit of genetic epistemology is this discovery that the only way in which we get knowledge is through continual construction, and that we can have no enduring knowledge without actively maintaining this

---

*Another way of putting this: The identity operation refers to the *past*, because nothing has been added or taken away; the compensation operation is oriented toward a continuous *present*, during which changes of one kind correspond to changes of another kind; the inversion operation refers to a hypothetical or anticipated *future*, in which the preexisting situation is restored. Taken altogether, these operations thus provide an account of the uninterrupted existence of the property in question, i.e., conservation.

process. Something else, therefore, will surely be constructed, something that still lies ahead, that will replace whatever the naïve realist
chooses to canonize today. And so on ad infinitum.

At this point the reader may wish to say, "Je m'en fous de la discussion. It is only philosophy and has nothing to do with psychology."
We do not wish to provide a facile answer to the ontological questions
posed above. But we do wish to stress the importance of Piaget's patient
transformation of difficult philosophical questions into manageable psychological ones. In the particular instance, his lifelong strategy has been
to transform seemingly unmanageable ontological questions (what is
reality? what exists?) into manageable epistemological questions (how
do we know? how do we get knowledge?).

The Concept of Stage in Piaget's Theory: Some Questions

That there are definite stages of development, which occur universally
in a fixed order, is now probably the best known of Piaget's ideas, and
seems to be central to his theory. But there are some important questions not easily answered by reading Piaget's work, because, although
he has used it for a long time, in fact he has not written a great deal
about the stage concept.

RANGE OF APPLICATION

Does the stage concept apply only to the three major "periods" of
development (sensorimotor, concrete operations, formal operations), or
does it also apply to the progressive steps or substages in the attainment
of a cognitive structure within a stage? A repeated theme in his frequent
brief discussions of the stage concept is the inclusion of attainments of
earlier stages in the structures of later stages: an earlier stage is neither
discarded nor displaced nor "grown out of"—rather, a later stage is
"grown into," and depends on the prior attainment of earlier stages,
hence the idea of necessary order. This is an easy enough point to
establish convincingly if one considers the relations among the three
major stages. It seems self-evident, for example, that the idea of the
conservation of matter (attained between 6 and 10 years) rests on and
includes the idea of object permanence (attained between 1 and 2
years). But it is not so self-evident that the substages described in the
Origins of Intelligence (dealing with the first 1–2 years of life) necessarily follow in the order described, or just what attainments of the
earliest substages are retained in the later ones. This point is of particular
significance to teachers of children in the age range 5–11, the period in
which concrete operations are being acquired. It is not very helpful to
know that a 6 year old must some years ago have developed the semiotic
function to the point where he can talk, or that some years later, in
adolescence, if all goes well, he may reach the stage of formal operations.
It is helpful to know that developments *within* the period of concrete

operations generally follow certain lines, display certain substages; and it would be important to establish that this is a necessary order. Piaget's own work in Geneva established the existence of the basic sequences under discussion; beginning one or two decades later, the work of various followers established that much the same sequence indeed occurs in widely varying cultures; the demonstration that this sequence is logically necessary remains to be done. It might be added here that experiments that attempt to accelerate the child's movement through a well-known sequence, whether they succeed or fail, do not touch the question of the immutability of the order itself.

When the period of formal operations is reached in adolescence, does stagewise development cease? If so, does this mean that all development ceases, or, alternatively, that later cognitive development is so individualized or has other properties such that it cannot be described in terms of an orderly progression of universal stages? Neither alternative is very satisfying. The one disposes of developmental change for the greater part of the life span; the other proposes that development need not be stagewise. To say either we can have life without development or we can have development without stages seems quite unlike Piaget.

EVIDENCE FOR STAGES

The one point that Piaget has made most insistently is that developmental stages occur in a *constant order*. On the empirical side, the main evidence for this is that the number of children displaying a certain way of thought or kind of behavior increases with age. To show that the sequence is *universal*, the same observations must be repeated under widely differing circumstances. When such cross-cultural studies were done, and were found in the main to support Piaget's views as to the universality of cognitive stages, he was not dissatisfied. To show that the sequence is *orderly* requires a kind of work that has not yet been done on any important scale; to show that any sequence is orderly means to show that the observed sequence corresponds in some way to another sequence which is deemed orderly. Thus, growth in stature is orderly in the sense that the observed sequence of heights corresponds to a sequence of increasing numbers, i.e., age. If children grew and shrank and grew again, the way snowbanks do, we would have to look elsewhere for a criterion of order. To show that the logical structures underlying thought grow in an orderly way, we must have a method for ordering logical structures that is independent of any observations we may make of children's growth. Piaget has concentrated much of his effort on showing that the thought of the child at a given age (or stage) corresponds to a given logical model; this is something less than showing orderly growth.

A thoroughgoing empirical defense of the stage concept would require an investigation of the stability and the coherence of any hypothesized stage. To demonstrate *stability*, we would have to show that the same child exhibits the same characteristics over the period of time presupposed in the definition of the stage. Piaget has done this very impressively even if nonquantitatively in his studies of his own three children, especially in *Origins of Intelligence* and in *Construction of*

Reality. But in the vast panorama of his later works, nothing resembling test-retest reliability can be found because the same child is not seen twice in one study. On the other hand, a certain estimate of stability is built into testing procedures developed by Piaget and his group. The child's initial responses to a given task are not the only evidence adduced; the child's resistance to countersuggestions is routinely tested as well. Moreover, the decision that a given child is at a given stage in the development of a concept is often not based on one narrowly circumscribed task, but on her performance on a group of closely related tasks, so that even if there is no evidence for stability over periods of time such as a week or a month, there is a kind of evidence for consistency in performance.

Another argument in favor of the stability of performance within stages emerged as a result of a series of experiments on the learning of cognitive structures, performed in Geneva in the late 1950s. A group of Piaget's collaborators conducted a series of experiments, often with great ingenuity, intended to show that the child could progress more rapidly in the development of certain cognitive structures if she were subjected to a carefully worked out training program. The results were disappointing: little or no such rapid change could be detected. But Piaget was not disappointed. These results supported his claim that the structures under discussion develop slowly and primarily through an internal process of construction, rather than representing direct and immediate copies of environmental events.

To demonstrate *coherence*, we would have to show that the same underlying logical model underlies the child's performance in widely differing tasks. Again, this requires testing the same child in different situations, which has not generally been done. Different groups of children are used in different studies, making such comparisons impossible. This leaves us with the plausible but not demonstrated inference that *if* we had tested the same child on a wide variety of tests she would have behaved in a way governed by the same logical model. If all children developed at the same rate we could, of course, substitute one child for another of the same age, and thus avoid testing the same child too often. But if, as is generally agreed, children develop at different rates or if each child shows a certain amount of unevenness in his development, such substitutions are invalid.

The unevenness of development, under the name of *horizontal décalage*, has entered Piaget's theory both as a matter of fact and of theory. On the factual side, although there has been no thoroughgoing systematic effort to define the amount of coherence a stage would need to have in order to qualify as a stage, or exhaustive empirical effort to study intertest correlations, there has been an accumulation of evidence showing that development is local, spotty, and uneven. A concept may appear in one form, but take a year or more to extend itself over its possible range. On the theoretical side, this unevenness, or *décalage*, has been used by Piaget as one explanatory principle for development: the very coexistence of the more highly developed and the less highly developed structures generates disequilibrium or conflict that leads to further growth. But how much unevenness is acceptable within a stage theory without undermining the very concept of stage?

FUNCTION IN THE THEORY

Is the stage concept an essential part of Piaget's theory? If it were essential, we would expect him, sometime in the fifty year period in which he used it, to have elaborated it at the same length and with the same care he has given to other ideas: this he has not done. It is reasonable to ask, what would remain undisturbed in Piaget's theory if the hypothesis of a single, orderly, and universal succession of stages of cognitive development were dropped? There is, of course, a great deal more to Piaget besides the stage concept, but it cannot be clear without a major theoretical effort how other parts of the theory would be affected. It seems plausible to suggest that Piaget's interactionism, his ideas of assimilation and accommodation, his recent equilibration model, the idea of progressive decentering, and his elaboration of the idea of intellectual operations—all these might stand without the stage concept. On the other hand, his search for a progression of different logical models underlying thought at different points in development and his emphasis, especially in later years, on the hierarchical growth of cognitive structures seem more closely linked to the stage concept.

Another possibility worth considering would be to weaken the definition of stage by dropping the idea of universality. Intellectual growth could be orderly and could correspond to series of logical models without following one universal developmental pathway. Piaget himself well understands that it takes a complex system of forces to maintain development on its observed course; he has borrowed Waddington's concept of homeorhesis to express this idea.* It takes only one further step, also proposed by Waddington, to recognize that development is eminently polymorphic, and that when the forces making for one choice of developmental pathway (*creode*) are not strong enough, the organism will develop in another way. This step can be taken without admitting that development is helter-skelter, subject to every wind of chance. The proposal that there is more than one *creode* available does not undermine the central idea of orderly growth.

If Piaget's stage concept be not essential to his theory, what role does it play? We propose two major functions. First, it is a descriptive tool. The biologist must first describe and classify the major forms of life before he can even raise the question, how does one form evolve into another? Piaget began his career as a biologist working in just this way. When he moved into psychology, he took this strategy along with him. Describing the stages of growth, even in a first approximation, gave him the point of departure he needed for raising the dynamic and genetic questions: how does the organism maintain its present structure and how does it change?

Second, Piaget's use of the stage concept is an expression of his remorseless anti-empiricism. During a given stage, the person does thus and so, and he can do no other. To change as a mere reaction to environmental pressure would be to violate the organized integrity of

---

*For a brief sketch of some of C. H. Waddington's ideas, see his chapter, "The Theory of Evolution Today," in *Beyond Reductionism: New Perspectives in the Life Sciences*, ed. Arthur Koestler and J. R. Smythies (Boston: Beacon Press, 1969).

the individual in his given stage of development. Change is a serious matter; to accomplish it the individual must reconstruct himself.

When we question the central role of the concept of a universal series of ordered stages in Piaget's theory, we do not mean to question the importance of the idea to Piaget's work. One looks in vain through his writings, all the way to 1955, for an extended discussion of the stage concept. (See Selection 43.) Even this paper is brief and does not go into very great detail. But Piaget takes the idea of stages for granted, and uses it vigorously as a framework on which to organize his findings during the whole of the 36 year period from 1923 (*"Language and Thought of the Child"*) to 1959 (*"The Early Growth of Logic in the Child"*). In the *Origins of Intelligence*, the opening chapter is a theoretical sketch of Piaget's views, recapitulated in the closing chapter of the companion volume, *The Construction of Reality*. In neither place does Piaget elaborate on the concept of stage as a theoretical idea. But throughout the body of these two great and seminal works, all of Piaget's observations are presented in the form of a series of stages. What shall we conclude: Theory is as theoretician says, or as empirical scientist does?

In the longer reaches of time over which science evolves, we may find a firmer basis for deciding whether there are fixed and universal stages of cognitive growth, whether these have sudden or gradual onsets and offsets, whether they are coherent and unitary characteristics of the intellect as a whole or uneven in their development over a rather disjointed intellect, whether they can be much modified by variations in experience, and what determines whether the individual remains in a stable phase or undergoes a period of change. Meanwhile, without our having firm answers to any of these questions, Piaget's work stands as a major landmark in the history of knowledge, because within the framework of the unexamined concept he has given brilliant description one after another of the changing intellect of the child.

Piaget's Theory of Intellectual Process

By this time the reader may well believe we are arguing that Piaget's theory is unimportant and only his observations matter.* Not at all. We propose only that other parts of Piaget's theory are far more important than the stage concept, and we hope to draw the reader's attention to them. Piaget offers a theory of *how* the intellect grows: at any point in its development, it may be described as a set of organized structures or schemes; as the individual encounters his world, he assimilates objects and events to these structures (thus they function and expand without structural change); when this is not possible because the existing structures are inadequate, they modify themselves or accommodate

---

*In Piaget's view this would be almost a mortal sin, since he has devoted so much of his energy to the struggle against just such an empiricist view of the growth of knowledge, both in the child and among scientists.

(thus they undergo structural changes). At first the child is unaware of himself or the world or the distinction between them, but he becomes increasingly aware, and finally conscious of and capable of reflecting upon his own intellectual processes; thus he gains a new level of command over his thought and its growth. There is much more to the theory, but we refrain from expanding on it here. Throughout this volume there are theoretical passages which we have not slighted in our selection.

Here we wish only to stress the point that for Piaget the growth of the intellect, rather than something that happens to the child from the outside, is a process of self-construction, governed by existing formations of cognitive structures. To be sure, it happens in relation to the world, and it is a process that has evolved in such fashion that its results are biologically and socially adaptive; the world plays its regulative function. But it is not a matter of stimulus and response, push and pull. Rather, environmental events are assimilated as well as they can be to existing structures, chewed over and digested, and, finally, only occasionally do they result in fundamental changes in such structures.*

Piaget is not the only case in the history of science where great theoretical interest attaches to the interplay between the description of fixed entities, such as species or stages, and the process of change. Darwin, in developing the theory of evolution, had to use as his point of departure whatever was already known about species, especially as organized in a masterly array by his great predecessor, Linnaeus, a century before. Marx, in developing his theory of social change and the functioning of the capitalist system, drew on what was known of the major stages in the evolution of economic forms. Both Darwin and Marx had to argue against earlier theories of change in which a fixed order was given in a metaphysical law of progress. There were evolutionary theorists before Darwin who believed that the explanation of evolutionary change lay simply in a tendency toward progress inherent in the natural order (and perhaps preordained by the Creator). Darwin's alternative was that change grows out of the functioning of the system of living things as it is.†

Similarly, there was a current among nineteenth-century social theorists to explain history as a series of necessary and foreordained economic stages (such as food gathering, pastoral, slavery, feudal, bourgeois, socialist, and so on). Like Darwin, whom he greatly admired, Marx argued that social change grows out of the struggles inherent in the existing social order: "*History* does *nothing*, it possesses no immense wealth, it wages no battles. It is *man*, real living man, that does all that, that possesses and fights; 'history' is not a person apart, using

---

*There is some room for discussion as to whether Piaget believes that change is continuous or sporadic. In our view he makes a distinction on this score between assimilation and accommodation: "assimilation, the fundamental fact of psychic development," he writes in his theoretical introduction to the *Origins of Intelligence* (p. 42); we believe he treats assimilation more thoroughly than accommodation and regards it as more fundamental. Maybe it is true that in some sense it is more characteristic of an organism to go on functioning as it has done, to preserve its identity, than it is for it to change.

†See Howard E. Gruber, *Darwin on Man: A Psychological Study of Scientific Creativity together with Darwin's Early and Unpublished Notebooks*, transcribed and annotated by Paul H. Barrett (New York: E. P. Dutton, 1974).

man as means for its own particular aims; history is *nothing but* the activity of man pursuing his aims."*

Freud, in developing his theory of the growth of personality, postulated a series of psychosexual stages (oral, anal, phallic, latent, genital), which he then proceeded to explain by a group of psychodynamic principles. It is instructive in Freud's case that one can separate his stage theory from his psychodynamics. We have been suggesting that the same is true of Piaget. But there is a difference. Freud's theory of psychosexual stages was a rather long-range inference about children, based on his work with adult patients.† Piaget's theory of cognitive stages is based on years of work with the children to whom it refers. We may also note that Darwin did not have to assemble the evidence for the existence of species or to construct a taxonomy *de novo*, nor did Marx have to demonstrate the existence of different social forms and classes. Thus, Piaget had a truly Herculean labor to perform: he had to discover and describe the very rudiments of the course of cognitive growth at the same time as he developed a theory to explain it.

One has only to compare Piaget's efforts with others of similar intent to see how much needed to be done. Piaget succeeded in transforming each of the Kantian categories of knowledge from a first principle into a subject of scientific investigation to which he contributed the first significant monograph. Enormous energy, persistence, and the privileged position of a university professor were important requirements, but by no means enough to explain his feat. Piaget was guided by certain abiding philosophical and biological concerns that gave him the sense of abiding purpose that was indispensable for the task.

Structures and Operations

It is the great task of science to search for unifying descriptions and explanations, to illuminate likenesses that underlie apparent differences in the manifold of nature. There are three great stategies of search: to look for laws, elements, or structures. Our knowledge of the laws of physics, the elements of chemistry, and the structures of biology represents the fruits of such efforts. Of course, the three strategies are not kept in separate portfolios, to be brought out exactly as needed. As we begin to explore a domain of nature, we do not know what to expect or how to proceed, what strategy or combination of strategies will be most helpful. There is, moreover, a constant interplay of strategies. For instance, the gas laws (relating pressure, volume, and temperature) are general laws that describe the behavior of quantities of gas in closed

---

*Karl Marx, *The Holy Family*. Quoted in *Marx in His Own Words*, ed. Ernst Fischer (Harmondsworth, Middlesex, England: Penguin Books, 1970), p. 87.

†This is not intended as a deep criticism of Freud, since he was not primarily interested in children, and wanted mainly to use the stages to help develop his psychodynamic ideas.

containers, but these quantities are made up of elementary particles or molecules, and when we understand the nature of these elements, we understand why the gas laws must be modified in significant ways. But what do we mean by the "nature" of an element? In good part, its internal structure.*

In the social sciences, nothing is as familiar as Adam Smith's law of supply and demand. This is quite similar to the gas laws in that it describes the reciprocal relationships between variables that determine the form of a complex event, the fluctuation in price of a commodity. But the elements in this process are the individual buyers and sellers, and their social and psychological characteristics must be examined if we are to understand the conditions under which the law operates. Furthermore, these individuals are not isolated human particles who just happen to be brought together in a container called the market place; they are part of a complex social structure, a class system with a certain distribution of rights of property and exploitation, institutions of education and law enforcement to ensure that individuals play their roles within the system. Without all this the market would not function as it does. Thus, law, element, and structure are indissociable.

Nevertheless, in the work of an individual scientist or of a group in a particular epoch, we may find a penchant for one or another strategy. Piaget is widely known as a structuralist, but his structuralism takes a specific and interesting form. To understand it, it will be helpful to examine the theoretical scene in psychology and to distinguish Piaget's concern for structures from others.

Psychology as an organized science got its start in the middle of the nineteenth century and was less than a century old when Piaget began his psychological studies in Paris in 1921. During the period about 1875–1925 one of the dominant currents of thought was an introspective variety of elementarism: first find the elementary sensations of which experience is composed, then see how more complex structures are built up from these elements.

Beginning about 1912, Gestalt psychologists, challenging the very existence of such elementary sensations, argued that experience occurs as structured wholes and that the task of psychology is to study the properties of such wholes. The properties to search for are those underlying invariants that help to explain why experience is not a chaos of diversity, but has organization, unity, stability. Consider the problem of spatial orientation: why does an object ever appear stable and upright? At any one moment, depending on the position of the head, it may stimulate this or that set of retinal receptors, or "elements," which may or may not be aligned with a major bodily axis. Yet the object does not seem to change its orientation with every movement of the head. What remains *invariant* is the relation of the object to its background, in

---

*The approach which we have called *introspective elementarism* has sometimes been called *structuralism*; among its leading exponents were Wundt at Leipzig and Titchener at Cornell; it is not to be confused with the contemporary movement known as Structuralism, with which we deal below. The latter began its rise to prominence early in this century and includes such figures as Ferdinand de Saussure in linguistics, Nicolai Bourbaki (pseudonym for an intellectual collective) in mathematics, and Claude Lévi-Strauss in anthropology.

particular to the major lines of the visual field. Such invariants are structural properties of the total perceptual configuration, not any localizable element or set of elements. There is no need to invent elements out of which structured experiences are built; experience is structured in the first place.

Piaget, in his interest in psychological structures, has much in common with Gestalt theory. Indeed, his summaries of it are sympathetic, full, and accurate. But he has one central criticism: the lack of concern for the genesis of the structures under discussion. Thus, in the example given above, Piaget's research has focused on the emergence in the child's thought of the operation of a coordinate system or frame of reference with respect to which things may have an invariant orientation. There would be no necessary contradiction between these two approaches, if these perceptual invariants did not change with age; we might simply have two independent systems of knowledge, conceptual and perceptual. But Piaget has given considerable effort to show that the developing concepts do indeed control the perception of space. In this sense, Piaget is not merely concerned with structures, he is structur*alist:* he wants to show the general regulative functions of structures, their pervasiveness in controlling experience and action, and the psychological coherence of the individual as the expression of a few very general structures.

To sum up this historical movement of ideas, the elementarists said, "from elements, structures," the Gestaltists answered "no elements, only structures," and Piaget rejoined, "out of structures, new structures."

In spite of his kinship with Gestalt psychology, there are some important differences. Piaget's structures are not things or beliefs, but coherent sets of mental operations which can be applied to things or beliefs or to anything else in the individual's psychological space. For example, the belief in the conservation of matter when shapes are deformed is not, in this sense, a "structure." Rather, the set of operations by which this belief is arrived at is a structure. Piaget does not claim that 8-year-old children all over the world spontaneously discover the conservation of matter; rather, they develop a set of operations that permits them to make this discovery when presented with a problem that can be solved if they do so. What matters is not a particular set of beliefs but a general set of operations.

A second special character of Piaget's structuralism is concern for change. He is not only interested in showing that, at each stage of development, a great variety of acts express the same structure; he is also interested in the way in which structures are transformed from stage to stage. He has given fuller attention to and been more successful at the first of these tasks. But there is no questioning that his aim is a developmental or genetic structuralism. In this respect his intentions are quite distinct from the contemporary structuralist movement that explicitly avoids genetic or historical explanations, choosing instead to elaborate ahistorical analyses of structures as they are at a given moment or period.

If the introspective elementarists were attacked from "above" by Gestalt psychologists, they were at the same time attacked from "below" by behaviorists. Behaviorism is in its own right an outstanding form of elementarism, hoping to explain complex behavior as the chaining together of simpler habits. The introspective elementarists were mentalists in the highest degree: the task of psychology was to explain mental life, and the method was to examine it directly with the tool of mentation itself, trained introspection. The Gestaltists were also interested in mental life and certainly used a type of introspection, or direct examination of experience as one of their tools. But they were also prepared to study the functioning of the intellect by the observation of behavior. One of the great classics of Gestalt psychology is a study of the problem-solving behavior of primates who could not at that time report to psychologists about their inner lives.*

The behaviorists, as is well known, would have none of this. The whole project of describing inner experience seemed unscientific to them: science deals with observable events, all we can observe and study directly is overt behavior, therefore scientific psychology must restrict itself to the study of behavior. "Inner experience," "consciousness," and all other subjective phenomena have no place in science.

Piaget has rarely bothered to criticize the introspective elementarists. He had no quarrel with their mentalistic aims, and, besides, by the time his career in psychology began, the importance of this school of thought had faded considerably. Why then has he often stopped to criticize the claims of behaviorists? Not to defend his interest in mental life. On the pragmatic American scene that might have seemed necessary, but not in the heart of Europe. We think there are two reasons for Piaget's interest in behaviorism, its focus on action, which Piaget shares, and its empiricism, which he loathes.

First, Piaget's own theory and behaviorism both begin with interest in action. Theoretically, both begin with the simple reflexes of the newborn and aim at explaining development by studying the developmental fate of these reflexes. From this point on, the theoretical differences are profound. Behaviorists aim at explaining all behavior as the modification of simple reflexes through the formation of habits, and the chaining together of these elements to form more complex units of behavior. It would be incorrect to say that behaviorists are not interested in structures, since chains and simple hierarchies are certainly structures; but they are structures of such primitive kind as practically to bypass the problem of organized, complex behavior.†

In Piaget's approach, the units of behavior, or schemes of action, are always seen as evolving structures. Thus complex behavior is not built up out of simple elements that retain their identity; instead, structures grow and change. Insofar as they are hierarchically organized, lower structures are governed and regulated by higher ones: rather than the primordial dominating the more highly evolved, the reverse is the case. Finally, Piaget's concern has always been to show how action is interiorized, transformed into mental life, and he insists that in the course

*W. Köhler, The Mentality of Apes (London: Routledge and Kegan Paul, 1925).

†This description of behaviorism is somewhat oversimplified and does not do justice to certain modern trends. See, for example, D. Berlyne, Structure and Direction in Thinking (New York: Wiley, 1965) for an explicit attempt to integrate behaviorism and Piagetian theory. See also Piaget's commentary on Berlyne's efforts in D. Berlyne and J. Piaget, Études d'Épistémologie Génétique XII: Théorie du comportement et opérations (Paris: Presses Universitaires de France, 1960).

of this transformation action becomes qualitatively distinct from its primitive origins. As actions become operations, they form structured groups that give to thought its flexibility, its versatility, its ability to deal with novelty, its creativity.

In some sense everything has a structure. If we wanted to develop a theory pertaining to a unique structure, unlike any other, it would have to be an analysis of the elements composing the structure or an account of the laws linking the variables within the structure. The third alternative, comparing the given structure to some ideal structure, necessarily admits the existence of more than one structure. Piaget's way has been the structuralist way, comparing structures with each other, in the first place to show the underlying similarities among seemingly different intellectual acts, and in the long run hopefully to discover the laws of transformation governing the relationships between structures.

The stage concept is necessarily linked to the idea of structure. Whatever we mean by a stage in the development of anything must be a set of relations prevailing at one time. But this is not enough to separate stage from flux. The set of relationships must be stable.*

Since we are talking about mental operations, or an activity of an organism that is always changing, we mean something more general than a single, frozen structured act. We mean the similarities or correspondences among different acts. That is why we can speak of the structure as underlying or regulating the acts in question.

A key feature of the kind of structure we are discussing is its coherence and unity: there is one set of rules for passing from state to state, and any transformation or series of transformations that follows these rules is an expression of the structure. Unless the intellect as a whole is completely coherent at each stage of development, we cannot expect to find a clearcut set of stages (series of structures) without delimiting the domains to which the structures apply.

This leads directly to another consideration, the distinction between structure and system. Suppose we find that there are a number of distinct structures coexisting at any moment of development. These coexist in one individual, and they must have some relation to each other. One possibility is to search for a more general structure, of which each of the seemingly distinct ones is but an expression. The effort to exhaust this strategy, to carry it as far as possible, is the heart of the movement known as *structuralism*.

An alternative strategy is to accept the structures as different and to search for ways of understanding their interconnections; this approach is characteristic of a movement known as *systems theory*. As we discussed above in another context, scientific theories are rarely pure cases of any one strategy. Moreover, the approaches in question are not contradictory but complementary, and we may expect to find an individual scientist using first one then the other. But it is fair to describe Piaget as a structuralist rather than a systems theorist. To take only one example, when Piaget turned his attention to mental imagery and

---

*This might be enough to say if we could restrict ourselves to a series of stages of long duration. The notion of a brief stage (the measure of brevity depending on the time scale we are using, which is not the same for the life of both a subatomic particle and a child) really depends on our ability to show that it appears reliably within a series of more stable structures.

memory, he did not delight in showing how different these are from logical thinking, and then seek to understand the relations among these functions. Rather, he sought to demonstrate that at each stage the child's imagery and memory express the same logical structures as had been found earlier in his studies of the child's thinking.*

It might reasonably be objected here, that Piaget did not seek to demonstrate, but attacked a problem objectively, and these were his empirical findings. This objection is not entirely available to Piaget himself, since he has strenuously criticized the empiricist view of science. The finding of some similarities, of course, does not conflict with the finding of some differences. The similarities in question were genuine discoveries, and this work is a good example of the fruitfulness of Piaget's approach. At the same time, it should be noted that he did not seek out whatever differences may exist between these functions precisely because he is a structuralist rather than a systems theorist.

The suggestion that a general point of view, such as structuralism or systems theory, may be a causal agent affecting the work of a scientist is compatible with either of the approaches under discussion. Put more generally, the two have one key point in common, the idea of self-regulation; this applies as much to the mind of a scientist as it does to the behavior of any other living system.†

Interaction, Construction, and Logical Determinism

No issue touches the thinking person more deeply than the relation of the individual to the world. Discussion takes many forms and gives rise to a number of questions, the answers to which never quite seem to stay put. The role of the individual in history, the individual's place in the family, and the relative contributions of heredity and environment in determining intelligence—all these raise questions that bear on one's general conception of the relation of organism and environment.

Piaget's approach to the general issue has been open to some misunderstanding. His insistence on the slow development of fundamental concepts and operations has sometimes been interpreted as meaning that the child "learns" these things primarily through commerce with the environment: stimulus evokes response, and, depending on the outcome, future response tendencies are altered, habits built up, but slowly. This is the position Piaget labels "empiricism," and he is very far from agreeing with it. To return to the example of the conservation of matter, what evidence could the child possibly have that amount remains the same when shape is deformed? No one talks about it, or

---

* A similar point can be made with respect to Gestalt psychologists, who have stressed the likenesses among different mental functions, such as perception, memory, and thinking. For them, perception plays the role of the central metaphor; for Piaget, logic plays that role.

†As will be especially evident in the final section of this volume, Piaget lays great stress on the idea of self-regulating systems. But systems theories aim to do more than that.

tells her, or asks her about it, or rewards her for giving the right answer. Even more implausible is the suggestion that the child learns the reasons she gives to defend her answer; if we could believe that the child learned the right answer, how would we explain where she had gotten the wrong answer and reasons, only a few months before? When we turn to the history of science, as Piaget is fond of doing, we see many examples of resistance to evidence because it does not fit into previously constructed ways of thought. Why, then, credit the child with a facile empiricism, readily fitting thought to experience?

If Piaget has been persistent and relentless in his criticism of empiricism, how does it happen that he remains open to this interpretation? The plain fact is, as he admits, that he has never succeeded in giving a satisfactory explanation of the production of a novel response. This leaves an opening for the application of an old and almost intractable thought-form: if a pattern of responses changes slowly, it must be due to learning.

Piaget has not only insisted on the slowness of development, but on the universality of its main stages. Since children grow up in such varied environments, the question arises, how can they all develop in the same way unless they are impervious to environmental influences, in other words, unless development is determined by hereditary factors? This is the position Piaget labels *preformism* when it refers to matters of general biology, and *apriorism* when it refers to the growth of intelligence.

Every study Piaget has ever made of children's concepts and mental operations shows how far the child's mentality is from being preformed in adult ways of thought, how he must during his own lifetime reinvent these ways. What the child brings to the world makes this growth possible, but the child himself must accomplish it through his own activity.

Nevertheless, if children everywhere do this in much the same way, does it not support the idea that development is an unfolding of inherent structures that are incipiently present in the germ plasm? And is this not a sort of apriorism, only extended over time?*

Piaget has been vulnerable to this interpretation of his work because of his insistence on the universality of stages. It would seem incumbent on the interactionist to produce evidence that commerce with the environment does affect the course of development. For this reason, in the 1950s, studies of the learning of Piagetian concepts and operations came to occupy an important place in the theoretical discussion. We have already mentioned the first group of such studies. To say the least, they demonstrated that it is not easy to invent a way of accelerating the child's movement through the stages of cognitive growth, existing structures resist change, the child's mind is no direct copy of the external reality presented to him by experimenter or teacher.

Insofar as this result supported Piaget's anti-empiricism, it seemed quite satisfactory. But it did leave the way open to the "unfolding" interpretation. In recent years, there has been a concerted effort in many quarters to show that Piagetian concepts and operations are indeed

---

*For an account of the vicissitudes of the same kind of question in another discipline, during the eighteenth and nineteenth centuries, see J. Needham, with the assistance of A. Hughes, *History of Embryology*, 2nd ed. (Cambridge: Cambridge University Press, 1959).

amenable to change through learning experiments. And modest results
have now been achieved. So long as the experiment is planned in ways
that respect the child's existing structures and elicit the child's own intellectual activity, some acceleration of growth can be achieved.* Since
no one actually believes that it is possible to transform a young child
overnight into an adult, modest effects are theoretically satisfactory. It
should be added, however, that acceptance of this point implies a tacit
acceptance of much of the structuralist approach.

To contrast it with empiricism and apriorism, Piaget has sometimes
labeled his own position *interactionism*. But this term has often been
used in a sense which does not quite fit Piaget. Hardly anyone who considers the subject goes to either extreme: it is widely accepted that the
child's mentality is neither entirely inherited nor entirely determined by
environmental forces. A compromise seems in order, and the question is
then transformed: what are the proportionate contributions of heredity
and environment in the determination of intelligence?† Someone formulating the issue in this way may well call himself an interactionist.

This formulation has at least two aspects that are entirely unacceptable to Piaget. First, the idea that intelligence is an "amount" that can
be measured, rather than a structure which must be described and
whose functioning must be understood. Second, the idea that heredity
and environment are, for each individual, fixed components that determine the intellectual outcome without affecting each other, rather than
vectors whose developmental significance changes incessantly, depending on the structures already achieved.

There are two features of Piaget's approach to the environment that,
although not unique in Piaget, are characteristic of him and worth
pointing out. The environment is not conceived as something that
"happens" to the child, not a stimulus that elicits a response. Rather the
child seeks out those features of the environment to which he can mean-
ingfully respond, both by assimilating them to existing structures and
by accommodating those structures to make continued assimilation
possible. The initiative belongs to the child.

The ordinary conception of the environment as determining behavior
rather than behavior determining the environment is an extreme expression of a commonplace adult achievement, that highly cultivated
paralysis summed up in the phrase, "I only followed orders." We must
admit that this is a state that can be attained, but it is not typical of
childhood.

For Piaget, moreover, the environment is "nonspecific." One does
not need clay balls or jars of water to learn about conservation. The
materials are everywhere and unavoidable; clenching and unclenching
the fist is just as good as flattening out a ball of clay. But even such
simple events are so rich, so open to varied logical structurings that it is
the child who sees in each experience that which he can draw upon for
his growth as it must be at that moment.

Piaget has sometimes labeled his position *constructivism*, to capture

*For an account of work in this vein conducted in Geneva see B. Inhelder,
H. Sinclair, and M. Bovet, *Learning and the Development of Cognition* (Cambridge: Harvard University Press, 1974).
†More precisely, what are the proportionate contributions of *variations* in
heredity and in environment to variations in intelligence.

the sense in which the child must make and remake the basic concepts and logical thought-forms that constitute his intelligence. Piaget prefers to say that the child is inventing rather than discovering his ideas. This distinction separates him both from empiricism and from apriorism. The ideas in question do not preexist out there in the world, only awaiting their discovery by the child: each child must invent them for himself. By the same token, since the ideas have no a priori external existence, they cannot be discovered by simple exposure; rather, they must be constructed or invented by the child. Thus, Piaget's book dealing with the growth of the concepts of object, space, time and causality in the first year of life is not called *The Discovery of Reality*, but *The Construction of Reality in the Child*.

But we do not think the term constructivism goes far enough in characterizing Piaget's position. It is possible to believe that the child constructs his own mentality through his own activity without any preoccupation whatsoever with the development of logical structures underlying intellectual life. Indeed, this describes the romantic ideal of many progressive educators. There is something more austere in Piaget's constructivism. It goes beyond mere logicism, or the attempt to characterize each stage of development by a logical model. He proposes that the functioning of the logic of each stage determines the structure of the stage that follows. Without wanting to engage in a neologistic tournament, we suggest that the term *logical determinism* captures this essential aspect of Piaget's thinking. Interactionism, constructivism, logical determinism—to summarize the entirety of his position Piaget has come to call it *genetic epistemology*.

If learning were very fast and our resulting image of the world a very accurate copy of an unambiguous reality, we would all be empiricists. If there were no learning at all, whatever intelligence we possessed could be due only to preformed structures, and we would all be apriorists. The conception of learning therefore occupies a strategic role in discussions of the relation between organism and environment, and it is important to understand what Piaget has done with it. First, he has defined learning as having only a limited role within a larger process of the functioning and growth of structures. Second, he insists that learning of specific behaviors or contents can only take place within existing structures: the individual's action upon the world is itself the operation of a structure, and in the process he assimilates new information to that structure, which sometimes requires changing the structure. Third, structures grow according to laws which are not given in the behavioristic associationism of stimulus-response psychology, or in the Gestalt laws describing the direct perception of an organized world. The function of cognitive growth is not to produce schemes that are more and more veridical copies of reality, but to produce more and more powerful logical structures that permit the individual to act upon the world in more flexible and complex ways.

Having said this much, let us reexamine a problem that has suffused and troubled this whole discussion. To arrive at a comfortable alternative to preformism, is it really necessary to demonstrate empirically that Piagetian stages are affected by variations in the environment? Biologists do not need to raise some children in an oxygen-deficient environment in order to demonstrate that the blood carries oxygen all over the body, and that the complex of mechanisms for the formation of blood and assimilation of oxygen is indispensable for normal development.

Similarly, it is at least possible that there are some aspects of intellectual growth that are both indispensable for normal functioning and dependent for their development on properties of the environment that are to be found everywhere on earth. It is hard to imagine a planet that could support life that did not have permanent objects, and it is equally hard to imagine a high level of intelligent functioning (e.g., mammalian?) without the idea of the permanent object.*

If you were a scientist interested in studying the growth of ideas, generally speaking it would make sense to begin by studying fundamental ideas rather than trivial ones. What is a fundamental idea? Indispensability would seem to be one of its more evident characteristics. Piaget followed an almost unique path in choosing what he hoped were fundamental concepts and operations for study, stepping outside of psychology and relying heavily on a certain philosophical tradition for guidance.† To the extent that he was successful in his choices, it would be difficult to demonstrate that the variables of growth he has chosen are accessible to environmental manipulation.

This is not to say that confirmed interactionists, Piaget among them, do not ultimately face the task of specifying the way in which the environment influences development. But one can imagine two quite different strategies for attacking this problem. At a primitive stage of science, techniques of measurement are crude, and it may be extremely difficult to detect variations in fundamental organs, concepts, operations: the basic requirements of development make such variations small. If we insist on searching for small and subtle effects in such fundamental variables, we must expect many failures.

An alternative strategy is to choose as objects of study things that obviously vary, even if they are not so fundamental. At first sight, this approach looks trivial (like the story of the drunk who looks for his keys under the lamp post, where the light is, rather than twenty yards away where he dropped them in the dark). Yet in biology it has yielded high rewards. Geneticists interested in mutations were willing to study *any* detectable mutation; one that could be produced at will by environmental manipulation would be a geneticist's dream (and would have no simple bearing on the nature-nurture dispute!) whether it affected the formation of the blood itself or only the most trivial morphological characteristic.

No psychologist worth his salt would use the preceding remarks to justify entirely abandoning the study of the interplay of organism and environment with regard to fundamental intellectual characteristics. Certainly Piaget has not done so. Only, at the present stage of scientific knowledge it may be that such study can best be pursued at a theoretical level. In any event, it must be admitted that the variational method that has characterized all empirical efforts thus far, while it has produced a

*See Selection 20 for Piaget's examination of object permanence.
†No one can read Piaget without thinking of Kant. He is not, of course, Kantian in his solutions, but a very considerable portion of his work has gone into studying the development of just those fundamental ideas that Kant identified and claimed were given a priori.

few interesting results in these last twenty years, has nothing staggering to show.

To take one last leaf from the biologist's notebook, what sort of approach could we hope for in studying organism-environment relationships with regard to well-protected fundamentals? A method that produced some very easily detectable effect *without* disturbing normal functioning or development would be ideal. The use of isotopic tracers comes to mind as a plausible analogy. Thus far, psychologists have not approached the subject in this way and have no similarly subtle tools at their disposal.

In closing this introduction we return to a point made in the Preface, the collaborative aspect of Piaget's work. From a very early age, even as an adolescent in *Le Club des Amis de la Nature*, Piaget presents the double aspect of the lonely intellect going his own way and the social being, seeking out others for real collaboration, and still others on whom to try out his ideas. His first psychological book, *Language and Thought of the Child*, was accomplished with the aid of 6 collaborators. The pursuit of discussion has often led to public controversy with other scientists; a few well known names that come to mind are Vygotsky, Wallon, Michotte, and Bruner—a Russian, a Frenchman, a Belgian, and an American.

As Piaget's career developed, or rather, as he constructed it, he evolved a characteristic style of working with assistants and other collaborators. This is most evident in the functioning of the Centre International d'Epistémologie Génétique, founded in 1955. Each year Piaget selects the topic to be investigated. Through a process of discussion, involving a large amount of give and take, the details of up to 20 specific experiments are worked out. These are discussed incessantly while being executed throughout the year by the resident members of the Centre, working in small groups which report frequently to the larger group and even more frequently to "Le Patron." At the end of the academic year, at an annual Symposium, the same work is once more presented, now in nearly finished form, and discussed with a group of invited participants. Most of these visitors are habitués, who return to Geneva periodically—not only for the Symposium, but for their own purposes, to help think through some of their own intellectual problems in fields as varied as biology, philosophy, education, physics, psychology, logic, mathematics, and the history of science.

It is this complex, multi-layered process of socialized reflection and explanation that gives the work we call Piaget's its full complexity, its somewhat involuted character, its extraordinary variety. After the Symposium, Piaget retires to a mountain retreat for a summer of writing. It is he who produces the final synthesis of all this discussion and empirical research. This too takes a double form. On the one hand, it is a factual account of the research. On the other hand, it is an exploration of ideas, a restructuring of the *problematique* as Piaget sees it. The research has not necessarily produced any definite answers, but it has certainly changed the questions.

Summary

There are at least three Jean Piagets. There is the austere theoretician, turning the thought of children into formal constructions of logic. There is the playful empirical scientist, who led a whole generation of psychologists into a new way of listening to children. There is the doubter, driven onward to new research by the feeling that he has not yet explained the emergence of novelty, which must lie at the core of any account of the growth of thought.

To know only one of these is not to know Piaget. One must persevere through the logical and other theoretical difficulties, listen to the children, and let some of the same questions take hold. And in reading Piaget, it is important to stop often and try to work out some of the ideas for yourself: ". . . real comprehension of a notion or a theory implies the reinvention of this theory by the subject."*

Note: In citing Piaget's works, we have used a shortened reference form. For complete citations the reader should consult the Bibliography of Piaget's works at the end of this volume.

---

*J. Piaget, "Comments on Mathematical Education," in *Developments in Mathematical Education, Proceedings of the Second International Congress on Mathematical Education.*

CHRONOLOGY

Our introduction to this volume is a discussion of issues, rather than a biographical sketch of Piaget's life. The reader can, however, easily discover that the book as a whole *is* such a sketch. As a life-long intellectual, all the important events in Piaget's life are intellectual acts. The table of contents of this volume, and the introductions to the selections, add up to a tolerably full account. For more biographical detail the reader should turn to Piaget's own brief autobiography.*

1896: August, 9: birth in Neuchâtel (Switzerland) of a first child and only son, Jean, to Arthur and Rachel Piaget. He has two younger sisters.

1907: First article on an albino sparrow.

1918: Doctor of Natural Sciences with a thesis on molluscs presented at the University of Neuchâtel.
Publication of *Recherche*, a novel.

1919–1920: Studies in psychology in Zürich under Lipps and Wreschner for experimental methodology and measurement and under Bleuler for psychiatric clinic.
Studies and practicum in Paris at the Alfred Binet Institute.
Publication of a paper on psychoanalysis.

1921: Director of studies (Chef de travaux) at the Jean-Jacques Rousseau Institute in Geneva.
First articles on cognitive child psychology.

1923: Married to Valentine Châtenay.
Publication of *The Language and Thought of the Child.*

1924: Publication of *Judgment and Reasoning in the Child.*

1925–1929: Professor of psychology, sociology and philosophy of sciences at the University of Neuchâtel.

1925: Birth of daughter Jacqueline.

1927: Birth of Lucienne, the second daughter.
Publication of *The Child's Conception of Physical Causality.*

1929–1939: Associate Professor of History of Scientific Thought at the University of Geneva.

1929–1967: Director of the International Bureau of Education.

1931: Birth of Laurent, a son.

1932: *The Moral Judgment of the Child.*

*See bibliography, this volume, pp. 447–450.

1933–1971: Director of the Institute for Educational Sciences of the University of Geneva.
1936: *The Origins of Intelligence in Children.*
1937: *The Construction of Reality in the Child.*
1938–1951: Professor of Psychology and Sociology at the University of Lausanne.
1939–1952: Professor of Sociology at the University of Geneva.
1940–1971: Professor of Experimental Psychology at the University of Geneva.
1941: *The Child's Conception of Number* with Alina Szeminska.
1942: *The Child's Construction of Physical Quantities* with Bärbel Inhelder.
1945: *Play, Dreams and Imitation in Childhood.*
1946–1948: Books on the child's representation of movement, speed, time and space.
1949: *Traité de logique.*
1950: *Introduction à l'épistémologie génétique.*
1952–1963: Professor of Developmental Psychology at the Sorbonne.
1955 to present: Director of the International Center for Genetic Epistemology (University of Geneva).
1967: *Biology and Knowledge.*
1971: Professor Emeritus of the University of Geneva.
1975: *L'Equilibration des structures cognitives.*

The idea of equilibrium first appeared explicitly in Piaget's writings in *Recherche* (1918). Much later, it became the subject of a monograph, *Logique et Equilibre* (1957). Still later, dissatisfied with his previous efforts, Piaget reworked the whole subject in *L'Equilibration des structures cognitives: problème central du développement* (1975). The following year, he proposed to present this volume as his thesis for a doctorate in psychology, which he had never received. The officials of the University of Geneva refused him this privilege, but graciously, on the grounds that a man of Piaget's breadth should not be classified in any one discipline. Nevertheless, in honor of his eightieth birthday, it was arranged that the new volume on equilibration should be the theme of a day of reflection.

PART I
Early Biology

INTRODUCTION

In these earliest papers by Piaget we see a pattern of movement: first description, then correlation of facts with each other, and finally beginning efforts to construct scientific explanations. Even the simplest descriptions are not mere fact gathering, but are governed by a point of view. The correlations among facts that he advances involve him in what may be fairly described as interdisciplinary activity, since he looks for connections among zoological, geographical, and geological observations. His first theoretical effort (Selection 7) is not so much a full-blown effort at theory construction as a criticism of and reply to another scientist; nevertheless it is truly theoretical in intention, and closes with a prediction that is clearcut, albeit not testable in the author's lifetime.

Piaget's work in these years can be classified under three main headings, taxonomy (primarily molluscs, but one study of batrachians), zoogeography, and the process of adaptation. Although his first printed theoretical effort bears on a straightforward biological question, the definition of species in relation to Mendelian theory, it is striking that he is led into these considerations through a study of animal behavior.

"An Albino Sparrow" is Piaget's first published effort, written in 1907 when he was 11 years old. Brief and modest as it is, it is worth noting the systematic style emerging. He does not say that he saw an albino sparrow; he says he saw a sparrow that has the characteristics of an albino; thus he is already one definite step away from simple realism. In the second selection, we see again that he is interested in the unusual specimen, that he has enough experience to notice it among the ordinary, and that he is interested in explaining its origins.

The third selection is a paragraph from a twenty-two page article on the *Limnaea* (a type of mollusc that recurs often in Piaget's later work) of three Swiss lakes. The article reviews the literature of the subject, traces geographical origins and probable course of migrations of the species of the region, and examines fossil species of Switzerland. He gives examples of protective coloration and other adaptations. The main burden of the article is an attempt to rework the existing system of classification of these species, and to reduce the taxonomy to the simplest plausible scheme. This was Piaget's first printed publication, the earlier ones having been mimeographed in *Le Rameau de Sapin* (The Fir Branch). In this excerpt we catch a pleasing glimpse of Piaget's relation with his teacher, Dr. Paul Godet. And from the sure-handed way with which he announces his intentions, we can almost feel his scientific aspirations growing.

In the fourth selection, on albinism in a species of *Limnaea*, the key point is Piaget's interest in the coherence of the organism: if one part is modified, other modifications follow.

In the fifth selection we see the beginnings of a controversy that would engage Piaget's attention over the next few years. Another investigator, Rozkowski, had proposed that the molluscs living on the lake bottom in deep water were really the same species as those found in shallow waters along the shore, this in spite of behavioral and morphological differences. In Rozkowski's view the deep-water specimens, having migrated (probably fallen) to their new surroundings, adapt only a little to the changed conditions of life and then die out, to be replaced by a fresh supply falling to the bottom. Piaget argues that the two groups are distinct species. The significance of the disagreement only emerges in the following selections. Piaget concludes the general introduction to this article with a list in parallel columns showing the pairwise correspondences between deep-water and littoral forms that have evolved from the same ancestral species. After these opening remarks, Piaget gives one of his many extensive descriptions of collections of molluscs; in this case there are ten species and fourteen variants, making twenty-four descriptions in all, most of them accompanied by drawings. We have omitted this catalogue.

When shore-dwelling molluscs are suddenly precipitated to the bottom of a deep lake, for example by accidental currents, they must make a rapid adaptation to radically changed conditions of pressure, temperature, light, availability of air, and type of food supply. Without this rapid adaptation they cannot survive or evolve into a species better adapted to deep-water life. In the sixth selection Piaget studies the reverse adaptation, deep-water specimens dredged up from the bottom and placed in an aquarium—technically a much easier experiment and shedding some light on the same general problem. The fact that he is interested in rapid adaptation leads naturally to the behavioral emphasis of this paper.

Piaget observes the animals carefully and reports on their breathing, climbing, food-seeking, and reproductive behavior. In some respects they change within a few days toward a greater resemblance to the habits of littoral species, in others they retain the habits of deep-water animals.

In his discussion Piaget argues against Rozkowski's Mendelian position that distinguishes between fluctuating and hereditary variations, the former being due to changes in the intensity of some environmental variable and the latter to the introduction of a wholly new factor. By the same token Piaget is arguing against saltatory evolutionary changes, insisting that all changes are gradual.

We have omitted the theoretical section of this article because the same theme is taken up in the next selection. But one passage from his conclusion should be quoted, because it is so pertinent to issues Piaget developed later on in other contexts:

If the transformation is not immediate, the distinction between fluctuating and hereditary variations obviously falls, and good species [i.e., well defined and stable]* will always begin by being hereditary only in their given milieu, capable of being brought back to some already existing type, if they are transported somewhere else. Time alone will have a real effect. Moreover, it is not the factors which must be new, but the ensemble of factors, their relationships, their synthesis. In other words, a new species is from its beginnings not characterized by its properties, its acquired characteristics, but by its tendencies, as more than one philosopher has remarked.

* [Throughout this volume, brackets have been reserved for our—the volume editors[3]—use. Exceptions are rare and are evident from the context, e.g., in equations, or are indicated by an appropriate footnote.]

"Has the Mendelian Species an Absolute Value?" proceeds by a kind of *reductio ad absurdum*. First Piaget accepts Rozkowski's distinction between hereditary and fluctuating species. Then he marshals evidence to show that many species thought to be hereditary can in some sense be considered as fluctuating. "At this rate, there will be nothing left in nature but fluctuating varieties!" He thinks of this conclusion as an obvious absurdity, which therefore proves his point: "good" species arise gradually; the same processes of adaptation that first produce fluctuating variations, if continued, produce stable or hereditary species. It is interesting that he does not even consider the alternative conclusion that the concept of species is indeed entirely artificial, an idea advanced by one of his predecessors in theoretical biology, Lamarck.

He takes up three types of case: species that appear to be hereditary now, but that in some paleontological past were only fluctuating varieties; species that appear to be hereditary in one locale, but that can be seen as fluctuating in another place; and species that have become distinct through adaptation to a gradual change in the environment, such as those that make the transition from salt water to a brackish pond and then to a freshwater pond. Such environmental changes are readily ascertainable, and corresponding to them are adaptive changes in the species inhabiting these milieux; some of these changes are reversible, or "fluctuating," others—especially those long-continued—become irreversible, or "hereditary," in the terms used in this paper.

Having prepared the way, he now turns to the point at issue. In certain obvious cases isolation leads to speciation, for example when islands are separated from the mainland through geological processes. Isolation does not occur suddenly in nature, because such geological processes are gradual; by the same token, the adaptive changes accompanying isolation must be gradual, so that fluctuating variations *become* hereditary species differences. This argument, which may not be entirely convincing, has certainly a long and honorable history; it can be found in very similar form in *The Origin of Species* by Charles Darwin.

The dispute between Piaget and Rozkowski arose over their different taxonomic decisions in classifying deep water *Limnaea*. But the reader may note that in his last sentence Piaget meets his adversary halfway; rather than insisting that these species *are* hereditary he predicts that they will *become* hereditary, or Mendelian. Thus the particular taxonomic issue can be put aside: it has served its purpose in provoking a critical examination of the fundamental issue of gradual versus sudden change.

An Albino Sparrow*

1907†

At the end of last June, to my great surprise, in the Faubourg de l'Hôpital at Neuchâtel, I saw a sparrow presenting all the visible signs of an albino. He had a whitish beak, several white feathers on the back and wings, and the tail was of the same color. I came nearer, to have a closer look, but he flew away; I was able to follow him with my eyes for some minutes, then he disappeared through the Ruelle du Port.

I have just seen today in the *Rameau de Sapin* of 1868 that albino birds are mentioned; which gave me the idea to write down the preceding lines.

Neuchâtel, the 22nd of July 1907

Jean Piaget
élève du Collège Latin

---

*Professor Piaget informs us that he published this observation in order to show the curator of the Neuchâtel Museum of Natural Sciences that he was active in the field, so that he might be granted permission to work at the museum out of regular hours. The 11-year-old boy wanted to be taken seriously by the curator, who was to become his master in the field of zoology.

† From J. Piaget, Un moineau albinos. *Le rameau du sapin*, Organe du Club Jurassien, Neuchâtel, 41: 36. Translated by H. E. G. and J. J. V.

Xerophila Obvia in the Canton of Vaud*

1909

Xerophila obvia (Htm) (Helix, Hartm.—H. candicans, Zgl.) belongs to the family of *Helicidae* and to the subfamily of *Xerophilinae*. This shell originated in Western Europe and was imported into Germany where it multiplied much.

In February 1909, I found it at Le Chanet (near Neuchâtel); having brought it to Professor Paul Godet, he was kind enough to let me know that this mollusk had been imported from Germany along with fodder-plant seeds.

At the beginning of April 1908, how great was my astonishment when I saw a whole colony of *Xerophila obvia* at Prangins (Canton of Vaud). I picked some specimens for my collection. It is likely that the *X. obvia* from Prangins have been imported in the same way. However, they must have escaped from the meadow where they had been brought at first, because they were in a completely arid spot covered with some sparse shrubs and grass turned yellow by the sun.

Jean Piaget
élève du Collège Latin

* La xerophila obvia au canton de vaud. *Le rameau du sapin.* Organe du Club Jurassien, Neuchâtel, 43: 13; 44 (1910): 4. Translated by H. E. G. and J. J. V.

The *Limnaea* of the Lakes of Neuchâtel, Bienne,

Morat, and Their Surroundings*

1911

When, after having vainly attempted to classify certain ill-defined specimens of *Limnaea*, I would bring them to my revered master, the late Dr. Paul Godet, he would not miss the opportunity to repeat to me all the aversion he felt for these unbearable animals that are the despair of malacologists because of their variability. Then he would light up a cigar, saying that he needed strength, examine the shells that I was showing him, and give his opinion with an extreme circumspection.

That variability was what interested me most, and I have wondered whether it would not be possible to reduce the number of species as it has been done for *European Anodontae*. I would like, then, in this little work, to take up the question of *Limnaea*, to which M. Godet grants only five pages in his 1907 catalogue, to modify the classification of the forms of the subspecies of *Gulnaria*, to add the results of my research about distribution, mimicry, previously unobserved stations, and to indicate some new varieties in the area.

*From J. Piaget, "Les Limnées des Lacs de Neuchâtel, Bienne, Morat et des environs," *Journal de Conchyliologie*, 59, (1911): 311–332. Translated by H. E. G. and J. J. V.

Albinism in *Limnaea Stagnalis**

1912

Limnaea Stagnalis, L. has a blackish color and a more or less dark, horn-colored shell, but in some of our small lakes the color is much lighter. For instance, the specimens from the Doubs valley at Les Brenets are much paler than those from the lake of Etalières. Moreover, the variety, *Lacustris, Stud,* specific to our three large lakes, has a lighter color than normal individuals, for the shell as well as for the animal. In 1907, in their monograph on the lake of St.-Blaise, Les Amis de la Nature mentioned at Loclat some albino specimens, that is, pure white shell and very dark animal: M. Godet says the same in his catalogue. This curious fact contradicts Moquin-Tandon's observations, according to which, when the shell presents the modification, the animal is more or less affected too. In a pond located near Epagnier, I have even observed the reverse phenomenon: among large individuals, slightly paler than usual, but with normal shell, there was one whose limbs, head and foot were of a dirty white color in contrast with the horn color of the shell. I have observed an exactly similar case in Cudrefin, in the lake, among specimens belonging to the variety *Lacustris*.

*This is the whole text of J. Piaget, "L'Albinisme chez la *Limnéa Stagnalis*," *Le Rameau du Sapin*. Neuchâtel, Organe du Club Jurassien, 46: 28. Translated by H. E. G. and J. J. V.

Recent Malacological Draggings in the
Lake of Geneva by Professor Emile Yung[*]

1912

The important preliminary materials which Professor Emile Yung has kindly entrusted to me for examination include a certain number of new forms. I intend to publish their diagnoses below. The late Professor Forel had already, in 1910, communicated to me four unpublished varieties, of which two have been found again by Professor Yung. I will also give the descriptions of these two. Finally, I cannot thank enough M. Henri Fischer, whose advise has been most valuable.

It is known that only six species of molluscs, without the least variation, had been found in the deep-water fauna of the Lake of Geneva: *Limnaea profunda*, *abyssicola*, and *Foreli*; *Valvata lacustris*; and *Psidium Foreli* and *profundum*—described either by Brot or by Clessin.

Genus Limnaea Lam.

In the fortieth volume of *Zoologischer Anzeiger* M. Waclaw Rozkowski has published a preliminary work of the greatest interest. Basing himself primarily on the anatomy of the organs of reproduction, the author concludes that *L. profunda*, *L. Foreli*, and *L. abyssicola* cannot be regarded as species: the first two are *L. ovata* and the last is *L. palustris*. Moreover, he agrees with Forel that the abyssal fauna derives from the littoral fauna by way of migration, either active or passive. "The representatives of the littoral species emigrating to the depths adapt only imperfectly to the conditions of their new milieu; they vegetate there for several generations and end by disappearing to be replaced by newcomers."

While recognizing the value of certain of the author's assertions, in particular his very justifiable opinion on the affinities of *L. profunda* and *L. ovata*, I cannot accept his fundamental interpretations. Nothing proves that the present-day deep-water forms derive from the present-

[*]From J. Piaget, Les récents dragages malacologiques de M. Le Prof. Emile Yung dans le lac Léman. *Journal de Conchyliologie*, Paris, 60: 205–232. Translated by H. E. G. and J. J. V.

day littoral forms, or vice versa. On the contrary, I believe it is a matter of much older transformations.

It seems probable to me that the separation between littoral and deep-water forms dates from the appearance of *Limnaea* in the Lake of Geneva. The ancestral *Limnaea*, having populated the whole body of these waters from the moment of these origins, has given rise to, by evolution, in the deep-water fauna, *L. profunda* and *L. Foreli*, and at the same time these same ancestral forms have produced, in a parallel evolution in the surface waters, *L. stagnalis* (and its variant, *lacustris*), *L. palustris*, and *L. limosa*, without these two evolutionary streams having any relation between them.

This hypothesis explains perfectly the resemblance of the receptaculum seminis, observed by Rozkowski, in *L. palustris* and *L. abyssicola*, an organ of this nature being obviously much less subject to the influence of the milieu than are morphological characteristics of the animal, or than the shell, or than those organs whose physiology is directly modified by external conditions.

Let us consider now the whole group of *Limnaea* evolved in these deep waters; it is natural that, being submitted to very uniform actions of the milieu, they exhibit, on the one hand, very close affinities among them, but, on the other, very constant specific characteristics. In contrast, surface forms, being subject to very variable external influences, have given rise to species whose variability is considerably greater, but which are also more unstable.

This is why *L. stagnalis* and *L. lacustris* are very polymorphic and exhibit many intermediaries, whereas the two corresponding deep-water forms, *L. Yungi* and *L. profunda*, have characteristics that are less divergent and better defined.

But, if deep-water species exhibit closer affinities among themselves than do littoral species, this results from another type of influence: the action of deep water having varied much less than the action of surface water—either because of the difference in the transformations of nature itself, which is almost immutable in the depths in comparison with surface regions, or because of the ease with which littoral *Limnaea* change their milieu, in contrast with the uniformity of conditions over wide stretches of abyssal waters—it is probable that the deep-water species have evolved relatively little. In other words, each deep-water species is closer to its ancestral form than is its corresponding littoral form.

On the hypothesis advanced by M. Rozkowski, it is difficult to understand how *L. ovata* (*sensu stricto*) alone could produce two deep-water forms as different as *L. profundis* and *Foreli*. It is even harder to understand, in applying his theory to the new *Limnea* dragged by M. Yung, how present-day surface forms so polymorphic as *L. stagnalis* and *lacustris* could have furnished only two deep-water forms, *L. Yungi* and *L. profunda* (and even the latter would be an *ovata*), whereas in the other way of reasoning, things are easily explained.

There are, in addition, some curious details of bathymetric distribution: *L. limosa* var. *sublittoralis*, which, judged by its shell is a purely littoral form, was dragged by M. Yung as deep as 30 to 50 meters, while *L. Foreli*, an abyssal species, is found as high as 30 and even 15 meters off Morges, from where Prof. Forel sent it to me. Only the first of these two forms follows the law announced by the great limnologist, but applied by M. Rozkowski to the deep-water *Limnaea* known until now; that is to say that, of all the abyssal forms now known, only *L. sublittoralis* derives directly from a littoral *Limnaea*. (It is undoubtedly identical with the variety dragged by Doctor André at the Geneva end of the Lake of Geneva, at 40 meters of depth, and identified by him as *L. contracta Kob.*)

It remains for me to say a few words about the peculiarities of distribution, the reason for which still escapes us: all the sub-genera among which are distributed our present-day indigenous species of Limnaea are represented in the deep waters, with the exception of the sub-genus *Fossaria*. There is no abyssal form comparable to *L. truncatula*.

To sum up, I maintain that the deep-water species are distinct from the surface species, contrary to the opinion of the author cited, and I propose that each deep water form corresponds to one littoral form having the same ancestral origin, according to the following table:

Littoral Forms	Deep-water Forms
L. stagnalis	*L. Yungi*
L. stagnalis, var. *lacustris*	*L. profunda*
L. palustris	*L. abyssicola*
L. limosa	*L. Foreli*

Limnaea Yungi Piaget, m dredged opposite Cully depth of 247 meters (m.).

Limnaea Yungi var. *humilis* Piaget, between Cully and Lutry (30–50 m.).

Limnaea Yungi var. *intermedia* Piaget, between Cully and Lutry (30–50 m.).

Limnaea Yungi var. *ventriosa* Piaget, between Cully and Lutry (30–50 m.)

Limnaea Yungi var. *acella* Piaget, opposite Cully (247 m.).

Jawbones of *L. Yungi.*

Closed mouth of *L. Yungi.*

Tentacles of *L. Yungi* (a) of the var. *intermedia* and (b) of the form.

Limnaea abyssicola Brot var. *macrostoma* Piaget, dredged between Lutry and Cully (30–50 m.).

Limnaea Foreli Cless. var. *obtusiformis* Piaget, between Lutry and Cully (30–50 m.).

Limnaea Foreli Cless. var. acutispirata Piaget, opposite Morges (15–30 m.).

Limnaea limosa (L.) var. *sublittoralis* Piaget, between Lutry and Cully (30–50 m.).

Ancylus fluviatilis (Müll.) var. *achromata* Piaget, opposite Morges (from 15–30 m.).

Ancylus fluviatilis (Müll.) var. *achromata* Piaget, seen from above (top).

Valvata lacustris Cless. var. *Foreli* Piaget, opposite Morges (from 50 m.).

Valvata lacustris Cless. var. *Yungi* Piaget, found with the preceding (one).

Pisidium (Clessinia) Yungi Piaget, between Lutry and Cully (30–50 m.).

Pisidium (Clessinia) infimum Piaget, opposite Cully (247 m.).

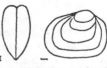

Pisidium (Clessinia) var. *noviodunensis* Piaget, Nyon (47 m.).

Pisidium (Clessinia) candidum Piag between Lutry and Cully (30–50 m

Notes on the Biology of Deep-water *Limnaea**

1914

It is well known that the bottoms of our lakes are populated by an infinity of animals of all sorts, which adapt more or less to the very difficult biological conditions of this milieu. The dark, the cold, the pressure, are significant factors reducing vital activity and leading naturally to great difficulty in the search for food. In addition, there is a great lack of vegetation, because of the lack of sunlight. Finally, the complete nakedness of the great depths, without any rocks, or other means of shelter such as are available to littoral animals, is also an obstacle, especially with regard to egg-laying and the safety of the young.

The molluscs in question in the present work have to struggle especially against all sorts of biological difficulties. It is only by the force of circumstances independent of their will that they have been recently precipitated to the depths. The rising of rivers, or the more or less sudden elevation of the level of the lakes, has contributed to the genesis of these species, some time after the first peopling of our sub-alpine regions. These animals, thus forced to emigrate, have necessarily had to adapt themselves to their new conditions. They have exhibited such suppleness in their remarkable evolution that today these races withstand their exile very well and sometimes survive being brought back to the surface.

When abyssal animals are removed from their milieu, they differ considerably in their behavior, depending on the genera or the species. . . .

The few individuals that I have studied in preparing this note were caught either by Professor Emile Yung in the Lake of Geneva, or by Professor Fuhrmann of Neuchâtel, at a depth of 50 meters. These last, which I have specially studied, belong to *Limnaea Foreli Cless* and were very young on their arrival in my jars, reaching only 3 to 6 meters in

*From J. Piaget, Notes sur la biologie des Limnées abbyssales. *Internationale Revue des gesamten Hydrobiologie und Hydrographie*, Leipzig, *Biologisches* supplement, 6: 15 pp. Translated by H. E. G. and J. J. V.

length. Dragged the 15th of May, they were brought to me the 19th, at 11 o'clock in the morning, and immersed in a small aquarium, which was at a temperature of about 11°C. It is known that the deep-water fauna live continually at 4°, and that at a depth of 50 meters, the pressure must reach five atmospheres.

Immediately after their arrival, they began to explore their domicile, very slowly climbing the walls, the thermometer, and the aquatic plants, but especially moving about the bottom, covered with sandy leaf mould and a little lake mud. During the whole day they were somewhat dormant, more active after sunset. The next day, two of them—the youngest—having no doubt suffered from the trip and from my handling, died. The others, on the contrary, quickly habituated to their new milieu, spread out everywhere and displayed very great activity, as they continued to do from then on.

It appears interesting to study in an aquarium the biology of these animals, highly specialized by their habitat, since we cannot observe them in nature. But we will only emphasize those points where their customs and instincts differ from those of littoral races.

It is known that the *Limnaea* are "pulmonated" molluscs [containing a cavity that functions like a lung], inhabiting our marshes, ponds, lakes, and sometimes our streams, normally air-breathing when conditions permit, but being quite able to spend hours underwater, closing their pneumostome. They live under rocks, the leaves of waterlilies, on aquatic plants of all sorts; they are not very active, and they like cool temperatures. They know how to swim with the current, spreading their enormous foot, the shell upside down, and the moment there is any danger, they let themselves fall straight down, releasing the air which helps them float. Their food is vegetable, with their three large jaws they make large notches in the edges of submerged leaves and consume them over a period of hours. The shell is ordinarily thick and rather large, extraordinarily variable. Finally, they are hermaphrodites and ditremes, which permits them to copulate sometimes in long chains of individuals, at the surface of the water. They lay quantities of eggs, from 30 to 60 at a time, enveloped in long rolls of albumen, with which they adhere to plants or rocks.

In a few words, this is the modus vivendi of these animals, in their normal conditions. In the deep-water fauna, naturally, everything is changed. The dark and the lack of food render the animal minuscule and pale, the shell white and fragile. The layer of water above prevents all air-breathing, forcing, as Brot has observed, the lung to take in water and to function like a gill. They live on or in the mud, which profoundly modifies the form of the test [shell]; their food, distributed mainly in this mud, is necessarily animal and gives them crawling habits. For the rest, the lack of air and the depth prevent all efforts to swim in the manner practiced by littoral *Limnaea*.

But all that could be established by reasoning alone. Let us see now how individuals brought from these deep waters behave in an aquarium.

During the first hours of their captivity, my eight specimens did not rise to the surface, where free air would be available, but they did so beginning with the following morning. It is probable that they continued to breathe more or less as they did in deep water, but one could only be sure by means of dissecting them. Meanwhile, after awhile, one or two individuals arriving at the surface very visibly opened their pneumostomes to the free air. This habit spread little by little throughout the colony. But my subjects are far from returning frequently out of the water, and I have not seen those prolonged periods out of the liquid, so frequent among all the littoral *Limnaea* in an aquarium. Given their lack of assiduity and especially their interminable stays in the mud or at the bottom of the tank, it is even quite probable that my specimens made use of either mode of respiration with impunity.

I also observed a curious custom which they took up, with or without an aim. I noticed that some individuals buried in the mud—just along the edge of the aquarium and thus concealing themselves from observation—left behind them after their departure, empty spots filled with air bubbles more or less compressed. Some time later, one could see the *Limnaea* go back to the same spots, precisely to these underground reservoirs. Have we here an instinctive concern for conservation, or is this circumstance purely fortuitous?

Besides the displacements motivated by respiration or by the search for food, one can observe among these animals a penchant for the cool and the dark. Frequently, during moments of great heat, which arise sometimes rather suddenly because of the smallness of the tank and its position in the open air on a balcony, one can see the *Limnaea* descend all at once to the bottom of the aquarium, half bury themselves in the mud, or huddle in the corners, carefully avoiding the heat and sun. By contrast, they do not find light disagreeable, and they are extremely insensitive to it. It is undoubtedly because of this fact that the eyes of abyssal *Limnaea* have no peculiarities that distinguish them from surface *Limnaea*.

On this point, M. Yung has published, in the "Archives de Psychologie," the results of his experiments with snails. But it is more difficult to ascertain anything about the visual power of *Limnaea* than of *Sytlommatophores*, because there is no invagination of the tentacles, to register the impression received. All that I can report is that my *Limnaea*, plunged in complete darkness for an hour, acted as though nothing had happened; placed suddenly in the presence of a strong light, they gave no sign of astonishment, continuing their paths along the glass, the plants, or the surface.

The fact of air-breathing had as one consequence to give my *Limnaea* the possibility of resting above a current of water, inflating the pulmonary chamber. They did not do this right away, but when this behavior appeared, it did so all at once, as if it were instinctive. They also know how to let themselves drop straight down by the sudden expulsion of the air contained in the cavity of the lung. But these rapid descents also occur frequently against their will. They even seem to be afflicted by a considerable clumsiness. Shaking the tank gently often suffices to make all the *Limnaea* fall, whether they are swimming or creeping along the walls. Littoral *Limnaea* in an aquarium are far from being so unstable but know how to maintain themselves at the surface or against submerged objects, in spite of much more severe tremors. Even left entirely alone, my eight individuals constantly suffered failures of this nature. It very often happens that some specimens climb painstakingly up the walls, let go suddenly, only to begin again at once. This pattern is extremely frequent at the time of fertilization, and the future parents always miss each other two or three times when they pursue each other anywhere but on the bottom, before succeeding in meeting and coupling. These facts, which do not occur so frequently among surface *Limnaea*, show an ineptness, very natural moreover, in moving anywhere but in the mud. But the habit is quickly acquired, and at the end of a month they show more vivacity and skill in their ascents, although they are never very agile. The new generation will appear more sure of themselves.

The food eaten by my eight *Limnaea* does not seem to have changed much during their captivity. I have only once seen one of them attack an aquatic plant. They appear, on the contrary, to search for all their sustenance in the mud, which accounts for their habit of waiting interminably in one place, half buried or completely covered. I have also seen individuals traverse the walls, licking them conscientiously, undoubtedly for nourishment, since the glass is covered with a sticky crust, slightly wrinkled, which must be very rich in organisms.

The consequence of this persistence of carnivorous habits was visible in the growth of the test. The shell, which was from 3 to 6 mm. long at the beginning of my observations, grew to 6 to 7 mm., and the part that was formed in the aquarium did not differ at all from the older part: extremely fine, fragile, whitish, dull, a little shiny on the inside, transparent. These are the characteristics common to all the deep-water *Limnaea*, and to certain *Psidea*. As for the general shape, it does not yet show the modifications that will be seen in the following generations.

One curious fact that should be noted is a consequence of the form of the tank: my eight specimens exhibit a rather prominent protuberance just at the point where the growth in the aquarium began. Moreover, the outline is very slightly fuller from the same moment.

One might have expected that my subjects, cultivated as they were, would attain a rather large size, resulting from the improved environment, as compared with their natural milieu. But this was not at all the case, these individuals not surpassing the mean size of *Limnaea Foreli*. It should be added that they seem to eat very little, devoting far less time to this activity than their littoral congeners under equivalent conditions.

They do, however, devote considerable activity for reproduction, laying eggs very often, but few at a time. I did not see fertilization in a chain, but only between two individuals. My subjects began to lay eggs from June 21st, that is one month after their arrival and at a rather young age. The season does not seem to matter very much to abyssal *Limnaea*. I have seen coupling from the end of May, in June, July, on both warm and cold days. Moreover, I have found living, young specimens of all ages in the contents of draggings made in December, March, May, and June, in the lakes of Geneva and Neuchâtel, which shows clearly the slight influence of the seasons.

The eggs are rarely laid on plants, or at least not on the stems, since one sees them among the numerous little leaves of the small surface. The bundles of eggs are also not often seen stuck to the walls, to which these masses do not adhere very solidly. Several such groups came off by themselves, sinking to the bottom of the water. It is there, in the main, that one finds the bundles of eggs, simply deposited on the bottom surface, or half buried in the mud. It is quite evident that this originates in abyssal conditions, since the calm of the water offers safety enough.

In contrast, it is well known how solidly the eggs of littoral *Limnaea* hold fast, so that the waves and the currents do not detach them from the stones or the plants where they are moored. *Limnaea* eggs do not sustain displacements very well: they are readily damaged by being shaken, the envelope of the mass breaks, the eggs are set free and delivered to a certain death, due to their fragility and the inadequate protection of their thin, diaphanous membrane.

It is perhaps because of this danger that abyssal *Limnaea* multiply in bundles of no more than 9 eggs. This is the maximum number that I have observed, the majority having only 3, 4, 5, 6, 7, or even only 1. Among surface *Limnaea*, however, the agglomerations range from 15 to 60 eggs, and they hatch after about 20 days (19 to 26, depending on the temperature).

Among my abyssal specimens, unfortunately, I have been unable to make regular observations of the period of incubation. I have only retrieved two isolated cases: bundles laid June 21st and 22nd, 1913, both hatched July 15th, which makes 23 and 24 days, at a temperature of 11 °C to 28 °C, with sudden variations. . . .

We turn now to a new paragraph of my notes, and study briefly the development of the young of the first generation raised entirely in the aquarium. The little ones emerging from the egg have a size of about 1 mm. in length and ½ mm. in width. The shell is extremely pale, fragile, and transparent; and the animal itself is whitish with red viscera. They eat nothing the first hours and very little the first days.

Unfortunately, two days after their birth, I had to absent myself, and I put several individuals in a portable tank, which made the trip with me from Neuchâtel to Paris, then a little while later from Paris to Brittany. On my return to Switzerland, I could compare them with the specimens that had remained in a larger aquarium and at a different temperature. . . .

Let us note here the difference between the *Limnaea* which made the trip with me and those which I left in Neuchâtel, a difference that results from the conditions of the two tanks. In the original aquarium, the biology of *Limnaea Foreli* maintained itself perfectly among the new subjects, and had as a consequence the conservation of their morphological characteristics. The peculiarities of the shell and of the animal remained the same, the former sometimes taking a form slightly fatter, reminiscent of the variety *obtusiformis Piag.*, of the Lake of Geneva. By contrast, in the small portable tank, the complete absence of mud prevented the specimens from taking up their long stations in this substance, and thus permitted them to take on littoral habits, giving to the shell a form tending noticeably toward that of the typical *L. limosa*, that is, the ancestral species.

Such a fact cannot pass without comment. Notice first that this transformation takes place directly, without the animal passing through the sublittoral form, *Roszkowskiana*. This latter has been considered an intermediary between surface and deep-water races, but the direct return to type (*Foreli* → *limosa*) seems to confirm the theory according to which the sublittoral fauna would be an independent formation, rather than representing a continuous transformation between the other two bathymetric zones.*

I must add that, in conformity with the experiments of Forel on this subject, my specimens did not return entirely to the original type, and always exhibit a certain abyssal appearance. According to M. Rozkowski, it appears that this regression becomes complete after a certain number of generations.

One could multiply observations on the evolution in an aquarium of these forms derived from abyssal *Limnaea*. All these modifications are evidently very different, depending on the intensity of the factors, the form of the tank, the heat, the food, the season, etc. etc. But the important point to establish is the return to the original type, a fact which can have the highest philosophical importance.

We know that according to certain modern biologists of the Mendelian school, there would be a fundamental difference between fluctuating varieties and hereditary varieties, the former being produced only by the intensity of one or another preexisting factor, and the latter being determined by the appearance of a new factor. The former would correspond to varieties, and the latter would be the explanation for the genesis of species. . . .

---

*J. Piaget, "Nouvcaux dragages malacologiques de M. le Prof. Yung dans la faune profonde du Léman," *Zoologischer Anzeiger* 42 (1913): 216–223; J. Piaget, "Les mollusques sublittoraux du Léman recueillis par M. Prof. Yung," *Zoologischer Anzeiger* 42 (1913): 615–624.

Has the Mendelian Species an Absolute Value?*

1914

In a recent article in the *Zoologischer Anzeiger*, M. le Dr. Rozkowski does me the honor of criticizing my taxonomy of the *Limnaea* of the deep-water fauna of the Lake of Geneva.† I would certainly avoid taking up my pen if the question did not seem to me to have a more general interest. Purely specific discussions are always totally useless, and no one ever convinces anyone else, for lack of solid criteria. But M. Rozkowski attacks with a decisiveness denoting a remarkable search for scientific rigor in a domain so controversial as the philosophy of species. I have therefore tried to bring together some material to study the point in dispute as objectively as possible.

M. Rozkowski is a distinguished disciple of the Mendelian school. We know the remarkable results of recent researches of this school of biology, results that can be summed up as follows: there exists a fundamental difference between hereditary variations and variations called fluctuating. The former are determined by the appearance of a new factor in the habitat of the species, while the latter are only the result of the intensity of factors already present. The former alone are specific, while the latter are the property of simple varieties.

The Mendelian species is thus the ensemble of individuals presenting the same hereditary character or characters—subsisting in all milieux— and is most readily recognized by experiments, crossings, etc. Such is the criterion of M. Rozkowski and from this point of view he is perfectly correct: the deep-water *Limnaea* of the Lake of Geneva are only fluctuating varieties of littoral species.

But is this criterion absolute? I am going to try to show the contrary, and if I succeed my taxonomy will rest intact.

Let us begin with two isolated examples, taken from the facts of malacology. In central Europe two very closely related species of *Clausilia* are known, *Clausilia fimbriata* and *Clausilia laminata*, which differ in

---

*From J. Piaget, L'espèce mendelienne a–t–elle une voleur absolute? *Zoologischer Anzeiger*, Leipzig, 44: 328–331. Translated by H. E. G. and J. J. V.

†W. Rozkowski, A propos de Limnées de la faune profonde du lac Léman," *Zool. Anz.*, 43 (1913): 88–90.

certain stable characteristics of the folds of the aperture and of the clausilium. Everyone now considers them as two good species, and there is no difficulty in distinguishing between them (even though they sometimes live together). But paleontology reveals, in contrast, a long period during which, in a restricted region (Eastern Alps) these molluscs frequently exhibited transitory forms for which contemporary criteria provide no absolute basis of distinction.

What does the Mendelian school say? That only those characters are specific that are due to the appearance of a new factor, which implies a sudden transformation, and renders incomprehensible intermediaries distributed over several thousands of years. It should be added that even today one finds in Austria a variety which is quite intermediary, while in Switzerland, for example, the two species are always clearly separated. *Clausilia fimbriata* would therefore be a species in Switzerland and a fluctuating variety in Austria? The Mendelian species seems to me to be at fault.

I have taken this particular example, but there are many others. Let us cite the three *Tachea sylvatica*, *memoralis*, and *hortensis*, which were only fluctuating varieties at the time of the glacial invasions and for a long time after, and which are today so stable that their hybrids are not fertile. Let us cite *Pupa frumentum* and *variabilis*, *Xerophila candidula* and *striata*, *Planorbis rotundatus* and *spirobis*, etc., which are exactly in the same case.

Let us turn now to a second sort of exception, provided by the genera *Digeirydium* and *Belgrandia* (Paludinidae of the south of France). These groups of species, recognized if not as genera properly speaking at least as subgeneric categories, are spread over a vast enough scale (certainly the second) and exhibit very stable characters: spiral operculum and boursouflure belgrandienne. However, in a certain pond observed by M. Coutagne, one finds all the intermediaries between *Digeirydium* and *Bythinia* and I have confirmed the same fact at La Fontaine de Vaucluse between *Belgrandia gibba* and *Bythinella sorgica* (I will soon publish these observations), while everywhere else the limits are well defined and crossings unknown. Thus, in the environs of Geneva, where *Belgrandia marginata* lives with certain *Bythinella*, the genera remain independent. What can be said? That forms so dissimilar that they are considered as generically and a fortiori specifically distinct are only fluctuating variations because by chance one still finds one transitory form, completely exceptional? At that rate, there would be nothing but fluctuating variations in nature!

Let us turn to a third series of exceptions, much more general than the preceding, the ensemble of different faunules (restricted fauna) known under the name of residual fauna (fauna relicta). Let us take the phenomenon at the psychological moment, that is to say at its formation, for example in the lagoons of North Africa. In the great ponds progressively separated from the sea, there are produced different forms of brackish water, which gradually differentiate their species from their marine counterparts. These are evidently fluctuating varieties according to the Mendelian school, since if a junction with the sea is made again, the ancestral type reappears immediately by crossing (I have observed this fact in Brittany). But if the brackish pond remains autonomous and if it converts itself little by little (I emphasize "little by little" which is the negation of the fundamental difference between hereditary variations and fluctuating variations) into a freshwater lake, its fauna evolves slowly, as paleontology shows, and gives rise to species absolutely authentic and hereditary (fauna of the lakes of North Germany, etc.). It is clear that residual faunas are a major exception to the Mendelian laws of species.

This is even more striking in the case of insular faunas, which have become over a period of time absolutely autonomous. Here again, during the period of formation, none of the varieties which will later constitute the species and genera recognized by everyone, none of these varieties were hereditary (in the Mendelian sense) but all quite fluctuating. There was no new factor on the peninsula becoming a complete island and one could not understand the evolution of its fauna without progressive isolation. The proof of this is that islands recently detached from continents, like Great Britain, do not have an authochthonous fauna, while islands formed much longer ago are very differentiated zoologically (Ceylon, etc.). What does this mean if not that isolation is a factor more important than heredity (Mendelian), and here again our law fails?

Closer to home, cave fauna are another conclusive example. According to the Mendelian school, a grotto would constitute either an ensemble of "new factors" and all forms appearing in the milieu would invariably give rise to new species; or, on the contrary, the conditions as a whole offering no more than an intensification of existing factors,* the cave forms would be only fluctuating varieties. Unfortunately, one finds in the grottos, on the one hand, forms that are very differentiated specifically and even generically (*Zoospeum, Bythiospeum*, etc.) and, on the other hand, secondary varieties like certain Limnaea (*Limnaea truncatula* var. *spelaea*, etc.). Would this not be once more the rather considerable isolation of the grottos, which produces—just as in residual and insular fauna—variations at first fluctuating then hereditary and even generically distinct? It is self-evident.

This example brings us to the case in dispute, that is, to the case of the deep-water fauna. Here again, we observe species which, from the Mendelian point of view, are fluctuating varieties (M. Rozkowski has shown it very well for our *Limnaea*) and also very characteristic forms, like *Choanomphalus, Trachybaikala, Dybowskia*, etc., in the deep fauna of Lake Baikal, others of Lake Tanganyika, etc. Are there qualitative differences between the abyssal fauna of these lakes in relation to their littoral fauna, and the deep fauna of our Swiss lakes in relation to our littoral fauna?

Evidently not, but the former are much older than our lakes and here again, progressive isolation plays its capital role.

Here then are some materials that seem to me sufficient to prove that there is nothing absolute about the Mendelian species, and that it can be reduced, in certain cases, to a simple physiological species, or one produced by crossing.

*We see here how difficult it is to distinguish "new factors" from "factors already existing," a difficulty that I have emphasized elsewhere.

By what authority and in the name of which criteria would I then be forced to modify my taxonomy? I see none, and believe myself justified.

The experiments of M. Rozkowski are evidently very conclusive, but they are conducted outside the natural milieu of deep-water *Limnaea*. But we have seen in all our examples the role of isolation, a considerable role already illuminated by the work of Moritz Wagner. It is certainly on this criterion that we must base ourselves when the Mendelian school is defective. One sees, in effect, that so long as the abyssal *Limnaea* remain isolated from littoral forms, they can be considered as specifically distinct. This isolation is due naturally to distinct bathymetric distributions that prevent crossings and also to the fact the periods of reproduction of surface species are different from those of deep species.

If these factors remain as they are, it is permissible to predict that one day the *Limnaea* in dispute, very stable in their milieu, will be hereditary even when removed from their milieu, that is to say, they will acquire the fundamental character of a Mendelian species.

Neuchâtel (Switzerland), February 17, 1914.

PART II
Transitional Years: From Biology to Philosophy

INTRODUCTION

After his boyhood and early adolescence as a productive malacologist, Piaget went through a protracted period of religious, philosophical, and political searching. While this period corresponds well to Erikson's concept of moratorium, in Piaget's case it took a somewhat unusual form, productive in its own right and laying the basis for his later prodigious output: he wrote down almost everything he thought and published almost everything he wrote.

The first of several publications reflecting the musings of this period was "Bergson and Sabatier" (1914). This was a critical essay mainly intended to show the remarkable analogies between the two authors, but also showing us how early and how protracted were the preoccupations of this period of Piaget's life.*

We include in this section, three selections, which we have handled quite differently. The prose poem *La Mission de l'Idée* (1916) is translated in full, although rather freely. The novel *Recherche* is fully summarized rather than translated. The article "Biology and War" is translated in full and exactly.

---

* J. Piaget, "Bergson et Sabatier." The works discussed are A. Sabatier, *Esquisse d'une philosophie de la religion d'après la psychologie et l'histoire*, 2nd ed. (Paris: Fischbacher, 1897); H. Bergson, *Creative Evolution*.

The Mission of the Idea*

1915

INTRODUCTORY NOTES

The Mission of the Idea is a long prose poem written at the height of the First World War to castigate a Europe afflicted with a conservative spirit, nationalism, egoism, pride, and inertia. These are the evils seen as killing the Idea. As the work progresses, the identity of the Idea seems to change, or rather, the particulars chosen to exemplify it: justice, equality, women's rights, free expression of the human spirit in all its diversity, faith in Jesus, faith in the people, self-discipline, struggle for the good, peace, socialism, and so on. The Idea is all these things, and above all, the never-ending movement of thought toward them. The author expresses over and over his belief in the power of ideas, they "lead the world," govern action. If we must sum up his message in a few words, we can call it the outcry of youth against the smug hypocrisy of the Church and the bourgeoisie during the long suffering of the war, and a romantic, moralistic belief in Christian socialism.

Our translation is very free and considerably compressed, varying from about one-third the original to full length. Our omissions are simply intended to reduce repetition; we have not indicated them with ellipses because we wanted to retain the feeling of a flowing emotional expression. In a few places, our rendition is extremely compressed or too free to represent the original language fairly; in these cases we have put our summary in square brackets; within these brackets, however, there may be a quotation indicated that stays closer to the original. In reducing the translation, we have tended to eliminate a number (but not all) of the metaphoric passages using landscape and the emotional experience of a lonely traveller who reappears from time to time, and to retain passages more directly expressing ideas. Certain compressions may have made the tone of our version slightly less religious than the original.

Two words occur often and give special difficulty: *âme* is most literally translated as *soul*, but it does not necessarily have a supernatural connotation, it can also mean the spirit or essence of the person: we have sometimes translated it as soul, sometimes as spirit; *égoïsme* in French means both *self-*

---

*From J. Piaget, *La mission de l'idée*. Lausanne, Édition la Concorde (couverture, 1916), 68 pp. Translated by H. E. G. and J. J. V.

centeredness and *selfishness*, whereas in English the first of these meanings is more often intended: we have usually translated it as egoism, letting a slight ambiguity stand.

Hymn to the Idea

I

The Idea surges from the depths of our being. The Idea overthrows kings and priests, raises the masses, decides the outcome of battles, guides the whole of humanity. Everything is Idea, comes from the Idea, returns to the Idea. The Idea is an organism, is born, grows, and dies like organisms, renews itself ceaselessly. "In the beginning was the Idea," say the mysterious words of the Christian cosmogeny.

II

Think of the force of the idea of freedom, of the untold numbers who have fought for it, of all those giants of the Idea who have imposed on whole peoples the plans of their fertile brains. The same for the idea of country, of justice. These ideas are indestructible and yet always new. To the blind the Idea seems unchanging. Poor and cold, seen from the outside, no one who tries can grasp it all, so great is its richness, so infinite its diversity.

III

Woe unto him, be he young or old, who has not lived for the Idea, for country, liberty, humanity, justice, religion. At the end of time those who have lived for the Idea will be together with God, all in peace. Woe unto him who will have deserted the side of the Idea.

IV

Indignantly, revolted, the young man rejects hypocrisy, and egoism, seized by the Idea he is immensely free. This is the truly moral period of life. Later the compromises begin. But here and there a hero rises. Genius is the crystalization of the Idea in a man, the hero abandons himself to the Idea, gives vent to his rage against all that is mean, bourgeois, orthodox, conservative, in a word, reactionary.

V

Jesus is the Idea made flesh. The Idea grew in him, sometimes he was seized by sacred indignation, sometimes by pity and love. At last he understood the immensity of his own heroism to come, he knew that the Idea must destroy everything that seems respectable, legitimate, established. And this knowledge made him compassionate, made him suffer, for life for the Idea is struggle, renunciation, agony. A normal existence is such a life, but no one can attain it, only Jesus has realized the Idea.

VI

The Idea leads the world. Action is the servant of the Idea, the crude instrument with which our limited nature must be satisfied, the means toward the advent of that glorious end which is the Idea. In the words he must use, the poet expresses only a small part of the beauty within him, killing the rest. Likewise action only captures the Idea in one of its aspects, and thus destroys the beauty of the whole. Progress springs from the brains of wise men, not from the arms of men of action. The Revolution was made in Rousseau's contemplative walks and not in meetings or uprisings in the streets. When a man of action dies his work lives on just long enough to produce a few new men of action, paler and weaker than he. When a man of thought dies, his work sets off a thousand men of action, all armed with a new strength.

VII

Cursed be the ruling classes, the orthodox, the reactionaries, the utilitarians, the sceptics. The ideal lives only by destroying one after another each particular idea, because each is only a fragmentary and provisional view wrenched from the whole. Pride and egoism lead those who hold power to cling to what they have, to what exists, and thus they fetter the idea and betray their brothers. When the idea is on the point of affirming itself it destroys all equilibria, threatens those who are established in the past. Cursed be all those who fetter the idea.

VIII

The winter traveler sees the cold, still world around him, the snow-flakes falling crazily. By turns he senses the emptiness and sadness of the world, feels himself filled with the painful bitterness of his solitude, is united in an immense sympathy with the snow around him, finds the calm of the idea that brings him closer to God. We fear that our efforts may be all in vain, we do not see the ideal, but we construct it nevertheless. Such is life for the idea, painful, and fecund, for to suffer is truly to live.

IX

Sometimes, the great ascent which humanity pursues generation after generation seems to halt. The idea is dying. The lonely traveler is overcome with horror, feels all resistance in him melt, becomes suddenly a weak and suffering being shaken by the passion of his fright. When a facile lie kills the idea, the people, leaderless, rush toward carnage and catastrophe, then ask who is to blame for this madness and crime. The voice of orthodoxy tells the people, stop, do not change what is, conserve the heritage of the past. The shapeless flock of conservatives accept, agree. Insane, to believe that progress has come to a halt! Selfish, to cling to the comfortable nest of the past! Down with these hypocrites! They are the ones responsible for the faltering of progress, inertia and crises, the misery of the people, war among nations. They are the ones who make the evil that kills the world, the enfeeblement of the idea.

1914

X

It is not the politicians who are guilty of the war, not the peoples, not even the military fanatics, poor brutes, not the narrow patriots. It is everyone who has fettered the idea. To let the idea act, or rather to make it act, is to render impossible crises such as today's, because the Idea and life are naturally directed toward love and sacrifice. It is the conservative spirit which is guilty, which has arrested progress, forbidden work for world peace, maintained armies, destroyed faith and the dignity of man. Without the conservative spirit the people would not have remained in their misery, they would not have been faced with an obstinate bourgeoisie, ignorant of its duties. It is the conservative spirit which is guilty because without it woman would be equal to man, and never would the horrors of this century have withstood her. The conservative spirit killed the idea, it is the cause of war.

XI

The good is life. Life is a force which penetrates matter, organizes it, introduces harmony, love. Above the cells that it animates it creates the beings which link them, above these individual beings it creates the social beings, species. Above human groups it creates nations and above nations it creates Humanity. Everywhere life brings harmony, solidarity in the new and vaster units that it creates. The force of altruism and union, that is life. The good is the free action of this force. The good is not the good of the individual, or even of any of the higher groups. The struggle for existence is not the essence of evolution: the struggle results not from the action of the living force but from the encroachments of individuals or societies on the force of solidarity. To hasten evolution is to do good.

XII

Life is good, but the individual pursuing his self-interest renders it bad. Every individual instinctively, unconsciously serves its species, serves life. But self-interest may lead the individual to keep for himself some of the vital energy which he might bring to others. One day intelligence appeared, illuminated life, opened new domains to mankind, and through him God thought to attain his ends. But here again self-interest appeared, now armed with reason. Life is threatened, instinct evolves and is transformed into a sacred feeling which sets man on the right path again, and brings him back to God: moral consciousness. But man, having tasted of the fruits of the tree of life, remains caught in this conflict between self-interest and renunciation.

XIII–XVI

[The author continues in the same vein, condemning both individualism and collectivism so long as they are not turned toward the higher good, and further evolution of absolute humanity; progress is the growth of the human spirit, taking ever more embracing forms, first family, then tribes, clans, countries. In the divine symphony, "humanity is not a mere sum of individuals, it is the greater whole which goes beyond and coordinates the multiple resonances."]

XVII

There is an egoism of countries, even more terrible than that of individuals. It is immense, the harm it can do is frightful. Like the individual, the nation is capable of beauty, sublimity. And like the individual, it can only attain true life by sacrifice, by the force of the idea, harmony with life. A sign of progress: 1914 has shown us the highest manifestation of the sacrifice to duty, accomplished by the whole soul of one country, the Belgian nation. Let us all reject narrow national self-interest, have faith in a distant future. Just as with individuals, only nations that have lived renunciation and idealism will contribute to the construction of that absolute humanity which calls us onward.

XVIII

As he enters into life the young man has a force which nothing can withstand, a power of potentialities which, if ever realized, would uplift life, nourish the idea. He is not yet soiled, his virgin spirit is not yet crusted over with scorn or hate. But evil tells him, enjoy life, develop some one of your special talents and use it to seek pleasures more intense than you have yet known. The youth is deflected from his true course by pleasures unchained, and emotions once natural and sweet become passions both furious and false. But all is not lost, passion does not kill at once, he can turn away from it and back to the true use of his energies in the cause of life. That is why we exalt passion, because beneath its diabolical skin we sense the divine fruit.

XIX

[Against the conservative spirit, the partner of passion in the arresting of progress. It arises not from external causes but from our selfishness, lust for pleasure, intellectual pride, laziness.]

XX

There are maladies that are signs of life. The child on the point of becoming a man is irresolute and weak, his soul is in turmoil, painful no matter how beautiful its mysterious source. From this crisis comes a mature fruit. Thus is born humanity. After our present crisis, the murderous war, all humanity will be able to feel pride in having at last matured. An eternal remorse will weigh on us all if we do not act, because we have passed through and seen what has never before been seen. Our fathers sinned through ignorance. We, we know, and that condemns us. The war has taught us: the great criminal is conservatism. That is what raises us up and enlarges our duties.

The Betrayal of Christianity

XXI–XXII

[Condemns the churches for their orthodoxy, conservatism, for their failure to oppose the onrush of war. "It is you who are red with blood that flows in floods, it is on your sons that will weigh the consequences of the war. If the conservative spirit is responsible for the war, it is you who have incarnated it." Inveighs against the selfish quest for individual salvation, dreaming of heaven and forgetting earth.]

XXIII

Dogma has killed the Idea of Christianity. We can only discover reality by constantly destroying the dogmas of the past, by accepting the transitory, symbolic character of all our explanations. The Church refuses this path, because it is in the nature of human pride and individualistic egoism to believe what one has invented. Like a snake shedding its hardened skin every spring, ridding itself of this hindrance to growth, let us every hour reject the dogma of the past: it kills the élan in us.

XXIV

Power, possession, worldly concerns corrupt pure impulses such as the love of a man for a woman, or the pursuit of the idea. Idolatry is the result. Like other books inspired by the Idea, the Bible was written by men, with a breath of the divine; the Church has made it a unique, intangible book, dead.

XXV

[In praise of quiet humility, against the false pride of the Church.]

XXVI

Charity and forgiveness, that is the essence of Christian morality. "Judge not," Jesus said, but the Church rests its influence on sanctions and on the authoritarian use of an outdated, accusatory morality. Of atheists the Church has made criminals. Instead of appreciating the courage of these men, whose life without hope offers an example of unrewarded work, of selfless sacrifice, of sublime struggle, the Church has judged, condemned, abused. The self-serving, prideful use of its powers, especially moral sanctions, stems from the egoism of the conservative spirit, the quest for salvation, the immobility of dogma, the death of the Idea.

XXVII–XXX

[Against prayer for personal gain or personal salvation. Did Jesus pray for himself? Against the egoism and smugness of the Church. The way a man uses his power reveals his quality, prayer is the most glorious of all forces; in abusing it we plunge toward eternal death. Against fear-driven ritual, for the beauty of life for the Idea. Jesus was an idealist, a creator, a rebel, against orthodoxies. Yet in his name the Church has succeeded in making people fear that the wrath of God will descend on them if they stray from orthodoxy. Skillfully playing on the motives of fear, and desire for love and forgiveness, the Church has triumphed. But we can reject this "apparatus of death" and return to Christ as he really is. "Let us be better than the Church!" We can condemn all these abuses of the Church, and the bourgeoisie's errors of orthodoxy and self-interest, and at the same time, like Christ, forgive our enemies. "That is a lesson of the war: understand everything in order to forgive everything."]

The New Birth

XXXI

It was a stormy night, thunder and lightning shook the forests and the mountains. A man lost, frightened and trembling, sought his way in the solitude of the night, ran and then collapsed at the foot of a boulder. Little by little the storm abated, the air cleared, and between two clouds spread the first rays of dawn. The phantoms of night dissipated, and an immense hope lighted up the plain. The man rose, worshipped, and went away.

Such is the condition of Christianity caught in the stormy night of death. Such could be the day, if there is still time, a complete new birth. New blood would run through its veins, its heart beat more violently. The idea resuscitated would replenish its spirit and strengthen its arm. Let us rise up, bestir ourselves, throw ourselves into the unknown: it is to reawaken us. We will study the road and take up our journey with new certainty.

This reawakening is essential for the Church. It must recognize its sins, repent, and beg forgiveness of Christ. And who will accomplish this miracle? It is the Idea that will overturn dogmatism, overwhelm the conservative spirit, wipe out egoism. It is the Idea which is the engine of life, it is the Idea which will animate our corpse. Let us restore the idea, give up our old conceptions. From the new theory will spring action regenerated, the reconciliation of the Church and the people, the Church and thought. For the idea leads the world.

XXXII–XXXIII

[Christianity contains latent forces within it that can save the world, if only we can break through the dead shell to the obscure seed within, to the Idea. Dogma and superstition keep us from the reality that is Christ. The deeper we go in the search for truth the better we find God: "reason is not made to fight against the heart." The appearance of prayerful humility may simply express fear of the unknown and a stupefying self-abasement; better to doubt and reflect before praying, to have the courage to place truth before contentment. Scepticism often only means a respect for the truth; the search for truth is the only hope of escape from the thicket.]

XXXIV

Morality must be in constant flux. What was good yesterday is not today, what is good for one cannot be for another. Through its own evolution morality creates the soul of Humanity, and who does not participate in this flux, this work, must perish. Jesus is the one fixed point in this ascent. Humanity will only be itself as it is built on complete human souls, just as our souls are only built on the cells of our body. Jesus is the only absolute, and everything else must change. The first idea that we must suppress is moral sanction, for it is scandalous to the modern conscience. Because Jesus showed that few would be chosen, we have attributed the death of the sinner, not to a blind and necessary law against which God struggles, although powerless against it, but to God himself, rendered incapable of forgiving freely, and whose charity is not worth ours.

XXXV

[When we are not ready to sacrifice our possessions and comforts in order to do good, we do not give up our higher instincts. Instead, we construct a new ideal, a compromise between our aspirations and our egoism, legitimizing our conduct. And we think ourselves good. Very often, our doctrines are nothing but vast apologies for one or another of our vices. The Church is like that.]

XXXVI

In the search for rational truth there is a higher beauty which is almost religious. When the little child reaches the age where his curiosity becomes acceptable, he asks himself questions that his parents have until then evaded; and when he has more or less grasped the mystery himself, one evening his mother reveals to him the secrets of his birth. In his sacred turmoil, he feels all at once a pure and noble joy in this true knowledge and a grateful reverence for the beautiful truth. He feels himself grown because of what he has just learned, and better

able truly to live. For this is the first time that he rises to the sublimity of the human quest, to the point where knowledge and feeling
mingle in a religious act.

Such is the nature of metaphysics. Metaphysics is the supreme
manifestation of the idea, so long as it keeps a living sympathy and does
not become an arid dogmatism. In the effort to unite faith and reason
the believer expands his soul, he adds a new element, the force of
synthesis, which is a new energy marching toward the great goal. Thus
he achieves a supreme joy: the esthetic of reason is one hundred times
greater than the esthetic of sense. But this joy is nothing, one should
not pursue it. In the postwar world, once one has understood that the
Idea leads the world and that Christianity has abdicated, one has a great
duty: to throw oneself into the pursuit of a truth purer than we now live,
for that is the only way for the new birth to begin.

XXXVII

[The war raises once again the problem of evil. The Church has
many ways of justifying war. First, the barbarous notion of God-country,
which actually worships war. Second, a type of charity in which one
admits that war is bad, but it is an evil intended to punish the sinner.
Finally, the war is a method of education used by God. Let anyone who
thinks so visit a burned village or spend even one anguished night
hiding in the woods, and he will change his mind about such divine
pedagogy. Who knows, of all God's suffering, impotent before evil, perhaps the greatest is for him to see what the Church has done with his
immense love.]

XXXVIII

[Here the author includes the *Dies Irae*, Catholic prayer for the dead,
interspersed with some of his own prose, ending: "When will the God of
love and pity destroy the 'holy' God of vengeance? What an hour of
anguish under this heavy sky! Oh! how beautiful tomorrow's ideal!"]

The Idea and the People

XXXIX

The Church has betrayed the people. Jesus was a son of the people,
and if he wanted to save the world, it was by and for the people. Jesus
told us to look for the kingdom of God and his justice. But the Church
has taken the Idea of salvation and distorted it to mean individual, personal, salvation. That is why our Christiantity is bourgeois, why the
people regard the priest with horror. That is why socialism, a grandiose
and naive ideal, wants to be a religion but can only vegetate, because the
Christians divert what would be its force. And it is the death of the Idea

that has done this. Christian dogma has betrayed the people, and the people have deserted the Church.

The people are the force of tomorrow. Apparently inert, they contain all the potentialities that will arise one day. The war will give them birth.

XL

[A list of all the social evils about which the Church has done nothing: poverty, inequality, war, inhuman work, child labor, oppression of women, the monotony of the life of the people.]

XLI

Feminism is the duty of the Church, because everything that touches the health of society must be its mission. The problem of feminism is badly formulated. One speaks of rights when it is a matter of obligations. All contemporary society is built on this error. One enumerates the rights of the individual, the rights of the people, the rights of women, and the rights of liberty, when one should speak of the duties of the individual, the duties of the people, of the actions of women, and of responsibility. A duty presupposes a right, while a right does not presuppose duties. A duty is a real force, which wants to affirm itself and cut a road for itself. A right is only an empty place in which the first occupant can just as well be a bad man as a good man.

Woman should not demand rights. It is her duty that she pursues, her duty to regenerate the ruins of society into which the conservative spirit of man has precipitated it.

Such should be the Christian point of view. On obligations must be based the world to come, and no longer on rights. Men have made an infamous commerce of politics, corrupting countries; in their insanity they have not prepared a peace; with their narrow logic they have neglected the laws of philanthropy; they are incapable of life, of morality, and of beauty as soon as they are alone at the task.

It is from women's suffrage that will come peace, the death of the politics of interest, patriotic idealism, humanitarian laws, social regeneration, the uplifting of the proletariat. Women will make impossible, once they are conscious of their rights, a gigantic crisis that destroys today everything that was yesterday.

Such is the ideal, and an ideal once stated becomes a duty. Feminism might even compromise the grace of women and the tranquility of the family, that a duty would remain a duty and feminism remain the school of sacrifice to the idea, of painful struggle in the vanguard of progress.

But the Church, by its narrowness, has joined with conservatism, to struggle once more against the good and against life.

XLII

Science and the people are always as one. It is the same fault of the Church that strikes both. It is orthodox pride which has opposed its dogma to science at the same time as it opposed its morality to the public weal. It is Christian egoism which has refused science every just concession, at the same time as it has refused the people their most essential needs. Thus, now without the Church science and the people unite. Modern thought tends toward the relief of suffering humanity, as the people rising tend toward giving power to science. Science is becoming socialist, and socialism scientific.

And the Church, which should have been the link between these forces of tomorrow is a thousand times outstripped and its former slaves walk over it. Oh salutary humiliation, just reordering of things, which, if it was not demanded by destiny, would resemble the terrible sanction which the Church imputes to God!

But all is not lost, if the Church sees its errors. Let it humiliate itself, and let us see that superb event: science and the people uniting once again, to regenerate the Church and to greet Christ the eternal redeemer.

XLIII

Christian optimism is base and cowardly. The conservative spirit rests on optimism. To enjoy shamelessly what one has, to deny the existence of misery, to say that all is well, is easy, if one does nothing except for oneself. This optimism is also extended to an egoistical belief in the pleasures that lie ahead in paradise. But this was not the way of Jesus. He saw the evil around him, he believed in progress, and trusted in God, without knowing what awaited him in the heavens. He believed in immortality, but through good works.

XLIV

When the wheat grows in the springtime, the little green shoots stand straight on the soil with the vigor of youth. When the wind and the rain sweep the countryside or the sun dries out the earth, they engage each other in a struggle to the death, so hard is existence and so necessary is strife. And in the fray, the weak die, the strong suffer, and life diminishes itself. But when repose follows the blind thrusting, when the survivors of the struggle bloom, no longer harming anyone, then harmony reigns and the harvest is great.

Thus will come the peace.

Men have kept women in bondage, the bourgeoisie has oppressed the people, conservatism has killed life, orthodoxy the Idea, mean men have dirtied their countries, and nations are detested. And in this great disorder, a clamor is everywhere rising, groans, cries of hate or songs of hope. The mass rises and falls, gigantic convulsions shake the surface, followed by calm.

But it is the august growth of life, in which tomorrow's harvest slowly matures.

Courage then! Nothing is wrong, so long as the Idea lives. Let us rise up and build anew. A day will come when the opposed forces will reach equilibrium, when this chaos will give place to a harmonious organism, palpitating with beauty. That is the goal of Christianity.

When women will have risen, the people will again become aware of their duties. Nothing will resist them. In the people lies the future.

XLV

The Church of tomorrow will not be a church. True communion, that of sympathy and good works, will unite believers in one identical advance toward the ideal goal. And each believer, in his most intimate being, will construct the rational edifice which best suits him, which best contains the nucleus of life his heart will feel. For every individual there will be a doctrine, and their infinite diversity and their contradictions will forever prevent living ideas from becoming automatized, or from struggling amongst each other.

XLVI

. . . When the idea is reborn, every man now suffering in the shadows will find his place in the vast harmony which by its crescendo will make life grow, so high that it will see God. But the rebirth of the idea requires the help of everyone. Metaphysics is not an aristocratic art. The scientist, who finds hypotheses, must build over them a grand edifice that can contain them; the Christian, who in the depths of his heart has felt a life, must assimilate it by an interpretation which justifies it; the moral man, who wants a rule of conduct to govern his life, must construct an idea to justify it. The special mark of each man must be his idea and from these ideals, numerous as the cells, the true idea will come forth, like the soul from the body.

Oh! that the tears shed during the war bear this beautiful fruit: the new birth of Christianity.

For that is the mission of the Idea.

Biology and War*

1918

INTRODUCTORY NOTES

By 1918 Piaget had established himself as a biologist and also as a young man concerned with social issues, ready to take up his pen to write against war and for socialism. These were the two great issues claiming the passions of youth. The First World War was ending, with millions of soldiers dead, and the Bolsheviks, having overthrown the Czar, were establishing the world's first socialist government. The editors of *Zofingue*, journal of a Swiss student society, had recently opened their pages to a debate on pacifism, and they invited Piaget to write an article for them.

"Biology and War" can be read in two ways. As an expression of social opinion it is clearly antiwar and opposed to the doctrine that war is an inevitable consequence of human nature. As a discussion of the relation between heredity and environment, and of the mechanisms of evolutionary adaptation, the paper takes up issues that Piaget had already written about and that were to occupy much of his attention from then on.

The paper is interesting as an early statement of his third alternative, neither hereditarian nor environmentalist, neither Darwinian nor Lamarckian, and for his insistence upon altruism as a valid biological concept. His opposition to simple instinctivism and individualism, taken together, leads him also to reject Freud's image of man as guided by an instinctual bundle of irrational, egocentric impulses. But Piaget's rationalism in this paper is far from easy optimism. The peace of reason is not guaranteed by any direct biological fiat: it is simply part of the human condition to struggle for it.

You have asked me for a few lines on biology and war. If you want an article, no, I do not have the necessary documentation, and I do not believe that a naturalist will be able to say anything on the subject for a long time to come. It would take an objectivity and a detachment he cannot have. He can try literature, since it is alive and aims at human

*From J. Piaget, La biologie et la guerre. *Feuille centrale de la Société suisse de Zofingue* (zentralblatt des schweizerischen Zofinger-Vereins), 58: 374–380. Translated by H. E. G. and J. J. V.

and not scientific truth, but he cannot yet integrate his attitude as a human being and as a scientist. He is too much a human being to adopt an a priori attitude which would go against his loyalty to scientific knowledge. Romain Rolland's Nicolai in *Demain*, writing from the depths of a prison, certainly has the right to put his biology at the service of his ideal, but we who are not suffering and are looking for an answer in tranquility, we at least ought to keep our heads. So, if you are asking me for an opus, I refuse; if you just want my own modest opinion, I accept, for everything obliges us to search . . .*

In order to decide if war is or is not a part of the internal logic of biological evolution, I think it is a mistake to look at the problem from an a posteriori point of view, to restrict oneself to the facts and wonder at what point war is implied in them. For the facts are many and involved, and can, in themselves, be used to justify any number of theories. Darwin saw in the facts the struggle for life, struggle against the environment and struggle against competitors. From these findings, he drew only a biological doctrine, but it also contained a moral: one that has, since then, not been overlooked! Well, there is nothing conclusive about an argument like this until it has been shown that natural selection is the only possible process in evolution and, once this has been done, ethics can always maintain it has nothing to do with life. But let us stick to life, since we are discussing it. Kropotkine also looked at the facts, but with very different eyes than Darwin's. He saw mutual aid in nature and by virtue of this, thought himself justified in condemning war. In biological ethics, everything can be justified by the facts. From Guyau to Nietzsche, from Bain and Stuart Mill to Kropotkin, from Spencer to Cresson and Le Dantec, all of them appealed to the facts, and all of them were right. War is, love is, therefore war like love is good . . .*

Let us, however, look at things from an a priori point of view and reason on the basis of a sort of "pure biology" as mathematical physics is to experimental physics, and define the normal laws of evolution. Without worrying about the perpetual obstacle reality presents to the free play of evolution or about any of man's subjective aspirations, let us see if war is or is not included in this normal evolution. Only then will we have answered the question before us. We deal not with a moral problem, therefore, but with a biological one, and our solution will have no import for ethics unless ethics itself postulates that life and the good are identical.

Now, everything leads us to expect that the idea of a pure evolution like this will coincide with that which is deepest in man's consciousness—the materialists have taught us without knowing they were working on the side of idealism—which simply reflects the intimate physical-chemical reactions of a living organism. And, what is still more profound, moral aspirations.

Let us go on to the proof.

There are only two ways of justifying war by biology: by showing that Darwinism alone explains evolution or, if this theory is proved false, by reducing Lamarckism to the narrow conception Le Dantec gave to "functional assimilation."

*Piaget's ellipsis—trans.

It seems obvious to me that Darwinism, taken by itself as the complete explanation of evolution, justifies war. By this I mean neo-Darwinism, which denies the heredity of acquired traits and, thus, the influence of the environment, and which sees competition between individuals and entire species as the whole mechanism of evolution. Competition *is* struggle, and here there is no room for argument. It is true that a doctrine of harmony can be based on Weissmannism and related theories. Between the hereditary "particles," whatever they may be, a certain coordination which has an influence on relationships between individuals can be demonstrated. But this factor would necessarily be minimized by competition, since by definition no new adaptation could be transmitted by heredity. On the other hand, as Freudian psychoanalysis has done, one could see in the transmitted germ plasm a psychological force, one could call it *libido*, and show how the "sublimation" of such an unconscious energy leads to love, art, and religion. But this position can be held only at the price of a rather unscientific finalism (if one starts from neo-Darwinist hypotheses).

Conclusion: either particles and libido are mechanisms and, with selection alone being involved, only egoism and struggle can be deduced; or else they are entities, and we are off biological ground.

But natural selection cannot explain evolution. Weissmann himself had to admit this late in life. The heredity of acquired traits is an experimental fact. If the value of Brown Séquard's well-known experiments can be questioned, it seems difficult to doubt the findings of experiments in animal psychology: Hachet Souplet, by training cats, formed habits that were transmitted to later generations. If life continually escaped action of the environment by isolating the germ plasm for the thousands of centuries it has existed, it would be a miracle. It is already enough of a miracle without our adding that . . .*

We can then decide in favor of Lamarckism without any qualms, without excluding natural selection as a secondary or accidental factor.

Now, Lamarckism makes all of evolution amount to environmental influence, an influence which creates habits and preserves itself by heredity. This supposes, then, the stability of these new characteristics, once acquired; this in turn supposes assimilation, and Le Dantec, in basing all of biology on this factor, was only making the tenets of Lamarckism explicit. Assimilation is that property possessed by every living thing to reproduce a substance identical to itself. Thus, assimilation is a conservative factor and nothing else. The environment and not the living creature, or anything in it, is the source of variation.

Now, by the very fact that an individual assimilates, he is engaged in a struggle against his environment. Everything around him tends to act on him, deform him, while alone and withstanding the opposition of the whole universe, he tends to preserve his individuality. This is the most formidable struggle imaginable. And it is not limited to a struggle against the environment. All that is not self is hostile, and individuals of my own kind and of other species are included in this nonself, throughout the whole of life. Le Dantec has gradually exposed all the consequences for egoism of the struggle against the environment; he has gone through all the stages. Even the beings we love leave their

*Piaget's ellipsis—trans.

imprint on us, conquering us by the mark they leave, and in so doing, they diminish us. Instead of assimilating them according to our own formula, we "imitate" them as the eye is obliged to "imitate" the ray of light that strikes it, as an animal species "imitates" the new condition to which it is forced to adapt, as protoplasm "imitates" the toxin injected into it.

Conclusion: egoism is the basis of every society. Struggle is therefore the internal logic of life; war is necessary. Darwinism gives it a roughly legitimate status. Lamarckism, with subtler arguments, arrives at the same conclusions.

But if we analyze this "functional assimilation" at the basis of Le Dantec's system, we find a flaw which explains these deductions. This flaw consists of making assimilation and "imitation" inversely proportional to each other, in order to make a synthesis between them. While this conception holds a profound truth for the phenomena involved in digestion (assimilation being at its maximum and imitation at its minimum), it takes little reflection to see that just the opposite is true with regard to psychological phenomena. One is the more oneself the better one understands one's environment while, for Le Dantec, one is, at the most, either original but stupid, or intelligent but lacking in personality. This analysis could be taken much further to show that, in every conscious phenomenon, assimilation and imitation are in direct proportion to each other. More than that, I maintain that this is the case for all phenomena essential to life, but I cannot expand this idea without going into the details of a mechanism too specialized for our purposes here.

From this moment, our point of view on war changes completely. As far as intellectuality is concerned, understanding things does permit real assimilation (as common sense already indicates). As far as ethics are concerned, only love, *caritas*, permits the full development of the self. As far as society is concerned, only cooperation and peace contribute to the good of social groups.

I will stop here. I have said enough to make it understood that, the more one examines the mechanism of life, the more one discovers that love and altruism—that is, the negation of war—are inherent in the nature of living beings. Only later complications due to environmental inertia, and thus, competition, force living creatures to a restricted assimilation, that is, egoism, stupidity, struggle, and, in the human species, war. To struggle against war is therefore to act according to the logic of life against the logic of things, and that is the whole of morality.

20 January 1918 Jean Piaget*

---

*Mr. Jean Piaget is not a member of the Zofingue Society. The readers of the *Feuille centrale* will certainly be interested in a short study of so timely a question as "Biology and War." It is for this reason that we called upon Mr. Piaget, who is very knowledgeable about biological theories—[The Editors of Zofingue].

Recherche*

1918

INTRODUCTORY NOTES

It may seem strange that Piaget's first book should be a prose poem and his second a novel. But *Recherche* is not a novel in the usual sense of the word. It belongs to the same tradition of introspection as the works of two other Swiss writers, Rousseau and Amiel. *Recherche* means both "search" and "re-search"; the book is a personal journal in the form of a novel, having as its sole object, like all such journals, the ego.

The ego of Sebastian, the hero and only character of the book, is entirely absorbed in working out a few fundamental preoccupations: the relations between science and faith, the value of science as a theory of knowledge, the relations between science and morality, and, finally, social salvation.

The novel is quite classically divided into three parts: prelude to crisis, the crisis itself, and the reconstruction which follows the crisis and discovery of truth. Sebastian, who had previously been satisfied with a vague biological philosophy consisting of a universal sympathy for all life, experiences his own crisis of identity at the moment when the occidental world is collapsing in the tragedy of the First World War. He is conscious of this connection between his individual crisis and that of the world in which he lives; this gives a certain dramatic force to the first part of the novel. "Intelligence was thought to be the power that could lead humanity; we see it reduced to serving passions." Sebastian wants to remain, in the words of Romain Rolland, "above the battle." But there is nothing firm to which he can attach himself.

His need for logic tears him away from the churches, and directs him toward philosophy. "For he had always a faith that the power of reason was capable of breaking out of the circle of experience." But the philosophers disappoint him too, one after the other.

These metaphysical disappointments bring Sebastian back to science, in which he has an "unshakeable faith." This gives rise to a first formulation of the idea of the circle of sciences, which assures knowledge its own foundations, without external recourse.

*From J. Piaget, *Recherche*, Lausanne, Édition La Concorde, 210 pp. Summary, H. E. G. and J. J. V.

At the same time, the war obliges Sebastian to search for social salvation. He sees it in a scientific socialism, where an objective synthesis of scientific knowledge would give the objective laws of nature, of life, and of society.

Such is the crisis. Sebastian, alternating between phases of mania and depression, struggles to reconstruct a valid system. He begins from the biological problem of species, around which everything seems to organize itself: evolution, morality, and knowledge.

Then the "blinding discovery": "science gives knowledge of good and of evil." It can explain everything, but it says nothing about values. It is faith that speaks of them. Faith is not knowledge, it is action. The contradiction between faith and knowledge is thus resolved. The final phase of the search is reconstruction: science gives the laws of the world, faith is its engine; in obeying these two forces, social salvation is the equilibrated result.

What follows is a chapter by chapter resumé of the entire novel.

Part I: Prelude to Crisis

Chapter I. The hero of this novel is Sebastian, a young man between 16 and 20, born a Protestant in French-speaking Switzerland. The fundamental problem of his adolescence is the opposition between science and faith. For him, faith drowns reason in a troubled mysticism, while science is obedience to a scholasticism that suffocates liberty and truth. The difficult task Sebastian sets himself is the reconciliation of faith and science.

Chapter II. Sebastian observes that believers are numerous, especially among Catholic youth. But their faith is not real. For some, faith is life and life is faith. For others, faith is a remedy for doubt. For still others, faith is either pure snobbery or political necessity. Finally, there are the mystics for whom faith is pure revelation. But this revelation must come through the church, sole depository of true faith, and its guarantor through dogma. This dogma appears in the form of a symbolism clearly distinguished from discursive reason, to which it is opposed.

Chapter III. The reconciliation of science and faith is the origin of the disequilibrium of the twentieth century, just as the opposition between faith and philosophy troubled the eighteenth century. Dogma is the order of existence that mixes good and evil, while faith is the order of values and of life. The question is, to understand the justification of values. For the Catholic Church, values rest on the authority of the Church. This authority comes from Jesus Christ who is God. But Jesus is God because dogma affirms it. Thus, as had already been pointed out by Rousseau, the authority of the Church rests on a vicious circle:

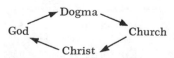

For the rest, since Kant, it has been known that all metaphysics is impossible. Faith cannot be based on reason. Pascal sought to base faith on the history of the Jewish people, and Lamennais on the consensus of nations. As for the neo-Thomism of the University of Louvain, it separates science and faith as being of two different orders.

Chapter IV. Sebastian therefore no longer believes in a revealed God, because a God who leaves man in ignorance of good and evil can do nothing against evil. At this point, Sebastian discovers the book by the pastor Monod, *To Believers and Atheists* and he discovers the essential idea that God struggles together with us. But Sebastian comes up against the difficulty of the multiplicity of Protestantisms, all bad copies of the Church of Rome, since they have not the inherent authority of Revelation, of which only the Church is the depository. In Protestantism, only the Bible guarantees faith. But its interpretation is open, therefore individual and anarchic; it is therefore mortal for faith and for society.

Chapter V. Sebastian hopes to find a solution in the liberalism of Protestant youth and in the symbolism of Sabatier, which distinguishes faith from its intellectual shell. But the illusion is of short duration: there are so many diverse tendencies within this liberal movement. There are the philosophers who search for a new metaphysics. There are the socialists who end by leaving their respective churches. There are the mystics who throw themselves into Catholicism. There are finally the students who affirm a living faith and the death of reason. The solution would be to conceive of faith as a pure form that is endowed with its contents by each according to his own hunger. This solution would be in equilibrium between a symbolism that is in vain alone and a dogmatism that becomes quickly sterile.

Chapter VI. To this end, Sebastian, who is a naturalist by training, throws himself into philosophy. Three philosophies claim to justify virtue without the aid of faith: positivism, pragmatism, and Bergsonism. Sebastian is attracted by the position of Fouillée, for whom the idea is the law of evolution. This leads, in the mental order, to a universal psychology, and, in the material order, to a universal mechanism. The idea is a force combined with material forces to form life. But this reasoning is vicious, because the idea is not a state of consciousness but a group of forces. An equilibrium achieved by these forces can never be other than real, and not ideal. Thus, it cannot be imperative. It is simply declarative and consequently cannot justify any faith whatsoever.

Chapter VII. This positivism of Fouillée is opposed to the position of Boutroux, who distinguishes between science, which is submitted to laws of mechanistic determinism, and religion, which penetrates the work of the Divine. Nevertheless, if it is possible to go from the lower toward the higher, the reverse is not possible. Consequently, if one cannot deduce the lower from the higher, one cannot begin with God and deduce the world. Once this is granted, no reconciliation is possible between faith and science, from the positivist point of view.

There remains the solution of Bergson: on the one hand, there is reason which engenders science which spatializes the world; on the other hand, there is vital intuition which is flux, élan, and as such temporalizes everything. But intuition can only be either an ineffable, mystical experience or an enlargement of reason. In the first case, it is incommunicable; In the second, it loses its special character. The solution proposed by Bergson, who saw the problem clearly, is a conception of time that permits unresolved oppositions, as contrasted with mathematical logic that, being discontinuous and nontemporal, excludes them.

For Sebastian, on the contrary, the solution resides in the creation of a new science of types, such as the biology of Aristotle.

There remains, meanwhile, one last obstacle to surmount: pragmatism. But pragmatism is only the twilight of philosophies, like a deceived husband wanting only that much of reality that is useful to him, for fear of discovering his misfortune. Pragmatism makes of value an evanescent thing, where positivism had made it unattainable and Bergsonism vital but inexplicable.

Chapter VIII. From now on, Sebastian thinks, since doctrines can vary infinitely, he must rely upon laws that are invariable and never false, even if they may be incomplete or ideal. This solution offers a double advantage: it shows that the dogmatism of the scholars is the proof of their ignorance, but above all it permits the demonstration of the circle of the sciences:

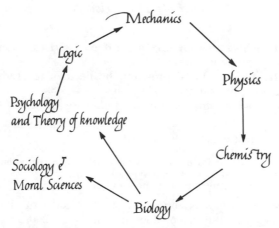

In this circle, the laws of one science are founded on those of another, passing through all the intermediaries from the idealist, nondogmatic pole of mathematics to the realist, dogmatic pole of biology.

Chapter IX. Literature, too, oscillates between the two poles of idealism and realism.

What Sebastian would like is more young Rousseaus and future Lamennais for ideas, and more Tolstois and Ibsens for social literature.

Chapter X. The world is led by the idea. Societies are organisms whose evolution depends on two causes, of which one, logic, is internal, and the other, chance, is external.

When internal causes are strong (logic or ideas) they destroy the accidents of history. When they are weak, they accommodate themselves to history and tend to enter into a relation of equilibrium with historical accidents. There is, therefore, a relation of cause and effect between disturbances in the world of ideas and social disturbances. The former are born of the disequilibrium between external and internal causes in the movement of societies. The Jewish people are a clear example. Exclusive and nationalist in their early history, they were the most religious people of antiquity. When they became internationalist, assimilation to all the cultures of the world made them the most intelligent and artistic of all peoples. It is necessary, therefore, to return to the internationalism of primitive Christianity.

The historical movement of ideas goes from the union of science and faith in the Middle Ages to the world harmony perceived by the Renaissance. In the eighteenth century, the French Revolution, provoked by the advent of the sciences of man, is the point at which faith ceases to be enriched by science. As a result, the Romanticism of the nineteenth century is a return to the self and a rejection of science. Romanticism engenders, in its turn, positivism which leads to social well-being by the objective synthesis of the sciences and the subjective synthesis of faith and its works. But positivism cannot prevail because it lacks a theory of knowledge.

Part II: The Crisis

Chapter I. Sebastian is in the grip of dark crises, alternating between agitation and depression.

Chapter II. To cure his depression, he decides to study a crucial problem in biology, the variation of species.

Meanwhile, he loses his faith in the following stages:

1. orthodoxy;
2. revolt against the absurdity of evil;
3. terror at the loss of faith;
4. reconstruction of faith on the basis of absolute symbolism;
5. loss of faith again, even this symbolic faith; and
6. health regained in pursuing the new science of types.

This science of types is conceived on the model of the biology of Aristotle. Every living unit is considered as an organization governed by a principle of equilibrium between qualities of the parts and qualities of the whole. Every real equilibrium is unstable, but tends toward an ideal of complete equilibrium. From now on, the science of types explains everything, since everything is a matter of equilibrium. At the same time, it cannot explain values.

Chapter III. A universe without values has no meaning, since action must have a minimal bearing on the universe, or else it is absurd.

Chapter IV. Values pose the question of choice between passion, which is a lie, and good, which is a sacrifice.

Chapter V. The search for the solution of such a problem is already faith.

Chapter VI. Science gives knowledge of good and evil and therefore provides the basis of morality. But it does not explain the roots of things. Faith, on the other hand, gives a meaning to life. Nothing develops without life. Therefore, nothing develops without faith. To live is to believe. This is the meaning of Pascal's wager. Consequently, science and faith are complementary. Sebastian is happy.

Chapter VII. He dreams: "a course synthesizing the sciences of life, a broadened equivalent of the course in positivist philosophy of Auguste

Comte" and claiming, as Comte does, to bring social well-being. He formulates a theory of genetic recapitulation in which progress is the work of those who know nothing of action, "who mingle fact and law" and tend toward the ideal of law. For there is an opposition between the abnegation of action, which is a descent into the imperfections of facts, and the abnegation of thought, which is the fulfillment of law.

Chapter VIII. Sebastian follows his calling of thinker and withdraws from action because of his pride and his desire for greatness, motivated by the three libidos: libido *sciendi*, which is the need for the ideal; libido *sentiendi*, which is the need for the real; and libido *excellendi*, which is the need to dominate. This discovery of self leads Sebastian to despair.

Chapter IX. This despair is mystical, for Sebastian believes in an attainable ideal.

Chapter X. Having withdrawn to a mountain, Sebastian can now accept his calling of thinker.

Chapter XI. But this vocation carries with it the obligation to follow his ideas to the very end.

Chapters XII and XIII. Sebastian experiences joy in having vanquished his passions and in listening to his vocation, which is the acme of his faith.

Part III: Reconstruction

LETTER TO YOUNG SOCIALISTS

This letter is essentially a proposal to create a third political force between a left without culture and a reactionary right, which are two forms of disequilibrium. Sebastian fears the loss of culture that may ensue in the struggles following the war. The general lines of his thought are to be presented in the following pages.

SCIENCE

Science has always concerned itself with the quantitative. It should turn to the qualitative. Every cell manifests itself in rhythmic movements, that is in mechanical equilibria and in parallel qualitative equilibria, according to the materialist hypothesis of a perfect psychophysical parallelism. These qualities differ according to the movements. Many movements engender many qualities. But these movements form parts of a totality. Their relation to the totality engenders a new form of equilibrium that implies them. This produces, on the one hand, the mode of laws that governs the physical sciences and the mode of types that governs the equilibria between the independent qualities of parts and a quality of the totality, which is also autonomous. "As such, the type forces the mind to proceed from the whole to the parts, and not from the part to the whole as does the mind of the physicist" (p. 153). As a result, while the simplest laws are the clearest, the most complex types are the clearest, which gives them the appearance of purposiveness (*finalité*). Everything is reduced, therefore, to a question of equilibrium between parts and whole. When the parts are compatible with the whole, there is conservation. When there is no such compatibility, the ensemble does not conserve itself in equilibrium, since in this case either only the parts or only the whole will be conserved.

Chapter I. Life is defined by assimilation, that is, by the reproduction of a substance identical to itself. As a result, the *quality of the ensemble* remains independent and stable. But this assimilation leads the organism to submit to the influence of the environment through the substances absorbed. From this arises heterogeneity, variation, and *qualities of the parts*. Thus, to raise the question of life is to raise the question of the ideas of equilibrium and of type, as Le Dantec clearly saw. But for Le Dantec the notion of equilibrium is an elementary form within which the whole and the parts are in opposition. This is expressed in the polar concepts of Le Dantec: assimilation and imitation. But these concepts are not contradictory, they are complementary. In a living equilibrium, the better an organism assimilates, the more sensitive it is to its milieu.

From this principle three laws can be deduced. (1) Every organization tends to conserve itself as such; this is the result of the equilibrium between whole and parts. (2) There are two types of equilibrium: (a) conserving, and (b) decomposing. Le Dantec envisages only the latter. (3) All possible equilibria are a combination of these two types. To these three laws must be added a fourth: all organic equilibria are of the conserving kind, which is an ideal type of equilibrium. The other kinds are unstable. They are the real equilibria.

The theory of equilibrium is distinguished from teleology in that it is a result and not a goal.

Chapter II. Life implies consciousness, within the framework of a general psychology. "Only the conception of a real, individual organization controlled by an ideal organization permits the understanding of consciousness as a pure internal translation of physico-chemical phenomena," without raising criticisms against the very idea of consciousness. The stream of consciousness of James or Bergson's intuition of time are steps toward a biological equilibrium that integrates the parts in the whole according to a hierarchical order.

Chapter III. Living organization implies thought. The three essential laws of thought are readily deducible from the nature of this organization. The self-conserving tendency of the organization is the origin of the principle of identity, from which the principle of contradiction can be deduced. The principle of sufficient reason characterizes an organization that maintains itself in its union with the whole.

Knowledge of space and of time proceed from the expansion and exteriorization of this organization. This suggests a vicious circle in which mind engenders reality and reality engenders mind. But one must avoid posing the question in these terms, and reformulate it in terms of common sense for which thought knows a part of reality by means of understanding, reasoning, autistic thought, and judgments of value.

Understanding is thought acting on quantity. Autistic thought, on the contrary, acts only on quality. Rather than grouping and depersonalizing objects, as does understanding, autistic thought conserves their originality, individualizing them in a sort of symbolism of which imagination, dreams, art, mysticism and metaphysics are examples. Reason is the synthesis of understanding and autistic thought; it can therefore express the universality of law and the qualitative grasp of types.

The judgment of value is the quality of that which can justify human activity. But the absolute remains unknowable. Thus the problem of value has no theoretical solution. Everything that thrusts toward life has value.

Chapter IV. For sociology, reconstruction is simple. The whole is society and the part is the individual, and their equilibrium becomes morality. There are two main schools of sociology: Tarde's, for whom the social is a composite of individuals, and Durkheim's, for whom the social is a new totality. Each is partially true. Both are based on the principle of organization, but one (Durkheim's) sees only the action of the whole on itself and on the parts, while the other (Tarde's) sees only the inverse, the action of the part on itself and on the whole. To understand society, these two schools can and must be reconciled.

Mass movements create a social unit at the expense of individuals, who lose their critical sense, their personality, and even their moral sense, even though there are positive social upheavals. But the question remains, of the equilibrium between society and the individual. The horde and the primitive clan accord primacy to the social over the individual, while liberalism favors the individual at the expense of society. The solution lies in an equilibrium between these two tendencies in a sort of "widened" socialism.

Chapter V. The links between the real organization of the individual and the ideal organization of society are of three kinds. There is the will, which is the experiential basis of morality; sentiment, which is the basis of esthetics; and their union, which engenders religion.

From the point of view of morality, in this new perspective, everything that represents life is good. Everything that is an obstacle to life is evil. For Guyau, evolutionary biology leads necessarily to altruism; for Nietzsche and Le Dantec, to egoism. Mill and Spencer seek a compromise in utilitarianism, which would be a coming to terms among egoisms. In fact, life is a kind of altruism, because life tends toward an ideal equilibrium. The good is neither individual nor interindividual; it is an ideal equilibrium governing both the person and society. This raises the question of liberty, but this should be reformulated as the problem of responsibility, since freedom is without interest for life.

Chapter VI. Beauty itself is integrated in this reconstruction, since "art organizes, constructs an ideal equilibrium. Beauty is the love of this equilibrium." But beauty begins with real organizations, which are never alike. Therefore, the beautiful does not lead to knowledge of any ideal organization, but only to sympathy (with all the risks of disequilibrium that this presupposes).

Chapter VII. Religion can also be explained by the equilibrium of the ideal organization. For individual sacrifice is the intensive realization of the ideal social equilibrium, while morality is its extensive realization. A true religion must realize an equilibrium between fanaticism, which is an excess of collective equilibrium, and mysticism, which is the opposite. Science will make a true and natural religion without contents and without metaphysics. For metaphysics can be entirely relegated to psychological mechanisms, in relation to individual affirmation or negation of absolute values.

Chapter VIII. Metaphysics and mysticism are forms of autistic thought, for they function by displacement and condensation, which are special modes of generalization and abstraction. They concentrate values, which are harmonies with the universal order, in a single ontological entity: God or the categorical imperative for monotheism; the Ideal Being of equilibrium for the pantheism of Spinoza or Marcus Aurelius; the annihilation of values for the pantheism of Epicurus.

FAITH

Faith is an absolute value, for it is at once transcendent because it is ideal, and immanent because it is everywhere.

SOCIAL SALVATION

Social salvation, as science teaches us, is the realization of the ideal equilibrium in oneself, in others, and in society.

All social reform must be based on the realization of the ideal type of organization in three ways: in each society, among neighbors, and in general. This last rule is opposed to nationalism, which favors the part over the whole, and to internationalism, which is the reverse; it leads to federalism, which is equilibrium between the whole and the parts.

The second rule teaches respect for equilibrium among neighbors, while the first preaches equality, liberty, and fraternity—in opposition to statism, to collectivism, and to liberalism.

PART III
The Paris Period

INTRODUCTION

Although it is easy to think of Piaget's work in psychology as beginning in Paris, in fact, his decision to go there matured over a period of some years. He had studied some psychology with the philosopher, Reymond, at the University of Neuchâtel. After receiving his doctorate in science in 1918, with a dissertation on the molluscs of certain Swiss mountain valleys, he spent several months in the spring of 1919 in Zurich, where he studied some experimental psychology and some psychopathology. Among his teachers were Lipps, Bleuler, and Jung. Nevertheless, up to this point his main exposure to the field had probably been his own reading and his writing of an abstract system exploring the forms of equilibrium in the relation between the part and the whole; this later led him to say that if he had known the works of Köhler and Wertheimer he would have become a Gestalt psychologist. In the fall of 1919 he went to Paris, determined to combine psychological research with philosophical studies.

Piaget, in his autobiographical sketch,* has always emphasized the importance of the time he spent in the school for boys in rue Grange-aux-Belles. It was there, in the laboratory left empty by the death of Alfred Binet and the departure for Rouen of Theodore Simon, that he had the leisure to initiate himself in his future vocation as a psychologist, working almost alone under conditions of great freedom. One can imagine his days. He spent his mornings at the celebrated National Library of Paris, reading works of logic by Couturat and Goblot, just at the time that Bertrand Russell and Alfred North Whitehead were putting the finishing touches on their intellectual nonviolent explosion, *Principia Mathematica*. In the afternoons, the young Piaget began by devoting himself to carrying out Dr. Simon's suggestion that he standardize the French version of certain tests of reasoning by Cyril Burt. Piaget could not restrain his intellectual curiosity from leading him where he really wanted to go.

Instead of administering the tests in a standardized way, he interviewed the children at length. The children did not complain. They found this "M'sieu" amusing. With him, one was not bored at all. Instead of simply noting the responses given by the children to the test items, the young Swiss biologist was interested in the how and the why of the answers. What had been at the outset nothing but a boring and annoying test situation became a real dialogue with suggestions and countersuggestions, an argument developed, a deepening of the child's thought, a new method of interrogating children was born. It leads the child to show how he formulates and solves a problem, how he thinks.

Selection 12, "The Child's Idea of Part," was a thirty-page research re-

* "Autobiography," *A History of Psychology in Autobiography*, ed. by. C. Murchison (Worcester, Mass.: Clark University Press, 1952).

port, illustrating an early phase in Piaget's development of the "clinical method" in experimental child psychology. We give only a brief excerpt showing something of the flavor of his thought at that time.

This is a long step from the hodgepodge of traditional testing. Intelligence is no longer a comparative and differential measuring instrument in which each child is assigned to a place in a statistical distribution. It has already become the ensemble of logical operations, owing its beginnings to the mornings spent reading logic in the Bibliothèque Nationale and to Piaget's earlier studies of French evolutionary theory. The title of the articles he wrote in this period are indicative of this state of affairs: the aforementioned "The Child's Idea of Part" (1921); "Essay on Logical Multiplication and the Beginnings of Formal Thought in the Child, a Case of Transition Between Predicative Judgment and Judgment of Relation" (1921); and "Symbolic Thought and the Thought of the Child" (1922).

There is nothing in this that surprises us now, both because we know the sequel in Piaget's career and because he has written it in his autobiographical sketch. But there is a third line of study that appeared at this time, which seems more and more forgotten as time passes, and our image of Piaget changes: psychoanalysis. It is a matter of some interest for the development of ideas that this domain attracted the young Piaget. In 1919, psychoanalysis was still a taboo subject. To approach it required a nonconformist spirit. Psychoanalysis is a branch of scientific knowledge that is also a clinical discipline. The basic technique was, at that time, free association, by means of which the patient himself discovers his own field of preoccupations and himself cuts the Gordian knot of his neurosis. Do we not find the same thoroughgoing analytical attention to the individual in Piaget's work, the same accent on patient, intelligent observation, the same going behind the observable to discover something more fundamental by means of a heightened form of critical analysis?

We include here (Selection 11) a somewhat abbreviated translation of an address by Piaget on psychoanalysis. The opening paragraphs of the text explain the somewhat unusual circumstances under which Piaget spoke. In our translation we have omitted Piaget's straightforward summary of aspects of psychoanalytic theory, and have retained primarily the passages in which he comments on it.

In his later work, Piaget's brief brush with psychoanalysis found echoes in *Play Dreams and Imitation* and in *The Moral Judgment of the Child*, and perhaps one might add, more recently, *The Grasp of Consciousness: Action and Conception the Young Child* (1976).

Psychoanalysis in Its Relations with Child Psychology*

1920

Ladies and gentlemen: I am perhaps the only one in this hall who is not a teacher. As for psychoanalysis, I am only a beginner. And I must speak to you about psychoanalysis in its relations with the psychology of the child! Those of you who know Dr. Simon, your congenial president, will understand how he could make me the victim of this hoax. But I am quits with him. "Psychoanalysis," he told me, "is little known in France. It is only studied by our psychiatrists. A sketch of psychoanalytic trends in pedagogy would be interesting." As a good Swiss, which I am proud to be, I could hardly believe him. I felt myself immediately absolved of the need to give you anything original. But I should have understood that a good presentation of my subject is beyond my power, especially in a lecture and in the little time available to me. Imagine my embarrassment: you know by heart everything I am about to say. Judge for yourself who is responsible.

The aim of psychoanalysis is very daring. It consists in rediscovering, in the individual's unconscious, the hidden tendencies which guide the person without his knowledge and which influence the actual contents of consciousness. These tendencies are of two kinds. First, there is the individual's own past which must be rediscovered, because systematic forgetting since the earliest years of childhood has rendered it unconscious. Secondly, there are hidden instincts whose role must be defined, and here we will see that psychoanalysts are engaged in the most suggestive controversies, to decide whether it is sexuality or the instinct of self-preservation which is the most important in the unconscious. On the one hand, psychoanalysis is a sort of individual history, an embryology of the personality; on the other hand, it is a theory of the unconscious; a science properly speaking.

Its methods are equally audacious. They consist in dissecting dreams,

*From J. Piaget, La psychanalyse dans ses rapports avec la psychologie de l'enfant. *Bulletin mensuel de la Société Alfred Binet*, Psychologie de l'enfant et pédagogie expérimentale, Paris, 20: 18–34; 41–58. Translated by H. E. G. and J. J. V.

the most direct products of the unconscious, and in trying to explain them.

The boundary between psychoanalysis and contemporary psychology seems clear. In reality, it is not at all. The conscious and the unconscious are everywhere entangled, often inextricably; if these two aspects of the life of the mind have been treated as in violent contrast with each other, and thus also psychoanalysis and the psychology of intelligence, this was a simplification of reality, undoubtedly useful at the beginning of research, but which is unnecessary to maintain today. . . .

The Freudian Doctrine: Analysis of Dreams and Theory of the Unconscious

. . . We can therefore say that between symbols properly speaking and the association of ideas every shade exists; but not a fundamental difference in their natures.

In this sense, the Freudian principle is correct, but only if reformulated in a broader form: *the dream is a coherent system of associations of ideas such that, in the waking state, each term is associated with new terms which lead eventually to the discovery of more and more profound psychic conflicts.* This principle is fecund in every case. The guiding threads of the search are sometimes hypothetical, but the conflicts uncovered are not. Moreover, this proposition is general. It is concerned not only with dreams, but with all forms of thought that are not strictly logical and objective. Now these two characteristics are not simultaneously present in consciousness except in a very special form, scientific thought in a broad sense of the term. All the rest participates in the psychic life in all its complexity, that is to say, in the passions, the desires, the fears of the unconscious itself. It is an inextricable network of symbol—associations whose only logic is that of the emotions. It is the thought of the child, of the neurotic, of the dreamer, of the artist, the mystic. It has also been studied by Lévy-Bruhl under the name of *prelogical thought*, of which the principal characteristic among primitive peoples is its fusion with magic.

Between symbolism, which scorns the framework of logic, and magic, which scorns the framework of reality, there is only a difference in contents. Psychoanalysis has done the great service of demonstrating the profound unity of these ways of thinking, and of showing that they all are governed by the laws of the dream itself. Following Bleuler's usage, we will call this general activity of the mind *autistic thought*, since as against scientific thought it is strictly personal and uncommunicable.

. . . Genuine repression leads to *sublimation*. This is not the annihilation of an existing tendency, but the deviation of its energy in new directions in relation to the conscious activity of the individual. It is thus an old story. It explodes in all its grandeur in that passage of Plato where Socrates shows that the love of beautiful bodies elevates itself to the love of beautiful souls, and from there to the very Idea of beauty. Out of the deaths of Beatrice and Laura, Dante and Petrarch drew an Image of the loved one which led them to the love of theology. Auguste Comte, having lost Clotilde de Vaux, felt the growth in himself of the worship of Humanity. Thus sublimation takes for its object a product of autistic thought itself, a poetic or mystical product, wholly impregnated with human significance. Here one grasps the admirable unity exhibited in the study of the same complexes throughout psychoanalysis, be it in the medical or pedagogical domains, or in what it makes of the psychology of art or religion.

Undeniably, the Freudian doctrine, of which we now conclude this rapid sketch, is of the highest interest. It poses new problems, it is very rich in suggestive perceptions, it provides a method of investigation. In brief, it has what it needs to flourish. Can we say, however, that the principle which seems to constitute its nerve center but which is in reality more theoretical than practical, I mean pansexualism, is so self-evident that it carries conviction? It is permissible to doubt this. There is something obsessive in wanting at any cost to reduce to the sexual instinct certain tendencies which seem even more primitive, such as the revolt of the son against his father, often a simple outcome of the instinct of self-preservation. At the same time, pansexualism has the merit of showing that, in psychology as elsewhere, everything is in everything ["tout est dans tout"]. There are no parts of the psychic life which do not nourish some relation with the whole of personality. But in reducing this complex whole to one fundamental tendency one exposes oneself to insurmountable difficulties. . . .

Adler and the Zurich School

One of the difficulties inherent in the Freudian system has been emphasized by the school of Adler. . . . If everything is sexual, from where does civilization and its morality come? From censorship. But from where does censorship come? From civilization. Adler, to break this circle, renounces pansexualism. He opposes to it a very interesting theory, unfortunately just as systematized, without any evident reason not to superpose it on Freudianism, rather than trying to exclude the latter.

Many psychasthenics are haunted by sexuality. They speak of nothing else. To listen to them, they have needs that nothing could satisfy. In reality, they are cold, it is only their imagination at work. Now there is only one hypothesis to explain such cases, that against their state of physical inferiority their psychology opposes an over-compensation. Could not this phenomenon be general? It seems so. Such, at least, is Adler's thesis. At the origin of all of the work of the unconscious, as much in healthy men as in psychoneurotics, there is to be found a feeling of organic inferiority, a feeling linked either to a particular organ or to a weak constitution. Such inadequacies, and in particular sexual impotency, can arise precisely from an unconscious complex, which explains the psychic turmoil which accompanies them. For childhood the psychology of Adler seems incontestable. The child necessarily suffers from feelings of inadequacy, because of his physical delicacy, his lack of stable psychic adaptations, or because of the incessant comparisons he makes, often correctly, between himself and his elders. Conscious life is born in fear and pain, and develops in the discomfiture of not yet being at that ideal age, so it seems, the age of adults. From this nostalgia, which is no longer for the past, as in Freud, but for the future, a comfortable psychic equilibrium does not arise. There is compensation in the form of the will to grow up. And the stronger this inadequacy, the stronger the overcompensation, resulting in a discharge of autistic imaginings to create an ideal world in which one plays the role one desires.

It is just as in Freudian narcissism, but the motor is no longer sexuality, it is the will to dominate. The injured instincts are the most fertile from the point of view of imagination. The stammerer sees himself as an orator (and this brings to mind Demosthenes or Camille Desmoulins), the myopic devotes himself to drawing, and so on. At a younger age, the very faults of autism are sometimes explainable, as Freud put it, by the desire to play a role. We can also see the value of such explanations in the case of kleptomania or in childhood lying. Infantile sexuality itself is clarified in a new way. Consider a little girl of 5 or 6 years who, having put her doll in her own bed, says that "you must always have a friend with you to sleep." Freud takes these childish naivetés at face value; for him they are direct expressions of unconscious wishes. Adler is certainly more subtle in saying that, in general, and the example that I have given seems good enough, sexuality is only a form, a language choosing its metaphors from characteristics peculiar to the adult world. This language is necessarily accompanied by a pleasure, often divinatory, which will play an essential role in the sexuality of a slightly more advanced age, and here Freud is perfectly correct; but this language conceals an element no less essential, which is the desire to grow, and to be in all ways like grownups. . . .

Religious orientation is one interesting consequence of infantile remorse. Hatred for the father readily provokes remorse, whether this hatred is due to the classical Oedipal complex or to nonsexual revolt. There ensues an overcompensation of respect which never finds a real object adequate to its needs. This leads to the gradual sublimation of the image of the father, which links itself with the image of the heavenly Father, whose features have already been formed by religious education. There is a very precocious infantile introversion, of which Jung has given some pretty examples. We see readily in the divine image, elements of paternal origin: respect full of love, but also fear, hidden hatred sometimes, from which springs the terrifying character which the child, in his religious remorse, can sometimes give to the face of his God.

For Adler, the dream is not necessarily a tissue of desires straining to revive past loves of which nothing remains but a complex. It is, rather, a way of planning one's life unconsciously, in which the projected conquests and the will to achieve have free rein. The past no longer determines the present, it no longer constitutes this sort of necessary ideal, forever immutable, which the unconscious strives to realize by no matter what trickery, it serves instead as the material to be reconstructed. . . .

Adler has remarked that the successive dreams of a single night represent repeated efforts to solve the same problem. This interpretation seems the more true in that the juxtaposition of two dreams does not appear arbitrary. One need, a need for internal unity, drives the subject to search his past in the first dream, and in the second to pose once again the problem of his present way of life. . . .

All things considered, there is a close agreement between the ideas of Adler and those ideas of Freud which are correct. A third doctrine, therefore, seems necessary to reconcile these two equally interesting tendencies in psychoanalytic thought. This is the task which the Zurich school has taken upon itself. . . .

The complex, for the Zurich school, is an autonomous ensemble of ideas and feelings, striving for its own development. It is a second ego, since the ego itself is a complex. Each complex, in its tendency to associate itself with ongoing representations, enters into rivalry with the ego and tends to supplant it in the field of consciousness. Censorship is the ego's resistance to this invasion. This is a solution to the vicious circle of Freud, perhaps a little too formalized, but interesting. . . .

Now, autistic thought, creator of personal symbols, remains essential in each of us throughout his life. Its role changes with age. In the child, autism is everything. Later, reason develops at its expense, but— and this is the real problem—does it ever extricate itself entirely? Apparently not. There remains, therefore, an extremely instructive psychological task to be undertaken in order to determine in each individual the relations between the state of his intelligence and the state of his autistic or unconscious life. And certainly, psychoanalysis is already full of insights in this regard.

12

The Child's Idea of Part*

1921

How shall we conceptualize this interaction [between logical and extra-logical factors]?

Before the phenomena which we have studied, the ideas of collection, part, etc., are formed by means of verbal schemas and especially those which are linked to substantives isolated from their context. With the insertion of these words and these schemas in the body of the language imposed by adults, conditions are changed. Tachistoscopic experiments and the analyses of M. Bergson have shown that sentences are not read and understood in detail, but in one inspection. In this regard, the phenomena of the limitation of the field of attention are fundamental: it is in part thanks to them that we have been able to characterize the three stages of our classification. Attention divides complete sentences into subwholes that logical forms can assimilate. There is, therefore, a relation of antecedent and consequent between the forms of the field of attention and logical forms. But this is a two-way interaction, because, as we have emphasized in discussing the "implicit" stage, the forms of the field of attention are shaped by logic itself. Each field of attention has a configuration such that the corresponding logical form collaborates in expanding the field of attention while attention works at constituting new logical forms. . . .

*From J. Piaget, Essai sur quelques aspects du developpement de la notion de partie chez l'enfant. *Journal de psychologie normale et pathologique*, Paris, *18*: 449–480. Translated by H. E. G. and J. J. V.

PART IV

Egocentric Thought in the Child

INTRODUCTION

Piaget sketched out a plan for four books in 1923, in the preface to the first one. There was to be a two-part work, *Studies in Child Logic*, of which *The Language and Thought of the Child* (1923) was the first volume, and *Judgment and Reasoning in the Child* (1924) the second. These were to be followed by another two-part work in which he planned to analyze causality and the function of reality in the child. *The Child's Conception of the World* (1926) and *The Child's Conception of Physical Causality* (1927) carried out this part of the plan with some dispatch. But there was a third part in the plan of 1923. Piaget hoped "in a few years' time to produce a work dealing with child thought as a whole, in which I shall again take up the principal features of child logic, and state their relation to the biological factors of adaptation (imitation and assimilation)." This part of the plan had a more complex fate and it took Piaget the whole of his career to pursue it. The themes of assimilation and accommodation (a broader concept than imitation) were opened up in the four books of the 1920s, and then became one of the central themes in his trilogy about infancy and very early childhood, based on his studies of his own three children. But these works dealt with the prelogical child, and say little about child logic. Rather, they take egocentric thought—the unifying idea of the books of the 1920s—and push back into infancy in a search for its origins, resulting in the concept of infant solipsism, another central theme in the trilogy. He returned to the attack on child logic in the middle 1930s, and the subject occupied a great deal of his attention from then on. Attempts to synthesize his ideas about biology and his ideas about thought occur throughout his career. "The Elaboration of the Universe" (Selection 20), the concluding chapter of *Construction of Reality* (1937), probably comes the closest of his writings to representing the synthesis spoken of in 1923. By the time he wrote *The Psychology of Intelligence* (1947, but based on lectures given in 1942) Piaget's interest in the formal models underlying childhood thinking had grown to the point where this subject was the central theme of the work. Of course he tried, in that work, to show how the intellectual operations of childhood grow out of infant thought and action; but his writings of the 1920s were not given much attention. Were they outgrown, or merely displaced by new interests? The question remains open.

Sometimes Piaget speaks of these four books, published between his twenty-seventh and thirty-first years, as belonging to his youth, almost as outgrown juvenilia. But when he was approached by an author and illustrator of children's books for advice on how to captivate the child's mind, it was to the methods and themes of these books that Piaget and his team turned. The result of this collaboration was a charming children's book about a young creature's discovery of the world.* In evaluating preliminary versions of the

---

* E. Delessert, *How the Mouse Was Hit on the Head & So Discovered the World*, foreword by Jean Piaget (New York: Doubleday, 1971).

text and illustrations, a research group adapted methods from Piaget, such as asking children to draw pictures representing the text, and then comparing these with the author's own sketches.

Besides their common subject matter, these four books share other characteristics that distinguish them from Piaget's later works. They all use the "clinical method"—interviewing each child at length about his ideas and thoughts (although it should be added that other methods are used as well); they do not insist on a clear progression of stages in the development of the child's intellect; and they do not appeal to explicit logical models that might be said to underlie the child's thought. In the years following, Piaget was to move away from the clinical method in favor of methods relying much less on the child's verbalizations, to emphasize stages of development, and to search for formal models.

13

The Language and Thought of the Child*

1923

INTRODUCTORY NOTES

The Language and Thought of the Child (1923) made its young author immediately famous, because it contrasted strongly with the favorite occupations of child psychologists of the time. Here was a book about language with very little word-counting in it. The subjects' ages were all above the age of language acquisition. On the other hand, as compared with today's psycholinguistics, there was very little concern for children's grammar or for grammatical structures in general.

Here was a book about children's thinking without mention of learning or imagery, with very little space given to habit formation, and no space given to conditioning, problem-solving, or creativity as we understand them now.

What then was the merit of the book? Clearly its provocative charge came from the point of view that was developed in it. It was a careful observation of the different functions of language among children and as such had something special to offer. It was also the first attempt to organize the material collected around the central concept of egocentrism. It examined language from the viewpoint of the subject and not from the cold external viewpoint of the objective observer. This position led Piaget to attempt to arrange his material into types of linguistic exchanges and stages in the development of the conversations among children aged from 4 to 7. This progression could then be compared with their verbal explanations, their understanding of order, cause, justification, reality, history, human action, and rules and regulations.

For Piaget, language serves multiple functions that develop with age. At first, language is plainly echolalic and repetitive. The child merely repeats what she has heard or understood from the speech of others. Next, the child is more interested in her own linguistic productions and repeats words for the pleasure of talking. This is still echolalia. Monologue takes place when

*From J. Piaget, *The Language and Thought of the Child*, Marjorie Gabain, translator. Reprinted by permission of Humanities Press, Inc., Atlantic Highlands, New Jersey, and Routledge & Kegan Paul Ltd., London. Originally published in French, 1923. (Collaborators: Alice Deslex, Germaine Guex, A. Leuzinger-Schuler, Hilda de Meyenburg, Valentine Piaget, Liliane Veihl.)

the child talks to herself as though she were thinking aloud. Collective monologue is a soliloquy in which the child uses the presence of others as a mere stimulus for his or her own verbal productions. These functions of speech are all egocentric as contrasted with socialized speech, which serves other functions such as the exchange of information, criticisms, commands, requests, threats, and questions and answers.

After having characterized the different functions of language during children's conversations, Piaget arranges the types of conversation in a developmental sequence. The explanations given by one child to another are egocentric. This means that explanations are not conceived of by children between 6 and 8 years of age as an effort at decentration, i.e., taking the position of someone who does not know. The child does not attempt at all to adapt her explanation to the viewpoint of the others. For instance, the child of this age will tell a story without putting the different sequences of the story in the right order. Rather, she will tell the story in the order in which she remembers the different passages, which is neither logical nor historical. In the same way, the necessary ordering of causes and effects will be altered. In sum, the child of this age behaves as if everyone already shares the same knowledge that she has.

From 9 to 11 years of age, egocentric speech gives way to a form of verbal and conceptual syncretism characterized by a need for justification at any price. In his desire for understanding, the child of this age jumps too fast from premises to conclusions, attempts to link everything with everything. In verbal syncretism the child tends to drop all the difficult words in a narration or a sentence and to link all the easy words with one another so that he can, afterwards, reinterpret the difficult words he missed in the first place. Conceptual syncretism is the incorporation of two propositions (that have been understood separately by the child) into a global picture in which, by adult standards, they may or may not fit. This need for justification at any cost leads the child to all sorts of fusions among propositions that he evaluates and understands correctly in isolation but tends to juxtapose uncritically with others in his desire for an explanation.

This first psychological book presents certain features that are exceptional in comparison with Piaget's later productions. All through the book, there is an effort at quantitative analysis of the material presented to the reader. For instance, there is an attempt at measuring egocentrism by means of a "coefficient of egocentrism" that can be calculated for any individual. This idea appears in the first chapter of the book and is tested later. The experimental method for the study of understanding and verbal explanations is carefully delineated and the numerical results presented.

Another interesting aspect of this book is the lack of differentiation of the notion of stage; Piaget does not clearly separate stage from type. He has not yet developed the harmonious progression à la Comte* from one level of behavior to the next that will be explicit, for the first time, in the *Origins of Intelligence* and that will become a central theme in his later work. Such a linear conception of development is not yet apparent here.

The Functions of Language in Two Children of Six†

The question which we shall attempt to answer in this book may be stated as follows: What are the needs which a child tends to satisfy when he talks? This problem is, strictly speaking, neither linguistic nor logical; it belongs to functional psychology, but it should serve nevertheless as a fitting prelude to any study of child logic.

At first sight the question may strike one as curious, for with the child, as with us, language would seem to enable the individual to communicate his thoughts to others. But the matter is not so simple. In the first place, the adult conveys different modes of thought by means of speech. At times, his language serves only to assert, words state objective facts, they convey information, and are closely bound up with cognition. "The weather is changing for the worse," "Bodies fall to the ground." At times, on the other hand, language expresses commands or desires, and serves to criticize or to threaten, in a word to arouse feelings and provoke action—"Let's go," "How horrible!" etc. If we knew approximately in the case of each individual the proportion of one type of speech to another, we should be in possession of psychological data of great interest. But another point arises. Is it certain that even adults always use language to communicate thoughts? To say nothing of internal speech, a large number of people, whether from the working classes or the more absentminded of the *intelligentsia*, are in the habit of talking to themselves, of keeping up an audible soliloquy. This

* Auguste Comte, leading exponent of positivism in France, was one of many nineteenth-century writers who searched for regular stages of development in the history of society.
†With the collaboration of Mlle. Germaine Guex and of Mlle. Hilda de Meyenburg.

phenomenon points perhaps to a preparation for social language. The solitary talker invokes imaginary listeners, just as the child invokes imaginary playfellows. This is perhaps an example of that return shock of social habits which has been described by Baldwin; the individual repeats in relation to himself a form of behavior which he originally adopted only in relation to others. In this case he would talk to himself in order to make himself work, simply because he has formed the habit of talking to others in order to work on them. Whichever explanation is adopted, it would seem that language has been sidetracked from its supposed function, for in talking to himself, the individual experiences sufficient pleasure and excitement to divert him from the desire to communicate his thoughts to other people. Finally, if the function of language were merly "communicate," the phenomenon of verbalism would hardly admit of explanation. How could words, confined as they are by usage to certain precise meanings (precise, because their object is to be understood), eventually come to veil the confusion of thought, even to create obscurity by the multiplication of verbal entities, and actually to prevent thought from being communicable? This is not the place to raise the vexed question of the relation between thought and language, but we may note in passing that the very existence of such questions shows how complex are the functions of language, and how futile the attempt to reduce them all to one—that of communicating thought. . . .

THE MATERIAL

The method we have adopted is as follows. Two of us followed each a child (a boy) for about a month at the morning class at the Maison des Petits de l'Institut Rousseau, taking down in minute detail and in its context everything that was said by the child. In the class where our two subjects were observed the scholars draw or make whatever they like; they model and play at games of arithmetic and reading, etc. These activities take place in complete freedom; no check is put upon any desire that may manifest itself to talk or play together; no intervention takes place unless it is asked for. The children work individually or in groups, as they choose; the groups are formed and then break up again without any interference on the part of the adult; the children go from one room to another (modeling room, drawing room, etc.) just as they please without being asked to do any continuous work so long as they do not themselves feel any desire for it. . . .

Once the material was collected, we utilized it as follows. We began by numbering all the subjects' sentences. . . .

Once the talk has been portioned out into numbered sentences, we endeavor to classify these into elementary functional categories. It is this method of classification which we are now about to study.

An Example of the Talk Taken Down. Let us first of all give one complete example of the documents collected in this way, and let us examine it in all its complexity:

23. Pie (to Ez who is drawing a tram-car with carriages in tow): *But the trams that are hooked on behind don't have any flags.* (No answer.)
24. (Talking about his tram). *They don't have any carriages hooked on* . . . (He was addressing no one in particular. No one answers him.)

25. (To Béa), *'T'sa tram that hasn't got no carriages.* (No answer.)
26. (To Hei), *This tram hasn't got no carriages, Hei, look, it isn't red, d'you see* . . . (No answer.)
27. (Lev says out loud, "A funny gentleman" from a certain distance, and without addressing himself to Pie or to anyone else). Pie: *A funny gentleman!* (Goes on drawing his tram.)
28. *I'm leaving the tram white.*
29. (Ez who is drawing next to him says, "I'm doing it yellow"), *No, you mustn't do it all yellow.*
30. *I'm doing the staircase, look.* (Béa answers, "I can't come this afternoon, I've got a Eurhythmic class.")
31. *What did you say?* (Béa repeats the same sentence.)
32. *What did you say?* (Béa does not answer. She has forgotten what she said, and gives Ro a push.)
33. (To Béa), *Leave him alone.*
34. (Mlle. B. asks Ez if he would like to come with her), *Come here Ez, it isn't finished. 34 bis. Please teacher, Ez hasn't finished.*
35. (Without addressing himself to anyone,) *I'm doing some black stones.* . . .
36. (Id), *Pretty . . . these stones.*
37. (To Ez), *Better than you, eh?* (No answer. Ez had not heard the previous remark.)

We have chosen this example from Pie (6½ years) because it is taken during the most sociable activity of which this child is capable: he is drawing at the same table as his bosom friend, Ez, and is talking to him the whole time. It would therefore be natural in a case of this kind if the sole function of speech were to communicate thought. But let us examine the matter a little more closely. It will be seen that from the social point of view the significance of these sentences or fragments of sentences is extremely varied. When Pie says: *"They don't have* . . . etc." (24), or *"I'm doing* . . . etc." (35) he is not speaking to anyone. He is thinking aloud over his own drawing, just as people of the working classes mutter to themselves over their work. Here, then, is a first category which should be singled out, and which in future we shall designate as *monologue.* When Pie says to Hei or to Béa: *"'T'sa tram* . . . etc." (25) or *"This tram* . . . etc." (26) he seems on this occasion to want to make himself understood; but on closer examination it will be seen that he cares very little who is listening to him (he turns from Béa to Hei to say exactly the same thing) and, furthermore, that he does not care whether the person he addresses has really heard him or not. He believes that someone is listening to him; that is all he wants. Similarly, when Béa gives him an answer devoid of any connection with what he has just been saying (30), it is obvious that he does not seek to understand his friend's observation nor to make his own remark any clearer. Each one sticks to his own idea and is perfectly satisfied (30–32). The audience is there simply as a stimulus. Pie talks about himself just as he does when he soliloquizes, but with the added pleasure of feeling himself an object of interest to other people. Here then is a new category which we shall call the *collective monologue.* It is to be distinguished from the preceding category and also from those in which thoughts are actually exchanged or information given. This last case constitutes a separate category which we shall call *adapted information,* and to which we can relegate sentences 23 and 34*b*. In this case the child talks, not at random, but to specified persons, and with the object of making them listen and understand. In addition to these practical and objective forms of information, we can distinguish others of a more subjective character consisting of commands (33), expressions of derision or criticism, or assertions of personal superiority, etc. (37). Finally, we may distinguish mere senseless repetitions, questions and answers.

Let us now establish the criteria of these various categories.

The Functions of Child Language Classified. The talk of our two subjects may be divided into two large groups—the *egocentric* and the *socialized.* When a child utters phrases belonging to the first group, he does not bother to know to whom he is speaking nor whether he is being listened to. He talks either for himself or for the pleasure of associating anyone who happens to be there with the activity of the moment. This talk is egocentric, partly because the child speaks only about himself, but chiefly because he does not attempt to place himself at the point of view of his hearer. Anyone who happens to be there will serve as an audience. The child asks for no more than an apparent interest, though he has the illusion (except perhaps in pure soliloquy if even then) of being heard and understood. He feels no desire to influence his hearer nor to tell him anything; not unlike a certain type of drawing-room conversation where everyone talks about himself and no one listens.

Egocentric speech may be divided into three categories: (1) *Repetition (echolalia):* We shall deal only with the repetition of words and syllables. The child repeats them for the pleasure of talking, with no thought of talking to anyone, nor even at times of saying words that will make sense. This is a remnant of baby prattle, obviously devoid of any social character.

(2) *Monologue:* The child talks to himself as though he were thinking aloud. He does not address anyone.

(3) *Dual or collective monologue:* The contradiction contained in the phrase recalls the paradox of those conversations between children which we were discussing, where an outsider is always associated with the action or thought of the moment, but is expected neither to attend nor to understand. The point of view of the other person is never taken into account; his presence serves only as a stimulus.

In *socialized speech* we can distinguish:

(4) *Adapted information:* Here the child really exchanges his thoughts with others, either by telling his hearer something that will interest him and influence his actions, or by an actual interchange of ideas by argument or even by collaboration in pursuit of a common aim.

Adapted information takes place when the child adopts the point of view of his hearer, and when the latter is not chosen at random. Collecive monologues, on the other hand, take place when the child talks only about himself, regardless of his hearers' point of view, and very often without making sure whether he is being attended to or understood. We shall examine this criterion in more detail later on.

(5) *Criticism:* This group includes all remarks made about the work or behavior of others, but having the same character as adapted information; in other words, remarks specified in relation to a given audience. But these are more affective than intellectual, i.e., they assert the superiority of the self and depreciate others. One might be tempted in view of this to place this group among the egocentric categories. But

"egocentric" is to be taken in an intellectual, not in an ethical sense, and there can be no doubt that in the cases under consideration one child acts upon another in a way that may give rise to arguments, quarrels, and emulation, whereas the utterances of the collective mono-logue are without any effect upon the person to whom they are addressed. The shades of distinction, moreover, between adapted information and criticism are often extremely subtle and can only be established by the context.

(6) *Commands, requests* and *threats:* In all of these there is definite interaction between one child and another.

(7) *Questions:* Most questions asked by children among themselves call for an answer and can therefore be classed as socialized speech, with certain reservations to which we shall draw attention later on.

(8) *Answers:* By these are meant answers to real questions (with interrogation mark) and to commands. They are not to be compared to those answers given in the course of conversation (category 4), to remarks which are not questions but belong to "information."

These, then, are the eight fundamental categories of speech. . . . Four people have been engaged in classifying the material in hand, and the results of their respective enquiries were found to coincide within 2 or 3 percent.

Let us now return to one of these categories in order to establish the constants of our statistical results.

Repetition (Echolalia). Everyone knows how, in the first years of his life, a child loves to repeat the words he hears, to imitate syllables and sounds, even those of which he hardly understands the meaning. It is not easy to define the function of this imitation in a single formula. From the point of view of behavior, imitation is, according to Claparède, an ideomotor adaptation by means of which the child reproduces and then simulates the movements and ideas of those around him. But from the point of view of personality and from the social point of view, imita-tion would seem to be, as Janet and Baldwin maintain, a confusion be-tween the I and the not-I, between the activity of one's own body and that of other people's bodies. At his most imitative stage, the child mimics with his whole being, identifying himself with his model. But this game, though it seems to imply an essentially social attitude, really indicates one that is essentially egocentric. The copied movements and behavior have nothing in them to interest the child, there is no adapta-tion of the I to anyone else; there is a confusion by which the child does not know that he is imitating, but plays his game as though it were his own creation. This is why children up to the age of 6 or 7, when they have had something explained to them and are asked to do it immediately afterwards, invariably imagine that they have discovered by themselves what in reality they are only repeating from a model. In such cases imitation is completely unconscious, as we have often had occasion to observe. . . .

(Mlle. E. teaches My the word "celluloid") Lev, busy with his·drawing at another table: "*Luloïd . . . le le loid . . .*" etc.
(Before an aquarium Pie stands outside the group and takes no interest in what is being shown. Somebody says the word "triton"). Pie: "*Triton . . . triton.*" Lev (after hearing the clock strike "coucou"): "*Coucou .. . coucou.*"

These pure repetitions, rare enough at the age of Pie and Lev, have no interest for us. Their sudden appearance in the midst of ordinary conversation is more illuminating.

Jac says to Ez: "Look, Ez, your pants are showing." Pie, who is in another part of the room immediately repeats: *"Look, my pants are showing, and my shirt, too."*

Now there is not a word of truth in all this. It is simply the joy of repeating for its own sake that makes Pie talk in this way, i.e., the pleasure of using words not for the sake of adapting oneself to the conversation, but for the sake of playing with them. . . .

There is no need to multiply examples. The process is always the same. The children are occupied with drawing or playing; they all talk intermittently without listening very much to each other; but words thrown out are caught on the bounce, like balls. Sometimes they are repeated as they are, like the remarks of the present category, sometimes they set in action those dual monologues of which we shall speak later on. The frequency of repetition is about 2 percent and 1 percent for Pie and Lev respectively. . . .

Monologue. Janet and the psychoanalysts have shown us how close in their opinion is the bond which originally connected word and action, words being so packed with concrete significance that the mere fact of uttering them, even without any reference to action, could be looked upon as the factor in initiating the action in question.

Now, independently of the question of origins, it is a matter of common observation that for the child words are much nearer to action and movement than for us. This leads us to two results which are of considerable importance in the study of child language in general and of the monologue in particular. (1) The child is impelled, even when he is alone, to speak as he acts, to accompany his movements with a play of shouts and words. True, there are silences, and very curious ones at that, when children work together as in the Maison des Petits. But, alongside of these silences, how many a soliloquy must take place when a child is alone in a room, or when children speak without addressing themselves to anyone. (2) If the child talks even when he is alone as an accompaniment to his action, he can reverse the process and use words to bring about what the action of itself is powerless to do. Hence the habit of romancing or inventing, which consists in creating reality by words and magical language, in working on things by means of words alone, apart from any contact either with them or with persons.

These two varieties belong to the same category, that of the monologue. It is worth noting that the monologue still plays an important part between the ages of 6 and 7. At this age the child soliloquizes even in the society of other children, as in the classrooms where our work has been carried on. We have sometimes seen as many as ten children seated at separate tables or in groups of two or three, each talking to himself without taking any notice of his neighbor.

Here are a few examples of simple monologue (the first variety) where the child simply accompanies his action with sentences spoken aloud.

Lev sits down at his table alone: *"I want to do that drawing, there . . . I want to draw something, I do. I shall need a big piece of paper to do that."*

Lev knocks over a game: *"There! everything's fallen down."*
Lev has just finished his drawing: *"Now I want to do something else."*

Lev is a little fellow who is very much wrapped up in himself. He is always telling everyone else what he is doing at the moment. In his case, therefore, monologue tends in the direction of collective monologue, where everyone talks about himself without listening to the others. All the same, when he is alone he goes on announcing what he is going to do, with no other audience than himself. It is in these circumstances that we have the true monologue.

In the case of Pie, the monologue is rarer, but more true to type; the child will often talk with the sole aim of marking the rhythm of his action, without exhibiting a shade of self-satisfaction in the process. Here is one of Pie's conversations with context, where monologue is interspersed with other forms of talk:

53. Pie takes his arithmetic copybook and turns the pages: *"1, 2 . . . 3, 4, 5, 6, 7 . . . 8 . . . 8, 8, 8, 8 and 8 . . . 9. Number 9, number 9, number 9* (singing) *I want number 9.* (This is the number he is going to represent by a drawing).

54. (Looking at Béa who is standing by the countingframe but without speaking to him): *Now I'm going to do 9, 9, I'm going 9, I'm doing 9.* (He draws).

55. (Mlle. L. passes by his table without saying anything). *Look, teacher, 9, 9, 9 . . . number 9.*

56. (He goes to the frame to see what color to choose for his number so that it should correspond to the 9th row in the frame). *Pink chalk, it will have to be 9.* (He sings).

57. (To Ez as he passes): *I'm doing 9, I am—*(Ez) What are you going to do?*—Little rounds.*

58. (Accident to the pencil) *Ow, ow!*

59. *Now I've got to 9."*

The whole of this monologue has no further aim than to accompany the action as it takes place. There are only two diversions. Pie would like to inform someone about his plans (sentences 55 and 57). But in spite of this the monologue runs on uninterrupted as though Pie were alone in the room. Speech in this case functions only as a stimulus, and in nowise as a means of communication. Pie no doubt enjoys the feeling of being in a room full of people, but if he were alone, his remarks would be substantially the same.

At the same time it is obvious that this stimulus contains a certain danger. Although in some cases it accelerates action, it also runs the risk of supplanting it. "When the distance between two points has to be traversed, a man can actually walk it with his legs, but he can also stand still and shout: 'On, on! . . .' like an opera singer."* Hence the second variety of child soliloquy where speech serves not so much to accompany and accelerate action as to replace it by an illusory satisfaction. To this last group belong certain cases of word magic; but these, frequent as they are, occur only in the strictest solitude.† What is more usual is that the child takes so much pleasure in soliloquizing that he forgets his activity and does nothing but talk. The word then becomes a command to the external world. Here is an example of pure and of

*P. Janet, p. 150.
†These cases will be dealt with elsewhere.

collective monologue where the child gradually works himself up into issuing a command to physical objects and to animals:

"Now then, it's coming (a tortoise). *It's coming, it's coming, its coming. Get out of the way, Da, it's coming, it's coming, it's coming. . . . Come along, tortoise!"*

A little later, after having watched the aquarium soliloquizing all the time: *"Oh, isn't it* (a salamander) *surprised at the great big giant* (a fish)," he exclaims, *"Salamander, you must eat up the fishes!"*

In short we have here the mechanism of solitary games, where, after thinking out his action aloud, the child, under the influence of verbal excitement as much as of any voluntary illusion, comes to command both animate and inanimate beings.

In conclusion, the general characteristic of monologues of this category is that the words have no social function. In such cases speech does not communicate the thoughts of the speaker, it serves to accompany, to reinforce, or to supplement his action. It may be said that this is simply a sidetracking of the original function of language, and that the child commands himself and external things just as he has learned to command and speak to others. . . . It should be remembered, however, that throughout the time when he is learning to speak, the child is constantly the victim of a confusion between his own point of view and that of other people. For one thing, he does not know that he is imitating. For another, he talks as much to himself as to others, as much for the pleasure of prattling or of perpetuating some past state of being as for the sake of giving orders. It is therefore impossible to say that the monologue is either prior to or later than the more socialized forms of language; both spring from that undifferentiated state where cries and words accompany action, and then tend to prolong it; and both react one upon the other at the very outset of their development.

But as we pass from early childhood to the adult stage, we shall naturally see the gradual disappearance of the monologue, for it is a primitive and infantile function of language. It is remarkable in this connection that in the cases of Pie and Lev this form should still constitute about 5 percent and 15 percent respectively of their total conversation. . . . The difference in the percentages, however, corresponds to a marked difference in temperament, Pie being of a more practical disposition than Lev, better adapted to reality and therefore to the society of other children. When he speaks, it is therefore generally in order to make himself heard. It is true, as we saw, that when Pie does talk to himself his monologue is on the whole more genuine than Lev's, but Pie does not produce in such abundance those rather self-satisfied remarks in which a child is continually announcing his plans to himself, and which are the obvious sign of a certain imaginative exuberance.

Collective Monologue. This form is the most social of the egocentric varieties of child language, since to the pleasure of talking it adds that of soliloquizing before others and of interesting, or thinking to interest, them in one's own action and one's own thoughts. But as we have already pointed out, the child who acts in this manner does not succeed in making his audience listen, because, as a matter of fact, he is not really addressing himself to it. He is not speaking to anyone. He talks aloud to himself in front of others. This way of behaving reappears in certain men and women of a puerile disposition (certain hysterical subjects, if hysteria be described as the survival of infantile characteristics) who are in the habit of thinking aloud as though they were talking to themselves, but are also conscious of their audience. Suppress the slightly theatrical element in this attitude, and you have the equivalent of the collective monologue in normal children. . . .

Here are a few more examples which show how little a child is concerned with speaking to anyone in particular, or even with making himself heard:

Mlle. L. tells a group of children that owls cannot see by day. Lev: *"Well, I know quite well that it can't."*

Lev (at a table where a group is at work): *"I've already done 'moon' so I'll have to change it."*

Lev picks up some barley-sugar crumbs: *"I say, I've got a lovely pile of eyeglasses."*

Lev: *"I say, I've got a gun to kill him with. I say, I am the captain on horseback. I say, I've got a horse and a gun as well."*

The opening phrase, "I say, I" which occurs in most of these sentences is significant. Every one is supposed to be listening. This is what distinguishes this type of remark from pure monologue. But with regard to its contents it is the exact equivalent of the monologue. The child is simply thinking out his actions aloud, with no desire to give anyone any information about it. . . .

The collective monologue represents about 23 percent of Lev's and 30 percent of Pie's entire conversation. But we have seen that it is harder to distinguish the pure from the collective monologue in Lev's case than in Pie's. Taking therefore the two types of monologue together, we may say that with Lev they represent 38 percent and with Pie 35 percent of the subject's sum of conversation.

Adapted Information. The criterion of adapted information, as opposed to the pseudo-information contained in the collective monologue, is that it is successful. The child actually makes his hearer listen, and contrives to influence him, i.e., to tell him something. This time the child speaks from the point of view of his audience. The function of language is no longer merely to excite the speaker to action, but actually to communicate his thoughts to other people, . . .

It is adapted information, moreover, that gives rise to dialogue. The dialogues of children deserve to be made the object of a special and very searching investigation, for it is probably through the habit of arguing that, as Janet and Baldwin have insisted, we first become conscious of the rules of logic and the forms of deductive reasoning. We shall therefore attempt in the next chapter* to give a rough outline of the different stages of conversation as it takes place between children. In the meantime we shall content ourselves with examining adapted information (whether it takes place in dialogue or not) in relation to the main body of talk indulged in by our two subjects, and with noting how small is the part played by this form of language in comparison to the egocentric forms and those socialized forms of speech such as commands, threats, criticisms, etc., which are not connected with mere statement of fact.

The form in which adapted information first presents itself to us, is that of simple information. Here are a few clear examples:

*[Omitted from this volume.]

Lev is helping Geo to play Lotto: *"I think that goes here."* Geo points to a duplicate card. Lev: *"If you lose one, there will still be one left."* Then: *"You've got three of the same,"* or: *"You all see what you have to do."*

Mlle. R. calls Ar "Roger." Pie: *"He isn't called Roger."*

Such remarks as these are clearly very different from dual monologues. The child's object is definitely to convey something to his hearer. It is from the latter's point of view that the subject speaks, and no longer from his own. Henceforward the child lays claim to be understood, and presses his claim if he does not gain his point; whereas in the collective monologue words were thrown out at random, and it little mattered where they fell.

In adapted information the child can naturally talk about himself as about any other subject of conversation. All that is needed is that his remarks should be "adapted" as in the following examples:

Ez and Pie: "I shall have one tomorrow (a season-ticket on the tramway)—*I shall have mine this afternoon."*

Ez and Pie are building a church with bricks: *'We could do that with parallels too. I want to put the parallels on."*

. . . Dialogue, in our view, occurs when the child who has been spoken to in a proposition, answers by talking about something that was treated of in this proposition (as in the example of the tram-way season-ticket), and does not start off on some cock-and-bull story as so often happens in collective monologue.

In conclusion, as soon as the child informs his hearer about anything but himself, or as soon as in speaking of himself, he enters into collaboration or simply into dialogue with his hearer, there is adapted information. So long as the child talks about himself without collaborating with his audience or without evoking a dialogue, there is only collective monologue.

These definitions and the inability of collective monologue to draw others into the speaker's sphere of action render it all the more remarkable that with Pie and Lev adapted information numbers only half as many remarks as collective monologue. Before establishing the exact proportion we must find out what sort of things our two subjects tell each other, and what they argue about on those rare occasions when we can talk of arguments taking place between children.

On the first point we may note the complete absence between the children of anything in the nature of explanation, if by this word we mean causal explanation, i.e., an answer of the form "for such a reason" to the question "why?" All the observed cases of information which might be thought to resemble explanation are statements of fact or descriptions, and are free from any desire to explain the causes of phenomena.

Here are examples of information which simply state or describe:

Lev and Pie: *"That's 420." "It isn't 10 o'clock." "A roof doesn't look like that"* (talking of a drawing). *"This is a village, a great big village,"* etc.

Even when they talk about natural phenomena, the information they give each other never touches on causality.

Lev: "Thunder rolls—*No, it doesn't roll—It's water— No it doesn't roll—* What is thunder?—*Thunder is . . ."* (He doesn't go on.)

This absence of causal explanations is remarkable, especially in the case of machines, motors, bicycles, etc., which the subjects occasionally discuss, but always from what we may call the factual point of view.

Lev; *"It's on the same rail. Funny sort of cart, a motor cart—A bicycle for two men."*

Now each of these children taken separately is able to explain the mechanism of a bicycle. Pie does so imperfectly, but Lev does so quite well. Each has a number of ideas on mechanics, but they never discuss them together. Causal relations remain unexpressed and are thought about only by the individual, probably because, to the child mind, they are represented by images rather than by words. Only the underlying factual element finds expression.

This peculiarity comes out very clearly when children collaborate in a game.

Here for instance are Pie and Ez occupied in drawing a house together. Pie: *"You must have a little button there for the light, a little button for the the light . . . Now I'm doing the 'lectric light . . . There are two 'lectric lights. Look we'll have two 'lectric lights. These are all squares of 'lectric lights."*

Questions of causality are therefore confined to conversations between children and adults, or to those between younger and older children. Which is the same thing as saying that most of these questions are kept hidden away by the child in the fastness of his intimate and unformulated thought.

Here are those of the remarks exchanged by Lev and Pie which approach most nearly to causal explanation. It will be seen that they are almost entirely descriptive:

Lev: *"We ought to have a little water. This green paint is so very hard, most awfully hard"* . . . *"In cardboard, don't you know? You don't know how to, but it is rather difficult for you, it is for everyone."*

Childish arguments, it is curious to note, present exactly the same features. Just as our two subjects never communicate their thoughts on the why and wherefore of phenomena, so in arguing they never support their statements with the "because" and "since" of logic. For them, with two exceptions only, arguing consists simply in a clash of affirmations, without any attempt at logical justification. It belongs to the type which we shall denote as "primitive argument" and which we shall characterize by just this lack of motivation.

The example given on page 76 (the argument between Lev and a child of the same age about thunder) proves this very clearly. Here are three more examples, the first two quite definite, the third of a more intermediate character.

Ez to Pie: *"You're going to marry me—Pie: No, I won't marry you—Oh yes you'll marry me—No—Yes . . . etc."*
"Look how lovely my 6 is going to be—Lev: Yes it's a 6 but really and truly it's a 9—No, it's a 6, Nought—You said nought, and it's not true, it's a 9. Really it is—No—Yes—It was done like that already—Oh no, that's a lie. You silly."
Lev looks to see what Hei is doing: *"Two moons—No, two suns.—Suns aren't like that, with a mouth. They're like this, suns up there—They're round—Yes they're quite round, but they haven't got eyes and a mouth.— Yes they have, they can see—No they can't. It's only God who can see."*

In the first two examples the argument is simply a clash of contrary affirmations, without mutual concessions and without motivation. The last is more complex. When Lev says *"It's only God who can see . . ."* or *"They are like this,"* he does seem at the first glance to be justifying his remarks, to be doing something more than merely stating facts. But there is no explicit justification, no attempt to demonstrate. Hei asserts and Lev denies. Hei makes no effort to give any reasons for believing that the sun has eyes, he does not say that he has seen pictures which have led him to such an idea, etc. Lev for his part does not attempt to get at Hei's point of view, and gives no explicit reason for defending his own. In the main then there is still only a clash of assertions, different enough from the two following little arguments, one of which, by the way, takes place between a child and an adult.

These indeed are the only examples we have found where the child tries to prove his assertions. They should be carefully examined, considering how seldom the fact occurs before the age of 7 or 8.

Lev talking to Mlle. G.: *"You've been eating paint—No, I haven't, which? —White paint—No—Oh, yes you have 'cos there's some on your mouth."*

The reader will note the correct use made of "because" at the age of 6½. In the three lists of complete vocabularies given by Mlle. Descoeudres* "because" is used by the 7-year-old but not by the 5-year-old child.

Here is another instance, again of Lev: *"That is 420—But it's not the number of the house—Why not?—The number of the house is on the door."*

Note here the use of "why" in the sense of "for what reason." The reader will see how superior these two arguments are to the preceding examples. . . .

Criticism and Derision. If we set aside questions and answers, the socialized language of the child in its nonintellectual aspect may be divided into two easily distinguishable categories: on the one hand commands, on the other criticism and derision. There is nothing peculiar about these categories in children; only their percentage is interesting. . . .

The percentage of this group is low: 3 percent for Lev, and 7 percent for Pie. This may be a question of individual types, and if this category is too weakly represented in subsequent research, we may have to assimilate it to one of the preceding ones.

Commands, Requests, Threats. Why is the ratio of adapted information so low in comparison to that of the egocentric forms of speech, particularly in comparison to collective monologue? The reason is quite simple. The child does not in the first instance communicate with his fellow-beings in order to share thoughts and reflections; he does so in order to play. The result is that the part played by intellectual interchange is reduced to the strictly necessary minimum. The rest of language will only assist action, and will consist of commands, etc.

Commands and threats, then, like criticisms, deserve a category to themselves. They are, moreover, very easy to recognize:

Lev (outside a shop): *"Mustn't come in here without paying. I shall tell Gé"* (if you come). *"Come here Mr. Passport," "Give me the blue one." "You must make a flag." "Come along, Ro. Look . . . you shall be the cart,"* etc.

*A. Descoeudres, "Le developpement de l'enfant de deux à sept ans," *Coll. Actual. Ped.* (1922): 190.

Pie: *"Ez, come and see the salamander." "Get out of the way, I shan't be able to see,"* etc. (About a roof): *"No, take it away, take it away 'cos I want to put on mine,"* etc.

We need not labor the point. The only distinction calling for delicate discrimination is that between requests which tend imperceptibly to become commands, and questions which contain an implicit request. All requests which are not expressed in interrogative form we shall agree to call "entreaties," and shall include in the present category; while for interrogative requests a place will be reserved in our next category.

. . . So long as we are agreed upon the conventions adopted, and do not take the statistics too literally, the rest need not detain us. It is not, moreover, the ratio of commands to orders that will be of most use to us, but the ratio of the bulk of socialized language to the bulk of ego-centric language. It is easy enough to agree upon these fundamental distinctions.

The percentage of the present category is 10 percent for Lev and 15 percent for Pie. Dialogue and information were for the same subjects respectively, 12 percent and 14 percent.

Questions and Answers. A preliminary difficulty presents itself in connection with these two categories which we propose to treat of together: do they both belong to socialized language? As far as answers are concerned, we need be in no doubt. Indeed, we shall describe as an "answer" the adapted words used by the person spoken to, after he has heard and understood a question. For instance:

"What color is that?—(Lev) *Brownish yellow."*—"What are you doing, Lev?—*The boat,"* etc.

To answers we shall assimilate refusals and acceptances, which are answers given not to questions of fact but to commands and requests:

"Will you give it back to me? (the ticket).—*No, I don't need it. I'm in the boat"* (Lev).

These two groups, which together constitute answers, obviously belong to socialized language. If we place them in a separate category instead of assimilating them to adapted information, it is chiefly because answers do not belong to the spontaneous speech of the child. It would be sufficient for his neighbors to interrupt him and for adults to question him all the time, to raise a child's socialized language to a much higher percentage. We shall therefore eliminate answers from our calculations in the following paragraph. All remarks provoked by adults will thus be done away with. Answers, moreover, constitute only 18 percent of Lev's language and 14 percent of Pie's. . . .

And the questions which children ask one another—do they too belong to socialized language? Curiously enough the point is one that can be raised, for many remarks are made by children in an interrogative form without being in any way questions addressed to anyone. The proof of this is that the child does not listen to the answer, and does not even expect it. He supplies it himself. This happens frequently between the ages of 3 and 5. At the age of our two subjects it is rarer. When such pseudo-questions do occur, we have classed them as monologue or information (e.g., *"Please teacher is half right? Yes, look"* Lev). For the present we shall therefore deal only with questions proper.

Questions make up 17 percent of Lev's language and 13 percent of Pie's. Their importance is therefore equal and even superior to that of information, and since a question is a spontaneous search for information, we shall now be able to check the accuracy of our assertions concerning this last category. Two of its characteristics were particularly striking: the absence of intellectual intercourse among the children on the subject of causality, and the absence of proof and logical justification in their discussions. If we jump to the conclusion that children keep such thoughts to themselves and do not socialize them, we may be met with the counter assertion that children simply do not have such thoughts, in which case there would be no question of their socializing them! This is partly the case as regards logical demonstration. With regard to causal explanation, however—and by this we mean not only the appeal to mechanical causality such as is made only after the ages of 7 or 8, but also the appeal to final, or as we shall call it, to pre-causality, i.e., that which is invoked in the child's "whys" between the ages of 3 and 7 to 8—as regards this type of explanation, then, there are two things to be noted. In the first place, the children of the Maison des Petits deal in their drawings and free compositions with animals, physical objects (stars, sky, rain, etc.), with machines and manufactured objects (trains, motors, boats, houses, bicycles, etc.). These might therefore give rise to questions of origin and causality. In the second place, "whys" play an important part in all questions asked of grown-ups by children under 7. Now among these "whys" a large number are "whys of explanation," meaning "for what reason" or "for what object." Explanation supplies about 18 percent of the subject matter dealt with in the questions of the child of 6 or 7. If, therefore, there are few questions of explanation in the talk of our two present subjects, this is strongly in favor of the interpretation we have given of information and dialogue between children in general. Intellectual intercourse between children is still factual or descriptive, i.e., little concerned with causality, which remains the subject of conversation between children and adults or of the child's own solitary reflection.

The facts seem to bear this out. Only 3 out of Pie's 173 questions are "whys." Out of Lev's 224 questions only 10 are "whys." Of these, only two "whys" of Lev's are "whys of explanation."

"Why has he turned round?" (a stuffed owl which Lev believes to be alive), and *"Why has he turned round a little?"* (the same).

The rest are "whys" not of causal but of psychological explanation, "intentions" as we shall call them, which is quite another matter:

"Why did he say: 'Hullo Lev'?" "Why was Rey crying?" "Why has he gone away?" etc.

In addition to these we have one "logical why" from Lev, that which we dealt with [above]. It is clear how rarely children ask each other "why?" and how little such questions have to do with causality.

Thus out of the 224 questions asked by Lev and the 173 asked by Pie only two are about explanation, and those two both come from Lev. All the rest can be divided as follows. First of all, we have 141 of Lev's [questions] and 78 of Pie's about children's activities as such, about "actions and intentions":

Lev: *"And my scissors, can you see them?"* *"Are we going to play at Indians?"* *"I'm working, are you?"* *"I didn't hurt you, did I?"* *"Do you know that gentleman?"* *"How shall I paint the house?"* *"How does this go?"* (a ball in the countingframe).

Pie: *"Are you coming this afternoon, Béa?"* *"I say, have you finished yet?"* etc.

This enormous numerical difference between the questions bearing upon children's activity as such, and those dealing with causal explanation is very remarkable. It proves how individualistic the child of 6 still shows himself to be in his intellectual activity, and how restricted in consequence is the interchange of ideas that takes place between children.

A second category of questions, made up of 27 of Lev's and 41 of Pie's, deals with facts and events, time and place.

Facts: *"Is your drum closed?"* *"Is there some paper, too?"* *"Are there snails in there?"* (Pie).
Place: *"Where is the blue, Ez?"* *"Where is she?"* (the tortoise).
Time: *"Please teacher, is it late?"* *"How old are you?"* (Pie).

It will be seen that these questions do not touch upon causality, but are all about matters of fact. Questions of place predominate in this category, 29 for Pie and 13 for Lev.

Another numerous category (51 for Pie, 48 for Lev) is made up of questions purely concerning matters of fact, questions of nomenclature, classification, and evaluation.

Nomenclature: *"What does 'behind' mean?"* *"What is he called?"* (a cook) (Lev).
Classification: *"What ever is that?"* *"Is that yellow?"* (Lev).
Evaluation: *"Is it pretty?"* (Lev, Pie).

We may add a few questions about number (5 by Lev, 1 by Pie):

"Isn't all that enough for 2fr.50?" *"And how much for 11?"* (Lev).

Finally, mention should be made of two questions by Pie and one by Lev about rules (writing, etc.).

"You put it on this side, don't you?" (the figure 3) (Lev).

The following table completely summarizes the questions asked by Lev and Pie, including their "whys."

		LEV		PIE	
Questions of causal explanation		2		0	
			2		0
Questions of Reality	Facts and events	7		8	
	Time	7		4	
	Place	13		29	
			27		41
Actions and intentions		—	141	—	78
Rules		—	1	—	2
Questions of Classification	Nomenclature	7		0	
	Classification and evaluation	41		51	
			48		51
Number		—	5	—	1
TOTAL			224		173

We shall not dwell upon the criteria of the different categories nor upon their functional interests. It will be enough if we conclude from this table that questions from one child to another (questions from children to adults play only a negligible part in this group), bear first and foremost upon actual psychological activity (actions and intentions). Otherwise, when they concern objects and not persons, they bear upon the factual aspect of reality, and not upon causal relations. . . .

CONCLUSIONS

The Measure of Egocentrism. Among the data we have obtained there is one, incidentally of the greatest interest for the study of child logic, which seems to supply the necessary guarantee of objectivity: we mean the proportion of egocentric language to the sum of the child's spontaneous conversation. Egocentric language is, as we have seen, the group made up by the first three of the categories we have enumerated —*repetition, monologue,* and *collective monologue.* All three have this in common that they consist of remarks that are not addressed to anyone, or not to anyone in particular, and that they evoke no reaction adapted to them on the part of anyone to whom they may chance to be addressed. Spontaneous language is therefore made up of the first seven categories, i.e., of all except *answers.* It is therefore the sum total of all remarks, *minus* those which are made as an answer to a question asked by an adult or a child. We have eliminated this heading as being subject to chance circumstances; it is sufficient for a child to have come in contact with many adults or with some talkative companion, to undergo a marked change in the percentage of his answers. Answers given, not to definite questions (with interrogation mark) or commands, but in the course of the dialogue, i.e., propositions answering to other propositions, have naturally been classed under the heading *information and dialogue,* so that there is nothing artificial about the omission of questions from the statistics which we shall give. The child's language *minus* his answers constitutes a complete whole in which intelligence is represented at every stage of its development.

The proportion of egocentric to other spontaneous forms of language is represented by the following fractions:

$$\frac{Eg.\ L}{Sp.\ L} = 0.47 \text{ for Lev,} \quad \frac{Eg.\ L}{Sp.\ L} = 0.43 \text{ for Pie.}$$

(The proportion of egocentric language to the sum total of the subject's speech, including answers, is 39 percent for Lev and 37 percent for Pie.)

. . . Moreover, these two coefficients do actually represent the average for children between the ages of 7 and 8. The same calculation based on some 1500 remarks in quite another classroom yielded the result of 0.45 (a.v. = 0.05).

This constancy in the proportion of egocentric language is the more remarkable in view of the fact that we have found nothing of the kind in connection with the other coefficients which we have sought to establish. We have, it is true, determined the proportion of socialized factual language (*information and questions*) to socialized nonfactual language (*criticism, commands,* and *requests*). But this proportion fluctuates from 0.72 to 2.23 with a mean variation 0.71 for Lev (as compared with 0.04 and 0.06 as the coefficients of egocentrism), and between 0.43 and 2.33 with a mean variation of 0.42 for Pie. Similarly, the relation of egocentric to socialized factual language yields no coefficient of any constancy.

Of all this calculation let us bear only this in mind, that our two subjects of 6½ have each an egocentric language which amounts to nearly half of their total spontaneous speech.

The following table summarizes the functions of the language used by both these children:

	Pie	Lev
1 Repetition	2	1
2 Monologue	5	15
3 Collective monologue	30	23
4 Adapted information	14	13
5 Criticism	7	3
6 Commands	15	10
7 Requests	13	17
8 Answers	14	18
Egocentric language	37	39
Spontaneous socialized language	49	43
Sum of socialized language	63	61
Coefficient of egocentrism	0.43±0.06	0.47±0.04

We must once more emphasize the fact that in all these calculations the number of remarks made by children to adults is negligible. . . .

Conclusion. What are the conclusions we can draw from these facts? It would seem that up to a certain age we may safely admit that children think and act more egocentrically than adults, that they share each other's intellectual life less than we do. True, when they are together they seem to talk to each other a great deal more than we do about what they are doing, but for the most part they are only talking to themselves. We, on the contrary, keep silent far longer about our action, but our talk is almost always socialized. . . .

Egocentrism must not be confused with secrecy. Reflection in the child does not admit of privacy. Apart from thinking by images or autistic symbols which cannot be directly communicated, the child up to an age, as yet undetermined but probably somewhere about 7, is incapable of keeping to himself the thoughts which enter his mind. . . . Does this mean that he socializes his thought more than we do? That is the whole question, and it is for us to see to whom the child really speaks. It may be to others. We think on the contrary that, as the preceding study shows, it is first and foremost to himself, and that speech, before it can be used to socialize thought, serves to accompany and reinforce individual activity. Let us try to examine more closely the difference between thought which is socialized but capable of secrecy, and infantile thought which is egocentric but incapable of secrecy.

The adult, even in his most personal and private occupation, even when he is engaged on an inquiry which is incomprehensible to his fellow-beings, thinks socially, has continually in his mind's eye his collaborators or opponents, actual or eventual, at any rate members of his own profession to whom sooner or later he will announce the result of his labors. This mental picture pursues him throughout his task. The task itself is henceforth socialized at almost every stage of its development. Invention eludes this process, but the need for checking and demonstrating calls into being an inner speech addressed throughout to a hypothetical opponent, whom the imagination often pictures as one of flesh and blood. When, therefore, the adult is brought face to face with his fellow-beings, what he announces to them is something already socially elaborated and therefore roughly adapted to his audience, i.e., it is comprehensible. Indeed, the further a man has advanced in his own line of thought, the better able is he to see things from the point of view of others and to make himself understood by them.

The child, on the other hand, placed in the conditions which we have described, seems to talk far more than the adult. Almost everything he does is to the tune of remarks such as "I'm drawing a hat," "I'm doing it better than you," etc. Child thought, therefore, seems more social, less capable of sustained and solitary research. This is so only in appearance. The child has less verbal continence simply because he does not know what it is to keep a thing to himself. Although he talks almost incessantly to his neighbors, he rarely places himself at their point of view. He speaks to them for the most part as if he were alone, and as if he were thinking aloud. He speaks, therefore, in a language which disregards the precise shade of meaning in things and ignores the particular angle from which they are viewed, and which above all is always making assertions, even in argument, instead of justifying them. Nothing could be harder to understand than the notebooks which we have filled with the conversation of Pie and Lev. Without full commentaries, taken down at the same time as the children's remarks, they would be incomprehensible. Everything is indicated by allusion, by pronouns and demonstrative articles—"he, she, the, mine, him, etc."—which can mean anything in turn, regardless of the demands of clarity or even of intelligibility. In a word, the child hardly ever even asks himself whether he has been understood. For him, that goes without saying, for he does not think about others when he talks. He utters a "collective monologue." His language only begins to resemble that of adults when he is directly interested in making himself understood; when he gives orders or asks questions. To put it quite simply, we may say that the adult thinks socially, even when he is alone, and that the child under 7 thinks egocentrically, even in the society of others.

What is the reason for this? It is, in our opinion, twofold. It is due, in the first place, to the absence of any sustained social intercourse between the children of less than 7 or 8, and in the second place to the fact that the language used in the fundamental activity of the child—play—is one of gestures, movement, and mimicry as much as of words. There is, as we have said, no real social life between children of less than 7 or 8 years. The type of children's society represented in a classroom of the Maison des Petits is obviously of a fragmentary character, in which consequently there is neither division of work, centralization of effort, nor unity of conversation. We may go further, and say that it is a society in which, strictly speaking, individual and social life are not differentiated. . . . The child is neither individualized, since he cannot keep a single thought secret, and since everything done by one member of the group is repeated through a sort of imitative repercussion by almost every other member, nor is he socialized, since this imitation is not accompanied by what may properly be called an interchange of thought, about half the remarks made by children being egocentric in character. If, as Baldwin and Janet maintain, imitation is accompanied by a sort of confusion between one's own action and that of others, then we may find in this fragmentary type of society based on imitation some sort of explanation of the paradoxical character of the conversation of children who, while they are continually announcing their doings, yet talk only for themselves, without listening to anyone else.

Social life at the Maison des Petits passes, according to the observations of Mlles Audemars and Lafendel, through three stages. Up till the age of about 5, the child almost always works alone. From 5 to about 7½, little groups of two are formed, like that of Pie and Ez (cf. the remarks taken down under the heading "adapted information"). These groups are transitory and irregular. Finally, between 7 and 8 the desire manifests itself to work with others. Now it is in our opinion just at this age that egocentric talk loses some of its importance, and it is at this age that we shall place the higher stages of conversation properly so called as it takes place between children. It is also at this age that children begin to understand each other in spoken explanations, as opposed to explanations in which gestures play as important a part as words.

A simple way of verifying these hypotheses is to reexamine children between 7 and 8 whose egocentrism at an earlier stage has been ascertained. This is the task which Mlle Berguer undertook with Lev. She took down under the same conditions as previously some 600 remarks made by Lev at the age of 7 and a few months. The coefficient of egocentricism was reduced to 0.27. . . .

If language in the child of about 6½ is still so far from being socialized, and if the part played in it by the egocentric forms is so considerable in comparison to information and dialogue, etc., the reason for this lies in the fact that childish language includes two distinct varieties, one made up of gestures, movements, mimicry, etc., which accompany or even completely supplant the use of words, and the other consisting solely of the spoken word. Now, gesture cannot express everything. Intellectual processes, therefore, will remain egocentric, whereas commands, etc., all the language that is bound up with action, with handicraft, and especially with play, will tend to become more socialized. . . .

Results and Hypotheses. Psychoanalysts have been led to distinguish two fundamentally different modes of thinking: *directed* or *intelligent thought*, and *undirected* or, as Bleuler proposes to call it, *autistic thought*. Directed thought is conscious, i.e., it pursues an aim which is present to the mind of the thinker; it is intelligent, which means that it is adapted to reality and tries to influence it; it admits of being true or false (empirically or logically true), and it can be communicated by language. Autistic thought is subconscious, which means that the aims it pursues and the problems it tries to solve are not present in consciousness; it is not adapted to reality, but creates for itself a dream world of imagination; it tends, not to establish truths, but to satisfy desires, and it remains strictly individual and incommunicable as such by means of language. It works chiefly by images, and in order to express itself, has recourse to indirect methods, evoking by means of symbols and myths the feeling by which it is led.

Here, then, are two fundamental modes of thought which, though separated neither at their origin nor in the course of their functioning, are subject, nevertheless, to two diverging sets of logical laws.* Directed thought, as it develops, is controlled more and more by the laws of experience and of logic in the stricter sense. Autistic thought, on the other hand, obeys a whole system of special laws (laws of symbolism and of immediate satisfaction) which we need not elaborate here. Let us consider, for instance, the completely different lines of thought pursued from the point of view of intelligence and from that of autism when we think of such an object as, say, water.

To intelligence, water is a natural substance whose origin we know, or whose formation we can at least empirically observe; its behavior and motions are subject to certain laws which can be studied, and it has from the dawn of history been the object of technical experiment (for purposes of irrigation, etc.). To the autistic attitude, on the other hand, water is interesting only in connection with the satisfaction of organic wants. It can be drunk. But as such, as well as simply in virtue of its external appearance, it has come to represent in folk and child fantasies, and in those of adult subconsciousness, themes of a purely organic character. It has in fact been identified with the liquid substances which issue from the human body, and has come, in this way, to symbolize birth itself, as is proved by so many myths (birth of Aphrodite, etc.), rites (baptism, the symbol of a new birth), dreams† and stories told by children.‡ Thus in the one case thought adapts itself to water as part of the external world, in the other, thought uses the idea of water not in order to adapt itself to it, but in order to assimilate it to those more or less conscious images connected with fecundation and the idea of birth.

Now these two forms of thought, whose characteristics diverge so profoundly, differ chiefly as to their origin, the one being socialized and guided by the increasing adaptation of individuals one to another, whereas the other remains individual and uncommunicated. Furthermore—and this is of the very first importance for the understanding of child thought—this divergence is due in large part to the following fact. Intelligence, just because it undergoes a gradual process of socialization, is enabled through the bond established by language between thoughts and words to make an increasing use of concepts; whereas autism, just because it remains individual, is still tied to imagery, to organic activity, and even to organic movements. The mere fact, then, of telling one's thought, of telling it to others, or of keeping silence and telling it only to oneself must be of enormous importance to the fundamental structure and functioning of thought in general, and of child logic in particular. Now between autism and intelligence there are many degrees, varying

---

*There is interaction between these two modes of thought. Autism undoubtedly calls into being and enriches many inventions which are subsequently clarified and demonstrated by intelligence.

†See H. Flournoy, "Quelques rêves au sujet de la signification symbolique de l'eau et du feu." *Intern. Zeitschr. f. Psychoan.*, p. 398 (cf. pp. 329 and 330).

‡We have published the case of Vo, a child of 9, who regards humanity as descended from a baby who issued from a worm which came out of the sea. Cf. Piaget, "La pensée symbolique et la pensée de l'enfant."

with their capacity for being communicated. These intermediate varieties must therefore be subject to a special logic, intermediate too between the logic of autism and that of intelligence. The chief of those intermediate forms, i.e., the type of thought which like that exhibited by our children seeks to adapt itself to reality, but does not communicate itself as such, we propose to call *egocentric thought*. This gives us the following table:

	Noncommunicable thought	Communicable thought
Undirected thought	*Autistic thought*	*(Mythological thought)*
Directed thought	*Egocentric thought*	*Communicated intelligence*

We shall quickly realize the full importance of egocentrism if we consider a certain familiar experience of daily life. We are looking, say, for the solution of some problem, when suddenly everything seems quite clear; we have understood, and we experience that *sui generis* feeling of intellectual satisfaction. But as soon as we try to explain to others what it is we have understood, difficulties come thick and fast. These difficulties do not arise merely because of the effort of attention needed to hold in a single grasp the links in the chain of argument; they are attributable also to our judging faculty itself. Conclusions which we deemed positive no longer seem so; between certain propositions whole series of intermediate links are now seen to be lacking in order to fill the gaps of which we were previously not even conscious; arguments which seemed convincing because they were connected with some schema of visual imagery or based on some sort of analogy, lose all their potency from the moment we feel the need to appeal to these schemas, and find that they are incommunicable; doubt is cast on propositions connected with judgments of value, as soon as we realize the personal nature of such judgments. If such, then, is the difference between personal understanding and spoken explanation, how much more marked will be the characteristics of personal understanding when the individual has for a long time been bottling up his own thoughts, when he has not even formed the habit of thinking in terms of other people, and of communicating his thoughts to them. We need only recall the inextricable chaos of adolescent thought to realize the truth of this distinction.

Egocentric thought and intelligence therefore represent two different forms of reasoning, and we may even say, without paradox, two different logics. By logic is meant here the sum of the habits which the mind adopts in the general conduct of its operations—in the general conduct of a game of chess, in contrast, as Poincaré says, to the special rules which govern each separate proposition, each particular move in the game. Egocentric logic and communicable logic will therefore differ less in their conclusions (except with the child, where egocentric logic often functions) than in the way they work. The points of divergence are as follows:

(1) Egocentric logic is more intuitive, more "syncretistic" than deductive, i.e., its reasoning is not made explicit. The mind leaps from premise to conclusion at a single bound, without stopping on the way. (2) Little value is attached to proving, or even checking propositions. The vision of the whole brings about a state of belief and a feeling of

security far more rapidly than if each step in the argument were made explicit. (3) Personal schemas of analogy are made use of, likewise memories of earlier reasoning, which control the present course of reasoning without openly manifesting their influence. (4) Visual schemas also play an important part, and can even take the place of proof in supporting the deduction that is made. (5) Finally, judgments of value have far more influence on egocentric than on communicable thought.

In communicated intelligence, on the other hand, we find (1) far more deduction, more of an attempt to render explicit the relations between propositions by such expressions as *therefore, if . . . then,* etc. (2) Greater emphasis is laid on proof. Indeed, the whole exposition is framed in view of the proof, i.e., in view of the necessity of convincing someone else, and (as a corollary) of convincing oneself whenever one's personal certainty may have been shaken by the process of deductive reasoning. (3) Schemas of analogy tend to be eliminated, and to be replaced by deduction proper. (4) Visual schemas are also done away with, first as incommunicable, and later as useless for purposes of demonstration. (5) Finally personal judgments of value are eliminated in favor of collective judgments of value, these being more in keeping with ordinary reason.

. . . In the child between 3 and 7 the five characteristics which have just been enumerated actually go to make up a kind of special logic which we shall have occasion to mention. . . . We are now in a position to realize that the fact of being or of not being communicable is not an attribute which can be added to thought from the outside, but is a constitutive feature of profound significance for the shape and structure which reasoning may assume. . . .

14

Judgment and Reasoning in the Child*

1924

INTRODUCTORY NOTES

Judgment and Reasoning in the Child (1924), published one year after *Language and Thought,* is primarily devoted to an analysis of the main features of children's thinking by means of three specific studies.

The first study deals with the relations between grammar and logic as Piaget understood them in 1924, long before generative grammar had an impact upon psychologists. It analyzes children's use and understanding of causality and discordance conjunctions, such as "because," "thus," "then," "but," and so on. Children seem to understand and use these conjunctions according to rules of logic that differ strongly from adult rules of logic for their use and understanding. In this work, Piaget states, for the first time, his position on the relations between language and thought. He not only suggests the primacy of thought over language but also places the origin of thought in action.

The second study approaches the constitution of formal reasoning by close examination of an intelligence test item. But instead of presenting the test in the standardized fashion in which the test is supposed to be administered, Piaget uses the test questions as an opportunity for an extended discussion with the child. During this conversation the experimenter tries to bring forth the best of the child's conception of a specific problem by following all the meanderings of the flow of thinking. The resemblance with certain elements of the psychoanalytic method is clear.

In the third study Piaget investigates notions of relativity: the brother relationship; the relativity of the notions of left and right; the definition of a family; and class inclusion as applied to country, state, and city.

Out of this apparent disparity of aims and goals, Piaget draws, nevertheless, interesting conclusions such as the absence of a principle of contradiction in children's reasoning, and reasoning by mere juxtaposition of elements of

*From J. Piaget, *Judgment and Reasoning in the Child.* Reprinted by permission of Humanities Press, Inc., Atlantic Highlands, New Jersey, and Routledge & Kegan Paul Ltd., London. Originally published in French, 1924. (Collaborators: Emmy Cartalis, Sophie Escher, Ulbrike Hanhart, L. Hahnloser, Olga Matthes, Suzanne Perret, and Marcelle Roud.)

thought or information. The most interesting of these conclusions is the focus on the problem of mental reversibility and its absence in prelogical children.

The book concludes with a theoretical essay on reasoning in the child at the preoperational level of development.

The Principal Features of Child Logic*

Rousseau loved to say that the child is not a small grown-up, but has needs of his own, and a mentality adapted to these needs. Contemporary studies of the language and drawing of children have often emphasized the truth of this view. Karl Groos, in his "theory of play," has given particular weight to this statement, and Claparède has developed it extensively from the functional point of view. The time, therefore, seems ripe for raising the question whether child thought, which differentiates itself from every other kind of thought, both by the interests which guide it, and by its means of expression, cannot also be distinguished by its logical structure and method of functioning. . . .

But what do we mean by explaining psychological phenomena? As Baldwin has shown in his subtle analyses, without the genetic method in psychology, we can never be sure of not taking effects for causes, nor even of having formulated problems of explanation aright. The relation of cause and effect must, therefore, be superseded by that of genetic progression, which adds the notion of functional dependence, in the mathematical sense of the word, to that of antecedent and consequent. This will give us the right to say of two phenomena, A and B, that A is a function of B, as B is a function of A, and yet leave us the possibility of taking the earliest phenomenon, i.e., genetically speaking, the most explicative, as the starting point of our description. What, then, are these explicative phenomena? The psychology of thought is always faced at this point with two fundamental factors, whose connection [must be explained]: the biological factor, and the social factor. The mind becomes conscious of itself, and consequently exists psychologically speaking only when it is in contact with objects or with other minds. We have here two different planes, theoretically independent of one another, and which logically one would wish to keep separate; but in practice, these two planes will always be associated, so long as the child has parents who represent society to him, and so long as he experiences sensations which constitute a biological environment. . . . These two poles must both be kept in view, and nothing must be sacrificed; but in order to make a beginning, we must needs choose one language at the expense of others. We have chosen the language of sociology, but wish to emphasize the point that there need be nothing exclusive in the choice. . . . All we have attempted to do as a beginning, was to order our description from the point of view of social psychology, taking the most characteristic phe-

*This chapter summarizes Volume I (*The Language and Thought of the Child*), and the present volume, which constitutes the conclusion of our "Studies in Child Logic." . . .

nomenon as our starting point, namely, egocentrism of child thought. We have sought to trace most of the characteristics of child logic to egocentrism; though of many of these it might just as well be said that their presence explains egocentrism. This is of no consequence to the object of our research; all we need do is to point out that these characteristics form a compact group, for it is this very group that defines the logic of the child.

EGOCENTRISM OF THOUGHT IN THE CHILD

Logical activity is not the whole of intelligence. One can be intelligent without being particularly logical. The main functions of intelligence, that of inventing solutions, and that of verifying them, do not necessarily involve one another; the first partakes of imagination, the second alone is properly logical. Demonstration, search for truth, is therefore the true function of logic.

But on what occasions do we experience the need to verify our thought? This need does not arise spontaneously in us. On the contrary, it appears very late, and for two reasons. The first is that thought puts itself at the service of the immediate satisfaction of desire long before forcing itself to seek for truth. [The] most spontaneous manifestation [of thought] is play, or at any rate that quasi-hallucinatory form of a imagination which allows us to regard desires as realized as soon as they are born. All the writers who have concerned themselves with the play, the testimony, and the lies of children, have realized this. Freud has restated it with vigor by showing that the *Lustprinzip* is prior to the *Realitätsprinzip*. Now the child's mind is full of these "ludistic" tendencies up to the age of 7–8, which means that before this age it is extremely difficult for him to distinguish between fabulation and truth.

But this is not all. Even when thought turns away from immediate satisfaction and play, and gives itself up to disinterested curiosity in things for their own sakes (and this curiosity appears very soon, certainly from the age of 3) the individual still has the peculiar capacity for immediate belief in his own ideas. It is, therefore, not for ourselves that we try to verify our statements. One of the most striking things one finds about the child under 7–8, is his extreme assurance on all subjects. When, according to one of the well-known Binet-Simon tests, a subject of 4 or 5 is shown two little boxes of the same volume, and is asked, "Which is [heavier]?" he immediately answers, "That one," without even having felt the weight of the boxes, and it is the same in everything. "I know!" . . . such is the only proof that is used for a long time in childish logic. . . .

It must be remembered, moreover, that experience itself does not undeceive minds orientated in this fashion. Things are in the wrong, not they. The savage who calls down rain by a magic rite explains his failure as the work of an evil spirit. He is, according to a famous saying, "impervious to experience." Experience undeceives him only on very special technical points (cultivation, hunting, or manufacture); but even this momentary and partial contact with facts does not react in any way upon the orientation of his thought. This applies even more strongly to the child whose every material want is anticipated by his parents' care. Only in his manual games does the child learn to understand the resistance of objects. On the plane of verbal thought, every idea pictures a belief. Round about the age of 6–7, for example, what Mr Brunschvicg calls the "artificialist" explanations given by children, of natural phenomena, are very frequent: rivers, lakes, mountains, sea, and rocks have been made by man. Obviously, this does not require the slightest proof: the child has never seen people digging lakes or building rocks, but this does not matter. He enlarges sensible reality (a bricklayer making a wall, or a labourer making a ditch) by means of the verbal and magic reality which he puts onto the same plane. These things are not sufficient in themselves to make the mind feel any need for verification, since things themselves have been made by the mind. On the contrary, the child never really comes into contact with things because he does not work. He plays with them, or simply believes them without trying to find the truth.

What then gives rise to the need for verification? Surely it must be the shock of our thought coming into contact with that of others, which produces doubt and the desire to prove. If there were not other people, the disappointments of experience would lead to overcompensation and dementia. We are constantly hatching an enormous number of false ideas, conceits, Utopias, mystical explanations, suspicions, and megalomaniacal fantasies, which disappear when brought into contact with other people. The social need to share the thought of others and to communicate our own with success is at the root of our need for verification. Proof is the outcome of argument. All this, moreover, is common knowledge for contemporary psychology. P. Janet has laid great stress on the psychological origin of reflection. Reflection is the act by which we unify our various tendencies and beliefs, in the same way as conversation and social intercourse unify the opinions of individuals, namely, by giving due weight to each, and extracting an average opinion from the lot. Argument is, therefore, the backbone of verification. Logical reasoning is an argument which we have with ourselves, and which reproduces internally the features of a real argument. Ch. Blondel has given an added importance to these views, by showing that pathological thought is the result of the given individual's inability to submit to social habits of thought. Discursive talk and reasoning are the product of intercourse between individuals. When a man cannot fit his personal thoughts and emotions into this schema, when he ceases to think socially, the mere fact of this isolation destroys the logical structure of his thought. Psychoanalysis arrives at a very similar result from a completely different angle, and it is to the lasting credit of this science that it has discovered two ways of thinking, one, social, communicable, guided by the need for adapting oneself to others, "logical thought," the other, personal, incommunicable as such, "autistic thought." Now Freud and his disciples have shown that by the mere fact of its "autism," this second way of thinking was bound to be confused, undirected, indifferent to truth, rich in visual and symbolic schemas, and above all, unconscious of itself and of the affective factors by which it was guided.

In order to understand child logic, we must therefore begin by asking in what degree children communicate their thought, and try to conform to that of others. In order to answer this question, the study of intercourse between children and adults will not at first be of very much use to us. Such intercourse is undoubtedly of fundamental importance, but it raises problems of its own, for the respective parts are not on an equality. The child feels he is inferior to the adult in every way, and is also for a long time under the delusion that the adult understands everything he says. Consequently, he never tries to express his thoughts clearly when he speaks to his parents, and conversely, he remembers only as much as he chooses of what is said by adults, because of his inability to enter into the world of "grown-ups." This is why we have no proof that childish beliefs held in solitude are the same as those which appear in his intercourse with adults. From this point of view, the unity of child thought is only a postulate. We shall, therefore, leave the question of intercourse between child and adult for the moment, and confine ourselves to the results of conversations between children; for if the child really feels any need to socialize his thought, he must be able to satisfy such a need to the full with friends of his own age, whom he sees every day, and with whom he plays in freedom from restraint or self-consciousness. Now, experiment shows that the child's way of thinking occupies a place situated exactly between the "autistic" and the social. We have therefore given it the name of egocentric, which indicates that this type of thought is still autistic in its structure but that its interests tend not merely toward organic or "ludistic" satisfaction as in pure autism, but toward intellectual adaptation as in adult thought. The egocentric character of child thought has been demonstrated by three special inquiries. In the first place (L.T.,* Chap. I), after making verbatim reports at the Maison des Petits (attached to the Institut J. J. Rousseau at Geneva) of the language of several children over a period of about one month each, we discovered that between the ages of 5–7, 44–47 percent of their spontaneous remarks were still egocentric, although these children were free to work, play, and talk exactly as they choose. . . .

A second study (L.T., Chap. II) showed that even in the socialized portion of childish language, conversation passed through a certain number of primitive stages before becoming a genuine interchange of ideas. . . .

Finally, a third study (L.T., Chap. III) served as a countertest and enabled us to specify the causes of this egocentrism. If children talk so little to each other, and if, in particular, their best thoughts toward adaptation to adult thought and to the external world are performed in solitude, this may be for two quite separate reasons. It may be either that they prefer their own company, or it may be that they are permanently under the impression that they understand each other, and have no suspicion of the egocentric character of their thought. As a matter of fact, the second solution is the right one. Not only do children believe that they are talking and actually listening to one another, but they also have a tendency to think that each of their thoughts is common to all the others, that they can all discern it, and understand it, even if it never finds distinct expression. For even if children are egocentric, they are ignorant of the nature of thought, or rather by the mere fact that they talk only for themselves, they are saying aloud everything

*[J. Piaget, The Language and Thought of the Child, hereafter, L.T. Section numbers, when given, refer to original translation.]

that they can express verbally, and therefore believe that they are always understanding one another.

. . . Our third study was devoted to the solution of this question of verbal understanding between children of the same age. Naturally, when children are playing together, or are all handling the same material, they understand each other, because, however elliptical their language may be, it is accompanied by gesture and mimicry which is a beginning of action and serves as an example to the interlocutor. But it can be questioned whether verbal thought and language itself are really understood among children, whether, in other words, children understand each other when they speak without acting. This problem is of fundamental importance, since it is on the verbal plane that the child makes the chief effort of adaptation to adult thought and to the acquisition of logical habits. . . .

For the solution of this problem, we [paired off] fifty children from the same class, between the ages [6 and 8], and we made them [tell] each other a set story, and the explanation of a drawing showing the mechanism of a tap and of a syringe. Now, it will be remembered that although the child who had to explain (and each did so in turn) generally had a clear idea of what he was explaining, his interlocutor generally failed to grasp this explanation, although of course he imagined he had been understanding it perfectly well. We need not recapitulate the numbers which enabled us to estimate the degree of understanding between child and adult, and between one child and another. We need only recall the fact that lack of understanding between children is due as much to faulty expression on the part of the explainer, whose very language is egocentric, as to faulty adaptation on the part of the interlocutor who does not listen because he thinks all along that he can understand everything, and because he assimilates everything he hears to his own point of view.

These are the three groups [of facts] in support of the hypothesis that the thought of the child is more egocentric than ours and that it is halfway between "autism" proper, and socialized thought. Such a statement is indeed hypothetical. There is still a great deal of work to be done on the intercourse between children of different ages, between brothers and sisters, and above all, between parents and children. But the hypothesis is close to common sense. However intimately the child may be connected to his surroundings in his affective life, there is still an enormous portion of his thought that is incommunicable, partly because the adult cannot turn himself into a child, partly because the child cannot measure the limits of adult understanding, nor find language that will logically convey his various shades of meaning. The fact of childish egocentrism, therefore, seems to us to be beyond dispute. The [whole] point is whether egocentrism [leads to] the difficulties in expression and the logical phenomena which we shall presently examine, or whether the reverse is the case. But surely from the genetic point of view, we must start from the child's activity, if we want to explain his thought. Now, this activity is unquestionably egocentric and egotistical. The social instinct is late in developing. The first critical stage occurs at the age of 7–8, and it is precisely at this age that we can place the first period of reflection and logical unification, as well as the first attempts to avoid contradiction.

THE DIFFICULTIES OF CONSCIOUS REALIZATION, AND THE

SHIFTING* OF OPERATIONS ONTO THE PLANE OF THOUGHT

Many adults are still egocentric in their way of thinking. Such people interpose between themselves and reality an imaginary or mystical world, and they reduce everything to this individual point of view. Unadapted to ordinary conditions, they seem to be immersed in an inner life that is all the more intense. Does this make them more conscious of themselves? Does egocentrism point the way to a truer introspection? On the contrary, it can easily be seen that there is a way of living in oneself that develops a great wealth of inexpressible feelings, of personal images and schemas, while at the same time it impoverishes analysis and consciousness of self. The work done by Ch. Blondel constitutes a complete demonstration of this view. The concept of autism in psychoanalysis throws full light upon the fact that the incommunicable character of thought involves a certain degree of unconsciousness. In short, the claim is not too bold that we became conscious of ourselves to the extent that we are adapted to other people. Our discovery that other people do not spontaneously understand us nor we them is the gauge of the efforts we make to mould our language out of the thousand and one accidents created by this lack of adaptation and the measure of our aptitude for the simultaneous analysis of others and of ourselves. . . .

Now a study which we made of certain types of arithmetical reasoning (J.R.,† Chap. IV, §1) brought us into close contact with a very interesting fact in this connection. When we questioned children between the ages of 7 and 9 about little problems connected with the notion of fractions or about certain verbal expressions, such as "x times more," "x times less," we discovered that the very diverse answers we received obeyed a law of development which we were able to state more and more definitely. But it was a long time before we were able to give an immediate interpretation of the children's answers, precisely because the child was incapable of telling us how he had set about the task in each particular case. He appeared in a manner to be unconscious of his own reasoning process, or at any rate incapable of immediate introspection or retrospection. To recall an example: the expression "5 times faster than 50 minutes" was sometimes identified with "45 minutes." As such, this answer has no particular interest for us. But the method and the degree of consciousness in the reasoning process are suggestive. As the number of questions was increased, analysis showed that the child simply takes away 5 minutes, as though "5 times less" meant "−5." But when he is asked to explain what he has done, he can neither describe his process of reasoning nor even say that he has "taken away 5" from 50. He answers, "I tried" or "I found 45." If we go on to ask "How did you find?" and press him to reveal the steps of his reasoning, the child invents a new calculation which is perfectly arbitrary and presupposes the answer 45. One boy, for example, told us: "I took 10 and 10, and then 10 and 10 and then I added 5."

*French décalage.
†[J. Piaget, Judgment and Reasoning in the Child, hereafter, J.R.]

In short, as soon as the problem contains ever so little complexity the child seems to conduct his reasoning process much as we do ours in the course of a purely empirical problem (such as a puzzle, etc.); i.e., he keeps no record of his successive attempts, and his mind proceeds by a series of fumbling movements, each of which is conscious, but that does not easily admit of retrospection as a whole. If after this is over we ask the child to describe his search, all he gives us is a device for finding the solution, and a device which presupposes the solution in question. Never does he succeed in describing his reasoning process as such.

The reader may consider these introspective difficulties insufficient to prove the faint degree of consciousness present in childish reasoning, but a number of other facts lead us to the same conclusion. One of the clearest is the inability of children to give definitions (J.R., Chap. IX, §2). . . .

This feature of children's arithmetical reasoning and of their definitions shows in itself that childish reasoning cannot consist of a deductive sequence about which the subject knows how and why he is carrying it out. It consists of a series of discontinuous judgments which determine one another extrinsically and not intrinsically, or, to put it differently, which entail one another like unconscious acts, and not like conscious judgments. Childish reasoning before the age of 7–8 is in the strict sense of the word the "mental experiment" of Mach. It resembles a physical action during which one arm-movement will bring about another arm-movement, but in which the subject is unaware of the determinism of these successive movements. In other words, the operations remain unconscious, and the determinism which rules them has not yet become logical necessity. Of course, it may be objected that in this determinism there is virtually contained a logical implication. But of such the child is not aware, so that we have no right to speak of logical deduction. There is here, if one likes, a logic of action but as yet no logic of thought.*

Claparède has shown in some exceedingly interesting experiments that consciousness of resemblance appears earlier in the child than consciousness of difference. As a matter of fact, the child simply adopts an identical attitude to all objects that lend themselves to assimilation, but does not need to be aware of this identity of attitude. He "acts" resemblance, in a manner of speaking, before "thinking it." Difference between objects on the other hand creates disadaptation, and this disadaptation is what occasions consciousness. Claparède has taken this fact as the foundation of the law which he had called *loi de prise de conscience:* the more we make use of a relation the less conscious we are of it. Or again: We only become conscious in proportion to our disadaptation.

This law seems to us fundamental for establishing relations between the functional factors of childish thought, particularly between egocentrism and the absence of social needs, and the structural features which define childish logic. For this "law of conscious realization" is

---

*The notion of "unconscious reasoning" is singularly elastic. Either we assign to the unconscious a logic similar to that of reflective thought in which we are making a gratuitous assumption, or else we are thinking of some special process analogous to that which will be described later on. But then the problem arises of how to distinguish this process from conscious "reasoning," and nothing but confusion can come from giving the same name at the outset to operations which are perhaps very different from each other.

alone in explaining why childish egocentrism should involve the inability to be conscious of logical relations. For insofar as he is thinking only for himself, the child has no need to be aware of the mechanism of his reasoning (J.R., Chap. I, §§2 and 4). His attention is wholly turned toward the external world, toward action, in no way directed toward thought as a medium interposed between the world and himself. Insofar, on the other hand, as the child seeks to adapt himself to others, he creates between himself and them a new order of reality, a new place of thought, where speech and argument will henceforth hold this sway, and upon which operations and relations which till then have been the work of action alone will now be handled by imagination and by words. The child will therefore have to become conscious to the same extent of these operations and relations which till then had remained unconscious because they were sufficient for the purposes of action.

How does this conscious realization take place? Claparède's law is a functional law, and only indicates when the individual does or does not require to become conscious. The structural problem remains. What are the means and the obstacles to this conscious realization? In order to answer this question, we shall have to introduce a second law, the law of "shifting." For to become conscious of an operation is to make it pass over from the plane of action to that of language; it is therefore to reinvent it in imagination in order to express it in words. As regards reasoning in particular, to become conscious of its operations means, as Mach, Rignano, and Goblot have said, to remake "mentally" mental experiments that one has already made in action. Consequently, given this perpetual necessity for reinvention, whenever a child attempts to speak an operation, he will probably relapse into the difficulties which he had already conquered on the plane of action. In other words, the process of learning an operation on the verbal plane will reproduce the same incidents as had arisen when this operation was being learned on the plane of action; a process of shifting will take place from one [learning situation] to the other. . . .

This shifting of external experience onto the verbal plane has not always received due attention. To associationism it is incomprehensible; for if our conscious reasoning were the direct result of previous experiences, then, clearly, once these experiences were over, the individual ought to be able to reenact them in thought or imagination upon the verbal plane. If, however, the mental experiment which appears at a given moment on the verbal plane is really, as Claparède maintains, due to a failure to adapt to new requirements, it will not be a mere translation of the subject's most recent and most highly evolved external experiments, but will, on the contrary, entail a whole process of relearning. It is in this sense in which the past is shifted onto the present. The evolution of intelligence is therefore not, as was claimed in the associationism of Taine and Ribot, continuous, but rhythmical; it seems at times to go back upon itself, it is subject to waves, to interferences, and to "periods" of variable length.

All these statements are the merest truisms nowadays, but they are truisms which it is dangerous to neglect when we are analyzing the reasoning processes of children. For we may either confuse verbal aptitude with an aptitude for handling relations in action, or neglect the verbal element altogether, as though all the operations of logic had not at one time or another to be learnt over again on the plane of discursive thought, if they are to be of any use in social intercourse.

Most of the phenomena of child logic can be traced back to general causes. The roots of this logic and of its shortcomings are to be found in the egocentrism of child thought up to the age of 7–8, and in the unconsciousness which this egocentrism entails. . . .

INABILITY TO HANDLE THE LOGIC OF RELATIONS, AND
NARROWNESS OF THE FIELD OF ATTENTION

One of the first results of childish egocentrism is that everything is judged from the individual's own point of view. The child experiences the greatest difficulty in entering into anyone else's point of view. Consequently, his judgment is always absolute, so to speak, and never relative, for a relative judgment involves the simultaneous awareness of at least two personal points of view.

Moreover, we are not speaking of any logical relations in general but solely of what the logicians call a "judgment of relation" in contrast to a "predicative judgment." Now a predicative judgment such as "Paul is a boy" only persupposes a single point of view, mine or Paul's, it does not matter which. A judgment of relation such as "Paul is my brother," on the contrary, presupposes at least two points of view: mine, for Paul is no one else's brother, not even his own, and Paul's, for in his mouth the judgment would change its form and become "I am the brother of. . . ." The same applies to all judgments of relation which connect at least two individuals and change in form according to the point of view of each. Now the child is so accustomed to thinking from his own individual point of view, and so incapable of taking that of anyone else, that such simple relations as those of brother and sister give rise in him to all sorts of difficulties, at any rate on the verbal plane. The child tends to deform relational judgments that are proposed to him, and to reduce them all to the simpler, because absolute, form of the predicative judgment.

Two of our former studies (J.R., Chaps. II and III) showed us that the child has a tendency, in connection with such statements as "I have brothers," to confuse the point of view of inclusion or of the predicative judgment ("We are x brothers") with that of relation. It is to such causes as these that we must attribute the difficulties arising out of the Binet-Simon test of absurd phrases ("I have three brothers, Paul, Ernest, and myself": a 10–11 years' test, [depending on] the district). In addition to this, up to the age of 10, three-quarters of the children are unable to indicate simultaneously both how many brothers and sisters there are in their own family and how many brothers and sisters each brother or sister possesses. The typical answer is as follows. The child says, for example, that there are two brothers in his family, which is correct. "And how many brothers have you got?—*One, Paul.*—And has Paul got a brother?—*No.*—But you are his brother, aren't you?—*Yes.*—Then he has a brother?—*No,*" etc. Such a phenomenon is clearly under the domination of egocentrism. There is no reasoning in the real sense of the word. The child has never asked himself the question and makes no attempt to answer by reasoning. The phenomenon consists rather in what might be called an illusion of point of view. The habit of thinking solely from his own point of view prevents the child from taking up that of others and consequently from handling the judgment of relation, i.e., from realizing the reciprocity of viewpoints.

A further inquiry showed us that this explanation can be made to cover phenomena connected with more complex relations, such as those of right and left (J.R., Chap. III). A 5-year-old child (in Geneva) can show his left and his right hand, but these qualities possess for him an absolute meaning. They are the names of the hands, and the names of all objects situated in a certain way in relation to the child's body. Thus, up to the age of 8, the child is unable to point to the left or right hand of anyone placed opposite him, for the same reason that his own point of view is felt to be the only one. At the age of 8, the child succeeds in adopting his interlocutor's point of view, but this does not mean that he can place himself at the point of view of the actual objects. If a pencil and a knife are placed on the table, he will be able to say whether the pencil is to the left or to the right of the knife, but this is still from his own point of view. It is not till he is 11 years old that he will know when presented with three objects in a row whether they are to the left or to the right of one another when they are taken in pairs. In short, his progress seems to run as follows: personal viewpoint, viewpoint of others, and finally, viewpoint of objects or of the relational judgment in general. . . .

In a recently published study* we had occasion to analyze in some detail a phenomenon of this kind in connection with a Burt test. Take three little girls, of whom the first is fairer than the second and darker than the third. The question asked is which of the three is the darkest. The children whose reasoning processes we analyzed make no attempt to compare by taking account of the relations that are indicated. They transform the relational judgments into predicative judgments, by means of a mechanism which may be schematized as follows. The first and the second of those little girls are fair, the first and the third are dark; therefore the third is the darkest of all, the second is the fairest, and the first stands midway between the two. The result is the exact opposite of what it would have been if the relational logic of the adult mind had been applied.

In order to explain this phenomenon, we simply appealed to the narrow field of attention in the child (although we reminded the reader that this was a static, and therefore a provisional way of describing things). For a far wider field of attention is required to handle a relational judgment than to handle a predicative judgment; or at any rate, as Revault d'Allonnes would put it, there is need for more complex "attentional schemas." Every relation requires that the subject be conscious of at least two objects at the same time. P. Janet has often drawn attention to this point. Supposing the child's field of attention to be narrower, i.e., less synthetic than ours, this means that he will be unable to take in all the data of the test at a single grasp. He will take the objects in one after another and not as a whole. This alone will be sufficient to transform relational judgments into a series of predicative judgments, and comparison will take place, not during the act of attention, but after it. We were able, moreover, to confirm this hypothesis

*"Un cas de comparaison verbale chez l'enfant."

by an examination of the different stages traversed by children from 7–8 up to 11–12 years old in connection with this comparison test.

But on this hypothesis it still remains to be explained why the child has a narrower field of attention than ours. We showed in the last section of this chapter that the child's awareness of his own thought and reasoning process is fainter than ours. But this is no reason why attention that is directed toward the external world (attention in perception, understanding of language, etc.) should obey the same law. Childish attention might very well, like childish memory or the memory of feebleminded persons, be more plastic than ours. The difference would then reside in the degree of organization, in the structure of the schema of attention. This is the solution we must look for.

. . . The egocentric way of thinking in relation to one's immediate neighbors (of which we have just been examining examples in connection with the notions of brother and sister, right and left) brings with it a certain number of habits or schemas which may be characterized as *realistic* in analogy to the many realistic illusions which occur in the early history of science (geocentric hypothesis, etc.) (J.R., Chap. III, §§5–7). The child therefore takes his own immediate perception as absolute. Most of the boys in Geneva go on believing till they are 7–8 years old that the sun or the moon follows them on their walks because they always happen to be above them. They are greatly perplexed when they have to say which of two boys walking in different directions is being accompanied by these heavenly bodies. (I was able to make sure that this was due neither to invention nor to deformation of adult talk.) This amounts to practically the same thing as ignorance of relational notions and avoidance of comparison. This is why, in the opinion of young Genevans up to the age of 7–8, wood floats upon water because it is light (in the absolute sense), and not because it is lighter than water. Their language alone is sufficient to make this clear. But what is most significant is that in the presence of equal volumes of water and wood they maintain that the wood is the heavier of the two. This estimate changes after the age of 8–9. In other words comparison and relation, even imagined, have no interest in connection with natural phenomena before this age. Immediate perception is the measure of all things.

Such habits of thought, acquired as they are over a period of many years, will naturally have some effect upon the schematism of attention. In the first place this realism prevents the child from looking at things as they are in themselves. He sees them always in terms of the momentary perception which is taken as absolute and, in a manner of speaking, hypostasized. He therefore makes no attempt to find the intrinsic relations existing between things. Again, by the mere fact of not being considered in their internal relations, but only as presented by immediate perception, things are either conglomerated into a confused whole (syncretism), or else considered one by one in a fragmentary manner devoid of synthesis. Herein lies the narrowness of the child's field of attention. The child sees a great many things, often many more than we do; he observes, in particular, a whole mass of detail which escapes our notice, but he does not organize his observations, he is incapable of thinking of more than one thing at a time. Thus he squanders his data instead of synthesizing them. . . .

SYNTHETIC INCAPACITY AND JUXTAPOSITION

This narrowness of the field of attention in children and the peculiar character of their schema of attention carry yet further consequences. They explain a whole set of phenomena such as the synthetic incapacity which appears in children's drawings, the inability to establish interference between logical classes, the inability to understand partitive relations, etc., all of which, in the verbal sphere, can be brought together under the heading of *juxtaposition* (J.R., Chap. I.)

For if things are perceived in the light of the moment, without order or organization, if the work of rational attention is to deal with them one by one and not in groups, then the child will naturally juxtapose things and events in his mind, without achieving their synthesis. . . . We have published a very clear example of this—the drawings of bicycles between the ages of 5 and 7. . . .

Synthetic incapacity survives for a long time after this, at least if the concept be extended so as to cover all the similar phenomena which we designate under the name of phenomena of "juxtaposition." Thus there is a tendency in childish reasoning to juxtapose classes and propositions rather than to establish their exact hierarchy. We went into this in connection with the difficulties raised by logical multiplication.* The child is given, for example, a test of the form: "If this animal has long ears it is a mule or a donkey; if it has a thick tail it is a mule or a horse. Well, this animal has long ears and a thick tail, What is it." Instead of finding the exact intersection of the two classes and saying that the animal in question is a mule, boys, even of 10 or 11 years old, add up the conditions and juxtapose the classes instead of excluding the unwanted elements. In this way, they reach the conclusion that the animal might just as well be a horse, a donkey, or a mule. This shows the true nature of the phenomenon of juxtaposition. The child begins by considering the existence of long ears, and concludes that the animal must be a donkey or a mule. He then considers the existence of the thick tail. If this new condition were made to interfere with the preceding one, the child would eliminate the donkey since it has not got a thick tail. But the child considers this new condition separately, he juxtaposes it instead of contrasting it with the former condition, and he concludes that the animal may be a horse or a mule. Each judgment is therefore juxtaposed and not assimilated to the judgment that precedes it. Finally, the child merges these two judgments into a single whole, but this whole constitutes a mere juxtaposition not a hierarchy. For the child comes to the conclusion that all three cases are possible. He therefore eliminates nothing. He juxtaposes without choosing. In a sense then, this is synthetic incapacity, since all synthesis implies choice and hierarchy, and differs from mere juxtaposition (J.R., Chap. IV, §2). . . .

But the tendency to juxtapose instead of synthesizing is not to be found only in the schematism of judgments as in the preceding examples, it also characterizes implication itself. What is meant by this was shown by our study of the conjunctions of logical and causal relation (because) and of the conjunctions of discordance (although) (J.R.,

*Journ. de Psych., 19 (1922): 222.

Chap. I.). In his language, the child frequently omits from between his successive judgments such relations as we would expect to find, and is content to juxtapose these judgments without any conjunctions or simply by means of the term "and." Thus in the explanations that take place between children (L.T., Chap. III, §1) there are hardly any explicit causal relations. Explanation takes on the character of a narrative. Relations are only indicated by "and then" even in connection with mechanical phenomena. This is why, when a child of 7–8 is asked to complete a sentence containing "because," he will sometimes do so correctly and sometimes invert the relation indicated by "because." For example, "The man fell off his bicycle *because he was ill afterwards.*" The word "because" is often used correctly by the child to indicate psychological relations (such as motivation: "because Daddy won't let me"). But instances of "because" indicating relations of physical causality or logical relations are almost completely absent from the spontaneous talk of the child, and when their use is induced, mistakes such as those we have quoted tend to occur. For a long time, finally, the word "therefore" (*donc*) does not exist in child language. It is replaced by the term "and then" (*alors*); but for a considerable period this term only indicates succession in time and not the relation of consequence.

All these facts agree in proving a certain synthetic incapacity in the thought of the child, and show that this incapacity bears primarily upon the schematism of judgment or upon the relations existing between judgments. But does this mean that the mind of the child is peopled with a multitude of juxtaposed ideas and judgments unconnected by any bond, as appears to be the case to an outsider? In other words, has the child himself a feeling of chaos and discontinuity? It is obvious that nothing could be farther from the truth, and that for any deficiency in objective relations there is a corresponding excess of subjective relations. This is shown to be the case by the phenomenon of syncretism which seems to be the opposite, but is really the complement of juxtaposition.

There is one particular feature in the structure of childish ideas which serves as a transition between juxtaposition and syncretism; we mean the relation which unites terms that have been separated by synthetic incapacity. When there is no occasion, such as drawing or language, for the child to break up objects by analysis, these are, as will be shown in a moment, perceived syncretically. But once they have been broken up and that synthetic incapacity renders their synthesis impossible, what is the relation which gathers the juxtaposed elements into a group? Luquet has noted with great truth that it is a relation of membership and not of inclusion, by which he means (no regard being paid to the logical meaning of these terms) that an arm drawn alongside of a manikin is conceived by the child as "going with" the manikin not as "forming part of" his body. We have often come across this relation in the ideas of children, and have given it the name of relation of *property*, so as to avoid confusion with the vocabulary of logic. This is how in the expression "A part of my posy" the term "of" indicates neither a partitive nor an attributive relation, but, as it were, a mixture of the two: "the part that is with my posy," such is the translation which a child gave us. And it is in the same way that our young Genevans, though they knew for the most part that Geneva is in Switzerland, yet declare themselves to be Genevan and not Swiss, because they cannot imagine being both at the same time (J.R., Chap. III, §6). For them, Geneva "goes with" Switzerland, but they see no sign here of a part and a whole, and make no attempt to define the spatial contacts. Finally— if comparison may be made between heterogeneous cases—this is how judgments of juxtaposition come to be accompanied by a "feeling of juxtaposition," although this feeling never becomes an awareness of causality or of implication. Children who draw a bicycle chain alongside of a gear wheel and a pedal know that these things "go together"; but if they are urged to be more precise in their statements, they will sometimes say that gear wheel sets the cogged chain in motion, sometimes that it is the other way about. These two statements coexist within the same individual, and prove very clearly that in this case the consciousness of causality does not go beyond a simple "feeling of relation."

Juxtaposition and synthetic incapacity do not therefore stand for disharmony. These phenomena are accompanied by relational feelings, either static (relation of property) or dynamic (feeling of causal relation), feelings of which the explanation is supplied by our analysis of syncretism. For they constitute a substitute for syncretism when the unity which the latter supplied has been broken up, and no fresh unity has been built up again.

SYNCRETISM

Syncretism is related to nearly all the phenomena we have been calling to mind. In the first place, as we said a moment ago, it seems like the contrary but is really the complement of juxtaposition. For if childish perception considers objects in their immediate, fragmentary, and unrelated aspect, and if either in language or in drawing these objects are simply juxtaposed instead of being arranged in a hierarchy, it is perhaps because these objects, before being broken up by the exigencies of drawing or conversation, were too intimately related to one another, too deeply sunk in comprehensive schemas, and too thoroughly implicated in one another to be broken up with impunity. The reason why this relatedness given in the original perception of objects offers so little resistance to the disintegrating effects of drawing or conversation is perhaps that it was exaggerated and, consequently, subjective. Now to say that child thought is syncretistic means precisely this, that childish ideas arise through comprehensive schemas and through subjective schemas, i.e., schemas that do not correspond to analogies or causal relations that can be verified by everybody. If, therefore, the child possesses neither the logic of relations nor the synthetic capacity which would enable him to conceive of things as objectively related to one another, it must be because his way of thinking is syncretistic. For in the mind of the child everything is connected with everything else, everything can be justified by means of unforeseen allusions and implications. But we have no suspicion of this wealth of relations, precisely because this very syncretism which causes it is without the means of expression that would render it communicable.

This last remark leads one to suppose that syncretism, besides being bound up with the phenomenon of juxtaposition and with inability to handle the logic of relations, is also the direct outcome of childish egocentrism. Egocentric thought is necessarily syncretic. . . . Syncretism is the expression of this perpetual assimilation of all things to subjective schemas and to schemas that are comprehensive because they are unadapted.

Syncretism therefore permeates the thought of the child. Claparède has pointed out its importance in perception. Cousinet has described, under the name of "immediate analogy," the prompt and unhesitating process by which the child identifies new objects with old schemas. In the meantime, we have discovered in the understanding and reasoning of the child under 7–8 and in the understanding and verbal thought of the child between 8 and 11–12, a tendency which is common to all syncretism. On the one hand, childish understanding undergoes a process which is completely unanalytic. A sentence heard is not broken up into distinct terms, but gives rise to a general schema which is vague and indissociable. On the other hand, the child does not reason by explicit inferences, but by projecting these schemas into one another, and by fusing images according to laws which are more often those of "condensation" than of logic. Let us recall [briefly] how syncretism makes its appearance before the age of 7–8, then what it becomes once it has been shifted onto the verbal plane between 7–8 and 11–12. Before the age of 7–8, syncretism may be said to be bound up with all mental events and with nearly all the judgments that are made. For any two phenomena perceived at the same moment become caught up in a schema which the mind will not allow to become dissociated, and which will be appealed to whenever a problem arises in connection with either of these two phenomena. . . .

Here are some examples: The sun does not fall down *"because it is hot. The sun stops there.—How?—Because it is yellow"* (Leo, age 6). "And the moon, how does it stop there?—*The same as the sun, because it is lying down on the sky*" (Leo). *"Because it is very high up, because there is no* (no more) *sun, because it is very high up"* (Béa, age 5), etc. Or again, if one shows the child a glass of water and if, after putting a small pebble into it so as to make the level of the water rise, one asks the child why the water has risen, the only explanation given will often be a simple description of what has happened; but because of syncretism this description will possess explanatory value for the child. In Tor's opinion (age 7½) the water rises because the pebble is heavy. When wood is used, the water rises because the wood is light, and so on. . . . What is most remarkable is that two contradictory reasons can be invoked by the same subject. Either such facts as these are due to the *n'importe quisme* of which Binet and Simon have spoken (and this would hardly apply to cases where the child is interested in the experiment in which he is taking part), or else description has a greater explanatory value for the child than for us, because features bound together within the raw material of observation seem to him to be related to one another by causal connections. This immediate relation is what constitutes syncretism.

In all these cases—and they are without number—syncretism seems to describe the following course. First of all two objects or two features are given simultaneously in perception. Henceforth the child perceives or conceives them as connected or rather as fused within a single schema. Finally, the schema acquires the strength of reciprocal implication, which means that if one of the features is isolated from the whole, and the child is asked for its reason, he will simply appeal to the existence of the other features by way of explanation or justification.

This facility in connecting everything with everything else, or to speak more accurately, this inability on the part of childish perception and understanding to isolate the elements of [global] schemas, is to be found again on the verbal plane after the age of 7–8. For after this age perception becomes more analytical, causal explanation begins to play its part in a mentality which up till then was precausal (see p. 105 and sel. 15); in short, syncretism tends to disappear from the subject's view of the external world. But on the verbal plane, which, with the increasing mental intercourse between children and between children and adults, becomes the habitual sphere of reasoning, the old difficulties survive and even reappear in new forms. For sentences and statements heard in the mouth of other people give rise to a mass of syncretistic verbal manifestations which are due, as before, to analytical weakness, and the tendency to connect everything with everything else. . . .

Another and very different case of syncretism which we discovered is equally suggestive from the point of view of the analytical weakness shown by the child whenever there is any question of connecting propositions or even of understanding words independently of the schemas in which they are enveloped (L.T., Chap. IV). The child is given a certain number of easy proverbs and a certain number of corresponding sentences jumbled together, but each meaning the same thing as one of the given proverbs. He is then asked to find the connection. Now up till the age of 11–12 the child chooses the corresponding sentence more or less at random, or at any rate by means of accidental and purely superficial analogies. But the significant thing is that at the moment of choosing the corresponding sentence the child fuses proverb and sentence into a single schema which subsumes them both and justifies the correspondence. We have here a syncretistic capacity which at first sight seems due to pure invention; but analysis shows that it comes from the child's inability to dissociate comprehensive perceptions or to restrain the tendency that wants to simplify and condense everything. For instance, a child of 9 assimilates the proverb "White dust will ne'er come out of sack of coal," to the corresponding sentence, "People who waste their time neglect their business." According to him, these two propositions mean "the same thing," because coal is black and can be cleaned. Similarly, people who waste their time neglect their children, who then become black and can no longer be cleaned. The uniformity shown by these answers to which we need not return at this point, excludes the hypothesis of invention. It shows how universal is the tendency of the child to create comprehensive schemas in his imagination, and to condense various images into each other.

Such, then, is syncretism: immediate fusion of heterogeneous elements, and unquestioning belief in the objective interimplication of elements condensed in this way. Syncretism is therefore necessarily accompanied by a tendency to justify things at any price. Now this is exactly what the facts show to be the case. The child can always find a reason, whatever may happen to be in question. . . .

TRANSDUCTION, AND INSENSIBILITY TO CONTRADICTION

Does reasoning in the child obey the laws of adult logic? Above all, does it obey the law of contradiction? If it be borne in mind, in the first place, that child thought is ignorant of the logic of relations, that addition and multiplication of logical classes are unknown to it (juxtaposition being constantly chosen in preference to hierarchical arrangement): if it be remembered, moreover, that the various relations created by syncretism are comprehensive and do not admit of analysis, then nothing will prevent us from concluding that the process of reasoning in the child is, as Stern has put it, neither inductive nor deductive, but *transductive*. By this Stern means that child thought proceeds neither by an amplifying induction nor by an appeal to general propositions which are designed to prove particular propositions, but that it moves from particular to particular by means of a reasoning process which never bears the character of logical necessity. For instance, a child of 7 who is asked whether the sun is alive, answers: *"Yes.—Why?—Because it moves* (moves along)." But he never says that "All things that move are alive." This appeal to a general proposition has not yet come into being. The child seeks neither to establish such a proposition by means of successive inductions, nor to postulate it for the purposes of deduction. [Moreover], if we try to make him aware of a general rule, we shall find that it is by no means the rule for which we were prepared. . . .

What seems to us the distinguishing feature of transduction is therefore its lack of logical necessity; the fact that this type of reasoning deals only with individual cases is certainly important, but cannot be said to be fundamental. As a result of his egocentrism, the child does not as yet feel any desire for demonstration; he makes no attempt to connect his judgments with bonds that bear the mark of necessity. . . . What welds these momentary judgments together is some one aim, external to the act of judging, or some one action carried out upon the world of reality. But outside such extrinsic systematization there exist between these judgments no conscious implication and no demonstrative links. The psychologist will certainly succeed in finding the logical reason for a child's judgment, but the child himself looks for no such filiation between his propositions. At this stage, therefore, implication constitutes a motor rather than a mental phenomenon, and it is no exaggeration in this sense to say that there is no logical reasoning before the age of 7–8. For the justifications arising out of syncretism are devoid of logical necessity. As to the motor implications which have produced the reasoning process, they are still below the level of consciousness.

For by the term "reasoning" should be understood the work of [verifying] and proving hypotheses, which work alone creates conscious implications among judgments. Claparède has distinguished with great clarity three distinctly separate moments in intellectual activity: question, invention of hypothesis, and [verification]. Now, the question is only the manifestation of a desire; the hypothesis is framed by the imagination to fill up the gap created by this desire. Reasoning therefore appears only at the moment when the hypothesis is verified. Up till then there has been no logical activity. How then does the [verification] take place? To use the current formula, by means of a mental experiment.

But this formula is slightly ambiguous and there are, in our opinion, three genetically distinct types of mental experiment: that which we find in the child before the age of 7–8, that which we find between 7–8 and 11–12, and finally, that of the adult. We also believe it necessary to point out that this third type of mental experiment is accompanied by an experiment which might be called "logical experiment.". . .

Mental experiment is a reproduction in thought of events as they actually succeed one another in the course of nature; or again, it is an imagined account of events in the order which they would follow in the course of an experiment which one would actually carry out, if it were technically possible to do so. As such, mental experiment knows nothing of the problem of contradiction; it simply declares that a given result is possible or actual, if we start from a given point, but it never reaches the conclusion that two judgments are contradictory of each other. Consequently, mental experiment, like actual physical experiment, is irreversible, which means that, starting from a and finding b, it will not necessarily be able to find a again, or if it does so, it will not be able to prove that what it has found is really a and not a become a'. Similarly, if it finds b again after starting from c or from d, and not from a, it will have no means of proving that what it has found is really b and not b become b'. And these defects in mental experiment are the same as those which characterize childish reasoning, for the latter is content to imagine or to reproduce mentally actual physical experiments or external sequences of fact.

The logical experiment which intervenes from the age of 11–12 is certainly derivative from this process and has no other material than that of the mental experiment itself. It also deals mostly with individual cases, and does no more than combine the different relations existing between things, with or without the aid of syllogisms. But this logical experiment which comes as the completion of mental experiment and which alone confers upon it the quality of true "experiment," introduces, nevertheless, a new element which is of fundamental importance: it is an experiment upon the subject himself as a thinking-subject, an experiment analogous to those which one makes upon oneself in regulating one's moral conduct. It is therefore an attempt to become conscious of one's own operations (and not only of their results), and to see whether they imply, or whether they contradict one another.

In this sense, logical experiment is very different from mental experiment. The first is the construction of reality and the awareness of this reality, the second is awareness and ordering of the actual mechanism of the construction. Now this ordering, which is the mark of logical experiment, has a considerable effect upon mental experiment: it makes it reversible. This means that the subject is led to lay down only such premises as are capable of entertaining reciprocal relations to each other and of remaining each identical with themselves throughout during the mental experiment. (This feature is one whose importance may not be evident to introspection, but is nevertheless fundamental from the genetic point of view, because it appears very late and is in no way implied in the mechanism of mental experiment pure and simple.) Premises which are the necessary requisite of logical experiment will therefore contain decisive judgments, which means that they will necessitate the use of conventional definitions, of assumptions, and so on, and that they will consequently extend beyond the sphere of mere fact and observation. This is the price of reversibility in mental experiment. Logical experiment is therefore an experiment carried out on oneself for the detection of contradiction. This process is undoubtedly founded on mental experiment, but on mental experiment which it fashions for itself, and which differs from primitive mental experiment as widely as does the work of the physicist from the observations of the man in the street. The necessity resulting from mental experiment is a necessity of fact; that which results from logical experiment is due to the implications existing between the various operations: it is a moral necessity due to the obligation of remaining true to oneself.

We are now in a position to understand how this first stage of childish reasoning is to be distinguished from logical reasoning proper. We were saying just now that the judgments of children before the age of 7–8 do not imply each other, but simply follow one another, after the manner of successive actions or perceptions which are psychologically determined without being logically necessitated by each other. For transduction is nothing but a mental experiment unaccompanied by logical experiment. It is either a simple account of events in succession, or a sequence of thoughts grouped together by one and the same aim or by one and the same action; it is not yet a reversible system of judgments, such that each will be found to have remained identical with itself after no matter what kind of transformation. . . .

The irreversibility of primitive reasoning may be recognized by the further circumstance (J.R., Chap. VI, §§4–5) that the subject cannot keep a premise, identical with itself throughout a mental experiment. This is because while he is "constructing" by means of this premise a whole series of new results, he has no means (unless he takes the decisions that regulate the experiment itself) of knowing whether this premise has varied or not in the course of the mental experiment. Or again, there is no means of knowing whether a concept to which one has been led by different paths is really the same under these different forms, and does not contain any contradictions. In reality, neither of these questions exists for the child before the age of 7–8, and his habit of reasoning only about individual cases, of applying judgments which, though universal in appearance are particular in fact, leaves him in almost complete ignorance of the problem.

. . . For instance, we can take a list of objects specially selected so as to avoid suggestion, and ask children of 7–8 whether such and such an object is alive, or has force, and so on. We shall then immediately realize that a concept like that of "life" is frequently determined by two or three heterogeneous components. For example, the same child will agree that the sun, the moon, wind, and fire are alive, because they "move," but that neither streams, nor lakes, nor clouds are alive, because the wind pushes them and they consequently have no movement of their own. On the other hand, clouds are alive, because they "make rain," the lake, because it "runs"; both, in short, because they perform some activity which is useful to man. Thus the two components "self-movement" and "useful activity" define between them the concept of life. But owing to the schematism of childish judgment which we have described, these components do not multiply, or to put it differently, they do not interfere, but remain juxtaposed without synthesis in such a way that they only act one at a time, and make the child say, for instance, sometimes that the lake is alive, and sometimes that it is not. The idea of force, again, is defined by movement, by solidity and by activity, all of them components that define the adult idea of force, but which in the child remain thrown together without any hierarchical order. It is in this sense that childish reasoning is irreversible. According to the turn taken by the mental experiment, the child will discover on the way facts which will cause him to alter his definitions, modify his premises, and which will completely change the nature of one and the same concept by reason of the path taken to reach it. . . . On the one hand, the logic of relations is foreign to the child along with all the adult habits of logical multiplication, of hierarchical arrangement of classes and of propositions. This is one cause of irreversibility. The child can certainly reach a conclusion from given premises, but he cannot perform the return journey without deviating from his path. On the other hand, syncretism, which makes the child connect everything with everything else, and prevents him from making the excisions and distinctions necessary to analytical thought, will have the natural consequence of making him concentrate heterogeneous elements within a single word. We have here a second cause of irreversibility. The concepts of children are systems which are not in equilibrium, to borrow a term from chemistry. They have a pseudo-equilibrium, which means that their seeming immobility is simply due to their viscosity. In consequence of this they do not remain identical, but vary imperceptibly throughout a reasoning process.

We can now lay our finger upon the real cause of contradiction in the child. There can be no doubt that up to the age of 7–8, child thought teems with contradictions. . . . And as these contradictions to which the child seems completely [insensitive] are of two kinds, it is important to distinguish very clearly between them.

To begin with, there is what may be called contradiction "by amnesia," which, incidentally, has no particular interest for us. The child has two contradictory opinions about one object, and hesitates between them. When he is questioned he will affirm one of these, but a moment later he will forget what he has said, and affirm the other, and so on. For instance, a child believes that rivers are dug out and made entirely by the hand of man. Then he learns that the water coming from their sources has been sufficient to produce them. But for a long time he fluctuates between these two explanations, neither of which he finds completely satisfactory, so that when questioned, he will give first one, then the other, forgetting each time what he has previously asserted. . . .

The second type of contradiction, on the other hand, strikes us as peculiarly characteristic of child thought. It is what might be called contradiction "by condensation." The child, unable to choose between two contradictory explanations of one and the same phenomenon, agrees to both simultaneously and even fuses them into each other. Nor must it be thought that this is in any way an attempt at synthesis. The child is never in the presence of two terms which are first conceived as separate and then condensed, *faute de mieux*. It is rather a certain lack of restraint that allows new elements to be constantly heaped on the old ones, regardless of synthesis. Such schemes inherit their character from these syncretistic habits of thought which lead the subject to simply add up and condense his impressions instead of synthesizing them. And this is the immediate consequence of what we were saying just now about the irreversibility of child thought. For one and the same concept being different according to the path along which the child has reached it, the various components of which this concept is the product are bound to be heterogeneous and to lead to incessant contradictions.

Let us recall an example. A boy of 7½ tells us that boats float because they are light. As to big boats, they float because they are heavy, Theoretically, this reasoning is legitimate. In the first case, the water is thought of as strong and supporting the boat, in the second case the boat is thought of as strong and supporting itself. But as a matter of fact, the child is not aware of this opposition. He is subject to contradiction because he is unable to resolve this condensation of heterogeneous explanations.

We may also conclude that transductive reasoning, insofar as it consists purely in mental experiment, is still irreversible and consequently powerless to detect contradiction. The reason for this is quite simple. Consciousness of contradiction arises from an awareness of mental operations, and not from observation of nature, whether this observation be actual or imaginary. Now, up to the age of 7–8, childish judgments entail each other without any awareness of implications. They succeed, but do not justify each other. It is therefore perfectly natural that contradictory judgments should be added straightaway to the pile by simple condensation. Only if the child became conscious of the definitions he has adopted or of the steps by which his reasoning proceeds, would these judgments seem to him to contradict one another.

After the age of 7–8, however, comes a stage lasting till about the age of 11–12, and during which the following fundamental changes take place. Little by little the child becomes conscious of the definition of the concepts he is using, and acquires a partial aptitude for introspecting his own mental experiments. Henceforward, a certain awareness of implications is created in his mind, and this gradually renders these experiments reversible, removing at least such contradictions as are the fruit of condensation. Does this mean that these are finally disposed of, and that the child is now fit to reason formally, i.e., from given or merely hypothetical premises? We have shown that this is not the case, and that formal thought does not appear till about the age of 11–12. From 7–8 till 11–12 syncretism, contradiction by condensation, etc., all reappear independently of observation, upon the plane of verbal reasoning, in virtue of the law of shifting. It is therefore not until about the age of 11–12 that we can really talk of "logical experiment." The age of 7–8, nevertheless, marks a considerable advance, for logical forms have entered upon the scene of the mind in perception.

Within the sphere of direct observation the child becomes capable of amplifying induction and of necessary deduction.

It is not without interest to recall that these advances in logic are connected with the definite diminution of egocentrism at the age of 7–8. The result of this last phenomenon is on the one hand to give birth to the need for proof and verification, and on the other to induce a relative awareness of the way thought moves. We have here a remarkable instance of the influence of social factors on the functioning of thought.

MODALITY OF CHILD THOUGHT, INTELLECTUAL

REALISM, AND INCAPACITY FOR FORMAL REASONING

The question of reasoning and particularly of contradiction in the child is closely bound up with the problem of modality or of the different planes of reality on which the child uses his thought. For if contradiction "by amnesia" is so frequent before the age of 7–8, in other words, if the child has the faculty for permanently hesitating between two contradictory views and of always forgetting the view he held a moment previously, this is to a great extent because he has the power of passing far more swiftly than we can from a state of belief to a state of invention or of play. In thinking about reality, the child has a whole scale of planes which are probably devoid of any sort of hierarchy, and therefore favorable to logical incoherence. We have here at any rate a problem worth discussing.

Before entering upon this discussion, two truths should be remembered. The first is that for egocentric thought the supreme law is play. It is one of the merits of psychoanalysis to have shown that autism knows of no adaptation to reality, because pleasure is its only spring of action. Thus the sole function of autistic thought is to give immediate and unlimited satisfaction to desires and interests by deforming reality so as to adapt it to the ego. For reality is infinitely plastic for the ego, since autism is ignorant of that reality shared by all, which destroys illusion and enforces verification. Insofar then as child thought is still permeated with egocentrism, the question of modality will have to be embodied in the following somewhat biased formula: Does there exist for the child only one reality, that is to say one supreme reality which is a touchstone of all others (as is the world of the senses for one adult, the world constructed by science, or even the invisible world of the mystic for another)? Or does the child, finding himself, [depending on whether] he is in an egocentric or in a socialized state of being, in the presence of two worlds which are equally real, and neither of which succeeds in supplanting the other? It is obvious that the second hypothesis is the more probable.

[Moreover]—and this is the second truth to remember—there is nothing to prove that the child is any the worse for this bipolar nature of reality. Seen from the outside his attitude seems disharmonious: at one moment he is believing, at the next he is playing. As Baldwin has said: "The object, therefore, not only exists, but always exists as fulfilling the interest which motives its apprehension."* But seen from the inside there may be nothing particularly uncomfortable about this attitude. For us adults lack of harmony and hierarchy between states of belief and play would be unbearable, but that is because of a desire for inner unity which is perhaps very late in appearing. For it is chiefly in relation to other people that we are obliged to unify our beliefs, and to place on different planes those that are not compatible with each other, so that we gradually build up within ourselves a plane of reality, a plane of possibility, a plane of fiction, and so on. The hierarchy of these planes

*J. M. Baldwin, *Thoughts and Things* (London: 1911).

is therefore determined by their degree of objectivity, and the capacity for objectivity depends in its turn upon the socialization of thought, since we have no other criterion of objectivity than the agreement of different minds. . . .

In [sum], there may be several realities for the child, and these realities may be equally real in turn instead of being arranged in a hierarchy as with us. It may be, moreover, that the disharmony resulting from this fact is in no way a source of discomfort to the child (L.T., Chap. V, §9). The facts show this very clearly. Four stages can be picked out in the evolution of modality. The first lasts till the age of 2–3, the second extends from 2–3 to 7–8, the third from 7–8 to 11–12, and the fourth begins at this age. During the first stage, reality may be said to be simply and solely what is desired. Freud's "pleasure principle" deforms and refashions the world to its liking. The second stage marks the appearance of two heterogeneous but equal realities—the world of play and the world of observation. The third marks the beginning of hierarchical arrangement, and the fourth marks the completion of this hierarchy, thanks to the introduction of a new plane—that of formal thought and logical assumptions.

Stern has noted that round about the age of 3 such expressions as "to think," "to believe," etc., begin to appear, which indicates that the child has detected a shade of difference between two kinds of existence —what is true and what is simply imagined. And as a matter of fact, from this date onward children distinguish better and better between ideas that are believed *pour de vrai* as the young Genevans say, and ideas that are believed *pour s'amuser*. But we must not allow ourselves to regard this as indicating two hierarchical planes. When the child is directed toward one of these poles, he turns his back on the other. Until he reaches the age of 7–8, the question of modality very rarely occurs to him at all. He does not try to prove whether such or such of his ideas does or does not correspond to reality. When the question is put to him, he evades it. It does not interest him, and it is even alien to his whole mental attitude. The rare cases when he spontaneously asks himself such a question ("Do they exist sometimes?" etc., 5 cases out of 750 questions asked by a boy of 6) are due to necessary friction with the thought of others. [Apart from] circumstances such as these, the child from 2–3 to 7–8 is certainly acquainted with two planes, or two orders of reality, that of play and that of observation, but they are juxtaposed and not hierarchisized, in the sense that when he is in the presence of one it seems to him the only true one, and he forgets the other.

In consequence, these two planes, that of play and that of sensuous observation, are very different for the child from what they are for us, and in particular they are less distinct. This probably explains the lack of hierarchy; for two still partially indifferentiated elements obstruct one another far more than when a clear differentiation has shed light upon their opposing qualities. In the first case the contradictions involved by the lack of differentiation produce antagonism, in the second case, the oppositions make synthesis possible.

For, for us, play rests on fiction. But for the child it is something much more. It is not enough to say, with Groos, that it is a "voluntary illusion," for this attitude presupposes in the child the power to resist illusion, or rather to contrast certain beliefs that are voluntary with certain others that are necessary. As a matter of fact play cannot be contrasted to reality, because in both cases belief is arbitrary, or rather devoid of logical reasons. Play is a reality which the child chooses to believe in by himself, just as reality is a game which the child chooses to believe in with grown-ups and with anyone else who believes in it. In both cases the belief is either very strong or very weak, [depending on whether] it is characterized by its momentary intensity or by its duration, but in neither case does it require any intrinsic justification. Childish play may therefore be said to constitute an autonomous reality, by which we mean that "true" reality to which it stands in contrast is far less true for the child than for us.

Thus, sensible or "true" reality is also quite different for the child from what it is for us. To us, this reality is given by experimentation, and its laws are submitted to incessant control. For the child, sensible reality is observed and experimented upon to a much lesser degree, and its laws are hardly submitted to any control whatsoever; it is made up almost in its entirety by the mind and by the decisions of belief.

We are dealing here with the phenomenon of "intellectual realism," as studied by specialists in children's drawings and by Luquet in particular, and which we have extended to cover the concept of child thought in general.*

For we have already seen (L.T., Chap. V, §3) that in consequence of his egocentrism, the child's picture of the world is always moulded on his immediate, sectional, and personal point of view. Relations between things will therefore not be what is yielded by experimentation or fashioned by comparison of viewpoints; they will be what child logic, and especially what syncretism makes them. By reason of the same cause which prevented him from adapting himself to other people, the child will fail to be adapted to the observation of the senses. He does not analyze the contents of his perceptions, but weighs it down with a load of previously acquired and ill-digested material. In short, he sees objects, not as they really are, but as he would have imagined them, if, before seeing them, he had *per impossibile* described them to himself. This is why the early stages of children's drawings are not characterized by visual realism, i.e., by a faithful copy of the model in question, but by intellectual realism, such that the child draws only what he already knows about things and copies only an "inner model." Childish observation follows the same lines. The child often sees only what he already knows. He projects the whole of his verbal thought into things. He sees mountains as built by men, rivers as dug out with spades, the sun and moon as following us on our walks. The field of attention seems wide in this sense that things are observed in large numbers, but it is narrow in the sense that things are schematized in accordance with the child's own point of view, instead of being perceived in their intrinsic relations.

Intellectual realism is the picture of the world that is most natural to egocentric thought. It points, on the one hand, to an incapacity for objective observation (visual realism). On the other hand, it is realism nonetheless, for the child is neither an intellectualist (his disregard of

*Journ. de Psych., 19 (1922): 256–257.

logical system is complete) nor a mystic. His egocentrism is, moreover, perpetually leading him into realistic delusions, such as confusing words and things, thought and the objects of thought, etc.; in a word, he is conscious of nothing but his own subjectivity.

In [sum], there exist before the age of 7–8 two planes of reality—play and the reality of ordinary life, but they are juxtaposed instead of being compared and ordered in a hierarchy, and each taken by itself is different from what it is for us. But at about the age of 7–8, certain changes take place in the modality of childish judgment which are in close relation to the appearance of a desire for a system and noncontradiction. This stage is characterized on the one hand by the beginnings of a positive observation of the external world, and on the other by an awareness of the implications contained in such reasoning as is connected with actual observation. These two facts tend to make the child dissociate objective reality from verbal reality, to dissociate, that is, the world of direct observation from that of stories, of fantasies, and of things conceived or heard of, but never seen. This is therefore the decline of intellectual realism, so far as actual observation is concerned.

But in virtue of the law of shifting, all the phenomena which up till now have stood in the way of complete adaptation to the external world (inability to handle relations, syncretism, juxtaposition, etc.), are shifted on to the verbal plane, and stand in the way of the child's awareness of his own reasoning process. This gives rise to two consequences which are closely bound up with each other, one being concerned with modality, the other with the structure of the reasoning process.

Here is the first. As regards the faculty of perception, the different planes of reality stand in hierarchical order. The categories of the possible and of the necessary in particular (which alone enable the different orders of reality to be grouped in relation to each other) appear in the conception of nature, and allow the child to conceive of some phenomena as due to chance (for this notion first appears at the age of 7–8), and of others as bound by a necessity that is physical and not moral. But as regards the verbal faculty, these different planes have not yet come to be distinguished, so that the child [remains] incapable of conceiving on the one hand of a purely logical necessity (If we say that . . . then we must say that . . .), [or] on the other hand of a plane [of] pure hypothesis or logical assumption (Let us say that . . .).

Childish reasoning between the years of 7–8 and 11–12 will therefore present a very definite feature (J.R., Chap. II): reasoning that is connected with actual belief, or in other words, that is grounded on direct observation, will be logical. But formal reasoning will not yet be possible. For formal reasoning connects assumptions—propositions, that is, in which one does not necessarily believe, but which one admits in order to see what consequences they will lead to.

At about the age of 11–12, on the contrary, modality in the thought of the child becomes more or less what it is with us, or at least, with the uneducated adult. The various planes of reality—play, verbal reality, observation—are set in a hierarchy that is defined in relation to a single criterion—experience. And this hierarchy is possible, thanks to the notions of necessity and possibility which are now extended to verbal thought.

This evolution in the structure of childish reasoning has very important consequences. We have already* put forward the view, which has since been confirmed by a more recent study, that formal thought does not appear till the age of 11–12, at the period, therefore, when the child comes to reason about pure possibility. For to reason formally is to take one's premises as simply given, without inquiring whether they are well-founded or not; belief in the conclusion will be motivated solely by the form of the deduction. . . . Between the years of 7–8 and 11–12, there is certainly awareness of implications when reasoning rests upon beliefs and not upon assumptions, in other words, when it is founded on actual observation. But such deduction is still realistic, which means that the child cannot reason from premises without believing in them. Or even if he reasons implicitly from assumptions which he makes on his own, he cannot do so from those which are proposed to him. Not till the age of 11–12 is he capable of this difficult operation, which is pure deduction, and proceeds from any assumption whatsoever. Take, for instance, the absurd-phrase test which Binet gives as one for 10 years, but is really an 11- or 12-year-old test: "If one day I kill myself from despair, it will not be on a Friday, because Friday is an unlucky day, . . . etc." Before the age of 11–12 the child cannot make the assumption. He either accepts the data and fails to see the absurdity, or else he rejects them as absurd and fails to see the formal absurdity of the argument.

11–12 is therefore the age at which we must situate the appearance of what a little earlier we called "logical experiment." Logical experiment, in conclusion, presupposes and may be defined by the two following conditions: (1) A "mental experiment" carried out on the plane of pure hypothesis or of pure possibility, and not as before on the plane of reality reproduced in thought; and (2) an ordering and awareness of the operations of thought as such, as for example of definitions or assumptions that one has made and has decided to retain identical with themselves.

It is not without interest to note that this new awareness is once again under the dependence [control] of social factors, and that conversely, incapacity for formal thought is very directly the result of childish egocentrism. For what prevents the child from reasoning from data that he does not agree to but is asked simply to "assume," is that he is untutored in the art of entering into other people's points of view. For him, there is only one comprehensible point of view—his own. Hence the fact that up till the age of 11–12, physical reality is not accompanied by subjective reality (the child being unaware of the personal character of his opinions, his definitions, and even his words), nor, consequently, even by a logical reality in which everything conceivable would be possible. Previous to this, there is only the real and the unreal. There is undoubtedly a plane of physical possibility, but there is no plane of logical possibility. The real alone is logical. At about the age of 11–12, on the contrary, social life starts on a new phase, and this obviously has the effect of leading children to a greater mutual understanding, and consequently of giving them the habit of constantly placing themselves at points of view which they did not previously hold. This progress in the

*Journ. de Psych., 19 (1922): 222. ("Essai sur la multiplication logique et les débuts de la pensée formelle chez l'enfant.")

use of assumptions is probably what lends greater suppleness to the child's conception of modality, and teaches him the use of formal reasoning.

PRECAUSALITY IN THE CHILD

We have now reached the end of our outline of child logic. We must nevertheless recall in a few short words a certain question which so far we have asked rather than answered. What is the picture of the world which goes hand in hand with such a logic? What are the notions of causality which the child constructs at his different stages of development? . . .

Egocentrism helps, as we saw, to make the child unconscious of himself. But this unconsciousness goes far beyond the difficulties in introspection which we described; it goes so far as to prevent the child under 7–8 from being aware of the phenomenon of thought as a subjective phenomenon, and even to prevent him from establishing the exact limit between his own ego and the external world. Baldwin has laid great stress upon this "adualistic" character of primitive thought. We have ourselves described a very definite phase (about the age of 7) during which the child knows that his dreams are subjective (a person standing beside him could neither see nor touch them), and nevertheless locates them in front of himself in the room.* A large number of facts of this order has led us to admit that the child is ignorant of his own thought, and projects it in its entirety into things. He is therefore a "realist" in the sense in which one talks of the realistic illusions of thought. But this realism keeps its possessor in ignorance of the distinction between the physical and the psychical, and consequently leads him to regard the external world as endowed with both these qualities at the same time. Hence the tendency to "precausality."

On the other hand, and for the same reasons, childish realism is intellectual and not visual (see preceding paragraph); the child only sees what he knows, and sees the external world as though he had previously constructed it with his own mind. Childish causality is therefore not visual, in other words is not interested in spatial contacts nor in mechanical causation. It is intellectual, that is to say, full of considerations that are foreign to pure observation: justification of all phenomena, syncretistic tendency to connect everything with everything else (see pp. 103–105), in short, confusion of physical causality with psychological or logical motivation. Hence, once again, precausality.

In this sense, then, precausal mentality, as we defined it above, will be seen to be the type of mentality most in agreement with egocentrism of thought and with all the logical peculiarities which this egocentrism entails.

But once again, we must remind the reader that we have just raised an enormous problem by drawing attention to these few characteristics of childish causality, and that we are still very far from guessing its solution.

*See *Arch. de Psych.*, 18 (1923): 288.

CONCLUSION

[We do believe, however,] that we have solved the problem which we set ourselves at the beginning of our inquiry. The features of child thought which we have described really do constitute a coherent whole, such that each of its terms partially implies a portion of the other terms. To be sure, child thought cannot be isolated from the factors of education, and all the various influences which the adult exercises upon the child. But these influences do not imprint themselves upon the child as on a photographic plate; they are "assimilated," i.e., deformed by the living being who comes under their sway, and they are incorporated into his own substance. It is this psychological substance, [in other words] this structure and functioning peculiar to [the child's] thought that we have tried to describe, and in a certain measure, to explain.

It is therefore our belief that the day will come when child thought will be placed on the same level in relation to adult, normal, and civilized thought, as "primitive mentality" as defined by Lévy-Bruhl, as autistic and symbolical thought as described by Freud. . . . But we must beware of the danger of drawing parallels in which functional divergencies are forgotten. Moreover, we have already taken our stand on the subject of the relations which exist between the thought of the child and symbolic thought; though perhaps we did not at the time sufficiently emphasize the differences which separate these two kinds of thought.* Let us therefore not be in too great a hurry to follow a path so full of the pitfalls of comparative psychology. Patient analysis of the child's mentality keeps on safer ground, which though not yet thoroughly cleared, offers so sure a realm of investigation that wisdom forbids us to leave it forthwith.

*"La pensée symbolique et la pensée de l'enfant," Arch. de Psych.

15

The Child's Conception of Physical Causality*

1927

INTRODUCTORY NOTES

The Child's Conception of Physical Causality (1927) was immediately and widely hailed by many child psychologists. In spite of this positive reception, Piaget grew gradually dissatisfied with the book and, after an interruption of forty years, started a new series of studies that have now become the substance of six monographs or books.†

In his early work on causality, Piaget took a merely observational and verbal approach. He was satisfied with the discovery of what children say about how things happen around them. The results obtained were explained in terms of children's indirect egocentrism. Indirect egocentrism consists of such an undue assimilation of the outside world to the self that properties of the self are granted to the universe too. I am animated, so is the world (animism). I am a toolmaker (Latin: *artifex*) so is the world (artificialism), etc. There is a spreading or extension of the self to include the rest of reality.

But the reasons for this overextension of the properties of the self did not seem clear enough to Piaget. In his later work he transformed his initial theory into an attribution theory. Any causal explanation, from the simplest to the most sophisticated, is and must be essentially an attribution to the universe of the level of cognitive operativity reached by the subject. So the quality of any causal explanation depends on the degree of cognitive development reached by its proponent, and on the awareness he has of this level

*From J. Piaget, *The Child's Conception of Physical Causality*, Marjorie Gabain, translator. Reprinted by permission of Humanities Press, Inc., Atlantic Highland, New Jersey, and Routledge & Kegan Paul Ltd., London. Originally published in French, 1927. (Collaborators: C. Bieler, A. Bodorurian, Daiber, Germaine Guex, L. Hahnloser, R. Hepner, M. Herzog, Hélène Krafft, J. Lebberz, Emile Margairaz, Valentine Piaget, H. Rehfous, M. Rodrigo, M. Roud, N. Swetlova, Versteeg, and Zwickhardt.)

†M. Bunge, F. Halbwachs, T. S. Kuhn, J. Piaget, and L. Rosenfeld, *Les théories de la causalité* (Paris: P.U.F., 1973); J. Piaget (with R. Garcia), *Causal Explanations* (New York: W. W. Norton, in press); J. Piaget (with seven collaborators), *La Transmission des mouvements*, (Paris: P.U.F., 1972); J. Piaget (with seven collaborators), *La Direction des mobiles lors des chocs et des poussées* (Paris: P.U.F., 1972); J. Piaget (with seven collaborators), *La Formation de la notion de force* (Paris: P.U.F., 1973); and *La Composition des forces et le problème des vecteurs* (Paris: P.U.F., 1974).

and of its basic features. Once a child has established certain invariant relationships between his own actions and events in the environment around him, he becomes capable, thanks to the tools so constructed, of working out causal links between these two worlds. Depending on the degree of awareness he has of his own action upon the world, he will attribute to it simple invariances such as rhythmic regularities, feedback systems or more complex ones such as mathematical groups as modern physicists do all the time.

In sum, in spite of the long time interval and their important differences, there is a continuity between the two theories of causality advanced by Piaget. The same mechanism of projection of the properties of the self accounts for the appearance of a causality principle in the child. But the fact remains—not too evident in Piaget's writings—that not all the properties of the self are attributed to the universe but only certain ones that have been carefully selected through experimentation and deduction. This fact prompted Arnold Reymond, Piaget's master of philosophy, to say that, with Piaget, one somehow remained in Bishop Berkeley's brave world where *esse est percepi*:* there is nothing beyond sensations and their ever-increasing organization by the mind. Is this the only way in which one could understand Piaget's central belief that experience shapes thought and thought experience?

Explanation of Machines†

The artificialist turn of mind, of which we have seen so many manifestations, may certainly be expected to go hand in hand with a systematic interest in industry and adult handicraft. Everyone will have had occasion to notice this. All workmen and especially mechanics excite the greatest interest in boys, and even in little girls, before their more feminine tastes have begun to predominate. Interest in machines, in particular, combined with interest in everything that moves, provokes in the child a universal curiosity about all the means of locomotion— motorcars, boats, trains, airplanes, etc. Considering the persistence with which the children of the Maison des Petits de l'Institut J.-J. Rousseau draw trains, boats, and airplanes, model them in clay, or build them with bricks and sticks, it seems as though this tendency were at root nothing but a variant of that joy in being a cause of which K. Groos has spoken —the joy of being a cause of movement.

But whatever may be the affective components of this interest, the important thing for us is to try and analyze the explanations which children give of how machines work. Are these explanations precausal or are they mechanistic in tendency? Does the correct explanation of machines come before the correct explanation of natural movements, or is the reverse the case? What are the relations between *homo faber*

*Reymond, *Philosophie spiritualiste* (Paris: Rouge/Vrin, 1942), Vol. 2, p. 343. *Esse est percepi*: to be is to be perceived. The remark is made about a book by J. Piaget and J. de la Harpe: *Deux types d'atitudes religieuses: Immanence et transcendance* (Geneva: Labor, 1928).

†[The following section is from the introduction to Section III.]

and *homo sapiens*? This is the last problem we have to solve, but it is the most fundamental of all.

It will perhaps be objected that the problem is one to be eliminated, since the spectacle of machinery has been imposed upon children by quite a recent civilization, and that the explanations given cannot supply us with results of any value for the psychology of the child in general. But this would be a strange objection to raise, for new as machines are, they nevertheless call forth, at least in the very young child, mental reactions which have always existed, if not always at the same age. . . .

The Mechanism of Bicycles*

One of the results that show most clearly the interest felt by boys for machines and the original mental reaction of any child when questioned on the subject, is the synchronism of ages marking the correct explanation of a bicycle in the various towns where we collected our material. In Paris and Geneva in particular, 8 is the average age of the boys who can give a complete explanation of this mechanism, supported by a spontaneous drawing. . . .

A bicycle is an excellent subject for questions. Every boy has observed its mechanism. All the pieces of this mechanism are visible. And above all, the combined use of drawing and speech enables the child who has been questioned to show all he has understood.

The technique to be adopted is as follows:

We say to the child: "Do you like looking at bicycles in the street? Very well then, draw me a bicycle on this piece of paper." The boy will often protest: "But I can't draw," etc. But we insist. "Do it as well as you can. I know it is difficult, but go ahead, your friends can do it and you'll be able to too." Care should be taken not to let the drawing be too small (7 cm. at least). If necessary, one can outline the two wheels for the youngest children (it is a question of explanation not of drawing!) and wait for them to finish the rest. Then we ask: "Well, and how does a bicycle go?" If the child answers "With wheels," we go on, "yes, but how, what happens when the gentleman sits there?" and so on, not suggesting the answer to the question one has set, but trying to get at everything that the child knows already. Finally, as a counter [example] we point to the parts that have been drawn, the pedals, the chain, the cogwheels, and ask about each in turn: "What is that for?" In this way we obtain a complete and unsuggested explanation, for we confine ourselves to such indications as are given by the drawing.

Thus the drawing is a perpetual and extremely valuable safeguard. Often even after 7 or 8 years it is sufficient to show the quality of the explanation. It is rare for a drawing to be complete without the corresponding understanding of the mechanism. I call complete a drawing that has, (1) the two wheels of the bicycle; (2) one cogwheel correctly placed, i.e., interposed between these two wheels; (3) one cogwheel situated in the center of the back wheel; (4) a chain surrounding the

*[The following section is from Chapter IX.]

two cogwheels in correct fashion; (5) the pedals fixed to the large cog-wheel. (See Figures 1 and 2.)

With very young children it is as well to make use of a sort of puzzle game. You cut out of cardboard a bicycle frame, wheels, and cogwheel, and lay beside them a piece of string which represents the chain. The pieces are explained to the child in detail, and he is required to put them in order. But the best way of all is, of course, to show the youngsters a real bicycle and ask for their explanation on the spot.

The stages we discovered are four in number. During the first stage, the cause of movement is entirely synthetic (*global*): sometimes the child says that what makes the bicycle is "the mechanism," sometimes "the lamp," "the light," etc.; but in neither case is the "how" of the movement in any way analyzed. The average age of this stage is 4–5 years. During a second stage (5–6), the pieces are examined in detail, each piece is mentally isolated and thought of as necessary. But the cause of the movement is still synthetic, for the action of the pieces upon one another is in no way made clear, and when the child is asked to make it

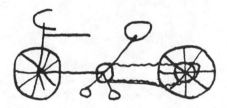

Figure 1

more definite, he takes refuge in a series of vicious circles which do not trouble him in the least. During the third stage, the action of the pieces is sought for, but the correct explanation has not been completely dis-covered. Finally, during a fourth stage (after 8 years) the complete explanation is given.

Figure 2

FIRST STAGE: THE CAUSE OF THE MOVEMENT IS SYNTHETIC

As Claparède has pointed out, perception in the very young child is syncretistic, that is to say, synthetic (*global*), confused, proceeding from the whole to the part. As far as causality is concerned, this synthetic perception tends to [lump] together all the elements of a given whole, but does not bring out the analysis of particular sequences. The child has the impression that each element "goes with" all the others or is "made for" all the others but does not inquire as to the "how" of the phenomenon. In the case of the bicycle, this first stage is very definitely marked. The child of 4–5 explains the movement of the bicycle by a sort of general forward impetus (*élan d' ensemble*) which is supposed to be released as soon as the cyclist moves his legs. If the child is asked to state things more clearly he explains the movement by bringing in "the mechanism,"

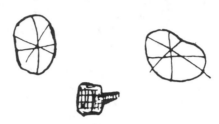

Figure 3

"the engine," the lamp, the pump, etc., in short any particularly striking piece which seems sufficiently charged with efficacy to account for the whole of the movement. The drawing corresponding to this conception consists essentially in two wheels between which the child has situated a pedal or anything else (see Figure 3).

Here are examples:

Schnei (4; 5): "How does this bicycle work? (a man's bicycle that we prop against a chair in front of Schnei)—*When you pedal*—What happens? —*It turns and then it goes.*—Why?—*Because the wheels turn.*—Why do the wheels turn?—*Because there's an engine.*—Where?—*In the bike.*—Where?— *In a spoke.*—What is a spoke?—*A wire.* (Schnei does actually show us a spoke and not the chain).—What does the engine do?—*When you pedal it makes it turn.*—How?—*When you turn the wheel.* (Shows the back wheel).— How does it make the wheel go?—*When you push the pedal.*—And then?— *It turns.*—Why?—*It goes.*—Why?—*If you lift up* (the pedal) *you push hard and then it goes.*—If there were no chain, would it go?—*Yes.*—Why is there a chain?— *Because you can pedal nicely.*—Why can you pedal nicely?— *Because if there wasn't a chain you couldn't pedal.*—Why not?—*Because that* (showing the bar of the pedals) *couldn't turn.*" The chain, therefore, is merely a support for the pedals and plays no part in the movement of the wheels: it is the turning of the pedals which directly causes the wheels to turn. And further, in connection with the pedals, Schnei says: "What happens when you pedal?—*It makes the wheels turn.*—Why?—*When the thing is lit.*—What thing?" (Schnei shows us the red light, i.e., the rear lamp). Thus the cause of the movement of the wheels is entirely synthetic, in that the movement of the pedals suffices, in the child's eyes, to explain that of the wheels, without the need for any intermediate links. . . .

Aub (4): "How does this bicycle move along?—*It's that.* (He points to the pedals.)—What does that do?—*You turn with your feet.*—How does it go?—*That. You put your feet on.*—And then?—*It goes.*—Why?—*It turns.* —How?—*That* (the pedals)." Through failing to understand our questions on the relation of the pedals to the wheels, Aub ends by saying that "wind" is put into the tires "*to make the bicycle go. Then you get on top. That makes the wheel go.*" In other words, the bicycle moves along as soon as the pedals are turned, the connection between the pedals and the wheels being entirely synthetic: he adds that the wheels contain "wind" which makes them turn more rapidly.

As for the children to whom we do not show a real bicycle, and from whom we merely ask for an explanation and a drawing from memory, they naturally give even less precise replies:

Mol (5; 3) says among other things: "*You must turn the pedals with your feet.*" But he claims that the pedals make the wheels go. "How do the pedals make the wheels go?—*They can, no, they can't make the wheels go. It's very hard to say. When you want them* (the wheels) *to go quickly, you turn your feet very fast.*" Mol, therefore, has quite realized a connection between the movement of the feet and that of the bicycle, but the "how" escapes his completely, and he does not trouble about it. The details of the mechanism are not at all necessary. "If you don't turn the pedals, can the bicycle go?—*Yes, you can do that.*—Uphill as well?—*Yes.*" In short, everything is possible. . . .

The drawing gives a very good schematic representation of the first stage. It consists of two wheels, and a pedal, a thread or a little wheel, etc., situated between the wheels without showing any attempt to insert or connect the pieces. . . .

The role assigned to lamps, to air, etc., is highly interesting, and shows how swiftly the child will establish relations between a given movement to be explained and some feature that happens to be particularly striking to immediate observation.

The few features essential to this stage may be summarized as follows.

In the first place these children are in no way concerned as to "how" the mechanism works. Essential parts like the cogwheel or the chain are not kept in mind by children who speak from memory. Those who have a real bicycle before them certainly make a note of the parts and they incorporate what they notice into their conception of the machine's motion by saying that these parts serve "to make it go" to "bike with" and so on. But in point of fact, nothing is changed. For, (1) these parts are thought to be [auxiliaries] to, not links in the movement. The role of the pedals is never even suspected of being connected with that of the wheels. (2) Some children regard these parts as unnecessary: Schnei, for example, says that the bicycle would go without a chain. (3) Others think that they are necessary, but only as supports: [One child] believes that the cogwheel and the chain help to keep the pedals in place. (4) Others, finally—and this leads us on to the second stage where the phenomenon will become more pronounced—think that the parts are necessary, but merely because they are there: [Another], says that there must be a chain, but does not know what purpose it serves.

Of the positive features of this stage we may signal out the following three. The first is explanation by moral determinism. [Each child], for example, is always saying: "It must go." The wheel may resist ("it doesn't want to go") but it is obliged to: "it must go." We have here a conception analogous to that which we emphasized in connection with the movements of the sun and moon and of the clouds.

The second positive feature is explanation without spatial contact: movement of the feet or of the pedals brings about that of the wheels, directly and without any contact. What conception does the child form of this relation? It seems as though the child thought that the mere movement of the feet was sufficient to set the bicycle going, just as though the cyclist were swimming or flying and used the bicycle only as a support to carry him over the ground. The cyclist is supposed to travel by himself, while the bicycle merely follows his movements. The wheels, in this case, are certainly bound to go round when the pedals go round, not because the pedals act by contact on the wheels but because both are carried along with the advancing cyclist.

Our reason for thinking this interpretation the most probable is that throughout the second stage we shall see this schema take more definite shape and give rise to explanations by reaction of the surrounding medium which recall the explanations of the movements of the heavenly bodies and of the clouds.

This is why expressions chiefly of a moral character come to be used in characterizing the movements of the various parts of the machine. When, for example, [one child] declares that: "It's the street that makes the bicycle go," what he means is obviously that the bicycle is forced to move along, whereas in a room it can resist. It was a conception analogous to this which made the children say that the stones make the river flow (by calling forth its impetus), or that the sun or night set the clouds in motion (by driving them away or by attracting them).

Finally, a third feature should be noted: the participation of "forces" or of a "current" shows that there exists in the child a form of causality compounded of phenomenism and dynamism. The lamp, the air in the tires, the spokes—all these are given without reason at the same time as the wheels, etc.: they are therefore efficacious in bringing about the movement.

SECOND STAGE: THE VARIOUS PARTS ARE NECESSARY BUT UNRELATED

The second stage begins from the moment when the child spontaneously draws chains, cogwheels, etc., or mentions their existence, and from the moment when he thinks of these parts as necessary to the bicycle's forward movement. This stage is distinguished from that which follows it by the fact that the action of one part on another is not supposed to follow any causal order properly so called, i.e., one which assumes regular antecedents and consequents. The bicycle's motion is still explained by means of syncretistic or synthetic relations, and when the child is pressed to enter into details, he only takes refuge in a series of vicious circles. The drawing at this stage is characterized by juxtaposition of the parts without correct insertions, often without even any connection between them.

Here are examples, beginning with some cases that are transitional between the first and the second stage:

Grim (5½): "How does the bicycle move along?—*With the brakes on top of the bike.*—What is the brake for?—*To make it go because you push.*—What do you push with?—*With your feet.*—What does that do?—*It makes it go.*—How?—*With the brakes.*—What are the pedals for?—*To make it go at the back.*" As Grim has noticed a chain, but without being able to explain its use, we show him a man's bicycle. Grim then says that the pedal makes the back wheel go, *"because you push like that* (on the pedal) *and it makes that* (the chain) *work.*—What is that chain for?—*It's to turn that wheel* (the cogwheel. Grim thus inverts the order) *and that makes the big one* (wheel) *turn with it.*—If there were no chain, would it go with the brakes?—*No.*—

And if there were no brakes, would the bicycle move?—*No.*" Grim then makes a drawing from memory analogous to that of Figure 4, i.e., a drawing in which all the parts are indicated, but in simple juxtaposition. "What makes the chain turn?—*The wheels.*—Which ones?—*That one* (the back wheel).— What makes that wheel turn?—*The wires* [the brakes].—What makes the cogwheel turn?—*The chain.*—What is the cogwheel for?—*To make it go.*—And the chain?—*Also.*—And the pedals?—*To make this wheel go* (cogwheel).— And what does the cogwheel do?—*It makes the wires work* (the brakes).— And the wires?—*They move and make the bicycle go.*—How do the wires make the bicycle go?—*At the same time as you make the wires go, you push with your feet.*—How do you make the wires work?—*With the brakes.*"

Ru (9, backward) is a good case of "synthetic incapacity." His drawing (Figure 4) shows the two wheels of the bicycle jointed correctly by a bar which serves as a frame, but between the two wheels are placed in a row, the chain, the cogwheel, and one pedal, without any relation between them. Questioning elicits the following: the pedals serve *"to make the back wheel go,"* the chains *"to make that go"* (the cogwheel), etc. . . .

Figure 4

Bern (7; 10) and Font (8; 6) each places the pedals, in his drawing, on the actual framework of the bicycle, stretches a chain between the two wheels and indicates the cogwheel, but without inserting them correctly. Yet they both explain the propulsion of the bicycle by a concerted movement. Bern: "How does the bicycle go?—*With the wheels and the pedals.*—How do the pedals make the wheels go?—*It's as he* (the man) *makes the bicycle move, that makes the wheels turn.*—Do the pedals make the wheels turn?—*No, because the pedals are to put your feet on.*—And how do you make the wheels work?—*By making the bicycle go.*—And how do you make the bicycle go?—With his hands. He pushes the bicycle. . . . He puts wind in the wheels and that swells the rubber and the bicycle goes better.*—What do your feet do?—Make the pedals turn.*—Why?—*I don't know* (he laughs). *It is because it makes the wheels turn. When you push the handlebar it makes them go even quicker. It makes the front wheel go.*"

Font, similarly: "*The pedals make the wheels go. The bicycle goes because of the wheels, and the pedals are to put our feet on, to hold us up. The person on top makes the pedals go. The pedal pushes the wheels. It's us that pushes it* (the wheels). *The wheels make the bicycle go. When you move your feet it gives a push. You have to push first* (before mounting): *the gentleman pushes first and then gets on.*" The separate parts have certainly been observed, but not as playing a distinctive role. Bern believes that the chain is worked by the back wheel, while the chain itself works the cogwheel. As for Font, he denies that there is a chain on the bicycle.

It will be noticed that the answers of the second stage are on certain points a continuation of those of the first, whilst on others they clearly introduce fresh features.

The chief residue of the first stage is the idea of a synthetic causality, the belief that the movement of a pedaling cyclist taken as a whole will be sufficient to make the wheels move along. For we do not find a single example at this stage of an intermediary link between the movement of the pedals and that of the wheels. The pedal makes the wheels go, not by a series of causes and effects, but directly. The intermediary factors are certainly seen to be there—the chain, the cogwheels, etc. But their movement is as much the effect as the cause of the movement of the wheels: here is no series taking place in time, but a syncretistic relation.

In some cases, this immediate action of the pedaling is made more definite. This can happen in the most interesting fashion, as with Font and Bern, and perhaps even with Grim. These children think much as follows: the cyclist who gives the bicycle a start before jumping on to it, once he is seated on the saddle, pushes the handlebars (or the brakes, which according to Grim, comes to the same thing) and in this way accelerates the impetus (*l'élan*). Besides this, he "moves his feet," which also gives an impetus. In short, the cyclist pushes himself by pushing the handlebars and moving his feet. He takes a start before mounting, and adds to it by pushing the handlebars.

Obviously, it is the same schema that lies at the back of the minds of the first stage children and enables them to be so easily satisfied with the idea that the pedals make the wheels go round without any intermediary factor.

It should be noted, moreover, that as in the first stage the child brings in helping forces:

Be (8): *"There's a current in the tires, because they are pumped up.—* Why do you pedal?—*To make the wheels go.—*And the current?—*It also makes them go when it* (the bicycle) *is started. It makes it go downhill, and along a straight road, but not uphill."*

Bot (8; backward): The bicycle goes round *"because the light* (the lamp) *is there."*

The fresh feature of this stage, as compared to the preceding one, is the presence of a certain analysis of detail. The child remembers the existence of the cogwheels and of the chain, and declares these parts to be necessary. If they did not exist, says the child, the bicycle would not go. It is interesting to note that this feeling of necessity comes long before any understanding of the "how," and consequently before causality properly so called. For at this stage, although the child declares the separate pieces to be necessary, he does not know what they are for. . . . The child says to himself quite simply: "They are necessary since they are there," and this is sufficient to make him feel very strongly the necessity of their existence. . . .

This absence of any concern about the "how" of things leads naturally to a complete absence of order in the relations subsisting between the parts. The same child will say at one time that the chain makes the cogwheel go round, and at another that the reverse is the case; at one time that the back wheel makes the chain go round, at another that the reverse is the case. There is, as yet, no irreversible succession.

Finally, the drawings show a mere juxtaposition of the parts, since the mind has not yet grasped their relations. We have here a very good example of correlation between what Luquet has called "synthetic incapacity" in the child's drawing, and what we have called "juxtaposition" in the child's mind. And this is yet another example of the necessary bond existing between juxtaposition and syncretism (see J.R., Chap. I, Conclusion):* it is because the cause of movement is synthetic that the pieces are simply juxtaposed, and it is because the pieces are simply juxtaposed that the explanation of the movement is still synthetic or syncretistic.

THIRD AND FOURTH STAGES: THE SEARCH

FOR CONTACTS AND MECHANICAL EXPLANATION

It is at about the age of 7 that the child passes from the second stage and sets out to find an irreversible order in the action of the parts upon each other. But, naturally, the correct explanation is not found straight-away, and it is necessary to distinguish a third stage before reaching that of complete explanation. The third stage is therefore characterized by the fact that the child gives up synthetic explanation and looks for an irreversible sequence of cause and effect in the detailed interaction of the parts.

Here are examples:

Jor (7; 9): "There's a high seat. It's made to join the pedals. When the pedal turns, I believe there are some little round things hidden away . . . when the pedal turns, the seat turns, and then comes down."

Dher (8; 1): "The gentleman makes the pedals turn. The wheels turn with them. There is a chain that is joined to the pedals and the wheels." But Dher draws the chain as in Figure 5, i.e., joining it directly to the tires and the pedals.

Ge (9) similarly imagines a chain joined to the tires, on which the pedals would work directly (see also Figure 5).

This shows a great advance on the preceding stages insofar as the contact is definitely sought for and leads to an irreversible causal sequence. But most of these children go no further than rudimentary explanations such as imagining that chains or bars are attached to the tires, and they are quite unperturbed by the unlikelihood of such suppositions. This fact alone shows how far removed were the subjects of the earlier stages from mechanical explanations, since the present subjects, who are far more advanced, still cling to schemas of such obvious absurdity.

It is only fair to add that this third stage is of short duration and serves chiefly as a transition to the next. Boys over 8 are able, as a rule, to give a correct explanation of the bicycle. Here are three examples:

In (8; 3): "You pedal and it makes a wheel (the cogwheel) go round. There's a chain, and it makes the back wheel go round" (see Ju's drawing from memory, Figure 2).

Ster (10; 1): "When you pedal, there's a chain, two (cog-) wheels and a cogwheel that makes the (back) wheel go."

Liv (10): "How do the pedals make the wheels go round?—With a chain. It goes round at the same time as the pedals. There's a thing like a cogwheel that makes the chain go round. The chain makes the (back) wheel go round. How many cogwheels are there?—Two."

*[J. Piaget, *Judgment and Reasoning in the Child*; hereafter, J.R.]

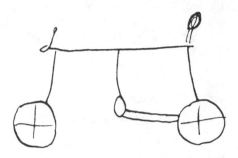

Figure 5

Here we have the first truly mechanical explanation that has occurred so far between the years of 8 and 9. To conclude, the evolution of answers about the bicycle shows a gradual progression from irrational dynamism to dynamism of the ἀντιπερίστασις* type, and from this more intelligible dynamism to a genuinely mechanistic view of causality.

Summary and Conclusion

We propose in this section† to inquire into the relations existing between the mind of the child and the external world. This should lead us into the very heart of the problem of knowledge. But we intend to approach the matter from an angle, and to formulate the problem so as to keep within the bounds of psychology and not encroach upon the domain of epistemology.

If we examine the intellectual development of the individual or of the whole of humanity, we shall find that the human spirit goes through a certain number of stages, each different from the other, but such that during each, the mind believes itself to be apprehending an external reality that is independent of the thinking subject. The content of this reality varies according to the stages: for the young child it is alive and permeated with finality, intentions, etc., whereas for the scientist, reality is characterized by its physical determinism. But the ontological function, so to speak, remains identical: each in his own way thinks that he has found the outer world in himself.

This being so, two points of view are possible in the study of intellectual evolution.

The first of these is to choose a system of reference and agree to call

---

*[Antiperistasis: An Aristotelian conception of violent motion in which the projectile flies because the air behind it pushes it, and this push derives from the motion of the cannonball which displaces the air.]

†We shall summarize in this section [Section IV] the conclusions reached in the present volume and in our last book *The Child's Conception of the World*.

"external reality," reality such as it is conceived to be during one of the stages of mental evolution. Thus it would be agreed upon to regard as the external world reality as it is postulated by contemporary science, or contemporary common sense. From this point of view, the relations of child thought to the external world would, in fact, be its relations to the universe of our existing scientific thought taken as the norm. In each explanation given by a child it would be possible to determine the part played by the activity of the subject and the part played by the pressure of objects, the latter being, by definition, objects as we now conceive them to be. And this would be psychology, for the statements which this method led to would not claim to have any decisive bearing upon the critical problem in general.

Or else, the attempt to regard any system of reference as absolute can be abandoned. Contemporary common sense or even contemporary science may be regarded as stages among other stages, and the question as to the true nature of external reality left open. And this would be theory of knowledge: this would be to place oneself above all the types of mentality that characterize the various stages of human development, and to seek to define the relations of the mind to reality without any preconceived notions as to what is mind and what is reality.

For our part, we shall confine ourselves to psychology, to the search, that is, for the relations between child thought and reality as the scientific thought of our time conceives it. And this point of view, narrow and question-begging though it appear, will enable us to formulate very clearly several outstanding problems. Does the external world (and by this we shall in future mean the world as it is viewed by science) impress itself directly on the child's mind, or are childish ideas the product of the subject's own mentality? If the child's mind is active in the process of knowing, how is the collaboration effected between his thought and the data of the external world? What are the laws which this collaboration will obey? All these are the traditional problems of the theory of knowledge, which we shall be able to transpose into the particular sphere which we have just defined.

More exactly, the problems we are about to study are biological problems. Reality, such as our science imagines and postulates, is what the biologists call environment. The child's intelligence and activity, on the other hand, are the fruit of organic life (interest, movement, imitation, assimilation). The problem of the relation between thought and things, once it has been narrowed down in this way, becomes the problem of the relation of an organism to its environment. . . .

These, then, are the terms in which we set the problem. And if, in describing the results we have obtained in child psychology, we occasionally use words like empiricism, apriorism, etc., it must be remembered that we are not giving to these terms their strictly epistemological meaning, but are using them in a restricted and, as it were, in a purely psychological sense.

But, be it said in passing, it might perhaps be possible to make use in the theory of knowledge of the results acquired by our restricted method. Let us suppose, for the sake of brevity, that intellectual growth takes place along a straight line, in a linear series such that the stages A, B, C, . . . N follow one another without either interferences or changes from one level to another. We shall take the external world corresponding to stage G as absolute, and compare to it the external world corresponding to stages $C, D, E, \ldots$ etc. Such a comparison is without any epistemological bearing, since there is nothing to prove that G is decisive. But if, now, we take into account this very possibility of variation and regard the series $C, D, E \ldots G$ as capable of being extended, on the one hand, backward, by the supposition of stages A and B, on the other hand, forward, thanks to the future stages $H, I, K \ldots N$, we shall discover the following: there will obviously exist a relation between the comparison of C, D, E to G and the comparison of G *to* H, I, etc.; and the fragmentary conclusions obtained by the comparison of C, D, E to G will become a particular case of the general conclusions obtained by comparison of all possible stages.

To put things more concretely, it may very well be that the psychological laws arrived at by means of our restricted method can be extended into epistemological laws arrived at by the analysis of the history of the sciences: the elimination of realism, of substantialism, of dynamism, the growth of relativism, etc., all these are evolutionary laws which appear to be common both to the development of the child and to that of scientific thought.

We are in no way suggesting, it need hardly be said, that our psychological results will admit straightaway of being generalized into epistemological laws. All we expect is that with the cooperation of methods more powerful than our own (historical, sociological methods, etc.), it will be possible to establish between our conclusions and those of epistemological analysis a relation of particular case to general law, or rather of infinitesimal variation to the whole of a curve.*

THE CHILD'S REALITY

How does the idea of reality constitute itself in the child's mind? Any direct analysis of its origin is beyond our power; the earliest stages precede language or are contemporaneous with the first spoken words, and any effort to reach the child's consciousness during these stages is fruitless, if one claims to go beyond mere hypothesis. But if we can content ourselves with conjecture, then it is best to try to extricate the laws according to which the idea of reality develops between the ages of 3 and 11, and to extrapolate the guiding lines thus obtained so as to reconstruct the earliest stages. Moreover, as soon as we put this method into practice, we find that we can learn enough from the laws of evolution between 3 and 11 years, and that there is no need to attach any special importance to the original stage.

Three complementary processes seem to be at work in directing the evolution of reality as it is conceived by the child between the ages of 3 and 11. Child thought moves simultaneously: (1) *from realism to objectivity*, (2) *from realism to reciprocity*, and (3) *from realism to relativity*. By *objectivity* we mean the mental attitude of persons who are able to distinguish what comes from themselves and what forms part of external reality as it can be observed by everybody. We say that

*The reader who wishes to pursue this subject further may be referred to a critical study which appeared under the heading "L'expérience humaine et la causalité physique de L. Brunschvicg," *Journ. de Psychol.*, 21 (1924): 586.

there is *reciprocity* when the same value is attributed to the point of view of other people as to one's own, and when the correspondence can be found between these two points of view. We say that there is *relativity* when no object and no quality or character is posited in the subject's mind with the claim to being an independent substance or attribute.

Let us examine these processes more closely. In order to be objective, one must have become conscious of one's "I." Objective knowledge can only be conceived in relation to subjective, and a mind that was ignorant of itself would inevitably tend to put into things its own prenotions and prejudices, whether in the domain of reasoning, of immediate judgment, or even of perception. An objective intelligence in no way escapes from this law, but, being conscious of its own "I," it will be on its guard, it will be able to hold back and criticize, in short it will be able to say what, roughly, is fact and what is interpretation.

So that in stating that the child proceeds from realism to objectivity, all we are saying is that originally the child puts the whole content of consciousness on the same plane and draws no distinction between the "I" and the external world. Above all we mean that the constitution of the idea of reality presupposes a progressive splitting-up of this protoplasmic consciousness into two complementary universes—the objective universe and the subjective.

We have met with many examples of this realism of the first kind and of its progressive reduction. Children's ideas about thought may be taken as a first illustration of the phenomenon in question. The feeling of subjectivity and inwardness felt by the adult is, to a great extent, connected with the conviction of being the owner of a thought that is distinct from the things thought about, distinct from the physical world in general, and more internal and intimate than the body itself. This conviction only comes late in the child's development. During the earliest stages, the child believes that he thinks with his mouth, that thought consists in articulating words, and that these words themselves form part of the external things. The voice, being thus identified with thought itself, is regarded as a breath which participates with the surrounding air, and some children go so far as to say that it is identical with the wind in the trees, and that dreams are made of "wind." They are quite incapable of distinguishing between thought and the things thought about. To use the expression chosen by M. H. Delacroix, the sign "adheres" to the thing signified. Later on, the child gives up this realism and localizes thought inside his mouth, then in a little voice placed in the head; he then gives up materializing thought and makes of it something *sui generis* which characterizes the self as spirit.

The evolution of ideas about names is particularly suggestive from this same point of view. Word and name are about all that the child knows of thought, since he identifies thought with the voice. Now, names are, to begin with, situated in objects. They form part of things in the same way as does color or form. Things have always had their names. It has always been sufficient to look at things in order to know their names. In some cases, this realism actually turns to magic: to deform the name is to deform the thing. Later on, names are situated in the adjoining air where the voice has uttered them, then in the voice, and finally in thought itself.

Dreams give rise to an equally definite realism. At first, they are thought to be pictures of air or light which come before our eyes from outside. At the earliest stage, the child thinks, naturally enough, that anyone could see the dream come into the room and go out again. Later on, the dream is believed to have an internal origin, but is conceived as coming out of the head or the stomach before appearing before the child. Finally, the child learns to distinguish between "being" and "seeming," and localizes the dream, first in the eyes, then in the head.

All these facts show that the localization of the objects of thought is not inborn. It is through a progressive differentiation that the internal world comes into being and is contrasted with the external. Neither of these two terms is given at the start. . . .

Consequently, during the gradual and slow differentiation of the initial protoplasmic reality into objective and subjective reality, it is clear that each of the two terms in process of differentiation will evolve in accordance with its own structure. In the case of every object there will be a displacement of values which will modify the character of the object. Take, for example, the notion of "air," or of "wind." During the earliest stages, air is conceived as participating with thought: the voice is air, and, in return, the wind takes notice of us, obeys us, is "good at making us grow," comes when we move our hands, and so on. When thought proper is localized in the self, and the participations between air and thought are broken, the nature of air changes by virtue of this fact alone. Air becomes independent of men, sufficient to itself, and living its own life. But owing to the fact that it is held to participate with the self, it retains at the very moment when it is severing these bonds, a certain number of purely human aspects: it still has consciousness, of a different kind perhaps than formerly, but its own nevertheless. Only very gradually will it be reduced to a mere thing.

This phenomenon is very general. During the early stages the world and the self are one; neither term is distinguished from the other. But when they become distinct, these two terms begin by remaining very close to each other: the world is still conscious and full of intentions, the self is still material, so to speak, and only slightly interiorized. At each step in the process of dissociation these two terms evolve in the sense of the greatest divergence, but they are never in the child (nor in the adult for that matter) entirely separate. From our present point of view, therefore, there is never complete objectivity: at every stage there remain in the conception of nature what we might call "adherences," fragments of internal experience which still cling to the external world.

We have distinguished at least five varieties of adherences defined in this way. There are, to begin with, during a very early stage, feelings of participation accompanied sometimes by magical beliefs; the sun and moon follow us, and if we walk, it is enough to make them move along; things around us notice us and obey us, like the wind, the clouds, the night, etc.; the moon, the street lamps, etc., send us dreams "to annoy us," etc., etc. In short, the world is filled with tendencies and intentions which are in participation with our own. This is what we have called dynamic participation, in contrast to substantial participation, to which, however, it may lead.

A second form of adherence, closely allied to the preceding, is that constituted by animism, which makes the child endow things with consciousness and life.

A third form is artificialism (see C.W., Sect. III).* The reader should be reminded at this point that artificialism in the child is not a theory which after reflection systematically takes man as the point of departure for everything. The terms must be reversed, and that is why artificialism has the same right to be classed among the adherences as animism. The child begins by thinking of things in terms of his own "I": the things around him take notice of man and are made for man; everything about them is willed and intentional, everything is organized for the good of men. If we ask the child, or if the child asks himself, how things began, he has recourse to man to explain them. Thus artificialism is based on feelings of participation which constitute a very special and very important class of adherences in the sense that we have defined.

A fourth form is finalism: the starting point and then the residuum both of animism and of artificialism; the deep and stubborn finalism of the child shows with what difficulty external reality frees itself from schemas due to internal and psychical experience.

A fifth form of adherence is constituted by the notion of force: things make efforts, and their powers imply an internal and substantial energy analogous to our own muscular force.

It is a striking fact that both the area of application and the strength of resistance of these adherences decrease progressively throughout the mental development of the child. And not only do these adherences lose ground little by little in correlation with each other, but their progressive disappearance seems to be proportional to the increasing clarity with which the child becomes conscious of his subjectivity. In other words, the better the child succeeds in dividing off the internal world from the external, the less stubborn are the adherences.

Three groups of facts may be mentioned in this connection. In the first place, as the child comes to notice the existence and the mechanism of his own thought, he separates signs from the things signified: thus, names cease to belong to the things named, thought is interiorized and ceases to participate with wind, dreams are no longer regarded as emanations of objects, and so on. Thus participations are loosened little by little, and even eliminated.

In the second place, insofar as the child discovers the existence and inwardness of his thought, animism, far from being strengthened, is, through this alone, compromised and even completely destroyed. The decline of animism brings with it a progressive reduction of child dynamism. For so long as things seem to be alive and consequently active, the forces of nature are multiplied by the child; and the elimination of life leads to a mechanization of force which means ultimately an impoverishment of the actual notion of force. . . .

Finally, as the child becomes conscious of his subjectivity, he rids himself of his egocentricity. For, after all, it is insofar as we fail to realize the personal nature of our own point of view that we regard this point of view as absolute and shared by all. Whereas, insofar as we discover this purely individual character, we learn to distinguish our

*[J. Piaget, The Child's Conception of the World; hereafter, C.W.]

own from the objective point of view. Egocentricity, in a word, diminishes as we become conscious of our subjectivity. Now the decrease of egocentricity means the decrease of anthropomorphic finalism, and consequently the decrease of all the feelings of participation that are at the bottom of artificialism.

Progressive separation of the outer from the inner world, and progressive reduction of the adherences, such, in brief, are the two fundamental aspects of the first process which we defined as a passage from realism to objectivity. What we have just said about the relations between egocentricity and artificialism takes us on to the analysis of the second process, for it goes without saying that all these processes are closely related to each other, so much so, indeed, that they may be said to be completely indissociable.

The second characteristic process in the evolution of the idea of reality is the passage *from realism to reciprocity*. This formula means that the child, after having regarded his own point of view as absolute, comes to discover the possibility of other points of view and to conceive of reality as constituted, no longer by what is immediately given, but by what is common to all points of view taken together.

One of the first aspects of this process is the passage from realism of perception to interpretation properly so called. All the younger children take their immediate perceptions as true, and then proceed to interpret them according to their egocentric prerelations, instead of making allowance for their own perspective. The most striking example we have found is that of the clouds and the heavenly bodies, of which children believe that they follow us. The sun and moon are small globes traveling a little way above the level of the roofs of houses and following us about on our walks. Even the child of 6–8 years does not hesitate to take this perception as the expression of truth, and, curiously enough, he never thinks of asking himself whether these heavenly bodies do not also follow other people. When we ask the captious question as to which of two people walking in opposite directions the sun would prefer to follow, the child is taken aback and shows how new the question is to him. Children of 9–10 years, on the other hand, have discovered that the sun follows everybody. From this they conclude that the truth lies in the reciprocity of the points of view: that the sun is very high up, that it follows no one, and that each sees it as just above him.

What we said just now about dreams is also to a certain extent germane to the present process: the child begins by regarding his own dreams as true, without asking himself whether everyone dreams the same as he does.

Side by side with this realism of perception and images, there is a logical realism which is far more important. We met with numerous examples of it in the course of our studies on child logic. Before the age of 10, on the average, the child does not know that he is a brother in relation to his own brothers. The ideas of right and left, of dark and fair, of the points of the compass, etc., are all subject to the law which is occupying us at the moment. These conceptions are at first regarded as absolute, so long as the personal point of view is accepted as the only possible one; after that, the reciprocity of relations gradually begins to make itself felt. In the present volume we have pointed to several fresh

examples of this process, examples which were of importance in forming the structure of reality.

Such are, above all, the ideas of weight and density. During the
earliest stages, an object is heavy or light according to the immediate
judgment implied by the child's own point of view: a pebble is light, a
boat is heavy. Later on, other points of view are taken into account, and
the child will say, for example, that such and such a pebble is light for
him but heavy for the water, and that a boat may be light for the lake
while it remains heavy for the child.

These last examples bring us to the third process which marks the
evolution of the child's idea of reality: thought evolves *from realism to
relativity*. This process is closely related to the last, and yet differentiates
itself from it on certain points. During the early stage, the child tends
to think of everything under the form of absolute substance and quality;
after that, bodies and their qualities seem to him more and more dependent upon each other and relative to us. Thus, substances become
relations, on the one hand, because the mutual connection of phenomena has been seen, and on the other, because the relativity of our
evaluations has been discovered. It would perhaps be as well to distinguish between these two aspects of "relativity," but the second is, as
a matter of fact, nothing but a combination of the first with the
"reciprocity" of which we spoke just now. . . .

The most striking example of this process is undoubtedly the evolution of the conceptions about life and movement. During the early
stages, every movement is regarded as singular, as the manifestation,
that is, of a substantial and living activity. In other words, there is in
every moving object a motor substance: the clouds, the heavenly bodies,
water, and machines, etc., move by themselves. Even when the child
succeeds in conceiving an external motor, which already takes away
from the substantiality of movement, the internal motor continues to be
regarded as necessary. Thus a leaf is alive, even though it moves with
the wind, i.e., it retains its spontaneity even though the wind is needed
to set it in motion. Similarly, a cloud or one of the heavenly bodies
remains master of its movements, even though the wind is necessary
to start it on its path. But later on, the movement of every body becomes the function of external movements, which are regarded no
longer as necessary collaborators but as sufficient conditions. Thus the
movement of clouds comes to be entirely explained by that of the wind.
Then these external motors are conceived as themselves dependent
upon other external motors, and so on. In this way there comes into
being a universe of relations which takes the place of a universe of
independent and spontaneous substances.

Closely analogous to this is the evolution of the idea of force, since
it is, as we saw, intimately connected with the idea of life.

The idea of weight supplies us with an excellent example of this
advance toward relativity, and the evolution in this particular case is
closely bound up with the advance toward reciprocity which we spoke
of just now. During the earliest stages, weight is synonymous with
strength and activity. A pebble sunk in water weighs on the water, even
when the latter is motionless, and produces a current toward the surface.
An object floats because, being heavy, it has the strength to keep itself

up. Weight is an absolute thing: it is a quality possessed by certain bodies, a variant of that life, or substantial force which we have described. Later on, weight is regarded as relative to the surrounding medium: bodies float because they are lighter than water, the clouds, because they are lighter than air, etc. But the relation is still vague: the child simply means that for the water in the lake, such and such a boat is light, but no comparison has been made which introduces proportional volumes. The wood of the boat is regarded as heavier than an equal volume of water. Finally, between the years of 9 and 10, "lighter than the water" begins to mean that the body in question is, taken at equal volume, lighter than water. Thus do the ideas of density and specific weight make their appearance: absolute weight is succeeded, in part at any rate, by relative weight.

The explanation of shadows and of night also offers an example of the progression from substantialism to an explanation founded on relations. During the earliest stages, night and shade are substances that emanate from clouds and bodies in general, and which come and go more or less intentionally. In the later stages, night and shade are nothing but the effects conditioned by the spatial relations which regulate the diffusion of light.

In every domain the substantialist realism of perception is succeeded by explanation through geometrical and cinematic relations. Running parallel with this growing relativity of phenomena in relation to each other, can be seen a growing relativity of ideas and notions in relation to ourselves and our evaluations. Thus the establishment of relativity between phenomena leads to a relativity between the measurer and what is measured. The evolution of the notion of weight brings out very clearly this double development. On the one hand, as we have just seen, the weight of the body becomes relative to the medium constituted by the other bodies, and presupposes the establishment of a relation between weight and volume. On the other hand, the words "light" and "heavy" lose the absolute meaning they had during the earliest stages, and acquire a meaning that is relative to the units of measurement that have been chosen: the pebble is heavy for the water, light for us, etc. The absolute concept has become a relation. In such cases, the advance toward relativity ends by converging absolutely with the advance toward reciprocity of viewpoints; in other words, the second and third processes as we distinguished them finally merge into one.

Such, then, is the evolution of the notion of reality in the child. Three processes help to make it emerge from its initial realism and to orientate it toward objectivity. In what relation do these three processes stand to one another? The first is of a purely social nature: the child replaces his own individual and egocentric point of view by the point of view of others and the reciprocity existing between them. The second of these three processes is of a purely intellectual order: substantialism of perception is replaced by the relativism of intelligence. The third process is both social and intellectual in character: in becoming conscious of his "I," the child clears external reality of all its subjective elements, and thus attains objectivity; but it is, above all, social life that has forced the child to become conscious of his "ego." Are we then to conclude that social factors determine the progress in the understanding of reality, or does this progress itself explain the development of social life? Let us note, in the first place, that the three processes synchronize. All three begin very early, all three are very slow, they remain uncompleted at the close of childhood and survive throughout the intellectual development of the adult. There is therefore every reason to believe that they are interdependent.

As a matter of fact, we have here, as in the case of child logic, to suppose that social life is necessary to rational development, but that it is not sufficient to create the power of reasoning. Without collaboration between his own thought and that of others, the child would not become conscious of the divergences which separate his ego from that of others, and he would take each of his perceptions or conceptions as absolute. He would therefore never attain to objectivity, for lack of having ever discovered his own subjectivity. Without social life, he would never succeed in understanding the reciprocity of viewpoints, and, consequently, the existence of perspectives, whether geometrical or logical. He would never cease to believe that the sun follows him on his walks. He would be ignorant of the reciprocity of the notions of right and left, of dependence, in short, of relations in general. It is therefore highly probable that the relativity of ideas would elude him.

But at the same time, it would seem that reason, while it presupposes a social environment in which to develop, at one point transcends it. Once it has liberated the appearance of the logical norms in the child, the social environment enables him to become "permeable" to experience. And when this faculty has been acquired, the collaboration of logical reason and experience itself suffices to account for the intellectual development that takes place.

With this last remark we are led to analyze the evolution of the idea of reality from the point of view of the influence of environment on intelligence. Here, we are at once confronted with a paradoxical fact: compared with ourselves, the child is both closer to immediate observation and further removed from reality. For, on the one hand, he is often content to adopt in his mind the crude forms of actuality as they are presented in observation: one boat will float because it is light, another, because it is heavy, etc. Logical coherence is entirely sacrificed in such cases to fidelity to fact. The causality which results from phenomenism of this kind is not unlike that which is to be found in primitive races and has been wittily compared by M. Brunschvicg to causality as it was understood by Hume. Anything can produce anything: so long as two facts are given together in raw observation, the one may be considered the cause of the other. We shall give this the name of *phenomenistic causality*. It is the starting point of a large number of childish notions. The moon that follows us, the clouds that go with the rain, the heaviness or lightness of floating bodies—all these are phenomenistic associations at the start, which later on lead the child to say: the moon moves along because I do, the clouds are the cause of rain, floating is determined either by heaviness or by lightness, etc. . . .

But, in another sense, the child is far farther away from reality in his thought than we are. Reality, for him, is still overgrown with subjective adherences: it is alive and artificial; words, dreams, and thought reside in external objects: the world is filled with forces. Phenomenistic relations themselves take place against a background of dynamism, either magical or animistic. Thus the fact that the moon follows us is immediately interpreted by means of prerelations, one of which makes the child think that he has power over the moon, the other that the moon is interested in him.

This paradoxical dualism of pure phenomenism on the one hand, and of magical dynamism, animistic or artificialist on the other, is a new manifestation of that dualism of juxtaposition and syncretism which we examined in our earlier volumes (L.T., Chap. IV, and J.R., Chap. I). Child thought proceeds by juxtaposition of its elements. There is a synthesis, but the terms juxtaposed in this way are embodied in subjective schemas, syncretism consisting in connecting everything with everything else in accordance with the hazards of a mental orientation that is subjective and egocentric.

The counterpart of this paradoxical dualism of phenomenism and egocentricity is the following: as it develops, the idea of reality tends to become both desubstantialized and desubjectified. Reality, as the child conceives it, is desubjectified with the years, in the sense that the adherences of animism, of artificialism, and of dynamism are progressively eliminated. But at the same time, reality becomes desubstantialized, in the sense that a universe of relations gradually takes the place of the universe of absolute substances which were assumed by primitive perception. Movement, weight, shadow, and night, force, etc., are all of them notions whose evolution is characteristic in this respect.

In short, from the point of view of the action of the physical environment upon the child, we are faced with a continual paradox: the child is both nearer to and farther from the world of objects than we are, and in evolving an adult mentality he both advances toward reality and recedes from it. . . .

The truth lies halfway between empiricism and apriorism: intellectual evolution requires that both mind and environment should make their contribution. This combination has, during the primitive stages, the semblance of confusion, but as time goes on, the mind adapts itself to the world, and transforms it in such a way that the world can adapt itself to the mind. . . .

CAUSALITY AND THE CHILD

The evolution of the idea of causality in the child follows very much the same lines as those we have just been observing in connection with the notion of reality. But it is important at this point to recall the facts in all their complexity. If we decide to do away with any arbitrary simplification, we shall find no less than 17 types of causal relation in child thought. Let us first make an analytical survey of these, and then try to establish the laws which control their evolution.

The first type is that of psychological causality, which is both causal and final; let us call it the *motivation* type. For example, God or men send us dreams because we have done things that we ought not to have done. This type is, no doubt, the most primitive, but it is also the one that survives the longest. Its scope is reduced, however, as mental development proceeds, since things in general cease to be thought of as conscious or as specially made by men. But during the primitive stages the motivating relation is omnipresent. Elsewhere we have designated as *precausality* this tendency to take a psychological motive as the true cause of everything: there are two Salève mountains, because there must be one for grown-ups and one for children, and so on.

The second type is that of pure *finalism*. This type overlaps with the preceding one to a certain extent, but it gradually separates itself from it. When the child says that the river flows so as to go into the lake, the river is not necessarily endowed with consciousness, nor the makers of things with a motive. There is simply finality, without either the origins or the consequences of this finalism being noticed by the child. It is much the same when we say, in accordance with ordinary common sense, that ducks have webbed feet so as to swim better. Implicitly, of course, there is present some idea of a divine plan, or of conscious and voluntary effort on the part of the duck. But these links with psychological causality are not perceived or made explicit, which shows that finalism is to be distinguished from motivation.

A third type is constituted by *phenomenistic causality*: two facts given together in perception, and such that no relation subsists between them except that of contiguity in time and space, are regarded as being connected by a relation of causality. A fire lit under an engine or alongside of it is regarded as the cause of movement, long before the child has attempted to find a single intermediary between this fire and the wheels of the engine. A child will say that one pebble sinks to the bottom of the water because it is white, that another pebble is light because it is black, that the moon remains suspended in the sky because it is yellow and bright, and so on. Anything may produce anything.

This form of causality is undoubtedly independent of the preceding forms, since the connections which it implies are imposed by the external world itself. But we cannot, as Hume would have liked to do, regard phenomenistic causality as the only original form of causality in the child. For phenomenistic causality is essentially unstable; as soon as it is established, a phenomenistic relation transforms itself into one that is animistic, dynamic, magical, etc. Thus the child who thinks that he is the cause of the movements of the moon always interprets this relation in a way that goes beyond the limits set by pure phenomenism. Up to the age of 4–5, he thinks that he is "forcing" or compelling the moon to move; the relation takes on an aspect of dynamic participation or of magic. From 4 to 5 he is more inclined to think that the moon is trying to follow him: the relation is animistic. The child who attributes to the fire the movement of the engine, immediately lends to the fire a force, the capacity for making air, etc.

The phenomenistic relation is therefore essentially vicarious; it clears the way for the dynamic and other forms of relations which follow immediately upon it. One even wonders whether the phenomenistic relation would exist if there were not other forms of relations to support it. Rather does it seem that the mind of the very young child, saturated as it is with dynamism, with finalism, with animism, with magic, with precausality, with artificialism, etc., when it is confronted with new phenomena establishes at random spatial and temporal contiguities, and sees relations between any one thing and another.

In short, though it cannot be reduced to causality by motivation, etc., phenomenistic causality, such as we find it in the child, would seem to be capable of existing in a mind already attuned to other forms of relation. Thus phenomenistic causality is to these other forms what,

in our case, induction is to deduction properly so called: we make inductions independently of any sort of deduction, simply by empirical groping, but we do so because we are perpetually on the lookout for some
possible deduction.

A fourth type of relation is *participation*. This type is more frequent
than would at first appear to be the case, but it disappears after the
age of 5–6. Its principle is the following: two things between which
there subsist relations either of resemblance or of general affinity, are
conceived as having something in common which enables them to act
upon one another at a distance, or more precisely, to be regarded one
as a source of emanations, the other as the emanation of the first. Thus
air or shadows in a room emanate from the air and shadows out of
doors. Thus also dreams, which are sent to us by birds "who like the
wind" (C.W., Chap. III, § 2).

Closely akin to participation is *magical causality* (a fifth type),
magic being in many respects simply participation: the subject regards
his gestures, his thoughts, or the objects he handles, as charged with
efficacy, thanks to the very participations which he establishes between
those gestures, etc., and the things around him. Thus a certain word
acts upon a certain thing; a certain gesture will protect one from a
certain danger; a certain white pebble will bring about the growth of
water lilies, and so on. . . .

A sixth type, closely related to the preceding ones, is *moral causality*.
The child explains the existence of a given movement or of a given
feature by its necessity, but this necessity is purely moral: the clouds
"must" advance in order to make night when men go to bed in order to
sleep; boats "have to" float, otherwise they would be of no use, etc.

Closely akin to psychological causality or finalism, but with an
added element of necessity, moral causality is also related to that form
of participation which we have called dynamic: external objects have
intentions which participate with ours, and in this way our desires force
them to obey us in accordance with purely moral or psychical laws.

The seventh type of relation is *artificialist causality*. Psychological
causality or precausality is at the start neither purely moral nor purely
physical. A given event is explained straightaway by the intention or
motive at the back of it, but the child does not ask himself how this
intention has worked itself out in action. Since all nature—both matter
and consciousness—is nothing but life, the problem does not arise. As
soon as the two terms come to be differentiated, artificialist causality
appears, at the same time as moral causality and in the nature of its
complement: the event or object to be explained is then conceived as
the object of human creative activity. This shows the family resemblance
to the preceding types which are all capable of growing into artificialism
or of finding themselves completed, thanks to this new type of relation.

An eighth type is *animistic causality*, or what might be called
causality by realization of form. The existence of a character or form
is explained by an internal biological tendency that is both alive and
conscious. The sun is what it is because, after having been made by
men, it grows. Mountains have grown, etc. Clouds and the heavenly
bodies move along because they are alive. This is the complement of
artificial causality; external motors act on things only if the latter

possess an internal motor capable of carrying out the directions and commands received from without.

A ninth type, which is simply left over from the preceding, is constituted by *dynamic causality*. Once animism proper has been eliminated, there still remain in objects forces that are capable of explaining their activity and their movements. Thus, primitively, force is confused with life itself, but dynamism outlives animism, just as finalism outlives precausality. We have had occasion to point to the very general character of childish dynamism.

A tenth type of relation is explanation by *reaction of the surrounding medium*. It is, properly speaking, the child's first genuinely physical explanation. For all the preceding forms appeal either to motives or to intentions, either to occult emanations or to mystical manufactures. But reaction of the surrounding medium implies, and, for the first time, the need for defining the "how" of phenomenon, i.e., the need for continuity and contact. At first reaction of the surrounding medium still goes hand in hand with animistic dynamism. Only it completes this dynamism with a more exact mechanism. Thus the clouds are regarded as setting themselves in motion, but once this movement is started, the clouds are driven along by the air which they produce by their flight. Later on, reaction of the surrounding medium will serve to explain purely mechanical movements. Thus projectiles which are supposed to be devoid of any spontaneous movement are pushed along by the air which they make in moving. The prime motor is thus the hand that throws the projectile, and not an internal force, as in the case of the clouds. We have seen what universal use children make of explanation by reaction of the surrounding medium. The movement of clouds, of the heavenly bodies, of water, of air, of projectiles, of bicycles, of airplanes, of boats, of tops, the effects of centrifugal force—all these are reduced to a schema which up till now was thought to be peculiar to Greek and medieval physics.

An eleventh type of causality is constituted by *mechanical causality* properly so called, i.e., explanation by contact and transference of movement: the wind pushes the clouds, the pedals make the bicycle go, etc. This form of causality appears between the years of 7 and 8. It is always the result of eliminating dynamism. The child who always begins by attributing these movements to the collaboration of two forces, one internal (the object's own force) and the other external, gradually comes to look upon the internal motor as unnecessary. At this point explanation becomes mechanical. Very often the schema of reaction of the surrounding medium serves as a transitional stage between the dynamic character of the early stages and the mechanical character of the later explanations which the child may offer of a given phenomenon.

A twelfth type of relation is what may be called *causality by generation*. The explanation of movement naturally admits much more easily of being reduced to the mechanical type than the explanation of how bodies are actually produced. And at the stage when children bring their ideas of movement in general under the heading of mechanism, they still look to artificialism and animism to explain the origin of things. How, then, will an attempt at a rational explanation of this origin first present itself? We saw that in the matter of the heavenly

bodies, of the clouds, etc., as soon as the child has given up the idea
that they were made by men, he tries to think of them as being born
out of each other. This is the type of relation which we shall call generation. The sun, for example, is regarded as a little living ball that has
come out of a fiery cloud; the clouds themselves have come out of smoke,
of air, of fire, etc. This is simply an extension of the animistic idea,
with the added notion of a transmutation of substances. The idea of
such transmutations is often imposed by relations of dynamic participation: the child feels that there is a relation between rain and clouds
long before knowing that the one comes out of the other. He begins by
saying that the clouds "come with" the rain, then, from the moment
that the rain ceases to be thought of as made by men, he imagines
that it comes out of the clouds. Thus a mere participation between
intentions and movements (clouds are at first believed to accompany
rain, just as the sun and moon accompany us, not for any reason, but
because they are made to) gives rise little by little to the idea of
generation proper.

From this type of explanation to the thirteenth, namely, to explanation by *substantial identification* there is but a step. We shall say that
there is identification when bodies that are born from each other cease
to be endowed with the power of growth as it exists in living beings. It
is not always easy to draw the line, but it is useful to note the difference. For instance, great progress has been made when the sun is no
longer believed to have been born of a cloud, but is regarded as a collection of clouds that have "rolled themselves up into a ball." In the
first case, the sun is looked upon as a living being that is very small at
first and gradually grows bigger. In the second case, it is regarded
merely as matter resulting from the fusion and burning of other inert
matters. It will be remembered how frequent were these explanations
by identification between the years of 8 and 10.

Once this thirteenth type of explanation has detached itself from
the preceding type, it quickly gives rise to the more subtle fourteenth
and fifteenth types. The fourteenth is characterized by the schemas of
condensation and *rarefaction*. For it is not enough for the child to say
that the sun has been made by clouds that have rolled themselves up
into a ball, or that a stone is formed of earth and sand. The qualitative
differences have to be explained, which separate bodies of similar origin.
The child then makes the following perfectly natural hypothesis. That
the qualities of the sun result from the fact that the clouds have been
"well packed" (*serrés*). That the hardness of the stone comes from the
fact that the earth is "close" (*serrée*). Thus the matter that makes up
bodies is more or less condensed or rarefied. Naturally, the child does
not seek, as did the early pre-Socratic thinkers, to reduce all qualitative
differences to differences of condensation. Nevertheless, between the
ages of 9 and 10, we can see a very general attempt at explanation by
condensation. This shows with particular clearness in the evolution of
the idea of weight. According to the very young children, bodies are
heavy in proportion to their size, and the child has no notion of differences in specific density. The older ones, on the contrary, say that the
water is light because it is "thin," or "liquid," whereas wood and stone
are heavy because they are "big," "thick," "full," and so on. In short,

putting aside mistakes in the evolution of weight, water is a rarefied matter, whereas wood and stone are condensed matters.

The fifteenth type of explanation is, in a sense, simply an extension of the last: it is that of *atomistic composition*. From the moment that bodies are regarded as the result of the condensation or rarefaction of original substances, it follows inevitably that sooner or later they will be conceived of as made up of particles tightly or loosely packed together. This is the conclusion which the child comes to with regard to stones: the stone is made of little stones, which are made of grains of earth, etc.

The sixteenth type of explanation is *spatial explanation*. Thus the explanation of the cone-shaped shadow appeals, in the later stages, to principles of perspective. Similarly, the explanation of the rise in the water level due to the immersion of solid bodies appeals, after the age of 9–10, to the volume of the immersed body. This is rather an advanced form of explanation and consequently only occasionally to be found in children.

Finally, the seventeenth type of explanation, the most subtle, but toward which most of the others tend, is *explanation by logical deduction*. A good example of this was supplied by the experiment of the communicating vessels: the level of the water is the same in both branches, so some of the children told us, because the water can go equally well in one or both directions, and this is what explains the final equilibrium. This is explanation by the principle of sufficient reason. All mechanical explanations, spatial, atomistic, etc., appeal sooner or later to the principle of deduction, and this type of explanation is therefore one of increasing frequency after the age of 10–11. For example, from the laws which he has observed in connection with the floating of boats, the rise in the water level, the child gradually draws explanations which imply concepts, such as density, specific weight, and so on. These concepts are pure relations; they are chosen in view of deductions to be made, and are not imposed by facts.

Having distinguished these seventeen types, we can now lay down three main periods in the development of child causality. During the first, all the explanations given are psychological, phenomenistic, finalistic, and magical (types I–VI). During the second stage, the explanations are artificialist, animistic, and dynamic (types VII–IX), and the magical forms (III and IV) tend to diminish. Finally, during a third period, the preceding forms of explanation disappear progressively and give place to the more rational forms (X to XVII). Thus the first two periods are characterized by what we have called precausality (in the widest sense of the word), i.e., by the confusion of relations of a psychological or biological type in general with relations of a mechanical type, and true causality does not appear till about the age of 7–8 (third period).

Three processes seem to us to characterize this evolution: the desubjectification of causality, the formation of series in time; and the progressive reversibility of the systems of cause and effect.

The first process is very definite. Causality, like the whole of reality, is at first teeming with subjective elements. No distinction is drawn between motivation and physical causality (types I, II, VI) or between muscular and manual activity and mechanical action (types VII and IX), or again between the influence of mind on body or of the body on itself, and the influence of external objects on each other (types III, IV, and VIII). As to phenomenistic causality, it is, as we saw, essentially vicarious and unstable. In the course of our studies on child psychology we had expected to fix upon 7–8 as the age before which no genuinely physical explanation could be given of natural phenomena. Our present inquiry entirely confirms this expectation. After 7–8 the more positive forms of causality gradually supplant the others, and we can say that at the age of about 11–12 the evolution is completed. There is, therefore, in the domain peculiar to causality a process of evolution exactly similar to that to which we drew attention in speaking of reality: confusion of the self and the universe, then progressive separation with objectification of the causal sequences.

The second process is peculiar to causality: it is the constitution of temporal series. What strikes one most about the child's more primitive forms of causality is the immediate and almost extratemporal character of the relation. It was the same with participation: the moment we have made a certain movement in a room, the air rushes into our hands through closed windows. As soon as we bring a copybook up to the table, the shadows of the sky or of the trees come and interpose themselves between our hand and the wood of the table. As soon as we walk along the street, the sun or the moon begins to move. Not a thought is given to the question of distance or of how long the action would have to take in traveling from the cause to the effect. Joined to this relative immediacy is a remarkable absence of interest as to "how" phenomena occur. Thus, according to the very youngest children, the pedals make the wheels go round without being in any way attached to them, simply by influence. The fire makes the wheel of the engine turn, even 50 cm. away. There is no contact, during the primitive stages, between cause and effect. Immediacy of relations and absence of intermediaries, such are the two outstanding characteristics of causality round about the age of 4–5. But such features are completely absent from children of 11–12 in subjects of which they know nothing. Thus, it is more or less impossible for a child of 10 to understand how a motorcar works. Nevertheless, the child presupposes pipes, cogwheels, chains, and belts to act as intermediaries between the [gas] and the wheels. From 7–8 onward, excellent explanations from memory are to be found concerning bicycles, whereas before this age, the various parts were believed to act on one another, but never in the same order. In the sphere of nature, the establishment of contacts and of series in time is also very definite. The step from precausality to mechanical causality in the explanation of movement is a good example; and the explanation by reaction of the surrounding medium—an explanation which serves as a transition between the two extreme types of causality—marks precisely the presence of a need for a chain of intermediate links between cause and effect. There is, therefore, in every sphere a constant progression toward the establishment of series of intermediaries, and series ordered in time. . . .

A third process in the evolution of causality is the progressive establishment of reversible series. At first sight this aspect of the question seems to be in contradiction with that which we have just been discussing, but it will soon be seen that this is not the case. If we examine a mechanism of any complexity that has been correctly understood by a child of 8–10, we shall always find that it is a reversible mechanism. When the stone has been understood to be composed of little particles of earth, the child admits that the stone can be decomposed into earth. When a child has understood how the pedal of a bicycle makes the wheel move round, he sees that by turning the wheel the pedals can be made to turn. The child believes that the cloud is made of smoke and that this is how it produces fire: from this he concludes, sooner or later, that the cloud can turn itself back into fire and in this way give rise to thunder and to the heavenly bodies. This reversibility does not exclude the existence of a series in time. Only, the series in question is one that can happen in two different directions.

Now, if we really look into the matter, we shall find that all the more advanced forms of explanation in the child are reversible. Mechanical causality is obviously so. So also is causality by substantial identification, i.e., by transmutation of the elements. Children, at any rate, have no doubts on this point: air produces fire, and fire, air; water produces smoke, and smoke, water, etc. Causality by atomic composition follows the same rule, so much so, indeed, that the child always becomes involved in vicious circles when he applies it for the first time: the stone is made of earth, and vice versa. Later on, these vicious circles cover more ground, i.e., a greater number of intermediaries are introduced between the extreme terms of the series. But the explanation is still circular. As to spatial and deductive explanations, it goes without saying that they are reversible, since they omit the time element.

The primitive forms of causality, on the contrary, are all irreversible. Take, for example, psychological, magical, finalist causality, etc.: an action or a motive explains a given phenomenon, but the reverse is inconceivable. Artificialism is in the same case: men made the universe, but the universe did not make men. Participation raises a special problem: its immediacy seems to imply reversibility. But in every participation there are emanations and there is the source from which they issue. This is therefore anything but reversibility. Of all the types of causality that come before that of mechanical causality, explanation by reaction of the surrounding medium is the one that points most clearly to a beginning of reversibility. But this is precisely the type that clears the way for the higher forms of explanation.

The progress from irreversibility to reversibility is thus continuous. This process, moreover, seems extremely natural if we bear in mind the manner in which the idea of reality grows up in the child. For the primitive universe is both strewn with subjective adherences and very near to immediate perception. Now, insofar as it is tinged with the child's subjectivity, this universe is irreversible: the flow of consciousness, psychological time, the whims of desires and actions which follow one another without order or repetition—all these things are projected in their entirety into the external world. Similarly, inasmuch as it is near to immediate perception, the child's universe is irreversible, for perception never shows us the same sun nor the same trajectory, nor the same movements twice. Events cannot happen over again in the same way. It is the mind that builds up reversible sequences underneath perception. To the extent that the child's universe is removed from these constructions and close to the immediately given, it is irreversible. Thus the advance toward reversibility shown by the development of child causality follows exactly the same lines as those underlying the processes defined in connection with the idea of reality. . . .

What conclusion are we to draw from our study of child causality as regards the influence of physical environment on the growth of intelligence? Here, again, we can only note that the more primitive the ideas of the child, the further removed are they from the physical environment as we know it. All the early forms of causality—magic, finalism, animism, artificialism, and, above all, dynamism, are inexplicable if we do not allow that between environment and consciousness there come to be interposed schemas of internal origin, i.e., psychophysiological schemas. The starting point of causality is a nondifferentiation between inner and outer experience: the world is explained in terms of the self.

[But] we have no more direct cognizance of the self than we have of external objects. Participation and magical causality show, on the contrary, that it is for lack of having discovered his own subjectivity that the young child feels his gestures, his words, and his thoughts, to be bound up with the objects themselves. We do not therefore, as Maine de Biran maintained, begin by discovering internal causality and then proceed to transfer it into objects. Causality is the result of a sort of bodily contact between the organism and the world, which is prior to consciousness of self, and this bodily contact takes us back to the notion of an assimilation of things by thought, a notion to which we shall return later.

On the other hand, to make causality into an a priori form, fixed once and for all in the structure of the mind, is to raise insuperable difficulties. For, after all, why should not causality appear from the first in its completed form? Why does it evolve to the extent of giving rise to 17 forms, distinguishable among children alone? Why is it dependent upon the influence of environment? If these are, in causality, signs of a structure which eludes empirical explanation, it will have to be admitted that this structure is plastic, and this leads us back once more to the hypothesis of an assimilation of external objects by the organism, such that the objects modify the organism, and such that the organism in its turn adapts things outside to its own peculiar structure.

THE CHILD'S IDEA OF LAW

The notion of law presents in the child, as indeed in the whole history of thought up to modern times, two complementary features— universality and necessity. Law is a constant and necessary relation. M. E. Meyerson has done very useful work in drawing attention to the difficulties of the position, and in distinguishing clearly between legality and causality, legality being simply generality, while causality alone could serve as a foundation for necessity. But from the genetic point of view, the concepts of natural and of social law have always reacted upon each other. For the child, who alone concerns us here, law is inconceivable without necessity. Let us therefore try, without the help of any preconceived ideas, to trace the development of these conceptions.

We can distinguish three periods in the evolution of law in the child. Each of these is characterized by the peculiar relationship in which generality and necessity stand to one another. During the first, generality is nonexistent; as to necessity, it is purely moral, physical determinism not having been separated from the idea of social obligation. During the second period, these two types of necessity are differentiated, and generality comes into being. During the third period, generality is established, and physical determinism is accompanied by logical necessity, which is the last term in the evolution from moral necessity.

The first period lasts till about the age of 7–8. During this time, there are no natural laws. Physical and moral determinism are completely confused with each other. More exactly, any law observed to hold among external objects is regarded as a social law, and things are believed to behave in accordance with rules that are imposed upon them from outside. This will be recognized as the combination, to which we have so often drawn attention, of animism and artificialism: nature is a society of living beings of whom man is the master and at the same time the creator. All recurring movements are explained primitively in this way. The movements of the sun and the moon, that of the clouds, the return of night, the course of rivers and of waves—all these are subject to the same principle: things have obligations toward us. Before the age of 7–8 we found no example of movement regulated by purely physical laws. There are always two motors which ensure the movement, thanks to their collaboration: an internal motor, which is the obedient will of the moving object, and an external motor, which is at first man himself, and then certain other bodies which play the part of masters or of more vigorous enemies (such as the sun driving away the clouds and the night summoning them). . . .

This is why for the child, as for Aristotle, the two notions which for us are to characterize the world of laws—violence and chance—come under no law whatsoever. With regard to violence, we cannot claim to have found in children any explicit belief that could be compared to the distinction made by Aristotle. But the whole of the moral conception of law of which we were speaking just now, shows that natural movements are, in the child's eyes, not violent, but harmonious and free. This implicit belief is constantly coming to the surface. Thus a boy of 6 told us that the sun is clever "because he wants to make it warm; we are clever "when we don't do what we ought not to do"; as to clouds, they are "not clever," because "they try to fight the sun."

We have dealt at great length elsewhere with the question of chance, and shall therefore content ourselves now with recalling our results. Before the age of 7–8 the child seeks, as far as possible, to eliminate chance from nature. The very way in which he formulates his "whys" shows that for him everything has a reason, even when to us it seems fortuitous and contingent. Now, whatever contradicts this conception provokes, by the mere fact of doing so, the maximum of curiosity on the part of the child. And this is why we find the child trying to find the reason or justification for a whole number of facts which for us are inexplicable because they are due to chance: why there is a big and a little Salève mountain, why pigeons are like eagles, why one person has smaller ears than another, etc. In short, law may be arbitrary in the sense that the will of gods or of men may be capricious; but chance is banished from nature, for everything admits of justification or of motivation, since everything in nature has been willed.

To conclude, during the first period the necessity of law is entirely moral, and physical necessity is simply the lining as it were of this moral necessity, i.e., it is simply dependent upon the force and authority of the masters of nature. What is the type of generality that could go hand in hand with such a conception of necessity as this? History has shown over and over again that to a moral conception of natural law there corresponds a belief in the possibility of numerous exceptions. These exceptions are of two kinds: miracles and the resistance of external things (monsters, etc., conceived by Aristotle as the resistance of matter in relation to form). The child thinks in exactly the same way. Corresponding to the confusion existing between natural and moral law, there is, during this first stage, a complete absence of generality in the laws of nature. . . .

The possibility of miracles is, of course, admitted, or rather, miracles form part of the child's conception of the world, since law is a moral thing. Children have been quoted who asked their parents to stop the rain, to turn spinach into potatoes, etc.

During the second period, on the contrary, we see two processes at work which are complementary to each other and take place between the years of 7–8 and 11–12; on the one hand, moral necessity and physical determinism become differentiated, and on the other hand, law becomes general.

We have seen numerous examples after 7–8 years of the manifestation of physical determinism. Thus the movements of water and clouds come fairly soon to be attributed to purely mechanical causes: the water cannot do otherwise than go down the slope, the cloud is bound to move forward when there is wind, and so on. At 8 years old on the average, the mechanism of a bicycle is completely understood, and this fact alone points to a mentality that is beginning to bend to the idea of uniform and physically determined causal sequences.

But the clearest index of all is the appearance of the idea of chance. At about 7–8 the child begins to admit that there are things which serve no particular purpose and events due solely to chance encounters. Thus the arbitrary and capricious element, which during the preceding period went hand in hand with the conception of law, has turned into chance, which means that it has lost its moral aspect and has taken on a purely physical character.

It goes without saying that moral necessity is not changed into physical determinism at a stroke. Up to the age of 11–12, many natural laws are still thought of as moral. The movements of the sun and the moon, for example, are those which are interpreted the longest as obeying purely moral laws. Moreover, determinism conquers only the details of events, whereas the body of natural laws taken in their most general aspect remains moral in character. For instance, the child may know that the formation of rain and the movement of clouds are due to purely physical processes, but he continues to believe that if there are clouds it is "for the gardens." Finalism dies hard.

As to the generality of law, it naturally grows in proportion as moral necessity decreases. As soon as the movement of rivers is interpreted physically, water is considered as always flowing in the same sense, etc. This is the age when the child seeks to avoid contradictions, and when he begins to understand that a law either is general or is not.

Finally comes the third period, which sets in at about 10–11. During this period, the generality of law naturally takes deeper root. But what becomes of necessity? For a general law is not, as such, necessary. The child may very well discover the absolute regularity of a given physical law (such as that light bodies float, and that heavy ones sink, etc.) but there is no physical necessity that can account in his eyes for this regularity. Apart from cases of apparent constraint (as when the wind pushes the clouds) there is no physical necessity. What makes a law necessary in our eyes is its deducibility: a law is necessary if it can be deduced with a sufficient degree of logical necessity from another law, or from sufficient geometrical reasons. Thus a paradox attends the evolution of law in the child: as the generality of laws increases their necessity grows less (insofar as this necessity, as during the first two periods, is moral). For as the child abandons the idea of moral necessity for justifying laws, he is faced with a mere generality of fact that is, however, devoid of any foundation whatsoever. When we ask the child why water goes down whereas smoke goes up, he can answer that heavy bodies fall whereas light bodies rise, which is certainly a general law; but when we question him further as to why this is so, he can answer nothing. The younger ones invent a moral reason to get out of the difficulty, but the older ones are nonplussed. Are we then to admit that moral necessity disappears without leaving a trace, or shall we, during this third period, find this necessity reappearing in a new form? We believe this last solution to be the right one, and that after the age of 10–11, moral necessity becomes logical necessity. . . .

But what possible affinity can we allow to exist between moral and logical necessity, two types which at first sight seem so radically distinct? Let us imagine a universe controlled by moral necessity. Now take from it all direct influence, all consciousness and will, and also all mystical activity exercised by man upon things. Much will still remain. There will still be the ideas of order, of organization, of regularity, coherence, and intelligibility. Thus there remains the possibility of explaining one group of phenomena by taking another group as our starting point. All this is characteristic of logical necessity: for at its root lies the conviction that every law that has been observed empirically must admit of justification by an appeal addressed no longer to the will and the emotions, but to reason.

What conclusions can we draw from our analyses from the point of view of the influence of environment? We cannot honestly account for the evolution of the idea of law by any direct action of the physical environment. The idea of law, like those of cause and reality, is much more remote from the child than it is from us. From the very first, we see that the feeling of the moral necessity of law comes before any exact knowledge of the law itself. From the first, we can observe a fusion of physical experience and internal feeling. No doubt only "conditioned reflexes" and motor anticipations will supply the contents of the most primitive laws discovered by the child, but this purely empirical attitude in no wise explains the "obligatory" character of law.

This feeling of obligation, thanks to which the child coordinates things as they are presented to him, can therefore only be of internal origin. Nothing in nature herself can give the child the idea of necessity. To immediate perception nature is full of whims, and there are no laws that do not admit of numerous exceptions. The child sees this himself when he begins by refusing to allow any generality to the laws of nature. . . .

If, then, the feeling of necessity is not due to the pressure of the physical environment, is it perhaps the outcome of social surrounding? For one may well wonder how a child would think who was removed from the authority of his parents. Is not the concept of nature simply the outcome of comparisons with family life rather than the result of prerelations properly so called?

Only one of the various theories put forward to account for the moral obligation attaching to the idea of law tends to make us subscribe to this hypothesis. We are thinking of the fine work done by Bovet on the conditions of obligation in the conscience.* There is obligation insofar as the orders are given by persons for whom we feel respect, respect being a *sui generis* mixture of fear and love. There is obligation in the measure that a relation exists, not between person and person, but between the small and the great.

It would therefore be in the relation of the child to its parents that we should have to look for the origins of law. Only, in Bovet's view, this relation would go a long way back. And indeed, observation shows the extreme importance and the great precocity of this attitude of mingled fear and love, which according to Bovet is precisely what constitutes respect. The child's conceptions about natural law would therefore seem to have their roots in a very universal and a very primitive reaction.

We must not therefore say that the child's concept of nature is based simply on an analogy with family life. What is at work is a genuine prerelation. Moral obligation forms part of the very structure of the child's mind, if we admit that the feeling of obligation is derived from the earliest contacts of the child's will with that of its parents, for these early contacts condition the whole of the child's mental life. . . .

LOGIC AND REALITY

Experience fashions reason, and reason fashions experience. Thus between the real and the rational there is a mutual dependence joined to a relative independence, and the problem is a singularly arduous one to know how much of the growth and elaboration of knowledge is due to the pressure of external things, and how much to the exigencies of the mind. This question belongs primarily to the theory of knowledge, but there exists from the genetic point of view a problem that is a very near neighbor to it, and concerning which we must add a few words. At each stage of intellectual development we can distinguish roughly two groups of operations: on the one hand, the operations of formal logic which condition the very structure of reasoning, and on the other hand, what Höffding calls the "real categories" (as opposed to

*"Les conditions de l'obligation de conscience," *Année Psychol.*, 18: 55–120, 1912.

formal categories), that is to say such notions as causality, reality, etc. We can now seek to find in what relation the logical structure characterizing each stage stands to the corresponding real categories. Do the logical relations condition the real categories, or is the converse the truth? In what measure are these two factors independent of each other?

We have endeavored in this volume to determine how the real categories evolved in the child's mind. In the preceding paragraph we were able to confirm the analysis we had made elsewhere of the formal development of thought in the child. We now hope to be able to show that there exists a parallelism between these two kinds of evolution.

In the first place, let us note the astonishing similarity of the general processes which condition the evolution of logic and that of the idea of reality. For the construction of the objective world and the elaboration of strict reasoning both consist in a gradual reduction of egocentricity in favor of the progressive socialization of thought, in favor, that is to say, of objectivation and reciprocity of viewpoints. In both cases, the initial state is marked by the fact that the self is confused with the external world and with other people; the vision of the world is falsified by subjective adherences, and the vision of other people is falsified by the fact that the personal point of view predominates, almost to the exclusion of all others. Thus in both cases, truth—empirical truth or formal truth such as forms the subject matter of argument—is obscured by the ego. Then, as the child discovers that others do not think as he does, he makes efforts to adapt himself to them, he bows to the exigencies of control and verification which are implied by discussion and argument, and thus comes to replace egocentric logic by the true logic created by social life. We saw that exactly the same process took place with regard to the idea of reality.

There is therefore an egocentric logic and an egocentric ontology, of which the consequences are parallel: they both falsify the perspective of logical relations and of things, because they both start from the assumption that other people understand us and agree with us from the first, and that things revolve around us with the sole purpose of serving us and resembling us.

Now, if we examine these parallel evolutions, logical and ontological, in greater detail, we shall distinguish three main stages in each. The first is that which precedes any clear consciousness of the self, and may be arbitrarily set down as lasting till the age of 2–3, that is, till the appearance of the first "whys," which symbolize in a way the first awareness of resistance in the external world. As far as we can conjecture, two phenomena characterize this first stage. From the point of view of logic, it is pure *autism*, or thought akin to dreams or daydreams, thought in which truth is confused with desire. To every desire corresponds immediately an image or illusion which transforms this desire into reality, thanks to a sort of pseudo-hallucination or play. No objective observation or reasoning is possible: there is only a perpetual play which transforms perceptions and creates situations in accordance with the subject's pleasure. From the ontological viewpoint, what corresponds to this manner of thinking is primitive *psychological causality*, probably in a form that implies *magic* proper: the belief that any desire whatsoever can influence objects, the belief in the obedience of external things. Magic and autism are therefore two different sides of one and the same phenomenon—that confusion between the self and the world which destroys both logical truth and objective existence.

The second stage lasts from the age of 2–3 to the age of 7–8, and is characterized, from the logical point of view, by egocentricity: on the one hand, there is an absence of the desire to find logical justification for one's statements, and on the other, syncretism combines with juxtaposition to produce an excess of subjective and affective relations at the expense of genuine logical implications. To this egocentricity corresponds, in the ontological domain, *precausality*, in the widest sense, meaning all the forms of causality based on a confusion between psychological activity and physical mechanism. For precausality is to physical causality what syncretism is to logical implication. Precausality confuses motive and cause, just as, in the sphere of logic, syncretism confuses subjective justification with verification.

Now among the various forms of precausality existing in this second period, two, of which one probably precedes the other, are particularly important: these are participation and dynamism. And each of these is dependent in its own way upon egocentric logic: participation is the ontological equivalent of transduction, and dynamism is closely connected with the predominance of conceptualism over the logic of relations, which predominance comes, as we saw, from the habits created by transduction.

With regard to transduction and participation, this is what we believe to be the truth: transduction passes from one singular or particular case to another, without bringing in any general laws or taking account of the reciprocity of relations. Thus to reason transductively about the formation of shadows is to dispense with laws altogether. To do so deductively, i.e., by means of generalization or an appeal to already established laws, would mean saying: "This copybook makes a shadow just like trees, houses, etc., etc. Now, what trees, houses, etc., have in common is that they block out the daylight. The shadow of the copybook must therefore also come from the fact that it shuts out the daylight." In this way, we should bring in (1) analogy between individual cases, and (2) a law stating what all these individual cases had in common. The child, on the contrary, reasoning transductively, brings in no general law. He begins, indeed, as we do, by feeling the analogy of the shadow cast by the book with the shadows of trees, houses, etc. But this analogy does not lead him to abstract any relation: it simply leads him to identify the particular cases with one another. So that we have here, not analogy proper, but syncretism. The child argues as follows: "This copybook makes a shadow; trees, houses, etc., make shadows. The copybook's shadow (therefore) comes from the trees and the houses." Thus, from the point of view of the cause or of the structure of the object, there is participation. . . .

Similar reflections can be made in connection with dynamism. One of the outstanding features of transduction is its conceptualism. Transduction is ignorant of the logic of relations, and therefore operates by means of concepts which have the appearance of being very general, such as "alive," "strong," etc., but are, in point of fact, merely syncretistic schemas resulting from the fusion of singular terms. Now from this to substantialism there is only a step. In *L'expérience humaine et la causalité physique* there is a remarkable chapter where Brunschvicg brings out the affinity existing between Aristotelian substantialism and the pseudo-ideal of traditional deduction. Something of the same kind happens, on an appropriate scale, in the mind of the child. Just as with Aristotle the logic of subject and predicate leads to the substantialism of substance and attribute and to the dynamism of form and matter, so with the child conceptualism leads him to "reify" everything, and consequently to see active and living substances in all around him.

But as soon as logical thought breaks away from transduction and becomes deductive, the idea of reality also breaks away from all these forms of primitive realism. Thus during the third great stage of child development, a new parallelism grows up between logic and the real categories.

Having established the fact of this parallelism, the question remains as to the mechanism of the various factors involved. Is it the real content of thought that fashions the logical form, or is the converse the truth? Put in this vague manner, it is obvious that the problem has no meaning. But if we are careful to distinguish logical form from what may be called psychological form (i.e., the factors of assimilation in the sense in which we defined the word), the problem may perhaps admit of a positive solution. For the moment, we must abstain from anticipating the answer. To establish its main features will be the task of a more searching study of the nature of assimilation.

16

Moral Feelings and Judgments*

1966

INTRODUCTORY NOTES

The Moral Judgment of the Child (1932) is a natural sequel to the four volumes on egocentric thought. Here we find a set of conceptions similar to those of the 1920s on thought itself, but now applied to a wide domain of practical life. Piaget can be described as a rationalist, not in the sense that he views the child as innately rational, but rather as becoming more and more rational. How? Not through an automatic unfolding, but through his interplay with other people: in relation to adults, first the acceptance of parental domination, followed by gradual liberation from it; in relation to other children, first the egocentric behavior of early childhood, followed by complete acceptance of the rules imposed by tradition (older children), and finally by the emergence of rational and reciprocal application of rules made by and agreed upon by the child and his peers.

We include in this section a brief selection from *The Psychology of the Child* (1969) which gives a brief account of the subject as Piaget and Inhelder saw it nearly forty years later. It follows the original book fairly closely but there is one interesting shift: the treatment of "moral feelings and judgment" is included in the chapter on the " 'concrete' operations of thought." Thus the leading concept is the growth of intellectual operations rather than the growth of socialization. The younger child is seen as nonoperational and therefore egocentric. This is not a change in Piaget's views so much as a clarification. By 1969 the work on concrete operations had been thoroughly developed and had become an international byword. In 1932 Piaget could only indicate that he believed that moral judgment must follow approximately the same lines of development as other forms of thought. By the later date he could show just what these other lines were like.

Moral Judgment reports research using an interesting combination of methods. We see the observational techniques of *Language and Thought*, but here extended in an important way. The experimenter functions as a participant

*From J. Piaget and B. Inhelder, *The Psychology of the Child*, Helen Weaver, translator, © 1969 by Basic Books, Inc., Publishers, New York, and Routledge & Kegan Paul Ltd., London. Originally published in French, 1966. Reprinted by permission of the publishers.

observer: he plays the game with the child in order to clarify the child's way of playing, the child's observance of rules. This study of moral *behavior* in "The Rules of the Game" of marbles is then amplified by quasi-clinical interviews, first to deepen our grasp of the child's *consciousness* of the rules he is following, and then in subsequent chapters to a series of other problems. Piaget takes up the child's relations with adults involving moral issues such as breaking rules or things, stealing, and lying. This is followed by studies of the child's understanding of his relations with other children, especially with regard to the emergence of genuine cooperation and mutual respect, and the development of the idea of justice.

Piaget is aware of a deep social question raised by his work. Although moral judgment develops in certain regular ways, it is by no means obvious that adult behavior lives up to the idealized norms of which children are capable. There are various plausible ways of understanding this disparity. For example, it may be that all mature adults are capable of high levels of moral judgment, but not necessarily of moral behavior, given the pressures of an often irrational and corrosive society. Or, it may be that living in such a world eventually erodes the capacity for moral judgment and even for rational thought.

These questions lead to another theoretical issue, the relation between practical reason and pure reason. The main line of Piaget's position is to insist that thought grows through action, but at the same time that actions of a given stage are determined by the intellectual level then achieved by the child. This position allows for minor disparities or *décalages* between thought in one domain and another, such as logico-mathematical thought and moral judgment. But major discrepancies do not accord well with the Piagetian vision of a person who uses intellectual achievements in limited domains to generate wider and more embracing structures of the same kind.

These are hard questions, and we do not have the answers, either empirically or theoretically. There is some experimental evidence that not all adolescents or adults reach the level of formal thought. Whether or not research eventually shows a strong correlation between higher types of moral judgment and the achievement of formal thought, no one can afford to blind himself to the historical facts: some of the world's most intelligent people have inflicted a great deal of evil on their fellow human beings. Only the crudest sort of elitism would insist that those of highest intellectual attainment have also the highest moral prerogatives.

On the other hand, this sense of history need not blind us to the potential utility of social ideals. Just as the unrealizable ideal of a frictionless machine helps physicists to think through physical problems, idealized social norms— such as the idea of justice founded on the best intellectual efforts of children in society—may help social scientists to solve their problems. Up to now educators interested in these matters have focussed their attention on fostering the growth of intelligence, working on the optimistic assumption that all good things would follow. If we are wiser now, and recognize the riskiness of this simplistic sequence, we should begin to search for ways of achieving a *synthesis* of morality and intelligence.

The affective relationship between the child and his parents, or the adults who play the parental role, engenders the specific moral feelings forced upon one by one's conscience. Freud popularized the notion of a "superego," or the internalization of the affective image of the father or parents, which becomes a source of duties, coercive models, remorse, and sometimes even of self-punishment. But this conception is older than Freud; it can be found, remarkably developed, in the work of Baldwin. This writer explained the formation of the self in terms of imitation (since imitation is necessary to provide first a complete image of the child's own body, then a comparison between the general reactions of the other and the self). Further, Baldwin showed that beyond a certain point, which is reached because of conflicts of will and the superior general powers of the adult, the self of the parents can no longer be imitated immediately, and thus becomes an "ideal self" which is a source of coercive models and of moral conscience.

The Genesis of Duty

Bovet* furnished a more detailed and accurate analysis of this process. According to him, the formation of the sense of obligation is subject to two conditions: (1) the intervention of orders given from the outside, that is, orders of indeterminate time span (don't tell lies, etc.); and (2) the acceptance of these orders, which presupposes the existence of a sentiment *sui generis* on the part of the person who receives the order toward the person who gives it (for the child does not accept orders from just anyone, for example a younger brother or sister or an unimportant person). According to Bovet, this sentiment is one of respect and consists of affection and fear. Affection alone could not suffice to produce obligation, and fear alone provokes only a physical or self-interested submission, but respect involves both affection and the fear associated with the position of the inferior in relation to the superior, and therefore suffices to determine the acceptance of orders and consequently the sense of obligation.†

The sentiment described by Bovet constitutes only one of two possible forms of respect. We shall call it "unilateral," since it binds an inferior to a superior who is regarded as such, and shall distinguish it from "mutual respect," which is based on reciprocity of esteem. Unilateral respect, if it is indeed the source of the sense of duty, begets in the young child a morality of obedience which is characterized primarily by a *heteronomy* that declines later to make way, at least partially, for the autonomy characteristic of mutual respect.‡

---

*P. Bovet, "Les Conditions de l'obligation de conscience," *Année psychologique*, 1912.

†This analysis, based on child psychology, is opposed to the theories of both Kant and Durkheim. Kant saw respect as a unique sentiment not attached to a person per se, but aroused by a person to the degree that he embodies or represents moral law. Durkheim thought along the same lines, but replaced "law" with "society." For both, respect was a result of obligation, and subsequent to it, whereas for Bovet it is its prerequisite. There is no question that Bovet is right insofar as the child is concerned. The child does not respect his father as a representative of the law or the social group but as a superior individual who is the source of compulsions and laws.

‡J. Piaget, *The Moral Judgment of the Child*.

Heteronomy

Heteronomy is expressed by a number of affective reactions and by certain remarkable structures peculiar to moral judgment before the age of 7 or 8.

From the affective point of view it should first be noted (as one of us and several collaborators of Lewin have done) that the power of orders is initially dependent upon the physical presence of the person who gives them. In his absence the law loses its force and its violation is accompanied only by a momentary uneasiness.

Later this power becomes permanent and the process of systematic assimilation occurs which psychoanalysts refer to when they speak of identification with the parental image or with authority figures. But the submission cannot be complete, and parental or authority figures give rise to ambivalence. The elements that make up respect become dissociated and the dissociation leads to a mixture of affection and hostility, sympathy and aggression, jealousy, etc. It is probable that the feelings of guilt that sometimes wreak havoc during childhood and later are related, at least in their quasi-neurotic form, to these ambivalences more than to the mere influence of the orders and of the initial respect.*

Moral Realism

From the standpoint of moral judgment, heteronomy leads to a systematic structure that is preoperatory both with reference to the relational cognitive mechanisms and to the processes of socialization. This structure is *moral realism*, according to which obligations and values are determined by the law or the order itself, independent of intentions and relationships.

One of us observed a young child who was habitually subjected to a maternal order of no moral importance (to finish a certain part of the meal). When one day this order was waived by the mother herself because the child was indisposed, the child could not help feeling bound by the order and guilty for not respecting it.

Moral realism leads to *objective responsibility*, whereby an act is

---

*Guilt begets feelings of anxiety, which have been studied, notably by Charles Odier (*L'Angoisse et la pensée magique*, Neuchâtel: Delachaux et Niestlé, 1947) and by Anna Freud (*The Ego and the Mechanisms of Defense*, rev. ed., New York: International Universities Press, 1967), along with the defense mechanisms that these anxieties provoke. The child feels guilty for having been hostile, and the anxiety born of this guilt leads to self-punishments, sacrifices, etc., and is sometimes combined, as Odier has shown, with certain quasi-magical forms of precausality (see selection 15.) as instruments of defense and protection. (Indeed, these mechanisms are not limited to moral anxieties: a young boy who was later to become a mathematician took a different route on his second visit to the dentist because the first visit had hurt—as if the pain depended on the route he took to get there.)

evaluated in terms of the degree to which it conforms to the law rather than with reference to whether there is malicious intent to violate the law or whether the intent is good but in involuntary conflict with the law.* The child, for example, is told not to lie long before he understands the social value of this order (for lack of sufficient socialization), and sometimes before he is able to distinguish intentional deception from the distortions of reality that are due to symbolic play or to simple desire. As a result, veracity is external to the personality of the subject and gives rise to moral realism and objective responsibility whereby a lie appears to be serious not to the degree that it corresponds to the intent to deceive, but to the degree that it differs materially from the objective truth. One of us set up the comparison of a real lie (telling your family you got a good mark in school when you weren't called on to recite) to a simple exaggeration (telling, after being frightened by a dog, that he was as big as a horse or a cow). For young children, the first lie is not "naughty," because (1) it often happens that one gets good marks; and above all (2) "Mama believed it!" The second "lie," however, is very naughty, because nobody ever saw a dog *that* size.

Autonomy

With advances in social cooperation and the corresponding operatory progress, the child arrives at new moral relationships based on *mutual respect* which lead to a certain *autonomy*. One must not, of course, exaggerate the importance of these factors in relation to the preceding ones. However, two important facts should be noted:

First, in games with rules, children before the age of 7 who receive the rules ready-made from their elders (by a mechanism derived from unilateral respect) regard them as "sacred," untouchable, and of transcendent origin (parents, the government, God, etc.). Older children, on the contrary, regard rules as the result of agreement among contemporaries, and accept the idea that rules can be changed by means of a democratically arrived at consensus.

Second, an essential product of mutual respect and reciprocity is the sense of justice, which is often acquired at the expense of the parents (on the occasion of an involuntary injustice, for example). As early as 7 or 8 and increasingly thereafter, justice prevails over obedience itself and becomes a central norm, equivalent in the affective realm to the norms of coherence in the realm of the cognitive operations.

---

*In primitive law, homicide is criminal even if it is accidental and not the result of negligence. Touching the ark of the covenant is a violation of a taboo, even in case of immediate danger.

17

Moral Judgment: Children Invent the Social Contract

1932

*The Rules of the Game**

. . . Now, most of the moral rules which the child learns to respect he receives from adults, which means that he receives them after they have been fully elaborated, and often elaborated, not in relation to him and as they are needed, but once and for all and through an uninterrupted succession of earlier adult generations.

In the case of the very simplest social games, on the contrary, we are in the presence of rules which have been elaborated by the children alone. It is of no moment whether these games strike us as "moral" or not in their contents. As psychologists we must ourselves adopt the point of view, not of the adult conscience, but of child morality. Now, the rules of the game of marbles are handed down, just like so-called moral realities, from one generation to another, and are preserved solely by the respect that is felt for them by individuals. The sole difference is that the relations in this case are only those that exist between children. The little boys who are beginning to play are gradually trained by the older ones in respect for the law; and in any case they aspire from their hearts to the virtue, supremely characteristic of human dignity, which consists in making a correct use of the customary practices of a game. As to the older ones, it is in their power to alter the rules. If this is not "morality," then where does morality begin? At least, it is respect for rules, and it appertains to an inquiry like ours to begin with the study of facts of this order. Of course the phenomena relating to the game of marbles are not among the most primitive. Before playing with his equals, the child is influenced by this parents. He is subjected from his cradle to a multiplicity of regulations, and even before language he becomes conscious of certain obligations. These circumstances even exercise, as we shall see, an undeniable influence upon the way in which the rules of games are

*From J. Piaget, *The Moral Judgment of the Child*, translator, Marjorie Gabain. First Free Press paperback edition, 1965. Reprinted with permission of Macmillan Publishing Co., Inc., New York, and Routledge and Kegan Paul Ltd., London. (Collaborators: N. Baechler, A. M. Feldweg, Marc Lambercier, L. Martinex-Mont, N. Maso, Valentine Piaget, and M. Rambert.)

elaborated. But in the case of play institutions, adult intervention is at any rate reduced to the minimum. We are therefore in the presence here of realities which, if not amongst the most elementary, should be classed nevertheless amongst the most spontaneous and the most instructive.

With regard to game rules there are two phenomena which it is particularly easy to study: first the *practice* of rules, i.e., the way in which children of different ages effectively apply rules; second the *consciousness* of rules, i.e., the idea which children of different ages form of the character of these game rules, whether of something obligatory and sacred or of something subject to their own choice, whether of heteronomy or autonomy. . . .

THE RULES OF THE GAME OF MARBLES

Three essential facts must be noted if we wish to analyze simultaneously the practice and the consciousness of rules.

The first is that among children of a given generation and in a given locality, however small, there is never one single way of playing marbles, there are [numerous] ways. . . . Every child is familiar with several games, a fact that may help according to his age to reinforce or to weaken his belief in the sacred character of rules.

In the second place, one and the same game, such as the Square game, admits of fairly important variations according to when and where it is played. . . . These variations according to time and place are important, because children are often aware of their existence. A child who has moved from one town, or merely from one school building to another will often explain to us that such and such a rule is in force in one place but not in the other. Very often, too, a child will tell us that his father played differently from him. . . .

Finally, and clearly as a result of the convergence of these local or historical currents, it will happen that one and the same game (like the Square game) played in the playground of one and the same school admits on certain points of several different rules. Children of 11 to 13 are familiar with these variants, and they generally agree before or during the game to choose a given usage to the exclusion of others. These facts must be borne in mind, for they undoubtedly condition the judgment which the child will make on the value of rules.

Having mentioned these points, we shall give a brief exposition of the rules of the Square game, which will serve as a prototype, and we shall begin by fixing the child's language so as to be able to understand the reports of the conversations which will be quoted later on. . . .

A marble is called *un marbre* in Neuchâtel and *un cœillu* or *un mapis* in Geneva. There are marbles of different value. The cement marble has the place of honor. The *carron* which is smaller and made of the more brittle clay is of less value because it costs less. The marbles that are used for throwing ["shooter"] and are not placed inside the square are called according to their consistency *corna* (if in carnelian), *ago*, or *agathe, cassine* (glass ball with colored veins), *plomb* (large marble containing lead), etc. Each is worth so many marbles or so many *carrons*. To throw a marble is to *tirer* (shoot) and to touch another marble with one's own is to *tanner* (hit).

Then comes a set of terms of ritual *consecration*, that is, of expressions which the player uses in order to announce that he is going to perform such-and-such an operation and which thus consecrate it ritually as an accomplished fact. For, once these words have been uttered, the opponent is powerless against his partner's decision; whereas if he takes the initiative by means of the terms of ritual *interdiction*, he will in this way prevent the operation which he fears.*

The Square game consists in putting a few marbles in a square, and in taking possession of them by dislodging them with a special marble, bigger than the rest. But when it comes to details this simple schema contains an indefinite series of complications. Let us take them in order, so as to get some idea of their richness.

First of all, there is the *pose*,† or outlay. One of the players draws a square and then each places his *pose*. If there are two players, each one puts down two, three, or four marbles. If there are three players, each puts down two marbles. If there are four or more players, it is customary to put down only one marble each. The main thing is equality: each one puts down what the others do. But in order to reach equality, the relative value of the marbles must be taken into account.

The game, regulated in this way by an indefinite number of rules, is carried on until the square is empty. The boy who has pocketed the largest number of marbles has won.

THE INTERROGATORY AND ITS GENERAL RESULTS

The rules that we have outlined above constitute a well-marked social reality, "independent of individuals" (in Durkheim's sense) and transmitted, like a language, from one generation to another. This set of customs is obviously more or less plastic. But individual innovations, just as in the case of language, succeed only when they meet a general need and when they are collectively sanctioned as being in conformity with the "spirit of the game." But while fully recognizing the interest attaching to this sociological aspect of the problem, it was from a different standpoint that we raised the questions which we are now going to study. We simply asked ourselves (1) how the individuals adapt themselves to these rules, i.e., how they observe rules at each age and level of mental development; (2) how far they become conscious of rules, in other words, what types of obligation result (always according to the children's ages) from the increasing ascendancy exercised by rules.

The interrogatory is easy to carry out. During the first part, it is sufficient to ask the children (we questioned about twenty boys ranging from 4 to 12–13) how one plays marbles. The experimenter speaks more or less as follows. "Here are some marbles." (The marbles are placed on a large baize-covered table beside a piece of chalk.) "You must show me how to play. When I was little I used to play a lot, but now I've quite forgotten how to. I'd like to play again. Let's play together. You'll teach me the rules and I'll play with you." The child then draws a square, takes half the marbles, puts down his *pose*, and the game begins. It is important to bear in mind all possible contingencies of the game and to ask

*[We have eliminated nearly three pages describing the intricate terminology of the local games of marbles.]

†[We have eliminated three pages of fascinating details about the rules of the game.]

the child about each. This means that you must avoid making any sort of suggestions. All you need do is to appear completely ignorant, and even to make intentional mistakes so that the child may each time point out clearly what the rule is. Naturally, you must take the whole thing very seriously, all through the game. Then you ask who has won and why, and if everything is not quite clear, you begin a new set.

It is of paramount importance during this first half of the interrogatory to play your part in a simple spirit and to let the child feel a certain superiority at the game (while not omitting to show by an occasional good shot that you are not a complete duffer). In this way the child is put at ease, and the information he gives as to how he plays is all the more conclusive. Many of our children became absorbed in the game to the extent of treating me completely as one of them. "You are dished!" cries Ben (10 years) when my marble stops inside the square.

In the case of the little ones, who find difficulty in formulating the rules which they observe in practice, the best way is to make them play in pairs. You begin by playing with one of them in the manner described above, and ask him to tell you all the rules he knows. Then you make the same request of the second boy (the first being no longer present), and finally you bring the two together and ask them to have a game. . . .

Then comes the second part of the interrogatory, that which bears upon the consciousness of rules. You begin by asking the child if he could invent a new rule. He generally does this easily enough, but it is advisable to make sure that it really is a new rule and not one of the many existing variants of which this particular child may already have knowledge. "I want a rule that is only by you, a rule that you've made up yourself and that no one else knows—the rule of N—— (the child's name)." Once the new rule has been formulated, you ask the child whether it could give rise to a new game: "Would it be all right to play like that with your pals? Would they want to play that way? etc." The child either agrees to the suggestion or disputes it. If he agrees, you immediately ask him whether the new rule is a "fair" rule, a "real" rule, one "like the others," and try to get at the various [reasons for his] answers. If, on the other hand, the child disagrees with all this, you ask him whether the new rule could not by being generalized become a real rule. "When you are a big boy, suppose you tell your new rule to a lot of children, then perhaps they'll all play that way and everyone will forget the old rules. Then which rule will be fairest—yours that everyone knows, or the old one that everyone has forgotten?" . . .

Having cleared up this point it will be easy enough to ask the two following questions. (1) Have people always played as they do today: "Did your daddy play this way when he was little, and your grand-dad, and children in the time of William Tell, Noah, and Adam and Eve, etc., did they all play the way you showed me, or differently?" (2) What is the origin of rules: Are they invented by children or laid down by parents and grown-ups in general?

Sometimes it is best to begin by these last two questions before asking whether rules can be changed; this avoids perseveration, or rather reverses its direction, and so facilitates the interpretation of the answers. All this part of the interrogatory requires extremely delicate handling; suggestion is always ready to occur, and the danger of romancing is ever present. But it goes without saying that the main thing is simply to grasp the child's mental orientation. Does he believe in the mystical virtue of rules or in their finality? Does he subscribe to a heteronomy of divine law, or is he conscious of his own autonomy? This is the only question that interests us. The child has naturally got no ready-made beliefs on the origin and endurance of the rules of his games; the ideas which he invents then and there are only indices of his fundamental attitude, and this must be steadily borne in mind throughout the whole of the interrogatory.

From the point of view of the practice or application of rules four successive stages can be distinguished.

A first stage of a purely *motor* and *individual* character, during which the child handles the marbles at the dictation of his desires and motor habits. This leads to the formation of more or less ritualized schemas, but since play is still purely individual, one can only talk of motor rules and not of truly collective rules.

The second may be called *egocentric* for the following reasons. This stage begins at the moment when the child receives from outside the example of codified rules, that is to say, some time between the ages of 2 and 5. But though the child imitates this example, he continues to play either by himself without bothering to find playfellows, or with others, but without trying to win, and therefore without attempting to unify the different ways of playing. In other words, children of this stage, even when they are playing together, play each one "on his own" (everyone can win at once) and without regard for any codification of rules. . . .

A third stage appears between 7 and 8, which we shall call the stage of incipient *cooperation*. Each player now tries to win, and all, therefore, begin to concern themselves with the question of mutual control and of unification of the rules. But while a certain agreement may be reached in the course of one game, ideas about the rules in general are still rather vague. In other words, children of 7–8, who belong to the same class at school and are therefore constantly playing with each other, give, when they are questioned separately, disparate and often entirely contradictory accounts of the rules observed in playing marbles.

Finally, between the years of 11 and 12, appears a fourth stage, which is that of the *codification of rules*. Not only is every detail of procedure in the game fixed, but the actual code of rules to be observed is known to the whole society. There is remarkable concordance in the information given by children of 10–12 belonging to the same class at school, when they are questioned on the rules of the game and their possible variations.

These stages must of course be taken only for what they are worth. It is convenient for the purposes of exposition to divide the children up in age-classes or stages, but the facts present themselves as a continuum which cannot be cut up into sections. This continuum, moreover, is not linear in character, and its general direction can only be observed by schematizing the material and ignoring the minor oscillations which render it infinitely complicated in detail. So that ten children chosen at random will perhaps not give the impression of a steady advance which gradually emerges from the interrogatory put to the hundred odd subjects examined by us at Geneva and Neuchâtel.

If, now, we turn to the consciousness of rules we shall find a progression that is even more elusive in detail, but no less clearly marked if taken on a big scale. . . .

During the first stage rules are not yet coercive in character, either because they are purely motor, or else (at the beginning of the egocentric stage) because they are received, as it were, unconsciously, and as interesting examples rather than as obligatory realities.

During the second stage (apogee of egocentric and first half of cooperating stage) rules are regarded as sacred and untouchable, emanating from adults and lasting forever. Every suggested alteration strikes the child as a transgression.

Finally, during the third stage, a rule is looked upon as a law due to mutual consent, which you must respect if you want to be loyal but which it is permissible to alter on the condition of enlisting general opinion on your side.

The correlation between the three stages in the development of the consciousness of rules and the four stages relating to their practical observance is of course only a statistical correlation and therefore very crude. But broadly speaking the relation seems to us indisputable. The collective rule is at first something external to the individual and consequently sacred to him; then, as he gradually makes it his own, it comes to that extent to be felt as the free product of mutual agreement and an autonomous conscience. And with regard to practical use, it is only natural that a mystical respect for laws should be accompanied by a rudimentary knowledge and application of their contents, while a rational and well-founded respect is accompanied by an effective application of each rule in detail. . . .

THE PRACTICE OF RULES

The First Two Stages. We need not dwell at any length upon the first stage, as it is not directly connected with our subject. At the same time, it is important that we should know whether the rules which come into being previous to any collaboration between children are of the same type as collective rules.

Let us give a handful of ten marbles to a child of 3 years and 4 months and take note of its reactions:

Jacqueline has the marbles in her hands and looks at them with curiosity (it is the first time she has seen any); then she lets them drop onto the carpet. After this she puts them in the hollow of an armchair. *"Aren't they animals? —Oh, no.—Are they balls?*—Yes." She puts them back on the carpet and lets them drop from a certain height. She sits on the carpet with her legs apart and throws the marbles a few inches in front of her. She then picks them up and puts them on the armchair and in the same hole as before. (The armchair is studded with buttons which create depressions in the material.) Then she collects the lot and lets them drop, first all together, then one by one. After this she replaces them in the armchair, first in the same place and then in the other holes. Then she piles them up in a pyramid: *"What are marbles?— What do you think?*— . . ." She puts them on the floor, then back onto the armchair, in the same holes.—We both go out onto the balcony: she lets the marbles drop from a height to make them bounce.

The following days, Jacqueline again places the marbles on the chairs and armchairs, or puts them into her little saucepan to cook dinner. Or else she simply repeats the behavior described above.

Three points should be noted with regard to facts such as these. In the first place, the lack of continuity and direction in the sequence of behavior. The child is undoubtedly trying first and foremost to understand the nature of marbles and to adapt its motor schemas to this novel reality. This is why [she] tries one experiment after another: throwing them, heaping them into pyramids or nests, letting them drop, making them bounce, etc. But once [she] has got over the first moments of astonishment, the game still remains incoherent, or rather still subject to the whim of the moment. On days when the child plays at cooking dinner, the marbles serve as food to be stewed in a pot. On days when [she] is interested in classifying and arranging, the marbles are put in heaps in the holes of armchairs, and so on. In the general manner in which the game is carried on there are therefore no rules.

The second thing to note is that there are certain regularities of detail, for it is remarkable how quickly certain particular acts in the child's behavior become schematized and even ritualized. The act of collecting the marbles in the hollow of an armchair is at first simply an experiment, but it immediately becomes a motor schema bound up with the perception of the marbles. After a few days it is merely a rite, still performed with interest, but without any fresh effort of adaptation.

In the third place, it is important to note the symbolism* that immediately becomes grafted upon the child's motor schemas. These symbols are undoubtedly enacted in play rather than thought out, but they imply a certain amount of imagination: the marbles are food to be cooked, eggs in a nest, etc.

This being so, the rules of games might be thought to derive either from rites analogous to those we have just examined or from a symbolism that has become collective. . . .

Symbols appear toward the end of the first year and in consequence of ritual acts. For the habit of repeating a given gesture ritually, gradually leads to the consciousness of "pretending.". . . Finally, when language and imagery come to be added to motor intelligence, the symbol becomes an object of thought. The child who pushes a box along saying "tuff-tuff" is assimilating in imagination the box's movement to that of a motorcar: the play symbol has definitely come into being.

This being so, can one seek among rites and symbols for the origin of the actual rules of games? Can the game of marbles, with its infinite complexity both with regard to the actual rules and to all that relates to the verbomotor system of signs in use—can the game of marbles, then, be conceived simply as the result of an accumulation of individual rites and symbols? We do not think that it can. We believe that the individual rite and the individual symbol constitute the substructure for the development of rules and collective signs, its necessary, but not its sufficient, condition. There is something more in the collective rule than in the motor rule or the individual ritual, just as there is something more in the sign than in the symbol.

With regard to motor or ritualistic rules, there can be no doubt that

*We use the term "symbol" in the sense given to it in the linguistic school of Saussure, as the contrary of sign. A sign is arbitrary, a symbol is [not]. It is in this sense, too, that Freud speaks of symbolic thought.

they have something in common with rules in the ordinary sense, namely the consciousness of regularity. When we see the delight taken by a baby of 10 to 12 months or a child of 2–3 in reproducing a given behavior in all its details, and the scrupulous attention with which it observes the right order in these operations, we cannot help recognizing the *Regelbewusstsein* of which Bühler speaks. But we must distinguish carefully between the behavior into which there enters only the pleasure of regularity, and that into which there enters an element of obligation. It is this consciousness of obligation which seems to us, as to Durkheim* and Bovet,† to distinguish a rule in the true sense from mere regularity.

. . . The individual rite develops quite naturally, as we have just shown, into a more or less complex symbolism. Can this symbolism be regarded as the starting point of that system of obligatory verbomotor signs which are connected with the rules of every collective game? As with the previous problem, we believe that the symbol is a necessary, but not a sufficient condition of the appearance of signs. The sign is general and abstract (arbitrary), the symbol is individual and motivated. If the sign is to follow upon the symbol, a group must therefore strip the individual's imagination of all its personal fantasy and then elaborate a common and obligatory imagery which will go hand in hand with the code of rules itself. . . .

Jacqueline (after the observations given above) is playing with Jacques (2 years, 11 months and 15 days), who sees marbles for the first time. I. Jacques takes the marbles and lets them drop from a height one after another. After which he picks them up and goes away. II. Jacques arranges them on the ground, in a hollow and says, *"I'm making a little nest."* Jacqueline takes one and sticks it in the ground in imitation. III. Jacques also takes one, buries it and makes a mud-pie above it. He digs it up and begins over again. Then he takes 2 at a time which he buries. Then 3, 4, 5, and up to 6 at a time, increasing the number of marbles systematically each time by one. Jacqueline imitates him: she first puts one marble down and makes a mud-pie over it, then two or three at random and without adopting a fixed system of progression. IV. Jacques puts all the marbles on a pile, then he places an india-rubber ball beside them and says: *"That's the Mummy ball and the baby balls."* V. He piles them together again and covers them up with earth which he levels down. Jacqueline imitates him but with only one marble which she covers up without leveling the earth. She adds: *"It's lost,"* then digs it up and begins over again.

This example shows very clearly how all the elements of individual fantasy or symbolism remain uncommunicated; as soon as the game takes on an imaginative turn each child evokes its favorite images without paying any attention to anyone else's. It will also be observed how totally devoid of any general direction are the ritualized schemas successively tried. But as soon as there is reciprocal imitation (end of II and whole of III) we have the beginnings of a rule: each child tries to bury the marbles in the same way as the other, in a common order only more or less successfully adhered to. In bringing out this aspect, the observation leads us to the stage of egocentrism during which the child learns other peoples' rules but practices them in accordance with his own fantasy. . . .

*L'Education Morale.
†"Les Conditions de l'Obligation de la Conscience," *Année Psychol.*, 1912, vol. 18, pp. 55–120. or Bovet, 1912 *op cit.*

The second stage is the stage of *egocentrism*. In studying the practice of rules we shall make use of a notion which has served on earlier occasions in the descriptions we have given of the child's intellectual behavior; and, in both cases, indeed, the phenomenon is of exactly the same order. . . . Through imitation and language, as also through the whole content of adult thought which exercises pressure on the child's mind as soon as verbal intercourse has become possible, the child begins, in a sense, to be socialized from the end of its first year. But the very nature of the relations which the child sustains with the adults around him prevents this socialization for the moment from reaching that state of equilibrium which is propitious to the development of reason. We mean, of course, the state of cooperation, in which the individuals, regarding each other as equals, can exercise a mutual control and thus attain to objectivity. In other words, the very nature of the relation between child and adult places the child apart, so that his thought is isolated, and while he believes himself to be sharing the point of view of the world at large he is really still shut up in his own point of view. . . .

Similarly, with regard to the rules of games, it is easy to see, and greater authorities than ourselves* have already pointed [it] out, that the beginnings of children's games are characterized by long periods of egocentrism. The child is dominated on the one hand by a whole set of rules and examples that are imposed upon him from outside. But unable as he is, on the other hand, to place himself on a level of equality with regard to his seniors, he utilizes for his own ends, unaware even of his own isolation, all that he has succeeded in grasping of the social realities that surround him.

To confine ourselves to the game of marbles, the child of 3 to 5 years old will discover, according to what other children he may happen to come across, that in order to play this game one must trace a square, put the marbles inside it, try to expel the marbles from the square by hitting them with another marble, start from a line that has been drawn beforehand, and so on. But though he imitates what he observes, and believes in perfect good faith that he is playing like the others, the child thinks of nothing at first but of utilizing these new acquisitions for himself. He plays in an individualistic manner with material that is social. Such is egocentrism.

Let us analyze the facts of the case. . . .

Baum (6½) begins by making a square and puts down 3 marbles, adding: "*Sometimes you put 4, or 3, or 2.—Or 5?—No, not 5, but sometimes 6 or 8.—Who begins when you play with the boys?—Sometimes me, sometimes the other one.—Isn't there a dodge for knowing who is to begin?—No.* —Do you know what a *coche* [starting line] is?—*Rather!*" But the sequel shows that he knows nothing about the *coche* and thinks of this word as designating another game. "And which of us will begin?—*You.*—Why?—*I want to see how you do it.*" We play for a while and I ask who has won: "*The one who has hit a mib [marble] well, he has won.*—Well! who has won? —*I have, and then you.*" I then arrange things so as to take 4 while he takes 2: "Who has won?—*I have, and then you.*" We begin again. He takes two, I none. "Who has won?—*I have.*—And I?—*You've lost.*" . . .

*Stern in his *Psychology of Early Childhood* notes the identity of the stages we have established in children's conversations with those he has himself established with regard to play, pp. 177 and 332.

Let us now see how two children, who have grown accustomed to playing together, set about it when they are left alone. They are two boys of whom one (Mae) is a very representative example of the present stage, while the other (Wid) stands at the borderline between the present stage and the next. The analyses of these cases will be all the more conclusive as the children in question are no mere beginners at the game.

Mae (6) and Wid (7) declare that they always play together. Mae tells us that they both *"played again, yesterday."* I first examine Mae by himself. He piles his marbles in a corner without counting them and throws his shooter into the pile. He then places 4 marbles close together and puts a fifth on top (in a pyramid). Mae denies that a square is ever drawn. Then he corrects himself and affirms that he always does so: "How do you and Wid know which is to begin?—*One of the two throws his shooter and the other tries to hit it. If he hits it, he begins."* Mae then shows us what the game consists in: he throws his shooter without taking into account the distances or the manner of playing (*piquette*), and when he succeeds in driving a marble out of the square he immediately puts it back. Thus the game has no end. "Does it go on like that all the time?—*You take one away to make a change* (he takes a marble out of the square, but not the one that he has touched). *It'll only be finished when there's only one left* (he 'fires' again twice). *One more shot, and then you take one away."* Then he affirms: *"every third shot you take one away."* He does so. Mae removes a marble every third shot independently of whether he has hit or missed, which is completely irregular and corresponds to nothing in the game as habitually played, or as we have seen it played in Neuchâtel or Geneva. It is therefore a rule which he has invented then and there but which he has the impression of remembering because it presents a vague analogy with what really happens when the player removes the marble he has just "hit" (touched). This game of Mae's is therefore a characteristic game of the second stage, an egocentric game in which "to win" does not mean getting the better of the others, but simply playing on one's own.

Wid, whom I now prepare to question and who has not assisted at Mae's interrogatory, begins by making a square. He places 4 marbles at the 4 corners and one in the middle (the same disposition as Mae's, which was probably a deformation of it). Wid does not know what to do to decide which is to begin, and declares that he understands nothing of the method which Mae had shown me as being familiar to both of them (trying to hit one's partner's shooter). Wid then throws his shooter in the direction of the square, knocking out one marble which he puts in his pocket. Then I take my turn, but fail to touch anything. He plays again and wins all the marbles, one after the other, keeping them each time. He also declares that when you have knocked a marble out, you have the right to play another shot straightaway. After having taken everything he says: *"I've won."* Wid therefore belongs to the third stage if this explanation is taken as a whole, but the sequel will show that he takes no notice of Mae's doings when they are playing together. Wid stands therefore at the boundary line which separates the stage of egocentrism from the stage of cooperation.

I then tell Mae to come into the room and the two children begin to play with each other. Mae draws a square and Wid disposes the marbles in accordance with his habitual schema. Mae begins (he plays *roulette* whereas Wid most of the time plays *piquette*) and dislodges four marbles. *"I can play four times, now,"* adds Mae. This is contrary to all the rules, but Wid finds the statement quite natural. So one game succeeds another. But the marbles are placed in the square by one child or the other as the spirit moves them (according to the rules each must put his *pose*) and the dislodged marbles are sometimes put straight back into the square, sometimes retained by the boy who has won them. Each plays from whatever place he chooses, unchecked by his partner, and each "fires" as many times as he likes (it thus often happens that Mae and Wid are playing at the same time).

I now send Wid out of the room and ask Mae to explain the game to us for a last time. Mae places 16 marbles in the middle of the square. "Why so many as that? *So as to win.*—How many do you put down at home with Wid?—*I put five, but when I'm alone, I put lots."* Mae then begins to play and dislodges a marble which he puts on one side. I do the same. The game continues in this way, each playing one shot at a time without taking the dislodged marbles into account (which is contrary to what Mae was doing a moment ago). Mae then places five marbles in the square, like Wid. This time I arrange the five marbles as Mae himself had done at the beginning of the interrogatory (four close together and one on top) but Mae seems to have forgotten this way of doing things. In the end Mae plays by taking away a marble every three shots, as before, and says to us: *"It's so that it should stop."*

We have quoted the whole of this example in order to show how little two children from the same class at school, living in the same house, and accustomed to playing with each other, are able to understand each other at this age. Not only do they tell us of totally different rules (this still occurs throughout the third stage), but when they play together they do not watch each other and do not unify their respective rules even for the duration of one game. The fact of the matter is that neither is trying to get the better of the other: each is merely having a game on his own, trying to hit the marbles in the square, i.e., trying to "win" from his point of view.

This shows the characteristics of the stage. The child plays for himself. His interest does not in any way consist in competing with his companions and in binding himself by common rules so as to see who will get the better of the others. His aims are different. They are indeed dual, and it is this mixed behavior that really defines egocentrism. On the one hand, the child feels very strongly the desire to play like the other boys, and especially like those older than himself; he longs, that is to say, to feel himself a member of the very honorable fraternity of those who know how to play marbles correctly. But quickly persuading himself, on the other hand, that his playing is "right" (he can convince himself as easily on this point as in all his attempts to imitate adult behavior) the child thinks only of utilizing these acquisitions for himself: his pleasure still consists in the mere development of skill, in carrying out the strokes he sets himself to play. It is, as in the previous stage, essentially a motor pleasure, not a social one. The true "socius" of the player who has reached this stage is not the flesh and blood partner but the ideal and abstract elder whom one inwardly strives to imitate and who sums up all the examples one has ever received.

It little matters, therefore, what one's companion is doing, since one is not trying to contend against him. It little matters what the details of the rules may be, there is no real contact between the players. This is why the child, as soon as he can schematically copy the big boys' game, believes himself to be in possession of the whole truth. Each for himself, and all in communion with the "Elder": such might be the formula of egocentric play. . . .

Third and Fourth Stages. Toward the age of 7–8 appears the desire for mutual understanding in the sphere of play (as also, indeed, in the conversations between children). This felt need for understanding is what defines the third stage. As a criterion of the appearance of this stage we shall take the moment when by "winning" the child refers to the fact of getting the better of the others, therefore of gaining more marbles than the others, and when he no longer says he has won when he has done no more than to knock a marble out of the square, regardless of what his partners have done. As a matter of fact, no child, even from among the older ones, ever attributes very great importance to the fact of knocking out a few more marbles than his opponents. Mere competition is therefore not what constitutes the affective motive-power of the game. In seeking to win the child is trying above all to contend with his partners *while observing common rules*. The specific pleasure of the game thus ceases to be muscular and egocentric, and becomes social. Henceforth, a game of marbles constitutes the equivalent in action of what takes place in discussion in words: a mutual evaluation of the competing powers which leads, thanks to the observation of common rules, to a conclusion that is accepted by all.

As to the difference between the third and fourth stages, it is only one of degree. The children of about 7 to 10 (third stage) do not yet know the rules in detail. They try to learn them owing to their increasing interest in the game played in common, but when different children of the same class at school are questioned on the subject the discrepancies are still considerable in the information obtained. It is only when they are at play that these same children succeed in understanding each other, either by copying the boy who seems to know most about it, or, more frequently, by omitting any usage that might be disputed. In this way they play a sort of simplified game. Children of the fourth stage, on the contrary, have thoroughly mastered their code and even take pleasure in juridical discussions, whether of principle or merely of procedure, which may at times arise out of the points in dispute. . . .

Ross (11; 1): *"First, everyone puts two marbles on the square. You can make the square bigger when there are more playing."* Ross knows the method of the *coche* for knowing who is to begin. He allows both *roulette* and *piquette* [two marble games with different rules]. He also allows what is not only contrary to all established usages but also to the sense of the words, a way of playing which he calls *femme-poussette* which consists in carrying one's hand along with the marble as one throws it (push stroke in billiards). Now this is always forbidden, and the very word that Ross has deformed says so— *fan-poussette* [pushing forbidden]. According to Ross, you play from the place you have reached with the last shot, and when you have won a marble you have the right to another shot straightaway. To change your place you must say *du mien*. *"If a stone gets in our way, you say 'coup-passé' and have another shot. If it slips (if the marble slips out of your hand) you say 'laché'* [gone]. *If you don't say that, you can't have another turn. It's the rules!"* . . . Finally, Ross knows of a rather peculiar custom. . . . *"If you stay in the square you can be hit and then he picks up the marbles* (= If your shooter stays inside the square and is touched by your opponent's shooter, he is entitled to all the marbles in the square). *He* (the opponent) *can have two shots* (to try and hit the shooter in question) *and if he misses the first he can take* (at the second shot) *the shooter from anywhere* (though of course only from the outside of the square) *and make the marbles go out* (= take them)." This rule has generally only been described to us by children of the fourth stage, but the rest of Ross's interrogatory is typically third stage.

Such then is the third stage. The child's chief interest is no longer psychomotor, it is social. In other words, to dislodge a marble from a square by manual dexterity is no longer an aim in itself. The thing now is not only to fight the other boys but also and primarily to regulate the game with a whole set of systematic rules which will ensure the most complete reciprocity in the methods used. The game has therefore become social. We say "become" because it is only after this stage that any real cooperation exists between the players. . . .

As yet, however, this cooperation exists to a great extent only in intention. Being an honest man is not enough to make one know the law. It is not even enough to enable us to solve all the problems that may arise in our concrete "moral experience." The child fares in the same way during the present stage, and succeeds, at best, in creating for himself a "provisional morality," putting off till a later date the task of setting up a code of laws and a system of jurisprudence. Nor do boys of 7 to 10 ever succeed in agreeing amongst themselves for longer than the duration of one and the same game; they are still incapable of legislating on all possible cases that may arise, for each still has a purely personal opinion about the rules of the game.

To use an apter comparison, we may say that the child of 7 to 10 plays as he reasons. We have already* tried to establish the fact that about the age of 7 or 8, precisely, that is to say, at the moment when our third stage appears, in the very poor districts where we conducted our work,† discussion and reflection gain an increasing ascendancy over unproved affirmation and intellectual egocentrism. Now, these new habits of thought lead to genuine deductions (as opposed to primitive "transductions") and to deductions in which the child grapples with a given fact of experience, either present or past. But something is still lacking if deduction is to be generalized and made completely rational: the child must be able to reason formally, i.e., he must have a conscious realization of the rules of reasoning which will enable him to apply them to any case whatsoever, including purely hypothetical cases. In the same way, a child who, with regard to the rules of games, has reached the third stage, will achieve momentary coordinations of a collective order, but feels no interest as yet in the actual legislation of the game, in the discussions of principle which alone will give him complete mastery of the game in all its strictness. A well-ordered game may be compared on this point to a good discussion. From this point of view the juridico-moral discussions of the fourth stage may be compared to formal reasoning in general.

It is, on an average, toward the age of 11 or 12 that these interests develop. . . .

Rit (12), Gros (13), and Vua (13) often play marbles. We questioned them each separately and took steps to prevent them from communicating to each other during our absence the contents of our interrogatory.

With regard to the square, the *pose*, the manner of throwing, and generally speaking all the rules we have already examined, these three children are naturally in full agreement with each other. To know who is to play first, Rit, who has lived in two neighboring villages before coming to town, tells us that various customs are in usage. You draw a line, the *coche*, and whoever gets nearest to it plays first. If you go beyond the line, either, according to some, it does not matter, or else *"there is another game: when you go beyond the line, you play last."* Gros and Vua know only of this custom, the only one that is really put into practice by the boys of the neighborhood.

*J.R., Chap. IV.

†We take this opportunity of reminding the reader of what has not been sufficiently emphasized in our earlier books, viz. that most of our research has been carried out on children from the poorer parts of Geneva. In different surroundings the age averages would certainly have been different.

But there are complications about which the younger boys left us in the dark. *"Whoever,* according to Gros, *says 'queue' plays second. It's easier because he doesn't get 'hit'* (= if a player's shooter lands near the square, it is exposed to hits from the other players)." In the same way, Vua tells us that *"whoever says 'queue de deux' plays last."* And he adds the following rule, also recognized by Gros: *"When you are all at the same distance from the coche whoever cries 'egaux-queque' plays second"* (the problem is therefore to play sufficiently soon still to find marbles in the square, but not first, for fear of being hit).

On the other hand, Gros tells us: *"Whoever takes out two* (two of the marbles placed inside the square, i.e., the equivalent of the player's 'pose') *can say 'queue-de-pose.' In that way he can play second from the coche in the next game."* And Vua: *"When there are two outside* (when two marbles have been knocked out of the square) *you can dare to say 'queue-de-pose,' and you can play second from the coche again in the second game."* Rit gives us the same information. . . .

In addition, there is a whole set of rules, unknown to the younger boys, which bear upon the position of the marbles in the square. . . .

Our three legal experts also point the measures of clemency in use for the protection of the weak. According to Vua *"if you knock out three at one shot and there's only one left* (one marble in the square) *the other chap* (the opponent) *has the right to play from halfway* (halfway between the coche and the square) *because the first boy has made more than his 'pose.' "*

The number of shots at the disposal of each player also gives rise to a whole series of regulations on which the three boys lay stress, as before, in full agreement with each other.

There is only one point on which we saw our subjects differ. Rit who, it will be remembered, has known the game in three different districts, tells us that the boy whose shooter stays inside the square may generally come out of it. He added, it is true, that in some games the player in such a plight is "dished" (Fr., *brulé*), but this rule does not seem to him obligatory. Vua and Gros, on the contrary, are of opinion that in all cases *"when you stay inside the square you are dished."* We think we may confuse Vua by saying: "Rit didn't say that!—*The fact is,* answers Vua, *that sometimes people play differently. Then you ask each other what you want to do.*—And if you can't agree?—*We scrap for a bit and then we fix things up."*

These answers show what the fourth stage is. Interest seems to have shifted its ground since the last stage. Not only do these children seek to cooperate, to "fix things up," as Vua puts it, rather than to play for themselves alone, but also—and this undoubtedly is something new—they seem to take a peculiar pleasure in anticipating all possible cases and in codifying them. Considering that the square game is only one of the five or ten varieties of the game of marbles, it is almost alarming in face of the complexity of rules and procedure in the square game, to think of what a child of 12 has to store away in his memory. These rules, with their overlapping and their exceptions, are at least as complex as the current rules of spelling. It is somewhat humiliating, in this connection, to see how heavily traditional education sets about the task of making spelling enter into brains that assimilate with such ease the mnemonic contents of the game of marbles. But then, memory is dependent upon activity, and a real activity presupposes interest. . . .

In conclusion, the acquisition and practice of the rules of a game follow very simple and very natural laws, the stages of which may be defined as follows: (1) Simple individual regularity. (2) Imitation of seniors with egocentrism. (3) Cooperation. (4) Interest in rules for their own sake. Let us now see whether the consciousness of rules describes in its evolution an equally uncomplicated curve.

Consciousness of Rules

The First Two Stages. As all our results have shown, consciousness of rules cannot be isolated from the moral life of the child as a whole. . . .

Thus the great difficulty here, even more than with the practice of rules, is to establish the exact significance of the primitive facts. Do the simple individual regularities that precede the rules imposed by a group of players give rise to the consciousness of rules, or do they not? And if they do, is this consciousness directly influenced by the commands of adults? . . . With regard to consciousness of rules, we shall designate as the first stage that which corresponds to the purely individualistic stage studied above. . . . Not only does every act of adaptation extend beyond its content of intellectual effort into a ritual kept up for its own sake, but the baby will often invent such rituals for its own pleasure; hence the primitive reactions of very young children in the presence of marbles.

But in order to know to what consciousness of rules these individual schemas correspond it should be remembered that from its tenderest years everything conspires to impress upon the baby the notion of regularity. Certain physical events (alternation of day and night, sameness of scenery during walks, etc.) are repeated with sufficient accuracy to produce an awareness of "law," or at any rate to favor the appearance of motor schemas of [anticipation]. The parents, moreover, impose upon the baby a certain number of moral obligations, the source of further regularities (meals, bedtime, cleanliness, etc.) which are completely (and to the child indissociably) connected with the external regularities. From its earliest months the child is therefore bathed in an atmosphere of rules, so that the task of discerning what comes from itself in the rites that it respects and what results from the pressure of things or the constraint of the social environment is one of extreme difficulty. In the content of each ritual act it is certainly possible to know what has been invented by the child, what discovered in nature, and what imposed by the adult. But in the consciousness of rules, taken as a formal structure, these differentiations are nonexistent from the point of view of the subject himself.*

An analysis of the rites practiced by older children, however, will allow us to introduce a fundamental distinction at this point. On the one hand, certain forms of behavior are, as it were, ritualized by the child himself (e.g., not to walk on the lines that separate the paving stones from the curb of the pavement). Now, so long as no other factor intervenes, these motor rules never give rise to the feeling of obligation proper. . . . On the other hand, certain rules—it matters not whether they were previously invented by the child, imitated, or received from outside—are at a given moment sanctioned by the environment, i.e., approved of or enjoined. Only in such a case as this are rules accompanied by a feeling of obligation. . . .

*E.g., heat burns (physical law), it is forbidden to touch the fire (moral law), and the child playing about in the kitchen will amuse himself by touching every piece of furniture except the stove (individual ritual). How can the subject's mind distinguish at first beween these three types of regularity?

What then does consciousness of rules amount to during our first stage? Insofar as the child has never seen anyone else play, we can allow that it is engaged here upon purely personal and individual ritual acts. . . . At the same time, and this is where the analysis becomes so difficult, it is obvious that by the time a child can speak, even if it has never seen marbles before, it is already permeated with rules and regulations due to the environment, and this in the most varied spheres. . . . It is therefore quite possible that when the child comes across marbles for the first time, it is already convinced that certain rules apply to these new objects. And this is why the origins of consciousness of rules even in so restricted a field as that of the game of marbles are conditioned by the child's moral life as a whole.

This becomes clear in the second stage, the most interesting for our thesis. This second stage sets in from the moment when the child, either through imitation or as the result of verbal exchange, begins to want to play in conformity with certain rules received from outside. What idea does he form of these rules? This is the point that we must now try to establish.

We made use of three groups of questions for the purpose of analyzing the consciousness of rules in this second stage. Can rules be changed? Have rules always been the same as they are today? How did rules begin? Obviously the first of these questions is the best. It is the least verbal of the three. Instead of making the child think about a problem that has never occurred to him (as do the other two), it confronts the subject with a new fact, a rule invented by himself, and it is relatively easy to note the child's resulting reactions, however clumsy he may be in formulating them. . . .

Now, as soon as the second stage begins, i.e., from the moment that the child begins to imitate the rules of others, no matter how egocentric in practice his play may be, he regards the rules of the game as sacred and untouchable; he refuses to alter these rules and claims that any modification, even if accepted by general opinion, would be wrong.

Actually, it is not until about the age of 6 that this attitude appears quite clearly and explicitly. Children of 4–5 seem, therefore, to form an exception and to take rules rather casually, a feature which, if judged purely externally, recalls the liberalism of older children. In reality, we believe that this analogy is superficial, and that little children, even when they seem not to be so, are always conservative in the matter of rules. If they accept innovations that are proposed to them, it is because they do not realize that there was an innovation. . . .

Let us now pass on to the typical cases of this stage, i.e., to children who out of respect to rules are hostile to any innovation whatsoever.

We must begin by quoting a child of 5½ years, Leh, whose reaction was among the most spontaneous that we had occasion to note. Leh was telling us about the rules of the game before we had questioned him about consciousness of rules. He had just begun to speak and was showing us how to play from the *coche* (which was about the only thing in the game that he knew) when the following dialogue took place. We asked Leh quite simply if everyone played from the *coche* or whether one could not (as is actually done) put the older ones at the *coche* and let the little ones play closer up. "No, answered Leh, *that wouldn't be fair.—Why* not?—*Because God would make the little boy's shot not reach the marbles and the big boy's shot would reach them.*" In other words, divine justice is opposed to any change in the rules of marbles, and if one player, even a very young one were favored in any way, God Himself would prevent him from reaching the square.

Pha (5½): "Do people always play like that?—*Yes, always like that.*—Why?—*'Cos you couldn't play any other way.*—Couldn't you play like this (we arrange the marbles in a circle, then in a triangle)?—*Yes, but the others wouldn't want to.*—Why?—*'Cos squares is better.*—Why better?— . . ." We are less successful, however, with regard to the origins of the game: "Did your daddy play at marbles before you were born?—*No, never, because I wasn't there yet!*—But he was a child like you before you were born.—*I was there already when he was like me. He was bigger.*" "When did people begin to play marbles?—*When the others began, I began too.*" It would be impossible to outdo Pha in placing oneself at the center of the universe, in time as well as in space! And yet Pha feels very strongly that rules stand above him: they cannot be changed. . . .

Geo (6). The case of Geo comes as a beautiful confirmation that for little children inventing a game comes to the same thing as finding in one's head a game that has already been anticipated and classified by the most competent authorities. Geo attributes the game he has invented to divine inspiration, and supposes it to be already known to the "Gentlemen of the Commune." As soon as we undeceive him he undervalues his own invention and refuses to regard it as right even if ratified by general usage. . . .

. . . The result is clearly paradoxical. Here are children playing more or less as they choose; they are influenced, it is true, by a few examples that have been set before them and observe roughly the general schema of the game; but they do so without troubling to obey in detail the rules they know or could know with a little attention, and without attributing the least importance to the most serious infringements of which they may be guilty. Besides all this, each child plays for himself, he pays no attention to his neighbor, does not seek to control him and is not controlled by him, does not even try to beat him—"to win" simply means to succeed in hitting the marbles one has aimed at. And yet these same children harbor an almost mystical respect for rules: rules are eternal, due to the authority of parents, of the Gentlemen of the Commune, and even of an almighty God. It is forbidden to change them, and even if the whole of general opinion supported such a change, general opinion would be in the wrong: the unanimous consent of all the children would be powerless against the truth of Tradition. . . .

In reality, however, this paradox is general in child behavior and constitutes, as we shall show toward the end of the book, the most significant feature of the morality belonging to the egocentric stage. Childish egocentrism, far from being asocial, always goes hand in hand with adult constraint. It is presocial only in relation to cooperation. In all spheres, two types of social relations must be distinguished: constraint and cooperation. The first implies an element of unilateral respect, of authority and prestige; the second is simply the intercourse between two individuals on an equal footing. Now egocentrism is contradictory only to cooperation, for the latter alone is really able to socialize the individual. Constraint, on the other hand, is always the ally of childish egocentrism. Indeed it is because the child cannot establish a genuinely mutual contact with the adult that he remains shut up in his own ego. The child is, on the one hand, too apt to have the illusion of agreement where actually he is only following his own fantasy; the adult, on the other, takes advantage of his situation instead of seeking equality. . . .

As far as the game of marbles is concerned, there is therefore no contradiction between the egocentric practice of games and the mystical respect entertained for rules. This respect is the mark of a mentality fashioned, not by free cooperation between equals, but by adult constraint. When the child imitates the rules practiced by his older companions he feels that he is submitting to an unalterable law, due, therefore, to his parents themselves. Thus the pressure exercised by older on younger children is assimilated here, as so often, to adult pressure. . . .

Ben (10 yrs.), whose answers we have given with regard to the practice of rules (third stage), is still at the second stage from the point of view that is occupying us just now: "Can one invent new rules?—*Some boys do, so as to win more marbles, but it doesn't always come off. One chap* (quite recently, in his class) *thought of saying 'deux empans'* (two spans) *so as to get nearer* (actually this is a rule already known to the older boys). *It didn't come off.—* And with the little ones?—*Yes, it came off all right with them.*—Invent a rule.—*I couldn't invent one straight away like that.*—Yes you could. I can see that you are cleverer than you make yourself out to be.—*Well, let's say that you're not caught when you are in the square.*—Good. Would that come off with the others?—*Oh, yes, they'd like to do that.*—Then people could play that way?—*Oh, no, because it would be cheating.*—But all your pals would like to, wouldn't they?—*Yes, they all would.*—Then why would it be cheating?—*Because I invented it: it isn't a rule! It's a wrong rule because it's outside of the rules. A fair rule is one that is in the game.*—How does one know if it is fair?—*The good players know it.*—And suppose the good players wanted to play with your rule?—*It wouldn't work. Besides they would say it was cheating.*—And if they all said that the rule was right, would it work?— *Oh, yes, it would. . . . But it's a wrong rule!"* . . .

Borderline cases like these are particularly interesting. Ben stands midway between the second and third stages. On the one hand, he has already learned, thanks to cooperation, the existence of possible variations in the use of rules, and he knows, therefore, that the actual rules are recent and have been made by children. But on the other hand, he believes in the absolute and intrinsic truth of rules. . . . Older children cease to believe in the intrinsic value of rules, and they do so in the exact measure that they learn to put them into practice. Ben's attitude should therefore be regarded as a survival of the features due to constraint.

Generally speaking, it is a perfectly normal thing that in its beginnings cooperation on the plane of action should not immediately abolish the mental states created on the plane of thought by the complexus, egocentricity and constraint. Thought always lags behind action, and cooperation has to be practiced for a very long time before its consequences can be brought fully to light by reflective thought. This is a fresh example of the law of *prise de conscience* or conscious realization formulated by Claparède and of the time lag or [*décalage*] which we have observed in so many other spheres. A phenomenon such as this is, moreover, well fitted to simplify the problem of egocentrism in general since it explains why intellectual egocentrism is so much more stubborn than egocentrism in action.

Third Stage. After the age of 10 on the average, i.e., from the second half of the cooperative stage and during the whole of the stage when the rules are codified, consciousness of rules undergoes a complete transformation. Autonomy follows upon heteronomy: the rule of a game appears to the child no longer as an external law, sacred insofar as it has been laid down by adults; but as the outcome of a free decision and worthy of respect in the measure that it has enlisted mutual consent.

This change can be seen by three concordant symptoms. In the first place, the child allows a change in the rules so long as it enlists the votes of all. Anything is possible, so long as, and to the extent that you undertake to respect the new decisions. Thus democracy follows on theocracy and gerontocracy: there are no more crimes of opinion, but only breaches in procedure. All opinions are tolerated so long as their protagonists urge their acceptance by legal methods. Of course some opinions are more reasonable than others. Among the new rules that may be proposed, there are innovations worthy of acceptance because they will add to the interest of the game (pleasure in risks, art for art's sake, etc.). And there are new rules that are worthless because they give precedence to easy winning as against work and skill. But the child counts on the agreement among the players to eliminate these immoral innovations. He no longer relies, as do the littles ones, upon an all-wise tradition. He no longer thinks that everything has been arranged for the best in the past and that the only way of avoiding trouble is by religiously respecting the established order. He believes in the value of experiment insofar as it is sanctioned by collective opinion.

In the second place, the child ceases ipso facto to look upon rules as eternal and as having been handed down unchanged from one generation to another. Thirdly and finally, his ideas on the origin of the rules and of the game do not differ from ours: originally, marbles must simply have been rounded pebbles which children threw about to amuse themselves, and rules, far from having been imposed as such by adults, must have become gradually fixed on the initiative of the children themselves.

Here are examples:

Ross (11) belongs to the third stage in regard to the practice of rules. He claims that he often invents new rules with his playmates: *"We make them (up) sometimes. We go up to 200. We play about and then hit each other, and then he says to me: 'If you go up to 100 I'll give you a marble.'* Is this new rule fair like the old ones, or not?—*Perhaps it isn't quite fair, because it isn't very hard to take four marbles that way!*—If everyone does it, will it be a real rule, or not?—*If they do it often, it will become a real rule.* —Did your father play the way you showed me, or differently?—*Oh, I don't know. It may have been a different game. It changes. It still changes quite often.*—Have people been playing for long?—*At least fifty years.*—Did people play marbles in the days of the 'Old Swiss'?—*Oh, I don't think so.*—How did it begin?—*Some boys took some motor balls* (ball bearings) *and then they played. And after that there were marbles in shops.*—Why are there rules in the game of marbles?—*So as not to be always quarreling you must have rules, and then play properly.*—How did these rules begin?—*Some boys came to an agreement amongst themselves and made them.*—Could you invent a new rule?—*Perhaps . . .* (he thinks) *you put three marbles together and you drop another from above on to the middle one.*—Could one play that way?—*Oh, yes.*—Is that a fair rule like the others?—*The chaps might say it wasn't very fair because it's luck. To be a good rule, it has to be skill.*— But if everyone played that way, would it be a fair rule or not?—*Oh, yes, you could play just as well with that rule as with the others."*

Malb (12) belongs to the fourth stage in the practice of rules: *"Does everyone play the way you showed me?—Yes.*—And did they play like that long ago?—*No.*—Why not?—*They used different words.*—And how about the rules?—*They didn't use them either, because my father told me he didn't play that way.*—But long ago did people play with the same rules?—*Not quite the same.*—How about the rule not hitting for one?—*I think that must have come later.*—Did they play marbles when your grandfather was little?—*Yes.*—Like they do now?—*Oh, no, different kinds of games.*—And at the time of the battle of Morat?—*No, I don't think they played then.*—How do you think the game of marbles began?—*At first, children looked for round pebbles.*—And the rules?—*I expect they played from the coche. Later on, boys wanted to play differently and they invented other rules.*—And how did the coche begin?—*I expect they had fun hitting the pebbles. And then they invented the coche.*—Could one change the rules?—*Yes.*—Could you?—*Yes, I could make up another game. We were playing at home one evening and we found out a new one* (he shows it to us).—Are these new rules as fair as the others?—*Yes.*—Which is the fairest, the game you showed me first or the one you invented?—*Both the same.*—If you show this new game to the little ones what will they do?—*Perhaps they will play at it.*—And if they forget the square game and only play this one, which will be the true game, the new one that will be better known, or the old one?—*The best known one will be the fairest."* . . .

[From now on] a rule is conceived as the free pronouncement of the actual individual minds themselves. It is no longer external and coercive: it can be modified and adapted to the tendencies of the group. It constitutes no revealed truth whose sacred character derives from its divine origin and historical permanence; it is something that is built up progressively and autonomously. But does this not make it cease to be a real rule? Is it perhaps not a mark of decadence rather than of progress in relation to the earlier stage? The facts, however, seem definitely to authorize the opposite conclusion: it is from the moment that it replaces the rule of constraint that the rule of cooperation becomes an effective moral law.

In the first place, one is struck by the synchronism between the appearance of this new type of consciousness of rules and a genuine observation of the rules. . . . These are simply two aspects of the same reality: when a rule ceases to be external to children and depends only on their free collective will, it becomes incorporated in the mind of each, and individual obedience is henceforth purely spontaneous. True, the difficulty reappears each time that the child, while still remaining faithful to a rule that favors him, is tempted to slur over some article of the law or some point of procedure that favors his opponent. But the peculiar function of cooperation is to lead the child to the practice of reciprocity, hence of moral universality and generosity in his relations with his playmates.

This last point introduces us to yet another sign of the bond between autonomy and true respect for the law. By modifying rules, i.e., by becoming a sovereign and legislator in the democracy which toward the age of 10–11 follows upon the earlier gerontocracy, the child takes cognizance of the raison d'être of laws. A rule becomes the necessary condition for agreement. "*So as not to be always quarreling,*" says Ross, "*you must have rules and then play properly* (= stick to them)." The fairest rule, Gros maintains, is that which unites the opinion of the players, "*because* (then) *they can't cheat.*"

Thirdly, what shows most clearly that the autonomy achieved during this stage leads more surely to respect for rules than the heteronomy of the preceding stage is the truly political and democratic way in which children of 12–13 distinguish lawless whims from constitutional innovation. Everything is allowed, every individual proposition is, by rights,

worthy of attention. There are no more breaches of opinion, in the sense
that to desire to change the laws is no longer to sin against them. Only—
and each of our subjects was perfectly clear on this point—no one has
the right to introduce an innovation except by legal channels, i.e., by
previously persuading the other players and by submitting in advance
to the verdict of the majority. There may therefore be breaches but they
are of procedure only: procedure alone is obligatory, opinions can always be subjected to discussion. Thus Gros tells us that if a change is
proposed "*Some want to and some don't. If boys play that way* (allow an
alteration) *you have to play like they do.*" As Vua said in connection with
the practice of rules "*sometimes people play differently. Then you ask
each other what you want to do. . . . We scrap for a bit and then we fix
things up.*"

In short, law now emanates from the sovereign people and no longer
from the tradition laid down by the Elders. And correlatively with this
change, the respective values attaching to custom and the rights of
reason come to be practically reversed.

In the past, custom had always prevailed over rights. Only, as in all
cases where a human being is enslaved to a custom that is not part of
his inner life, the child regarded this Custom imposed by his elders as a
sort of Decalogue revealed by divine beings (i.e., adults, including God,
who is, according to Fal, the oldest gentleman in Neuchâtel after his
own father). With the result that, in the eyes of a little child, no alteration of usage will exempt the individual from remaining faithful to the
eternal law. . . . And yet he is all the time enslaved to custom and not
to any juridico-moral reason or reality distinct from this custom and
superior to it. Nor indeed is this way of thinking very different from that
of many conservative adults who delude themselves into thinking that
they are assisting the triumph of eternal reason over present fashion,
when they are really the slaves of past custom at the expense of the
permanent laws of rational cooperation.

But from now on, by the mere fact of tying himself down to certain
rules of discussion and collaboration, and thus cooperating with his
neighbors in full reciprocity (without any false respect for tradition nor
for the will of any one individual) the child will be enabled to dissociate custom from the rational ideal. For it is of the essence of cooperation as opposed to social constraint that, side by side with the body
of provisional opinion which exists in fact, it also allows for an ideal of
what is right functionally implied in the very mechanism of discussion
and reciprocity. . . . For if there is to be any reciprocity between players
in the application of established rules or in the elaboration of new rules,
everything must be eliminated that would compromise this reciprocity
(inequalities due to chance, excessive individual differences in skill or
muscular power, etc.). Thus usages are gradually purified in virtue of
an ideal that is superior to custom since it arises from the very functioning of cooperation.

This is why, when innovations are proposed to the child, he regards
them as fair or unfair not only according as they are likely or not to
rally the majority of players in their favor, but also according as they
are in keeping with that spirit of the game itself, which is nothing more
or less than the spirit of reciprocity. Ross tells us, for instance, concerning his own proposition, "*Perhaps it isn't quite fair, because it isn't*

very hard to take four marbles that way," and again, *"The chaps might say it wasn't very fair because it's luck. To be a good rule, it has to be skill.".* . . .

In a word, as soon as we have cooperation, the rational notions of the just and the unjust become regulative of custom, because they are implied in the actual functioning of social life among equals. During the preceding stages, on the contrary, custom overbore the issue of right, precisely insofar as it was deified and remained external to the minds of individuals. . . .

One more fundamental question must still be discussed. How is it that democratic practice is so developed in the games of marbles played by boys of 11 to 13, whereas it is still so unfamiliar to the adult in many spheres of life? Of course it is easier to agree upon some subjects than on others, and feeling will not run so high on the subject of the rules of the "Square" as in an argument about the laws of property or the legitimacy of war. But apart from these questions (and after all, is it so obvious that social questions are more important to us than are the rules of a game to the child of 12?) there are others of greater psychological and sociological interest. For it must not be forgotten that the game of marbles is dropped toward the age of 14–15 at the latest. With regard to this game, therefore, children of 11–13 have no seniors. Since they no longer have to endure the pressure of playmates who impose their views by virtue of their prestige, the children whose reactions we have been studying are clearly able to become conscious of their autonomy much sooner than if the game of marbles lasted till the age of 18. In the same way, most of the phenomena which characterize adult societies would be quite other than they are if the average length of human life were appreciably different from what it is. Sociologists have tended to overlook this fact, though Auguste Comte pointed out that the pressure of one generation upon the other was the most important phenomenon of social life.

We shall have occasion to see, moreover, that toward the age of 11 the consciousness of autonomy appears in a large number of different spheres. . . .

CONCLUSIONS

Motor Rules and the Two Kinds of Respect. In order to pursue our analysis with any profit we shall have to draw from the material that has been presented above certain conclusions which will serve as guiding hypotheses. In other words, we shall try to find in the various stages we have examined certain evolutionary processes which are likely to reappear in our future inquiries. . . .

Between the various types of rules which we shall give there will therefore be at once continuity and qualitative difference: continuity of function and difference of structure. This renders arbitrary any attempt to cut mental reality up into stages. The matter is further complicated by the "law of conscious realization" and the resulting time lag. The appearance of a new type of rule on the practical plane does not necessarily mean that this rule will come into the subject's consciousness, for each mental operation has to be relearnt on the different planes of action and of thought. There are therefore no inclusive stages which define the whole of a subject's mental life at a given point of his evolution; the stages should be thought of as the successive phases of regular processes recurring like a rhythm on the superposed planes of behavior and of consciousness. A given individual may, for example, have reached the stage of autonomy with regard to a certain group of rules, while his consciousness of these rules, together with the practice of certain more subtle rules, will still be colored with heteronomy. We cannot therefore speak of global or inclusive stages characterized as such by autonomy or heteronomy, but only of phases of heteronomy or autonomy which define a process that is repeated for each new set of rules or for each new plane of thought or reflection. . . .

With these reservations in mind, let us then try to outline the processes which govern the evolution of the idea of rules. And if language and discursive thought which, according to a famous metaphor, are necessarily cinematographic in character, tend to lay too much emphasis on discontinuity, let it be understood once and for all, that any oversharp discontinuities are analytical devices and not objective results.

To continue, our inquiry into the nature of games would seem to reveal the existence of three types of rules, and the problem before us will be to determine the exact relations between them. There is the *motor rule*, due to preverbal motor intelligence and relatively independent of any social contact; the *coercive rule* due to unilateral respect; and the *rational rule* due to mutual respect. Let us examine these three rules in succession.

[*The motor rule.*] In its beginnings the motor rule merges into habit. During the first few months of an infant's life, its manner of taking the breast, of laying its head on the pillow, etc., becomes crystalized into imperative habits. This is why education must begin in the cradle. To accustom the infant to get out of its own difficulties or to calm it by rocking it may be to lay the foundations of a good or of a bad disposition. But not every habit will give rise to the knowledge of a rule. The habit must first be frustrated, and the ensuing conflict must lead to an active search for the habitual. Above all, the particular succession must be perceived as regular, i.e., there must be judgment or consciousness of regularity (*Regelbewusstsein*). The motor rule is therefore the result of a feeling of repetition which arises out of ritualization of schemas of motor adaptation. The primitive rules of the game of marbles (throwing the marbles, heaping them, burying them, etc.) which we observed toward the age of 2–3 are nothing else. . . .

But is this early behavior accompanied by consciousness of obligation or by a feeling of the necessity of the rule? We do not think so. Without the feeling of regularity which goes to the formation of any intelligence and already so clearly characterizes motor intelligence, the consciousness of obligation would no doubt never make its appearance. But there is more in this consciousness of obligation than a mere perception of regularity, there is a feeling of respect and authority which, as Durkheim and Bovet have clearly shown, could not come from the individual alone. One might even be tempted to say that rules only begin when this consciousness of obligation, i.e., when the social element has made its appearance. But the material we have collected all goes to show that this obligatory and sacred character only marks an episode in the evolution of rules. After being unilateral, respect becomes mutual.

In this way, the rule becomes rational, i.e., it appears as the fruit of a mutual engagement. And what is this rational rule but the primitive motor rule freed from individual caprice and submitted to the control of reciprocity?

Let us therefore turn to the influence of interindividual relations in the constitution of rules. In the first place, we repeat, the social element is to be found everywhere. From the hour of its birth certain regularities of conduct are imposed upon the infant by the adult, and, as we have shown elsewhere (C.W. and C.C.), every regularity observed in nature, every "law" appears to the child for a long time as both physical and moral. . . . A baby of 10–12 months, which elaborates all sorts of ritual acts connected with the objects it handles, may be influenced indirectly by its feelings for the adult, but neither the baby nor anyone observing it could distinguish these influences from the rest of what constitutes its universe. But the same child at about 2, once he is able to speak or to understand what is said to him, will be acutely conscious of the rules that are imposed upon him . . . and will distinguish them perfectly well from the motor rules or rituals which he has himself established in the course of his games. It is the increasing constraint exercised upon the child by those around him that we regard as the intervention of the social factor.

In the case of play rules, the discontinuity between this process and the purely motor processes is obvious. On a given occasion, the child meets with others, older than himself, who play marbles according to a code. Immediately he feels that he *ought* to play in the same way himself; immediately he assimilates the rules adopted in this way to the totality of commands which control his way of living. In other words, he immediately places the example of children older than himself on the same plane as the hundred and one other customs and obligations imposed by adults. . . . A rule imitated in this way is felt from the first as something obligatory and sacred.

Only, the main result of our inquiry, and one which will receive repeated confirmation in the latter part of this book, is that the social factor is not just one thing. If there is relative discontinuity between the early motor activity and adult intervention, the discontinuity is no less marked between the unilateral respect which accompanies this intervention and the mutual respect which gradually comes into being later on. Once again, let there be no misunderstanding: the qualities in question are not more important than the proportions in which they are mixed. Between the unilateral respect of the little child who receives a command without even the possibility of disagreement and the mutual respect of two adolescents who exchange their points of view there is room for any number of intermediate stages. Constraint is never unadulterated, nor, therefore, is respect ever purely unilateral: the most submissive child has the feeling that he can, or could, argue that a mutual sympathy surrounds relationships that are most heavily charged with authority. And conversely, cooperation is never absolutely pure: in any discussion between equals, one of the disputants can always exert pressure on the other by making overt or hidden appeals to custom and authority. Cooperation, indeed, seems rather to be the limiting term, the ideal equilibrium to which all relations of constraint tend. As the child grows up, his relations with adults approximate to equality, and as communities develop, their group ideas leave more room for free discussion between individuals. . . .

[*The coercive rule.*] Let us begin with *unilateral respect* and the *coercive rule* to which it leads. The outstanding fact here, and what differentiates this type of respect from its successor, is the close connection which we have noted between respect due to the constraint of older children or adults and the egocentric behavior of the child between 3 and 7. . . .

. . . In the first place, let us remind the reader that the behavior of children of 3 to 7 with regard to the game of marbles is comparable on all points to the behavior of children of the same age in regard to their conversations or to their social and intellectual life in general. But the egocentrism common to all these types of behavior admits of at least two interpretations. Some people think—and in all our previous works we have claimed to be of their number—that egocentrism is presocial in the sense that it marks a transition between the individual and the social, between the motor and quasi-solipsistic stage of the baby and the stage of cooperation proper. However closely connected with unilateral respect egocentrism may be, this mixture of coercion and subjectivity which characterizes the stage lasting from 2 to 7 years does seem to us less social than cooperation (which is the one determining factor in the formation of the rational elements in ethics and in logic). Other thinkers, on the contrary, consider egocentric behavior to be in no way presocial —the social element remaining identical with itself throughout all the various stages—but take it to be, as it were, parasocial behavior, analogous to what occurs in the adult when private feeling obscures his objectivity or when he is left out of a conversation from which he is precluded by his incompetence or stupidity.* Thinkers belonging to this second group can see no essential difference between cooperation and coercion; hence their view that the social factor is a permanent element throughout the whole course of mental development.

The data with which the present discussion is concerned would seem to be of a nature to remove these ambiguities. Egocentrism is both presocial, in view of the eventual cooperation, and parasocial, or simply social, in relation to the constraint of which it constitutes the most direct effect.

To understand this we need only analyze the relations of the younger to the older children. Every observer has noted that the younger the child, the less sense he has of his own ego. From the intellectual point of view, he does not distinguish between external and internal, subjective and objective. From the point of view of action, he yields to every suggestion, and if he does oppose to other people's wills a certain negativism which has been called "the spirit of contradiction"† this only points to his real defenselessness against his surroundings. . . . From the intellectual point of view, he mingles his own fantasies with accepted opinions, whence arise pseudo-lies (or sincere lies), syncretism, and all the features of child thought. From the point of view of action, he interprets in his own fashion the examples he has adopted, whence the

*See Blondel, "Le Langage et la Pensée chez l'enfant d'après un livre récent." *Revue Hist. Phil. Rel.* (Strasbourg), 4 (1924): 474 ff.
†See Reynier, "L'esprit de contradiction chez l'enfant," *La Nouvelle Education*, 5 (1926): 45–52.

egocentric form of play we were examining above. The only way of avoiding these individual refractions would lie in true cooperation, such that both child and senior would each make allowance for his own individuality and for the realities that were held in common.

But this presupposes minds that know themselves and can take up their positions in relation to each other. It therefore presupposes intellectual equality and reciprocity, both of them factors that are not brought about by unilateral respect as such.

Egocentrism insofar as it means confusion of the ego and the external world, and egocentrism insofar as it means lack of cooperation, constitute one and the same phenomenon. So long as the child does not dissociate his ego from the suggestions coming from the physical and from the social world, he cannot cooperate, for in order to cooperate one must be conscious of one's ego and situate it in relation to thought in general. And in order to become conscious of one's ego, it is necessary to liberate oneself from the thought and will of others. The coercion exercised by the adult or the older child is therefore inseparable from the unconscious egocentrism of the very young child. . . .

To return, however, to our analysis of the game of marbles, it is a highly significant fact that it is the younger and not the older children who believe in the adult origin of rules, although they are incapable of really putting them into practice. The belief here is analogous to that prevalent in conformist communities, whose laws and customs are always attributed to some transcendental will. And the explanation is always the same. So long as a practice is not submitted to conscious, autonomous elaboration and remains, as it were, external to the individual, this externality is symbolized as transcendence. Now in the case of the child, exteriority and egocentrism go hand in hand insofar as egocentrism is preserved by the constraint exercised from outside. If, therefore, the children of the earlier stages were those who showed the maximum respect for rules together with the most pronounced belief in their transcendental origin, this was not due to any fortuitous resemblance. The two features coexisted in virtue of an inner logic which is the logic of unilateral respect.

[*The rational rule.*] Let us now deal with *mutual respect* and *rational rules*. There is, in our opinion, the same relation between mutual respect and autonomy as between unilateral respect and egocentrism, provided the essential qualification be added, that mutual respect far more than unilateral respect, joins forces with the rationality already incipient in the motor stage, and therefore extends beyond the phase that is marked by the intervention of constraint and egocentrism.

We have, in connection with the actual facts examined, pointed to the obvious correlation between cooperation and the consciousness of autonomy. From the moment that children really begin to submit to rules and to apply them in a spirit of genuine cooperation, they acquire a new conception of these rules. Rules become something that can be changed if it is agreed that they should be, for the truth of a rule does not rest on tradition but on mutual agreement and reciprocity. How are these facts to be interpreted? In order to understand them, all we have to do is to take as our starting point the functional equation uniting constraint and egocentrism and to take the first term of the equation through the successive values which link up constraint and cooperation.

At the outset of this genetic progression, the child has no idea of his own ego; external constraint works upon him and he distorts its influence in terms of his subjectivity, but he does not distinguish the part played by his subjectivity from that played by the environmental pressure. Rules therefore seem to him external and of transcendental origin, although he actually fails to put them into practice. Now, insofar as constraint is replaced by cooperation, the child dissociates his ego from the thought of other people. For as the child grows up, the prestige of older children diminishes, he can discuss matters more and more as an equal and has increasing opportunities (beyond the scope of suggestion, obedience, or negativism) of freely contrasting his point of view with that of others. Henceforward, he will not only discover the boundaries that separate his self from the other person, but will learn to understand the other person and be understood by him. So that cooperation is really a factor in the creation of personality, if by personality we mean, not the unconscious self of childish egocentrism, nor the anarchical self of egoism in general, but the self that takes up its stand on the norms of reciprocity and objective discussion, and knows how to submit to these in order to make itself respected. Personality is thus the opposite of the ego* and this explains why the mutual respect felt by two personalities for each other is genuine respect and not to be confused with the mutual consent of two individual "selves" capable of joining forces for evil as well as for good. Cooperation being the source of personality, rules cease, in accordance with the same principle, to be external. They become both the constitutive factors of personality and its fruit, in accordance with the circular process so frequently exemplified in the course of mental development. In this way autonomy succeeds heteronomy.

This analysis will have shown how new in quality are the results of mutual respect as compared with those that arose out of unilateral respect. And yet the former is the outcome of the latter. Mutual respect is, in a sense, the state of equilibrium toward which unilateral respect is tending when differences between child and adult, younger and older are becoming effaced; just as cooperation is the form of equilibrium to which constraint is tending in the same circumstances. . . .

We are faced, then, with three types of rules: the motor rule, the coercive rule founded on unilateral respect, and the rational rule (constituted or constitutive) due to mutual respect. We have outlined above the relation in which the last two types stand to each other. We have examined elsewhere how the first two succeed one another. It remains for us to show what are the relations of the rational rule to the motor rule.

Generally speaking, one can say that motor intelligence contains the germs of completed reason. But it gives promise of more than reason pure and simple. From the moral as from the intellectual point of view, the child is born neither good nor bad, but master of his destiny. Now, if there is intelligence in the schemas of motor adaptation, there is also the element of play. The intentionality peculiar to motor activity is not a search for truth but the pursuit of a result, whether objective or subjective; and to succeed is not to discover a truth.

*See R. Fernandez, *De la Personnalité*, Au Sans Pareil (Paris), 1928.

The motor rule is therefore a sort of experimental [lawfulness] or rational regularity, and at the same time a play ritual. It will take one or other of these two forms according to circumstances. Now, at the moment when language and imagination are added to movement, egocentrism directs the child's activity toward subjective satisfaction, while, at the same time, adult pressure imposes on his mind a system of realities which at first remains opaque and external. . . . It is at this point that the motor rule is followed by the coercive rule, a crystalized social product which shows the sharpest contrast with the fragile tentative products of the initial motor intelligence, though, as we have seen, egocentric play continues in a sense the early gropings of the motor stage.

But as the element of constraint is gradually eliminated by cooperation, and the ego is dominated by the personality, the rational rule so constituted recaptures the advantages of the motor rule. The play of 11-year-old children is in some ways closer to the motor accommodation of the one-year-old child in all its richness and truly experimental qualities than to the play of 7 year olds. The boy of 11 plans his strokes like a geometrician and an artist in movement, just as the baby acts as a mechanician in handling objects and as an experimenter in inventing its rules. At the age of 6 or 7, on the contrary, the child is apt to neglect this element of invention, and to confine himself to imitation and the preservation of rites. But the immense superiority of the 11-year-old player over the one year old, a superiority perhaps acquired by passing through the intermediate stage, is that his motor creations are no longer at the mercy of individual fantasy. The 11-year-old has rediscovered the schema of experimental [lawfulness] and rational regularity practiced by the baby. But the motor rule found by the baby tends constantly to degenerate into play ritual, [while] the 11-year-old invents nothing without the collaboration of his equals. He is free to create, but on condition of submitting to the norms of reciprocity. The motor being and the social being are one. Harmony is achieved by the union of reason and nature, whereas moral constraint and unilateral respect oppose super-nature to nature and mysticism to rational experiment.

The discussion of the game of marbles seems to have led us into rather deep waters. But in the eyes of children the history of the game of marbles has quite as much importance as the history of religion or of forms of government. It is a history, moreover, that is magnificently spontaneous; and it was therefore perhaps not entirely useless to seek to throw light on the child's judgment of moral value by a preliminary study of the social behavior of children amongst themselves. . . .

The Idea of Justice

To bring our inquiry to a close let us examine the answers given to a question which sums up all that we have been talking about. We asked the children, either at the end or at the beginning of our interrogatories, to give us themselves examples of what they regarded as unfair.*

* As a matter of fact this term is not understood by all, but it can always be replaced by "not fair" (Fr. *pas juste*).

The answers we obtained were of four kinds: (1) Behavior that goes against commands received from the adult—lying, stealing, breakages, etc.; in a word, everything that is forbidden. (2) Behavior that goes against the rules of a game. (3) Behavior that goes against equality (inequality in punishment as in treatment). (4) Acts of injustice connected with adult society (economic or political injustice). Now, statistically, the results show very clearly as functions of age:

	Forbidden	Games	Inequality	Social Injustice
6–8	64%	9%	27%	—
9–12	7%	9%	73%	11%

Here is an example of the identification of what is unfair with what is forbidden:

AGE 6: *"A little girl who has a broken plate," "to burst a balloon," children who make a noise with their feet during prayers," "telling lies," "something not true," "it's not fair to steal,"* etc. . . .

Here are examples of inequalities:

AGE 6: *"Giving a big cake to one and a little one to another."* . . .
AGE 10: *"When you both do the same work and don't get the same reward." "Two children both do what they are told, and one gets more than the other." "To scold one child and not the other if they have both disobeyed."* . . .
AGE 12: *"A referee who takes sides."*

And some examples of social injustice:

AGE 12: *"A mistress preferring a pupil because he is stronger, or cleverer, or better dressed."* . . .
"A mother who won't allow her children to play with children who are less well dressed."
"Children who leave a little girl out of their games, who is not so well dressed as they are."

These obviously spontaneous remarks, taken together with the rest of our inquiry, allow us to conclude, insofar as one can talk of stages in the moral life, the existence of three great periods in the development of the sense of justice in the child. One period, lasting up to the age of 7–8, during which justice is subordinated to adult authority; a period contained approximately between 8–11, and which is that of progressive equalitarianism; and finally a period which sets in toward 11–12, and during which purely equalitarian justice is tempered by considerations of equity.

The first is characterized by the nondifferentiation of the notions of just and unjust from those of duty and disobedience: whatever conforms to the dictates of the adult authority is just. As a matter of fact even at this stage the child already looks upon some kinds of treatment as unjust, those, namely, in which the adult does not carry out the rules he has himself laid down for children (e.g., punishing for a fault that has not been committed, forbidding what has previously been allowed, etc.). But if the adult sticks to his own rules, everything he prescribes is just. In the domain of retributive justice, every punishment is accepted as perfectly legitimate, as necessary, and even as constituting the essence of morality: if lying were not punished, one would be allowed to tell lies, etc. In the stories where we have brought retributive justice into conflict with equality, the child belonging to this stage sets the necessity for punishment above equality of any sort. In the choice of punishments, expiation takes precedence over punishment by reciprocity, the very principle of the latter type of punishment not being exactly understood by the child. In the domain of immanent justice, more than three-quarters of the subjects under 8 believe in an automatic justice which emanates from physical nature and inanimate objects. If obedience and equality are brought into conflict, the child is always in favor of obedience: authority takes precedence over justice. Finally, in the domain of justice between children, the need for equality is already felt, but is yielded to only where it cannot possibly come into conflict with authority. For instance, the act of hitting back, which is regarded by the child of 10 as one of elementary justice, is considered "naughty" by the children of 6 and 7, though, of course, they are always doing it in practice. (It will be remembered that the heteronomous rule, whatever may be the respect in which it is held mentally, is not necessarily observed in real life.) On the other hand, even in the relations between children, the authority of older ones will outweigh equality. . . .

The second period does not appear on the plane of reflection and moral judgment until about the age of 7 or 8. But it is obvious that this comes slightly later than what happens with regard to practice. This period may be defined by the progressive development of autonomy and the priority of equality over authority. In the domain of retributive justice, the idea of expiatory punishment is no longer accepted with the same docility as before, and the only punishments accepted as really legitimate are those based upon reciprocity. Belief in immanent justice is perceptibly on the decrease and moral action is sought for its own sake, independently of reward or punishment. In matters of distributive justice, equality rules supreme. In conflicts between punishment and equality, equality outweighs every other consideration. The same holds good a fortiori of conflicts with authority. Finally, in the relations between children, equalitarianism obtains progressively with increasing age.

Toward 11–12 we see a new attitude emerge, which may be said to be characterized by the feeling of equity, and which is nothing but a development of equalitarianism in the direction of relativity. Instead of looking for equality in identity, the child no longer thinks of the equal rights of individuals except in relation to the particular situation of each. In the domain of retributive justice this comes to the same thing as not applying the same punishment to all, but taking into account the [extenuating] circumstances of some. In the domain of distributive justice it means no longer thinking of a law as identical for all but taking account of the personal circumstances of each (favoring the younger ones, etc.). Far from leading to privileges, such an attitude tends to make equality more effectual than it was before.

Even if this evolution does not consist of general stages, but simply of phases characterizing certain limited processes, we have said enough to try to elucidate now the psychological origins of the idea of justice and the conditions of its development. With this in view, let us distinguish retributive from distributive justice, . . . and let us begin with distributive judgment, whose fate in the course of mental development seems to indicate that it is the most fundamental form of justice itself.

Distributive justice can be reduced to the ideas of equality or equity. From the point of view of epistemology such notions cannot but be regarded as a priori, if by a priori we mean, not of course an innate idea, but a norm, toward which reason cannot help but tend as it is gradually refined and purified. For reciprocity imposes itself on practical reason as logical principles impose themselves morally on theoretical reason. But from the psychological point of view, which [considers] what is, not what should be, an a priori norm has no existence except as a form of equilibrium. It constitutes the ideal equilibrium toward which the phenomena tend, and the whole question is still to know why, the facts being what they are, their form of equilibrium is such and no other. . . . The two* will coincide only when mind and reality become coextensive. In the meantime let us confine ourselves to psychological analysis, it being understood that the experimental explanation of the notion of reciprocity can in no way contradict its a priori aspect.

From this point of view it cannot be denied that the idea of equality or of distributive justice possesses individual or biological roots which are necessary but not sufficient conditions for its development. One can observe in the child at a very early stage two reactions which will play a very important part in this particular elaboration. Jealousy, to begin with, appears extremely early in babies: infants of 8 to 12 months often give signs of violent rage when they see another child seated on their mother's knees, or when a toy is taken from them and given to another child. On the other hand, one can observe in conjunction with imitation and the ensuing sympathy, altruistic reactions and a tendency to share, which are of equally early date. An infant of 12 months will hand his toys over to another child, and so on. But it goes without saying that equalitarianism can never be regarded as a sort of instinct or spontaneous product of the individual mind. The reactions we have just alluded to lead to a capricious alternation of egoism and sympathy. It is true, of course, that jealousy prevents other people from taking advantage of us, and the need to communicate prevents the self from taking advantage of others. But for true equality and a genuine desire for reciprocity there must be a collective rule which is the *sui generis* product of life lived in common. There must be born of the actions and reactions of individuals upon each other the consciousness of a necessary equilibrium binding upon and limiting both "alter" and "ego." And this ideal equilibrium, dimly felt on the occasion of every quarrel and every peace-making, naturally presupposes a long reciprocal education of the children by each other. . . .

Now on this point the results of our analysis seem to leave no room for doubt. Authority as such cannot be the source of justice, because the development of justice presupposes autonomy. This does not mean, of course, that the adult plays no part in the development of justice, even of the distributive kind. Insofar as he practices reciprocity with the child and preaches by example rather than by precept, he exercises here, as always, an enormous influence. But the most direct effect of adult ascendancy is, as Bovet has shown, the feeling of duty, and there

*[I.e., the a priori norm and the psychological fact.]

is a sort of contradiction between the submission demanded by duty and the complete autonomy required by the development of justice. For, resting as it does on equality and reciprocity, justice can only come into being by free consent. Adult authority, even if it acts in conformity with justice, has therefore the effect of weakening what constitutes the essence of justice. Hence those reactions which we observed among the smaller children, who confused what was just with what was law, law being whatever is prescribed by adult authority. Justice is identified with formulated rules—as indeed it is in the opinion of a great many adults, of all, namely, who have not succeeded in setting autonomy of conscience above social prejudice and the written law.

Thus adult authority, although perhaps it constitutes a necessary moment in the moral evolution of the child, is not in itself sufficient to create a sense of justice. This can develop only through the progress made by cooperation and mutual respect—cooperation between children to begin with, and then between child and adult as the child approaches adolescence and comes, secretly at least, to consider himself as the adult's equal.

In support of these hypotheses, one is struck by the extent to which, in child as well as in adult society, the progress of equalitarianism goes hand in hand with that of "organic" solidarity, i.e., with the results of cooperation. For if we compare the societies formed by children of 5–7 with those formed at the age of 10–12, we can observe four interdependent transformations. In the first place, while the little ones' society constitutes an amorphous and unorganized whole, in which all the individuals are alike, that of the older children achieves an organic unity, with laws and regulations, and often even a division of social work (leaders, referees, etc.). In the second place, there exists between the older children a far stronger moral solidarity than among the younger ones. The little ones are simultaneously egocentric and impersonal, yielding to every suggestion that comes along and to every current of imitation. In their case the group feeling is a sort of communion of submission to seniors and to the dictates of adults. Older children, on the contrary, ban lies among themselves, cheating, and everything that compromises solidarity. The group feeling is therefore more direct and more consciously cultivated. In the third place, personality develops in the measure that discussion and the interchange of ideas replace the simple mutual imitation of the younger children. In the fourth place, the sense of equality is, as we have just seen, far stronger in the older than in the younger children, the latter being primarily under the domination of authority. Thus the bond between equalitarianism and solidarity is a universal psychological phenomenon, and not, as might appear to be the case in adult society, dependent only upon political factors. With children as with adults, there exist two psychological types of social equilibrium—a type based on the constraint of age, which excludes both equality and "organic" solidarity, but which canalizes individual egocentrism without excluding it, and a type based on cooperation and resting on equality and solidarity.

Let us pass on to retributive justice. In contrast to the principles of distributive justice, there does not seem to be in the ideas of retribution or punishment any properly rational or a priori element. For while the idea of equality gains in value as intellectual development proceeds, the idea of punishment seems actually to lose ground. To put things more precisely, we must, as we have already done, distinguish two separate elements in the idea of retribution. On the one hand there are the notions of expiation and reward, which seems to constitute what is most specific about the idea of punishment, and on the other, there are the ideas of "putting things right" or making reparation, as well as the measures which aim at restoring the bond of solidarity broken by the offending act. These last ideas, which we have grouped under the title of "punishment by reciprocity," seem to draw only on the conceptions of equality and reciprocity. It is the former set of ideas that tends to be eliminated when the morality of heteronomy and authority is superseded by the morality of autonomy. The second set are of far more enduring stuff, precisely because they are based upon something more than the idea of punishment. . . .

It cannot be denied that the idea of punishment has psychobiological roots. Blow calls for blow and gentleness moves us to gentleness. The instinctive reactions of defense and sympathy thus bring about a sort of elementary reciprocity which is the soil that retribution demands for its growth. But this soil is not enough in itself, and the individual factors cannot of themselves transcend the stage of impulsive vengeance without finding themselves subject—at least implicitly—to the system of regulated and codified sanctions implied in retributive justice.

Things change with the intervention of the adult. Very early in life, even before the infant can speak, its conduct is constantly being subjected to approval or censure. . . . During the years that follow, the child is watched over continuously, everything he does and says is controlled, gives rise to encouragement or reproof, and the vast majority of adults still look upon punishment, corporal or otherwise, as perfectly legitimate. It is obviously these adult reactions due generally to fatigue or impatience, but often, too, coldly thought out on his part that are the psychological starting point of the idea of expiatory punishment. If the child felt nothing but fear or mistrust, as may happen in extreme cases, this would simply lead to open war. But as the child loves his parents and feels for their actions that respect which Bovet has so ably analyzed, punishment appears to him as morally obligatory and necessarily connected with the act that provoked it. Disobedience is a breach of the normal relations between parent and child; some reparation is therefore necessary, and since parents display their "righteous anger" by the various reactions that take the form of punishments, to accept these punishments constitutes the most natural form of reparation. The pain inflicted thus seems to reestablish the relations that had momentarily been interrupted, and in this way the idea of expiation becomes incorporated in the values of the morality of authority. In our view, therefore, this "primitive" and materialistic conception of expiatory punishment is not imposed as such by the adult upon the child, and it was perhaps never invented by a psychologically adult mind; but it is the inevitable product of punishment as refracted in the mystically realistic mentality of the child.

If, then, there is such close solidarity between the idea of punishment and unilateral respect *plus* the morality of authority, it follows that all progress in cooperation and mutual respect will be such as to gradually eliminate the idea of expiation from the idea of punishment, and to reduce the latter to a simple act of reparation, or a simple measure of reciprocity. And this is actually what we believe we have observed in the child. As respect for adult punishment gradually grows less, certain types of conduct develop which one cannot but class under the heading of retributive justice. We saw an example of this in the judgments made by our subjects on the topic of "hitting back"; the child feels more and more that it is fair that he should defend himself and to give back the blows he receives. This is retribution without doubt, but the idea of expiation seems not to play the slightest part in these judgments. It is entirely a matter of reciprocity. So-and-so takes upon himself the right to give me a punch, he therefore gives me the right to do the same to him. Similarly, the cheat gains a certain advantage by the fact of cheating; it is therefore legitimate to restore equality by turning him out of the game or by taking back the marbles he has won.

It may be objected that such a morality will not take one very far, since the best adult consciences ask for something more than the practice of mere reciprocity. Charity and the forgiving of injuries done to one are, in the eyes of many, far greater things than sheer equality. Moralists have often laid stress on the conflict between justice and love, since justice often prescribes what is reproved by love and vice versa. But in our view, it is precisely this concern with reciprocity which leads one beyond the rather shortsighted justice of those children who give back the mathematical equivalent of the blows they have received. Like all spiritual realities which are the result, not of external constraint but of autonomous development, reciprocity has two aspects: reciprocity as a fact, and reciprocity as an ideal, as something which ought to be. The child begins by simply practicing reciprocity, in itself not so easy a thing as one might think. Then, once he has grown accustomed to this form of equilibrium in his actions, his behavior is altered from within, its form reacting, as it were, upon its content. What is regarded as just is no longer merely reciprocal action, but primarily behavior that admits of indefinitely sustained reciprocity. The motto "Do as you would be done by," thus comes to replace the conception of crude equality. The child sets forgiveness above revenge, not out of weakness, but because "there is no end" to revenge (a boy of 10). Just as in logic, we can see a sort of reaction of the form of the proposition upon its content when the principle of contradiction leads to a simplification and purification of the initial definitions, so in ethics, reciprocity implies a purification of the deeper trend of conduct, guiding it by gradual stages to universality itself. Without leaving the sphere of reciprocity, generosity—the characteristic of our third stage—allies itself to justice pure and simple, and between the more refined forms of justice, such as equity and love properly so called, there is no longer any real conflict.

In conclusion, then, we find in the domain of justice, as in the other two domains already dealt with, that opposition of two moralities to which we have so often drawn the reader's attention. The ethics of authority, which is that of duty and obedience, leads, in the domain of justice, to the confusion of what is just with the content of established law and to the acceptance of expiatory punishment. The ethics of mutual respect, which is that of good (as opposed to duty), and of autonomy, leads, in the domain of justice, to the development of equality, which is the idea at the bottom of distributive justice and of reciprocity. Solidarity between equals appears once more as the source of a whole set of complementary and coherent moral ideas which characterize the rational mentality. The question may, of course, be raised whether such realities could ever develop without a preliminary stage, during which the child's conscience is molded by his unilateral respect for the adult. As this cannot be put to the test by experiment, it is idle to argue the point. But what is certain is that the moral equilibrium achieved by the complementary conceptions of heteronomous duty and of punishment properly so called, is an unstable equilibrium, owing to the fact that it does not allow the personality to grow and expand to its full extent. As the child grows up, the subjection of his conscience to the mind of the adult seems to him less legitimate, and except in cases of arrested moral development, caused either by decisive inner submission (those adults who remain children all their lives), or by sustained revolt, unilateral respect tends of itself to grow into mutual respect and to the state of cooperation which constitutes the normal equilibrium. . . .

PART V
The Mind of the Baby: From Action to Thought

INTRODUCTION

When Piaget's first child was born he was immediately drawn to a series of careful and highly original observations of her mental development. This work led eventually to three volumes dealing with the mental life of babies, based almost entirely on his study of his own three children. This effort was well under way in 1927, when he was just finishing his early studies of the thinking of children from about 3 to 8 years of age. In that year, he gave two papers in England, one on his work on causality,* and the one presented here in Selection 18, based on his observations of his daughter. We also include selections from *The Origins of Intelligence* and from *The Construction of Reality*, his more fully elaborated works on the mind of the baby. Selections from *Play, Dreams, and Imitation*, the third volume of the trilogy, are deferred to Part VII: although that work deals with the same three children in the same period of life, it does so from a somewhat different perspective, focusing on representation and the development of symbolic activity, rather than, as is the case here, treating action and experience.

---

* J. Piaget, "La causalité chez l'enfant." An address given at Cambridge, March 4, 1927, under the auspices of the Cambridge Education Society.

18

The First Year of Life of the Child*

1927

INTRODUCTORY NOTES

"The First Year of Life of the Child" (1927) provides us with two valuable views of Piaget's thought. First, it gives us his attempt at a synthesis of his earlier work on childhood with his newer work on infancy. His central proposition is that childhood egocentrism must necessarily grow out of infant solipsism. The focus of his efforts is the close examination of a few key observations of infant behavior, to show the nature of this solipsistic mentality in which self and world have not yet parted company, or even emerged as distinct facets of experience.

Second, the paper gives a rapid and fresh panoramic view of the trilogy about his own babies that he was to write over the next twenty years. Most of the major themes are already present, such as constructive repetition, imitation, assimilation and accommodation, and the intertwining of object, space, and causality. Among the many differences, it is notable that the growth of the idea of causality plays a more central role in this paper than in the work as it later developed. Causal relationships are concerned with objects in space; they therefore imply the existence of such objects. By the time Piaget wrote *Construction of Reality* he put the chapter on the "The Development of Object Concept" before the chapter on causality. But in 1927, probably because this was the transition from his earlier work on children, he put the greater emphasis on causality. This is seen in the present paper in his choice of illustrative material, as well as in the other major address he gave in England that year, "Causality in the Child."

In this paper Piaget uses, without much change, the principle of "circular reaction," borrowed from his American contemporary, J. M. Baldwin. The systematic elaboration of the idea, distinguishing among primary, secondary, and tertiary circular reactions, was not introduced until 1936 in *The Origins of Intelligence* (see Selection 19). Perhaps this development merely awaited

*From J. Piaget. "La première année de l'enfant." *British Journal of Psychology*, 18 (1927–28): 97–120. Paper read before the British Psychological Society, March 7, 1927. Reprinted by permission of Cambridge University Press. Translated by H. E. G. and J. J. V.

Piaget's accumulation of observations of somewhat older babies, since especially the tertiary circular reaction typically appears in the second year of life.
On the other hand, the progressive elaboration of a central concept over a
period of years is characteristic of Piaget's work.

The child's first year of life is unfortunately still an abyss of mysteries
for the psychologist. If only we could know what was going on in a
baby's mind while observing him in action, we could certainly understand everything there is to psychology. Unfortunately, this knowledge
will always be denied us. Certain authors scorn the primitive mind as a
subject unfit for study, limiting themselves to the study of observable
gestures. But it cannot be denied that adults do think, and that children
of all ages think, and very differently from us. This leads us to the
unavoidable even if exceptionally difficult question of how thought
originates, and particularly of how thought begins in babies.

I begin with the question of method. We watch babies doing things,
gesticulating, grabbing objects and moving them about. Since our
interest lies in what they are thinking, we use our own adult knowledge
of states of awareness gleaned from experience, drawing analogies
between them and what we see babies doing. Unfortunately, this leads
us nowhere, both because it has been a long time since we acted that
way and also because our states of consciousness are so complex that
in projecting them onto a baby we feel quite rightly that we are mis-
representing his state of mind. Here, we hit upon a first methodological
rule: beware of comparing infant with adult behavior, or, if you wish,
of a certain "adulto-centrism." Luckily, there are two sides to the coin.
We are, it is true, adult. But between us and babies, there are many
intermediate steps: the adolescent, the 11 year old, the 7 year old, and
the 2 year old. There are developmental laws that govern each of these
successive mentalities, and there are ways of studying each one. For
instance, the behavior of little children exhibits many carryovers from
infant behavior. Some light might be thrown on the shadowy first year
of life if we could manage, by a method of backwards reasoning, to
piece together the meaning of particular sorts of behavior and the states
of mind with which they seem to occur. For my part, watching my little
girl during her first months always gave me the impression of finding
the key to phenomena observed only as vestiges in the behavior and
thought of older children. While such a method can be dangerous, it is
the one used in biology. The biologist very frequently compares superior
animals to inferior ones using the one to understand the other. This
game of give and take, used with discretion, eliminates such over-
ambitious evolutionary notions as the fixity of genetic constituents.

That much said, let us look for a working hypothesis. From our
studies of the thought of children from 3 to 15 years of age, we have
come to the conclusion that the most important characteristic of children's thinking—that which influences all the other characteristics—
can be called the *egocentrism* of the child. Carrying this to its extreme,
we can speak of the baby as exhibiting an absolute egocentrism, which
can be called the *solipsism* of the first year of life. We will attempt to
explain the attitudes of the baby as solipsism, just as we have interpreted children's thinking as egocentrism.

The plan of our presentation will be simple. First, we will compare primitive solipsism with egocentrism in children. Then, from this point of view we will examine a privileged case, the baby's idea of causality.

The Egocentrism of the Child and the Solipsism of the Baby*

We can now move on to the study of babies and the first year of their mental development. If our method is viable, we should find the same two paradoxes that exist in children's thinking likewise present in babies' thought, and even more pronounced.

The first paradox is the solipsistic state in which infants live. A baby appears to be completely directed toward the world around him. Most probably, he is not at all aware of his own existence as a separate entity. He first discovers his own body as a thing outside himself. Nevertheless, if the younger a child is, the more egocentric he is, babies are even more so. Freud discussed narcissism in babies as if they were interested in nothing but themselves. We could go so far, especially in studying the origins of causality, as to hypothesize that the baby experiences the universe as himself, the way a solipsist identifies the world with his representation of it.

Second paradox. Babies' thinking is made up of a set of movements of accommodation adapted to the world outside. Yet, in other respects, this thinking also resembles a sort of perpetual waking dream, with all the characteristics of unadulterated autism.

Let us begin with the first paradox, and try to understand what solipsism means in the first year of life. When a baby opens his eyes for the first time and begins to conquer the universe little by little, what he finally discovers is himself as a person, something of which he has not the slightest idea in his first months. J. M. Baldwin seems to have established the existence of this process of gradual self-knowledge beyond the shadow of a doubt with his well-known analysis of the projective stage. As Baldwin explains it, self-awareness is acquired by successive differentiations; during the primitive stages, all awareness of self is on the same level, without any distinction between an inner and an outer world. Thus, most likely, when a baby is happy or sad, he colors his whole universe with his joy or grief; when he eats or nurses, everything that he sees seems to participate in his experience of sucking; and conversely, when a baby discovers his own body— his fingers, feet, arms—he looks at them no differently than he regards other objects, without any idea that he himself is the one responsible for moving the particular objects that he is admiring. Along with Baldwin, we grant that to begin with a baby has no sense of self at all.

A troubling question arises with regard to the regressive method that we intended to use to interpret the facts discovered by observing primitive behavior: if a baby has no sense of self, is it possible to speak

*[We have deleted two pages at the beginning of this section, which summarize Piaget's work on egocentric thought in children.]

of solipsism in babies and, can narcissism be called a baby's obvious self-love for himself, as Freud has done? There seems to be a contradiction in terms here, denying self-consciousness and speaking of narcissism or solipsism in the same breath. If this is the case, is it legitimate to compare egocentrism in older children with solipsism in babies? May we look at the behavior and thinking of babies to find the roots of the general phenomena characteristic of egocentric thought?

I intend to reply in the affirmative to all these questions. Why not admit that a baby is solipsistic and that this is the source of childish egocentrism? We will see shortly that this working hypothesis is a good one for interpreting the facts we are going to present. It remains for us to agree on what these concepts mean.

It is of course absurd to call a baby a solipsist if by solipsism is meant a philosophic attitude that regards the whole universe as contained in the self, since just what a baby lacks is this sense of himself. This definition of solipsism, however, is not the only possible one. There are no really solipsistic philosophers, and those who think they are deceive themselves. The true solipsist feels at one with the universe, and so very identical to it that he does not even feel the need for two terms. The true solipsist projects all his states of mind onto things. The true solipsist is entirely alone in the world, that is, he has no notion of anything exterior to himself. In other words, the true solipsist has no idea of self. There is no self: there is the world. It is in this sense that it is reasonable to call a baby a solipsist: the feelings and desires of a baby know no limits since they are a part of everything he sees, touches, and perceives.

Babies are, then, obviously narcissistic but not in the way adults are, not even Spinoza's God, and I am a little afraid that Freud sometimes forgets that the narcissistic baby has no sense of self.

Given this definition of solipsism, egocentrism in children clearly appears to be a simple continuation of solipsism in infants. Egocentrism, as we have seen, is not an intentional or even a conscious process. A child has no idea that he is egocentric. He believes everybody thinks the way he does, and this false universality is due simply to an absence of the sense of limits on his individuality. In this light, egocentrism and solipsism are quite comparable: both stem from the absence or the weakness of the sense of the self.

We should expect to find the main traits of egocentric thought in babies, where they should be much more accentuated. This brings us to the second paradox we mentioned. Egocentric children are both more empiricist and more under the sway of autistic logic than we adults. In solipsistic babies, we would expect to find a mixture *sui generis* of accommodation by pure trial and error and autism, something like an animal's practical intelligence combined with a sort of incessant waking dream. This is what we are now going to attempt to show.

If a baby really has no awareness of himself and is totally thing-directed and at the same time all his states of mind are projected onto things, our second paradox makes sense: on the one hand, thought in babies can be viewed as pure accommodation or exploratory movements, but on the other this very same thought is only one, long, completely autistic waking dream.

To take exploratory behavior first: an excellent description of this sort of behavior has been given by numerous authors. It begins with what Baldwin called the *circular reaction*, the first step toward all other accommodations. The child docs something at random, and when he gets an interesting result, he repeats the action indefinitely. In this way, he learns to suck his thumb, to seize objects, to make noises by knocking hard things together, and so on. The circular reaction is therefore the utilization of chance. Next, the baby learns to imitate by means of processes we do not want to elaborate upon here, and this imitation plays a large role in the child's motor accommodation. In our opinion, it is this very imitation of people and objects that gives children the ability to construct mental images. Just as reflection is the product of the interiorization of language, so mental images grow out of the interiorization of imitation. Both motor accommodation and the imitation-image prolong themselves in memory: it is common knowledge what an extraordinary memory little children over a year old have. In short, we have here a series of steps that characterize the first-mentioned aspect of primitive thought: babies think by mental and motor accommodations that, thanks to the ability to imitate themselves and others and to interiorize their imitations, give them a collection of direct or indirect copies of things. These are the materials practical intelligence uses beginning right at birth.

This accommodation babies make to things, usually considered to be the whole story behind the growth of intelligence, is really only one aspect of the process. Another aspect is just as essential: one can consider the thought of the baby as a sort of waking dream, the starting point of autism. The paradox involved in early thought is that two such contradictory aspects are actually in close interaction.

From an examination of the facts, three main characteristics of autism in general and of the dream in particular meet the eye: first, the assimilation of the world to the self; second, the formation of emotional schemas charged with images; third, the special orientation of thought by emotional association and not by logical systematization. These traits correspond to the principal characteristics of solipsistic thinking in babies.

Take *assimilation* first: the essence of intelligence is the mind's adaptation to things, a sort of intellectual accommodation prepared by the motor accommodation that we just discussed. Autism or dreams, on the other hand, adapt things to their own ends, without any attempt to be objective. This is precisely how babies proceed; it is striking to see how accommodation is completely under the sway of a sort of constant assimilation by young babies of the external world to the self.

From the moment a baby is born, he most likely experiences a variety of states of awareness related to his first reflexes such as taste sensations connected to nursing, tactile sensations that go with sucking or manual reflexes, visual and auditory sensations, and so on. The basic law of dawning psychological activity could be said to be the search for the maintenance or repetition of interesting states of consciousness.

With all this activity, a baby naturally hits upon lots of new elements. Not always does he successfully find the breast: his mouth sometimes finds his hand, the pillow, the covers, or something else. The assimilation of the world to the self is the phenomenon most typical of psychic behavior in its beginnings. Just as the organism transforms its environment to assimilate it to its own substance, so the developing sense of consciousness works on the new elements it meets to include them in its particular tendencies: a foreign body with which the mouth of a baby comes in contact is not interesting in itself but only from the point of view of its place in the baby's scheme of things, that is, as something suckable that activates sucking. Thus, the object is assimilated by the schema of sucking.

From this point of view, virtually everything offers material for assimilation. The newborn's whole universe is divided into things to suck, things to grab, things to look at, things to listen to, and the like. Now, one particular aspect of this world view is diametrically opposed to intelligent behavior and identical to dream activity. When we dream of a far-off land that we are traveling through, the function of our thinking is not to inform us about the country but simply to satisfy a desire: the desire to be great, sexual desire, or any other wish. The dream deforms things in order to satisfy its desire. Primitive thought does the same.

The tendency to assimilate everything, so evident in the first months, persists less obviously for quite a long time in little children. Take, for example, an 8-month-old baby confronted with a new object. I once gave my little daughter (8 months, 16 days) a cigarette case. She took it with both hands, looked at it, and went *pff pff*, a sound she had a habit of making that made people laugh. Next, she rubbed the case along the edge of her crib (to make a noise). After that, she looked at it again and arched her body (for her, this was a sort of magical procedure that we will examine later when we discuss causality and that she used to make things move when she could not reach them directly herself). Next, she held it above her and, in the end, put it in her mouth. She had tried to incorporate this new object into five different schemas of assimilation. This is how babies consistently greet new objects. After classifying them according to their elementary reflexes, which is what psychic assimilation amounts to in its initial stages, babies learn to make new schemas by combining these basic cycles of assimilation: for instance, seizing objects to put them into their mouths, shaking things or rubbing them against something to make a sound, and so on; and they spend their time and their days trying to fit the universe inside these new schemas.

Of course, this is not just a case of pure assimilation, since learning and accommodation are always going on at the same time. In this activity lies the crux of the paradox and the problem: at every moment, reality is breaking down the frames of reference of assimilatory schemas and provoking new adaptations, while assimilation is continually restoring the balance by reestablishing continuity between new and old.

Let us turn to the second point: emotional schemas charged with images. Intelligence is made up of concepts, first generalizations from motor experience and finally abstract relations, thanks to the progressive growth of thought from concrete to abstract reasoning. Autism, unlike intelligent reasoning, consists of the condensation of images guided by feeling. Accommodatory schemas in babies obviously contain embryonic concepts but, mixed with these schemas, are what can be termed *symbols* (symbolic thought is considered here the opposite of thinking with *signs*, that is, language and intelligence). The autistic symbols so typical of small children's games stem from the assimilatory schemas we were just discussing.

While it is undeniably difficult to say just at what point play begins in children, the question itself is probably meaningless, since the process of assimilation we have just described can be considered as the point from which play develops. A more pertinent question is at what moment babies are able to imagine that a particular object is something else. Once the child talks, it is easy to observe this playful attitude. My daughter, when she was only 21 months old, would push a box in front of her saying, "Car," or make believe she was eating paper, saying, "Very good." Two months earlier, she would tell her dog to cry and herself mimic someone crying. Such behavior is a simple extension of assimilation. Whether a child, before he can speak, uses any available object to satisfy his need to suck or grab, etc., or whether, knowing how to talk, he uses a box to represent a car he would like to see, the process is really the same: the object is not considered for itself but in relation to a specific desire. Once a child can speak, however, there is proof that these assimilations result in the formation of symbols analogous to those of autistic thought in general.

An analogy has often been made between dreaming and children's play. When a 22-month-old girl takes a shell, puts it to bed, washes and dresses it, the shell becomes the symbol of an array of feelings and interests; the only difference between it and a dream symbol is that it is a much more conscious phenomenon. But, as is well known, autistic thought can exist in all sorts of states of mind, from the transparent symbol used in play or art to the obscure symbols of dreams or insanity. What is important here is that the formation of symbols is predetermined already in the most primitive mental habits that we have just described under the name of assimilation.

In the third place, it is easy enough to show that thinking in babies is "undirected," that is, that it has the same orientation as a state of deep dreaming, and not that of intelligent activity, which functions uniquely in order to attain a given goal. Take the example of a 9-month-old infant trying to reach an object hanging from the top of his bassinet. He does things aimed at getting it, but, seeing the top of the bassinet shake, forgets his original goal and concentrates on making the whole bassinet move. Then, he goes back to his original intention, pulls on a cord, but then notices his hands as he does so. At this, he loses interest in anything but his hands and shakes them. This movement gives him the idea of taking his pillow and shaking it, too, in the air. Then, he happens to notice the fringe on the edge of the pillow and starts to suck it. This activity reminds him of the position he takes to go to sleep, which he immediately assumes, etc. Here is an example of infant thought made up of a series of schematized cycles of behavior linked and mutually activating each other by association. Each cycle has a definite goal, and the means to reach it, and in this sense the process of thinking is partially directed. But there is no hierarchy governing these cycles in relation to each other. They simply succeed each other at the beck and call of circumstances and assimilation.

There is no need to continue at greater length with examples of the parallel between thinking in the baby and autistic thought in general. It can be seen that while the baby's behavior is just one continual motor accommodation to things, the whole of his activity is still a sort of long waking dream. The baby is both closer to things and farther away from them than we are. If we remember our hypothesis of primitive solipsism, this paradoxical situation becomes understandable. The essence of primitive thought is that there is no difference between the self and the world. For the baby, nothing exists apart from himself or, if you prefer, all his desires and feelings are projected onto things. With this state of affairs, everything is assimilated to subjective desires and tendencies. A perpetual motor accommodation insures this adaptation of things to the self, and that is the reason the baby is constantly learning new behavior instead of just marking time. Still, he is always trying to fit new elements into the old ones and to assimilate the entire universe to the demands made by the self.

All this discussion must seem terribly schematic so long as we avoid concrete details. To clarify these hypotheses, let us take a look at one particular domain of the behavior that can be observed in the first year of life: the domain of causality. If our deductions are correct, we should come to at least two conclusions: first, that the only kind of causality that solipsistic thought can admit is a sort of primitive magic in which desires, accompanied by movements, are considered as acting on reality; second, that if the baby really is both nearer and farther from things than we are, this magic nonetheless arises only due to chance encounters that result from the most empirical and least rational experiences.

This is what we shall try to demonstrate.

Primitive Causality

For egocentric children between the ages of 3 and 8, causality is obviously a sort of constant assimilation of physical phenomena to processes that form a part of the child's psychological experience. Explanation, for the child, presupposes that behind the phenomenon there lies a deliberate intention modeled on human intentions and a force that realizes this intention modeled on human capabilities. Children's causal notions, or precausality, are thus a direct product of egocentrism.

What about the solipsistic baby? To understand him, let us once again carry egocentrism to its extreme. By hypothesis, a baby has no consciousness of self and in this way cannot think of things as semipersonal beings distinct from each other. There is total continuity between internal and external experience. Every phenomenon is perceived as charged with both physical qualities (taste, resistance, sound, color, shape, and so on) and psychic qualities (pleasure or pain, desire, sentiment, effort, efficacity, resistance, waiting, anxiety, and so on). In short, all movement outside seems to be the prolongation of feelings and kinesthetic sensations. This gives rise to causal relations even more primitive than causal concepts in children (finalism, animism, artificialism, dynamism, and so on), and which can be very roughly

compared to a sort of magic that we will call *efficacious causality*:* it
is characterized by a liaison between physical sensation (or rudimentary feelings) and movements in the world outside without there being
any spatial contact or any other obvious connection between the two.

But these connections made by efficacious causality do not of course
appear out of the blue in the baby's mind; their source is in chance
encounters in his experience. From an external view, from the point
of view of a pure reaction, primitive causality appears *phenomenistic*.
Psychologically speaking, however, it is likely that with these phenomenistic liaisons go feelings of efficacity, for many vestiges of this
sort of behavior can be seen in 2, 3, and 4 year olds and in even older
children, in which they can be analyzed directly. As far as the first
year is concerned, the facial expressions of babies leave almost no
room for doubt that they feel responsible for certain events and very
happy about it indeed.

Let us turn to the fact themselves. The first causal experience the
baby has is certainly what Baldwin has called a circular reaction, which
we have already touched upon from another point of view: the child
does something by chance, takes pleasure in the result, and does it over
and over again as if he wants to reproduce the same result (it matters
little if this desire for reproduction is the cause or the result of the act
reproduced). For example, near the end of the second month and
during the third, a baby begins to slip his thumb into his mouth no
longer by chance but deliberately and sucks it for long periods of time.
During the fourth month, I saw my daughter watch her fingers moving
for a long time, repeating the same movements countless times. At
6 months, she started grabbing objects and bringing them into her line
of vision. At 8 months, she watched endlessly the opening and closing
of her hands. At the same age, she loved to watch the movements of
her feet, etc.

It is certainly dangerous to want to guess what a baby is thinking
while he is watching the movements of his hands and feet. Yet, a baby
at this age does such amazing things in order to act on the outside
world that we must try to unravel the meaning of his elementary acts.
For example, still at the age of 8 months, my little daughter moved
her hand or raised herself up on her shoulderblades, falling back with
all her might, in order to make objects she saw in the distance move.
Another baby, only slightly older, blinked his eyes when he saw a lamp
cord in order to switch the lamp on, etc. Unless all psychology is to be
constructed with conditioned reflexes, as used to be done with the
association of ideas, we should try to understand. Let us go back to
the baby who is looking at his hands and feet moving to try to put
ourselves in his place, leaving our own frame of reference behind.

At least two things emerge clearly from the baby's behavior here.
On the one hand, he wants to have the movement he sees continue
and he makes an effort toward that end. There is nothing mysterious

---

*[We translate *causalité par efficace* as *efficacious causality*; this does
not have the same meaning as "efficient causality." Piaget later used *magico-
phenomenistic causality* instead of efficacious causality: magical because
there is no realistic link between the child's actions and their supposed effects,
phenomenistic because any event (phenomenon) can thus be linked with any
other event. See *Construction of Reality*, pp. 229 ff.]

about this (unless perhaps in the relation between the desire and the act). On the other hand, he is amazed by what he sees and he looks at his own body the way we look at a strange animal. It would be a real miracle if the baby said to himself: "This hand is mine; my desire to see it move is also mine; therefore I must be the one who is moving it." It is infinitely more likely (given what we know of the problems posed by the thought of older children, and, in general, by the relations between awareness and activity) that a baby has no such feeling, but a much simpler reaction. Let us assume, prudently, that no state of consciousness accompanies the first repetitions of a movement. It still must be supposed that sooner or later the tendency to repeat is translated into consciousness as a desire or an awareness of an effort, no matter how vague or without any representation of the aim of the movement. By the very fact of this repetition, the desire or sense of effort will necessarily occur between two perceptions of the hand moving, although the infant will have no idea of any intermediary between his feeling of making an effort and his desire and the spectacle that interests him. Thus, an immediate liaison between the feeling or desire and the perception of the movement will be created. If we could make a baby talk, as William James does his crab, we would make him say: "This thing here I see moving and the incredible feeling that just filled the entire universe are one and the same!"

Our working hypothesis is that every movement a baby makes in the universe that surrounds him, and every movement that follows an effort on his part, will be regarded as the same up until the moment when the resistance of things and of people will bring the child to divide the world into several centers of action and to construct parallel to the notion of his own self the notion of beings outside himself considered as other "selves."

Perhaps these hypotheses seem complicated. In my opinion, however, they are as simple as possible, and vital to an understanding of the origins of imitation and the consequent development of causality. If one starts with the idea that a baby is innately conscious of his own existence as an individual separate from the rest of the world, or if one postulates a precocious localization of his states of consciousness (localization of feelings of muscular effort, etc.), it is impossible to understand both why babies start imitating others at all or why they do such strange things in an effort to act at a distance on the outside world. According to our hypothesis, on the contrary, the baby is submerged in a chaos of interesting impressions without there being any distinction between his internal states and things outside. He is limited to associating nonlocalized sensations of muscular effort and other actions with movements he sees in the universe around him. What is more, as soon as the baby finds a way to maintain and reproduce any one of these movements he sees, he tries to do so as much as possible. As has been seen, life in psychological terms begins with this tendency to prolong and repeat experienced realities just as organic life is made up of the constant self-maintenance of the organism. At first, only psychological activity that works, or "the circular reaction" as Baldwin puts it, is noticeable; but this is only a special case. I propose now to continue with other examples for, if our hypothesis is correct, the baby will try to continue and recreate the totality of movements he sees.

The baby begins merely as a particularly interested witness to a multitude of events; a picture passing through his visual field, a sound he hears, a sound that occurs at the same time as he sees something, and so on. The efforts a baby will make to follow something with his eyes and head, and then with his hands, to grab and especially to imitate as soon as he can, are proof enough that he is no passive spectator. What he thinks while he is looking is impossible to say. But why not suppose that the baby projects all his feelings and especially those of making of an effort and of having accomplished something onto everything he perceives? Such a process would be analogous to circular reactions. We will come back to this hypothesis when we discuss the origins of imitation.

One thing that is certain is that, as soon as some chance event results in the slightest coincidence between a movement of the baby's body and another movement, he will seize upon this contingency to reactivate the outside movement he has noticed. Here is an example:

At the age of 5 months, 8 days, my daughter was moving her whole body, her feet most of all, although she had not caught sight of them moving; by chance, she hit a doll hanging above her. At that same moment, she noticed that the doll was moving, took an interest in it, and started to make it happen again, first, by chance, and then, so it seemed, in self-imitation by agitating her body and legs. She kept this up for a minute; then, I removed the doll from her line of vision, to put it back a second or two later. At that, she started moving around again, although she had stopped moving when the doll left her field of vision. Once again, I took the doll away, then brought it back, not to the usual place but beneath it, out of reach of the infant's feet. Despite the change of place, the baby resumed her wriggling about as before, looking at the doll (and not at her feet) all the time. It would appear here that she had established a general relationship between her movements and the doll's, and not a precise relationship between the movements of her feet and those of the doll. Now, she knew her own movements only as a collection of muscular sensations and feelings of pleasure that she undoubtedly did not localize, but simply associated with seeing the doll. This vague relation, very definitely real from the baby's expressions of satisfaction, shows clearly the existence of what we call efficacious causality.

A possible objection to this idea is that nothing prevents the baby from localizing her muscular sensations in her foot, thus becoming aware of the impact that permits this foot to make the doll move. If the baby really is conscious of such spatial relations, however, we fail to understand why she moved her feet both when far away and when near the doll, nor do we understand another phenomenon: babies indiscriminately apply a newly acquired procedure to the outside world, paying not the slightest heed to spatial relations. By this kind of unconscious motor assimilation, a baby generalizes every new procedure upon which he happens.

Here are some examples:

I.   At the age of 7 months, 16 days, my daughter inadvertently pulled on a string attached to a doll hanging by another string at the top of her bassinet and saw that this made the top move. By a simple circular reaction, she repeated this again and again. A minute later, I showed her my watch, a short distance away from the string holding the doll to the bassinet. She tried to grab the watch, raising herself up and twisting her body, all to no avail. Since this did not work, she seized the string attached to the doll with her right hand, keeping her left hand stretched out toward the watch. Then, she pulled hard on the string while still obviously wanting the watch toward which she continued to hold out her other hand.

II. Five days later (when she was 7 months, 21 days), I made the top of the bassinet shake, without the baby's seeing me. As soon as I stopped, she took the string hanging down from the top and pulled on it. Notice that she had absolutely no need to understand this technique in order to use it. All she had to do to pull on the string was to assimilate what she saw to what she had seen five days earlier; at that time, she had discovered by pure chance what happened when she pulled on the string. Next, I took a book and moved it back and forth for a while over the baby's head at the same height as the bassinet top, but some distance away from it. When I stopped, she immediately grabbed the string and pulled it hard about ten times. While she was busy doing this, I kept the book still, but began to move it again when she stopped. As soon as I stopped, she pulled on the string, but not as many times as before. I made two other tries and, with each one, the baby pulled on the string, but with less and less conviction.

You could tell me that these facts do not prove a thing. I view them, however, as examples of efficacious causal relations stemming from phenomenistic relations. The baby gets a result from some accidental gesture, which in turn produces a certain feeling: for example, pulling on a string makes the bassinet top move, all of which is permeated with feelings of effort and success. When the baby wants to get a new result such as the swinging movement of a watch or a book, her desire sets off the action of pulling on the string as it would set off anything she had previously done, provided that the action chosen had previously been linked to a feeling of efficacity. A much more rational behavior—a sort of elementary process of induction based on an awareness of certain relationships—could be invoked here: the baby pulls the string because she has seen the relationship between it and the bassinet top when she pulled the string before; this interpretation implies that she recognizes some sort of spatial relationship between the string, the watch, and the book. While this explanation may seem simpler than ours at first glance, it is really far more complicated, for it takes for granted the presence in the infant's mind of groups of geometrical and physical concepts that, for us, are almost certainly the result and not the cause of the experiments babies make.

Two counter examples may help to justify our point of view:

First, we need to show that causal relationships such as we have described are established without there being any intelligible spatial link between the things involved. Second, we need to show that what seems to be only a question of causality by physical contact is a case of exactly the same phenomenon.

To begin with the first point, we will see that even the slightest parallel between a gesture made by a baby and a movement he sees gives him the idea that his gesture has caused the movement. Here are some examples:

I. At the age of 7 months, 30 days, my daughter was watching the top of her bassinet which I was shaking without her seeing me. When I stopped, she had no idea of pulling on the string hanging there, but moved her hand gently against the inside lining of the bassinet. She did this as soon as I stopped my shaking, and then looked fixedly at the bassinet top as if the movement of her hand could make it move. She moved her hand this way a great many times.

The next day, I clapped my hands in front of her. As soon as I stopped, she rubbed her hand the way she had the day before on the inside of her bassinet, watching my hands attentively. When I took up clapping again, she stopped what she was doing, only to begin again the moment I stopped.

Several hours later, I made a hat go back and forth one meter above her head. When I stopped, she took up the same hand movement.

II.   At the age of 8 months, 9 days, the baby was watching a small plate moving in front of her. Over the preceding days, she had developed the habit of expressing joy in the following way: she would raise her body up, leaning on her shoulderblades and heels and then letting herself fall with all her force. When she saw the plate, she went through this routine simply for the pleasure of it, without any special intention. But at the moment that she arched her body, I happened to move the plate. From that time on, as soon as I would stop moving it, she would arch her body, stopping whenever the plate began moving again. Without any doubt, she had the impression that she was causing the plate's movements by arching her body.

Four days later, she was looking at the roof of her bassinet while I was jiggling it. As soon as I stopped, she would arch her body—again, undoubtedly, to prolong the movement of the plate.

Finally, a month later, after the beginning of this series, she arched her body in front of an object she wanted to see jiggle.

These instances show with what ease a feeling of causal connection can be established without any intelligible spatial link!*

III.   At the age of 11 months, the son of Dr. R. de Saussure was dazzled by a lamp switched on in the dark by pulling on a cord and blinked his eyes instinctively. As soon as accustomed to the light, however, he blinked his eyes deliberately in front of the cord several times, each time looking at the lamp to see if it was on again. This activity went on and on. After four months of not doing this at all, the infant reproduced the same behavior in broad daylight when he was shown the cord.

These examples of behavior can certainly be interpreted as simple responses as long as the baby himself does not seem to establish any causal connection between his own movement and a movement he perceives. But, while such simple reactions are undoubtedly at the root of such behavior, they gradually take on a causal meaning. On the one hand, a movement is executed not while a spectacle is going on, but only after it stops, in order to make it continue. On the other hand, the baby's obvious expectancy and delight clearly demonstrate the feelings directing his activity.

These examples seem to indicate that, for a baby, as Hume once said, "anything can produce anything": that a movement can be associated arbitrarily with a perception of a physical event and that this movement can be seen as the cause of the event. Such phenomenism, however, can never be pure. While a baby considers his activity to be the cause of a particular movement, it is only thanks to his solipsistic illusion that he draws no lines between the external world and the self: kinesthetic sensations and feelings appear directly connected with things and so, without any objective link being present between his gesture and an outside event seen at the same time, the baby develops a subjective link in his consciousness which shows up in his expressions of expectation and then of pleasure.

Let us turn now to the second counterexample that illustrates how

*See a further discussion of this point in J. Piaget, *Année Psychologique*, 31 (1926): 57–64.

even relationships that seem obviously spatial and physical and nothing else really fall into the same category as those discussed previously. Our examples will come from 2 year olds, since it is particularly convincing to find phenomena of efficacious causality at this late age.

I.   At the age of a year, 28 days, my daughter learned by imitating to use a stick to make a cork put on the edge of her crib fall into it. She managed in this way to get the cork, which was too far away for her to seize it directly with her hand. Two days later (at 13 months), she was holding a doll that I made disappear over the edge of the bassinet. She looked for it, tried to catch a glimpse of it and, unsuccessful, took the stick and hit the edge of the crib in exactly the same place where the doll had disappeared! It would be difficult to interpret this action differently than an attempt to make the doll come back.

II.   At the age of 18 months, 8 days, my little girl was sitting up in a double bed in front of a big eiderdown humped up into a sort of mountain. I put a toy on top of it and tapped the quilt so that the toy slid down toward her little by little. She imitated this action very well. A minute later, I put the toy on a table a meter away, separated from the bed by a good space. Despite the distance the child began to tap on the quilt, while looking at the toy, as if calling it to come!

The same thing happened several times.

III.   Three days later, I saw the same sort of behavior, but completely spontaneous. The baby was in a room with some chairs. She moved one whose back was touching an open window, saw that this made the window change place and began moving the chair again, all the time watching the window. A minute later, she bumped into another chair, a meter and a half away, shook it and then looked quickly at the window to see if it had moved again. . . .

Causal sequences independent of the child's activity also deserve examination. Take the example of a child who notices that two bodies hitting each other produce a noise. How does he picture this to himself? We have, unfortunately, no way of finding out. All we can say, given a child's behavior in general, is that either such sequences do not strike him as causal, or else he uses a model of efficacious causality to imagine the relation involved, at least until he has a sufficient understanding of the resistance put up by the outside world in order to establish an elementary distinction between himself and other things.

Before concluding our presentation, we would like to refute one more possible objection. It could be thought that if babies use any procedure at all to get any result at all, depending on the associations experience provides, they count on their parents to satisfy their every desire. In line with this hypothesis, a baby's way of acting on things would be simply a special kind of language used by people familiar to him. There would be no magic involved, only a prayer offered to all-powerful gods. For instance, around the age of 1½ or 2 years, a child will go looking for one of his parents as soon as he wants something, asking for it with a simple "please," without trying to explain more exactly what it is he wants, so strong is his conviction that his parents know all his desires.

If this hypothesis becomes plausible once a child begins to talk, it is impossible earlier in development for three reasons.

The first reason is that, around the age of 7 or 8 months, when the baby begins to imitate (interestingly enough, this age coincides with phenomena typical of efficacious causality), there is as yet no distinction felt by the baby between himself and others. This very confusion is responsible for the birth of imitation. No matter what explanation can be given of the mechanism or technique of imitation, there remains the problem of why the child imitates. Seen as a special case of the basic need of primitive psychic activity—that is, to prolong everything that is felt or perceived—imitation is easy to understand. We have seen how this need is the point of departure of a child's progressive conquest of the world. This same need sets off the circular reaction in which a baby reproduces movements it has already made and sets in motion behavior based on efficacious causality where movements other than those of the baby's own body are concerned. In cases where the movements a baby sees can be directly assimilated to something he has previously done with his own body (as in the case where a baby hears a noise he knows how to make or sees a movement he can make happen), his need to repeat the action is translated by imitation. In this respect, at the beginning, imitation is simply a matter of confusing the self and the world, due to the sense of identification a baby has with everything around him. Imitation in these first stages is in no way a social behavior although, later on, it leads a child to an awareness of certain aspects of his self. Thus, at the moment in which causal ideas begin to develop, social behavior does not yet exist, only solipsistic behavior.

In the second place, as soon as a child learns to imitate, he does so in order to act on the outside world; here lies the connection between the parallel growth of imitation and causality. When my daughter was 8 or 9 months old, she would frequently imitate a sound or an action until it was repeated, or else would try to make people or things imitate her. When she wanted to get this kind of effect, moreover, she was just as apt to use either imitation or magical procedures (shaking her hand, arching her body, and so on). This fact seems to speak in favor of the hypothesis we have been trying to refute, namely that efficacious causality behavior is simply a way to influence people, similar to using a private kind of language. This causality by imitation however (a sort of dawning imitative magic) is used just as much with things as with people. For instance, my daughter at the age of 9 months, 9 days, was watching a parrot I was swinging in front of her (the same motion as saying "hello") without her seeing me or knowing I was there. As soon as I would stop, she would imitate the movement with her hand, stop, begin again, obviously trying to make the parrot swing. When it did not, she finally hit it as if in order to make it start moving again. This shows how children fail to distinguish between persons and things.

The third and strongest argument in favor of solipsistic primitive behavior is that, much later, people still exhibit residues of these quasi-magical procedures of early childhood. Here is a typical example: when she was 22 months old, my little girl was hitting the bottom of a basket with a key; each time, I would make a funny noise that made her laugh. She knew very well that it was I making the noise, but she could not see me. (I was hiding behind a partition in the wall from which I could observe her.) After a moment, I stopped making the noise at the appropriate time. The child, in order to make the noise start again, redoubled her efforts and, seeing it was no use, moved the basket a little way, then put it back in place and began to hit it again. I cried out once more, then stopped. She moved the basket around as before and began again. She had no conception of my noise as intentional behavior that I could make or not as I liked. For her, it was not the response of one person to another but a sort of necessary physical reaction from the force of the key hitting the basket, combined with the basket's position. In view of the fact that confusions like this still occur close to the age of 2, behavior in the first year of life cannot legitimately be considered as social.

We need now to go into our analysis in greater depth and study the facts of phenomenism accompanied by efficacious causality, which continue to show up in children up to 4 or 5 years of age. It will come to light that the common belief of little children that they can make the sun, moon, and stars (not to speak of clouds and the entire sky) move has a psychological structure similar to the other attitudes we have studied. Our remarks will be brief since I had the honor of presenting a talk on causal notions in children from 3 to 12 years of age several days ago before the Cambridge Education Society.*

To conclude this quick sketch of causal notions in babies, the preceding discussion leads to two results. First, the dualism of motor accommodation and autistic assimilation in the first year of life seems to be confirmed by the notions of causality we have found in infants of that age. Second, the same findings seem to indicate again that, as far as a baby's consciousness is concerned, motor accommodation and autistic assimilation are undifferentiated, thanks to a solipsism in which the self identifies completely with the world; in other words, that there is close overlapping of motor and affective states of consciousness in the total complex of visual, tactile, and auditory representations of things themselves.

The first point seems to present no difficulty. Primitive causality is both motor accommodation and autistic assimilation. It is motor accommodation to the degree that it is phenomenistic. A child does something, gets a certain result, tries to repeat the action in order to get the same result: this cycle of movements is simply a continuation of the same process that occurred when the baby learned to follow a moving body with his eyes, grab, bring things up to his mouth or into his visual field, and so on. In this sense, as Hume says, causality derives from motor habit. But primitive causality is also assimilation, as we have defined this term, and here the feeling of being the cause of a movement plays a role. Motor accommodation in fact does not take place without corresponding states of consciousness (whether these appear at the very beginning of mental development or along the way; whether these come before or after or along with the act of accommodation matters little here). There are desires, feelings of effort, waiting, uneasiness, satisfaction, success, and the like. It is clear, given these elements of consciousness, that a baby is not going to establish a completely objective relationship between his actions and their results, like a scientist who notices a simultaneity and asks himself if there is a causal relationship involved. The baby's emotional states will always be embedded in the totality of his perceptions; his awareness of the efficacious action will be far more the awareness of feelings that accompany it than the knowledge of its objective characteristics (trajectory,

*[Published as "La causalité chez l'enfant," *The British Journal of Psychology*, 18 (1927–1928): 276–301.]

spatial contacts, and so on). Once a baby knows how to talk, he will explain this state of affairs like this: "I am the one who is making this happen . . . ," etc. Before he can speak and, a fortiori, before he is conscious of himself, he feels something like: "this desire or awareness of making an effort, etc., goes with this result . . . ," etc. If this is indeed the case, then causality involves autistic assimilation as well as motor accommodation. When a baby sees an object moving in the distance, a watch swinging, and so on, he includes this perception in a schema he already knows: he arches his body, for example, because this action previously has led to the satisfaction of his desires. In other words, the desire to have an interesting spectacle continue sets off the action that usually makes this happen. In this mode of causality there is of course as much an element of accommodation as there is assimilation: the baby is trying to reproduce something he sees (as in imitating, which is a sort of accommodation) and not to change it to suit his needs. But inasmuch as primitive causality involves a sense of efficacity, there is also assimilation, since the means the baby uses to act on things are not adapted to them, but are only actions that are usually associated with his desires. This dualism can be seen in the later development of causal notions. To the degree that the element of assimilation is eliminated from these processes, causal ideas obviously become completely empirical or phenomenistic. But to the degree that the element of accommodation is eliminated from certain other processes (under the influence of emotion, for example), causal notions become magical: a child under the sway of assimilation will invent an absurd procedure so as not to die, to grow up, to get a particular wish, not to be punished, and so on. His use of causality is not at all adapted but completely autistic.

The important thing to note is that in the growth of causal notions, one cannot say whether accommodation precedes assimilation or vice versa. From the very first inklings a baby has of her own power, she considers the thing on which she is acting as subject to her desire, that is, as dependent on her emotional states, or even as participating in them—assimilation in action; and at the same time, she does and repeats as well as she can whatever has accidentally just been connected with a particular pleasing result—accommodation in action. Primitive causality consists of this intimate fusion of the organism's purely empirical accommodation to things and systematic assimilation of things to subjective states of being, like all activity in general in the first year of life.

It now seems clear that this paradox implies solipsism. The later evolution of causality would make no sense unless the baby failed to make a distinction between the self and the world. If primitive causality boiled down to pure phenomenism, causal notions ought to develop in the direction of unadulterated empiricism. The fact is, causality in children from 3 to 8 years of age is in a sense only one long projection of the self into things: animism and dynamism really amount to endowing things with intelligence and the ability to make efforts. Where could this attitude come from, once a child sees the world as composed of beings and persons separate from himself, if the baby had not previously regarded the pictures constituting his universe as simple continuations of his own desires and groping actions?

19

The Origins of Intelligence in Children[*]

1936

INTRODUCTORY NOTES

The Origins of Intelligence in Children (1936) and *The Construction of Reality in the Child* (1937) constitute Piaget's fundamental contribution to the study of infancy.

To simplify an enormously complex problem, Piaget divided his work into two tasks, leading to one book dealing with the early growth of the child's capacity for intelligent action, and another with the early growth of his ideas about the world he lives in.[†] This distinction corresponds roughly to the distinction between plans and images advanced much later by Miller, Galanter, and Pribram in *Plans and the Structure of Behavior*.[‡]

In choosing excerpts from *Origins of Intelligence* and *Construction of Reality*, we have lost some of Piaget's emphasis on the continuity of development; we have tried to compensate for this by providing an introductory sketch of each work as a whole. At the same time, Piaget's own division of his work has not yet led to any clearcut synthesis of the two parts. How coherent is the child's development? What is the most fruitful way to conceive of the developing relation between knowledge and action? Such questions remain largely unexplored. Our rapid summary of these two parallel aspects of development will be useful if it at least helps to bring into clearer focus the existence of such questions.

[*]From J. Piaget, *The Origins of Intelligence in Children*, Margaret Cook, translator. Reprinted by permission of International Universities Press, Inc., and Routledge & Kegan Paul Ltd., London. Originally published in French, 1936.

[†]The reader may want to read first "The First Year of Life of the Child," an earlier article in which this separation of issues is not yet fully evident. That article also gives some concrete examples of the "primary circular reaction," which have been omitted from the present selection. See Selection 18.

[‡]G. A. Miller, E. Galanter, K. H. Pribram. *Plans and the Structure of Behavior* (N.Y.: Holt, Rinehart, Winston, 1960).

Sensorimotor Intelligence

This first period of mental development, the sensorimotor period, extending broadly from birth to the appearance of language, traces the path, in six stages, from infancy to representation.

Two basic mechanisms are supposed to account for development, assimilation and accommodation. Psychological assimilation as well as biological assimilation is the transformation of the external world in such a way as to render it an integral part of oneself. In the case of intelligence, it is the integration of external objects to the schemata of subjective actions, fusing a preexisting schema and a new object. Any object is then perceived in terms of the actions using it. Any schema tends to assimilate any object. But there are limits and obstacles to this principle of universal assimilation. These limits are imposed upon the voracity of schemata by the external world. This resistance of the external world to assimilation exacts the modification of schemata, thus adapting them to the environment. Accommodation is therefore a tendency of the organism to compensate for resistance of the object to assimilation by creating a new alternative, or *tertium*, between the application and the nonapplication of a schema to a certain object. Assimilation and accommodation are the two poles of the same activity of adaptation that characterizes any biological organism.

Since every schema tends to assimilate every object, schemata tend also to assimilate each other. This reciprocal assimilation leads to the coordination of schemata, which takes place whenever the subject intends to reach a new goal requiring the combination of actions not previously related to one another.

With this rather simple set of fundamental mechanisms of development, Piaget then proceeds to the study of the different stages of development during the sensorimotor period. He recognizes essentially six stages:

1. birth to 6 weeks: reflexes;
2. 6 weeks to 4 to 5 months: habits;
3. 4 months to 9 months: coordination between vision and prehension;
4. 9 months to 12 months: coordination between means and goals;
5. 12 months to 18 months: discovery of new means; and
6. 18 months to 24 months: insight.

STAGE I: REFLEXES

What Piaget means by reflexes is somewhat different from what Pavlov and his followers meant by it. A reflex, in the Piagetian sense, is a reaction of the organism that is hereditary and not acquired by experience.

Unlike the concept of the innate releasing mechanism advanced by ethologists such as Lorenz, the Piagetian reflex is at first global and undifferentiated, becoming progressively more differentiated through exercise. For instance, what has been acquired in the palmar reflex is conserved in intentional grasping. Reflexes form schemata that function by means of three forms of assimilation: (1) assimilation by repetition, or reproductive assimilation, which consists of the mere repetition of the same functional exercise; (2) assimilation by recognition, or recognitive assimilation, which implies discrimination in the application of the schema; (3) assimilation by generalization, which implies extension of the schema to an increasing number of objects.

At this stage, Piaget focuses his attention on three important reflexes: (1) sucking; (2) eye-movements; and (3) palmar reflex.

STAGE II: THE FIRST HABITS OR ACQUIRED ADAPTATIONS

Piaget distinguishes two forms of habits: active and passive. The active pole consists of circular reactions that either reproduce or continue a result obtained by chance. This elementary form of conservation is a typical example of reproductive assimilation. It can take three different forms, distinguished according to the locus of activity and the degree of intentionality. Primary circular reactions involve only the individual's own body, as in bringing the hand before the face repeatedly. Secondary ones involve external objects. Tertiary circular reactions are actions upon objects reproduced in order to see what happens when some movements are slightly different from their initial equivalents.

Primary circular reactions appear in the second stage, secondary ones in the third stage, and tertiary ones in the fifth stage.

The passive pole (which is only apparently passive) is formed by conditioned reflexes. Such habits seem to be imposed upon the subject by the external world. But a pressure from within must correspond to a pressure from without in order to maintain a conditional reflex. If a conditioned reflex is no longer associated with reward or satisfaction of need, extinction of the reflex occurs quickly, in spite of exercise. In order to be reinforced, a reflex has to be the object of an active assimilation on the part of the subject. This assimilation by generalization creates a new schema of habit. This feedback process constitutes the course of cognitive growth and adaptation.

STAGE III: COORDINATION BETWEEN VISION AND PREHENSION

This stage is characterized by three novelties: (1) intentional grasping; (2) secondary circular reactions; and (3) first differentiations between means and ends.

The practice of visual schemata and grasping schemata leads to a coordination between them, a clear example of reciprocal assimilation. This mutual assimilation is made possible not only by practice but also by maturation of the nervous system. The role of the nervous system, both its structure and development, is not underestimated by Piaget. But maturation without practice, its functional counterpart, is useless according to Piaget.

Secondary circular reactions consist of repetitions of chance discoveries made about external objects, or of the reproduction of movements producing initially unexpected results.

Intelligence is defined by Piaget as the use of certain means to reach certain goals. The early differentiation of means from ends is marked by a form of behavior that is intermediate between mere habits and intelligence. At this stage the goal is imprecise at first. It consists essentially in making interesting sights last. A typical example of such conduct is given by Laurent who, after having produced some rattling noise from the top of his cradle by pulling the ropelet hanging from it, pulls the same rope in order to have his mother stay in the room.

STAGE IV: COORDINATION BETWEEN MEANS AND ENDS

This stage is the first one in which intelligence properly speaking appears. The infant applies schemata from his repertoire to novel situations. He sets out to obtain a certain result and coordinates his acquired schemata in order to reach the fixed goal. Characteristic of this stage is the removal of one object in order to get another object located out of reach behind or upon the removed object.

Piaget insists on the novelty of the situation because otherwise it would not be intelligence but mere learning at work in the child's behavior. He insists also on the combination of two things, the coordination of schemata and the discrimination of goals, in order to characterize a behavior as intelligent.

The result of this distinction of means and goals is an increased mobility of action for the growing infant and a parallel extension of his field of action.

STAGE V: DISCOVERY OF NEW MEANS

This stage is marked by the emergence of tertiary circular reactions. In this, the infant demonstrates for the first time that he is a young scientist, since he actively replicates successful results with a quasi-systematic variation of conditions. This variation leads to the elaboration of new schemata and a wider coordination of an increasing number of schemata for the discovery of new means.

From the observer's point of view, this leads to groping, a new form of behavior primarily resulting in the formation of a network of meanings. For Piaget, the real role of groping in the development of the child is one of maintaining a balance between the necessary accommodations to objects and the assimilatory coordinations, this balance forming the essence of intelligence. Groping is directed both by the schema assigning a goal to the action and the schema chosen as initial means; it is also oriented, during trials and errors, by the schemata that are likely to give a meaning to fortuitous events occurring in the course of action, which are then used with intelligence.

Among the behavior patterns characteristic of this stage, three examined closely by Piaget deal with reaching a distant object by means of an intermediary: a stick, a rope, or the support (such as a rug) on which the object is placed. In such instances, the child—groping for the object he desires—accidentally discovers how to use the intermediary object as a means to attain his end, and then incorporates this action into his already existing schemata of reaching and grasping. In Piaget's treatment of these cases, the coordination of schemata is involved in this development, since the child has also been developing the schemata of pushing and pulling necessary to use the objects.*

---

*It is interesting to note that H. G. Birch ["The relation of previous experience to insightful problem-solving." *Journal of Comparative Psychology* 38 (1945): 295–317] later showed experimentally that much the same was true of chimpanzees who discover the use of a stick as a rake to reach an otherwise unattainable object. The actual discovery seems to come as a sudden insight, but only if the animal has previously built up a backlog of experience with the more general properties of sticks.

STAGE VI: INVENTION OF NEW MEANS

At this stage, new means are discovered with much less initial groping. There are two distinct phases: (1) no or very brief groping at the beginning; and (2) insight during a period of no activity from the observer's viewpoint. This period is interpreted by Piaget as a period of internal coordination of the schemata that are most adequate to solve the puzzle presented to the child.

This stage marks the passage from sensorimotor actions to mental representation, since an internal coordination of schemata requires at least a minimum of mental imagery.

The Construction of Reality

Paralleling the acquisition of sensorimotor intelligence, the mastery of the environment is constructed in six stages, too, which form the core of *The Construction of Reality*, published one year after *The Origins of Intelligence*. Taking over a Kantian framework, Piaget distinguishes four categories of understanding at the sensorimotor level: object concept, space, time, and causality.

STAGE I

Object Concept. The baby has no idea of a permanent object sitting "out there" with its own properties. At this stage, he recognizes "things" thanks to sensorimotor recognition. This means, in fact, that he is more skilled at recognizing a posture, a sight, or a noise than at responding to a thing out there entirely given to him from the outside. This very fact indicates the limits of his world made, in Piaget's terms, of the residues of his sensorimotor schemata.

Space Concept. As William Stern had observed before Piaget, the notion of space at this stage is fragmentary, since objects dissolve into nothingness. There is a juxtaposition of different and local spaces without intercoordination: a mouth-space, a visual space, a tactile space, a postural space, and so on.

Causality. Since there are no permanent objects that can influence each other, and no articulated space and time in which events can occur, there can be no causal relations among events. There is no causality. Similarly, there is no differentiation of ends from means, and therefore no possibility of intentional behavior.

STAGE II

Object Concept. During this stage, the infant begins to search for an object that has been grasped for a while when contact with it is interrupted. This behavior pattern is in sharp contrast with the previous stage characterized by the reabsorption of "object," or better, figure, in the background.

The child continues to search for it for awhile if it is still in sight, but he does not search for it if it disappears, nor does he in any other way indicate that something has vanished. There are no permanent things yet: if it has vanished it is not.

Space Concept. The different spaces mentioned above are still kept separated, but there is a beginning of coordination among them, without, however, reaching the level of a general container of objects.

There is also an early concept of time. The child gives the impression that he is waiting for periodical repetitions of the same rituals such as bathing or eating.

Causality. The appearance of the first acquired behavior patterns, habits, does not provoke any change in the notion of causality, since the principal character of a habit is that its parts are not hierarchically organized into means and ends, the entire sequence of individual movements and acts being fused into one undifferentiated lump.

STAGE III

Object Concept. With the coordination between vision and prehension, reaching out for an object becomes intentional and an interrupted prehension is resumed as long as the object remains in the visual field of the subject. There is still no specific behavior pattern toward an object that has disappeared from perception.

Space Concept. This stage marks the beginning of a general coordination of the different spaces. Not only are mouth and tactilo-kinesthetic spaces coordinated through sucking, but all the separate spaces are unified into a general container centered around the infant's own body. An object has no independent trajectory; its movement is linked to the action of the child, of which it is a prolongation. A typical consequence of this limitation is the child's inability to anticipate the movement of a rolling ball.

Causality. This stage marks the beginning of causality that is limited to one universal cause: the infant's own action. Although the child of this stage smiles, handles objects according to various schemata (swinging, striking, rubbing, shifting, and so on) she does not locate the cause of some phenomenon she enjoys in the object itself but, on the contrary, fuses it with her own action. The infant pulling the cord of her cradle to produce pleasant sights of all sorts is typical of this stage. This form of causality has been labeled by Piaget magico-phenomenist causality, magical in the sense that it produces anything and phenomenist in the sense that it is produced by any temporal contiguity between any two events.

STAGE IV

Object Concept. With the coordination between means and ends, the infant becomes capable of removing a screen that is placed over an object in front of her just as she reaches out for the object. In order for her to look for the hidden object, she has literally to be caught in the act of reaching for it.

All through this stage, the child will improve her performance and look for objects under different screens. But this search does not take into account all the displacements of the object. For instance, after having hidden the object, first under a cushion placed to the left of the child and then under one placed to the right, Piaget observes that the child looks first under the cushion from under which she has just seen the object removed, seems puzzled not to find it there, then looks under the cushion where it is to be found.

Space Concept. The very fact that the child looks for an object hidden behind a screen indicates that he conceives of space as a general container in which things are. But this space remains very self-centered since the child's belief about the location of an object depends on his search procedure more than on the independent changes of position of the object. This search indicates, in addition, the beginning of reversibility in the organization of the displacements, since an object that lies *behind* a screen can be brought *before* it by an action that removes the screen or reverses the respective positions of the screen and the object. Unless the object has acquired some degree of permanence one can hardly speak of reversibility; since there are no objects there can be no previous arrangement of them to be restored.

Time Concept. The beginning of search for a hidden object coincides with the initial ordering of instants into "before" and "after" as crude as "before" and "behind" in space.

Causality. At this stage, the causality system is still entirely magico-phenomenist and the child still thinks of himself as the cause of everything around.

STAGE V

Object Concept. At this stage, the infant responds to all the displacements of the object and he looks for a lost object where it was seen last as long as all the movements of the object have so far remained perceptible.

Space Concept. The child takes into consideration the total organization of displacements provided that they are all simultaneously visible. There is a progressive decentration of space from his own action. Objects begin to be considered as independent; they have their own movements of translation and rotation. This means, for Piaget, that the practical group of displacements is being structured by the child.

Causality. When objects become permanent, causality becomes differentiated and objective, an object is no longer the direct prolongation of an action but becomes perceived in itself. This means that the subject becomes able to recognize not only the causes situated in his own actions but also in various objects, as well as the causal relations between two objects. This presupposes that he attributes to these objects some spatial and physical connections independent of his own action on them.

STAGE VI

Object Concept. At this stage, the child conserves the object in a stable permanence that is a function of its objective location in a world where the subject does not occupy a privileged position anymore, but is simply one object among others.

Now the child is able to use all the displacements and movements to reconstitute the actual position of an object. Displacements are so well organized that the child uses practical transitivity in his own displacements in space or in his anticipation of the changes of position of other objects.

Space Concept. Poincaré's group of displacements is attained at the sensorimotor level. The child is now capable of structuring space in the following coherent way: (1) return to departure point (corresponding to reverse operation in a mathematical group); (2) conservation of the initial point of departure (or identity operation); and (3) detour behavior pattern (or associativity). This does not mean that the child has this group in mind, but simply that he behaves accordingly.

Causality. Causal relations and connections have not improved during this period.

These two books generated considerable interest when they were initially published. Child psychology at the time was deeply concerned with questions such as the discrimination of individual abilities, the nature-nurture controversy, and the establishment of scientific procedures of investigation. Piaget was completely against the mainstream of ideas about children when he offered these two books to the public. Here we find no discussion of heredity and environment, virtually no attempt at showing individual differences among the three subjects, no statistics, and no fancy experimental design. Only careful observations and a bit of informal experimentation. Nevertheless, the author manages to demonstrate fascinating facts about infants: the notion of the permanence of objects in space, that seems so natural to adults and older children, is acquired progressively by the infant; the passage from innate reflexes to the capacity for insight is gradual; causality is constructed more slowly than space and time. In sum, the fundamental categories of understanding are not innate or acquired by learning as commonly understood. Probably, here we reach the root of the interest of these two books for its first readers. At a time when learning psychologists were confronting Gestalt psychology with its nativistic claims, here was a book showing that the road from reflexes to insight existed and was built with remarkable milestones. A third way was offered to replace the simple opposition between nativism and environmentalism.

The First Stage: The Use of Reflexes*

If, in order to analyze the first mental acts, we refer to hereditary organic reactions, we must study them not for their own sake but merely so that we may describe *in toto* the way in which they affect the individual's behavior. We should begin, therefore, by trying to differentiate between the psychological problem of the reflexes and the strictly biological problem.

Behavior observable during the first weeks of life is very complicated, biologically speaking. At first there are very different types of reflexes involving the medulla, the bulb, the optic commissures, the ectoderm itself; moreover, from reflex to instinct is only a difference of degree. Next to the reflexes of the central nervous system are those of the autonomic nervous system and all the reactions due to "protopathic" sensibility. There is, above all, the whole group of postural reflexes whose importance for the beginnings of the evolution of the mind has

*[The following section is from Chapter I.]

been demonstrated by H. Wallon. It is hard to envisage the organization of the foregoing mechanisms without giving the endocrine processes their just due as indicated by so many learned or spontaneous reactions. Physiological psychology is confronted at the present time by a host of problems which consist of determining the effects on the individual's behavior of each of these separate mechanisms. . . .

The psychological problem begins to pose itself as soon as the reflexes, postures, etc., are considered no longer in connection with the internal mechanism of the living organism, but rather in their relationships to the external environment as it is subjected to the individual's activity. Let us examine, from this point of view, the various fundamental reactions in the first weeks: sucking and grasping reflexes, crying and vocalization, movements and positions of the arms, the head or the trunk, etc.

What is striking about this is that such activities from the start of their most primitive functioning, each in itself and some in relation to others, give rise to a systematization which exceeds their automatization. Almost since birth, therefore, there is "behavior" in the sense of the individual's total reaction and not only a setting in motion of particular or local automatizations only interrelated from within. In other words, the sequential manifestations of a reflex such as sucking are not comparable to the periodic starting up of a motor used intermittently, but constitute an historical development so that each episode depends on preceding episodes and conditions those that follow in a truly organic evolution. In fact, whatever the intensive mechanism of this historical process may be, one can follow the changes from the outside and describe things as though each particular reaction determined the others without intermediates. This comprises total reaction, that is to say, the beginning of psychology.

SUCKING REFLEXES

Let us take as an example the sucking reflexes or the instinctive act of sucking; these reflexes are complicated, involving a large number of afferent fibers of the trigeminal and the glossopharyngeal nerves as well as the efferent fibers of the facial, the hypoglossal and the masseteric nerves, all of which have as a center the bulb of the spinal cord. First here are some facts:

Observation 1.—From birth suckinglike movements may be observed: impulsive movement and protrusion of the lips accompanied by displacements of the tongue, while the arms engage in unruly and more or less rhythmical gestures and the head moves laterally, etc.

As soon as the hands rub the lips the sucking reflex is released. The child sucks his fingers for a moment but of course does not know either how to keep them in his mouth or pursue them with his lips. Lucienne and Laurent, a quarter of an hour and a half hour after birth, respectively, had already sucked their hand like this: Lucienne, whose hand had been immobilized due to its position, sucked her fingers for more than ten minutes.

A few hours after birth, first nippleful of collostrum. It is known how greatly children differ from each other with respect to adaptation to this first meal. For some children like Lucienne and Laurent, contact of the lips and probably the tongue with the nipple suffices to produce sucking and swallowing. Other children, such as Jacqueline, have slower coordination: the child lets go of the breast every moment without taking it back again by himself or applying himself to it as vigorously when the nipple is replaced in his mouth. There are some children, finally, who need real forcing: holding their head, forcibly putting the nipple between the lips and in contact with the tongue, etc.

Observation 2.—The day after birth Laurent seized the nipple with his lips without having to have it held in his mouth. He immediately seeks the breast when it escapes him as the result of some movement.

During the second day also Laurent again begins to make suckinglike movements between meals while thus repeating the impulsive movements of the first day: His lips open and close as if to receive a real nippleful, but without having an object. This behavior subsequently became more frequent and we shall not take it up again.

The same day the beginning of a sort of reflex searching may be observed in Laurent, which will develop on the following days and which probably constitutes the functional equivalent of the gropings characteristic of the later stages (ascquisition of habits and empirical intelligence). Laurent is lying on his back with his mouth open, his lips and tongue moving slightly in imitation of the mechanism of sucking, and his head moving from left to right and back again, as though seeking an object. These gestures are either silent or interrupted by grunts with an expression of impatience and of hunger.

Observation 3.—The third day Laurent makes new progress in his adjustment to the breast. All he needs in order to grope with open mouth toward final success is to have touched the breast or the surrounding teguments with his lips. But he hunts on the wrong side as well as on the right side, that is to say, the side where contact has been made.

Observation 4.—Laurent at 0;0(9)* is lying in bed and seeks to suck, moving his head to the left and to the right. Several times he rubs his lips with his hand which he immediately sucks. He knocks against a quilt and a wool coverlet; each time he sucks the object only to relinquish it after a moment and begins to cry again. When he sucks his hand he does not turn away from it as he seems to do with the woolens, but the hand itself escapes him through lack of coordination; he then immediately begins to hunt again.

Observation 5.—As soon as his cheek comes in contact with the breast, Laurent at 0;0(12) applies himself to seeking until he finds drink. His search takes its bearings: immediately from the correct side, that is to say, the side where he experienced contact.

At 0;0(20) he bites the breast which is given him, 5 cm. from the nipple. For a moment he sucks the skin which he then lets go in order to move his mouth about 2 cm. As soon as he begins sucking again he stops. In one of his attempts he touches the nipple with the outside of his lips and he does not recognize it. But, when his search subsequently leads him accidentally to touch the nipple with the mucosa of the upper lip (his mouth being wide open), he at once adjusts his lips and begins to suck.

The same day, same experiment: after having sucked the skin for several seconds, he withdraws and begins to cry. Then he begins again, withdraws again, but without crying, and takes it again 1 cm. away; he keeps this up until he discovers the nipple.

Observation 6.—The same day I hold out my crooked index finger to Laurent, who is crying from hunger (but intermittently and without violence). He immediately sucks it but rejects it after a few seconds and begins to cry. Second attempt: same reaction. Third attempt: he sucks it, this time for a long time and thoroughly, and it is I who retract it after a few minutes.

Observation 7.—Laurent at 0;0(21) is lying on his right side, his arms tight against his body, his hands clasped, and he sucks his right thumb at length while remaining completely immobile. The nurse made the same observation on the previous day. I take his right hand away and he at once

---

*[0;0(9) = year; month (days).]

begins to search for it, turning his head from left to right. As his hands remained immobile due to his position, Laurent found his thumb after three attempts: prolonged sucking begins each time. But, once he has been placed on his back, he does not know how to coordinate the movement of the arms with that of the mouth and his hands draw back even when his lips are seeking them.

At 0;0(24) when Laurent sucks his thumb, he remains completely immobile (as though having a nippleful: complete sucking, pantings, etc.) When his hand alone grazes his mouth, no coordination.

Observation 8.—At 0;0(21): Several times I place the back of my index finger against his cheeks. Each time he turns to the correct side while opening his mouth. Same reactions with the nipple.

Then I repeat the same experiments as those in Observation 5. At 0;0(21) Laurent begins by sucking the teguments with which he comes in contact. He relinquishes them after a moment but searches with open mouth, while almost rubbing the skin with his lips. He seizes the nipple as soon as he brushes against it with the mucosa of his lower lip.

That evening, the same experiment, but made during a nursing which has been interrupted for this purpose. Laurent is already half asleep: his arms hang down and his hands are open (at the beginning of the meal his arms are folded against his chest and his hands are clasped). His mouth is placed against the skin of the breast about 5 cm. from the nipple. He immediately sucks without reopening his eyes but, after a few moments, failure awakens him. His eyes are wide open, his arms flexed again and he sucks with rapidity. Then he gives up, in order to search a little further away, on the left side which happens by chance to be the correct side. Again finding nothing, he continues to change places on the left side, but the rotary movement which he thus gives his head results in making him let go the breast and go off on a tangent. In the course of this tangential movement he knocks against the nipple with the left commissure of his lips and everything that happens would seem to indicate that he recognizes it at once. Instead of groping at random, he only searches in the immediate neighborhood of the nipple. But as the lateral movements of his head made him describe a tangential curve opposite and not parallel to the curve of the breast, he oscillates in space guided only by light, haphazard contacts with the breast. It takes a short time for these increasingly localized attempts to be successful. This last phase of groping has been noteworthy for the speed with which each approach to it has been followed by an attempt at insertion of the nipple, while the lips open and close with maximum vigor; and noteworthy also for the progressive adjusting of the tangential movements around the points of contact.

At 0;0(23) a new experiment. Laurent is 10 cm. from the breast, searching for it on the left and on the right. While he searches on the left the nipple touches his right cheek. He immediately turns and searches on the right. He is then moved 5 cm. away. He continues to search on the correct side. He is brought nearer as soon as he grasps the skin; he gropes and finds the nipple.

Same experiment and same result that evening. But, after several swallows, he is removed. He remains oriented to the correct side.

At 0;0(24) Laurent, during the same experiments, seems much faster. To localize his search it suffices for the nipple to be brushed by the outside of his lips and no longer only by the mucosa. Besides, as soon as he has noticed the nipple, his head's lateral movements become more rapid and precise (less extensive). Finally, it seems that he is henceforth capable not only of lateral movements but also of raising his head when his upper lip touches the nipple.

Observation 9.—At 0;0(22) Laurent is awakened an hour after his meal, and only cries faintly and intermittently. I place his right hand against his mouth but remove it before he begins to suck. Then, seven times in succession he does a complete imitation of sucking, opening and closing his mouth, moving his tongue, etc.

Observation 10.—Here are two facts revealing the differences in adaptation according to whether the need for nourishment is strong or weak. At .0;0(25) Laurent is lying on his back, not very hungry (he has not cried since his last meal) and his right cheek is touched by the nipple. He turns to the correct side but the breast is removed to a distance of 5 to 10 cm. For a few seconds he reaches in the right direction and then gives up. He is still lying on his back, facing the ceiling; after a moment his mouth begins to move slightly, then his head moves from side to side, finally settling on the wrong side. A brief search in this direction, then crying (with commissures of the lip lowered, etc.), and another pause. After a moment, another search in the wrong direction. No reaction when the middle of his right cheek is touched. Only when the nipple touches his skin about 1 cm. from his lips does he turn and grasp it.

On reading this description it would seem as though all the practice of the last weeks were in vain. It would seem, above all, that the excitation zone of the reflex stops about 1 cm. from the lips, and that the cheek itself is insensitive. But on the next day the same experiment yields opposite results, as we shall see.

At 0;0(26) Laurent is lying on his back, very hungry. I touch the middle of his cheek with my index finger bent first to the right, then to the left; each time he immediately turns to the correct side. Then he feels the nipple in the middle of his right cheek. But, as he tries to grasp it, it is withdrawn 10 cm. He then turns his head in the right direction and searches. He rests a moment, facing the ceiling, then his mouth begins to search again and his head immediately turns to the right side. This time he goes on to touch the nipple, first with his nose and then with the region between his nostrils and lips. Then he twice very distinctly repeats the movement observed at 0;0(24) (see Obs. 8): He raises his head in order to grasp the nipple. The first time he just catches the nipple with the corner of his lips and lets it go. A second or two later, he vigorously lifts his head and achieves his purpose.

The way in which he discerns the nipple should be noted; at 0;0(29) he explores its circumference with open and motionless lips before grasping it. . . .

THE USE OF REFLEXES

Concerning its *adaptation*, it is interesting to note that the reflex, no matter how well endowed with hereditary physiological mechanism, and no matter how stable its automatization, nevertheless needs to be used in order truly to adapt itself, and that it is capable of gradual accommodation to external reality.

Let us first stress this element of *accommodation*. The sucking reflex is hereditary and functions from birth, influenced either by diffuse impulsive movements or by an external excitant (Obs. 1); this is the point of departure. In order that a useful function may result, that is to say, swallowing, it often suffices to put the nipple in the mouth of the newborn child, but, as we know (Obs. 1), it sometimes happens that the child does not adapt at the first attempt. Only practice will lead to normal functioning. That is the first aspect of accommodation: contact with the object modifies, in a way, the activity of the reflex, and, even if this activity were oriented hereditarily to such contact, the latter is no less necessary to the consolidation of the former. This is how certain instincts are lost or certain reflexes cease to function normally, due to the lack of a suitable environment.* Moreover, contact with the

*Thus Larguier des Bancels (*Introduction à la Psychologie*, 1921, p. 178), after recalling Spalding's famous experiments concerning the decline of instincts in newly hatched chickens, adds: "The sucking instinct is transitory. A calf which has been separated from its mother and fed by hand for a day

environment not only results in developing the reflexes, but also in coordinating them in some way. Observations 2, 3, 5, and 8 show how the child, who first does not know how to suck the nipple when it is put in his mouth, grows increasingly able to grasp and even to find it, first after direct touch, then after contact with any neighboring region.*

How can such accommodations be explained? It seems to us difficult to invoke from birth the mechanism of acquired associations, in the limited sense of the term, or of "conditioned reflexes," both of which imply systematic training. On the contrary, the examining of these behavior patterns reveals at once the respects in which they differ from acquired associations: Whereas with regard to the latter, including conditioned reflexes, association is established between a certain perception, foreign to the realm of the reflex, and the reflex itself (for example, between a sound, a visual perception, etc., and the salivary reflex), according to our observations, it is simply the reflex's own sensibility (contact of the lips with a foreign body) which is generalized, that is to say, brings with it the action of the reflex in increasingly numerous situations. In the case of Observations 2, 3, 5, and 8, for example, accommodation consists essentially of progress in the continuity of the searching. In the beginning (Obs. 2 and 3) contact with any part of the breast whatever sets in motion momentary sucking of this region, immediately followed by crying or a desultory search, whereas after several days (Obs. 5), the same contact sets in motion a groping during which the child is headed toward success. It is very interesting, in the second case, to see how the reflex, excited by each contact with the breast, stops functioning as soon as the child perceives that sucking is not followed by any satisfaction, as is the taking of nourishment (see Obs. 5 and 8), and to see how the search goes on until swallowing begins. In this regard, Observations 2 to 8 confirm that there is a great variety of kinds of accommodation. Sucking of the eiderdown quilt, of the coverlet, etc., leads to rejection, that of the breast to acceptance; sucking of the skin (the child's hand, etc.) leads to acceptance if it is only a matter of sucking for the sake of sucking, but it leads to rejection (for example when it involves an area of the breast other than the nipple) if there is great hunger; the paternal index finger (Obs. 6) is rejected when the child is held against the breast, but is accepted as a pacifier, etc. In all behavior patterns it seems evident to us that learning is a function of the environment.

---

or two and then is taken to another cow, more often than not refuses to nurse. The child behaves somewhat similarly. If he is first spoon-fed, he subsequently has great difficulty in taking the breast again."

*See Preyer (L'Ame de l'Enfant, translated by Variguy, 1887, pp. 213–217), in particular the following lines: "To be sure, sucking is not as fruitful the first as the second day and I have often observed in normal newborn children (1869) that attempts at sucking were completely vain in the first hours of life: when I made the experiment of putting an ivory pencil in their mouth, they were still uncoordinated" (p. 215). Also: "It is well known that newborn children, when put to the breast do not find the nipple without help; they only find it by themselves a few days later (in one case only on the eighth day), that is to say, later than animals" (pp. 215–216). And: "When the child is put to the breast the nipple often does not enter his mouth and he sucks the neighboring skin; this is still evident in the third week . . ." (p. 216).

Surely all these facts admit of a physiological explanation which does not at all take us out of the realm of the reflex. The "irradiations," the "prolonged shocks," the "summations" of excitations, and the inter-coordination of reflexes probably explains why the child's searching becomes increasingly systematic, why contact which does not suffice to set the next operation in motion, does suffice in doing so a few days later, etc. Those are not necessarily mechanisms which are superposed on the reflex such as habit or intelligent understanding will be, later. But it remains no less true that the environment is indispensable to this operation, in other words, that reflex adaptation is partly accommodation. Without previous contact with the nipple and the experience of imbibing milk, it is very likely that the eiderdown quilt, the wool coverlet, or the paternal index finger, after setting in motion the suck-ing reflex, would not have been so briskly rejected by Laurent.*

But if, in reflex adaptation, allowances must be made for accom-modation, accommodation cannot be dissociated from progressive *assimi-lation*, inherent in the very use of the reflex. In a general way, one can say that the reflex is consolidated and strengthened by virtue of its own functioning. Such a fact is the most direct expression of the mechanism of assimilation. Assimilation is revealed, in the first place, by a growing need for repetition which characterizes the use of the reflex (functional assimilation) and, in the second place, by this sort of entirely practical or sensorimotor recognition which enables the child to adapt himself to the different objects with which his lips come in contact (recognitory and generalizing assimilations).

. . . Why does Lucienne suck her fingers soon after birth for ten minutes in succession? This could not be because of hunger, since the umbilical cord had just been cut. There certainly is an external excitant from the moment the lips touch the hand. But why does the excitation last, in such a case, since it does not lead to any result except, precisely, to the use of the reflex? It therefore seems that, from the start of this primitive mechanism, a sort of circular process accompanies the func-tion, the activity of the reflex having augmented due to its own use. If this interpretation remains doubtful, insofar as the point of departure is concerned, it obtains increasingly, on the other hand, with regard to subsequent behavior patterns. After the first feedings one observes, in Laurent (Obs. 2), suckinglike movements, in which it is difficult not to see a sort of autoexcitation. Besides, the progress in the search for the breast in Observations 2–5 and 8 seems also to show how much the function itself strengthened the tendency to suck. The counterproof of this is, as we have seen, the progressive decay of reflex mechanisms which are not used. How to interpret these facts? It is self-evident that "circular reaction," in Baldwin's sense of the term, could not yet be involved, that is to say, the repetition of a behavior pattern acquired or in the process of being acquired, and of behavior directed by the object to which it tends. Here it is only a matter of reflex and not acquired movements, and of sensibility connected with the reflex itself and not with the external objective. Nevertheless the mechanism is comparable

---

* In animals every slightly complicated reflex mechanism occasions re-actions of the same kind. The beginnings of copulation in the molluscs, for example, give way to very strange gropings before the act is adapted.

to it from the purely functional point of view. It is thus very clear, in Observation 9, that the slightest excitation can set in motion not only a reflex reaction but a succession of seven reactions. Without forming any hypothesis on the way of conserving this excitation, or a fortiori, without wanting to transform this repetition into intentional or mnemonic behavior, one is compelled to state that, in such a case, there is a tendency toward repetition, or, in objective terms, cumulative repetition.

This need for repetition is only one aspect of a more general process which we can qualify as assimilation. The tendency of the reflex being to reproduce itself, it incorporates into itself every object capable of fulfilling the function of excitant. Two distinct phenomena must be mentioned here, both equally significant from this particular point of view.

The first is what we may call "generalizing assimilation," that is to say, the incorporation of increasingly varied objects into the reflex schema. When, for example, the child is hungry but not sufficiently so to give way to rage and to crying, and his lips have been excited by some accidental contact, we witness the formation of this kind of behavior pattern, so important due to its own future developments and the innumerable analogous cases which we shall observe in connection with other schemata. Thus, according to chance contacts, the child, from the first two weeks of life, sucks his fingers, the fingers extended to him, his pillow, quilt, bedclothes, etc.; consequently he assimilates these objects to the activity of the reflex.

To be sure, we do not claim, when speaking of "generalizing" assimilation, that the newborn child begins by distinguishing a particular object (the mother's breast) and subsequently applies to other objects the discoveries he has made about this first one. . . . We simply maintain that, without any awareness of individual objects or of general laws, the newborn child at once incorporates into the global schema of sucking a number of increasingly varied objects, whence the generalizing aspect of this process of assimilation. . . . The assimilation of objects to its activity will gradually be generalized until, at the stage of acquired circular reactions and even at the stage of intentional movements, it gives birth to a very complex and strong schema. From the end of the second month the child will suck his thumb systematically (with acquired coordination and not by chance), then at nearly 5 months his hands will carry all objects to his mouth and he will end by using these behavior patterns to recognize bodies and even to compose the first form of space (Stern's "buccal space"). . . .

How to interpret this generalizing assimilation? The sucking reflex can be conceived as a global schema of coordinated movements which, if it is accompanied by awareness, certainly does not give rise to perception of objects or even of definite sensorial pictures but simply to an awareness of attitudes with at most some sensorimotor integration connected with the sensibility of the lips and mouth. Now this schema, due to the fact that it lends itself to repetitions and to cumulative use, is not limited to functioning under compulsion by a fixed excitant, external or internal, but functions in a way for itself. In other words, the child does not only suck in order to eat but also to elude hunger, to prolong the excitation of the meal, etc., and lastly, he sucks for the sake of sucking. It is in this sense that the object incorporated into the sucking schema is actually assimilated to the activity of this schema. The object sucked is to be conceived, not as nourishment for the organism in general, but, so to speak, as aliment for the very activity of sucking, according to its various forms. From the point of view of awareness, if there is awareness, such assimilation is at first lack of differentiation and not at first true generalization, but from the point of view of action, it is a generalizing extension of the schema which foretells (as has just been seen) later and much more important generalizations.

But, apart from this generalizing assimilation, another assimilation must be noted from the two first weeks of life, which we can call "recognitory assimilation." This second form seems inconsistent with the preceding one; actually it only reveals progress over the other, however slight. What we have just said regarding the lack of differentiation which characterizes generalizing assimilation is, in effect, true only with respect to states of slight hunger or of satiety. But it is enough that the child be very hungry for him to try to eat and thus to distinguish the nipple from the rest. This search and this selectivity seem to us to imply the beginning of differentiation in the global schema of sucking, and consequently a beginning of recognition, a completely practical and motor recognition, needless to say, but sufficient to be called recognitory assimilation. . . . How is this kind of recognition to be explained?

Of course there could be no question, either here or in connection with generalizing assimilation, of the recognition of an "object" for the obvious reason that there is nothing in the states of consciousness of a newborn child which could enable him to contrast an external universe with an internal universe. Supposing that there are given simultaneously visual sensations (simple vision of lights without forms or depth), acoustic sensations, and a tactile-gustatory and kinesthetic sensibility connected with the sucking reflex, it is evident that such a complexus would in no way be sufficient to constitute awareness of objects: the latter implies, as we shall see,* characteristically intellectual operations, necessary to secure the permanence of form and substance. Neither could there be a question of purely perceptive recognition or recognition of sensorial images presented by the external world, although such recognition considerably precedes the elaboration of objects (recognizing a person, a toy, or a linen cloth simply on "presentation" and before having a permanent concept of it). If, to the observer, the breast which the nursling is about to take is external to the child and constitutes an image separate from him, to the newborn child, on the contrary, there can only exist awareness of attitudes, of emotions, or sensations of hunger and of satisfaction. Neither sight nor hearing yet gives rise to perceptions independent of these general reactions. As H. Wallon has effectively demonstrated, external influences only have meaning in connection with the attitudes they arouse. When the nursling differentiates between the nipple and the rest of the breast, fingers, or other objects, he does not recognize either an object or a sensorial picture but simply rediscovers a sensorimotor and particular postural complex (sucking and swallowing combined) among several analogous

*Vol. 2, *The Construction of Reality in the Child* [Selection 20].

complexes which constitute his universe and reveal a total lack of differentiation between subject and object. In other words, this elementary recognition consists, in the strictest sense of the word, of "assimilation" of the whole of the data present in a definite organization which has already functioned and only gives rise to real discrimination due to its past functioning. But this suffices to explain in which respect repetition of the reflex leads by itself to recognitory assimilation which, albeit entirely practical, constitutes the beginning of knowledge. More precisely, repetition of the reflex leads to a general and generalizing assimilation of objects to its activity, but, due to the varieties which gradually enter this activity (sucking for its own sake, to stave off hunger, to eat, etc.), the schema of assimilation becomes differentiated and, in the most important differentiated cases, assimilation becomes recognitory.

In conclusion, assimilation belonging to the adaptation reflex appears in three forms: cumulative repetition, generalization of the activity with incorporation of new objects to it, and finally, motor recognition. But, in the last analysis, these three forms are but one: The reflex must be conceived as an organized totality whose nature it is to preserve itself by functioning and consequently to function sooner or later for its own sake (repetition) while incorporating into itself objects propitious to this functioning (generalized assimilation) and discerning situations necessary to certain special modes of its activity (motor recognition). . . .

The progressive adaptation of the reflex schemata, therefore, presupposes their *organization*. In physiology this truth is trite. Not only does the reflex arc as such presuppose an organization but, in the animal not undergoing laboratory experimentation, every reflex system constitutes in itself an organized totality. . . . From the psychological point of view, on the other hand, there is too great a tendency to consider a reflex, or even a complex instinctive act such as sucking, to be a summation of movements with, eventually, a succession of conscious states juxtaposed, and not as a real totality. But two essential circumstances induce us to consider the sucking act as already constituting psychic organization: The fact that sooner or later this act reveals a meaning, and the fact that it is accompanied by directed searching.

Concerning the meanings, we have seen how much sucking acts vary according to whether the newborn child is hungry and tries to nurse, or sucks in order to calm himself, or whether in a way he plays at sucking. It seems as though they have a meaning for the nursling himself. The increasing calm which succeeds a storm of crying and weeping as soon as the child is in position to take nourishment and to seek the nipple is sufficient evidence that, if awareness exists at all, such awareness is from the beginning awareness of meaning. But one meaning is necessarily relative to other meanings, even on the elementary plane of simple motor recognitions.

Furthermore, that organization exists is substantiated by the fact that there is directed search. The precocious searching of the child in contact with the breast, in spite of being commonplace, is a remarkable thing. Such searching, which is the beginning of accommodation and assimilation, must be conceived, from the point of view of organization, as the first manifestation of a duality of desire and satisfaction, consequently of value and reality, of complete totality and incomplete totality, a duality which is to reappear on all planes of future activity and which the entire evolution of the mind will try to abate, even though it is destined to be emphasized unceasingly.

Such are, from the dual point of view of adaptation and organization, the first expressions of psychological life connected with hereditary physiological mechanisms. This survey, though schematic, we believe suffices to show how the psyche prolongs purely reflex organization while depending on it. The physiology of the organism furnishes a hereditary mechanism which is already completely organized and virtually adapted but has never functioned. Psychology begins with the use of this mechanism. This use does not in any way change the mechanism itself, contrary to what may be observed in the later stages (acquisition of habits, of understanding, etc.). It is limited to strengthening it and to making it function without integrating it to new organizations which go beyond it. But within the limits of this functioning there is room for a historical development which marks precisely the beginning of psychological life. This development undoubtedly admits of a physiological explanation: if the reflex mechanism is strengthened by use or decays through lack of use, this is surely because coordinations are made or unmade by virtue of the laws of reflex activity. But a physiological explanation of this kind does not exclude the psychological point of view which we have taken. In effect, if, as is probable, states of awareness accompany a reflex mechanism as complicated as that of the sucking instinct, these states of awareness have an internal history. The same state of awareness could not twice reproduce itself identically. If it reproduces itself it is by acquiring in addition some new quality of what has already been seen, etc., consequently some meaning. But if, by chance, no state of awareness yet occurred, one could nevertheless speak of behavior or of behavior patterns, given, on the one hand, the *sui generis* character of their development and, on the other, their continuity with those of subsequent stages. We shall state this in precise terms in our conclusion.

The true character of these behavior patterns involves the individual utilization of experience. Insofar as the reflex is a hereditary mechanism it perhaps constitutes a racial utilization of experience. That is a biological problem which, while of highest interest to the psychologist, cannot be solved by his particular methods. But, inasmuch as it is a mechanism giving rise to use, and consequently a sort of experimental trial, the sucking reflex presupposes, in addition to heredity, an individual utilization of experience. This is the crucial fact which permits the incorporation of such a behavior pattern into the realm of psychology, whereas a simple reflex, unsubordinated to the need for use or experimental trial as a function of the environment (sneezing, for example) is of no interest to us. Of what does this experimental trial consist? An attempt can be made to define it without subordinating this analysis to any hypothesis concerning the kinds of states of consciousness which eventually accompany such a process. Learning connected with the reflex or instinctive mechanism is distinguished from the attainments due to habits or intelligence by the fact that it retains nothing external to the mechanism itself. A habit, such as that of a 2- or 3-month-old baby who pens his mouth on seeing an object, presupposes a mnemonic fixation related to this object. A tactilomotor schema is formed according to the variations of the object and this schema alone explains the uniformity of the reaction. In the same way the acquisition of an intellectual operation (counting, for instance) implies memory of the objects themselves or of experiments made with the objects. In both cases, therefore, something external to the initial mechanism of the act in question is retained. On the other hand, the baby who learns to suck retains nothing external to the act of sucking; he undoubtedly bears no trace either of the objects or the sensorial pictures on which later attempts have supervened. He merely records the series of attempts as simple acts which condition each other. When he recognizes the nipple, this does not involve recognition of a thing or of an image but rather the assimilation of one sensorimotor and postural complex to another. If the experimental trial involved in sucking presupposes environment and experience, since no functional use is possible without contact with the environment, this is a matter of a very special kind of experimental trial, of an autoapprenticeship to some extent and not of an actual acquisition. . . .

But the great psychological lesson of these beginnings of behavior is that, within the limits we have just defined, the experimental trial of a reflex mechanism already entails the most complicated accommodations, assimilations, and individual organizations. Accommodation exists because, even without retaining anything from the environment as such, the reflex mechanism needs the environment. Assimilation exists because, through its very use, it incorporates to itself every object capable of supplying it with what it needs and discriminates even these objects thanks to the identity of the differential attitudes they elicit. Finally, organization exists, inasmuch as organization is the internal aspect of this progressive adaptation. The sequential uses of the reflex mechanism constitute organized totalities and the gropings and searchings apparent from the beginnings of this period of experimental trial are oriented by the very structure of these totalities. . . .

ASSIMILATION: BASIC FACT OF PSYCHIC LIFE

In studying the use of reflexes we have ascertained the existence of a fundamental tendency whose manifestations we shall rediscover at each new stage of intellectual development: the tendency toward repetition of behavior patterns and toward the utilization of external objects in the framework of such repetition. . . .

Three circumstances induce us to consider assimilation the fundamental fact of psychic development. The first is that assimilation constitutes a process common to organized life and mental activity and is therefore an idea common to physiology and psychology. In effect, whatever the secret mechanism of biological assimilation may be, it is an empirical fact that an organ develops while functioning (by means of a certain useful exercise and fatigue). But when the organ in question affects the external behavior of the subject, this phenomenon of functional assimilation presents a physiological aspect inseparable from the psychological aspect; its parts are physiological whereas the reaction of the whole may be called psychic. Let us take for example the eye which develops under the influence of the use of vision (perception of lights, forms, etc.). From the physiological point of view it can be stated that light is nourishment for the eye (in particular in primitive cases of

cutaneous sensibility in the lower invertebrates, in whom the eye
amounts to an accumulation of pigment dependent on environing
sources of light). Light is absorbed and assimilated by sensitive tissues
and this action brings with it a correlative development of the organs
affected. Such a process undoubtedly presupposes an aggregate of
mechanisms whose start may be very complex. But, if we adhere to a
global description—that of behavior and consequently of psychology—
the things seen constitute nourishment essential to the eye since it is
they which impose the continuous use to which the organs owe their
development. The eye needs light images just as the whole body needs
chemical nourishment, energy, etc. Among the aggregate of external
realities assimilated by the organism there are some which are incorporated into the parts of the physico-chemical mechanisms, while others
simply serve as functional and general nourishment. In the first case,
there is physiological assimilation, whereas the second may be called
psychological assimilation. But the phenomenon is the same in both
cases: the universe is embodied in the activity of the subject.

In the second place, assimilation reveals the primitive fact generally
conceded to be the most elementary one of psychic life: repetition. How
can we explain why the individual, on however high a level of behavior,
tries to reproduce every experience he has lived? [This] is only comprehensible if the behavior which is repeated presents a functional
meaning, that is to say, assumes a value for the subject himself. But
whence comes this value? From functioning as such. Here again, functional assimilation is manifest as the basic fact.

In the third place, the concept of assimilation from the very first
embodies in the mechanism of repetition the essential element which
distinguishes activity from passive habit: the coordination of the new
with the old which foretells the process of judgment. In effect, the reproduction characteristic of the act of assimilation always implies the
incorporation of an actual fact into a given schema, this schema being
constituted by the repetition itself. In this way assimilation is the
greatest of all intellectual mechanisms and once more constitutes, in
relation to them, the truly basic fact. . . .

The Sixth Stage: Invention of New Means
through Mental Combinations*

The ensemble of intelligent behavior patterns studied hitherto—secondary circular reaction, application of familiar means to new situations,
tertiary circular reaction and discovery of new means through active
experimentation—characterizes a single big period. To be sure, there
is progress from one type to another behavior pattern and so one can
consider the three main groups which we have delineated in the preceding chapters as forming three sequential stages (it being understood

*[The following section is from Chapter VI.]

that the advent of each new stage does not abolish in any way the behavior patterns of the preceding stages and that new behavior patterns are simply superposed on the old ones). But the facts remain so complicated and their sequence can be so rapid that it would be dangerous to separate these stages too much. On the other hand, with the behavior patterns, which we are now going to describe, begins a new period which everyone will concur in considering as appearing tardily, much later than the preceding behavior patterns. We can therefore speak of a sixth stage which does not mean that the behavior patterns hitherto under study will disappear, but merely that they will henceforth be completed by behavior patterns of a new type: invention through deduction or mental combination.

This new type of behavior patterns characterizes systematic intelligence. Now it is the latter which, according to Claparède, is governed by awareness of relationships and no longer by empirical groping. It operates, according to Köhler, by sudden structurizations of the perceptual field or, according to Rignano, is based on purely mental experience. In short, all writers, whether associationists like Rignano, believers in "structures" like Köhler or, like Claparède, believers in a more or less directed groping, agree that there exists an essential moment in the development of intelligence: the moment when the awareness of relationships is sufficiently advanced to permit a reasoned prevision, that is to say, an invention operating by simple mental combination.

We are consequently confronted by the most delicate problem which any theory of intelligence has to treat: that of the power of invention. Hitherto the different forms of intellectual activity which we have had to describe have not presented particular difficulties of interpretation. . . . As soon as real invention arises the process of thought baffles analysis and seems to escape determinism. Will the schemata to which the preceding facts have accustomed us fail in the task, or will the new facts which we are about to describe appear once more to be prepared by all the functional mechanism of earlier activities? . . .

THE FACTS

First, here is a series of observations beginning with those most reminiscent of the discoveries due to directed groping. It happens that the same problem, such as that of the stick to be brought through the bars, can give rise to solutions through real invention as well as to solutions involving simple experimental groping. Analysis of such cases will enable us to see right away both the originality of the new behavior patterns and their relationship to the preceding ones. This relative contrast of solutions can be observed either in passing from one child to another or in the same child several months later.

Observation 177.—In order to explain the difference between the present and preceding behavior patterns it can be instructive to examine the way in which Laurent all at once discovered the use of the stick after not having known how to utilize that instrument for several months.

In contradistinction to Jacqueline and Lucienne whom we know were subjected to numerous experiments during which they had opportunity to "learn" to use the stick, Laurent only manipulated it at long intervals until the time when he knew how to use it spontaneously. It is therefore worthwhile, in order to characterize that moment, briefly to retrace the ensemble of Laurent's earlier behavior patterns relating to the stick.

As early as 0;4(20), that is to say, at the beginning of the third stage, Laurent is confronted by a short stick which he assimilates to some object. He shakes it, rubs it against the wicker of his bassinet, draws himself up, etc. In a general way he makes it the equivalent of the paper knife in Observation 104. But, at 0;4(21), when Laurent is holding the stick, he happens to strike a hanging toy and immediately continues. But during the next hours Laurent no longer tries to reproduce this result even when I put the stick back into his hand.—This first situation, then, is not an example of the "behavior pattern of the stick." Laurent confined himself to momentarily inserting a new element in an already constructed schema (the schema of striking). But the fortuitous intervention of the latter gave rise to no immediate comprehension or even experimentation. The following days I give him the stick again and try to make him associate it to the activity of the various schemata. But Laurent does not react then or in the following weeks. The "behavior pattern of the stick," that is to say, the utilization of the stick in the capacity of intermediate or instrument, does not seem able to be acquired during the stage of the secondary circular reactions, even when chance has favored the momentary insertion of the stick in an already existing schema.

In the course of the fourth stage, characterized by the coordination of the schemata, the use of the stick makes no progress. However, during this stage, the child comes to use the hand of another person as an intermediate to act upon distant objects, thus succeeding in spatializing causality and preparing the way for experimental behavior. But when, at 0;8 or even 0;9 I give Laurent the stick, he only uses it to strike around him and not yet to displace or bring to him the objects he hits.

At 1;0 (0)—that is to say, well into the fifth stage (it is during this stage that Jacqueline and Lucienne succeeded in discovering the utilization of the stick)—Laurent manipulates a long wooden ruler for a long time, but only arrives at the three following reactions. In the first place, he turns the stick over systematically while transferring it from one hand to the other. Then he strikes the floor, his shoes and various objects with it. In the third place, he displaces it by pushing it gently over the floor with his index finger. Several times I place, at a certain distance from the child, some attractive objective to see whether Laurent, already holding the stick, will know how to use it. But each time Laurent tries to attain the object with his free hand without having the idea of using the stick. Other times I place the stick on the floor, between the objective and the child, in order thus to provoke a visual suggestion. But the child does not react to that either.—There does not yet exist, therefore, any trace of the "behavior pattern of the stick."

At 1;0(5), on the other hand, Laurent is playing with a little child's cane which he handles for the first time. He is visibly surprised at the interdependence he observes between the two ends of his object. He displaces the cane in all directions, letting the free end drag along the floor, and studies the coming and going of this end as function of the movements he makes with the other end. In short, he begins to conceive of the stick as a rigid entity. But this discovery does not lead him to that of the instrumental signification of the stick. Having by chance struck a tin box with the cane, he again strikes it but without the idea either of making it advance in that way or of bringing it to him.—I replace the box with various more tempting objectives: the child's reaction remains the same.

At 1;2(25) I give him back the stick because of his recent progress. He has just learned to put objects on top of one another, to put them into a cup and turn it upside down, etc.: the relationships which belong to the level of the behavior pattern of the stick. He grasps the stick and immediately strikes the floor with it, then strikes various objects (boxes, etc.) placed on the floor. He displaces them gently but it does not occur to him to utilize this result systematically. At a given moment his stick gets caught in a rag and drags it for a few moments in the course of its movements. But when I put various desirable objectives 50 cm. or 1 m. away from Laurent he does not utilize the virtual instrument he holds.—It is apparent that, if I had repeated such experiments at this period, Laurent, like his sisters, would have discovered the use of the stick through directed groping and learning. But I broke off the attempt and only resumed it during the sixth stage.

At 1;4(5) Laurent is seated before a table and I place a bread crust in front of him, out of reach. Also, to the right of the child I place a stick about 25 cm. long. At first Laurent tries to grasp the bread without paying attention to the instrument, and then he gives up. I then put the stick between him and the bread; it does not touch the objective but nevertheless carries with it an undeniable visual suggestion. Laurent again looks at the bread, without moving, looks very briefly at the stick, then suddenly grasps it and directs it toward the bread. But he grasped it toward the middle and not at one of its ends so that it is too short to attain the objective. Laurent then puts it down and resumes stretching out his hand toward the bread. Then, without spending much time on this movement, he takes up the stick again, this time at one of its ends (chances or intention?), and draws the bread to him. He begins by simply touching it, as though contact of the stick with the objective were sufficient to set the latter in motion, but after one or two seconds at most he pushes the crust with real intention. He displaces it gently to the right, then draws it to him without difficulty. Two successive attempts yield the same result.

An hour later I place a toy in front of Laurent (out of his reach) and a new stick next to him. He does not even try to catch the objective with his hand; he immediately grasps the stick and draws the toy to him.

Thus it may be seen how Laurent has discovered the use of the stick almost without any groping when, during the preceding stages, he handled it without understanding its usefulness. This reaction is therefore distinctly different from that of his sisters.

Observation 178.—We recall Jacqueline's gropings at 1;3(12) when confronted by a stick to be brought through the bars of her playpen (Obs. 162). Now it happens that the same problem presented to Lucienne at 1;1(18) gives rise to an almost immediate solution in which invention surpasses groping. Lucienne is seated in front of the bars and I place against them, horizontally and parallel to the bars (half way up them) the stick of Observation 162. Lucienne grasps it at the middle and merely pulls it. Noticing her failure, she withdraws the stick, tilts it up, and brings it through easily.

I then place the stick on the floor. Instead of raising it to pull it directly, she grasps it by the middle, tilts it up beforehand and presses it. Or else she grasps it by one end and brings it in easily.

I start all over again with a longer stick (30 cm. long). Either she grasps it by the middle and tilts it up before pulling it, or else she brings it in by pulling on one end.

Same experiment with a stick 50 cm. long. The procedure is obviously the same but, when the stick gets caught, she pulls it away briefly, then lets it go with a groan and begins over again in a better way.

The next day, at 1;1(19), same experiments. Lucienne begins by merely pulling (once), then tilts up the stick and so rediscovers the procedures of the day before. At 1;2(7) I resume the observation. This time Lucienne tilts up the stick before it touches the bars.

It may thus be seen how these attempts are reminiscent of Jacqueline's, taking place through groping and learning. Lucienne begins by merely pulling the stick and repeats this once the next day. But, in contrast to her sister's prolonged efforts, Lucienne at once profits from her failure and uses a procedure which she invents right away through simple representation.

Observation 179.—The example of the watch chain to be put into an aperture 16 × 34 mm. is more complex. Here again we remember Jacqueline's gropings (Obs. 173 and 173 repeated). But Lucienne has solved the problem by sudden invention:

At 1;4(0) without ever having contemplated this spectacle, Lucienne looks at the box which I bring nearer and return without her having seen the contents. The chain spreads out on the floor and she immediately tries to put it back into the box. She begins by simply putting one end of the chain into the box and trying to make the rest follow progressively. This procedure

which was first tried by Jacqueline, Lucienne finds successful the first time
(the end put into the box stays there fortuitously), but fails completely at
the second and third attempts.

At the fourth attempt, Lucienne starts as before but pauses, and after a
short interval, herself places the chain on a flat surface nearby (the experiment takes place on a shawl), rolls it up in a ball intentionally, takes the ball
between three fingers, and puts the whole thing in the box.

The fifth attempt begins by a very short resumption of the first procedure. But Lucienne corrects herself at once and returns to the correct
method.

Sixth attempt: immediate success.

Thus one sees the difference between the behavior patterns of Jacqueline
and of Lucienne. What was, in the former, the product of a long apprenticeship, was suddenly invented by the latter. Such a difference is surely a question of the level. So it is that at 2;6(25) Jacqueline, with whom I repeat the
experiment, solves the problem unhesitatingly. By grasping the chain in both
hands she puts it in with her left hand while holding the remaining part in
her right, to prevent it from falling. In the event that it gets caught, she
corrects the movement.

Observation 180.—Another mental invention, derived from a mental combination and not only from a sensorimotor apprenticeship was that which
permitted Lucienne to rediscover an object inside a matchbox. At 1;4(0),
that is to say, right after the preceding experiment, I play at hiding the chain
in the same box used in Observation 179. I begin by opening the box as wide
as possible and putting the chain into its cover (where Lucienne herself put
it, but deeper). Lucienne, who has already practiced filling and emptying her
pail and various receptacles, then grasps the box and turns it over without
hesitation. No invention is involved of course (it is the simple application of
a schema, acquired through groping) but knowledge of this behavior pattern
of Lucienne is useful for understanding what follows.

Then I put the chain inside an empty matchbox (where the matches
belong), then close the box leaving an opening of 10 mm. Lucienne begins by
turning the whole thing over, then tries to grasp the chain through the opening. Not succeeding, she simply puts her index finger into the slit and so
succeeds in getting out a small fragment of the chain; she then pulls it until
she has completely solved the problem.

Here begins the experiment which we want to emphasize. I put the chain
back into the box and reduce the opening to 3 mm. It is understood that
Lucienne is not aware of the functioning of the opening and closing of the
matchbox and has not seen me prepare the experiment. She only possesses
the two preceding schemata: turning the box over in order to empty it of its
contents, and sliding her finger into the slit to make the chain come out. It is
of course this last procedure that she tries first: she puts her finger inside
and gropes to reach the chain, but fails completely. A pause follows during
which Lucienne manifests a very curious reaction bearing witness not only
to the fact that she tries to think out the situation and to represent to herself
through mental combination the operations to be performed, but also to the
role played by imitation in the genesis of representations. Lucienne mimics
the widening of the slit.

She looks at the slit with great attention; then, several times in succession, she opens and shuts her mouth, at first slightly, then wider and wider!
Apparently Lucienne understands the existence of a cavity underneath the
slit and wishes to enlarge that cavity. The attempt at representation which
she thus furnishes is expressed plastically, that is to say, due to inability to
think out the situation in words or clear visual images she uses a simple
motor indication as "signifier" or symbol. Now, as the motor reaction which
presents itself for filling this role is none other than imitation, that is to say,
representation by acts, which, doubtless earlier than any mental image, makes
it possible not only to divide into parts the spectacles seen but also to evoke
and reproduce them at will. Lucienne, by opening her mouth thus expresses,
or even reflects, her desire to enlarge the opening of the box. This schema
of imitation, with which she is familiar, constitutes for her the means of

thinking out the situation. There is doubtless added to it an element of magico-phenomenistic causality or efficacy. Just as she often uses imitation to act upon persons and make them reproduce their interesting movements, so also it is probable that the act of opening her mouth in front of the slit to be enlarged implies some underlying idea of efficacy.

Soon after this phase of plastic reflection, Lucienne unhesitatingly puts her finger in the slit and, instead of trying as before to reach the chain, she pulls so as to enlarge the opening. She succeeds and grasps the chain.

During the following attempts (the slit always being 3 mm. wide), the same procedure is immediately rediscovered. On the other hand, Lucienne is incapable of opening the box when it is completely closed. She gropes, throws the box on the floor, etc., but fails.

Observation 181.—At 1;6(23) for the first time Lucienne plays with a doll carriage whose handle comes to the height of her face. She rolls it over the carpet by pushing it. When she comes against a wall, she pulls, walking backward. But as this position is not convenient for her, she pauses and, without hesitation, goes to the other side to push the carriage again. She therefore found the procedure in one attempt, apparently through analogy to other situations but without training, apprenticeship, or chance.

In the same kind of inventions, that is to say, in the realm of kinematic representations, the following fact should be cited. At 1;10(27) Lucienne tries to kneel before a stool but, by leaning against it, pushes it further away. She then raises herself up, takes it, and places it against a sofa. When it is firmly set there she leans against it and kneels without difficulty.

Observation 181 repeated.—In the same way Jacqueline, at 1;8(9) arrives at a closed door—with a blade of grass in each hand. She stretches out her right hand toward the knob but sees that she cannot turn it without letting go of the grass. She puts the grass on the floor, opens the door, picks up the grass again, and enters. But when she wants to leave the room things become complicated. She puts the grass on the floor and grasps the doorknob. But then she perceives that in pulling the door toward her she will simultaneously chase away the grass which she placed between the door and the threshold. She therefore picks it up in order to put it outside the door's zone of movement.

This ensemble of operations, which in no way comprises remarkable invention, is nevertheless very characteristic of the intelligent acts founded upon representation or the awareness of relationships.

Observation 182.—At 1;8(30) Jacqueline has an ivory plate in front of her, pierced by holes of 1–2 mm. in diameter and watches me put the point of a pencil in one of the holes. The pencil remains stuck vertically there and Jacqueline laughs. She grasps the pencil and repeats the operation. Then I hold out another pencil to her but with the unsharpened end directed toward the plate. Jacqueline grasps it but does not turn it over and tries to introduce this end (the pencil is 5 mm. in diameter) into each of the three holes in succession. She keeps this up for quite awhile even returning to the smallest holes. On this occasion we make three kinds of observations:

(1) When I return the first pencil to Jacqueline she puts it in the hole correctly at once. When I hand it to her upside down, she turns it over even before making an attempt, thus revealing that she is very capable of understanding the conditions for putting it in. On the other hand, when I hold out the second pencil correctly directed (the point down) she also puts it in by the point. But if I offer it to her upside down she does not turn it over and recommences wishing to put it in by the unsharpened end. This behavior pattern remained absolutely constant during thirty attempts, that is to say, Jacqueline never turned the second pencil over whereas she always directed the first one correctly. Everything happens as though the first attempts had given rise to a sensorimotor schema which persisted in acting during the whole series: the two pencils were accordingly conceived as being in contrast to each other, the first being that which one puts into the hole easily and the second that which resists. However, the pencils are of course identical from the point of view of the facility with which they can be put in the hole; the first is merely shorter than the second and is green and the second is brown (both have hard, black lead).

(2) Several times Jacqueline, seeing the second pencil will not go in, tries to put it in the same hole as the first one. Hence, not only does she try to put it in by the unsharpened end but also she wants to put it into a hole which is already filled by the other pencil. She resumed this strange procedure several times despite total failure. This observation shows very well how, in a child of this age, representation of things is still ignorant of the most elementary mechanical and physical laws and so makes it possible to understand why Jacqueline so obstinately tries to put in the second pencil by the wrong end. Ignorant of the fact that two objects cannot occupy the same small opening, there is no reason for her not to try to put an object 5 mm. in diameter in a 1–2 mm. hole.

(3) At about the thirtieth attempt, Jacqueline suddenly changes methods. She turns the second pencil over as she does the first and no longer tries a single time to put it in by the wrong end. If the series of these new attempts is compared with the first series, one has the impression of a sudden understanding, as of an idea which arises and which, when it has suddenly appeared, definitively imposes itself. In other words, the second pencil has suddenly been assimilated to the first. The primitive schema (connecting the two pencils by contrast) has dissociated itself and the pencil which one did not turn over has been assimilated to the particular schema of the pencil that one had to turn over. This kind of a process is consequently again capable of making us understand the mechanism of invention.

The respect in which these behavior patterns are original in relation to the preceding ones may thus be seen. The child finds himself in a situation which is new to him, that is to say, the objects arising between his intentions and the arrival at an end demand unforeseen and particular adaptation. It is therefore necessary to find adequate means. Now these means cannot be brought back to the procedures acquired earlier in other circumstances (as in the "application of familiar means to new circumstances"); it is therefore necessary to innovate. If these behavior patterns are compared to all the preceding ones, they resemble most the "discovery of new means through active experimentation." Their functional context is exactly the same. But, contrary to the latter, the present behavior patterns do not appear to operate by groping or [learning], but by sudden invention; that is to say, that instead of being controlled at each of the stages and a posteriori by the facts themselves, the searching is controlled a priori by mental combination. Before trying them, the child foresees which maneuvers will fail and which will succeed. The control of the experiment therefore bears upon the whole of this deduction and no longer, as before, upon the details of each particular step. Moreover, the procedure conceived as being capable of succeeding is in itself new, that is to say, it results from an original mental combination and not from a combination of movements actually executed at each stage of the operation.

INVENTION AND REPRESENTATION

The two essential questions raised by such behavior patterns in relation to the preceding ones are those of *invention* and *representation*. Henceforth there exists invention and no longer only discovery; there is, moreover, representation and no longer only sensorimotor groping. These two aspects of systematic intelligence are interdependent. To invent is to combine mental, that is to say, representative, schemata and, in order to become mental the sensorimotor schemata must be capable of intercombining in every way, that is to say, of being able to give rise to true inventions.

How can this transition from directed gropings to invention, and from motor schema to representative schema be explained? Let us begin by establishing the continuity between the extremes in order subsequently to account for the differentiations.

It must be understood, with regard to the first point of view, that the contrast between directed groping and actual *invention* is primarily due to a difference in speed. The structuring activity of assimilation only operates step by step in the course of experimental groping, so that it is not immediately visible, and one is tempted to attribute the discoveries which result from it solely to fortuitous contact with external facts. In invention, on the contrary, it is so rapid that the structurization seems sudden. The structuring assimilatory activity thus once again passes unnoticed at first glance and one is tempted to consider the "structures" as organizing themselves. Thereafter the contrast between the empiricism of simple groping and the intelligence of deductive invention seems to be complete. But if one thinks about the role of intellectual activity peculiar to combined assimilation and accommodation, one perceives that this activity is neither absent from empirical groping nor useless to the structuring of representations. On the contrary, it constitutes the real motor of both, and the primary difference between the two situations stems from the speed at which the motor goes, a speed slowed down in the first case by the obstacles on the road and accelerated in the second case by the training acquired.

But this continuous increase of speed entails a differentiation in the very procedure of the functioning. At first cut up and visible from the outside, it becomes regularized and seems to be internalized by becoming rapid. In this respect, the difference between empirical groping and invention is comparable to that which separates induction from deduction. The empiricists have tried to reduce the second to the first, thus making induction the only genuine reasoning. Induction being, according to them, only a passive recording of the results of experience, deduction then became a sort of internal replica of this experience, a "mental [experiment]" as Mach and Rignano put it. In contrast to this thesis is that of a certain logicism according to which induction and deduction have nothing in common, the former consisting, according to the empiricists, in a catalogue of statements, and the second in purely formal combinations. At last came the sound [logical] analysis which showed the relationship as well as the contrast between these two complementary processes. Both consist in constructions of relationships, induction thus involving deduction and resting upon its constructive activity. But in the first, construction is ceaselessly controlled from without and so can appeal to those extralogical procedures of anticipation which appeared to the empiricists to constitute the essence of thought, whereas in the second, construction is regulated from within, solely by the play of operations. So also, empirical groping already presupposes the mechanism of invention. As we have seen, there is no pure accommodation, but accommodation is always directed by a play of schemata whose reorganization, if it were spontaneous, would become identified with the constructive deduction of the present behavior patterns. But as this reorganization peculiar to accommodation is unable, when the problem transcends the subject's level, to dispense with a continuous external control, it always works through cumulative assimilation; that is to say, the structuring activity keeps a slow pace and only intercombines the sequential data of assimilation. In the present case, on the contrary, in which the question raised is addressed to a mind sufficiently furnished with already constructed schemata so that the reorganization of these schemata operates spontaneously, the structuring activity no longer needs always to depend on the actual data of perception and, in the interpretation of these data, can make a complex system of simply evoked schemata converge. Invention is nothing other than this rapid reorganization, and representation amounts to this evocation, both thus extending the mechanisms at work in the ensemble of the preceding behavior patterns.

From this point of view let us again take up Observations 177–182, comparing them to the mechanism of empirical gropings. As before, the point of departure of these behavior patterns consists in the impetus given by the schema assigning an end to the action; for instance, in Observation 180, sight of the chain in the matchbox sets in motion the schema of grasping. This schema of the goal immediately arouses a certain number of schemata which the child will utilize as initial means and which he must accommodate, that is to say, differentiate according to the variations of the new situation. In Observation 180, Lucienne tries to turn the box over or to slide her finger into the slit in order to extract the chain. But in utilizing these schemata the child perceives at the same time the difficulties of the present situation. In other words, there occurs here, as in the course of empirical groping, an encounter with the unforeseen fact which creates an obstacle (the slit is too narrow to admit the finger). Now in both cases, this encounter entails a new intervention of earlier schemata. It is due to the latter that these unforeseen facts acquire meaning. The only difference is that, henceforth, such encounters with the obstacle no longer take place in the course of discovery (since the latter is no longer groping and consists in sudden invention) but beforehand, at the moment when the first procedures tried out as hypotheses fail, and when the problem is clarified by virtue of that very failure. In Observation 180, these auxiliary schemata which attribute a meaning to the facts are those that permit the child to understand what the slit is that he sees before him (= sign of a subjacent opening) and how it is troublesome (because it is too narrow). The child often opens and closes boxes, wants to put his hand through very small openings, etc. Those are the schemata which confer a meaning on the present situation and which at the same time direct the search. They intervene, therefore, as secondary means and hence are subordinated to the initial procedure. It is then that invention comes in, in the form of sudden accommodation of the ensemble of those schemata to the present situation. How does this accommodation work?

It consists, as always, in differentiating the preceding schemata according to the variations of the present situation, but this differentiation, instead of operating through actual groping and cumulative assimilation, results from a spontaneous assimilation, hence more rapid and operating by means of simply representative attempts. In other words, instead of exploring the slit with his finger and groping until he has discovered the procedure which consists in drawing to him the inner side (of the box) in order to enlarge the opening; the child is satisfied to look at the opening, except for experimenting no longer on it directly, but on its symbolic substitutes. Lucienne opens and closes her mouth while examining the slit of the box, proving that she is in the act of assimilating it and of mentally trying out the enlargement of the slit; moreover, the analogy thus established by assimilation between the slit perceived and other openings simply evoked leads her to foresee that pressure put on the edge of the opening will widen it. Once the schemata have thus been spontaneously accommodated on the plane of simple mental assimilation, Lucienne proceeds to act and succeeds right away.

An interpretation of this sort applies to each of our observations. In Observation 179, for example, if Lucienne rolls the chain up into a ball to put in into the box after having noted the failure of the direct method, it is because the schemata acquired in putting the chain into a pail or a necklace into a watering can (Obs. 172) or again in squeezing materials, putting her pillow or handkerchief in her mouth, etc., afford her sufficient assimilation of the new situation. Instead of groping she mentally combines the operations to be performed. But this mental experience does not consist in mnemonic evocation of already manufactured images; it is an essentially constructive process the representation of which is only a symbolic adjuvant, since genuine invention exists and it never perceived a reality identical to the one it is in the process of elaborating. In Observations 180 and 180 repeated there also exists spontaneous functioning of the schemata of displacement, by analogy, to be sure, with the experiments the child was able to make in reality, but this analogy entails imagination of new combinations. Finally, in Observation 182, we see how an initial schema can be differentiated, without progressive groping, through sudden dissociation and assimilation.*

*In order better to understand the mechanism of this assimilation which has become deductive while remaining on the plane of sensorimotor operations, let us again analyze a case of elementary practical invention observed in an adult and consequently capable of correct introspection. While driving an old automobile I am bothered by oil on the steering wheel which makes it slippery. Lacking time to stop, I take out my handkerchief and dry the spots. When putting it in my pocket I observe that it is too greasy and look for a place to put it without soiling anything. I put it between my seat and the one next to me, as deeply as possible in the crevice. An hour later the rain forces me to close the windshield but the resulting heat makes me try to open it a little. The screws being worn out, I cannot succeed; it only stays wide open or completely shut. I try to hold the windshield slightly open with my left hand, but my fatigue makes me think that some object could replace my hand. I look around me, but nothing is in evidence. While looking at the windshield I have the impression that the object could be put, not at the bottom of the windshield (one pushed it at the bottom to open it), but by wedging it in the angle formed by the right edge of the windshield and the vertical upright of the body of the car. I have the vague feeling of an analogy between the solution to be found and a problem already solved before. The solution then becomes clarified. My tendency to put an object into the corner of the windshield meets a sort of motor memory of having just a few minutes before placed something into a crevice. I try to remember what it was, but no definite representation comes to mind. Then suddenly, without having time to imagine anything, I understand the solution and find myself

But how can we account for the mechanism of this spontaneous reorganization of schemata? Take, for example, the construction of the schema of "rolling into a ball" in Observation 179, or that of "widening the slit" in Observation 180; does this construction consist in a sudden structurization of representations or of the perceptual field, or is it the result of assimilatory activities prior to invention? As we have just recalled, a certain number of already acquired schemata direct the search at the moment of invention without, however, any one of them containing in itself the correct solution. For example, before rolling the chain up into a ball to put it in the narrow opening, Lucienne has already: (1) squeezed the material, (2) put the chain in a wide opening, and (3) compared large objects to inadequate openings (as when she tried to bring objects through the bars of her playpen). In Observation 180 she also possesses the earlier schemata we have already emphasized. The question raised is therefore to find out how these schemata will inter-coordinate in order to give rise to invention: Is it by a structuring independent of their genesis or due to the very activity which engendered them and which is now pursued without any longer depending on the external circumstances in which it began? One might as well ask whether ideas organize themselves in the course of theoretical invention or whether they are organized as a function of implicit judgments and of the potential intelligent activity they represent. We do not doubt that the second of these two theses is in both cases (in sensorimotor intelligence as well as in reflective thought) much the most satisfying to the mind, the first only consisting in a manner of speaking which veils the dynamism of the facts with static language.

But how is this reorganization of schemata to be conceived if it must fulfill the dual condition of extending their assimilatory activity and of liberating itself from the external circumstances in which this activity began? It is due to the process of reciprocal assimilation but insofar as it is henceforth extended on a plane independent of the immediate action.

Here we rediscover a remark already made in connection with the "application of familiar means to new circumstances"; it is that, in the act of practical intelligence, means are subordinated to ends through a coordination analogous to that of the heterogeneous schemata in the case of intersensorial coordinations (hearing and sight, etc.), hence through reciprocal assimilation of the schemata. In other words, each schema tends to extend the assimilatory activity that gave rise to it (just as every idea tends to extend the judgments from which it derived), and consequently applies to the ensemble of the situations which lend them-

---

already in the act of searching with my hand for the hidden handkerchief. Therefore the latter schema directed my search and directed me toward the lateral corner of the windshield when my last idea was a different one.

This trite observation demonstrates very well how a sensorimotor search can arouse schemata previously acquired and make them function independently of internal language and clear representation. The tendency to introduce an object into a slit, in this example, is modeled exactly on a schema remaining in an almost purely motor state, and the conjunction thus produced suffices to insure discovery of a solution. One therefore understands how a sensorimotor deduction is possible in the small child through simple practical evocation of the schemata and independently of a well-defined system of representations.

selves to it. Thereafter, when there is a watch chain to be put into a narrow opening, the schemata presenting some analogy to the situation and so capable of assimilating the data will enter into activity by themselves. We have constantly met with examples illustrating this process. But, until the present time, the activity thus set in motion has always given rise to real actions, that is to say, to immediate applications ("application of familiar means to new circumstances") or to empirical gropings. The novelty of the case of invention consists, on the contrary, in that henceforth the schemata entering into action remain in a state of latent activity and combine with each other before (and not after) their external and material application. This is why invention seems to come from the void. The act which suddenly arises results from a previous reciprocal assimilation instead of manifesting its vicissitudes before everyone. Introspection enabled us to observe clearly how the schema of the handkerchief wedged down into a slit assimilated progressively and mentally the schema of the object to be slid into the opening of the windshield and vice versa, this reciprocal assimilation bringing with it the invention of the correct solution. With respect to Lucienne, Observation 180 also shows this explanation to be well founded. The gesture of opening and closing the mouth in the presence of the opening to be widened indicates sufficiently clearly how the internal reorganization of the schemata works through assimilation. G. Tarde's* well-known formula illustrates this mechanism: Invention, Tarde said, results from the interference of independent currents of action. The process of this interference could only be, in our language, that of reciprocal assimilation.

    . . . Once the goal has been set and the difficulties encountered by the use of initial means have been perceived, the schemata of the goal, those of the initial means and the auxiliary schemata (evoked by awareness of the difficulties) organize themselves into a new totality, without there being need of external groping to support their activity.

    It is therefore inaccurate to speak, as does the empiric theory of "mental experiment," of a simple internalization of earlier actual experiences; what has been internalized is solely the knowledge acquired due to these experiences. But actual or external experience involves from the outset, as does simply mental deduction, an internal assimilatory activity which forms schemata, and it is this activity, internal from the very beginning, which henceforth functions by itself without having any further need of external alimentation. Let us keep the term "mental experiment" to designate these primitive deductions. But this is on condition that we remember that all experience, including empirical groping, presupposes a previous organization of assimilatory schemata and that contact with the facts is nothing, at any level, outside of accommodation to these schemata. The baby who mentally combines the operations to be performed in order to widen the slit of the matchbox is in the same situation as the older child who no longer needs to count apples with his fingers in order to establish that "2 + 2 are 4" and who confines himself to combining the numbers. . . . Deduction thus appears at its beginnings as the direct extension of earlier mechanisms of assimi-

*G. Tarde, *Les lois sociales* (Paris; Alcan).

lation and accommodation, but on a plane which begins to become differentiated from direct perception and action.

Thereafter can one state, as does the theory at the opposite extreme, that invention is due to an immediate structuring of the perceptual field independently of any [learning] and of earlier actions? The foregoing observations do not seem to favor so radical a thesis any more than the thesis of "mental experiment" of the pure empiricists. The defect of the empirical thesis is that it does not explain the creative element of invention. By making all deduction the internal repetition of external gropings, it ends by negating the existence of a constructive activity remaining internal (at all levels) and which alone accounts for the progressive purification of reasoning. But the theory of "structures," by emphasizing the originality of invention too much, leads to the same result and, in order to account for novelties without invoking the activity belonging to combined assimilation and accommodation, finds itself obliged to attribute them to a structural preformation. While empirical associationism considered all constructive deduction as being the internal replica of external experiences already completely organized, according to the theory of structures it is an outward projection of internal forms also completely prepared in advance (because they are connected with the nervous system, with the a priori laws of perception, etc.). But analysis of the assimilatory activity leads us to doubt this. . . . The assimilatory schema is not an entity separable from assimilatory and accommodating activity. It is only formed by functioning and it only functions in experience. The essential is, therefore, not the schema insofar as it is a structure, but the structuring activity which gives rise to the schemata. Thereafter if, at a given moment, the schemata reorganize themselves until they bring about inventions through mental combination, it is simply because the assimilatory activity, trained by many months of application to the concrete data of perception, finally functions by itself by only using representative symbols. That does not mean at all, let us repeat, that this purification is a simple internalization of earlier experiences: Gestalt psychology has happily emphasized this point by showing that the reorganization peculiar to invention creates the new. But that means that the reorganization is not produced by itself, as though the schemata were endowed with a structure independently of the assimilatory activity which gave rise to them; the reorganization that characterizes invention simply extends this activity. So it is that, in observing our children (Obs. 177–182) and doubtless every time the history of the subjects examined is known in detail, it is possible to discover which old schemata intervened in the course of invention. Invention is no less creative, for all this, but it also presupposes a genetic process which functioned long before it.

What is now the role of *representation* in these first sensorimotor deductions? At first it seems vital: due to representation, reciprocal assimilation can remain internal instead of giving rise, from the outset, to empirical gropings. It is therefore due to representation that "mental experiment" succeeds actual experimentation and that assimilatory activity can be pursued and purified on a new plane, separate from that of immediate perception or action properly so called. That explains how Köhler, in his research concerning animal intelligence, was led to place all emphasis on the reorganization of the field of perception, as though it were that reorganization which brought intellectual invention after it, and not the reverse.* Representation is, in effect, a novelty essential to the formation of the behavior patterns of the present stage; it differentiates these behavior patterns from those of earlier stages. As we have seen, the most complex behavior patterns of the preceding stages, including the "discovery of new means through active experimentation," can dispense with representations, if one defines the latter as the evocation of absent objects. The motor anticipation peculiar to the mobile schemata of assimilation suffices to insure the comprehension of signs and the coordination of means and ends, without need for perception to substitute for representation. Rolling a chain up into a ball to put it in a narrow opening (when the subject never had occasion to roll anything up in such circumstances), combining in advance the positions of a stick before bringing it through bars (when the experiment is new to the child), widening a slit in advance in order to pull a hidden object out of it (when the child comes to grips with such a problem for the first time), all that presupposes that the subject represents the data offered to his sight otherwise than he perceives them directly. In his mind he corrects the thing he looks at; that is to say, he evokes positions, displacements, or perhaps even objects without actually contemplating them in his visual field.

But if representation accordingly constitutes an essential acquisition, characteristic of this stage, we should not, however, exaggerate its scope. Representation is surely necessary for invention, but it would be erroneous to consider it the only cause. Furthermore, it can be maintained, with at least as much verisimilitude, that representation results from invention. The dynamic process belonging to the latter precedes the organization of images, since invention arises from spontaneous functioning of the schemata of assimilation. The truth seems to be that between invention and representation there is interaction and not simply a connection. What can be the nature of this interaction?

Things are clarified as soon as, with the theory of signs, one makes of the visual imagery peculiar to representation, a simple symbolism serving as "signifier," and of the dynamic process peculiar to invention the signification itself, in other words, the signified. Representation would thus serve as symbol to inventive activity which takes away nothing from its utility, since the symbol is necessary for deduction, but which relieves it of the burden of the too difficult role it is sometimes made to play of being the motor of invention itself.

Here it is necessary to distinguish between two cases. The first is that in which the child merely evokes a movement or an operation already performed previously. For instance, when Lucienne perceives that her stick does not enter through the bars and that she tilts it up before trying to bring it through (Obs. 178), it is very possible that, in combining the new movements required by the operation, she visually evokes the movements of the stick previously performed (either just before or during other experiments). In that case representation plays the role of simple visual memory and one might think that invention

---

*This role attributed to visual representation is not essential to Gestalt explanations, as revealed by the applications made by K. Lewin of the theory of form to the activity itself.

consists in merely intercombining these image memories. Unfortunately this simple hypothesis, [on which alone] the associationist theory of mental experiment rests, encounters serious obstacles. Observation does not seem to show at all that during the first year of life the visual image extends action so easily. The observations described in connection with the "invention of new means through active experimentation" (Obs. 148–174) would be unexplainable if visual imagery formed itself by itself as a function of perception. How can it be explained, for example, that in Observation 165 Jacqueline had so much difficulty in profiting from her experiences (impossibility of bringing the rooster through the bars) if an adequate visual representation allowed her to record what she sees? It seems, on the contrary, in such a case as though the [learning] were of a motor kind and the image did not yet extend the movement. It would seem difficult to interpret invention through mental combination as a simple reorganization of the perceptual field. That reorganization results from the organization of the movements themselves and does not precede it. If images intervene it is therefore in the capacity of symbols accompanying the motor process and permitting the schemata to depend on them to function by themselves, independently of immediate perception. Images are not in this case elements but simply the tools of nascent thought. . . .

In short, the fact that invention is accompanied by representation does not speak in favor either of the associationist theory of mental experiment or even of the thesis of a spontaneous reorganization of the perceptual field, the thesis maintained by certain famous works derived from the Gestalt theory. All representation admits of two groups of elements which correspond to words or symbols, on the one hand, and to the concepts themselves, on the other, with regard to theoretical representation: Those are the signs and significations. Now the image is to be classed in the first group, whereas the second group is formed by the schemata themselves whose activity engenders invention. This shows that if invention presupposes representation, the converse is true, because the system of signs could not be elaborated independently of that of significations.

The manner of this advent of the image still remains to be clarified, inasmuch as it is derived from the activity of the schemata. But this is not the place to discuss it, for an important question must first be taken up: the problem of imitation. If it is true that the image does not, from the outset, accompany the movement, an intermediate term must be able to explain the transition from the motor to the representative and the image must in some way be acted before being thought. This intermediate is none other than imitation. . . .

. . . On the one hand, due to the progress of accommodation (which, as we shall state later on, is perforce extended in imitation), signs are modeled increasingly upon the characteristics of things and so tend to form "images." On the other hand, due to the progressive detachment of signs [from] immediate action for the benefit of mental combination, these images are liberated from direct perception and become "symbolic."

One observes this dual movement in the facts of imitation and of play. Imitation characteristic of the sixth stage becomes representative as much because the child begins to imitate new movements by means of parts of his body invisible to him (imitation relating to head movements, etc., which leads to a representation of his own face), as because of the "deferred imitations" which presage symbolism (imitating absent persons, etc.). On the other hand, play, during the same period, becomes symbolic inasmuch as it begins to involve the "as if."

Now, from the point of view of meanings and of intelligence in general, the development of representations is not only predicated on the "invention of new means through mental combination" but on a series of other behavior patterns bearing witness to the existence of representative images necessary for the evocation of absent objects. Here is one example:

Observation 183.—At 1;6(8) Jacqueline plays with a fish, a swan and a frog which she puts in a box, takes them out again, puts them back in, etc. [At one point she loses] the frog. She places the swan and the fish in the box and then obviously looks for the frog. She lifts everything within reach (a big cover, a rug, etc.) and (long after beginning to search) begins to say *inine, inine* (= *"grenouille"* = "frog"). It is not the word which set the search in motion, but the opposite. There was therefore evocation of an absent object without any directly perceived stimulus. Sight of the box in which are found only two objects out of three provoked representation of the frog, and whether this representation preceded or accompanied the act is of little importance.

Thus may be seen the unity of the behavior patterns of the sixth stage: Mental combination of schemata with possibility of deduction surpassing actual experimentation, invention, representative evocation by image symbols, so many characteristics marking the completion of sensorimotor intelligence and making it henceforth capable of entering the framework of language to be transformed, with the aid of the social group, into reflective intelligence.

20

The Construction of Reality in the Child

1937

*The Development of Object Concept**

To understand how the budding intelligence constructs the external world, we must first ask whether the child, in its first months of life, conceives and perceives things as we do, as objects that have substance, that are permanent and of constant dimensions. If this is not the case, it is then necessary to explain how the idea of an object (object concept) is built up. The problem is closely connected with that of space. A world without objects would not present the character of spatial homogeneity and of coherence in displacements that marks our universe. Inversely the absence of "groups" in the changes of position would be equivalent to endless transformations, that is, continuous changes of states in the absence of any permanent object. In this first chapter, then, substance and space should be considered simultaneously, and it is only through abstraction that we shall limit ourselves to object concept.

A question of this sort conditions all other questions. A world composed of permanent objects constitutes not only a spatial universe but also a world obeying the principle of causality in the form of relationships between things, and regulated in time, without continuous annihilations or resurrections. Hence it is a universe both stable and external, relatively distinct from the internal world and one in which the subject places himself as one particular term among all the other terms. A universe without objects, on the other hand, is a world in which space does not constitute a solid environment but is limited to structuring the subject's very acts; it is a world of pictures each one of which can be known and analyzed but which disappear and reappear capriciously. From the point of view of causality it is a world in which the connections between things are masked by the relations between the action and its desired results; hence the subject's activity is conceived as being the primary and almost the sole motive power. As far as the boundaries

*From J. Piaget, *The Construction of Reality in the Child* by Margaret Cook, translator, © 1954 by Basic Books, Inc., Publishers, New York. Reprinted with permission of Basic Books and Routledge & Kegan Paul Ltd., London. Originally published in French 1937.

Note: [The following section is from Chapter I.]

between the self and the external world are concerned, a universe without objects is such that the self, lacking knowledge of itself, is absorbed in external pictures for want of knowing itself; moreover, these pictures center upon the self by failing to include it as a thing among other things, and thus fail to sustain interrelationships independent of the self.

Observation and experimentation combined seem to show that object concept, far from being innate or given ready-made in experience, is constructed little by little. Six stages can be discerned, corresponding to those of intellectual development in general. During the first two stages (those of reflexes and the earliest habits), the infantile universe is formed of pictures that can be recognized but that have no substantial permanence or spatial organization. During the third stage (secondary circular reactions), a beginning of permanence is conferred on things by prolongation of the movements of accommodation (grasping, etc.) but no systematic search for absent objects is yet observable. During the fourth stage ("application of known means to new situations") there is searching for objects that have disappeared but no regard for their displacements. During a fifth stage (about 12 to 18 months old) the object is constituted to the extent that it is permanent individual substance and inserted in the groups of displacements, but the child still cannot take account of changes of position brought about outside the field of direct perception. In a sixth stage (beginning at the age of 16 to 18 months) there is an image of absent objects and their displacements.

FIRST TWO STAGES: NO SPECIAL BEHAVIOR

RELATED TO VANISHED OBJECTS

Among all the impressions which assail his consciousness, the child distinguishes and quickly recognizes certain stable groups which we shall call pictures. That is why we have stated that every schema of reproduction assimilation is extended sooner or later in generalizing assimilation and recognitory assimilation combined, recognition being derived from assimilation.

The most elementary example of this process is incontestably that of sucking. The nursling, from the second week of life, is capable of finding the nipple and differentiating it from the surrounding teguments; therein is proof that the schema of sucking in order to nurse begins to be dissociated from the schemata of empty sucking or of sucking at random, and thus results in recognition through acts. So also, after the fifth to the sixth week of life, the child's smile reveals that he recognizes familiar voices or faces whereas strange sounds or images astonish him. In a general way, every functional use (hence all primary circular reaction) of sucking, of sight, of hearing, of touch, etc., gives rise to recognitions.

But none of that proves or even suggests that in the first weeks of life the universe is really cut up into objects, that is, into things conceived as permanent, substantial, external to the self, and firm in existence even though they do not directly affect perception. . . .

Observation 4.—Just as the child seems to expect to see again that which he has just seen and to hear again the sound which has just ceased, so also, when he begins to grasp, he seems to be convinced of the possibility that his hand will rediscover the object it has just relinquished. Thus during the behavior patterns described in O.I.,* Obs. 52–54, Laurent, considerably before knowing how to grasp what he sees, constantly lets go and recaptures the objects he is handling. At 0;2(7) in particular, Laurent holds a sheet in his hand for a moment, then lets it go and grasps it again soon afterward. Or he holds his hands together, separates them, holds them together again, etc. Finally it may be recalled that as soon as coordination between prehension and sight has been established, the child brings before his eyes everything he grasps outside the visual field, thus revealing expectation comparable to that which we have noted in connection with hearing and sight.

Observation 5.—A reaction slightly more complex than these is that of the child who stops looking at a certain picture and directs his glance elsewhere and who then returns to the first picture; that is the equivalent, in the realm of primary circular reactions, of the deferred reactions which we shall analyze in connection with the second stage.

Thus Lucienne, at 0;3(9) sees me at the extreme left of her visual field and smiles vaguely. She then looks in different directions, in front of her and to the right, but constantly returns to the place in which she sees me and dwells on it every time for a moment.

At 0;4(26) she takes the breast but turns when I call her and smiles at me. Then she resumes nursing, but several times in succession, despite my silence, she turns directly to the position from which she can see me. She does it again after a pause of a few minutes. Then I withdraw; when she turns without finding me her expression is one of mingled disappointment and expectation. . . .

At first these facts and analogous ones which it would be easy to accumulate seem to indicate a universe similar to ours. The gustatory, visual, auditory, or tactile images that the child ceases to suck, see, hear, or grasp seem to exist for him in the capacity of permanent objects which are independent of the action and which the action simply finds again. But in comparing these same behavior patterns with those we describe in connection with subsequent stages, it is apparent how superficial this interpretation would be and how phenomenalistic this primitive universe remains, far from constituting from the outset a world of substances. An essential difference contrasts these early behavior patterns with the true search for objects True search is active and causes the intervention of movements which do not solely extend the interrupted action, whereas in the present behavior patterns either there is simple expectation, or else the search only continues the earlier act of accommodation. . . .

THIRD STAGE: BEGINNING OF PERMANENCE

EXTENDING MOVEMENTS OF ACCOMMODATION

The behavior patterns of the third stage are those which are observable between the beginnings of prehension of things seen and the beginnings of active search for vanished objects. Hence they still are earlier than object concept but mark progress in the solidification of the universe depending on action.

Between 3 and 6 months of age, as we have seen elsewhere (O.I., Chap. II, §4), the child begins to grasp what he sees, to bring before his eyes the objects he touches, in short to coordinate his visual universe with the tactile universe. But not until the age of 9 or 10 months does

*[J. Piaget, *The Origins of Intelligence in Children*; hereafter, referred to as O.I.]

active search for vanished objects occur in the form of the use of grasping to remove solid objects that may mask or cover the desired object. This intermediate period constitutes our third stage.

But, if this long lapse of time is necessary for transition from prehension of an object at hand to true search for a missing object, it is because the interim is filled with the acquisition of a series of intermediate behavior patterns all of which are necessary to proceed from the mere perceived image to the concept of permanent object. In this connection we can distinguish these five types of behavior: (1) "visual accommodation to rapid movements"; (2) "interrupted phehension"; (3) "deferred circular reaction"; (4) the "reconstruction of an invisible whole from a visible fraction"; and (5) the "removal of obstacles preventing perception." The first of these behavior patterns merely extends those of the second stage, and the fifth fulfills those of the fourth stage.

Visual accommodation to rapid movements makes possible the anticipation of future positions of the object and consequently endows it with a certain permanence. This permanence of course remains related to the act of accommodation itself, and thus the behavior patterns merely extend those of the second stage; but there is progress in the sense that the anticipated position of the object is a new position and not one observed a moment ealier to which the eyes merely return. Two particular instances are of special importance: reaction to the movement of bodies which disappear from the visual field after having induced a lateral turn of the head, and reaction to falling movements. Both these behavior patterns seem to have developed under the influence of prehension.

Observation 6.—Laurent's reaction to falling objects still seems to be nonexistent at 0;5(24): he does not follow with his eyes any of the objects which I drop in front of him.

At 0;5(26), on the other hand, Laurent searches in front of him for a paper ball which I drop above his coverlet. He immediately looks at the coverlet after the third attempt but only in front of him, that is, where he has just grasped the ball. When I drop the object outside the bassinet Laurent does not look for it (except around my empty hand while it remains up in the air).

At 0;5(30) no reaction to the fall of a box of matches. The same is true at 0;6(0), but then when he drops the box himself he searches for it next to him with his eyes (he is lying down).

At 0;6(3) Laurent, lying down, holds in his hand a box five cm. in diameter. When it escapes him he looks for it in the right direction (beside him). I then grasp the box and drop it myself, vertically and too fast for him to be able to follow the trajectory. His eyes search for it at once on the sofa on which he is lying. I manage to eliminate any sound or shock and I perform the experiment at his right and at his left; the result is always positive.

At 0;6(7) he holds an empty matchbox in his hand. When it falls his eyes search for it even if they have not followed the beginning of the fall; he turns his head in order to see it on the sheet. Same reaction at 0;6(9) with a rattle, but this time he has watched the initial movement of the object. The same is true at 0;6(16) when his eyes have followed the beginning of the fall, at 0;6(20) etc., etc.

At 0;7(29) he searches on the floor for everything I drop above him, if he has in the least perceived the beginning of the movement of falling. At 0;8(1) he searches on the floor for a toy which I held in my hand and which I have just let drop without his knowledge. Not finding it, his eyes return to my hand which he examines at length, and then he again searches on the floor.

Observation 7.—At 0;7(30) Lucienne grasps a small doll which I present to her for the first time. She examines it with great interest, then lets it go (not intentionally); she immediately looks for it in front of her but does not see it right away.

When she has found it, I take it from her and place a coverlet over it, before her eyes (Lucienne is seated); no reaction.

At 0;8(5) Lucienne searches systematically on the floor for everything that she happens to drop. When an object is released in front of her, sometimes she searches for it also with her eyes, but less often (an average of one out of four times). The need to grasp what was in her hand therefore plays a role in this reaction to movements of falling; the permanence belonging to the beginnings of the concept of tactile object (of which we shall again speak in connection with interrupted prehension) thus interferes with the permanence arising from visual accommodation.

At 0;8(12) I again observe that Lucienne tries harder to find fallen objects with her eyes when she has previously touched the objects.

At 0;9(25) she looks at my hand which I at first hold motionless and then suddenly lower; Lucienne searches for it on the floor for a long time. . . .

However commonplace these facts may be they are important in forming object concept. They show us that the beginnings of permanance attributed to images perceived arise from the child's action in movements of accommodation. In this respect the present behavior patterns merely extend those of the second stage but reveal essential progress: the child no longer seeks the object only where he has recently seen it but hunts for it in a new place. He anticipates the perception of successive positions of the moving object and in a sense makes allowance for its displacements. But precisely because this beginning of permanence is only an extension of the action in progress, it could only be very limited. The child cannot conceive of just any displacements or just any objective permanence. He is limited to pursuing, more or less correctly, with his eyes or with his hand the trajectory delineated by the movements of accommodation peculiar to the immediately preceding perception; and it is only in the measure in which, in the absence of the objects, he continues the process begun in their presence that he is able to endow them with a certain permanence. . . .

Observation 31.—At 0;9(7) Lucienne tries to grasp a celluloid goose, which I cover either completely or partially. We have seen, in Obs. 23, the beginning of these reactions: Lucienne is able to grasp the goose with precision when she perceives the beak (in this case she extricates it from the coverlet and even raises the latter in advance) but she remains incapable of searching for the object when it is entirely covered up.

At the end of the experiment I facilitate things as follows: the animal is lying under the coverlet and Lucienne has withdrawn her hand; I tap on the goose which then rattles very distinctly. Lucienne imitates me at once, taps harder and harder, and laughs; but it does not occur to her to raise the screen. Then I again let the beak emerge; Lucienne at once raises the coverlet to look for the animal. I cover it up again; she taps, laughs, looks at my hands for a moment, but does not again touch the screen.

Observation 32.—Laurent, as we have seen (Obs. 24), ceases to cry at 0;6(19) and until about 0;9, at the time when he sees the bottle he desired disappear; everything occurs as though the child believed that it ceased to exist in substance. In particular, at 0;7(3), when Laurent has been on a diet for a week, he cries from hunger after each meal and clings frantically to his bottle; however if I hide it slowly behind my arm or my back this is enough to calm Laurent. He screams on seeing it disappear, but at the precise moment when he can no longer see it at all he ceases to react.

At 0;7(28) I offer him a little bell behind a cushion (the cushion in

Obs. 27); so long as he sees the little bell, however small it may be, he tries to grasp it from above the screen which he lowers more or less intentionally. But if the little bell disappears completely he stops all searching.

I then resume the experiment, using my hand as a screen. Laurent's arm is outstretched and about to grasp the little bell at the moment I make it disappear behind by hand (which is open and at a distance of 15 cm. from him); he immediately withdraws his arm, as though the little bell no longer existed. I then shake my hand, always revealing the back of it and gripping the little bell in my palm; Laurent watches attentively, greatly surprised to rediscover the sound of the little bell, but he does not try to grasp it. I turn my hand over and he sees the little bell; he then stretches out his hand toward it. I hide the little bell again by changing the position of my hand; Laurent withdraws his hand. In short, he does not yet have the concept that the little bell is "behind' my hand for he has no concept of the "reverse side" of it (see Obs. 24, reaction 3).

Afterward I put the little bell before him, but at the moment he is about to grasp it with outstretched hand I cover it with a thin cloth; Laurent withdraws his hand. He taps on the little bell with his index finger, through the cloth, and the little bell rings; Laurent watches this phenomenon with great interest, then his eyes follow my hand as I withdraw it open and look at it for a moment (as though the little bell were going to arise from it). But he does not raise the cloth.

Observation 33.—From about 0;8, as we have seen (Obs. 27), Laurent begins to remove the screen or even to lean forward to look over it. But during this entire phase intermediate between the third and the fourth stage he never once succeeds in raising the screen when the object has entirely disappeared. Thus at 0;8(8) he is incapable of finding my watch under his little pillow, placed before him. This is all the more curious because he has just searched with his hand (outside the visual field) for the watch which escaped him ("tactile object" and "interrupted prehension": see Obs. 17). But when I put the watch under his eyes, and at the moment he is about to grasp it I cover it with his small pillow, he withdraws his hand, whimpering. It would, however, be very easy for him to raise his pillow as he always does in play.

At 0;8(25) Laurent watches me when I place a cushion against my face. He begins by pushing himself up in order to look at me over the screen, then he pulls the screen away (therefore he knows I am there). But when I lie down before him with the cushion over my head he does not raise it, even if I say "coucou." He simply looks at my shoulder at the place where I disappear under the cushion and no longer reacts. Similarly, the objects he sees me hide under the cushion give rise to no reaction. It is only after 0;9 that he applies himself to searching for the object in such circumstances.

In short, so long as the search for the vanished object merely extends the accommodation movements in progress, the child reacts to the object's disappearance. On the other hand, as soon as it is a question of doing more, that is, of interrupting the movements of prehension, of visual accommodation, etc., in order to raise a screen conceived as such, the child abandons all active search; he is content to look at the examiner's hand as though the object should emanate from it. Even when he hears the object under the cloth which serves as a screen he does not seem to believe in its substantial permanence.

How, then, can the whole of the behavior patterns of this stage be interpreted? They surely mark notable progress over those of the preceding stage. A greater degree of permanence is attributed to vanished images, since the child expects to find them again not only in the very place where they were left but also in places within the extension of their trajectory (reaction to falling, interrupted prehension, etc.). But in comparing this stage to the following ones we prove that this permanence remains exclusively connected with the action in progress and does not yet imply the idea of a substantial permanence independent of the organism's sphere of activity. All that the child assumes is that in continuing to turn his head or to lower it he will see a certain image which has just disappeared, that in lowering his hand he will again find the tactile impression experienced shortly before, etc. Moreover he shows impatience or disappointment in the event of failure. He always knows, in the end, how to search for the image in its absolute position, that is, where he saw it at the beginning of the experiment (in the hands of the experimenter, for instance); but this return to the initial position is still determined by the activity itself, the advantage of this position rising merely from the fact that it characterized the beginning of the action in progress. . . .

In effect, at this stage the child does not know the mechanism of his own actions, and hence does not dissociate them from the things themselves; he knows only their total and undifferentiated schema (which we have called the schema of assimilation) comprising in a single act the data of external perception as well as the internal impressions that are affective and kinesthetic, etc., in nature. So long as the object is present it is assimilated in that schema and could not therefore be thought of apart from the acts to which it gives rise. When it disappears, either it is forgotten because it is not sufficiently dynamogenic or else it gives way to a feeling of disappointment or expectation and to the desire to continue the action. Then that which is the essential of circular reaction or reproductive assimilation is produced: a conservation effort. This effort radiates as always in movements extending the action in progress, and if the vanished image is rediscovered it appears merely as the completion of that action. None of this implies substantial permanence: the permanence in question is still only that with which circular reaction in general is impregnated, that is to say definitively the assimilatory activity itself. The child's universe is still only a totality of pictures emerging from nothingness at the moment of the action, to return to nothingness at the moment when the action is finished. There is added to it only the circumstance that the images subsist longer than before, because the child tries to make these actions last longer than in the past; in extending them either he rediscovers the vanished images or else he supposes them to be at [his] disposal in the very situation in which the act in progress began.

Proof that this interpretation is the right one, however painful it may be to our realism, is that the child makes no attempt to search for the object when it is neither within an extension of the gesture made, nor in its initial position; here Obs. 28–33 are decisive.

But could not the latter facts be accounted for simply by the lack of motor skill or defects of the child's memory? We do not at all see how. On the one hand it is not difficult for a baby of seven to nine months to lift a cloth, a coverlet, etc. (as he does in Obs. 26 and 27). On the other hand we shall see in studying the behavior patterns of the fourth stage that the formation of the object is far from finished when the child begins to look under screens; at first he does not take account of the displacements perceived and always searches for the object in its initial position!

But then could it not be said that the object exists in substance from the very beginning, only its localization in space being subject to difficulties? As we shall see later such a distinction is in fact devoid of meaning; to exist as object is to be ordered in space, for the elaboration of space is precisely the objectification of perceived images. A reality which merely remains at [the] disposal of the action without being situated in objective displacement groups is therefore not an object; it is only a potential act. . . .

FOURTH STAGE: ACTIVE SEARCH FOR

VANISHED OBJECT BUT WITHOUT TAKING

ACCOUNT OF THE SEQUENCE OF VISIBLE DISPLACEMENTS

An essential acquisition marks the beginning of this fourth stage. The child is no longer content to search for the vanished object when it is found in the extension of accommodation movements; henceforth he searches for it even outside the perceptual field, that is, behind screens interposed between the subject and the image perceived. This discovery rises from the fact that the child begins to study displacements of objects (by grasping them, shaking them, swinging them, hiding and finding them, etc.) and thus begins to coordinate visual permanence and tactile permanence, which remain unlinked during the preceding stage.

But such discoveries, however it may seem, do not yet mark the definitive advent of object concept. The experiment shows that when the object disappears successively in two or more distinct places, the child still confers on it a sort of absolute position; he does not take note of the sequential displacements, although they are quite visible, and seems to reason as if the place where the object was found the first time remains where he will find it when he wants to do so. In the fourth stage, therefore, the object remains intermediate between the thing at disposal of the preceding stages and the object properly so called of the fifth and sixth stages.

At what age does the child begin to search for the object hidden behind a screen? According to our observations, this occurs between the ages of 8 and 10 months.* But it is hard to determine with precision the boundary between the third stage and the fourth and, if one adheres to a precise criterion, that is, the advent of the behavior pattern which consists in raising the screen in order to find the objective, it is only around 0;9 that the present stage begins, that is, with a well-marked temporal displacement as compared to the corresponding stage of the development of intelligence (O.I., Chap. IV).

Observation 34.—At 0;8(29) Laurent plays with a tin box (see O.I., Obs. 126). I take it from him and place it under his pillow; whereas four days previously the child did not react in a similar circumstance (see Obs. 33), this time he grasps the pillow and perceives the box of which he immediately

---

*See Obs. 0;9 cited by Stern, Psychol. der frühen Kindheit (4th ed.), p. 97. In their Kleinkindertests Mmes. Bühler and Hetzer consider as characteristic of the ninth and tenth months the behavior pattern which consists in finding a toy under a folded cloth when this toy has been hidden before the child's eyes (see test 7 of Series IX, p. 49). After the eighth month, it is true, the children observed by these writers can find an object half hidden in a pocket (test 8 of Series VIII, p. 47, Figure 15), but as part of the toy remains visible it involves a behavior pattern comparable to our third stage.

takes possession. Same reaction at the second test. But is this chance or is the behavior intentional? It is doubtless merely an attempt on Laurent's part and not yet real anticipation. Proof of this is his inertia as soon as I slightly modify the conditions of the experiment. At the third test I place the box 15 centimeters away from him, and as soon as he extends his hand I cover the object with the same pillow as before; he immediately withdraws his hand.

The next days, analogous reactions, difficult to interpret. At 0;9(17) on the other hand, it suffices that he see a cigar case disappear under a cushion for him to raise the screen and discover the object. At the first attempts the case was completely hidden; nevertheless Laurent found it easily. Then I let a fraction of the object appear; the effort is increased tenfold, Laurent displacing the cushion with one hand and trying to catch the case with the other. In a general way, when the object disappeared completely Laurent showed less animation but the search continued until the end.

At 0;9(20) in the same way he finds my watch under a quilt, under a cloth, etc. At 0;9(24) he searches for a little duck under his pillow, under a spread cloth, etc. The behavior pattern has now been acquired and is accompanied by a growing interest.

Observation 35.—As we have seen, up to 0;9(22) Jacqueline has manifested reactions typical of the third stage (see Obs. 8–9, 13–14, 25, and 28–29). Nevertheless, from 0;9 and even from 0;8(15) some sporadic searching for the hidden object is observable.

The most elementary searches derive merely from the removal of obstacles preventing perception, of which we have spoken in connection with Obs. 26 and 27; at a given moment instead of removing a pillow or sheet only when it covers her own face, she manages to remove it when it covers someone else.

For example, at 0;8(14) Jacqueline is lying on my bed beside me. I cover my head and cry "coucou"; I emerge and do it again. She bursts into peals of laughter, then pulls the covers away to find me again. Attitude of expectation and lively interest.

At 0;8(16) she faces a coverlet raised between her and me, within reach of her hand but not touching it. I am behind this screen and call her. She responds to each sound but it does not occur to her to lower the coverlet. I rise and reveal myself as briefly as possible, then disappear behind the coverlet. This time she pulls it down with her hand and stretches her head to see me. She laughs at her success. I recommence, lowering myself still further; she again pulls the coverlet down. Jacqueline finally removes it when it completely conceals me.

Obviously these two behavior patterns belong to the fourth stage with regard to the mechanism of intelligence since there is subordination of means to ends with coordination of heterogeneous schemata. On the other hand, with regard to object concept (the elaboration of which naturally lags behind the progress of the intellectual function in general, since it results from this progress instead of engendering it by itself), these behavior patterns remain midway between the third and fourth stage; it is evident that Jacqueline assumes my presence in the sheets or the coverlet, and in this she is already in the fourth stage, but the movements she makes to find me again extend those of Obs. 26–27 in such a way that they still belong to the third stage. Let us note, furthermore, that the object searched for in the course of these two behavior patterns is a person, and that persons are obviously the most easily substantiated of all the child's sensorial images; hence it is natural that as early as 0;8(15) Jacqueline behaves as we have just seen toward her father when she does not find some toy hidden under a screen. . . .

The chief interest of this stage is that the active search for the vanished object is not immediately general, but is governed by a restrictive condition: the child looks for and conceives of the object only in a special position, the first place in which it was hidden and found. It is this peculiarity which enables us to contrast the present stage with the succeeding stages and which should be emphasized now.

The procedure is as follows, at least in the most characteristic period of the stage. Suppose an object is hidden at point A: the child searches for it and finds it. Next the object is placed in B and is covered before the child's eyes; although the child has continued to watch the object and has seen it disappear in B, he nevertheless immediately tries to find it in A! We shall call this the typical reaction of the fourth stage. Toward the end of the stage a reaction appears which we shall consider residual. It is as follows: the child follows with his eyes the object in B, searches for it in this second place, and if he does not find it immediately (because the object is buried too deeply, etc.) he returns to A.

Let us begin by describing the typical reaction. It is noteworthy that this reaction was presaged from the third stage by a series of signs which were doubtless noticed. It has been observed, for example, that in Obs. 28–30, showing that the child at the third stage gives up searching for the object hidden behind a screen, the subject does not actually abandon all investigation but searches for the object in the same place where it was found before it was put under the screen. Thus Jacqueline, in Obs. 28, searches for the duck on top of her quilt and even resumes wriggling to make it fall, although she saw it slide down under a fold in the sheet. In Obs. 30 Lucienne, after having seen me place a stork under a cloth, looks at my hand to see if the stork is still there. Such behavior patterns seem to show us that the object is not yet at this stage a substantial thing remaining in the place to which it was moved but a thing at disposal in the place where the action has made use of it. This is precisely what happens during the whole of the fourth stage: the child learns to search for the object behind a screen—and thereby makes progress over the second stage—but he always returns to the same screen, even if one moves the object from one location to another, because the original screen seems to him to constitute the special place where the action of finding is successful.

Observation 39.—At 0;10(3) after the events recorded in Obs. 37 on that day, Jacqueline looks at the parrot on her lap. I place my hand on the object; she raises it and grasps the parrot. I take it away from her and, before her eyes, I move it away very slowly and put it under a rug, 40 cm. away. Meanwhile I place my hand on her lap again. As soon as Jacqueline ceases to see the parrot she looks at her lap, lifts my hand and hunts beneath it. The reaction is the same during three sequential attempts.

I then simplify the experiment in the following way; instead of hiding the parrot under the rug I place it in plain view on the edge of a table, 50 cm. away. At the first attempt Jacqueline raises my hand and obviously searches under it, always watching the parrot on the table.

Second attempt: She raises my hand from her lap without looking under it and without taking her eyes from the parrot.

Third attempt: She stops looking at the parrot on the table for a moment and searches carefully under my hand. Then she again looks at the object while removing my hand.

Fourth attempt: She removes my hand without looking at it any more. As this last reaction might be due to automatism I give up the experiment and several days later devise the following:

Observation 40.—At 0;10(18) Jacqueline is seated on a mattress without anything to disturb or distract her (no coverlets, etc.). I take her parrot from her hands and hide it twice in succession under the mattress, on her left, in A. Both times Jacqueline looks for the object immediately and grabs it. Then I take it from her hands and move it very slowly before her eyes to the corresponding place on her right, under the mattress, in B. Jacqueline watches this movement very attentively, but at the moment when the parrot disappears in B she turns to her left and looks where it was before, in A.

During the next four attempts I hide the parrot in B every time without having first placed it in A. Every time Jacqueline watches me attentively. Nevertheless each time she immediately tries to rediscover the object in A; she turns the mattress over and examines it conscientiously. During the last two attempts, however, the search tapers off.

Sixth attempt: She no longer searches. . . .

Observation 51.—At 1;3(9) Lucienne is in the garden with her mother. Then I arrive; she sees me come, smiles at me, therefore obviously recognizes me (I am at a distance of about 1 meter 50). Her mother then asks her: "Where is papa?" Curiously enough, Lucienne immediately turns toward the window of my office where she is accustomed to seeing me and points in that direction. A moment later we repeat the experiment; she has just seen me 1 meter away from her, yet, when her mother pronounces my name, Lucienne again turns toward my office.

Here it may be clearly seen that if I do not represent two archetypes to her, at least I give rise to two distinct behavior patterns not synthesized nor exclusive of one another but merely juxtaposed: "papa at his window" and "papa in the garden."

At 1;6(7) Lucienne is with Jacqueline who has just spent a week in bed in a separate room and has gotten up today. Lucienne speaks to her, plays with her, etc., but this does not prevent her, a moment later, from climbing the stairs which lead to Jacqueline's empty bed and laughing before entering the room as she does every day; therefore she certainly expects to find Jacqueline in bed and looks surprised at her own mistake.

At 2;4(3) Lucienne, hearing a noise in my office, says to me (we are together in the garden): "That is papa up there."

Finally, at 3;5(0) after seeing her godfather off in an automobile, Lucienne comes back into the house and goes straight to the room in which he slept, saying, "I want to see if godfather has left." She enters alone and says to herself, "Yes, he has gone."

We know the little game which consists in saying to children: "Go look in my room and see if I am there," and we know how often the child yields to the suggestion. Jacqueline and Lucienne have never been taught the custom by us, but Lucienne has let herself be taken in by it after the foregoing observation. It seems probable that there is here some residual reaction analogous to the preceding.

Observation 52.—Let us cite an observation made not on our children but on an older cousin who suggested to us all the foregoing studies. Gérard, at 13 months, knows how to walk, and is playing ball in a large room. He throws the ball, or rather lets it drop in front of him and, either on his feet or on all fours, hurries to pick it up. At a given moment the ball rolls under an armchair. Gérard sees it and, not without some difficulty, takes it out in order to resume the game. Then the ball rolls under a sofa at the other end of the room. Gérard has seen it pass under the fringe of the sofa; he bends down to recover it. But as the sofa is deeper than the armchair and the fringe does prevent a clear view, Gérard gives up after a moment; he gets up, crosses the room, goes right under the armchair and carefully explores the place where the ball was before.

The general fact common to all these observations is that the child, after seeing an object disappear under a screen B, goes to look for it under screen A under which he searched for it and found it a moment before. In Obs. 39 to 45, characterizing what we have called the typical reaction of this fourth stage, the child searches for the object in A as soon as he has seen it disappear in B and without first trying to find it in B. In Obs. 46 to 50 characterizing the residual reactions, the child searches first in B and, if he fails, returns to A. Or again, accustomed to searching indiscriminately in A or in B, he does not search in C if the object has been put in this third place, but returns to A or to B (Obs. 49 and 50). Finally, in Obs. 51 and 52 the child, even after having transcended this fourth stage (this is certain with respect to Lucienne and very probable with respect to Gérard) relapses, in certain circumstances, into residual reaction.

How are these facts to be interpreted? Three interpretations seem possible to us according to whether one attributes these strange behavior patterns to difficulties of memory or of spatial localization, or to the incomplete formation of object concept.

The first explanation seems to be the simplest from the point of view of adult psychology. Everyone, in a moment of absentmindedness, has behaved somewhat like our children. For example I take my clothesbrush out of the small bag in which it is usually kept and place it on a table; afterward when I want to use it I look for it in its bag and cannot understand its disappearance. Or else I go to look for a necktie in my closet, place it before me, and when ready to put it on, return to my tie rack; I see my pipe on my desk, put in in my pocket, then hunt for it on the desk, etc. This is not, fortunately, either confusion related to the constitution of objects as permanent substances or confusion related to spatial localization; I have merely forgotten the sequential displacements of the object, and left without it, I search for it in the place where my attempts are ordinarily crowned with success or else in the place where I noted its presence on the last occasion. So also it could be stated that Gérard (Obs. 52), having known perfectly well at first that the ball had left the armchair and was to be found under the sofa, little by little lost all memory of the events; no longer knowing very well what he was doing under the sofa, he remembered having found the ball under the armchair and immediately followed his impulse. In the example in Obs. 51, there is no doubt that the habit of seeing her father at the office window, of seeing Jacqueline in bed or of seeing her godfather in the guest room is important in Lucienne's reactions; it could therefore be affirmed that she forgets what she has just seen and reverts to her habitual schema. In residual reactions in general it is permissible to think that the child, after having failed to find the object in B, no longer remembers the order of events very well and tries at all events to seek the object in A. In typical reactions one could go so far as to believe that, faced with the disappearance of the object, the child immediately ceases to reflect; in other words, he does not try to remember the sequence of positions and thus merely returns to the place where he was successful in finding the object the first time.

The second explanation pertains to the constitution of space. It can be asserted that between the ages of 9 and 12 months the child still has too much difficulty in elaborating objective displacement groups for him to take note of the localization of invisible objects. Surely, if he saw the object uninterruptedly, nothing would be easier for him than to form the two following groups (we shall designate by M the position of the object when it is at rest in the child's hand and by A and B the other positions of the same object):

$$(1) \quad M \to A; \quad A \to B; \quad B \to M, \text{ or}$$
$$(2) \quad M \to A; \quad A \to M; \quad M \to B; \quad B \to M.$$

But precisely because in normal times he sees the object uninterruptedly, the child does not need to be aware of such groups; he puts them into action without thinking about them. In other words, the child grasps the object where he sees it or else where he has just seen it without needing to retrace his itinerary mentally. If such were the case, that is, if the "group" remained chiefly practical without being a concept to him, it could very well be that the localization of objects in space would remain a matter of mere sensorimotor schemata, hence of immediate and not considered actions. There would, consequently, be no image of localizations but merely an empirical use of localization. The hierarchy of behavior patterns would therefore be the following: the object would first be sought where it is seen, then where it was seen, and finally where it was found behind a screen for the first time. But when the object disappears behind a second screen the child would use up the series of these behavior patterns in the first place before searching for it behind this new obstacle; no longer seeing it, but having already seen and found it in a first position, the child would therefore return to A merely through failure to vary his action of searching and to vary it in relation to the sequential positions. This is seen, for example, when the subject manages to search in B but refuses to search in C (Obs. 49 and 50): the search in A and in B having been successful, it is useless to try in C! In other words, there would be no localization from the point of view of object but solely from the point of view of action. The object would have a special position merely because the group remains practical or subjective and is not yet entirely objective or representative.

With this hypothesis it would be easy to explain the chronological order of the behavior patterns observed. The child would begin with the typical reaction for the reasons just demonstrated: having previously found the object in A and not trying to imagine its localization in B, he would return to A as soon as the object disappears in B. In the second place the child, discovering gradually and empirically the failure of his procedure, would begin to search for the object also in B; but unaware as he still is of objective localization, if he did not succeed at once he would return to his search in A. Residual reaction would therefore indicate the persistence of practical or subjective localization or its primacy in relation to objective localization. Finally, in Obs. 51, the belated resurrection of this behavior pattern would stem from the fact that, as the object has a very unyielding practical or subjective localization (for reasons of habit), the objective and representative localizations would momentarily pass over to the second plane.

But still a third explanation is possible with regard to the constitution of object concept. It is possible that during this third stage the object is still not the same to the child as it is to us: a substantial body, individualized and displaced in space without depending on the action context in which it is inserted. Thus the object is, perhaps, to the child, only a particularly striking aspect of the total picture in which it is contained; at least it would not manifest so many "moments of freedom" as do our images. Hence there would not be one chain, one doll, one watch, one ball, etc., individualized, permanent, and independent of the child's activity, that is, of the special positions in which that activity takes place or has taken place, but there would still exist only images such as "ball-under-the-armchair," "doll-attached-to-the hammock," "watch-under-a-cushion," "papa-at-his-window," etc. Certainly the same object reappearing in different practical positions or contexts is recognized, identified, and endowed with permanence as such. In this sense it is relatively independent. But, without being truly conceived as having several copies, the object may manifest itself to the child as assuming a limited number of distinct forms of a nature intermediate between unity and plurality, and in this sense it remains a part of its context. Obs. 51 permits us to understand this hypothesis: when Lucienne looks for me at the window when she knows that I am beside her two behavior patterns are obviously involved, "papa-at-his-window" and "papa-in-front-of-oneself"; and, if Lucienne does not hesitate to consider the two papas as being one and the same person, she nevertheless does not succeed in abstracting this person from the total pictures with which he is connected sufficiently to refrain from looking for him in two places simultaneously. A fortiori, in Obs. 52, the child who does not find the "ball-under-the-sofa" does not hesitate to look for the "ball-under-the-armchair" since here there are two distinct totalities. Whereas we think of the ball as able to occupy an infinitude of different positions, which enables us to abstract it from all of them at once, the child endows it with only a few special positions without being able, consequently, to consider it as entirely independent of them. In a general way, in all the observations in which the child searches in A for what he has seen disappear in B, the explanation should be sought in the fact that the object is not yet sufficiently individualized to be dissociated from the global behavior related to position A.

Such then are the three possible explanations for the phenomenon: defect of memory, defect of spatial localization, or defect of objectification. But far from trying to choose among them, we shall on the contrary try to show that these three explanations, seemingly different, in reality constitute only a single explanation, seen from three distinct points of view. It is only if one retained one of the three explanations to the exclusion of the two others that it would be disputable. But if all three are accepted, they are complementary.

First, the defect of memory. The great difference between the behavior of the 10-month-old child and our own seemingly analogous behavior (looking for the brush in its usual place when we have just put it somewhere else) is that we could very well keep the memory of the sequential displacements if we paid attention whereas, by hypothesis, the child cannot. If we change the order of movements of the brush, the necktie, or the pipe, it is because we are absentminded; but being otherwise quite capable of remembering the sequential displacements of the things which surround us, we attribute to them by virtue of this fact an objective structure, and by extension we conceive of the brush, etc., in an identical way even in moments of the worst absentmindedness. On the contrary, in Obs. 39 to 52 the child manifests the *maximum* of attention and interest of which he is capable, and if one may refer to absentmindedness in certain events of Obs. 51, this could not be involved when the child is trying by every means to find the hidden object he wants. In particular in the instances of typical reaction (Obs. 39 to 46), the child is watching the object with the greatest fixity as it disappears in B, yet immediately afterward he turns to A; it would therefore be unrealistic to admit that he forgets the displacements out of

mere absentmindedness. Thereafter to the extent that a defect of
memory intervenes it would only involve a systematic difficulty in arranging events in time and, consequently, in noting the sequence of displacements. Seeing the object disappear, the child would not try to
reconstruct its itinerary; he would, without reflection or memory, go
straight to the position where his action had already succeeded in
finding it. But then in this hypothesis, the spatial and objective structure
of the universe would become, at the same stroke, entirely different
from what it is for us. Let us suppose the existence of a mind which
retained no memory of the order of displacements: its universe would
consist in a series of total pictures whose coherence would pertain to the
action itself and not to the relations sustained by the elements of the
different pictures with each other. This first interpretation is tantamount
to the next two: the construction of objective groups of displacements
presupposes time and memory, just as time presupposes a universe
spatially and objectively organized.

With regard to the second explanation, it is equally true, provided it
includes the first and third. It is perfectly accurate to say that the child
searches for the object in A when it has disappeared in B, simply because
the practical schema prevails over the objective group of displacements.
The child does not take note of those displacements and when (in the
residual reactions) he begins to note them, he still subordinates them to
the schemata of immediate action. But if that is the case it must be concluded, first, that the memory of the positions does not play a decisive
role and, second, that the object remains linked with a global context
instead of being individualized and substantiated as an independent and
permanent body in motion.

Hence we are brought to the third solution inasmuch as it really
involves the first two solutions and vice versa. In a word, during this
fourth stage the object remains a practical object rather than a substantial thing. The child's reactions remain inspired in whole or in part
by a sort of phenomenalism mixed with dynamism. The object is not a
thing which is displaced and is independent of those displacements; it
is a reality at [his] disposal in a certain context, itself related to a certain
action. In this respect the behavior patterns of the present stage merely
extend those of the preceding one. They are phenomenalistic since the
object remains dependent on its context and not isolated in the capacity
of a moving body endowed with permanence. They are dynamic, moreover, since the object remains in the extension of the effort and of the
feeling of efficacy linked with the action by which the subject finds the
object again. From this dual point of view the progress made by the
child in learning to search for the object behind a screen has not yet
sufficed to cause him to attribute an objective structure to the things
which surround him. In order that these things really become objects the
awareness of relations of position and displacement must be acquired.
The child will have to understand the "how" of the appearance and disappearance of these objects and thus will have to abandon belief in the
possibility of their mysterious reappearance at the place they have left
and where action itself has discovered them. In short, a truly geometric
rationalism will have to supersede the phenomenalism of immediate
perception and the dynamism of practical efficacy.

FIFTH STAGE: CHILD TAKES ACCOUNT OF

SEQUENTIAL DISPLACEMENTS OF OBJECT

From the end of the first year of life until toward the middle of the second there extends a stage characterized by the progressive acquisition of spatial relations whose absence during the stage just passed prevents the definitive formation of object concept. In other words, the child learns to take account of the sequential displacements perceived in the visual field; he no longer searches for the object in a special position but only in the position resulting from the last visible displacement. This discovery we consider the beginning of the fifth stage.

Thus characterized, the behavior patterns of the present stage are of great interest in connection with the questions raised with respect to the fourth stage. To the extent that these behavior patterns bear upon visible displacements they reveal a nascent geometric rationalism; this constitutes the new element peculiar to them. True, to the extent that they remain incapable of making allowance for invisible displacements (those which the child does not see) they conserve an element of mixed phenomenalism and dynamism. But such a complication does not alter in any way the regularity of the development. Far from disappearing entirely the practical and egocentric object defends foot by foot the terrain which the geometric relationships will conquer. . . .

The first acquisition of the fifth stage (which marks its advent) is signified by the success of the tests whose initial failure is described in Obs. 39 to 52: when the object is hidden under a first screen under which the child finds it, and then under a second screen, the subject no longer searches for the object under the first screen, but only under the second one.

Observation 53.—At 1;0(20) Jacqueline watches me hide my watch under cushion A on her left, then under cushion B on her right; in the latter case she immediately searches in the right place. If I bury the object deep she searches for a long time, then gives up, but does not return to A.

At 1;0(26), same experiment. At the first attempt Jacqueline searches and finds in A where I first put the watch. When I hide it in B Jacqueline does not succeed in finding it there, being unable to raise the cushion altogether. Then she turns around, unnerved, and touches different things including cushion A, but she does not try to turn it over; she *knows* that the watch is no longer under it.

Subsequent attempts: Jacqueline never succeeds in finding the watch in B because I hide it too deep, but neither does she ever try to return to A to see if it is still there; she searches assiduously in B, then gives up.

At 1;1(22) new experiments with different objects. The result is always the same.

Observation 54.—Laurent, at 0;11(22), is seated between two cushions A and B. I hide the watch alternately under each; Laurent constantly searches for the object where it has just disappeared, that is, sometimes in A, sometimes in B, without remaining attached to a privileged position as during the preceding stage.

It is noteworthy that the same day Laurent reveals a very systematic mind in searching for the vanished object. I hide a little box in my hand. He then tries to raise my fingers to reach the object. But, instead of letting him do this and without showing the box, I pass to him with two fingers of the same hand a shoe, a toy, and finally a ribbon; Laurent is not fooled and always returns to the proper hand despite its displacements, and at last opens it and takes the box. When I take it from him to put it in the other hand, he searches for it there immediately.

At 1;0(20) likewise, he searches sequentially in both my hands for a button I am hiding. Afterward he tries to see behind me when I make the button roll on the floor (on which I am seated) even though, to fool him, I hold out my two closed hands.

At 1;1(8) etc., likewise, he takes note of all the visible displacements of the object.

Observation 54a.—Lucienne also, at 1;0(5), no longer looks for the object only in B and does not return to the initial place, even in the event of continuous failure.

Same observations at 1;0(11) etc.

On this point phenomenalism has certainly yielded to awareness of relation; the child takes account of all the visible displacements he has observed and dissociates the object from its practical context.

But if we interpose the simplest possible of invisible displacements the phenomena of the preceding stage immediately reappear. In this connection we have tried the following experiment: hiding an object not directly under the screen, but in a box without a lid; box and object are made to disappear under a screen and the box brought out empty. The child does not succeed in understanding, except by luck, that the object can have been left behind under the screen.

Observation 55.—At 1;6(8) Jacqueline is sitting on a green rug and playing with a potato which interests her very much (it is a new object for her). She says "po-terre" and amuses herself by putting it into an empty box and taking it out again. For several days she has been enthusiastic about this game.

I.   I then take the potato and put it in the box while Jacqueline watches. Then I place the box under the rug and turn it upside down thus leaving the object hidden by the rug without letting the child see my maneuver, and I bring out the empty box. I say to Jacqueline, who has not stopped looking at the rug and who has realized that I was doing something under it: "Give papa the potato." She searches for the object in the box, looks at me, again looks at the box minutely, looks at the rug, etc., but it does not occur to her to raise the rug in order to find the potato underneath.

During the five subsequent attempts the reaction is uniformly negative. I begin again, however, each time putting the object in the box as the child watches, putting the box under the rug, and bringing it out empty. Each time Jacqueline looks in the box, then looks at everything around her including the rug, but does not search under it.

II.   At the seventh attempt, I change the technique. I place the object in the box and the box under the rug but leave the object in the box. As soon as I remove my empty hand Jacqueline looks under the rug, finds and grasps the box, opens it and takes the potato out of it. Same reaction a second time.

III.   Then I resume the first technique: emptying the box under the rug and bringing it forth empty. At first Jacqueline looks for the object in the box, and not finding it there, searches for it under the rug. Hence the attempt has been successful. This occurs a second time but from the third attempt on, the result becomes negative again, as in I. Is this due to fatigue?

Observation 56.—The next day, at 1;6(9), I resume the experiment but with a celluloid fish containing a rattle. I put the fish in the box and the box under the rug. There I shake it and Jacqueline hears the fish in the box. I turn the box upside down and bring it out empty. Jacqueline immediately takes possession of the box, searches for the fish, turns the box over in all directions, looks around her, in particular looks at the rug but does not raise it.

The next attempts yield nothing further. I do not use technique II of the preceding observation.

That evening I repeat the experiment with a little lamb. Jacqueline herself puts the lamb in the box and when the whole thing is under the coverlet she says with me, "Coucou, lamb." When I take out the empty box she says, "Lamb, lamb," but does not look under the coverlet.

Whenever I leave the whole thing under the coverlet she immediately searches for the box and brings out the lamb. But when I start again, using the first technique, she no longer looks under the coverlet!

Observation 57.—At 1;0(16) Lucienne looks at my watch chain which I place in my own hand; she opens my hand and takes the chain. I recommence, but after having closed my hand I place it on the floor next to the child (Lucienne is seated), and cover my fist with a coverlet. I take out my fist and extend it to Lucienne, who has watched the whole thing most attentively; Lucienne opens my hand, finds nothing, looks all around her but does not raise the coverlet.

Attempts 2–4: Same reaction.

Fifth attempt: Lucienne raises the coverlet mechanically or by chance, and perceives the chain. This must not have been intentional since it did not affect the rest of the behavior.

Attempts 6–10: Return to the initial reaction. Lucienne searches attentively around my hand, looks at the coverlet but does not raise it. This reaction could not, however, be attributed to boredom; Lucienne seems to be very much interested.

These first failures are significant. For example, Jacqueline knows very well how to search for an object hidden behind a screen, as we have established to be the case for more than six months. But she succeeds in keeping track of only the visible displacements of the object and locates it only where she has actually seen it. In the experiment now under discussion an invisible displacement is involved (the object leaves the box or the hand when both are under the rug) and the object occupies a space where it has not been directly perceived (under the rug); these are two new conditions of the experiment. In effect, so long as the child sees the box or the hand disappear under the rug he knows that the object is in the box and the box under the rug; but from this he does not succeed in concluding that, when the box comes out empty, the object has been left under the rug. Hence the search for the object as yet makes allowance only for observed displacements and positions in which the object has actually been seen. . . .

SIXTH STAGE: REPRESENTATION OF INVISIBLE DISPLACEMENTS

After the sixth stage the child becomes capable of constructing objects when the displacements are not all visible. That of course does not signify that this discovery is immediately generalized to include the whole universe, since we have just seen that during the years following this is still not the case. It merely means that the child succeeds in resolving the problems raised in the course of the preceding experiments and has resolved them by means of a new method: that of representation. This success became systematic in Jacqueline's case at 1;7(20) and in Lucienne's at 1;3(14).

Observation 64.—(1) At 1;7(20) Jacqueline watches me when I put a coin in my hand, then put my hand under a coverlet. I withdraw my hand closed; Jacqueline opens it, then searches under the coverlet until she finds the object. I take back the coin at once, put it in my hand, and then slip my closed hand under a cushion situated at the other side (on her left and no longer on her right); Jacqueline immediately searches for the object under the cushion. I repeat the experiment by hiding the coin under a packet; Jacqueline finds it without hesitation.

II. I complicate the test as follows: I place the coin in my hand, then my hand under the cushion. I bring it forth closed and immediately hide it under the coverlet. Finally I withdraw it and hold it out, closed, to Jacqueline. Jacqueline then pushes my hand aside without opening it (she guesses that there is nothing in it, which is new), she looks under the cushion, then directly under the coverlet where she finds the object.

During a second series (cushion and jacket) she behaves in the same way.

I then try a series of three displacements: I put the coin in my hand and move my closed hand sequentially from A to B and from B to C; Jacqueline sets my hand aside, then searches in A, in B, and finally in C.

Lucienne is successful in the same tests at 1;3(14). . . .

From the point of view of object formation each of our observations thus leads to the same conclusion: the object is no longer, as it was during the first four stages, merely the extension of various accommodations, nor is it, as in the fifth stage, merely a permanent body in motion whose movements have become independent of the self but solely to the extent to which they have been perceived; instead, the object is now definitely freed from perception and action alike and obeys entirely autonomous laws of displacement. In effect, by virtue of the very fact that it enters the system of abstract or indirect images and relations, the object acquires in the subject's consciousness, a new and final degree of liberty. It is conceived as remaining identical to itself whatever may be its invisible displacements or the complexity of the screens which mask it. Doubtless this representation of the object which we call the characteristic of the sixth stage is already budding in the preceding stages. As soon as the child at the fourth stage begins to search actively for the vanished object it can be claimed that there exists a sort of evolution of the absent object. But never until the present stage has this behavior led to real evocation, because it has merely utilized a system of signs linked with the action; searching for an object under a screen when the subject has seen it disappear there (stages IV and V) does not necessarily presuppose that the subject "imagines" the object under the screen but simply that he has understood the relation of the two objects at the moment he perceived it (at the moment when the object was covered) and that he therefore interprets the screen as a sign of the actual presence of the object. It is one thing to assume the permanence of an object when one has just seen it and when some other object now in sight recalls its presence, and it is quite another thing to imagine the first object when there is nothing in sight to attest its hidden existence. True representation therefore begins only when no perceived sign commands belief in permanency, that is to say, from the moment when the vanished object is displaced according to an itinerary which the subject may deduce but not perceive. That is why up to the fifth stage inclusively as soon as the displacements are not all visible the child searches for objects in the place where they were found the first time, as though they were always at the subject's disposal, whereas from this sixth stage he takes account of all possible displacements, even if they are invisible.

Can it be said that this difference between the behavior patterns of the sixth stage and those of the fifth concern only the construction of space and not the permanence of the object as such? In this hypothesis an object whose displacements it is impossible to reconstruct would nevertheless be conceived as being as invariant and as identical to itself as if all its movements were known. For example, even though I cannot imagine or deduce the course of a small stone which I toss down the irregular slope of a mountain, I know that it remains somewhere· as an object and that its properties (or those of its parts, in the event of fragmentation) have remained identical to what they were at the moment of the fall. But let us beware of too facile comparisons. If the adult can lend the quality of objects to bodies whose trajectory he does not know or to bodies he has seen only for a moment, it is by analogy with others of whose displacements he is already aware, whether these are absolute or related to the movements of the body itself. But, sooner or later, representation and deduction enter into this knowledge. With regard to the baby at the fifth stage, to the extent that he does not know how to imagine or to deduce the invisible displacements of bodies he remains incapable of perceiving these bodies as objects truly independent of the self. A world in which only perceived movements are regulated is neither stable nor dissociated from the self; it is a world of still chaotic potentialities whose organization begins only in the subject's presence. Outside the perceptual field and the beginnings of objectivity which are constituted by the organization of perceived movements, the elements of such a universe are not objects but realities at the disposal of action and consciousness. On the contrary, the representation and deduction characteristic of the sixth stage result in extending the process of solidification to regions of that universe which are dissociated from action and perception; displacements, even invisible ones, are henceforth envisaged as subservient to laws, and objects in motion become real objects independent of the self and persisting in their substantial identity.

A final consequence essential to the development of representation is that henceforth, the child's own body is regarded as an object. Thanks to imitation, for example, and in particular to the behavior patterns of the present stage (these are characterized by the fact that imitation becomes embedded in representation), the child is now able to see his own body as an object by analogy with that of another person. Moreover, nascent spatial, causal, and temporal images permit him to locate himself in a space and time reaching beyond him everywhere, and to consider himself as mere cause and mere effect among the totality of the connections he discovers. Having thus become an object among other objects at the very moment when he learns to conceive of their true permanence even outside all direct perception, the child ends by completely reversing his initial universe, whose moving images were centered on an activity unconscious of itself, and by transforming it into a solid universe of coordinated objects including the body itself in the capacity of an element. Such is the result of object construction on the sensorimotor plane, until reflection and conceptual thought pursue this elaboration on new planes of creative intelligence.

CONSTITUTIVE PROCESSES OF OBJECT CONCEPT

We have hitherto limited ourselves to describing merely the historical development of object concept. The time has come to attempt an explanation of this development by attaching it to the whole of the intellectual evolution peculiar to the child's first two years of life.

To understand the formation of initial sensorimotor objects it may not be useless to compare the elementary processes of the child's intelligence to those used by scientific thought to establish the objectivity of the beings it elaborates. For if the structures employed by thought vary from one stage to another and, a fortiori, from one mental system to another, thought remains constantly identical to itself from the functional point of view. It is therefore not illegitimate to elucidate one of the terms of intellectual evolution by the directly opposite term, that is, the construction of practical objects by that of scientific objects, provided that the first term, when it is sufficiently understood, elucidate the second in return.

Now three criteria seem to us to contribute to the definition of the object peculiar to the sciences: in the first place, every objective phenomenon permits anticipation, in contrast to other phenomena whose advent, fortuitous and contrary to all anticipation, permits the hypothesis of a subjective origin. But, as subjective phenomena also can give rise to anticipation (for example, the "illusions of the senses") and moreover as unexpected events are sometimes those which mark the failure of an erroneous interpretation and thus entail progress in objectivity, a second condition must be added to the first: a phenomenon is the more objective the more it lends itself, not only to anticipation, but also to distinct experiments whose results are in accordance with it. But that is still not enough, for certain subjective qualities may be linked with constant physical characteristics, as qualitative colors with luminous waves. In this case, only a deduction of the totality succeeds in dissociating the subjective from the objective: only that phenomenon constitutes a real object which is connected in an intelligible way with the totality of a spatio-temporal and causal system (for example, luminous waves constitute objects because they have a physical explanation, whereas quality is dissociated from the objective system).

These three methods are found to be the very same which the little child uses in his effort to form an objective world. At first the object is only the extension of accommodation movements (anticipation). Then it is the point of intersection, that is, of reciprocal assimilation of multiple schemata which manifest the different modalities of the action (concordance of the experiments). Finally, the object is fully constructed in correlation with causality to the extent that this coordination of schemata results in the formation of an intelligible spatio-temporal world endowed with permanence (comprehension related to a deductive system of the totality).

. . . To the extent that things are detached from action and that action is placed among the totality of the series of surrounding events, the subject has power to construct a system of relations to understand these series and to understand himself in relation to them. To organize such series is to form simultaneously a spatio-temporal network and a system consisting of substances and of relations of cause to effect. Hence the construction of the object is inseparable from that of space, of time, and of causality. An object is a system of perceptual images endowed with a constant spatial form throughout its sequential displacements and constituting an item which can be isolated in the causal series unfolding in time. Consequently the elaboration of the object is bound up with that of the universe as a whole. To understand this genesis it would thus be necessary to show how displacement groups as well as temporal and causal structures are formed. But since, inversely, it is only by achieving belief in the object's permanence that the child succeeds in organizing space, time, and causality, we must begin our analysis by trying to explain the behavior patterns which tend to construct the object as such. How then does the child come to search for the object not only in a special place but by taking account of displacements observed sequentially, then even displacements occurring ouside the perceptual field?

. . . How are we to account for object construction from the laws of the schemata of assimilation? Such construction is not the act of an a priori deduction, nor is it due to purely empirical gropings. The sequence of the stages which we have distinguished testifies much more strongly to progressive comprehension than to haphazard achievements. If there is experimentation, the experiments are directed: in finding the object the child organizes his motor schemata and elaborates his operative relationships rather than submitting passively to the pressure of events.

The solution to the problem, therefore, seems to us to be the following: the permanence of the object stems from the constructive deduction which from the fourth stage is constituted by reciprocal assimilation of the secondary schemata, that is, the coordination of schemata which have become mobile. Until this level has been reached the object merely extends the activity itself; its permanence is only practical and not substantial, because the universe is not detached from the action nor objectified in a system of relationships. The coordination of the primary schemata, in particular that coordination between sight and prehension which gives rise to the secondary circular reactions, does indeed result in a relative externalization of things; but so long as the secondary schemata remain global or undifferentiated instead of being dissociated the better to unite, this externalization does not go far enough to constitute a substantial permanence. On the contrary, from the fourth stage onward the secondary schemata become mobile through a reciprocal assimilation which permits them to combine among themselves in different ways; it is this process of complementary dissociation and regroupment which, by engendering the first acts of intelligence properly so called, enables the child to build a spatio-temporal world of objects endowed with causality.

As we have seen (O.I., Chap. IV, §3), the mobile schemata resulting from the coordination of secondary reactions constitute not only some kinds of motor concepts that may be arranged in practical judgments and reasonings, but also some systems of relations that permit an increasingly precise elaboration of the objects on which these behavior patterns bear. The reciprocal assimilation of the schemata therefore entails the construction of physical connections and consequently of objects as such. Thus the union of the schemata of prehension with those of striking, which explains the behavior pattern consisting in removing obstacles (O.I., Chap. IV, §1–2), permits the child to construct the relations "above," and "below," "hidden behind," etc., and leads him to base his belief in the permanence of the object on truly spatial relations. But above all, the combinations of the mobile schemata make possible a better accommodation of behavior to the specific characteristics of objects. The fact that the schemata can henceforth adjust themselves to each other leads the child to observe the detail of objects much more closely when his action bears upon them than when the objects are absorbed in the acts as a whole and remain undifferentiated. For this reason the behavior patterns of "exploration of new objects" appear at the fourth stage and, during the fifth, are extended in tertiary circular reactions, that is, in experiments in order to see. It is in this context that, from the fifth stage on, the true object will be elaborated.

It may be recalled that the specific behavior patterns of the fifth stage—"discoveries of new means through active experimentation"—are explainable precisely by this union of the coordination of schemata and of tertiary reactions. The union of this progressive accommodation with the reciprocal assimilation of the schemata constitutes, with respect to the intelligence, a process of learning which should not be considered as either purely experimental or purely deductive, but which partakes simultaneously of experience and mental construction. Sensorimotor intelligence, having arrived at this level, is therefore essentially the construction of relations or constructive deduction.

This process explains, it seems to us, the discovery of the object's real permanence. After having established during the fourth stage that the vanished object remains behind a screen, the child succeeds during the fifth stage in bestowing on that object an autonomous trajectory and consequently a truly spatial permanence. This discovery simultaneously presupposes two things: (1) experience, since only the failure of his initial search teaches the child that the object is no longer where it was found the first time but rather where it was last hidden, and (2) deduction, since without the reciprocal assimilation of schemata the child would not succeed in assuming the existence of objects hidden behind the screen nor in postulating their permanence, once and for all, particularly when he has not found them where he first looked for them. In short, object conservation, which is the first of the forms of conservation, results like all the others in the close union of a rational or deductive element and an empirical element, indicating that deduction is constantly at work in close relation to things or at their suggestion. . . .

Finally, during the sixth stage, the coordination of the schemata is internalized in the form of mental combinations, while accommodation becomes representation. Thereafter deduction of the object and of its spatial characteristics is achieved in the construction of a collective universe in which displacements that are merely indicated are inserted among observed movements and complete them in a truly coherent whole.

The Elaboration of the Universe*

ASSIMILATION AND ACCOMMODATION

The successive study of concepts of object, space, causality, and time has led us to the same conclusions: the elaboration of the universe by sensorimotor intelligence constitutes the transition from a state in

*[The following section is from the Conclusion.]

which objects are centered about a self which believes it directs them, although completely unaware of itself as subject, to a state in which the self is placed, at least practically, in a stable world conceived as independent of personal activity. How is this evolution possible?

It can be explained only by the development of intelligence. Intelligence progresses from a state in which accommodation to the environment is undifferentiated from the assimilation of things to the subject's schemata to a state in which the accommodation of multiple schemata is distinguished from their respective and reciprocal assimilation. To understand this process, which sums up the whole evolution of sensori-motor intelligence, let us recall its steps, starting with the development of assimilation itself.

In its beginnings, assimilation is essentially the utilization of the external environment by the subject to nourish his hereditary or acquired schemata. It goes without saying that schemata such as those of sucking, sight, prehension, etc., constantly need to be accommodated to things, and that the necessities of this accommodation often thwart the assimilatory effort. But this accommodation remains so undifferentiated from the assimilatory processes that it does not give rise to any special active behavior pattern but merely consists in an adjustment of the pattern to the details of the things assimilated. Hence it is natural that at this developmental level the external world does not seem formed by permanent objects, that neither space nor time is yet organized in groups and objective series, and that causality is not spatialized or located in things. In other words, at first the universe consists in mobile and plastic perceptual images centered about personal activity. But it is self-evident that to the extent that this activity is undifferentiated from the things it constantly assimilates to itself it remains unaware of its own subjectivity; the external world therefore begins by being confused with the sensations of a self unaware of itself, before the two factors become detached from one another and are organized correlatively.

On the other hand, in proportion as the schemata are multiplied and differentiated by their reciprocal assimilations as well as their progressive accommodation to the diversities of reality, the accommodation is dissociated from assimilation little by little and at the same time insures a gradual delimitation of the external environment and of the subject. Hence assimilation ceases merely to incorporate things in personal activity and establishes, through the progress of that activity, an increasingly tight web of coordinations among the schemata which define it and consequently among the objects to which these schemata are applied. In terms of reflective intelligence this would mean that deduction is organized and applied to an experience conceived as external. From this time on, the universe is built up into an aggregate of permanent objects connected by causal relations that are independent of the subject and are placed in objective space and time. Such a universe, instead of depending on personal activity, is on the contrary imposed upon the self to the extent that it comprises the organism as a part in a whole. The self thus becomes aware of itself, at least in its practical action, and discovers itself as a cause among other causes and as an object subject to the same laws as other objects.

In exact proportion to the progress of intelligence in the direction of differentiation of schemata and their reciprocal assimilation, the universe proceeds from the integral and unconscious egocentrism of the beginnings to an increasing solidification and objectification. During the earliest stages the child perceives things like a solipsist who is unaware of himself as subject and is familiar only with his own actions. But step by step with the coordination of his intellectual instruments he discovers himself in placing himself as an active object among the other active objects in a universe external to himself.

These global transformations of the objects of perception, and of the very intelligence which makes them, gradually denote the existence of a sort of law of evolution which can be phrased as follows: assimilation and accommodation proceed from a state of chaotic undifferentiation to a state of differentiation with correlative coordination.

In their initial directions, assimilation and accommodation are obviously opposed to one another, since assimilation is conservative and tends to subordinate the environment to the organism as it is, whereas accommodation is the source of changes and bends the organism to the successive constraints of the environment. But if in their rudiment these two functions are antagonistic, it is precisely the role of mental life in general and of intelligence in particular to intercoordinate them.

First let us remember that this coordination presupposes no special force of organization, since from the beginning assimilation and accommodation are indissociable from each other. Accommodation of mental structures to reality implies the existence of assimilatory schemata apart from which any structure would be impossible. Inversely, the formation of schemata through assimilation entails the utilization of external realities to which the former must accommodate, however crudely. Assimilation and accommodation are therefore the two poles of an interaction between the organism and the environment, which is the condition for all biological and intellectual operation, and such an interaction presupposes from the point of departure an equilibrium between the two tendencies of opposite poles. The question is to ascertain what forms are successively taken by this equilibrium which is being constituted.

If the assimilation of reality to the subject's schemata involves their continuous accommodation, assimilation is no less opposed to any new accommodation, that is, to any differentiation of schemata by environmental conditions not encountered up to then. On the other hand, if accommodation prevails, that is, if the schema is differentiated, it marks the start of new assimilations. Every acquisition of accommodation becomes material for assimilation, but assimilation always resists new accommodations. It is this situation which explains the diversity of form of equilibrium between the two processes, according to whether one envisages the point of departure or the destiny of their development.

At their point of departure they are relatively undifferentiated in relation to each other, since they are both included in the interaction which unites the organism to the environment and which, in its initial form, is so close and direct that it does not comprise any specialized operation of accommodation, such as the tertiary circular reactions, behavior patterns of active experimentation, etc., will subsequently be. But they are nonetheless antagonistic, since, though each assimilatory schema is accommodated to the usual circumstances, it resists every new accommodation, precisely through lack of specialized accommodative technique. It is therefore possible to speak of chaotic undifferentiation. It is at this level that the external world and the self remain undissociated to such a point that neither objects nor spatial, temporal, or causal objectifications are possible.

To the extent that new accommodations multiply because of the demands of the environment on the one hand and of the coordinations between schemata on the other, accommodation is differentiated from assimilation and by virtue of that very fact becomes complementary to it. It is differentiated, because, in addition to the accommodation necessary for the usual circumstances, the subject becomes interested in novelty and pursues it for its own sake. The more the schemata are differentiated, the smaller the gap between the new and the familiar becomes, so that novelty, instead of constituting an annoyance avoided by the subject, becomes a problem and invites searching. Thereafter and to the same extent, assimilation and accommodation enter into relations of mutual dependence. On the one hand, the reciprocal assimilation of the schemata and the multiple accommodations which stem from them favor their differentiation and consequently their accommodation; on the other hand, the accommodation to novelties is extended sooner or later into assimilation, because, interest in the new being simultaneously the function of resemblances and of differences in relation to the familiar, it is a matter of conserving new acquisitions and of reconciling them with the old ones. An increasingly close interconnection thus tends to be established between the two functions which are constantly being better differentiated, and by extending the lines this interaction ends, as we have seen, on the plane of reflective thought, in the mutual dependency of assimilatory deduction and experimental techniques.

Thus it may be seen that intellectual activity begins with confusion of experience and of awareness of the self, by virtue of the chaotic undifferentiation of accommodation and assimilation. In other words, knowledge of the external world begins with an immediate utilization of things, whereas knowledge of self is stopped by this purely practical and utilitarian contact. Hence there is simply interaction between the most superficial zone of external reality and the wholly corporal periphery of the self. On the contrary, gradually as the differentiation and coordination of assimilation and accommodation occur, experimental and accommodative activity penetrates to the interior of things, while assimilatory activity becomes enriched and organized. Hence there is a progressive formation of relationships between zones that are increasingly deep and removed from reality and the increasingly intimate operations of personal activity. Intelligence thus begins neither with knowledge of the self nor of things as such but with knowledge of their interaction, and it is by orienting itself simultaneously toward the two poles of that interaction that intelligence organizes the world by organizing itself.

A diagram will make the thing comprehensible (Figure 1). Let the organism be represented by a small circle inscribed in a large circle which corresponds to the surrounding universe. The meeting between the organism and the environment takes place at point A and at all analogous points, which are simultaneously the most external to the

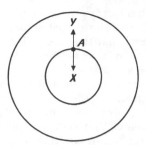

Figure 1

organism and to the environment itself. In other words, the first knowledge of the universe or of himself that the subject can acquire is knowledge relating to the most immediate appearance of things or to the most external and material aspect of his being. From the point of view of consciousness, this primitive relation between subject and object is a relation of undifferentiation, corresponding to the protoplasmic consciousness of the first weeks of life when no distinction is made between the self and the nonself. From the point of view of behavior this relation constitutes the morphologic-reflex organization, insofar as it is a necessary condition of primitive consciousness. But from this point of junction and undifferentiation A, knowledge proceeds along two complementary roads. By virtue of the very fact that all knowledge is simultaneosuly accommodation to the object and assimilation to the subject, the progress of intelligence works in the dual direction of externalization and internalization, and its two poles will be the acquisition of physical experience ($\rightarrow Y$) and the acquisition of consciousness of the intellectual operation itself ($\rightarrow X$). That is why every great experimental discovery in the realm of exact sciences is accompanied by a reflexive progress of reason on itself (of logico-mathematical deduction), that is, by progress in the formation of reason insofar as it is internal activity, and it is impossible to decide once for all whether the progress of the experiment is due to that of reason or the inverse. From this point of view the morphologic-reflex organization, that is, the physiological and anatomic aspect of the organism, gradually appears to the mind as external to it, and the intellectual activity which extends it by internalizing it presents itself as the essential of our existence as living beings.

In the last analysis, it is this process of forming relationships between a universe constantly becoming more external to the self and an intellectual activity progressing internally which explains the evolution of the real categories, that is, of the concepts of object, space, causality, and time. So long as the interaction between subject and object is revealed in the form of exchanges of slight amplitude in a zone of undifferentiation, the universe has the appearance of depending on the subject's personal activity, although the latter is not known in its subjective aspect. To the extent, on the contrary, that the interaction increases, the progress of knowledge in the two complementary directions of object and subject enables the subject to place himself among objects as a part in a coherent and permanent whole. Consequently, to the extent that assimilation and accommodation transcend the initial state of "false equilibrium" between the subject's needs and the resistance of things to attain a true equilibrium, that is, a harmony between internal organization and external experience, the subject's perspective of the universe is radically transformed; from integral egocentrism to·objectivity is the law of that evolution. The relations of assimilation and accommodation thus constitute, from the time of the sensorimotor level, a formative process analogous to that which, on the plane of verbal and reflective intelligence, is represented by the relations of individual thought and socialization. Just as accommodation to the point of view of others enables individual thought to be located in a totality of perspectives that insures its objectivity and reduces its egocentrism, so also the coordination of sensorimotor assimilation and accommodation leads the subject to go outside himself to solidify and objectify his universe to the point where he is able to include himself in it while continuing to assimilate it to himself.

TRANSITION FROM SENSORIMOTOR INTELLIGENCE TO

CONCEPTUAL THOUGHT

This last remark leads us to examine briefly, in conclusion, the relations between the practical universe elaborated by the sensorimotor intelligence and the representation of the world brought about by later reflective thought.

In the course of the first two years of childhood the evolution of sensorimotor intelligence, and also the correlative elaboration of the universe, seem, as we have tried to analyze them, to lead to a state of equilibrium bordering on rational thought. Thus, starting with the use of reflexes and the first acquired association, the child succeeds within a few months in constructing a system of schemata capable of unlimited combinations which presages that of logical concepts and relations. During the last stage of their development these schemata even become capable of certain spontaneous and internal regroupings which are equivalent to mental deduction and construction. Moreover, gradually as objects, causality, space, and time are elaborated, a coherent universe follows the chaos of the initial egocentric perceptions. When in the second year of life representation completes action by means of the progressive internalization of behavior patterns, one might therefore expect that the totality of sensorimotor operations would merely pass from the plane of action to that of language and thought and that the organization of schemata would thus be directly extended in a system of rational concepts.

In reality, things are far from being so simple. In the first place, on the plane of practical intelligence alone, the excellent studies of André Rey* show that not all the problems are solved by the child by the end of his second year. As soon as the data of problems become complicated and the subjects are obliged to attain their ends by means of complex contacts or displacements, in the solution of these new problems through a sort of temporal displacement in extension we rediscover all the obstacles analyzed in this volume apropos of the elementary stages of the first two years of life. Furthermore, and this is valuable to the

*A. Rey, *L'Intelligence pratique chez l'enfant* (Paris: Alcan, 1934).

theory of temporal displacements, these obstacles reappear in the same order despite the gap which separates the ages of birth to 2 years, studied here, from the ages of 3 to 8 years studied by André Rey. Thus in Rey's experiments the child begins by revealing a sort of "dynamic realism," "in the course of which the movement (pulling, pushing, etc.) would possess a quality independent of any adaptation to the particular data of the environment."* Then he goes through a phase of "optical realism" analogous to that which we observe among chimpanzees, in which he substitutes for the physical relations of bodies the visual relations corresponding to the apparent data of perception. How is it possible not to compare these two preliminary steps to those which characterize the beginnings of sensorimotor intelligence and of the practical universe resulting from them? Dynamic realism is the residue of the assimilation of things to actions that accounts for practical groups and series, for the magico-phenomenistic causality and the object-less universe peculiar to our elementary stages. Before being able to structure a complex situation, the child from 3 to 4 years of age, like the baby a few months old who is confronted by a situation that is simpler but from his point of view obscure, is limited to assimilating it to the act which should be performed. Because of a residual belief in the power of his personal activity, he still confers upon his gestures a sort of absolute value, which is tantamount to forgetting momentarily that things are permanent substances grouped spatially, seriated temporally, and sustaining among themselves objective causal relations. With regard to optical realism it seems clear that it constitutes a residue of behavior patterns which are intermediate between the primitive egocentric stages and the stages of objectification, behavior patterns characterized by subjective groups and series or by transitional behavior relating to the beginnings of the object and of spatialized causality. Optical realism, too, consists in considering things as being what they appear to be in immediate perception and not what they will become once they have been inserted in a system of rational relations transcending the visual field. Thus the child imagines that a stick can draw an object because it is beside it or touches it, as though optical contact were equivalent to a causal link. It is precisely this confusion of immediate visual perceptions with physical realities that characterizes the subjective groups or series, for example, when the baby does not know how to turn over a nursing bottle because he cannot conceive of the object's reverse side, or when he imagines himself able to rediscover objects where he saw them the first time, regardless of their actual trajectory.

Hence, between the sensorimotor intelligence which precedes the advent of speech and the later practical intelligence which subsists under verbal and conceptual realities, there is not only a linear continuity but also there are temporal displacements in extension, so that in the presence of every truly new problem the same primitive processes of adaptation reappear, although diminishing in importance with age.

But above all, even if these obstacles encountered in action by the 2- to 7-year-old child are destined to be overcome finally, through the instruments prepared by the sensorimotor intelligence during the first

---

*Ibid., p. 203.

two years of life, the transition from the merely practical plane to that of speech and conceptual and socialized thought brings with it, by nature, obstacles that singularly complicate the progress of intelligence.

At the outset, two innovations place conceptual thought in opposition to sensorimotor intelligence and explain the difficulty of transition from one of these two forms of intellectual activity to the other. In the first place, sensorimotor intelligence seeks only practical adaptation, that is, it aims only at success or utilization, whereas conceptual thought leads to knowledge as such and therefore yields to norms of truth. Even when the child explores a new object or studies the displacements he provokes by a sort of "experiment in order to see," there is always in these kinds of sensorimotor assimilations, however precise the accommodation they evidence, the concept of a practical result to be obtained. By virtue of the very fact that the child cannot translate his observations into a system of verbal judgments and reflexive concepts but can simply register them by means of sensorimotor schemata, that is, by outlining possible actions, there can be no question of attributing to him the capacity of arriving at pure proofs or judgments properly so called, but it must be said that these judgments, if they were expressed in words, would be equivalent to something like, "one can do this with this object," "one could achieve this result," etc. In the behavior patterns oriented by an actual goal, such as the discovery of new means through active experimentation or the invention of new means through mental combinations, the sole problem is to reach the desired goal, hence the only values involved are success or failure, and to the child it is not a matter of seeking a truth for itself or reflecting upon the relations which made it possible to obtain the desired result. It is therefore no exaggeration to say that sensorimotor intelligence is limited to desiring success or practical adaptation, whereas the function of verbal or conceptual thought is to know and state truths.

There is a second difference between these two types of activity: sensorimotor intelligence is an adaptation of the individual to things or to the body of another person but without socialization of the intellect as such; whereas conceptual thought is collective thought obeying common laws. Even when the baby imitates an intelligent act performed by someone else or understands, from a smile or an expression of displeasure, the intentions of another person, we still may not call this an exchange of thoughts leading to modification of those intentions. On the contrary, after speech has been acquired the socialization of thought is revealed by the elaboration of concepts, of relations, and by the formation of rules, that is, there is a structural evolution. It is precisely to the extent that verbal-conceptual thought is transformed by its collective nature that it becomes capable of proof and search for truth, in contradistinction to the practical character of the acts of sensorimotor intelligence and their search for success or satisfaction. It is by cooperation with another person that the mind arrives at verifying judgments, verification implying a presentation or an exchange and having in itself no meaning as regards individual activity. Whether conceptual thought is rational because it is social or vice versa, the interdependence of the search for truth and of socialization seems to us undeniable.

The adaptation of intelligence to these new realities, when speech and conceptual thought are superimposed on the sensorimotor plane, entails the reappearance of all the obstacles already overcome in the realm of action. That is why, despite the level reached by the intelligence in the fifth and sixth stages of its sensorimotor development, it does not appear to be rational at the outset, when it begins to be organized on the verbal-conceptual plane. On the contrary, . . . the child does not at first succeed in reflecting in words and concepts the procedures that he already knows how to carry out in acts, and if he cannot reflect them it is because, in order to adapt himself to the collective and conceptual plane on which his thought will henceforth move, he is obliged to repeat the work of coordination between assimilation and accommodation already accomplished in his sensorimotor adaptation. . . .

It is easy to prove: (1) that the assimilation and accommodation of the individual from the time of the beginnings of speech present a balance less well developed in relation to the social group than in the realm of sensorimotor intelligence; and (2) that to make possible the adaptation of the mind to the group these functions must proceed again over the same steps, and in the same order, as during the first months of life. From the social point of view, accommodation is nothing other than imitation and the totality of the operations enabling the individual to subordinate himself to the precepts and the demands of the group. With regard to assimilation it consists as before in incorporating reality into the activity and perspectives of the self. On the plane of adaptation to the sensorimotor universe the subject, while submitting to the constraints of the environment from the very beginning, starts by considering things as dependent on his actions and succeeds only little by little in placing himself as an element in a totality which is coherent and independent of himself. [Similarly], on the social plane the child, while at first obeying someone else's suggestions, for a long time remains enclosed in his personal point of view before placing it among other points of view. The self and the group therefore begin by remaining undissociated in a mixture of egocentrism and submission to environmental constraints, and subsequently are differentiated and give rise to a cooperation between personalities which have become autonomous. In other words, at the time when assimilation and accommodation are already dissociated on the plane of sensorimotor adaptation, they are not yet dissociated on the social plane, and thus they reproduce there an evolution analogous to that which has already occurred on the former plane. . . .

In the first place, just as practical intelligence seeks success before truth, egocentric thought, to the extent that it is assimilation to the self, leads to satisfaction and not to objectivity. The extreme form of this assimilation to personal desires and interests is symbolic or imaginative play in which reality is transformed by the needs of the self to the point where the meanings of thought may remain strictly individual and incommunicable. . . .

In all the social behavior patterns of thought it is easy to see how much more easily the child is led to satisfy his desires and to judge from his own personal point of view than to enter into that of others to arrive at an objective view. But in contrast to this powerful assimilation of reality to the self we witness during the earliest stages of individual thought the child's astonishing docility with respect to the suggestions and statements of another person; the little child constantly repeats what he hears, imitates the attitudes he observes, and thus yields as readily to training by the group as he resists rational intercourse. In short, assimilation to the self and accommodation to others begins with a compromise without profound synthesis, and at first the subject wavers between these two tendencies without being able to control or organize them.

In the second place, there arises a series of intellectual structures peculiar to these beginnings of infantile thought and which reproduce through temporal displacement the initial sensorimotor structures. Thus the first concepts the child uses are not at the outset logical classes capable of operations of addition, multiplication, subtraction, etc., which characterize the logic of classes in its normal functioning, but rather kinds of preconcepts proceeding by syncretic assimilations. So also the child who succeeds in handling relationships on the sensorimotor plane begins on the verbal and reflexive plane by substituting for relationships absolute qualities. [He lacks the] ability to coordinate the different perspectives and to emerge from the personal point of view to which he assimilates everything. Thereafter the primitive infantile reasoning seems to return to the sensorimotor coordinations of the fifth and sixth stages: not yet familiar with classes or relations properly so called, it consists in simple fusions, in transductions proceeding by syncretic assimilations. It is only in the course of a laborious development which transforms egocentric assimilation into true deduction, and accommodation into a real adjustment to experience and to perspectives surpassing the personal point of view, that the child's reasoning becomes rational and thus extends, on the plane of thought, the acquisitions of sensorimotor intelligence. . . .

FROM SENSORIMOTOR UNIVERSE TO

REPRESENTATION OF CHILD'S WORLD

Space and Object. The understanding of spatial relations is a particularly clear first example of the parallelism with temporal displacement between the sensorimotor acquisitions and those of representative thought.

We recall how, starting with purely practical and quasi-physiological groups, the child begins by elaborating subjective groups, then arrives at objective groups, and only then becomes capable of representative groups. The groups of this last type constitute the culminating point of practical space and thus insert in sensorimotor spatial relations the representation of displacements not occurring within the direct perceptual field. [But these groups] are far from marking the beginning of a complete representation of space, that is, a representation completely detached from action. What will happen when the child is called upon, apart from any current action, to represent to himself a group of displacements or a system of coherent perspectives? It is from this decisive moment that we witness, on the plane of thought properly so called, a repetition of the evolution already accomplished on the sensorimotor plane.

Take, for example, the following problem.* The child is presented with a model, about one square meter in size, representing three mountains in relief; he is to reconstruct the different perspectives in which a little doll views them in varying positions that follow a given order. No technical or verbal difficulty impedes the child, for he may simply point with his finger to what the doll sees, or choose from among several pictures showing the possible perspectives, or construct with boxes symbolizing mountains the photograph the doll could take from a given point of view. Moreover, the problem posed to the child consists in representing to himself the simplest of all the spatial relations which transcend direct action and perception, that is, to represent to himself what he would see if he were in the successive positions suggested to him. At first it would seem as though the child's answers would merely extend the acquisitions of the sixth stage of sensorimotor space and arrive immediately at the correct representations.

But interestingly enough the youngest of the children capable of understanding the problem of the mountains and of responding without difficulties of a verbal or technical kind reveal an attitude which, instead of extending the objective and representative groups of our sixth stage, on the contrary, regresses to the integral egocentrism of the subjective groups. Far from representing the various scenes which the doll contemplates from different viewpoints, the child always considers his own perspective as absolute and thus attributes it to the doll without suspecting this confusion. In other words, when he is asked what the doll sees from a particular position the child describes what he himself sees from his own position without taking into account the obstacles which prevent the doll from seeing the same view. When he is shown several pictures from among which he is to choose the one which corresponds to the doll's perspective, he chooses the one which represents his own. Finally, when he is to reconstruct with boxes the photograph the doll might take from its place, the child again reproduces his own view of things.

Then, when the child disengages himself from this initial egocentrism and masters the relationships involved in these problems, we witness a totality of transitional phases. Either the child who begins to understand that the perspective differs according to the doll's position effects various mixtures between those perspectives and his own perspective ("prerelations"), or else he takes into account only one relation at a time (left-right or before-behind, etc.) and does not succeed in multiplying the interrelations. These transitions correspond to the limited groups of displacements belonging to the fourth of the sensorimotor stages. Finally, complete relativity is attained, corresponding to stages V–VI of the same series.

How then can this temporal displacement be explained, as well as this return to the phases which have already been transcended on the plane of sensorimotor space? To act in space the child is certainly obliged to understand little by little that the things which surround him have a trajectory independent of himself and that their displacements

---

*This problem was studied at our request by our assistant, Miss E. Meyer; see E. Meyer, "La Représentation des relations spatiales chez l'enfant," *Cahiers de Péd. exp. et de Psych. de l'Enfant de l'Institut des Sciences de l'Education*, 8 (1935).

are thus grouped in objective systems. From a purely practical point of view the child is therefore led to emerge from an initial egocentrism, in which things are considered to depend solely on his personal activity, and to master a relativity which is established between displacements successively perceived or even between certain perceived moments and others which have simply been represented. But the egocentrism and objective relativity in question here concern only the relationships between the child and things, and nothing in sensorimotor action forces him to leave this narrow realm. So long as the problem is not to represent to himself reality in itself, but simply to use it or to exert an influence upon it, there is no need to go beyond the system of relations established between objects and self or among objects as such in the field of personal perspective; there is no need to assume the existence of other perspectives and to interconnect them by including his own among them. To be sure, the act by which one confers an objectivity on the displacements of things already implies an enlargement of the initial egocentric perspective. It is in this sense that, apropos of the fifth and sixth sensorimotor stages, we have been able to speak of a change in perspective and the mastery of a universe in which the subject locates himself instead of bringing the universe illusively to him. But this is only the first step, and even in this objective, practical universe, everything is related to a single frame of reference which is that of the subject and not that of other possible subjects. Hence there is objectivity and even relativity, but within the limits of a realm which is always considered absolute, because nothing yet induces the subject to transcend it. If we may be permitted to make a somewhat daring comparison, the completion of the objective practical universe resembles Newton's achievements as compared to the egocentrism of Aristotelian physics, but the absolute Newtonian time and space themselves remain egocentric from the point of view of Einstein's relativity because they envisage only one perspective on the universe among many other perspectives which are equally possible and real. On the contrary, from the time when the child seeks no longer merely to act upon things, but to represent them to himself in themselves and independently of the immediate action, this single perspective, in the midst of which he had succeeded in introducing objectivity and relativity, no longer suffices and has to be coordinated with the others.

This is true for two reasons, one relating to the subject's intention in his attempt at representation, the other to the requirements of representation. Why at a given moment in his mental evolution does the subject try to represent spatial relations to himself instead of simply acting upon them? Obviously in order to communicate to someone else or to obtain from someone else some information on a fact concerning space. Outside of this social relation there is no apparent reason why pure representation should follow action. The existence of multiple perspectives relating to various individuals is therefore already involved in the child's effort to represent space to himself. Moreover, to represent to himself space or objects in space is necessarily to reconcile in a single act the different possible perspectives on reality and no longer to be satisfied to adopt them successively. Take, for example, a box or some object upon which the child acts. At the end of his sensorimotor evolution he becomes perfectly capable of turning the box over in all directions, of representing to himself its reverse side as well as its visible parts, its contents as well as its exterior. But do these representations connected with practical activity, with the "concrete active behavior" of which Gelb and Goldstein have spoken in their fine studies on space, suffice to constitute a total representation of the box, a pattern of "formal conceptual behavior?" Surely not, for to achieve that the box must be seen from all sides at once, that is, it must be located in a system of perspectives in which one can represent it to oneself from any point of view whatever and transfer it from one to the other point of view without recourse to action. Now, if it is possible for the child to imagine himself as occupying several positions at one time, it is obvious that it is rather by representing to himself the perspective of another person and by coordinating it with his own that he will solve such a problem in concrete reality. In this sense one can maintain that pure representation detached from personal activity presupposes adaptation to others and social coordination.

Therefore we understand why, in the problem of the mountains which is typical in this respect, the child 4 to 6 years of age still reveals an egocentrism reminiscent of the beginnings of sensorimotor intelligence and the most elementary subjective groups; it is because, on the plane of pure representation to which this experiment pertains, the subject must compare various points of view with his own, and as yet nothing has prepared him for this operation. Besides, the attitudes which have already been transcended in the relations between things and himself reappear when connections are established with other persons. . . .

. . . On the occasion of movements near at hand, after having constructed the groups of displacements studied above, the child finds himself confronted by analogous problems raised by the observation of more distant movements: displacements relating to bodies situated on the horizon or to celestial movements. For many years we have observed the child's attitude toward the moon and often toward clouds, stars, etc.; until he is about seven years old he believes that he is followed by these bodies and considers their apparent movements real. From the point of view of space, this is only an extension of the behavior patterns relating to nearby objects observed during the first sensorimotor stages. The child, by taking appearance for reality, links all displacements to himself, instead of locating them in an objective system that includes his own body without being centered on it. Similarly, we have observed in our children analogous illustrations relating to mountains, on an excursion in the Alps or in an automobile going up and down the hills. At four or five years of age the mountains still seem to be displaced and actually to change shape in connection with our own movements, exactly like the nearby objects in the subjective groups of the baby.

These last remnants of primitive space in the child of school age lead us to the temporal displacements of processes relating to the object. It is self-evident that in proportion as the groups of displacements require new constructive work on the plane of representation or of conceptual thought to complete them, the object, in its turn, cannot be considered as entirely elaborated once it has been formed on the sensorimotor plane. At the time of displacements in extension, of which we have spoken apropos of the moon and the mountains, the matter is

clear. The mountains which move and change shape with our movements are not objects, since they lack permanence of form and mass.
So also a moon which follows us is not "the" moon as object of simultaneous or successive perceptions of different possible observers. The
proof is that at the period in which the child believes he is being followed
by the stars he believes in the existence of several moons rising over
and over again and capable of occupying different regions of space
simultaneously.

But this difficulty in attributing substantial identity to distant objects
is not the most interesting residue of the processes of objectification
peculiar to the stages of sensorimotor intelligence. . . . The construction of the object seems to be not only a continuous process unremit-
tingly pursued throughout the evolution of reason and still found in
the most elaborate forms of scientific thought, but also a process constantly passing through phases analogous to those of the initial sensorimotor series. Thus the different principles of conservation whose progressive formation occupies the whole development of the child's physics
are only successive aspects of the objectification of the universe. For
example, the conservation of matter does not seem necessary to the
child 3 to 6 years old in cases of changes of state or even changes of
form. Sugar melting in water is believed to be returning to the void,
only taste (that is, a pure quality) being supposed to subsist and that
only for a few days. So also, when one offers the child two pellets of the
same weight and mass and then molds one of them into a long cylinder,
this one is considered to have lost both weight and mass. When one
empties the contents of a large bottle of water into small bottles or
tubes, the quantity of liquid is conceived as having been changed,* etc.
The child subsequently arrives at the concept of a necessary conservation of matter, independently of changes of form or of state. But having
arrived at this level, he nevertheless continues to believe that the weight
of bodies can change with their form; thus the pellet by becoming
elongated loses weight while conserving the same quantity of matter.
Around 11 or 12 years of age, on the other hand, the child is so convinced of the conservation of weight that he attributes to the particles
of sugar dissolved in water the same total weight as to the initial lump.†

Thus we see that, from the point of view of conservation of matter
and weight, the child again, this time on the plane of conceptual and
reflective thought, passes through stages analogous to those he traverses
on the sensorimotor plane from the point of view of conservation of the
object itself. . . .

How then can we explain this temporal displacement; how can we
explain why thought, at the moment it gathers up the work of sensorimotor intelligence and in particular the belief in permanent objects,
does not at the outset attribute to objects constancy of matter and of
weight? As we have seen, it is because three formative processes are
necessary to the elaboration of object concept: the accommodation of
the organs which makes it possible to foresee the reappearance of bodies;

*This excellent experiment is thanks to our assistant, Miss A. Szeminska;
see A. Szeminska, "Essai d'analyse psychologique du raisonnement mathématique," *Cahiers de Ped. Exp. et de Psych. de l'Enfant*, 7 (1935).

†See B. Inhelder, "Observations sur le principe de conservation dans la
physique de l'enfant," *Cahiers de Ped. Exp. et de Psych. de l'Enfant*, 9 (1936).

the coordination of schemata which makes it possible to endow each of these bodies with a multiplicity of interconnected qualities; and the deduction peculiar to sensorimotor reasoning which makes it possible to understand displacements of bodies and to reconcile their permanence with their apparent variations. These three functional factors—foresight, coordination, and deduction—change entirely in structure when they pass from the sensorimotor plane to that of speech and conceptual operations, and when systems of classes and thoughtful relations are substituted for simple practical schemata. Whereas the substantial object is a mere product of action or practical intelligence, the concepts of quantity of matter and conservation of weight presuppose on the contrary a very subtle rational elaboration. In practical object concept there is nothing more than the idea of a permanence of qualities (form, consistency, color, etc.) independent of immediate perception. There is, however, in the concept of the conservation of matter such as sugar, the clay pellet which changes shape, or the liquid poured from a large receptacle into several small ones, a quantitative relation which as soon as it is perceived seems essential; this is the idea that despite changes of state or of form (real form and no longer merely apparent form) something is conserved. This something is not at the outset weight, but it is volume, occupied space, and only later is it weight, that is, a quality that is quantified insofar as it is considered invariant. But for their construction these qualitative relationships do not solely involve a foresight which remains practical in kind (foresight of the water level when the sugar is dissolved, of the weight of the pellet made into a cylinder, etc.); they involve primarily a coordination of classes and of logical relations as well as true deduction, for on the plane of thought foresight gradually becomes the function of deduction instead of preceding it.

In the case of the sugar which dissolves in water, how does the child succeed in postulating the permanence of matter and even in making the atomic hypothesis of invisible particles of sugar permeating the liquid, particles whose total volume equals that of the initial lump, to the point of explaining that the water level remains above the original level? From all the evidence this is not a simple lesson of experience or, as in the case of the permanence of the practical object, an intelligent structuring of experience, but rather a deduction which is primarily due to thought and in which a complex series of concepts and relations intervenes. So also, the idea that the pellet conserves its weight while becoming a cylinder is a deductive construction which experience does not suffice to explain, for the child has neither the means to perform the delicate weighing that verification of such a hypothesis would necessitate nor, above all, the curiosity to attempt such a verification, because its affirmation seems to him self-evident and because as a general rule the problem does not arise for him. What is most interesting in the child's reaction is the fact that, having doubtless never thought about the problem, he solves it at once a priori and with such certainty that he is surprised it was raised, whereas a year or two earlier he would have solved it in precisely the opposite direction and would not have had recourse to the idea of conservation!

In short, the development of the principles of conservation can only be explained as the function of an internal progress in the child's logic in its triple aspect of an elaboration of deductive structures, of relations, and of classes, forming a corporate system. This is the explanation of the temporal displacement under discussion here. Through speech the child [reaches] the plane of representative thought, which at the same time is the plane of socialized thought; to the extent that he must now adapt himself to other persons, his spontaneous egocentrism, already overcome on the sensorimotor plane, reappears in the course of this adaptation, as we have shown with the examples concerning space. From this arises a series of consequences with regard to the structure of thought. On the one hand, in proportion as the child does not succeed in coordinating with his own perspective the perspectives peculiar to different individuals, he cannot master the logic of relationships, although he knows how to handle practical relations on the sensorimotor plane. . . . Moreover, the child begins by utilizing only syncretic pseudo-concepts before elaborating true logical classes, because the operations formative of classes (logical addition and multiplication) require a system of definitions whose stability and generality transcend the personal point of view and its subjective attachments (definitions by usage, syncretic classifications, etc.). From this stems the conclusion that a deductive structure on the plane of reflective thought presupposes a mind freed from the personal point of view by methods of reciprocity inherent in cooperation or intellectual exchange, and that reason, dominated by egocentrism on the verbal and social plane, can only be "transductive," that is, proceeding through the fusion of preconcepts located midway between particular cases and true generality.

If the conquest of the object on the sensorimotor plane is not at once extended on the conceptual plane through an objectification capable of insuring rational permanence, it is because the egocentrism reappearing on this new plane prevents thought from attaining at the outset the logical structures necessary for this elaboration. Let us try again to define this mechanism by analyzing some examples chosen from the periods of the beginning of speech and of reflective thought; these will show us both how difficult it is at first for the child to form true logical classes and how those pseudo-concepts and primitive transductions lead us back to a stage which, from the point of view of the object, seemed to be surpassed by sensorimotor intelligence and which reappears on the conceptual plane.

First of all it is currently observed that the first generic concepts utilized by the child, when they do not designate certain ordinary objects related to daily activity but totalities properly so called, remain midway between the individual and the general. For a long time, for instance, one of my children, to whom I showed slugs on successive walks, called each new specimen encountered "the slug"; I was unable to ascertain whether he meant "the same individual" or "a new individual of the slug species." While it is impossible to furnish definitive proof, in such a case everything seems to indicate that the child himself neither succeeds in answering nor tries to answer the question and that "slug" is for him a sort of semi-individual and semigeneric type shared by different individuals. It is the same when the child encounters "lamb," "dog," etc.; we are confronted by neither the individual nor the generic in the sense of the logical class but by an intermediate state which is precisely comparable on the conceptual plane to the primitive state of the sensorimotor object floating between the unsubstantial perceptual image and permanent substance.

Interpretation may seem hazardous when observations of this kind are involved because one can always attribute them to mere mistakes by the subject, but it becomes more certain when these pseudo-concepts come into operation in transductions properly so called, that is, in the analytical or classificatory reasoning proceeding by fusion of analogous cases. Let us refer, for example, to the explanations given us by the youngest of our subjects concerning the phenomenon of the shadow or the draft:* the shadow produced on a table before their eyes comes, according to them, from "under the trees" or other possible sources of darkness, just as the draft from a fan emanates from the north wind which blows outside the room. The child thus likens, as we do ourselves, the shadow from a notebook to that of the trees, the draft to the wind, etc., but instead of simply placing the two analogous phenomena in the same logical class and explaining them by the same physical law, he considers the two compared terms as participants of each other from a distance and without any intelligible physical link. Consequently, here again the child's thought wavers between the individual and the generic. The shadow of the notebook is not a pure singular object since it emanates from that of the trees, it "is" really that of trees arising in a new context. But an abstract class does not exist either, precisely since the relation between the two shadows compared is not a relation of simple comparison and common [membership in] the same totality, but of substantial participation. The shadow perceived on the table is therefore no more an isolable object than is, on the sensorimotor plane, the watch which disappears under one cushion and which the child expects to see appear under another. But if there is thus an apparent return to the past it is for an opposite reason to that which obstructs objectification in sensorimotor intelligence; in the latter case the object is difficult to form in proportion as the child has difficulty in intercoordinating perceptual images, whereas on the plane of conceptual thought the object, already elaborated, again loses its identity to the extent that it is coordinated with other objects to construct a class or a relation.

In conclusion, in the case of the object as in that of space, from the very beginnings of verbal reflection there is a return of the difficulties already overcome on the plane of action, and there is repetition, with temporal displacements, of the stages and process of adaptation defined by the transition from egocentrism to objectivity. And in both cases the phenomenon is due to the difficulties experienced by the child, after he has reached the social plane, in inserting his sensorimotor acquisitions in a framework of relationships of logical classes and deductive structures admitting of true generalization, that is, taking into account the point of view of others and all possible points of view as well as his own.

Causality and Time. The development of causality from the first months of life to the eleventh or twelfth year reveals the same graphic curve as that of space or object. The acquisition of causality seems to be completed with the formation of sensorimotor intelligence; in the measure that objectification and spatialization of relations of cause and effect succeed the magico-phenomenistic egocentrism of the primitive connec-

*J. Piaget, *The Child's Conception of Causality.*

tions, a whole evolution resumes with the advent of speech and representative thought which seems to reproduce the preceding evolution before really extending it.

But among the displacements to which this history of the concept of cause gives rise, distinction must again be made between the simple temporal displacements in extension due to the repetition of primitive processes on the occasion of new problems analogous to old ones, and the temporal displacements in comprehension due to the transition from one plane of activity to another; that is, from the plane of action to that of representation. It seems useless to us to emphasize the former. Nothing is more natural than the fact that belief in the efficacy of personal activity, a belief encouraged by chance comparisons through immediate or phenomenistic experience, is again found throughout childhood in those moments of anxiety or of desire which characterize infantile magic. The second type of temporal displacements, however, raises questions which it is useful to mention here.

During the first months of life the child does not dissociate the external world from his own activity. Perceptual images, not yet consolidated into objects or coordinated in a coherent space, seem to him to be governed by his desires and efforts, though these are not attributed to a self which is separate from the universe. Then gradually, as progress is made in the intelligence which elaborates objects and space by spinning a tight web of relations among these images, the child attributes an autonomous causality to things and persons and conceives of the existence of causal relations independent of himself, his own body becoming a source among other sources of effects integrated in this total system. What will happen when, through speech and representative thought, the subject succeeds not only in foreseeing the development of phenomena and in acting upon them but in evoking them apart from any action in order to try to explain them? It is here that the paradox of displacement in comprehension appears.

By virtue of the "why" obsessing the child's mind, as soon as his representation of the world can be detached without too much risk of error, one perceives that this universe, centered on the self, which seemed abolished because it was eliminated from practical action relating to the immediate environment, reappears on the plane of thought and impresses itself on the little child as the sole understandable conception of totality. Undoubtedly the child no longer behaves, as did the baby, as though he commanded everything and everybody. He knows that adults have their own will, that the rain, wind, clouds, stars, and all things are characterized by movements and effects he undergoes but cannot control. . . . But this does not at all prevent the child from representing the universe to himself as a large machine organized exactly by whom he does not know, but organized with the help of adults and for the sake of the well-being of men and particularly of children. Just as in a house everything is arranged according to a plan, despite imperfections and partial failures, so also the raison d'être for everything in the physical universe is the function of a sort of order in the world, an order both material and moral, of which the child is the center. Adults are there "to take care of us," animals to do us service, the stars to warm us and give us light, plants to nourish us, rain to make the gardens grow, clouds to "make night," mountains to climb on,

and lakes for boats, etc. Furthermore, to this more or less explicit and
coherent artificialism there corresponds a latent animism which endows everything with the will to play its role and with just the force and
awareness needed to act with regularity.

Thus the causal egocentrism, which on the sensorimotor plane disappears gradually under the influence of spatialization and objectification, reappears from the time of the beginnings of thought in almost as
radical a form. Doubtless the child no longer attributes personal causality to others or to things, but while endowing objects with specific
activities he centers all these activities on man and above all on himself.
It seems clear that in this sense we may speak of temporal displacement from one plane to another and that the phenomenon is thus comparable to the phenomena which characterize the evolution of space
and object.

But it is in a still deeper sense that the primitive schemata of
causality are again transposed in the child's first reflective representations. If it is true that from the second year of life the child attributes
causality to others and to objects instead of reserving a monopoly on
them for his own activity, we have still to discover how he represents to
himself the mechanism of these causal relations. We have just recalled
that corresponding to the egocentric artificialism which makes the universe gravitate around man and child is an animism capable of explaining the activity of creatures and things in this sort of world. This
example is precisely of a kind to help us understand the second kind
of temporal displacement of which we now speak: if the child renounces
considering his actions as the cause of every event, he nevertheless is
unable to represent to himself the action of bodies except by means of
schemata drawn from his own activity. An object animated by a "natural"
movement like the wind which pushes clouds, or the moon which advances, thus seems endowed with purposefulness and finality, for the
child is unable to conceive of an action without a conscious goal. Through
lack of awareness, every process involving a relation of energies, such
as the rising of the water level in a glass in which a pebble has been
dropped, seems due to forces copied from the model of personal activity;
the pebble "weighs" on the bottom of the water, it "forces" the water
to rise, and if one held the pebble on a string midway of the column
of the water the level would not change. In short, even though there
is objectivity on the practical plane, causality may remain egocentric
from the representative point of view to the extent that the first causal
conceptions are drawn from the completely subjective consciousness of
the activity of the self. With regard to spatialization of the causal connection the same temporal displacement between representation and
action is observable. Thus the child can acknowledge in practice the
necessity for a spatial contact between cause and effect, but that does
not make causality geometric or mechanical. For example, the parts of
a bicycle all seem necessary to the child long before he thinks of establishing irreversible causal series among them.

[During] these primitive stages of representation one sees reappear
on the plane of thought forms of causality [corresponding to] those of
the first sensorimotor stages and which seem surpassed by the causal
structures of the final stages of sensorimotor intelligence. [Subsequently]
one witnesses a truly reflective objectification and spatialization, whose

progress is parallel to that which we have described on the plane of action. Thus it is that subsequent to the animism and dynamism we have just mentioned, we see a gradual "mechanism" taking form, correlative to the principles of conservation described (pp. 285–287) and to the elaboration of a relative space. Causality, like the other categories, therefore evolves on the plane of thought from an initial egocentrism to a combined objectivity and relativity, thus reproducing, in surpassing, its earlier sensorimotor evolution.

With regard to time, we have tried to describe on the purely practical plane of the first two years of life the transformation from subjective series into objective series; there is no need to emphasize the parallelism of this evolution with that which, on the plane of thought, is characterized by the transition from internal duration, conceived as the sole temporal model, to physical time constituted by quantitative relations between spatial guidemarks and external events. . . .

CONCLUSION

The formation of the universe, which seemed accomplished with that of sensorimotor intelligence, is continued throughout the development of thought, which is natural, but is continued while seeming at first to repeat itself, before truly progressing to encompass the data of action in a representative system of the totality. . . .

We have tried to show how, on the sensorimotor plane, assimilation and accommodation, at first undifferentiated but pulling behavior in opposite directions, gradually became differentiated and complementary. From what we have seen with regard to space, object, causality, and time it is clear that on the plane of representative thought, which is at the same time that of social relationships or coordination among individual minds, new assimilations and accommodations become necessary and these in turn begin with a phase of chaotic undifferentiation and later proceed to a complementary differentiation and harmonization.

During the earliest stages of thought, accommodation remains on the surface of physical as well as social experience. Of course, on the plane of action the child is no longer entirely dominated by the appearance of things, because through sensorimotor intelligence he has managed to construct a coherent practical universe by combining accommodation to objects with assimilation of objects to intercoordinated structures. But when it is a question of transcending action to form an impersonal representation of reality, that is, a communicable image destined to attain truth rather than mere utility, accommodation to things finds itself at grips with new difficulties. It is no longer a matter only of acting but of describing, not only of foreseeing but of explaining, and even if the sensorimotor schemata are already adapted to their own function, which is to insure the equilibrium between individual activity and the perceived environment, thought is obliged to construct a new representation of things to satisfy the common consciousness and the demands of a conception of totality. In this sense the first contact of thought with the material universe constitutes what may be called "immediate experience" in contradistinction to experimentation which is scientific or corrected by the assimilation of things to reason.

Immediate experience, that is, the accommodation of thought to the surface of things, is simply empirical experience which considers, as objective datum, reality as it appears to direct perception. In the numerous cases in which reality coincides with appearance this superficial contact with the object suffices to lead to truth. But the further one departs from the field of immediate action to construct an adequate representation of reality, the more necessary it is, to understand the phenomena, to include them in a network of relations becoming increasingly remote from appearance and to insert appearance in a new reality elaborated by reason. In other words, it becomes more and more necessary to correct appearance and this requires the formation of relationships among, or the reciprocal assimilation of, various points of view. In the example cited (pp. 282–284) of the groups of displacements relating to mountains, it is obvious that a whole structuring of experience, that is, a rational assimilation and coordination of many possible points of view, is indispensable to make the child understand that, despite appearance, mountains do not displace themselves when one moves in relation to them and that the various perspectives on them do not exclude the permanence of their form. The same applies to attributing stationary banks to a river or a lake when the boat advances and, in a general way, to organizing distant space no longer depending on direct action. Concerning objects let us consider the difference between immediate experience relating to the stars, that is, simple accommodation of perception to their apparent size and movements, [and] the experience which the mind acquires when it combines that accommodation with an assimilation of the same data to the activity of reason. From the first of these points of view, the stars are little balls or spots located at the same height as clouds; their movements depend on our own walking and their permanence is impossible to determine. . . . From the second point of view, on the contrary, real dimensions and distances no longer have any relation to appearance, the actual trajectories correspond with the apparent movements only through relationships of increasing complexity, and the identity of celestial bodies becomes the function of this system of totality. What is true on a large scale of the stars is always true, on every scale, of objects on which direct action does not bear. With regard to causality, the first example seen, like that of the floating of boats so suggestive to the child, gives rise to the same considerations. By following the course of immediate experience the child begins by believing that small boats float because they are light; but when he sees a tiny piece of lead or a little pebble gliding along at the bottom of the water, he adds that these bodies are doubtless too light and small to be held back by the water; moreover big boats float because they are heavy and can thus carry themselves. In short, if one remains on the surface of things, explanation is possible only at the price of continuous contradictions, because, if it is to embrace the sinuosity of reality, thought must constantly add apparent connections to one another instead of coordinating them in a coherent system of totality. . . . Let us also be satisfied, in the realm of time and duration, with a single example, that of the dissociation of the concept of speed into relations between the concepts of time and the space traversed. From the point of view of immediate experience, the child succeeds very soon in estimating speeds of which he has direct awareness, the spaces traversed in an identical time or the "before" and "after" in arrival at a goal in cases of trajectories of the same length. But there is a considerable gap between this and a dissociation of the notion of speed to extract a measurement of time, for this would involve replacing the direct intuitions peculiar to the elementary accommodation of thought to things by a system of relations involving a constructive assimilation.

In short, thought in all realms starts from a surface contact with the external realities, that is, a simple accommodation to immediate experience. Why then, does this accommodation remain, in the true sense of the word, superficial, and why does it not at once lead to correcting the sensory impression by rational truth? Because, and this is what we are leading up to, primitive accommodation of thought, as previously that of sensorimotor intelligence, is undifferentiated from a distorting assimilation of reality to the self and is at the same time oriented in the opposite direction.

During this phase of superficial accommodation to physical and social experience, we observe a continuous assimilation of the universe not only to the impersonal structure of the mind—which is not completed except on the sensorimotor plane—but also . . . to individual experience, and even to the desires and affectivity of the subject. Considered in its social aspect, this distorting assimilation consists, as we have seen, in a sort of egocentrism of thought so that thought, still unsubmissive to the norms of intellectual reciprocity and logic, seeks satisfaction rather than truth and transforms reality into a function of personal affectivity. . . .

The superficial accommodation of the beginnings of thought and the distorting assimilation of reality to the self are therefore at first undifferentiated and they operate in opposite directions. They are undifferentiated because the immediate experience which characterizes the former always, in the last analysis, consists in considering the personal point of view as the expression of the absolute and thus in subjecting the appearance of things to an egocentric assimilation, just as this assimilation is necessarily on a par with a direct perception that excludes the construction of a rational system of relations. But at the beginning, however undifferentiated may be these accommodative operations and those in which assimilation may be discerned, they work in opposite directions. Precisely because immediate experience is accompanied by an assimilation of perceptions to the schemata of personal activity or modeled after it, accommodation to the inner workings of things is constantly impeded by it. Inversely, assimilation of things to the self is constantly held in check by the resistances necessitating this accommodation, since there is involved at least the appearance of reality, which is not unlimitedly pliant to the subject's will. So also, on the social plane, the constraint imposed by the opinion of others thwarts egocentrism and vice versa, although the two attitudes of imitation of others and assimilation to the self are constantly coexistent and reveal the same difficulties of adaptation to reciprocity and true cooperation.

Gradually, as the child's thought evolves, assimilation and accommodation are differentiated and become increasingly complementary. In the realm of representation of the world this means, on the one hand, that accommodation, instead of remaining on the surface of experience, penetrates it more and more deeply, that is, under the chaos of appearances it seeks regularities and becomes capable of real experimentations to establish them. On the other hand, assimilation, instead of reducing phenomena to the concepts inspired by personal activity, incorporates them in the system of relationships rising from the more profound activity of intelligence itself. True experience and deductive construction thus become simultaneously separate and correlative; [meanwhile] in the social realm the increasingly close adjustment of personal thought to that of others and the reciprocal formation of relationships of perspectives insures the possibilty of a cooperation that constitutes precisely the environment that is favorable to this elaboration of reason.

Thus it may be seen that thought in its various aspects reproduces on its own plane the processes of evolution we have observed in the case of sensorimotor intelligence and the structure of the initial practical universe. The development of reason, outlined on the sensorimotor level, follows the same laws, once social life and reflective thought have been formed. Confronted by the obstacles which the advent of those new realities raises, at the beginning of this second period of intellectual evolution assimilation and accommodation again find themselves in a situation through which they had already passed on the lower plane. But in proceeding from the purely individual state characteristic of sensorimotor intelligence to the cooperation which defines the plane on which thought will move henceforth, the child, after having overcome his egocentrism and the other obstacles which impede this cooperation, receives from it the instruments necessary to extend the rational construction prepared during the first two years of life and to expand it into a system of logical relationships and adequate representations.

PART VI

*Logico-Mathematical
Operations*

INTRODUCTION

We often think of the domain of logic and mathematics as representing the extreme in the separation of form and content. An argument is logically *valid* if the conclusions follow from the premises; this has nothing to do with the *truth* of the premises and the conclusion as measured by events in the real world. The contents are irrelevant—only the form of the argument counts. "Nativists" believe that these logical and mathematical forms spring directly from innately given laws of thought about which there can be no valid dispute. But there has long been another "empiricist" way of looking at the relations of logic and mathematics with real contents: that these formal structures arise through human experience in the real world, and that they are therefore historical products that change as the world changes.

Piaget's position borrows something from each of these perspectives. Since he has interested himself almost entirely in those aspects of human experience that are well-nigh universal in the contemporary world, he can be seen as a nativist. This impression is enhanced by the fact that he has often taken, as his point of departure for research, categories of experience and thought that occur in classical logic from Aristotle to Kant. On the other hand, he conceives of laws of thought as developing in each child's mind through its own commerce with the world. In that sense he is an empiricist. Because of this complexity, Piaget is best referred to as an interactionist.

This position is directly reflected in Piaget's work on logico-mathematical aspects of thought. To separate these aspects from their roots in the activity of the child is almost impossible. As the reader goes through Part VI he will see neither a progression from the concrete to the abstract nor its reverse, but rather a constant interplay between the laws of thought and the laws of action. The very term *operation* is chosen by Piaget (among others) to bring home the idea that thought and action are one.

21

The Child's Conception of Number*

1941

INTRODUCTORY NOTES

The Child's Conception of Number, co-authored with Alina Szeminska†
(whose name was somehow deleted from the American translation), is certainly one of Piaget's most important works.

Here the reader finds the first articulated study of Piaget's well-known
work on the child's notion of conservation of matter, in addition to a more
thorough study of the genesis of the concept of number.‡ The book is indeed
devoted more to the development of the conservation of number than to the
conservation of physical quantities.

By conservation, Piaget means logical operations by means of which the
subject maintains magnitudes and relations despite displacements and perceptual transformations of all sorts. The existence of these operations renders
conservation à la Piaget irreducible to mere perceptual constancies and makes
it even contradictory of perceptual impressions. Conservation implies a fixed
system of reference independent to a large extent of perceptual, representational, and linguistic information and deeply rooted in the subject's awareness
of her own actions (*prise de conscience*).

A good example of this conception of conservation is given by the formation of the notion of number in the child around the age of 7–8 years. Pre-

---

*From *The Child's Conception of Number*, Jean Piaget and Alina
Szeminska, translated by Caleb Gattegno and Francis Mary Hodgson. Re-
printed by permission of Humanities Press, Inc., Atlantic Highlands, New
Jersey, and Routledge & Kegan Paul Ltd., London. Originally published in
French, 1941. (Collaborators: Zahara Glikin, Juan Jaen, Tatiana Katzaroff-
Eynard, Refia Mehmed-Semin, Zoe Trampidis, Edith Vauthier, and Florentine
Zakon.)

† Alina Szeminska, a Polish psychologist who first worked with Piaget in the years
before World War II. When her country was invaded by the Nazis she returned home.
She was eventually imprisoned in a concentration camp but survived, and resumed
her collaboration with Piaget after the war.

‡ Since *Le Dévelopement des Quantités chez l'Enfant (Conservation et atomisme)*
has only recently been translated into English, this is the most common source of information for English-speaking psychologists interested in the notion of conservation;
which explains certain misgivings of some of Piaget's critics and followers alike about
his conception of this notion.

sented with a collection of items, the young child pays attention mostly to specific physical properties of these items. Thus, 4-year-old Don, asked to compare two rows of counters (six blue ones close together versus seven red ones further apart), vacillates between the perceptual qualities of density and spatial extent. A child giving such responses may well be able to "count" in the sense of reeling off the numbers from 1–10 or 20, but his *conception* of number is still in an early stage of formation: "*I've got more* (7 red ones) *because it's bigger. No, Myriam's got more* (6 blue ones).—Why?—*Because they're close together; there are a lot.*" (See pp. 317–322.) An older child abstracts all the specific properties of the objects in front of him except for their existence; thus, these objects are denied any individuality, any quality, in such a way that they become equivalent to one another. The only distinction left after such an operation of abstraction is the *order* of the objects. One object is followed by another either in space, time, or, more generally, in the enumeration told by the subject. Mere counting supposes ordering, and ordering requires abstraction of individual qualities.

But this is not enough, according to Piaget, to reach the level of conservation of number. Such enumeration is, for him, equivalent to a mere seriation of objects that would indicate order but not quantity. What is needed is a hierachical classification system in which the class containing only one object is included in the class that counts two, which in turn, is included in the class that counts three, and so on.

Consequently, the conservation of integers supposes the synthesis of seriation and classification into a single system that is richer than the mere juxtaposition of its two components, since each number is, at the same time, ordinal (the first, the second, the third . . . *or one and one and one* . . .) and cardinal (the first is in the second is in the third . . . *or the class containing one element is contained in the class containing two elements, the class containing two elements is contained in the class containing three elements, and so on*).

The construction of this synthesis is not possible immediately after the installation of seriation on the one hand and of classification on the other. First the child must reflect on the relations of order and of inclusion as well, and he must abstract the common properties of classes, relations, and numbers. This reflective abstraction takes some time and explains the relatively late advent of number conservation compared to the relative precocity of seriation, one-to-one correspondence, and mere counting as imitative behavior.

The order of composition of the chapters of this book appears extremely logical after this introduction to the notion of number. The first part of the book explains how the child attains the notion of invariance of continuous and discontinuous physical quantities. The second part analyzes children's behavior in tasks requiring bijective applications between elements of two or more sets (the well-known one-to-one *correspondence* of Piaget's language). The third part is devoted to qualitative and quantitative comparisons between finite sets and subsets, and to additive and multiplicative compositions of classes and relations.

Conservation of Continuous Quantities*

Every notion, whether it be scientific or merely a matter of common sense, presupposes a set of principles of conservation, either explicit or implicit. It is a matter of common knowledge that in the field of the empirical sciences the introduction of the principle of inertia (conservation of rectilinear and uniform motion) made possible the development of modern physics, and that the principle of conservation of matter made modern chemistry possible. It is unnecessary to stress the importance in everyday life of the principle of identity; any attempt by thought to build up a system of notions requires a certain permanence in their definitions. In the field of perception, the schema of the permanent object presupposes the elaboration of what is no doubt the most primitive of all these principles of conservation. Obviously conservation, which is a necesary condition of all experience and all reasoning, by no means exhausts the representation of reality or the dynamism of the intellectual processes, but that is another matter. Our contention is merely that conservation is a necessary condition for all rational activity, and we are not concerned with whether it is sufficient to account for this activity or to explain the nature of reality.

This being so, arithmetical thought is no exception to the rule. A set or collection is only conceivable if it remains unchanged irrespective of the changes occurring in the relationship between the elements. For instance, the permutations of the elements in a given set do not change its value. A number is only intelligible if it remains identical with itself, whatever the distribution of the units of which it is composed. A continuous quantity such as a length or a volume can only be used in reasoning if it is a permanent whole, irrespective of the possible arrangements of its parts. In a word, whether it be a matter of continuous or discontinuous qualities, of quantitative relations perceived in the sensible universe, or of sets and numbers conceived by thought, whether it be a matter of the child's earliest contacts with number or of the most refined axiomatizations of any intuitive system, in each and every case the conservation of something is postulated as a necessary condition for any mathematical understanding.

[Piaget then points out that although conservation is a "necessary condition for all rational activity" it may be or may not be an a priori structure or innate idea preceding all "numerical or quantifying activities." He intends to show, by the experiments reported in this book, that conservation is not an innate idea but is constructed by the child over the same period of development and in an inseparable unity with the ideas of quantity and number. He then goes on to describe the well-known *transvasement* experiment in which a liquid is poured from one container into another of a different shape (e.g., from a short, squat cylinder into a tall, narrow one). He gives a very close and interesting analysis of the growth of the idea of conservation. Although we have omitted most of this discussion because much the same ground

*J. Piaget, *The Construction of Reality in the Child*, Chapter One.

is covered elsewhere in this volume, we urge the serious investigator to consult this passage.]

TECHNIQUE AND GENERAL RESULTS

This [discussion] and the one that follows will be devoted to experiments made simultaneously with continuous and discontinuous quantities. It seemed to us essential to deal with the two questions at the same time, although the former are not arithmetical and were to be treated separately in a special volume,* since it was desirable to ascertain that the results obtained in the case of discontinuous sets were general.

The child is first given two cylindrical containers of equal dimensions (A_1 and A_2) containing the same quantity of liquid (as is shown by the levels). The contents of A_2 are then poured into two smaller containers of equal dimensions (B_1 and B_2) and the child is asked whether the quantity of liquid poured from A_2 into ($B_1 + B_2$) is still equal to that in A_1. If necessary, the liquid in B_1 can then be poured into two smaller, equal containers (C_1 and C_2), and in case of need, the liquid in B_2 can be poured into two other containers C_3 and C_4 identical with C_1 and C_2. Questions as to the equality between ($C_1 + C_2$) and B_2, or between ($C_1 + C_2 + C_3 + C_4$) and A_1, etc., are then put. In this way, the liquids are subdivided in a variety of ways, and each time the problem of conservation is put in the form of a question as to equality or nonequality with one of the original containers. Conversely, as a check on his answers, the child can be asked to pour into a glass of a different shape a quantity of liquid approximately the same as that in a given glass, but the main problem is still that of conservation as such.

The results obtained seem to prove that continuous quantities are not at once considered to be constant, and that the notion of conservation is gradually constructed by means of an intellectual mechanism which it is our purpose to explain. By grouping the answers to the various questions, it is possible to distinguish three stages. In the first, the child considers it natural for the quantity of liquid to vary according to the form and dimensions of the containers into which it is poured. Perception of the apparent changes is therefore not corrected by a system of relations that ensures invariance of quantity. In the second stage, which is a period of transition, conservation gradually emerges, but although it is recognized in some cases, of which we shall attempt to discover the characteristics, it is not so in all. When he reaches the third stage, the child at once postulates conservation of the quantities in each of the transformations to which they are subjected. Naturally this does not mean that this generalization of constancy extends at this stage beyond the limits of the field studied here.

In our interpretation of these facts, we can start from the following hypotheses, some of which directed the research of this chapter while others arose in the course of our experiments. The question to be considered is whether the development of the notion of conservation of

*J. Piaget and B. Inhelder, *Le Développement des Quantités chez l'Enfant: Conservation et Atomisme* (Neuchâtel & Paris, Delachaux & Niestlé, 1942), 344 pp.

quantity is not one and the same as the development of the notion of quantity. The child does not first acquire the notion of quantity and then attribute constancy to it; he discovers true quantification only when he is capable of constructing wholes that are preserved. At the level of the first stage, quantity is therefore no more than the asymmetrical relations between qualities, i.e., comparisons of the type "more" or "less" contained in judgments such as "it's higher," "not so wide," or etc. These relations depend on perception, and are not as yet relations in the true sense, since they cannot be coordinated one with another in additive or multiplicative operations. This coordination begins at the second stage and results in the notion of "intensive" quantity, i.e., without units, but susceptible of logical coherence. As soon as this intensive quantification exists, the child can grasp, before any other measurement, the proportionality of differences, and therefore the notion of extensive quantity. This discovery, which alone makes possible the development of number, thus results from the child's progress in logic during these stages.

STAGE I: ABSENCE OF CONSERVATION

For children at the first stage, the quantity of liquid increases or diminishes according to the size or number of the containers. The reasons given for this nonconservation vary from child to child, and from one moment to the next, but in every case the child thinks that the change he sees involves a change in the total value of the liquid. . . .

It might of course be argued that the child may not really have grasped the question. Does he always understand that it refers to the total quantity, or does he think he is merely being asked about changes in the number, level, or size of the glasses? But the problem is precisely to discover whether the child is capable of grasping a quantity as being a whole, as a result of the coordination of the various relationships he perceives. The fact that these children isolated one of these relationships may therefore be due as much to lack of understanding of the notions in question as to failure to grasp the verbal question.

On the other hand, it might be suggested that when the liquid is poured from one container to another before the eyes of the child there are certain illusions of perception that counteract his judgment as to conservation.* We are well aware that perception of the quantifiable qualities such as length, weight, etc., leads to systematic distortions, and that the child finds it extremely difficult to perceive the constancy of these qualities. Hence, when the constancy is directly perceived, there is no problem as far as we are concerned. Our only problem is to discover by what means the mind succeeds in constructing the notion of constant quantity in spite of the indications to the contrary provided by immediate perception. Judgment comes into play precisely when perception proves inadequate, and only then. For instance, the discovery that a given quantity of liquid does not vary when poured from a container A into one or two containers B of a different shape, requires on the part of the child an effort of intellectual understanding which will

*E. Brunswik, *Wahrnehmung und Gegenstandwelt*, Leipzig and Vienna: 1939.

be the greater and the more easily analyzable the more deceptive the immediate perception. We are therefore not concerned to discover why this perception is deceptive, but why children at a certain level accept it without question, whereas others correct it by the use of intelligence. Moreover, either perception must be studied "from the angle of the object," in which case intelligence will in the final resort be the origin of the constancy, or else perception presupposes an organization which elaborates the constancy on its own plane, in which case the functioning and the successive structures of perception imply a sensorimotor activity that is intelligent from the start. If the latter is the case, the development of the notion of invariant quantities (like that of "object") would be a continuation, on a new, abstract plane, of the work already undertaken by sensorimotor intelligence in the field of conservation of the object.

We shall attempt to interpret the examples given above from this second point of view. What is most striking at this first stage is the inadequate quantification of the perceived qualities, and the lack of coordination between the quantitative relations involved in the perception. For example, Blas (4;0) begins by thinking that the quantity of liquid diminishes when the contents of a large glass three-quarters full are poured into two smaller glasses, but that it increases when poured from these small glasses into a long, narrow tube. It is therefore only the level and not the number or the cross section of the glasses which seems to be Blas's criterion. But a moment later he thinks there is more liquid in three small glasses than in two medium-sized ones filled with the same quantity. There are two noteworthy features in this reaction. In the first place, the child continually contradicts himself. At one moment he thinks there is more orangeade than lemonade, at another he thinks the opposite, and yet it does not occur to him to question his previous assumption. Obviously, if it is accepted that a liquid is capable of expansion or contraction and has no constancy, there is no contradiction. The real contradiction lies in the fact that the child attempts to justify his opposing statements by resorting to explanations that he cannot coordinate one with another, and that lead to incompatible statements. Thus Blas sometimes finds his evidence in the level of the liquid and thinks that the quantity diminishes when it is poured from a large glass into several small ones: sometimes he bases his statement on the number of glasses involved, in which case the same operation is thought to imply an increase in quantity. Alternatively, the child will use the cross section of the containers in his estimate of the change, disregarding the number of glasses and the level, and will then take one of these factors into account and arrive at the opposite conclusion. This brings us to the second feature of the reaction: the child behaves as though he had no notion of a multidimensional quantity and could only reason with respect to one dimension at a time without coordinating it with the others. . . .

Conservation of Discontinuous Quantities and Its
Relation to One-to-One Correspondence*

The experiments described in the previous chapter can all be repeated with discontinuous quantities that can be evaluated globally when the elements are massed and counted when they are separated. Sets of beads, for instance, can be used. If they are put into the containers used in Chapter I, they can serve for the same evaluations as the liquids (level, cross section, etc.), and in addition they are material for a further global quantification with which children are familiar: that of the length of necklaces made from the beads. The evaluation of this length can thus be used in each case to check the quantification of the contents of the various containers used. [Moreover], when the beads are considered as separate units they can be used in operations of correspondence. If the child is told, for instance, to put beads into a container, one by one, at the same time as the experimenter is putting beads one by one into another container, he can then be asked whether the total quantities are the same, with or without identity in the shape of the two containers.

In going on from the analysis of continuous quantities to that of discontinuous quantities we are therefore not merely checking our earlier findings. We are also making a preliminary study of the relationship between conservation of quantities and the development of one-to-one correspondence, which is, as is well known, one of the origins of number. We shall then be in a better position to approach the question of cardinal and ordinal correspondence as such.

It should be noted that the stages we shall find here correspond exactly to those of the previous chapter.

STAGE I: ABSENCE OF CONSERVATION

During the first stage there is no conservation of the sets of beads, just as there was no conservation of the quantity of liquid. The child not only thinks that the total quantity changes when a set of beads is poured from one container into another of a different shape, but he also thinks that a necklace made of the beads will not be of the same length in the two cases.

Port (5;0): "What are these?—*Little green* (A_2) *and red* (A_1) *beads.*—Is there the same amount in the two glasses?—*Yes.*—If we made a necklace with the red ones and another with the green ones, would they be the same length?—*Yes.*—Why?—*Because there's the same height of green and red.*— If we put the beads in there (L), what would happen?—*They would be higher.*—Would there be the same amount?—*No.*—Where would there be more?—*There* (L).—Why?—*Because it's narrow* (A_1 was poured into L).— Do you really think there are more beads there (L) than here (A_2)?—*Yes.*— Why?—*Because it's narrow and they go higher.*—If I poured them all out (making as though to pour the red beads on one side and the green on the other), would they be the same or not?—*More red ones.*—Why?—*Because that one* (L) *is narrow.*—And if I make a necklace with the red beads and

*With the collaboration of M. Juan Jaen. [The following section is from Chapter II.]

one with the green beads, will they be the same, or not?—*The red one will be longer.*—Why?—*Because there'll be more in there* (L).—(The red beads were put back into A_1.) And now?—*They're the same height again.*—Why?—*Because you've poured them into that one* (A_1).—Are there more red ones or green ones?—*The same.*—(The red ones were poured from A_1 into M.)—*It's higher.*—But does it make the same amount?—*No. There* (M), *there are more.*—Where did the extra beads come from?—*From there* (A_1).—And if I pour the red beads back into that glass(A_1), what will happen?—*They'll be the same* (red and green).—If I make a necklace with those (M) and those (A_2)?—*There'll be more red beads.*—And if I pour this glass (M) into that one (G)?—*It'll be the same as there* (A_1) *because you'll have poured it into a thing that's too big.*—Where will there be more?—*There'll be less there* (G) *then there* (M) *because you'll have poured that one* (M) *into this one* (G) *and it's bigger.*—(The beads in M were poured into G.) If I made two necklaces, one with those (the red ones in G), and the other with those (the green ones in A_2), would they be the same?—*It would be bigger green* (A_2) *than red* (G).—Which would be longer?—*The red would be longer because before we had them here* (M) *and there were more. If you pour the green ones into this one* (M) *and then into that one* (G), *we'll see if there are more green or red ones.*—And if I pour that one (A_2 green) into this one (E), what will happen?—*It'll be a smaller necklace because you've poured them into a smaller glass.*—And if I take these green beads (A_2) to make a necklace, and measure it, and then pour the beads into this one (E) and then make the necklace again? *It'll be shorter because you've poured them into a very small glass* (E).—But will there be more beads, or less, or the same?—*Less beads.*—(The green beads were then poured into E, without comment.) *Oh! there are more!*—And what did you think?—*That there'd be less.*—Why?—*Because this one* (E) *is smaller than that one* (M) *and it's higher than that one. No, it's narrower.*—Are there more or less beads than before, or the same?—*More, because you've poured them out.*—And if we made a necklace with these beads, would it be the same as the other?—*Longer!*"

Port was then told to put a red bead into A_1 with her right hand every time she put a green one into A_2 with her left hand. After a moment she was stopped: "Have you got the same amount in the two glasses?—*Yes.*—(A_1 was poured into B.) Are they the same?—*No, less there* (B) *and more there* (A_2). —Why?—*Because you poured them into a little glass.*" Etc.

. . . As soon as the beads are poured from one container to another of different shape and dimensions, the child thinks that the quantity increases or diminishes, basing his estimate now on the level of the beads, now on the width of the glass, now on the number of glasses. In other words, as in the case of the liquids, the quantities are estimated merely from perceptual relationships uncoordinated one with another. This initial lack of coherence explains both the continual contradictions in the various judgments of the child, and the absence of any criterion for conservation.

. . . As long as we were considering continuous quantities such as the liquids used in the experiments in Chapter I, we might perhaps have thought that the child's failure to see that there was conservation was due rather to physical than to mathematical reasons, since liquids might be imagined to contract or expand according to the shape of the containers. But when we come to discontinuous quantities, a new feature intervenes. In spite of the fact that the elements of the sets are discrete, the child thinks that they increase or diminish in number with the change in the shape of the set in passing from one container to another. When therefore he assumes that the same set can be made now into a longer, now into a shorter necklace, there is definitely nonconservation in the mathematical sense.

Moreover, as we have seen, in order that the child may be well aware that the elements in the two sets to be compared are equal, he himself is made to put one bead into a given container each time the experimenter puts one into the other container. Even this one-to-one correspondence, which amounts to a practical enumeration, is not sufficient for conservation to be assumed. The child grasps that the two corresponding sets are equal only so long as the containers are equal. . . .

. . . Obviously, if there is no conflicting factor, the one-to-one correspondence between two sets ought to lead to equivalence of the corresponding sets. This is what we find at the second stage, during which the conflict is between the correspondence and the perceptual appearances. But at the first stage, quantification is so little developed that there is no conflict; perception completely overrules the correspondence. Goc [5;0], for instance, thinks that A_1 and A_2 are equal "because the two glasses are the same" rather than because the two corresponding beans are put in at the same time, as if the first criterion were more reliable than the second. As for Bab [4;6], although he says "it's the same" each time the two corresponding beans are put in, he disregards this estimate once L is half full, and judges only by the levels. Moreover, in spite of having counted six beads in both E and P, he still concludes that the necklace made from the beads in E will be longer, because in E there are "a lot, quite full." Thus not only the one-to-one correspondence, but also the actual enumeration, seems to the child at the first stage to be less sure means of quantification than direct evaluation through global perceptual relationships (gross quantities). . . .

STAGE II: BEGINNINGS OF CONSTRUCTION OF PERMANENT SETS

As in the case of continuous quantities, we can distinguish here also a second stage characterized by intermediary solutions. In general, the situation is as follows. On the one hand, the child tends to think that there is conservation, either because the two sets are put into two identical containers (A_1 and A_2) or because the two sets have been built up by a one-to-one correspondence. But on the other hand, this tendency comes into conflict with the appearance of the sets, i.e., with the difference in level, cross section, etc. Two new features are then observable, as distinct from the reactions of the first stage. In the first place, there is a real conflict; the factors of conservation do not immediately give way before the factors of change, and the struggle between the two is most instructive. Secondly, as a result of this conflict, the perceptual relationships are coordinated as relations, and are integrated in a system susceptible of justifying conservation while taking into account the concomitant variations.

Marg (5;6): "Is there the same number of beads (in A_1 and A_2)?—*Yes, the same.*—And if we made necklaces, etc.?—*The same length.*—Why?— . . . —And if I pour this into that (A_1 into L)?—*There are more there (A_2).*— Why?—*Because it gets bigger here* (pointing to the narrower column in L). —Where is there more?—*In the big one* (= the wide one, A_2).—And if we make two necklaces(with L and A_2)?—*They'll be the same length.*—And if we pour these (L) into those ($M_1 + M_2$)?—*There'll be more in the two little ones.*—Why?— . . . —And if we make a necklace?—*It will be longer with the two little ones* (than with A_2).—And before, when the beads were here (A_1 and A_2)?—*The necklaces were the same length.*—And if I put those (A_2) here ($E_1 + E_2 + E_3 + E_4$), will the two necklaces be the same (i.e., $2M$ and $4E$)?—*No, it'll be longer from the little ones ($4E$).*" . . .

The first point to notice here is that, as in the case of continuous quantities, the child at this level is capable of postulating conservation when there is only a slight change in pattern, but not when the change is more significant. Thus Marg and Ari think that the two necklaces will still be the same length if the beads in A are poured into L, but not if they are poured into $2M$ or $4E$. But this is not all. By the very fact that he hesitates to assume conservation because of the change in shape, the child comes to distinguish between evaluations based on mere perception of the relationships of height and width and those which result from representation of the length of the necklaces. For instance, although Marg and Ari think that the quantity changes in passing from A to L because the level rises, they still think that the necklace made from the beads in L will be the same length as the one made from those in A. Hence there is conservation when the child is thinking of the row of discontinuous elements, and nonconservation when he is thinking of one or other of the dimensions of the set as a whole. Such distinctions between the various evaluations are extremely instructive. On the one hand they indicate how many and varied are the operations that the child has to coordinate in quantification. On the other hand, the fact that the evaluations based on representation of the necklace are more correct than the others suggests that the notion of conservation involves decomposition into elements. We shall now see whether this is borne out by the facts:

Tis (5;1) put one bead into V_1 each time the experimenter put one into V_2: "Are they the same?—*Yes, because I put the same as you every time.—* If we make two necklaces, etc.?—*They'll be the same length, because there are a lot of beads, and you've got a lot as well.—*(V_1 was poured into $L + M$.) Are they still the same?—*In yours* ($L + M$) *there are a lot.—*And in yours? *—Not many.—*And if we make two necklaces, etc.?—*Yours will be longer; mine won't be so long.—*Why?—*Because there are more beads in yours.—* But how did we put the beads in?—*Two each time.—*Then why have I got more?—*There are two big lots in yours, look.*" So far then, Tis's reaction is characteristic of the first stage, but we shall now see the transition from this reaction to the conflicts typical of the second stage.
Tis put one bead into L every time the experimenter put one into P. He counted each bead as he put it in and reached the correct total of 12. L was then full, and Tis cried spontaneously: "*I've got more.—*Why?—*There are more in mine.—*And if we make two necklaces?—*This one* (L) *will be longer —*Why?—*The glass is bigger, and that one* (P) *is smaller* (pointing to the height).—But are there more beads?—*In that one* (L).—Why?—*It's bigger. —*How did we put the beads in?—*We put two every time.—*Have we got the same, or have you more or less?—*Both the same.—*Why?—*Because we put two every time.—*What will the necklaces be like?—*Yours will be long and mine will be the same length.—*Why?—*Because this one* (L) *is big, and mine* (P) *is little. You've got a lot of beads in yours.—*And what about you? *—Not as many, but a lot all the same.*" It is clear that as soon as the child is reminded of the one-to-one correspondence there is a conflict between it and his perception of the dimensions, the former tending toward equality and the latter toward difference, with the result that no real synthesis is achieved. . . .

There is obviously a systematic conflict in the . . . cases typical of this stage, between a factor of equalization and conservation and a factor of difference. Every one of these children concludes that there is equality if the same number of elements is dropped, one at a time, into two containers, irrespective of the shape of the containers, but when the child afterward considers the result obtained when the shapes are different, his belief in the equivalence is shaken by an evaluation based on the perceptual relationships. Although he himself has just made the one-to-one correspondence, he reacts like the child at the first stage and thinks that any variation in height or width entails a change in the quantity as a whole. But whereas at the first stage his belief in the equivalence was destroyed, now there is merely a conflict between the two tendencies, neither of which definitely triumphs. When the child considers the sets of beads he thinks that there is nonequivalence, and when he remembers the correspondence he again thinks that the sets are equivalent. Even when, as in the case of Tis, a final decision appears to have been reached, the words the child uses express his doubt ("You have got a lot. . . . I've not got so many, but a lot all the same").

How is the child going to reconcile these two opposing tendencies? It is interesting to find that he solves the problem of the beads in exactly the same way as that of continuous quantities. The synthesis of the real equivalence and the apparent variations is achieved through co-ordination of the relations in question, and here again this coordination first takes the form of mere logical multiplication, which rapidly develops into true proportionality. This is begun at the second stage and completed during the third. Von [5;10], for example, who begins by accepting the equivalence because of the correspondence, explains the apparent variations in quantity by saying that the width of P compensates for the height of L. But his attempt at the operation of multiplication of relations ("They're the same . . . because here (L) it's round and long, and there (P) it's round and bigger"), is as yet so ill founded that the second time he does it he forgets to correlate the height of L with the width of the other container and suddenly decides that L "is longer and bigger and so there's more"!

STAGE III: CONSERVATION AND QUANTIFYING COORDINATION

Let us now examine how the intensive and extensive quantification begun during the second stage reaches completion. . . .

Lin (6;0) recognized the equality of A_1 and A_2. "Suppose I pour this one (A_1) into that one (L)?—*It'll still be the same.*—And if I pour that one (L) into this one (G)?—*Still the same.*—Will it really?—*Of course, because there, in the little one* (i.e., L, the narrow one), *there's more* (pointing to the height, and thus indicating that the increase in height compensated for the narrowing of the column).". . .

It is at once obvious that the difference between these answers and all those given earlier lies in the fact that the child no longer needs to reflect in order to be certain that there is conservation of the total quantities: he knows it a priori. At first sight, therefore, is might seem that the notion of the invariance of the whole results merely from a global judgment, counteracted hitherto by perceptual factors, but standing out plainly once the perceptual factors are overcome. Yet the arguments used by these children show that the coordinations of relations achieved during the preceding stage are still the essential factors, but are now a single act instead of being constructed step by step. Lin, for example, simply says "in the little one (L) there is more" to justify the total invariance of which he is convinced. . . .

In order to see the real significance of the discovery of the invariance of wholes—which is a decisive stage in quantification—it is therefore essential to make a further analysis of the operations of co-ordination involved in the earlier reactions. It is, however, no longer sufficient to oppose the one-to-one correspondence to the changes in shape, since at this stage the factor of equivalence overrides that of change. Our technique will therefore be to some extent modified. We shall give the child two sets of different shapes whose equivalence he cannot check, and we shall ask him whether he thinks they are or are not equivalent, afterward checking by one-to-one correspondence, with retrospective explanation, the hypothesis he makes. Here are some examples:

Sum (6;10) compared glasses L and P (each containing 18 beads) without having counted or made the correspondence between the beads. "Are they the same or not?— . . . —How can we find out?—*There are more in that one* (P).—Why?—*Because it's bigger. You can't put as many in this one* (L)."
L and P were emptied, and Sum put one bead into L each time the experimenter put one into P. "*They're the same.*—Why?—*That one* (P) *is bigger, but it's not full, and this one's narrower but it's quite full.*—How do you know they're the same?—*Because we put them in together.*"
Sum was then given glass G containing a single layer of beads and was asked to put the same number in L. He filled L ⅔ full and said: "*I don't know how to do it, I think there are more there* (G).—(We then filled up L.) —*I think they're the same.*—Why?—*That one* (G) *is bigger, but if we made it long* (making as though to elongate G and so to make the beads vertical), *it would be the same as there* (L)." . . .

Dur (7;8), after thinking that L "had more" than P, put in one bead each time the experimenter put one into P. "*They're both the same.*— How do you know?—*Because we finished together; we began at the same time and we finished at the same time.*—But is that one (L) narrower?—*It's narrow, but it's higher, and this one* (P) *is low but it's bigger.*"
Dur was then asked to put into G ($= 4E$) a quantity equal to that in E (full). He pointed to a level that was about ⅓G. "How do you know?— *I fill it in my mind and I can see where it comes up to.*—What do you mean by 'where'?—*I lay the glass* (E) *on its side, and then I can see that there's more here* (G), *because there's still some room left.*" . . .

Gar (8;2): "*There* (P), *they're close together, in a heap.*—Well, what difference does that make?—*Here* (P), *they're spread out. If I put them close together, they'd be the same as there* (L)."

Kor (8;6): "*That glass* (P) *is wider, it goes out more at the sides, so they don't go up so fast* (as in L)." In comparing G and E, Kor said at once that G contained more than E. "Why?—*If we wanted to make it* (G) *narrow and high, it would be as narrow as the other* (E) *but higher.*" These remarks were accompanied by gestures indicating that by compressing the broad column in G we could make a narrow column like that in E, but taller.

Gui (9;0): "*In the little glass* (L), *there's only one bead on another, and there* (P), *there are more at a time: there are only two layers, but it's the same* (as in L)." In the case of E and G, "*It goes 4 times.*—How do you know?—*I cut it in the middle, and then again. I make quarters, I fill up each quarter and then I see that it goes 4 times.*" On the other hand, Gui thought G was bigger than L, as a result of the following reasoning: "*I cut it* (G) *into lines* (the last gesture he made to illustrate what he meant showed the circumference of G divided into four sections each corresponding to the width of L), *and then afterward I compared with that one* (L). *I put it like that* (L on its side) *and then measured with one portion of it* (L divided into two unequal parts, one of which corresponded to the width of G). He was therefore comparing the width of G with the height of L. As for the width of

L and the thickness of *G*, he finally made the following comparison: "*I cut this one* (G) *like that* (into two layers), *and I saw that that layer is just right if we cut that one* (L) *in two* (lengthwise)." Hence half a column in *L* was equal to one layer in *G*!

These various methods of comparison—all of them discovered spontaneously by the child—enable us both to verify the interpretations of the previous chapter and to see the problem of correspondence more clearly. . . .

In the first place, it should be observed that each of these reactions, like those quoted at the beginning of this section, has as its starting point logical multiplication of the relations of height and cross section. In order to remove the contradiction between the one-to-one correspondence of the elements of the two sets and the apparent variations, the child at once assumes that the latter constitute a whole. Thus for Sum, *P* is "bigger but not full," while *L* is "narrower but quite full," and for Lea, *L* is "not so wide but higher," etc., each relation being multiplied by another, usually its inverse.

But as was clearly apparent when the comparison between *L* and *P* was made without the equivalence of their contents being previously verified, such an operation is quite inadequate for the constitution of the notion of a permanent quantity or the equality of two quantities. It merely enables the child to deduce, provided that he already knows that the two quantities are equal, that an increase in height necessarily corresponds to a decrease in width, and conversely. This explains the fact that it is when the child is already conscious of the invariance owing to the one-to-one correspondence, and only has to explain the apparent variations, that he resorts to multiplication of the relations, thereby coordinating all the relationships in question in an intensive quantification. This coordination does not of itself result in that case in the construction of the notion of invariance, since it could only do so if the relations of height and width were merely permuted. But as soon as the child has mastered the operation of coordinating the differences, i.e., when he multiplies the relations, he assumes that the differences can be equated. As we have just seen, he even formulates this hypothesis very clearly. For Sum, for instance, the set in *G* is equal to that in *L* because "if we made it long it would be the same," or in other words, because the difference in cross section between *G* and *L* is exactly equivalent to the difference in height. . . .

Most of the children at this stage show clearly that this proportion, which constitutes the beginning of extensive quantification, goes hand in hand with arithmetical partition, as we assumed in the previous chapter. For instance, for Lea, *L* contains more than *P* (when *P* is full), because "if we cut it (*L*) in the middle and put the two bits in there (*P*), it would still be not so wide," and Chai [7;8] divided the height of *G* into two, and equated each section to *E*. The case of Kor, who was older, shows how far such decomposition can lead in the absence of any enumeration of the elements.

Generally speaking, it can be seen that these proportions, this equating of differences, and these numerical partitions come into being as a result of the inverse operations which the child can now perform, precisely because the transformations hitherto considered to be mere perceptual relationships have become "operational." When, for instance,

Lea says "if I emptied this one (P) into that one (L), or that one (L) into this one (P), they'd be the same," he is expressing the reversibility characteristic of any logical, mathematical operation, and it is this reversibility that makes possible the notion of equalization and decomposition. . . .

The conflict between the one-to-one correspondence and the perceptual relationships thus comes to an end only during the third stage, with the triumph of correspondence over perception. But what is the connection between one-to-one correspondence and coordination of the perceptual relationships?

So far, we have approached the problem from one point of view only. We have considered the progressive coordination of relations merely as means by which the child explains the changes in shape of the sets from the two angles of intensive and extensive quantification, and thus reconciles these changes with the invariance of the corresponding sets, the correspondence thus being viewed as the initial reason for the invariance. But one considerable difficulty still remains: how is it that it is not until the third stage that the one-to-one correspondence implies lasting equivalence in the sets, and that during the first two stages it is inadequate to override perceptual appearances? As far as the first stage is concerned, it might be argued that since coordination is lacking, the perceptual relationships make so firm an impression on the mind that the equivalence is conceived of as not lasting. But during the second stage, coordination of the relationships does take place and yet the equivalence still does not triumph over perceptual appearances.

The truth of the matter may be that coordination of the relationships occurs as soon as correspondence itself has been constructed, and that the mechanisms involved in this evolution form a much more integrated whole than has hitherto appeared. It may in fact be that the correspondence that leads to lasting equivalence is not the same operation as the one-to-one correspondence without lasting equivalence between corresponding sets. If by further experiments it were found possible to distinguish between these two forms of correspondence, it would then be natural that the perceptual correspondence of the first stage should be subordinated to the apparent changes, and that only the correspondence of the third stage should develop into coordination of the relationships, because the latter are already implied in it. The intermediary stage would then be merely the period during which the correspondence itself is being organized.

Spontaneous Correspondence, Cardinal Value of Sets*

In the previous chapter, we tried to show that there are various types of correspondence, which can be distinguished by their relationship to the idea of equivalence they entail. While the highest level can be

*With the collaboration of Mlle. Zoé Trampidis and Mme. Rafia Mehmed-semin. [The following section is from Chapter IV.]

termed "quantifying correspondence" because it results in the notion of necessary, lasting equivalence, the lower levels are intuitive, because the equivalence of the sets is recognized only when the correspondence is actually perceived, and ceases to exist when it is no longer in the field of perception.

Before going any further, we must now analyze the mechanism of correspondence, no longer considering its results, but examining its spontaneous development, i.e., in situations in which the child is compelled to find the correspondence of his own accord and to make what use of it he can. . . .

For this purpose, what is most suitable is correspondence between like objects, the child being required to find a quantity equal to that contained in a given model. A problem of this kind is, of course, similar to those we examined in the previous chapter, [but] here our material will not be of such a kind that the correspondence is suggested by the fact that the objects are qualitatively complementary; the objects will be similar, and this may make some difference. In the second place, and more important, the child will not be told to "put one A opposite (or into) each B," or to "exchange one A for each B." We shall say to him: "There is a number of objects: pick out the same number," without suggesting any method. . . .

These were the techniques used. In the first place, we presented the child with a succession of figures made with counters, and asked him to take the same number of counters as each figure contained. . . . There were five [categories] of figures: I, "badly-structured" figures, e.g., a collection of counters distributed at random, but neither touching nor overlapping: II, open series, e.g., two parallel rows of counters; III, closed figures, the shape of which did not depend on the number of elements used, e.g., a circle, a house, a right angle; IV, closed figures of which the shape depended on the number of counters, e.g., a square, a cross, etc.; V, more complex closed figures, less familiar to the child, e.g., a rhombus, etc.*

With one of these figures in front of him, the child was told to look at it, and to pick out of a box the same number of counters.

In the second place, the child was shown a row of six beans, representing sweets or pennies, one to two cm. apart, and he was asked to pick out the same number. . . .

The results obtained with these two kinds of test can be classified into three types, corresponding to the three stages found in the earlier chapters. During the first stage, the child uses only global comparison, imitating the configuration of the model without attempting exact quantification. When he is dealing with rows, he makes a row of the same length as the model, but of different density. During the second stage, there is one-to-one correspondence, but it ceases to exist when the figure is distorted. Finally, in the third stage, there is exact correspondence and lasting equivalence.

*When the counters are presented to the child in this way, care must be taken to avoid stressing the figure. Otherwise the test would become the reproduction of the figure rather than the estimate of the number of elements.

REPRODUCTION OF FIGURES

W. A. Lay* made a detailed study of the way in which various figures made with three, four, five, etc., objects arranged as triangles, squares, etc., are distinguished by the child, from the point of view of perception of number. The number four, for instance, is more easily recognized when the objects are placed at the four corners of a square than when they are placed at random. A. Descoeudres† and O. Decroly‡ made use of these investigations in their interesting research into the development of number. Our point of view here will be different, for while these authors examined what has come to be called perception of number, i.e., the application of already existing numerical schemata to discrete objects perceived in the same field, we shall examine what might be called quantifying operations, i.e., the elementary operations of correspondence, equating, etc., which constitute the logic of number. In a word, we shall ignore the problems of perception and shall concentrate on the problem of the genesis of operations as such. This being so, our analysis of the reproduction of figures will serve merely as an introduction to the study of the mechanism of correspondence. . . .

Stage I: Global Comparison. The characteristic feature of children at the first stage is that they do not as yet feel the need for a quantitative evaluation, since they have no precise notions of the cardinal number. They therefore confine themselves, in evaluating the given sets, to global qualitative comparisons, without coordination of the qualities that are compared. Our first examples are cases of nonstructured figures:

Pa (4;6). To find the required number of counters to correspond to a collection of 15 elements, he took small handfuls of them and tried to arrange them so that they looked the same: "Are they the same?—*No.*—Why?—*There are more here* (the collection he had just made did in fact contain 2 extra elements).—Well then?—(He did not remove any of the counters, but moved the ones that were too close together, so as to produce a configuration more like that of the model.)—Is there the same number of counters?—*No, yes, I've the same amount.*". . .

In the case of the series, children at this stage attempt to reproduce both the configuration and the dimensions of the model, but are not concerned with details:

Li (4;9), in order to reproduce the model first put 5 counters in a row, then made 4 of them into pairs by adding 4 more: "Are they the same?—*Yes.*—Why?—(She made a movement of the hand to indicate the direction of the row.)—Are there as many?—*Yes.* (She looked at the model and saw that her copy was a little shorter. She added 2 counters: her series was then composed of 11 counters instead of 8 as in the model, but it was the same length.)—Where are there more?—*There* (pointing to her copy).—I want them to be the same.—(She removed the 2 counters, leaving 9 as against 8, but the model series was longer, so she spaced out her counters to make hers longer.)—Is there the same number?—*Yes.*"

In the case of closed figures, children at this stage can reproduce correctly those which require a definite number of elements, provided

Führer durch Rechnen Unterricht gegründet auf didaktische Experimente, 2nd ed. (Leipzig: Nemnich, 1907).

†A. Descoeudres, *Le Développement de l'Enfant de 2 à 7 ans* (Delachaux & Niestlé, S.A., 1920.)

‡O. Decroly, *Etudes de Psychogenèse* (Lamertin, 1932).

that the form is familiar (category IV), but if the shape is unfamiliar (V), or does not involve a definite number of elements (III), the copy is no longer numerically correct:

Mül (4;1), in attempting to find the same number of elements as there were in a circle of 10 counters, made a circle of 14. Similarly, for a circle made by 6 matches arranged as radii, he made one with 12 matches: "Is there exactly the same number of matchsticks?—*Yes.*—Where are those (indicating on the copy some that were particularly close together)?—*There* (pointing at random to those of the model)."

For a right angle with 6 counters (sides of 4 and 3 elements), Mül made, three times in succession, angles with 4 counters (sides of 3 and 2): "Is there the same number of counters?—*No. I don't know.*—Try again.—(He then made an angle with 8 counters.)—Is there exactly the same number?—*Yes.*—Who has more?—*Me.*—Well then, take away the extra ones.—(He removed two and altered the spacing of the counters to make them like the model.)—Are they the same?—*Yes.*—Who has more?—*Me* (which was incorrect since there were 6 in both. He then put back the 2 he had removed.)" Similarly, for a house of 6 counters, Mül made one of 13, then removed 1 "so that it should be just right," etc.

In the case of figures whose shape depended on the number of elements, Mül successfully reproduced a square of 4 counters and a triangle of 6, but made a cross with 6 instead of 5. He also failed with a square of 9 counters, being careful to make the elements at the 4 corners correspond, but putting 1 counter too many in between. The rhombus of 13 counters was copied as a vague quadrilateral containing 15 elements. . . .

The reactions of this first stage are of great importance to the psychology of number. It might at first seem that these children feel no need for a quantitative evaluation, and that they merely make a more or less correct copy of the model. Such an assumption would be too sweeping. Even if the child sometimes forgets, in making his copy, that he was told to "put the same number of counters," he shows by his answers to the questions put to him that he understood perfectly what he had to do. Pa, for instance, says "there are more here," and Li recognizes the differences and attempts to correct them. But the expressions "more counters" and "less counters" have a quite different meaning for the child of this stage than for us, and do not as yet represent a cardinal evaluation.

For the adult, cardinal evaluation always presupposes that units have been added or merged in order to form the whole obtained by correspondence with the set to be evaluated. For the child of this stage, on the contrary, the evaluation is based merely on the global qualities of the sets in question, these qualities being quantified by comparison as "more" or "less," without coordination of the comparisons. . . . The child does not coordinate the global qualities he perceives, but focuses on one at a time in comparing his copy with the model. . . . Mül thinks that a circle of twelve has the same number as one of six, because the diameter is the same.

This experiment, unlike the earlier ones, provides us with evidence that this failure to coordinate the quantitative relationships only makes its appearance when there are explicit judgments of comparison. The child's initial procedure is to coordinate the perceived qualities, but this coordination has not yet become operational or logical. It is still purely intuitive, and consists only in the attempt to produce a general resemblance between the model and the copy. This is why, when the child tries to find the same number of counters as he has been shown, he contents himself with a rough reproduction of the configuration of the model. The copy is only approximate precisely because the child cannot analyze the figure, i.e., he cannot find the relationships which, when logically composed, constitute its qualities. . . .

To sum up, the most general characteristic of this stage is the irreversibility of the reactions. The evaluations of children at this level are purely perceptual, with the result that qualities that are not comparable are related and the synthesis can only be global. This means, in other words, that the child's intuitive judgment is not yet combined with operations through which the elements isolated by his analysis can be put together again. It is precisely because the judgments of the child at this stage lack mobility, that his thought is essentially irreversible.

Stage II: Intuitive Correspondence. We shall apply the term *qualitative* to correspondence that is based only on the qualities of the corresponding elements, as for example, when the child puts angles in his copy when there are angles in the model, irrespective of whether he knows how many there are, or whether there is the same number as in the model. *Numerical* correspondence, on the other hand, will be that in which each element is considered as a unit, irrespective of the qualities, e.g., n blue counters corresponding to n red counters, whatever their distribution. We shall call *intuitive* any correspondence that is entirely based on perception (or possibly on representative images) and is consequently not preserved outside the actual field of perception (or of clear recollection). We shall say, on the other hand, that correspondence is *operational* when it is based on relationships of an intellectual nature, its distinctive characteristics therefore being the fact that it is preserved independently of actual perception, and its "reversibility." Qualitative correspondence may therefore be either intuitive or operational, whereas numerical correspondence is essentially operational (except perhaps in the case of the first three or four numbers).

Having clearly defined our terms, we shall find that the second stage, that of intuitive qualitative correspondence, is merely a continuation of the first. As the copying of the models becomes more exact, it leads to one-to-one correspondence susceptible of greater precision. But by the very fact that this correspondence is based on perceptual comparison, it is not numerical from the start, in spite of appearances, but remains qualitative and intuitive. This can easily be proved by altering the configuration of the corresponding sets. As soon as this is done, the child no longer accepts the equivalence. This intuitive correspondence without lasting equivalence justifies our assertion that there is a second stage, which differs from the first in that there is systematic use of correspondence, and from the third in that the correspondence does not yet involve necessary equivalence. We must point out also that, while children at the first stage usually begin by putting a pile of counters on the table and then arrange them to imitate the model (adding or removing elements where they think necessary), children at the second stage usually begin by making the correspondence, taking the counters one by one to reproduce the various parts of the model.

First we have some examples related to category I:

Ha (4;5) first looked carefully at the pile of 15 counters, then put down 16 elements one at a time, copying the configuration of the model bit by bit, looking to see that he was making the correspondence (his one error being due to the fact that he counted one element twice): "Are they the same?— *That one* (copy) *is bigger. I'll take some away* (removing the extra counter). —Are they the same?—*Yes.*—Are you sure?—(The elements of the model were then spaced rather further apart.) Is there the same number of counters?—*Yes . . . no* (he added some counters to the model in order to imitate the new configuration of the copy)."

We then distributed 13 counters in front of Ha, some in groups of 3 or 2, but making the configuration a recognizable whole. He was then asked to find as many matches as there were counters. He arranged 11 matches in groups of 3 and 2 so as to reproduce certain details of the model.—"Are there as many?—*There* (counters), *there aren't many, here* (matches), *there are a lot.*—Make it so that there's the same number in both. (Ha then spaced out the counters)."

Finally, 8 matches were distributed in front of him: "Find the same number of counters.—*I don't know how to make the pattern.*—Never mind, try." He spaced out the matches a little, then took 14 counters one by one and tried to reproduce the pattern of the model. The correspondence thus broke down when the difference in shape of the objects prevented an exact copy of the model, whereas the copy was an exact reproduction of the model when counters only were used. . . .

The next example [is in response to figures] of category II: . . .

Gis (5;5) provides an example of the distinction between verbal numeration and actual operations. She counted correctly up to 27, pointing to each counter in the row in turn. After 27, there ceased to be any coordination between the counters to which she pointed and the number she said, but she continued from memory up to 54. This verbal enumeration did not however correspond to any systematic colligation except in the case of the first few numbers, because although she said that $12 > 8$ and $10 > 7$, she also said that $9 > 13$ and $19 > 21$: "Where are there more (with the counters she had just counted in front of her)?—*19.*—Why?—*Because there are a lot.* —And there?—*21.*—Well then?—*That's less because there aren't many.*"

It is interesting to note that, on the plane of actual operations, Gis was at the second stage: correct correspondence, but without lasting equivalence. For example, she made the correspondence between four or more pairs correctly, but no longer thought they were equivalent when one set was spaced out.

We find the same reactions for categories III–V:

Nil (5;0) began by putting 2 extra elements in copying a cross of 9 counters, but corrected himself by pointing to the corresponding terms. He at once correctly reproduced the square of 9 counters, a house of 11 and a circle of 10. In copying the circle, he kept the same diameter. When he was asked if it was exactly the same, he pointed with his finger to the one-to-one correspondence. One counter was then put opposite each element of the model so that the one-to-one correspondence would produce a concentric circle larger in diameter: "Will there be enough counters to put opposite each one?—*Yes.*—Why?—*They're the same.*" But once the bigger circle was completed, he no longer thought they were equivalent: "Is there the same number of counters?—*No.*—Why?—*Because it's bigger.*" . . .

These then are the reactions of the second stage. There is one-to-one correspondence, but it is always based on the particular properties of the figure, for without the figure, the child no longer thinks the two sets are equivalent.

Stage III: Operational Correspondence. During the third stage, the correspondence no longer depends on the intuitive figure, and the child begins to use spontaneous operations as a check, breaking up the figures himself and arranging them in series. The correspondence thus becomes either qualitatively or numerically operational. . . .

Fav (5;6) had no difficulty in reproducing the figures in categories III and IV. He copied the figure, and also assumed the equivalence of the sets when the configuration was changed. For a figure of type V, he began by copying the model, and then counted aloud: "I must put 3 more," etc., then, getting confused, he stopped both copying the figure and counting, and adopted a procedure very typical of this stage, i.e., he made an "arbitrary" correspondence. He separated the elements of the model, arranged them 2 by 2 in two vertical rows, then did the same with the counters of his own set, but placed these horizontally. He then saw at once that there was one missing and added it. . . .

It is obvious that Fav and Maw [6;0] believed in the equivalence of corresponding sets, since they themselves destroyed the figures in order to check their numerical equality.

. . . We can therefore distinguish a stage characterized by operational correspondence, with recognition of the equivalence of corresponding sets, and conservation of quantities. This stage is intermediary between mere intuitive correspondence and correspondence between the objects and the numerals used to count them. This last type of correspondence, which is characteristic of a fourth stage, in which practical correspondence is replaced by the ability to use numeration correctly, does not concern us here, since the object of this volume is the study of the genesis of number, and it is only when operations are logically established on the practical plane that counting becomes truly numerical.

SINGLE ROWS

Before proceeding to discuss the reactions given above, it will be useful to analyze correspondence between single rows. This study will not be a repetition of that in Chapter III, since then we were concerned only with investigating why one-to-one correspondence, even between objects that are qualitatively complementary, does not entail the notion of necessary and lasting equivalence of corresponding sets. Here, on the contrary, our object will be to place correspondence among the various processes of cardinal evaluation, i.e., to study, making use of like objects, how the child makes two sets of equal value. Moreover, although in the preceding sections we have already seen these processes at work, we feel that it is desirable to simplify the problem, in order to discover whether the same results are achieved when single rows are used instead of complex figures.

Stage I: Global Comparison. In the case of single rows, the reactions are very similar to those observed earlier. Instead of making the one-to-one correspondence, the child bases his evaluations on only one or other of the two global qualities of the row, its length or the density of the elements, without coordinating them. Here we have some examples:

Don (4;1) had a sister, Myriam: "Mummy is giving Myriam all those pennies to go to the fair. Now you take the same number of pennies as Myriam.—(He took a handful at random (5), but arranged them so that his row was longer than the model.) *It's bigger, it's not right!*—Why? Is one of you richer, or have you both got the same?—*Yes, I'm richer.*—Well then, make it so that it's right.—(He put them all back into the box, then took out 4 which he put close together, then 1 more which he put close to the others.)

But this will be smaller (his row). *I'll have to put some more.* (He added 1 at each end, thus obtaining a row of 7, the same length as the model).—Are they the same like that, or will one of you be richer?—*They're exactly the same.*" . . .

More rarely, the evaluation is based on the density of the elements, as in the following examples:

Don (4;1), just after the experiment quoted above, put 7 red counters close together under 6 blue ones: "Are they the same?—*Yes.*—(The model row was then closed up and his copy spaced further apart.)—And now?—*I've got more* (7 red ones) *because it's bigger. No, Myriam's got more* (6 blue ones).—Why?—*Because they're close together; there are a lot."*
Lin (5;3) also, although most of his estimates were based on the length of the row, said more than once that 6 elements close together were more than *n* elements spread out *"because it's bigger."*

Although the result of these estimates based on density is the converse of those based on the length of the row, the principle is obviously the same: the criterion of the evaluation is not the number of elements or the one-to-one correspondence, but perception of a global quality.

What is the nature of this quantification prior to one-to-one correspondence, and why is one-to-one correspondence impossible at the level of the first stage?

Our conclusions are the same as before: elementary or "gross" quantities are nothing else than the relationships expressing "more," "equal to," or "less" immediately perceived in the given qualities, but not yet coordinated. The two qualities inherent in any row of objects, irrespective of the nature of the objects, are the total length and the density of the elements. Now it is impossible to compare any two rows without relating the qualities of one to those of the other, i.e., without one of the rows being seen as longer, shorter, or the same length as the other, or as more compact, less compact, or of the same density. It is therefore these relationships, which are as elementary as the qualities themselves, that are used by children at this level in their precardinal evaluations. When Don, for instance, says "I've got more because it's bigger," and Ler thinks that six pennies spread out are more than eight close together "because it's bigger," they are directly expressing the length of the rows in terms of quantity. . . . It is clear that the child is also capable of comparing two rows from the point of view of the intervals separating the elements. He recognizes that in one row the elements are more (or less) compact than in the other, and he can translate this perception into elementary quantitative relationships. For Don, for instance, "because they're close together, there are a lot," and for Lin, there are more when "it's bigger." Each of these two relationships of total length and density thus constitutes a beginning of what will later be cardinal evaluation, both of them being, from the start, inseparable from the quantity.

For the adult, a row of *n* spaced out elements keeps its cardinal value *n* if its length is diminished by closing up the elements. It is therefore the relation between the length of the row and the intervals between the elements which determines the conservation of the whole, whereas the relationships of length and density are variable. It is precisely this coordination, or logical composition of the two relationships in question, that the child of this level cannot make, and that is why the notion of conservation of the sets and even of one-to-one correspondence is still impossible. The elementary quantitative relationships are merely practical schemata which are still prelogical because there is not as yet any operation properly so called.

Now why is it that one-to-one correspondence is not possible during the first stage? We must, of course, distinguish between intuitive and operational correspondence. Operational correspondence presupposes the intervention of special operations which we shall discuss later, but intuitive correspondence, when it is qualitatively correct, is the result of elementary multiplication of the relations, and we have seen that the relationships of total length and density are not susceptible of composition at this first level. . . . It is only when two rows are of equal length and density that their equivalence implies their correspondence and goes beyond global evaluation. It can be seen, therefore, that correspondence is the expression of a construction in the true sense, even at the level of intuitive qualitative correspondence (i.e., before there is any question of numerical correspondence), the operation then being partially replaced by perception of the figures.

This construction can be analyzed as follows. First, there must be a decomposition, so that composition may become possible. If the global relationships of length and density of a row are to be merged in a single whole, it must first be understood that the total length is formed by the sum of the intervals separating the elements, and that consequently, in a compact row the intervals will be shorter and more numerous, while in a scattered row of the same length the intervals will be longer and less numerous. Secondly, when the two rows are compared, the construction on which the correspondence rests will presuppose a multiplicative composition of relationships: the two rows will correspond to one another spatially if they are at the same time equal in length and density, i.e., if each element of the one can be placed opposite an element of the other.

In this connection, the hesitations of the most advanced children of this stage, and the means they finally use to discover the correspondence, are most revealing. Having made their evaluation, like the other children, from the point of view of the length only, they begin to notice the density, hesitate for a moment between the two possible points of view, then, disconcerted by the contradictions involved, attempt to take account of both at once. They are thus led to make a spatial correspondence between both the elements and the intervals in the two sets. . . .

Thus for Stu [5;11], it was the discovery that a compact row of six elements may contain more than a longer row of four elements, that made her try to combine the relationships of length and density, and consequently to decompose the sets, thereby discovering the one-to-one correspondence.

Stage II: Intuitive Correspondence, Without Lasting Equivalence. When children at the second stage are asked to pick out a number of elements equal to those in a model row of six, they react immediately (or almost immediately) by making an optical spatial correspondence with the model, but they no longer accept the equivalence of the two rows when the correspondence cannot actually be perceived: . . .

Per (5;7) had no difficulty in making a row of 6 sweets corresponding to the model. The model was then closed up: *"I've got more.—Why?—Because it's a longer line.—*(The process was reversed.)*—Now there are more there, because it's a big line."* But a moment later, Per said the opposite: "Are there more here (spaced out)?*—No.—*Why not?*—Because it's long.—*And there (closed up)?*—There are more there, because there's a little bundle* (= close together).—Then are there more in a little bundle than in a big line?*—Yes."* After this Per went back to using length as the criterion, made the two rows the same length again, and said: *"Now they're both the same."* . . .

These examples clearly confirm our hypothesis as to the origin of qualitative correspondence. Elementary though this form of correspondence is on the purely intuitive plane, it nevertheless constitutes a complex relation involving a system of comparisons, i.e., of logical multiplications or divisions. . . . Such relationships obviously belong to a more advanced level than the undifferentiated, globally perceived relationships of the previous stage. In the case of our two rows, it is the coordination of the relationships of length and density of the rows that leads to correspondence. As long as the child judges the quantity by length or density alone, there is no possibility of correspondence. The children quoted above are now able to make a copy of the same length and density as the model, the twofold equality being ensured by the fact that each element of the copy is placed opposite an element of the model. . . . Moreover, when one of the rows is closed up or spaced out, and the child is asked to restore the equivalence in which he no longer believes, the reaction at this stage is different. Children at the first stage usually merely add or remove elements in order to have the same length or density again, whereas Jon, for instance, closes up the elements and gives as his reason for thinking the sets are equivalent: "because I pushed mine together." . . .

. . . The question then arises: how is it that the equivalence lasts only as long as the correspondence is perceived and ceases to exist when it is no longer perceived? Why is it that coordination of the two relationships does not lead to necessary lasting equivalence? In order to find the answer, we must distinguish two aspects of the matter: that of the general coordination, and that of the nature of the operations involved.

As regards the first, it is clear that, while there is here a continuous process of coordination, its stages indicate the existence of successive planes of structuration. First there are the elementary, global, perceptual relationships that are inherent in perception of the length and density of the rows. Then, when these perceptual relationships begin to be coordinated by means of seriations and logical multiplications, the coordination takes place first of all on an intuitive and still perceptual plane, and is only semioperational. This is precisely what happens during the present stage. The child certainly considers the relationships of length and density simultaneously, since he can produce a copy equal in length and density to the model, but the coordination does not go beyond the plane of perception, i.e., as soon as the perceived figure, which made the correspondence possible, is altered, not only does the correspondence vanish, but also the coordination between length and density.*

*We shall see later that the conservation of correspondence presupposes numerical, and not merely qualitative, operations.

Indeed, when one of the rows is contracted or expanded, the child does not say: "it's shorter, but closer together, so we can't tell," but chooses one of the two criteria at random, and judges the total quantity by it alone. . . .

Even at this second level, however, there are signs of a beginning of operational coordination. For if, as it is the purpose of this book to prove, an operation is indeed a reversible action, it is clear that the reactions of [4–5 year old children] who space out or close up the elements in order to restore the equivalences, are forerunners of the construction of true operations.

Coming now to the second aspect, we find that the global relations "more or less long," "more or less close together," which characterize the rows themselves and not the detail of the relationships between the elements, correspond to the first level, that of uncoordinated perceptual relationships. The coordination between these two kinds of relationships, which takes place during the second stage on the intuitive plane only, is both additive (seriation) and multiplicative (correspondence), and thus corresponds exactly to the beginnings of operations which we described in Chapters I and II in connection with the second stage of conservation of quantities. Indeed, on the one hand, the density of a row is nothing more than the succession (perceived or grasped) of the intervals separating the elements, and the sum of these lengths is identical with the total length of the row. Hence, to coordinate total length and density is merely to decompose the former into segments which define the latter, and this constitutes an additive seriation. On the other hand, to make the one-to-one correspondence between two rows is to construct two series whose elements are exactly opposite one another, i.e., to multiply the relations "situated at a certain distance along" by the relations "situated above." What the child discovers in making the perceptual one-to-one correspondence is the beginning of seriation and of multiplication of the qualitative relations of position, but nothing more. When the density or total length of one of the rows is altered, he ceases to believe in the correspondence, because he cannot understand that the displacements compensate one another and that the differences can be equated, an understanding which requires a higher level than that of mere qualitative grouping. All that the child can do is to restore the equality of the two rows, but he does not as yet deduce from this empirical return to the initial position that operational reversibility is always possible.

Stage III: Operational Correspondence and Lasting Equivalence. At the third stage, on the contrary, we find correspondence freed from perceptual or spatial limitations, and persisting in spite of any displacement of the elements. One-to-one correspondence thus becomes really quantifying, and from now on, expresses numerical equality and not merely qualitative equivalence. . . .

Lan (6;2), to reproduce a row of 6 matches, picked up 4, without counting, but looking at the corresponding elements. Having reached this point, he put his finger on the fourth match of the model, took 2 more, then put his 6 matches in front of the model row, but in a heap, so that there was no spatial contact. We then spread out his matches in a row and made the others into a bundle: "Are they the same?—*Of course.*—Why?—*Because before, those* (his own) *were in a bundle, and now you've put them like that* (spread out), *and these* (the model) *were spread out before, and now you've made them into a bundle."*

The contrast between these children and those of the preceding stage is obvious. In the first place, they do not rely on the perceptual contact between the elements, even when they make the one-to-one correspondence. . . . Lan put his six matches in a heap opposite the model row. What is more important, however, is that these children can relate the succesive configurations of the corresponding sets by correctly coordinating their relationships. For example, in order to prove that the pennies in the model are still equivalent to those in his copy, Fet [5;5] uses the same argument that the younger children used to prove the contrary: "because you've put them closer together." This justification can have one meaning only: when the pennies are put closer together, if none are added or removed the total length decreases but the density increases. The child is therefore now capable of considering simultaneously the relationships of length and density, not only when the series to be compared are similar, but also (and this is the progress over the second stage) when they differ in both length and density. . . . We can say that the third stage indicates the completion of the multiplication of these two relationships. Even at the second stage, there is already a beginning of this multiplication, but at that level the child either compares two corresponding rows correctly because they are equal in length and density respectively, or, when one of these qualities is the same in both, concludes correctly as to the other. When the two qualities vary together, at the second stage the child's estimate is wrong, while at the third stage, by multiplication of the two relationships, he grasps for the first time that a row which is both shorter and more compact than another can be equal to it.

. . . There is therefore, in reality, a freeing from perception in general, since each perception of the configuration takes its place in a coherent system of transformations governed by the logic of relationships, each composition corresponding to a possible perception of the sets.

It is this freeing from perception that marks the beginning of operations properly so called, which are thus seen to be the result of the progressive reversibility of thought. The terms used by Lan to explain the relationships between the two corresponding sets might be translated as follows: heap becomes row = row becomes heap. In other words, the two sets are still equivalent because their transformations are only reversible changes of position, i.e., they are the result of operations that can be reversed. . . .

The assumption that a short, compact row corresponds term for term with a longer and less compact row, involves the understanding of two facts essential to the construction of number. Hitherto, the elements of the corresponding rows have been considered by the child as being determined by their intuitive spatial qualities: the first counter on the left in the upper row, the counter next to it on the right, and so on. But once the correspondence is accepted as lasting irrespective of these positions, the elements merely become units, each equivalent to the others, and the correspondence then rests only on the notion of equal units, differing one from the other only by their relative order of enumeration. In other words, the correspondence is now the application of the same order of enumeration to two sets of equal units. From the point of view of the intervals between the units, we find the same mechanism. Up to the third stage, the child accepted the one-to-one correspondence between two rows of elements only if the total lengths and also the density, i.e., the intervals between the elements, were both equal. From the third stage onward, however, he recognizes that the correspondence persists when one of the rows is more compact, the difference in length being compensated by the difference in the intervals. The discovery of truly arithmetical correspondence thus always pre-supposes a new operation as compared with mere qualitative logic, this operation being the equating of the differences, or to put it more concretely, the seriation of units seen as equal in all respects except the temporary relative position of each one in the series.

CONCLUSIONS

The facts contained in this chapter are remarkably in agreement one with another and with those of the previous chapter. They provide us with the general picture of the stages through which correspondence passes, and thereby enable us to attempt a general explanation of the successive methods of quantification.

We have seen, in the course of our analysis, that the problem has gradually become more and more precise. In Chapters I and II we saw that the child does not at first assume conservation of either continuous or discontinuous quantities when the perceptual configuration is changed. We then examined the question of whether one-to-one correspondence, in its more familiar forms (correspondence between container and content, and one for one exchange) was sufficient to ensure conservation, i.e., necessary lasting equivalence, of corresponding sets. Chapter III led us to give a negative answer to this question. There is a level of perceptual correspondence which is characterized by the disappearance of the equivalence as soon as the corresponding elements are no longer in contact. Reactions of this kind are a relic of a first stage during which the one-to-one correspondence is not grasped even when it is imposed by the external situation, the equivalence resulting from a global estimate of the space occupied. We found it necessary, therefore, to study the spontaneous processes of quantification used by the child in order to determine the cardinal value of sets, and we therefore devoted Chapter IV to the question of spontaneous correspondence.

The tests used in Chapter IV involved the children in an activity which was a direct continuation of their everyday experience, and this activity yielded a rich crop of spontaneous procedures following a regular order: global evaluation, correspondence without lasting equivalance, and numerical correspondence with lasting equivalence. Three questions then arose. Why does the child not feel the need, from the beginning, to decompose the global totalities that he thinks he can evaluate? How does the first form of decomposition or intuitive qualitative correspondence make its appearance? In what condition does operational qualitative correspondence become numerical correspondence?

We outlined [above] the answer to these problems in the case of rows, but we must now generalize it. In so doing, we shall distinguish between psychological analysis, which is causal and genetic, and analysis of the logical construction of operations, though, as will eventually appear, the two kinds of interpretation are parallel.

All the preceding experiments have shown that at a first level (usually at about the age of 4½–5), the child evaluates discontinuous quantities as if they were continuous, i.e., extended, quantities. His quantitative judgments are thus based only on the general shape of the set and on global relationships such as "more or less long," "more or less wide," etc. . . .

Hence the child who is asked to pick out "as many" counters as there are in a given set is in no way equipped by his intellectual structure to consider the set as being a union of units, i.e. $1 + 1 + 1$ . . . etc., which would imply that he already possessed the notion of whole number. For the child, therefore, "as many" merely means a set similar to the model with respect to its overall qualities. But if he does not feel the need for decomposition, does this mean that he is incapable of it? To our mind, the preceding reactions have given a decisive answer to this question.

The only principle of synthesis at the disposal of the child at the first level is the intuitive global preception of the general configuration itself, in the absence of "operations" which would enable him to put together again the various parts of the perceptual intuition if it were broken up. That is why, as soon as there is an alteration in the data, children of the first stage apparently base their evaluations on one criterion only: length of the rows, width of the figures, density, etc.

But might it not be said that in the very action of copying there is coordination of the global qualities, and therefore at least a suggestion of decomposition, since the model is roughly reproduced? There precisely is the point: the copy is only roughly correct. Closed figures depending on a given number of elements are well reproduced, because they involve a "good" configuration, but collections, rows, open figures, and even closed figures with an arbitrary number of elements, are not correctly copied. Linear series, in particular, are evaluated by their total length only, irrespective of their density.

Although the method of global comparison allows of a rough comparison between two sets of the same form, covering the same area, and having approximately the same density, it becomes inadequate as soon as these properties differ substantially. . . . He cannot understand that when there is a change in the shape, and therefore in the distribution of the parts, something remains invariant, namely, the number of elements. The reason is that he has not yet acquired the notion of number, but only of perceptual wholes. . . .

The method of global comparison is therefore not only vague, but lacking in mobility, since there is no operational mechanism by which the various succesive states can be linked into a dynamic whole or system of relationships. Hence the characteristic feature of this first stage is the almost complete irreversibility of thought. It is true that each of the global qualitative relationships established by the child, e.g., "longer," etc., is capable of giving rise to an inverse relationship, "less long," etc., but as these relationships are not decomposable into units and are not coordinated one with the other, but merely put together in a nonstructured whole, they cannot yet form a reversible system, and perceptual intuition therefore holds sway, operations being as yet impossible.

The second method, which is characteristic of the second stage, and which consists in comparison of figures by intuitive qualitative correspondence, indicates some progress, but this is less than might at first appear. The progress lies in the precision brought to the analysis of shapes and qualities, which results in a deeper understanding of the intuitive data. At the previous level, the only details noticed are those necessary for the construction of the overall shapes: angles, ends of rows, etc., but from now on there are no privileged details. Each part of the whole is perceived and taken into account, and the child begins to coordinate the various criteria. It is because he is puzzled at finding that he arrives at different evaluations according as he stresses one or other of the criteria, that he eventually comes to coordinate them.

The child's success in thus reproducing the various geometrical configurations of the sets is achieved through a new semioperational method, or rather through the development of a schema which already existed within the global comparison, but which comes to the fore at this level, i.e., intuitive qualitative correspondence. Psychologically, to make a correspondence is merely to systematize judgments of resemblance and difference. The child perceives the details of one figure only through their resemblance to, or difference from, those of the other to which he is comparing it. He therefore works out the correspondence between all the analogous parts, and no longer concentrates only on certain outstanding details and the general configuration. This qualitative correspondence, or "comparison of the parts," is the tool used by the child for the reproduction of all the figures whose shape depends on the number of elements, and although it is not always successful in other cases, it constitutes a new and much more efficient method of reproducing the sets.

Yet this second method, although more precise than the first, is not much more mobile. It enables the child to compare only certain privileged static states of the sets in question, i.e., those which give the figures their particular shape. . . . From the point of view of coordination of relationships and conservation of quantity, there is only a slight progress, since displacement of the elements, resulting in a change in the figure, is sufficient to make the child think that the total number of elements has changed.

There is, indeed, a beginning of coordination of the relationships of length, width, density, etc., but it takes place only on the purely practical or intuitive plane. The tool used for the coordination of these relationships is not yet the operation as such, but the configuration itself. In order to make his own figure correspond to the model, the child must of course take into account simultaneously dimensions, density, shape, etc. As compared with the first stage, the progress lies in the fact that in the actual construction of the figure these relationships are coordinated, but as soon as the figure is changed, the child is incapable of abstract operational coordination of the relationships involved, and has recourse to the only available principle of unification: the figure he perceives. This explains why the child at this stage ceases to believe in the constancy or correspondence of the sets when the configuration of one is changed, and why he then again bases his evaluation on one criterion only, forgetting the others.

. . . With this semioperational character goes progress in reversibility of thought, reversibility being the psychological expression of the operation. This can be seen from the fact that although children at this level think that the number of elements changes with a change in the configuration, they nevertheless assume that a return to the original figure is possible. Thus in order to restore the equality between two rows, they merely space out or close up the elements of one of them, and do not add or remove any elements. But obviously this reversibility is incomplete and the relationships still do not constitute a reversible system. In other words, they are not yet independent of perception.

The third method, on the other hand, represents a definite progress: correspondence leads to necessary and lasting equivalence. The sets are now assumed to be equivalent, whatever the configuration or the distribution of the elements. The progress takes place gradually as a continuous process, the correspondence depending less and less on the figure itself, i.e., on perceptual intuition. As soon as qualitative correspondence is to any extent independent of the precise form of the respective parts of the two figures, the elements become interchangeable units, and the correspondence thus acquires a numerical character. . . .

The fundamental factor of this development is, in our view, the complete reversibility of the action involved in the child's procedure. The operation he performs is no longer immediately absorbed in the intuitive result obtained. . . . Each transformation can be compensated by its inverse, so that any arrangement may give rise to any other, and conversely. Thus instead of relying on an all-important figure, the child proceeds exclusively by reference to the one-to-one correspondence, and thereby succeeds for the first time in decomposing the wholes and coordinating the relationships. From now on, therefore, his actions constitute a reversible system involving constancy of the set. . . . in which each element, irrespective of its qualities, is considered as a unit equal to the others and differing from them only by its temporary position in the series. . . .

At the second stage, the child is still on the intuitive plane. He sees that the length and density of the rows are variable and he is perfectly coherent from the point of view of perception in assuming that this variation involves variation in the number, and this prevents him from attempting composition. Where he ceases to be logical, however, is in failing to grasp that in a contracted series the decrease in length carries with it increase in density. Instead of deducing that the result of composition is uncertain, he then dissociates length and density and makes the mistake of assuming that the number of elements depends on one of the two only.

How then does the child at the third stage succeed in overcoming this difficulty and discovering the constancy of number? Here there is a distinction to be made. On the one hand, if the comparison of two sets is merely a matter of "more or less numerous" (e.g., all the blue counters that correspond to the red counters), it is obvious that generalization of logical multiplications will suffice to establish the constancy of the sets, because of the operational reversibility of qualitative correspondence. The correspondence can be made and unmade, i.e., the two sets, which are two series of relationships, can be multiplied by another relationship which links them together and which can then be disregarded. Through this relationship, the two sets become, and remain, equivalent, which constitutes a certain constancy. When, for instance, a set of blue counters has been placed term for term below a set of red counters, the two series remain linked by the relationship "below" or "above," which ensures their equivalence from this particular point of view. . . .

But this constancy of classes or series of relations is not as yet constancy of number, and the equivalence to which we have just referred is not numerical equality. For example, there will be qualitative correspondence between three blue counters forming a triangle and three red counters also arranged in a triangle. If the red counters are then arranged in a row, the possibility of arranging them in a triangle still remains, and from that point of view, and that only, they are still equivalent to the blue ones. This equivalence is therefore of a special kind, depending on the same configuration. This is understood by the child in the third stage when, like Lan, he says that two sets which formerly corresponded are still "the same" because the heap can be made into a row as easily as the row can be made into a heap. A further step involves the assumption that the three counters in a row still correspond to the three in the triangle, and to any other set of three counters, whatever their distribution. This also is grasped by children at the third stage, since they frequently succeed in making the correspondence without troubling about the shape of the sets.

This brings us to the third stage in the logical construction of correspondence, that of numerical correspondence proper, which is parallel to what we called "extensive quantities" in Chapters I and II and reaches its apex at the same time as the operations of logical multiplication, i.e., at the same time as the discovery of the constancy of classes and series of relations takes place.

The explanation of the transition from qualitative to numerical correspondence can perhaps best be given in terms of classes. Let us again consider the case of the three blue counters in a triangle with a corresponding set of three red counters also in a triangle. Obviously any one of the counters can be used to start the correspondence, but once it is in the figure, its position is defined absolutely, and the correspondence is defined by the spatial properties of the counter chosen. Order in no way intervenes in the definition of the total classes formed by the corresponding elements. Such is the qualitative correspondence used by the child (and also frequently by adults). If, instead of making a triangle with the red counters, the child puts them in a heap or a row, or distributes them at random, the one-to-one correspondence he makes is of a new type, since each counter no longer carries with it qualities that distinguish it from the others, but becomes a unit equal to the others. Each red counter can then correspond to any one of the blue counters, but to one only. Hence the set of red counters acquires its quality of number three, and is no longer the class of counters forming a triangle, just as a pair of counters acquires the number two and is no longer the class of counters forming the ends of one side of the triangle. Moreover, any union of a pair of counters will produce the same class containing two elements irrespective of their qualities.

In this numerical correspondence, how are the elements distinguished one from another? It is merely by the order in which they appear in the correspondence, an order which is relative, and varies from one operation to another, and which we shall therefore call "vicariant." For instance, in order to find the number of red counters corresponding to the blue ones in a complex figure, one child will point to each blue counter in turn, in any order (provided he does not count any element twice and does not omit any) and each time he will add a red counter to his row; another child will make a pile of red counters, and a third will merely take one each time from his reserve pile and put them aside at random, and so on. The only order common to all is in the act of pointing, but this order is essential if the correspondence is to be correct.

The correspondence therefore ceases to be qualitative and becomes numerical when the elements are grasped as being equivalent in all respects, and when the differential properties that distinguished them within the set are replaced by the only difference compatible with their equality, i.e., their relative position in the order of the correspondence. Once again, therefore, we find that it is the equating of differences that is the origin of the unit, and consequently of number.

We find the same mechanism of arithmetization when we examine the evolution of relationships. Children at the third stage accept the fact that there is equivalence in spite of the distortion of one of the corresponding rows, without feeling the necessity for a return to the initial state. This means that they replace qualitative correspondence by mathematical correspondence, and that they understand that the decrease in length is exactly compensated by the increase in density. The multiplication of qualitative relationships is thus from now on completed by a higher operation, that of the equating of differences. This being so, the length of the row and the size of the intervals lose their significance, and it is only the constant relationship between the two which counts for the child. Each interval becomes a unit equivalent to the others and the relation that represents the shift caused by the interval is then equivalent to "plus one."

It is clear, therefore, that whether it be the elements as such or the relations that are being considered, in order that there shall be the transition from qualitative to numerical correspondence, a process of reasoning that goes beyond mere qualitative logic is necessary. It is the construction of units which are at the same time equal to one another and susceptible of seriation, and this construction takes place through the equating of differences. A class is, in fact, a union of terms seen as equivalent irrespective of their differences. For instance, all the counters of a series form a class to which those at the ends belong on the same terms as the others; red and blue counters are counters irrespective of their color, i.e., two classes are united to form a third by disregarding their difference, in this case the color. An asymmetrical relation, on the other hand, is the expression of a difference, e.g., when counter B is on the right of A and a certain distance away, A and B are conceived as different. To unite two asymmetrical relationships in one is to add the differences. Symmetrical relationships are those which unite the elements of the same class, without thereby adding anything. None of these qualitative compositions, therefore, would make it possible to define units properly so called. The union of two classes in a third does not constitute two units, because their union results from their common qualities, and in the new class their differences are disregarded. The union of two asymmetrical relationships also does not produce two units, since the partial differences which are composed are not necessarily equivalent. The construction of number, however, consists in the equating of differences, i.e., in uniting in a single operation the class and the asymmetrical relationship. The elements in question are then both equivalent to one another, thus participating of the class, and different from one another by their position in the enumeration, thus participating of the asymmetrical relationship. Moreover, since these differences are differences only of order, they are all equivalent one to the other. It therefore follows that the criterion for the transition from an arbitrary qualitative series to the corresponding numerical series is that each elementary relationship shall be considered as equivalent to the others.

Additive and Multiplicative Composition of Relations and Equalization of Differences*

In the previous chapter, we examined the procedure used by the child, when required to make a set Y correspond successively to two others, X and Z, in discovering that if X = Y, and Y = Z, then X = Z. This composition of relations of equivalence leads, as we saw, to the development of numerical multiplication, in the same way as the composition of qualitative correspondence of classes leads to multiplication of classes.

It now remains to analyze additive and multiplicative compositions of asymmetrical relations in relation to number. The best field for such an investigation is the one we used at the beginning of this book: that of the relationships between continuous quantities. It is true that by adding two sets or two lengths we obtain a total set or a total length, but these evoke a different idea from that of their components, whereas when a liquid is poured from one container into another, or when two units are added in a single glass, they essentially remain identical. . . .

It is satisfying to the mind to return, in this last chapter, to our starting point, and to utilize what we have discovered in the course of our investigation. There could be no better way of seeing the interdependence and deep-seated unity of the mechanisms that explain the psychological construction of number.

*[The following section is from Chapter X. Chapters V–IX are omitted from this volume.]

PROBLEMS AND RESULTS

In the questions put to the children during this investigation there are six distinct problems.

Problem I, that of conservation of quantities, has already been studied in Chapter I. If $A = B$, and B is poured into a number of containers, will the new quantities C, D, E, etc., remain identical with A? Since we have already analyzed the reactions to this problem, all that concerns us here is to discover what level has been reached by each child, from the point of view of conservation, when he is required to consider composition and measurement.

Problem II is that of spontaneous numerical measurement. The child is given two or three quantities of liquid in two or three containers of different shapes, such that he cannot estimate their ratio by direct perception. He is asked to say whether one of the quantities is equal to, greater than, or less than, one or both of the others, and is given some empty containers which he can use at will for the solution of the problem. Our particular concern is to discover whether the child is capable of constructing a definite unit.

Problem III is similar to Problem II, but this time a common measure is [provided by the instructions given to the child]. Using E_1, a small low, narrow glass, we pour the same quantity of liquid into three containers, the first wide and tall, the second wider but lower, and the third narrower and taller. The child is then asked whether the three quantities are the same. This experiment is useful mainly as a control test, when the child has failed with Problem II, to discover whether his failure is due to incapacity to understand measure, or merely to lack of initiative in using the empty containers.

For Problem IV, the child is given a certain quantity of liquid in container U_1 (wide and low), and is asked to put the same amount into L (tall and narrow). This coordination of inverse relations, already studied in Chapter I, is here considered in connection with Problems II–III and V–VI.

Problem V involves coordination of relationships of equivalence: if $L = A$ and $A = G$, will $L = G$?

Lastly, with Problem VI, it is a question of numerical additive or multiplicative composition resulting from these relationships. From the above equation it can easily be deduced that $L + G = 2A$, and that if A is filled with $2L$, then $G = \frac{1}{2}A$, etc.

The replies given to these various questions can be classified according to three stages, corresponding to those we have found throughout our investigations. At the first stage, when there is primacy of immediate perception, we find: no conservation (I); no notion of common measure (II); disregard of the common measure used by the experimenter, and evaluation through perception only (III), and consequently complete incapacity to compose perceived relationships (IV–VI).

During the second stage, the child discovers that there is conservation in certain cases only, and cannot generalize (I). He is partially successful in measuring, but does not always choose the right container (II). When he is given a unit of measurement (III), he continues to use perceptual criteria. Problems IV and V confront him with the same difficulty, and Problem VI proves that he is still incapable of any general composition.

At the third stage, the child has grasped the fact that there is conservation (I), he is capable of measuring, making use of a common unit (II–III), and is successful with all the elementary compositions (IV–VI).

DEVELOPMENT OF THE NOTION OF MEASURE (PROBLEMS I–III)

For the sake of clarity, we shall study separately the questions involving measure (I–III) and those involving composition (IV–VI), but remembering that theoretically the first differ from the second only by the practical character of the activity they involve.

Our procedure is as follows. We give the child two or three containers of different shapes, in which there is the same quantity of liquid. He is first asked to make an evaluation by looking at them. All children, at whatever stage, are then naturally victims of the perceptual illusions due particularly to the inequality of the levels. We then say: "What can we do to make sure? You've got all those empty glasses; pour it out and see." If there is no reaction from the child, we ourselves show him what we mean, by pouring out the liquid from the first two containers. There are two possible alternatives. Either the child does not yet believe in conservation, in which case measurement is impossible since he thinks that any change from one container to another involves a change in quantity, or else he has sufficient grasp of conservation for the questioning to be continued so as to see the various compositions he makes.

Here are some examples of the first stage:

Bo (6;0): Problem II. He was given G_1 (blue) $= W_1$ (pink) $= L_1$ (green). "Are they the same?—*No, there's more here* (L_1) *than there* (W_1), *but here* (G_1) *there's a little less than there* (W_1).—*How do you know?*—*I can see.*— Would it help you to make sure if you used the other glasses?—*Yes, one other* (taking P_1 and putting it next to W_1). *I'll pour the green into it* (L_1 into P_1). —And then what are you going to do?—*Would that one* (L_2) *be any use?*— (He did not understand.)—Suppose you poured this one (W_1) into that one (L_2)?—*Yes.*—How far up would it come?—(He pointed to the same level in L_2 as in W_1.)—Why?— . . . —And suppose I poured this one into there (W_1 into A_1)?—(He still pointed to the same height.)—(W_1 was then poured into A_1 and Bo saw that the level was higher.) And suppose I poured this (W_1) into that (L_2)?—*No, it won't come up as high* (as in A_1).—(W_1 was poured into L_2.) Is there more green (L_1) or more pink (L_2)?—*The same.*—And if I pour this (L_2) back into that (W_1)?—*It'll come up higher. There's more.*— (This was then done.) Is there the same amount of pink (W_1) and green (L_1)?—*No, there's more green.*—If I drink this (W_1) and you drink that (L_1), shall we both have drunk the same amount?—*No, not the same.*—And if I pour this (W_1) into that (L_2)?—*The same.*—And into that one (W_1)?—*No.*"

"Look, I'm putting the same here (W_1) and there (W_2). Is there the same amount?—*Yes.*—And now that I've poured that one (W_2) into those (C_1 and C_2)?—*No. It's higher, and there are 2 glasses. That makes more.*"

Problem III. "I'm putting that and that and that (3 times E_1) into each of these glasses (P, very wide and low, T, less wide and a little taller, and L, tall and narrow.) Now tell me what I did.—*You poured it with that one* (E_1). —Is there the same amount in the three glasses?—*Here* (L) *it's more than there* (T), *and there* (T) *it's more than there* (P).—Can you do it again?— (Bo poured E_1 three times into each of the large glasses.)—So if we give 3 glasses to each of these little girls, they'll have the same amount, will they? —*No, that one has a lot* (L), *and that one hasn't* (T). *And that one's got less still* (*P*).—But what did you pour with?—*With that one* (*E₁*) *I poured three times in each one.*—Then aren't they the same?—*No, there's more there* (*L*), *then there* (*T*), *then there* (*P*)." . . .

These reactions of the first stage are extremely important for the understanding of measure. There could be no more striking evidence that measure is impossible without conservation of the quantities to be measured, for the very good reason that quantities that are not conserved cannot be composed.

These children not only provide a clear confirmation of our findings in Chapter I with regard to conservation in general, but they also indicate in the most obvious way their prelogical attitude. For instance, Bo thinks there is more liquid in L_1 than in W_1. When W_1 is poured into L_2 (identical with L_1), he agrees that they are equal, and yet when L_2 is poured back into W_1 he no longer accepts the equality. . . .

Obviously in such a situation measure has no meaning, and the child does not understand what he is supposed to do when he is asked to verify his evaluations by means of the empty glasses given to him. Thus Jol [6;0], in order to compare L_1 and W_1, wanted to pour L_1 into L_2 and W_1 into W_2, regardless of the fact that it would make no difference. Then, when it was suggested that L_1 should be poured into W_2 he completely failed to see any use in such a transfer.

The position is even clearer in the case of Problem III, which involves the simplest form of measure through additive composition, glass E being poured three times into each of the containers G, U, and L, or P, T, and L. The children understand the data perfectly, and Bo himself repeats the operation correctly. But at this level the child does not conclude from the fact that the distribution was equal that the resulting quantities are also equal. Jol says explicitly that the same amount was taken with E, but that there is not the same amount in G, U, and L. If the terms "prelogical" and "prenumerical" have a meaning, they must surely be used to qualify a behavior in which there is complete negation of the axioms of equivalence.

We now come to the reactions of the second stage:

Vis (6;9), Problem II. G_1 (blue) $= W_1$ (pink) $= L_1$ (green): "Are they the same?—*No. There's more here* (*L₁*) *than there* (*W₁*)*and this one* (*W₁*) *is more than that* (*G₁*).—How do you know?—*I can see.*—Take these empty glasses and see if you're right.—(He took L_2). *It's the same size as that one* (*L₁*).—Well then, what must you pour into it?—*The pink* (pouring W_1 into L_2). *Oh! There's just the same amount. I thought there was more green.*— (L_2 was poured back into W_1.)—Is there the same amount of pink and green? —*No* (hesitating). *I don't know.*—If I drink this (*W₁*) and you drink that (*L₁*), shall we both have the same amount to drink?—*No, I'll have more* (*L₁*).—And if I pour this (*W₁*) back into that (*L₂*)?—*Both the same.*—And if I drink it out of this one (*W₁*)? *No, not the same.*"

Similarly, after recognizing that "*there's just the same amount*" in A_1 (pink) and A_2 (green), when A_2 was poured into $B_1 + E_1 + E_2 + E_3 + E_4$ there was more green (while if A was poured into $B_1 + B_2$ the green remained constant.) "And when all the green was in there (*A₂*)?—*It was the same* (as the pink).—And if I put all the green back into there (*A₂*), where will it come up to?—*The same height.*—Then are the green (*B₁ + 4E*) and the pink (*A₁*) the same?—*Yes, the same* (hesitating and pouring $B_1 + 4E$ into A_2).—Why are you pouring it out?—*To see if they're the same. No, it'll come up higher. . . . No, it'll be the same. Yes, it is.*" . . .

As far as conservation is concerned, these reactions fully confirm our findings in Chapter I. There is conservation when the changes are only slight and not too easily perceptible, nonconservation when the changes are more obvious, then gradual belief in constancy as a result of successive verifications. Vis, for instance, does not at first think that $L_1 = W_1$, although he agrees that $L_1 = L_2$ when W_1 is poured into L_2. He sees that $A_1 = B_1 + B_2$ if A_2 is poured into $B_1 + B_2$, but refuses at first to recognize that $A_1 = B_1 + 4E$ when B_2 is poured into $4E$, etc.

In such circumstances, measurement begins to be possible, but without as yet any systematization. Unlike the children of the first stage, these children spontaneously make use of the empty glasses as instruments for measurement, and even (toward the end of the stage) as common measures. Thus Vis, when told to see whether the quantity in L_1 was equal to that in W_1, poured W_1 into L_2. . . .

In spite of the fact that these children spontaneously discover the notion of measure, which makes its appearance at the same time as the notion of conservation, it is essential to notice the limitations of their metrical capacity. In the first place, as the construction of conservation is not yet completed, their estimate of the measurement depends on the elements taken into account (as for instance, when Vis judges the quantity in W_1 by comparing its level with that in L_2). In the second place, as there is no rigorous composition, there cannot be coordination of successive measurements. Thus Ree [6;0], after using L_2 to measure W_1 and seeing that L_1 and W_1 are equal, also measures W_1 and G_1 but is incapable of deducing that $L_1 = G_1$. It is obvious that this incapacity to combine equivalent relationships affects measurement. W_1 ought to be the common measure between L_1 and G_1, [but] since composition is lacking, there can be no general unit. In comparing W_1 and L_1 by means of L_2 these children were not measuring in the true sense, because L_2 was not a mean term distinct from L_1, but a duplicate identical with it. When the [middle] term is different in shape and dimensions, these children find great difficulties. The same Ree, for instance, when he had to compare G and P without duplicate glasses, was unable to find a common measure without assistance.

This brings us to the third limitation, which is revealed in Problem III. At the second stage, there are not yet "units" of measurement, i.e., there is no common measure susceptible of being added or multiplied. Thus, when E is poured three times into various containers which the child has to compare, he encounters great difficulties. Even Pos and Cot, who for the other problems were on the borderline between stages two and three, declined to accept E as the unit of measurement and estimated the quantities by the level reached in the various containers. Pos, for example, knew that the same quantity had been poured out from E, but did not deduce that there was the same amount of liquid in the four containers. Cot was unaware that an equal quantity had been distributed until he was made to repeat the process in detail. . . .

We now come to the third stage, at which the child is capable of operational constructions. . . .

San (6;3). Problem II. $L_1 = A_1 = G_1$. San thought that $L_1 > A_1 > G_1$. "Try with these glasses.—(He poured A_1 into L_2.) *They're the same.*—(L_2 was poured back into A_1.) And those (A_1 and L_1)?—*The same.*—How do you know?—*I measured it with the same one.*—And those (A_1 and G_1)?— *I think they're the same. We must measure.* (He poured G_1 into L_2 then L_2 into A_2.) *They're the same* (pouring back).—And those (G_1 and L_1)?—*They're the same, because we've measured: we could see that those* $(G_1$ *and* A_1) *were the same.*—Yes, but what about these two $(L_1$ and G_1)?—*Because we measured that* (A_1) *with that* (L_2)."

Problem III: E was poured twice into G, P, and L: "Is there the same amount in all three?—*Yes, you put* 2 *in each time.*" . . .

The difference between these reactions and those of the second stage is obvious. There is no need to point out that all these children assume that there is conservation, but in addition to this, they can measure of their own accord, Ar [6;8] with some hesitation, but the others systematically. The most interesting case is that of Van [7;0], who spontaneously discovers a common measure A_1 for D_1 and A_2 and for $L_1 + L_2 + D_1$. Even when there are no duplicates of G and P Van and Jan [6;6] find a solution to their problem, Van by a common measure, and Jan by calculation. Moreover, the coordination of the measurements is spontaneous, as is shown by the case of San, who at once assumes that $L_1 = G_1$ if $L_1 = A_1$ and $A_1 = G_1$, without being asked about them. What is still more important is that Problem III is solved without hesitation, which means that the child at once discovers the relation "in each container, so many units." In a word, what is new at this stage is the discovery of the common measure and the unit, and these define operational composition as distinct from mere intuitive coordination.

COMPOSITION OF RELATIONS AND OF NUMERICAL UNITS

From what has been said above it is clear that there is a logic of measurement: in measuring, we compose units that are conserved, and introduce a system of equivalences between these compositions. We shall therefore now analyze the logical and numerical compositions that intervene, not only in the preceding questions, but also in Problems IV, V, and VI, each of which has a specific lesson to teach in this respect. Here [is an] example of the first stage: . . .

Mol (6;0). Problem IV (U_1 was ½ full): Mol filled L_1 to the same level. U_1 was then tilted, and Mol looked at the slanting surface of the liquid: "*There's more here* (U_1). *No, there's more here* (L_1), *because it's higher.*"

Problem V (simplified): "Take that one (W_1) and pour it into there (G_1) and then into there (A_1).—(He did so.)—Tell me what you did.—*I poured with that* (W_1) *into that one and that one.*—Then is there the same amount to drink in both?—*No. There's more here* (A_1) *than there* (G_1) *because it's higher.*—But how much was there in that one (W_1)?—*It was quite full, but it doesn't make the same amount.*"

Problem VI (simplified): "Is there the same amount here (L_1) and there (L_2)?—*Yes.*—Watch (pouring L_2 into $E_1 = E_2$).—*It's the same, because that one* (E) *is half those* (pointing to $2E$).—And if I do this (L_1 poured into P)?—*Oh no! I've got more* ($2E$).—But where did I get this (P) from?—*From there* (L_1), *but it's not the same any more.*" . . .

Further examples are unnecessary to show that children at this level are incapable of any composition, either logical or numerical. They are not capable of multiplying the two inverse relations of height and cross section of the columns of liquid. . . .

This absence of composition is so amazing that one constantly wonders whether there is not some misunderstanding on the part of the child, i.e., whether when he says "there's more" or "less" he is not merely thinking of the level, instead of the total quantity. This interpretation must, however, be excluded, for we have always taken the greatest care to see that the instructions were understood, and specified "more (or less) to drink" in order to ensure that there was no ambiguity. Moreover, when the child thinks of the level, it is precisely because he is unable, for want of adequate logical tools, to picture the total quantity otherwise than by means of one of its aspects, without coordinating this particular relationship with the others. He frequently attempts to take the cross section into consideration, but he then forgets the level. Generally speaking, there can be no doubt that the child understands what is required of him, since he spontaneously transfers the liquids from one container to another in his attempts to measure and verify his results.

We now come to the reactions of the second stage: . . .

Lois (7;0). Problem V: He measured the equality of G_1 and W_1, then of W_1 and L_1. "And will there be the same amount to drink in these two (G_1 and L_1)?—*I think so.*—Why?—*Because here (G_1) it's more spread out. That's why it's low down.*"
Problem VI: "Look, those ($E_1 + P_1$) are for you. This one (A_1 into which $2E_2$ was poured) is for me. Tell me what I did when I poured it out.—*You poured twice with that one (E_2).*—And is there the same amount in this (P_1) and that (E_1)?—*Yes.*—And in that (E_2)?—*The same.*—Then have we both got the same amount to drink, if this (A_1) is mine and those ($P_1 + E_1$) are yours?—*I've got more because I'll drink two glasses and you only that (A_1).*— But is that (P_1) the same amount as that (E_1)?—*Yes.*—And what about these two (E_1 and E_2)?—*Oh yes! It's the same. These two ($E_1 + P_1$) are the same, and you poured out that (E_1) twice, so that makes the same amount.*"
"And if I pour that (P_1) into there (A_2), how far up will it come?— (He pointed to ¾.)—And that one (E_1)?—*The same height* (¾).—And both of them?—*The same height as that* (level in A_1)."

These reactions show, as usual, that at the second stage there is a beginning of coordination, but that it is merely intuitive, without operational composition.

This can be clearly seen in the solutions given to Problem IV. These children, in contrast to those at the first stage, consider simultaneously height and cross section, and expect the level in the narrow container to be higher than in the wide one. Instead, however, of finding a principle of composition and measurement, they confine themselves to empirical evaluations.

The results obtained in the case of Problem V are exactly parallel. At the earlier stage, the children were not capable of deducing the equality $G_1 = L_1$ from the equalities $G_1 = W_1$ and $W_1 = L_1$, since any notion of conservation or measurement was absent. At the present stage, on the contrary, the child succeeds in discovering the equalities $G_1 = W_1$, and $W_1 = L_1$, gradually comes to recognize their constancy, and finally concludes that $G_1 = L_1$. Nevertheless, in spite of appearances, it would be wrong to assume that the child reaches this conclusion as a result of true deduction, which would consist in composing the general equalities $L_1 = W_1$; $W_1 = G_1$; therefore $L_1 = G_1$. He discovers the correct result merely by virtue of an inductive analogy. In establishing the equalities $L_1 = W_1$ and $W_1 = G_1$ he has to establish at least four equivalences, and when he is further questioned as to whether $L_1 = G_1$ he is inclined to think that probably the equivalence will continue, but for him it is a matter of probability and not of logical necessity. Ree, for example, thinks that "perhaps" L_1 will equal G_1, but is not prepared to make a categorical statement about it until he has verified it empirically. Bor also accepts the equivalence, but merely because "there was always the same amount" on other occasions, and Vis, Gis, and Lois use the same type of reasoning.

A comparison of the reactions to Problems V and VI shows that in both cases there is composition of the relations of height and cross section, and also of equivalences. In Problem IV, however, the equivalence is given and the multiplicative relation has to be constructed, while in Problem V the situation is the opposite. It is therefore of interest to find that at this level the same method of intuitive coordination, and not deduction, is used in both cases.

The key to these reactions is to be found in the answers given to Problem VI, for here the correct solution requires an arithmetization of the additive and multiplicative compositions of the relations in question. None of the children quoted had any difficulty in understanding that $E_1 = U_1$, all of them remembered that $2E_1$ had been poured into A_1, and yet none of them arrived at a complete deductive solution.

As for the equality $E_1 + U_1 = A_1$, Ree, for example, is torn between the idea of equivalence and that of nonequivalence, because U_1 "is a little glass with only a little in it." The struggle between reasoning, which strongly suggests that $E + E = 2E$, and perception, which suggests that there is inequality, finally leads Ree to the conclusion that "we must try it." Later, he understands almost at once that to obtain a quantity equal to $E_1 + U_1 + A_1$ it will be necesary to pour $4E_1$ into A_2, but is still anxious to verify it, and when he has poured $E_1 + U_1 + A_1$ into B_2 he fails to see why the level in the narrower container B_2 differs from that in A_2.

These children, then, are not yet capable of composing three or four elements into two equivalent totalities. Or rather, while they find no difficulty in so doing when there is no opposition between the relations and perception (e.g., when $E_1 + E_2 = E_3 + E_4$) they have not yet reached the point at which rational composition triumphs over perception.

The position is even clearer in the second part of the problem which involves decomposition. All these children are aware that $A_1 = 2E_1$, and that $E_1 = P_1$, and yet when asked about the level of the liquid in E_1 if it is poured into A_2 (which is placed next to A_1), none of them are certain that it will be half the level in A_1, that the same will be true of the contents of P_1, and that $E_1 + P_1$ will give the same level as in A_1. Ree alone says "halfway because it's the same amount as there" (E_1), but he at once adds "I don't know if it's exactly halfway," as if to make quite clear that it is not a matter of deduction but of intuitive probability. Bor also begins by attributing half the height of A_1 to E_1, and also to P_1 but for $E_1 + P_1$ he indicates a level much higher than that in A_1 (more than three times the unit E_1), because "if we measured that (P_1) it would get higher." Thus for Bor $1 + 1$ does not give 2 if the two units differ too much in appearance. Gis thinks that when he has $P_1 + E_1 = B_1$, if $E_1 = P_1$, the contents of E_1 will reach the same level in B_2 as in E_1, while $P_1 + E_1$ will reach a higher level than in B_1. Then, when he grasps that $P_1 + E_1$ poured into B_2 will reach the present level in B_1, he thinks that E_1 alone represents five-sixths of the amount, and that the same is true of P_1 alone. Thus for Gis, each of the two halves of a whole, when taken separately, is equivalent to five-sixths of the whole. . . .

The contradiction in these compositions is a further and even more striking proof of the conflict between perception and reasoning at this stage. It shows more particularly that the construction of the unit, necessary for measurement, involves equalization of differences, and this we now see to be the essential condition for the transition from compositions of purely qualitative relations to truly numerical compositions.

We now come to the reactions of the third stage: . . .

Chou (7;0). Problem V. L_1 (blue) $= W_1$ (pink) and $W_1 = G_1$ (green). "There (G_1), there's as much as there (L_1). They're both the same.—Why?— I looked at all three of them.—But did you look at these two together (blue and green)?—No, but I saw by the pink."

Problem VI. $P_1 = E_1$ and $A_2 = 2E_1$: "You'll have all those $(P_1 + E_1 + A_1)$. How many little ones (E_2) must I take so as to have the same amount here (A_2)?—6—Why?—(He pointed to the 3 glasses one after the other.) 2, 4, 6 . . . Oh no! I thought there were two everywhere (his reasoning was therefore correct)."

If we compare these reactions with those of the previous stage the contrast between operation and intuition is clearly to be seen. At this stage, Problem IV no longer presents any difficulty and there is extreme precision in the solution of Problem V. Chou, for instance, is well aware that he used glass W_1 as a common measure in comparing L_1 and G_1 as his words indicate: "I looked at all three of them . . . I saw by the pink."

A comparison of Problem VI with the two earlier ones clearly proves that when the child becomes capable of rigorous composition of elementary operations of logic or relations, he also becomes capable of numerical composition involving the same relations.

From the point of view of logic of relations, Problem VI is indeed only the synthesis of Problems IV and V, since in order to establish that $E_1 + U_1 = A_1$, where $A_1 = 2E_1$ and $U_1 = E_1$, it must be understood: (1) that the increase in height of the liquid in a narrow container is compensated by the decrease in cross section, and conversely (Problem IV), and (2) that if $U_1 = E_1$ and $E_1 = \frac{1}{2}A_1$, then $U_1 = \frac{1}{2}A_1$ (Problem V). Something more, however, is involved in Problem VI, since it also presupposes the constitution of units susceptible of addition and multiplication.

It is in fact, when Problems IV and V are solved operationally that Problem VI also is solved. Fol's certainty of the equivalence of the units or of their sums is proof against a whole series of successive transformations. In the case of Nao, Schen, San, and Chou, composition of the type $E + E + E$ . . . acquires a character that is both multiplicative and additive, as Chou, for example, shows when he thinks that the sum is equal to six because two units were poured into each glass. Conversely, we find that these same children indicate half, and even a third, of a given column of liquid as corresponding to the units. To sum up, in contrast to those of the earlier stages, these children can combine the units of measure obtained by a rigorous equalization of differences.

CONCLUSIONS

We must emphasize, if the relation between numerical operations and qualitative logical relations is to be understood, that the compositions dealt with in this chapter are already implicit in the elaboration of conservation itself. In the case of the problem of conservation, however, the child is unaware of their existence, whereas in the present case he has to discover and "think" them.

The problem we put to the children in Chapter I, using exactly the same material as in this chapter, was that of deciding whether a quantity A_1, equivalent to A_2, remains equivalent when subdivided or poured into a different container. Obviously the solution of such problems requires on the part of the child the capacity to unite parts into a whole, to divide a whole into parts, to coordinate equivalences and to multiply relationships. In other words, it involves all the additive and multiplicative compositions studied in this chapter. It is therefore in no way surprising that the stages of the construction of conservation are exactly synchronic with those of the development of these compositions. It may even have seemed to the reader that we were merely repeating, with only slight changes in the language used, the tests of Chapter I. But it is one thing to postulate the equivalence of A_1 and A_2 from the point of view of perception and to discover whether the equivalence is conserved in spite of successive transformations, and it is quite another thing to construct the equivalence by measurement (Problems II and III of this chapter) or by various deductions (Problems IV–VI). In the first case, the child has to justify a given solution, while in the second he has to find the solution. The same compositions are thus the result, in the first situation, of an analysis which may involve varying degrees of awareness, and in the second, of a synthesis which demands clear and precise thinking. This fact explains why for the child the problems of operational composition appear to be new, while for the adult they are immanent in every problem of quantification.

What we have just said is equally applicable to each of the investigations in Chapters VII to IX concerning additive and multiplicative compositions. Addition and multiplication of classes, relations, and numbers are implicit in the construction of every class, every relation, and every number. But it is not at all the same thing to construct such elements without any knowledge of the operations involved, as it is to link the elements, once they have been constructed, by means of the same operations explicitly and consciously performed. In both cases the same "groupings" or the same "groups" are in question, but in the first case the mind is proceeding from the result to the analysis of its composition, while in the second it proceeds from the synthetic composition to its results.

The reason why the stages of composition are the same as those of conservation is now clear, since the latter is at the same time the result of composition and the invariant that makes composition possible.

At the first stage, the child is unaware of both conservation and composition. Perceived relationships, which change with each change of container, are not coordinated operationally, or even intuitively, with the result that the child's evaluation is based entirely on the qualities and their immediate relationships (gross quantity), awareness of one relationship preventing awareness of others, coordination thus being impossible.

With the progress of intuition, the perceptual relationships gradually begin to be coordinated, provided that the transformations are not too great, and this beginning of intuitive coordination characterizes the second stage. Until coordination of relationships becomes generalized, however, there can be no rigorous system of compositions, and as at the second stage the relationships resulting from extensive transformations are not coordinated, the child relying on his actual perception rather than on any rule of composition, this stage remains intuitive, intuition being merely representation constructed by means of interiorized, fixed perceptions. How then are we to explain the transition from this intermediary stage to the rigorous composition to be found in all the various fields we have examined?

It seems that the third stage only becomes possible with the constitution of two interdependent systems, the "grouping" of multiplications of relations, and the "group" of numerical multiplications, both of which coordinate into a closed and reversible whole the operations involved, the one on the qualitative and the other on the numerical plane.

What is lacking in the multiplications of asymmetrical relations characteristic of the second stage is the possibility of their grouping. At the third stage, on the contrary, grouping is achieved. Let us take as a typical example the case of Fol, who is capable of coordinating a sequence of equivalences which it is difficult for the reader to follow without putting them on paper: $U_1 = U_2$; then $U_2 = L_1$; $L_1 = E_1 + E_2$; then $E_1 = M_1$; therefore $E_2 + M_1 = U_2$; then $\frac{1}{2}U_2 = M_2$; therefore $\frac{1}{2}U_2 + M_2 = M_1 + E_1$; and if $E_2 = M_2$, then $\frac{1}{2}U_2 + E_2 = M_1 + E_1$, etc. It is clear that, in addition to the equating of differences and the constitution of mathematical operations, this sequence involves as a minimum the following logical operations:

1. Composition of multiplications of relationships.
2. A sequence of equivalences such that two successive transformations are reducible to a single one.
3. Generalization, which consists in passing from an intuitive relationship between two objects to an operational relationship between three objects, then four, and so on. These complete the grouping of multiplications of asymmetrical relations.

The progress of the third stage does not, however, consist merely in the completion of the qualitative coordinations (in this particular case, grouping of the multiplications of relationships), but also in the synchronic constitution of the group of arithmetical multiplications through the process of equalization of differences.

This process can clearly be seen in the correct solutions to Problem II. When, in comparing L_1 and G_1, the child spontaneously pours G_1 into L_2, or, in comparing G and P, pours G into W_1 and P into W_2, he is not merely seriating the differences between G_1 and L_1 or between G and P, but is trying to reduce the relations of difference to equalities, and this is characteristic of measurement. The simplest form of this equalization consists in pouring G into L_2 in order to compare it with L_1, thus showing that the decrease in cross section from G to L is compensated by the increase in level. In this case, the equating of differences consists merely in the reduction of G to L, L serving as the measure for G. When, however, G is poured into W_1 and P into W_2 the differences between G and P are canceled out through the use of a common measure W, which thus constitutes an elementary unit, distinct from the terms to be compared, but not yet composed with itself through additions or multiplications.

With the correct solutions to Problem III, the equalization of differences is completed by the constitution of units that can be additively and multiplicatively composed, i.e., of a common measure in the ordinary sense.

At the third stage, when the child is capable of solving Problem VI in its form $P (= E) + E = A$ (if $A = 2E$), he also understands that the successive levels in A are susceptible of graduation into a system of units and fractions according to the number of E poured into A.

Thus by children at this level, questions III, V, and VI are regarded as multiplicative problems. When, for instance, in the case of Problem VI, San says that for $P + L + A$, glass L must be poured in "four times . . . because there (A) there are two," we have a particularly explicit example of the process that takes place in all measurement, the very notion of a common measure depending on that of multiplicative equivalence.

We thus find that while multiplication of classes and multiplication of relations are two distinct operations, the one bringing into correspondence terms that are qualitatively equivalent, and the other asymmetrical relations between nonequivalent terms, all that is necessary in order to make the terms of these relations equivalent and thus to fuse multiplication of relations and that of classes into a single operational whole, is that the differences shall be equalized. We then have multiplication of numbers. Once again, therefore, number is seen to be the synthesis of class and asymmetrical relation. This general conclusion is supported by the whole of our analysis of number in the preceding pages.

Glossary

a priori analytic deduction—deduction which is not based on any experiment (a priori) and which does not say anything about its object that is not contained in its premises (analytic).

extensive quantity—the name given to any magnitude that is susceptible of actual addition, as for example mass or capacity—the mass of a body formed of two bodies is the sum of the masses of the original bodies.

intensive quantity—the name given to any magnitude which is not susceptible of actual addition, as for example temperature. Two quantities of water at 15° and 25° respectively do not produce a mixture at 40°.

logical groupings—by this expression the author understands a type of organization of propositions such that the four following conditions are satisfied: (1) there exists a law of composition; (2) this law is associative; (3) there exists an inverse for each operation; (4) there exists an identical operation.

logical multiplication—expresses the fact that two or more attributes are considered simultaneously. Thus, to consider red round beads as opposed to red square beads or black round beads, is to make use of the logical multiplication of two attributes; red, round; red, square; black, round.

22

Intellectual Operations and Their Development*

1963

INTRODUCTORY NOTES

The Development of Physical Quantities in the Child: Conservation and Atomism† was an expansion of a lecture given by Piaget in 1936 in Cambridge at the tricentennial of Harvard University. It deals with some problems that Piaget had touched lightly in the *Construction of Reality* and in the first two chapters of *The Child's Conception of Number*. The growth process through which the child constructs the idea of the conservation of matter is one of Piaget's most famous discoveries. We give as our selection, to represent this essential aspect of Piaget's work, a summary published in 1963, "Intellectual Operations and their Development." These two titles taken together suggest the scope and aim of the work: to apply the fundamental theoretical ideas about intellectual operations to the domain of physical quantities.‡ The key point is not merely that the child attains the idea of conservation, or even the particular arguments she uses to defend her belief, but rather that she constructs the idea through the use of certain intellectual operations; and, moreover, that she does so at the same time as she is mastering these operations.

When an object is put out of shape, the child becomes able to dissociate the deformation of the shape from the conservation of the object itself. The objective shape has become different but the object has in some sense remained the same. A hat is, for instance, put out of shape by a clumsy person who sits on it, but the hat remains of course the same in spite of the distortion. Is that clear? Not really: take a square, turn it 45° so that it rests on a

---

*From *Experimental Psychology: Its Scope and Method*, edited by Paul Fraisse and Jean Piaget, VII. Intelligence, by Pierre Oléron, Jean Piaget, Bärbel Inhelder, and Pierre Greco, translated by Thérèse Surridge, © 1963 Presses Universitaires de France, English translation © Routledge & Kegan Paul, 1969, Basic Books, Inc., Publishers, New York. Reprinted with permission of Basic Books and Routledge & Kegan Paul Ltd., London. Originally published in French, 1963.

†*The Development of Physical Quantities in the Child: Conservation and Atomism*. Arnold Pomerans, translator. London, Routledge & Kegan Paul, 1974. Originally published in French in 1941.

‡We do not mean that theory developed before application; as with the child, so with the scientist they developed hand in hand.

corner. It is not a square anymore. It is a diamond. This use in the English language of different words to characterize the same object is a vestigial evidence of the difficulty our ancestors had in conserving the invariance of objects through their transformations. The same difficulty exists for children under the age of 7 in our own culture of today. Presented with two equal clay balls the child denies their equality after one of them is flattened or undergoes any other transformation. For her, the quantity of matter is altered when the shape is altered.

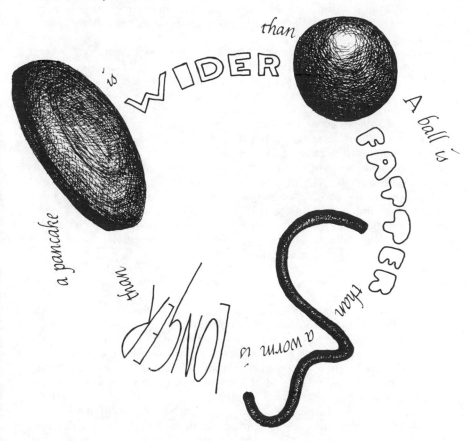

The same holds true for weight and volume. The younger subjects simply deny the conservation of these physical or material properties after any transformation, whereas the older subjects admit it first for substance in general, then for weight, and finally for volume.*

In this research Piaget and Inhelder conducted similar experiments not only with clay balls, but also with liquids poured from one container to another of a different shape. They also imagined more paradoxical situations such as the conservation of sugar after its dissolution in water, the dilation of mercury, or the popping of corn. Finally, they constructed materials requiring the formal composition of many elements to obtain the desired results or effects.

* But not everyone attains conservation of volume, even in a qualitative sense.

In sum, all the forms of invariances of three basic physical properties are investigated here in a systematic fashion. The results thus obtained are interesting and useful in three different ways. First of all, they show increasing complexity of the system of invariants with age. At 6 months roughly, the child masters perceptual constancies. At 18 months, the child attains permanence of the object after it has disappeared from the perceptual field. Around the age of 6 years, the child admits the identity of an object that undergoes certain changes in its color, size, and position. But this construction remains fragile until the child attains command of the invariance of transformation with respect to an external standard that is left unchanged all through the experiment.

This attainment is the sign of a new stage of development or of a complete restructuration, on a more advanced plane, of the subject's criteria for truth. This reconstruction is marked, according to Piaget, by the emergence of what he calls concrete operations. In Piaget's language an operation is an internalized action that is reversible and part of an ensemble. (See below, pp. 456–463.) For the moment, it suffices to say that operations cannot occur without representation; when actions become mental acts they can be reorganized in more mobile fashion than real actions, since the person can group them together into one coherent set or contemplate at the same time an act and its opposite (reversibility). All these factors explain why the child becomes more and more capable of compensating the changes of the object by reversed changes performed as mental actions and easily checked up through direct experimentation. This solidarity of direct and reversed actions into one unitary synthetic system solidifies the child's thinking into a logical structure that Piaget calls *groupement* (grouping) that we shall study under the rubric of logic. This construction once again takes some time to be completed. This explains the existence of *décalages* among the different acquisitions of invariants.

The second important effect of the notion of conservation on the development of the child is the construction of new theories about matter such as the development of atomism (in Piaget's sense of the notion) in the case of the dissolution of sugar in fine particles. The combination of these particles explains why the quantity of sugar is conserved despite the apparent disappearance of the initial big domino. It accounts also for the conservation of the quantity of corn before and after popping it. This composition of particles makes possible the construction of density as a notion relevant to matter.

The third contribution of these experiments is the information that they provide about the genesis of quantification in children. Piaget, after Kant, distinguishes two sorts of quantities: intensive and extensive. Intensive quantification deals only with the relation between the part and the whole. It is clear without counting that a part of something numerable is smaller than the whole. Or in more general terms, that a subclass of a class contains fewer elements than the class itself. The principle of transitivity is deducible from this rule. If A is larger than B and B larger than C, A is larger than C and the difference between A and C is larger than the difference between A and B.

Extensive quantification appears when the differences themselves are compared. A special case of extensive quantification is metric quantification in which all differences are compared to a standard measure of which they are either a multiple or a fraction.

Completely new horizons open to the child as he masters conservation, this simple but clever principle to keep invariant a constantly changing reality.

For Piaget, a child has not attained conservation merely because he gives the right answer (same amount of clay). He must be able to defend it with arguments, entailing fundamental intellectual operations. (See pp. 453–458.) Of course, conservation cannot be seen or sensed. What is seen and sensed is change and transformation.

Consequently, there is nothing empirical in conservation. It is not a physical property of an object like its color, shape, or size. It is the result of all the possible manipulations that can be made with reality.

Some questions are in order. Why have the conservation experiments become so famous, almost as the apotheosis of Piaget's work? Is it because there is some special mystery in the universal discovery by children of an idea that is neither taught in school nor visible to the senses?

Compared with the other fields of mental life, the field of intellectual operations has given rise to a relatively limited number of experimental studies. And yet, insofar as all behavior simultaneously comprises cognitive and affective aspects, one would think that the operations which alone make it possible to distinguish the true from the false would have attracted the attention of researchers at every phase of scientific psychology. The fact that this has not been the case is probably due to [three] reasons.

The first reason is that everyone (including, sometimes, psychologists) believes that he has adequate insight into his own intellectual operations. As introspection is linked to verbal habits and to socially acquired notions, it has naturally encouraged the belief that the descriptions of thought mechanisms given by philosophers and by classical logic are adequate (the analyses of modern logic have failed to attract attention partly because of their technical character). Thus, the tests proposed by Toulouse and Piéron in 1911 contained as yet no other means of measuring intellectual operations than a set of syllogisms. The premises were given and the subjects had to deduce the conclusion.

The second reason is that insofar as experimental psychologists have attempted to give a fresh interpretation of intellectual operations, they have begun by giving in to "reductive" tendencies, hence the effort made by associationism to reduce these operations to a mere play of associations between images, etc. Finally there was a reaction against reductionism, strongly evident in the Würzburg school but resulting in a return to logicism.

The main reason that experimental work on intellectual operations has not flourished must be sought elsewhere. These operations are linked in normal adults to complex structures which escape introspection and which in the analysis of behavior (in problem-solving techniques, etc.) either still pass unnoticed or else give rise merely to descriptions. The only really fruitful method consists in studying their genesis and this implies different techniques. That is why experimental psychology has taken so long to approach the central problem in this field: that of the progressive construction of operational structures in the course of development from birth to maturity.

It is therefore fitting to begin with a brief historical survey indicating the main methods that have been adopted and showing why recourse to the genetic dimension is necessary. Following this, it will be sufficient to describe some typical experiments, taking each level of mental development in turn so as to show how the main operational structures become organized. Finally a retrospective study will assist us in adopting a position on several general problems. It would be unwise to discuss and even to state these before examining the facts, for in a field so fraught with philosophical reminiscences, it is essential that the psychologist should learn to avoid every a priori interpretation. He should pose problems only insofar as he is led to do so in following the development of genetic processes.

Caution is very necessary as misunderstandings can arise from the language that one is led to use. When describing the results of a particular experiment, concerning perception or factor analysis, etc., the mathematical language used is unlikely to lead to confusion, since it is relatively easy to dissociate the mathematical form of the expressions from their psychological content (although the famous discussions between C. Spearman and G. Thomson on the role of such and such a "factor" already showed that not everyone views the dissociation in the same way). When it comes, however, to describing the structure of particular intellectual operations from the qualitative angle independently of their measurable (or metrical) performance, one has no option but to use, as a language, the general theory of structures which in mathematics goes by the name of general algebra and which includes the algebra of modern logic. In a case of this kind, one must naturally remain on one's guard to avoid a confusion between the psychological content (which in a sense constitutes a logic, since it concerns the intellectual operations of the subject, hence his logic) and the form used to describe it (which is also a logic, but of the kind formulated by algebraists). It would be unreasonable at this point to accuse the psychologist of dealing with logic and not with psychology. He is simply using a precise language, as he may be led to do in statistics, and no one would ever think of saying that calculating a correlation is mathematics and not psychology. The discussion between Spearman and Thomson shows that with more advanced probabilistic analyses, things are not always straightforward. Similarly, the description of operational structures in terms of qualitative algebra requires constant care in order to avoid interference between the intellectual operations of the observed subject (e.g., the child at such and such a level), those of the psychologist who is observing him and above all those which are involved in the language used by the psychologist, when it is that of logical or algebraic structures generally.

Historico-critical Survey

The proof that this is not an imaginary danger is that on comparing the various experimental studies on the psychology of thought, it becomes apparent that for want of genetic perspective they either simply ignore the existence of operational structures or merely employ those used in classical logic. It is only by systematic genetic study that it has been possible to reveal the existence of structures that had not been noticed until then, some presenting a certain amount of psychological interest but little logical interest* (cf. the "grouping" structure, p. 465), others both a logical and a psychological interest (cf. the "INRC group," pp. 395–399).

It is striking to note that even studies which have not arrived at the notion of operational structures offer glimpses, under various names, of the reality of "operations." This is very significant since one could wonder whether the concept of "operation" is an authentic psychological reality or merely a term borrowed from logicians.† The only studies which have long remained totally foreign to the idea of operation are those inspired by classical or contemporary associationism. But, as we shall see, the very history of these studies, taking into account their recent transformations and especially the "conversions" which they have brought about, points to certain notions which are definitely operational in character.

FROM ASSOCIATIONISM TO "STRATEGIES"

Thus, Binet, after having admitted in *The Psychology of Reasoning* that inferences are due to simple associations between images later stressed in his *Étude expérimentale de l'intelligence*‡ the specific character of affirmations and negations, of judgments expressing relations, etc.—in short of what we shall term "operations" as against imaged representations. In so doing, he resolutely left behind him his original associationism.

Similarly, modern associationism has led, particularly in the case of Hull and those who followed him, to an interpretation of the acquisition of notions (number, etc.) which is based on the stimulus-response schema, on generalizations of stimuli or of responses, on external reinforcements and on the hypothesis of habit-family hierarchies. One of Hull's successors, D. Berlyne, recognized as a result of personal experience the cogency of our distinction between representation of states or configurations and operations referring specifically to transformations. He added to Hull's conception by introducing a new duality: he distinguished between copy-responses, relating to states, and transformation-responses which modify the former and thus correspond to our "operations."**

Above all, within the context of "behavior theory" on which are based the many American conceptions of learning, a particular technique for analyzing intellectual mechanisms has developed. It is known as the problem-solving method. It consists in setting the subject a

---

*Because they are not general enough.
†Let us note here that apart from certain exceptions (Curry's combinatorial logic and Lorenzen's operational logic), logicians avoid the notion and even the term of "operation" and speak of "functors," etc. Couturat used to accuse the notion of operation of being "manifestly anthropomorphic," in other words of being psychological!
‡A. Binet, *The Psychology of Reasoning* (London: Kegan Paul, 1899); A. Binet, *"L'étude expérimentale de l'intelligence"* (Paris: Schleicher, 1903).
**D. E. Berlyne, "Les équivalences psychologiques et les notions quantitatives," in *Théorie du comportement et opérations*, E.E.G., Vol. 12 (Paris: P.U.F., 1960), pp. 1–76.

problem that is new to him and which may be of any level (ranging from sensorimotor intelligence to the higher thought processes). His behavior sequence up to the discovery and consolidation of the solution is then analyzed. Although most interpretations of this kind of data have begun by being linked to associationism and thus foreign to the idea of operation, the most remarkable achievement arising from the use of this method is a definitely antiassociationist work: *A Study of Thinking*,* which opens up new perspectives. According to these authors, the successive steps taken by a subject as he grapples with problems are not "associations" simply determined by previous experience. They are "decisions" made by the subject as he comes to grips with, or matches himself against, objects or events. The appropriate language in this case is that of "strategies" used in game theory and one sees at once the kinship between these decisions or strategies and what we call operations (as J. Bruner himself indicates).

CLAPARÈDE'S "IMPLICATION"

Although research arising out of associationism (as a continuation or as a reaction against it, but using the methods arising from it) has not led to an analysis of operational structures, it has nonetheless arrived on several occasions at notions close to that of operation. This is also true of an allied standpoint which however lays more stress on the subject's activities. It tends to reduce acts of intelligence to a succession of groping attempts which may be actual physical attempts, in the form of trial and error with selection arising from the pressure of facts, or internalized attempts in the form of "hypotheses," controlled by acquired consciousness of relations. This interpretation, inspired by the work of Jennings and Thorndike, was adopted by Claparède. He proceeded to devise an ingenious method for analyzing acts of intelligence. This method, known as "spoken reflection," consists in observing the successive steps taken by subjects who have previously been trained to think aloud while solving everyday problems (such as finding the caption of a cartoon or the end of a story).

In [a] fine study† in which he recorded the results obtained by this method, Claparède went beyond his original views on groping and arrived at a fundamental conclusion. Groping, he tells us, is never purely random, but is to some extent directed from the beginning by certain connections. Furthermore, it is not the most elementary form of behavior but appears only when a number of primitive connections have been invalidated. What are these connections which precede groping or impose a direction upon it? They are not associations, according to Claparède, but connections asserting themselves with a sort of internal necessity. These he calls "implications." That is how "cat" implies "miaowing" even to a baby, once he has simultaneously seen and heard a cat. At the level of acts of thought, every act of comprehension relies on such implications and, in the case of actual research, all groping is directed or framed by implications.

*J. Bruner, J. J. Goodnow, and G. A. Austin, *A Study of Thinking* (New York: Wiley, 1956).
†E. Claparède, "La genèse de l'hypothèse, *Arch. Psychol.*, 24 (1933): 1–155.

Although Claparède did not yet regard implication as the product of operational or preoperational activities (since he believed that it was due to a kind of elementary syncretism), it is nevertheless easy to show that this interpretation necessarily follows. It is not at the first perceptual contact that "cat" implies "miaowing." The cat miaows and this is no more than a fact. But from the second contact, when the baby recognizes a cat, he can infer that it will miaow. Implication is thus subordinated to an act of assimilation. Assimilation means construction of schemata (implication in the broad sense is in fact the expression of these schemata) and it is this schematization which probably constitutes the point of departure of operational activities and of their structurizations.

SPEARMAN'S "NOEGENESIS"

From a totally different standpoint, the studies carried out by C. Spearman* culminated, even more clearly, in the recognition of operations, but without involving as yet the recognition of integrated operational structures. It is well known that Spearman's work on intelligence evolved on two planes: a probabilistic analysis of "factors" on the one hand, and a qualitative analysis of "noegenesis" on the other. The factor analysis of intelligence led to nothing further than a distinction, to which the great English psychologist attached great importance, between general intelligence and particular factors. He did not reconstitute the actual genesis of general intelligence by directly studying mental development but was content to retrace an ideal genesis as it were. This is nevertheless of undoubted interest because, despite his empiricism, Spearman in part revealed the operational nature of acts of intelligence. He believed that intelligence develops in three stages: the "apprehension of experience," the "eduction" of relations and the "eduction" of "correlates." As all knowledge is supposed to be drawn from experience and from experience alone, there is as yet no question of "structuring" experience, but only of "apprehending" it. Similarly, relations are not constructed but simply "educed," that is drawn from an experience that contains them in advance. As for "correlates," that is, relations between relations, (e.g., feathers are to birds what hair is to mammals), Spearman considers that they are also drawn from reality by "eduction," but this is incorrect since it goes without saying that in reaching this degree of complexity, eduction assumes the form of a genuine operation. It amounts in fact to a multiplicative coordination of relations, corresponding to a matrix or table of double entry.

Spearman, however, did not become altogether conscious of the operational character of his "eductions." He omitted to ask himself whether those he had observed did not necessarily require to be completed by others and especially whether collectively these possible operations did not obey the general laws governing structures. It is nonetheless highly significant that the inventor of factor analysis should have come so close to an operational conception of intelligence. Indeed it was probably only his empiricist underestimation of the part played by the subject's activities that prevented Spearman from formally elaborating this conception.

*C. Spearman, *The Nature of Intelligence* (London: Macmillan, 1923).

"GESTALT" STRUCTURES

With the Gestalt psychologists came the discovery of integrated structures. With Wertheimer in particular, they begin to take on an explicitly operational character. The Gestaltists, it is true, were willing to recognize only one type of structure (the Gestalt in the particular sense ascribed to the term). In spite of this, their discovery was far-reaching in that, for the first time, logical structures made an appearance in psychology not because they had been postulated in advance but as a result of a general interpretation based on experimentation.

It is well known that [Gestalt] theory has renewed our knowledge of perception. It began as a field hypothesis and went on to refute atomic associationism. W. Köhler, Meili, Duncker,* and Metzger viewed problem-solving as a restructuring of perceptual data, passing from a less good to a better form and obeying the same laws as the Gestalt, that is laws of totality according to which the whole is distinct from the sum of its parts and appears as an organization with properties of its own by virtue of being a totality. The decisive moment in the assimilation of the structures of intelligence to Gestalt laws came when Wertheimer† began to study higher acts of intelligence: the solving of mathematical problems or of deductive problems in general. According to Wertheimer, deductions like these are simply restructurizations such as Koehler had already claimed to have found in the sphere of practical intelligence. In a syllogism of the type " All B's are C's, A is a B, therefore A is a C," the act of thought consists only in fusing into a new whole AC the partial wholes AB and BC, by "recentering" A in C after dissociating it from its one original link B. In his posthumous work, when Wertheimer wanted to describe the successive acts of this process of restructuring, he used the term "operation" which we ourselves had used to describe the construction by the child of his first concrete logical structures. Thus he also regards these operations as bound up with integrated structures.

A difficulty remains concerning the nature of these. The notion of Gestalt brings together into a single concept: (1) the idea of a whole whose properties are those of a total system and are thus distinct from those of the parts, and (2) the idea of a whole differing from the sum of its parts (nonadditive composition). Logico-mathematical structures possess the first of these characteristics in that their properties are those of integrated systems. They do not possess the second, however, since they are rigorously additive. The series of whole numbers, for instance, is an admirable integrated system which has laws *qua* system (laws of "groups," of "sets," of "rings," of "lattices," etc.) and yet 2 + 2 are rigorously 4 and not a little more or a little less as in probabilistic or perceptual compositions. Logico-mathematical structures are thus not Gestalten, as these are of a nonadditive and therefore irreversible nature.

*W. Köhler, *The Mentality of Apes* (London: Kegan Paul, 1927); R. Meili, "'Experimentelle Untersuchungen über das Ordnen von Gegenständen," *Psychol. Forsch.*, 7 (1926): 155–193; K. Duncker, *Zür Psychologie des produktiven Denkens* (Berlin: Springer, 1935).
†M. Wertheimer, *Productive Thinking* (New York: Harper, 1945).

To define operations, it is necessary to go beyond the category of Gestalten and to conceive the existence of other psychological integrated structures, which are reversible.

"THOUGHT PSYCHOLOGY"

A solution that is simpler than the *Gestalttheorie*, while also in reaction against associationism, was outlined as early as the beginning of the century and could be drawn upon to overcome the above difficulty; it is that of the German *Denkpsychologie*. Having discovered at the same time as Binet the existence of imageless thought, the Würzburg school then tried to characterize it. They used a method of induced introspection (for instance subjects were asked to produce supraordinate associations, such as bird → animal or plumtree → tree and to describe the accompanying states of consciousness). From the very beginning, Marbe, failing to find states of consciousness corresponding bi-univocally to [acts] of judgment, introduced a logical factor claiming that it was at once causal and "nonpsychological" as if a logical structure could play a part in the mental context and could modify it without resulting from it! Those who followed him, Messer, Watt, and especially Bühler,* renounced this position with its dangerous methodology, but turned toward a kind of logico-psychological parallelism. According to this, there exists a correspondence between certain well-defined states (that have indeed been very subtly described, as for instance K. Bühler's *Regelbewusstsein* or "consciousness of rules") and given logical structures. Finally, the main heir to this tradition, O. Selz† (whose work breaks away from induced introspection and seeks instead to analyze, in behavior itself, the process of "reproductive" and of "productive" thought) regarded thought with all its interconnections as a "mirror of logic."

But this point of view, which seems at first sight to avoid all conflicts by adopting a cautious principle of parallelism in fact fails to resolve anything, for two reasons. The first is that there is nothing to prove the existence of isomorphism between the subject's logic, with which the psychologist is concerned, and that of the logician, which goes far beyond it. Even if there is partial isomorphism, nothing proves that the function of thought is to reflect a logic that has appeared out of the blue. It is much more likely that logic is in fact an axiomatization of the forms of equilibrium that characterize thought, an autonomous axiomatization, it goes without saying, but one which, like all axiomatizations, serves to formalize preliminary data. Thereafter, the data are of no further concern in logic but fall within the province of the corresponding concrete science (in this instance, the psychology of thought). Secondly, if *Denkpsychologie* was content with a somewhat facile parallelism between logical structures and acts of thought, this was because it confined itself to the analysis of adult thought. In con-

---

*K. Bühler, *Die geistige Entwicklung der Kinder* (Leipzig: Hirzel, 1931).
†O. Selz, *Ueber die Gesetze des geordneten Denkverlaufs*, 2 vols. (Stuttgart, 1913; Bonn, 1922); *Die Gesetze der produktiven und reproductiven Geistestätigkeit* (Bonn, 1924).

sidering the child and his development, the real problem is to discover how structures are constructed and not how they appear when completely formed. More exactly, knowledge of the final states can only arise out of knowledge of how they come to be constructed.

METHOD TO BE FOLLOWED

The lesson that we learn from these two observations is that for our methods to be sound, we must not refer to any preexisting logical structure (although we may use the instruments of the logician to describe with precision what we observe, but that is another question, affecting the language adopted and not the facts themselves). We must first try to find out whether spontaneous intellectual operations exist or whether such operations are only learnt socially, or again whether the term "operation" is of interest only to logicians and embraces a psychological complexity too great to serve as a natural psychological unit. We must then establish whether operations develop in isolation (along similar lines to Spearman's "educations") or whether they are always bound up with integrated structures. Finally it is most important that we should determine whether these operations and their integrated structures are present at all levels of development or, if not, when and how they are constituted, which amounts to asking of what they consist.

In order to solve these problems we must use material studied by American psychologists under the heads of *problem-solving* and *concept formation*. A combination of data from both areas is necessary since a problem that is really new to the subject demands an elaboration of concepts. These studies need to be supplemented by a systematic study of concept formation from birth to adolescence. Only then do we discover the essentials and find that the laws of progressive structurization reveal the simultaneous formation of operations and of their integrated structures.

Our genetic studies, of which we shall give a few examples, have been going on for forty years. The main finding has proved different from what our knowledge of the psychology of adult thought and of logistic axiomatization would have led us to expect. It is that, underlying language and at a level far below conscious reflection, there exists a logic of coordinations of actions, if one rates as logical the relations of order, inclusion, etc., which regulate actions as they are later to regulate thought. The notion of operation is thus psychologically natural. This is so not only if one calls by that name internalized actions (uniting, dissociating, ordering, etc.) which can be performed in both directions (reversibility)* but also if one characterizes internalized actions by their most specific genetic property which is that they are abstracted from the most general coordinations of actions. Operations are thus only a higher form of regulations, and that is enough to guarantee their psychological authenticity, despite their convergence with what are known as operations in mathematics and logic. Logico-mathematical activities are thus to be conceived psychologically as an inexhaustibly fruitful prolongation of the coordination of actions. The second funda-

---

*For example, the action of uniting (addition) can be inversed into an action of dissociating (subtraction), etc.

mental characteristic of operations, which follows directly from the first, is that they are always structured in integrated systems. Here again, genetic analysis has produced unexpected results in that (1) the large structures described in general algebra (groups and lattices, with their derivatives) are led up to, from the time of concrete operations (which provide a bridge between coordinations of actions and formalizations of thought), by much more elementary structures. These, however, are already mixed in character and we shall call them "groupings." (2) The transition from these concrete structures to abstract structures is made possible by a group of four transformations. There are many manifestations of these at the preadolescent and adolescent levels yet the part they play in adult thought had escaped logicians. We ourselves owe the discovery of the existence of this group of transformations entirely to our genetic studies.

Notions of Conservation

INTRODUCTION

Let us assume for a moment that there is a researcher who doubts the existence of operations as experimental facts and considers that they belong to a type of interpretation which goes beyond psychology. He will ask that they should be shown to him as observable processes, spontaneous activities, modes of functioning that "really" play a part when the subject is presented with a stimulus and makes a response.

We have just assumed, however, that operations are a higher form of regulations of action. This amounts to saying that the reversibility characterizing operational structures is in fact the culmination of the approximate compensations appearing in regulations. A regulation cannot be observed directly, but its effects are recorded objectively in "responses" to given stimuli. In the field of sensorimotor or perceptual regulations, there is a particularly famous example which several Gestaltists (Katz, etc.) have compared to a form of homeostasis: it is the constancy of magnitude, form, color, etc. In such cases, it is true that one cannot follow regulations in detail but one can see when they occur (for instance with the colors of figures), and when they do not (for instance with background colors: experiment by Kardos). One can also assess their degree of effectiveness. Can it be said that all this is only a measure of performances and not an analysis of functioning? One can pass from the consideration of performance to that of functioning by analyzing the factors, by measuring for example (at various levels of development) the estimation of apparent magnitudes, of distances, and of real magnitudes. All this will give a preliminary approximate idea of the functioning of constancy of magnitude.

The example of perceptual constancies is a remarkable prefiguration, at the level of elementary regulations, of the manner in which operations appear at the level of thought. There is one difference in that when regulations have become operational they reveal themselves not only by their performances—judgments of conservation corresponding to evaluations of constancy—but also in their actual functioning, since the subject is able to justify in part the reasons for his affirmations and thus to describe the process of reversibility.

The best criterion of the emergence of operations at the level of concrete structures (toward the age of 7) is, in fact, the constitution of invariants or notions of conservation. Observation shows, as we shall see from several examples, that a child who can internalize an action or imagine its result is not necessarily able to visualize ipso facto the possibility of performing the same action in reverse and thus canceling the result. In other words, an action does not at once transform itself into a reversible operation. There are a number of intermediates such as imagining reversal, but on request or as a new action distinct from the first and not implied by it (this we shall call "empirical reversal"). It is therefore not easy to recognize in the subject the beginnings of reversibility as such, except by its results. Yet, one has only to listen to what the subject says once he has mastered the notion of reversibility, to obtain an expression of reversibility and consequently of operations (internalized actions that have become reversible) which is remarkably simple and exact. Moreover, it coincides with the best of logical definitions: an operation is that which transforms a state A into a state B leaving at least one property invariant throughout the transformation and allowing the possibility of return from B to A thereby canceling the transformation. It so happens—and this time diagnosis is easy—that at preoperational levels the transformation is conceived as modifying all the data at once, without any conservation. This of course makes it impossible to return to the point of departure without a new action transforming the whole once more (re-creating what has been destroyed, etc.) and consequently differing from the first instead of remaining the same action but inversed. That is why we feel that tests dealing with conservation give the best indication of the natural, and not merely the logical, reality of operations. We shall therefore begin with these.

THE BALL OF CLAY

Let us now examine the first of the forms of nonconservation followed by conservation which we observed.* The results have been re-examined and controlled by various authors.

The subject is shown a ball of clay and asked to make another ball of the same size and weight. One ball, A, is left on the table as evidence and the other is transformed into a sausage, a pancake, a number of pieces, etc. The subject is asked first whether there is still the same amount of substance in B as in A and why. The procedure is the same whether the child answers "yes" or "no." In either case, his answer and the reason that he gives (for instance, in the case of the sausage: "There is more stuff because it is longer") serve to prompt further modifications of the object (in this case, making the sausage longer or

---

*J. Piaget, "Principal Factors Determining Intellectual Evolution from Childhood to Adult Life"; J. Piaget and B. Inhelder, Le Développement des Quantités physiques chez l'enfant, Chapters I–III.

shorter). This is done to see whether he will continue to reason in the same way or will change his opinion. The stage that the child has reached is noted (no conservation of substance, ungeneralized and uncertain conservation, or necessary conservation) and also the kind of arguments he uses (see below). One then passes to the conservation of weight, but if possible not immediately afterward, so as to avoid verbal perseverations. Questions are asked about the same transformations as in the case of substance (sausage, etc.), but the child is asked whether or not the weight remains the same. To make the questions more concrete, he is given a balance with two scales and the ball is put on the first scale. He is asked to anticipate what will happen when the other (modified) object is placed on the second scale. Finally, the same questions are asked about the conservation of volume, but it is not sufficient to use the terms "large," "big," etc., as these remain ambiguous in relation to the amount of substance (it took us a long time to realize that, to the child, substance is not equivalent to volume.) The ball of clay A is therefore immersed in a narrow* cylindrical jar three-quarters full. The child is asked whether the sausage, etc. B will take up "as much room in the water and will make the water rise" to the same level in another container identical with the first.

QUALITATIVE AND QUANTITATIVE RESULTS

Three kinds of results were obtained. In the first place, three successive stages can be observed in the case of each of the notions studied. At first there is lack of conservation when the object is modified. This is followed by transitional reactions (conservation is assumed but without certainty and in the case of some transformations only). Finally conservation comes to be affirmed and regarded as evident throughout the various transformations of the ball of clay.

Secondly, we find that three arguments are advanced by the child on reaching the third stage and these are characteristic of an operational approach. Longitudinal analysis carried out by one of us (Inhelder) in collaboration with G. Noelting on 12 subjects who were examined every three months, has shown that these three arguments do not correspond to three substages but are interdependent and do not always appear in the same order. The first is based on simple reversibility: there is in B as much (substance, weight, or volume) as in A because the ball A can be remade from B. The second rests on a more subtle kind of reversibility† based on compensation: object B is longer but thinner, etc. (composition of two seriations in inverse order: longer × thinner = same quantity). The third argument appears less sophisticated and is simply based on identity: the quantity (or the weight, etc.) does not change "because it's the same stuff," "because it has only been rolled," "because it has only been flattened," or "because nothing has been taken away or

---

*A narrow jar is used so that the change of level may be sufficiently perceptible. In addition, to dissociate the action of volume from that of weight (often wrongly adduced by the child), the ball of plasticine A is replaced by a metal ball of the same volume but of greater weight.

†Or reversibility through "reciprocity," as distinct from simple reversibility or reversibility through "inversion."

TABLE 1

Percentage Success in Tests on the Conservation of Substance,
Weight, and Volume*

Ages	5	6	7	8	9	10	11
Substance							
Nonconservation	84	68	64	24	12	—	—
Transitional	0	16	4	4	4	—	—
Conservation	16	16	32	72	84	—	—
Weight							
Nonconservation	100	84	76	40	16	16	0
Transitional	0	4	0	8	12	8	4
Conservation	0	12	24	52	72	76	96
Volume							
Nonconservation	100	100	88	44	56	24	16
Transitional	0	0	0	28	12	20	4
Conservation†	0	0	12	28	32	56	82

*Each of the 175 subjects underwent the three tests, but on different days so as to avoid verbal perseverations.

†Out of the numbers given for conservation, 12 percent of the 7 year olds, 12 percent of the 8 year olds, 16 percent of the 9 year olds, 28 percent of the 10 year olds and 26 percent of the 11 year olds foresaw that the displacement of water would be the same with the ball that has been pulled out of shape as with the round ball but attributed this to the conservation of weight.

added." The remarkable character of this identity is that it ranks as an argument of conservation only when the other two arguments have been discovered. Young children at the preoperational level also knew that it was the "same stuff" and that nothing had been taken away or added, but did not conclude from this that there was conservation. It therefore seems clear (chronologically and functionally) that the arguments are interdependent and that they lead to the construction of an integrated operational structure, of the "grouping" type in which conservation constitutes the invariant.

In the third place, the results obtained at Geneva and at Saint-Gall show a time lag between the child's acquisition of the notion of the conservation of substance (toward the age of 8), of weight (age 9–10), and of volume (age 11–12). At least, that is what we had observed in the past in the course of clinical analysis.* One of us† found when studying 159 mental deficients ranging in age from 7 to 30 that conservation of weight was never present without that of substance, nor conservation of volume without that of weight. This did not apply the other way round.‡ In their standardization of operational tests, Vinh-Bang and Inhelder** obtained the following percentage with 25 subjects per age group:

*J. Piaget and B. Inhelder, *Le développement physiques chez l'enfant.*

†B. Inhelder, *Le diagnostic du raisonnement chez les débiles mentaux* (Neuchâtel and Paris: Delachaux and Niestlé, 1943).

‡Inhelder also showed that the conservation of volume is found only in subjects suffering from retarded development and never in true mental deficients (probably because the notion of volume implies the notion of proportion and this is attained by formal operations of which they are incapable).

**Vinh-Bang and B. Inhelder, unpublished work on the standardization of operational tests.

TABLE 2

Percentage Success in Tests on the Conservation of Substance,
Weight, and Volume
(according to D. Elkind, U.S.A.)

Ages	5	6	7	8	9	10	11
Substance	19	51	70	72	86	94	92
Weight	21	52	51	44	73	89	78
Volume	0	4	0	4	4	19	25

TABLE 3

Percentage Success in Tests on the Conservation of
Substance and Weight
(according to Lovell and Ogilvie)

Tests	Substance (322 subjects)			Weight (364 subjects)		
	Non-conservation	Transitional	Conservation	Non-conservation	Transitional	Conservation
Class I (age 7–8)	31	33	36	91	5	4
Class II (age 8–9)	20	12	68	29	36	36
Class III (age 9–10)	11	15	74	32	20	48
Class IV (age 10–11)	5	9	86	13	13	74

AMERICAN AND ENGLISH CONTROLS

As a control, here are the results obtained in the United States by D. Elkind* with 25 subjects per age group:

Elkind stresses the fact that 70–75 percent of the subjects show a definite time lag between acquiring the notion of the conservation of weight and that of substance. In the case of volume, there is still no conservation at the age of 11 with most subjects. This last result, according to him, is to be explained by a slight difference in technique: he himself asked whether the two objects (ball and sausage, etc.) took up the same amount of *space* in the water. When the question is worded (as ours was) in terms of displacement of water level, the problem is more quickly solved.

Lovell and Ogilvie† obtained the results shown in Table 3 concerning substance and weight in four primary school classes in Leeds, in which the children's ages ranged from 7–8 to 10–11

It is clear that evolution is broadly the same, with the same time lag between weight and substance (and between volume and weight, but the authors used a different test for volume). On the other hand, Laurendeau and Pinard‡ found scarcely any inversion in the order:

*D. Elkind, "Children's Discovery of Conservation."

†K. Lovell and E. Ogilvie, "Conservation of Substance"; "Growth of Concept of Volume."

‡M. Laurendeau and A. Pinard,

substance, weight, and volume (12 aberrant cases out of 441) but observed that their Canadian subjects acquired the notion of the three conservations in a much shorter space of time, particularly in the case of weight and volume. This interesting result seems linked in part to the techniques which they used. According to one technique, each of the five transformations of the ball (into a ring, a cube, a sausage, a filament, and finally ten rounded pieces) was followed by questions on volume, weight, and substance in turn. In our technique, these three aspects were dealt with in separate questionnaires and each questionnaire referred to the modifications of the ball as a whole. Laurendeau and Pinard followed this pattern with their other technique, but with no interval between the three questionnaires. It is therefore probable that systematic transfers occurred and it is all the more remarkable that subjects who attained the notion of conservation in the case of all the transformations studied retained the order of succession: substance, weight, and volume, the last two being acquired earlier. . . .

23

The Early Growth of Logic in the Child: Classification and Seriation*

1959

INTRODUCTORY NOTES

The Early Growth of Logic in the Child: Classification and Seriation (1959) examines two fundamental aspects of the logic of the child, classification and seriation. Classification, the fundamental act of the logic of classes, simply means systematically putting together things that belong together on the ground that they share the same property or properties. Seriation, an aspect of the logic of relations, refers to arranging a collection of things systematically with regard to some dimension along which they differ, for example, in order of size or of desirability.

The activities of classification originate in the organizing activities of the child. These begin very early: they organize the diversity of sensations as objects, and then objects as categories governed by the same schemas of action. This organizing activity permits, for example, a child to distinguish between objects that can be grasped and those that cannot.

These initial categories prefigure classifications properly speaking without being their equivalent, for they are only classifications-in-action. They last only during the moment of immediate manipulation which occasions them and is their raison d'être. They are an integral part of the action and do not lead directly to the formation of concepts by successive abstractions from the accidental. Unstable and ephemeral, they appear only on the occasion of a given activity. They are therefore always imprecise, provisional, and temporary, because they depend narrowly on the here and now of the immediate situation and on the momentary intentions of the subject. Finally, they lack logical stability because they have no adequate definition.

In logic, a class may be defined in two ways. The definition by *intension* specifies the properties shared by members of the class; the definition by *extension* lists the members of the class. Either one, taken alone, will be

*From pp. 1–260 in *The Early Growth of Logic in the Child: Classification and Seriation*, by Bärbel Inhelder and Jean Piaget. © 1964 by Routledge & Kegan Paul Ltd., London. Reprinted by permission of Harper & Row, Inc., and Routledge & Kegan Paul. Originally published in French, 1959.

rather limited. The child may grasp the definition of some class by intension without applying it systematically to all members of the class, for example if he were to announce a plan to put together all the red things on the table, but then omit one red thing because it is too small, another because it has the wrong shape, and another "just because." On the other hand, the child might make a list of all the things he sees that he wishes to class together without specifying the defining properties of the class. Even if he behaves consistently for the moment, this approach would not have the generality of true classification, because it would not indicate how to classify a new object. Thus, only the joint application of intension and extension leads to true classification.

Typically the child in the sensorimotor period never knows exactly which objects belong to a given class and which do not.

How does a child between 2 and 4 years act when confronted with a heterogeneous collection of objects? This is the question posed by Piaget and Inhelder in the first chapters of the present work. They find that the child's behavior differs appreciably from true classification. Criteria of class membership among young children are not like ours. A child will put together, for example, a tree and a house "because, like that, the tree will shade the house in summer," while an adult in a similar situation will spontaneously put the houses in one pile and the trees in another. The child will put the woman among the farm animals "so she can look after them," the man with the sheep "because he's a shepherd," the little boy on a bench under the trees near the house. If the child is given a collection of geometrical forms to classify, he puts one circle with one triangle with one square in such a way as to make a figure of a person, perhaps repeating the design with the remaining material; or he will put a triangle just above a square to make a "house." Piaget calls such collections of disparate objects *graphic collections.*

Between 4 and 7 years, the child becomes capable of classification in the sense of an occidental adult. He can, for example, put all the red things together, or all the square things together. But he remains incapable of coordinating two such dimensions with each other to put together all the red squares: the forms and colors remain incommensurable dimensions at this age. However, the distinction between classes and subclasses already makes its appearance: rectilinear objects can be correctly divided into squares, triangles, rectangles, and so on. Such *nongraphic collections,* as Piaget calls them, do not yet form classes properly speaking, because they are limited and constructed by the child step after step, without a clear anticipation or explicit comprehension of the definition of the class.

The next stage is achieved when the child succeeds in coordinating these classifications with each other both hierarchically and multiplicatively. The hierarchical aspect of classification refers to the systematic arrangement of classes and subclasses, etc., and to the understanding of the relations among these sets of things. The child must be able to understand *class inclusion,* the way in which the members of a subclass are members of a class, but not necessarily the reverse. To accomplish this, the child must be able to handle adequately the relations between *all* and *some.* He must know that (1) *all* daisies are flowers and (2) only *some* flowers are daisies. This asymmetry in the relation between the including class and the class included poses serious problems for children before the age of 10 in Piaget's studies. They have a tendency to read symmetry into the relation between class and subclass. For example, if one says that all the Jews of Hamburg were gassed in World War

II, the child may think that there is no one alive in Hamburg because everyone there was gassed. When one says, "All the Hamburg Jews," one means implicitly that *all* the Hamburg Jews are *some* of the inhabitants of Hamburg. According to Piaget, such relationships cannot be managed without an adequate reciprocal adjustment between intension (the predicate of a proposition) and extension (specification of the items to which this predicate applies). Inhelder and Piaget conducted several experiments to demonstrate such phenomena.

In a first study, the child is asked to reproduce a row of five blue circles interspersed with three red squares. The younger children tend to focus their attention on one property at a time, form or color, neglecting the other property and therefore incorrectly reproducing the row of the model. In a second step, the child correctly reproduces the rows shown him, but remains incapable of reversing the order of all and some. For, if he can readily see that some red things are squares, in a row of red squares and blue circles, he does not manage to grasp that all the squares are red. At this age, the proposition, "Some reds are squares," carries with it automatically its inverse, "Some squares are reds"—an error of intension.

When Piaget and his collaborators ask the child what he means by the word "some," the responses are quite varied. For the youngest children, the words "all" and "some" are equivalent. Somewhat later, some is used for one or two objects, if the whole set is not very large, and for four or five objects if the set is larger. There is, in other words, no exact idea of the exact extension of *some* in relation to all.

Once this logical quantification of the predicate has been acquired, the child becomes capable of class inclusion. Class inclusion necessarily raises the problem of *complementary* classes: these are classes which, united with another class, exhaust the contents of a superior class. For example, if A is the class of ducks, B of birds, and C of animals, A' will be the class of birds that are not ducks, B' of animals that are not birds. Such complementary classes are always defined negatively, by hierarchical inclusion.

The idea of complementary classes leads to that of the number of elements in a class. The child before 7 years has difficulties with the singular class: a class made of one single object. He does not know, for example, if one ought to say *the* moon or *a* moon. Similarly, children carefully avoid having recourse to such classes in their spontaneous classifications until about 9 years.

One finds the same reticence when faced with empty classes. A child less than 10 years, given the task of classifying cards, some of which have pictures and some of which are blank, refuses to give a particular status to the blank cards. He slips them under the others, or he leaves them to one side as leftovers of the process of classification, or he classifies them by their outline shapes. But he refuses to recognize the negative character of these null classes.

Something similar occurs in the analysis of the number of members of a complementary class. Let us suppose a singular class A, myself, and its complementary non-A, everything that is not myself. This class A is included in a class B, mankind, that is larger than A. In turn, class B has a complementary, non-B, which is smaller than non-A since it includes only nonhumans, whereas non-A included, in addition, all humans that are not me. This symmetrical relationship between a class and its complementary is not understood by the child until the appearance of formal operations.

Myself   —   World

| Myself | — | Man | — | World |

Not myself > not man
              = man + rest of world
Not man   = rest of world

All the classes envisaged so far are called simple or additive classes by opposition to multiplicative classifications which involve more than one discussion to be taken into consideration at the same time.

As compared with simple or additive classes multiple classifications require arrangement of things in the form of matrices, or multiple entry tables. Thus, in constructing a double entry table, if each item in a collection has both a color and a shape, all the items of one color can be arranged in one row, etc., and all the items of one shape can be arranged in one column, etc; the intersection of a given row and a given column would therefore define exactly which items go together, i.e., have the same color and the same shape. Such tables have the interesting special characteristics of being at the same time logically more complex than simple additive classifications, and dependent on spatial arrangement. From the logical point of view, to establish these tables one must compose two or more criteria, while from the spatial point of view one must place the objects correctly in their respective cells. The figurative factor therefore plays an important role in these classifications. (See Table I.) This is why we see uneven performance (*décalage*), depending

$$W \quad \underline{W} \quad w \quad \underline{w}$$

$$X \quad \underline{X} \quad x \quad \underline{x}$$

$$Y \quad \underline{Y} \quad y \quad \underline{y}$$

$$Z \quad \underline{Z} \quad z \quad \underline{z}$$

on the number of criteria to be considered together, the actual material, and the information provided to the child. Figurative factors introduce a greater variation in performance but they remain, in Piaget's eyes at least, a secondary factor, because multiplicative structures cannot be considered as arising directly out of the earlier graphic collections; rather, they develop at the same time as and in close relation with additive classification. In both cases, the movement goes from graphic collections to rudimentary classes, and then to true classification, no matter how many criteria are involved.

In the second part of this work, Inhelder and Piaget study the formation of structures of seriation. The experimental situations are all designed on the same model. The child must construct a series of objects in accordance with a criterion of serial order: size, color, or form. In multiplicative seriation (Table II), the child must compose several criteria at once, which again requires multiple entry tables. The stages of cognitive development brought to light correspond to those which appear in the work on classification. There is a conjunction of these two kinds of elementary logical structures, which paves the way for the construction of the idea of number, which is, according to Piaget, the synthesis of seriation and classification.

Introduction

This volume as a whole incorporates the results obtained from the examination of a total of 2,159 children. The introductory chapter which follows consists of a general outline of the problems to be discussed, a number of essential definitions, and, finally, a résumé of the previous research which led up to the present work.

We propose to study the formation of operations of classification (Chaps. I–VIII) and seriation (Chaps. IX–X). Although we already know something about the stages shown in their development, we know next to nothing about the mechanisms which account for this development. The study of these mechanisms was first undertaken by A. Szeminska, so that this is a continuation of her work.

The greater part of this volume deals with classification, because the problems which it raises are far more complex. But we cannot afford to neglect problems of seriation altogether. Had we examined only one of these structures, we might easily have been led to systematic errors of interpretation by exaggerating the role of some factors and underestimating others. Thus, the part played by language would seem greater for classification than for seriation, while perceptual factors are probably more important in seriation. By comparing the two situations, we can discover the mechanisms which are common to both. These we may justifiably regard as the essential formatory mechanisms.

In order to elucidate the causal mechanism of a given process, we must first discover the structures which are there to begin with, and then show how and why these structures come to be transformed. All development presupposes an initial structure. The development consists in the completion and differentiation of this structure.

. . . We propose first of all to list the various forms or structures which could provide a starting point for the construction of classification and seriation. But we will also point out what they lack of the final structures which we wish to explain. In the main body of the book, we can then study the way in which the gap is bridged, bearing in mind whatever ideas we have gleaned from our analysis of these initial structures.

LANGUAGE

Both the syntax and the semantics of language involve structures of classification and seriation. That this is true of classification is immediately obvious. All nouns and adjectives divide reality into classes. Insofar as children use words with the same meaning as adults, these may be directly transmitted to them when they learn to talk. In any case, words inevitably force a beginning of classification on the child. On the other hand, seriations are rarely completely elaborated in any language (as they are for certain series like that leading from "great-grandfather" to "grandfather," "father," "son," "grandson," etc.). But seriations are sometimes suggested in a language by special grammatical forms like the comparative and the superlative.

One possible hypothesis would be to attribute the formation of classification and seriation exclusively to language. Alternatively, we could give language no more than an auxiliary role (e.g., that of an accelerator). We might even say that while language is necessary for the completion of these structures, it is insufficient for their formation. If this view were found correct, their formation would have to be explained by operational mechanisms which underlie linguistic activity but are themselves independent of their verbal expression.

A number of avenues of research seem open for deciding between these possibilities. These are (1) the study of the deaf; (2) an analysis of the first verbal patterns (or "preconcepts"); and (3) the study of certain operational patterns which occur in the everyday use of language.

We have not ourselves carried out any research on the deaf. But the excellent work of P. Oléron,* together with the articles of M. Vincent† on the intellectual development of the deaf, suggest the following conclusions, which are further borne out by the research of our colleague, F. Affolter, who studied the development of operational structures among deaf children, following our own work with normal children:

1. The development of seriation is not noticeably different in the deaf.
2. Deaf children carry out the same elementary classifications as do normal children, but are retarded in their handling of more complex classifications (e.g., changing from one criterion to another, using the same elements). In other words, deaf children undoubtedly show signs of operational thinking, as we understand the term; and this may be due to the fact that they use symbols (e.g., sign language). So it looks as if the social transmission of spoken language is not essential for the formation of operational structures. But it certainly helps; and it may well be a necessary, although not a sufficient, condition for the completion of these structures in their generalized forms.

Piaget,‡ in his description of the first verbal patterns or "preconcepts," showed that learning how to talk does not imply that children immediately adopt the collective classifications embodied in their mother tongue. Language merely accelerates the formation of classes.

Children assimilate the language they hear to their own semantic structures, which are a function of their level of development. Adult language may help to modify these, in the long run, yet at any given moment, it is always interpreted in terms of them. Thus, the generality of a word (i.e., a noun or an adjective) may be very weak for a child, so that symbolically the word is closer to an image than a concept, or it may approximate to a true conceptual generality—and there is every shade in between. In other words, the fact that a child calls a cat a cat does not prove that he understands the "class" of cats. The name is borrowed from the language of adults (for whom it signifies the class of cats, included in that of animals, of living creatures, etc.); but, to a child, it may be the schematic equivalent of an image, which is halfway between the individual and the generic.

For instance, a child of 3–5 years will talk about the "wind" made by a fan and then be unable to decide whether this "wind" is the *same*

*P. Oléron, *Recherches sur le développement mental des sourds-muets* (Paris: C.N.R.S., 1956).

†*Enfance*, (4) 1951: 222–238; 1956: 1–20 and 1957: 443–464.

‡J. Piaget, *Play, Dreams and Imitation in Childhood*. First French publication, 1945.

object as the breeze which blows the leaves, or whether these are two distinct terms belonging to the *same class.* . . .

From the beginning language favors a series of assimilations, and these imply a notion of similarity. (In the same way, unsuccessful attempts at assimilation create a notion of dissimilarity.) But for a long time these relationships cannot be made concrete and precise. Little children cannot arrange a set of objects in such a way as to bring out the relation of inclusion, which is a part-whole relation. Yet this relation is essential to an understanding of classification in the strict sense. We are bound to conclude that, although language is an important factor in building logical structures, it is not the essential factor, even for children with normal hearing.

We have made a closer study of the role of language . . . by analyzing the operational schema involved in the correct use of the verbal quantifiers "all" and "some." This implies the quantification of inclusion: if all A are B and some, but not all, B are A, then B exceeds A. The main finding of these investigations may be stated thus: the fact that the language of adults crystallizes an operational schema does not mean that the operation is assimilated along with the linguistic forms. Before children can understand the implicit operation and apply it, they must carry out a structurization, or even a number of successive restructurizations. These depend on logical mechanisms. They are not passively transmitted by language. They demand an active construction on the part of the subject.

What research has proved is that language accelerates the processes of classification and seriation and helps to complete them. We do not propose to study how it does so in detail. In the first place, the importance of language is a commonplace. Secondly, we have concentrated more on the formation of structures than on their end state. But, even when we look at their end state, we will see that the development of seriation is almost exactly parallel to that of classification, and tends to precede it step by step. This shows conclusively that the development of these operations is largely independent of language. For, while the structures of classification are largely mirrored by verbal structures, serial structures are far less closely connected with language. . . .

PERCEPTUAL FACTORS

If the operational structures of classification and seriation cannot be attributed exclusively to language and maturation, it follows that their origin must lie in the most elementary cognitive structures, i.e., perceptual and sensorimotor structures.

Long before they learn to classify objects or to arrange them in order, children perceive objects in terms of relations of similarity and dissimilarity. It is tempting to look for the origin of classification and seriation in these perceptual relationships. Psychologists today agree that the perception of relationships is elementary. Perception itself is not confined to isolated terms which must then be brought together by a higher mechanism (association, judgment, etc.). Classification implies a relation of resemblance between members of the same class, and one of dissimilarity between members of different classes. Seriation is the product of a set of asymmetrical transitive relations connected in series.

Hence, one may reasonably ask how far purely perceptual relationships can provide a starting point for these operations.

. . . Two different hypotheses are possible. We need not decide between them for the moment; but it is essential to have them in mind. Otherwise we might easily be led astray in our search for possible analogies between perceptual structures and those of classification and seriation.

The first of the two hypotheses is that perceptual knowledge exists prior to any other form of knowledge and is independent of anything else. Perceptual knowledge is taken to be "elementary" (this would not imply sensory atomism; the same thing might also be expressed in terms of "Gestalt"). All intelligent structurization (sensorimotor intelligence, conceptual intelligence, etc.) is then a matter of extending these initial perceptual structures, or of expanding them and making them more supple. Alternatively, we can still allow that these higher forms of structurization involve new structures, but the content of these new structures will consist of perceptual data and these will be ready-structured. In other words, we will still refuse to allow that these undergo any substantial modification by virtue of their integration into structures of a higher order.

But there is an alternative hypothesis. This is to assume that, at every level, perception is bound up with action schemata of a higher order, and that these structures can influence those of perception. This would mean that knowledge of objects cannot be considered as being "first" perceptual and "afterward" super-perceptual. All knowledge of objects is a function of those action schemata to which the object is assimilated; and these range from the earliest reflexes to the most complex elaborations acquired by learning. Perceptual structures are bound up with more extensive structures right from the beginning. If we adopt this second hypothesis, we might still begin our study with an analysis of perceptual structures, but only because these are simpler, and not because they are more "elementary."

The perceptual structures which interest us are those which change least with age and are relatively independent of other factors. These include simple geometrical shapes as well as certain visual structures which we shall call "primary"—"primary" because they operate within the field of one centration and do not involve an interplay of successive centrations. These perceptual structures include certain relations which are partly analogous to the operations of classification and seriation. But the analogy is only partial, and even if we assume that such relations are the [perceptual] forerunners of operations, we are still left with the whole problem of how they develop into complete and coordinated operational schemata.

What kinds of perceptual relations are most relevant to this inquiry? To answer this question, we could begin by drawing up an exhaustive list of all the various ways in which perceptions are organized, and then select those that we need. But it is more economical to work backwards by first defining the most general relations involved in classification and seriation, and then seeking their nearest perceptual analogues.

Classes. Classes may be defined both by their "intension" and by their "extension." This distinction is not perfected until the stage of equilibrium reached at 9–10 years. As far as intension is concerned, we know from the Binet and Simon test on definitions that children below this age tend to give definitions by use rather than definitions by genus and differentia. As far as extension is concerned, our experiments on "all" and "some" (Chaps. III and IV) show that younger children have an imperfect grasp of the quantitative relations involved.

We will therefore pose the following as criteria for the operational existence of classes: (1) The subject can give an intensive definition of a class in terms of a more general class and one or more specific differences. (2) He can handle their extension in accordance with the structure of inclusion, as shown by his mastery of the quantifiers "all," "some," "one," and "none."

We will begin by giving a definition of each of these terms:*

Definition 1. Given a family of classes, A, A', and B, such that $B = A + A'$ and $A \times A' = 0$ (A' being therefore the complement of A with respect to B, since A and A' are disjoint), the "intension" of a class is the set of properties common to the members of that class, together with the set of differences which distinguish them from another class.

Definition 2. We shall call "relations of resemblance" (a for the elements of A, and b for those of B) all those properties which are common to the elements of one class, even though the relation of resemblance as such is not explicit. Thus, the statement "All grasses (A) are green (a)" implies that they resemble one another in being green and so present a relation of "co-greenness."

Definition 3. The "complementarity" a' of a class A' is the sum of the differences between its members and those of another class A where A and A' also have similarities by virtue of their common membership of B. For instance, if A is a group of brothers, then A', the first cousins of A, are the grandchildren of the same grandfather (and therefore B), although they do not have the same father: i.e., $a' = b$ *not* a. Again, vegetables are living things which are not animal, where the difference, nonanimal, is the complementarity.

Definition 4. To define a class by genus and specific difference is to characterize its members as: both b and a or both b and a'.

Definition 5. The "extension" of a class is the set of members (or individuals) comprising that class (as defined by its intension).

Definition 6. Intensive quantification is given by the use of one or more of the quantifiers "all," "some," and "none." Thus, the statement "All A are B" implies that there are more B than A, without specifying the quantitative relationships between A and A' (where $A' = B - A$).

Definition 7. The conditions of "class inclusion" are satisfied if and only if the following propositions both obtain: (1) All A are some B; (2) $A < B$. (Some subjects do not understand the second of these, although they appear to agree to the first.)

Definition 8. The relation of "class membership" (denoted by the symbol ϵ) is the relation between an element x and the class A to which it belongs. This relationship will be written as: $(x) \epsilon (A)$. We distinguish this relationship from "partitive membership," in which an element x is only a spatial part or a "piece" of a continuous whole (as the nose is to the face), and also from "schematic membership," where an element x is identified with a perceptual or sensorimotor schema as a result of assimilation by recognition.

How far can these relations, so defined, be paralleled in perception? Such perceptual equivalents can be found, and one of the writers has called these "partial isomorphisms."† But in order to bring out their implications we must also point out the essential difference between

---

*These definitions do not themselves contain any hypotheses. They simply specify how these terms will be used.

†J. Piaget and A. Morf, "Les isomorphismes partiels entre les structures logiques et les structures perceptives." 1958.

perceptual sets or aggregates and logical classes. It is this. There is an exact correspondence between the predicates or intensive properties of a logical class and the extensive distribution of its elements. But perceptual aggregates do not require a regular correspondence between the perceived qualities of individual elements and their grouping in more or less extended totalities. The reason is that the extension of a perceptual set depends on spatial proximity (for visual and haptic perception) or temporal proximity (for auditory perception), while the extension of a logical class is independent of the proximity of its members. We may therefore note the following three points (taking visual perception as an example):

1. Perception allows the relation of partitive membership (but not that of class inclusion, Def. 8), and even extends it to collections or collective objects which are united by their spatial proximity. Thus, in Figure 1, the element x is seen as part of the total set, but only because it is close to the set, and because it supplies a gap in the general configuration of the set as a whole. If there were no gap and x were further removed, it would no longer be seen as a part of the set (see x in Figure 2).

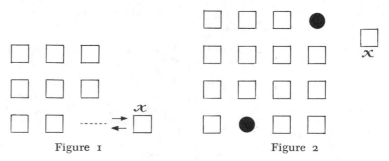

Figure 1   Figure 2

2. Perception also allows relations of similarity, whether it is applied to parts of the same figure which are perceived simultaneously (e.g., the sides of a square or the two black circles in Figure 2), or whether it involves successive assimilations, as when we see the same object again after looking around, or when an object is presented several times in succession, or in general, whenever we recognize a shape from previous perceptual experience. Wherever there is perception of resemblance between objects seen successively, its occurrence involves an assimilation to a perceptual or sensorimotor schema (Def. 8).

3. The relations of partitive membership and similarity do not always coincide. Thus, in Figure 2, the black circles are seen as a part of the main collection, although they are different from the other elements, while the small outside square x does not seem to belong to it although it is similar to them.

It follows from (3) that perception does not recognize the relations of class inclusion (Def. 7) and class membership (Def. 8), since both demand the coordination of intensive and extensive properties. Hence, it makes no sense to speak of "perceptual classes."

Nevertheless, J. Bruner is not wholly wrong in maintaining that perception is an act of classification,* i.e., that its essential function is to

---

*J. Bruner, "Les processus de préparation à la perception," in "*Logique et perception,*" E.E.G., Vol. 6, Chapter I. [E.E.G. refers to *Etudes d'épistémologie génétique.*]

identify an object by attaching it to a known class (for instance, "This is an orange"). In effect, he is doing no more than to emphasize the role of similarity in successive perceptions.

But this does not mean that the class has been constructed by perception alone, nor that the subject perceives the class as such (as, for instance, the union of "all oranges"), nor even that he perceives a class membership. A class cannot be constructed by perception, for it presupposes a series of abstractions and generalizations, from which it derives its meaning or intension, together with additive operations, governing its extensive relations. A class can never be perceived as such, since it is generally of indefinite extension; and even when its extension is restricted, what the subject perceives is not the class itself but a certain spatial configuration of the elements which compose it. When we see an orange and say, "This is an orange," the connection between the object and the class is not directly perceived. What we are doing is to assimilate the orange we see to a perceptual schema of the sort described by Brunswik as an "empirical Gestalt." The orange is perceived as presenting the familiar configuration of an ovoid with a corrugated skin and an orange color. This configuration has acquired its stability as a result of previous perceptual experience. But it is closely linked to a number of sensorimotor schemata: peeling the fruit, cutting and chewing it, squeezing out the juice, etc.

The class of oranges is *based* on schemata of this kind, both perceptual and motor, and is further enriched by various botanical analogies. But what the subject *perceives* when he says: "This is an orange," is a "schematic membership" (Def. 8) and not a class membership. For the adult, the first leads to the second through verbalization and the conceptual judgment that verbalization makes possible.

As for the schema itself, this is certainly not a class; it is not even a distinct perception which can be referred to a definite point in time, since it develops over a period, as a result of successive assimilations.

Thus the only structures attributable to perception which come near to classificatory behavior are (1) perceptual similarity in schematic membership—where the schema itself is not a product of immediate perception, and (2) partitive membership based on spatial proximity.

In neither of these structures is there coordination between intension and extension. Schematic membership is an intensive quality of objects in perception, and is quite separate from partitive membership which is an extensive property. Conceptual classification is developed out of the sensorimotor schema which governs the former, but, unlike perception, it involves the coordination of intension and extension.

Relations. Although we cannot perceive classes directly, we do perceive relations. As stated above, we have an immediate perception of similarity, which is a symmetrical relation. But we also perceive differences (e.g., differences in size), which are asymmetrical relations.

Is there a difference between an operational structure of relations and the way in which they are organized in perception? To begin with, a serial arrangement of a set of elements (e.g., strips of wood arranged in increasing order of length) is a "good" perceptual form. It is even "better" if the differences between elements are equal ($C - B = B - A$, etc. where $A, B, C, \ldots$ are the elements of the series). We may therefore ask what operational seriation adds to this perceptual configuration.

The difference is threefold. In the first place, operational seriation implies transitivity ($C > A$ if $B > A$ and $C > B$), while the perceptual configuration of a series is tied to the image. The transitivity of the image is a "preinference."* Second, there is no perceptual series unless the elements are arranged in a particular way. From the operational point of view, this graphic arrangement is not essential; it is no more than a symbolic representation of the series, in the same way as Euler's circles symbolize class-inclusions. Third, what makes seriation operational is the fact that it deals with the transformation of asymmetric transitive relations ($A < B < C$ . . . , implies $a + a' = b$, etc., if $a = A < B$; $a' = B < C$ and $b = A < C$)† and recognizes their reversibility ($b - a' = a$, etc.). For perception, only results of these transformations are meaningful; the transformations themselves are simply a matter of the visible displacement of elements. The operation is an integrated whole involving both the various end states and the transformations leading from one to the other.

Hence we shall find that it takes children nearly as long to achieve operational seriation on the basis of perceptual configurations as it does to achieve operational classification. Although perceptual anticipation is easier in seriation, the advantage accruing to *operational* seriation is comparatively slight.

SENSORIMOTOR SCHEMATA

Clearly, there is a considerable difference between perceptual structures and the operational structures involved in classification and seriation. In fact the difference is even greater than would appear from the previous section. For we cannot assume that there is a linear evolution beginning with primary perception and ending with logical operations: primary perception → perceptual activities → sensorimotor schemata → preoperational representation → operations. Field effects shown in primary perception may not be the "simplest" form of cognitive organization. There is certainly no proof that they represent the point of departure out of which higher forms are evolved. It is altogether more probable that these "good forms" are themselves the outcome of more complex sensorimotor schemata which are not confined to perception, and, still less, to immediate perception. We will now have to bear in mind our second hypothesis: that the operations of classification and seriation have their origin not in perception alone but in the development of sensorimotor schemata as a whole. We should then have to postulate a continuous modification of perception itself. The highest level of perception would then be a late development, and we would have to look for more primitive stages of perception corresponding with more primitive stages of intelligence.

Take the perception of a square as an example of a "good form." We‡ studied the resistance of this form at various ages [and] found that the tendency to see a shape as a square was not constant but

---

*J. Piaget and A. Morf, *Les préinférences perceptives.*

†This may be read: ". . . if a is the increment from point A to point B; a' is the increment from point B to point C . . ." etc.—trans.

‡J. Piaget, F. Maire, and F. Privat, "La résistance des bonnes formes à l'illusion de Müller-Lyer," 1954.

increased with age. The primary perception of the square is integrated into a schema of perceptual activity involving not only the immediate recognition of the square as a familiar shape, but a systematic comparison of sides and angles to see if they are equal. The application of the schema amounts to a transposition of exploratory movements, leading to the verification, for each perceived object, of the properties which constitute the intension of the class of squares. At the same time the extension of the class can never be realized in perception, since this would imply the simultaneous presentation of the set of squares, which is infinite. But the close parallelism between the perceptual schema and the class involves far more than primary perception. In older children and adults the perceptual schema is able to transform the character of primary perception by a process of active comparison based on transpositions and generalizations, which are wider than mere perception. The similarity of different squares (based on the equality of their sides, of their angles, etc.) is bound up with the similarity of the subject's exploratory actions. That is why, between the age of 5 and 9 or 10, there is a threefold increase in the stability of this "good form."

Any one sensory modality can operate only in close connection with others. Visual perception is intimately bound up with haptic (or tactile-kinesthetic) perception. The coordinations between sight and the action of gripping are established at about 4–5 months. From then onward, if not before, the visual perception of objects is inextricably bound up with haptic perception: the meaning recognized in perception is a function of the entire sequence of actions. The perceptual schema is never independent; right from the start, perception is subordinated to action. It follows that, genetically, sensorimotor schemata are as elementary as primary perceptions. A schema is not just a rearrangement of past and present perceptions. Perceptions are no more than signals which enter into the construction of the schema (and they include proprioceptive signals). As such, they are necessary but not sufficient. Nor can the schema be interpreted purely on the basis of exteroceptive and proprioceptive signals. The action itself which causes the signal is a vital factor in the organization of the schema as a whole. In other words, the subject does not perceive objects and his own movements separately; he perceives objects as things which are modified, or are capable of being modified, by his own actions. A cube is perceived as a thing which can be handled and turned over or turned round. Those portions which are invisible to the senses are still present in perception because of the way in which it is integrated with action. . . .

We therefore come to our final hypothesis, that the origins of classification and seriation are to be found in sensorimotor schemata as a whole (which include perceptual schemata as integral parts).

Between the ages of 6–8 and 18–24 months, which is well before the acquisition of language, we find a number of behavior patterns which are suggestive both of classification and of seriation. A child may be given a familiar object: immediately he recognizes its possible uses; the object is assimilated to the habitual schemata of rocking, shaking, striking, throwing to the ground, etc. If the object is completely new to him, he may apply a number of familiar schemata in succession, as if he is trying to understand the nature of the strange object by determining whether it is for rocking, or for rattling, or rubbing, etc. We have here a sort of practical classification,* somewhat reminiscent of the later definition by use. But this rudimentary classification is realized only in the course of successive trials and does not give rise to a number of simultaneous collections. However, even these latter are foreshadowed very early when children pile a number of similar objects together or when they construct a complex object. These two kinds of behaviors may be regarded as preverbal precursors of the graphic collections of Chapter I.

As for seriations, some approximation to these can be found in various constructions. One such example is a tower made up of nesting boxes. [At first] children may choose the boxes at random but in time they manage to arrange them approximately in order of decreasing volume.

The fact that we can observe various prototypes of classification and seriation at the sensorimotor and preverbal stage of development proves that the roots of these structures are independent of language. Nevertheless, these elementary organizations are still far removed from the corresponding operational structures. A sensorimotor schema is the functional equivalent of a concept inasmuch as it results in intelligibility and generalization, but from a structural point of view the two are by no means identical. It is characteristic of the sensorimotor schema that its various possible applications cannot be realized simultaneously, so that "extension" and "intension" cannot be coordinated by reference to one another.

A sensorimotor schema consists of a stable pattern of movements together with a perceptual component geared to the recognition of appropriate signals. The schema can be applied to a series of new objects if these are sufficiently similar to one another, or to situations which are analogous with one another: e.g., swinging suspended objects, or obtaining an object on a sheet of paper or a cloth by pulling the support.

Following is an analysis of the intensive and extensive properties of a sensorimotor schema:

1. From the intensional point of view, there is the construction of equivalence relations governing the properties of the various objects to which the schema is applied. The child recognizes that an object can be swung if he sees that it is suspended and that it can be pulled toward him if he sees it lying on a movable support which he can reach.
2. The extension of a sensorimotor schema is the series of objects and situations to which it can be applied.

But from the point of view of the subject there is still no systematic correspondence between intension and extension because the elements to which the schema is applied do not form a simultaneous collection. Where there is operational classification, this condition is met by a material collection for a limited class of objects, and by a mental collection for open classes based on the manipulation of symbols. Properties 1 and 2 may be further analyzed as follows:

1a. Intensional properties which are internal relations of an object in perception (e.g., the relation of being suspended, of resting on a "support," etc.).

*Cf. J. Piaget, *The Origins of Intelligence in the Child*, pp. 236–252.

1b.   Relations of similarity between a perceived object and other objects
      to which the schema has been applied in the past.
2a.   Partitive membership relating a part of the perceived object to the
      whole.
2b.   Schematic membership relating the object actually perceived to the
      sensorimotor schema.

1a is an intensive property while 2a is the corresponding extensive
property. These two are integrated in the sensorimotor schema inasmuch as the potential uses of an object are seen as a function of the
relation of its parts to the whole. Similarly, the intensive property (1b)
corresponds to the extensive property (2b). But these properties fail to
coincide in the schema. Because there is no representaion at this level,
the child cannot evoke the set of objects to which the schema applies.
Hence the similarity between the object actually perceived and the
objects to which the schema has already been applied (1b) cannot be
evoked, although the latent experience determines recognition. It follows that schematic membership (2b) cannot take the form of extensive
inclusion. The predication of a given property to a particular object,
which should establish an extensive relation between that object and
the entire class defined by the predicate, is confined to the indivdual
object and therefore remains intensive. At the very least, we shall say
that there is a more or less complete lack of differentiation between
extension and intension.

The rudimentary seriation shown at the sensorimotor level is less
static and therefore closer to operational seriation than a perceptual
configuration. But it has yet to achieve the complete mobility which
engenders reversibility. Because there is no reversibility, the subject is
unable to construct the series systematically by coordinating the relations $>$ and $<$.

In all likelihood, the nearest approach of these sensorimotor schemata to the structure of logical thinking is the differentiation of schemata
into subschemata, with a resultant hierarchical organization. In this
respect, the sensorimotor system foreshadows future operational hierarchies. Thus, the schema of pulling a support to obtain a coveted
object will tend to the eventual differentiation of a subschema where the
support is rigid like a plank: it can then be pivoted on its axis. The
subject will then have a general schema of using a support to gain an
object, subdivided into two subschemata, one of which consists in simply
pulling the support while the other involves pivoting it or sliding it.
However, both the differentiation and the hierarchical structure remain implicit. The situations in which the schema and subschema are
applicable are not realized simultaneously either in practice or in principle. So once more there is no classification in the strict sense of the
term.

The upshot of this chapter is to suggest that the origins of classification and seriation can be traced prior to the evolution of language and
symbolic representation. . . . While an early and rudimentary recognition of similarity and dissimilarity is highly suggestive of the "intensive" qualities of these later systems, "extension" is limited to the sublogical form of a spatial distribution of the parts of a single object,
which may be collective. There is no extension as yet in the prelogical
form of a nongraphic collection or in the logical form of a class. The

central problem of classification must therefore be the differentiation and progressive coordination of extension and intension.

This process is a complex elaboration dependent on several inter-related factors. We will endeavor to study the problem in terms of the actions of the child at various levels of development in order to discover how he comes to construct the necessary operations by successive stages.

Class-Inclusion and Hierarchical Classifications*

The nongraphic collections of Chapter II are the immediate precursors of classes involving a structure of inclusion. The construction of such classes implies a thorough grasp of "all" and "some," no mean achieve-ment. We can now turn to a discussion of stage III, which is charac-terized by class-inclusion, and we shall be describing new experiments bearing on the transition from stage II to stage III.

Knowing what difficulties the child encounters in coordinating exten-sion and intension, we shall not restrict ourselves to analyzing his clas-sificatory behavior. We shall also try to elucidate how he understands the extension of a class (or collection), i.e., how far he succeeds in quantifying the extension. But this time we will avoid questions of "all" and "some." These would be tedious for the reader and tiring for the children (as a matter of fact, that problem of ours was the only one in which our subjects failed to show a genuine interest!). We therefore chose the following form of question: suppose one class A to be included in another class B, without being equal to the whole of B, are there more As than Bs or more Bs than As?

The question can be made very concrete. The last subject in Chap. II Cla ($7;0$) told us that six small toys consisting of four birds (A) and two horses (A') were "all animals" and that that made "six animals" (B). Nevertheless, he said that there were more birds than animals, i.e., $A > B$ instead of $A < B$! Now this sort of problem forms the topic of an earlier experiment, with beads.† It is all the more interesting to see whether the fact that the present subjects carry out their own classifica-tions spontaneously will materially affect the results.

But there is a small paradox which we ought to clear up first to avoid possible misunderstandings. We have seen that "All the As are Bs" tends to be understood at stage II as "All the As are all the Bs." We now propose to ask whether there are more As than Bs or less As than Bs taking it for granted that "All the As are b." But this is precisely what a child is denying when he answers the [following] questions: "Are all the circles (A) blue counters (B)?—No, because there are also blue squares (A')." We expect our stage II subjects to say that there are more As than Bs (if $A > A'$), al-though by rights they ought to say that there are the same number or less if their answers are to be in line with those they gave in Chapter III. So there would seem to be a contradiction between the answers given to questions

*With the collaboration of Vinh-Bang, B. Matalon, and B. Reymond-Rivier. [The following section is from Chapter IV.]

†J. Piaget and A. Szeminska, *The Child's Conception of Number*, Chapter VIII.

about "all" and "some" as described in Chapter III, and the basis of our questioning when dealing with the quantitative relations between A and B.

But the contradiction is purely formal. In neither case should the children's statements be taken literally; and in both it is the negative aspect which is significant. When answering "Are all the As Bs?" the child at stage II does not see the relation, "All the As are some of the Bs," which is why he fails to understand inclusion. When answering "Are there more of the As or of the Bs?" he cannot compare the As with the Bs, and he compares them with the A's, precisely because he cannot handle class-inclusion. When he evaluates the Bs correctly, he is unaware of the As and A's (so that "all" is then applied correctly to B without reference to its divisions). Alternatively, he can compare A and A' forgetting about B (so that "all," and even "some," are applied correctly to A). But he cannot compare A and B. He cannot think simultaneously of the part and the whole (precisely because he cannot deal with inclusion), and this is reflected both in the incorrect usage of "all" and in the false quantifications. Thus the child will readily agree to a qualitative demonstration that all the As are B, even though he is perplexed when the problem is presented in purely quantitative terms "Are all the As Bs?" just because his grasp of the term "all" is lacking in precision.

CLASSIFICATION OF FLOWERS (MIXED WITH OTHER OBJECTS)

In this experiment 20 pictures were used, of which four represented colored objects and 16 represented flowers. Eight of these were primulas, four being yellow and the others being of four different colors. This arrangement gives rise to the following sequence of inclusions:

A (yellow primulas) < B (primulas) < C (flowers) < D (flowers and other objects). Beads were used as well, to allow comparisons with the earlier experiment already mentioned. The beads consisted of the following classes: A (red square ones) < B (red beads, round and square) < C (wooden beads with various colors) < D (wooden beads and glass ones).

The following problems were put and will subsequently be referred to by the appropriate Roman numeral:

(I) Spontaneous classification. (II) General questions on inclusion: If you make a bouquet out of all the primulas, will you use these (the blue primulas)? (III) Four types of question all bearing on the quantification of inclusion: (IIIA) Is the bunch made of all . . . (e.g., the yellow primulas) bigger or smaller or the same as the bunch of all . . . (e.g., the primulas)? (IIIB) Are there more . . . (primulas) or . . . (flowers)? (IIIC) If you take all the . . . (primulas), will there be any . . . (flowers) left? (IIID) If you take all the . . . (flowers), will any . . . (primulas) be left?

Here are some examples of stage I and stage II, when subjects fail all the questions in group III. Usually they will either fail the simpler type II questions as well, or else they cannot coordinate their answers to the thinking required for later questions (type III).

Gae (4;9). I. He puts four yellow and two blue primulas in Class A, adding the other blue flowers; a pink primula, another pink flower, and a cherry then form A': "The pink ones go together"; the lily of the valley and green hat go in C' (he remarks on the lily's green stalk): "The colors go well."

Questions II: "Can one put (this) in the bouquet made of (these)?" Whatever the question his answer is always "Yes." This means that the As can be part of the Bs (= A + A'), the A's are part of the As, while the B's are part of the As as well as the A's, etc.

Questions III are not understood in any of the three forms. . . .

Ter (5;8). I. He first classifies the objects by their color, and subsequently puts the primulas in A, the remaining flowers in A', and the other objects in B'. II. "Can I put an (A') in (A)?—*Yes, it's a flower.*—And an (A) with the (A')?—*Yes, it's also a flower.*—And is a pink flower (A') one of the primulas (A)?—*Yes, you can put all the flowers together.*" Thus Ter accepts the fusion of Class A and Class A', but fails to understand the inclusion relation (A < A + A'). Questions III: "Are there more yellow primulas or more primulas?—*No, there are more yellow primulas.*—And are there more primulas or more flowers?—*More flowers* (but he points to A' and not to A + A')." . . .

Ric (6;6) puts all the primulas and the yellow flowers in A, the rest of the flowers (grouped according to color) in A', and the other objects in B'. He then transfers the other yellow flowers to A'. Questions II: "Can I put an (A') in (A)?—*No, it isn't a primula*—And is an (A) one of these (B = A + A')?—*Yes, a primula is a flower too.*—Does that mean I can put primulas in a bunch of flowers?—*Yes, you can put a primula in the big bunch.*" Question III: "How would I be making a bigger bunch, by taking the primulas or by taking the yellow primulas?—*They're both the same.*—And a bunch of flowers or a bunch of primulas?—*It's the same.*"

In the simple classification of problem I, there is a continuous development toward logical arrangements. The most immature of these subjects, who is Gae, can manage no more than four little parallel collections and his criteria tend to fluctuate. (Although he puts the primulas together, he adds other blue flowers to the blue primulas, while another of his collections is based on color alone, and so on.) . . . Our older subjects, at their first or second attempt, are spontaneously able to construct collections which are clearly differentiated by logical criteria: A = the primulas; A' = the other flowers; B (= A + A') = all the flowers; B' = the other objects; and C (= B + B') = all the objects. Our problem is to decide whether this classification amounts to a true "grouping," comprising both inclusion and reversibility (A = B − A', etc.) or whether it is no more than a set of nongraphic collections because there is no class-inclusion.

The type II questions give some information on this point, in that the answers obtained are not up to the apparent level of the classifications. We can distinguish three phases. During the first, everything is a part of everything else (Gae) or nothing is a part of anything else (Fav and Breg, although Breg's spontaneous classification suggested a higher level). In the second phase (Ter), the subject agrees to combine A and A' to obtain B, but without understanding that, although all the As are Bs, not all the Bs are As. In the final phase (Rap and Ric), he seems to understand the relations of class-inclusion. For example, when Ric says that a primula "is also a flower," he seems to have constructed the relation A < B; and his answer to the next question (is an A' one of the As?) appears to confirm this.

Nevertheless, the type III questions show that none of these subjects can make a genuine quantitative comparison of the part A and the whole B. The reason is that in order to compare A and B, they would need to separate B into A and A' and still retain its identity. In other words, the relation A < B implies the inverse relation A = B − A', so that the whole B continues to exist even while its components A and A' are separated in thought. But as soon as these are separated, our subjects lose sight of B, which is why they compare A and A'. Some (like Far) decide that there are more primulas A than flowers (meaning

A' = the other flowers), others that there are more A' than A (Ter), and others again that they are the same (Breg, Ric).*

This reaction is quite characteristic of stage II, but what is interesting here is that the type II questions precede the type III ones, and ought to make them easier. Moreover, the present experiment differs from the earlier experiment with beads in that A and A' are numerically equal. (In the earlier experiment these classes were in the ratio of 10 to 1 or 2, as compared with our four yellow primulas and four of other colors, etc.) Why is it then that so many subjects (e.g., Ric) succeed with type II questions and fail with type III? We cannot accept the answer that they did not understand the language we used. In every single case we took good care that they did.† On the other hand if there was a systematic verbal misunderstanding this would itself require an explanation in terms of logical structures. The results of Chapter III suggest that when a child at stage II gives the right answers to the type II questions his thinking is qualitative, or at most it is halfway to quantitative thought: the yellow primulas belong to the primulas because "they are primulas." Spatial extension is the only kind of extension available to our subjects ("you can put a primula in the big bunch"). "All" then becomes an intensive quality which belongs to the whole taken as a unit. When he has to deal with extension in the strict sense, the child is lost, which means that his achievement in solving questions of type II is strictly limited. Type III questions are not answered in terms of extension. And this is crucial, because the essential characteristic of class-inclusion is the fact that this relation generates a hierarchical nesting structure which is extensive. It is therefore quite different in scope from a mere qualitative differentiation.

However, the situation is paradoxical in one respect. Between 50 percent and 90 percent of these subjects (ages 5–7) who fail questions IIIA and B, answer IIIC and D correctly. Thus the same child will tell us that there are more primulas than flowers in a bunch, while admitting that there would still be some flowers left in a garden if he picked all the primulas, but if he picked all the flowers there would be no primulas left. . . .

Aub (6;9). "Are there more primulas or more flowers in this bunch?— *More primulas, because here there are two* (other flowers) *and here there are three* (primulas).—And are there more yellow primulas (2) or more primulas (3) in this one?—*More yellow primulas. There is only one purple one.*—You pick all the primulas in a field. Are any yellow primulas left?—*No.*—And if you pick all the yellow primulas, are any primulas left?—*No.*—And are there more primulas or more yellow primulas in this bouquet?—*More yellow ones, because there are two yellow ones and there is one purple one.*" . . .

Although some of these answers are still wrong (e.g., Aub with primulas and yellow primulas), they are usually right, although the very same subjects consistently deny that a collection ("all the flowers") is bigger than a subcollection ("all the primulas"). At first sight, this would seem to contradict our assumption that they cannot compare a sub-

---

*A and A' can, of course, be replaced by B and B' (included in C), etc.

†The experiment with beads has been repeated by educational psychologists in Paris, who obtained similar results using bunches of grapes ("are there more grapes or more black grapes?" etc.).

collection A with the collection B without destroying B (so they compare A and A'). Indeed, it would seem to contradict all the findings of Chapter III. One is tempted to argue that not only the wrong answers given to questions IIIA and B, but also the errors found in relation to "all" and "some," are all instances of verbal misunderstanding. When questions are formulated in a concrete and familiar way the subject seems perfectly capable of handling class-inclusion, and he also seems to understand the subtraction $B - A = A'$ (the flowers minus the primulas = the other flowers).

We find the same thing with beads.* We show a child a box containing red beads, some round and some square, and ask him: "if you take all the red beads from this box, will there be any square ones left?" Naturally enough, he answers "No." When we ask him: "If you take the square beads, will there be any red beads left?" he usually answers that the round ones would be left. This does not stop him from saying that the square beads are as numerous as the red ones or even outnumber them, in spite of the fact that he can see for himself that all the beads are red and says so explicitly.

In effect, the two statements (1) "If one takes away all the primulas (B), there will be no yellow primulas (A) left" and (2) "If one takes away the yellow primulas (A), the purple ones (A') will be left," should express the operations $A + A' = B$ and $B - A = A'$ applied to the classes A, A', and B. Is this true of the child? To prove that it is, one would have to show that B is retained in the child's mind, i.e., that the apparent logical subtraction really is the inverse of the apparent addition. Now all we know from (1) is that B (the primulas) has two different parts A (yellow) and A' (mauve), and taking the whole means taking both parts. (2) merely implies that the part A' remains when the part A is taken. It does not necessarily imply that in spite of that separation B retains its identity as the union of these two parts. The union $A + A' = B$ can exist without (a) mobility of parts, (b) reversibility of the transformations (+ and −), or (c) preservation of the whole (B). But unless all these are present in thought, such a union is tantamount to an intuitive apperception of the fact that the given collection consists of unlike parts. Only when all three are present can we legitimately speak of operational addition. The only decisive test is to ask the subject to compare the extension of B with that of A. If he recognizes that there are more primulas (B) than yellow primulas (A) in a bunch, he must be aware of B as the sum of $A + A'$ and he must simultaneously be aware of A as the difference $B - A'$. Such simultaneous awareness, which is characteristic of operational thinking, implies the conservation of the whole B. It is not surprising that a subject at stage II can be intuitively aware that the whole is the union of its parts (statement 1), and that one part is distinct from another, even though he cannot compare the extensions of the part and the whole. For this comparison is not implied by statements 1 and 2. The fact that the subject only succeeds in comparing A and A' (for B is momentarily nonexistent) shows that statement 2

---

*We shall not weary the reader with the details of the bead experiment. The stages observed were the same as in the experiment with flowers, and they occurred at the same average ages. The quantification of the inclusions $A < B$ and $B < C$ (only $A < B$ had been studied previously) was also similar. The beads were, if anything, a shade easier.

does not express the logical subtraction of classes, but only a simple intuitive separation of A and A'.

When the problem of inclusion cannot be solved, the most frequent error is to compare A and A', instead of A and B. But it is not the only one possible. The reduction of B to A' is not always automatic and unconscious; it may be motivated by the fact that one cannot use the same elements in two different ways. A child, for example, may say: "If I make a bunch out of the primulas (A), the bunch of flowers (B) will no longer contain any primulas because these will be in the first bunch." (B is then reduced to A' by the conscious substraction of A.) We might add that where there are more A's than As the subject often appears to be giving the right answer, although in fact when he tells us that there are more Bs than As, what he means is that there are more A's than As and he is simply calling the A's Bs.

Rather more interesting are the following two sorts of answers. The first reply appears to be right, and in fact is wrong. The subject agrees that $B > A$ on the ground that B, represented by A', is more heterogeneous than A ("there is more than one color"). This, of course, is not inclusion, even if the whole class B is intended; for instead of being thought of as a higher ranking class it is simply being looked on as a variegated unit. Finally, in some cases, when a child replies: "They're both the same" to the question "Are there more As or more Bs?" he is not thinking of the A's: he says they are the same because he thinks that "if all the As are Bs" then "all the Bs are As." This is a clear instance of the incorrect quantification of the predicate.

Here are two examples of subjects who decide that A and B are equal.

Per (8;3) has already constructed three classes: yellow primulas, primulas, and flowers. "Can one put a primula in the box of flowers (without changing the label)?—*Yes, a primula is also a flower.*—Can I put one of these flowers, say a tulip, in the box of primulas?—*Yes, it's a flower like the primula.*" When the experimenter does so, she changes her mind, and puts it back with the other flowers. "Can one make a bigger bunch with all the flowers or with all the primulas?—*It's the same thing. Primulas are flowers, aren't they?*—Suppose I pick all the primulas, will there be any flowers left? —*Oh yes, there will still be violets, tulips, and the other flowers.*—Well, suppose I pick all the flowers, will there be any primulas left?—*No, primulas are flowers. You're picking them too.*—Are there more flowers or more primulas?—*The same number. Primulas are flowers.*—Count the primulas. —*Four.*—And the flowers?—*Seven.*—Are there the same number?—(Astonished.) *The flowers are more . . .*".

Did (7;5) first classes the objects as follows: A = the yellow primulas; A' = the other primulas and an orange flower; B' = the other flowers; C' = the other objects. "Is that right?—*No, this one* (the orange flower in A') doesn't really fit in (he puts it in B'). Questions III (given before II): "If one boy wanted to pick all the flowers and another boy wanted to pick all the primulas, who would have more?—*Both the same: they're both 8.* (This shows residual traces of stage II, as does the initial error in classification.)— How about one who wants to pick all the primulas and another who wants to pick the yellow primulas?—*The one who takes all the flowers; because he takes the yellow primulas as well.*" Questions II: "Can one put an (A) among the $(B$s$)$?—*Of course, it's a primula.* —And this one (an orange primula) among the $(A$s$)$?—*No.*—Could you put the primulas in a bunch made up out of all the flowers?—*Yes.*—And this one (a blue flower)?—*Of course.*— And can I put this lily of the valley among these $(A + A')$?—*No, it isn't the same.*" Question III (repeated): "All the flowers or all the primulas?—*The one who takes all the flowers takes the primulas too, so he'll have more.*" . . .

Trev (8;6). Questions III: "Which will be bigger: a bunch made out of all the primulas or one made out of all the yellow primulas?—*The one with all the primulas.*—Why?—*Because it's all the primulas.*—Suppose you make a bunch out of all the flowers and I make one out of all the primulas. Whose will be bigger?—*Mine.*—Which ones will you take?—(Correctly indicates $A + A' + B'$): *All those.*—Are there more flowers there (indicating all the objects) or more primulas?—*There are more flowers, yes.*—What about in the wood (a new question not previously asked), are there more flowers or more primulas?—*More primulas.*—Suppose someone picks all the flowers, will there be any primulas left?—*There won't be any left.*—So are there more flowers or more primulas in the wood?—*More primulas.*—Show me all the flowers here.—(He now indicates the *B*'s alone!)—What if I take all the yellow primulas and you take all the primulas, who will have more?—*Me. I'll have all the primulas here (A) and there (A').*—Count them.—*No* (as much as to say, it isn't worth it), *there are more primulas!*"

Needless to say questions IIIC and D were always answered correctly.

Among 69 subjects, aged from 5–10 years, the following percentages of answers were correct. The [row] heading $A < B$ denotes the question: "Are there more primulas or more yellow primulas in this bunch?" and $B < C$ the question: "Are there more flowers or more primulas?"

The following results were obtained with questions IIIC and D. *BA* denotes: "If all the *B*s are picked, are any *A*s left?"; $\overline{AB}$ denotes: "If all the *A*s are picked, are any *B*s left?"; and $\overline{CB}$ and $\overline{BC}$ denote the corresponding questions for *B* and *C*.

We note that subjects aged 8 years and above differ markedly from those at stage II (5–7). Not only do they classify correctly in the form of additive groupings, but they recognize the inclusions implied by that structure. ($A + A' = B$; $B + B' = C$; $C + C' = D$.) Questions of type II no longer present any difficulty whatever. What is more, in this situation, subjects at stage III can compare the extension of a part with that of the whole. This means that the whole retains its identity although it is conceptually separated into its component parts. Most of the answers are quite explicit. Did, for example, says "The one who takes

TABLE 1

Percentage of correct answers to questions on the inclusions of classes of flowers*

Ages (no. of subjects)	5–6 (20)	7 (19)	8 (17)	9–10 (13)
$A < B$	30	38	67	96
$B < C$	46	47	82	77
Both questions	24	26	61	73

* The total number of answers varied slightly from one subject to another.

TABLE 2

Percentage of correct answers to questions $\overline{BA}$, $\overline{AB}$, $\overline{CB}$, $\overline{BC}$

Age	BA	AB	CB	BC
5–6 years	71	83	71	71
7–8 years	66	75	85	88

all the flowers (will have more) because he takes the primulas as well." Extension is at last coordinated with intension!

Nevertheless there are times when the reasoning of these subjects lags far behind. A subject like Trev may reason perfectly correctly with the objects right in front of him, yet one has only to ask him to apply the relation of inclusion to the flowers and primulas "in a wood" to find the same incorrect reasoning as before! Although Trev tells us without the slightest hesitation that "there are more flowers than primulas" among those in front of him, he compares the primulas growing in a wood with the other flowers (not primulas), and cannot compare the class of primulas with the higher ranking class of flowers which includes it. Nonetheless he can tackle question IIIC: "Suppose someone picks all the flowers (in the wood), will there be any primulas left?" This raises a problem which will be taken up in the next section.

CLASSIFICATION OF ANIMALS

The three kinds of questions were put to another group of children, numbering 117 in all, with the only difference that we used pictures of animals instead of flowers. Ages ranged from 7 to 13 or 14 years. The reason for presenting these results separately is that they systematically lag behind those already given, even though the stages are basically the same. We have here a remarkable instance of the way in which the emergence of concrete operational reasoning depends very closely on the intuitive character of its content. We have to ask why this is so. It does not appear to be true of formal operations, so long as they are elementary.

That different results are obtained when animals are used must be due to the fact that these classes are more remote from everyday experience and therefore more abstract. It is true that circles and squares, or primulas and flowers, are designated by words which evoke verbal concepts of a general kind and are therefore abstract. But children do play about with circles and squares between the ages of 5 and 9; and unless they are city dwellers they often pick flowers or just primulas either in their gardens or when they go for a walk. Now using pictures of ducks and other birds and animals should make precious little difference if the questions are still confined to the actual pictures on the table. Each one of these represents a perfectly familiar object and there is no difficulty about naming them. There is certainly no explicit reference to the highly generalized conceptual structure which lies behind this nomenclature. But in fact (this is our a posteriori explanation of the results), a child cannot say that ducks are birds and birds are animals by simply relying on experience drawn from his own actions, as he can for squares and circles which he has drawn and for flowers which he has picked. He is compelled to rely far more on purely linguistic concepts and he may need to structure and develop these in the course of the actual experiment. This explains the time lag. In effect the problem we are faced with is this: What is the effect of introducing this kind of material, which is finite and perceptible but relies on a more abstract kind of knowledge? More particularly, how will hierarchical classification and the quantification of class-inclusion differ as compared with the previous situation where the objects could readily be handled.

Figure 3

The following objects were used for this part of the study: (1) series I contained three or four ducks (class *A*), three to five other birds (class *A′*: cock, sparrow, parrot, etc.), and five animals other than birds (class *B′*: snake, mouse, fish, horse, poodle). This series is illustrated in Figure 3. The primary classes* were ducks (*A*), birds (*B*), and other animals (*C*). (2) Series II consisted of three ducks (*A*), four other birds (*A′*), four winged animals which were not birds (*B′*: bee, butterfly, dragon-fly, and bat), and three inanimate objects (*D′*). The primary classes here were ducks (*A*), birds (*B*), flying animals (*C*), animals (*D*), and the universal class (*E*). We used transparent boxes of different sizes (these were kept transparent so that the relationships would remain perceptible), which fitted inside one another to correspond with the primary classes *A*, *B*, *C*, etc. As each class was named by the subject, so this name was written on the appropriate label-card. The procedure for the interview was identical with that used for the flower experiment. The question "Has one the right to put *A* in *B* or *B* in *A*?" was particularly emphasized.

We found that neither the hierarchical system (*A* < *B* < *C*, etc.) nor the quantification of inclusion was properly understood until the second half of stage III. A number of subjects were nearly at the stage of formal

*The primary classes are those which define the sequence of inclusions: $A < B < C < \ldots$, and the secondary classes are the complements defined by this sequence: $A′ = B - A$, $B′ = C - B$, $\ldots$

operations by the time they showed such understanding. Subjects who answered other questions at the level of stage III often gave replies equivalent to those of stage I when dealing with animals. We shall denote the stages found in the animal experiment by DI, DII, DIII,* these being stages which lag behind those found in other situations.

DI, then, is the stage at which the preliminary classification is inadequate and there is no understanding of relations in terms of extension; there may, however, be some partial successes with questions IIIC and D.

Pie (7;11). Series I. "This one is one of the . . . —*Animals.*—Can you make two piles?—(She puts the ducks on one side, and the other animals on the other.)—Now can you make two new piles with these (the other animals)?—*Yes, birds and animals* (as though birds were not animals).—Are the ducks birds?—*Yes . . . no.*—They all have feathers?—*Yes.*—If I put them all in this box, what would you write on the label?—*Animals."* Pie puts the ducks in *A* and the other birds in *B.* "Are the ducks animals?—*Yes.*—Are the birds animals?—*Yes*—Can one put the ducks (*A*) in (*B*)?—*No, they aren't birds.*—Can one put them in (*C*)?—*No.*—What is (*C*)?—*All the animals.*—So can one put the ducks (*A*) in (*C*)?—*No."*

"If a fox killed off all the ducks, would there be any other feathered animals left?—*Yes, the birds.*—If he killed the ducks, would there be any other animals left?—*Yes, the birds, the cat,* (etc.)—If one killed all the animals, would any ducks be left?—*Yes . . . no, they'd all have been killed.*—If one kills all the animals, will any feathered animals be left?—*No, because one kills all the animals."*

"Are there more birds or more animals in this box?—*More birds.*—Why? —*No, it's the same thing.* (Four birds and four other animals.)" . . . .

These replies are very much of a piece with those given by children of 4–6 years, for the problems of flowers and geometrical shapes. Yet there is no doubt that these same subjects, had they been given that material, would have been able to reason correctly in terms of a hierarchical classificatory structure using the relations of class-inclusion.

Yet here they cannot even answer question IIIC (If one took away all the As would there be any Bs left?) and IIID (If one took away all the Bs would there be any As left?). One is therefore not surprised to find that they cannot quantify the relations of inclusion.

Seriation†

. . . Let us now see whether the development of seriation shows any parallel to what we have found in classification.

STATEMENT OF THE PROBLEM

There are two main differences between seriation and classification. The first is that a relation can be perceived while a class as such cannot, and the second is that a serial configuration constitutes a "good form"

---

*The symbols DI, DII, DIII have no connection with the class *D.* The letter D stands for the French *décalé* i.e., delayed—trans.

†With the collaboration of M. Zanetta. [The following section is from Chapter IX.]

perceptually, which is apparently simpler and more elementary than the structure of a matrix. If perceptual structures are to be regarded as the sole source of operational structures, seriation ought to appear long before classification. It does not. It is a little earlier, but neither develops much before the age of 7 or 8.

The two main problems which arise are the following: (1) Does the perceptual configuration of a series constitute the initial datum from which operational seriation is abstracted? (2) In what way does operational seriation differ radically from perceptual seriation, and is this sufficient to account for its relatively late development?

The first problem really calls for an analysis of perception, and such a study lies beyond our terms of reference. All that we can do is to remind the reader of a few facts which are of obvious relevance to the solution of the second problem. . . .

One investigation relevant to this question was that of Piaget and Morf.* We presented children aged 4–10 with a variety of serial arrangements of sticks of different lengths. Some of these had equal differences so that the series went up in a straight line, while others had unequal differences. But these were still regular: when the sticks were ordered along a straight line, the tops of the sticks described either a positively accelerated or a negatively accelerated parabola, i.e., the differences increased regularly from left to right or they decreased regularly. The operative question is to ask the subject to compare the differences between two pairs of adjacent elements. The first pair is near the beginning of the series while the second is near the end. Now younger children (5–7 years) need to compare the two differences by measuring one pair against the other, while older children (9–10 years) can tell at once whether the differences are equal or unequal by taking the configuration of the series into account (i.e., by referring to the shape of the line across the top). This experiment seems to prove that children do not use the configuration of the whole until a comparatively late age. . . .

The known facts seem to indicate that the perceptual schema corresponding to a serial configuration is not a primary datum but is itself influenced by the subject's activities. These would include perceptual activities, but they would also include the actions involved in ordering objects, which are sensorimotor. In other words even when a subject has this immediate perception of a serial configuration, it is because he recognizes the structure as one which he himself can construct or reconstitute. Serial operations are simply an interiorized result of previous activities. Their origin must therefore be sought in sensorimotor schemata rather than in a purely perceptual schema.

The second problem can now be reformulated as follows. We take it that the schema which underlies the recognition of serial configurations is a sensorimotor schema, i.e., one that arises from activity as a whole and not from perception alone. We should therefore be in a position to trace the intermediate steps leading from graphic to operational seriation. This will help us to determine what the second adds to the first, as we did in the case of classification. The present situation is different in that perceptual serial configurations correspond more closely to the

*Cf. J. Piaget and A. Morf, "Les préinférences perceptives et leurs relations avec les schèmes sensori-moteurs et opératoires."

relevant operational organization than do graphic collections to classifications based on inclusion. Since operational seriation does not, in fact, occur appreciably earlier than operational classification, we have to study those intermediate stages where the serial configuration is more advanced than operational seriation. In so doing we should be able to bring out the differences between the two, and this might help to explain why operational seriation does not appear earlier.

Intermediate steps of this type can be observed. Because of their graphic character, series tend to be recognized as good perceptual forms. Therefore serial configurations give rise to a sort of semianticipation at 5–6 years which has no equivalent in the domain of classification, since classes cannot be perceived as such.

We have already seen something of the relation between anticipation and the operations involved in the addition and multiplication of classes. Now we propose to study the semianticipation of a serial configuration in order to find out how and why it arises at a preoperational level. But we shall also see why the semianticipation is not enough to permit the operational organization of the mental actions involved in seriation.

There is one way of separating aspects of seriation which arise from graphic factors from those which are bound up with operations as such. We can analyze the seriation of objects which are perceived by touch alone, and then compare these "tactile seriations" with ordinary visual ones. Even in tactile seriation, we can ask the subject to touch the sticks and then draw a picture of the configuration that he intends to construct. We can then compare the graphic anticipations that arise in tactile tests with those that arise in visual ones.

SERIATION AND ANTICIPATION OF SERIAL CONFIGURATIONS

WITH ELEMENTS PERCEIVED VISUALLY

Many years ago, Piaget and Szeminska studied the development of seriation in an experiment using 10 small rods ranging from 9 16.2 cm. together with a set of rods of intermediate lengths for subsequent insertion in the completed series.* We found three distinct stages. In the first, the child cannot arrange the ten initial elements in order. He arranges them in subseries of 2, 3, or 4 elements, which he cannot then put together. At the second stage, he manages the initial seriation empirically by a process of trial and error. He can only insert the additional elements by further trial and error, and he usually has to start again from the beginning. At the third stage, which starts at 7–8 years, the child proceeds systematically by looking for the smallest (or largest) element first, then for the smallest among those remaining, etc. This procedure, and this alone, may be regarded as properly operational, because it implies an awareness that any given element is both larger than the preceding and smaller than those that succeed it (e.g., $E > D, C$, etc. and $E < F, G$, etc.). This operational reversibility is accompanied by the ability to insert the new elements correctly, without trial and error.

*Cf. J. Piaget and A. Szeminska, *The Child's Conception of Number*, Chapter VI.

TABLE 3
Development of Seriation
(in percentage)

Age (no. of subjects)	4 (15)	5 (34)	6 (32)	7 (32)	8 (21)
Stage IA. No attempt at seriation	53	18	7	0	0
Stage IB. Small uncoordinated series	47	61	34	22	0
Stage II. Success by trial and error	0	12	25	15	5
Stage III. Success with operational method	0	9	34	63	95

We repeated this experiment in order to confirm the age at which the final third stage is reached and the order of succession of the three stages. . . .

Systematic seriation is not reached until 7–8 years, at least with this set of objects [see Table 3]. This age is dependent in part on the particular experiment. As we noted elsewhere,* the seriation of weight develops about two years later than that of length. Again, we might have found a marked improvement in the seriation of length had we used fewer elements, or if there had been greater differences between the elements. But either of these variations would mean that we were measuring a perceptual adjustment to an intuitive whole instead of operational reasoning. In point of fact, this sort of perceptual adjustment is a fairly early development, as we shall soon see.

On the other hand, had we increased the number of elements without altering the difference between elements (i.e., keeping it small enough to make the child compare the rods by actually measuring one against the other) it is probable that the average age by which stage III is reached would still be the same: once a systematic method is found, it can be generalized.

Knowing that seriation is not operational until about the same age as classification, we can now turn to the anticipation of seriation, in order to try to separate the intuitive and operational factors relevant to the formation of this logical schema.

We must first emphasize that the operational schema of seriation is necessarily anticipatory. The subject knows in advance that by choosing the smallest element among those that remain, he will eventually build a series in which each term is larger than the preceding ones, which is why he is able to avoid any errors or inconsistencies. The anticipatory nature of the seriation schema is confirmed in a neat experiment by A. Rey.† Rey showed his subjects a square sheet of paper measuring 10–15 cm.² with a small square drawn on it, some 2–3 cm.², asking them to draw the biggest possible square and the smallest possible square on the same paper. Children aged 7–8 immediately drew one tiny square (1–2 mm.²) and another square along the edges of the paper. Younger subjects, however, simply drew other squares near the model, trying to make them slightly bigger or slightly smaller. Strangely enough, they did not

*J. Piaget and B. Inhelder, *Le développement des quantités chez l'enfant.*
†A. Rey, "Le problème psychologique des 'quantités limites' chez l'enfant," *Revue suisse de psychologie,* 2 (1943): 238–249.

even succeed in doing this, and oscillated about the dimensions of the one they could see. Since they have no anticipatory schema, they cannot envisage the limiting sizes of squares drawn on the given sheet of paper. . . .

Our own problem is rather different. In Rey's experiment, the subject is shown one single element and he has to imagine the two extremes of an entirely imaginary series. In our experiment the subject perceives all the elements of the series, and is then asked to imagine (or to draw) the serial arrangement before constructing it. The only thing which he has to work out is the form of the series, for he can actually perceive every one of its constituent elements, whether visually, as in this section, or by touch, as in the next.

The first question is whether children cannot anticipate the series until the operational level at 7–8 years, or whether there is a stage at which they can anticipate the framework of the series, (e.g., by drawing an ordered set of elements), but cannot then seriate the elements themselves so as to conform with it. If indeed this does prove to be the case, we shall want to find out how this sort of semianticipation arises, and why it is not enough to give rise to an operational organization. There is a certain paradox in admitting that children can construct a seriation in a drawing, but cannot carry it out in fact, since ordering abstract graphic symbols can hardly be easier than ordering material objects!

In point of fact, the paradox does exist, for the second hypothesis proves to be right. Our method of experiment is as follows. First of all we show the subject four dolls of different sizes, and ask him to arrange them in order. This is to give him an idea of what is required. He is then given ten small colored rods 0.5 cm. in cross section and increasing in length from 9–16.2 cm. (the differences being 0.8 cm.). These are in jumbled order, and the child is asked to arrange them in the same way as the dolls. Before he does so, he is asked to "guess" what the arrangement will be and to make a drawing of it. There are two ways in which the drawing can be done. We may ask for a drawing in color; each rod has its own color, and the child is given a crayon to match each one, as well as additional crayons in other colors. He is allowed to touch the rods to check the correspondence between each rod and the crayon used to represent it, but the rod must then be put back in its place immediately afterward. He is not allowed to rearrange the rods at this stage. If the colored drawing is incorrect, he is asked for a drawing in ordinary pencil. This is particularly useful for younger subjects. When the drawing is done, he tries the actual seriation. This means that we can compare the level of his graphic anticipation with the level of his performance.

Here are the results for 88 subjects [see Table 4]. We found three levels of anticipation in the drawings: (1) complete and analytic anticipation, i.e., an exact correspondence of colors and sizes together with a correct seriation of the latter; (2) a global anticipation, i.e., a correct pencil drawing or a correct seriation of size in the colored drawing, but without correspondence between the colors and those of the real objects; (3) failure. In the actual seriation, we distinguish between a correct solution achieved operationally, a correct solution achieved by trial and error, and an incorrect solution.

TABLE 4
Anticipation and performance in seriation
(in percentages)

Age (no. of subjects)	4 (19)	5 (33)	6 (19)	7 (10)	8–9 (7)
Drawings					
Failure in anticipation	89	42	5	0	0
Global anticipation	11	55	73	20	0
Analytic anticipation	0	3	22	80	100
Arranging rods					
Failure in seriation	84	54	42	0	0
Success by trial and error	16	40	36	20	14
Operational seriation	0	6	22	80	86

It is well to bear in mind that the graphic anticipation provides a certain amount of practice for the actual seriation. That is why the results of the latter are slightly better here than in Table 3 for subjects of 4–7 years. There is no appreciable difference for subjects of 8–9 years, but we saw only 7 subjects in that age-group. However, the important point is that the graphic anticipation is clearly in advance of the actual seriation at 5–6 years. . . . These results are all the more striking when it is remembered that, although "analytic" anticipation corresponds obviously enough with operational seriation (with one exception, these occurred together), "global" anticipation bears little similarity to seriation by trial and error. Global anticipation means drawing the serial configuration quite correctly, and without trial and error, although the individual lines do not match the colors of the rods to which they should correspond. So it looks as if children of 5 or 6 can anticipate the form of a series well before they can seriate objects in an operational manner, and, at least at 6, the anticipation is ahead even of correct solution by trial and error.

Before trying to explain the discrepancy, we may well study a few protocols to bring out the qualitative differences between these stages.

Stage I: No Anticipation. At this stage, children cannot anticipate the series in their drawings, nor can they construct it later on. Neither the drawing nor the action can be said to be more advanced: each results in small unconnected groups of two or three elements.

Fra (4;0). Given colors, Fra draws seven lines of the same length going from one edge of the paper to the other, and two small lines which are more than ten times smaller than the others. The pencil drawings are: (1) a long line and a short one; (2) five lines, three short alternating with two long. The actual seriation is a set of uncoordinated pairs. . . .

Hil (4;5) orders the dolls correctly. "And now I'd like you to draw me the sticks, but in order, starting with the smallest, then one that's a little bigger, then a little bigger, till you get to the biggest one of all.—(Pencil drawing: 2, 1, 4, 10; then 10, 2, 6, 8, 7. Actual seriation: 1, 3, 7; then 8, 7; then the two uncoordinated series 1, 3, 7, 10 and 2, 4, 8, 9.)" . . .

There is no anticipation in these drawings apart from small uncoordinated sequences of two or three elements. The actual seriations are of the same type. The partial series in the drawings might be thought of as anticipations, but in actual fact the same simple type of activity is at work both in the drawings and in the arrangements of the objects themselves. Neither is more advanced than the other. That is why it sometimes happens that at stage I children establish a better correspondence of lengths as between the rods and the colors used to represent them than at stage II. For they are only copying two or three of the elements at a time. Later on, when they begin to anticipate the total structure, the drawing depicts a configuration which is ahead of actual performance, and this leads to a dissociation between color and size.

Stage I raises a curious problem. In the case of classification, stage I is the stage of graphic collections, while the prelogical collections of stage II are no longer tied to a particular spatial configuration. In the case of seriation, however, stage I is the stage of small uncoordinated sequences, while it is only at stage II that we find a graphic anticipation of the total serial configuration. In other words there are apparently no graphic serial structures at the stage which corresponds to the graphic collections in classification, and the graphic anticipation of a series arises only when classificatory collections begin to lose their graphic character. However if we pose the problem in terms of "intension" and "extension," the "intension" of a series being its order and the "extension" being the set of its elements, the paradox disappears. We know that graphic collections arise out of a lack of coordination between intension and extension, due to the fact that the intension is based on relations of similarity which are only constructed through successive comparisons, while the extension depends on the actual spatial perception. Now this is also true of the small uncoordinated series of elements constructed at stage I. The subject fails to anticipate a complete seriation, just as he fails to carry it out, for the very good reason that both would involve building up a spatial totality out of a sequence of successive comparisons. What he does is to make isolated comparisons yielding tiny series of two or three elements. Then he simply puts these together in a line. There is the same lack of coordination between intension and extension as we found in classification. So these little series do correspond to the graphic collections and the "complex objects" with which we are familiar. Conversely, in order to anticipate the serial configuration, as children do at stage II, they have to achieve some coordination between intension and extension, however incomplete. Once again, the same is true of nongraphic collections in classification.

Stage II: Semianticipation. Substage IIA: No correspondence Between the Colors in the Anticipatory Drawing and Those of the Actual Objects. Actual Seriation Is by Trial and Error and May Be Unsuccessful. Stage II is extremely interesting. At this stage the child can depict the correct seriation in his drawing, occasionally after one or two shots, but sometimes immediately. But at the same time his actual performance is usually only approximate, and even if it is entirely correct, he still requires a good deal of trial and error. We shall first describe a substage IIA, during which there is no relation between the color and size of the lines in the drawing. There are a good many individual variations, depending on the regularity or irregularity of the differences between the lines and on the extent to which the colors interfer with the accuracy of the form. . . .

Bad (5;2). (In the early stages of this investigation we used 9 rods of the same color.) "You try to arrange them from the biggest to the smallest. Can you guess what they will be like?—*Yes.*—Well draw these sticks.—

(Draws a house.)—No, these sticks.—(Draws eight elongated rectangles.)"
The drawing is a good series with the rectangles increasing in height: 7, 11,
19, 27, 57, 65, 82, and 91 mm. The differences are irregular, but the increase
is consistent. Bad looked at the objects after each drawing, althought it was
impossible to tell whether he was trying to copy each object or merely to
gain a global impression. The experimenter now points to the first and the
last elements in the drawing, and asks him to show the corresponding rods.
Bad puts these on top of his drawing, and continues by placing the others
on his drawing, so that eventually he obtains a correct seriation of all the
objects. He is then asked to repeat the seriation without the drawing, and
this time he finishes with 1, 5, 2, 6, 3, 9, 4, 7, 8! "Is that like the drawing
you made?—Yes.—Have you arranged them from the smallest to the biggest?
—Yes.—(The experimenter corrects the first two choices by placing 1, 2 at
the beginning.)—(Bad continues and ends with 1, 2, 3, 5, 4, 8, 7, 6, 9.)" . . .

Bar (5;3) says she will put the small ones on one side and the large ones
on the other. The first drawing, which is colored, is a good seriation with
regular differences between the elements. But there is no attempt at representing the real objects (by looking at them), and there are twelve of them
instead of ten. The actual seriation results in short series of the smaller elements only. She cannot seriate all ten.

Man (5;6) also draws a regularly ascending series at the first attempt,
which does not correspond with the objects themselves. He is then presented
with five elements only and asked to choose the right colors: He can only
do so at the expense of the seriation. The actual seriation results in small
uncoordinated series.

Bor (5;9) first tries to make his drawings correspond in size and color
to the objects. He achieves this approximately, but without any seriation. The
second drawing is a regularly decreasing series, but does not correspond with
the objects (there is one element too many and green is used three times).
When asked once again to keep to the right colors, he produces them like
the first time, without the seriation. The actual seriation results in 1, 7, 2, 8,
6, 3, 4, 5, 9, followed by 1, 3, 2, 6, 4, 5, 7, 9, 8, 10, which he now proceeds to
correct bit by bit until the seriation is right. . . .

In spite of considerable individual differences, these reactions have
a great deal in common. Every one of these subjects can draw a perfectly
good series of nine or ten elements, but when it comes to the actual
seriation he fails outright or else he has to resort to trial and error. Yet
he draws the seriation correctly at the first attempt when all the objects
are of one color, or when he is using a black pencil, or again, when he
does use colors but is not concerned that these should correspond with
sizes. When the correct anticipation of the series is not produced at
once, we invariably find that the subject has been trying to take the
colors into account, and could not do both together. As soon as he ne-
glects the colors, he succeeds in drawing the seriation right away, using
a black pencil or using colors at random. But, although the anticipation
is both immediate and correct, the actual seriation is inadequate or far
from immediate. In other words, there is a sharp contrast between the
systematic nature of the drawings and the total lack of system in the
actual seriations. The problem is that we know that it is not the colors
of the rods which prevents children from actually arranging a series of
rods in order of increasing size. The seriation is often incorrect at this
stage, and always halting, even when we use rods of the same color (see
Table 4).

The solution of this problem is really very simple. We have seen that the systematic method of carrying out a seriation implies reversibility: finding the smallest element, and then the smallest among those that remain, etc., means bearing in mind that a given element, say E, is both longer than those already in the series $(E > D, C)$ and shorter than the ones yet to follow $(E < F, G)$. Now a drawing does not require anything of the sort. A child draws the lines one after another simply following one direction of the size variable, and he has no need to make any comparisons between pairs. The relation he imposes is one-directional and therefore irreversible. The anticipation expressed in these drawings is an incomplete anticipatory schema because it is preoperational. There is no anticipation of the comparisons involved in the operational seriation of the actual objects (which implies the coordination of the two directions $<$ and $>$). The only anticipation is that of the global result, and the child cannot anticipate the steps which are necessary to obtain it. This is a *semianticipation*, in a very precise sense, because it applies to one direction of variation only instead of to both. It is very natural that this semianticipation should be a whole stage in advance of operational seriation and of the complete anticipatory schema which this implies.

But although our first problem has been solved, there is still a second one: the problem of explaining the formation of this semianticipation. It is not there at stage I. This is where we come back to the relation between the "intension" and the "extension" of series which, as we have seen, remain uncoordinated at the stage I level, since the "intension," or the order, involves a sequence of successive comparisons while the extension corresponds to an actual spatial configuration. As the ability to relate objects to one another develops (and this sort of development depends on the progressive coordination of actions which is going on all the time) so a stage is eventually reached when the child finds it easy to envisage the indefinite repetition of the same relationship, in particular the relationship $<$, $<$, etc., or $>$, $>$, etc., and to represent this repetition by drawing a spatial pattern. But one thing that is very obvious is the fact that the coordination of intension and extension is fairly easy only because the intension can be fashioned by the subject as he chooses. When he has to take the actual objects and arrange them, the attempt at coordination is brought up against the resistance of real things with all their multiplicity of relations in both directions $(< and >)$. That is why the coordination of intension and extension is far from being complete at stage IIA when real objects have to be arranged, even though there is anticipation to the extent of a simple graphic representation.

When we have finished our description of the different stages, we shall come back to the nature of these graphic images and the mental imagery behind them.

Stage II. Substage IIB: Beginnings of Correspondence Between Graphic Anticipation and Individual Objects. Actual Seriation is by Trial and Error, but Successful. There is some advance in that the subject tends to take the colors and sizes of the actual rods into account in his drawing, instead of being satisfied with an entirely abstract design. The actual seriation, too, is always correct, but the method is trial and error and not systematic or operational.

Rac (5;2) draws a series of colored lines decreasing regularly from 15–7.5 cm., and with colors corresponding to the rods in the order 2, 1, 4, 3, 6, 10, 7, 5, 9. He is trying to make colors and sizes correspond, but he cannot help making a number of inversions. This case is intermediate between stages IIA and IIB. Actual seriation: first 2, 1, corrected to 1, 2; then 1, 2, 4, 3 corrected to 1, 2, 3, 4, etc. The correct solution is eventually achieved. . . .

Wal (6;10) draws 1, 3, 5, 7, 9, 10, 8 (8 being drawn as the smallest, so that its size and color do not correspond). There is a regular seriation from 5.5–1.7 cm. "Have you forgotten anything?—(Only looks at the elements of the drawing, one by one.)—No.—Why is this one (8) after this one (10)?— I don't know (corrects it).—Is that what the sticks will look like when they are arranged?—Yes.—Are you sure?—Not altogether." The actual seriation: 1, 3, 5, 7. He then measures 4 against 7, and puts 4 aside. He eventually constructs 1, 3, 5, 7, 6, 2, 4, 8, 9, 10 (i.e., two separate series), and finally corrects this to reach the correct solution.

The advance is substage IIB is that the graphic image is no longer a semianticipation only, for it is more than a global one-directional schema. Although imperfect, it is an anticipation in the true sense, since it bears not only on the result of the seriation, but also on the details of its construction. The graphic anticipation and the actual seriation of these subjects should therefore be at the same level, as indeed they are.

Stage III: Anticipation Correct in Detail, Together with an Operational Method in the Actual Seriation. At this stage, the anticipatory graphic image is completely correct (when mistakes occur they are due to distraction and not to any error in method), and the actual seriation is entirely operational. There is a remarkable correlation between these two properties (cf. Table 4). Nearly every subject who shows one of them shows the other. (There are only two exceptions, one at 5, the other at 8.) This agreement is not surprising, because both the analytic graphic anticipation and the correct performance depend on one and the same method, which is the culmination of this developmental process.

Here are examples, starting with an intermediate case:

Mil (6;2) starts with 2, 3, 1, 4, 5, . . . , 10, so that the sizes of the first three elements do not correspond with their colors. The actual seriation: he starts by copying his drawing, and then corrects the first elements to 1, 2, 3. "It was wrong, the green one should have come before the red one." He then continues correctly, without looking at the drawing any more. . . .

Ben (7;1). His drawing and actual seriation are immediately correct. The latter is disarranged, and a new element is added to be inserted in the series. Ben compares it systematically to the smallest elements, and places it between 5 and 6, without reconstructing the series. "Why there?—(Reconstructing the series to prove his point.) There!"

At stage III, the graphic anticipation and the actual seriation are at the same level, just as they were at stage I, but for the opposite reasons. Both are incorrect at stage I, because there is no coordination of intension and extension. Both are analytically correct at stage III, because these two aspects of the series have been coordinated. At stage II, and particularly stage IIA, there is a semianticipation applying only to the global schema of the series, because extension and intension are more easily coordinated in an "abstract" drawing than in the real arrangement of objects.

There is one question we have yet to consider, and that is the precise nature of this sort of anticipatory graphic image (whether global as at level IIA, or analytic as at level III, or transitional as at level IIB). In particular, how is this sort of image related to mental images as such, or, in general, to perceptual schemata. The reader will no doubt recall that although classes are not perceived as such, relations are often perceptible. In particular a regular seriation constitutes a "good form." For the reasons given earlier, we would not allow that this sort of perceptual schema is a primary datum from the start, but it is nevertheless probable that the marked differences in the development of anticipation, as between seriation and classification, are bound up with the fact that only the former is perceptible. What we need to know are the relations between anticipation and imagery, or between imagery and perception. One possible solution would be to explain the early anticipation of seriation by arguing that this global semianticipatory schema is abstracted from the "good" perceptual form, or, it might be, from a child's perceptual experiences, and the same would no doubt apply to the operational schema itself. The alternative solution is that not only the operational schema but the anticipatory image which precedes it are both abstracted from the subject's own actions in relation to seriable objects instead of being directly abstracted out of his perception. This means recognizing imagery as an interiorized imitation of actions, while operations are then regarded as extended forms of interiorized actions with the added richness that comes from a more or less complete structurization. Now to accept this second solution does not entail denying the role of perception altogether. We may quite well agree that perception influences actions reciprocally, just as actions influence perceptual schemata. In other words, where the relations have an obvious perceptual correlate, the subject will have less difficulty in evolving a corresponding schema based on his actions (both at the level of semianticipation and at the operational level): so the anticipation of seriation is easier than that of classification. But it still remains that the "good form" of an ordered series only becomes perceptually apparent because of the corresponding sensorimotor action schema and its development as a whole.

[The authors go on to argue for the second hypothesis: "the perception of serial configurations is something which develops in line with activity as a whole, including operational reasoning, so that the relation between perception and action (including interiorized action) is a two-way relation." The line of argument is similar to that developed in Selection 31, Mental Images.]

24

The Preadolescent and the Propositional Operations*

1966

INTRODUCTORY NOTES

We usually think of adolescence as marked primarily by emotional crises caused jointly by the physiological changes of puberty and the altered social demands placed on the individual. But, perhaps starting just before puberty and extending well into adolescence, a profound intellectual change takes place as well, the appearance of formal operational thought.† We use the term *preadolescent* to describe the child who is just achieving formal operations, because there is no evidence that the physiological and social changes directly provoke the intellectual ones, which in fact sometimes precede them. The following selections describe a pioneering effort to delineate the nature of the intellectual change, which, as will be seen, has its own special emotional concomitants.

Five transformations mark the passage from the concrete operational level of thought to the stage of formal operations.

(1) The first and most important transformation is the capacity for reasoning on hypotheses. This mode of reasoning, often called hypothetico-deductive, is used by scientists in their work: formulate certain hypotheses about the nature of the universe, deduce some logical consequences from these hypotheses, then observe the universe to see whether it behaves according to expectations.

To a superficial observer, the concrete operational subject seems capable of reasoning on hypotheses, since he uses various "maybes" to account for his observations. But, in the end, these numerous "maybes" boil down to mere fictions that are submitted neither to verification nor experimental proof.

*From *The Psychology of the Child* by Jean Piaget and Bärbel Inhelder, translated from the French by Helen Weaver, © 1969 by Basic Books, Inc., Publishers, New York. Reprinted with permission of Basic Books, Inc., and Routledge & Kegan Paul Ltd., London. Originally published in French, 1966.

†At this writing there are various studies suggesting that not everyone reaches this level. But it is by no means clear whether, for those who do not, intellectual development simply comes to a halt or veers off in another direction.

Without hypothetical thinking, the idea of proof has no meaning. It happens that some fortunate preadolescents grasp the idea of proof at the very moment in their development that they are exposed to the system of proofs of Euclidean geometry. This can be an exciting moment in life.

(2) The second transformation is the use of propositional logic. At the concrete operational level, the child is capable of reasoning on what Piaget calls *intra*propositional operations such as relations, classes, and numbers (see Selections 21, 22, 23, and 26). The preadolescent reasons on *inter*propositional operations. He has become capable of evaluating the validity of a train of reasoning independently of its factual content. He has become interested in establishing the logical link between premises and conclusions independently of the nature of these propositions.

(3) This new capacity leads to the third transformation marking this new stage of development, the capacity to dissociate completely form from contents, which is the logical consequence of the second transformation. The preadolescent is capable of replacing any concrete proposition by an arbitrary sign such as the *p* and *q* of symbolic logic; he is also capable of replacing the concrete relations between propositions by all sorts of cabalistic signs that logicians invent every day for their apparent utmost satisfaction.

(4) The fourth transformation deals with the combinatorial nature of operations. Given two propositions, *p* and *q*, that can be either true or false, the concrete operational child is capable of grouping them into four types of associations: (1) both true; (2) both false; (3) *p* true and *q* false; (4) *p* false and *q* true. For Piaget this elementary form of association differs fundamentally from true combination which would fully develop the sixteen subsets of the four associations of two initial propositions (see selections 25 and 26). This combinatorial system can be extended from the sixteen binary operations to the 256 ternary operations (see Selection 26). The point of this combinatorial system is that the operations in question form a closely knit system in which passage from one element of the structure to another is always possible.*

(5) Thanks to this closed system of transformations, the preadolescent becomes capable of inserting real cases in the set of all possible cases that can be generated logically. Reality has become a special case of possibility. The system of all possible combinations forms the logic of propositions whose use and mastery constitute the fifth basic transformation of the formal operational stage of thought.

For Piaget, these five transformations derive from one single identifiable mental structure: the INRC group where I stands for identity, N for negation, R for reciprocity, and C for correlative or dual operation. Many things can be described with these operations, for instance, the functioning of an hydraulic press where I would stand for the pressure of the piston; N for the elimination of the pressure; R for the resistance of the pressurized liquid; and C for the elimination of the resistance. These four operations form a group; there is a

---

* For example, in the number system, one can always pass from one element, or number, to another by the operation of addition, and the result of such operations will always be an element of the system, i.e., a number. Similarly, in a combinatorial system, the combination of elements and operations always produces an element that is a member of the system. Thus in a propositional system composed only of statements that can be either true or false, a true statement combined with the operation of negation produces a false statement.

complete passage from one element of the system to another and the result of such an operation is always an element of the group. According to Piaget, this fascinating new mental structure results from the fusion of two different structures, the lattice and the group of reversibilities, into one coherent structure, the INRC group. Let us consider these points separately.

Piaget speaks of two kinds of reversibility, inversion and reciprocity. For Piaget, pouring a liquid from a container into another and back is an operation. If the act of pouring the liquid into the new container is called the direct operation, the action of pouring it back into the initial one can be called the reverse operation. This operation of reversibility is called negation or *inversion*, because it cancels the whole thing out just like inverted movement in a film cancels the whole action out: divers plunge back up the diving board, etc. This sort of reversibility is different from reversibility by *reciprocity* where the combination of the direct operation with the reverse one results in an equivalence rather than a cancellation. For instance, if John and Mary are the same size, saying that John is as tall as Mary (direct operation) and that Mary is as tall as John (reverse operation) amounts to saying that they both are of equivalent size.

These two operations play their roles in two different logical domains. Reciprocity bears upon relations and inversion bears upon classes. The coordination of these two domains is not achieved by the concrete operational subject but only by the preadolescent.

This new construction goes hand in glove with the emergence of the lattice structure that pushes the combinatorial system toward its own limits by allowing the association of any element of a structure with any other.

Consequently, the INRC group, which encompasses all this, provides the child with a formal structure capable of ruling the entire domain of knowledge as it stands today; a tremendous achievement indeed.

The experimental studies of Inhelder and Piaget are organized in two ways. The first part of the book, *The Growth of Logical Thinking*, focuses on the development of propositional logic. The central empirical question is the growth of the ability to formulate and test hypotheses. The experiments are analyzed with regard to the mental operations involved, such as reciprocal implication, exclusion, and disjunction. The products of this growth are the capacity to separate variables, to eliminate contradictions, and to orchestrate a number of operations in solving problems.

The second part of the book focuses on the operational schemata of formal logic. The central empirical question is the growth of the ability to solve a set of physical problems, each of which draws attention to a particular schema.

Each of these schemata has the following properties: it is a *general* idea, applicable to a variety of contents; it is an *abstract* idea, derived from intellectual operations upon operations, rather than upon objects themselves; and it depends on the lattice structure and the INRC group. Below is a list of such schemata, and an example of an experimental problem dealing with each.

In each case, the authors show that the preadolescent solves the problem thanks to a systematic exploration of the table of all possibilities, isolating factors and varying them or suppressing their actions one by one. The inherent suggestion that one might achieve complete domination over nature often leads the adolescent to grandiose ideas about himself and the world around him, and these speculations lead in turn to huge depressions when not confirmed by experience (see Selection 25).

Schema	Experiment
Combinations	Chemical combinations, in a system containing a substance to be colored, a dye, an inhibitor, and a neutral agent
Proportionality	Equilibrium on a balance beam, where the multiplicative relation between length and weight must be dealt with
Correlations and probability	Discovering the relations between a pair of imperfectly correlated variables (hair and eye color)
Conservation beyond empirical experience	Conservation of movement in a system containing some friction, i.e., rolling balls on a horizontal plane
Inversion and reciprocity coordinated in maintenance of equilibrium	Behavior of liquid in communicating vessels (equality of water levels, relation between water pushed out of one tube and into the other)
Mechanical equilibrium	Hydraulic press (a more quantitative version of the preceding)
Coordination of two reference systems	Snail moving on moving platform
Equilibrium of work, mechanical proportions	Behavior of wagon on variably inclined plane counterbalanced by variable weight on pulley
Geometrical proportionality	Predicting size of shadow cast with objects varying in size and distance, screen and source varying in distance
Compensation of interacting variables	Behavior of balls on rotating platform, relation between weight and distance from center in determining centrifugal motion

The same unity or behavior encountered earlier in the various stages is found again between 11 or 12 and 14 or 15, when the subject succeeds in freeing himself from the concrete and in locating reality within a group of possible transformations. This final fundamental decentering, which occurs at the end of childhood, prepares for adolescence, whose principal characteristic is a similar liberation from the concrete in favor of interest oriented toward the nonpresent and the future. This is the age of great ideals and of the beginning of theories, as well as the time of simple present adaptation to reality. This affective and social impulse of adolescence has often been described. But it has not always been understood that this impulse is dependent upon a transformation of thought that permits the handling of hypotheses and reasoning with regard to propositions removed from concrete and present observation.

This new structure of thought is formed during preadolescence, and it is important to describe and analyze it as a structure, something which the devisers of "tests" too often forget, overlooking the common and general characteristics in favor of individual differences. There is only one way to get at the structures as such, and that is by isolating their logical aspects. This does not mean falling prey to logicism, but simply using a general and qualitative algebra instead of (or before) resorting to statistical qualification. The particular advantage of this algebra is that it provides a table of the potentialities that a normal subject may utilize—though, of course, every subject does not realize all of them. Moreover, their realization is subject to accelerations or retardations, according to the scholastic or social milieu.

The study of these preadolescent substructures is particularly important to an integrated picture of child psychology, for they constitute a natural culmination of the sensorimotor structures and of the groupings of concrete operations. Although in a sense these new transformations mark the end of childhood, they are no less essential to this discussion. They not only open up new perspectives into later stages of psychological development, but they also represent a completion of the preceding stages. Indeed, it is not a question of adding another story to an edifice to which it bears no relation; rather, we have here a group of syntheses or structurations which, although new, are a direct and natural extension of the preceding ones and fill in some of the gaps left by them.

Formal Thought and the Combinatorial System

The concrete operations relate directly to objects and to groups of objects (classes), to the relations between objects and to the counting of objects. Thus, the logical organization of judgments and arguments is inseparable from their content. That is, the operations function only with reference to observations or representations regarded as true, and not on the basis of mere hypotheses. The great novelty of this stage is that by means of a differentiation of form and content the subject becomes capable of reasoning correctly about propositions he does not believe, or at least not yet; that is, propositions that he considers pure hypotheses. He becomes capable of drawing the necessary conclusions from truths which are merely possible, which constitutes the beginning of hypothetico-deductive or formal thought.

THE COMBINATORIAL SYSTEM

The first result of this "disconnection" of thought from objects is to liberate relations and classifications from their concrete or intuitive ties. Up to now both were bound by the essentially concrete condition of a step-by-step progression based on graduated resemblances; and even in a zoological classification (for these remain on the level of the "grouping") you cannot extract two noncontiguous classes, like oysters and camels, and make them into a new "natural" class. With the liberation of form from content, however, it becomes possible to establish any relations or classes that are desired by bringing together any elements singly, in twos, threes, etc. This generalization of the operations of classification and of relations of order culminates in a *combinatorial system* (combinations, permutations, etc.), the simplest of which consists in the actual combinatorial operations, or classification of all classifications.

This combinatorial system is of prime importance in the extension and reinforcement of the powers of thought. Once established, it enables the subject to combine among themselves objects with objects or factors with factors (physical, etc.), or similarly ideas or propositions (which gives rise to a new logic), and, consequently, to reason about a given reality (a segment of physical reality, an explanation based on factors, or a theory in the simple sense of a group of related propositions) by considering this reality no longer in its limited and concrete aspects but in terms of some or all of the possible combinations. This considerably reinforces the deductive powers of intelligence.

COMBINATIONS OF OBJECTS

One can ask the child, for example, to combine colored counters in twos, threes, etc., or to subject them to permutations according to the various possible orders. At the level of the concrete operations, these combinations always remain incomplete, because the subject adopts a step-by-step method, without generalizing. At the preadolescent level, however, the child manages easily (after the age of 12 for combinations, a little later for permutations) to find an exhaustive method—without, of course, discovering the formula (which he is not asked to do), but by working out a system that takes account of all possibilities. . . .

The Two Reversibilities

At the formal level, the liberation of thought mechanisms from content results in the formation of a combinatorial system and also in the elaboration of a fundamental structure that marks both the synthesis of the previous "groupings" and the starting point for a series of new advances.

The groupings of concrete operations are of two kinds and exhibit two fundamental forms of reversibility that, at the age of 7 to 11, are the culmination of a process going back to the sensorimotor schemes and the preoperatory representative regulations.

The first of these forms of reversibility is *inversion* or negation; its characteristic is that the inverse operation combined with the corresponding direct operation cancels the whole thing out: $+A - A = 0$. Negation has its origins in the most primitive forms of behavior: a baby can put an object in front of himself, then push it away; when he starts to talk, he is able to say "no" before he says "yes." At the level of the first preoperatory classifications he is able to add an object to others, or take it away. The generalization and particularly the exact structuration of such behavior patterns of inversion characterize the first operations and their strict reversibility. In this respect, inversion characterizes class groupings, whether additive (the elimination of an object or group of objects) or multiplicative (the inverse of the multiplication of two classes is the "abstraction" or elimination of an intersection).*

The second form of reversibility is *reciprocity* or symmetry. Its characteristic is that the original operation combined with its reciprocal results in an equivalence. If, for example, the original operation consists introducing a difference between A and B in the form of $A < B$, and the reciprocal operation consists in canceling out this difference or expressing it the other way around, you end up with the equivalence

*For example, white crows, apart from their whiteness, are still crows.

$A = A$ (or if $A \leqslant B$ and $B \geqslant A$, then $A = B$). Reciprocity is the form of reversibility which characterizes relational groupings, but it also has its source in early behavior patterns of a symmetrical nature. There are spatial symmetries, perceptive symmetries, representative symmetries, motor symmetries, etc. At the level of the preoperatory representative regulations, a child will say that when a ball of dough is rolled into a sausage it contains more dough because it is longer. If you keep making the sausage longer, however, he will change his opinion, by regulatory and not operatory reciprocity, and he will say that the sausage contains less dough because it is so thin. Both kinds of reversibility exist at the level of concrete operations. Lengthening can be negated by shortening or compensated for by thinning.

At the level of the groupings of concrete operations, each of the two forms of reversibility rules its separate domain, the system of classes or that of relations. The child does not yet have at his disposal an integrated system that would enable him to pass deductively from one set of groupings to another and to compose thereby the inverse and reciprocal transformations. The concrete operations, whatever their advances over the preoperatory regulations, remain incomplete, and the combinatorial system makes it possible to fill in one of the gaps.

The combination of inversions and reciprocities into a single system is attended by a process analogous to and inseparable from that which occurs in the constitution of the combinatorial system.

The liberation of the formal mechanisms from content leads the child to free himself from the step-by-step groupings and to try to combine inversions and reciprocities. The combinatorial system leads him to superimpose on the elementary operations a new system of operations on operations, or propositional operations (whose content consists of operations of class, of relation, or of number, whereas their form constitutes a combinatorial system that includes them all). The new operations, being combinatory, include all the combinations—inversions and reciprocities as well.

The new system which now emerges clearly involves synthesis or completion, though it too will be integrated into a larger system. There is not merely a juxtaposition of inversions and reciprocities, but an operatory fusion into a whole. Henceforth every operation will at once be the inverse of another and the reciprocal of a third, which gives four transformations: direct, inverse, reciprocal, and inverse of the reciprocal, the latter also being the correlative (or dual) of the first.

Let us take as an example the implication $p \supset q$, and let us imagine an experimental situation in which a child between 12 and 15 tries to understand the connections between phenomena which are not familiar to him but which he analyzes by means of the new propositional operations rather than by trial and error. Let us suppose then that he observes a moving object that keeps starting and stopping and he notices that the stops seem to be accompanied by the lighting of an electric bulb. The first hypothesis he will make is that the light is the cause (or an indication of the cause) of the stops, or $p \supset q$ (light implies stop). There is only one way to confirm the hypothesis, and that is to find out whether the bulb ever lights up without the object stopping, or $p \cdot \bar{q}$ ($p \cdot \bar{q}$ is the inverse or negation of $p \supset q$). But he may also wonder whether the light, instead of causing the stop, is caused by it, or $q \supset p$

(now the reciprocal and not the inverse of $p \supset q$). To confirm $q \supset p$ (stop implies light), he looks for the opposite case which would disconfirm it; that is, does the object ever stop without the light going on? This case, $\bar{p} \cdot q$, is the inverse of $q \supset p$. It is at the same time a correlative of $p \supset q$. The object stopping every time the light goes on is quite compatible with its sometimes stopping for some other reason. Similarly, $p \cdot \bar{q}$, which is the inverse of $p \supset q$, is also the correlative of $q \supset p$. If every time there is a stop the bulb lights up $(q \supset p)$, there can be lights without stops. Similarly, if $q \supset p$ is the reciprocal of $p \supset q$, then $\bar{p} \cdot q$ is also the reciprocal of $p \cdot \bar{q}$.

Thus, without knowing any logical formula, or the formal criteria for a mathematical "group" (any more than the baby knows this definition when he discovers the sensorimotor group of displacements), the preadolescent of 12 to 15 is capable of manipulating transformations according to the four possibilities: I (identical transformation), N (inverse transformation), R (reciprocal transformation), and C (correlative transformation). In the case of $p \supset q$ these four operations are:

$$I = p \supset q; N = p \cdot \bar{q}; R = q \supset p; \text{ and } C = \bar{p} \cdot q.$$

But $N = RC, R = NC, C = NR,$ and $I = NRC,$* which constitutes a group of four transformations, labeled the 4-group, combining inversions and reciprocities into a single system, and thus achieving a synthesis of the hitherto partial structures.

The Formal Operatory Schemes

[In this section the authors stress the extremely general nature of the 4-group, showing how it can be understood as the source of structural affinity among seemingly diverse operatory schemes. We have deleted this section because most of the examples used are taken up in greater detail in our selections from *The Growth of Logical Thinking*.]

The Induction of Laws and the Dissociation of Factors

The propositional operations are naturally much more closely related than the "concrete" operations to a precise and flexible manipulation of language, for in order to manipulate propositions and hypotheses, one must be able to combine them verbally. It would be erroneous to imagine, however, that the only intellectual advances of the preadolescent and the adolescent are those marked by improvement in language. . . . Combinatorial system and double reversibility affect the conquest of reality as well as the capacity for clear formulation.

*This means that $N = (p \cdot q)$ is the reciprocal $\bar{R}$ of $\bar{C} = (p \cdot q)$; that $R = (q \cdot p)$ is the inverse N of the correlative $(p \cdot q)$; etc.

There is one remarkable aspect of thought at this stage which was largely overlooked because traditional instruction in schools almost totally ignored it (in defiance of the most obvious technical and scientific requirements of modern society), namely, the spontaneous development of an experimental spirit, which is impossible to establish at the level of concrete operations but which the combinatorial system and the propositional structures render accessible, once the proper occasion is provided. Here are examples:

ELASTICITY

One of the authors presented subjects with mechanisms, the problem being to discover the laws that governed their functioning. The situations presented involved several factors, among which the child had to choose those that were effective. Once he had made this more or less complex induction, he was asked to furnish detailed proof of his conclusions—in particular, proof of the effective or noneffective role played by each of the factors spontaneously enumerated. Thus, by observing successively the inductive process and the method of verification, the experimenter is in a position to judge whether the subject has arrived at an adequate experimental method involving dissociation of factors and respective variation of each of them while neutralizing the others.

For example, the subject is presented with a number of metal rods which he can fasten at one end, the problem being to account for their differences in flexibility. The factors involved in this experiment are the length of the rods, their thickness, their cross section, and the material they are made of (in our experiment, steel and brass, whose moduli of elasticity are quite different). At the level of concrete operations, the subject does not attempt to make a preliminary inventory of the factors but proceeds directly to action by means of seriation and serial correspondence: examining longer and longer rods and seeing whether they are increasingly flexible, etc. In case of interference between two factors, the second is analyzed in turn by the same method, but without systematic dissociation.

When asked to furnish proof, subjects of 9 or 10 will choose a long thin rod and a short thick one to demonstrate the role of length, because in this way, as a boy of 9½ told us, "you can see the difference better"! From 11 or 12 onward (with a leveling off at 14 to 15), subjects, after a little groping, make a list of factors by way of hypothesis, and then study them one by one. The advance over the earlier performance is shown by the fact that they dissociate each from the others. That is, they vary each factor alone, keeping all the other factors constant. For example, they choose two rods of the same width, the same cross section (square, rectangular, or cylindrical), and the same substance, varying only the length. This method, which becomes fairly general at about 14, is all the more remarkable in that none of the subjects we interviewed had received instruction in this method in school.

It is not taught in school (and if it were, it would still have to be assimilated by the necessary logical structures), and must be the direct result of propositional operations. On the one hand, the dissociation of factors presupposes a combinatorial system; that is, the variation of one factor at a time (which is sufficient in the experiment in question, where all factors act positively), two at a time, etc. On the other hand, in a complex system of influences, the concrete operations of classification, seriation, correspondence, measurement, etc., are not sufficient, and it is necessary to introduce implications, disjunctions, exclusions, etc., which belong to the propositional operations and which presuppose both a combinatorial system and coordinations of inversion and reciprocity (4-group system).

THE PENDULUM

A second example will help to explain the logical complexity which is inevitably introduced whenever there is concurrence of *real* and *apparent* factors. (It is not for nothing that experimental physics has always been centuries behind mathematics and logic.) The pendulum in the experiment can be made to swing faster or slower by varying the length of the string, the rate of oscillation remaining unaffected by differences in the attached weight, the height from which the weight is dropped, or the initial impetus. Subjects at the level of concrete operations vary everything at the same time and are convinced that varying the weight has an effect (most adults start with the same idea). The children have great difficulty in excluding the weight factor, for when they simultaneously vary the length of the cord and the weight, they generally find "good" reasons to justify the influence of weight. The preadolescent, however, by dissociating the factors, observes that the weight can vary without altering the frequency of oscillation and vice versa, so he excludes the weight factor; and the same is true of the height of the fall and the initial impetus which the subject can impart to the weight.

The Affective Transformations

It has long been thought that the affective changes characteristic of adolescence, beginning between the ages of 12 and 15, are to be explained primarily by innate and quasi-instinctive mechanisms. This is assumed by psychoanalysts who base their interpretations of these stages of development on the hypothesis of a "new version of the Oedipus complex." In reality, the role of social factors (in the twofold sense of socialization and cultural transmission) is far more important and is favored more than was suspected by the intellectual transformations we have been discussing.

Indeed, the essential difference between formal thought and concrete operations is that the latter are centered on reality, whereas the former grasps the possible transformations and assimilates reality only in terms of imagined or deduced events. The change of perspective is as important for affective as for cognitive development, for the world of values also can remain bound by concrete and perceptible reality, or it can encompass many interpersonal and social possibilities.

Adolescence (15 to 18) is the age of the individual's introduction into adult society much more than it is the age of puberty. Preadolescence is characterized both by an acceleration of physiological and somatic growth and by the opening up of new possibilities for which the subject is preparing himself, for he can anticipate them by means of the deductive capabilities he has acquired.

Each new mental structure, by integrating the preceding ones, succeeds both in partly liberating the individual from his past and in inaugurating new activities which at the formal operatory level are mainly oriented toward the future. Yet clinical psychology, and especially the kind of psychoanalysis currently in vogue, often sees nothing in affectivity but a series of repetitions or analogies with the past (new versions of the Oedipus complex, narcissism, etc.). It is true that Anna Freud* and E. Erikson† stressed "successive identifications" with elders who serve as models, thus liberating children from infantile choices (with the concomitant danger of identity diffusion according to Erikson), but they have neglected the role of the "concrete autonomy" acquired during later childhood and above all the role of cognitive constructions that pave the way for an anticipation of the future and a receptiveness to new values.

The moral autonomy which emerges on the interpersonal level between the ages of 7 and 12 acquires, with formal thought, an added dimension in the application of ideal or supra-individual values. . . . As a result of the acquisition of such values, decisions, whether in opposition to or in agreement with the adult, have an altogether different significance than they do in the small social groups of younger children. This is particularly true within the high-school community. The possibilities opened up by these new values are obvious in the adolescent, who differs from the child in that he is not only capable of forming theories but is also concerned with choosing a career that will permit him to satisfy his need for social reform and for new ideas. The preadolescent has not yet reached this stage, but there are many indications, in this transitional phase, of the beginnings of the creation of ideas and the formation of values related to plans for the future. Unfortunately, few studies have been made that are directly relevant to this subject.

One reason [for this neglect] among others is the extent to which well-known studies on adolescence (G. Stanley Hall, O. Spranger, Charlotte Bühler, M. Debesse, and others) are bound up with our society and even with certain social classes, so that the question arises whether the "crises" so often described do not amount to a kind of social artifact. Margaret Mead in Samoa, and B. Malinowski among the Trobrianders of New Guinea, did not find the same affective manifestations, and Schelsky, in his investigation of *Die skeptische Generation*, shows how these manifestations vary within our own society. Certainly an essential sociological factor is the attitude of adult society toward the adolescent and preadolescent. Negligible in conservative societies, the adolescent is the man of tomorrow in countries in the throes of change. . . .

*Anna Freud, *The Ego and the Mechanisms of Defense* (rev. ed.; New York: International Universities Press, 1967).

†E. Erikson, *Childhood and Society* (2nd ed.; New York: W. W. Norton, 1963).

25

The Growth of Logical Thinking
from Childhood to Adolescence*

1955

The Oscillation of a Pendulum and the
Operations of Exclusion†

We have just seen [omitted chapters] how the subject goes about separating out factors in order to determine their respective effects in a multi-
factor experimental setup. The present chapter [Chapter IV] takes up
the reactions of the child and adolescent in an analogus situation‡ with
the difference that only one of the possible factors actually plays a causal
role; since the others have no effect they must be excluded after they
have been isolated. Such is the case for the pendulum. The variables
which, on seeing the apparatus, one might think to be relevant are: the
length of the string, the weight of the object fastened to the string, the
height of the dropping point (= amplitude of the oscillation), and
the force of the push given by the subject. Since only the first of these
factors is actually relevant, the problem is to isolate it from the other
three and to exclude them. Only in this way can the subject explain and
vary the frequency of oscillations and solve the problem.

Stage I. Indifferentiation Between Subject's Actions and Motion of
Pendulum. The preoperational stage I is interesting because the subjects'
physical actions still entirely dominate their mental operations and because the subjects more or less fail to distinguish between these actions

*From The Growth of Logical Thinking by Bärbel Inhelder and Jean
Piaget, translated by Anne Parson and Stanley Milgram, © 1958 by Basic
Books, Inc., Publishers, New York. Reprinted by permission of Basic Books,
Inc., and Routledge & Kegan Paul Ltd., London. Originally published in
French, 1955.

†With the collaboration of A. Morf, research assistant, Laboratory of Psychology and Institut des Sciences de l'Education; F. Maire, former research
assistant, Laboratory of Psychology; and C. Lévy, former student, Institut des
Sciences de l'Éducation. [The following section is from Chapter IV.]

‡The technique consists simply in presenting a pendulum in the form of
an object suspended from a string; the subject is given the means to vary the
length of the string, the weight of the suspended objects, the amplitude, etc.
The problem is to find the factor that determines the frequency of the
oscillations.

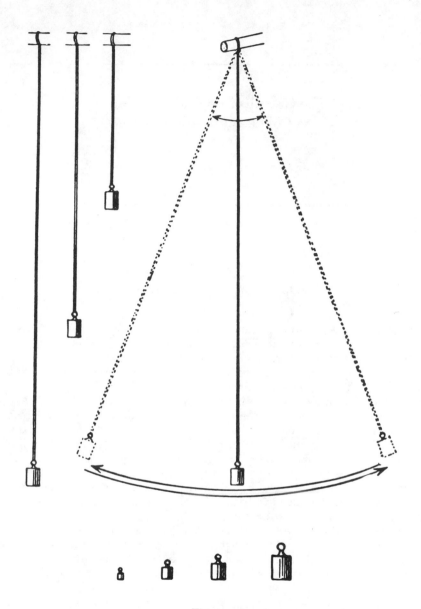

Figure 1

The pendulum problem utilizes a simple apparatus consisting of a string, which can be shortened or lengthened, and a set of varying weights. The other variables which at first might be considered relevant are the height of the release point and the force of the push given by the subject.

and the motion observed in the apparatus itself. In fact, nearly all of the explanations in one way or another imply that the impetus imported by the subject is the real cause of the variations in the frequency of the oscillations:

Hen (6;0) gives "some pushes" of varying force: *"This time it goes fast . . . this time it's going to go faster."*—"That's true?"—*"Oh! Yes"* (no objective account of the experiment). Next he tries a large weight with a short string: *"It's going faster* (he pushes it). *It's going even faster."*—"And to make it go very fast?"—*"You have to take off all the weights and let the string go all by itself* (he makes it work but by pushing). *I'm putting them all back, it goes fast this time"* (new pushes). As for the elevation: *"If you put it very high, it goes fast"* (he gives a strong push). Then he returns to the weight explanation: *"If you put on a little weight, it might go faster."*— Finally we ask him if he really thinks that he has changed the rate.—*"No, you can't; yes, you can change the speed."* . . .

One can see, then, that because of the lack of serial ordering and exact correspondences the subject cannot either give an objective account of the experiment or even give consistent explanations which are not mutually contradictory. It is especially obvious that the child constantly interferes with the pendulum's motion without being able to dissociate the impetus which he gives it from the motion which is independent of his action.

Stage II. Appearance of Serial Ordering and Correspondences but Without Separation of Variables. Stage II subjects are able to order the lengths, elevations, etc., serially and to judge the differences between observed frequencies objectively. Thus they achieve an exact formulation of empirical correspondences but do not manage to separate the variables, except insofar as the role of the impetus is concerned.

At substage IIA serial ordering of the weights is not yet accurate. . . . Since the ordering serially of the other factors is accurate, the subject discovers the inverse relationship between the length of the string and the frequency of the oscillations at this and succeeding levels. However, since he does not know how to isolate variables, he concludes that [length] is not the only relevant one in the problem. Moreover, if he attributes causal roles to the weight and the dropping point as well, it is because he varies several conditions simultaneously.

In spite of the marked progress seen at substage IIB, which is due to an accurate ordering of the effects of weight (in the raw data), the factors cannot always be separated: . . .

Per (10;7) is a remarkable case of a failure to separate variables: he varies simultaneously the weight and the impetus; then the weight, the impetus, and the length; then the impetus, the weight, and the elevation, etc., and first concludes: *"It's by changing the weight and the push, certainly not the string."*—"How do you know that the string has nothing to do with it?"— *"Because it's the same string."*—He has not varied its length in the last several trials; previously he had varied it simultaneously with the impetus, thus complicating the account of the experiment.—"But does the rate of speed change?"—*"That depends, sometimes it's the same. . . . Yes, not much. . . . It also depends on the height that you put it at* (the string). *When you let go low down, there isn't much speed."* He then draws the conclusion that all four factors operate: *"It's in changing the weight, the push, etc. With the short string, it goes faster,"* but also *"by changing the weight, by giving a stronger push,"* and *"for height, you can put it higher or lower."*—"How can you prove that?"—*"You have to try to give it a push, to lower or raise the string, to change the height and the weight"* (He wants to vary all factors simultaneously).

These cases* are extremely instructive because they show the difference between concrete and formal operations. From the first standpoint, the subjects can handle all the forms of serial ordering and correspondence which make the variation of the four factors possible and assure the reporting of the result of these variations, but they know how to draw from these operations nothing more than inferences based on their transitiveness (from the model $A < C$ if $A < B$ and $B < C$). They remain inept at all formal reasoning. From the second standpoint, they commit the following two errors: (1) In varying several factors simultaneously so that A_1, A_2, A_3, A_4 are transformed to A'_1, A'_2, A'_3, A'_4 and in ascertaining the change from the result X to X', they think they have shown that each one of the factors in turn implies X'. Put into propositional language, the error amounts to concluding from $(p \cdot q \cdot r \cdot s) \supset x$ that $(p \supset x) \cdot (q \supset x) \cdot (r \supset x) \cdot (s \supset x)$, without suspecting the existence of other possible combinations. . . . (2) Reciprocally, subject Per, having varied all of the factors except one (the length of the string) and not being very sure whether or not the result has been modified, concludes that the single constant factor must be ineffective ("Anyway it's not the string . . . because it's the same string!"). In other words, from $p \cdot q \cdot r \cdot s (x) \vee p \cdot \bar{q} \cdot \bar{r} \cdot \bar{s} (x \vee \bar{x})$ he concludes $p \overline{\supset} x$.

Thus it is evident that the subjects still lack some logical instrument for interpreting the experimental data and that their failure to separate out the factors is not simply the result of mental laziness. Just as Bau (Chap. III) varied two factors simultaneously in the comparison of the flexibility of rods so that the results would be "more different," so do Mat [10;6] and the preceding subjects explicitly propose to modify all factors simultaneously so as to accomplish more impressive transformations. At this stage the subjects lack a formal combinatorial system. Since they are accustomed to operations of classification, serial ordering, and correspondences, they are limited to simple tables of variation and do not conceive of the multiplicity of combinations which can be drawn from them. Since they have no combinatorial system based on the "structured whole," they do not even begin to isolate the relevant variables.

Substage IIIA. Possible but not Spontaneous Separation of Variables. At the lower formal level, substage IIIA, the child is able to separate out the factors when he is given combinations in which one of the factors varies while the others remain constant. In this case he reasons correctly and no longer according to the kinds of inference of which we have just seen several examples. But he himself does not yet know how to produce such combinations in any systematic way—i.e., formal operations are already present in a crude form, making certain inferences possible, but they are not yet sufficiently organized to function as an anticipatory schema. . . .

Lou (13;4) also compares 20 grams on a short string to 50 grams on a long string and concludes that *"it goes faster with the little weight."* Next, rather curiously, he performs the same experiment but reverses the weights

*[Several cases illustrating the same points found in Per have been omitted in the present volume.]

(50 grams with a long string and 100 grams with a short one). However, this time he concludes that *"when it's short it goes faster"* and *"I found out that the big weight goes faster";* however, he does not conclude that the weight plays no role.—"Does the weight have something to do with it?-"—"*Yes* (he takes a long string with 100 grams and a short one with 20 grams). *Oh, I forgot to change the string* (he shortens it, but without holding the weight constant). *Ah, no, it shouldn't be changed.*"—"Why?"—"*Because I was looking at* (the effect of) *the string.*"—"But what did you see?"—"*When the string is long, it goes more slowly.*" Lou has thus verified the role of the length in spite of himself but has understood neither the need for holding the nonanalyzed factors constant nor the necessity for varying those which are analyzed.

These transitional cases are of an obvious interest. They demonstrate, even better than the examples from substage IIB, the difficulty which arises in distinguishing factors and in the method "all other things being equal." In the first place, as among the substage IIB subjects, we find the tendency deliberately to vary two factors simultaneously, and even (as for Lou) the tendency not to vary the particular factor under consideration. But almost in spite of themselves and under the influence of nascent formal operations, these same subjects feel that in proceeding as they do they are not proving anything, so they manage either actually to transform the factor which they want to leave unchanged (as for Lou) or to vary all factors by turns without knowing how to focus their analysis on the point being analyzed. In such cases, the conclusion is accurate insofar as it relates to the factor of length, the only effective factor; but because the subjects lack combinations which would make exclusion possible, it is not accurate for weight or impetus, etc. In other words, the formal logic in the process of formation is for these subjects superior to their experimental capacity and has not yet adequately structured their method of proof; consequently, they are able to manipulate the easiest operations, those which state that which is and establish the true implications. But they fail in the case of the more difficult ones, those which exclude that which is not and deny the false implications.

Substage IIIB. Separation of Variables and Exclusion of Inoperant Links. For the pendulum problem, as for flexibility (Chap. III), substage IIIB subjects are able to isolate all of the variables present by the method of varying a single factor while holding "all other things equal." But, since only one of the four factors actually plays a causal role in this particular problem, the other three must be excluded. This exclusion is a new phenomenon that contrasts sharply with substage IIIA, where such an operation was still impossible, and with the flexibility experiment where it was unnecessary. . . .

Egg (15;9) at first believes that each of the four factors is influential. She studies different weights with the same string length (medium) and does not notice any appreciable change: *"That doesn't change the rhythm."* Then she varies the length of the string with the same 200-gram weight and finds that *"when the string is small, the swing is faster."* Finally, she varies the dropping point and the impetus (successively) with the same medium length string and the same 200-gram weight, concluding for each one of these two factors: *"Nothing has changed."*

The simplicity of these answers is in contrast to the hesitation found at substage IIIA, but this must not mislead us. The answers are the result of a complex elaboration whose operational mechanism must now be isolated.

Let p be the statement that there is a modification in the length of the string and $\bar{p}$ the absence of any such modification; q will be the statement of a modification of weight and $\bar{q}$ the absence of any such modification; likewise r and s state modifications in both the height of the drop and the impetus and $\bar{r}$ and $\bar{s}$ the invariance of these factors. Finally, x will be the proposition stating a modification of the result—i.e., of the frequency of the oscillations—and $\bar{x}$ will state the absence of any change in frequency.

When Eme [15;1] varies the length of the string with equal weights (and successively for three different weights), she states the truth of the following combinations:

$$(p \cdot q \cdot x) \, \text{v} \, (p \cdot \bar{q} \cdot x) \, \text{v} \, (\bar{p} \cdot q \cdot \bar{x}) \, \text{v} \, (\bar{p} \cdot \bar{q} \cdot \bar{x}). \tag{1}$$

This is to say that the modification of the length corresponds, with or without modification of weight, to a modification of the frequency and the absence of the first transformation corresponds, with or without modification of weight, to the absence of the result x.

On the other hand, none of the four combinations $(p \cdot q \cdot \bar{x}) \, \text{v}$ $(\bar{p} \cdot q \cdot x) \, \text{v} \, (p \cdot \bar{q} \cdot \bar{x}) \, \text{v} \, (\bar{p} \cdot \bar{q} \cdot x)$ is verified because when p is present $\bar{x}$ is never present and reciprocally when x is present $\bar{p}$ is never present.

But expression (1) can be broken down into two operations. First, when the subject says: "It's the length of the string which makes it go faster or slower," he expresses the reciprocal implication between p and x—i.e., $p \gtrless x$. Second, between q and x there is no single linkage, since the four possible combinations $(q \cdot x) \, \text{v} \, (q \cdot \bar{x}) \, \text{v} \, (\bar{q} \cdot x) \, \text{v} \, (\bar{q} \cdot \bar{x})$ all occur. (This can be written in the form $(q * x)$, in which case we say there is a tautology or "complete affirmation.") This is what the subject expresses when he says: "The weight has no effect." As for the relationship between p and q, it can be written $p \cdot (q \, \text{v} \, \bar{q})$ or, abbreviated, $p \, [q]$ —i.e., there is affirmation of p with or without q; likewise, we have $\bar{p} \cdot (q \, \text{v} \, \bar{q})$—i.e., negation of p with or without q. (The affirmation and negation brought together are the same as $p * q$.)

Thus expression (1) can be written:

$$(p \gtrless x) \cdot (q * x) = p \cdot (q \, \text{v} \, \bar{q}) \quad x, \text{or, abbreviated,}$$
$$p \, [q] \gtrless x. \tag{2}$$

We see in these formulae that the exclusion of weight as a cause of variation in the frequency of oscillations results simply from the subject's realization of $(p * x)$—i.e., from the fact that all of the combinations possible between q and x occur: to exclude weight means to exclude the choice of any particular linkage between q and x.

The reasoning process is the same for the exclusion of height of the drop and impetus. However, since the subject takes both the length and the weight into account when he analyzes the role of the height of the drop (r and $\bar{r}$), there are eight true combinations:

$$(p \cdot q \cdot r \cdot x) \, \text{v} \, (p \cdot q \cdot \bar{r} \cdot x) \, \text{v} \, (p \cdot \bar{q} \cdot r \cdot x) \, \text{v} \, (p \cdot \bar{q} \cdot \bar{r} \cdot x) \, \text{v}$$
$$(\bar{p} \cdot q \cdot r \cdot \bar{x}) \, \text{v} \, (\bar{p} \cdot q \cdot \bar{r} \cdot \bar{x}) \, \text{v} \, (\bar{p} \cdot \bar{q} \cdot r \cdot \bar{x}) \, \text{v} \, (\bar{p} \cdot \bar{q} \cdot \bar{r} \cdot \bar{x}) \tag{3}$$
$$= (p \gtrless x) \cdot (q * x) \cdot (r * x) = p \, [q \, \text{v} \, r] \quad x,$$

where the expression $p \, [q \, \text{v} \, r]$ stands for $p \cdot (q \, \text{v} \, r) \, \text{v} \, p \cdot (\bar{q} \cdot \bar{r})$.

Furthermore, when he studies the role of the impetus (s or $\bar{s}$) the subject also takes into account the length, the weight, and the height of the drop. In this case, he finds sixteen true combinations:

$$(p \cdot q \cdot r \cdot s \cdot x) \vee (p \cdot q \cdot r \cdot \bar{s} \cdot x) \vee (p \cdot q \cdot \bar{r} \cdot s \cdot x)$$
$$\vee (p \cdot q \cdot \bar{r} \cdot \bar{s} \cdot x) \vee (p \cdot \bar{q} \cdot r \cdot s \cdot x) \vee (p \cdot \bar{q} \cdot r \cdot \bar{s} \cdot x)$$
$$\vee (p \cdot \bar{q} \cdot \bar{r} \cdot s \cdot x) \vee (p \cdot \bar{q} \cdot \bar{r} \cdot \bar{s} \cdot x) \vee (\bar{p} \cdot q \cdot r \cdot s \cdot \bar{x}) \qquad (4)$$
$$\vee (\bar{p} \cdot q \cdot r \cdot \bar{s} \cdot \bar{x}) \vee (\bar{p} \cdot q \cdot \bar{r} \cdot s \cdot \bar{x}) \vee (\bar{p} \cdot q \cdot \bar{r} \cdot \bar{s} \cdot \bar{x})$$
$$\vee (\bar{p} \cdot \bar{q} \cdot r \cdot s \cdot \bar{x}) \vee (\bar{p} \cdot \bar{q} \cdot r \cdot \bar{s} \cdot \bar{x}) \vee (\bar{p} \cdot \bar{q} \cdot \bar{r} \cdot s \cdot \bar{x})$$
$$\vee (\bar{p} \cdot \bar{q} \cdot \bar{r} \cdot \bar{s} \cdot \bar{x}) = (p \quad x) \cdot (q * x) \cdot (r * x) \cdot (s * x)$$
$$= p \, [q \vee r \vee s] \gtreqless x.$$

Thus we see that the exclusion of the three inoperant factors (which at first seemed so simple) as well as the reciprocal implications of the length and the result x actually presuppose a complicated combinatorial operation which the subject cannot master except by ordering seriately the factors which are to be varied one-by-one, each time holding the others constant. For example, in expression (4), the first two combinations $(p \cdot q \cdot r \cdot s \cdot x) \vee (p \cdot q \cdot r \cdot \bar{s} \cdot x)$ are sufficient for the subject to deduce that frequency does not imply the operation of impetus $(s \cdot x)$ and it is sufficient that he add the last two combinations to conclude $(s * x)$—i.e., to exclude completely the role of this factor. But it goes without saying that, in order to choose the conclusive combinations in this way, he must have at least an approximate idea of all the rest. This fact explains why the isolation of variables by the method "all other things being equal" and the exclusion of inoperant factors appear at such a late date, being reserved for substage IIIB.

The best proof that such a combinatorial system is needed is that the substage IIIB subject is not satisfied with drawing exact conclusions from the demonstrative combinations that he conceives of in the course of the experiment with such apparent simplicity. He avoids as well all of the paralogisms that we have noted at substages IIB and IIIA. But, in comparing the correct inferences found at substage IIIB with the earlier false ones, we see that the choice is again dictated by the presence of one or two conclusive combinations. Once more they presuppose a degree of mastery of the system of all possible combinations.

For example, in the case of the hypothesized influence of weight (q), the subject may hesitate between operation (3), $p \, [q] \gtreqless x$ and the operations $(p \vee q)$ or $(p \cdot q)$ $x \ldots$ assumed at substage IIIA and signifying that the change of frequency is due either to the length or the weight or to both at once $(p \vee q)$ or else that it is always due to both at once $(p \cdot q)$. In such cases, we would have:

$$[(p \vee q) \gtreqless x] = (p \cdot q \cdot x) \vee (p \cdot \bar{q} \cdot x) \vee (\bar{p} \cdot q \cdot x) \vee (\bar{p} \cdot \bar{q} \cdot \bar{x}), \quad (5)$$
and
$$[(p \cdot q) \gtreqless x] = (p \cdot q \cdot x) \vee (p \cdot \bar{q} \cdot \bar{x}) \vee (\bar{p} \cdot q \cdot \bar{x}) \vee (\bar{p} \cdot \bar{q} \cdot \bar{x}). \quad (6)$$

Here we see that expression (5) does not differ from expressions (1) and (2), themselves mutually equivalent, except for the presence of $(\bar{p} \cdot q \cdot x)$ and the absence of $(\bar{p} \cdot q \cdot \bar{x})$. And expression (6) does not differ except for the presence of $(p \cdot \bar{q} \cdot \bar{x})$ and the absence of $(p \cdot \bar{q} \cdot x)$. But the adolescent at substage IIIB certainly knows how to exclude $(\bar{p} \cdot q \cdot x)$ and $(p \cdot \bar{q} \cdot \bar{x})$, since he verifies accurately the falsehood of $\bar{p} \cdot x$ and $p \cdot \bar{x}$ (= changes of frequency without modification of length or the reciprocal) even while admitting the truth of $q \cdot x$ and of $\bar{q} \cdot \bar{x}$ (= simultaneous variation of frequency and weight or invariance of both) when the length factor operates at the same time.

Analyzing all the inferences accepted by a substage IIIB subject and all of those which he rejects, one must assume that he has knowledge of the combinations of expression (4). This knowledge itself presupposes a knowledge of the sixteen other rejected combinations—i.e., a choice among thirty-two basic combinations.* Such choices imply, after all, a selection among a set of basic combinations. Once more we see that this selection implies the operation of the formal combinatorial system based on the "structured whole," whereas concrete operations amount simply to constructing correspondences from which these basic combinations are composed. . . .

Combinations of Colored and Colorless Chemical Bodies†

We have constantly seen that the formation of propositional logic, which itself marks the appearance of formal thought, depends on the establishment of a combinatorial system. The *structured whole* depends on this combinatorial system which is manifested in the subjects' potential ability to link a set of base associations or correspondences with each other in all possible ways so as to draw from them the relationships of implication, disjunction, exclusion, etc. Faced with an induction problem in which subjects at concrete stage II would be limited to classifications, serial ordering, equalizations, and correspondences, the substage IIIB adolescents combine all of the known factors among themselves in terms of all the possible links. But the problems given the subjects up to this point have involved factors which can be disassociated and combined at will or simply made to correspond without going beyond the level of observation or of "raw" experiment. One may wonder what would happen if we posed a problem that involved combinations directly—i.e., one that involved elements or factors whose combination is indispensable if [observable] results are to be obtained. Will subjects at substage IIB or even IIA discover a combinatorial system to meet the requirements of the experiment, one which would demonstrate the independence of this combinatorial system in relation to propositional logic? Must one await the formal stage for the establishment of this experimental combinatorial system, and will the stage II children accomplish nothing more than scattered empirical combinations without a total system such as

---

*In the case of flexibility (five factors and the result) there are even more —i.e., sixty-four basic combinations. But to give proof of the influence of each factor it is sufficient to retain them separately by couples of combinations, whose model is furnished by operation (3) presented in Chapter III, which can be taken in turn.

†With the collaboration of G. Noelting, research assistant, Laboratory of Psychology, and doctor in chemistry. [The following section is from Chapter VII.]

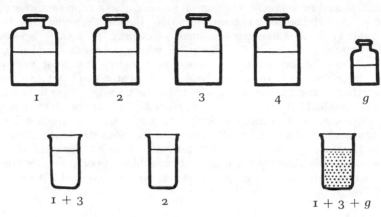

Figure 2

This diagram illustrates Experiment I in the problem of colored and color-less chemicals. Four similar flasks contain colorless, odorless liquids: (1) diluted sulphuric acid; (2) water; (3) oxygenated water; (4) thiosulphate. The smaller flask, labeled *g*, contains potassium iodide. Two glasses are presented to the subject; one contains 1 + 3, the other contains 2. While the subject watches, the experimenter adds several drops of *g* to each of these glasses. The liquid in the glass containing 1 + 3 turns yellow. The subject is then asked to reproduce the color, using all or any of the five flasks as he wishes.

we have seen elsewhere (in studying the formation of the mathematical operations of combinations, permutations, and arrangements)?*

The best technique with regard to this matter is to ask subjects to combine chemical substances among themselves. [See Figure 2.] In experiment I, the child is given four similar flasks containing colorless, odorless liquids which are perceptually identical. We number them: (1) diluted sulphuric acid; (2) water; (3) oxygenated water; (4) thiosul-phate; we add a bottle (with a dropper) which we will call *g*; it contains potassium iodide. It is known that oxygenated water oxidizes potassium iodide in an acid medium. Thus mixture (1 + 3 + *g*) will yield a yellow color. The water (2) is neutral, so that adding it will not change the color, whereas the thiosulphate (4) will bleach the mixture (1 + 3 + *g*). The experimenter presents to the subject two glasses, one containing 1 + 3, the other containing 2. In front of the subject, he pours several drops of *g* in each of the two glasses and notes the different reactions. Then the subject is asked simply to reproduce the color yellow, using flasks 1, 2, 3, 4, and *g* as he wishes. . . .

Stage I. Empirical Associations and Precausal Explanations. At the preoperational level subjects are limited to randomly associating two elements at a time and noting the result in explaining it by simple phenomenalism or by other forms of prelogical causality. . . .

Preoperational thinking of this type contains neither proof nor even hypothesis. The apparent hypotheses of "maybe it's because . . ."—are nothing more than fictions, for they make no reference to verification and she simply replaces or fills in the real world with imagery. Since they

*J. Piaget, *The Origin of the Idea of Chance in Children,* Chapters VII to IX.

are not placed in a precise context of actions, these representations re-main precausal; the color is a sort of active element that emanates from the water (it's the water that "changes") but may "go away," "go down to the bottom," "flatten out" to the point where it becomes invisible, or fly away to a beaker more than one meter away. The color can also "come back" but only to certain beakers of "water" and not to others. Appropriately, the subject may even shake the uncooperative beakers.

Substage IIA. Multiplication of Factors by "g." At the time concrete operations appear it is interesting to note the extent to which subjects spontaneously and systematically associate the element g with all of the others (in the case of experiment I) but without any other combination. If the subject is directly encouraged to combine several factors simul-taneously, a few tentative empirical procedures are elicited but they are not followed up:

Ren (7;1) tries $4 \times g$, then $2 \times g$, $1 \times g$, and $3 \times g$: *"I think I did everything. . . . I tried them all."*—"What else could you have done?"—*"I don't know."* We give him the glasses again: he repeats $1 \times g$, etc.—"You took each bottle separately. What else could you have done?"—*"Take two bottles at the same time"* (he tries $1 \times 4 \times g$, then $2 \times 3 \times g$, thus failing to cross over between the two sets (of bottles), for example 1×2, 1×3, 2×4, and 3×4).—When we suggest that he add others, he puts $1 \times g$ in the glass already containing 2×3 which results in the appearance of the color: "Try to make the color again."—*"Do I put in two or three?* (he tries with $2 \times 4 \times g$, then adds 3, then tries it with $1 \times 4 \times 2 \times g$). *No, I don't remember any more,"* etc. . . .

Cur (8;11) also proceeds one by one with g: *"Nothing happens. You can't do it unless you put everything in the same glass."* He mixes the four without success, then hypothesizes not that he has put in too much but that he should have chosen another order: *"Nothing happens. I should have started with that one"* (2). He does this, but since he does not control the permutation operations any better than the combination operations, he fol-lows the sequence 2, 3, 4, 1, g, then he adopts any sequence whatsoever: *"The color doesn't come because I did it in reverse."* . . .

The reactions at this stage are of interest because, although these subjects are in possession of logical multiplication operations of one-by-one correspondence, the idea of constructing combinations two-by-two or three-by-three, etc., does not occur to them.

From the standpoint of combination operations, the only spontaneous reactions of the subject are either to associate each one of the bottles 1 to 4 in turn to the dropper g or to take all four at the same time. In both cases combinations are involved, but only the elementary and limited combinations that operate in multiplicative "groupings" of classes and relations (i.e., associations or correspondences between one term and all the others).

Even when he sees he has failed, the subject does not use two-by-two combinations without prompting by the experimenter. On the other hand, his two hypotheses are either purely quantitative ("too much water" or not enough, the result being a new distribution of drops) or have to do with serial ordering (Cur). But this appeal to order is also prompted by a grouping structure, since the serial ordering which is acquired from 7 years on rests on sequences. But here again the sub-ject's reaction is to introduce a single change in order or to invert this sequence; he fails to try all of the possible sequences that combinatorial permutation operations allow. In sum, no true combinatorial operation has appeared as yet, but only correspondences and serial ordering—i.e., first-degree combinations based on fixed class inclusions.

Another interesting point is that, with the color already formed, the subject is well aware that liquid 4 is "a kind of water which takes away the color." But when he is in the process of bringing together the four elements $1 \times 2 \times 3 \times 4 \times g$ and the color, which has appeared after he has combined the first three elements with g, disappears under the influence of 4, he no longer has the idea of a possible exclusion between 4 and the color; he simply declares that the color has disappeared for various reasons.

Because it helps to point up the opposition between noncombinatorial and combinatorial structures, we should note that at this level the child does not think of attributing color to the combination of several elements as such. Rather, he thinks in terms of such and such an element taken by itself, whether or not it combines with others. For example, Gay [7;6] thinks that the color is in 3; then he withdraws it from 3 in order to assign it to g, as if it could be linked to only one liquid at a time. . . .

Substage IIB. Multiplicative Operations with the Empirical Introduction of n-by-n Combinations. The substage IIB reactions are analogous to the preceding ones but with a visible progress, namely, the appearance of *n*-by-*n* combinations. However, the subject does not as yet discover any system; only tentative empirical efforts are involved: . . .

Tur (11;6) begins with $1 \times g$, etc. *"That doesn't work. You have to mix all four* (he does this). *That doesn't work either* (he changes the order several times without success, then tries two-by-two combinations: $1 \times 4 \times g$, $2 \times 3 \times g$, $3 \times 4 \times g$, then $2 \times 1 \times g$). *I wonder if there isn't water in all of them!"* Then he spontaneously moves on to three-by-three combinations $(\times g)$, but without order: $3 \times 4 \times 1 \times g$, then $2 \times 3 \times 4 \times g$, then $1 \times 4 \times 2 \times g$, then $3 \times 1 \times 2 \times g$. *"That's it."*—"What do you have to do for the color?"—*"Put in 2."*—"All three are necessary?"—*One at a time* (always with g) *it doesn't work. It seems to me that with two it doesn't work; a liquid is missing."*—"Are you sure that you have tried everything with two?" —*"Not sure* (he tries in addition $2 \times 1 \times g$, already attempted, then $3 \times 1 \times g$). *It works! It's 1 and 3!"*—"Tell me what effect the bottles have."—*"1 is a colorant, 2 prevents the color; no it doesn't prevent it because it worked. 3 takes away the effect of 2, and 4 doesn't do anything."*

We see that, as at substage IIA, these subjects begin by multiplying each element by g or by taking them all at once, but finally they spontaneously use two-by-two or three-by-three combinations (each time with g). This is the true innovation of this substage, since at substage IIA this type of combination had to be called forth by the experimenter. But the fact that these combinations are not systematic defines the upper limit of this substage: Tur, who is the most advanced of the cases cited, does not even attain the six possible two-by-two $(\times g)$ combinations.

As for the cause of the color, it is still sought in particular elements rather than in their combination; Tur locates the color in 1 only and misinterprets the roles of 2, 3, and 4. Others discover the negative effect of 4 but by direct (and fortuitous) formulation and without having a specific method of proof. . . .

Substage IIIA. Formation of Systematic n-by-n Combinations. The two innovations which appear at the formal level are the systematic method in the use of *n*-by-*n* combinations, and an understanding of the fact that the color is due to the combination as such:

Sar (12;3): "Make me some more yellow."—*Do you take the liquid from the yellow glass with all four?*"—"I won't tell you."—(He tries first with $4 \times 2 \times g$, then $2 \times g \times 4 \times g$) "*Not yet.* (He tries to smell the odor of the liquids, then tries $4 \times 1 \times g$) *No yellow yet. Quite a big mystery!* (He tries the four, then each one independently with *g*; then he spontaneously proceeds to various two-by-two combinations but has the feeling that he forgot some of them.) *I'd better write it down to remind myself:* 1×4 *is done;* 4×3 *is done; and* 2×3. *Several more that I haven't done* (he finds all six, then adds the drops and finds the yellow for $1 \times 3 \times g$). *Ah! it's turning yellow. You need* 1, 3, *and the drops.*"—"Where is the yellow?"— . . . "In there?" (*g*)—"*No, they go together.*"—"And 2?"—"*I don't think it has any effect, it's water.*"—"And 4?"—"*It doesn't do anything either, it's water too. But I want to try again; you can't ever be too sure* (he tries $2 \times 4 \times g$). *Give me a glass of water* (he takes it from the faucet and mixes $3 \times 1 \times$ water $\times$ *g*—i.e., the combination which gave him the color, plus water from the faucet, knowing that $1 \times 2 \times 3 \times 4 \times g$ produces nothing). *No, it isn't water. Maybe it's a substance that keeps it from coloring* (he puts together $1 \times 3 \times 2 \times g$, then $1 \times 3 \times 4 \times g$) *Ah! There it is! That one* (4) *keeps it from coloring.*"—"And that?" (2).—"*It's water.*"

Cha (13;0): "*You have to try with all the bottles. I'll begin with the one at the end* (from 1 to 4 with *g*). *It doesn't work any more. Maybe you have to mix them* (he tries $1 \times 2 \times g$, then $1 \times 3 \times g$). *It turned yellow. But are there other solutions?* . . .

We see the complete difference in attitude between these subjects and those at substage IIB, in spite of the fact that the latter attempt some *n*-by-*n* combinations. The new attitude found at substage IIIA can be noticed both in the combinatorial methods adopted and in the reasoning itself.

From the point of view of method, two achievements are worthy of note. The first is the establishment of a systematic *n*-by-*n* combinatorial system complete for the numbers involved in this experiment. For example Sar, who is afraid of forgetting certain associations, makes out a written list, and Cha works out the six two-by-two combinations without hesitation. . . . The second achievement is just as important from the point of view of the utilization of these combinations (for it is obviously the needs linked to this use or, in other words, functional considerations which determine the completion of the corresponding structure): once the combination $1 \times 3 \times g$ which brings about the color is found, the subject, not satisfied with a single solution to the problem, does not stop there but looks for others. Thus his main interest is not success by the intermediary of a particular combination but an understanding of the role which this combination plays among the total number of possible combinations.

This leads us to the advances made in reasoning. The way subjects use combinatorial operations demonstrates that they are not concerned with particular mathematical operations at this point (moreover, the required operations have not yet been taken up in class by these subjects); but certainly we are dealing with a general logical structure, analogous to that of the multiplicative groupings utilized at substage IIA and tending to round out the structure after substage IIB.

At the same time as they combine the factors involved in the experiment among themselves (the liquids presented in the four flasks), stage III subjects form their judgments according to a combinatorial system having the same form, that of the sixteen binary propositions (combinations one-by-one, two-by-two, three-by-three, four, or zero of the four base possibilities $p \cdot q \vee p \cdot \bar{q} \vee \bar{p} \cdot q \vee \bar{p} \cdot \bar{q}$). In other words, when these subjects combine factors in the experiment, by the same token they generate a combinatorial system which corresponds to the observed facts. This is how they determine the links of conjunction, implication, exclusion, etc., by means of which they interpret the experimentally established combinations. Moreover, this fact explains the progress—correlated with that of the combinatorial operations themselves—which is noted in their deductive reasoning and in the formulation of verbal statements.

This reasoning bears on elements 2 and 4 in particular. Element 2 is judged neutral because it is sometimes present, sometimes absent, in a colored combination as well as in others. If p designates the presence of color and q the presence of element 2, then the subject sees that one can have:

$$(p \cdot q) \vee (p \cdot \bar{q}) \vee (\bar{p} \cdot q) \vee (\bar{p} \cdot \bar{q}) = (p * q), \qquad (1)$$

thus excluding the possibility of any positive or negative effect for 2: "It's water," conclude Sar and Cha. On the other hand, between liquid 4 and the color there is reciprocal exclusion or incompatibility, as Cha says clearly:

$$(p \cdot \bar{q}) \vee (\bar{p} \cdot q) = (p \vvv q), \text{ or} \qquad (2)$$
$$(p \cdot \bar{q}) \vee (\bar{p} \cdot q) \vee (\bar{p} \cdot \bar{q}) = p/q \qquad (3)$$

(where q now designates liquid 4).

But, from the fact that he has formulated the association $p \cdot q$ (in combinations 1×4; 3×4; etc.), at first Sar believes that 4 is neutral, just as is 2, so he replaces 2 with 4 in a combination ($1 \times 3 \times 2 \times g$) and perceives that $1 \times 3 \times 4 \times g$ fades, whence the associations $(p \cdot \bar{q}) \vee (\bar{p} \cdot q)$ which characterize reciprocal exclusion.

Secondly, this formal mode of reasoning—i.e., founded on the combinations of factors and consequently on combinations of the statements themselves—naturally leads the subject to a new conception of the cause of the color. This cause is no longer sought in one or another of the elements but in their being brought together—or, more precisely, in the very fact of their combination. For example, Sar refuses to locate the color in g because "they go together" (= it's the whole [mixture] $1 \times 3 \times g$ as such which is the cause); Cha refers to elements which make "or don't make any color together"; and another subject, Sie (12;6), declares: "This one (3), joined to 1 and to g, gives the color: 3 all alone does nothing and 1 alone does nothing either." From this, if p, q and r = the statements concerning the effects of 1, 3, and g— and if x = the statement that the color appears:

$$x \supset (p \cdot q \cdot r) \text{ and no longer } x \subset r. \ldots \qquad (4)$$

Substage IIIB. Equilibration of the System. In [this] experiment the difference between substages IIIA and IIIB is only one of degree, actually it is not at all necessary in this case to apply the method "all other things being equal," since the factors are already presented in a dissociated state. Thus, the only innovations of substage IIIB are that the combinations, and more particularly the proofs, appear in a more systematic fashion—i.e., this level appears as a point of equilibrium in relation to the preceding level which is a phase of organization:

Eng (14;6) begins with $2 \times g$; $1 \times g$; $3 \times g$; and $4 \times g$: *"No, it doesn't turn yellow. So you have to mix them."* He goes on to the six two-by-two combinations and at last hits $1 \times 3 \times g$: *"This time I think it works."*— "Why?"—*"It's 1 and 3 and some water."*—"You think it's water?"—*"Yes, no difference in odor. I think that it's water."*—"Can you show me?"—He replaces g with some water: $1 \times 3 \times$ water. *'No, it's not water. It's a chemical product: it combines with 1 and 3 and then it turns into a yellow liquid* (he goes on to three-by-three combinations beginning with the replacement of g by 2 and by 4—i.e., $1 \times 3 \times 2$ and $1 \times 3 \times 4$). *No, these two products aren't the same as the drops: they can't produce color with 1 and 3* (then he tries $1 \times 3 \times g \times 2$). *It stays the same with 2. I can try right away with 4* ($1 \times 3 \times g \times 4$). *It turns white again: 4 is the opposite of g because 4 makes the color go away while g makes it appear."*—"Do you think that there is water in (any of the) bottles?"—*"I'll try* (he systematically replaces 1 and 3 by water, trying $1 \times g \times$ water and $3 \times g \times$ water, having already tried $1 \times 3 \times$ water). *No, that means 3 isn't water and 1 isn't water."* He notices that the glass $1 \times 3 \times g \times 2$ has stayed clearer than $1 \times 3 \times g$. *"I think 2 must be water. Perhaps 4 also?* (He tries $1 \times 3 \times g \times 4$ again) *So it's not water: I had forgotten that it turned white; 4 is a product that makes the white return."*

Thus the results are the same as in IIIA (save that the neutral character of 2 had not been established systematically at the earlier level). But they are discovered by a more direct method because, from the start, the experiment is organized with an eye to proof. This method may be described as a generalization of substitution and addition. For example, having established the fact that the color is due to $1 \times 3 \times g$, the subject replaces g by 2 then by 4 to see if they play equivalent roles; then he immediately goes back to $1 \times 3 \times g$ and adds 2 and 4 alternately to the mixture in order to determine the effects of these additions. But it should be understood clearly that substitution as well as addition is already operating in the stage IIIA combinatorial system. When the subject constructs the combinations 1×2, 1×3, and 1×4, the very construction of these associations implies the substitution of 3 and then of 4 for 2; and when he makes the transition from two-by-two to three-by-three combinations, he adds the alternative elements 3 and 4 to a given couple (for example 1×2)—i.e., $1 \times 2 \times 3$ and $1 \times 2 \times 4$. Moreover, as we have seen, substage IIIA subjects already use these substitutions and additions to prove certain effects. Thus, the only innovation appearing at substage IIIB is the greater speed with which the subject understands the use he may make of these substitutions and additions in the determination of the respective effects of the elements during the actual construction of these combinations. Thus, first and foremost, progress is to be sought in the organization of the proof and in the integration of methods of discovery and methods of proof. From the start, the combinatorial system becomes an instrument of conclusive deduction.

On a more general level, the lesson to be drawn from this experiment is that it points up the close correlation that exists between the mode of organization or the overall structure of the combinatorial operations on the one hand and those of the formal or interpropositional operations on the other. At the same time that the subject combines the elements or factors given in the experimental context, he also combines the propositional statements which express the results of these combinations of facts and in this way mentally organizes the system of binary operations consisting in conjunctions, disjunctions, exclusions, etc. But this coincidence is not so surprising when we realize that the two phenomena are essentially identical. The system of propositional operations is in fact a combinatorial system, just as from the subject's point of view the only purpose of the combinatorial operations applied to the experimental data is to make it possible for him to establish such logical connections. Nevertheless, we had to show empirically that such an intimate relationship between the combinatorial operations and the propositional operations does exist. In order to do this we have had to examine the reactions of the child and the adolescent to an experimental situation that did not impose either kind of operation by any sort of instructions but in which they would have to be discovered and organized in a completely natural and spontaneous way.

Equilibrium in the Balance*

In a problem using a simple balance-type weighing instrument, a seesaw balance, we find the operational schema of equilibrium between action and reaction. The experiment was set up in a way that would force the question of proportionality. When two unequal weights W and W' are balanced at unequal distances from an axis L and L', the amounts of work WH and $W'H'$ needed to move them to heights H and H' corresponding to these distances are equal. Thus, we have the double (inverse) proportion:

$$W/W' = L'/L = H'/H$$

The result is that finding the law presupposes the construction of the proportion $W/W' = L'/L$ and spelling out its explanation implies an understanding of the proportion $W/W' = H'/H$. It seemed to us that it would be interesting to study how this proportionality schema develops as it is linked with the equilibrium schema. As a result of previous research we know that in all realms (space, speed, chance, etc.) the notion of proportions does not appear until formal substage IIIA. Now we are going to find out why this is so.

Stage I. Failure to Distinguish Between Subject's Action and External Process (IA) Followed by Integration of Intuitions in Direction of Compensation of Weights (IB). From about 3 to 5 years, subjects give responses which, given our interests, are instructive. As we have said before, in general causality is an assimilation of external processes either to the subject's own actions or to his operations, but with the delegation [attribution] of one or the other to reality itself. In the case of an apparatus such as a balance scale, the notion of an equilibrium between

*With the collaboration of F. Matthieu, former research assistant, Institut des Sciences de l'Education, and J. Nicolas. In reference to the same subject, see the previous study of Mme. Refia Ugurel-Semin, *Istanbul University Yayinlari*, 110 (1940), pp. 77–211. [The following section is from Chapter XI.]

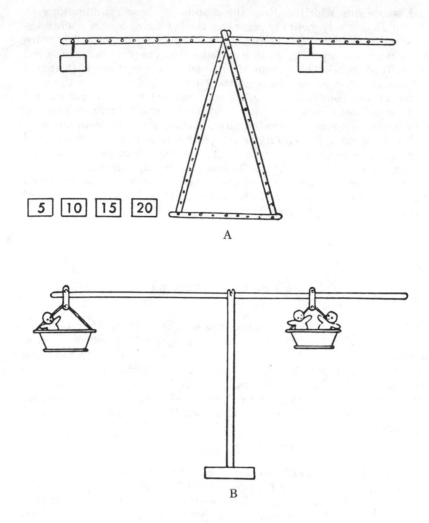

Figure 3

The balance scale is here shown in two forms: (A) a conventional balance with varying weights which can be hung at different points along the cross-bar; (B) a balance equipped with baskets which can be moved along the crossbar to different points and in which dolls are used as weights.

one's body weight and other weights is constructed very early, but the notion is undifferentiated and extends beyond weight itself to include the muscular force of an upward or even a downward push. Weight is thought to be linked with the actions of pushing up or pressing down. The balance is first assimilated to this sort of undifferentiated action and not to a system of compensation operations between weights nor a fortiori to weight × length. In fact, no form of concrete operations exists at this level for there are only representational regulations—i.e., instruments of global compensation without systematic reversibility. The result of this situation is that the substage IA subjects cannot guarantee equilibrium simply by distributing weights but intrude in the working of the apparatus with their *own* actions, which they fail to distinguish from the actions of the *objects* that they are trying to control.

. . . The lack of differentiation does not preclude his making predictions about some more or less constant effects. The most striking aspect of these predictions is their negative aspect. For example, at this level the child does not yet think that equilibrium implies the equality of weights (even at equal distances); thus Mar puts two weights on one side and none on the other in order to attain the horizontal. The heavy side moves upward and the light one downward, as well as the reverse. The relationship between weights is not formulated; the epithet "too heavy" may be applied to a single weight suspended to one arm without its counterpart, "too light," being used. There is no conservation of weight. The subject tries constantly to repeat with new weights what he has just accomplished by chance with others, without paying any attention to differences in weight. However, through improved regulation these subjects come to see that weight has a relative influence. Generally they suspend at least one weight [on] each side for purposes of symmetry. Often they add new weights to the others to improve the equilibrium, but they add them not to the side where weight is lacking (which would tend to equalize the weights) but to the side where the weight already is largest with the idea that several weights will improve the situation.

But the adding characteristic of this level is not yet operational. Although it does constitute the beginning of the additive operation, the operation is not achieved because of lack of equalization between parts $(A + A')$ and the whole B (compensating $A + A'$ on the other arm). Most important, it is not an operation, because reversibility is lacking; at this point elements are not removed with the deliberate aim of equalizing the weights. When the subject removes a weight, it is only in order to try a new and different course of action after earlier attempts have failed.

Generally, the subject is not concerned with the question of the distances from the axis and does not look for any equality or coordination between the distances and the weight. Nevertheless, operations may start to take form here in that the subject may establish a preliminary form of symmetry. Once again this is not an operation in the strict sense. First, coordination with the weight is lacking; secondly, this symmetry is related generally to the two extremities of the arms and does not include equalizations for the intermediate distances.

In contrast, from about 5 to 7–8 years (substage IB) one can see increasing integration of these intuitive representations moving toward reversible operations.

Mal (5;8) notes that the arms are not horizontal: *"You have to put another* (weight) *on the other side. I know what has to be done; put still another one there because there isn't any weight here* (she adds it). *These here must be lighter than those over there. You have to take two that have the same weight."* Next: *You could take one off"* (because it is too heavy on one side). Mal does not spontaneously discover the influence of distance, but when a weight is moved in front of her she says: *"You brought that one up closer, that makes more weight. If it were at the end, it wouldn't work and there it makes more weight."* . . .

Thus, from this point on the child understands that weight is needed on both sides to achieve a balance and even that the weights should be approximately equal. But he does not yet know how to proceed toward this equalization in a systematic way. Similarly, henceforth he succeeds in adding and subtracting, but without accurate equalizations. His actions are successive corrections (thus regulations) and are not yet strictly reversible.

We see how these two sorts of regulations—by equalizations and by addition or subtraction—furnish the starting point for future transformations by reciprocity (symmetries) and by inversion, relative to the weight. As for the distances, there is progress in the tendency toward symmetry (the weights are no longer put at equal distances only at the extremities but also in the region close to the axis). Sometimes the subject discovers the role played by changes in distance (cf. Mal). But there are as yet no systematic correspondences of the type further = heavier.

Substage IIA. Concrete Operations Performed on Weight and Distance but Without Systematic Coordination Between Them. From this point on, weights are equalized and added exactly, while distances are added and made symmetrical. But coordination between weights and distances as yet goes no further than intuitive regulations. The subject discovers by trial-and-error that equilibrium between a smaller weight at a greater distance and a greater weight at a smaller distance is possible, but he does not yet draw out general correspondences:*

Mas (7;7) begins with E_3 and D_3, then replaces them with G_3 and F_3 (thus equal distance and an attempt to find equal weights), adds two other weights, takes off some, then all, and finally weighs two equal weights (E) in his hands, counts equal numbers of holes (14) and places E_{14} at each side. Afterward he looks for other forms of equilibrium; he adds the weights, moves them, takes off some, and finally has GED on one side and P_3 on the other: *"That's it* (empirical compensation of weight and distances). *It's just like when there weren't any* (when the arms were horizontal without weight); *it's the same weight on each side."* He begins again with large weights (for which there are no matched pairs). *"I should have put one on each side. Since there aren't any, I had to put three on one side and two on the other. It stays straight because it's the same weight on each side."* He predicts that equal distances are necessary for two unequal weights, but he does not find the law: heavier $\rightleftarrows$ nearer.—"If you put on C and E, where would you have to place them?"—"*I would say one hole and another hole* (= two different distances), *but they shouldn't go the same way* (at equal distances) *or it wouldn't make the same weight."*

Nem (7;4) discovers empirically that C on the left at a distance of 10 balances E on the right at a distance of 5. We ask him to place C on the right

*From now on we will indicate objects of increasing weight by the letters *A, B, C,* etc. Increasing distances (which are measured for the child at three equidistant points where the hooks for the weights are attached) are indicated by the numbers 1, 2, 3, etc.

and E on the left, but he does not succeed in inverting the distance relationship. After the experiment, he exclaims, *"Ah! You have to do the same thing as before but in the opposite way!"*

Thus, from this point on the subject can order serially the weights he comes across as well as determine whether they are equal. He can add them in a reversible manner and correctly compare one pair of weights with another pair. What is more, he knows how to make use of the transitiveness of the relations of the equality or inequality of the weights. Moreover, all these operations reappear when he compares distances, but with the additional correspondence between distances oriented in opposite directions (symmetries relative to the axis).

On the other hand, in the case of unequal weights A_1 and B_2 and of unequal distances L_x and L_y, coordination is not yet possible at substage IIA. Even when the subject discovers by experimentation that a large weight at a small distance to the right of the axis balances a small weight at a large distance to the left, he does not know how to invert these relations from one side to the other and discovers too late that he should have "done the same thing but in the opposite way" (Nem).

Substage IIB. Inverse Correspondence of Weights and Distances. The example just described (unequal weights and distances) is resolved at substage IIB, not yet by metric proportions . . . but by qualitative correspondences bordering on the equilibrium law: "The heavier it is, the closer to the middle."

Fis (10;7) sees that P does not balance F *"because it's heavy: that one (F) is too light."*—"What should be done?"—*"Move it forward* (he moves P toward the axis and attains equilibrium). *I had to pull it back from 16 holes* (arbitrary) *to see if it would lower twice* (arbitrary) *the weight."*—"What do you mean by that?"—*"It raises the weight."*—"And if you put it back over there?" (moves P away).—*"It would make the other one go up."*—"And if you put it at the end?" (P).—*"It would go up still more"* (F), etc. Conclusion: When you have two unequal weights *"you move up the heaviest"* (toward the median axis). But Fis does not measure the lengths even for the relations of 1 to 2. . . .

The difference between these reactions and those of substage IIA is clear. At the earlier stage, when the subject comes across two weights which do not come into equilibrium, he works mostly with substitutions —additions or subtractions. In this way he achieves certain equalizations by displacement, but only exceptionally and by groping about (regulations). On the other hand, at the present stage the subject who comes to two unequal weights tries to balance them by means of an oriented displacement on the hypothesis that the same object "will weigh more" at a greater distance from the axis and less when brought closer to it. He is working toward the law, but without metrical proportions and by simple qualitative correspondences.

Thus, the new operation mediating the determination of the conditions of equilibrium is a double serial ordering of weights $A < B < C <$ . . . and distances $L_1 > L_2 > L_3 > $ . . . but with bi-univocal inverse correspondences:

$$
\begin{array}{ccc}
A & < B & < C < \ldots \\
\updownarrow & \updownarrow & \updownarrow \\
L_1 & > L_2 & > L_3 > \ldots
\end{array}
\qquad (5)
$$

which can be translated into reciprocities (expressed in the language of relational multiplication):

$$(A \times L_1) = (B \times L_2) = (C \times L_3) = \ldots, \text{etc.} \qquad (6)$$

But it is clear that such qualitative operations are inadequate to establish the law. The logical multiplications of type (6) allow some inferences but leave certain cases indeterminate:

> heavier × same distance = greater force,
> less heavy × same distance = less great force,
> same weight × further (from the axis) = greater force,
> same weight × less far = less great force; but $\qquad$ (7)
> heavier × further = indeterminate,
> less heavy × less far = indeterminate; and
> heavier × less far = less heavy × further
> (but only under certain metrical conditions).

At this level the subject can quantify the weights (he knows that $B = 2A$; etc.) as well as the distances (measurable by the number of holes). Given these facts, why must we await formal stage III before the schema of proportions is organized? We might say that it is a matter of book-learning, but, in contradiction, we are able to present some examples (analogous to those which we have already published elsewhere*) in which the proportionality schema is organized before any academic knowledge enters. Thus, it is probable that this schema requires, as a necessary and sufficient condition, a qualitative operational system that is both differentiated and unified, analogous to the INRC group. . . .

Stage III. Discovery and Explanation of the Law. When the experimenter restricts himself to a procedure such as the foregoing, where the subject is allowed to hang the weights simultaneously on the two arms of the balance, subjects start to discover the law at substage IIIA. It takes the form of the proposition $W/W' = L'/L$ (where W and W' are two unequal weights and L and L' the distances at which they are placed); this law is so immediately obvious that it does not give rise to a particular causal explanation even during substage IIIB. ("It's a system of compensations," as Chal will tell us.) But, when the experiment proceeds by successive and alternate suspensions of the weights, the subject's attention turns to the inclinations and the distances in height to be covered; this may lead him to an explanation in terms of equal amounts of work (displacement of forces). It is true that, although this explanation is already possible at substage IIIA, it is only rarely appears before substage IIIB. Nevertheless we have observed it in several cases and think it worth analyzing.

First, we will present a case of the discovery of the law at substage IIIA:

Rog (12;11): for a weight P placed at the very tip of one arm (28 holes), he puts $C + E$ in the middle of the other arm, measures the distances, and says: *"That makes 14 holes. It's half the length. If the weight $(C + E)$ is*

*See Piaget and Inhelder, *The Child's Conception of Space*, Chapter XII, no. 9; Piaget, *The Child's Conception of Movement and Speed*, Chapter IX, nos. 2 and 3; Piaget and Inhelder, *The Origin of the Idea of Chance in Children*, Chapter VI, nos. 5 and 6.

halved, that duplicates" (P).—"How do you know that you have to bring the weight toward the center?" (to increase the weight).—"*The idea just came to me, I wanted to try. If I bring it in half way, the value of the weight is cut in half. I know, but I can't explain it. I haven't learned.*"—"Do you know other similar situations?"—"*In the game of marbles, if five play against four, the last one of the four has the right to an extra marble.*" He also discovers that for two distances of 1 and ¼ you have to use weights 1 and 4; that for two distances of 1 and ⅓ you need weights 1 and 3, etc.: "*You put the heaviest weight on the portion that stands for the lightest weight* (which corresponds to the lightest weight), *going from the center.*"

The rapidity with which the subject makes the transition from the qualitative correspondence to the metrical proportion seems at first to indicate the presence of an anticipatory schema. However, the analogy that the subject established between the balance and the game of marbles shows that this schema is taken from notions of reciprocity or of compensation. So we have to examine how, starting with substage IIIB, the subjects proceed from the same conception to a search for an *explanation* in the strict sense of the term (with the apparatus using alternate suspensions): . . .

Sam (13;8) discovers immediately that the horizontal distance is inversely related to weight.—"How do you explain that?"—"*You need more force to raise weights placed at the extremes than when it's closer to the center . . . because it has to cover a greater distance.*"—"How do you know?" —"*If one weight on the balance is three times the other, you put it a third of the way out because the distance* (upward) *it goes is three times less.*"— "But once you referred to the distance (horizontal gesture) and once to the path covered?"—"*Oh, that depends on whether you have to calculate it or whether you really understand it. If you want to calculate, it's best to consider it horizontally; if you want to understand it, vertically is better. For the light one* (at the extremity) *it changes more quickly, for the heavy one less quickly.*" . . .

These reactions, found at both substages of stage III, bring us back to the now familiar schemata of the INRC group. But, above all, they show us how the general equilibrium schema is differentiated in the present case by constructing the proportions $W/W' = L'/L$ and $W/W' = H'/H$. Thus we have two questions to discuss—first, how is the proportion schema organized; second, how does it relate to the INRC group?

In these responses the INRC group first appears in a form which we could have described earlier when dealing with the problem of the oscillations of a liquid in communicating vessels. One of the arms of a balance will lower when a weight is hung on it at a given distance from the axis; when an equal weight is placed on the other arm in a symmetrical position (= at the same distance from the axis as the first weight), this second arm will lower. "One goes up and then the other," says Chal [13;6], "and if it's inclined (below the horizontal plane) it comes back to the middle and goes down on the other side."

In other words, a reciprocal relation operates in this case ($p \supset \bar{q}$) $= R(q \supset \bar{p})$ in which p and q stand for the upward motion of the arms. But there is something new in the case of the balance: two·factors are operative and they compensate each other; operating alone, a weight W at a distance L produces the same inclination as a weight $W' = nW$ at a distance $L' = L/n$. Chal is astonished by this fact ("the same angles"), then finds it quite natural because "the distance is compensated by the weight."

. . . Two kinds of operations for reestablishing equilibrium can correspond to the operation in which a weight is placed on one of the arms at a given distance—the inverse N which consists of taking off this weight or the reciprocal R which consists of putting on equal weight at an equal distance on the other arm of the balance. Moreover, whereas the inverse N cancels the original operation, the reciprocal R compensates it without canceling it; still, N and R have the same final result—i.e., they bring the arms back into the horizontal plane. . . .

The Proportion Schema and the INRC Group. First, we should remember that an understanding of proportions does not appear until substage IIIA; this is true in all spheres and not only in the balance scale experiments. During substage IIB it has often been noted that subjects search for a common denominator of the two relations that they compare, but this common relation is thought to be additive. Thus, instead of the proportion $W/W' = L'/L$ one would have an equality of differences $W - W' = L' - L$. Clearly, the formation of the notion of proportions presupposes that [in place of] simple relations of difference [there] be substituted the notion of the equality of products $WL = W'L'$. But we must also note that the transition from the difference to the product rarely takes place from the start in a form that is metrical. The numerical quantification of the proportion is usually preceded by a qualitative schema based on a conception of logical product—i.e., by the idea that two factors acting together are equivalent to the action of two other factors added together. "The larger the distance, the smaller the weight," says Chal, using simple qualitative correspondence (cf. prop. [5]). But he adds, "They go together."

In other words a small weight combined with a great distance is equivalent to a large weight with a small distance. These logical multiplications are outlined at substage IIB (cf. props. [6] and [7]), but the subjects fail to generalize to all possible cases. Where does the generalization found at substages IIIA and IIIB come from? Without doubt, this is where the notions of compensation and reciprocity connected with the INRC group come in.

It is clear that when the subject at stage III becomes able to understand transformations by inversion (N) and reciprocity (R) and to group them into a single system (I, N, R, and NR = C), by the same token he becomes able to make use of the equality of products in a more general form than in the multiplication of relations (6) and (7). Moreover, this form already implies the notions of compensation and cancellation. The possibility of reasoning in terms of a group structure—INRC—indicates an understanding of the equalities NR = IC, RC = IN, NC = IR, etc., the equalities between the products of two transformations. The result is that the INRC group is itself equivalent to a system of logical proportions:

$$\frac{Ix}{Cx} = \frac{Nx}{Rx} \text{ or } \frac{Rx}{Ix} = \frac{Cx}{Nx}$$

since IN = RC (where x = the operation transformed by I, N, R, or C).

For example, let us examine the subjects' reasoning on the changes of weight and horizontal distance (to simplify notation we shall disregard the constant weights and distances). Let p be the statement of a fixed increase of weight and q of a fixed increase of distance; let us call $\bar{p}$ and $\bar{q}$ the propositions stating a corresponding diminution of weight and distance on the same arm of the balance. Propositions p' and q' correspond to p and q, and $\bar{p}'$ and $\bar{q}'$ correspond to p' and q' on the other arm. The subjects understand the following relations of inversion and reciprocity (the INRC group but with $p \cdot q$ chosen as the identical operation I):

I $(p \cdot q) =$ to increase simultaneously the weight and the distance on one of the arms;

N $(\bar{p} \, v \, \bar{q}) = (p \cdot \bar{q}) \, v \, (\bar{p} \cdot q) \, v \, (\bar{p} \cdot \bar{q}) =$ to reduce the distance while increasing the weight or diminish the weight while increasing the distance or diminish both;   (8)

R $(p' \cdot q')$ compensates I by increasing both weight and distance on the other arm of the balance;

C $(\bar{p}' \, v \, \bar{q}') = (p' \cdot \bar{q}') \, v \, (\bar{p}' \cdot q') \, v \, (\bar{p}' \cdot \bar{q}') =$ cancels R in the same way that N cancels I.

But, since R $(p' \cdot q')$ is equivalent to compensating action I $(p \cdot q)$ with a reaction (symmetry) on the other arm of the balance, we find that it can be written $\bar{p} \cdot \bar{q}$; and since $(\bar{p}' \, v \, \bar{q}')$ is also equivalent to compensating the action N by symmetry, we can write it $(p \, v \, q)$. Therefore proposition (8) can be formulated as follows:

$$
\begin{aligned}
&\text{I } (p \cdot q) \\
&\text{N } (\bar{p} \, v \, \bar{q}) \\
&\text{R } (\bar{p} \cdot \bar{q}) \\
&\text{C } (p \, v \, q).
\end{aligned}
\qquad (8a)
$$

The system of these transformations, which states only the equilibrium of weights and distances, is in itself equivalent to the proportionality:

$$
\frac{p \cdot q}{\bar{p} \cdot \bar{q}} = \frac{p \, v \, q}{\bar{p} \, v \, \bar{q}} \text{ thus } \frac{\text{I}x}{\text{R}x} = \frac{\text{C}x}{\text{N}x} \text{ (where } x = p \cdot q). \qquad (9)
$$

In other words, an understanding of the system of inversions and reciprocities (8) and (8a) follows directly from an understanding of this proportional relation; an increase of weight and distance on one arm of the balance is to the symmetrical increase on the other arm as an increase of weight or distance on one arm is to a reciprocal operation on the other.

Undoubtedly, this qualitative schema of logical proportions corresponds to the global intuition of proportionality with which the subject begins. And it is easy to pass on from this qualitative schema to more detailed logical proportions (involving a single proposition) and from there to numerical proportions.

In this respect, remember that, for a single proposition p, the correlative C is identical with I and the reciprocal R identical with N. From proportion (9) one can construct:

$$
\frac{p}{q} = \frac{\bar{q}}{\bar{p}}, \text{ whence } p \, v \, \bar{p} = q \, v \, \bar{q}. \qquad (10)
$$

In other words, the increase of weight is to the increase of distance as the decrease of distance is to the decrease of weight.

Secondly, beyond the direct proportions of types (9) and (10) the INRC group includes what can be called reciprocal proportions, where one of the cross-products is the reciprocal R of the other:

$$\frac{p \cdot q}{\bar{p} \cdot \bar{q}} = R \frac{\bar{p} \vee \bar{q}}{p \vee q}, \text{ thus}$$
$$[(p \cdot q) \cdot (p \vee q) = p \cdot q] = \tag{11}$$
$$R [(\bar{p} \cdot \bar{q}) \cdot (\bar{p} \vee \bar{q}) = \bar{p} \cdot \bar{q}].$$

Hence, by virtue of (10) and (11), the reciprocal proportion:

$$\frac{p}{q} = R \frac{\bar{p}}{\bar{q}}, \text{ thus } (p \cdot \bar{q}) = R (\bar{p} \cdot q). \tag{12}$$

The formulae demonstrate that the two logical proportions (11) and (12) are isomorphic to the numerical propositions which can be obtained by giving the same coefficient n either to an increase in weight (p) or to an increase in the distance (q). In other words, if $p = nW$ and $q = nL$, then:

$$\frac{p}{q} = \frac{\bar{p}}{\bar{q}} \text{ corresponds to } \frac{nW}{nL} = \frac{n:W}{n:L}, \text{ for example}$$
$$\frac{2 \times 4}{2 \times 8} = \frac{2:8}{2:4}; \tag{13}$$

and

$$\frac{p}{q} = R \frac{\bar{p}}{\bar{q}} \text{ corresponds to } \frac{nW}{nL} = \frac{W:n}{L:n}, \text{ for example}$$
$$\frac{2 \times 4}{2 \times 8} = \frac{4:2}{8:2}. \tag{14}$$

Formulae (9) to (14) may seem much too abstract to account for the actual reasoning of our subjects. Actually, this is in part an independent result of the symbolism which we have introduced; nevertheless this is how proportions are discovered. Before introducing numbers as measurements for weight and distance, the subject usually begins by assuming:

$$p \cdot \bar{q} = R (\bar{p} \cdot q) \tag{15}$$

(increasing the weight and reducing the distance on one of the arms is the same as reducing the weight and increasing the distance on the other arm).

However, proposition (15) is none other than proportion (12), which then implies (10) and (9) and leads to metrical proportion (14). Thus we are justified in considering the preceding formulae symbolic expressions of the actual reasoning of our subjects.

As for the proportion between weight and height, as soon as they encounter alternating suspensions in the apparatus all the subjects understand that an increase in distance (q) implies a determinate increase in height (r), thus:

$$q \gtrless r. \tag{16}$$

Consequently proportions (10) and (12) imply:

$$\frac{p}{r} = \frac{\bar{r}}{\bar{p}}, \tag{17}$$

and

$$\frac{p}{r} = R\frac{\bar{p}}{\bar{r}}. \tag{17a}$$

Finally, the transfer of a weight to a higher point constitutes work. This is expressed by our subjects in their own words, as they do not have the technical vocabulary of physics at their disposal: "There is more distance to pull" (Chal) or "More force to raise the weight" (Sam). Actually, if a heavy weight hung at a small distance from the axis balances a weight n times smaller at a distance n times larger, it is because the same amount of work is needed to raise the first to a given height and to raise the second to a level n times higher than that height. As Fis says, there is compensation "between the force and the height." This idea of an equivalent amount of work, half-understood during stage III, provides the explanation of the phenomenon of equilibrium. Since the reaction of these subjects is not completely spontaneous on this point, we must turn to the next experiment. There we replaced the overly simple apparatus of the balance scale with one for hauling a weight on an inclined plane; we can see from this experiment how the concept of work is elaborated beginning with the concrete substage IIB; and we can see how it is used in the explanations of the formal stage III.

[For the reader who may not have had an elementary course in physics we point out that a number of fundamental concepts must be distinguished from each other: work, force, energy, and power. Work is defined as the operation of a given force through a given distance $W = f \times d$. This simply means that it takes the same amount of work to lift a 100 lb. weight 1 foot as it takes to lift a 10 lb. weight 10 feet, or a 1 lb. weight 100 feet; in all three cases $f \times d = 100$ foot lb. But there is a psychological point which is even more important to bring out. Inhelder and Piaget do not intend to argue that the untutored adolescent necessarily "has" the concept of work in this form, but rather that he can develop it when confronted with a suitable problem under the circumstances permitting free and spontaneous thought because he has available the logical structures of formal operations. A similar qualification, of course, applies to all the physical concepts dealt with in this book.]

Random Variations and Correlations[*]

Problems of chance are relevant to the study of formal thought from two standpoints. In a general way, formal thought has the property of dealing with what is possible and not only with what is real. But the prob-

[*] With the collaboration of Vinh-Bang and S. Taponier, research assistant, Institut des Sciences de l'Education. [The following section is from Chapter XV.]

ability that an event will occur is nothing more than the relationship between the possible instances of an event and those which actually occur. Moreover, a probability estimate of relations or laws presupposes certain special operational instruments such as the calculation of "correlations" or "associations." In its simplest form, the notion of correlation is a formal operational schema related to those we have just studied—particularly the proportionality schema. The aim of this chapter is to analyze the two-sided problem of how subjects from 5 to 15 years react to chance fluctuations that occur during the experiments and how they construct the correlation schema.

RANDOM VARIATIONS

Nearly all the phenomena studied in the foregoing experiments involve chance fluctuations. We have emphasized elsewhere* that one of the essential tasks of experimental reasoning *or* induction is that of separating the deducible from the random. The earlier chapters have shown how the child and adolescent organize the deducible; now we shall examine how they react to chance and how they assimilate it to the deducible, though they do so indirectly through probability.

. . . The subject must first fit a probability law to the fluctuations. Secondly, he has to isolate the laws or causes of the phenomenon under study in spite of the fluctuations. But the first task is precisely the problem of the probability of random variations, and the second that of correlations.

Stage I. Neither Conservation nor Law of Distribution. At the preoperational level, the subjects' attitudes toward chance are paradoxical. They expect that under similar conditions given phenomena will be repeated either identically or in terms of a definite progression, etc. When they do realize that there are small fluctuations, they first deny the conservation of the relevant quantities (matter, etc.) and then conclude that the stopping points are completely arbitrary:

Mey (6;8), in the stopping-point problem, sees that the large aluminum ball stopped at a given point (20 cm.): "And if we throw it again, where will it go?"—*"Further"* (experiment: 21 cm.).—"And if you throw it again?"—*"A little further because it already went further."* (experiment: 19 cm.).—"Why did it stop there?"—*"Because the little flag* (that marks the stopping points) *is still there."*—"And if you throw it again?"—*"A little further because it goes a little further every time."* . . .

These responses are familiar ones in the protocols of the young children. They deny chance, but when faced with fluctuations they believe anything is possible or look for a hidden order (effect of the flag for Mey) or a temporary disorder masked by invisible reasons which have to be divined. In both cases, the subject's attitude is reinforced by his lack of notions of conservation; the box can become heavier in moving more quickly, the water can increase in quantity or weight, etc.

Stage II. Diffuse Probabilistic Responses (IIA) then Determination of a Zone of Distribution (IIB). After 7–8 years of age, the subject's responses are quite different. Not only does he cease to be surprised by variability, but his predictions often take it into account ("it will go

*See Piaget, *Introduction a l'épistémologie génétique*, Vol. 2, Chapter 6.

about the same place"). As usual, the appearance of the notion of chance is at first characterized by a generally negative attitude based on caution and a feeling that it is hard to make predictions:

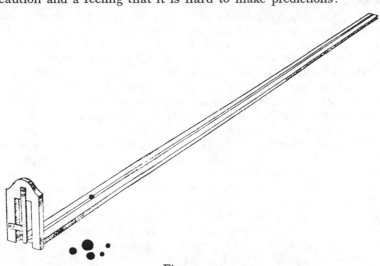

Figure 4

Conservation of motion in a horizontal plane is demonstrated with a spring device which launches balls of varying sizes. These roll on a horizontal plane, and the subjects are asked to predict their stopping points.

Bout (7;6): "If you throw it (the same ball on the horizontal plane) 10 or 20 times?"—"(It can get) *there* (1.60 m.), *there* (1.79), *or there*" (1.80). —"Do you think it will ever go all the way to the end?"—"No." . . .

CORRELATIONS

Thus, this latent correlation schema, which may be present at stage III, needs a more detailed analysis. To study it, we have devised an apparatus such that the subject can easily count the cases that confirm and those that fail to confirm a hypothesized relationship between two variables. It will allow us to see what relationships will be established between confirming and nonconfirming cases and if these relationships resemble any of the "association" formulae used in the calculation of correlations.

The problem set for the subjects involves simply a correlation between eye and hair color. Subjects are shown 40 cards, each with a face drawn on it. The eyes and the hair are colored according to the following four associations:

$$a = \text{blue eyes and blond hair} \quad (= p \cdot q),$$
$$b = \text{blue eyes and brown hair} \quad (= p \cdot \bar{q}),$$
$$c = \text{brown eyes and blond hair} \quad (= \bar{p} \cdot q),$$
$$d = \text{brown eyes and brown hair} \quad (= \bar{p} \cdot \bar{q}).$$

The subject is then given a set number of cards and asked whether he thinks there is a relationship between eye color and hair color (i.e., not whether there is such a relationship in real life, but whether one can be discovered in the given data). At the start, it is possible to proceed in either one of two different ways; one can let the subject form his own classification (construct the four boxes of a double-entry table) or give him the cards already classified according to the four possibilities. The latter method puts more emphasis on the possible numerical combinations. For example, we might apply combinations *abcd* to 4, 0, 0, and 4 faces respectively; or to 4, 4, 4, 4; 6, 6, 2, 2; or 13, 8, 3, 8; etc., asking the subject in each case to estimate the relevant relationships. In addition, the subject can be shown two different sets (i.e., 6, 4, 2, 4, and 4, 4, 4, 4) and asked which shows the clearest correlation. Finally, the subject can be asked to remove cards in such a way as to strengthen the correlation; then he can be asked to discuss which of the four associations he used as a basis for eliminating cards.

This is the experimental situation; it provides us with a number of interesting responses to examine from the standpoint of propositional logic—the only standpoint we are concerned with now—as opposed to questions of calculation or induction in the narrow sense of the term. If we let p stand for the presence of blue eyes and q for the presence of blond hair, cases favorable to the correlation will correspond to equivalence $(p \cdot q) \vee (\bar{p} \cdot \bar{q})$ and nonconfirming cases will correspond to reciprocal exclusion $(p \cdot \bar{q}) \vee (\bar{p} \cdot q)$. If one is to show a correlation one must first establish two classes of individuals, each class corresponding to the conditions stated in one of the two kinds of links we discussed, $(p = q)$ and $(p \, \vee\!\!\vee \, q)$; then, one has to determine the relationship between these two classes. . . .

Substage IIIA. Probabilistic Interpretation of Frequencies Considered in Isolation but Without Relating the $(a + d)$ Cases and the $(b + c)$ Cases. As we would expect, the substage IIIA subject can estimate probabilities as relationships between positive confirming cases and the cases which are possible relative to the characteristic under consideration. Consequently, he knows how to judge the chance that a given individual has blue eyes if he has blond hair by comparing the number of a cases to the number of b cases or the sum $a + b$. But in spite of this, he cannot yet add up the set of positive and negative confirming cases $(a + d)$ and relate them to the nonconfirming cases $(b + c)$ or to the set of all possible cases. Below are some examples:

Lyn (12;4): "Can you find a relationship between hair color and eye color in the cards?" (6, 0, 0, 6).*—"*Yes. These (d) have the same color eyes as hair.*"—"But for the group as a whole (all of the cards are shown), is there a relationship between the color of the eyes and the hair?"—"No."— "Here?" (d).—"*Here it's only brown.*"—"And here?" (a).—"*It's blue. They are all blue.*"—"And here (6, 2, 4, 4), is there a relationship?"—"No. Yes, the four (subsets) *separately, but not when they are together.*"—"Why?"— "*Because some are yellow* (blond) *and blue, and some yellow and brown.*"— "And like that?" (4, 4, 4, 4,).—"*You have more chances here; they are all 4. There if you go wrong, there are* 2 (b) *while here there are 4 and 4*" (indicates a and b).—"How many chances do you have of finding blond hair if you only see blue eyes?"—"*Four and 4; the chance is the same*" (a and b).

She is given all the cards to classify; she does it immediately according to the four associations. Then she is asked to form two groups so that the chances are higher of finding a relationship between eye color and hair color in one than in the other. She gives 3, 3, 4, 4 and 3, 6, 6, 4:

*The number of cards in each set corresponding to the four possible combinations are indicated in the order, *a, b, c, d.*

"The chances are higher here (3, 3, 4, 4) *because you have 3 and 3, and 4 and 4, while there, 6 and 4, and 6 and 3."* In other words, although Lyn has organized the sets correctly, she organized them and justified her view by reasoning about relations a/b and c/d and not in terms of the diagonal relations $(a + d) / (b + c)$. . . .

These cases suffice to bring out the two main difficulties that stand in the way of the substage IIIA subjects. The first, shown clearly in Lyn's case, is that when she encounters the four combinations a $(= p \cdot q)$, b $(= p \cdot \bar{q})$, c $(= \bar{p} \cdot q)$ and d $(= \bar{p} \cdot \bar{q})$, she has no difficulty in understanding the relationship between brown hair and brown eyes or between blond hair and blue eyes, but she does not understand that it is the same or the reciprocal relationship $(p \cdot q$ and $\bar{p} \cdot \bar{q})$. She places the a cases in opposition to the b cases and the d cases in opposition to the c cases without seeing that the a and d cases reinforce each other and form a single whole—i.e., composed of the cases which are favorable to a *general* relationship between eye and hair color.

A second difficulty stems from the same source as the first but its effect lasts longer. Once the subject sees that cases a and d confirm the relationship he seeks, and that cases b and c oppose it, he does not calculate the ratio of confirming cases to nonconfirming or to possible cases by comparing the sum $(a + d)$ to the sum $(b + c)$. Instead, unless he is limited to one of the pairs (either ab or cd, neglecting the other), he compares only a to b and d to c. For example, when Mor compares the two equal ratios $(8 + 8 / 4 + 4$ and $11 + 5 / 1 + 7)$ he finds the second more favorable because he compares $1 / 11$ to $4 / 8$. Lyn does the same when she limits herself to the relationships between a and b and d and c.

One of the interesting facets of the reasoning from relations ab or cd rather than from diagonals ad and bc is the reaction of the subjects [when the total number of confirming cases is equal to the total number of nonconfirming cases]: $ad = bc$. The subjects are a long way from understanding that the correlation is exactly zero in such cases. On the contrary, at this level they tend to assign them special importance, because when they reason about a and b only (or d and c only), the positive and negative chances are equal.

In contrast, toward the end of substage IIIA, we find a level intermediate between IIIA and IIIB in which the subject gradually comes to the diagonal relationship and begins to consider combined probabilities $(a + d)$ and $(b + c)$ even though he starts off with the same kind of reasoning found at substage IIIA. Below are some examples:

Bab (14;3) when he is given the set (5, 2, 1, 4) says: *"There are several with blond hair and blue eyes, but there are others too"* (he shows cases b, d, and c in order).—"Is there a relationship?"—*"There's a relationship anyway; most of the ones who have blue eyes have blond hair and most of the ones who have brown eyes have brown hair."*—"How many chances do you have of being right?"—*"In this group (a) 5 chances and here (d and c) 4 chances of being right and 1 of being wrong."*—"And on the whole?"—*"Three chances out of 12 of being wrong* [thus $(b + c)/(a + b + c + d)$]* . . . 3·chances out of 12."*

"And here?" (6, 0, 0, 6).—*"You have an equal number of chances. . . . No, you will always be right."*—"And there?" (5, 1, 3, 3)—*"One chance in 12 of being wrong; no, there are those too (c); no, 4 chances in 12."*—"In

*[Brackets in original.]

which of these two groups (5, 2, 1, 4 and 5, 1, 3, 3) are you most likely to be right?"—*"The same: 5 and 5* (he counts the *a* cases). *It doesn't make any difference."*—"And how many chances of being wrong?"—*"Three chances in 12 and 4 chances in 12."*

"And in these two groups?" (4, 2, 2, 4 and 3, 3, 1, 5).—He classifies the cards, then compares the *a* cases with each other and the *d* cases with each other, then counts the whole: *"Four out of 12 come out wrong here and there!"* Finally he is asked to form a set such that no prediction can be made. He chooses 1, 1, 1, 1, then 2, 2, 2, 2, etc.; he must understand that the correlation is zero in such cases. . . .

One can see how much progress has been made since the beginning of substage IIIA. Although Bab begins by reasoning about the blue eyes (*a*) independently of the brown (*d* cases), he soon realizes that the *a* and *d* cases make up a single whole confirming the same law, as opposed to the *b* and *c* cases which oppose it. . . . But there is still a tendency, of varying strength, to reason about either the *a* and *b* or the *c* and *d* cases in isolation. . . . But as soon as they are reminded of the totality of possible cases, the subjects of this intermediate level start to compare the (*a* + *d*) cases added to the (*b* + *c*) cases or (*a* + *b* + *c* + *d*). This addition marks the appearance of the idea of correlation in the strict sense of the word. The distinctive feature of substage IIIB is that the subjects succeed in performing it at the start and spontaneously.

Adolescent Thinking*

It is surprising that in spite of the large number of excellent works which have been published on the affective and social life of the adolescent . . . so little work has appeared on the adolescent's *thinking*. . . .

From the standpoint of logical structures, [the present] work seems to imply that the thinking of the adolescent differs radically from that of the child: The child develops concrete operations and carries them out on classes, relations, or numbers. But their structure never goes beyond the level of elmentary logical "groupings" or additive and multiplicative numerical groups. During the concrete stage, he comes to utilize both of the complementary forms of reversibility (inversion for classes and numbers and reciprocity for relations), but he never integrates them into the single total system found in formal logic. In contrast, the adolescent superimposes propositional logic on the logic of classes and relations. Thus, he gradually structures a formal mechanism (reaching an equilibrium point at about 14–15 years) which is based on both the lattice structure and the group of four transformations. This new integration allows him to bring inversion and reciprocity together into a single whole. As a result, he comes to control not only hypothetico-deductive reasoning and experimental proof based on the variation of a single factor with the others held constant but also a number of operational schemata which he will use repeatedly in experimental and logico-mathematical thinking.

*[The following section is from Chapter XVIII.]

But there is more to thinking than logic. Our problem now is to see whether logical transformations fit the general modifications of thinking which are generally agreed—sometimes explicitly but often implicitly—to typify adolescence. We should like to show briefly not only that they do but also that the structural transformation is like a center from which radiate the various more visible modifications of thinking which take place in adolescence.

However, we must begin by eliminating a possible source of ambiguity. We take as the fundamental problem of adolescence the fact that the individual begins to take up adult roles. From such a standpoint, puberty cannot be considered the distinctive feature of adolescence. On the average, puberty appears at about the same ages in all races and in all societies. . . . But the age at which adult roles are taken up varies considerably among societies and even among social milieus. For our purposes, the essential fact is this fundamental social transition.

Thus we will not attempt to relate formal thinking to puberty. There are, of course, a number of links between the rise of formal structures and transformations of affective life which we shall consider in greater detail presently. But these relations are complex and are not one-way affairs. Even at this point, our thinking would be muddled before we started if we wished to reduce adolescence to the manifestations of puberty. For example, one would then have to say that love appears only in adolescence; but there are children who fall in love and, in our societies, what distinguishes an adolescent in love from a child in love is that the former generally complicates his feelings by constructing a romance or by referring to social or even literary ideals of all sorts. But the fabrication of a romance or the appeal to various collective role models is neither the direct product of the neuro-physiological transformations of puberty nor the exclusive product of affectivity. Both are also indirect and specific reflections of the general tendency of adolescents to construct theories and make use of the ideologies that surround them. And this general tendency can only be explained by taking into account the two factors which we will find in association over and over again—the transformations of thought and the assumption of adult roles. The latter involves a total restructuring of the personality in which the intellectual transformations are parallel or complementary to the affective transformations.

Even though the appearance of formal thought is not a direct consequence of puberty, could we not say that it is a manifestation of cerebral transformations due to the maturation of the nervous system and that these changes do have a relation, direct or indirect, with puberty? Given that in our society the 7–8-year-old child (with very rare exceptions) cannot handle the structures which the 14–15-year-old adolescent can handle easily, the reason must be that the child does not possess a certain number of coordinations whose dates of development are determined by stages of maturation. . . . It seems clear that the development of formal structures in adolescence is linked to maturation of cerebral structures. [But] the exact form of linkage is far from simple, since the organization of formal structures must depend on the social milieu as well. The age of about 11–12 years, which in our society we found to mark the beginning of formal thinking, must be extremely relative, since the logic of the so-called primitive societies appears to be without such structures. Moreover, the history of formal structures is linked to the evolution of culture and collective representations as well as [to] their ontogenetic history. Since Greek adults became aware of some of these structures only in their logical and mathematical reflection, it is probable that the Greek children were behind our own. Thus the age of 11–12 years may be, beyond the neurological factors, a product of a progressive acceleration of individual development under the influence of education, and perhaps nothing stands in the way of a further reduction of the average age in a more or less distant future.

In sum, far from being a source of fully elaborated "innate ideas," the maturation of the nervous system can do no more than determine the totality of possibilities and impossibilities at a given stage. A particular social environment remains indispensable for the realization of these possibilities. . . .

. . . We [may well] wonder whether the individual manifestations of formal thinking are not simply imposed by the social group as a result of home and school education. But the psychological facts allow us to reject this hypothesis of complete social determinism. Society does not act on growing individuals simply by external pressure, and the individual is not, in relation to the social any more than to the physical environment, a simple tabula rasa on which social constraint imprints ready-made knowledge. For, if the social milieu is really to influence individual brains, they have to be in a state of readiness to assimilate its contributions. . . .

Two observations arise out of this circular process which characterizes all exchanges between the nervous system and society. The first is that the formal structures are neither innate a priori forms of intelligence which are inscribed in advance in the nervous system, nor are they collective representations which exist ready-made outside and above the individual. Instead, they are forms of equilibrium which gradually settle on the system of exchanges between individuals and the physical milieu and on the system of exchanges [among] individuals themselves. Moreover, in the final analysis the two systems can be reduced to a single system seen from two different perspectives. . . .

The second observation is that between the nervous system and society there is individual activity—i.e., the sum of the experience of an individual in learning to adapt to both physical and social worlds. If formal structures are laws of equilibrium and if there is really a functional activity specific to the individual, we would expect adolescent thinking to show a series of spontaneous manifestations expressing the organization of formal structures as it is actually experienced. . . . In other words, formal development should take place in a way that furthers the growth of the adolescent in his daily life as he learns to fill adult roles.

First we must ask what it means to fill adult roles? As opposed to the child who feels inferior and subordinate to the adult, the adolescent is an individual who begins to consider himself as the equal of adults and to judge them, with complete reciprocity, on the same plane as himself. But to this first trait, two others are indissolubly related. The adolescent is an individual who is still growing, but one who begins to think of the future—i.e., of his present or future work in society. Thus, to his current activities he adds a life program for later "adult" activities. Further, in most cases in our societies, the adolescent is the individual who in attempting to plan his present or future work in adult society also has the idea (from his point of view, it is directly related to his plans) of changing this society, whether in some limited area or completely. Thus it is impossible to fill an adult role without conflicts, and whereas the child looks for resolution of his conflicts in present-day compensations (real or imaginary), the adolescent adds to these limited compensations the more general compensation of a motivation for change, or even specific planning for change.

Furthermore, seen in the light of these three interrelated features, the adolescent's adoption of adult roles certainly presupposes those affective and intellectual tools whose spontaneous development is exactly what distinguishes adolescence from childhood. If we take these new tools as a starting point, we have to ask: what is their nature and how do they relate to formal thinking?

On a naive global level, without trying to distinguish between the student, the apprentice, the young worker, or the young peasant in terms of how their social attitudes may vary, the adolescent differs from the child above all in that he thinks beyond the present. The adolescent is the individual who commits himself to possibilities—although we certainly do not mean to deny that his commitment begins in real-life situations. In other words, the adolescent is the individual who begins to build "systems" or "theories," in the largest sense of the term.

The child does not build systems. His spontaneous thinking may be more or less systematic (at first only to a small degree, later, much more so); but it is the observer who sees the system from outside, while the child is not aware of it since he never thinks about his own thought. . . . In other words, the child has no powers of reflection—i.e., no second-order thoughts which deal critically with his own thinking. No theory can be built without such reflection.

In contrast, the adolescent is able to analyze his own thinking and construct theories. The fact that these theories are oversimplified, awkward, and usually contain very little originality is beside the point. From the functional standpoint, his systems are significant in that they furnish the cognitive and evaluative bases for the assumption of adult roles. . . . They are vital in the assimilation of the values which delineate societies or social classes as entities in contrast to simple interindividual relations.

Consider a group of students between 14–15 years and the *baccalaureat*.* Most of them have political or social theories and want to reform the world; they have their own ways of explaining all of the present-day turmoil in collective life. Others have literary or aesthetic theories and place their reading or their experiences of beauty on a scale of values which is projected onto a system. Some go through religious crises and reflect on the problem of faith, thus moving toward

Translators' note: baccalaureat—a French examination taken at the end of secondary school or about 18–19 years of age. Although, in its details, the analysis of the adolescent presented below fits the European better than the American pattern, one might suggest that even if metaphysical and political theories are less prominent, the American dating pattern and other phenomena typical of youth culture are a comparable "theoretical" or "as if" working out of types of interpersonal relations which become serious at a later point; thus the difference is one of content but not of structure.

a universal system—a system valid for all. Philosophical speculation
carries away a minority, and for any true intellectual, adolescence is
the metaphysical age par excellence, an age whose dangerous seduction
is forgotten only with difficulty at the adult level. A still smaller minority
turns from the start toward scientific or pseudo-scientific theories. But
whatever the variation in content, each one has his theory or theories,
although they may be more or less explicit and verbalized or even implicit. Some write down their ideas, and it is extremely interesting to
see the outlines which are taken up and filled in in later life. Others
are limited to talking and ruminating, but each one has his own ideas
(and usually he believes they are his own) which liberate him from
childhood and allow him to place himself as the equal of adults.*

If we now step outside the student range and the intellectual classes
to look at the reactions of the adolescent worker, apprentice, or peasant,
we can recognize the same phenomenon in other forms. Instead of
working out personal "theories," we would find him subscribing to ideas
passed on by comrades, developed in meetings, or provoked by reading.
We would find fewer family and still fewer religious crises, and especially a lower degree of abstraction. But under different and varied
exteriors the same core process can easily be discerned—the adolescent
is no longer content to live the interindividual relations offered by his
immediate surroundings or to use his intelligence to solve the problems
of the moment. Rather, he is motivated also to take his place in the
adult social framework, and with this aim he tends to participate in
the ideas, ideals, and ideologies of a wider group through the medium
of a number of verbal symbols to which he was indifferent as a child.

But how can we explain the adolescent's new capacity to orient himself toward what is abstract and not immediately present (seen from
the outside by the observer comparing him to the child), but which
(seen from within) is an indispensable instrument in his adaptation to
the adult social framework, and as a result his most immediate and
most deeply experienced concern? There is no doubt that this is the
most direct and, moreover, the simplest manifestation of formal thinking. Formal thinking is both thinking about thought (propositional logic
is a second-order operational system which operates on propositions
whose truth, in turn, depend on class, relational, and numerical operations) and a reversal of relations between what is real and what is
possible (the empirically given comes to be inserted as a particular
sector of the total set of possible combinations). These are the two
characteristics—which up to this point we have tried to describe in the
abstract language appropriate to the analysis of reasoning—which are
the source of the living responses, always so full of emotion, which
the adolescent uses to build his ideals in adapting to society. The adolescent's theory construction shows both that he has become capable of reflective thinking and that his thought makes it possible for him to escape
the concrete present toward the realm of the abstract and the possible.
Obviously, this does not mean that formal structures are first organized
by themselves and are later applied as adaptive instruments where they
prove individually or socially useful. The two processes—structural

---

*Of course, girls are more interested in marriage, but the husband they
dream of is most often "theoretical," and their thoughts about married life as
well often take on the characteristics of "theories."

development and everday applications—both belong to the same reality, and it is *because* formal thinking plays a fundamental role from the functional standpoint that it can attain its general and logical structure. Once more, logic is not isolated from life; it is no more than the expression of operational coordinations essential to action.

But this does not mean that the adolescent takes his place in adult society merely in terms of general theories and without personal involvement. Two other aspects of his entrance into adult society have to be considered—his life program, and his plans for changing the society he sees. The adolescent not only builds new theories or rehabilitates old ones; he also feels he has to work out a conception of life which gives him an opportunity to assert himself and to create something new (thus the close relationship between his system and his life program). Secondly, he wants a guarantee that he will be more successful than his predecessors (thus the need for change in which altruistic concern and youthful ambitions are inseparably blended).

In other words, the process which we have followed through the different stages of the child's development is recapitulated on the planes of thought and reality new to formal operations. . . . Even at the sensorimotor level, the infant does not at first know how to separate the effects of his own actions from the qualities of external objects or persons. At first he lives in a world without permanent objects and without awareness of the self or of any internal subjective life. Later he differentiates his own ego and situates his body in a spatially and causally organized field composed of permanent objects and other persons similar to himself. This is the first decentering process; its result is the gradual coordination of sensorimotor behavior. But when symbolic functioning appears, language, representation, and communication with others expand this field to unheard-of proportions and a new type of structure is required. For a second time egocentrism appears, but this time on another plane. It still takes the form of an initial relative lack of differentiation both between ego's and alter's points of view, between subjective and objective, but this time the lack of differentiation is representational rather than sensorimotor. When the child reaches the stage of concrete operations (7–8 years), the decentering process has gone far enough for him to be able to structure relationships between classes, relations, and numbers objectively. At the same stage, he acquires skill in interindividual relations in a cooperative framework. Furthermore, the acquisition of social cooperation and the structuring of cognitive operations can be seen as two aspects of the same developmental process. But when the cognitive field is again enlarged by the structuring of formal thought, a third form of egocentrism comes into view. This egocentrism is one of the most enduring features of adolescence; it persists until the new and later decentering which makes possible the true beginnings of adult work.

Moreover, the adolescent manifestation of egocentrism stems directly from the adoption of adult roles, since (as Charlotte Bühler has so well stated) the adolescent not only tries to adapt his ego to the social environment but, just as emphatically, tries to adjust the environment to his ego. In other words, when he begins to think about the society in which he is looking for a place, he has to think about his own future activity and about how he himself might transform this society. The result is a relative failure to distinguish between his own point of view as an individual called upon to organize a life program and the point of view of the group which he hopes to reform.

In more concrete terms, the adolescent's egocentrism comes out in a sort of Messianic form such that the theories used to represent the world center on the role of reformer that the adolescent feels himself called upon to play in the future. To fully understand the adolescent's feelings, we have to go beyond simple observation and look at intimate documents such as essays not written for immediate public consumption, diaries, or simply the disclosures some adolescents may make of their personal fantasies. For example, in the recitations obtained by G. Dumas from a high-school class on their evening reveries, the most normal students—the most retiring, the most amiable—calmly confessed to fantasies and fabulations which several years later would have appeared in their own eyes as signs of pathological megalomania. Without going into the details of this group, we see that the universal aspect of the phenomenon must be sought in the relationship between the adolescent's apparently abstract theories and the life program which he sets up for himself. Then we see that behind impersonal and general exteriors these systems conceal programs of action whose ambitiousness and naiveté are usually immoderate. We could also consider the following sample taken from the dozen or so expupils of a small-town school in French Switzerland. One of them, who has since become a shopkeeper, astonished his friends with his literary doctrines and wrote a novel in secret. Another, who has since become the director of an insurance company, was interested among other things in the future of the theater and showed some close friends the first scene of the first act of a tragedy—and got no further. A third, taken up with philosophy, dedicated himself to no less a task than the reconciliation of science and religion. We do not even have to enumerate the social and political reformers found on both right and left. There were only two members of the class who did not reveal any astounding life plans. Both were more or less crushed under strong "superegos" of parental origin, and we do not know what their secret daydreams might have been.

Sometimes this sort of life program has a real influence on the individual's later growth, and it may even happen that a person rediscovers in his adolescent jottings an outline of some ideas which he has really fulfilled since. But in the large majority of cases, adolescent projects are more like a sort of sophisticated game of compensation functions whose goals are self-assertion, imitation of adult models, participation in circles which are actually closed, etc. Thus the adolescent takes up paths which satisfy him for a time but are soon abandoned. . . .

Essentially, the process, which at any one of the developmental stages moves from egocentrism toward decentering, constantly subjects increases in knowledge to a refocusing of perspective. Everyone has observed that the child mixes up subjective and objective facts, but if the hypothesis of egocentrism did nothing more than restate this truism it would be worth next to nothing. Actually, it means that learning is not a purely additive process and that to pile one [newly] learned piece of behavior or information on top of another is not in itself adequate to structure an objective attitude. Objectivity presupposes a decentering —i.e., a continual refocusing of perspective. Egocentrism, on the other hand, is the undifferentiated state prior to multiple perspectives, whereas objectivity implies both differentiation and coordination of the points of view which have been differentiated.

But the process found in adolescence on the more sophisticated plane of formal structures is analogous. The indefinite extension of powers of thought made possible by the new instruments of propositional logic at first is conducive to a failure to distinguish between the ego's new and [unexpected] capacities and the social or cosmic universe to which they are applied. In other words, the adolescent goes through a phase in which he attributes an unlimited power to his own thoughts so that the dream of a glorious future or of transforming the world through Ideas (even if this idealism takes a materialistic form) seems to be not only fantasy but also an effective action which in itself modifies the empirical world. This is obviously a form of cognitive egocentrism. Although it differs sharply from the child's egocentrism (which is either sensorimotor or simply representational without introspective "reflection"), it results from the same mechanism and appears as a function of the new conditions created by the structuring of formal thought.

There is a way of verifying this view; namely, to study the decentering process which later makes it possible for the adolescent to get beyond the early relative lack of differentiation and to cure himself of his idealistic crisis—in other words, the return to reality which is the path from adolescence to the true beginnings of adulthood. But, as at the level of concrete operations, we find that decentering takes place simultaneously in thought processes and in social relationships.

From the standpoint of social relationships, the tendency of adolescents to congregate in peer groups has been well documented—discussion or action groups, political groups, youth movements, summer camps, etc. Charlotte Bühler defines an expansive phase followed by a withdrawal phase, although the two do not always seem clearly distinguishable. Certainly this type of social life is not merely the effect of pressures toward conformity but also a source of intellectual decentering. It is most often in discussions between friends, when the promoter of a theory has to test it against the theories of the others, that he discovers its fragility.

But the focal point of the decentering process is the entrance into the occupational world or the beginning of serious professional training. The adolescent becomes an adult when he undertakes a real job. It is then that he is transformed from an idealistic reformer into an achiever. In other words, the job leads thinking away from the dangers of formalism back into reality. Yet observation shows how laborious and slow this reconciliation of thought and experience can be. One has only to look at the behavior of beginning students in an experimental discipline to see how long the adolescent's belief in the power of thinking endures and how little inclined is the mind to subjugate its ideas to the analysis of facts. (This does not mean that facts are accessible without theory, but rather that a theoretical construction has value only in relation to empirical verification.)

From this standpoint, the results of Chapters I–XV of this work raise a problem of general significance. The subjects' reactions to a wide range of experimental situations demonstrate that after a phase of development (11–12 to 13–14 years) the preadolescent comes to handle certain formal operations (implication, exclusion, etc.) successfully, but he is not able to set up an exhaustive method of proof. But the 14–15-year-old adolescent does succeed in setting up proofs (moreover, spontaneously, for it is in this area that academic verbalism is least evident). He systematically uses methods of control which require the combinatorial system—i.e., he varies a single factor at a time and excludes the others ("all other things being equal"), etc. But, as we have often seen, this structuring of the tools of experimental verification is a direct consequence of the development of formal thought and propositional logic. Since the adolescent acquires the capacity to use both deduction and experimental induction at the same time, why does he use the first so effectively, and why is he so late in making use of the second in a productive and continuous task (for it is one thing to react experimentally to an apparatus prepared in advance and another to organize a research project by oneself)? Furthermore, the problem is not only ontogenetic but also historical. The same question can be asked in trying to understand why the Greeks were limited (with some exceptions) to pure deductive thought* and why modern science, centered on physics, has taken so many centuries to put itself together.

We have seen that the principal intellectual characteristics of adolescence stem directly or indirectly from the development of formal structures. Thus, the latter is the most important event in the thinking found in this period. As for the affective innovations found at the same age, . . . as usual, we find that they are parallel to intellectual transformations, since affectivity can be considered as the energetic force of behavior.

First, feelings relative to ideals are added to interindividual feelings. Secondly, personalities develop in relation to social roles and scales of values derived from social interaction, and no longer only by the coordination of exchanges which they maintain with the physical environment and other individuals.† . . .

First, we are struck by the fact that feelings about ideals are practically nonexistent in the child. A study of the concept of nationality and the associated social attitudes‡ has shown us that the child is sensitive to his family, to his place of residence, to his native language, to certain customs, etc., but that he preserves both an astonishing degree of ignorance and a striking insensitivity not only to his own designation or that of his associates as Swiss, French, etc., but toward his own country

*No one has yet given a serious explanation of this fact from the sociological standpoint. To attribute the formal structures made explicit by the Greeks to the contemplative nature of one social class or another does not explain why this contemplation was not confined to metaphysical ideologies and was able to create a mathematical system.

†*Translators' note:* "Interindividual" and "social" are used as oppositional terms to a greater extent in French than in English. The first refers to face-to-face relationships between individuals with the implication of familiarity, and the second to the relationship of the individual to society as a whole, to formal institutional structures, to values, etc. Here the meaning is that the child relates only to small groups and specific individuals while the adolescent relates to institutional structures and to values as such.

‡J. Piaget and A. M. Weil, "Le développement chez l'enfant de l'idée de patrie et des relations avec l'etranger."

as a collective reality. This is to be expected, since, in the 7–11-year-old child, logic is applied only to concrete or manipulable objects. There is no operation available at this level which would make it possible for the child to elaborate an ideal which goes beyond the empirically given. The notions of humanity, social justice (in contrast to interindividual justice which is deeply experienced at the concrete level), freedom of conscience, civic or intellectual courage, and so forth, like the idea of nationality, are ideals which profoundly influence the adolescent's affective life; but with the child's mentality, except for certain individual glimpses, they can neither be understood nor felt.

In other words, the child does not experience as social feelings anything more than interindividual affects. Even moral sentiments are felt only as a function of unilateral respect (authority) or mutual respect. But, beginning at 13–15 years, feelings about *ideals* or *ideas* are added to the earlier ones. . . . Of course, an ideal always exists in a person and it does not stop being an important interindividual element in the new class of feelings. The problem is to find out whether the idea is an object of affectivity because of the person or the person because of the idea. But, whereas the child never gets out of this circle because his only ideals are people who are actually part of his surroundings, during adolescence the circle is broken because ideals become autonomous. No commentary is needed to bring out the close kinship of this affective mechanism with formal thought.

As for personality, there is no more vaguely defined notion in psychological vocabulary, already so difficult to handle. The reason for this is that personality operates in a way opposite to that of the ego. Whereas the ego is naturally egocentric, personality is the decentered ego. The ego is detestable, even more so when it is strong, whereas a strong personality is the one which manages to discipline the ego. In other words, the personality is the submission of the ego to an ideal which it embodies but which goes beyond it and subordinates it; it is the adherence to a scale of values, not in the abstract but relative to a given task;* thus it is the eventual adoption of a social role, not ready-made in the sense of an administrative function but a role which the individual will create in filling it.

Thus, to say that adolescence is the age at which adolescents take their place in adult society is by definition to maintain that it is the age of formation of the personality, for the adoption of adult roles is from another and necessarily complementary standpoint the construction of a personality. Furthermore, the life program and the plans for change which we have just seen as one of the essential features of the adolescent's behavior are at the same time the changing emotional force in the formation of the personality. A life plan is above all a scale of values which puts some ideals above others and subordinates the middle-range values to goals thought of as permanent. But this scale of values is the affective organization corresponding to the cognitive organization of his work which the new member in the social body says he will undertake. A life plan is also an affirmation of autonomy, and the moral autonomy finally achieved by the adolescent who judges himself the equal

---

*For the relationship between personality and the task, see I. Meyerson, *Les fonctions psychologiques et les oeuvres* (Vrin).

of adults is another essential affective feature of the young personality preparing himself to plunge into life.

In conclusion, the fundamental affective acquisitions of adolescence parallel the intellectual acquisitions. To understand the role of formal structures of thought in the life of the adolescent, we found that in the last analysis we had to place them in his total personality. But, in return, we found that we could not completely understand the growth of his personality without including the transformations of his thinking; thus we had to come back to the development of formal structures.

26

Logic and Psychology*

1952

INTRODUCTORY NOTES

Piaget has written substantially on logic and its relations with psychology, not only in his empirical books but also in specialized books entirely devoted to logic. These have not gained the same acceptance among logicians as his psychological essays have gained among psychologists.

Piaget does not take an existing psychological theory and reformulate it in axiomatic, logical terms. On the one hand, existing psychological theories are too vague to be submitted to such rigorous treatment. On the other hand, formal logic as it stands cannot be readily applied to the course of cognitive development because it is just such logical structures that are developing, and, therefore, other logics must be sought that correspond to the child's mentality at any given stage. Moreover, axiomatic logic is atomistic and linear, whereas natural thought is structural, cyclical, and dialectical. Logical systems with these characteristics are not yet well enough developed to be applied to a psychological theory of development, even if such a theory were ready for them.

Consequently, Piaget prefers a *psycho-logic*, as he calls it, which is just emerging as a science, and which would stand between logic and psychology.

This position has led to some criticism of Piaget, either on the ground of "psychologism" or of "logicism," although what Piaget tries to establish is a collaboration between psychology and logic. The collaboration should ideally take the following form: the psychologist would observe the facts that the subject, in the course of his development, takes as normative, and as psychologist attempt to coordinate them in such a way as to account for the passage from one stage of norms or criteria to another. The logician, on his side, would use his own methods of work to verify the validity or invalidity of these successive normative systems.

Implicit in this proposition is the idea that cognitive development is not a matter of overcoming contradictions, but of completing cognitive structures.

*From *Logic and Psychology* by Jean Piaget, with an introduction on Piaget's logic by W. Mays. Published in the United States by Basic Books, Inc., by arrangement with Manchester University Press; first printing, 1957. Reprinted by permission of the publishers. Original publication was in English.

In other words, the evolution of ideas is not explained by their history, but by an appeal to a future logical equilibrium.

Classes, relations et nombres (1942) is an attempt at normalizing the activities proper to the level of concrete operations by means of the structure, invented by Piaget, of *groupements*, which is supposedly isomorphic to the thought processes of the ages 7–8 to 11–12. Piaget defines the central notion of *operation* both from a logico-mathematical and a psychogenetic standpoint. He distinguishes *seriation* and *classification*, notes their articulation in additive or multiplicative systems, and separates simple operations from secondary ones. He then proceeds to develop the eight typical groupements marking the stage. The last part of the book is devoted to the passage from logical groupements to arithmetic ones (number).

The *Traité de logique* (1949) aims at introducing the reader to Piaget's formalization of thought processes in general. It presents Piaget's theses about the reversibility of thought and the holistic structure of intelligence. The book was not well received by logicians who did not understand the reason for such an essay halfway between axiomatization and psychology.

A second edition, revised by J. B. Grize, was published in 1972. This revision clarifies some obscure passages. Looked at as a formalization of the *child's* thinking the "essay on operatory logistic" remains a very conservative and at the same time intuitive effort to account for certain mental processes in terms of a logic that is probably surpassed by more recent developments. Looked at as the work of a man trying to put some order into his *own* thinking the book takes on a very different light and becomes even fascinating.

There is a third volume in this series that should be mentioned: the *Essai sur les transformations des opérations logiques* (1952). Piaget analyzes the 256 ternary operations of the bivalent logic of propositions by means of substitutions, permutations, negations, additions, and so on. It is, in its own fashion, an "exercice de style" to persuade the readers that operatory logic, as Piaget understands it, will become the equivalent for psychology of what physical mathematics became to physics, a fertile hybrid that will carry the evolution of human thought one species further.

The piece selected to represent this part of Piaget's manifold activity is a series of lectures given at the University of Manchester in England.

The introduction and notes by Wolfe Mays make the three lectures easily readable for someone without much training in either modern mathematics or logic. It would be advisable for the reader to refer to it whenever, in the course of reading the rest of Piaget's work, he or she encounters a difficulty with some logical term.

An Elementary Introduction to Piaget's Logic[*]

From about 1939 onward Piaget has, at Geneva, been applying the techniques of symbolic logic to the study of the intellectual behavior of the child in an attempt to obtain some insight into the way in which the child's logical, mathematical, and physical concepts arise. In his *Traité de logique* he has outlined systematically the logical principles used in

---

[*][The following is from the Introduction by W. Mays.]

these investigations. And since the logical treatment of this book is largely based upon the above work, a short introductory survey is given of some of its more important concepts.

This account falls under five headings. In (1) the elements of symbolic logic are briefly dealt with together with the concept of a logical calculus; (2) deals with the class interpretation of this calculus and with classificatory systems; (3) with the propositional interpretation and the logical relations holding between any two propositions. In (4) some account is given of the nature of a mathematical group, since the system of propositions resembles such a group, whilst (5) deals with lattices, since Boolean algebra, upon which modern logic is based, is in its mathematical treatment subsumed under lattice theory.

It is Piaget's claim that psychologists have in symbolic logic an instrument as useful as statistics. Symbolic logic has already been applied to diverse fields—to language, to the design of logical and mathematical computers, to biology, and to nerve networks. Piaget has shown how it may be fruitfully applied to the analysis of the intellectual activities of the child.

ELEMENTS

In symbolic logic we make use of variables similar to those used in algebra (i.e., x, y, z), but instead of referring to numbers, they refer in the propositional calculus solely to propositions, e.g., "The sun is shining," "Mary is singing." We represent them by the letters p, q, r, s, etc. Just as we use such operations as $+$, $-$, $\times$, $\div$ in algebra, so in symbolic logic we use similar signs to refer to relations between propositions.

They are

    (1) not (negation) $-$
    (2) and (conjunction) $\cdot$
    (3) or (disjunction (either or both))   v
    (4) if . . . then (implication)   ⊃

Any logical operation can be expressed in terms of either $\cdot$ and negation or v and negation.

From this we can build up other relations such as equivalence $=$ ($p = q$) or incompatibility / (p/q), e.g.: "It is not the case both that it is raining (p) and the pavement is dry (q)." Further, there is a resemblance between the $+$ and $\times$ of ordinary algebra and the v and $\cdot$ operations of symbolic logic. This identification was first made by George Boole in his algebra of logic; p v q and $p \cdot q$ are therefore sometimes called the logical sum and logical product and the operations v and $\cdot$ logical addition and logical multiplication. Boolean algebra is really an algebra of 1 and 0, since in this system propositions can only have two values: truth and falsity.

CLASSES

The abstract algebra of logic can be given a number of interpretations. The propositional and class interpretations are alone considered here. In the class-calculus we start with the concept of a class of objects. A class may be defined as all those entities having a certain property; for example, the class of all men, or the class of all tigers. We may start

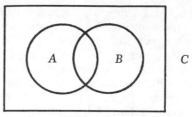

Figure 1

with a class C, and denote subclasses of C by A, B. Thus C might be a square and A, B, the subclasses of points in different regions of C (Figure 1). In mathematics the concept of a class is referred to as a *set*.

Similar relations hold between classes as between propositions, but to avoid confusion different symbols are used. Piaget uses the arithmetical sum and product signs $+$, $\times$.

The division of a class C may also be depicted as follows:

Table (a) Example:

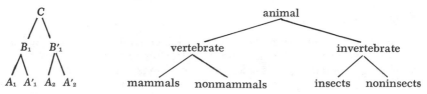

Consider another method of classification. Suppose B_1 and B_2 are two distinct classes, such that all the individuals of B_1 are part of B_2 and reciprocally.

Let B_1 be animals, A_1 vertebrates, A'_1 invertebrates. Let B_2 be the distribution of animals according to their habitat, A_2 terrestrial and A'_2 aquatic. We thus get four different combinations:

Table (b)

$A_1 A_2$	$A'_1 A_2$
$A_1 A'_2$	$A'_1 A'_2$

vertebrates terrestrial $(A_1 A_2)$
vertebrates aquatic $(A_1 A'_2)$
invertebrates terrestrial $(A'_1 A_2)$
invertebrates aquatic $(A'_1 A'_2)$.

The multiplication of $B_1 \times B_2$ therefore gives us animals distributed according to whether they live on land or in the sea and have the characteristic of being either vertebrate or invertebrate. As Piaget expresses it

$$B_1 \times B_2 = A_1 A_2 + A_1 A'_2 + A'_1 A_2 + A'_1 A'_2.$$

Type (a) classifications in terms of dichotomous divisions are found in botanical and zoological classifications. Piaget has such systems in mind when he speaks of additive groupements of classes.

Type (b) two-way classificatory systems, expressing qualitative correspondences, are used as above in zoology. Such systems form Piaget's multiplicative groupements of classes.

In the case of (b), Piaget points out that there is a correspondence between the multiplication of classes and the conjunction of propositions, since of any two propositions p and q each can be either true or false.

Combining these two at a time, we obtain

$$p \cdot q \vee p \cdot \bar{q} \vee \bar{p} \cdot q \vee \bar{p} \cdot \bar{q},$$

which may be read off from the following diagram:

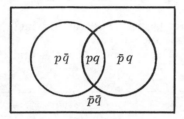

Figure 2

As each of these pairs may itself be either true or false, we obtain sixteen possible arrangements. Each type of relation between propositions may be translated in terms of one of these arrangements.

Examples:
$$p \vee q = p \cdot q \vee p \cdot \bar{q} \vee \bar{p} \cdot q \quad [\bar{p} \cdot \bar{q} \text{ is false}]$$
$$p \cdot q = p \cdot q \quad [p \cdot \bar{q} \vee \bar{p} \cdot q \vee \bar{p} \cdot \bar{q} \text{ are false}]$$
$$p \supset q = p \cdot q \vee \bar{p} \cdot q \vee \bar{p} \cdot \bar{q} \quad [p \cdot \bar{q} \text{ is false}].$$

The pairs which are false are shaded in the resultant diagrams, thus we have

$p \vee q$

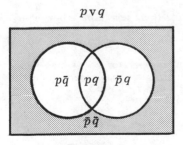

Figure 3

$p \cdot q$

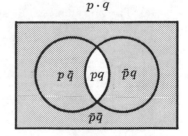

Figure 4

Piaget states that every such relationship has an inverse (complementary), a reciprocal and a correlate.

I. Inverse (N). If, e.g., the proposition is $p \vee q$ it has for its complementary $\bar{p} \cdot \bar{q}$ (if we negate $\bar{p} \cdot \bar{q}$ thus $\bar{p} \cdot \bar{q}$ we arrive back at $p \vee q$).

$$p \supset q$$

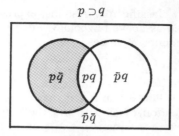

Figure 5

2. Reciprocal (R) of p v q is the same proposition but with negation signs added, i.e., $\bar{p}$ v $\bar{q}$.

3. Correlate (C) is the proposition obtained when we substitute a v whenever a · occurs, and vice versa. Thus p · q becomes p v q, and p v q becomes p · q.

4. Identity operator (I) is the operation which, when performed on any proposition, leaves it unchanged.

The following table (c)* shows how the first three operations are related

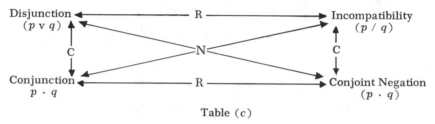

Table (c)

GROUPS

The above set of transformations N, R, C together with I constitute an abstract group. One example of a group† is the system of positive and negative numbers characterized by the operation $+n$ (addition of an integer).

It obeys the four conditions.

1. Two operations of the system have for their resultant a new operation of the system $+1 +1 = 2$.

2. Every operation of the system can be annulled by an inverse operation $+2 - 2 = 0$.

3. There exists one, and only one, identity operator (0) which is the resultant of every operation and its inverse, and such that when applied to any operation it does not change it: $+1 - 1 = 0$ and $1 \pm 0 = 1$.

4. The operations are associative $(4 + 2) - 3 = 4 + (2 - 3)$.

LATTICES

Boolean algebra may be considered as a special case of certain abstract mathematical systems called lattices. A lattice has certain limiting conditions—*join* and *meet*. In the case of any two classes X and Y, the

*Piaget, *Traité de logique*, p 271.
†Ibid., p. 92.

join is the smallest of the classes in which X and Y are both included, and the *meet* is the largest class included both in X and in Y.

The following classificatory system (Table (*d*))* can be considered as a semilattice. A branch leading from one element to another means that the latter is included in it.

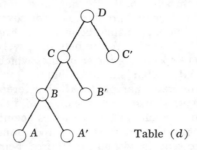

Table (*d*)

Each pair of classes possesses a *join*, B for A and A', C for A and B', or C for A' and B', etc., since it is the smallest class which includes both. As for the *meet*, A is the *meet* of A and of B, or of A and of C, etc., since it is the largest class included in both. On the other hand, the *meet* of two disjunctive classes is null, which is, of course, the definition of disjunction (i.e., they are excluded from each other), e.g., A and A', A and B', A' and B' all = 0.

Author's Introduction

The aim of this book is not to discover how psychological theories may be formalized by means of logic,† but to study the application of logical techniques to the psychological facts themselves, and especially to the thought structures found at different levels of intellectual development.

This problem is of both theoretical and practical interest.

Theoretically, it is important to ask what sort of correspondence exists between the structures described by logic and the actual thought processes studied by psychology. The question whether the structures and operations of logic correspond to anything in our actual thought, and whether the latter conforms to logical laws, is still an open one.

Practically, it is important to discover in what way logic can advance psychological research. In our opinion its chief value does not lie in axiomatizing psychological theories; a great gap still exists between the relative imprecision of such theories and the deductive rigor of logical systems. On the other hand, the algebra of logic can help us to specify psychological structures, and to put into calculus form those operations and structures central to our actual thought processes. Psychologists have no hesitation in using mathematics for calculating correlation coefficients, for factor analysis, etc. Now the algebra of logic is a subsystem of one of the most general fields of mathematics, that of "abstract algebra." The fact that it is concerned with qualitative structures

*Ibid., p. 95.
†F. B. Fitch and C. L. Hull are among the best known of those who have attempted such a formalization.

in no way detracts from its mathematical character; modern mathematicians are coming more and more to emphasize the importance of such structures. The psychologist for his part welcomes the qualitative character of logic, since it facilitates the analysis of the actual structures underlying intellectual operations, as contrasted with the quantitative treatment of their behavioral outcome. Most "tests" of intelligence measure the latter, but our real problem is to discover the actual operational mechanisms which govern such behavior, and not simply to measure it. The algebra of logic can therefore help the psychologist, by giving him a precise method of specifying the structures which emerge in the analysis of the operational mechanisms of thought.

To give a concrete example to which reference will be made again: psychologists have shown that at the age of 12 the child is able to discover elementary combinatorial operations (combinations 2 by 2, 3 by 3, or 4 by 4 in the random drawing of colored counters, etc., from a bag).* This the child discovers without, of course, being aware of the mathematical formulae involved, by finding a systematic method of completing the combinations at the same level of intellectual development at which he begins to use propositional operations (such as $p \supset q$, i.e., "if then," or $p \vee q$, p/q, etc.). We may then inquire why these two kinds of operations, which at first sight seem quite unrelated, nevertheless appear simultaneously in the child's behavior. The algebra of logic makes it immediately clear that propositional operations are based upon a combinatorial system not involved, for example, in the elementary structures of classes and relations which children aged 7 to 12, on the average, use. By submitting the operational structures to logical analysis, we can thus easily explain why such varied types of behavior occur simultaneously. In this way, the algebra of logic can constantly aid the psychologist in his studies.

However, at the present time there is little collaboration between logicians and psychologists. Indeed, there is a mutual distrust which makes cooperation difficult. A brief historical survey will explain how this has come about.

History and Status of the Problem†

In the nineteenth century before Boole, de Morgan, Jevons, etc., developed the algebra of logic, and before experimental psychology became a science, no such conflict between logic and psychology existed. Classical logic believed it was possible to discover the actual structure of thought processes, and the general structures underlying the external world as well as the normative laws of the mind. Classical philosophical psychology, in its turn, considered the laws of logic and the laws of ethics to be implicit in the mental functioning of each normal individual. These two disciplines then at no point had grounds for disagreement.

*See Piaget and Inhelder, *The Origin of the Idea of Chance in Children*, Chapter VII.
†[The following section is from Chapter I.]

But with the development of the young science of experimental psychology logical factors were excluded; intelligence was explained by sensations, images, associations, and other mechanisms. The reaction to this approach was unfortunate; for example, certain members of the Würzburg school of *Denkpsychologie* introduced logical relations to complete the action of psychological factors in judgment.

Logic was thus used in the causal explanation of the psychological facts themselves. To this fallacious use of logic in psychology the name of "logicism" has been given, and, if psychologists generally are distrustful of logic, it is due mainly to their fear of falling into this fallacy. Most present-day psychologists try to explain intelligence without any appeal to logical theory.

At about the time that psychologists were trying to divorce their science from logic, the founders of modern logic or "logistic" asked for it to be separated from psychology for similar reasons. It is true that Boole, the inventor of the algebra that bears his name, still believed he was describing "The Laws of Thought," but this was because he held these to be essentially algebraic in nature. With an increase in the deductive rigor and formal character of logical systems, one of the chief tasks of the later logicians has been to eliminate from the field of logic any appeal to intuition, that is to say, to any kind of psychological factor. When there is recourse to such factors in logic the fallacy is called "psychologism." This term has been used by logicians to refer to insufficiently formalized logical theories, just as psychologists have used the term "logicism" to refer to psychological theories insufficiently tested by experience.

Most logicians today are no longer concerned with whether the laws and structures of logic bear any sort of relation to psychological structures. A French disciple of Bertrand Russell, at the turn of this century, even asserted that the concept of an "operation" was essentially anthropomorphic, and that logical operations were, in fact, only formal operations having no resemblance whatever to psychological operations. As logic has perfected its formal rigor, logicians have ceased to interest themselves in the study of actual thought processes. Bernays held, for example, and from the standpoint of a perfectly formalized axiomatic logic he is undoubtedly right, that logical relations are strictly applicable only to mathematical deduction, since every other form of thought merely has an approximate character.

When we try to discover the entities to which these logical structures correspond, we find that the progressive formalization of logic has given rise to four possible solutions, which must be briefly examined from the point of view of their bearing on psychology.

First, there is *platonism*, which was a feature of the early work of Bertrand Russell and A. N. Whitehead, which stimulated the work of Scholz, and which remains either the confessed or unconfessed ideal of a large number of logicians. Logic on such a view corresponds to a system of universals existing independently of experience and nonpsychological in origin. However, we still have to explain how the mind comes to discover such universals. The platonic hypothesis only shelves this problem and brings us no nearer a solution.

The second solution is *conventionalism*, which holds that logical entities owe their existence and laws to a system of conventions, or generally accepted rules. But this leaves us with the problem of why these conventions should be so successful, and so surprisingly effective in their application.

The notion of convention has therefore given place to that of a *well-formed language*. This third solution, put forward by the Vienna Circle, has strongly influenced logical empiricism. It distinguishes empirical truths, or nontautological relationships, and tautologies or purely syntactical relationships, which, with the aid of an appropriate semantics, may be used to express empirical truths. We have here, for the first time, a theory having psychological significance which may be tested empirically. Psychologically, however, it entails several difficulties.

In the first place, we cannot speak about pure experience or "empirical truths" apart from logical relationships. In other words, experience cannot be interpreted in abstraction from the conceptual and logical apparatus which makes such an interpretation possible. In our experiments with Mlle Inhelder,* in which young children were asked to say whether the surface of the water in inclined glass tubes was horizontal or not, we found that children do not perceive "horizontality" before they are able to construct a spatial framework of reference. Now, in order to construct such a framework, they require geometrical operations, and in the construction of such operations logical operations have to be used.

Secondly, logical relationships throughout the whole period of their development never appear as a simple system of linguistic or symbolic expressions but always imply a group of operations.†

For example, children from 5 to 8 years of age are shown an open box in which there are twenty wooden beads (the class formed by the whole twenty will be called B). Most of the beads are brown (forming a class A) but some are white (class A': therefore $B = A + A'$). The child is asked the simple question: "Are there more brown beads (A) in this box or more wooden beads (B)?" A disciple of the Vienna Circle would reply that we have here a simple empirical fact of which even the youngest child can take note, and which is based on the propositions "all the beads are made of wood, but they are not all brown" (as a matter of fact the child immediately agrees with these two assertions). We have also a system of logical relationships by means of which this "empirical truth" may be expressed in terms of a precise symbolism, giving us in this case a simple inclusion between two classes, $A < B$, i.e., "the part A is smaller than the whole B."

Now psychological experiments definitely show that the child between 5 and 7 years is unable to construct this inclusion $A < B$. His own interpretation of the facts leads him to conclude (and once again this demonstrates that the interpretation of perceptual data presupposes a previous logical elaboration) that $A > B$ because $A > A'$. His answer is: "There are more brown beads (A) than wooden beads (B) because there are only two or three white ones (A')." What this answer really means is: either the question deals with the whole class (B), and then all the beads are wooden ones, or it deals with a part (A); but if the whole is split up into its constituent parts we no longer have a whole. In this case

---

*Piaget and Inhelder, *La Représentation de l'espace chez l'enfant*.
†This also remains true when the subjects have arrived at maturity.

it is reduced to the other part (A'), hence $A > B$ because $B = A'$. In other words, children find it difficult to reason about the whole and the parts at the same time. If they think of the whole, they forget the parts and vice versa.* In order to construct the inclusion $A < B$, which, on the average, can be done between the ages of 7 and 8 years, the child has not simply to carry out a verbal or symbolic translation of the perceptual data, but an operational composition or decomposition† of its elements: $B = A + A'$, hence $A = B - A'$ and $A' = B - A$, hence $A < B$. The logical relationship is, consequently, much more than a linguistic expression which translates the empirical properties of objects. It is the resultant of the *reversible actions of composition and decomposition*, which consist of actual operations of grouping or regrouping carried out on objects.

A third difficulty prevents us from accepting the thesis that logic is merely a language. If this hypothesis were valid, logic ought to be an essential feature of the child's intellectual make-up. We would expect, on the one hand, a simple interpretation of the perceptual facts, and, on the other, a simple verbal translation of these facts as basic as language itself. But if perceptions presuppose a preliminary conceptual interpretation involving logical relationships, and if these relationships presuppose actions and organized operations, there is an interaction between perceptions and operations which ought to take a lengthy period of time to establish itself. And, in fact, logic appears relatively late in the thinking of children: the first operations dealing with classes occur between 7 and 8, on the average, and those concerned with propositions between 11 and 12. From 8 to 9, for example, the child will state that a brass bar A weighs the same as another bar B, and that as the latter weighs the same as a lead ball C, $A = B$ and $B = C$. But he rejects the conclusion that $A = C$ since from past experience he expects the relation $A < C$, and says "B certainly weighs as much as the ball C, but with A it will be different!" Transitivity is therefore still absent from the picture (i.e., there is no duplication of a formal pattern), and this state of affairs continues as long as the weight relationships remain unstructured by a preliminary group of operations (seriation, etc.).

This brings us to the fourth and last of the ways of interpreting logical relationships; *operationalism*. Championed at first by Bridgman in the United States, it has today a following in many countries (cf. the Italian operationalist movement, of which Ceccato and others are members). Unlike the preceding interpretations, operationalism provides real ground on which logic and psychology can meet. Operations (in spite of Couturat!) play an indispensable role in logic, since logic is based on an abstract algebra and made up of symbolic manipulations. On the other hand, operations are actual psychological activities, and all effective knowledge is based on such a system of operations.

In order to determine the relations between logic and psychology we need, therefore, (1) to construct a psychological theory of operations in

---

*See Piaget, *The Child's Conception of Number*, Chapter VII.

†*Translator's note:* In the mathematical theory of sets, the operation of composition refers to that operation which, when applied to, say, two elements A, A', produces a new set B. Conversely, the operation of decomposition refers to that operation which, when applied to the set B, splits it up into its constituent elements A, A'.

terms of their genesis and structure; (2) to examine logical operations, treating them as algebraic calculi and as *structured wholes*;* and (3) to compare the results of these two kinds of inquiries.

Psychological Development of Operations†

Psychologically, operations are actions which are internalizable, reversible, and coordinated into systems characterized by laws which apply to the system as a whole. They are actions, since they are carried out on objects before being performed on symbols. They are internalizable, since they can also be carried out in thought without losing their original character of actions. They are reversible as against simple actions which are irreversible. In this way, the operation of combining can be inverted immediately into the operation of dissociating, whereas the act of writing from left to right cannot be inverted to one of writing from right to left without a new habit being acquired differing from the first. Finally, since operations do not exist in isolation they are connected in the form of *structured wholes*. Thus, the construction of a class implies a classificatory system and the construction of an asymmetrical transitive relation, a system of serial relations, etc. The construction of the number system similarly presupposes an understanding of the numerical succession: $n + 1$.

From the point of view of psychology, the criterion for the appearance of such operational systems is the construction of invariants or concepts of conservation. In the case (see pp. 454–455) of inclusion $A < B$ of brown beads in the larger class of wooden beads, the appearance of the operations $A + A' = B$ and $A = B - A'$ is marked by the conservation of the whole B. Before the stage at which operations are formed, however, B is destroyed as soon as it is divided into its parts A and A'. Conservation has thus to be conceived as the resultant of operational reversibility.

There are four main stages in the construction of operations, and these extend over the period from birth to maturity.

(1) *The Sensorimotor Period (0 to 2 Years).* Before language appears the small child can only perform motor actions, without thought activity, but such actions display some of the features of intelligence, as we normally understand it; for example, the child will draw a coverlet toward itself, so as to obtain an object placed on it.

Sensorimotor intelligence is not, however, operational in character, as the child's actions have not yet been internalized in the form of representations (thought). But in practice even this type of intelligence

---

**Translator's note:* By a *structured whole, structure d'ensemble,* Piaget refers to a system of elements defined by a general set of laws, such as the laws which define a group or a lattice. For example, a logical groupement is defined by a set of five operations, and in this sense forms a *structure d'ensemble* (since the laws define the system as a whole) and is thus to be distinguished from the individual operations themselves.

†[The following section is from Chapter II.]

shows a certain tendency toward reversibility, which is already evidence of the construction of certain invariants.

The most important of these invariants is that involved in the construction of the permanent object. An object can be said to attain a permanent character when it is recognized as continuing to exist beyond the limits of the perceptual field, when it is no longer felt, seen, or heard, etc. At first, objects are never thought of as permanent; the infant gives up any attempt to find them as soon as they are hidden behind or under a screen. For example, when a watch is covered with a handkerchief the child, instead of lifting the handkerchief, withdraws his hand. When the child begins to look behind the screen, he does not at first note the object's successive changes of position. If, for example, it was at A when he rediscovered it, he will continue to look for it at A after it has been moved to B, etc. Only toward the end of the first year does the object become permanent in its surrounding spatial field.*

The object's permanent character results from the organization of the spatial field, which is brought about by the coordination of the child's movements. These coordinations presuppose that the child is able to return to his starting point (reversibility), and to change the direction of his movements (associativity), and hence they tend to take on the form of a "group." The construction of this first invariant is thus a resultant of reversibility in its initial phase. Sensorimotor space, in its development, attains an equilibrium by becoming organized by such a "group of displacements," from which H. Poincaré assumed it originated, but which, in fact, is its final form of equilibrium.† The permanent object is then an invariant constructed by means of such a group; and thus even at the sensorimotor stage one observes the dual tendency of intelligence toward reversibility and conservation.

(2) *Preoperational Thought (2 to 7 Years)*. Toward 1½ to 2 years the "symbolic function" appears: language, symbolic play (the beginning of fictional invention), deferred imitation, i.e., occurring some time after the original event, and that kind of internalized imitation which gives rise to mental imagery. As a result of the symbolic function, "representation formation," that is to say, the internalization of actions into thoughts, becomes possible. The field in which intelligence plays a part becomes considerably enlarged. To actions occurring in the child's immediate spatial environment, are added actions occurring in the past (as engendered by storytelling), and elsewhere, e.g., in distant space, as well as the mental division of objects and collections into parts, etc. The practical reversibility of the sensorimotor period no longer suffices for the solution of all problems, as most of them now require the intervention of definite psychological operations.

However, the child cannot immediately construct such operations; several years of preparation and organization are still required. In fact, it is much more difficult to reproduce an action correctly in thought than to carry it out on the behavioral level. The child of 2 years, for example, is able to coordinate his movements from place to place (when he walks about the room or in the garden) into a group, as well as his movements when he turns objects round. But a lengthy period of time

*See Piaget, *The Construction of Reality in the Child*, 1937.
†Ibid., Chapter II.

will elapse before he will be able to represent them precisely in thought; in reproducing, for example, from memory with the help of objects, a plan of the room or garden, or in inverting the positions of objects in thought by turning the plan round.

Throughout the period from 2 to 7 years, on the average, there is an absence of reversible operations, and an absence of concepts of conservation on any level higher than the sensorimotor. For example, when the child aged 4 to 6 pours liquid or beads from one glass bottle into another of a different shape, he still believes that the actual quantity in the recipient bottle is increased or diminished in the process. He believes two sticks of equal length are equal if their end points coincide; but if we push one of them a little way in front of the other, he thinks that the stick has been lengthened. And he believes the distance between two objects changes if a third object is put between them. When equal parts are taken away from two equal whole figures, he refuses to believe that the remainders are equal if the perceptual configurations are different.* In all fields which involve continuous or discrete quantities, one comes across the same phenomenon: when the most elementary forms of conservation are absent, it is a consequence of the absence of operational reversibility. This becomes immediately apparent as soon as there is a conflict between the perceptual configuration and logic. The child's judgments of quantity thus lack systematic transitivity. If given two quantities A and B, and then afterward two quantities B and C, each pair can be recognized as equal ($A = B$ and $B = C$) without the first quantity A being judged equal to the last C.

We once regarded this period as "prelogical." Mrs. Isaacs, Miss Hazlett, and many others rightly criticized this view, since some of the early evidence which we thought satisfactory was too verbal in character. Starting from the postulate that all logical problems arise in the first place from manipulations of objects, we can now say that this period is preoperational. Our position is then identical with theirs, if we consider logic as being based essentially on operations; but with the proviso that the first operations only appear between 7 and 8 years, on the average, and in a concrete form (i.e., they are carried out on objects), whilst verbal or propositional operations only arise toward 11 and 12.

(3) *Concrete Operations (7 to 11 Years).* The various types of thought activity which arise during the preceding period finally attain a state of "mobile" equilibrium, that is to say, they acquire the character of reversibility (of being able to return to their original state or starting point). In this way, logical operations result from the coordination of the actions of combining, dissociating, ordering, and the setting up of correspondences, which then acquire the form of reversible systems.

We are still dealing only with operations carried out on the objects themselves. These concrete operations belong to the logic of classes and relations, but do not take into account the totality of possible transformations of classes and relations (i.e., their combinatorial possibilities). A careful analysis of such operations is therefore necessary, so as to bring out their limitations as well as their positive features.

*For a fuller account see Piaget, *The Child's Conception of Number*, 1941; and Piaget, Inhelder, and Szeminska, *The Child's Conception of Geometry*, 1948.

One of the first important operational systems is that of *classification* or the inclusion of classes under each other: for example, sparrows (A) < birds (B) < animals (C) < living beings (D); or we may take any other similar system of class-inclusions. Such a system (cf. p. 465) permits the following operations:

$$A + A' = B; B + B' = C; \text{ etc. (where } A \times A' = 0; B \times B' = 0, \text{ etc.)}$$
$$B - A' = A; C - B' = B; \text{ etc.}$$

We have seen why these operations are necessary for the construction of the relation of inclusion.

A second equally important operational system is that of *seriation*, or the linking of asymmetrical transitive relations into a system. For example, the child is given a certain number of unequal rods A, B, C, D . . . to arrange in order of increasing length. If the rods are markedly unequal, there is no logical problem and he can construct a series by relying on observation alone. But if the variation in length is small, so that the rods have to be compared two at a time before they can be arranged in such a series, the following is observed. Before the age of 7, on the average, the child proceeds unsystematically by comparing the pairs BD, AE, CG, etc., and then corrects the results. From 7 years onward, the child uses a systematic method; he looks for the smallest of the elements, then the smallest of those which are left over, etc., and in this way easily constructs the series.* This method presupposes the ability to coordinate two inverse relations: $E > D, C, B, A$ and $E < F, G$, H, etc. If we call a the relation expressing the difference between A and B; b the difference between A and C; c the difference between A and D; etc., and a' the difference between B and C; b' the difference between C and D; c' the difference between D and E; etc., we have the following operations:

$$a + a' = b; \quad b + b' = c; \text{ etc.}$$
$$b - a' = a; \quad c - b' = b; \text{ etc.}$$

Other systems appear during the same period having a multiplicative character. For example, the child can classify the same objects taking account of two characteristics at a time, square (A_1) or nonsquare (A'_1) and red (A_2) and nonred (A'_2). From this we can construct a table of double entry or matrix; the following four cells result from the multiplication:

$$B_1 \times B_2 = A_1A_2 + A_1A'_2 + A'_1A_2 + A'_1A'_2.$$

In a similar fashion, the child acquires the capacity for multiplying relations using tables of different kinds, correspondences, etc.

These different systems of logical operations are of especial importance in the construction of the concepts of number, time, and motion; and in the construction of different geometrical relations (topological, projective, and Euclidean).† In this respect, it is of particular interest to analyze how the system of positive and negative integers and the system of linear measure are constructed in close association with

*Piaget, *The Child's Conception of Number*, Chapter VI.
†Piaget, *The Child's Conception of Time* and *The Child's Conception of Movement and Speed*. Piaget and Inhelder, *The Child's Conception of Space*.

the operations of class and relation, but according to methods sometimes differing markedly from those of the logician. For our present purpose, however, details of such a construction are unnecessary.

On the other hand, it is important to emphasize the fact that despite everything acquired in the way of logical techniques during this period of concrete operations, it is, compared with the period which follows, restricted in two essential respects.

The first of these restrictions stems from the insufficiently formal character of the operations at this level. The formal operations are not yet completely dissociated from the concrete data to which they apply. In other words, the operations develop separately field by field, and result in a progressive structuralization of these fields, without complete generality being attained.

For example, when we show a child two balls of modeling clay of similar dimensions and weight, and shape one of them to look like a sausage or a pancake, three kinds of conservation problems arise: (i) does the altered ball still contain the same quantity of substance as the unaltered one; (ii) does it still have the same weight; (iii) does it still have the same volume, measured by the amount of water it is seen to displace?

The conservation of substance, which in the first period was denied because of the change of perceptual configuration (by the use of such arguments as, "there is more clay than before, because the thing is longer," and "there is less because it is thinner," etc.), is from 7 to 8 years onward felt as a logical necessity and is supported by the following three arguments. (a) The object has only been lengthened (or shortened), and it is easy to restore it to its former shape (simple reversibility); (b) it has been lengthened; but what it has gained in length it has lost in thickness (composition of relations by reversible composition); (c) nothing has been added or taken away (operation of identity which brings us back to the initial state, the product of direct and inverse operations). But these same children deny the conservation of weight for reasons similar to those they used when under 7 to deny the conservation of substance; it is longer, or thinner, etc. Toward 9 to 10 years they admit the conservation of weight, and use by way of proof the same three arguments (a), (b), (c) formulated in exactly the same terms as before! But we find, however, these same children denying at this age the conservation of volume for the very same reasons they formerly used to deny the conservation of substance and weight. Finally, when they are 11 to 12 they once again use the same three arguments to assert the conservation of volume!*

The same results are obtained if we study the conservation of substance, weight, and volume with other techniques,† for example, by dissolving a piece of sugar or by soaking popcorn in water. But curiously enough, with respect to all the operations, one finds exactly the same lack of correspondence. For example, children from 7 to 8 onward are able to order serially objects according to length or size, but it is not until about 9 to 10, on the average, that the serial ordering of objects by weight becomes possible (cf. the seriation of weights in the Binet-Simon tests).

*For a fuller discussion see Piaget and Inhelder, Le Développement des quantités chez l'enfant.
†Ibid. Chapter IV et seq.

From 7 to 8 children become aware of the transitive character of equalities in the case of lengths, etc., but only toward 9 to 10 in the case of weight and toward 11 to 12 for volume.

In short, each field of experience (that of shape and size, weight, etc.) is in turn given a structure by the group of concrete operations, and gives rise in its turn to the construction of invariants (or concepts of conservation). But these operations and invariants cannot be generalized in all fields at once; this leads to a progressive structuring of actual things, but with a time lag of several years between the different fields or subject matters. Because of this, concrete operations fail to constitute a formal logic; they are incompletely formalized since form has not yet been completely divorced from subject matter.

Operational systems at this level are restricted in another way—they are fragmentary. We can, with the aid of concrete operations, classify, order serially, form equalities or set up correspondences between objects, etc., without these operations being combined into a single *structured whole*. This fact also prevents concrete operations from constituting a purely formal logic. From the psychological point of view, this means that operations have not yet completely achieved an equilibrium; and this will only occur in the following stage.

(4) Propositional or Formal Operations (from 11–12 to 14–15 Years). The final period of operational development begins at about 11 to 12, reaches equilibrium at about 14 to 15 and so leads on to adult logic.

The new feature marking the appearance of this fourth stage is the ability to reason by hypothesis. In verbal thinking such hypothetico-deductive reasoning is characterized, *inter alia*, by the possibility of accepting any sort of data as purely hypothetical, and reasoning correctly from them. For example, when the child has read out to him the following sentences from Ballard's nonsense-sentence test: "I am very glad I do not eat onions, for if I liked them I would always be eating them and I hate eating unpleasant things," the subject at the concrete level criticizes the data, "onions are not unpleasant," "it is wrong not to like them," etc. Subjects at the present level accept the data without discussion, and merely bring out the contradiction between "if I liked them" and "onions are unpleasant."

But it is not only on the verbal plane that the subject reasons by hypothesis. This new capacity has a profound effect on his behavior in laboratory experiments. Subjects at the propositional level, when shown apparatus of the sort used by my colleague Mlle Inhelder in her investigations into physical inference,* behave quite differently from those at the concrete level. For example, when they are given a pendulum and allowed to vary the length and amplitude of its oscillations, its weights and initial impulse, subjects of 8 to 12 years simply vary the factors in a haphazard way and classify, order serially and set up correspondences between the results obtained. Subjects of 12 to 15 years, on the other hand, endeavor after a few trials to formulate all the possible hypotheses concerning the operative factors, and then arrange their experiments as a function of these factors.

The consequences of this new attitude are as follows. In the first

*B. Inhelder, "Le Raisonnement expérimental chez l'adolescent," *Proceedings and Papers of the Thirteenth Inter. Congress of Psychology at Stockholm* (1951), p. 153.

place thought no longer proceeds from the actual to the theoretical, but starts from theory so as to establish or verify actual relationships between things. Instead of just coordinating facts about the actual world, hypothetico-deductive reasoning draws out the implications of possible statements and thus gives rise to a unique synthesis of the possible and necessary.

From this it follows that the subject's logic is now concerned with propositions as well as objects. A group of propositional operations, such as implication $p \supset q$ (if ... then), disjunction $p \lor q$, incompatibility p/q, etc., is thus constructed. It must be emphasized that it is not simply a case of new linguistic forms expressing, at the level of concrete operations, already known relationships between objects. These new operations, particularly those which concern the mechanism of proof, have changed the whole experimental attitude. Mlle Inhelder has, for example, been able to show that the method of difference which varies a single factor at a time, the rest being kept constant, only appears between 12 and 15 years.* It is easy to demonstrate that this method implies propositional operations, since it presupposes a combinatorial system, which arises from something other than the simple setting up of concrete correspondences.

The logic of propositions is especially helpful in that it allows us to discover certain new kinds of invariants, which fall outside the range of empirical verification. For example, in studying the movement of balls of different weights and mass on a horizontal plane, some adolescents are able to state the problem in terms of factors of resistance or rest. If q, r, s, etc., are the statements expressing friction, air resistance, etc., and if p is the statement expressing the fact that the balls have come to rest, their reasoning runs, $p \supset (q \lor r \lor s \lor \ldots)$ from which $(\bar{q} \cdot \bar{r} \cdot \bar{s} \cdot \ldots) \supset \bar{p}$ (its contrapositive). Hence this deduction (contraposition of the implication) leads them to believe that without the intervention of the factors causing the balls to come to rest (their absence being represented by $(\bar{q} \cdot \bar{r} \cdot \bar{s} \cdot \ldots)$), the movement would continue indefinitely $(\bar{p})$, which is a disguised form of the principle of inertia.

The construction of propositional operations is not the only feature of this fourth period. The most interesting psychological problem raised at this level is connected with the appearance of a new group of operations or "operational schemata," apparently unrelated to the logic of propositions, and whose real nature is not at first apparent.

The first of these operational schemata deals with combinatorial operations in general (combinations, permutations, aggregations). Reference has been made in the introduction to the ability of subjects of 12 years and over to construct all the possible combinations in an experiment based on the random drawing of counters from a bag. Many other examples could be quoted; in particular, the way subjects of 12 to 14 years come to combine in all possible ways n by n five colorless and odorless liquids of different chemical composition, three of which give a colored product, whilst the fourth removes the color and the fifth is neutral. While subjects of a lower level mix these liquids at random, the older subjects try them out systematically and keep a strict control over the experiment.

*Ibid., p. 154.

The second operational schema is that of proportions. We have been led to conclude from a large number of different kinds of experiments (dealing with motion, geometrical relations, probabilities as a function of the law of large numbers, proportions between the weights and distances on the two arms of a balance, etc.) that subjects from 8 to 10 are unable to discover the proportionalities involved. From 11 to 12 onward, on the average, the subject constructs a qualitative schema of proportions which very quickly leads him on to metrical proportions, often without learning about these in school. But why should the understanding of proportions be found at this level and not earlier?

Another operational schema whose construction can be profitably analyzed is that of mechanical equilibrium, involving equality between action and reaction. In a system wherein a piston exerts pressure on a liquid contained in two communicating vessels, the subject can only understand the alteration in the level of the liquid by distinguishing four processes, which can most readily be described in terms of operations. (a) The direct operation—i.e., the increase in pressure in the system resulting from the addition of weights to the piston; (b) the inverse operation—i.e., a decrease in pressure resulting from the removal of weights; (c) the reciprocal operation—i.e., the increased resistance of the liquid caused, for example, by an increase in density; (d) the inverse of the reciprocal—i.e., a decrease in the resistance in the liquid. Whereas subjects aged 14 to 15 can easily distinguish these four operations and can correctly coordinate them, young children do not understand that the pressure of the liquid, as shown by its level in the vessel, acts in opposition to the pressure of the piston.

We need only mention the other operational schemata relating to probabilities, correlations, multiplicative compensations, etc. The foregoing examples indicate how they may be translated into logical operations.

This fourth period therefore includes two important acquisitions. Firstly, the logic of propositions, which is both a formal structure holding independently of content and a general structure coordinating the various logical operations into a single system. Secondly, a series of operational schemata which have no apparent connection with each other or with the logic of propositions.

Operational Structures of the Algebra of Logic*

We will now see whether by using the operational techniques which logic provides we can discover (or construct by their means) structures which can be put into correspondence with the operational structures of psychology.

However, in attempting to compare such mental structures and the structures of modern logic, a difficulty faces us comparable to that which we would find if we tried to compare the intuitive geometry of the child (or of the nonspecialist adult) with the axiomatic geometry of

*[The following section is from Chapter III.]

Hilbert. Though they are related, we need to introduce intermediate systems and distinguish different levels of formalization in order to make the relationship clear.

As far as formalization is concerned, logic can be conceived from two distinct points of view: (1) logic as an *operational algebra* with its procedures of calculation, its structures, etc.; (2) *axiomatic logic* as the science of truth-conditions, or the theory of formalization itself—this we will call pure or formalized logic.

Axiomatic logic is useless for the particular purpose we have in mind. If we wished to formalize psychological *theories* it would be the only suitable method, but our present aim is to disengage the logical structure of psychological or mental *facts*. We are prevented from using axiomatic or formalized logic for this purpose by three fundamental difficulties.

The first difficulty would be sufficient by itself. It arises from the fact that even the ordinary thinking of the adult is unformalizable. We agree with Bernays that only mathematical thought in its most developed forms permits of a formalization that modern theories of axiomatic logic would recognize as adequate. A fortiori the thought of the adult or young child is unformalizable.

The second difficulty is that the order inherent in axiomatization reverses in certain respects the genetic order of the construction of operations. For example, from the axiomatic standpoint the logic of classes is to be deduced from that of propositions, whilst from the genetic point of view propositional operations are derived from the logic of classes and relations. Similarly, for purposes of formalization the axioms precede the algebraic calculus, whilst genetically the axioms are the product of conscious intuition or reflection, directed in the first place by underlying operational mechanisms.

A third difficulty is that axiomatic logic is atomistic in character and the order of its demonstrations necessarily linear. A formalized theory starts from atomic elements (propositions, classes, operations, independent axioms, undefined concepts, etc.), and ends with a closed or completed system built up from these atomic elements. Operational mechanisms, however, have a psychological existence, and are made up of *structured wholes*, the elements of which are connected in the form of a cyclical system irreducible to a linear deduction. In fact, we have here something that resembles more a system involving biological organization than a linear sequence of demonstrations. Thus in our investigation of mental life we must start from the operational structures themselves.

These three difficulties force us to interpolate between psychology and axiomatic logic a *tertium quid*, a "psycho-logic" or logico-psychology, related to these in the same way as mathematical physics is related to pure mathematics and experimental physics.

Physics is primarily an experimental science concerned exclusively with the study of the material world, and its criterion of truth is agreement with empirical fact. Mathematics, on the other hand, is not based on experiment nor explainable by reference to physical facts; it is a formal science whose sole criterion of truth is the internal consistency appropriate to a rigorous deductive system. The need for explanation in physics itself has led to the application of mathematics to physics and thus given rise to mathematical physics, which has for its object the construction of a deductive theory which will explain the experimental findings.

Without pressing the parallel too far, and without concealing the fact that psychology is some centuries behind physics, we can say that, like physics, it is an experimental science, but one concerned with the study of mental life, whilst its criterion of truth is also agreement with empirical fact. Logic based on the axiomatic method is, on the other hand, a formal science whose sole criterion of truth is deductive rigor.

The need for explanatory schemata in psychology leads us to apply axiomatic logic to psychology itself, and in this way to construct a psycho-logic.* Its task would not, however, be to base logic on psychology, but rather to construct by means of the algebra of logic a deductive theory to explain some of the experimental findings of psychology.†

We will now try to construct logical or algebraic schemata without troubling about the axiomatic requirements of formalized logic, applying simply the two following criteria: (1) these schemata should be logically valid; (2) they should have an adequate application to the findings of experimental psychology.

To construct such schemata we need to start with the most *elementary* structures (not to be confused with the most general), and show by what sort of operations the higher structures are derived from these. We will begin with the first operational structures appearing in the course of the child's intellectual development (period 3: concrete operations), and try to disengage the corresponding algebraic structures; then go on to propositional structures, returning finally to preoperational structures.

"ELEMENTARY GROUPEMENTS"

The operations of classes and relations at mental level (3) correspond to the simple structures which we call "elementary groupements" and which are definitely limited in scope, if compared to lattices or to the groups characterizing propositional operations or the operations of classes and relations in their most general form (Boolean algebra, etc.).

Simple classification (A included in B, B included in C; etc.) is, for example, based on a system defined by the following five operations:

(1) $A + A' = B; B + B' = C$; etc. (where $A \times A' = 0; B \times B' = 0$; etc.).
[*Composition*]

(2) $-A - A' = -B$; etc., from which $A = B - A'$ and $A' = B - A$.
[*Inversion*]

(3) $A - A = 0$. [*Identity*]

(4) $A + A = A$ from which $A + B = B$. [*Tautology*]

(5) $A + (A' + B') = (A + A') + B'$ but $A + (A - A) \neq (A + A) - A$.
[*Associativity*]

*Mr. N. Isaacs in his review of my *Traité de logique*, *Brit. Journ. of Psychol.* (1951): 185–188, has suggested the term "psychologic" to bring out this meaning. This I think to be right, but unfortunately, at the time of writing, I was not sufficiently aware of the need for these three disciplines.

†See Piaget, "La Logique axiomatique ou pure, a logique opératoire ou psychologique, et les réalités auxquelles elles correspondent."

We see that such compositions of elements into classes can only be carried out *contiguously*, that is to say, by successive inclusions and as a function of the partial complementaries A', B', etc. To take an example:

$$A' + C' = D - A - B'.$$

Similarly, in zoological classification (which conforms to the same schema) the addition of the classes "sparrows" and "snails" does not correspond to any elementary class, since they are mutually exclusive. Its only meaning is: "the class of vertebrates except all classes other than birds and except all birds other than sparrows" + "the class of invertebrates except all classes other than molluscs and except all molluscs other than snails."

The structure of this "elementary groupement" is only a semilattice as the *meets* between classes of the same rank are all null: $A \times A' = 0$; $B \times B' = 0$; etc.

Since its associativity is incomplete, it forms an imperfect group, restricted by the tautological operation $A + A = A$.

The *seriation* of asymmetrical transitive relations (or system of serial ordering) exhibits an analogous structure. This may be seen if we express by a, b, c, etc., the differences in their respective order between the first term of the series (A or 0) and each successive term, and by a', b', c', etc., the differences between each term in the series and its immediate successor (i.e., between each pair of terms). Hence, $a + a' = b$; $b + b' = c$, etc., and $b - a' = a$; $a - a = 0$; etc.

In a multiplicative groupement, such as the bi-univocal multiplication of classes, the system is defined by the following operations:

(1) $A_1 \times A_2 = A_1 A_2$; $B_1 \times B_2 = A_1 A_2 + A_1 A'_2 + A'_1 A_2 + A'_1 A'_2$; etc.
  [*Composition*]

(2) $B_1 B_2 : B_2 = B_1$ (where $:B_2$ means "eliminating B_2."). [*Inversion*]

(3) $B_1 : B_1 = Z$ (where Z is the most general class of the system obtained by eliminating the inclusion B_1). [*Identity*]

(4) $B_1 B_2 \times A_1 A_2 = A_1 A_2$. [*Tautology*]

(5) Associativity restricted by the operations of (4).

Now it is the *join* (between the component classes) which is not general, and once again the complete structure of the lattice is absent.

We can thus construct four groupements of classes and four groupements of relations, which express the totality of operations at the psychological level of concrete operations. We need not refer to them in detail,* but it is useful to point out that these various groupements exhibit two very distinct forms of reversibility.

(a) *Inversion*, which consists in negating a class ($-A$) or an inclusion ($:A$). The product of an operation and its inverse is therefore either the null class ($A - A = 0$), or the most general class of the system ($A:A = Z$, since A is a subdivision of Z and if this subdivision is eliminated we arrive back at Z).

(b) *Reciprocity*, which consists in eliminating, not a class, or an inclusion (subdivision), but a difference. The product of an operation and its reciprocal gives us not a null class or a universal class but a

*See our *Traité de logique*.

relation of equivalence: $(A < B) + (A > B) = (A = B)$. We have expressed reciprocity in the language of inversion by formulating it (with respect to seriation) under the form $a - a = 0$.

But if a represents a difference (for example, $A < B$), then o represents the null difference, that is to say, we obtain this equivalence again.

Inversion is the form of reversibility concerned with the operations of classes, and reciprocity the form concerned with the operations of relations. No groupements are present at the level of concrete operations to combine these two kinds of reversibility into a single system. From the standpoint of mental development, inversion (negation or elimination) and reciprocity (symmetry) form two kinds of reversibility, whose beginnings are already to be seen at the lower developmental levels. At the level of concrete operations, they appear in the form of two distinct operational structures (groupements of classes and groupements of relations), and finally form a unique system at the level of propositional operations.

THE TRANSITION FROM "ELEMENTARY GROUPEMENTS" OF

CLASSES AND RELATIONS TO PROPOSITIONAL STRUCTURES

The multiplicative groupement of classes, e.g.,

$$A_1 \times A_2 = A_1A_2; B_1 \times B_2 = A_1A_2 + A_1A'_2 + A'_1A_2 + A'_1A'_2; \text{etc.},$$

arises from the multiplication of two simple classifications. If we make the proposition p correspond to A_1, the proposition q to A_2, the proposition $\bar{p}$ to A'_1, and the proposition $\bar{q}$ to A'_2, the multiplication $B_1 \times B_2$ then corresponds to:

Classes: $(A_1 + A'_1) \times (A_2 + A'_2) = A_1A_2 + A_1A'_2 + A'_1A_2 + A'_1 A'_2$
Propositions: $(p \vee \bar{p}) \cdot (q \vee \bar{q}) = (p \cdot q) \vee (p \cdot \bar{q}) \vee (\bar{p} \cdot q) \vee (\bar{p} \cdot \bar{q})$
Product number: 1   2   3   4.

Propositional operations are thus constructed simply by combining n by n these four basic conjunctions. The 16 binary operations of two-valued propositional logic therefore result from the combinations given below (written in numerical form):

o; 1; 2; 3; 4; 12; 13; 14; 23; 24; 34; 123; 124; 134; 234 and 1234.

Elementary groupements are distinguished from the higher groupements which form the system of propositional operations by the fact that the latter is based upon a combinatorial system. Elementary groupements have not yet a complete combinatorial character. For example, multiplicative groupements of classes or relations are solely based on the multiplication of elements 2 by 2 or 3 by 3, etc., but not on combinations among the resultant products (1 to 4 or 1 to 9, etc.), as in the case of the 16 binary propositional operations formed from the products 1 to 4. Another way of expressing the fundamental difference between the two kinds of structures is to say that elementary groupements are based only on simple sets (the included classes $A < B < C$, etc.) or on product sets (the multiplicative classes A_1A_2; $A_1A'_2$; etc.), whilst propositional structures are based on what is called in the theory of sets a *set of all subsets*, combinations taken n by n among the product sets.

We could, of course, easily construct such a combinatorial system, hence a *set of all subsets* by means of classes alone. In the case of mental operations at the concrete level, however, such a construction does not take place; which is why combinatorial operations are not included among elementary groupements.

We may therefore ask what operations produce these combinations which make possible the transition of elementary groupements to the *set of all subsets*, which is a feature of propositional operations. If we wish to construct algebraic structures which are isomorphic with mental structures, we cannot simply introduce a new operation by the back door. It has to be explained as a function of the preceding operations.

Now the combinatorial system is only a generalization of classification applied to the multiplicative products 1, 2, 3, and 4. In the classification $A_1 + A'_1 = B$, we can substitute for the complementary class A'_1 (if A'_1 is not null) a class A_2, and for A_1 the complementary class of A_2, i.e., A'_2, such that (if $<$ represents inclusion)

$$A + A'_1 = A_2 + A'_2 = B \text{ where } A_2 < A'_1 \text{ and } A_1 < A'_2.$$

This operation, which we call *vicariance*, gives rise to a *groupement* already present at the level of concrete operations; for example "(the French + the non-French) = (the Chinese + the non-Chinese) = (all men)." In classifying the products $p \cdot q$, $p \cdot \bar{q}$, $\bar{p} \cdot q$, and $\bar{p} \cdot \bar{q}$ in all possible ways, using the operation of vicariance, we obtain a combinatorial system n by n and a *set of all subsets*.

We can therefore say that the characteristic combinatorial structure of propositional operations forms a groupement of the second order, and consists in applying classification generalized by vicariance to the product sets of the multiplicative groupement. In other words, elementary groupements are groupements of the first order: consisting of (a) simple classifications, (b) vicariances or reciprocal substitutions within the classifications, and (c) the multiplication of two or n classifications. On the other hand, the combinatorial structure of propositional operations which applies operations (a) and (b) to the products of operation (c), is a groupement of the second order; and hence of a more general form and corresponds to later mental structures.

PROPOSITIONAL STRUCTURES

In contrast to elementary groupements, which have the structure of semilattices and imperfect groups, the *set of all subsets* upon which propositional operations are based has the dual structure of a (complete) lattice and a group. The lattice and group structures are combined into a single system which obeys the laws of groupements, since it is a groupement of the second order, without the restrictions noted above (contiguity, etc.).

It is unnecessary to stress the fact that this structure forms a lattice whose *join* is $(p \vee q)$ and whose *meet* is $(p \cdot q)$.

As against this, the "group" aspect of the structure of propositional operations is generally neglected. Now this structure is subject to the laws of a group of four transformations (*Vierer-gruppe*), which, from the point of view of operational mechanisms, is of great importance.

An operation such as $(p \vee q)$ has an *inverse* N distinct from it, namely $(\bar{p} \cdot \bar{q})$ and which in relation to the set $(p \cdot q) \vee (p \cdot \bar{q}) \vee$

$(\bar{p} \cdot q) \vee (\bar{p} \cdot \bar{q})$ is its complementary. It also has a reciprocal R (distinct or not), which is the same operation between negated propositions. In the case of $p \vee q$, the reciprocal R is distinct, and is $\bar{p} \vee \bar{q}$, that is to say, p/q. Finally, it has a correlate C (distinct or not) resulting from the permutation of (v) and of ($\cdot$) in the corresponding normal form: the correlate in this case is $(p \cdot q)$. On adding the identity transformation (I) to these three transformations they form a commutative group:

(1) CR = N; RN = C; NC = R; and (2) NRC = I.

Other examples are: if $I = (p \supset q)$, then $N = (p \cdot \bar{q})$, $R = (q \supset p)$, $C = (\bar{p} \cdot q)$.

If $I = (p = q)$, then $N = (p \text{ w } q)$, $R = (\bar{p} = \bar{q}) = (p = q)$, $C = (\bar{p} \text{ w } \bar{q}) = (p \text{ w } q)$; etc.

(where w symbolizes the reciprocal exclusion $p = \bar{q}$ and $\bar{p} = q$).

Thus the two forms of reversibility, inversion (N) and reciprocity (R), are found combined in a single system, while they remain separate in the field of elementary groupements.

To bring out the close connection between the lattice and group aspects of propositional operations, we can arrange these operations in the form of a single table. The elements of this table (numbered from the top horizontally starting from the left) are formed from four unary operations.

$$q \cdot \bar{q} \; (=0); q; \bar{q}; q \vee \bar{q}$$

multiplied by p or by $\bar{q}$:

1 (o)	2 $(p \cdot q)$	3 $(p \cdot \bar{q})$	4 $p \cdot (q \vee \bar{q})$
5 $(\bar{p} \cdot \bar{q})$	8 $(p = q) \vee (\bar{p} \cdot \bar{q})$	11 $(p \cdot \bar{q}) \vee (\bar{p} \cdot \bar{q})$	14 $(q \supset p)$
6 $(\bar{p} \cdot q)$	9 $(p = q) \vee (\bar{p} \cdot q)$	12 $(p \cdot \bar{q}) \vee (\bar{p} \cdot q)$	15 $(p \vee q)$
7 $\bar{p} \cdot (q \vee \bar{q})$	10 $(p \supset q)$	13 (p/q)	16 $(p \cdot q) \vee (p \cdot \bar{q}) \vee (p \cdot q) \vee (\bar{p} \cdot \bar{q})$

We observe that:

1. Elements 8 to 16 are each the logical sum (v) of the element at the top of the same column, and the element at the extreme left of the same row. For example: 8 $(p = q) = 2$ $(p \cdot q) \vee 5$ $(\bar{p} \cdot \bar{q})$.

2. Elements 1 to 3; 5, 8 and 11; 6, 9 and 12 are the logical product ($\cdot$) of the element at the extreme right of the same row and the element at the foot of the same column. For example: 8 $(p = q) = 14$ $(q \supset p)$ $\cdot$ 10 $(p \supset q)$.

3. Each element has for its inverse N its symmetrical in relation to the center of the table: for example 2 $(p \cdot q)$ and 13 (p/q), or 14 $(q \supset p)$ and 6 $(\bar{p} \cdot q)$.

4. Each element has for its reciprocal R its symmetrical in relation to the diagonal $\searrow$: for example, 14 $(q \supset p)$ and 10 $(p \supset q)$.

5. Each element has for its correlate C its symmetrical in relation to the diagonal $\diagup$: for example, 2 $(p \cdot q)$ and 15 $(p \vee q)$.

6. The elements of the diagonal $\searrow$ (therefore 1, 8, 12, and 16) exhibit the properties I = R and C = N. For example, the R of 8 is 8 and the N of 8 is 12 which is also its C.

7. The elements of the diagonal $\diagup$ (therefore 7, 9, 11, and 4) exhibit the properties I = C and R = N. For example, the N of 9 is 11, which is also its R and the C of 9 is 9.

We can construct a similar table, with the same seven properties (and several others besides) by means of the 256 tertiary operations, the 65,536 quaternary operations, etc.*

Now from the group INRC, we can deduce a system of *logical proportions* (restricting ourselves to the group transformations and without introducing the tautological operations $p \cdot p = p$ or $p \vee p = p$).

We shall say that the four operations α, β, γ, and δ are proportionals if we have:

$$\frac{\alpha}{\beta} = \frac{\gamma}{\delta} \text{ if } (1) \; \alpha \cdot \delta = \beta \cdot \gamma \quad \text{and} \quad (2) \; \alpha \vee \delta = \beta \vee \gamma$$

and if in these two equations we can transpose from one side to the other by transforming $(\vee x)$ into $(\cdot \bar{x})$ or $(\cdot x)$ into $(\vee \bar{x})$.

From which we get the properties (3–6) deduced from (2) and (7–10) deduced from (1):

(3) $\alpha \cdot \bar{\beta} = \gamma \cdot \bar{\delta}$ (5) $\bar{\alpha} \cdot \beta = \bar{\gamma} \cdot \delta$ (7) $\alpha \vee \bar{\beta} = \gamma \vee \bar{\delta}$ (9) $\bar{\alpha} \vee \beta = \bar{\gamma} \vee \delta$
(4) $\alpha \cdot \bar{\gamma} = \beta \cdot \bar{\delta}$ (6) $\bar{\alpha} \cdot \gamma = \bar{\beta} \cdot \delta$ (8) $\alpha \vee \bar{\gamma} = \beta \vee \bar{\delta}$ (10) $\bar{\alpha} \vee \gamma = \bar{\beta} \vee \delta$.

We then observe that four operations are to be found in the relationships I, N, R, and C which always satisfy these conditions:†

(1) $[\alpha \cdot \delta = \beta \cdot \gamma]$ $I \cdot N = R \cdot C$. E.g. $(p \vee q) \cdot (\bar{p} \cdot \bar{q}) = (p / q) \cdot (p \cdot q)$.
(3) $[\alpha \cdot \bar{\beta} = \gamma \cdot \bar{\delta}]$ $I \cdot \bar{R} = C \cdot \bar{N}$. E.g. $(p \vee q) \cdot \overline{(p / q)} = (p \cdot q) \cdot \overline{(p \cdot q)}$.

$$\frac{I}{R} = \frac{C}{N}, \text{ for example } \frac{p \vee q}{p/q} = \frac{p \cdot q}{\bar{p} \cdot \bar{q}}$$

since: (1) $(p \vee q) \cdot (\bar{p} \cdot \bar{q}) = (p / q) \cdot (p \cdot q) = 0$
(3) $(p \vee q) \cdot \overline{(p / q)} = (p \cdot q) \cdot \overline{(\bar{p} \cdot \bar{q})} = (p \cdot q)$ etc.

Proportionality may be extended to elements between which the relationships I, N, R, C do not hold, subject to the condition that the group transformations apply. We can, for example, add $(\vee x)$ to α if we add $(\cdot \bar{x})$ to δ, but only if x has no common part with α. Similarly, $(\vee x)$ may be eliminated in α, if $(\cdot \bar{x})$ is eliminated in δ, provided that x is wholly part of α.

From $\dfrac{p \vee q}{p \cdot q} = \dfrac{\bar{p} \vee \bar{q}}{\bar{p} \cdot \bar{q}}$ we can therefore deduce $\dfrac{p}{q} = \dfrac{\bar{q}}{\bar{p}}$ by eliminating

$(\vee q)$ in α and $(\cdot \bar{q})$ in δ, and by eliminating $(\vee \bar{p})$ in γ and $(\cdot p)$ in β.

In the same way a system of reciprocal proportions may be deduced from the preceding conditions,

$$\frac{\alpha}{\beta} = R\frac{\gamma}{\delta} \text{ if } \begin{array}{l} (1) \; \alpha \cdot \delta = R(\beta \cdot \gamma) \\ (2) \; \alpha \vee \delta = R(\beta \vee \gamma) \end{array} \quad (3) \; \alpha \cdot C\beta = R(\gamma \cdot C\delta) \text{ etc.}$$

For example $\dfrac{p}{q} = R\dfrac{\bar{p}}{\bar{q}}$ since $p \cdot \bar{q} = R(\bar{p} \cdot q)$ and $p \cdot q = R(\bar{p} \cdot \bar{q})$; etc.

It should be noted that these unary proportions correspond to numerical proportions:

---

*See our book, *Essai sur les transformations des opérations logiques. Les 256 opérations ternaires de la logique bivalente.*
†*Translator's note:* To take two examples:

$\dfrac{p}{q} = \dfrac{\bar{q}}{\bar{p}}$ corresponds to $\dfrac{nx}{ny} = \dfrac{n:y}{n:x}$ and $\dfrac{p}{q} = \mathrm{R}\dfrac{\bar{p}}{\bar{q}}$ corresponds to $\dfrac{nx}{ny} = \dfrac{x:n}{y:n}$.

Finally, we should note that from the proportion $\dfrac{\mathrm{I}}{\mathrm{C}} = \dfrac{\mathrm{R}}{\mathrm{N}}$ with the help of the preceding transformations and the deductions therefrom, we easily arrive at the following well-known proportion of lattice theory:

$$\frac{x \cdot y}{x} = \frac{y}{x \vee y} \quad \text{for example,} \quad \frac{p \cdot q}{p} = \frac{q}{p \vee q}.$$

The above proportion exhibits the same properties as the proportion $\dfrac{\mathrm{I}}{\mathrm{C}} = \dfrac{\mathrm{R}}{\mathrm{N}}$, but is naturally subject to the condition of asserting,

$$p = (p \cdot q) \vee (p \cdot \bar{q}) \quad \text{and} \quad q = (p \cdot q) \vee (\bar{p} \cdot q).$$

It would be easy to specify many other properties of this combined group and lattice structure, especially in the case of the 256 ternary operations, which contain numerous other kinds of transformations. But for the purpose of explaining the mental operations described the above account is adequate.

Translator's Notes

(1) *Logical Groupements.* Unlike a mathematical group (cf. pp. 450–451), a logical groupement is defined by five operations (cf. principles 1–5, pp. 465–467) and includes the restrictive condition of tautology (principle 4). In arithmetic a unit added to itself gives a new number $1 + 1 = 2$, but repeating a logical element only gives a tautology $A + A = A$.

(2) *The table of 16 propositional operations* (p. 469). This is isomorphic with a truth-value table for two propositions, in which all the possible products are listed. The relationships between the elements of the above table (the set of transformations INRC) form a commutative group.

(3) *Logical proportions.* This resembles Spearman's principle of the "eduction of correlates" (cf. Piaget, *Classes, Relations et Nombres*, pp. 97–99 (Vrin, 1942)). We proceed by establishing a relationship between two pairs of terms on the model of an arithmetical ratio (e.g. $\frac{2}{4} = \frac{3}{6}$), such that the relation existing between the first pair recurs in the case of the second pair and thus determines the choice of the fourth term.

Conclusion: The Psychological Meaning of
These Logical Structures[*]

We have described the operational structures from a psychological point of view, and analyzed a certain number of structures in terms of the algebra of logic, but we still have to bring out the correspondence between these two systems, and explain how algebraic structures can be used in psychological explanation. For this purpose it will be convenient to deal with the higher structures first, and then come back to the simpler ones.

PROPOSITIONAL STRUCTURES

To give a complete account of these structures we would have to show that the 16 binary operations of two-valued propositional logic are present in the intuitive thought of adolescents aged 12 to 15. But it is unnecessary to give examples here, as we have already shown that adolescents do, in fact, use these 16 binary operations, as well as a certain number of ternary operations or operations of a higher rank.

Further, and this is extremely important, the subject can proceed from any one of these operations to any other. On the other hand, the child aged 7 to 11 when given an inductive problem in physics, as in the case of Mlle Inhelder's problems, limits himself to the raw experimental data. He classifies, orders the data in series, sets up correspondences between them, etc., but does not isolate the factors involved or embark upon systematic experimentation. The adolescent, however, after several preliminary attempts tries to discover all possible combinations, so as to select the true and discard the false. In the course of this selective activity he intuitively constructs a combinatorial system. It is for this reason that he repeatedly passes from one propositional operation to another. The method of solution in each actual problem situation then consists in the selection of the true combination (or combinations) out of the whole set of possible combinations.

Propositional operations do not therefore appear in the adolescent's thought as unrelated discrete operations; they form a system or *structured whole*. What we have to discover is in what manner this structure is given for the subject.

As we have seen, the fact that the logic of propositions proceeds from the possible (i.e., theoretical) to the actual and consists in truth-selections, leads to a very simple hypothesis as to the psychological meaning of the system of propositional operations; and consequently, as to the way in which the *structured wholes*, such as the lattice or the group INRC, which are a feature of these operations, appear in the child's mind.

If this hypothesis were not accepted, what other explanation could we give for these structures? By way of a first hypothesis they might be regarded as the cumulative product of past experience. But such an interpretation seems improbable since they are completely unconscious.

---

[*][The following section is from Chapter IV.]

The adolescent is not conscious of the system of propositional operations. He undoubtedly uses these operations, but he does this without enumerating them, or reflecting on them or their relationships, and he only faintly suspects that they form such a system. He is unaware of this, in the same way that in singing or whistling he is unaware of the laws of harmony. The view that such unconscious structures result from a summation of acquired experiences is thus quite unacceptable.

A second hypothesis would be to treat these structures as a priori forms of the mind; for such forms, if they exist, can remain unconscious and nevertheless still influence the development of thought. But if we really are concerned here with a priori forms why do they appear at so late a stage?

A third hypothesis might be to regard them as arising from the late maturation of certain neural connections (we know, for example, that it is possible to apply propositional operations to neural networks).* But if the logical *structured wholes* exist as ready-made traces in the nervous system, they ought to appear in their entirety during thinking. This is simply not the case: only certain parts of such structures are actualized, the rest remain in the form of possible transformations.

We thus come to our fourth and last hypothesis, already touched upon, in which the lattice and the group INRC are regarded as structures belonging to the simple forms of equilibrium attained by thought activity. In the first place these structures appear psychologically in the form of a few concrete operations, but what is more important they provide a field of possible transformations.

A state of equilibrium, it should be remembered, is one in which all the virtual transformations compatible with the relationships of the system compensate each other. From a psychological point of view, the logical structures correspond precisely to this model. On the one hand, these structures appear in the form of a set of virtual transformations, consisting of all the operations which it would be possible to carry out starting from a few actually performed operations. On the other, these structures are essentially reversible, that is to say, the virtual transformations which they permit are always self-compensatory as a consequence of inversions and reciprocities.

In this way, we can explain why the subject is affected by such structures, without being conscious of them. When starting from an actually performed propositional operation, or endeavoring to express the characters of a given situation by such an operation, he cannot proceed in any way he likes. He finds himself, as it were, in a field of force governed by the laws of equilibrium, carrying out transformations or operations determined not only by occurrences in the immediate past, but by the laws of the whole operational field of which these past occurrences form a part.

We can now understand the paradox resulting from the simultaneous appearance of operational schemata (such as combinations, proportions, the schema of mechanical equilibrium) and of propositional operations, whose connection remains unperceived by the subject, and whose kinship the psychologist is unable to appreciate in his ignorance of algebraic structures. Operational schemata are thus to be thought of as actualized

*W. S. McCulloch and W. Pitts, *Bull. Math. Biophys.*, 5 (1943): 115–133.

structures, implying the diverse possibilities implicit in the *structured whole*, that is to say, in the form of equilibrium of the propositional operations.

Mathematical combinatorial operations are formed systematically from the first, whenever the situation or problem demands it; since the subject, when he coordinates experiential data and especially when he selects out of all the possible propositional operations those which fit this particular arrangement of data, is concerned with an implicit combinatorial system. This combinatorial system implied by the lattice of propositional operations is therefore derived by abstraction from the operational constructions intuitively arrived at by the subject. Hence, it is not due to chance that this system appears at the same level of intellectual development as the logic of propositions.

The concept of mechanical equilibrium, too, is only understood at the same period except of course, when all the given data are simultaneously visible in an intuitively simple system. We have seen that subjects have difficulty in distinguishing four transformations: increase or decrease of action and increase or decrease of reaction. The reaction (for example, the resistance of a liquid to the pressure of a piston) is not understood by small children as occurring in an inverse sense to that of action (resistance), but as a force which adds itself to the latter (the heavier the liquid the higher it can rise). To be able to solve this problem, the child has to coordinate the inversions (increase and decrease of action or reaction) and reciprocities. In fact, the reaction conceived as equal to the action but occurring in an inverse sense is a typical example of the relation of reciprocity. It is then natural to assume that the capacity for coordinating these inversions and reciprocities into a single system is based on an understanding of the logical relationships of inversion (CN) and reciprocity (R); therefore of the group INRC. Reciprocity can, in fact, have the same resultant as inversion, without necessarily becoming confused with it; similarly, the inversion of reciprocity (C) can without confusion have the same resultant as the identity transformation (I). The above assumption has a good deal to support it as subjects at this level (12 to 15 years) after having failed at the lower levels, are able to coordinate the four transformations INRC in quite different problems; such as those of relative motion, i.e., the prediction of changes in position of a moving body within a framework of reference itself in motion in relation to a fixed system (for example, the changes in position of a snail on a moving board).* All this seems to occur as if the acquisition of the logic of propositions went together with an understanding of the group INRC, not, of course, *in abstracto*, but as applied to various problems.

An important application of this "group" logic occurs, as we have seen, in the scheme of logical proportionality. It is striking once again to observe that this schema appears at the level of development at which the child begins to understand mathematical proportions. No doubt it will be objected that, since mathematical proportions are equalities between two relationships, they are much simpler than propositional proportions and can be constructed independently of them. But the following two facts need noting. In the first place, if the child had

*See Piaget, *The Child's Conception of Movement and Speed*, 1946.

directly understood the mathematical concept without the aid of the system of propositional operations, there would be no reason why this mathematical concept should not already be implicit in his thinking at the level of concrete operations, since the concept of a fraction is derivative from that of inclusion, and the equality of two fractions merely presents an additional difficulty of a trivial kind.

But, in all the fields we have examined, the schema of proportionality is only understood at the level of propositional operations. Further, all these systems of proportions which the child discovers for himself without schooling are found by means of a logical qualitative schema. The child begins by noting certain compensations, or equivalences; for example, the weight on a balance may be increased whilst its distance from the fulcrum remains unchanged, or the distance may be increased and the weight left constant. He then coordinates the inversions and reciprocities, and thus arrives at a qualitative statement of the proportion which he verifies by measuring, and in this way finally discovers the metrical proportion.

What therefore has to be explained is this anticipatory qualitative schema, which is why we believe that, psychologically, proportionality

begins through the logical schema $\dfrac{p}{q} = \dfrac{\bar{q}}{\bar{p}}$ or $\dfrac{p}{q} = R\dfrac{\bar{p}}{\bar{q}}$, which in turn is

based on the group INRC.

The above interpretation is made more plausible by the fact that, in many fields, the subject aged 12 to 14, without recourse to measurement or other quantitative methods, arrives at a qualitative schema—that of "multiplicative compensations"—which is closely akin to that of proportions. For example, in the case of changes in the form of an object it may be asked why the conservation of volume is only acquired in a general form toward the age of 12? The reason for this is that an increase in one of the dimensions is compensated by a corresponding decrease in the two others, in accordance with a multiplicative system implying proportionality. Once again, reasoning is shown to be dependent on an anticipatory schema, whose connection with the preceding schemata is fairly evident.

Other examples might be given, such as the combinatorial probabilities (assuming that it is through such combinations that possibility and fact are brought together), correlations (based on the quantification of the four conjunctions $p \cdot q$, $p \cdot \bar{q}$, $\bar{p} \cdot q$, and $\bar{p} \cdot \bar{q}$), etc. But we do not need to enter into details here.

What we have already said justifies the following conclusion: the construction of propositional operations is accompanied by a series of changes in the subject's capacity to perform operations. The different schemata which he acquires are shown to imply not merely isolated propositional operations, but the *structured wholes* themselves (the lattice and the group INRC) which the propositional operations exemplify. The *structured whole*, considered as the form of equilibrium of the subject's operational behavior, is therefore of fundamental psychological importance, which is why the logical (algebraic) analysis of such structures gives the psychologist an indispensable instrument of explanation and prediction.

CONCRETE OPERATIONAL STRUCTURES AND

PREOPERATIONAL STRUCTURES

The use of the algebra of logic is not, however, restricted to an analysis of psychological activities at the level of propositional operations. The eight groupements of classes and relations, constructed at the level of concrete operations, are of equal value in the study of behavior at this earlier level. The psychological problem at this stage is to construct a catalogue of possible operations for a mode of thought to which the combinatorial system implied by the lattice structure is still alien; and to explain why this mode of thought is unable to achieve a general formal mechanism independently of its content. The system of eight groupements answers these two questions. In the first place, it gives an exhaustive catalogue of concrete operations, since their number is not arbitrary, but is made up as follows: classes and relations (2), addition and multiplication (2), symmetry and asymmetry (2), hence $2 \times 2 \times 2 = 8$. Secondly, we have here eight interdependent systems, and not a single system enabling us to pass from one operation to any other, and this explains the absence of a general formal mechanism.

At the concrete level (7 to 11 years), elementary groupements, such as the group and lattice structure of propositional operations, make up the form of equilibrium of operational behavior, but an equilibrium less stable and covering a less extended field. We thus have to find out how this equilibrium comes about. Though we know that the final equilibrium is prepared and partly organized at the preoperational level (2 to 7 years), we still have to show what mechanisms at this preoperational level are the precursors of the future operations.

In term these mechanisms "regulations." They are to be conceived of as partial compensations or partial returns to the starting point, with compensatory adjustments accompanying changes in the direction of the original activity. Such regulations are found in the sensorimotor field (perceptions, etc.), and they come more and more to govern the representations preceding the operational level. For example, when we stretch a sausage-shaped piece of modeling clay, the child assumes there has been an increase in the amount of the material. Finally when it becomes very thin he gets the impression that the amount of material has diminished.

Such regulations which apply to the fields of perception and representation can also be formulated in terms of the algebra of logic. All we need to do is to express the transformations in terms of groupements, and transform the resultant logical inequalities into equalities, by adding the "noncompensated transformations" $+P$ or $-P$ as the case may be.

The particular advantage of this kind of formulation is that it brings out the difference between the changes (irreversible or not wholly reversible) occurring in perception or representation, and the corresponding reversible transformations which characterize operations. We have, for example, made use of this method in the analysis of perceptions, in spite of the absence of additive composition and logical coherence which is a feature of this mode of experience. The concrete operations which belong to the 7 to 8 level can then be considered as the resultant of these regulations when they reach a state of equilibrium, the point where equilibrium is reached being that of complete compensation. In other words, at the point where complete reversibility is achieved, "regulations of representations" are ipso facto transformed into operations. This is therefore the final form of equilibrium of regulations, and bears some resemblance to the way in which *feedback* (regulation) operates in a servo-mechanism as long as there is disequilibrium, and as soon as equilibrium is reached, takes on the form of a group.

Thus, even in those fields in which logic does not normally play a part, there exist *outline structures* which are the precursors of logical structures, and which can be formulated in terms of the algebra of logic. From a comparative point of view, these *outline structures* are of great interest. It is not inconceivable that a general theory of structures will at some future date be worked out, which will permit the comparative analysis of structures characterizing the different levels of development. This will relate the lower level *outline structures* to the logical structures characteristic of the higher stages of development. The use of the logical calculus in the description of neural networks on the one hand, and in cybernetic models on the other, shows that such a program is not out of the question.

Though the preceding discussion is concerned only with certain levels of the intellectual development of the child and adolescent, I should be glad if it could be regarded as a contribution to such studies.

PART VII

The Representation of Reality: Action, Space, and Geometry; Time, Movement, and Speed

INTRODUCTION

During the early 1940s Piaget turned much of his attention toward discovering the logical models corresponding to the child's thought at different stages of development, as well as to the actual use of logical reasoning by the child. Both of these aspects of the logicalization of developmental psychology bring to the foreground the problem of representation. Logical operations cannot be performed on anything like raw or immediate experience, but only on highly refined mental products, that is, the signs that stand for such experiences. Later in the 1940s, therefore, Piaget virtually doubled in his tracks and went more deeply into this problem of representation. Seemingly it is developmentally prior to logical operations; as it turns out, Piaget shows how the two strands of development occur in tandem. In *Play, Dreams and Imitation*, Piaget deals mainly with one aspect of representation: how the child represents his own and others' actions to himself. In the studies of action, space and geometry, time, and movement and speed, Piaget deals with children's deepening and enlarging knowledge of the universe around them. Are the major dimensions adults use to describe their world—such as distance, time, and rate—immediately self-evident ideas, or are they constructed in the same slow and complex way that Piaget has shown to be the case for other matters?

How does the child come to represent the world to himself? How does he attempt to measure it and master it, by what operations and representations? In order to make sense out of the universe the child must possess the instruments that make these questions possible. These instruments are the logical operations of classification and seriation. They bear upon discrete, whole objects whose position in space is unimportant. Their temporal ordering can always be reversed. These logical operations are not read directly off the environment: they are the product of reflection and abstraction by the subject upon his own actions and their coordination into a meaningful system.

In the sensorimotor construction of reality, we have already seen the crucial role played by the enactive schemata of intelligence in the elaboration of the here-and-now universe of the infant. Symbolic representation and cognitive operations play the same role in the conception of objects at this new level of mental development.

Piaget begins with the question: how does this set of mental operations help the child in his construction of reality? This question is then transformed into a different one: how does a logic that is built upon individual, discrete entities (objects) help in the construction of objects that are at once unitary totalities and divisible along the crucial dimensions of spatial position, temporal order, and speed?

The genesis of the representation of reality will, then, be the story of the adaptation of logical schemata and operations to *infralogical* materials. These operations do not deal any more with the domain of class inclusions but with inclusions of the parts of an object into one single totality, the whole object.

This substitution of domains leads to a substitution of notions: the notion of resemblance is replaced by that of vicinity or proximity, the notion of difference by that of order and displacement, and that of number by that of measurement.

Consequently, the prefix *infra* carries no negative meaning. Infralogical operations are developmentally neither inferior nor prior to logical ones. On the contrary, for Piaget, logical and infralogical operations develop roughly at the same time. But the former concern the discontinuity of individual objects, whereas the latter concern the partition of a continuum. Hence the separation of domains. But in both cases, the external observer witnesses the development of the same basic system of operations in which number at the logical level corresponds to measure at the infralogical one. If number results from the synthesis of classification and seriation, measurement results from the synthesis of partition and displacement, partition being equivalent to classification, and displacement to seriation.

Once one understands this whole system of correspondences among cognitive notions in Piaget's psychological theory, one can see how much Piaget owes to structuralism, which reduces reality to a vast system of correspondences and oppositions; in Lévi-Strauss's words "it is the logic of oppositions and correlations, exclusions and inclusions, compatibilities and incompatibilities, which explains the laws of association, not the reverse."* Piaget strongly believes in such a view "based on a system of operations which would not be without similarities to Boolean algebra."†

The problem of representation touches on every aspect of mental life. This is reflected in the structure of this part of the book. We begin it with a sketch, by the editors, of *Play, Dreams and Imitation*. This is followed by a chapter on the semiotic function from *The Psychology of the Child*, giving an excellent synthesis of the whole subject. Part VII also includes selections from works on the child's conceptions of movement, on time, and on space. The reader is also advised to turn to Selection 18, where can be found some of Piaget's earliest observations on the growth of imitation in the young baby. In his writings on moral development (Selections 16 and 17) Piaget also deals with aspects of play and imitation. While all this seems quite a miscellany, it is held together by one central concern, the problem of representation.

In discussing the growth of thought in children, Piaget wrote of the importance of argument: "It may well be that it is disputes that lead children to the need to make themselves understood."‡ Something similar might be said of Piaget himself. He has been involved in a number of controversies, and he has even sometimes changed his thinking as a result. In Selection 28, his reply to Wallon, he goes as far as to admit such a change, although grudgingly. We include here Piaget's reactions to two critics, one on imitation, the other on play. Brian Sutton-Smith's recent work on play is well known. Henri Wallon was a great French psychologist, especially known both for his Marxist views and for his efforts to integrate emotional and intellectual aspects of child development. Although he and Piaget exchanged intellectual blows, they remained good friends, and had great respect for each other.**

* Claude Lévi-Strauss, *Totemism* (Boston: Beacon Press, 1963), p. 90.
† *Ibid.*
‡ Piaget, *Language and Thought of the Child*, 1923.
** See *Henri Wallon: His World, His Work*, edited by Gilbert Voyat and Beverly Birns, *International Journal of Mental Health*, vol. 1, 1972–73, whole number 4 devoted to Wallon.

27

The Semiotic or Symbolic Function*

1966

INTRODUCTORY NOTES

La formation du symbole chez l'enfant: Imitation, jeu et rêve; image et représentation. This was the original French title of one of Piaget's three books based on observations of his own children. The title was shortened in English translation to *Play, Dreams and Imitation.* This change of name reflects the complexity of Piaget's goals and a certain difference in point of view. To be sure, in one focus the study makes use of the materials of children's play, dreams, and imitation, but Piaget's goals in writing this book were more general and more subtle. He himself refers to the book as *La Formation du Symbole,* because for him its major focus is the period of childhood from 2 to 7–8 years, during which the child is rapidly developing not only language, but all other aspects of the symbolic function or, more accurately, the semiotic function: the ways in which the individual represents his world, his actions, and his experiences to himself. As Piaget himself puts the relation between these two foci, "Only after discussing the problems of imitation, play, and unconscious symbolic thought can we then . . . place within the whole structure the beginnings of cognitive representation and draw the resulting conclusions as to the mechanism of representational activity or the symbolic function."† Thus, play, dreams, and imitation are the means, but the goal beyond them is the growth of the symbolic function.

This is the last of the works in which Piaget uses his own children as subjects. In another way, too, it forms a link with his earlier work. He is still concerned here with the growth of the child from the solipsism of infancy to the egocentric thought of early childhood; he makes considerable use of these concepts as well as the related categories of experience, such as animism, phenomenism, and artificialism, which can all be grouped under the general heading of "magical thought." Again, however, Piaget had a goal that lay beyond his examination and reexamination of these issues. By the end of

*From *The Psychology of the Child* by Jean Piaget and Bärbel Inhelder, translated from the French by Helen Weaver. © 1969 by Basic Books, Inc., Publishers, New York. Reprinted by permission of Basic Books, Inc., and Routledge & Kegan Paul Ltd., London. Originally published in French, 1966.

† J. Piaget, *Plays, Dreams and Imitation in Childhood,* p. 2.

this period of development the child will have gotten a firm foothold on the stage of concrete operations. But these operations do not spring from nowhere; they become possible precisely because the representative function has reached a certain level of effectiveness: "What now therefore requires to be done is to bridge the gap between sensorimotor activity prior to representation, and the operational forms of thought. The problem again becomes that of describing the beginnings of representational thought. . . ."*

By the end of this period the child will be both more socialized and more logical in her thinking. It may help to clarify Piaget's goals if we contrast his treatment of the relation between these two poles with that of many other psychologists. One common way of looking at the question is to propose that the child learns adult forms of logical thought by becoming more socialized, and this mainly through the process of imitation (and reinforcement for correct imitation). This formulation puts all the emphasis on the child's accommodation of her available cognitive structures to the demands of external reality. For Piaget, however, the primary relationship runs the other way: "Though obviously social life plays an essential role in the elaboration of concepts and of the representational schemas related to verbal expression, it does not in itself explain the beginnings of the image or the symbol as they are to be seen in deferred imitation or in the first imaginative games of the one year-old child. . . . the social fact is for us a fact to be explained, not to be invoked as an extra-psychological factor."†

This difference in point of view is dramatically expressed in contemporary research emphases. Imitation (now often called "modeling"), seen as the child's copying the behavior of others or the starkest sort of social accommodation, is widely studied, but the growth of imitation hardly at all. And the development of play, the assimilative pole of children's activity, is practically invisible in contemporary psychological research. In contrast, Piaget devotes considerably more space to play than to imitation, and he views the possibility of successful accommodation as entirely dependent on its coupling with assimilation in ever-increasing complexity. In one mood we may emphasize the accommodation of schemata to reality; in another mood we may emphasize the inner life of the child, in which she assimilates what she wants and what she can to her personal repertoire of these schemata. Piaget leaves no doubt that he sees these processes as indissociable functions of development and adaptation:

> Progressive equilibrium between assimilation of objects to individual activity and accommodation of activity to objects results in the reversibility which characterizes the operations of reason, while the primacy of accommodation characterizes imitation and the image, and the primacy of assimilation explains play and the "unconscious" symbol.‡

We turn now to a brief sketch of the book itself.

This period differs from the preceding one (sensorimotor level) in three ways: speed of the processes, spatial and temporal distances, and immediacy. At the sensorimotor level, the articulations of actions are necessarily successive, since one action must take place after another, each step serving as an index guiding the next. At the semiotic level or, as Piaget calls it, in a very revealing way, the preoperational period, the child, because of the growth of

* Ibid., p. 1.
† Ibid., p. 4.
‡ Ibid.

representation, becomes able to form a whole picture of a given situation, holding at once all the represented successive actions to be taken to reach a certain goal. Thought processes have been sped up and what were successive steps become a simultaneous totality.

The infant was capable only of actions in the here and now of his actual experience, with little anticipation of the future or recourse to the past. Now, the child is able to locate himself in a space that goes beyond perceptual space and in a field of time that permits the coordination of past, present, and future. Representation is the presentation, in thought, of what is perceptually absent.

At the sensorimotor level, the infant needs immediate contact with objects as apprehended through his available schemata. At the preoperational level, the child enters in contact with the objects via language and representation, that is to say, through the mediation of concepts.

This book deals with selected portions of the semiotic function. Language, which had been studied earlier by Piaget, is not mentioned. Mental imagery will be studied only much later. The subject matter is symbolic play, imitation, and to some extent, dreams. Early reasoning and preconcepts will be the object of several other books.

Piaget's theory of symbolization is rooted in Peirce's and Saussure's theories of signification, although little reference is made to these authors. Meaning is understood as the relationship between a signified, which is an object or an action, and a signifier, which stands for it. He distinguishes three sorts of signifiers: the *index*, which is an integral part of the signified; the *sign*, which is arbitrarily linked with the signified; and the *symbol*, which exhibits some analogical correspondence with the signified. For instance, the ringing of the telephone is an index, a word is a sign, and using a stick as a gun is a symbol. In addition, signs are always social signifiers, whereas symbols can be social or individual signifiers. The symbolism of dreams is individual; in contrast, the symbolism of games is social.

The book is divided into three parts: part one, on imitation, emphasizes the pole of accommodation that is inherent in any adaptive behavior pattern; part two, dealing with play and to some extent with dreams, emphasizes the pole of assimilation. The third part of the book is somewhat different, since it treats the problem of cognitive representation.

Piaget distinguishes six stages in the development of imitation.

Stage I: Preparation through Reflex. During this stage, infants imitate through contagion at the reflex level, as in echolalia and echopraxia. But this does not mean that all contagious phenomena, such as yawning, are reflex reactions. Contagious yawning appears rather late during the sensorimotor period of development. In this period imitation, in the sense of copying someone else, is absent.

Stage II: Sporadic Imitation. The infant imitates sporadically and unsystematically auditory and tactilo-kinesthetic models, provided that the model accomplishes a sound or a movement that the baby has already performed himself.

Stage III: Beginnings of Systematic Imitation. Systematic imitation of sounds and movements belonging to the infant's repertoire of noises and gestures. Here, Piaget, more careful in his observations than other psychologists who have studied imitation after him, observes that apparently imitative behavior patterns of infants do not constitute a modeling after an adult or an older child. In the first months of life, the infant does not make a clear distinction between what is his own body and what is his environment. Consequently, he does not dissociate his own actions from those of others, his own limbs from those of others. This is the stage that Piaget, after Baldwin, calls "adualism"; Freud, narcissism; Wallon, symbiosis.

Stage IV: Imitation of Movements Already Made but Not Visible on His Body by the Subject. The child imitates movements that he has seen in others but not seen in himself. These movements already belong to his natural repertoire of gestures and movements. They are movements of the mouth, showing the tongue, sucking one's thumb, etc. These imitations are usually gross attempts at imitating. For instance, instead of protrusion of the tongue, a child will bite his lips. Instead of closing and opening his eyes, the child will open and close his mouth. In addition, the child becomes capable of good imitations of sounds and movements that can be kept under perceptual control all the time such as tapping with two blocks, hitting a xylophone with a mallet, using tools and objects, and so on.

Stage V: Systematic Imitation of New Models Including Those Involving Movements Not Visible to the Child. At this stage, the child imitates with perseverance and precision. He accommodates his schemata according to the demands of the models but not in order to utilize them. This difference in attitude marks the difference between intelligence and imitation for Piaget. In the act of intelligence, the child accommodates his schemata to the demands of the objects only in order to use them toward some goal. In imitation, the act of accommodation is pursued for its own sake, i.e., for the sake of the object.

Stage VI: Deferred Imitation. This stage is marked by a drastic change in the way in which the child imitates. Now, his imitations take place in the absence of the model, because of internalization by the child of his own movements. This last form of imitation is a symbolic evocation, because it does not lean upon the presence of the model.

Imitation plays a central role in the construction of signifiers because it is the link between the sensorimotor and the semiotic periods, and because it is the link among the various signifiers appearing during the latter period: language, symbolic play, mental imagery, and representational drawing. Because of its social nature, language necessarily entails a good deal of imitation. Symbolic play, with its emphasis on make-believe, supposes deferred imitation of actual behavior patterns. Mental images and drawings have always been considered as imitative; witness the surprise and confusion many adults experience when confronted with abstract painting. When nonimitative, unusual images such as centaurs or minotaurs arise in consciousness, they are often elevated to divine status.

The study of symbolic play forms the second part of this book.

Piaget distinguishes three sorts of play: rule games, exercise games, and symbolic play. Rule games form an important portion of *Moral Judgment* and are therefore not discussed here. Exercise games are those actions that infants repeat just for the fun of it, for what the Bühlers called *Funktionlust* (pleasure of functioning). This sort of play activity goes on all through adult life where it is often socialized into activities such as sports. Such practice play is not restricted to motor activity, but also takes linguistic and symbolic forms such as confabulation, nonsense chanting, or the "why" games where no answer is expected from anyone.

Symbolic play starts around the last two stages of sensorimotor development, when a child begins to apply a sensorimotor schema in the absence of the appropriate object or outside of its habitual context. The child makes believe that he sleeps, cries, sings, or eats; and he invents imaginary situations. These pretendings do not last long and are limited to short segments of actions. Around the age of five, the child starts to organize all these activities in a coherent world in which he lives. He imitates real situations such as he encounters in school or stressful events of the recent past.

This last point, the functions of symbolic play, leads Piaget to discuss contemporary explanations of play: G. S. Hall's recapitulation theory, Groos's preexercise theory, and Buytendyk's infantile dynamics theory.

His examination of the functions of play in the global economy of a child's life leads also to a discussion of secondary symbolism in play and children's dreams. This gives Piaget occasion to specify his position toward psychoanalysis, at least as it is represented by Freud, Adler, and Jung. Piaget rejects the psychoanalytic position according to which the child is innately equipped with a complex cognitive superstructure. He simplifies notably theories of unconscious processes by means of his theory of schemata. For Piaget, affective schemata remain unconscious not because instinctual impulses are censored, but because assimilation, to the extent that it is not matched with equivalent accommodation, remains an unconscious process. The application of old schemata to novel situations is almost completely unconscious, be it in problem-solving or in emotional conflicts. There is no need for representative memory in the unconscious, since affective and cognitive schemata assure this mechanism of relating the past to the present in a continuous, unconscious way. There is no need for censorship, since the process of knowing is mainly unconscious. For Piaget, there is no mystery in ignorance. Ignorance is simply ignorance, ignorance, ignorance.

The rejection of the concept of censorship, however, does not entail the elimination of the concept of repression or other psychoanalytic mechanisms. Since Piagetian schemata tend to assimilate each other all the time, there is a constant shifting around of these schemata before they fall correctly into place, so to speak. This mutual assimilation results in all sorts of emotional displacements. In such a perspective, the psychoanalytic concepts of projection and identification are nothing but preconceptual assimilations. For instance, identification with the father becomes, for Piaget, a simple form of prelogical participation of the schemata of the self in the schemata of the father due to the mutual assimilation of these two schemata. The schema, or, as psychoanalysts would tend to say, the image, of the father swallows up the schema of the self (identification) that, in turn, absorbs the schema of the father (projection). This mutual assimilation eventuates in two different forms of thought: logical thought and autistic thought. Logical thought is the form of thought that reaches a certain equilibrium between the inner solicitations of assimilation and the external demands of accommodation. It is intelligent and adaptive. Autistic thought is entirely wrapped up in the exorbitant needs of assimilation and it produces all sorts of fantasies and disadaptations.

In sum, for Piaget, unconscious symbolic thought obeys the general rules of thought as expressed by him in his theory of assimilation. This coherence, at the functional level, of all forms of thought becomes even more striking if one examines the beginning of conceptual thought or cognitive representation.

Cognitive representation enables the child to represent an action instead of or before performing it. Acting upon the world is no more an immediate

and direct intervention upon the situation, but, rather, a reflective intervention. But, at this stage, the representional competence of the child is limited
by the specific features of every single situation that must be more or less
known to her as well as being located in her immediate space and time. This
limitation makes the child more sensitive to states than to transformations, to
static perceptual configurations than to conceptual operations such as, for
example, actually counting objects in an array.

At the same time, the child becomes capable of designating objects by
symbolic systems and not only by direct action. The child learns that things
have a name, but these names no longer exactly belong to the things to which
they refer. For instance, the same cat is called several names by the people
around the child: cat, pussy, Felix, beast. But the same name is given to
different objects: there are other cats than my pussy, Felix, beast; other
pussies, Felixes, beasts. These distinctions are not very clear to the child. For
instance, Lucienne Piaget calls "big girls" "Jacquelines" after her older sister
and girls her own age "Luciennes" after herself. Looking at a picture of
Jacqueline when she was her own age, Lucienne exclaims: "Oh, oh, this is
Jacqueline when she was a Lucienne."

In the same way, there is some hesitancy in the child this age about the
system of class inclusion: "This is *not* a bee. It's a *bumble*-bee. Is it a beast?."
The use of articles is not very precise either. A worm and *the* worm are confused by Jacqueline. Having seen a worm during a walk in the woods, she
says upon encountering another, "Here it is," and a third, "The worm again."

In short, the child of this age uses preconcepts instead of real concepts.
Preconcepts are characterized by the fusion of the individual and the collective into one, the confusion of the whole and the part as well as the
diffusion of the subjective and the objective. In the same way, relations are
only prerelations: the child says, "Mothers are ladies," flatly, without even
touching the specific difference between mothers and ladies, namely, that
mothers are ladies with children. This mode of reasoning in the child was
called "transduction" by William Stern to mark the fact that it lies between
induction and deduction, between the general and specific, and between
objective and subjective. The child goes from one undifferentiated entity to
another: "No, it's not afternoon, I didn't take my nap" or, from Lucienne
Piaget, all babies must be baby brothers, because it is so in her own case
with baby-brother Laurent.

This egocentrism appears also in the child's conception of causality.
Animism, artificialism, moralism, and finalism are different forms of the same
mentalism in the child. By assimilation to one's own action, animism is the
animation of everything that displays an activity. This animation is progressively reduced to self-moving objects (for instance, clouds), living objects, and
finally only some of them. Artificialism is the belief that all objects are constructed on the model of "the construction of babies." Moralism results from
the lack of differentiation between moral and physical laws. The floating of
boats is thus explained by the fact that, though they are heavy, boats are intelligent enough to keep their heads above water. Finalism explains everything in terms of the goal to be reached; clouds, for instance, move to bring
about the dark of night. Thus, it is obvious that, in all forms of causality presented here, there is a mentalization of material phenomena. But, in sharp
contrast with this, there is also a strong materialism in the child of this
period: dreams and ideas are, for instance, real material things that one could
touch with the finger, if one wanted to.

This excess of both idealism and materialism is the best evidence in favor of the child's egocentrism. Being so forcefully egocentric, the child has no need for logical proof or for objectivity in her dealings with the world. Her egocentrism takes care of all the problems and this last trait makes the preconceptual child so pleasant to adults who have lost most but not all of their own egocentrism. A preconceptual child reminds them that the virtue of egocentrism is the primacy of satisfaction over verification, as we see in Piaget's analysis of play, in this and the succeeding two papers.

At the end of the sensorimotor period, at about one and a half to two years, there appears a function that is fundamental to the development of later behavior patterns. It consists in the ability to represent something (a signified something: object, event, conceptual scheme, etc.) by means of a "signifier" which is differentiated and which serves only a representative purpose: language, mental image, symbolic gesture, and so on. Following H. Head and the specialists in aphasia, we generally refer to this function that gives rise to representation as "symbolic." However, since linguists distinguish between "symbols" and "signs," we would do better to adopt their term "semiotic function" to designate those activities having to do with the differentiated signifiers as a whole.

The Semiotic Function and Imitation

The sensorimotor mechanisms are prerepresentational, and behavior based on the evocation of an absent object is not observed until during the second year. When the scheme of the permanent object is in process of being formed, from about nine to twelve months, there is certainly a search for an object that has disappeared; but since it has just been perceived, the search is part of an action already under way, and a series of clues remains to aid the child to find the object again.

Although representation does not yet exist, the baby forms and uses significations, since every sensorimotor assimilation (including perceptual assimilations) already implies the attribution of a signification, of a meaning. Significations and consequently also a duality between "signified" (the schemes themselves with their content; that is, the action) and "signifiers" are already present. However, these "signifiers" remain perceptual and are not yet differentiated from the "signified." This makes it impossible to talk about semiotic function at this level. An undifferentiated signifier is, in fact, as yet neither a "symbol" nor a "sign" (in the sense of verbal signs). It is by definition an "indicator" (including the "signals" occurring in conditioning, like the sound of the bell that announces food). An indicator is actually undifferentiated from its signified in that it constitutes an aspect of it (whiteness for milk), a part (the visible section for a semihidden object), a temporal antecedent (the door that opens for the arrival of Mama), a causal result (a stain), etc.

THE APPEARANCE OF THE SEMIOTIC FUNCTION

In the course of the second year (and continuing from Stage 6 of infancy), however, certain behavior patterns appear which imply the representative evocation of an object or event not present and which consequently presuppose the formation or use of differentiated signifiers, since they must be able to refer to elements not perceptible at the time as well as to those which are present. One can distinguish at least five of these behavior patterns whose appearance is almost simultaneous and which we shall list in order of increasing complexity:

1. First there is *deferred imitation*, that is, imitation which starts after the disappearance of the model. In a behavior pattern of sensori-motor imitation the child begins by imitating in the presence of the model (for example, a movement of the hand), after which he may continue in the absence of the model, though this does not imply any representation in thought. But in the case of a little girl of sixteen months who sees a playmate become angry, scream, and stamp her foot (new sights for her) and who, an hour or two after the playmate's departure, imitates the scene, laughing, the deferred imitation constitutes the beginning of representation, and the imitative gesture the beginning of a differentiated signifier.

2. Then there is *symbolic play* or the game of pretending, which is unknown at the sensorimotor level. The same little girl invented her first symbolic game by pretending to sleep—sitting down and smiling broadly, but closing her eyes, her head to one side, her thumb in her mouth, and holding a corner of the tablecloth, pretending that it was the corner of her pillow, according to the ritual she observes when she goes to sleep. Shortly afterward she put her stuffed bear to sleep and slid a shell along a box while saying "meow" (she had just seen a cat on a wall). In all these cases the representation is clear-cut and the deferred signifier is an imitative gesture, though accompanied by objects which are becoming symbolic.

3. The *drawing* or graphic image is at first an intermediate stage between play and mental image. It rarely appears before two or two and a half years.

4. Then, sooner or later, comes the *mental image*, no trace of which is observed on the sensorimotor level (otherwise discovery of the permanent object would be greatly facilitated). It appears as an internalized imitation.

5. Finally, nascent language permits *verbal evocation* of events that are not occurring at the time. When the little girl says "meow" after the cat has disappeared, verbal representation is added to imitation. When, some time afterward, she says "Anpa bye-bye" (Grandpa went away), pointing to the sloping path he took when he left, the representation is supported either by the differentiated signifier, consisting of the signs of the nascent language, or by both language and mental image.

THE ROLE OF IMITATION

Given these first manifestations of the semiotic function, the problem is to understand the mechanism of its formation. This is greatly simplified by the fact that the first four of these five forms of behavior are based on imitation. Moreover, language itself, which, contrary to the preceding behavior patterns, is not invented by the child, is necessarily acquired in a context of imitation. (If it were learned solely by means of a series of conditionings, as is often maintained, it would appear as early as the second month.) Imitation constitutes both the sensorimotor prefiguration of representation and the transitional phase between the sensorimotor level and the level of behavior that may properly be called representative.

Imitation is first of all a prefiguration of representation. That is to say, it constitutes during the sensorimotor period a kind of representation in physical acts but not yet in thought.*

At the end of the sensorimotor period the child has acquired sufficient virtuosity in the mastery of the imitation thus generalized for deferred imitation to become possible. In fact, representation in action is then liberated from the sensorimotor requirements of direct perceptual copy and reaches an intermediary level where the action, detached from its context, becomes a differentiated signifier and consequently already constitutes in part a representation in thought. With symbolic play and drawing, this transition from representation in action to representation in thought is reinforced. The "pretending to sleep" of the example cited above is still only an action detached from its context, but it is also a symbol capable of generalization. With the mental image, which follows, imitation is no longer merely deferred but internalized, and the representation that it makes possible, thus dissociated from any external action in favor of the internal sketches or outlines of actions which will henceforth support it, is now ready to become thought. The acquisition of language, rendered accessible in these contexts of

---

*Imitation makes its appearance (with Stages 2 and 3 of infancy) through a kind of contagion or echopraxis. When someone performs in front of the child a gesture the child has just made, the child will repeat the gesture. A little later, the child will imitate any gesture made by an adult, provided that at some time or other this gesture has been performed by the child himself. There is thus at first an assimilation of what the child sees to his own schemes, and a triggering of these schemes. Then a little later the subject attempts to reproduce these models for the sake of the reproduction itself and no longer by automatic assimilation. This marks the appearance of the "prerepresentative" function fulfilled by imitation. Then the child advances rather quickly to the point where he copies gestures that are new to him, but only if they can be performed by visible parts of his own body. An important new phase begins with the imitation of facial movements (opening and closing the mouth or eyes, etc.). The difficulty is then that the child's own face is known to him only by touch and the face of the other person by sight, except for a few rare tactile explorations of the other person's face. Such explorations are very interesting to note at this level, when the child is forming correspondences between the visual and tactilo-kinesthetic sensations in order to extend imitation to the nonvisible parts of his body. Until these correspondences are elaborated, imitation of facial movements remains impossible or is accidental. For example, yawning, so contagious later, is not imitated until about the age of one, if it is silent. Once the correspondences have been established by means of a series of indications (auditory, etc.), imitation is generalized and plays an important role in the child's knowledge of his own body in analogy with the bodies of others. It is no exaggeration, therefore, to regard imitation as a kind of representation in action. Baldwin goes one step further, seeing it as an essential instrument in the complementary formation of the other and the self.

imitation, finally overlays the whole process, providing a contact with other people which is far more effective than imitation alone, and thus permitting the nascent representation to increase its powers with the aid of communication.

SYMBOLS AND SIGNS

Broadly speaking, the semiotic function gives rise to two kinds of instruments: *symbols*, which are "motivated"—that is, although they are differentiated signifiers, they do present some resemblance to the things signified; and *signs*, which are arbitrary or conventional. Symbols, being motivated, may be created by the individual by himself. The first symbols of the child's play are good examples of these individual creations, which obviously do not exclude later collective symbolisms. Deferred imitation, symbolic play, and the graphic or mental image thus depend directly on imitation, not as transmissions of readymade external models (for there is an imitation of oneself as well as of others, as is shown by the example of the game of simulating sleep), but rather as transitions from pre-representation in action to internal representation, or thought. Signs, on the other hand, being conventional, are necessarily collective. The child receives them, therefore, through the medium of imitation, but this time as an acquisition of external models. However, he immediately fashions them to suit himself and uses them, as we shall see later.

Symbolic Play

Symbolic play is the apogee of children's play. Even more than the two or three other forms of play which we shall discuss, it corresponds to the essential function that play fulfills in the life of the child. Obliged to adapt himself constantly to a social world of elders whose interests and rules remain external to him, and to a physical world which he understands only slightly, the child does not succeed as we adults do in satisfying the affective and even intellectual needs of his personality through these adaptations. It is indispensable to his affective and intellectual equilibrium, therefore, that he have available to him an area of activity whose motivation is not adaptation to reality but, on the contrary, assimilation of reality to the self, without coercions or sanctions. Such an area is play, which transforms reality by assimilation to the needs of the self, whereas imitation (when it constitutes an end in itself) is accommodation to external models. Intelligence constitutes an equilibration between assimilation and accommodation.*

Furthermore, the essential instrument of social adaptation is language, which is not invented by the child but transmitted to him in readymade, compulsory, and collective forms. These are not suited to expressing the child's needs or his living experience of himself. The

*Jean Piaget, *Play, Dreams and Imitation in Childhood* (New York: W. W. Norton, 1951; London: Routledge and Kegan Paul, 1951).

child, therefore, needs a means of self-expression, that is, a system of signifiers constructed by him and capable of being bent to his wishes. Such is the system of symbols characteristic of symbolic play. These symbols are borrowed from imitation as instruments, but not used to accurately picture external reality. Rather, imitation serves as a means of evocation to achieve playful assimilation. Thus, symbolic play is not merely an assimilation of reality to the self, as is play in general, but an assimilation made possible (and reinforced) by a symbolic "language" that is developed by the self and is capable of being modified according to its needs.*

The function of assimilation fulfilled by symbolic play is manifested in a great variety of forms, most of them primarily affective, but sometimes serving cognitive interests. A little girl who while on vacation had asked various questions about the mechanics of the bells observed on an old village church steeple, now stood stiff as a ramrod beside her father's desk, making a deafening noise. "You're bothering me, you know. Can't you see I'm working?" "Don't talk to me," replied the little girl. "I'm a church." Similarly, the child was deeply impressed by a plucked duck she'd seen on the kitchen table, and that evening was found lying on a sofa, so still that she was thought to be sick. At first she did not answer questions; then in a faraway voice she said, "I'm a dead duck!" The symbolism of play, then, may even fulfill the function of what for an adult would be internal language. Rather than simply recalling an interesting or impressive event, the child has need of a more direct symbolism which enables him to relive the event.†

*There exist three principal categories of play, and a fourth which serves as a transition between symbolic play and nonplayful activities or "serious" adaptations. (1) *Exercise play*, a primitive form of play, and the only kind that occurs at the sensorimotor level and is retained in part. It does not involve symbolism or any specific play technique, but consists in repeating, for the pleasure of it, activities acquired elsewhere in the course of adaptation. For example, the child, having discovered by chance the possibility of swinging a suspended object, at first repeats the action in order to adapt to it and understand it, which is not play. Then, having done this, he uses this behavior pattern for simple "functional pleasure" (K. Bühler) or for the pleasure of causing an effect and of confirming his newly acquired skill (something the adult does too, say, with a new car or a new television set). (2) *Symbolic play*, whose characteristics we have seen, reaches its apogee between two to three and five to six. (3) *Games with rules* (marbles, hop-scotch, etc.), which are transmitted socially from child to child and thus increase in importance with the enlargement of the child's social life. (4) Finally, out of symbolic play there develop *games of construction*, which are initially imbued with play symbolism but tend later to constitute genuine adaptations (mechanical constructions, etc.) or solutions to problems and intelligent creations.

†It is, primarily, affective conflicts that reappear in symbolic play, however. If there is a scene at lunch, for example, one can be sure that an hour or two afterward it will be re-created with dolls and will be brought to a happier solution. Either the child disciplines her doll more intelligently than her parents did her, or in play she accepts what she had not accepted at lunch (such as finishing a bowl of soup she does not like, especially if here it is the doll who finishes it symbolically). Similarly, if the child has been frightened by a big dog, in a symbolic game things will be arranged so that dogs will no longer be mean or else children will become brave. Generally speaking, symbolic play helps in the resolution of conflicts and also in the compensation of unsatisfied needs, the inversion of roles (such as obedience and authority), the liberation and extension of the self, etc.

These multiple functions of symbolic play have inspired several theories that attempt to explain all forms of play. They are today quite out of date. (An extreme example is G. S. Hall's hypothesis of hereditary recapitulation, which in the realm of play anticipated Jung's most adventurous ideas on unconscious symbols.) The most important of these early theories is that of Karl Groos, who was the first to discover that the play of children (and of animals) has an essential functional value and is not simply a diversion. He saw play as preliminary training for the future activities of the individual—which is true but obvious if you say that play, like every general function, is useful to the individual's development, but which becomes meaningless if you go into details. Is the child who plays that he is a church preparing to become a church warden, and the child who plays that he is a dead duck preparing to become an ornithologist? A much more profound theory is that of F. J. J. Buytendijk, who relates play to the laws of "infantile dynamics." However, these laws are not in themselves laws of play and in order to account for the specific nature of play it seems necessary, as we proposed above, to refer to a pole of assimilation to the self as distinct from both the accommodative pole of imitation and the equilibrium between the two (intelligence).* In symbolic play this systematic assimilation takes the form of a particular use of the semiotic function— namely, the creation of symbols at will in order to express everything in the child's life experience that cannot be formulated and assimilated by means of language alone.

This symbolism centering on the self† is not limited to formulating and nourishing the child's conscious interests. Symbolic play frequently deals with unconscious conflicts: sexual interests, defense against anxiety, phobias, aggression or identification with aggressors, withdrawal from fear of risk or competition, etc. Here the symbolism of play resembles the symbolism of the dream, to such a degree that child psychoanalysis makes frequent use of play materials (Melanie Klein, Anna Freud, and others). However Freudian theory has long interpreted the symbolism of the dream (not to mention the perhaps inevitable exaggerations involved in the interpretation of symbols when one does not possess sufficient means of checking results) as a disguisement based on mechanisms of repression and censorship. The vague boundaries between the conscious and the unconscious as evidenced by the child's symbolic play suggest rather that the symbolism of the dream is analogous to the symbolism of play, because the sleeper loses at the same time the rational use of language, the sense of reality, and the deductive or logical instruments of his intelligence. Involuntarily, therefore, he finds himself in the situation of symbolic assimilation which the

*In a penetrating and lively work, Jeux de l'esprit (Paris: Editions du Scarabée, 1963), J. O. Grandjouan finds fault with the interpretation of play in terms of the primacy of assimiliation. He puts the emphasis on games with rules, whereas the play characteristic of early childhood, it seems to us, is symbolic play, which is related by all the intermediate stages to nonplayful thought and which differs from it, therefore, only in the degree of assimilation of reality to the self.

†We no longer call it "egocentric," as one of us once did, in deference to the criticisms from many psychologists who are still not familiar with the practice in the exact sciences of using a term only in accordance with the definitions proposed, irrespective of its popular meanings and associations.

child seeks for its own sake. Jung saw that this oneiric symbolism consists of a kind of primitive language, which corresponds to what we have just seen of symbolic play, and he concentrated on certain symbols and showed their universal nature. But, without any proof (lack of concern for verification is even more noticeable in the Jungian school than it is in the Freudian schools), he argued from the universality of these symbols that they are innate and went on from there to the theory of hereditary archetypes. Yet one would no doubt find the same universality in the laws of the child's play symbolism; and since the child is anterior to the man and was so even in prehistoric times, it may be in the ontogenetic approach to the formative mechanisms of the semiotic function that the solution to the problem will be found.

Drawing

Drawing is a form of the semiotic function which should be considered as being halfway between symbolic play and the mental image. It is like symbolic play in its functional pleasure and autotelism, and like the mental image in its effort at imitating the real. G. H. Luquet classifies drawing as a game. Yet, even in its initial forms, there is no question of a free assimilation of reality to the subject's own schemes. Like the mental image, it is closer to imitative accommodation. In fact, it constitutes sometimes a preparation for, sometimes a product of imitative accommodation. Between the graphic image and the internal image (Luquet's "internal model") there exist innumerable interactions, since both phenomena derive directly from imitation.*

In his celebrated studies on children's drawings, Luquet† proposed stages and interpretations which are still valid today. Before him, two contrary opinions were maintained. One group held that the first drawings of children are essentially realistic, since they keep to actual models, and that drawings of the imagination do not appear until rather late. The other group insisted that idealization was evidenced in early drawings. Luquet seems to have settled the dispute conclusively by showing that until about eight or nine a child's drawing is essentially realistic in intention, though the subject begins by drawing what he *knows* about a person or an object long before he can draw what he actually *sees*. This observation is a fundamental one whose full significance will become apparent when we consider the mental image, because it too is a conceptualization before it culminates in good perceptive copies.

The realism of drawing thus passes through different phases. Luquet

---

*Actually, the very first form of drawing does not seem imitative and has characteristics of pure play, but it is a play of exercise: this is the scribbling the child of two to two and a half engages in when he is given a pencil. Very soon, however, the subject thinks he recognizes forms in his aimless scribble, with the result that soon thereafter he tries to render a model from memory, however poor a likeness his graphic expression may be from an objective point of view. As soon as this intention exists, drawing becomes imitation and image.

†G. H. Luquet, *Le Dessin enfantin* (Paris: Alcan, 1927).

uses the phrase "fortuitous realism" to refer to the realism of the scribble whose meaning is discovered in the act of making it. Then comes "failed realism," or the phase of synthetic incapacity, in which the elements of the copy are juxtaposed instead of being coordinated into a whole: a hat well above the head or buttons alongside the body. The little man, one of the commonest first drawings, passes through an extremely interesting stage: that of the "tadpole man," which consists of a head provided with threadlike appendages (the legs), or with arms and legs, but without a trunk.

Then comes the period of "intellectual realism," where the drawing has already evolved beyond the primitive scribblings, but where it pictures the conceptual attributes of the model, without concern for visual perspective. For example, a face seen in profile will have a second eye because a man has two eyes, or a horseman, in addition to his visible leg, will have a leg which can be seen through the horse. Similarly, one will see potatoes in the ground, if that is where they are, or in a man's stomach.*

At about eight or nine, "intellectual realism" is succeeded by "visual realism," which presents two new features. First, the drawing now represents only what is visible from one particular perspective. A profile now has only one eye, etc., as would be seen from the side, and the concealed parts of objects are no longer visibly represented. (Thus, one sees only the top of a tree behind a house, and no longer the whole tree.) Also, objects in the background are made gradually smaller (receding lines) in relation to objects in the foreground. Second, the objects in the drawing are arranged according to an overall plan (axes of coordinates) and to their geometrical proportions.

The value of Luquet's stages is twofold. They constitute a remarkable introduction to the study of the mental image, which, as we shall see, obeys laws that are closer to those of conceptualization than to those of perception. Moreover, they attest to a remarkable convergence with the evolution of the spontaneous geometry of the child.†

The first spatial intuitions of the child are, in fact, topological rather than projective or consistent with Euclidean metric geometry.‡

---

*In addition to this "transparency," one observes that children draw configurations as if seen from different angles and as if a three-dimensional object were flattened out (pseudo-rabatment). Luquet mentions a drawing of a cart in which the horse is seen from the side, the inside of the cart is seen from above, and the wheels are flattened out into a horizontal plane. A similar procedure is used to represent a narrative. Whereas adult imagery conventionally presents only one segment of many simultaneous events per drawing, without introducing, within the same drawing, actions that are chronologically successive, the child, like some primitive painters, uses one drawing to present a chain of chronological events. Thus one will see a mountain with five or six figures on it, each of which represents the same person in successive positions.

†Jean Piaget and Bärbel Inhelder, The Child's Conception of Space (London: Routledge and Kegan Paul, 1956).

‡Editor's Note: For the sake of the reader who may not be familiar with mathematics, let us briefly describe topology, projective geometry, and Euclidean geometry. Topology, sometimes nicknamed "rubber-sheet geometry," is concerned with the relationships between points, lines, and regions that are not disturbed when the space is stretched or compressed or distorted. If two regions drawn on a sheet of rubber have a common boundary, that fact re-

Up to the age of four, for example, squares, rectangles, circles, ellipses, etc., are all represented by a closed curve without straight lines or angles. Topologically, squares and circles are the same figure. Crosses, arcs, etc., are all represented by an open curve. At this same age, however, children can produce quite accurate copies of a closed figure with a little circle inside. The topological relation of the inside circle to the enclosing one, or even the relation between a closed figure and a circle on its boundary is represented by children who are quite incapable of copying a square correctly.

Although the "intellectual realism" of the child's drawing shows no awareness of perspective or metrical relationships, it does show topological relationships: proximity, separation, enclosure, closedness, and so on. And these topological intuitions are followed, after the age of seven or eight, by both projective intuitions and a sense of Euclidean metric geometry. At this age there appear the two essential elements of "visual realism" in drawing. Moreover, at this age the child discovers the end-on sighting methods for guaranteeing the projective straight line and also understands elementary perspective. The child becomes capable of drawing an object not as he sees it but as it would be seen by an observer located to the right of or opposite the child. At nine to ten the child is able to choose correctly from among several drawings all representing three mountains or three buildings as they would appear from specified viewing points. At this time too the child becomes aware of the vectorial straight line (conservation of direction), the group structure representing displacements, and measurement. He can also realize that similar figures may not be identical in size but they must be proportional. Finally he can understand measurement in two and three dimensions by means of a system of coordinates. From the age of nine or ten (but, interestingly, seldom before that) the average child becomes capable of anticipating that the water surface in a jar will be horizontal even if the jar is tilted at various angles, and that the line of the mast of a boat floating on this water will stay vertical. (The experimenter draws the outlines of the jars and the child indicates the horizontal and vertical lines by way of references external to the figure.*

---

mains true no matter how the rubber sheet is stretched. The straightness of a line or the shape of a region is changed if the sheet is stretched; therefore these are not topological properties.

Projective properties of a figure are those that are not changed if the figure is projected onto any plane surface as when it casts a shadow. The shadow of a straight line is always straight, but its shadow may be shorter or longer depending upon the slant of the surface on which its shadow is projected. The shadow of a circle is not circular, but it is always some form of ellipse.

Euclidean properties are those actual lengths and measurements of a figure constant, as when a figure is merely translated or copied in another spot.

*Thus we see that the evolution of drawing is inseparable from the whole structuration of space, according to the different stages of this development. It is not surprising, then, that the child's drawing serves as a test of his intellectual development. In this connection, F. Goodenough, A. Rey, and others have made useful studies, with standardized scales that concentrate particularly on development as seen in the "draw-a-man test." Drawing has also been used as an affective index, notably by the psychoanalyst S. Morgenstern in the case of children afflicted with selective autism.

Mental Images*

Associationist psychology regards the image as an extension of perception and thinking as consisting of the association between sensations and mental images. We have seen that in fact "associations" are always assimilations. There are at least two good reasons to doubt the derivation of mental images from perception. Neurologically, an imagined bodily movement is accompanied by the same pattern of electrical waves, whether cortical (EEG) or muscular (EMG), as the physical execution of the movement. That is, the imagining of a movement involves a kind of sketch of that movement. The second objection is genetic; if the image were merely a prolongation of a perception, it would appear from birth. Yet no evidence of it is observed during the sensorimotor period. It seems to begin only at the time of the appearance of the semiotic function.†

THE PROBLEMS RAISED BY THE IMAGE

It would seem, therefore, that mental images are relatively late in appearing because they are the result of an internalized imitation. Their resemblance to perception does not attest to a direct derivation from perception but is, rather, due to the fact that the imitation involved in imagery actively copies the perceptual data, and may even elicit sensations in the same way as an imagined movement elicits muscular contractions.

As for the relationship between images and thought, Binet and the German psychologists of the Wurzburg school (from K. Marbe and O. Külpe to K. Bühler) have shown the existence of what they call imageless thought. One can imagine an object, but the judgment that affirms or denies its existence is not itself characterized by an image. This finding implies that judgments and operations are not images, but it does not rule out the possibility that the image can play a role in thinking as a complementary symbolic auxiliary to language. Language itself never represents anything but concepts or concrete objects seen as classes with only one member (for example, "my father"). The adult, as does the child, needs a system of signifiers dealing not with concepts

---

*Jean Piaget and Bärbel Inhelder, *L'Image mentale chez l'enfant* (Paris: Presses Universitaires de France 1966).

†Psychoanalysts assume a very precocious capacity to hallucinate the realization of desires, but they have yet to furnish proof of this. Recently there have been indications that such verification would be possible, for N. Kleitman and E. Aserinsky have succeeded in taking electroretinograms during sleep which seem to correspond to visual images of dreaming (rapid eye movements distinct from the habitual slow movements). W. Dement has applied this technique to newborn babies, but he finds a much greater incidence of rapid eye movements than at later stages in the individual's development. A greater incidence of these movements has been observed in the opossum (a living fossil) than in the cat or in man. This seems to indicate that rapid eye movements have other functions (cleansing or detoxication) and do not necessarily involve actual visual imagery. Dement concludes, therefore, that his and E. A. Wolpert's studies do not confirm the psychoanalytic interpretation of the dream.

but with objects as such and with the whole past perceptual experience of the subject. This role has been assigned to the image, and its quality of "symbol" (as opposed to "sign") permits it to acquire a more or less adequate, although schematized, resemblance to the objects symbolized.

The problem, then, throughout the child's development, is to describe the relationship between imaginal symbolism and the preoperatory or operatory mechanisms of thought.*

TWO TYPES OF IMAGES

The studies we have conducted for several years on the development of mental images in the child between four or five and ten or twelve indicate a clear-cut difference between images characteristic of the preoperatory level (before seven or eight) and those of the operatory levels, which at this stage appear to be strongly influenced by the operations.

First of all, it is necessary to distinguish two broad categories of mental images: *reproductive images*, which are limited to evoking sights that have been perceived previously, and *anticipatory images*, which envisage movements or transformations as well as their results, although the subject has not previously observed them (as one can envisage how a geometric figure would look if it were transformed). Reproductive images may include static configurations, movements (changes of position), and transformations (changes of form), for these three kinds of realities occur constantly in the perceptual experience of the subject. If the image proceeded from perception alone, one would then find at every age these three classes of reproductive image (static, kinetic, and transformational) in frequencies corresponding to those actually occurring in the child's environment.

Our studies indicate, however, that the mental images of the child at the preoperatory level are almost exclusively static. He has systematic difficulties in reproducing in imagery movements or transformations he has observed. It is not until the level of concrete operations (after seven to eight) that children are capable of reproducing movements and transformations, and by this stage the child can also anticipate in his imagery movements and transformations. This seems to prove (1) that imaginal reproduction even of well-known movements or transformations involves either anticipation or a reanticipation, and (2) that both reproductive and anticipatory images of movements or transformations depend on the operations that make it possible for the child to understand these processes. The formation of mental images cannot precede understanding.

*This problem is parallel to the problem of the relationship between perception and intelligence, for perception, imitation, and the image correspond to the figurative aspects of the cognitive functions, as opposed to the operative aspects (actions and operations). In both cases, the ·need is first of all to determine whether the figurative element (image and perception alike) prefigures certain operatory structures (concepts, etc.), and in what sense, filiation or analogous formation. Next we must determine whether the evolution of the figurative elements (images and perceptions) follows an independent course in the form of a simple internal development, or whether it depends upon the help of external such as operatory factors.

COPY IMAGES

To introduce some clarity into this complex situation, let us begin by examining what we may call "copy images," in which the model remains in view of the subject or has just been perceived the instant before. There is here no deferred evocation after several days or weeks, as there is in tests relating to the translations or rotations of models present in the child's experience but not shown when he is questioned.*

In an experiment made with B. Matalon, for example, a horizontal rod 20 centimeters long was placed on a sheet of paper and the child was asked three times to draw it immediately to its right without leaving any intervening space: (1) after imagining that it describes an arc of 180° to arrive at this position, (2) after imagining that it is simply pushed (translation) into this same position, and (3) as a simple graphic copy without allusion to any movement, and still in the same position. (Naturally, the order is varied: 1, 2, 3; 3, 2, 1; etc.)

The first thing we observe is in fact a widespread phenomenon: at the age of five the graphic copy (3) is shorter than the model by about −13.5 percent (a 20-centimeter rod is drawn 17.3 centimeters long on the average). This systematic shortening diminishes with age (−10.5 percent at seven, etc.) and disappears in the adult. This phenomenon is also observed when young subjects are asked to draw with their fingers on the desk without a pencil, but it is not present when the child is asked to show the length in the air by means of two raised index fingers. A shortening of this kind, which is found in all the other experiments, seems to have only one explanation. Accustomed to judging lengths in an ordinal rather than in a metrical fashion, that is, by the order of the points of arrival rather than by the interval between the extremities (except in the case of the raised index fingers), the young subjects concentrate on not going beyond the terminal boundary of the model. It does not matter if the copy is shorter (for in this case it is still within the length of the model); the essential thing is that it not be too long.

In the case of conditions (1) and (2), the drawings produced are even shorter (−20.5 percent for rotation and −19 percent for translation at the age of five). In these cases, graphic imitations of the length of the model are even shorter, although the model remains in the child's sight and the copy is made in the same place as in (3). Thus we see the complexity of even a simple pencil stroke. The intention to imitate the length of the model requires a plan of execution whose laws are closer to conceptualization than they are to simple perception.†

*The copy image consists of a simple physical imitation (graphic or gestural), as opposed to the mental image, which is an internalized imitation.
†To turn to gestural copies, relating this time to kinetic models (for the kinetic copy image is naturally easier than the deferred evocation of a movement by means of mental images as such)—together with A. Etienne, we asked children from three to six to reproduce different, very easy models. Two checkers were set in motion in such a way as to describe movements of launching or pulling, symmetrical backward and forward movement, crossing, etc., and the subjects were requested to reproduce these movements, also with checkers, either while the movements were being slowly executed or immediately afterward. We observed numerous errors in the copies because of the predominance of "good forms" (symmetrical movements) over random

KINETIC AND TRANSFORMATIONAL IMAGES

Turning to mental images proper, let us remember first how difficult it is to measure them experimentally, since they are internal. We have to resort to indirect methods, within which cross-checking affords some degree of certainty: the child's drawing, the child's choices from among drawings prepared in advance, gestural indications, and his verbal comments (hazardous, but possible if used along with the other three techniques). From this point of view, the simplest of the kinetic reproductive images seems to us, as to F. Frank and T. Bang, to be one square placed on top of another (the upper side of the second being adjacent to the lower side of the first). The problem is to anticipate a slight movement on the part of the top square. One has first made sure that the child knows how to draw a fairly exact copy of the model; that is, of one square partially superimposed on another and partially projecting beyond the edge. After five and a half, the child can do this; yet, on the average, he is unable to make an anticipatory drawing of the same situation until he is seven or older. The young subjects confine themselves to drawing the square in its initial position, or beside the other square. When they succeed in drawing a slight change of position, they shorten the top (mobile) square or lengthen the bottom one so that the mobile square does not go beyond the boundary of the stationary one!*

Equally surprising in view of the frequency of the everyday models, which might have assured an accurate representation, are the reproductive images made of a 90-degree rotation of a rod (like the movements of the hand of a watch or an upright stick that falls to the ground) or of the "somersault" of a tube that describes a rotation of 180

---

forms. In addition, and more important, until the age of five a gap was observed (very obvious at three and diminishing afterward) between simultaneous reproductions and reproductions done immediately afterward. Those do not become as accurate as simultaneous reproductions until the age of six. This is a first and very significant indication of the difficulty of kinetic images.

*When the squares are presented so that one entirely covers the other (an experiment made with F. Frank and J. Bliss, using transparent squares, one with red edges and the other with black edges), the child, when invited to anticipate a gradual change of position, has no difficulty drawing the projecting of the red-edged square beyond the black-edged square, but he refuses to draw the parallel side of the red-edged square which can be seen through the middle of the black-edged one. This reaction is all the more curious since in his spontaneous drawings the child often indicates "transparencies," to use Luquet's expression. Such "transparencies" are illegitimate, however, as when the invisible leg of a horseman is "seen" through a horse drawn from the side. When the squares are actually transparent, the refusal to draw the red side which divides the black-edged square is related to a problem of boundary, this time with reference to an intersection. The child has the impression that by dividing the black-edged square in two through the introduction of a red line belonging to the other square, he would alter the image of the black-edged square, whose surface must remain intact. As in the case of the refusal to go beyond the boundary, we have here a kind of "pseudo-conservation" peculiar to the image which is all the more curious in that it is respected at the expense of the conservation of the surface (one square above the other) or the conservation of one side (one square covering the other overlapping squares).

degrees. In the first, the rod is nailed at its base so that it moves steadily around a fixed pivotal point. But the young subjects pay no attention to this fact, although it is clearly pointed out to them, and draw trajectories forming right angles (as if the rod traveled the length of its initial and final positions or the length of their opposites in the form of a square) or intersecting at any angle no matter which. In the case of the tube, it is colored red and blue at the ends and projects beyond the edge of a box, responding to a pressure of the finger on the free end which causes it to turn upside down and fall in an inverted position a few centimeters from the box. Subjects who anticipate rather well the transposition of the colored ends (about 50 percent at five and 100 percent at eight) do not manage until a later age to draw two or three of the intermediary positions of the tube (42 percent succeed at seven and 60 percent at eight) and, remarkably enough, are not much more successful in imitating the movement of inversion by a slow-motion gesture while holding the tube in their hands (45 percent at seven and 70 percent at eight, as shown in studies made with E. Schmid-Kitsikis). We see that movements of the most ordinary kind (for what child has not himself turned somersaults?) give rise to rather poor kinetic reproductive images up to and even after the onset of the concrete operations (seven to eight).

As an example of a transformational image, we can cite a detailed study carried out with F. Frank, involving the unbending of an arc (of flexible wire) into a straight line or, conversely, the bending of the straight line into an arc. Here again, children have great difficulty in imagining the intermediary positions. In imagining the outcome of the transformation, young subjects (until about seven) draw figures with a marked boundary effect. They draw the straight line so that its ends correspond to those of the arc: Thus the straight line resulting from the unbending of the arc is underestimated by −34 percent at five. Similarly, the arc resulting from the curving of the straight line is overestimated by +29 percent at five, so that its ends will meet those of the straight line.

It is no exaggeration, then, to speak of the static quality of preoperatory images. Kinetic and transformational images are possible only after seven or eight, and this as a result of anticipations or reanticipations which are no doubt themselves based on operatory comprehension.

IMAGES AND OPERATIONS

Turning now to direct analysis of the relationship between imaginary representation and the operation, we shall consider only two examples, for they all demonstrate similar phenomena. The technique consists in presenting the customary tests for conservation of quantity, but instead of questioning the subject about the transformations he has just observed, you ask him to anticipate what is going to happen by imagining the phases and results of the transformations. In the test of the conservation of liquids in which there is a standard glass A, a narrower glass B, and a wider glass C, subjects are asked to anticipate the result of pouring the liquid from A to B and C, and in particular to indicate the levels that will be reached by the water. Two interesting results (ob-

tained by S. Taponier) are observed in the reactions of preoperatory subjects (five to seven). The majority anticipate that the levels in the three
glasses will be the same and thus they predict that the quantity of liquid
will be unchanged (conservation but for the wrong reason). It is after
they actually see the results of the pouring—that is, the water rises
higher in B than in A and less high in C—that they begin to deny all
conservation of quantity.

However, a second group of subjects, smaller than the first, foresee
correctly that the water will rise higher in B and less high in C than in A,
but conclude from this in advance that the quantity of liquid is not the
same. When you ask these children to pour equal amounts of water in
A and B, they maintain the same level in both glasses. Even if the
reproductive image of the levels is accurate, this is not sufficient for a
judgment of conservation, as there is a lack of understanding of compensation. The child may say the water will rise higher in B "because
the glass is narrower," but he does not therefore conclude that "higher ×
narrower = same quantity." For him, the narrowness of B is only an
empirical indication that enables him to foresee (but not to understand)
the rise in the level of the water.

Another experiment gives parallel results. A child of five or six places
twelve red counters opposite twelve blue ones to make sure there is an
equal number of each. Yet if you space out either the blue or the red
counters, he concludes that the longer row contains more elements. The
question arises whether this lack of conservation is due to a difficulty in
imagining these displacements and a possible return of the displaced
elements to their original positions. We therefore constructed a fan-
shaped apparatus designed so that each blue counter in the compressed
upper row communicated with a red counter in the spaced-out lower row
by means of a lane within which the lower counter could move upward
until it met its blue counterpart. This arrangement in no way altered the
child's ideas. Even when he imagines the movements perfectly, he
nevertheless concludes, placing himself at a crosswise rather than a
lengthwise vantage point, that the number of counters increases when
the row grows longer and decreases when it grows shorter. After S.
Taponier had studied the effects of successive displacements, M.
Aboudaram introduced a mechanism whereby the twelve counters of
the mobile row could move up or down as a unit. The reactions remained the same.

From these and other facts, one can conclude that mental images are
merely a system of symbols which provide a more or less accurate but,
generally speaking, delayed translation of the subjects' preoperatory or
operatory level of comprehension. The image is far from sufficient to
give rise to operatory structurations. At the very most, the image, when
it is sufficiently adequate (cf. the representation of water levels in the
second group of subjects cited above), can serve to refine the subjects'
awareness of states which the operation will later connect by means of
reversible transformations. But the image in itself remains static and
discontinuous (cf. the "cinematographic process" which Bergson attributed to the intelligence itself, ignoring the operation, and characterizing
only image-representation). After the age of seven or eight, the image
becomes anticipatory and so better able to serve as a base for the opera-

tions. This progress is not the result of an internal or autonomous modification of the images, however, but rather of the intervention of external factors due to the development of the operations. These have their source in action itself, and not in image-symbolism, or in the system of verbal signs or language that we shall now discuss. . . .

Language

In the normal child, language appears at about the same time as the other forms of semiotic thought. In the deaf-mute, on the other hand, articulate language does not appear until well after deferred imitation, symbolic play, and the mental image. This seems to indicate that language is derived genetically, since its social or educational transmission presupposes the preliminary development of these individual forms of *semiosis*. However, this development, as is proved by the case of deaf-mutes, can occur independent of language.* Furthermore, deaf-mutes, in their collective life, manage to elaborate a gestural language which is of keen interest. It is both social and based on imitative signifiers that occur in an individual form in deferred imitation, in symbolic play, and the image, which is relatively close to symbolic play. Because of its adaptive properties rather than its playful purpose, this gestural language, if it were universal, would constitute an independent and original form of semiotic function. In normal individuals it is rendered unnecessary by the transmission of the collective system of verbal signs associated with articulate language.

EVOLUTION

Articulate language makes its appearance, after a phase of spontaneous vocalization (common to children of all cultures between six and ten or eleven months) and a phase of differentiation of phonemes by imitation (from eleven or twelve months), at the end of the sensorimotor period, with what have been called "one-word sentences" (C. Stern). These single words may express in turn desires, emotions, or observations (the verbal scheme becoming an instrument of assimilation and generalization based on the sensorimotor schemes).

From the end of the second year, two-word sentences appear, then short complete sentences without conjugation or declension, and next a gradual acquisition of grammatical structures. The syntax of children from two to four has been observed in some extremely interesting studies by R. Brown, J. Berko, and others, at Harvard and S. Ervin and W. Miller at Berkeley.† These studies, which were inspired by Noam

---

*One finds in the chimpanzee a beginning of symbolic function which enables him, for example, to save tokens with which to obtain fruits from an automatic dispenser (experiment by J. B. Wolfe) and even to offer them as gifts to less fortunate companions (H. W. Nissen and M. P. Crawford).

†U. Bellugi and R. Brown, eds., *The Acquisition of Language*, Monographs of the Society for Research in Child Development, No. 92 (1964).

Chomsky's hypothesis of the structure of grammatical rules, have shown that the acquisition of syntactical rules cannot be reduced to passive imitation. It involves not only an important element of generalizing assimilation, which was more or less known, but also certain original constructions. R. Brown isolated models of these. Moreover, he has shown that reductions of adult sentences to original infantile models obey certain functional requirements, such as the conservation of a *minimum* of necessary information and the tendency to add to this *minimum*.

LANGUAGE AND THOUGHT

In addition to this problem of the relationship of infantile language to linguistic theory, and to information theory, the great genetic problem raised by the development of infantile language concerns its relationship to thought, and in particular to the logical operations. Language may increase the powers of thought in range and rapidity, but it is controversial whether logico-mathematical structures are themselves essentially linguistic or nonlinguistic in nature.

As to the increasing range and rapidity of thought, thanks to language we observe in fact three differences between verbal and sensorimotor behavior. (1) Whereas sensorimotor patterns are obliged to follow events without being able to exceed the speed of the action, verbal patterns, by means of narration and evocation, can represent a long chain of actions very rapidly. (2) Sensorimotor adaptations are limited to immediate space and time, whereas language enables thought to range over vast stretches of time and space, liberating it from the immediate. (3) The third difference is a consequence of the other two. Whereas the sensorimotor intelligence proceeds by means of successive acts, step by step, thought, particularly through language, can represent simultaneously all the elements of an organized structure.

These advantages of representative thought over the sensorimotor scheme are in reality due to the semiotic function as a whole. The semiotic function detaches thought from action and is the source of representation. Language plays a particularly important role in this formative process. Unlike images and other semiotic instruments, which are created by the individual as the need arises, language has already been elaborated socially and contains a notation for an entire system of cognitive instruments (relationships, classifications, etc.) for use in the service of thought. The individual learns this system and then proceeds to enrich it.

LANGUAGE AND LOGIC

Must we then conclude, as has been suggested, that since language possesses its own logic, this logic of language constitutes not only an essential or even a unique factor in the learning of logic (inasmuch as the child is subject to the restrictions of the linguistic group and of society in general), but is in fact the source of all logic for the whole of humanity? These views derive from the pedagogical common sense characteristic of the sociological school of Durkheim and also the logical positivism still adhered to in many scientific circles. According to logical positivism, in fact, the logic of the logicians is itself nothing but generalized syntax and semantics (Carnap, Tarski, etc.).

We have available two sources of important information on this subject: (1) The comparison of normal children with deaf-mutes, who have not had the benefit of articulate language but are in possession of complete sensorimotor schemes, and with blind persons, whose situation is the opposite. (2) The systematic comparison of linguistic progress in the normal child with the development of intellectual operations.

The logic of deaf-mutes has been studied by M. Vincent* and P. Oléron,† in Paris, who have applied the operatory tests of the Genevan school, and by F. Affolter in Geneva. The results indicate a systematic delay in the emergence of logic in the deaf-mute. One cannot speak of deficiency as such, however, since the same stages of development are encountered, although with a delay of one to two years. Seriation and spatial operations are normal (perhaps a slight delay in the case of the former). The classifications have their customary structures and are only slightly less mobile in response to suggested changes of criteria than in hearing children. The learning of arithmetic is relatively easy. Problems of conservation (an index of reversibility) are solved with a delay of only one or two years compared with normal children. The exception is the conservation of liquids, which gives rise to special technical difficulties in the presentation of the assignment, since the subjects must be made to understand that the questions have to do with the contents of the containers and not with the containers themselves.

These results are even more significant when compared with the results obtained in studies of blind children. In studies made by Y. Hatwell, the same tests reveal a delay of up to four years or more compared with normal children, even in elementary questions dealing with relationships of order (succession, position "between," etc.). And yet in the blind children verbal seriations are normal (A is smaller than B, B smaller than C, therefore . . .). But the sensory disturbance peculiar to those born blind has from the outset hampered the development of the sensorimotor schemes and slowed down general coordination. Verbal coordinations are not sufficient to compensate for this delay, and action learning is still necessary before these children develop the capacity for operations on a level with that of the normal child or the deaf-mute.

LANGUAGE AND OPERATIONS

The comparison of progress in language with progress in the intellectual operations requires both linguistic and psychological competence. Our collaborator, H. Sinclair, who fulfills both conditions, undertook a group of studies of which we offer one or two samples.

Two groups of children were chosen. The first was clearly preoperatory; that is, these children did not possess the least notion of conservation. The children in the second group accepted one of these notions

*M. Vincent and M. Borelli, "La Naissance des opérations logiques chez des sourd-muets," *Enfance* (1951), pp. 222–238, and *Enfance* (1956), pp. 1–20.

† P. Oléron, "L'Acquisition des conservations et le langage," *Enfance* (1961), pp. 201–219.

and justified it by arguments of reversibility and compensation. Both groups were shown several pairs of objects (a large object and a small one; a group of four or five marbles and a group of two; an object that is both shorter and wider than another, etc.) and were asked to describe the pairs when one element of the pair is offered to one person and the other to a second person. This description is thus not related to a problem of conservation. The language of the two groups differs systematically. The first group uses "scalars" almost exclusively (in the linguistic sense): "this man has a big one, that man a small one; this one has a lot, that one little." The second group uses "vectors"; "this man has a bigger one than the other man"; "he has more," etc. Whereas the first group describes only one dimension at a time, the second group says: "This pencil is longer and thinner," etc. In short, there is a surprising degree of correlation between the language employed and the mode of reasoning. Similarly, a second study shows a close connection between the stages of development of seriation and the structure of the terms used.

How should this relationship be interpreted? A child at the preoperatory level understands the expressions of the higher level when they are integrated into orders or assignments ("Give that man a longer pencil," etc.), but he does not use them spontaneously. If you train him to use these expressions, he learns them but with difficulty, and the training seldom influences his notions of conservation (it does in approximately one case in ten). Seriation, on the other hand, is somewhat improved by verbal training, because then the linguistic process also relates to the act of comparison and therefore to the concept itself.

These data . . . indicate that language does not constitute the source of logic but is, on the contrary, structured by it. The roots of logic are to be sought in the general coordination of actions (including verbal behavior), beginning with the sensorimotor level, whose schemes are of fundamental importance. This schematism continues thereafter to develop and to structure thought, even verbal thought, in terms of the progress of actions, until the formation of the logico-mathematical operations. This is the culmination of the logic implied in the coordinations of actions, when these actions are ready to be internalized and organized into unified structures. We shall now attempt to explain this.

CONCLUSION

In spite of the astonishing diversity of its manifestations, the semiotic function presents a remarkable unity. Whether it is a question of deferred imitation, symbolic play, drawing, mental images and image-memories or language, this function allows the representative evocation of objects and events not perceived at that particular moment. The semiotic function makes thought possible by providing it with an unlimited field of application, in contrast to the restricted boundaries of sensorimotor action and perception. Reciprocally, it evolves under the guidance of thought, or representative intelligence. Neither imitation nor play nor drawing nor image nor language nor even memory (to which we might have attributed a capacity for spontaneous reproduction comparable to that of perception) can develop or be organized without the constant help of the structuration characteristic of intelligence.

28

The Role of Imitation in the Development

of Representational Thought*

1962

To pay tribute to the work of Henri Wallon, as well as to the man and the friend, . . . I have chosen an issue on which our positions converge and are complementary rather than contradictory.

Without a doubt, the most decisive turning point in the mental development of the child is that which marks the beginning of representational thought. Throughout his first year of life, the infant does not demonstrate representational thought in the sense of evocation of objects or events that are not directly perceived. . . . His behaviors are exclusively sensorimotor, emotional, etc. (and we should be quite aware of how much Wallon has contributed to our knowledge of these points). In particular, the child's intelligence is only sensorimotor intelligence or, according to Wallon's profoundly apt formulation, "an intelligence of situations." But during the second year, especially the second half, we witness an êvent of major importance for human intelligence: the birth of representational thought. From that point on, intelligence can become internalized as real thought. How can this emergence of representational thought be accounted for?

Representational thought implies the development of a symbolic function, i.e., the differentiation of signifiers and signified,† since it entails the evocation of what is not present, which it can do only by means of differentiated signifiers. To be sure, at the previous sensorimotor stages, every behavior makes use of significations ascribed to objects or to the gestures of others, etc., but the only signifiers used are perceptual "indices" or conditioned cues, i.e., signifiers that are still un-

*Jean Piaget, "The Role of Imitation in the Development of Representational Thought," in *Henri Wallon: His World, His Work*, ed. by G. Voyat and B. Birns, *International Journal of Mental Health*, vol. 1, no. 4, 1972/73, 67–74. Copyright © 1973 by International Arts and Sciences Press, Inc. Reprinted by permission of International Arts and Sciences Press, Inc. Piaget's article was originally published in French, 1962, in *Evolution Psychiatrique*, 1962, vol. 27, 141–150, a special issue honoring Henri Wallon (1879–1962).

†"Signifier" designates symbols or signs, "signified" refers to the object, action, or person in reality. (Editors' note)

differentiated from what is signified and thus constitute merely one of its aspects. A symbolic function, then, has not yet emerged, if by this is meant the differentiation of signifiers from signified. But with the birth of representational thought, this differentiation emerges and appears even as a necessary condition of the representational act as such.

Since one of the most specific forms of differentiated signifiers is the system of verbal "signs," one might assume that the development of representational thought is associated merely with the acquisition of speech; indeed, it is self-evident that this is a factor of major importance. But if speech, which is already fully organized within the social environment and transmitted to the child by education, does, in fact, play such a role in the development of representational thought and thought in general, one has not therewith said all, for two fundamental problems still remain to be resolved. The first is to understand why speech appears neither earlier nor later than it does, i.e., to determine the context in which its acquisition becomes possible. Conditioning is not a sufficient explanation, for it occurs much earlier. Consequently, we must consider a more precise concept, i.e., imitation. It remains necessary to determine the form of imitation that is relevant; for there are numerous forms, some of which also appear much earlier than, and others, concurrently with, the acquisition of speech.

The second problem is to determine whether the verbal sign is the only differentiated signifier implicated or if, in fact, others are also involved in the birth of representational thought and, if so, whether or not they are contemporaneous with the acquisition of speech, since if they are, a relationship would be indicated. It is striking that at the stage at which he learns to speak, the young child also begins to use a full symbolic system, based, however, no longer on "signs" but on "symbols" (the symbol being a "motivated" signifier or resembling what is signified, not "arbitrary" or a matter of convention, like the "sign"). This other system is the system of symbolic games, which follow functional or practical games, hitherto the only type of play engaged in. But the . . . symbolism of these fictive games consists essentially of imitation. Furthermore, it is noteworthy that a new form of imitation, usually called "deferred" imitation, appears at this stage (i.e., imitation initiated when the model is not in the perceptual field, thus involving a kind of recall through gestures and mimicry). Wallon considers this form of imitation the only authentic imitation, as opposed to sensorimotor imitation. Sensorimotor imitation is acquired only in the presence of models, even though it can continue after their disappearance. He regards this form as pseudoimitation, calling it "echokinesia," etc.

The involvement of imitation in all forms of the symbolic function that appear synchronously during the course of the second year (later we shall have occasion to observe another form with respect to the mental image) formerly led me (in *La naissance de l'intelligence chez l'enfant*, 1935*) to consider imitation as the process that ensures the transition from sensorimotor intelligence to representative imagery. Well before deferred imitation, from the age of 8–9 months on, sensorimotor imitation clearly testifies to an effort to copy a presented model, for example, in the case of imitation of movements relative to the fact of others,

*Pp. 334–335, etc.

without a visible equivalent on the child's own body. This behavior cannot be reduced to simple associative transfers induced by cues, in spite of the elegant observations of Guillaume. When at the age of 11 months and 14 days one of my children watched me open and close my eyes and responded by opening and closing his mouth, and then on the following days responded to my rubbing my eyes by passing his hand over his mouth, then his cheeks and ear, until finally, at the age of 11 months and 21 days, he was able to bring his hand to his eyes,* his mistakes could not be explained by false associations, but were evidence of systematic and controlled attempts, e.g., of an effort to achieve an equivalent behavior. From even before its deferred, strictly symbolic stage, imitation constitutes a kind of representation, but in the form of acts and in the strict sense of a material reproduction of the presented thing, still without any mental evocation or internal representation. It then becomes clear that once the imitative technique is acquired, particularly in the capacity to imitate new models (which is the case from 10 to 12 months for systematic efforts) . . . , imitation is no longer subject to the prior condition that it can be initiated for a new model only when that model is present in the perceptual field, and can give rise to deferred attempts, i.e., attempts initiated after the disappearance of the model. Indeed, it is in this stage that the act of intelligence, until then restricted by the necessity to proceed by trial and error, for the first time gives rise in the child to those momentary interruptions of action, followed by abrupt new reorganizations, that W. Köhler has described so well with respect to the chimpanzee. . . . It is striking, moreover, that these new acts of intelligence sometimes give rise, in the child of 15 to 18 months, to imitative representations of a future goal to be attained: slow opening of the mouth when faced with an aperture that must be enlarged to obtain access to the interior of a box; opening and closing of an empty hand in an analogous situation, etc. (Observations 56–58 in "La formation du symbole. . . ."). But, of course, to concede that sensorimotor imitation becomes internalized as deferred imitation is to assume that the new element mediating between the two, namely, the image, does not arise external to this process of internalization, but results directly from the internalization of imitation itself, in its accommodative capacity. Thus the image as such is itself a product of imitation.

However, it is noteworthy that Wallon, whose emphasis tends always toward discontinuities and crises, has also invoked imitation to explain the transition from the sensorimotor stage to the representational stage instead of positing a radical break between them, marked by the appearance of speech alone. In the charming and rich book *De l'acte à la pensée*, which he had the courage to publish in 1942 [that is, during the Second World War], Wallon writes:

Imitation becomes established as a latent capacity, a productive dynamism, a potential model, which initially consisted only of its effective execution, but which ultimately was able to detach itself from this act to become real representation. It is no longer strictly accommodation to others, but has become the imitation of scenes and events; it has become instrumental. . . . (P. 244)

*"La formation du symbole chez l'enfant," Observation 25. Another of my children, at 11 months and 5 days, in the presence of the model of opening and closing the mouth, opened and closed his hands first, and only later his mouth (Observation 29).

To be sure, in the entire chapter on imitation and representation, Wallon, as we have already remarked, uses the term "imitation" only from the onset of deferred imitation, i.e., beginning in the latter half of the second year, so that he may rate the preceding sensorimotor forms of imitation as echolalia, echokinesis, etc. But it is of some interest to note that Wallon, who ordinarily exhibits such deep distrust of the tendency to employ a genetic succession as the basis of an explanation, is not put off by such dangers when referring to the transition from lower to higher representational forms of imitation:

The successive stages of imitation thus correspond very precisely to the moment when *representation, which previously had not existed, must constitute itself.* These stages necessarily imply a state of movement in which movement no longer is confused with immediate reactions, and a state of representational thought in which *movement already contains representation before it is able to be transformed into an image* or to render explicit the features that should constitute it. (Pp. 134–135. My italics.)

The real reason why Wallon here glosses over the discontinuities he himself otherwise introduces is to be found in a fundamental aspect of his system, which we are indebted to him for stressing, namely, the role he ascribes to sensoritonic or postural reactions in affective and cognitive functions, from the most primitive emotional behaviors (which for him also have a cognitive meaning) to the collective "rituals" he describes so elegantly in his chapter on rites and representation. . . . In our opinion, this parallel is striking because it throws into relief the notion of causality through imitation in the doctrine of these image-ideas called "Eidos" or "forms."

But the involvement of the postural system exists prior to deferred imitation, inasmuch as it places a "bodily schema that is already quite complete and well delineated at the disposal of the latter. At this age,[*] in fact, the infant's sensorimotor play enables him to establish the broadest and most varied connections between his sensorial or exteroceptive fields and postural or proprioceptive fields. These are active connections, i.e., connections that are the result of mobile investigations and consequently involve a certain degree of anticipation or deduction" . . . In short, it is "perceptual-postural plasticity" . . . that for Wallon serves as the bridge between the sensorimotor and the representational stages, in spite of the relative discontinuities between its echokinetic and its "deferred" forms.

But if it is intellectually gratifying (and fitting also for an article in tribute to Wallon!) to stress this point of convergence between our two interpretations, it is no less satisfying to be able to underscore this essential fact (too seldom noted, it would seem): that the most marked difference between Wallon's work and mine is reducible in the long run to a complementarity rather than to an opposition. This difference derives from the dual nature of representational thought, which is such that the comments that are to follow are in direct continuity with those just made on the beginnings of symbolism.

At the level of scientific thought, representational thought exhibits a "figural" nature, i.e., it tends to provide an image that more or less conforms to represented realities, i.e., configurations. For example, geometry has long constituted a figural representation, and it is no

[*]Observations made on Guillaume's child, aged 1 year, 10 months.

accident that it enjoyed such an ascendancy among the Greeks over, for
example, algebra, and that the philosopher who reserved access to his
republic exclusively to geometricians constructed a theory of ideas whose
psychological kinship with a certain primacy of the image or apparition
Wallon so acutely perceived. . . .

But at the level of modern scientific thought, representation may
also involve transformations as such and deal more with operations and
constructions than with copying. Algebra rests entirely on systems of
transformations; and contemporary geometry tends, since the "Erlangen
program," to subordinate all varieties of space to basic "groups" of transformations that are themselves derived from one another. The overall
tendency leading from action and techniques to strictly operational
science obliges us, then, to distinguish an "operative" aspect of representation and thought as opposed to the preceding figural aspects.

It would even seem that the totality of cognitive functions derives
from such a dichotomy. Perceptions, imitation in all its forms, and the
manifold varieties of mental images, three great categories whose common trait is that they each deal exclusively with configurations (and
translate movements and even transformations, when the subject attempts to perceive or reproduce them, into figures or figural symbols),
may all be linked to the figural aspect of cognition. The operative aspect
of cognitive functions covers, in contrast, the continuous succession of
behaviors leading from sensorimotor actions, with their schemata, to
preoperational internalized actions, and finally to logico-mathematical
operations conceived as operations involving transformations. But the
operative mechanisms tend, on the one hand, to be subordinate to the
figural data, insofar as these refer to "states" that finally acquire meaning only when they are linked together through transformations. On the
other hand, these same mechanisms continually go beyond the figural,
inasmuch as they can never be adequately "reduced to static configurations." An action may be perceived proprioceptively and its result, ex-
teroceptively; but its schema, i.e., that aspect of an action that is generalizable and assimilable, is not perceptible. An operation may be
symbolized, but as a continuous act it can never be represented by an
image. It may even lose any direct bearing on objects except through a
very approximate act of symbolic imagination, as in pure mathematics.
Nevertheless, it is still impossible to think without some symbolic reference point; the most abstract mathematicians all agree that if "intuition"
(i.e., the figural aspect of mathematical thought) is divested of all
demonstrative value, it still remains indispensable as a heuristic device.

This being the case, it is clear that the genetic relationship on which
Wallon and I seem to agree in regarding imitation as the transitional
link between the sensorimotor stage and the representational stage is in
fact nothing more than an explanation of representational thought in
its figural aspect. It remains, then, to account for the formation, so
laborious, of "operations" for which, a series of studies in all areas of
elementary logical and mathematical thought . . . has demonstrated, the
groundwork is laid exclusively during the period between two and seven
years, during the course of a long process of *décentration* beginning with
action itself; and they do not reach completion until the two periods
from 7 to 11 and 11 to 15 years. But if the figural aspect of representational thought derives from the sensoritonic or postural system via

imitation and images, the operative aspect (actions and operations) . . . is explainable only in terms of coordinations between actions as such, coordinations that much more radically than those of speech already contain those elements of order found at all stages; thus it is the sensorimotor stage in its strict sense that must be invoked.

To return once again to the complementarity between Wallon's work and mine, which I believe I have succeeded in outlining . . . , we find that it is the result of interests that are divergent but are necessarily complementary to each other. The central idea in Wallon's work is the role of the postural system. In mine, it is the role of operations. Where Wallon speaks of a precategorial period in a child's thought. I see a preoperational period. Where Wallon, after discussing Plato, says that current science is also "to a certain extent the creation of its object" (P. 245), by which he means that if there is any direct relation between our thoughts and their object, it is that "they tend to reproduce the object" (P. 246), I would say that the primary end of science is to transform the object. Wallon continues, speaking of "representational thought, initially linked with myth, and later with experimental and scientific techniques. In its various forms, representational thought answers to the same need of figuration with a view toward action" (P. 246). I would say that figuration is merely one aspect of things and that systems of transformations are another, which subordinates itself to the first and distinguishes the specificity of science as opposed to the figural elements that it retains in common with myth.* In this same book *De l'acte à la pensée*, to which we are referring (Pp. 25–49), Wallon takes me extensively to task for having studied sensorimotor intelligence and the construction of reality from the vantage point of what he calls a "psychology of consciousness" and for projecting the intellect intact into sensorimotor schemata. With the serenity afforded by a distance of 20 years, I understand now that Wallon, conceiving representational thought as he describes it in the last chapters of his book, was correct in refusing to see in my sensorimotor schemata that which alone can provide an image—speech, and figural representation in general. But I was also correct in anticipating in the coordinations among action schemata the point of departure for later operations, and in the constitution of a schema for a permanent object, on the basis of a completely practical and active form of the "group of displacements," the first manifestation of these invariants (or conservational schemata) which our subsequent studies have shown to be inherent in operational transformations.

In a passage of remarkable lucidity, almost prophetic with respect to the later results of our respective research, Wallon writes:

Among the later effects of movement there are two kinds. First, those that are directed toward the external world and are still commonly regarded as being at the origin of mental life. . . . But a gesture modifies, along with the milieu, the person executing it, and in fact, it is this modification of the subject that is most immediately apprehended. Thus two orientations of activity are opened up, one addressed toward external objectives, and the other an activity directed toward the self, or "postural" activity, whose means and ends are the subject's own attitudes. This is a plastic activity. It is at the basis of imitation. . . . In the establishment of motor schemata, mutually overlapping and ordered and ultimately leading to representationl thought,

De l'acte à la pensée. Loc. cit.

they are arranged in a sort of mechanical progression, the utility of which will only later become evident. In contrast, the postural function contains within itself the source of its own progress. (Pp. 242–243)

One could find no better way to characterize the two forms of "representation," effectively quite distinct but precisely complementary, that have interested both Wallon and me: namely, the figural form, which gives rise to the image from the onset of imitation and derives from the postural system; and the operative form, which commences with sensorimotor schemata and ends in operations, properly so-called, of thought only much "later," as Wallon clearly states, since we must await the period between the ages of two and seven to eight years for the first operational representative structures or systems of transformations that no longer merely copy or reproduce the object, but also modify it, to be fully formed. But why is there this interval between sensorimotor schemata and operations? In the first place, it is precisely because a sufficient system of figural representations must previously have been constituted. And secondly, because between proper, material, and directly centered action and a system of coordinated and objective operations, a long process of *décentration* is still necessary. But as the English storyteller said, "That's another story"; and it would be useless to go into it here.

In summary, if Wallon and I have at times had discussions that our mutual friend Zazzo has recently compared to dialogues between the deaf, it has evidently been because in using the same words we have meant different things. Hence, after having searched (I confess, with some difficulty) for a point of agreement to present in this commemorative article, I found on rereading the fine writings of Wallon that the key word "representation" was just one of those difficult terms that separated us. Thus, since the figural aspect and the operative aspect of representational thought are basically complementary, as are the postural system and the sensorimotor system preceding representation, I am pleased to conclude this short note in tribute to Wallon by stating my conviction that our works themselves will also prove to be complementary.

29

Response to Brian Sutton-Smith*

1966

The interesting criticism that Sutton-Smith† has made of my play theory calls, I feel, for a brief reply. I must confess that I have some difficulty in recognizing the opinions that this author attributes to me, and I think that his formulations of them derive from the fact that he has only been able to assess that portion of my work that has been translated into English.

I have never, either implicitly or explicitly, expressed the view that knowledge is a copy of reality because such a view is contrary to my position with respect to the nature of intelligence. My whole conception of intellectual operations is based on the premise that to know or to understand is to transform reality and to assimilate it to schemes of transformation. In particular, I have never said that representative or symbolic thought, including concept formation, is derived from imitation (in the form of an accommodative copy). On the contrary, in my view, all concepts are derived first from the action and then from the operation, which is another way of saying that concepts are the expression of an assimilation by schemes of transformation.

In fact, the reality that intelligence tries to grasp consists of a series of states (A, B, C, etc.) and transformations which modify these states (A into B, B into C, etc.). One can, therefore, distinguish two components of cognitive functions:

There is first of all a figural component that does not itself constitute a copy but rather a more or less approximate description of reality states and their configurations. This figurative component is derived from perception, imitation, and imagery (graphic or mental) or from interiorized imitations.

There is secondly a cognitive component which takes account of transformations and which builds upon sensorimotor actions, interiorized actions, and finally, thought operations which are derived from actions and not at all from imitation.

*Jean Piaget, "Response to Brian Sutton-Smith." *Psychological Review*, vol. 73, 1966, 111–112. This paper was written in reply to "Piaget on play: a critique," by Brian Sutton-Smith, *Psychological Review*, vol. 73, 1966, 104–110. Copyright ©1966 by the American Psychological Association. Reprinted by permission.

†Brian Sutton-Smith, psychologist and folklorist, is the author of numerous works about play and games, including *The Folk Games of Children*, published for the American Folklore Society by the University of Texas Press (Austin, 1972).

In other words, when studying perception, mental imagery, etc. (research not yet published in English), I have tried to show that the figural aspects of cognitive functions are never sufficient to explain representative or conceptual knowledge. Indeed, the figurative components only play a useful role to the extent that they are subordinated to the cognitive component. It seems clear to me that knowledge of a "state" cannot be reduced to a copy of this state, but necessarily consists in an assimilation of this state to a preoperational scheme or a postoperational concept. In fact, to understand a state one must understand the transformations from which the state results which, let us repeat, excludes all types of copy knowledge.

The role of play in this system seems clear. Play is an exercise of action schemes and therefore part of the cognitive component of conception. At the same time, however, play manifests the peculiarity of a primacy of assimilation over accommodation which permits it to transform reality in its own manner without submitting that transformation to the criterion of objective fact. Regardless of what Sutton-Smith says, play fits into this system without becoming subordinated to accomodative imitation. Imitation only plays the role of a symbolic instrument from the moment that sensorimotor play becomes symbolic. This last point leads us to an examination of the symbolic function.

The sensorimotor functions (including sensorimotor play and perception) are not symbolic inasmuch as they only use undifferentiated signifiers (indexes or signals). The symbolic function begins around 1½–2 years of age with the appearance of differentiated signifiers (signs and symbols) and consists in representing various figurative and cognitive schemes by means of these signifiers. In other words, the symbolic signifiers are derived from imitation which, before becoming interiorized, is already a kind of symbolization in action. This fact, however, in no way implies that symbolic instruments should be confused with figural aspects of thought. Perception is figurative, but not symbolic, while language is symbolic (in the broad sense), but not figurative. Interiorized imitation and images are, on the contrary, at the same time figurative and symbolic. Mental imagery in particular is the product of interiorized imitation and not the simple residue of perception as it was previously believed.

If symbolic play uses imitation, it is exclusively as a symbolic instrument. This follows because there are only two ways that an absent situation can be represented; it can either be described by language or evoked by imitative gestures or images. This in no way means, however, that symbolic play can be reduced to imitation since play is exclusively an assimilation of reality to the self. Nonetheless, since it is symbolic it needs signifiers, and it borrows them either from language or from the only other source of symbols, that is to say, gestural or interiorized imitation.

It seems clear now that the criticisms that Sutton-Smith has made of our theory are unfortunately the result of a series of misunderstandings and that the opinions that he attributed to us, which indeed deserve to be criticized, are fortunately not our views. There remains, however, one other point that must be clarified. The author defends the idea that symbolic play does not diminish but rather differentiates during the course of development. This is certainly true in one sense of the word. In becoming differentiated, however, it at the same time becomes more and more adequately adapted to reality (construction games, etc.). This is the sense in which I speak of play as diminishing with age. And it does diminish if one takes, as I do, the essential property of play to be the deformation and subordination of reality to the desires of the self.

Finally, Sutton-Smith makes an allusion to Vygotsky's conception of egocentric language. I have already replied in length to Vygotsky's insightful remarks. However, if we are to take up the problem of egocentrism again, which goes hand in hand with the deforming processes of assimilation, we must also situate language and play in the overall context of the individual and social actions of the child. In studying the collaboration of children in collective actions, R. F. Nielsen has found an evolutionary law which resembles to a great extent what I used to call the passage from egocentrism to cooperation.

INTRODUCTORY NOTES

In The Child's Conception of Movement and Speed (1946) Piaget sees the origin of subjective activity in the notion of movement. Movements are supposed, in Piaget's theory, to generate both the physical notion of displacement and the practical group of geometric displacements (see these concepts in the introduction to the *Construction of Reality*). A movement being a change of position, it is a change of placement, a *dis-placement*.

But some movements are more than mere displacements. They are real actions involving effort on the part of the subject who *generates* the impressions of acceleration and duration through his own activity. This is the reason why an essay on the child's conception of movement necessarily entails the study of speed and time.

According to Piaget, the child constructs the basic operations of movement and speed in six different stages taking place between the last phases of the semiotic period and the end of the period of concrete operations or very early in the period of formal operations.

During the first two stages of this development, the child establishes the categories of placing objects (*placements*) or successive ordering, and of displacements, which are the changes of position of the objects themselves. The third and fourth stages bear upon the coordination of *placements* with displacements into one composed system of operations generating the notions of temporal succession, duration, and absolute speed in relation to a frame of reference. These notions allow "co-displacements": the composition of movements taking account of their relative speeds. At the fifth level, the establishment of proportions between spaces covered and times necessary to cover them becomes possible thanks to the formation of extensive operations. The sixth level is marked by the appearance of the metric system of operations on space and time, permitting, through the construction of an iterative unit, the measurement of distances and durations and, hence of the path traversed and the speed used.

The experimental data supporting this general theoretical viewpoint are ingenious. The child has to evaluate the consequences of rotations and translations of objects in space. Is the order of the components of an object conserved in translations or not? Is this order permuted by rotations and in what way? At first, the child pays attention to the extremes of these movements (points of departure and arrival), and to states of affairs rather than to transformations (in this case, displacements). The child remains unable to coordinate the movements of objects traversing different paths or to compose successive displacements of an object. He relies entirely upon what Piaget calls the intuition of overtaking, that is to say on the simple functional relationship between behind and before, and before and after. For a child that age, it is sufficient for a moving object to have been once behind and then before another to be considered as "having more speed." This ordinal concept of speed is, according to Piaget, very primitive in the child, and certainly anterior to the adult concept of speed as the ratio of the space covered to the time taken to cover it.

The experiments on this intuition of speed are of two types, synchronic and partially asynchronic movement. In the first, the objects considered are moving at the same time over distances of different lengths on rectilinear, circular, or concentric pathways; in the second, the objects may, for example, begin at different times and arrive at the same time, covering equivalent distances. The child is then required to estimate the relative speed of the objects. Simply from this description of the experiments one can see that a fully developed concept of speed as a dimension of an event that can be thought of separately from the event as one concrete totality—such a concept also requires a certain concept of time. This is the subject of another work.

30

The Child's Conception of Movement and Speed*

1946

Preface

These studies of the child's conception of movement and speed are a sequel to those recently published on the formation of the concept of time, with which they are closely bound up by the very fact that these three basic concepts are interdependent.

But is it not overrating them to devote an entire work solely to the notions of movement and speed in a child's mental development? In fact we are very well aware of this, and the primary object of this foreword must be to justify ourselves to the reader. Our only excuse is the still surprisingly unrefined state of the knowledge we have of children's intellectual growth. While botanists have catalogued all the world's plants, and zoologists have counted the hairs upon every little animal, and that at each stage of their growth, the science of child development, i.e., the embryology of the human spirit itself in effect, continues to be confined to general studies, upon which teaching techniques and therapy, etc. can be based only in the most empirical fashion.

Now the concepts of movement and speed especially touch upon the fields of mathematics and general science teaching, in which it would be of great value to know precisely the way in which these concepts develop; in other words, their psychological as well as their logical build-up.

But there is still more. The most fruitful use of psychology will not be found purely by seeking an immediate application. The gradual passage from intuitive thinking, still tied to the information of the senses,

*From *The Child's Conception of Movement and Speed* by Jean Piaget, translated by G. E. T. Holloway and M. J. Mackenzie from the French *Les Notions de Mouvement et de Vitesse chez l'enfant*, Presses Universitaires de France, 1946, English translation © Routledge and Kegan Paul Ltd., London, 1970, Basic Books, Inc., Publishers, New York. Reprinted by permission of the publishers. Originally published in French, 1946. (Collaborators: Barbara von Albertini, Madeleine Blanchet, Esther Bussman, M. and Mme. Claude Ferriere, Olga Frank, J. Frei, Monique Lagier, Madeleine Martin, A. Mauris, and Madeleine Reymond.)

toward operational thinking, which forms the basis of reasoning itself, may be studied in the light of the particularly simple examples which are to be found in the fields of movement and speed. It is this general position that we shall take up in the present work, and this is what justifies its size. Indeed when wishing to consider such questions, it is only by examining the facts step by step that one can hope to avoid indulging in mere verbal abstractions when one comes to making a synthesis.

In this work (as in previous works on the child's conception of number, quantity and time) we shall take the term "operations," in a limited and well-defined sense, to mean actions or transformations at once reversible and capable of forming systematic wholes. We have tried to show that prior to the formation of mathematical "groups," which always imply the occurrence of a metrical or at the least an extensive quantity, logical operations already form systems, which are likewise reversible and capable of synthesis (simple relations between the part and the whole), at the level of intensive quantity, though far less rich, which we have called "groupings." Such are the mechanisms which we shall find at the root of the first operational ideas of movement and speed, and that as a precondition of their subsequent mathematization.

We shall use the term intuition, or intuitive thinking, in an equally limited sense, and narrower than that of the mathematician in particular —for us it will mean preoperational thinking, i.e., thinking which relies only on perceptual configuration or on tentative empirical activity and is as yet unready for "grouping" or "groups." It is necessary, therefore, to speak here of "image-using intuition," or even "perceptual intuition" as opposed to rational intuition, but for brevity we shall confine ourselves to talking of intuition alone.

Thus, the essential problem which we shall study in relation to movement and speed is the passage from image-using or perceptual intuition to the forming of operational systems. We were earlier leading up to the study of a child's conception of movement through the analysis of his attempts to explain movement in nature and assign a cause to it. We laid stress on the child's animism in this respect, attaching as he does a consciousness and a purpose to moving things, and above all, on his finalism and his dynamism: all movement tends toward a goal and implies an inherent vital or creative power. Hence a number of curious analogies with Aristotle's physics, in particular the hypothetical need for two motive forces, one internal and the other external, to explain a movement like that of clouds or river water, and above all, a very systematic diagram of "environmental reaction" attributing the motion of missiles to the responsive action of the displaced air.

These facts will not be returned to in the present work, but it is useful to recall them, to illuminate the operational development of the conception of movement and speed. In fact, it is through this teleology, always more or less colored with animism, that one understands the important place given by children's intuition to the "point of arrival" of the movement and consequently to "overtaking" in the reckoning of speed. The ideas of order and "placing" which play, as we shall see, a fundamental role in the formation of these concepts are to be explained in this respect, as sharing in physics which are imbued with finalism and the idea of the proper place, and where purely qualitative or intensive operations long precede mathematical or extensive operations. But, to reiterate, our emphasis will be exclusively on this operational aspect of development.

The Problem of Alternative Directions of Travel*

Let us consider three elements A, B, and C, such that A precedes B, and B precedes C, during a movement from right to left $A \leftarrow B \leftarrow C$. We achieve this in three different ways: Technique 1. Three beads, $A =$ red, $B =$ black, and $C =$ blue are threaded on a small piece of wire; this is then placed within one's half-closed hand with the two ends of the wire projecting, then the beads are made to reappear on the other side in the same order ABC, then to retrace their path in inverse order CBA, etc. Technique 2. Three small wooden balls $A =$ red, $B =$ brown, and $C =$ yellow are placed in a chute made of cardboard in the order ABC and are guided with A leading, into a tunnel occupying the central part of the slide to emerge in the same order or to return in inverse order. Technique 3. Three little wooden dolls $A =$ blue, $B =$ green, and $C =$ yellow are strung on a wire and pass in the same order of $A \leftarrow B \leftarrow C$ behind a screen. The following questions are asked systematically, although giving way to free conversation insofar as may be profitable, depending on the child's reactions.

Q 1. In what order will the objects emerge at the other side of the hand, tunnel or screen?

Q 2. In what order will the objects reappear, on travelling through the tunnel (or passing behind the screen) in the opposite direction?
Note: The child draws the objects with suitably colored pencils in the direct order (either after or before Q 1) so as to serve as a reminder. To solve Q 2 then, he has only to look at his paper and read off the colors in reverse order. In this way the problem of reasoning is quite separate from memory.

Q 3. When the first two questions are solved (and if they are not at the first trial, the experiment is repeated until the child is sure of the answer), one then presents Q 3 and 4 (Q 3 applies only to the Technique 2). The objects are inserted in the direct order ABC into the tunnel, after which the child is asked to change places and sit at the other side of the table. If in his starting position the movement took place from right to left, it will now appear from left to right in the subject's new position: he is then asked in what order the balls will emerge on the right hand side and he should realize that this will be the direct order though he himself has changed his place in relation to the tunnel and so the balls seem to retrace their path. In other words the child must judge their order of progress from the starting point of the balls and not according to the left and the right of the tunnel. This question involves the two ways in which the child may judge the direction of travel when faced with the same objective order.

Q 4. The three objects are put back, in view of the child, in the order ABC, whether within the hand or into the tunnel or behind the screen, and a rotary movement 180° is described either with the hand and the wire jointly (Technique 1), or with the cardboard tunnel (Technique 2), or by

*[The following section is from Chapter I.]

the wire alone (Technique 3). Care is taken that the movement is fully visible, describing what is being done* and drawing attention, in Technique 1 and 3, to the ends of the wire visible in the process of turning on itself. This semirotation completed, one asks in what order the objects will emerge, in the same place as that where in Q 1 they came out in the direct order. This Q 4, thus bears, like Q 2 on the inverse order, but owing to the rotation of the apparatus, and no longer to a simple sending back as in Q 2.

Q 5. Same question as 4 but with two successive semirotations (in the same direction), either in two moves, 180° + 180°, or in one move: 360°.

Q 6. Same questions for a random number of semirotations, either [odd] (= emerging in inverse order) or even (= emerging in direct order).

Q 7. If up till now the child has not spontaneously thought that the middle object B could come out in first place, in any of the preceding situations, the question is then put as follows. A random number of semirotations is described (about 10 but without counting) and one asks which object "might emerge first? Could it be A? or C? or B?" Each time one asks why, or why not, and in the case of an affirmative for B, "How could that happen?" (it should be stated that the tunnel in Technique 2 is of a diameter hardly greater than the balls, to avoid any leap frogging).

Finally, the same Q 1 to 7 may be asked in relation to four or five objects, and not merely to three.

The following stages were observed among the responses made by about fifty children between 4 and 8 years of age. In stage I the child is able to answer Q 1 (which is without doubt the case from the second year on) but not Q 2, i.e., simple inverse order. In the course of stage II, Q 2 is solved, but not 3 to 5, at least not at the first attempt; during the second half of this stage (substage IIB), by contrast, Q 3 and 4 produce an immediate reply while 5 and 6 as yet only produce wavering attempts. During a third stage, finally, Q 1 to 5 are solved at once and soon after lead to a generalization in the form of a solution to Q 6. As for Q 7, which is concerned with the central object, at the start of stage I the child spontaneously allows that B could come out first or last as well as staying between A and C; toward the end of this stage he is seldom inclined to think of such a transformation himself, but it is enough for the question to be asked in the form already observed, for him to accept it without more being said. From stage II on he thinks it impossible for the order to be broken in the case of three objects, B staying in the middle in both directions of travel; for five elements, however, it still happens in the course of this stage that objects not at either end may spontaneously be thought capable of coming out first.

The First Stage: Path Retraced Without Inverting the Order and Displacement of Middle Object. This first stage ends on average toward 5 years of age but it is not unusual for examples to be found up to 5½ years. Here are some examples.

An (4 years). Technique 2. "Which will come first out of the tunnel? *The red one (A). And then? The brown one (B) and the yellow (C).* (dem). And now they are coming back, which one will come out first? *The red one, the brown, and the yellow one.* Look! (dem). *Oh, no, it's the yellow, then the brown and the red.* Why? *Because coming back it's the yellow one'.* Fine. And now, look, I'm turning the tunnel (Q 4). Which will be first this time? *The red, then the brown, then the yellow one.* Look! (dem). *It's the yellow one.* Why? *Because I didn't know.* We'll start again. *It will be the yellow one.* (dem). Why? *Don't know.*

*The semirotation is made on the horizontal or on the vertical plane.

"Right then, look: I am going to turn it twice, you see, one, two. Which will come first now? *The brown one* (*B*). Why? *Because you turned it two times.* But why is it the brown one first if it's turned twice? . . . (dem). Look! *The red one!* (*A*). Why? *Don't know.* And now I'm going to turn it three times, look. This will be? *The yellow one, no, the brown!* Why? *Because you did it three times.* (dem). Well? *Oh, the yellow one!* Why? *Don't know.* And now? (Five to six half turns). *The brown one* (*B*). Why? *Because you turned it lots of times.* Can the balls in the tunnel jump over each other? *No.* Why? *The hole is too little.* Good. And where is the brown one? *In the middle.* Then which is going to come out first? *The brown one.* Look! *Oh, dear no, it's the yellow one.* What does it mean when the brown one is in the middle? *That it is behind the red one and behind the yellow one.* Fine. Now look (several turns). Which will be first? *It's the yellow one.* And now? (several more turns). *The red.* And now (rep.)? *The yellow.* And now (rep.)? *And now it's the brown one!* Why? *Because you turned it I don't know how many times!* Look! *Oh, no, still not that one.*"

Technique 3. "Can these little fellows hop over each other? *No, because there's a wire.* Right; then which one will be first out there? (Q 1). *The blue* (*A*). And after that? *The green* (*B*) *and the yellow* (*C*). Is that right? (dem). *Yes.* And now, coming back? *The yellow one* (dem). And if I turn the wire this way? (Q 4). *The blue one.* (dem). *Oh, no, it's the yellow one because you turned the wire round.* And now, if I turn it twice? *The blue one.* And if I turn three times? *The blue* (dem). *No, the yellow one.* And if I turn it four times? *That will be the green one* (*B*) *first.* Why? *Because the green one* (*B*) *is after the blue one* (*A*). (dem). Is that right? *No, it's the blue.* And now? (turning some more) *The green one!* (*B*)." . . .

These responses in stage I are of some interest in connection with the psychology of the intuition of order, and for the study of the relation between intuition and operation.

We note first of all that all the subjects interviewed, from 4 years upwards, are able to solve Q 1, i.e., they have awareness of direct order and its conservation during a lateral movement: they are sure that three balls unable to overtake one another, and three manikins or three beads strung on a wire will be in the same order at the other end of a tunnel or cardboard screen. That this awareness is due, in part at least, to experience is obvious. An infant a few months old not yet possessed of the outlines of the conservation of the object would not, under the conditions we have just described, be able to foresee conservation of order. But once the invariability of objects, and the relations of cause and effect preventing them from travelling over one another out of one position into another inside the tunnel or along the wire are recognized, the conservation of order during a direct journey ("outward") is plain sailing for the child and fits intuitive evidence with three objects.

In contrast—and a very characteristic thing about preoperational intuition—from the beginning—the subjects in this stage I do not manage to deduce the order of the objects on the return journey to be the inverse of their order on the outward journey. Lasting for a longer or a shorter time according to the subjects, their mistake then consists in accepting that when the objects have moved off in the order *ABC* they can come back only in that same order, as though it were some sort of stroll during which the participants follow one another without ever changing places. It is obvious that no serious difficulty should prevent the child from visualizing their returning in the order *CBA*, the first one now last and vice versa, since experience might already have given the child numerous examples of these reversals. Moreover, it should be enough for the child to look more closely at the cardboard tunnel, or the fixing of the manikins, to see that on the way back the objects cannot resume direct order, since they cannot change places with one another; we stress in each interview the impossibility of overtaking and passing. Then why does the child not think of inverse order, preferring to keep direct order which, on reflection, would imply conditions impossible to fulfill with our apparatus? It is clearly, and this is the sole interest of these early replies to Q 2, that at this purely intuitive level, reasoning consists simply in retracing, by the act of representation, events just as they were perceived, instead of imagining an alteration or inversion. In the case of the order coming back, nothing would seem easier than to effect intuitively a "mental experiment" describing the process in detail. That is what the subject seems to do as soon as experience in reality has put him in contact with inverse order. . . . In other words, he is not yet able to anticipate intuitively this return in reverse, but only to recall and then to generalize it once it has been observed. In short, the subject refuses to imagine such a simple inversion because he is loath to attempt at all an act of representation other than a simple copy, and prefers therefore, from inertia, to preserve the perceptual figure ABC just as it is.

With Q 3 and 4 things change and the error observed is no longer due to this kind of mental sluggishness, but to a more stubborn and systematic difficulty. Q 3 presents no great interest in this stage because it implies the solving of Q 2, which happens only after two or three repetitions of the experience of the return journey. Nevertheless, once this training is acquired one notes the following suggestive fact: having learned, thanks to repeated observations, that object A always emerges from the left end of the tunnel and object C from the right end, [Jac (4;8)] does not reverse these results when he moves to the other side of the table, and now, seeing the former on his right, expects object C to emerge. In other words, he does not reason in terms of direction of travel in relation to the tunnel, but in terms of a static indication of which he simply records the *absolute* position relative to his own body. It is precisely both this lack of understanding of relative direction of travel, and this recourse to reference to *absolute* position which we find in the responses to Q 4 and 6.

Q 4 gives rise, in fact, to answers of a notable uniformity, which range from complete lack of understanding of the effect of the semi-rotation, to the commencement of an empirical understanding. The reason for this failure is quite clear: convinced that object A emerges first on the right-hand side and object C on the left, the subject no more takes into account the half-rotation of the tunnel or wire than he did his own change of place in Q 3. He thus judges once more in terms of the *static* indication established by the location of the extremity upon his right, and not in terms of the direction of travel, reversed by the semi-rotation of the line formed by the objects ABC or ABCDE. When the question is first given (with, of course, the child looking on while the tunnel or wire is turned, and only objects ABC out of sight) all subjects at this level expect that if the objects reappear on the right, the direct order ABC will plainly be maintained. But once the result of the experiment is observed, the child, while recognizing he was wrong, does not see why, or not immediately, and that is the essential difference from Q 2.

It is true that the subject, taking into account what he has just seen, usually expects object C to be first again when the question is tried again. But the rest of the questioning reveals this to be purely empirical association without understanding why. It is also true that some subjects reply: "it's because it was turned round," but this connecting of C in first place, with the half-turn, which was at the same time in his sight and brought explicitly to his notice, still does not prove his understanding of the reason: e.g., Fran, who gives this answer at the first trial (after his initial error based on absolute position: "the red one because it's over there," i.e., on the right), thinks that on two successive half-turns it is one more object C which will lead out first. As for Der, he is astounded by what he observes, after his mistaken forecast: "But over there (on right) it was yellow last and now over there it's yellow first (again on right)—how did it change?" To which he spontaneously answers: "Oh, it's because you turned the box round." He appears to understand perfectly, but subsequently he thinks that yellow (C) and red (A) will emerge by turns, irrespective of the number of half-turns. It is the same with Technique 3.

To sum up then, at this stage two constant responses are observed on Q 4. First, the child expects direct order to persist despite rotation, because he [predicts] the order of appearance of the objects in relation to one or other extremity of the tunnel, or wire, depending on whether this extremity is upon his right or his left, not according to the direction of travel itself. Secondly, when the experiment is made and the error noted, the child does attribute the reversed order to the half-turn, but in a purely empirical way (post hoc, ergo propter hoc), and without visualizing the inversion of the objects themselves. . . .

Q 5 [to] 7 form the natural complement of problem 4. If the subject understands that a half-turn of 180° reverses the order, he will thereby understand that a second semirotation of 180° cancels out this reversal, in other words that a complete rotation of 360° does not alter the order at all (Q 5). In fact if he thinks operationally, and not merely intuitively, he will see that a double inversion is a straightforward operation, i.e., that a double negative becomes a positive. On the other hand, if he abides by the empirical observation that a half-rotation alters the order, he cannot forecast the result of two half-rotations. Likewise Q 6 generalizes without elaboration on Q 5 and simply deals with the succession in turn of direct and inverse order.

Now the replies given during this stage to Q 5 and 6 are of great interest and reveal just how far the reactions of young children remain preoperational. E.g., An expects after two half-turns the middle ball B will appear first; with three operations he forecasts C or B, and when B still does not appear, he anticipates it after five or six semirotations. Der, seeing C leading the way after one half-turn thinks that with several rotations "it will be red because it was yellow before," as if there should be some compensation in favor of A regardless of the number of turns! He applies this principle so thoroughly that in the case of two semirotations he goes on to forecast that the middle object B will take the lead. . . . In short, the subject in no way understands the relationship between the successive rotations, . . . forecasts according to whim, manipulating frequency and compensation as if drawing lots among the objects.

This absence of any controlled mental representation, even in the way of intuitive anticipation, such as that of [mental experiment], is particularly striking in Q 7. Without any prompting on the part of the experimenter, subjects of 4 to 5 years spontaneously suppose that of three elements ABC in a straight line the median B can take precedence if the direction of travel is changed. It happens less often that the subject may expect to find B at the head, after a simple return journey, when he has noted from experience that it cannot be A. In contrast, when the tunnel or wire undergoes a semirotation the forecast for B is common. . . .

These facts, which are of great interest in the study of the geometry of the child as well as his understanding of movement, seem to us to involve two related conclusions, the first concerns the nature of the relationship expressed in "between," and the second preoperational intuition.

A celebrated axiom of Hilbert states that "if B is situated between A and C, it is also between C and A." In other words, the relationship "between" persists regardless of direction of travel, whether this continues to exist only in the mind, or takes form in an actual movement. Far from being an axiom for our subjects, this proposition begins by being quite unrecognized by them. Later it comes to be seen as a simple, experimental truth. Such an initial lack of understanding, may we say right away, brings to mind the behavior of infants of 10 to 12 months who in order to place a ring on a wire rod, do not slide the wire through the hole in the ring but merely touch the wire with the ring, as if it would encircle the former as a result of this: experience alone teaches them the topological relationship existing between a mass perforated by a hole, and a body passing through the hole. In the case of the relationship expressed by "between" what is the significance of its conservation irrespective of direction of travel? If A, B, and C are three objects placed along the same line, B could only cease to be between A and C by moving in a second dimension; if A, B, and C belong to a single surface of which no one part can move about on the same level relative to the others, B could only cease to be between A and C by moving in a third dimension; finally, if A, B, and C belong to the same mass, the order of whose parts cannot be rearranged (whether it be because of a box too narrow to allow leap-frogging, or a rod passing through rings or beads, etc.), B could only depart from its place in the middle by moving according to a fourth dimension, But one knows that objects may be taken from a box without opening it, left-hand gloves made into right-hand gloves, etc. So there is nothing intrinsically impossible in trying like the infant to slide a rod through a ring without using the opening in it, or in changing round the order of three balls in a narrow tunnel. . . . It is only impossible in our three-dimensional world, and therefore it is natural that it must be experience which teaches a child these different points. In the fairly common case of the ring and the rod, the experimental discovery takes place from the second year on. In the case, more remote from the child's life, of the balls in their tunnel or the beads strung on their wire rod, we must wait till the age of 5. But in all these cases, the impossibility is primarily of a physical order, as indeed is the actual existence of the three dimensions themselves. In contrast, as soon as it is granted that corresponding to the direct order ABC there is the inverse order CBA, it then becomes not only impossible but contradictory to allow that B could cease to occupy its median position: in fact, as soon as inverse order is conceived operationally as simply the reversal of direct order, without any changing around of the objects in their sequence, the relationship in "between" becomes symmetrical and expresses the invariable interval existing in relation to either order. Now, in this first stage, it has been seen that the inverse operation is, as yet, not logically constructed at all but merely discovered empirically: hence it is in the nature of things that the relationship "between," as an interval, shares the same preoperational and intuitive state.

. . . The lesson to be drawn from these reactions is therefore that . . . at a certain level of development the empirical or intuitive attitude sometimes raises such a complete barrier to operational grouping that it ends up in this bizarre and contradictory result, of unimaginable images, or intuitions incapable of being grasped intuitively. And the reason for it is simply that disconnected structures (each imagined whole being independently formed once and for all, according to the images which immediate experience has had to offer in one single field of perception) remain separated from each other by gaps impossible to bridge. . . . The relationships between intuitions which succeed each other are not themselves objects of which intuition is possible. . . . Operations will arrive at this result by using just those organizational *procedures*, applied to the gaps in relationships between intuitions. . . .

The Second Stage: Inverse Order on Return Journey and Beginnings of Invariability of the Median Object but No Understanding of the Effects of Semirotation (Substage IIa) then Forecasting of the First Effects of This, but Without Generalization (Substage IIb). This second stage is therefore that of the joining together of the intuitions, but without operational generalization, e.g., when going from three on to five objects, or from two to three on to a number of rotations. Here are examples of substage IIa:

Chri (5;4). Technique 1. "Look at these beads going into the tunnel. How will they come out on the other side? *Red (A) first, then black (B) and blue (C) last.* Good. And now I'm making them come back. So? *Blue (C) first, then black (B) then red (A).* Why are they the other way? *Because you're coming from the other direction.* Fine. Now, look: I'm sending them in as I did before, as on your drawing, then I'm going to turn the tunnel over. Which is first? *Red (A).* Why? *Because the wire is the other way.* And then? *Black (B) and blue (C).* Look: they're going in now and I'm turning the tunnel like that (half-turn). Which will be first? *Red (A).* (exp.). Is that right? *No. It's blue because you made it go the other way.* Let's start again (same exp.). Which first? *Red (A) because the wire is this side.* Look (exp.). *Oh, no, blue again because it was turned the other way.* (Start again). And now? *Blue* (correct). And now, listen: I'm going to turn it twice, not just once any more. Which first? *Blue.* Why? *Because it was turned the other way.* Look. (exp.). *Oh, no red! I thought it would come out on the other side.* (Several turns). Which would it be now? *Red or blue.* Why? *Or else black.* Why? *Oh, no, it couldn't because it's in the middle."* . . .

Wag (7;3). Technique 2. Return journey: "*Yellow (C). First because it was last before and they can't get mixed up.* (Half-turn). *Red (A).* Look. (exp.). *Yellow (C).* Why? *Because you changed the balls, you turned it round.* (360°). *Red.* (three half-turns). *Red.* Look! *No, yellow, because if you turn it four times it's red.* And brown (B)? (he smiles)."

Technique 3. Return and semirotation correct. Twelve turns. "Is the green one still in the middle? *No.* Why? *Yes, it's still there because you turned it round and you can't take it out."*

Mar (7;6). Technique 2. Return: correct. Semirotation: "*Red (A). Look! No, yellow.* Why? *Because you turned it round* (two half-turns). *Yellow, Oh, no, it's red.* (three times) *Red.* Look! *No, yellow* (four times)?*Red.* (random number). *Could be either red or yellow.* Not brown (B)? *No, because it's in the middle."*

It is interesting to compare these many intermediate reactions with the initial intuitions of stage I and with the foreshadowing of operations of substage IIb.

The only general progress to be noted is the correct forecast of return order (Q 2) and this applies to five objects as well as three. But one may wonder whether this discovery is still intuitive, or already operational, in other words whether it is a case of a return journey known only by experience, or of a reversibility that cannot be otherwise. Now, in order to understand inversion it is enough for the subject to imagine, by an intuitive anticipation or theoretical representation, the return of three people walking in single file who cannot overtake or change places with each other. This is what Chri says (it's back to front "because they're coming from the other direction") and especially Wag: "Yellow is first because it was the last one and they can't get mixed up together." It is true that operational reasoning would not state anything else, regarding Q 2 on its own, but [there is still a] difference between operations and articulated intuitions: the former give rise to generalizations, while the latter are restricted to the small area within which their association was brought about, without any generalization to other problems. . . .

Q 7 (invariability of the median position) is the one most rapidly solved as a result of the understanding of inversion: in fact, if direct order and inverse order are only conceivable in the absence of any leapfrogging, the intermediate objects can only remain as they are. But it is in fact extremely interesting to observe that the answer to Q 2 (inversion) does not always produce at the outset the answer to Q 7. When there are only three objects, the latter answer is generally found, but Wil (6;0) who at once solves the question on inversion and even the one on semirotation, expects in the case of rotation through 360° to see the median object appear first. . . . Pil (6;0) while foreseeing quite correctly the reversed order of five balls ("since they turned round about") and while refusing to allow that the median can appear first during this return journey, settles on D the penultimate object when he goes round to the other side of the table (Q 3), and on B, the second object, during semirotation, and on either of the extremes or the middle object in the case of a complete rotation: his mental experience of the return journey thus rests in a state of articulated intuition and in no wise at the level of an operation since none of the three intermediate positions is conceived as invariable. . . . If it were a question of operations properly so called, the answers to Q 2 and 7 together would in effect bring about without elaboration the solution of Q 3 up to 7.

Examination of the answers given in substage IIa, to Q 3 to 7, shows sufficiently what is wanting in these responses to lead to *grouped* operations. When the child, leaving out any sort of semirotation of the apparatus, has moved to the other side of the table (Q 3) we note at once that he cannot reverse left- and right-hand and cannot understand that object A will lead out on his left. Moreover, on the first semirotation (Q 4) the subject cannot foresee the inversion of the order (it is this absence of initial prediction which distinguishes substages IIa and IIb:

only Wil [6;0] is an exception, but as he does not solve Q 7, he belongs, as yet, clearly on the level of IIa). But the child, having observed that with one semirotation the order is reversed, at once takes this experience into account (except at the commencement of the stage) and thus expects that if we put everything back in its place and repeat one semirotation, then inversion will appear again. . . . It is only after observing the result of one, two, and three half-turns that Wag and Mar (the two most advanced subjects) begin to have an inkling that the order changes with each new half-turn, so announcing the reactions of substage IIb. Hence it is clear that in the course of substage IIa, Q 3 to 5 are solved only under pressure of a succession of experiences and without as yet any grouping of the transformations being brought into play.

The criterion of the existence of operations would then be their grouping, and it would be in the absence of this grouping (in the absence therefore of the solution to Q 3 to 5) that we should consider the correct replies given to Q 2 to 7, as being intuitive and not yet operational. But isn't this begging the question, and could we not concede that inversion of order and preservation of the intermediate elements are already operations, merely easier than the rest and only awaiting the appearance of these last, in order to result in grouping? And above all could we not say that rotations have nothing to do with relationships of order, and that the relationships in question in the case of problems 1 (direct order), 2 (inverse order), and 7 (relationship "between") are enough to constitute an autonomous grouping, that of "position," earlier than that of "change of position"?

These questions may be answered in two ways. Logically, it is clear that relationships of order imply a direction of travel, and that change of location likewise implies this, both [of these] relative to the system of positions in a series serving as points of reference, so much so that the two kinds of grouping are indissociable. Psychologically on the other hand it is essential, in establishing whether a subject is capable of inverting any kind of relationships of order, to have him change his place or to change the location of the objects in their series, according to the arrangement of Q 3, and 4 to 6, for in order to forecast a sequence of outward and return journeys upon the model of Q 1 and 2, the subject can content himself with anticipating the arrival of the outermost objects in terms of left-right or front-back, and this with automatic regularity: when Lan, e.g., foresees the appearance of object (C) upon the return journey (Q 2) he says quite simply "because (A) belongs to this side here" thus each object has once and for all "*its* side," which dispenses with any reasoning. It is therefore only on Q 3 to 7 that one can establish whether there actually is operational inversion.

It is nonetheless true that articulated intuition, which allows Q 2 and 7 to be solved, does act as transition between the early, static intuitions, and operations themselves, in the following manner. At first the child can succeed in imagining intuitively only certain exceptional situations, corresponding to what he has previously perceived as a function of his actions (in contradistinction to the sensorimotor level, where the subject does not actively imagine anything, but where that which he perceives immediately sets off motor programs prolonging the perception). These exceptional situations then constitute so many intuitive images acting as internalized models for actions, but there are gaps between these from the point of view of thinking, since the actions linking them remain impossible to imagine. This is the level of stage I, in the course of which the subject certainly intuits object *B* between *A* and *C*, then object *B* before or after *A* (or *C*), but without managing or even trying to visualize how *B* changes places with *A* or *C* in this way. Then comes an effort to bridge these gaps in intuitive representation, which consists in anticipating or reconstructing intuitively the action itself which might lead from one image to another. It is this sort of mental experience which constitutes articulated intuition, more mobile than the static intuition of the first simple perceptual reconstructions. It is in this way that the subject in stage II imagines the return journey of objects *ABC* in the inverse order *CBA* and above all how he discovers little by little (and not immediately) the impossibility of *B*'s changing places with *A* or *C*. But these articulated intuitions are not yet operations because the subject cannot manage to generalize nor, what comes to the same thing, to regulate them; they are still only adaptations or diffusions of the original islands of intuition, and thus they will remain in their preoperational state so long as they cannot be "grouped" in stable and reversible operational wholes.

Subjects at substage IIb, without arriving at a complete solution (Q 5 and 6 together), manage however to anticipate the order, when they themselves change places (Q 3) or upon one semirotation of the apparatus (Q 4) and even, at the end of this stage, upon two half-turns (Q 5).

Sul (5;6). Technique 2 with three objects: return journey correct. And if I turn it like that (Q 4)? *It will be yellow* (C) *then brown* (B) *then red* (A). Why yellow first? *Because you turned the tunnel round.* Look. (exp.). Correct. And now I'll turn it twice (from the starting point again) What first? *Yellow, because . . . I don't know.* Look: I turn it once (very slowly) and again once (same). Which? *Red, because that was first in the beginning, and you turned the tunnel twice round.* And three times? *I don't know.* Once? *Yellow.* Twice? *Red* (turning each time in sight of the child, but not showing the result). Three times? *Yellow.* Four? *Red.* Five? *Yellow.* Six? *Red.* Good. Now listen: if I turn two times? *Red.* Four times (turning the tunnel still in sight of the child)? *Yellow.* Six times? *Red.* Eight times? *Red.* Ten times? *Yellow.* And if I go on, will the brown one (B) ever be first one out? *No, because that's in the middle."* . . .

Pia (7 years). Technique 1. Return correct. 180° *"Yellow* (C) *because before it was the blue one* (A). Two turns. (360°)? *Blue or yellow.* Look. (1 + 1 slowly)? *Blue* (A) *because it starts off first and if you turn this once it's yellow* (C) *and if you turn it again it's blue* (A) *once more.* Four times? *Blue* (A) *because it's blue, yellow, blue, then yellow and blue again.* Five times? (He works it out again). *Yellow.* Six times? *Blue.* Three times? *Blue* (wrong). Eleven times? *Blue* (wrong). And black (B)? *No because that's always in the middle: it can't get out because of the others beside it."*

Od (7;6). Technique 2, same beginning. (Q 4–6): One time? *Yellow* (C). Two times? *Red* (A). Three times? *Yellow.* Four? *Red.* Five? *Yellow.* Six? *Red.* Twenty-five? *Yellow.* Forty? *Red.* Forty-eight? *Yellow.* Fifty-two? *Red.* Fifty-eight? *Yellow.* Once? *Yellow.* Twice. *Red.* Four? *Yellow.* .Six? *Red.* Eight times? *Yellow."*

It is of some theoretical interest (and might possibly become diagnostic) to note the constant regularity with which the child progresses in solving Q 4 to 6. . . . This development continues in IIb as follows. First of all, the child becomes able to solve spontaneously and by anticipation Q 4: one half-turn (vertically or horizontally) reverses the order. In correlation with this innovation, Q 3 is also solved (conservation of order upon observer changing place) and so too Q 7 (invariability of median positions). Likewise—and this is extremely interesting—when Q 4 (one half-turn) has once been solved spontaneously, Q 5 (two half-turns) is as well: the reversal of inverse order becomes once more direct order ("it's blue that started off first," says Pia: "if you turn this, it's yellow, and if you turn it once more it's blue again"). It is only in the case of five objects that hesitation persists. There is then yet another step, marked by the *simultaneous* solution to Q 4 and 5 since within substage IIa, Q 4 is solved only after the experiment, and when the solution has once been observed empirically it does not lead directly to that of Q 5 but only with a time lag. Now, once this step is reached, the upward climb begins to go forward again. First, in the case of three half-turns, the least advanced subjects of substage IIb do not have an immediate solution, while the most advanced of them answer correctly right away. Only, they do not succeed in finding the order corresponding to three half-turns except when the question about these follows immediately after the questions relating to one and two half-turns (e.g., Pia). Some children are found to be, as it were, exhausted after three half-turns and fail on four, even when questioned after each half-turn, and some are successful only when one proceeds in correct order. Finally, among these latter cases, distinction must be made between those who with five, six, seven . . . half-turns easily discover the alternating order (the most advanced, Od, etc.) and those who are finished after n half-turns, this number increasing gradually, therefore, with their development, just as has been seen in the advance to four.

Consequently what distinguishes substage IIb is that even subjects who can invert the order of the object upon each new half-turn, when the questions are asked following the series of whole numbers (1, 2, 3 . . . n half-turns), are lost as soon as one jumps from one number to any other number, once past the level of three or four half-turns, or upon counting backwards.

These then are the facts. One can see that they confirm the pattern sketched out earlier of the passage from intuitive to operational thinking. The problem is in fact to explain at the same time the failures which persist in substage IIb and the discovery characterizing this stage: the discovery at the same time, of inverted order upon one half-turn, and of the inversion of this inversion, in other words the return to direct order, upon one complete rotation. Now this double acquisition most certainly already verges on operations since it fits the two criteria of operational thinking, that of conceiving the operation of inversion (here inversion of order) and that of following through to an accurate "composition" (inversion of the inversion). But on the other hand it is not entirely operational since it does not lead to an immediate generalization of the solution which has been found; neither is the "composition" of the inversions jumping from one number of half-turns to any other yet possible for the subject who has to follow the succession of whole numbers in actual fact (and not just in imagination). We are therefore faced with the upper limit of "articulated intuition," as also, by this very fact, with the lowest limit of operations as such. In other words after having succeeded, from substage IIa, in imagining the return of the objects in the inverse direction (Q 2) then the invariability of the median objects (Q 7), the subject manages by a simple refinement of these articulated intuitions to make the experiment, mentally, of inverting the order by semirotation (Q 4). . . . But since the child, upon each half-turn, endeavors to follow the inversions in every detail in his thoughts he only gradually manages accurately to forecast the result of three, four, five half-turns. Once this game of visualizing the objects in alternation is set in train, he finally discovers (and this forms the ceiling of substage IIb) that upon each half-turn the order changes once more. Up to this upper limit the subject continues to rely on visualizing intuitively and therefore needs to imagine one by one the direct and indirect order of the objects upon each new half-turn: he is lost when a jump is made from one number of half-turns to any other, instead of keeping to the sequence of whole numbers.

What is this operational mechanism upon which the subjects of this level are verging without ever fully attaining? It may be understood by seeing exactly what they lack in order to generalize the solution found during orderly progression. Operations, one might say, are nothing other than articulated intuitions rendered adaptable and completely reversible since they are emptied of their visual content and survive as pure "intention"—taken in the sense fixed by Bühler in his celebrated analysis of thinking without imagery (*Bewusztheit*) (i.e., awareness). In other words, operations will come into being in their pure state when there is sufficient schematization. Thus instead of demanding actual representation, each inversion will be conceived of as a potential representation, like an outline for an experiment which could be performed but which it is not useful to follow to the letter, even in the form of performing it mentally. So one understands why the criterion of operations is "composition" or "calculation": detached from their representational content, operational schemes may no longer be based on the actual fact alone, even as imagined through a succession of reproductive or anticipatory intuitions, and will now only serve as a basis for deductions by resting on each other interdependently and this is just what "composition" consists of. But by the very fact that it frees itself from the bonds of intuition, this composition becomes endlessly fruitful and allows of any combination whatsoever of potential representations: whence the forecasting of the results of n half-turns independently of the order followed in choosing these numbers. . . .

The Third Stage: Operational Solving of Q 1 to 7 Inclusive. Some examples of entirely correct answers follow, allowing us to complete this analysis.

Gil (6;6). Technique 2: Q 1 to 4 answered correctly. And if I turn this twice? *It's red (A) first, because you turned it once and then a second time: that makes it the same side as at first.* And three times? *Yellow (C).* Four? *Red (A) because you turned it four times. It's easy. You don't know how I work it out. I can see through the cardboard* (really he moves his lips and works it out as he goes along). Six times? (But without actually turning it). *In any case it will not be brown (B) first because it cannot change.* Well? (he works it out in a low voice). *Red (A)* and five times? *Yellow.*

Lam (7; 4). Technique 2: Starting off the same. And if I turn it twice? *Red (A) because you turned it twice.* (Ten, twelve turns, very fast). Could it be brown (B)? *No, because it is in the middle of the other two.* And if I turn it all day on a motor? *It's always in the middle.* And three times? *Once yellow, twice red, three times yellow.* And five times? *Yellow.* Six times? *Red.* Twelve times? *Red.* Fifteen? *Yellow.* Eleven times? *Yellow.* What do we call numbers, 2, 4, 6, 8? *Don't know.* . . .

Thus we see that these subjects manage to forecast the order of the objects with any number of semirotations and whatever the order of the chosen numbers. Moreover, they quickly abstract from these forecasts the law according to which direct order corresponds to even numbers and and inverse order to odd numbers of semirotations.

The problem which arises at the culmination of this development is therefore to understand how the subject comes to deduce all the transformations in question, while each of them, without exception, has necessitated [experience] during previous stages.

. . . The role of experience in the construction of mathematical relationships is, therefore, of a very special nature and one which often escapes the attention of psychologists and epistemologists: experiments of order (number, space) are experiments the subject really makes on himself, i.e., on his own actions and not on the objects, as such, to which his actions simply are applied. That is why these actions once coordinated into coherent "groupings" may at a given moment dispense with any experiment and give rise to an internal and purely deductive composition, which would be inexplicable if the initial experience had consisted of extracting the knowledge from the objects themselves. But before this coordination is possible and composition of actions as such is translated into a "grouping" and hence becomes operational, it goes without saying that actions require experiences in order to coordinate themselves and consequently require objects to serve as a basis for these experiences. . . .

The Operations Constituting Movement and Speed*

The results of the foregoing studies show that instead of being immediately apprehended, movement and speed give rise to a long elaboration of responses at first sensorimotor, then intuitive, and finally operational. These operations themselves commence with a system of qualitative *groupements* before resulting in (extensive and above all metrical) quantitative groups. The concern of these conclusions is to give a total view of this development (setting aside purely perceptual questions), and to correlate this with the other closely related evolution studied in a complementary work: that of the conception of time.

Analyzing quite genetically, with no theoretical presuppositions, how the conceptions of movement and speed are elaborated, we were in fact led to distinguish six great operational systems, operating ever more closely together, of which four depend only upon qualitative logic, i.e., present a structure analogous to that of relations and classes, but applied to infralogical or internal transformations within the construction of the object. These are:

  1. Operations of "placement" which engender the ideas of succession in space or of order and which thus constitute a first type of qualita-

*[The following section is from Chapter XII.]

tive grouping, necessary for the construction of the idea of displacement.

2. Operations of "displacement" (or change of position) which from the qualitative point of view, form one single grouping with the foregoing. . . . but may however be distinguished from this as follows: in placement it is the subject who moves in order to place the objects in order, while in displacement it is actually the objects which change their position.

3. Operations of "co-displacement," i.e., correspondence between placements or displacements, operations which simultaneously engender the ideas of succession in time, or duration and of absolute speed (i.e., relative to a stationary system, or placement).

4. Operations of "relative displacements and co-displacements" permitting composition of correlative movements and their speeds.

5. Operations which are "extensive," i.e., mathematical and no longer qualitative, but still not metrical, which permit construction of relations of ratios, or proportions between times taken and lengths traveled.

6. Finally metrical operations permitting measurement (through the construction of repeatable units) of these distances and durations, hence of the paths traversed and the speeds.

OPERATIONS OF PLACEMENT: ORDER OF

SUCCESSION IN SPACE

Let us for a moment forget every mathematical fact we know, and confine ourselves to relating the data of experience in the simplest way such as they might be construed even by a young child without any presupposition: from such a point of view, movement appears to be above all not a distance traversed—an idea which analysis has shown to be much more abstract and derived than might be imagined—but a change of position or location. A pencil was on the table a moment ago, but it is not there any longer and is lying on the ground: so it has fallen, and this displacement is not seen as a precise path, evaluated in terms of distance, but in point of fact as a "change of position" in which the location "on the table" is replaced by the location "under the table." A marble thrown by a player rolls along the ground: the important thing is not the number of decimeters of space that it covers, but that its movement started from a base line and in particular that it arrived at the goal aimed for, i.e., reached a very definite final position. It is therefore positions or placements, and alterations of these which define movements [earlier] than intervals or distances traversed. This is why, when young children are asked to transfer a given linear trajectory on to a second line not parallel to the first, but with the same starting and stopping points, they concern themselves only with the stopping points and not with the distances traveled (Chap. III). This primacy of the terminal points is in any case the natural consequence of the "finalism" inherent in the earliest conception of movement.

Now, if displacement is thus to be conceived genetically as a "displacement" in the etymological sense of the word, i.e., as a change of position (A changes its position with reference to B, if at first it precedes the latter in a given direction, and later follows after it, or vice versa), it was appropriate to begin our study of movement with an analysis of "placements" themselves: the order of succession or orientation in any sequence of moving objects. This was the more necessary because all young children conceive of speed itself not in terms of relations of times and distances traversed, but simply of the intuition of overtaking: A travels faster than A' (when both move in relation to B simultaneously and in the same direction) if A, which was at first placed to the rear of A', or at the same point, is finally placed ahead of it. Because speed itself, as well as movement in general, is conceived at first in terms of relations of [placement], then surely the whole genetical structure which follows depends upon these relationships.

Let us then take the three balls A, B, and C, which follow one another along a tube or wire rod, in such a way that their order cannot be altered any more than that of any three points in a line. The operation constituting placement will consist of arranging them in a single direction, e.g., such as "A comes before B," and "B comes before C," etc. The composition of these two operations engenders a new operation: e.g., "A comes before C" is the product of the two placements AB and BC. Let us name the direction thus defined "direct." The inverse operation will therefore consist of arranging the elements in the inverse direction of travel, hence (from C to A) "C comes before B" and "B comes before A."*

One point remains to be noted. From the fact that the groupement of operations of placement is constituted by asymmetrical relations ("preceding" or "succeeding") of a transitive type, related to one another in the manner of a "qualitative seriation"† another grouping may be obtained: that of the nesting of intervals comprised between the elements in series. For example, there is an interval between A and B, which is nested within the interval comprised between A and C, etc. Now, if the relationships of order or placing are asymmetrical, the intervals consist of symmetrical relations: the interval is the same between A and B as between B and A. It is this symmetry of the intervals which allows a definition of the relationship of "between." E.g., between A and C there is an interval, occupied by the element B: it follows that B is also between C and A, and it is just this symmetry which is expressed in the famous axiom of Hilbert "if B is between A and C, it is also between C and A."

Regarding the acquisition of these two complementary groupings, observation furnished a decisive result: neither is present as an inborn mechanism of thought, and a construction is implied in both of these in which there is involved first perceptual activity, then intuition and its regulations, only completed by operations. These "grouped" operations which are thus found only at the end of this development, appear consequently as the final form of equilibrium of reasoning, this equilibrium being due to the fact that intuitive regulations have attained complete reversibility. The child is unable at the beginning of this evolution (as we saw in Chap. I) to deduce either the inverse order of the three balls, CBA, or that the middle object B will always stay "between" C and A as well as "between" A and C, whatever may be the operations carried out. In the course of a second stage the questions are solved, but only empirically, while in the course of stage III (toward 7 to 8 years) all the operations are grouped on the concrete level. As for formal operations,

---

*The equation would therefore be $(A \to C) + (C \to A) = (A = A)$. [Piaget means that the child cannot perform the task in question until a group has been formed in which the inverse operation and the identity operation function as a system.]

†See Piaget, *The Child's Conception of Number*, Chapters V and VI.

we were able to establish a very long time ago,* that one must wait till the age of 10 to 11 for the child to understand that *B* is necessarily at the same time "to the left of *A*" and "to the right of *C*" or vice versa.

Let us now suppose that the series is enclosed, in the order *ABCDABCDA* . . . etc. The same operations of order may of course be effected, in this new case, with just this difference that a cyclic order is then obtained such that the direct sequence gives the periodicity *A* . . . *DA* . . . *DA* . . . etc. and the inverse sequence the periodicity *D* . . . *AD* . . . *AD* . . . etc. Analysis of these operations represented concretely by the rotation of a series of colors on a cylinder, gave the same results and at the same ages (Chap. II).

Now, to explain the development of these operations of placement, linear as well as cyclic, it must certainly be recalled that from the sensori-motor level of intelligence and the preverbal level onward, the subject has contant opportunities of acquiring the practical schema of each of the relations involved in groupings. For example, he may sometimes watch a succession of objects first in one direction, then in the other; or he may move his own position with respect to this series of objects, first in one direction and then in the other: and he may see this series of objects changing position (or better still may move them himself), in one direction and the other, etc. In particular, and this has even been studied in detail on an earlier occasion,† he sometimes learns to turn objects round and round, thus discovering a cyclic order of succession, thanks to the rotation he gives them. In all these sensorimotor experiences, depending on a uniform organization of perceptions and habits under the direction of practical understanding, the different schemas of linear and cyclic "placement" are thus elaborated in a similar way to the experimental situations of Chapter I and II.

[But] it is quite clear that these practical schemas are not thoughts. In other words, seeing *A*, the subject learns to anticipate the perception of *B*, and seeing *B* after *A*, to anticipate the perception of *C*. It is more-over possible—though this is a new learning process which, at this psychological level, is by no means included in the previous one—that, seeing *C*, he learns to anticipate the perception of *B*, etc. This practical reversibility is not only accessible to the child of 10 to 12 months: it is even the necessary condition for construction of the schema of the permanent object, i.e., of the idea that it is possible for each modification of reality to return to its starting point. But this only constitutes a restoration in practice and not a deductive operation: the child of this level is by no means able to think of the series *ABC*, independently of the normal perceptual phases of the action under way.

The stage I envisaged in the present work, in other words that of the elementary intuitions preceding operational thought, is thus only a period of reconstruction of the relations already acquired on the purely practical level and which have to be translated into representations . . . independent of activity. . . . The progress of intuitive anticipations and reconstructions explains the regulation of the initial intuitions and the passage from stage I to stage II: the simple and irreversible intuition of stage I still attached to perception itself, becomes more supple through

---

*Piaget, *Judgment and Reasoning in the Child*, Chapter III, §4.
†Piaget, *Construction of Reality in the Child*, Chapter II.

articulated intuitions, the regulations of which herald reversible operations. Consequently of course [the latter] can only constitute a final form of equilibrium, and not an a priori structure, prior to any development.

Without experience no operations are possible, since operations proceed from actions, and it is activity which leads the child to discover direct and inverse orders, as well as the invariability of the symmetrical relation "between." . . . The relations of experience and deduction may be seen as follows. In the earliest stages the subject is concerned with actions which are not reversible or grouped, and which do not necessarily coincide with the properties of objective reality (subjective assimilation). Experience, with its modifications, constantly imposes new relationships which do not necessarily coincide with the expectations of the subject (accommodation to phenomena). These two kinds of transformation are thus orientated at the same time in different, often actually contradictory, and yet partly undifferentiated directions; while [assimilation] remains peripheral to the subject's activity and is [accommodation] on the surface of experience, they continually interrelate, and in a chaotic and unregulated way. As the subject becomes better able to coordinate his actions, he no longer only considers the actual and immediate experience, but every past experience, and possible future experiences.

There then ensue two correlated developments: (i). The subject succeeds in "composing" his actions. At first [he] anticipates their results more fully, and reconstructs their earlier phases (intuitive decentration and regulations) with greater accuracy; then [he] becomes aware of the actual conditions for coordination of actions and visualizations, and regulates his anticipations and reconstructions by means of operations of combination, of seriation, etc. This is how reversible groupements are formed, the final completion of the coordination belonging to the subject's activity. (ii). But then modifications of reality, instead of being perceived only in the narrow field of actual experience, produce the same anticipations and reconstructions, and so exceed the limits of perception in every way, often even the limits of what may be visualized, coinciding more and more with operations. This is why mathematical operations, which mark the final stage of this dual evolution, express equally well [both] the transformations of objective reality and the phases of the subject's activity: at this level of coordination operational transformations and modifications of reality are thus at the same time differentiated, yet in permanent equilibrium with one another.

OPERATIONS OF DISPLACEMENTS: MOVEMENTS

All that has just been reviewed in the case of operations of placement should be repeated for those of displacement, because in point of fact they are the same operations, and it is impossible to dissociate them psychologically. In order to study the order of succession of a series ABC .. the elements A, B, C . . . were set in motion outward and returning, and rotary movements imparted to the entire system in order to analyze better the invariability of the relation "between": movements from side to side, and rotation, are thus two displacements. We certainly could, and a mathematician would doubtless have insisted on this, have left the series immobile and traversed it mentally in the order *ABC* . . . or *CBA*. But what is meant by going over a sequence mentally? For the psychologist, who analyzes thinking instead of taking it as given, in the fashion of the mathematician, this necessarily involves movements. If it is a movement of one's gaze, or of some perceptual organ, onto each of the successive elements *A, B, C* . . . or . . . *C, B, A*, clearly the direction of travel of the series will be relative to a moving object, which is the eye or the hand, etc. If it is a question of a "pure" and "abstract" thought, such as that of the topologist who "traverses" in his mind's eye the infinity of the successive points of some line or other, or a Jordan curve, it is clear that the movement is still there, but internalized in the activity of the thinking subject, whose attention is centered successively upon some points *A, B, C* . . . or . . . *C, B, A*, and that without this internal movement, the very idea of "direction of travel" would have no meaning. Operations of placement are therefore always relative to a subject who changes the position of objects or of himself: this is the first point.

But what is a displacement if not in fact a change of position with respect to a system considered as immobile, hence a change of place with reference to a preliminary placing? A geometrical displacement is relative to a system of coordinates, i.e., to a previous placing of the points of reference, in the same way as the movement of a ball in a room is, even by a baby, referred to the placing of the furniture, doors, and walls. The operations of displacement are thus always relative to operations of placement: this is the second point.

This is why, even if the geometrician, reasoning as he must by setting aside the activity of the thinking subject, considers the group of displacements as a very restricted subgroup in a hierarchy of groups of which the most general is the principal group of pure topology, the psychologist, who studies the operations of the mind in their genetical order, definitely ought to consider the qualitative operations of placement and of displacement as unified from the start which in no way prevents him from recognizing that the metrical operations of displacement are much later in appearing, and far less general. This moreover is evidently the meaning the famous doctrine of H. Poincaré, for whom space was psychologically derived from a group of displacements made experimentally by each subject in terms of movements perceived in objects and his own displacements.

This said, the problem is then as follows: how is it possible, if the organization of displacements is begun with perceptions and bodily movements from the sensorimotor level of intelligence, that operational groupement is only completed so much later on the level of imaginative thought? In fact, one recalls the questions analyzed in the course of Chapters III and IV: comparison of the paths taken on two lines with the same starting and finishing points, but one of which is a straight line and the other zigzags: or else, a moving object setting off from *O*, making a series of zigzags *OC, CB, BA*, etc. between *O* and *D*, and finally reaching the starting point again—did it travel farther in the direction *OD* or in the direction *DO*? Up to around 7 years the child does not manage to dissociate the equality of the paths traveled from that of the stopping points (Chap. III); also up to 7 years he does not accept in every case the equality of a single journey *OD* with a single journey, *DO*, and one has to wait for the level of formal operations toward 10 to 11 years for him to understand that whatever the partial journeys (*OA, AB, BC, CB,* etc.) there will always be an equal distance in one direction as in the other if it returns to *O*.

But these curious results are self-explanatory if the close relation of operations of placement and displacement is recalled. In fact, the child at first conceives a displacement not in terms of the distance traveled, but only as changes of position, i.e., in essence the "placement" of its stopping point: it is in this way that he will judge two unequal paths to be equal if they stop together at the same point (Chap. III). Consequently if *D* is placed at a higher level than *O* instead of being situated on the same horizontal level, the journey *OD* will be considered as "longer" than the path *DO* because it ends in a qualitatively different stopping point (demanding more effort, etc.). In this same way, if *O* and *D* are on the same horizontal straight line, and *D* is farther away from the child, the journey *OD* will not have the same value as the journey *DO* (Chap. IV), etc. Toward 7 years on the other hand the path traversed will be defined by the interval between the starting and stopping points, or the segment *OD*, following the form of the path, when it is a wavy or zigzag line as well as as a straight line: the child will thus construct the equation *OD* = *DO* from the point of view of the interval, since this is symmetrical, unlike displacement viewed as a change of position, which is asymmetrical, i.e., $(O \rightarrow D) = - (D \rightarrow O)$. It is only at this level that displacements can be considered as operationally "grouped."* It only remains then to learn how to combine mentally complex journeys which cannot be visualized simultaneously and this will be the achievement of formal thinking (10 to 11 years).

Operations of displacement may therefore be represented as follows. Let there be a series of elements arranged in sequence, *ABCDE . . .* according to a linear order. Let us first withdraw all the surrounding space, i.e., other objects and in particular the kind of empty container in which objects are placed, which we call space. In other words this series *ABCDE* will at first form a space in itself, hence a one-dimensional space, and nothing is kept there (distances, etc.) other than the actual order. This posited, one element will be said to be displaced if it changes its sequence, and follows those terms which it formerly preceded: e.g., *A* will be displaced in relation to *B* and to *C*, if it comes to occupy the place situated behind *C* and if *ABCD . . .* is therefore transformed into *BCAD . . .* so that *A* which preceded *B* and *C* comes after them at the end of its displacement. The operation is moreover the same as if *A* remained stationary and *B* and *C* move on to the point where both are in front of *A* after coming behind it. It is at once evident that in a series *ABCDE*, each of these terms in turn, starting with *B* have only to be moved forward in relation to all those which precede it, in order to obtain the series *EDCBA*, i.e., the reverse order. From this point of view, the opera-

---

*This is why the sensorimotor "group" of displacements is only a groupement from the practical point of view: motor coordination of means and ends in terms of the finishing point, and not coordination of hypothetical displacements. An additional problem relating to the perception of distances has not yet been begun.

tions of placement and displacement form the same single "groupement": the inverse operation of the placing AB is the displacement BA and the inverse operation of this displacement, i.e., the reversal of the inversion is the replacement AB. Basically both kinds of operation therefore simply form a single operation, and this is actually what corresponds to their psychological origins.

However, instead of separating other objects foreign to the series $ABCDE$ . . . let us now reintroduce them: it can then be seen that the element A is not only "placed" relative to B, C, D, etc., but also in relation to all kinds of other factors: if, for example, it is a question of dolls on a table, A is indeed placed "in front" of B, C, D, etc., but it is also placed on the table, "after" a particular groove, "beside" a particular mark, etc. In short, it occupies a "position," clearly defined by a collection of other relations of order, and if this position is called A_0, we observe that in the case of a displacement of A, in relation to B, C, D, etc., the position A_0 does not move with it, but remains in situ, i.e., continues to be situated as before relative to the objects foreign to the series $ABCDE$. . . . It is this distinction between the moving objects and the stationary positions which permits operations of placement and displacement to be divided into two distinct subgroupements, in spite of their being identical at first. . . .

Consequently, to distinguish operations of placement from those of displacement, it will be enough to say that the arrangement of the former is relative to a movement (displacement) of a moving object or of the observer himself (the arranged or "placed" elements thus remaining by definition stationary), and that the movements of the latter are relative to a system of reference or placement, defined by the initial positions. But it must be fully understood that, in spite of this dissociation which in both cases separates the total reality into two compartments, one mobile and the other stationary, each of the groupements involved in fact remains dual; no order or placement exists without a movement which at the very least is that of the subject or observer and no displacement exists without an ordered system of reference.

The best proof that there is nothing artificial about this construction and that it really corresponds to the actual genetical development, is that it is easily found, not only in the facts described in our Chapters I to IV but also in all the child's behavior relating to geometry and movement in his spontaneous activities. The child does not learn to impart order or movement to objects at school or in the experiments imposed on him by the curiosity of psychologists: he does so by spontaneously handling solid and mobile objects. Now, the solid objects ABC . . . can only be moved by replacing one with another, and so the operations of placement and displacement come to life at the same time. Undoubtedly space itself is for a long time simply the system of these relations between solid objects. . . . Sooner or later, however, the fact of displacing objects involves the arrangement of their positions as such, $A_0 B_0 C_0$ . . . . : it is then that this system of stationary, unoccupied positions, distinct from the actual solid moving objects, begins to form a geometric space or a specifically spatial order, as opposed to the system of physical movements, which is characteristic of the moving elements or objects occupying the space. Consequently, after conceiving displacement simply as an empirical permutation, or change of place, the child will come to define it in relation to the positions alone and no longer to the other objects. This last system seems simpler to us, reasoning as we do more readily as geometricians than as physicists, than the system of correlative displacements, or of permutations of positions: but for the child the system of multiple, interrelated displacements of the objects *ABC* . . . is exactly equivalent in difficulty to the system of displacements of a single moving object in relation to unoccupied positions.

. . . In the course of the first stages the child is only worrying about the order of the stopping points but not about the order of the starting points. He defines the path traversed by the stopping point alone and is thus constantly misled for want of being able to construct the interval. Later (articulated intuitions), he certainly considers the interval, but still by no means dissociates it from the order of the stopping points: the interval is thus not conceived as symmetrical, hence the denial of the equality of the paths traversed on the outward and return journey. The accurate operational concept is only finally constructed when the groupement of nesting of intervals is accomplished in correspondence with the groupement of seriation of relations of order (placements and displacements to the extent that these are changes of order). But it is interesting that the concept of the distances traversed, to the extent that it is a pure distance, seems to remain for a long time in the background in relation to the ideas attached to the order of the starting and finishing points: the child will say, e.g., "stops farther ahead" in preference to "does a longer distance," etc. Now, this is self-explanatory in terms of what has just been seen of the duality of the qualitative operations of displacement: the first kind refer only to the changes of position among the elements *A, B, C* . . . in relation to one another, and then the interval recedes to the background, while the permutations play the vital role: the second kind, on the contrary, bear on the changes of order in relation to the "positions" themselves and then only are the ideas of distance and length of the intervals brought into the foreground.

OPERATIONS OF CO-DISPLACEMENTS: SPEEDS AND TIMES

We have observed so far the close solidarity of the operations of physical displacement and of spatial placement which are mutually formed in terms of one another, and so simultaneously shape the stable framework of space and its mobile content, i.e., the physical object at rest or in movement. But more is involved: this same coordination of placements and displacements explains the construction of the ideas of speed, of succession in time and of duration, and this is because two or more displacements are arranged at the same time, i.e., in correspondence with one another. It is this act of correlation which is named operations of co-displacement.

A single displacement and consequently a chain of displacements in turn is a movement having no speed: whether *A* goes from *A* to *D* in one hour, one second, or at an unlimited speed, it is still the same displacement. There is thus no absolute speed in the sense of the speed of a movement in isolation (there is moreover no absolute displacement either, since if *A* changes place in relation to *B*, *B* may equally well be considered to be the moving element and A to be stationary). On the other hand, if the successive positions of one moving object are ordered in relation to those of another object the concept of speed necessarily intervenes and this is in fact how it appears from the point of view of its psychological origins . . . for young children, speed is "overtaking," i.e., the reversal of the order of the respective positions of two moving objects in the course of a displacement. Now, however incomplete and even misleading this conception may be in its original intuitive form (which consists of judging speeds, like movements in general, according to the stopping points only), it becomes in fact the basic principle of groupement, through regulatory corrections, and the later operational corrections which it introduces, permitting interpretation of all the qualitative relations of speed (qualitative, as opposed to extensive and metrical). . . .

Let us first give the name of co-displacements to the distinct displacements which occur between two equal states I and II (hence in this example, the displacements of A_1 and A_2). On the other hand let us say that two displacements $A_1B_1C_1D_1$ . . . and $A_2B_2C_2D_2$ . . . are in one-to-one correspondence if a correspondence can be established between each element of the first and each element of the second in the same order, i.e., if one may recognize by an unambiguous criterion in the case of each term of the first placement what the term in the same order belonging to the other placement would be. And we shall say that two corresponding terms A_1 and A_2 are displaced "without *overtaking*" if their new placements are also in correspondence, while one of them is greater than the other if its new placement is farther ahead than the earlier one.

When these operations are possible (and it is at once evident what they represent in the true genesis of the child's conception of speed), four consequences necessarily follow: (i) Co-displacements are no longer characterized only by changes of position (placements), in the exclusively spatial sense of the term, but by *speeds*: displacements without overtaking will be of equal speeds while one displacement will have a greater speed than another according to the degree of overtaking. (ii) In addition to the spatial order of succession, ensured by the comparison which defines overtaking, there then appears a *temporal order* of succession, i.e., the order of the states themselves: state II comes after state I. This temporal order is distinct from spatial order since placements no longer correspond in the case of overtaking. Each state thus defines a system of "simultaneous phenomena" ($=$ the system of placements) "given" together in space, and the succession of two states defines a "before" and "after" in time. (iii) The interval in space between two successive placements of a single element (hence the interval between the points at either end of a single displacement) forms a "path traversed": every overtaking thus marks an inequality in the paths traversed and the greatest speed on the other hand is recognized by the fact that a longer distance has been covered between two equivalent states. . . . (iv) Finally, the duration forms the general interval given between two states, hence between the limits of the time passed as opposed to the spatial sequence. Thus duration is recognized by the path traversed related to the speed.* . . .

*Let us point out, in a general way, that the only interest of these various operations, which are literally childish by reason of their simplicity,

It is very interesting to observe that each of these operations occurs in the genetic development of the idea of speed. At the beginning of this evolution in fact only visible overtaking matters (stage I, Chaps. VI and VII) without the subject taking into account any comparison of the starting points, i.e., of paths traversed in the same times. In the course of the whole of stage II progress consists of generalizing the idea of overtaking by means of correlations allowing the extension of comparisons to cases where there is unseen overtaking and above all where the moving objects catch one another up without overtaking, or even do not completely catch up, travel from opposite directions, etc. In all these situations, the corrective mechanism of judgment, as we saw, consists of regulatory decentration which leads to attention being drawn to the starting points as much as on the stopping points, hence to anticipating the consequence of the movements up to a potential overtaking, or to the reconstruction of their earlier phases to the point where it is possible to establish the comparisons necessary for the establishment of potential overtaking. It is in terms of a process of this kind that the interval or path traversed begins to play a part, allowing speed to be gauged when the starting and finishing points are the same, but the paths are unequal: operational comparison then gradually supersedes merely visual comparison. Finally, in stage III speed is directly judged by comparison of starting and stopping points, i.e., by overtaking which is completely generalized, together with the intervals comprehended by these, i.e., by the paths traversed correlated with the duration.

But of course all the foregoing remains limited to the case of synchronous movements, in whole or in part, with simultaneous starting and stopping. The comparison of movements in succession on the contrary arises from extensive and metrical operations. (See Chaps. V and VI.) . . .

---

is just that they do call only for arrangement in series and qualitative articulation, with no appeal to extensive or metrical quantity. From a philosophical point of view, the following application might be drawn from them, to a hypothetical physical world, whose total viscosity would render all measurement impossible, and which would know no geometry other than pure topology. We know that in homeomorphy (topological correspondence) comparison is according to order alone, with no conservation of distances, because curves can expand and contract, intertwine (knots) and so on, but not become fragmented or form straight lines, angles, circles, etc. There is however conservation of the intervals in the sense that between two pairs of corresponding points one finds the same corresponding figures, since topological correspondence is a one-to-one correspondence in both directions. Let us then suppose that a process of expansion is transmitted from A_1 to C_1 on a first curve and from A_2 to D_2 on another curve (A_2 corresponds to A_1 but D_2 is farther ahead in order than C_1). If there existed a physical or psychological means (vision, etc.) of establishing this correspondence, one might say in this case that the speed of extension is greater along the second curve since 'overtaking' is present. In an entirely elastic world it is by this single criterion that one would recognize speed. On the contrary in our world of solid objects, perception gives the child the figures of straight line, parallels, angles, etc. long before the intellectual operations of a metrical order are constructed. This is why it is so difficult to reconstruct the genetical operations founding the major categories of space and time: in fact, it is a question of reconstructing operations which remain qualitative even while they are being applied to perceptual figures which anticipate metrical structures.

RELATIVE DISPLACEMENTS AND

CO-DISPLACEMENTS

[In this section Piaget deals with the case in which a "system of positions, while being fixed in relation to the movements considered may at the same time, itself be in motion in relation to another system of fixed positions.] It is then that there arises the need to 'compose' the two movements and their two speeds with one another."

EXTENSIVE OPERATIONS: PROPORTIONALITY OF

TIMES AND DISTANCES COVERED

The foregoing operations lead to purely qualitative groupements which the child masters between 7 years (concrete operations) and 11 years (formal operations) and which are accurate as far as they go, but they remain basically inadequate for the mastery of all the elementary problems of movement and speed. In the field of displacement, they lead solely to the deduction that a path traversed will be equal in both directions of travel (or that an inverse displacement cancels out the corresponding direct displacement), that two displacements added become one displacement, and finally that a partial displacement will always be smaller than an entire displacement. But they do not permit of measurement nor even of proportionality. In the field of speeds, they lead to the statement that in two synchronous durations, the moving object traveling along the longer path has a greater speed or in the case of equal distances traveled that the faster moving object is that which takes the shorter time—but in this latter case it is also necessary for the durations compared to start or finish at the same time. Finally, from these compositions may be deduced the least or greatest relative speed according to the movement of the observer. But in none of these cases do the qualitative operations described so far permit of the measurement of the speeds and they are not even capable of extending any of the relations we have just recounted to movements which are no longer simultaneous but in succession. Consequently they remain powerless to establish the concepts of uniform speed or acceleration, intuitive though these concepts are in some respects.

In other words, the operations considered until now in Sections 1 to 4, deal only with intensive quantity (comparison of the whole and the part, viz., $A < B$ if $B = A + A'$ as in pure qualitative logic) and not with extensive quantities (comparison of the parts with one another, viz., $A < A'$ or $A > A'$ if $B = A + A'$) nor, above all, with metrical quantities (repetition of a unit $A = A'$, then $B = 2A$ if $B = A + A'$). But as we saw in the course of Chapter IX to XI, as soon as intensive operations are formed, they expand by that very fact into extensive and metrical operations.

Particular mention must be made, in this connection, of the question of proportionality, which as we saw in Chapter IX appears in the comparison of the speeds of movements in succession. . . . Now, before trying to carry out any measurement it sometimes happens that the subject evinces a definite feeling for proportions and especially for disproportions, which poses an interesting psychological problem, i.e., the correlation of qualitative metrical operations.

We know, in fact, that the idea of proportion appears in two quite distinct forms in geometry: the metrical form, which is the equality of two numerical ratios $a/b = c/d$, and the form known as qualitative, or purely geometrical.* . . .

Nevertheless, this purely geometric form is basically different from a simple logical or qualitative proportion (the word "qualitative" being taken in different senses in logic and in geometry) such as "son is to father as grandson is to grandfather," or "Paris is to France as Rome is to Italy." These logical correlations, it is true, likewise form the equality of two ratios (inverse ratios in this first example, or the part qualifying the whole in the second) . . . But two fundamental differences make them contrast with mathematical proportions: (i) Logical correlations simply affirm the identical or equivalent nature of qualitative or intensive structures. . . . (ii) One can always translate a geometrical proportion . . . into a metrical ratio, . . . whereas logical ratios are not reducible to numbers. It follows that the multiplication (Paris × Italy = Rome × France) or (son × grandfather = father × grandson) has no meaning.

In short, even in its geometric form designated "qualitative" i.e., extensive and not metrical, proportion is an equation of two quantitative ratios which are not measured, but which are still capable of measurement, since they imply the concepts of straight line, parallels, and angles, whereas logical correspondence is an equation of two intensive ratios likewise not measured but in addition not capable of measurements.

How then does the child arrive at this conception? He must of course be in possession beforehand of qualitative operations, on the concrete level, but also on the formal level: on this latter level, he has mastered it as soon as he can compare movements in succession with unequal times and equal distances or with equal times and unequal distances. . . .

Now, where do these comparisons come from, of the parts a and a' with each other, which characterize proportion? Simply from a generalization of the qualitative operations [cited] earlier.

This is how proportionality appears: it constitutes, as we saw from the examples recalled above, a comparison of the parts with one another, hence a total comparison of two nested relations, whereas logical comparison is merely a double comparison of parts with the whole. But this last comparison, although limited, prepares the way for and leads to proportionality prior to any measurement. Comparing the way in which two parts belong to two wholes sooner or later prompts the comparison of these two parts with their complementary parts. It is this last relationship which marks the passage from the intensive to the extensive or from the qualitative to the mathematical. . . .

---

*Based on the theorem of Thales: the segments formed by two parallel straight lines intersecting the sides of an angle are proportional, or upon the theorem: the areas of two triangles are equal if they have one angle in common, and the sides adjacent to this angle are inversely proportional. These two theorems are self-evident without having recourse to the metrical concept of ratio.

31

The Child's Conception of Time*

1946

INTRODUCTORY NOTES

The construction of time is contemporary and roughly similar to the construction of space. After an earlier period of lack of differentiation, the child becomes capable of seriating a sequence of events in the course of a specific action. For instance, when looking for something she has lost, the child of the sensorimotor period explores the rooms of her house in a certain order. This is evidence of her mastery of space-in-action. But it is also good evidence of her mastery of time-in-action—she can order her displacements in time as well as in space. Around the sixth stage of the construction of reality, she even shows that she is capable of planning her actions, i.e., representing her displacements in a more or less systematic way. These behavior patterns anticipate the construction of time as it is studied in *The Child's Conception of Time* (1946).

The book begins with an experiment about ordering correctly a series of disordered pictures representing different phases of a sequence of events. At first, children are capable of ordering correctly pairs of pictures only. Afterward, they become capable of the coordinations necessary for a correct arrangement of longer series of events.

The next problem to be considered is the child's capacity to dissociate duration from space, and space from speed and motion. At first, children fuse these notions together. Then, they begin to understand the succession of perceptible events and they dissociate space from time. This does not imply that they fully understand complex notions such as ordering of events, comparing temporal intervals, simultaneity, succession, and synchronicity as being different components of a total structure. Lack of differentiation results in a certain incapacity to combine these notions with one another correctly. This explains children's incapacity to compare durations of events beginning

*From, J. Piaget, *The Child's Conception of Time* A. J. Pomerans, translator, *Le Développement de la Notion de Temps chez l'Enfant*, Presses Universitaires de France, 1946, English translation © Routledge and Kegan Paul Ltd., London, 1969, Basic Books, Inc., Publishers, New York, 1970, Reprinted by permission of the publishers.

at the same time but ending at a different time, as well as their failure to recognize that objects can move simultaneously but at different speeds.

Once the children become capable of dissociating the factors at work in the system, they also become capable of recomposing the various relations existing between speed and duration as well as the relations uniting duration, space, and speed. They understand, for instance, that slow motion and long duration are equivalent to fast motion and short duration with respect to the amount of space covered.

Such a discovery leads the child to the construction of an objective time independent of "inner time" or the time of subjective experience that depends on feelings, effort, work, concentration, and other factors of this sort. This dissociation between a time of personal activity and a physical time that is independent of these impressions comes after physical time has become measurable in a metric system.

The major difficulty in the elaboration of a metric system of time is due to the absence of an inner standard unit for the measure of time. This meter, or invariant, has to be found in an external referent that could serve as a unit. For Piaget, this external reference is the direct intuition of speed that the child has and considers as uniform. This intuition becomes the invariant of the temporal system of transformations. In the case of nonsynchronic time, the unit becomes the amount of space covered at a given speed. In the end, measuring time becomes equivalent to numbering; the unit of time is iterated on the continuum of time thanks to the fusion in one single set of the operations of inclusion of durations and the operations of seriation of successions.

Foreword

This work was prompted by a number of questions kindly suggested by Albert Einstein more than fifteen years ago* when he presided over the first international course of lectures on philosophy and psychology at Davos. Is our intuitive grasp of time primitive or derived? Is it identical with our intuitive grasp of velocity? What if any bearing do these questions have on the genesis and development of the child's conception of time? Every year since then we have made a point of looking into these questions, at first with little hope of success because, as we quickly discovered, the time relationships constructed by young children are so largely based on what they hear from adults and not on their own experiences. But when, after trying to apply the idea of "groupings" to the development of the child's conception of number and quantity,† we went on to apply it to the concepts of motion, velocity, and time, we discovered that the problems of duration and temporal succession had become greatly simplified. The results are presented in this volume; those bearing on the child's conception of motion and speed are reserved for a later work.‡

*The French original was published in 1946—trans.
†Piaget and Szeminska, *La Genèse du Nombre chez l'Enfant* [The Child's Conception of Number]; Piaget and Inhelder, *Le Développement des Quantités chez l'Enfant*.
‡Piaget, *The Child's Conception of Movement and Speed*, 1946.

Now, the study of the child's conception of time is not simply the psychological analysis of the development of scientific concepts. Bergson's entire philosophy, as well as the large number of purely psychological works influenced by it, have stressed the great importance of the concepts of inner duration and of psychological time. Yet far from seizing on the possible convergence of Einsteinian time and "lived duration," Bergson himself tried to contrast them in a little work that caused quite a stir at the time.* In the third part of our study we shall see what genetic research has to say on the subject of this apparent dichotomy.

Moreover, psychopathologists, too, often come face to face with the problem of time. Now, it is fairly well known to what extent the interpretation of pathological concepts is conditioned by the genetic study of corresponding concepts in child psychology. As far as time itself is concerned, J. de la Harpe has endorsed the claim of a well-known psychiatrist that the analysis of duration must be based exclusively on Bergsonian ideas and on phenomenology, and that the problem of the development of the conception of time in children must be ignored on principle.† We nevertheless hope that the results we are about to present will prove of use to all those psychopathologists who wish to base their work on the laws of real development rather than on a priori dialectics.

Finally, teachers and educational psychologists constantly come up against problems raised by the failure of schoolchildren to grasp the idea of time. A clearer understanding of the constructive processes that go into the development of the fundamental concepts of temporal order, simultaneity, and the equality and colligation of durations, at a stage when the child does not yet suspect that time is common to all phenomena, will no doubt prove helpful to them in their work. It is partly because of the possible educational applications that we shall be quoting so many concrete examples.

The first part of this book is entirely devoted to a discussion of a laboratory experiment (flow of liquid from one flask into another and reconstruction of successive levels of the liquid by means of diagrams) and to the methods young children use in ordering successive events and in estimating durations. The second part deals with various operations in physical time (order, simultaneity, synchronization, colligation and addition of durations, and measurement). The third part, finally, analyzes "lived time" (the notion of age and psychological duration) in the light of the first two sections, i.e., in the light of the analysis of the time schemata constructed by the subjects in the course of their adaptation to the outside world.

*H. Bergson, *Durée et simultaneité* (Paris: Alcan).
†J. de la Harpe, *Genèse et Mesure du temps* (Neuchâtel: Trav. Fac. Lettres, 1941), pp. 10ff.

Elementary Operations: Time and Motion*

The aim of this section is to set the development of the concept of time in the kinetic context outside which it can have no meaning. We are far too readily tempted to speak of intuitive ideas of time, as if time, or for that matter space, could be perceived and conceived apart from the entities or the events that fill it. Much as space is often conceived as an empty box into which bodies are fitted, so time is conceived as a moving film consisting of stills that follow one another in quick succession.

But space is not just a simple "container." It is the totality of the relationships between the bodies we perceive or imagine, or rather, the totality of the relationships we use to endow these bodies with a structure. Space is, in fact, the logic of the apparent world or at least one of the two essential aspects (the other being time) of the logic of things: the process of fitting its parts into a meaningful whole (colligation)† is analogous to the colligations and series that classes and relations introduce among concepts, and its metric system is that of numbers and numerical operations. Because it is a form of logic, space is above all a system of concrete operations, inseparable from the experiences to which they give rise and which they transform. But as the mind gradually learns to perform these operations outside their factual context, the operations may become "formal" and it is at this level, at which geometry becomes pure logic, that space appears as a container or a "form" independent of its content.

Now, exactly the same thing happens with time, the more so as time and space form an inseparable whole. As we shall see again and again throughout this book: no matter whether we are dealing with physical displacements or motions in space, or with those inner motions that memory recalls or anticipates, we shall find that time plays the same part in regard to them, as space does [with respect to] stationary objects. More precisely, space suffices for the coordination of simultaneous positions, but as soon as displacements are introduced, they bring in their train distinct, and therefore successive, spatial states whose coordination is nothing other than time itself. Space is a still of time, while time is space in motion—the two taken together constitute the totality of the ordered relationships characterizing objects and their displacements.

But though, in the case of space, we can ignore time to construct geometrical relationships (to do so we need merely postulate a fictitious simultaneity and describe motions as pure displacements at infinite velocity or as displacements independent of their velocity), when it comes to time, we cannot abstract the spatial and kinetic relationships, i.e., we cannot ignore velocity. It is only once it has already been constructed that time can be conceived as an independent system, and even then, only when small velocities are involved.

*[The following section is from the introduction to Part I.]

†[This is the translator's approximation for *emboîtement*, which Piaget uses to mean the inclusion of one class in another. In this volume the main use of the term expresses the idea that the class of people who are 20 years old includes all those who have been 19 years old, etc.]

. . . If time is really the coordination of motions in the sense that space is the logic of objects, we must expect to discover the existence of *operational time*, involving relations of succession and duration based on analogous operations in logic. Operational time will be distinct from *intuitive time*, which is limited to successions and durations given by direct perception. Operational time itself may be *qualitative* or *quantitative*, depending on whether the operations involved are analogous to those involved in classes and logical relations, or whether a numerical unit comes into play.

[What] then are the elementary operations that lead us to simultaneity and succession as well as to durations of different order? The answer will be attempted in the first section of this book, where we shall analyze the reaction of children at various stages of mental development to a simple experimental situation: the flow of liquid by successive stages from one container to another. Two simple motions are involved: a drop of level and a rise of level. The time operations involved are: (1) fitting the various levels into the series $A + B + C$, etc., by means of "before" and "after" relationships (seriation is impossible if the relations are "simultaneous"); and (2) fitting together the respective intervals (terms) AB, AC, etc. (AB is of shorter duration than AC, etc., and A_1 and B_1 or A_2 and B_2 are synchronous).

If temporal relations resulted from direct intuitions or from intellectual abstractions independent of their content, it is clear that these problems would not face the child with any fresh difficulties—after all, the events take place before [his] very eyes. But if time, as we suggest, is the operational coordination of the motions themselves, then the relations between simultaneity, succession, and duration must first be constructed, one by one. It is the general nature of this construction that we shall [now] examine.

The Sequence of Events*

In our attempt to determine the role of time in human experience generally, and that of children in particular, we invariably discover that temporal ideas are linked to memories, to complex causal processes, or to clearly defined motions. One might suppose that memory involves the direct intuition of time; that Bergson's pure memory and intuitive ideas of duration constitute an absolute reference system on which every psychological analysis of the concept of time must be based. But memory is a reconstruction of the past, a "narrative" as P. Janet has put it, and this applies at the higher and verbal planes no less than at the sensorimotor level. As such it necessarily involves causality. Thus when one memory seems earlier than another, the former is deemed to be causally anterior to the event recalled by the latter. If, for example, I recall that, ten days ago, I put on my tie before giving my morning lectures, this is not because these two memories are indelibly engraved on my mind in a precise order of succession; it is because I

*[The following section is from Chapter I.]

am certain that the first of the two acts is a necessary preparation for the second. The order of succession of two independent events is purely fortuitous, in the sense that Cournot defines chance as the mutual interference of two distinct causal series. . . . Because it is involved in chance, i.e., in a tangle of causal series, a given sequence of events is difficult to remember. We can only recall it by reference to inner causes or to indirect connections, i.e., to other causal series. . . .

To determine time, we must therefore appeal to causal operations, i.e., establish a chain between causes and effects by explaining the latter in terms of the former. Time is inherent in causality. It is to explicative operations what logical order is to implicative operations.

That is why we decided to begin our analysis of the child's conception of time with an examination of the way in which children link two events into a simple causal chain, for instance the motion of falling objects:* the child is presented with photographs of the falling body at various phases of its descent chosen at random and asked to put these into the right order. Now this technique, which we shall be discussing in some detail in the next chapter, has enabled us to demonstrate an apparently paradoxical fact: The operational, nonintuitive way in which children grasp time sequences—in effect, the reconstruction of an irreversible succession of events—presupposes a reversibility of thought, i.e., the performance of operations that make it possible to run through each sequence in both directions. In particular, we observe that up to the age of 7 or 8, the child, having adopted any sort of sequence (which in general is the one first presented to him) has great difficulties in changing his mind when presented with a better one (84 percent of our 6-year-old subjects but only 15 percent of the 8-year-olds). Clearly, before the age of 7 or 8, children are not yet capable of reasoning about several possibilities at the same time. In other words, they lack the power of operational reversibility needed for the selection of various possible orders, whereas 8-year-olds can make use of that power and thus reconstruct the true and irreversible order of events.

If time is linked to causality and to the irreversible course of events, it follows that the temporal operations needed for the construction of a particular order of succession must be akin to explicative operations in general, i.e., precisely to those operations that enable one to reconstruct the displacement of objects in space. What, in effect, is causality if not the coordination in time-space of motions of which time is one dimension? . . .

The Succession of Perceptible Events†

As we saw in Chapter I, children have great difficulty in reconstructing the correct succession of even so simple a series of events as the flow of a liquid. This is because two distinct problems are involved: (1) the

---

*Krafft and Piaget "La notion de l'ordre des événements et le test des images en désorde," *Arch. de Psychol.*, 19(1925): 309–349.
†In collaboration with Mlle. Esther Bussmann. [The following section is from Chapter III.]

reconstruction of the correct order after the event and (2) the correct perception of this order while the event is actually taking place.

We shall look at the second problem first. To that purpose, we could present the child with two bodies starting side by side, moving with the same speed, and stopping (a) successively and (b) simultaneously. At each of the three stages we have described, the child would have no difficulty in establishing the succession or simultaneity of the stopping points—since the two motions are similar and concurrent, they are no more complicated than a single motion. Now, in that case the temporal order remains undifferentiated from the spatial order so that [whatever] replies the child makes to our questions would bear on the geometrical course rather than on time as such. If, therefore, we wish to analyze the child's idea of temporal succession as such, we must introduce bodies moving at different velocities. . . . To simplify the problem, we can retain the parallel tracks and start or stop the two bodies simultaneously. In putting the questions, it is important to ensure that the child makes a clear distinction between temporal and spatial succession.

Once these precautions are taken, we can go on to find out whether or not the child is capable of fitting motions at different velocities into a single space-time framework. This is what we shall now go on to do.

EXPERIMENTAL METHODS AND GENERAL RESULTS

The two experimental arrangements we use in the analysis of the child's concept of succession (Chap. III) and simultaneity (Chap. IV) as he perceives them, are extremely simple. The first, which is more concrete but less precise, serves as a simple introduction to the second, which gives far more accurate results. In the first, the experimenter and the child run through the laboratory together. The experimenter gives three raps as the signal for the simultaneous start of the runs, and stops before, after, or at the same time as the child, but at a given distance from him. The child is then asked if the starting and finishing points of the two runs were simultaneous, or which one came first. Since, in this experiment, the child is spectator and actor all at once, his answers are generally biased. We accordingly use this question merely as an introduction to the second experiment.

Here we present the child with two small figures or mechanical snails moving across a table either at different but continuous velocities or else, and this is generally preferable, by fits and starts, each start being accompanied by a rap on the table. In this case there can be no failure to perceive the synchronism of the two runs or the order of succession or simultaneity of the final stopping points. We then ask the child:

(1) Whether one of the figures (II) was still moving when the other (I) had stopped (in practice this question is generally put last to make sure that the child has grasped the data; the reader will note that it does not necessarily bear on the child's grasp of time as such). Let A_1, B_1, C_1, etc., be points along the path of I, and A_2, B_2, C_2, etc., those along the path of II, with $A_1B_1 = A_2B_2$, $B_1C_1 = B_2C_2$, etc.; let I cover the distance A_1D_1 while II covers the distance A_2B_2, and let II

subsequently cover the distance B_2C_2 while I remains in D_1. The child will have no difficulty in grasping that when I stops in D_1, II keeps moving forward (from B_2 to C_2). We shall see that the child nevertheless fails to conclude that I stopped before II, and, in fact, will generally take the opposite view. Sometimes he will even go so far as to assert that the duration A_1-D_1 is greater than that of A_2-C_2, simply because D_1 is further from the starting point, etc. The question of whether I was still moving when II had stopped, and vice versa, thus involves only one, clearly defined, aspect of time: what one might call perceptive time by contrast to the intellectual time which is constructed at the moment of perception and which alone concerns us in this book. Perceptive time, in effect, is exclusively involved in what can be directly distinguished as being successive or simultaneous, but involves no comprehension of these concepts, much as the ear can distinguish chords from single notes without the mind having to grasp that the chord consists of two or more elementary sounds.

(2) Let I proceed from A_1 to D_1 while II proceeds from A_2 to B_2. Next, let II proceed from B_2 to C_2 while I has stopped. The child is then asked which of the two figures has stopped "first." Now this question introduces a linguistic problem—in trying to present our subjects with the idea of a temporal as distinct from a spatial succession, we find that it lacks a word to distinguish the two. If we say "which one stopped before the other?" the word "before" may mean "in front of" as well as "earlier." To avoid this pitfall we can explain that I stops at lunchtime and go on to ask if II stopped before or after lunch.

(3) We next ask the child if I and II moved for "the same length of time," or if not, which of them moved "longer."

(4) Let I stop in C_1 when II stops in B_2, both having started simultaneously from A_1 and A_2. We now ask the child whether I and II stopped "at the same time" or "at the same moment," and if not, which one stopped first.

We can finally vary the questions by introducing different starts with simultaneous stops, or simultaneous starts from different points with simultaneous stops in the same point, etc.

The results of all these tests fit easily into the three stages we have been distinguishing. During stage I, successions and durations remain undifferentiated from distances: "longer" is equivalent to further; "first" may mean "before" or "after," and differences in speed are thought to preclude synchronous processes and lead to confused estimates of duration. During the second stage, the initial intuitions slowly become differentiated or articulated, either because "before" and "after" in time and space become differentiated from each other, or else because simultaneity becomes recognized independently of positions or velocities, or finally because duration is understood to be inversely proportional to velocity. The point at which intuition becomes articulated varies from one subject to the next, nor does the initial step lead to the immediate articulation of temporal relations in general. In other words, at stage II, intuitions, even if articulated, cannot yet be combined into a general grouping, whence the incoherent reactions of our subjects. Finally, at stage III, the subjects become capable of applying the technique of operational grouping to all the relations involved, and go on to construct a coherent system involving both durations and successions.

THE FIRST STAGE: CONFUSION OF TEMPORAL

WITH SPATIAL SUCCESSIONS

During stages I and II, simple or even articulated intuitions of succession and duration give rise to constant contradictions—whence their continual readjustment and the fact that correct answers alternate quite arbitrarily with wrong ones. Let us nevertheless try to fit these answers into some sort of scale.

Here, first of all, are a few examples obtained at the lowest level:

Hes (4;5). The yellow figure (I) stops in D_1 while the blue figure (II) keeps moving on from B_2 to C_2: "Did they stop at the same time? *No.* Which one stopped first? *The blue one* (II). Which moved longer? *The yellow one* (1). When (I) stopped it was lunchtime, so did (II) stop before or after lunch? *Before lunch.* But which stopped first? *The yellow one* (1). *No, it was the blue one, the yellow one* (I) *went on longer.* Let's do it again. (The race is rerun.) *The yellow one* (I) *stopped first, the blue one was still moving, so the yellow one went on longer.* But did one stop before the other? *The blue one* (II)." . . .

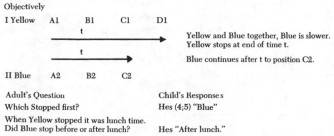

Objectively

I Yellow   A1   B1   C1   D1

Yellow and Blue together, Blue is slower.
Yellow stops at end of time t.

Blue continues after t to position C2.

II Blue   A2   B2   C2

Adult's Question	Child's Responses
Which Stopped first?	Hes (4;5) "Blue"
When Yellow stopped it was lunch time. Did Blue stop before or after lunch?	Hes "After lunch."

Cor (5;6). Same arrangement: "What did you see? *The yellow one* (I) *stopped and the other one* (II) *kept moving.* So which one stopped first? *The blue one* (II). Which one moved longer? *The yellow one* (I). Let's say that (I) stops at lunch. So when did this one (II) stop? *Before . . . no, at lunch.*" By way of control, we now let the two figures run in opposite directions, both starting at A. When I reaches D_1 on the right, II reaches B_2 on the left and continues as far as C_2. This time the subject has no difficulty in grasping that I stopped first. . . .

Arl (7 years): "(II) *stopped before the other one and* (I) *went on longer because it was further.* But which went on for the most time? *That one* (II), *no, this one* (I). And which went on longest? (I). Which one stopped first? (II). If (I) stopped at lunch when did (II) stop? *Before lunch.* Why? *Because it stopped in front of that one* (points to the space separating the two figures)."

It should be emphasized that these reactions are in no way due to errors of perception: all our subjects were agreed that when figure I had stopped, II kept on moving, and that when II stopped I had stopped moving as well. Why then do they obstinately assert that II stopped "first," "sooner," or "before" I, etc.?

One might argue that the whole thing is purely a matter of words, that the child uses the words "before" and "after" in a spatial sense, that he fails to appreciate that our questions have any bearing on time. [But] whenever we checked the answers by reversing the direction of the paths, we obtained (e.g., in Cor's final answer) the correct reply without hesitation, simply because, no longer able to compare the velocities, the child tries to coordinate the two displacements, and comes to look upon several of the motions as episodes in a single history. If, on the other hand, the two bodies I and II move in the same direction, the child confuses time, space, and velocity, which demonstrates that his errors are of a logical and not of a verbal kind.* This becomes particularly obvious in the case of duration, for when our subjects assert that I goes on "longer" because it finishes "further," they couple verbal differentiation to a lack of a logical differentiation between time and space.

What precisely accounts for this lack of differentiation between time and space? As far as duration is concerned, the explanation is quite simple, and agrees with the one we gave [elsewhere]: the child simply confuses time with velocity. Its argument runs roughly as follows: (1) If you go more quickly you necessarily cover more space (i.e., velocity is proportional to distance); (2) if you cover more space, you need more time to do so (hence distance is proportional to time); and (3) if you go more quickly you need more time because you cover more space. Each of these three "mores" entails the other two.

Once all these assumptions are granted, it follows that the child's confusion of temporal with spatial succession does not result from the fact that he bases his concepts of succession on those of duration or vice versa, but from the fact that he constructs both by the same logical methods. This emerges more clearly when we introduce the idea of lunch time. Having granted that the figure stops at lunch, the child will invariably go on to assert that, though II continues to move, it nevertheless stops before lunch. Why? The answer was given by Arl when he explained that II stopped "before lunch" because "it stopped in front of that one (I)." In other words, since it is at noon that you generally come home for lunch, the fact that you have not reached home by then, far from implying that you are late, simply means that time itself cannot possibly have reached the hour of lunch. This is why children use the terms "before," "first," "earlier," etc., arbitrarily in their spatial and temporal senses, and why they equate the failure to reach a place at the normal time with failure to reach the normal time itself. Now since the orders of spatial and temporal succession coincide in the case of a single body moving with uniform velocity, the child thinks that he can apply the same idea to the case of two bodies moving with distinct velocities. In other words, children at this stage apply the time-space framework of the single body to the joint motion of two bodies by egocentric assimilation, instead of [considering] the temporal relations [separately] from the spatial order of each of the motions. As a result, they fail to construct a time scale common to the two displacements.

In brief, they are no more capable of reconstructing temporal successions than are the subjects examined in Chapter I, and for the same reason: to reconstruct the phases of a motion when it is no longer perceptible (seriation of drawings) or to coordinate two perceptible motions with different velocities, calls for the dissociation of time and space, i.e., for mental reversibility. In the first case, when the order of events is no longer visible, the child has to select the correct temporal order from two possible spatial orders; in the second case, he

*Cf. Chapter IX for a similar error with respect to age.

must connect the positions of the two bodies by a relation distinct from that of the spatial successions: in either case, he must construct a unique and homogeneous time scale. The study of the child's conception of succession as applied to directly perceptible processes is therefore of greater expository value than even the analysis presented in Chapter I. . . .

Simultaneity*

We shall now look at the reactions of children when presented with the same experimental set-up but under the following new conditions: the two figures I and II are set off together from the same starting line (A_1 and A_2), move in the same direction and stop together, but I is moved more quickly than II, with the result that they come to rest at a distance of some 3 to 4 cm. from each other [I stops in C_1 while II stops in B_2].†

By their answers, the subjects can be clearly fitted into the three stages we have described. At stage I, they fail to grasp the simultaneity of the end points (and often even that of the starting points) and also the fact that the two figures move for the same length of time. Moreover, they argue that I takes longer than II because it goes further or more quickly, and think that II stops "first" because it covers a smaller distance. During substage IIA, they still deny the simultaneity and equality of the two synchronous durations, but contend that II goes on for a longer time because it moves less quickly, or else discover the simultaneity of the motions but still deny the equality of the synchronous durations; a very few subjects at this substage may, however, under certain conditions, grasp both the equality of the synchronous durations and also the simultaneity of the starting and end points. At substage IIB, these various advances begin to become coordinated. At stage III, finally, simultaneity and the equality of synchronous durations are appreciated and correlated straightaway.

THE FIRST STAGE: NO SIMULTANEITY. DURATION

JUDGED PROPORTIONAL TO DISTANCE

Here are a few examples:

Mar (4;6). To make certain that the subject understands the questions we put to him, we begin with two equal runs, i.e., with I and II starting simultaneously from A_1 and A_2 and stopping simultaneously in B_1 and B_2: "Did they start at the same time? *Yes.* Did they stop at the same time? *Yes.* Did one of them go on longer than the other? *No. It was the same for both.*"

I proceeds from A_1 to C_1 while II proceeds from A_2 to B_2: "Did they start at the same time? *Yes.* Did they stop at the same time? *No.* Did they stop at the same moment. *No.* Did they go on for the same amount of time? *No.* Which one went on longer? (I). Why? *Because it went further.*"

*In collaboration with Mlle. Esther Bussmann. [The following section is from Chapter IV.]

†[Brackets in original translation.]

We repeat the runs over the two equal distances A_1B_1 and A_2B_2: "Did the two stop at the same time? *Yes.* And what about these two (A_1C_1 and A_2B_2)? *No.* But didn't they start at the same time? *No.* Now look again. (Simultaneous departures from A_1 and A_2 and simultaneous arrivals in C_1 and B_2.) *No.* Which one started first? (I)."

Mic (4;9). We run with the child through the room, starting and stopping simultaneously but leaving the child some 1.50 meters behind us: "Did we start together? *Yes.* Did we stop together? *Oh no.* Which one stopped first? *I did.* Did one stop before the other? *I did.* When you stopped was I still running? *No.* And when I stopped were you still running? *No.* So did we stop at the same time? *No.* Did we run for the same length of time? *No.* Who went on longer? *You did."* . . .

Objectively

Experimenter   A1   B1   C1

                                    t   Experimenter and Child start and stop
                                                       at same moment. Experimenter goes
                                                       faster, passes child.

                              t

Child   A2   B2

Child's Responses   Lil (5;5). The experimenter passes the child: "Did we start at the same time? *Yes.* Did we stop at the same time? *No.* Did one of us stop before the other? *Yes, you did.* When I stopped, were you still going? *No.* And when you stopped was I still going? *No.* So did we stop at the same time? *No.* Did we walk for the same length of time? *No. You took longer because you went further."*

Luc (5;9). The child overtakes the experimenter, and both stop simultaneously on a given sound signal: "Did we start at the same time? *Yes.* Did we stop at the same time? *No.* Who stopped first? *You stopped a little earlier.* Did we take the same time? *No. Because you were walking and I was running.* Who stopped before the other one? *You did, because you were walking* (and did not run)."

Don (6 years): I is in C_1 and II in B_2: "Did they start at the same time? *Yes.* And stop at the same time? *No.* Which one stopped first? (II). Did they take the same time? *No.* (I) *took longer.* Why? *It went further."*

Arl (7 years). Same answers. . . . To make doubly sure, we place two glasses in C_1 and B_2 which the two moving figures reach and strike simultaneously. The child is told that the figures are coming home for dinner and ring the bell as soon as they come to the door: "Did they both reach home at the same time? *No.* Did they knock the glasses at the same time? *No."*

All these answers are characteristic. We can sum them up very simply as follows: when two moving bodies traveling with the same speed start out from, and end up in, the same spot, the simultaneity of their departures and arrivals is readily appreciated; when they start out simultaneously from two opposite points and arrive simultaneously at the same spot but travel with different speeds, the simultaneity of the departures may be denied or not, but the simultaneity of their end points is quite generally affirmed. On the other hand, if the two bodies start from the same point and finish up simultaneously at different end points (different speeds on parallel tracks) the simultaneity of their arrivals is generally denied.* Now this may not happen if the child ignores the differences in speed and distance, but as soon as he pays heed to these factors it invariably does occur. What are the reasons for this confusion? Certainly not a lack of perception or rejection of

---

*Sometimes even the simultaneity of the departures is denied, but this is by false analogy with the arrivals. Thus Ger (5;4) believed that of two bodies starting simultaneously, the second set out before the other; this was because it quickly overtook the first.

the perceived facts: every one of the subjects was agreed that when I had stopped, II was no longer moving, and vice versa. Things are therefore very much the same as we found them to be in the case of succession: simultaneity is, so to speak, perceived but not yet intellectually grasped. Could this be due to a purely verbal failure, i.e., to a systematic confusion of the terms "at the same time" or "at the same moment" with "in the same place," and of "for the same length of time" with "over the same distance"? Now this hypothesis, far from solving the problem, merely shifts it, since we would still have to explain why the child lacks words to express simultaneity at a distance when the velocities differ, while he is perfectly familiar with adult usage when it comes to the simultaneous or successive lighting of two lamps placed 2 meters apart (the distance between the figures I and II is only a few centimeters). Since, therefore, the child's answers are due neither to a lack of perception nor to verbal confusion, there remains only one possible interpretation of his failure: two motions at unequal velocities lack a common time, i.e., there is no single "moment" which two bodies separated in space can share. Arl put all this very clearly when, having granted that I has stopped running when II had stopped and vice versa, he nevertheless denied that they stopped "at the same time." When asked for his reasons, he explained that "this one (I) went further and the other one (II) didn't go so far."

All this would seem quite incomprehensible had not the analysis of succession accustomed us to this lack of differentiation between time and space. Now if "before" and "after" in time are confused with spatial succession, and if duration is identified with distance, it goes without saying that simultaneity at a distance, or with different velocities, can have no meaning for the child: he cannot possibly grasp that bodies moving in different places with different velocities can be fitted into a unique and homogeneous time scale. This negation of simultaneity therefore explains better than all our previous findings the purely "local" character of primitive time concepts: as long as it remains intuitive, the conception of time must, in fact, remain a subjective evaluation of every motion or action considered separately. As a result, simultaneity cannot possibly be grasped in the case of motions or actions proceeding at different speeds. This applies a fortiori to the equalization of synchronous durations. . . .

The Equalization of Synchronous Durations and the Transitivity of Equal Time Relations*

Having looked at the subject of succession, we must now make a closer analysis of duration and of simultaneity, and quite particularly of the equalization of synchronous durations.

We have seen that even when the child appreciates that two bodies start and stop simultaneously, he does not necessarily conclude that

*[The following section is from Chapter V.]

their motions are of equal duration. Before trying to explain this strange behavior, we must first show that it occurs quite generally. To do so, we shall use an experiment that is far more precise than those we have met in the earlier chapters of this book.

A large vessel (the reservoir) is allowed to empty through an inverted and tapering tube yielding two identical jets of water. The water is collected in small bottles or glasses of different shapes and dimensions. A single tap controls both branches of the Y-tube so that the water can clearly be seen to start and stop running simultaneously.* If the two bottles are of the same shape and dimensions, the water will obviously rise to the same level in both; in that case, the equality of the synchronous durations is invariably recognized. On the other hand, if the two bottles do not have the same shape, and equal quantities do not rise to the same level, children at the lower stages will deny the equality of the time of flow. We can then ask them a number of questions, not only about synchronization as such but also about the logical construction of the equality of durations, and about the relation between time and the amount of water run out.

We begin by asking, before the tap is turned on, which of the two dissimilar bottles will be filled more quickly and if it would take more or less time to fill than the other one.

When the water in one of the bottles (which we shall call A, B, C, etc., in order of increasing size) has risen to A_1 (in the case of the smallest bottle the subscript I means full to the top) the water in the second bottle will have risen to B_1 (A_1 and B_1 represent equal quantities of water). We then put our next question (simultaneity): "Did the water start and stop flowing at the same time from both tubes?"

Third question: "Did the water take some time to go from here (A_0 = the bottom of A, empty) to there (A_1)? And did it take the same, or more or less time to go from B_0 to B_1?"

We next make quite certain that the child fully understands that the two flows are simultaneous by saying: "As you can see, the water runs out the same way from both these taps, and we started it running into the two bottles at the same time, and stopped the flow in both at the same time." Once this is agreed, we ask the fourth question: "Is there the same amount (or the same water) in here (A_0-A_1) as there is in there (B_0-B_1) or is there more water in one of the bottles?" Then, to check the answer, we ask: "If we poured that lot (A_1) into B' (= another vessel identical to B) how high would it rise? And if we poured that lot (B_1) into here (A') how high would that rise?" Finally we might add another question: "If we poured this lot (A_1) into L (= an elongated tube) and that lot (B_1) into L' ($L' = L$) would it rise to the same height or not?"

Our fifth question (or rather set of questions) bears on the logical coordination of synchronous or colligated durations. We fill two vessels X and Y, of different shape, simultaneously to the top, so that $X = Y$. Now, if $Y = Z$, will the child be able to conclude that $X = Z$? And if $Z_2 > Y$, will it conclude that $X < Z_2$, i.e., that it takes longer to fill Z_2 than X?

---

*To make the simultaneity of the terminal points even more obvious, both bottles can be pulled away from under the taps at the same moment.

Now the stages of development represented by the answers to these questions (and especially questions 3 and 4) are generally comparable to those described in Chapters I to IV. Hence we need not dwell too long on the results, and can concentrate instead on the construction of the concept of synchronous duration.

THE FIRST STAGE: FAILURE TO GRASP SIMULTANEITY AND SYNCHRONIZATION, AND FAILURE TO QUANTIFY THE FLOW

Here, first of all, are a few reactions:

Per (4½): Question I: "Look at these two bottles (B and F). We are going to put both under these two taps at the same time and remove them at the same time. How far will the water rise in both? *They'll be full at the same time.* Just look. (Experiment) *Only one is full.* Why? . . ."
Question 2: "Did we start at the same time? *Yes.* Did we stop at the same time on both sides? *No.* Didn't we take the bottles from under the taps at the same time? *No.* (wrong) (The experiment is repeated.) Did we stop them together? *Yes.* So did we stop them at the same time? *No, because this bottle (F) is not full.* (We start again, counting this time.) 1 . . . , 2 . . . , 3. Did we stop at the same time? *No.*"
Question 3: "How long does it take from here to there (B_0 to B_1)? *Don't know.* A short time? *Yes.* And from here to there (F_0 to $F_1 = \frac{1}{3}$)? Was it a short time as well? The same time? *No, more for that bottle (B) because it was full.* (We now take a run together through the hall and stop together, but Per denies that we did so.) What was I doing while you were running? *You were walking.* The same time? *No. I took longer because I was running.* But wasn't I walking for the same time? *No.* (We go back to the bottles.) Did we stop the water at the same time? (We have been counting.) *No. . . . Yes.* Did that one (B) take some time to fill? *Yes, a long time.* And how long did that one take to rise from here (F_0) to there (F_1)? *Not a long time.* Why? *Because that bottle (B) has lots of water.*"
Question 4: "If that were syrup, which bottle would you like? *The full one, because it's bigger.* (false: B is smaller than F) What happens if I pour the water in B into (the empty) F? *It would go right up to the top.* And if I pour (F_1) into (the empty) B? *Up to here.* (the same level, i.e., half of B!)." . . .

Jack (5;10) predicts (question 1) that two bottles E and C (E visibly larger than C) "*will fill up together.* (Experiment) How much time for C_1? *One minute.* And for E_1 (= $\frac{2}{3}$)? *1 second. That's less.* The same time for both? *No, that one (C) took more time.* Why? *Because it is small and the other one is bigger.* (Similarly with B and F): (B) *is fuller and smaller, it gets filled more quickly because it's smaller.* So does it take more or less time? *More time.*"
Question 4: the fuller one "*contains more water, this one (C) will go higher* (in L) *than that one (E).*" After observing that the levels in L and L' are equal, Jack nevertheless continues to think that if the contents of E were poured into C they would only fill it to $\frac{2}{3}$.

As for running in the hall, he fails to appreciate the simultaneity of the stopping points, and makes the time proportional to the speed and the distance.

These . . . subjects produced the most primitive reactions we obtained by this method, i.e., failure to grasp simultaneity and synchronization and above all, a complete inability to quantify the work done (the flow of the water).

As regards the first point, though all these children realized quite clearly that by shutting off the tap we stop the flow into either bottle, and that the two bottles were withdrawn together from underneath the jets of water, they were nevertheless almost unanimous in denying the simultaneity of the end of the flow. This fully confirms what we have said in Chapter IV, and Per shows us precisely why: ignoring the different dimensions and capacities of the two small bottles B or C and of the two larger bottles F or G, the child, aware that the two taps give off water at an equal rate, expects the two bottles to be filled simultaneously ("they will be full at the same time" as Per put it). Now, when he saw that one of the bottles was filled before the other, he simply concluded that the flow could not have stopped "at the same time," simply " . . . because this (the other) bottle is not full." Here we have yet another example of the fact that children conceive of time as the complete course of a single action and not as the relation between, or common frame of, different actions. Now since, in our experiment, the taps are obviously turned on at the same time, the child treats the beginning of the flow as a single, simultaneous action. [But] since one of the bottles fills up more quickly than the other, in much the same way as one of the runners mentioned in Chapters III and IV overtakes his competitor, the child now faces two quite distinct actions with seemingly distinct end points in time. More precisely, he fails to appreciate the simultaneity of the end points because he fails to attribute a common time to these separate actions—having predicted that the two bottles will be "full at the same time," and seeing that one is filled before the other, the child simply denies that the flow has stopped "at the same time," meaning that there is no such thing as the "same time," and that times cannot be compared for lack of a common duration.

This explains our subjects' peculiar reaction to the synchronization of durations, i.e., their denial that the small bottle gets filled to the top in the same time that the big bottle gets filled to a third of its capacity, and their claim that it takes longer to fill the small bottle. According to Per, this happened because "it was full"; according to Luc [4;6] it took longer because "it went very quickly (at the end)"; and Jack gave both reasons when he said "It is fuller and smaller, it gets filled more quickly because it's smaller." Luc summed it all up when he claimed that the small bottle "took a little longer . . . because it's smaller." In brief, we are back with the general idea that time is proportional to velocity, the greater the speed, the greater the work done (distance covered, etc.). In our particular experiment, there is the added complication that the small bottle seems to contain more liquid because it becomes filled to the brim.

This brings us to the third reaction characteristic of this stage: the fact that failure to grasp simultaneity goes hand in hand with failure to synchronize durations, simply because time is thought to belong to each action separately and because the child thinks that actions can only be coordinated by their results (the work done). Now, since the results cannot yet be quantified, they cannot serve the child as objective criteria.

[With respect to] question 1, we saw that our subjects completely overlooked the obvious differences in the size of the bottles B or E, F or G, and so predicted that all of them would be "full at the same time" (Per). Here we have the old misconception about synchronous processes, i.e., the evaluation of duration by the results of the action alone

joined to a rather subjective or egocentric quantification of these results based, not on the actual work done, but on the final objective
(filling the bottles to the top). This also explains the curious reactions
to question 4: the full bottle, however small, is thought to contain
more water than the unfilled bottle, however big. Per even combined
this misconception to his erroneous views of duration, when he argued
that it takes longer to fill *B* "because the bottle has lots of water"; "the
full one is the bigger one." Similarly, Luc declared that "there's more
water there (*C*) because it's bigger," and this despite the fact that he
also claimed that (*C*) takes "a little longer (to fill) because it's smaller."

In brief, we are back with the same primitive intuition we met in
previous chapters: duration is evaluated by the results of an action,
and these results do not depend on the interval between the starting
and finishing points, but on the finishing point alone. In the case of
two runs, the latter was represented by a point in space, in the case
of the flow of liquid, the amount of water run out is judged by the
levels irrespective of the size of the bottles—even if the water is poured
back into equal vessels before the children's very eyes, they stick to
their old evaluations. As for the use of a watch, we saw from Luc's
reaction that the motion of the hand is simply incorporated into the
general system of interpretation. . . .

The Concept of Age*

The analysis of children's ideas of age raises a number of important
questions. Does the child look upon aging as a continuous process in
time? Is this time the same for all individuals? And, above all, does
he associate differences with the order of births?

The child's idea of age has been the subject of a highly evocative
study by O. Decroly† who, after observing the spontaneous reactions
of his daughter S. between the ages of 4 and 6, concluded that young
children tend to confuse age with height—as if aging were tantamount
to growing. Moreover, when he asked several groups of children how
old they were last year, how old they would be next year, and how old
they were at birth, he discovered that 75 percent of his subjects below
the age of 7 failed to give the correct answers to questions 1 and 2, and
that question 3 eluded even older children—not surprisingly when we
consider that it is of a metric rather than qualitative kind. From the
answers elicited by Decroly, it would also appear that young children
fail to grasp the relation between age and the order of succession of
births. The most typical reactions were those of Claire, aged 4, who
"no longer remembered" her age at birth—"it was much too long ago";
and of Jacqueline (5;6): 'I can't remember. . . . Oh yes, 'I was two

*In collaboration with Mlle. Myriam Van Remoortel. [The following
section is from Chapter IX.]
†O. Decroly, *Etudes de psychogenèse* Brussels: 1932, Chapter V.

months old!" In what follows we, too, shall find clear signs of this initial lack of coordination between the ideas of duration and succession.

THE AGE OF PERSONS

The First Stage. All our studies of the development of the concept of physical time have shown us that young children behave as if duration varied as the distance covered by moving bodies and as their velocity, i.e., as if physical time were heterogeneous. This brings us to our first two questions, namely whether children realize that age differences are preserved throughout life or whether they rather believe that, as people grow older and bigger they catch up with their elders; and secondly whether young children grasp the connection between age and the order of birth. As we saw in our discussion of physical time, the second question impinges upon the relation between duration and succession, though with the added difficulty that, since the idea of age is more frequently discussed in the home . . . than any other temporal concept, few children will give unprejudiced answers. For that reason, we have thought it best to question them on the age of plants and animals rather than on their own age and that of their near relatives. Nevertheless, we have found that, by dwelling upon personal age differences, we can bring to light a number of systematic difficulties, and so discover agreement between the results obtained in this field and in those we have already covered.

One thing in particular strikes one directly, namely the essentially static and almost discontinuous character of the child's idea of age. To him, aging is not a perpetual and continuous process, but rather a process of change tending toward certain states: time ceases to flow once these states are attained. That is precisely why young children equate aging with growing up: when growing stops, time apparently ceases to operate. Their conception is reminiscent of the ancient Greeks' idea of "becoming," and this similarity is yet another indication that childish thought resembles the static, and relatively unoperational, approach of the Ancients.

We can distinguish three stages in the development of the child's conception of age. During the first, age is independent of the order of birth, and age differences are thought to become modified with time conceived as a heterogeneous flux. During the second stage, the child believes either that, though age differences are not maintained throughout life, age depends on the order of births, or else that age differences are maintained but do not depend on the order of births. In the third stage, finally, duration and succession have become coordinated, and their relations are preserved by virtue of this very fact.

We shall now look at a few examples from stage I.

Rom (4;6) does not know her birthday. She has a small sister called Erica: "How old is she? *Don't know.* Is she a baby? *No, she can walk.* Who is the older of you two? *Me.* Why? *Because I'm the bigger one.* Who will be older when she starts going to school? *Don't know.* When you are grown up, will one of you be older than the other? *Yes.* Which one? *Don't know.* Is your mother older than you? *Yes.* Is your Granny older than your mother? *No.* Are they the same age? *I think so.* Isn't she older than your mother? *Oh no.* Does your Granny grow older every year? *She stays the same.* And your mother? *She stays the same as well.* And you? *No, I get older.* And your little sister? *Yes!* (categorically).

"Who was born first, Erica or you? *Don't know.* Is there a way of finding out? *No.* Who is younger, Erica or you? *Erica.* So which one was born first? *Don't know.* How many years older are you than Erica? . . . One year? *No.* Two years? *More.* Three years? *Yes.* When you are a lady will you still be three years older than Erica? *Don't think so.* Were you alive when your little sister came? *Yes.* And who was born first, your mother or you? *Mummy.* Your Granny or your mother? *Don't know.* Your father or your little sister? *Don't know.* Your father or you? *Can't say.*" . . .

Pti (4;9): "How old are you? *4½.* Is it a long time since your birthday? *It hasn't been yet, it will be in June.* How old will you be? *8 years.* Come, come! *No, 5 years.* Have you any brothers or sisters? *I have a big brother. He goes to the school in Secheron* (the "big school"). Were you born before or after him? *Before.* So who is older? *My brother, because he is bigger.* When he was small, how many years older was he than you? *Two years.* And now? *Four years.* Can the difference change? *No.* . . . *Yes. If I eat a lot of soup I shall grow bigger than him.* How can one tell which one is the older? *The one who is bigger.* Who is older your father or your grandfather? *They're both the same age.* Why? *Because they are as big as each other.*

"Pierre and Paul are two brothers. Pierre was born first. Can you tell which one is the elder? *It's Pierre.* But look, Pierre is the smaller of the two. *Then Paul is the older: the older one is the one who dies first.*" . . .

Aud (6 years) has a friend: "Is he older or younger than you? *He's bigger.* Was he born before or after you? *After.* Is your father older or younger than you? *Older.* Was he born before or after you? *I don't know.* Who came first, you or him? *Me.* Are you going to stay the same age all the time or will you grow older? *I shall grow older.* And your father? *He'll remain the same age.* And will your mother grow older? *No.* Why? *Because she is old already.*"

These stage I reactions are in remarkable agreement with those of the corresponding stage in the child's conception of physical time: failure to grasp the ideas of succession and duration operationally, and inability to coordinate pre-operational intuitions with respect to them.

As regards the idea of succession, it is surprising to find that children not only fail to affirm that they were born after their parents, but that many of them claim anteriority—one might almost say priority, with all the value judgments that term implies. While the more prudent subjects, e.g., Rom and Myr [5 years] (*It's possible to tell, but I myself don't know*) confess their ignorance, the more audacious are uncompromising, and, like Aud, insist that they preceded their father into the world. Such replies would be incomprehensible had we not learned (Chaps. III and IV) that these children fail to grasp temporal succession whenever the starting and end points of a process do not coincide in space. Hence the children who reply "I don't know" when asked about the order of births in their family, are speaking the truth: the problem has no meaning for them. As for those who attribute anteriority to themselves, they stress another kind of truth: from their point of view, time, and hence the existence of older people, begins with the dawn of their own memory. This explains why Myr could not "remember" whether her mother was born before her, or why Bor [4;9], asked about the birth of his older brother, declared: "Oh sure, I was there"—and, indeed, for as far as his memory stretched back he was always "there" to record his brother's presence. Here we have a temporal egocentrism that clearly reflects the incoherent nature of the intuitive and pre-operational idea of temporal succession.

This egocentric conception of intuitive time in no way reflects the predominance of the inner life over the organization of spatial objects, but [rather] a lack of differentiation between subject and object. [The best proof of this] is that our subjects' ideas about duration (age itself) are based on a confusion between time and the spatial or physical data serving as its content: age is equated with size, so that age differences can be annulled or reversed by growth in height. That was why Rom thought that her mother was the same age as her grandmother, and that neither grew any older. By contrast, she herself and her sister were still growing older, but at different rates. Jear [4;9] will always stay young, while his grandfather was born "old straight away," and though he appreciates that he himself is older than his juniors, he is not at all certain that he will grow up into a man before them (here temporal egocentrism goes hand in hand with emotional insecurity or feelings of inferiority, which seems paradoxical until we remember that this attitude is based on a lack of intellectual, and not of moral, differentiation). Pti believes that his older brother used to be his senior by two years, that the difference has now increased to four years, but that he himself will grow older than his brother if only he eats enough soup. Myr did not know if she would always remain younger than her sister, etc.

In brief, children at stage I have an egocentric and pre-operational conception of succession and duration, and therefore cannot base the former on the latter or vice versa. In other words, they are quite unable to say that A was born before B because A is older, or that A is older than B because he was born before him.

The Second and Third Stages. The similarity between the development of the concept of age and that of physical time is even more striking at stage II. The reader will recall that this stage is characterized by the emergence of articulated intuitions, either of succession (the past in time becomes divorced from the past in space) or of duration (more quickly = less time), which, however, remain uncoordinated. Now, in the case of age as well, the grasp of successions may precede that of durations (type I), or vice versa (type 2). In the first case, the child is able to order the births but fails to deduce the permanence of age differences, in the second case, he discovers that age differences persist but fails to deduce the order of succession of the births.

Here are some examples of type 1:

Filk (4;11) (precocious) has an older sister: "Are you the same age? *No, because we weren't born at the same time.* Who was born first? *She was.* Will you be the same age as her one day or will the two of you never be the same age? *Soon I shall be bigger than her, because men are bigger than women. Then I shall be older.*"

Vet (7;10): "*I have a little sister, Liliane, and a 9-month-old brother, Florian.* Are you the same age? *No. First of all there's my brother, then my sister, then me, then Mama and then Papa.* Who was born first? *Me, then my sister and then my brother.* When you are old, will Florian still be younger than you? *No, not always.* Does your father grow older every year? *No, he remains the same.* And you? *Me, I keep growing bigger.* When people are grown-up, do they get older? *People grow bigger and then for a long time they remain the same, and then quite suddenly they become old.*"

We conclude with a subject who nearly succeeds in coordinating birth with age, but nevertheless keeps to the idea that age is defined by size:

Clan (7;10): "How old are you? *7 years. I am big, people say I am 8 years old.* Have you a sister? *Yes, she's 6 years old.* Were you born before or after her? *Oh! Before!* When you will be a young man, will both of you be the same age? *No, when I'm 9 she'll be 8, when I'm 10, she'll be 9, when I'm 18 she'll be 17, there will always be a difference. My sister reaches up to here* (to his chin). *Me, I'm growing bigger all the time. When she reaches up to here* (to his forehead), *then I'll be there* (above his head), *and then afterward we'll be here and there,* etc. Who is younger, your father or your mother? *My father.* (wrong) Was he born before or after your mother? *After.* (wrong) So why is he the younger? *My mother is the tallest in our family.*" Despite his brilliant beginning, Clan thus sticks to his confusion of age with size.

As we can see, all these children give the correct replies to questions involving the succession of births, equating "older" with "born earlier" and "younger" with "born later." But, curiously enough, their grasp of this correspondence is restricted to the *actual* age of people, and does not imply a realization that age differences persist throughout life: it is therefore nonoperational and simply represents an "articulated intuition.* . . . Now the reason for these strange opinions is very simple: though the subjects grasp the order of succession of births, they always think of duration in terms of spatial or physical developments and hence confuse age with size. It follows that their conception of lived duration or age is discontinuous: as Vet put it so suggestively "people grow bigger and then for a long time they remain the same and then quite suddenly they become old."

Unlike these subjects, those of type 2 fully grasp the fact that age differences persist but fail to deduce the correct order of births (which is extraordinary from the operational point of view, but is easily explained when we remember that they still proceed by intuitive steps):

Dour (7;5): "How old are you? *7½.* Have you any brothers or sisters? *No.* Any friends? *Yes, Gerald.* Is he older or younger than you? *A little older, he's 12 years old.* How much older is he than you? *Five years.* Was he born before or after you? *I don't know.* But think about it, haven't you just told me his age? Was he born before or after you? *He didn't tell me.* But is there no way of finding out whether he was born before or after you? *I could ask him.* But couldn't you tell without asking? *No.* When Gerald will be a father, will he be older or younger than you? *Older.* By how much? *By five years.* Are you getting old as quickly as each other? *Yes.* When you will be an old man what will he be? *A grandfather.* Will he be the same age as you? *No, I'll be five years less.* And when you will be very, very old, will there still be the same difference? *Yes, always.*" . . .

The reader will note the paradoxical character of these replies, which are not only much rarer than those of type 1, but also far more instructive. . . . Their recognition of the conservation of age differences must be based on articulated intuitions (dissociation of age differences from physical growth, i.e., differences in height), while their grasp of the order of succession remains based on direct intuition.

Toward the end of stage II, we can, moreover, distinguish a sub-

---

*See the case of visual correspondences at stage II in the child's construction of number in *The Child's Conception of Number*.

stage IIB, representing a clear advance from stage II (types 1 and 2) toward stage III. Children at this substage set out with the same reactions as those at stage II, but then reach the correct answers by trial and error:

Phi (7;8): "Have you got a brother? *No, but I shall have one in February.* Which will be the older one? *I, because I was born first.* What will be the difference? *Seven years.* And when you become a father, what age difference will there be between him and you? *I don't know.* The same as now? *Oh yes.* Why? . . . And what about your mother, is she older than you? *Yes.* When you will be an old gentleman, will there be the same difference as now? *Yes . . . no, less . . . no, the same as now.* Is your father older than your mother? *Yes, one year older.* And when you were born, was there the same difference between them? *Mama was younger.* But the same difference? *No; yes; oh yes, the same."*

We see therefore that before it is fully taken for granted, the conservation of age differences can be adopted gradually, as an increasingly probable induction.

Here, finally, are some reactions at stage III, showing complete coordination between the order of succession of births and the colligation of ages:

Gilb (7;9) is an only child: "Have you a friend? *Yes, he's seven years old.* Is he older or younger than you? *He's the same age as me, he was born in the same year,* [so] *he must be the same age.* Have you got another friend? *Remy. He's 15 years old.* Is he older than you? *Yes, much.* What's the difference? *Eight years.* Was he born before or after you? *Before.* How long before? (Brief hesitation). *Oh well, eight years.* When both of you will be men, will you be the same age? *He'll be older because he was born first.* And you and your mother? *She is older.* And when you grow up? *There will still be the same difference.* Why? *It never changes.* Don't all old men have the same age? *It all depends on when they were born, some are 50 others are 60. . . ."*

Pol (8;3): "*I have two small brothers, Charles and Jean.* Who was born first? *Me, then Charlie and finally Jean.* When you are grown up, how old will you all be? *I'll be the oldest, then Charlie and then Jean.* How much older will you be? *The same as now.* Why? *It's always the same. It all depends on when one was born.*

We see that, for these subjects, the order of succession (seriation of births) and durations (the ages themselves) are related by logical necessity, so much so that the conservation of age differences is no longer merely asserted but deduced from the very order of the births.

All in all, the facts described [earlier] fully bear out the general progress with which we have become familiar in the course of this work. At stage I, the order of succession and duration remains completely uncoordinated and gives rise to egocentric and distorting intuitions, determined both by the subjective viewpoint and by a spatial and physical phenomenalism from which time has not yet become differentiated. During stage II, progress in intuitive regulation leads to the grasp of either the order of births or else of the permanence of age differences. During stage III, finally, the simultaneous use of these two types of articulated intuition helps to transform the regulations on which they are based into operations proper, whose "groupings" combine the succession and duration into a coherent, deductive system.

It is a striking fact that despite its verbal character, and though it is so strongly influenced by adult remarks, the child's conception of age should develop along paths precisely parallel to those described in Chapters III and IV for the case of physical time. The problem is, moreover, the same in both cases: the construction of time calls for the coordination of motions and velocities: growth is, in effect, comparable to the spatial trajectories we met in our discussion of physical time, and the rate of growth (aging) to differences in the velocity of two runners. Now, in both spheres, duration is at first confused with the path traversed—thus all children at stage I define age by size. In both cases, moreover, there is a complete failure to grasp the order of events, due to lack of differentiation between temporal and spatial succession: the spatial "before" along the track is, in effect, equivalent to an egocentric "before" on the age scale. Then, at stage II, the emergence of articulated intuition results, in both cases, from the partial correction of the primitive intuitions, and hence from a regulation and not directly from reversible operations. Finally, stage III sees the appearance of operational coordination: thanks to the grouping of the relations involved, the subject succeeds in deducing ages from the order of birth and the order of succession of births from the colligation of ages. . . .

Conclusions

From all the preceding discussions, we have learned that time is the coordination of motions at different velocities—motions of external objects in the case of physical time, and of the subject in the case of psychological time. [Before] the conception of time [has been] grasped operationally, i.e., as the ratio of the distance covered (or the work done, etc.) to the velocity, the temporal order is confused with the spatial order and duration with the path traversed. Conversely, before the temporal order has been constructed, the idea of velocity is often bound up with that of overtaking, i.e., with a purely spatial intuition involving a change in the respective positions of two moving bodies. The construction of time proper therefore begins with the correlation of velocities, be it in the case of human activity or of external motions. . . .*

Now all these operations presuppose a new relationship between durations and the order of successions, i.e., they involve an operational synthesis of the two and thus go beyond simple complementarity. In effect, whereas in qualitative time, durations are colligated rigidly and the order of succession allows of no permutations, in the case of quantitative time the equalization of successive durations introduces a mobile standard of duration whose identity is unaffected by the order of the real successions. In that case, the only difference between the unit α and another unit α is that one precedes the other in the order of denumeration, which order is quite arbitrary inasmuch as, if the second unit were counted first, it would become the first unit. We can

---

*[Approximately twenty pages are omitted.]

therefore say that the quantitative addition $\alpha + \alpha = 2\alpha$ is both serial and commutative, and that its serial character does not prevent it from being commutative.

In brief, in the sphere of time as in all other spatial and physical spheres, measurement appears as a synthesis of two fundamental systems of operation: displacement and partition. The reader may recall that number is the synthesis of the colligation of classes and the seriation of asymmetrical relations. Now similarly, when logico-arithmetical operations are replaced by spatio-temporal operations, and when the colligation of classes becomes the partition or colligation of parts into hierarchic wholes, and the seriation of relations becomes a spatio-temporal succession or placement (including changes in placement or displacement), measurement will result from the . . . displacement of a standard part chosen as a common unit. In the case of time, this unit is a motion at constant velocity that can be reproduced at will, i.e., that can be displaced in time and synchronized with the partial durations to be measured.

Now this is precisely how quantitative time is elaborated as the child develops its mental powers. To begin with, the child has great difficulties in admitting that a given partial duration, e.g., the time necessary for water to run between two levels (Chapters I and II), can be equal to a prior or subsequent duration: before he can do so, he must be able to divorce the duration from its qualitative context and feel free to reproduce it in a context that did not exist during the first duration, and that subsequently abolishes the earlier context. When faced with problems of this kind children react as if they had been asked to equate an hour spent at enjoyable play with an hour spent on tedious calculations. And, indeed, the two are not comparable unless they have first been divorced from the actual events and related to, say, the motion of a clock.

This leaves us with the construction of the concept of motion at uniform velocity, which, as we saw, is an indispensable adjunct to the elaboration of quantitative time. Now, this construction seems to introduce a vicious circle: while the measurement of time rests on uniform velocity the latter rests on the fact that two equal distances are covered in two equal durations. Hence how is it possible to establish that a given motion is uniform if we lack a unit of time? This particular psycho-genetic problem is the more interesting in that the same vicious circle appears in the scientific measurement of time: the adjustment of clocks rests on the regularity of natural motions, i.e., on the isochronism of small oscillations and the majestic periodicity of celestial orbits, but all we can say about this natural chronology is based on our own chronometry.* In point of fact, and this is characteristic of the operational organization of thought: the child discovers the conservation of uniform velocity simultaneously with the measurement of time, and by the identical operations.

This new correlation between the construction of the concepts of velocity and of time leads us to the psychological processes involved in

*See J. G. Juvet, *La Structure de nouvelles théories physique* (Paris: Alcan, 1935).

the operational grouping of temporal relations and in the elaboration of the three fundamental attributes of rational time: homogeneity, continuity, and uniformity.

Now, just as the intuitive conception of time results from the ego-centric and irreversible thought of young children, so the operational construction of time is the direct result of reversible correlations. The reversibility of thought is, in fact, marked by the correction of two tendencies, or, if you like, by the decentration of two types of centration. On the one hand, whereas the natural tendency of thought is to follow the course of the action itself, reversibility involves the retracing of that course: whence the operational construction of the concept of succession or order. On the other hand, while the personal point of view constitutes a privileged centration, reversibility, in the field of symmetrical relationships, leads to the construction of reciprocal view-points: whence the emergence of the concept of synchronous durations. In brief, the two chief results of decentration and the resulting reversibility of temporal concepts are the unfolding of time in two directions, after the discovery that the present is but a single moment in a continuous process, and the coordination of all the intersecting trajectories that, at any given moment, form a medium common to a host of simultaneous events.

Even on the qualitative plane, therefore, temporal operations lead to two remarkable results: they render time homogeneous and they also make it continuous. Quantitative operations, for their part, help to render the flow of time uniform (at least in the case of the small velocities characteristic of our everyday world).

Since homogeneous time is common to all phenomena, it is no longer the local time of intuition. But homogeneity does not imply the uniformity of successive durations: time could be common to the entire universe, even if its flow were constantly accelerated or slowed down, and even if it varied from one epoch to the next. . . .

As for the continuity of time, it is a remarkable fact that it, like homogeneity, should not be taken for granted at all levels of mental development: for young children, in effect, time is discontinous as well as local, since it stops with any partial motion. That is why adults are thought to have stopped aging, why a tree is thought to age if it still grows but not otherwise, etc. It is only with the introduction of operational time that duration is treated as a continuous flux, which shows that, far from being an intuitive concept, the continuity of time calls for a special construction. Now this construction is simply the system of qualitative colligations, which leads to the partition of durations and ensures that it can be continued indefinitely and at all times. . . . Since the idea of continuous time is not grasped at the earlier stages of mental development, it follows that the mind must construct a qualitative continuum (intensive quantity) based on colligations before the latter can give rise to mathematical quantification.

As for the uniform flow of time, it is based on uniform velocity, and its construction therefore calls for quantitative rather than qualitative operations. In the temporal as in all other spheres we have been investigating (number, mass, weight, and volume), quantitative, and extensive operations emerge the moment the grouping of qualitative or intensive operations has been achieved; [consequently] the uniformity of time is recognized just as soon as its homogeneity and continuity have been constructed.

Reversibility of thought thus helps the child to unfold successions or asymmetries in two directions and, by gradual progress in decentration, to construct a general grouping, both qualitative and quantitative, of temporal relations that ensure the homogeneity, continuity, and uniformity of time (on our scale). As Kant put it so profoundly, time is not a concept, i.e., a class of objects, but a unique schema, common to all objects, or, if you like, a formal object or structure. On the grounds that time is not a logical class, Kant argued that it is an "intuition," i.e., an "a priori form of sensibility" like space, and hence unlike the categories of the understanding, e.g., unlike quantity. Now, genetic analysis has led us to a quite different conclusion, namely that time must be *constructed* into a unique scheme by operations and, moreover, by the same groupings and groups as go into the construction of logical and arithmetical forms. The only difference is that, with time, the operations are not wholly logical (colligation of classes or seriation of relations) or arithmetical (correlation of invariant objects) but infralogical (partitions and displacements), i.e., identical with the operations used in the very construction of objects, or rather in their colligation into that total object which is the universe of space-time.* This is why time, though forming a unique object, or one of its structures, is operational nevertheless. This is equally true of space, with which, however, we are not concerned in this volume.

When it comes to psychological time, finally, we saw that it is not simply intuitive, as so many authorities claim, but that it involves the same operations as physical time: the evaluation of "lived" duration calls for a host of conscious or unconscious comparisons that lead to continuous progress from the level of perceptive or intuitive regulations to that of operational grouping.

The seriation of instants, first of all, is as essential in psychological as it is in physical time. The well-known idea of the "flow of consciousness" should not be allowed to disguise the fact that every particular moment in this inner flux does not represent a point on a line, but a multiple and complex state resulting from the intermingling of a great many diverse currents. At any particular moment, we can be happy about our work, unhappy about the political situation, confident about the welfare of a near relative, etc., all at once, so that each slice of our inner time continuum appears as a tissue of simultaneous events, or as a snapshot. The reconstruction of a series of inner events thus invariably involves the process of co-seriation.

But it is [with respect to] durations that the operational character of psychological time is most often overlooked. This is due to the common error of confusing the implicit qualitative operations with intuitions, and of the explicit qualitative operations with measurements: since inner durations generally lack a common measure, we imagine that they do not involve operational colligations. [But] it must

---

*For a further discussion of infralogical or spatio-temporal operations see *Le Développement des Quantités chez l'Enfant*, "Conclusions."

be clear that, whenever we are able to arrange internal events in their order O, A, B, C, etc., we are introducing the duration α (between O and A), α' (between A and B), β' (between B and C), etc. Now while we may not be able to evaluate these durations in numerical terms, or even tell if they are uniform, or what precisely is the relation between α, α', and β, we do know that $\alpha + \alpha' = \beta$ (β being the duration between O and B); $\beta + \beta' = \gamma$ (the duration between O and C), etc., and hence that $\alpha < \beta < \gamma$ . . . etc., i.e., that these durations can be colligated. One might say that this is very little knowledge, indeed, but it is, in fact, all that is needed for the logic of classes in general. And above all, it is this knowledge which, joined to the seriation of successive moments, enables the child to construct physical time before it can tell hours and minutes.

Nor is that all. Lived durations are not simply intervals but, as Bergson so rightly put it, the "very stuff of reality." [But] this in no way differentiates them from physical durations, since the real content of both is identical, i.e., the work done at a given rate. True, in the case of psychological time, the work does not take the form of a distance traversed, because inner time is not spatialized, nor is it usually measurable since we never count our ideas or perceptions, but it can nevertheless be [approximated]. "Time is creation, or it is nothing at all," Bergson said, and this is perfectly true, provided only we remember that mental, unlike physical, creation can only be translated into duration in terms of power (and hence of rapidity). That this translation is subject to systematic errors, as a result of which intense work seems short while it is being done and long in retrospect, no one will deny, but these illusions are partly corrected—thanks precisely to those operational comparisons which the mind performs incessantly and almost automatically.

Operations in psychological time would therefore seem to be mainly of a qualitative kind. Does that mean that there is no such thing as quantitative inner time? Bergson borrowed most of his imagery from music and, whenever this master of introspection wished to show that creative duration involved irreducibly intuitive and antirational factors, he did so in terms of melody, rhythm, and symphony. But what else is music than an inner mathematics? Long before Pythagoras discovered the numerical ratios which determine the principal musical intervals, ancient shepherds, singing their songs or playing an air on their pipes, busily constructed musical scales and realized, without being able to put into so many words, that a minim equals two crotchets and a crotchet equals two quavers. Musical rhythm is, in fact, the most intuitive of all time measurements and is most certainly not imposed on us from outside.* The same is true of stress in common speech and quite particularly of meter in poetry. Here, too, it was not the theorists who invented the meter but the bards. . . . The case of meter provides us with a good example of the continuous links between perceptive rhythms and spontaneous temporal operations.

*In his suggestive "Sur les opérations de la composition musicale" (*Archives de Psychologie*, Vol. 27, p. 186), A. Mercier has tried to show that tone and rhythm represent two fundamental musical "groups."

All this points to the common nature of temporal operations in all spheres, and to the close relationship between psychological and physical time: both are coordinations of motions with different velocities, and both involve the same "groupings." This is only to be expected since both are derived from practical or sensorimotor time which, in its turn, is based on objective relations and on personal actions. As the external universe is gradually differentiated from the inner universe, so objects and actions become differentiated as well, but remain closely interrelated.

It goes without saying that the development of psychological time involves physical time, since the coordination of actions performed at different rates presupposes that some work has been done in the first place, and since all work is sooner or later incorporated into the external world. Hence personal memory is the memory of things and actions in the external world as much, if not more so than, the memory of things and actions in the inner world. What is far less clear is that physical time implies psychological time: the succession of psychological phenomena can only be grasped by an observer who goes beyond them and so resurrects a physical time that is no longer. . . . In fact, the two are closely interrelated and both alike involve reconstructions of the causal order of events. Time, in both cases, is therefore the coordination of motions, and the direction of its flow can only be deduced from the causal chain, because causes necessarily precede their effects. Now, if causality is the general system of operations enabling us to correlate physical events, it is clear that before we can establish the existence of a causal relationship by experiment, we must first be able to correlate our measurements and this involves appealing to our memory or to reconstructions characteristic of psychological time. This is precisely what we mean when we say that physical time implies psychological time, and vice versa.

As for the time of relativity theory, far from being an exception to this general rule,* it involves the coordination of motions and their velocities even more clearly than the rest. Let us recall first of all that relativity theory never reverses the order of events in terms of the observer's viewpoint: If A precedes B when considered from a certain point of view, it can never follow B when considered from a different standpoint, but will at most be simultaneous with it. Einstein's refinements of the concept of time bear solely on nonsimultaneity at a distance, and consequently on the dilation of durations at very great velocities. Now both these consequences follow directly from our definition of simultaneity as a limiting case of succession, i.e., as the result of two signalling motions in opposite directions, whose relative successions cancel out. Simultaneity must therefore be relative to an organic or physical instrument (moving eye or optical signals, etc.). Now, since the relative velocity of light is constant and so constitutes a kind of absolute standard, simultaneity, in the case of great velocities, depends purely on the relative motions of the observer and the phenom-

---

*It is significant that Bergson, far from applauding the fact that Einsteinian time presents physics with a much closer model of psychological time (we might say of Bergsonian time) than Newtonian time did, challenged relativity theory with the claim that relative time was a characteristic of life alone.

enon he observes, as well as on their distance apart. And if simultaneities are indeed relative to velocities, it follows that the measurement of durations will itself depend on the coordination of these velocities. Relativistic time is therefore simply an extension, to the case of very great velocities and quite particularly to the velocity of light, of a principle that applies at the humblest level in the construction of physical and psychological time, a principle that, as we saw, lies at the very root of the time conceptions of very young children.

32

The Child's Conception of Space*

1948

INTRODUCTORY NOTES

At the end of the sensorimotor stage of development, the child is already in possession of a practical space that allows him all sorts of compositions of displacements such as the detour behavior pattern that he shares in common with apes and other mammals. While the child of this age is capable of planning his movements around his immediate space, this is only possible in the course of action and is not the fruit of a *representation* of space qua space. Four- and five-year-old children, though perfectly capable of going to school and coming back from it by themselves, have no representation of that space. In practice, the child does not get lost in his neighborhood, but he is completely unable to tell somebody how to go from his home to his school or to any other place in that very well-known neighborhood.

A representation and, even more so, a metric of space rely essentially upon a system of conservation of certain recognized properties of the space. The different geometries formalized by mathematicians are distinguished from one another on the basis of the set of properties that is conserved or kept invariant in each of them. For instance, Euclidean geometry allows measurement and conserves distances, angles, and parallel and straight lines. Projective geometry takes the viewpoint into consideration; it is the geometry of perspective and it conserves only straight lines. Topological geometry is strictly qualitative and it conserves only the most general properties of space: inside and outside, vicinity. All obey a principle of colligation that includes the more restricted in the more general: topological geometry is more general than projective, which is in turn more general than Euclidean.

Writing about the evolution of spatial representation and conception in *The Child's Conception of Space* (1948), Piaget notes that the child con-

*From Jean Piaget and Bärbel Inhelder *The Child's Conception of Space* F. J. Langdon and J. L. Lunzer, translators. (Atlantic Highlands, N. J.: Humanities Press, Inc., 1956). Reprinted by permission of Humanities Press, Inc., and Routledge & Kegan Paul Ltd., London. (Collaborators: Hans Aebli, G. Ascoli, E. Bussman, B. Demetriades, Marianne Denis-Prinzhorn, U. Galussen, M. Gantenbein, J. Halperin-Goetschel, E. DeJongh, T. Kiss, G. Lewinnex, Edith Meyer, Albert Morf, J. Nicholas, E. de Planta, Ch. Renard, M. Roth, and E. Sontag.)

serves at first only topological properties of spatial objects. He draws squares, circles, and rectangles as vague shapes that share the common property of being always *closed*; he represents crosses and rings with an opening by the same vague *open* figure. This distinction between open and closed figures is paralleled by a distinction between inside and outside. Two circles, or two squares, one enclosing the other, will be represented correctly as far as their respective positions are concerned; enclosing will be conserved, but not circularity, squareness, and so on.

Children become capable of distinguishing false knots from true knots and of recognizing reconstitutions of simple spatial orders such as the succession of colors of stringed beads. But they still lack the operatory reversibility that would permit them to reconstruct such sequences in the reversed order or to represent them when they are hidden or rotated.

In the second phase of concrete operations, the child becomes capable of coordinating different points of view of observers looking at the same object (three mountains) from different perspectives. He also takes into account apparent deformations of an object that changes position. In short, the child constructs a projective space.

At the same time, the child starts to really measure objects by means of a unit of measurement that is iterated on the object to be measured. A good example of the development of this notion is given in an experiment in which the child must construct a tower the same size as a model (Figure 1). All these

---

Figure 1

Building a tower: spontaneous development of measurement
Task: build a tower of the same size as the model with these blocks.
Situation: The tables are two metres apart and one is 90 cm higher than the other; the child cannot see the model while working.
Stages: I: (4 to 6) the child measures the height by eye: "I'm sharp-eyed, me"
        II: (5 to 7) tries to measure the model against his own work by carrying one of the two.
       III: (7 to 9) uses a measuring rod but it must be the same size as the model "to work," then eventually longer but not shorter. At the end of this stage, he becomes capable of using any rod arbitrarily selected as a measure to be iterated on the model and on his construction.

---

developments end up in the construction of a space that has the properties of Euclidean space in geometry, and in the generalization of measurement to the system of coordinates: horizontal and vertical, natural landmarks of a landscape, and arbitrary cues selected as references. These attainments make the representation of the group of displacements possible, as well as the measurement of solids, and the measurement of proportions in the case of similar figures.

In *The Child's Conception of Geometry* (1948) Piaget and Inhelder analyze the ways in which children between their fourth and tenth years come to master the concepts of measurement and metrical geometry. They trace the emergence and development of such geometrical notions as relationships of distances, subdividing a straight line, measuring angles, representing circles and curves, locating a point in two- and three-dimensional space, fractions, subdividing areas, and measuring volumes.

The development of all these notions follows the same general pathway as in the following example: First, the younger child is unable to describe changes of position because he cannot coordinate landmarks. Later, he starts to organize his landmarks but the coordination remains incomplete. At last, landmarks are fully coordinated and changes of position are represented as a comprehensive group.

The evolution of spontaneous measurement is illustrated in the "Building a Tower" experiment (Figure 1).

The relations of distance are not conserved at all by younger children when a screen is interposed between two objects. Later, they think that the function of the screen is to bring the two objects closer to each other. So distance relations are not yet conserved. At last distances become conserved. The same holds true for lines. The conservation of length of two equally long lines is asserted by younger children only if their extremities are aligned. When they are not, one line is longer than the other. At last, the child becomes capable of operational conservation.

These experiments give the flavor of The Child's Conception of Geometry, which concentrates on spatial measurement, whereas The Child's Conception of Space, as its name indicates, deals with the different conceptions of space that the child masters in the course of his cognitive development.

Perceptual Space, Representational Space, and the Haptic Perception of Shape*

The chief obstacle to any developmental study of the psychology of space derives from the circumstance that the evolution of spatial relations proceeds at two different levels. It is a process which takes place at the perceptual level and at the level of thought or imagination.

The common-sense approach to the problem, which is also that adopted by many mathematicians, assumes that the idea of space develops under the influence of motor and perceptual mechanisms; and so far as it goes this is quite correct. But this view goes on to assume that representational images and geometrical ideas are no more than a mere copy of existing sensorimotor constructs. This, however, oversimplifies and completely misrepresents the facts.

Kant considered space an a priori structure of "sensibility," the function of thought being merely to submit the data of space perception to a process of logical deduction capable of analyzing them indefinitely without ever exhausting their content. Poincaré, too, ascribed the formation of spatial concepts to sensory impressions, endeavoring to apply his theories on the group of displacements to the interplay of actual sensations, as if sensorimotor space furnished the basis for geometrical thought whilst the intellect elaborated this previously prepared material.

Now it is perfectly true that such a sensorimotor space begins to evolve right from the child's birth, and together with perception and motor activity it undergoes considerable development up until the appearance of speech and symbolic images, i.e., the symbolic functions in general. This sensorimotor space is superimposed upon various pre-existing spaces such as the postural, etc., though it is by no means a

*In collaboration with Mlles. E. de Jongh, U. Galluser, B. Demetriades, and M. A. Morf. [The following section is from Chapter I.]

simple reflection or repetition of them. On the contrary, it has its own course of development which can be traced fairly easily, and in addition, the spatial organization of sensorimotor behavior results in new mental constructs, complete with their own laws.*

At this juncture, however, there appears a rather curious phenomenon which tends to complicate the task of analysis. Though in a sense profiting from the achievements of perception and motor activity (which at their own level provide experience of straight lines, angles, circles, squares, projective systems, and so on), representational thought or imagination at first appears to ignore metric and perspective relationships, proportions, etc. Consequently, it is forced to reconstruct space from the most primitive notions such as the topological relationships of proximity, separation, order, enclosure, etc., applying them to the metric and projective figures yielded by perception at a level higher than that of these primitive relationships themselves.

Through failing to observe the discrepancy between the form of these initial relationships and the perceptual content to which they refer, outwardly at a more advanced stage, one tends to reduce everything to one common level and imagine that geometrical concepts are based directly on sense data. . . .

Knowing nothing of the stages which led up to this transformation, the adult assumes [for example], that perception involves coordinate systems or vertical-horizonal relations right from the outset, when in fact such systems are extremely complicated and are only fully developed by the age of 8 or 9. And such an illusion naturally tends to reinforce the misconception mentioned earlier, regarding the way perception is related to representation, a misconception which has influenced current explanations of geometrical concepts. . . .

Perception and Movement: the Role of "Perceptual Activity." The bare statement that sensorimotor structures anticipate in many ways the future achievements of spatial representation, whilst being a necessary preliminary, is not enough to indicate just exactly where the perceptual data discussed above stand in relation to representational space.

Thus the child can already perceive things projectively and grasp certain metric relationships by perception alone, long before he can deal with perspective in thought, or measure objects through operations. In addition, his ability to perceive forms in this way (straight lines, curves, squares, circles, etc.) is far in advance of his capacity to reconstruct them at the level of mental images or representational thought.

Thus thought has the task of reproducing at its own level (of representation as distinct from direct perception) everything that perception has so far achieved within the limited field of direct contact with the object. Besides this, there is a gap of several years separating the two constructions. For it is not until after 7–8 years of age that measurement, conceptual coordination of perspective, understanding of proportions, etc., result in the construction of a conceptual space marking a real advance on perceptual space. All the same, it is worth noting that despite their differences and the time lag which separates them, both perceptual and representational construction are to some extent repetitive and

*See *The Child's Construction of Reality*, Chapter I and II (here referred to as C.R.).

possess a factor in common. This common factor is motor activity. Having already been the governing factor in representational images and, in all probability, the most elementary perceptions, motor activity now becomes the fountainhead of the operations themselves. The fact of its continuous existence through all the stages renders motor activity of enormous importance for the understanding of spatial thinking.

At each level, spatial thinking appears in two quite distinct forms. Sometimes it concentrates on static patterns, as when a triangle or a straight line is conjured up, at other times it expresses possible transformations, such as a change in shape of the triangle or a rotation of the line about its middle. Are these two forms indissolubly linked together, or does one precede the other? Are they of equal importance, or does one govern the other? These are questions of the utmost importance, for our characterization of geometrical thought depends entirely on how they are answered. We may regard geometrical thought as "intuitive" in the usual etymological sense; as the contemplation of quasi-sensuous images. Or we may take it in the sense of something active and constructive, pre-operational at the outset but culminating finally with the *operation* as its specific form of equilibrium.

At each stage of development we shall see that it is the second interpretation which appears correct. For although the figural element and the purely motor element in spatial thinking are always associated and always co-present, we shall notice that it is always the latter which controls the former and not the reverse.

. . . There can be no movement occurring in any conceivable type of behavior which does not rest on perception. Neither can there be a perception taking place without activity which involves motor elements. It is the total "sensorimotor schema" which must constitute the starting point for the analysis of behavior, and not perception or movement considered in isolation.

From this point of view, a perception (such as the sight of a feeding bottle turned wrong way round) is a system of relationships organized in an immediate whole. But the equilibrium of this whole depends not only upon real (i.e., actually perceived) relations but also, like a mechanical equilibrium, upon virtual relations which refer to earlier or contingent perceptions (for instance, anticipation of the result of semi-rotation of the feeding bottle). The intervention of such virtual relationships presupposes motor activity, since it is always this last which dictates the transition from one perception to the next.

But what, in fact, is a movement? Gestalt psychology, it is true, noted its close linkage with perception, but only in the sense of being determined by perception. This point of view has been put very clearly by Guillaume*: "*Sensorium* and *motorium* constitute a single mechanism, and the dynamic play of the reaction is directly linked to that of the receptor field." Contrary to this view, however, we believe that if movement really marks the transition from one perception to another, then one must recognize the existence of reciprocity between a transformation as such—namely, movement; and successive states arising from the transformation—namely, perception. In this sense, every movement may

*P. Guillaume, *La psychologie de la forme* (Paris, 1937), p. 126.

be regarded as a transformation of the perceptual field and every perceptual field as a group of relationships determined by movements.

Thus an 8–10-month baby seeing half of a toy as it emerges from beneath a blanket will tend to lift the blanket to see the whole object. This movement transforms the first perceptual field (which gave only a partial view of the object) into a second field (one including the toy and the blanket which now covers other things). In all probability the movement of lifting the blanket was itself determined by the disequilibrium of the field, relative to the needs of the subject; or simply because of the perceptual disequilibrium occasioned by seeing only half of the object (hence an asymmetry and tension resolved by movement, reestablishing symmetry and equilibrium). This is the aspect of the situation stressed by Gestalt theory. But this formulation still leaves unanswered the question of whether such states, including those of equilibrium, can be conceived of, independent of the transformations leading from one to another, i.e., independent of the movements themselves.

Actually the whole process of development, starting out with perception and culminating in intelligence, demonstrates clearly that transformations continually increase in importance, as opposed to the original predominance of static perceptual forms.

But we go further than this and maintain that from the commencement of perception itself it is necessary to analyze most carefully the function of movement. For our interpretation of spatial thought depends entirely on the relation of figural to motor elements. Take, for example, a cube seen in perspective so that none of the sides appears as a square. The moment an observer grasps the fact of constancy of shape in this object it is impossible for him to perceive it without the intervention, in the present perception, of the movements he could make in obtaining a head-on view of the cube. In this way, even for direct perceptual recognition of objects, movements are involved in the guise of virtual relationships intimately linked with the real relationships. These movements, essential to the construction of shape constancy in general, cannot be ignored in the resultant perception, since they condition its equilibrium (in the same way as a mechanical equilibrium presupposes virtual speeds and displacements). In this sense, every perception implies a sensorimotor schema which brings the sum total of previous constructions to bear on the actual situation.

The perception of a simple plane figure such as a rectangle gives rise to similar considerations. To the extent that vision is centered on one point rather than another, or is centered to one side or one relationship rather than another, the width or the height will be overestimated, etc.* The shape of the figure as such, thus implies some optimal point of fixation or *centration* involving the minimum of distortion, and in this sense perception does determine eye movements. But conversely, the actual point chosen is only a matter of greater or lesser probability and one can calculate the probable perceptual effect of a particular shape

---

*Together with Lambercier we have shown that every area on which vision is centered is, so to speak, dilated, so that centration of vision results in the relative overestimation of that element of relationship. Cf. Piaget, and Lambercier, "La comparaison visuelle des hauteurs à distances variables dans le plan parallèle".

relative to the different combinations of possible points of fixation.*
Hence we find visual perception itself made up of a system of relationships determined by probable movements of the eyes, and we shall find in
the same chapter the exact analogy to these processes in connection with
tactile exploration as it occurs in "haptic" perception.

Generally speaking, side by side with purely passive perception such
as results from a particular centration, one must recognize the existence
of "perceptual activity" commencing with changes in centration (or
decentration) and consisting of comparisons, transpositions, anticipations, and the like. The need for this distinction is shown by the fact that
whilst the effects of simple perceptions remain relatively constant at all
ages (e.g., simple geometrical illusions diminish only very little in the
course of development) the effects of perceptual activity are progressively augmented as the child develops. A good example of this will be
seen in the phenomenon of "haptic" perception, which becomes vastly
more sensitive in the course of development of tactile-kinesthetic perceptual activity. . . .

Thus we can say that not only is movement active from the very
beginning of perception, but that the importance of its role is enormously
increased by perceptual activity. And in the transition from perception
to representation we shall again see this factor at work.

THE RECOGNITION OF SHAPES ("HAPTIC" PERCEPTION)

Perception is the knowledge of objects resulting from direct contact
with them. As against this, representation or imagination involves the
evocation of objects in their absence or, when it runs parallel to perception, in their presence. It completes perceptual knowledge by reference
to objects not actually perceived. Thus as an example, one may recognize
a "triangle" and liken the given figure to the entire class of comparable
shapes not present to perception.

Hence if representation can be said to extend perception, it can also
be said to introduce a new element peculiar to itself. What is distinctive
[in] representation is a system of meanings or *significations* embodying
a distinction between that which signifies and that which is signified.
Admittedly, perception itself contains significations [but] they are merely
signs or pointers, part and parcel of the sensorimotor schema. In contrast to this, representational signification draws a clear distinction between the *significants* or signifiers which consist of signs (ordinary or
mathematical language) and symbols (images, imitative gestures,
sketches), and the things they signify (in the case of spatial representation; spatial transformations, spatial states, etc.). The transition from
perception to representation is a twofold problem, embracing that which
signifies and that which is signified; that is to say, both image and
thought. . . .

We may outline the problem in this way. As a result of internalized

*Cf. Piaget, "Essai d'interprétation probabiliste du loi de Weber et de
celle des centrations relatives," p. 95. It is in relation to just such factors that
geometrical illusions such as the Delboeuf, Muller-Lyer, etc., are to be explained. [See also *The Mechanisms of Perception* (New York: Basic Books,
1969)].

imitation, the mental image benefits from the attainments of perceptual construction and is sooner or later (though much later than is generally thought) able to avail itself of ready-made forms, such as straight lines, curves, parallels, angles, squares, circles, and the like. Not that this stamps representational space as being Euclidean or projective right from the start, for it is in truth more directly linked with symbolic imagery than with genuinely conceptual relationships. In the case of the latter, as opposed to the imitative images on which they depend, it may well be that spatial representation has to begin by once more establishing the topological relationships of which perception itself was part. Only later can it embrace both projective and metrical relationships, and last of all embark upon the construction of a comprehensive space of coordinates and coordinated perspectives.

The Recognition of Shapes by Means of "Haptic" Perception. Technique and General Results. We thought it worthwhile to repeat a well-known experiment on children aged 2–7 as a suitable introduction to the study of spatial intuition, since it deals with the borderline between perception and the image. . . .

A child is presented with a number of objects, familiar solids or flat geometrical shapes, and touches or feels around each one without being allowed to see it. It must then be named, drawn, or pointed out from a collection of visible objects or drawings of them. Clearly, the reaction involves translating tactile-kinesthetic impressions from an invisible object into a spatial image of a visual kind. Thus the study of such data can be used to analyze the construction of the intuitive image as well as the mechanisms involved in tactile perception.

The child is placed before a screen behind which it feels the objects handed to it. By following this procedure rather than the conventional one of placing objects beneath a table, the experimenter can see the methods of tactile exploration employed. . . .

The following objects are offered in succession: (1) For very young children (older children find these too easy), a series of common objects: pencil, key, comb, spoon, etc., which they must identify among a corresponding series of objects which they can see. (2) A series of cardboard cutouts in the shape of geometrical figures. (a) Simple and symmetrical: circle, ellipse, square, rectangle, rhombus, triangle, cross, etc.* (b) More complex but also symmetrical: star, Cross of Lorraine, swastika, simple semicircle, semicircle with notches along the chord (see Figure 1), etc. (c) Asymmetrical but with straight sides: trapezoids of various shapes, etc. (d) A number of purely topological forms: irregular surfaces pierced by one or two holes, open or closed rings, two intertwined rings, etc.

In order to eliminate the element of chance, when the child has named the objects it has felt it is asked to identify them among a collection of figures. Alternatively the child may be shown a collection of drawings, or simply asked to draw the objects it has felt. We also employed (though simply as auxiliaries) shapes made of matchsticks stuck on a flat surface in the form of squares, triangles, etc., and letters of the alphabet cut out of cardboard. Outlines chiselled in wood worked even better than the matchsticks. The child has only to follow the grooves

---

*Circle 11.5 cm. diameter, square 10 cm. side, etc.

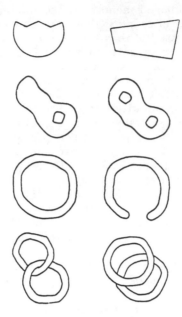

Figure 1

Toothed semicircle, trapezoid, irregular surfaces pierced by one or two holes, open and closed rings, intertwined and superimposed rings.

instead of making a complete tactile exploration, and in this case one can study the correspondence between the image or drawing and the simple movements themselves.

The problems set before the children face them with two distinct tasks. First, the translation of tactile-kinesthetic perceptions into visual ones. Second, the construction of a visual image incorporating the tactile data and the results of exploratory movements.

The subject is confronted with the first of these tasks when he has to recognize among several objects he can see, one he can feel but cannot see. The translation from tactile-kinesthetic into the visual mode is by no means a new task for the 2–4-year-old child. A baby of 3–5 months (the age of coordination of touch and vision) is already becoming accustomed to making visual perceptions of its hand or objects it manipulates correspond to tactile or kinesthetic perceptions of the same.* Apart from this, the general development of imitation, especially imitation of facial movements, leads to the achievement of such correspondence. For the parts of its own body which the baby cannot see correspond to the parts it can see of the bodies of other people, and which it can only come to know in its own case by tactile-kinesthetic means.† Hence we may expect to find the ability to recognize objects simply by means of tactile exploration developed at a very early age. The only new feature in this task for the child at the level of representation lies in the fact that it is now presented differently; namely with the aid of speech.

*See Piaget, *The Origin of Intelligence in the Child.*
†See Piaget, *Play, Dreams and Imitation in Childhood.*

As regards the second task, the construction of an image confronts the child with a new problem, and it is with this problem that the present study is exclusively concerned. What we find is that as soon as objects become too complex to be recognized (particularly the moment cardboard cutouts of two-dimensional geometrical shapes are met with) the child can no longer identify the figure simply by touching it. Instead, he is forced to make a tactile exploration of it. In this case, to identify or draw the object the child has to construct for himself a visual image of it.* What we are seeing here, then, is not only the transition from a tactile-kinesthetic to a visual percept, but in particular the transition from tactile-kinesthetic perception to the visual image.

Because it demonstrates how perceptually known forms are more or less rapidly exploited by imagination, and at the same time how the spatial relationships arising in the latter lag behind those already known perceptually, the analysis of this transition seems to us particularly interesting as an introduction to the study of conceptual space. It shows how early the mental image appears, but at the same time reveals its superficial character as regards the understanding, even from the intuitive standpoint, of the relationships themselves.

The results of these experiments were as follows. During the first stage, extending on an average up to 3;6–4 years, one finds familiar objects more or less easily recognized, but not geometrical Euclidean figures. During the second stage (4;6–6 or 7 years) Euclidean figures are progressively differentiated. Only during the third stage (after 6;6–7 years) is the synthesis of complex forms achieved.

Below the age of 2;6 years (stage 0) experimentation with hidden figures is not possible, although this by no means precludes the existence of spontaneous tactile recognition outside our experimental conditions, which are rather trying for the very young (bandaging the eyes was found even worse).

Stage I can be divided into two distinct substages. In substage IA one finds familiar objects recognized but not shapes—even visual correspondence between shapes, by simple superimposition, is only possible with practice (the children studied never having done any drawing nor having had experience of Montessori exercises). In substage IB (3;6–4 years) one finds, however, the beginnings of abstraction of shapes. But, curiously enough, the shapes first recognized are not Euclidean but topological. Thus the circle and the square cannot be distinguished because both are closed forms, although they are distinguished from open forms, etc. Neither straight lines nor angles are as yet identified.

Throughout stage I tactile exploration remains relatively passive. The child simply grasps the object, often with both hands, and responds to chance discoveries, such as when it pokes its finger through the hole in the key-handle, etc. In substage IB, shapes are explored as if they were three-dimensional objects.

In stage II one can distinguish three successive levels following one on the other. Between substages IB and IIA (4–4;6 years) there begins a crude differentiation of rectilinear from curvilinear shapes, whilst different rectilinear shapes (square, rectangle, etc.) or curvilinear shapes

---

*It is interesting to note that drawing the object and identifying it were found to be of about equal difficulty.

(circles, ellipses, etc.) are not differentiated among themselves. Representation by means of drawings is possible (beginning in stage IB) but lags somewhat behind identification by choice. Tactile exploration remains global but use is made of chance indications as they are encountered. In the course of substage IIA (4;6–5 or 5;6 years on average) one can observe a progressive differentiation of shapes according to their angles and even their dimensions (circle and ellipse or square and rectangle). There still remains a slight gap between recognition and drawing but the latter is becoming more precise. Tactile-kinesthetic exploration shows signs of a search for significant clues to identity. Finally, during substage IIB (5–5;6 years) one sees the successive discoveries, attended by much hesitation, of the rhombus and trapezium. Crosses and stars begin to be differentiated but many errors still occur in the representation of complex forms. Exploration becomes more active but it is not always systematic.

Lastly, stage III commencing at 6;6–7 years is notable for methodical exploration, doubtless influenced by what may now properly be called operations, which by this stage exist in all fields. The child can now [distinguish] complex forms, such as the swastika, and simultaneously take account of order and distance. . . .

Stage I. The Recognition of Familiar Objects, then of Topological, but Not of Euclidean Shapes. What is interesting about this stage is that the child, whilst recognizing with ease the things it touches, is at first unable to abstract shape for want of sufficient exploration. Later, when the child develops the ability to abstract shape he cannot get beyond topological relations and is unable to reconstruct Euclidean shapes. This raises [a] first question as to why the exploratory movements are absent when one might have expected them to be guided by the shapes offered as models, since nothing would appear easier than to follow the contour of a square or a circle with one's finger. A second question is also raised by the reactions observed during this stage as to just what abstraction of shape consists of, and why it is that topological shapes appear psychologically more simple than Euclidean ones.

Here are a few examples from substage IA.

Cri (2;10) recognizes a ball, a pencil, a key, a second pencil, scissors (but misses a spoon). But he cannot identify a cardboard circle from a collection of models, nor draw it. For the ellipse, semi-circle with or without notches, the reaction is the same.

Dan (3;0) recognizes objects in the same way—takes hold of them, passing them from hand to hand. Takes hold of a triangle but makes no attempt to explore it. "Have you any idea which one it is?—No—Keep trying—(He seizes it in both hands and turns it over). Can you draw it?—Yes—(scribbles). (Given several models to choose from) Is this it? (square)—Yes—Or is it this one? (rhombus)—No—Look at them; which is it?—This one (square)".

Ellipse: Takes hold of it in his left hand and feels the surface, then thinks he can recognize the semicircle with notches among the models. "Not this (ordinary semicircle)?—No, that one (with notches)."

Square: "I can't see anything—Draw it—(scribbles)—(round, oval and square models shown) Which is it?—That one (oval)."

Circle: At first remains passive, not making the slightest movement. Then explores it with the palm of the hand without touching it with the fingers. Drawing (scribble). From three models (oval, circle, square) chooses the oval one.

Semicircle with notched chord: Takes hold of it and places his fingers in the notches. From four models he chooses the triangle because of the point. "Take a good look—*That one* (oval)—Not that one? (rhombus)—*No* —Feel it again—(Moves his hand over the round part)—*That* (points to the ellipse).

Ordinary semicircle: Chooses the triangle after taking hold of the semi-circle by one of its angles. . . .

The main features of these reactions are clear. The child understands the questions since he shows himself capable of recognizing most of the familiar objects set before him. But when geometrical shapes are involved he cannot reconstruct the complete figure and, according to whether he has felt a curved or straight side or a point, he likens the shape touched to a visual shape possessing the same characteristic, not bothering about the rest of the object or attempting to put together the total structure. Thus Dan identifies the triangle with the square because of one of its angles, the ellipse with the notched semicircle on account of its curved outline, the square and the circle with an ellipse (not distinguishing straight from curved lines) and the notched semicircle with the triangle because of its points, etc.

It is obvious that these errors are due to inadequate exploration of the objects. The exploration required to identify geometrical shapes is not the same as avails for the recognition of familiar objects. The latter are in the main no more than prehensile gestures, or movements barely distinct from such: seizing in both hands, rolling from one hand to the other, touching, pressing the hands against both ends, sticking the finger in the hole of the key-handle, etc.

But to recognize geometrical shapes the child has to explore the whole contour, whereas he is content merely to take hold of the cards, feel their surfaces, and touch only part of the contour. . . .

But this remains only a partial explanation, since we have still to find out why exploration is not taken far enough to permit recognition of detailed geometrical shape. . . .

The act of seizing a ball, pencil, key, or a comb automatically in-volves some sort of tactile-kinesthetic adaptation or accommodation which at the same time makes it possible to distinguish the object con-cerned. Then why is such a mechanism not brought into play in ex-ploring the contours of geometrical shapes, discerning straight lines and angles, recognizing divergent or parallel lines or estimating the number or size of triangles, etc.? The usual answer is that the child cannot "analyze" its perceptions and is incapable of "abstraction." But what do such notions really mean?

It is in connection with "analysis" that the distinction between per-ception and perceptual activity, becomes relevant. Perceptual activity begins with "decentration." Touching any one part of a square involves centration and results in an initial tactile perception. Touching another portion involves another centration, producing a second perception, and so on. But being incomplete, each centration must lead to the overem-phasis of the part contacted at the expense of parts peripheral to the area of centration.

The passage from one centration to another (or *decentration*) thus tends to the correction or regulation of centrations by each other, and the more numerous the decentrations, the more accurate becomes the resulting perception. But such a process correspondingly implies an activity to some extent motor in character (going beyond pure perception) and consequently underlying many other active movements such as the "transfers" of perceptual data one to another, "comparisons" (reciprocal transfers), "transpositions" (temporal transfers), etc. It is this combination which constitutes perceptual activity and which is often referred to under the rather vague term "analysis."

The lack of exploration on the part of children at this stage may therefore be explained as the result of a general deficiency in perceptual activity itself. This means that the child's perceptions are still passive or static instead of being integrated in a system of sensorimotor coordinations tending to bind them together.

By working back one can thus understand what most probably takes place during the child's first few months, in the case of visually perceived shapes. Exploration by eye is much easier than exploration by touch, for the simple reason that a visual centration can embrace many more elements simultaneously than a tactile centration, and hence visual shapes are more rapidly constructed than tactile ones. But the process of construction is doubtless much the same in both cases, despite the gap of a year or two between them. . . .

The next question is whether "abstraction" of geometrical shape takes place on the basis of the object alone or on the basis of the subject's movements relative to the object. Substage IB enables us to answer this question by revealing the nature of the first geometrical shapes recognized, as distinct from the grasping of familiar objects. For during this substage a very instructive reaction is observable. The first geometrical shapes recognized by the child are remarkable, not for the properties apparent to ordinary sense perception, such as straight lines, curves, angles, etc., but rather for those properties which abstract mathematical analysis shows to be much more primitive, such as closed, open, intertwined, etc.: . . .

Don (3;6) recognized all the shapes by visual superimposition. After this we pass over to tactile perception. He recognizes the circle (holds it in both hands, turns it slightly, touching it across the diameter), but not the ellipse, etc., nor even the notched semicircle (which he holds both by the points and the curved side). As against this he distinguishes the ring from the circle, likewise the open half-ring and the surfaces with one or two holes.

Mar (3;10) recognizes the surface with one hole and also the closed ring without hesitation, and after some hesitation the open ring and the intertwined rings. In the case of the circle he sometimes makes the right choice but sometimes chooses the ellipse. Both the rectangle and the triangle are likened to an elongated ellipse. . . .

Thus we can say quite definitely that each of these children easily distinguishes an open from a closed figure, a surface with one or two holes from one without holes, a ring from a circle, intertwined rings from separate rings, etc. In other words the topological relations of open and closed shapes, intertwined and separate shapes, give rise to correct identification. On the other hand, simple Euclidean shapes remain undifferentiated, apart from the case of the circle where the beginnings of differentiation may be seen, although how far this extends has yet to be determined. . . .

We can now answer very simply the question of the "abstraction" of shapes raised in connection with substage IA. If abstraction meant no more than extracting from the object its most striking morphological features, what is the likelihood that topological relationships will be the ones singled out in the first place, and in particular, what is the likelihood of this choice being consistent? Does a rectilinear side or an angle present features so much more complex than the relationships of openness or closure, or interlacement, etc.?

But inasmuch as the shape is abstracted from the object by virtue of the actions which the subject performs on it, such as following its contour step by step, surrounding it, traversing it, separating it and so on, these relationships of proximity and separation (from which openness and closure derive) and interlacement take on a far greater importance, from the point of view of perception, than even the simplest Euclidean relationships.

It is similarly quite understandable how, being associated with the most rudimentary forms of action, especially one as crude as exploration at this passive and global level, these fundamental relationships have for a long time escaped the attention of geometry. For geometrical science began with the problem of measurement and only embarked on the study of these primitive notions comparatively late in its history.

Stage II. The Progressive Recognition of Euclidean Shapes. We have just observed, apropos of substage IB, that the first discriminations made by prehensile movement constitute the beginning of tactile-kinesthetic activity. In spite of its global and undifferentiated character it nevertheless makes possible the abstraction of elementary topological shapes. During stage II with the progress of this perceptual activity coordinating tactile centrations, which are retained as graphic and mental images, Euclidean shapes come gradually to be recognized by haptic perception. Similarly, the ability to draw also shows signs of progress.

. . . This transitional phase can be placed somewhere between the ages of 4 and 4;6 years:

Lou (4;1) recognizes immediately the pencil, key, and comb. He also recognizes without hesitation the surfaces with one or two holes, open and closed rings, etc.

He recognizes the circle and is able to draw it, likewise the ellipse (which is drawn slightly elongated). In the drawing of the square, one corner is more or less a right angle, the others being shown as curved, but it is only recognized among the models on one of two occasions. Triangles, rhombuses, etc., are all lumped together. His reaction to the notched semicircle is interesting: Lou draws a complete circle with points adorning the circumference. . . .

The features of this intermediate level are thus well marked. First of all exploration is more active than in stage I, the child being no longer content to grasp or simply feel the surface of an object without making any further movement.

He probes and explores it, though still in a global and haphazard fashion with no attempt at following the complete contour. But in this way he does happen on a number of cues or pointers, whose significance he is able to keep in mind.

As a result of this increase of perceptual activity, not only are the one or two topological relationships present in these experiments completely mastered, but we also see the beginnings of discrimination between rectilinear and curved shapes, the former being recognized by their angles. Lou demonstrates this discrimination in an extremely simple form, distinguishing the circle and ellipse from the rectilinear shapes but remaining unable to discriminate between the latter, while his drawings represent them all by means of a single prototype, a closed shape with one right angle. . . .

The information gained first from tactile recognition, and second from drawing, brings to light a new element which is involved in the abstraction of shape. There is no doubt that it is the analysis of the angle which marks the transition from topological relationships to the perception of Euclidean ones. It is not the straight line itself which the child contrasts with round shapes, but rather that conjunction of straight lines which go to form an angle. Now is not the discovery of the angle a typical case of abstraction direct from the object? As Volkelt* has shown, drawing and modeling often exhibit a multisensory character at this level, at once tactile, kinesthetic, and visual, quite apart from haptic perception. And Leo's remark "It's something that pricks" is a definition of the angle which illustrates Volkelt's thesis at the same time as it reveals the importance of "feeling out" the object in constructing the first representational Euclidean shapes.

But this by no means disposes of the matter. To consider the angle as two intersecting straight lines (Lam's drawing), and especially to incorporate it in a closed figure, the child has to be able to reconstruct it, and this necessarily implies that abstraction comes from the action rather than direct from the object itself. In this respect the angle is the outcome of a pair of movements (of eye and hand) which conjoin. Without bringing in notions such as these which include the idea of straight lines the child can never get beyond the simple impression of "something that pricks." Admittedly, the object with its spatial, physical properties must play some part in the appreciation of shape. But these properties, owing to the prior construction of topological relations, are made part and parcel of a system of coordinated movements, of which drawing is the visible manifestation. This being the case, Euclidean shapes, like the previous ones, are at least as much abstracted from particular actions as they are from the object to which the actions relate. Thus it is the coordination of the child's own actions which from the outset confers on these structures a geometrical character and not simply a physical one.

In the course of substage IIA progress is visible in two fields. Exploration becomes more active, particularly in probing for significant clues, although it is not yet exhaustive or systematic. As a result we see a progressive differentiation of angular shapes but no overwhelming success in their recognition. Similarly, drawing shows an advance on the previous level, but still lags somewhat behind recognition. On the average this substage begins about the age of 4 years, 6 months.

Ast (3;2, very precocious) recognizes the circle: "a ball"; the notched semicircle: "a rake"; the rhombus (by sliding her thumb and index finger along two sides, starting from the middle so that they meet): "a church"; the triangle, cross, and a four-pointed star. She fails with the ellipse (likened to a circle) and more complex shapes. But she recognized much more easily

*H. Volkelt, and J. Rabe, Einleitung zu Rabe: "Umgang mit Körpern von verschiederen Form und Farbe in frühester,"Kindheit, VII/4, 1938, München.

the irregular shapes involving only topological relations, such as the surfaces with holes and the open or closed rings. Of an open ring Ast immediately says: *"No, it wasn't that* (closed ring) *because it was open."*

Although Ast succeeds in making these comparisons, quite remarkable for her age, her drawing of Euclidean shapes still belongs to the earlier stage. Her shapes are curved so that the square is represented by an ellipse which is elongated to denote the rectangular sides. . . .

Has (5;8 up to 5;11) was the subject of repeated observations aimed at comparing the results of various techniques. From among the cardboard figures he recognizes the circle, ellipse, square, and rectangle, and all the irregular shapes involving topological relationships, and is able to draw them all correctly. But he does not at first recognize the triangle and draws it as an incomplete cross with only three arms! Then he has another try and this time draws it with three angles and curved sides. The rhombus he first draws as a square, then as a rectangle with two little figures in the middle of the long side intermediate between a square and a triangle. He draws the Cross of Lorraine just like an ordinary cross but identifies it correctly.

After this, while still at the age of 5;8, he is given the same shapes formed in relief by means of strips of plasticine stuck on a wooden board. This brings about a simplification of the child's movements which are then expressed exactly by the drawings. The square is drawn first as a right-angled triangle, then correctly. Conversely, the triangle is drawn first as a square, then correctly. The rectangle is drawn as an elliptical shape bisected by a straight line. The rhombus is shown first as a square with a triangle on top, to which is then added another triangle. The final drawing shows two triangles base to base. The cross produces drawings of uncoordinated right-angles. A further rhombus is represented by a square bisected diagonally, and then by a square standing on one corner.

At the age of 5;11 Has is given the same models, this time engraved on wood, his movements thus being guided by the grooves. The square and the triangle are now drawn correctly straightaway. The cross is drawn first as a right angle and subsequently as a double right angle, thus giving it three arms. The rectangle is drawn correctly whilst the rhombus once more appears as a square.

For a proper understanding of these results one really needs to appreciate in advance the remarkable similarity between these drawings obtained by means of tactile exploration, and those based on ordinary visual perception which we shall analyze in Chapter II. . . . This phenomenon of parallelism accompanied by a slight time lag would seem to throw light both on the problem of the formation of the image through perceptual activity, and on that of the "abstraction" of shape.

In the case of the representational image, it is clear that the drawings described above express not so much the model visually or tactilely perceived, as perceptual activity itself. In other words the drawing, like the mental image, is not simply an extension of ordinary perception, but is rather the combination of the movements, anticipations, reconstructions, comparisons, and so on, that accompany perception and which we have called perceptual activity. . . . Like a mental image, a drawing is an internal or external imitation of the object and not just a perceptual "photograph," whilst by its very nature imitation has the effect of prolonging the muscular accommodation or adaptation involved in perceptual activity. This explains the affinity between the adaptive movements involved in the children's tactile-kinesthetic exploration and their drawings (the time lag between the two may be explained by the technique required). In this connection the case of Has is particularly striking. Every one of his drawings is in some respect a direct continuation of his exploratory movements, modified by the different techniques employed.

In the case of "abstraction" it is worth noticing how the child, even at this relatively advanced level of shape discrimination, extracts from the object only that which he is able, not merely to reconstruct in imagination, but actually to construct through his own actions. The object is acted upon, and it is from this action that its shape is extracted. In the case of simple shapes, such as squares, rectangles, circles, etc., the actions consist in the grouping together of identities (such as equality of sides of the square, of the opposite sides of the rectangle, of the radii of the circles, right angles, etc.). In these simple cases, however, the reconstruction results in the object being imitated to such a degree that it produces the illusion of a representation abstracted directly from the object. On the other hand, in the more complex figures the element of construction is directly visible.

The most suggestive example is that of the rhombus, because of the dual difficulties in recognition and drawing which it occasions. From the perceptual point of view the rhombus would seem a relatively "good" shape, because it is doubly symmetrical. . . . The child first draws it as either a square or a rectangle, but adorned with a point or triangle . . . or flanked by two appendages halfway up the sides to represent the obtuse angles (Has), or else as a square bicepted diagonally, or a rectangle left open (probably to indicate the slope of the sides), and finally as two triangles facing in opposite directions but having a common base (which is in fact correct). . . .

In the course of substage IIB analysis becomes well-nigh complete. Thus, for example, the child is no longer content merely to locate the extremities of the arms of a cross or a star, but goes on to explore the recesses, and notices whether they are right-angled or acute. Nevertheless although capable of being carried to completion, this analysis remains empirical, so that in the case of complex shapes it fails to achieve a synthesis based on reasoning with which to coordinate the perceptual data. Only toward the age of 7 does the development of the operation proper enable deductive reasoning to direct exploration.

Mar (5;2) explores the rhombus and says of each side in turn: *"It's leaning, it's leaning, it's leaning, and this is leaning too."* He refuses to try drawing it but identifies it correctly among the visual models, and later draws it successfully. . . .

Ulr (6;11) turns the cardboard figures round in a clockwise direction: *"I've got the hang of it; I turn them like this and feel them."* The rhombus: *"It's almost like an egg, but it's pointed."* He draws it with four angles, each pair symmetrical, but makes the sides slightly convex. He is successful with the trapezium. Given a half-swastika he can neither draw nor identify it among a few models.

These few examples should be sufficient to show what a complete exploration amounts to so long as it lacks operational guidance. The child explores everything but keeps moving ahead all the time (*vide* Ulr's explanation of his method), never returning systematically to obtain a stable point of reference. . . . The responses obtained in stage III, to which we now come, show how this process of development is completed through the reversible coordination of the exploratory procedures.

Stage III. Operational Coordination. An operation may be defined as an action which can return to its starting point, and which can be integrated with other actions also possessing this feature of reversibility.

Now even within the limited sphere of simple actions typified by tactile-kinesthetic exploration, it is interesting to notice that as drawing or representation grows more exact so it begins to react upon the process of perceptual activity from which it first arose. As a result, perceptual activity becomes increasingly complex until by the age of 7 or 8 reversible coordination is achieved, though naturally, only in a very rudimentary form. Nevertheless, our experiments show that prior to this, reversible coordination cannot be achieved at all. At this level it takes the form of a systematic return to the point of departure in such a way as to group all the parts of a figure around one or more stable points of reference. The swastika (of whose notorious symbolic associations the children seemed quite unaware) constituted a particularly good demonstration of this point, because with such a figure it is essential to return to the starting point of exploration in order to coordinate the parts correctly. . . .

Tus (7;9) draws crosses, half-crosses, etc., correctly, Six-pointed star; explores the six arms, returning systematically to the center to coordinate them. He draws it correctly, checking each arm in turn by going back to the central reference point.

Swastika; "*I don't know what it is* (same method of exploration). *It has bends but I've already forgotten what they're like.* (First draws a horizontal line with pieces at each end placed at right angles, then makes another exploration.) *No, that's wrong. I felt it; it's the same all the time.* (He begins a fresh drawing which bit by bit approaches an accurate copy, except that one of the end pieces faces the wrong way.)" He is then shown a collection of models and recognizes all the figures. He points to the swastika and laughs: "*So that was it!*" . . .

The difference between these reactions and those of the previous level is obvious. The exploration is of course carried out by means of the same type of perceptual activity as at earlier stages. But this activity, instead of depending solely upon its own initial resources, is from now on directed by an operational method which consists of grouping the elements perceived in terms of a general plan, and starting from a fixed point of reference to which the child can always return. Now this reversible coordination is nothing more nor less than the form of equilibrium reached by the movements of exploration and imitative adaptation once they are related in such a way that every element explored is at the same time distinct, yet connected with all the rest in a single coherent whole. In the preceding stage these movements merely succeeded one another, earlier members of the series being obliterated by subsequent ones. At its present level therefore, the construction of shape is clearly quite separate from its perception and from its imitative or pictorial representation. It may be regarded as preceding both of these functions by a prior assembly of their data according to an anticipatory schema, which embodies the various possibilities of grouping afforded by different features, such as straight or curved lines, angles, parallels, order, and equal or unequal lengths. In other words, every perceived shape is assimilated to the schema of the [coordinated] actions required to construct it. This is why the pictorial image so accurately reflects the constructional process, in the same way as perceptual activity is governed by the operations. . . .

The Treatment of Elementary Spatial Relationships in Drawing. "Pictorial Space"*

In the first part of the preceding chapter we tried to show that perceptual space is organized in three successive stages. The first of these is based on topological, the second on metric and projective, the third on overall relationships bearing upon displacement of objects relative to one another.

We next endeavored to show that the transition from perception to mental representation—in other words, to notions which are no longer perceptual but imaginal—implied reconstruction of the relationships already grasped at the perceptual level, with functional continuity preserved between the new construction and the earlier perceptual one. For both constructions employ sense data by way of signs (perceptual pointers, or symbolic images of a pictorial nature) and both make use of movement and sensorimotor assimilation in the actual construction of the relationships to which they refer, i.e., to the "shapes" themselves.

Indeed, we have gone further in showing that at both levels the constructional process follows the same order of succession. It begins with topological relationships and only later arrives at Euclidean ones, with an interval of months or years between visual perception and mental representation based on haptic perception.

Now this sequence of events is in no way inevitable. In fact, so little does it correspond with generally accepted views with regard to representation of space that, so far as we know, it has never before been recognized. For this sequence could just as easily have been reversed. Perception having by degrees arrived at the level of projective and metric relationships (constancy of size and shape) and overall relationships (dimensions coordinated in terms of objective displacements), representational space might then have begun with general Euclidean coordination, passing to the development of projective relationships (perspective) and arriving at the abstraction of simple topological relationships last of all. There would be no inherent absurdity in imagining representational space developing in the reverse order to perceptual space, for this is the course followed by the historical development of formal geometry. The *Elements* of Euclid dealt only with metric geometry and similarities, projective geometry did not arise until the seventeenth century (Desargues), eighteenth century (Monge), and nineteenth century (Poncelet), while Analysis Situs or Topology is an entirely modern development.

It could thus have been the case that mental representation develops in the reverse order from actual perception, following instead the path traced out by formal analysis. . . .

It is therefore essential to find out whether, after some years interval, the reconstruction of conceptual space really does pass through the same phases as does construction of perceptual space. In particular, we must verify whether it is actually the case that the reconstruction of

*In collaboration with M. A. Morf and Mlle. B. Demetriades. [The following section is from Chapter II.]

topological relations at the level of mental imagery comes first, followed by the refashioning of metric and projective concepts, with construction of overall systems of coordinates and coordinated perspectives coming last of all.

Now such a verification is extremely difficult to carry through, and for a reason which, incidentally, explains why this alternative explanation has been so neglected. It is obvious that once the child can picture things to himself, he has at his disposal the achievements of perceptual activity and sensorimotor intelligence. In terms of perception he knows what distance is, what constitutes a straight line or a perspective or a metric figure such as a square. Nevertheless, he is unable as yet to translate these entities into thought or imagination the moment his efforts to do so are no longer supplemented by direct perception. Consequently, if in drawing or visualizing objects he can only avail himself of topological notions, then he will use them to supplement his existing projective or Euclidean perceptions. . . . In order to reconstruct the true formative order of conceptual space, it is essential not only to separate perception from representation, but within the realm of the latter to separate the element of imagery from the relationships actually grasped and applied. . . .

SPACE IN SPONTANEOUS DRAWINGS

The three principal stages characteristic of children's drawing once the level of mere scribbling is left behind are quite well known, and have been termed by Luquet* (1) synthetic incapacity, (2) intellectual realism, and (3) visual realism. It is these three stages of development that we shall endeavor to examine from the point of view of spatial representation.

Stage I. "Synthetic Incapacity." In his work, Luquet† cites the example of a boy aged 3;6 who draws a man in the shape of a large head to which are appended four strokes, two representing the arms and two the legs, as well as a small trunk separate from the limbs. The head contains two eyes, a nose and a mouth, but the latter is placed above the former. What is the meaning of such a drawing, which is quite typical of "synthetic incapacity," when one tries to interpret it in terms of the spatial representation of a 3–4-year-old child?

Obviously it cannot teach us anything about the child's perception as such, for when looking at the object the child sees the arms and legs attached to the trunk and not to the head, the mouth below the nose rather than above it. Why then does the drawing fail to correspond with the perception? [Piaget goes on to summarize Luquet's work and to suggest how the development of children's spontaneous drawings follow the same principles as those revealed in the experiments, reported below, on their drawings of geometrical figures. To save space we have had to cut this section radically.]

Briefly, if each of the most primitive topological relationships begin to be defined as soon as drawing of shapes really begins to appear, they nevertheless fail to be generalized when applied to complex structures.

*Luquet, *Le Dessin Enfantin*, p. 154, 1927.
†Ibid., Figure 85.

And these are just the structures children are most likely to produce in their spontaneous drawings; little men, animals, houses, etc. It can therefore be understood that at this stage pictorial space is necessarily lacking in Euclidean relationships of distance, proportions, and particularly in general axes in terms of three dimensions, as well as perspective relations, etc. But this predominance of topological features over all others, together with the failure to master these relationships themselves, is it really evidence of a law of pictorial space, similar to what we thought ourselves able to perceive in the development of perception? Or is it to be ascribed merely to technical ineptitude of a motor character? . . .

Stage II. "Intellectual Realism." We saw in Chapter I, through the experiments on haptic perception of shapes, that progress in exploration is followed very closely by pictorial synthesis. Here once again, as soon as the child becomes capable of such a synthesis he concentrates for a considerable period on one particular type of drawing, which has been described by all authorities and which Luquet analyzed extremely accurately. We refer of course to "intellectual realism" which consists in drawing not what the child actually sees of the object (this would be visual realism based on perspective) but "everything 'that is there.'"*
Consequently, there can be no question of ascribing the features of pictorial spatial representation apparent at this level to want of technical skill or lack of attention. On the contrary, we have here a schema that is in part deliberate and undoubtedly systematic and lasting. What then is its geometrical or spatial significance?

Without exaggerating their powers in any way, or crediting the children at this second level with any real geometry which they could formulate or develop, it is nevertheless possible to see that "intellectual realism" constitutes a type of spatial representation in which Euclidean and projective relationships are just beginning to emerge, though as yet in an inchoate form as regards their interconnections. But the topological relationships only sketched in at the previous stage are now universally applied to all shapes, and in the case of conflict prove stronger than more recently acquired ones.

. . . Intellectual realism marks the appearance of straight lines, angles, circles, squares, and other simple geometrical figures, though naturally without any exact measurements or proportions. But at this stage, their construction cannot in any way result in a comprehensive, Euclidean organization of space. On the contrary, the distinctive features of intellectual realism are as remote from such a structure as they are from the coordination of perspective viewpoints. For instance, when a child draws a profile head with two eyes, or a horseman in profile with two legs, or a group of houses seen from various points of view concurrently, his drawings are equally at odds with Euclidean as with projective structures. The object is distorted just as if it were plastic; distances and, consequently, coordinates play no more part in it than do perspectives.

Thus intellectual realism in children's drawings may be defined in geometrical terms by saying that while this particular structure derives its elements from concepts which are just becoming projective and

*Ibid., p. 224.

Euclidean, nevertheless its relationships are expressive of a representational space belonging to a level of understanding which is mainly topological and consists primarily of relationships of proximity, separation, order, surrounding, and continuity. Jumbling up different points of view necessarily implies the prior development of a certain number of projective relationships—though not necessarily coordinated with one another. And this point applies equally to the Euclidean properties of these constructions—they too are dealt with separately and are not yet integrated into a single whole. Thus with this kind of drawing, resemblance to the model amounts to no more than a crude sort of "homeomorphism"; that is to say, a point to point, term for term correspondence, remaining purely intuitive and qualitative without any coordination of projective or metrical relationships, although these begin to be separated out within the topological complex. This is why, at the level of intellectual realism, we find the tentative beginnings of the accurate copying of Euclidean shapes and a start made in the construction of projective relationships (see Chap. VI, on the straight line in projection), but as yet no coordination of perspective in the drawing as a whole (Chap. VIII), no understanding of proportions (Chap. XII), and especially a lack of coordinate systems (Chap. XIII) capable of application to a complex layout (Chap. XIV).

Stage III. "Visual Realism." Toward the age of 8 or 9, on the average, there finally appears a type of drawing which endeavors to take perspective, proportions, and distance into account all at once.

. . . Visual realism shows by its very contrast to intellectual realism the real nature of projective and Euclidean relationships as compared with topological ones. The latter proceed step by step, remaining tied to each shape considered as a single entity and not related to other shapes. On the other hand, projective relationships determine and preserve the true relative positions of figures, as distinct from the medley of viewpoints, pseudo-rotations, etc., found in the preceding stage. Finally, Euclidean relationships determine and preserve the relative or coordinate distances between figures. Hence in both cases, comprehensive systems replace empirical constructions, a development which is confirmed throughout the rest of this work.

THE DRAWING OF GEOMETRICAL FIGURES

Having broadly summarized the way pictorial space develops we must now try to analyze the construction of a few simple geometrical figures. For this purpose it is necessary to study the way these figures are drawn, both as regards their topological and Euclidean properties.

. . . What we wish to submit to detailed examination in the present section are the geometrical relationships themselves, together with the "abstraction of shape." From this standpoint, the copying of geometrical figures by children between 2–7 years yields results which are extremely important for the psychological theory of representational space. Although familiar with Euclidean figures such as circles, squares, triangles, rhombuses, etc., these children do not primarily express in their drawings the perceptual features of "good gestalt" which such figures present, but rather the topological characteristics of proximity, closure, surrounding, etc., as already seen in the case of haptic perception.

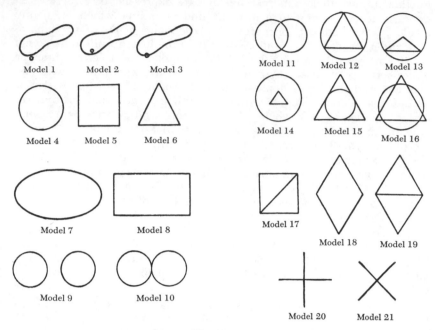

Figure 2

Figures to be copied by drawing (21 shapes).

Technique and General Results. We begin by asking each child to draw a man from memory, both to put the child at his ease and to give ourselves some idea of his natural drawing ability. Next we ask him to copy, either wholly or partly, the following series of models (see Figure 2). It will be noticed that some of the models emphasize topological relationships while others are simple Euclidean shapes. A third group combine both types of relationship (total or partial interlacing of Euclidean figures, etc.). . . .

In order to eliminate the element of skill and motor habits from spatial representation proper, we supplemented the task of drawing with another. The children were given a number of matchsticks with the heads removed with which to reconstruct the straight-sided models. Thus to form a square, twelve matchsticks are dealt out and if the task proves too difficult the number is reduced. This method often facilitates a better estimate of the child's intentions, though it is not without its disadvantages, for when the number of matches corresponds to the number of sides there is an element of suggestion, and when it is greater than the number of sides the construction is usually more difficult to execute than a drawing.

Finally, it should be noted that with very young children, who for the most part produce pure or only very slightly varied scribbles, it is necessary to scrutinize the drawings extremely closely to discover in them any possible influence of the visual model. It is also possible to introduce a motor stimulus by guiding the child's movements and then study a further copy made unassisted.

   Allowing for the special features deriving from the nature of the
experimental set-up, the results obtained are remarkably similar to
those of experiments in haptic perception.

   During stage o (at which no experiments in haptic perception were
possible) no purpose or aim can be discerned in the drawings. They are
simply scribbles (Figure 3) which shows no variation whatever the
model (up to the age of 2;6–2;11).

Figure 3

Pure scribble.

   Stage I can be divided into two distinct substages. In the first,
substage IA (up to 3;6–3;10), the scribbles appear to vary according
to the model being copied, open shapes being distinguished from closed
ones. Thus without being able to copy a cross or a circle, the child produces different types of scribble according to whether he is looking at
one or the other shape (see Figure 4). At the level of substage IB

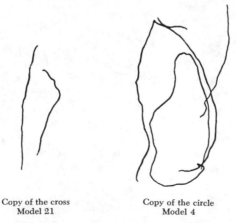

Copy of the cross   Copy of the circle
    Model 21   Model 4

Figure 4

Varied scribbles (substage IA).

(average 3;6–4 years) however, one can begin to speak of real drawings, though curiously enough it is only topological relationships which are indicated with any degree of accuracy, Euclidean relationships being completely ignored (see Figure 5). Thus the circle is drawn as an irregular closed curve, while squares and triangles are not distinguished from circles. That is to say, they are all shown as closed curves with perhaps an occasional symbolic suggestion, such as wavy lines jutting out to indicate angles, and so on. Only the open shapes are distinguished from these, like the cross (as two more or less intersecting lines, though not necessarily drawn straight). While there is no distinction as yet between straight-sided and curved figures, there is, however, a correct rendering of the topological properties of models 1–3, the closed figures with attendant small circles, and the enclosed figures are represented by means of enclosed circles also.

Stage II (starting about the age of 4) is marked by progressive differentiation of Euclidean shapes. At at level midway between substages IB and IIA curved shapes begin to be distinguished from straight-sided ones, though the latter still remain undifferentiated from each

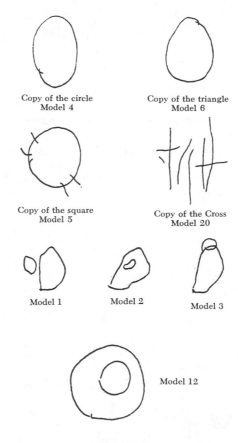

Copy of the circle
Model 4

Copy of the triangle
Model 6

Copy of the square
Model 5

Copy of the Cross
Model 20

Model 1   Model 2   Model 3

Model 12

Figure 5

Sample drawings from substage IB.

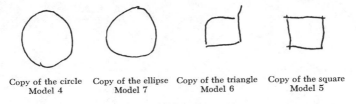

Copy of the circle   Copy of the ellipse   Copy of the triangle   Copy of the square
     Model 4   Model 7   Model 6   Model 5

Figure 6

Drawings midway between substages IB and IIA.

other (notably the square and the triangle), so that these figures are given straight sides but no regard is paid to how many. It is most frequently the rectangle which is reproduced correctly (for this intermediate stage, see Figure 6).

During substage IIA (Figure 7) shapes are gradually distinguished according to their angles, and even their dimensions. The square is separated from the triangle, as is the circle from the ellipse. Squares ʾnd rhombuses with diagonals (17 and 19) are reproduced with success, though not the ordinary rhombus (18). The two crosses are distinguished, marking the discovery of oblique lines. The circumscribed

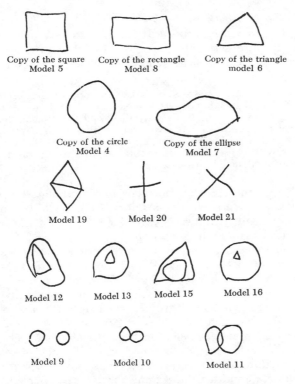

Copy of the square   Copy of the rectangle   Copy of the triangle
     Model 5   Model 8   model 6

Copy of the circle   Copy of the ellipse
     Model 4   Model 7

Model 19   Model 20   Model 21

Model 12   Model 13   Model 15   Model 16

Model 9   Model 10   Model 11

Figure 7

Sample drawings from substage IIA.

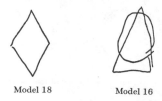

Model 18   Model 16

Figure 8

Sample drawings from substage IIB.

figures are drawn correctly enough as regards their actual shapes but the points of contact are not properly represented (as contrasted with the contiguous circles (10) which are successfully reproduced). Lastly, during substage IIB the rhombus is drawn correct and the circumscribed figures are gradually mastered, except for No. 16 (see Figure 8).

At stage III (from 6;6–7 years) all the problems are overcome, including the composite figures such as No. 16 (circle emerging from a triangle at three places).

It is thus apparent that the process of development is very similar to that which occurs with spontaneous drawing, with a constant bias in favor of geometrical shapes which are easier to draw than natural figures.

Stage 0, Simple Rhythmic Movements. Stage I, Beginnings of Discrimination (IA), then Appearance of Closed Curved Shapes (IB). Stage 0 is marked by pure scribbling, complete inability to close a line in order to form a shape, even with help from the experimenter.

Ther (1;9) and Mar (2;8) when asked to copy circles produced only shapeless scribbles. Their hands were then guided and made to describe four or five circles of 2–3 cm. They were then asked to repeat this unaided. The result was a mixture of vaguely straight lines with rhythmic in and out swerves, together with curved though never closed lines. Comparison of these drawings with those produced spontaneously fails to disclose any influence of the visual models whatsoever.

. . . Although the child cannot copy any figure at this stage, his scribbles, whether spontaneous or resulting from a fruitless attempt to copy a shape, present features of particular interest for the psychology of more advanced spatial representation.

The first of these has nothing whatever to do with space as such, even in the form of pictorial space. What it does relate to is the mode of operation of ideo-motor behavior, from whose subsequent stages will arise increasingly accurate drawings, and which will finally result in true operational construction of geometrical shapes. This is particularly the case if, as was suggested in Chapter I, shape is abstracted from the subject's own movements rather than from the object which occasions them. The primary feature of the children's drawings or scribbles is their simple rhythm. This very primitive expression of ability to draw is the product of a continual hither and thither movement of the hand across the paper, and it is from such a rhythmic pattern of movement that the first shapes come to be distinguished at stage I.

This point requires to be stressed because every mental mechanism passes from rhythm to "grouping" by means of regulatory processes which begin by coordinating the component parts of the initial rhythms and culminate, as an outcome of their increasing reversibility, in various types of groupings.* This is absolutely clear in the construction of geometrical shapes. It is on the basis of the rhythmic movement which the scribble constitutes that the rectilinear and curved shapes will later be gradually differentiated, through a series of perceptual-motor and intuitive regulatory processes. . . .

These rhythmic movements already contain in an undifferentiated state all those elements which will later go to make up the drawing of straight lines, curves, and angles, even though the child cannot yet extract or "abstract" these from the rhythmic complex. When the rhythmic action consists of a simple outward and return movement it results in a roughly straight line. As soon as the return fails to follow the outward path exactly or, after moving from left to right, the child's hand moves down the page and back again, acute, obtuse, or right angles result where these lines intersect. At the opposite extreme, when the child tries to cover the greatest possible area with his rhythmic movements, he ends up with a quasi-circular pattern like the threads of a ball of wool.†

Hence from these various drawings one could extract pieces of real straight lines, different angles, ellipses, and very near circles. The child Luc is in fact so near to possible differentiation at this point that for some moments after her hand has been guided in drawing a circle or a square she carries on with the curved or rectilinear shape, though she soon relapses into mere scribbling. But from the next stage on we shall encounter the beginning of real differentiations of shape. In fact, one of the main features of stage I is that after beginning with scribbles which, like those of stage o, remain similar irrespective of different visual models, the child can with very little practice, and especially after guidance by the experimenter, begin to vary the primary rhythmic movements in a way which tends toward a fairly clear reproduction, not of the model itself, but at least some aspect of it.

Rol (3;0) in his spontaneous scribbling at first produces the up and down and left to right lines at various angles, likewise the circular movements present in stage o. His hand is then guided in making discontinuous parallel lines, first horizontal and then vertical (the rhythmic movement is clearly interrupted at frequent intervals as against the original interlacing of the lines). The horizontal lines are nearly level, though not quite straight, whilst the verticals are not entirely parallel and slant at various angles though approximating to the vertical. As for the circles, after a little practice they result in purely circular movements which are kept up indefinitely according to a continuous rhythm without ever reaching a point of closure.

The topological shapes (1) and (2) (large closed curves with a small circle inside or outside) are clearly distinguished. The first is represented by a curved-in line, and at the spot where the small circle is located (clearly outside the boundary) Rol makes a small scribble which is accurately placed although shapeless. As for shape (2) (circle inside), the whole of the figure is represented by a tangle of circular sweeps without any distinction between the exterior curve and the enclosed circle, but clearly distinct from shape (1).

*Piaget, *The Psychology of Intelligence*, 1950, Conclusions.
† These rhythms, among others, have been studied by Krotzsch, *Rhythmus und Form in der freien Kinderzeichnungen* (Leipzig) 1917.

. . . One must draw a distinction between the way in which the child appears to divide the perceived figures into open or closed shapes, and the manner in which he tries to interrupt the rhythm of his own continuous movements in attempting to express the different features of each model. Now these two processes do not necessarily coincide, because in drawing a closed shape the child has first of all to interrupt his own motor rhythm and is thereby forced to recognize discontinuity of an objective, involuntary character.

The problem with which the child is faced actually amounts to producing a given shape through rhythmic movements which tend to oscillate between vague zig-zags and curved paths. Consequently, the child has to break this continuous rhythm even to draw a simple circle, while at the same time taking advantage of its bends and natural closures. [The children] form their circles from a number of spirals more or less intertwined, begun and ended so that the extremities cannot possibly meet, yet interrupted more sharply than in the case of a haphazard scribble. The circle is produced by interrupting the rotary movement and the failure to close it is entirely due to want of skill in drawing. This is shown by the enormous difference between the drawings of the circle and those of discontinuous lines or crosses where an open appearance is aimed at. But before passing on to the latter shapes it should also be noted that the squares, triangles, etc., are drawn, very similar to the circle, though there is some attempt at differentiation by way of inward and outward as against circular movements, and with more frequent breaks in the line (foreshadowing the appearance of straight lines and angles). . . .

In all these cases it is possible to see a distinct effort on the part of the child looking at the model to reproduce either the closed (circle, square, triangle, etc.) or open shape (parallels and crosses), by a species of extraction, on the basis of his own initial rhythmic movements. The features which tend thus to be extracted from these initial shapes are primarily topological. The feature which strikes the children first and foremost is whether a shape is open or closed, and also, as in the case of Rol (Models 1 and 2), whether there is anything inside or outside the closed contour.

[The] transition from [rhythmic] scribbling [to] varying the scribble according to particular features of the earliest definite shapes indicates the appearance of substage IB.

At this level are found the first properly closed circles, the first crosses with true intersection of lines, together with some appreciation of the relationships of inside and outside (Models 1–3). These begin to be clearly distinguished for the first time a little before the age of 4 on average, and this corresponds fairly closely to the developmental stages of spontaneous drawing. . . .

Fra (3;6). The men he draws may be described as of the "newt" type. That is, a head containing two very large eyes with everything else represented by long wavy lines. In response to the square he draws a well-formed ellipse (at one stroke and properly closed); the circles, triangles, rectangles, etc., produce the same result. The shapes circumscribing a figure (12, etc.) produce ellipsoids enclosing smaller ones. The contiguous circles are not made to touch, but the intersecting circles result in a chain of 10–12 circles with clearly defined links. The irregular closed figures with a small circle inside or outside them (1 and 2) are reproduced successfully, whilst the one with a small circle on the boundary (3) gives rise to an attempt correct in principle but technically a failure. Lastly, both crosses have four distinct arms but a complete cross (Red Cross on a white ground) is represented by a circle. . . .

Mal (4;4) is successful with shapes 1–3 and consequently with the circle, which is represented by a closed curve. But the square is shown in exactly the same way. The triangle is very similar but contains one almost straight side and two curved angles. The ellipse is not distinguished from the rectangle, except that the latter is drawn as an oval with a thin line at each end to mark the angles. The rhombus is drawn in the same fashion as the rectangle except that the thin lines are placed laterally to show the obtuse angles.

The separate, intersecting and contiguous circles are performed successfully, the last being separate, technically speaking, but joined together by means of a line to show their contiguity. The diagonalized square is represented by an elliptical figure having vague angles and bisected by a median. The upright cross, however, is reproduced quite successfully. . . .

Now why are the same children who can reproduce Models 1–3 unable to distinguish rectangles, squares, and triangles from circles and ellipses, and among the rectilinear shapes are only successful with the cross? Can this be explained by attributing it to a simple motor difficulty? For the circle does correspond to a single natural movement since it is curved, whereas squares and triangles are made up of straight lines which are harder to draw. Squares and triangles also require the deliberate location of these lines in a particular direction, according to a given angle, and their closure must be brought about by joining up a number of separate elements instead of merely following an unbroken line. But firstly, we have seen that on occasion the circle is constructed by means of composition, as with Ber [3;9] who adjusts the ends of two separate curves. Secondly, one finds just as many straight or nearly straight lines as curved ones among the children's spontaneous scribbles, and Gen [4;0] can even manage to draw a pine with a trunk and branches at right angles and thus disposes of all he needs to construct a square which he is nevertheless unable to copy. Finally, as regards deliberate combination of lines, the reproduction of Models 1–3 shows that this can be done. For to put a small circle astride the boundary of a closed shape seems just as complicated as adjusting four straight lines, although the children master the first of these tasks and fail with the second.

We may therefore take it that the problem is not one which depends upon mere motor ability, but rather on the method of composition itself, in other words, on the type of regulatory mechanism which will result in the construction of a shape on the basis of elements isolated from the original pattern. . . .

Thus it comes about that as soon as the rhythmic movement has been broken down into discrete elements, the very fact of connecting or not connecting them together results in relationship of proximity and separation, enclosure and open-ness, ordered succession and continuity. At this level drawing expresses in the simplest terms the relationships inherent [in] the actual organization of the earliest compositions, as distinct from the more complex types of organization which involve directions, such as parallels, angles, straight as against curved lines. In short, topological relationships are first in order of appearance because they are inherent [in] the simplest possible ordering or organization of the actions from which shape is abstracted.

In line with this, it is interesting to observe the success with which the upright cross is drawn, as compared with the failure to distinguish the squares, rectangles, and triangles from circles and ellipses. The explanation lies clearly in the fact that the cross is an open shape, no more than a couple of intersecting lines, whereas all the other shapes (including the tri-dimensional cross likened to a circle by Fra) are closed. As regards the closed shapes it would be incorrect to say that the circle and ellipse are copied accurately earlier than the square, or that the square is likened to the circle. It would be nearer the truth to say that at this stage children are not influenced in any way by the metrical and projective peculiarities of the circle. Although their perception of these figures naturally registers an accurate distinction between them, their representation retains only the topological characteristics; that is, the fact of their both being closed shapes. It is a "Jordan curve"; that is to say, the topological equivalent of a circle, and not a circle which these children are really drawing. For the same reason the triangle, square, etc., are also depicted by means of closed curves, since from this primitive point of view they have the same shapes as the circle. They become differentiated from the circle only very gradually, as in the case of Mal who represents the rectangle by a closed curved shape adorned with two wavy lines (see also his rhombus). Fran also shows the triangle by means of a similar rounded shape with a single wavy line added. . . . Even the ordinary upright cross is started off in this way by Ber (ellipsoid with long wavy lines) before being drawn correctly as an open figure with lines that cross.

The representation of figures containing inscribed shapes is similarly based on topological relationships. They are all drawn as closed curved figures containing other curved figures with no regard to accurate rendering of shape or size. As for the two large circles, separate, contiguous, and intersecting, whilst the last of these is shown correctly contiguity is most often indicated by one or two strokes connecting separate closed shapes. But oddly enough, these models present somewhat more difficulty than Models 1–3 although they are in fact their analogues, because while these last make up a single whole in each case, the large circles give the impression of two separate wholes as the thing to be reproduced.

In sum, topological relations universally take priority over Euclidean relations, which are not as yet differentiated from them. . . . It is obvious that in substage IB, as throughout stage I, pictorial representation does not in any sense correspond to the perceptual data at this level, for this data has long since acquired a projective and Euclidean character. Far from being something determined by perceptual [laws of] "good Gestalt," pictorial representation expresses in essence the basic requirements for the composition of figures: the active rather than the perceptual aspect of their construction. Similarly, the "abstraction of shapes" is not carried out solely on the basis of objects perceived as such, but it is based to a far greater extent on the actions which enable objects to be built up in terms of their spatial structure. . . .

Stage II. Differentiation of Euclidean Shapes. . . . In order to connect a given straight line with others at certain angles one has to take into account their inclinations, parallelity, numbers of lines, points of conjunction, and their distances. It can therefore be easily understood that the organization of this whole complex is vastly more complicated than simple topological relationships such as are found at stage I, or the angles taken as a whole, as in the processes of differentiation just described. This is why [one child] forms his rectangle simply of two lines which each contain an angle of 90°. But it is also the reason why so many shapes are incomplete, for the angles which the child first draws are merely closed by curved lines and cannot be coordinated with other lines.

These coordinations begin to take place during substage IIA as a result of various detail adjustments concerned mainly with sizes and inclinations of lines giving rise to differentiation of the square, the triangle, and the rectangle from each other, and the circle from the ellipse, etc.

Alb (4;1, advanced) produces accurate squares right away, but shows a process of gradual differentiation in the case of the triangle. He draws first a rectangle but with one of the short sides extended by an open acute angle outside the rectangle. This is followed by a trapezoid with two right, one obtuse, and one acute angle extended by a line at an angle to one side as in the previous figure. Then a similar figure is drawn, and finally a true triangle by closing the external angle and eliminating all the rest. The ellipse and rectangle are drawn correctly. The figures inscribed in circles begin to be more precisely defined. The points of contact with the circle are not shown but Alb points out his mistake accurately.

The rhombus is an open quadrilateral. The diagonal is not yet distinguished from the upright cross and the diagonalized square is fumbled. The diagonalized rhombus is shown as an ellipse with a median.

Bert (4;6) is successful with the circle, square, and rectangle. The triangle is also formed correctly straightaway, from an angle made with one stroke and closed with a straight line. The triangle inscribed in a circle (Model 12) is drawn after two attempts and so is the triangle inscribed but not touching the circle (Model 14), but Model 13, the triangle touching the circle at the base with the apex at the center, is a failure. Model 16, a triangle which protrudes from the circle at its extremities, is almost correct at first try and the diagonalized square is also a success. The rhombus results in many attempts, all unsuccessful. For instance, a three-sided square with a re-entrant angle in place of a fourth side (something like a bishop's miter), then a rectangle drawn obliquely, then a pentagon, then a square extended by a line at one corner, then a triangle, and so on. On the other hand, the diagonalized rhombus results in a square surmounted by a triangle, then two opposing triangles on a common base. The two types of cross are distinguished.

Bert was given a trial of the rhombus using matchsticks, but he was no more successful than he was with his drawings. He finishes up with the same open quadrilateral and is reduced to closing it with a fifth match, thus producing a pentagon. But the rhombus with a diagonal gives rise to two correct triangles.

Dav (5;2) is successful with the square, the triangle (through three separate lines later joined together), the ellipse, as distinct from the circle, and the rectangle. But he fails to indicate any points of contact in the case of the inscribed triangles (Models 12 and 13) and similarly so for the circles inscribed in triangles, though he renders their shapes correctly. He succeeds with the diagonalized square and distinguishes the two kinds of cross. But the rhombus results at the first attempt in a rectangle opening on a trapezoid, then by two opposed acute angles whose extremities are joined by a pair of parallel straight lines (without which it would have been correct!). After this he draws an acute angle and tries to locate its twin counterpart. "It

ought to be like the top half but I can't get it!" The diagonalized rhombus becomes a pentagon, also with an attempt to construct its counterpart. *"It ought
to be like this!"* then follows a triangle mounted on a square; but with an
awareness of having failed, he says *"Here it ought to be pointed as well."* . . .

These are the typical reactions of substage IIA. In the preceding
stage the global discrimination of angles and rectilinear sides was
achieved on the basis of curved shapes and elementary rhythmic movements. Subsequent to this there can be seen an effort at composition
based on the differentiated elements themselves. But as yet this process
of composition, which is the real mainspring in the "abstraction" of
shape, is not carried out by means of reversible operations, as it is
from stage III onward, but only by a series of tentative adjustments
governed by regulatory mechanisms simultaneously perceptual-motor
and inherent to imaginal intuition. Of these regulatory mechanisms
three in particular are worthy of mention.

The first is concerned with length and distance. The successful
drawing of the square and its discrimination from the rectangle, likewise beginning of an attempt to take account of equalities and irregu-
larities of length. Thus the square is given for equal sides, the circle
tends to have equal radii, the ellipse is slightly more elongated, and so
on. The belated appearance of these relationships in drawing is worth
noting. Although long since known in the realm of perception they
are only applied to graphic representation after a distinction has been
drawn between curved and rectilinear figures. . . .

Secondly, one should note the effort, not always successful, to apply to the Euclidean shapes themselves the relationships of contiguity
and separation which determine the position of figures inscribed within
others. So long as only indefinite closed shapes were involved we saw,
in relation to boundaries and enclosures, how precocious were these
topological relationships. But it goes without saying, that no sooner is
an attempt made to relate them to definite metrical shapes than they
have to be reconstructed on the Euclidean level. This is what we have
already seen in the case of the two circles (Models 9–11) noted above
and what we meet with again in all the various combinations of inscribed figures.

The third and most interesting process of regulation to examine at
this level is that of inclinations, previously unknown, but essential for
the discrimination of the triangle from the square, the two types of
cross, and especially for the construction of diagonals and the rhombus.
Indeed, up to substage IIA the child can neither represent the different
inclinations of the two crosses nor draw diagonals successfully. Because
of his inability to master inclinations he cannot even distinguish the
triangle from the square and vice versa. At this stage however, about
the age of 4;6 to 5;6 years, one sees a systematic effort to master the
drawing of inclinations in spite of considerable difficulties. In fact this
problem of inclinations will recur frequently in our studies, particularly, in connection with the horizontal and vertical axes themselves,
and with systems of coordinates, notions which are not worked out
until much later (not until 8–9 years). At this point, therefore, we must
make an important distinction. When it is a question of two completely
separate figures, ability to judge their inclination (e.g., to estimate
horizontals by finding some point of reference outside the figures them-

selves) is never in the least acquired prior to the appearance of operations, and such problems are only mastered after the age of 7. On the other hand, the kind of inclination we are dealing with at present and which begins to be constructed at this stage is purely internal to a single figure, for example, the inclination of one side of a triangle to the other. . . .

Although a few simple problems of inclination, such as angular coordination of sides belonging to the same figure or a pair of figures, are solved, the construction of the rhombus is by no means mastered at this stage. This is extremely interesting from the point of view of the abstraction of shape. The fact that *at least* 2 years work is required (as much as 3 according to Terman) in order to pass from copying the square to copying the rhombus . . . shows pretty clearly that to construct an Euclidean shape something more than a correct visual impression is required. Such a task really involves an extremely complex interplay of actions on the part of the subject.

Furthermore, the actions involved in drawing a rhombus are the same as are needed for its haptic exploration and recognition, and they recur in the technique of matchstick construction. This demonstrates that it is not mere skill in drawing, but abstraction of shape in general which is involved. What is the nature of the difficulty presented by the rhombus? It is a problem, besides that of closing the figure and drawing the straight sides, of adjusting their tilt to certain acute and obtuse angles. But over and above this, what is most difficult to achieve is the symmetry between the two triangles from which the rhombus is formed. For this involves reversing the relative order of the parts lying each side of the central axis.

Now these are precisely the relationships whose construction could be followed step by step through the successive levels which we have so far examined. At substage IB the rhombus is little more than a closed curve, after having been confused with the wandering open lines by which the children of substage IA distinguish shapes from spontaneously produced scribbles. But occasionally in substage IB the rough oval representing the rhombus is provided with a threadlike appendage denoting an acute angle. At the level midway between substages IB and IIA the rhombus acquires angles and straight sides though the slope of these cannot be controlled. Thus it is confused either with the square and rectangles or else with the triangle. Nevertheless, the acute angles together with the inclinations they govern are suggested in various ways, such as by lengths of straight line running from one corner of the square at an angle of 45°, or a triangle (beaks, hats, etc.) placed over the square. Alternatively, the obtuse angles may be indicated by means of little triangles or even curves (ears, etc.) on two sides of the square or rectangle. (For all these stages, see Figure 9.)

Finally, at substage IIA the child begins to attempt to represent the inclination itself, from which result the various trapezoids, pentagons, and the like, as the fruits of this activity. Similarly, figures are left open, not intentionally of course, but for lack of being able to close them in a way consistent with the desired inclination. Now what is missing at this stage? What would enable the rhombus to be mastered, after allowing for the fact that the problem of slopes has already been overcome in other figures? The answer is symmetry, which necessitates

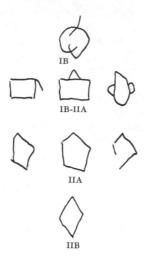

Figure 9

Development of drawings of the rhombus from stage IB to stage IIB.

the inversion of order. "It must be like the top," says Dav speaking of the lower half of the rhombus, "but I can't manage it!" That is the reason why most of the children succeed with the rhombus on a horizontal axis, for this axis enables them to grasp the reversed order more easily whereas the ordinary rhombus is as yet beyond their powers.

During substage IIB the rhombus is at last conquered and the problems of contact and separation, external and internal in circumscribed figures, are also resolved, though still by adjustments rather than by instantaneous organization. . . .

The analogy with exploration described in Chapter I is clearly evident, especially with Mar's remark when successively discovering the four sides of the rhombus: "It's leaning, it's leaning, it's leaning, and this one's leaning too!" Adjustment of the inclination according to the reverse order of the symmetries, such is the principle underlying these achievements. But with the more difficult figures it is still a matter of trial and error adjustments rather than operational anticipation.

Stage III and Conclusions. It will be recalled that our study of exploration in conditions of haptic perception indicated stage III as starting at the point where the movements through which the shape is abstracted could be defined as operational. That is, as being flexible and reversible enough to return constantly to the point of reference on which the subsequent construction is based.

. . . The development of geometrical drawing has enabled us to study in detail the actual problems posed by the abstraction of shape, in terms of the interesting theory proposed by Brunschvicg; namely, that the origin of the idea of spatial form was to be found in the effort to follow the contour made by a person drawing an object. But it must be stated categorically that in drawing, even more than with tactile-kinesthetic exploration in haptic perception, the mental abstraction of spatial form is not just a matter of extracting the morphological features of an object through the activity of the subject, even though such a process does in fact take place—and acts as a constant stimulus to the corresponding physical construction.

Geometrical space is not simply a "tracing" made over a simultaneously developed physical space, temporarily corresponding with it point for point. The abstraction of shape actually involves a complete reconstruction of physical space, made on the basis of the subject's own actions and to that extent, based originally upon a sensorimotor, and ultimately on a mental, representational space determined by the coordination of these actions. This is the main conclusion to be drawn from the study of drawing, whether it is a question of topological relationships or Euclidean relationships. From beginning to end of the process just recapitulated, all these structures are invariably derived from the general coordination of physical actions.

. . . The reconstruction of shapes is not just a matter of isolating various perceptual qualities, nor is it a question of extracting shapes from the objects without more ado. The reconstruction of shapes rests upon an active process of *putting in relation*, and it therefore implies that the abstraction is based on the child's own actions and comes about through their gradual coordination. . . . ·

The Study of Knots and the Relationship of "Surroundings"*

The relation of order exemplified by three elements arranged in a series ABC also entails a specific relationship expressed by the word "between." Thus B is "between" A and C, and at the same time "between" C and A. . . . Now the relation "between" is one particular instance of the more general relationships of "surrounding." These are, of course, elementary spatial relationships, just as much as proximity, separation, or order. Indeed, as regards the construction of space, they are even more important, since it is most probably these relationships which lead the child by the most direct route, to differentiate and build up the three initial topological dimensions. . . .

It is therefore our next task to examine these relationships of surrounding (or intertwining), the mental analogues of the action of surrounding, in the same way that we have analyzed the relationship of order; namely, in terms of the action of following or assembling one element after another. . . .

Moreover, certain types of behavior, such as surrounding a stick with a ring, have already evolved at the sensorimotor level,† which would tend to make such tasks too easy by the age of 4 or 5.

It so happens that in the case of "surrounding," there is one area in

---

*In collaboration with Mlle. G. Ascoli, Mme. J. Halperin-Goetschel, and M. A. Morf. [The following section is from Chapter IV.]

†Not without difficulties however. The children begin by simply pushing the ring against the stick, as if it would encircle the stick merely by contact. See *The Origins of Intelligence in the Child*, p. 320 (Obs. 174), 1953.

which perceptual relationships have not yet been developed and hence ideally suited for studying the main features of representation. This is the province of knots, which possess the added advantage of having been the subject of extremely detailed geometrical analysis. It will be recalled that the most elementary branch of geometry, topology, or analysis situs, does not deal with straight lines, distances, angles, and the like, but only with forms which are elastic and capable of deformation, though without breaks or overlapping. The basis of topology as a branch of geometry is formed by the operation of "homeomorphisms" or point-to-point, bicontinuous correspondences (i.e., correspondences which retain unchanged the proximities, separations, and in the case of lines, the relative order). One of the types of correspondence studied by topologists in this connection is precisely that covered by the theory of knots.* From the standpoint of mental development, the knot is something which the child learns to form at an early age and it is therefore eminently suited to psychogenetic investigation. The value of such an approach is considerably enhanced by the fact that, in addition to their not originating perceptual metric relationships, knots do not form visual or sensorimotor gestalten, and in consequence their transformations only come to be understood by degrees.

In this chapter we therefore propose to study children's responses to the very simplest kinds of knot, the "overhand" knot (an ordinary single-looped knot), laying particular stress on the idea of surrounding (the relationship of enclosure or intertwinement) and homeomorphic correspondence or noncorrespondence between simple shapes such as may be formed with an ordinary piece of string. For example, a circle, a figure of eight, a pseudo-knot, left and right overhand knots, taut or slack according to circumstances.

Technique and General Results. The technique employed is simple in the extreme. To start with, the child is shown an ordinary simple knot (see Figure 10) tied tightly and asked to state what it is, solely

Figure 10

to ensure that he understands the meaning of the word. He is then asked to make a similar knot.

(1) If the child cannot tie a knot he is asked to form one round a thick stick or bobbin and his method of learning studied. If he cannot succeed in this after a few attempts a knot is formed slowly whilst he watches and he is then asked to imitate the actions he sees. If this also fails, he is shown a piece of string in two colors (half blue, half red) and the process is explained as a story ("the red goes underneath, then on top, then inside," etc.) as the action gradually unfolds, after which he is invited to do the same.

(2) Once the knot has been formed, the child is shown one which is

*A knot is a closed curve lacking multiple points; that is to say, with no intermediate breaks. See L. Godeaux, *Les Géométries*, Paris, p. 188.

similar in pattern but more loosely tied so that it is enlarged or expanded
(Figure 10) and is asked if it is the same knot as the first. He is asked to
copy this second knot and is again asked if it is like the first, "if it was
made the same as the earlier one, etc." We next ascertain whether the
child knows what will happen if the two ends of the slack knot are pulled.

(3) The same knot is expanded still further in such a way that the
two wings or half-loops become clearly visible in the pattern used conventionally to represent the "clover" in geometry textbooks (Figure 11).

Figure 11

The same questions are then put once again. . . .

(4) The child is shown a "left-hand clover" (Figure 11) and a
"right-hand clover" (Figure 12) and asked if the knots are identical.

Figure 12

He can either judge this by eye or by running his finger over the string
from one end to the other. The problem may be rendered a little clearer
by threading a bead on the string and asking what course it will follow,
or by pretending that the string is a pipe inside which there is an ant
crawling from one end to the other. If the child still fails to appreciate
the difference between the two knots, he is asked to push the bead from
one end of the string to the other, or to copy the knots. . . .

(5) Using similar methods the children are asked to compare a true
and a false "overhand" (the false "overhand" is a pseudo-knot, homeomorphic with the circle when the ends of the string are joined, see
Figure 13).

Figure 13

(6) In the same way, the children are shown what we will term,
for the sake of brevity, a false and a true figure of eight. The false
figure of eight is a simple "overhand" knot whose ends are joined together

Figure 14

and arranged in such a way that the knot separates two loops which appear identical (Figure 15). The true figure of eight is, of course, homeomorphic with the circle (Figure 14).

Figure 15

(7) The children are shown two pairs of circles made of string, the first pair being merely superimposed, the second pair intertwined (Figure 16), and are asked what would happen if the two opposite sides

Figure 16

of the two loops were pulled in different directions (obviously, the first pair will separate and the second pair will remain linked together).

The reactions to these questions can be divided into the same three stages as were found to hold in previous chapters. The first stage, below the age of 4, is taken up by the learning of simple knots. Among the social strata from which our subjects are drawn, children learn to tie knots around the age of 4, on average. It is obviously interesting, however, to investigate how younger children approach the task of copying the model knots which they are shown, for in this respect a knot is directly comparable to the drawings of Chapter II or the ordered series of Chapter III. It was found that during substage IA the children could not copy knots, despite being able to watch a visible model or listen to a verbal explanation, because they cannot grasp the principle of intertwinement. Thus they either wind one end of the string round the other, but without managing to insert either end in the loop; or else they insert one end in a half-loop without superimposing it. In neither case is there the necessary "surrounding" and, consequently, no knot.

During substage IB the children learn how to copy the knots but are unable to follow the various sections of a slack knot with one finger, nor are they able to distinguish true from false knots. At stage II they can reproduce the simple taut knot (1) because they now understand intertwinement and are able to distinguish between complete loops and half-loops* when these are not superimposed. But at substage IIA they cannot yet perceive the identity of two similar knots when one is taut and the other left slack and hence expanded (2), nor when it is arranged in the shape of the clover (3). Neither can they distinguish false from true knots at sight.

At this stage, therefore, we find a simple mental correspondence between a pair of taut knots, or between a pair of loose knots. But this is lost as soon as the situation alters through the tightening or slackening of one of the knots, even though each of the pair is homeomorphic.

During the subsequent period (substage IIB), the children recognize the homeomorphism between the taut (1) and the slack (2) knots, but not between these and the knot arranged as a clover (3), nor can they distinguish false from true knots at sight. As soon as they have discovered the identity of taut and slack knots, however, they are able to follow the path of the string continuously, whereas at the previous substage they simply jumped from one loop to the next.

After a transitional level, midway between substage IIB and stage III, in which the right answers are only forthcoming after trial and error, stage III proper appears (between 7–7;6 years). At this point the correspondence between knots (1), (2), and (3) is generally recognized with the result that these become reversible, and thereby operational. It necessarily follows that all these knots, whether taut or slack, are distinguished correctly from the false overhand knot, just as the false figure of eight is distinguished from the true one. Moreover, these children are able to distinguish left from right overhand knots and to understand that when pulled tight they do not produce the same knot.

Stage I. Learning to Tie Knots. The first stage lasts up to the age of 4 on average but includes a number of children aged 4–5. None of these children yet understands how a knot is formed. At substage IA, of which a few examples are given below, the child cannot even tie a knot after he has watched it formed before his eyes. . . .

What is the meaning of this failure in motor activity, from the geometrical point of view? Simply this; a string, considered as a linear series, is composed of consecutive portions or one-dimensional "surroundings" (such that if B is "between" A and C, it is actually surrounded by A and C along one dimension only). But the knot which has to be tied with this same piece of string is a three-dimensional "surrounding," a complex of intertwinements. Although children have a clear idea of three dimensions at this age, nevertheless the transition from a single to a three-dimensional surrounding presents an obvious difficulty when it occurs through the agency of one and the same object. As proof of this we have the inability of Gab and Jac to follow slack knots with their fingers while at the same time following a continuous path when they get to the point where one part of the knot passes over another, likewise their failure to distinguish visually between intertwined and superimposed circles.

Stage II. Partial Intuitive Correspondence Between Knots Which Can Be Reproduced in Practice. From the very beginning of this stage

*We term "half-loops" the circles made by the string when the ends are not twisted one over the other.

the child can copy a knot which he can see, and without receiving any help from the experimenter. But at the start, in substage IIA, the knot needs only to be tightened or loosened a little for it to become unrecognizable. In addition, the child is frequently unable to tell a false from a true knot. . . .

The reason for these difficulties is easy to see. To start with, let us remind ourselves that at any age knots are troublesome things to deal with mentally, for they do not give rise to strong visual patterns or tend to produce metrical perceptions. Consequently there is always some difficulty in trying to visualize the changes which would ensue from tightening or slackening a knot. . . .

The outstanding thing about the various shortcomings most typical of substage IIA is their identical character. In the first place, although these children are able to reproduce the taut (1) and slightly loose (2) knots (the last sometimes only after hesitation, though all children succeed ultimately) they nevertheless fail to recognize their identity. In the second place, and this is most likely part and parcel with the first shortcoming, they cannot trace the course of the string whilst respecting its continuity. Even in the case of a partly slackened clover knot (3), they leave the section of string passing underneath as soon as they arrive at the intersection, and go straight on to the upper part without considering the true order of succession.

These two reactions obviously derive from the selfsame cause; namely, that though these children have been able to achieve a three-dimensional surrounding on the plane of action (after overcoming the difficulties we encountered in stage I), they cannot achieve it on the representational plane, nor even in that semiactive, semirepresentational form of behavior consisting of tracing the course of an already formed, visible knot with one's finger. . . .

This brings us to the core of the problem of homeomorphism. In studying how the child actually formed knots we saw that his difficulties arose when he tried to pass from a one-dimensional surrounding (one part of the string passing through the loop formed by the other two parts) via the agency of one and the same linear object. But no sooner has this particular problem been overcome in practice and the child has learned to tie a knot, than the paradoxical situation arises, in which the knot being placed on the table and loosened slightly, the child no longer recognizes it, is no longer able to distinguish the surroundings in terms of the three dimensions (above-below, left-right, before-behind). And when he endeavors to trace them through with one finger, he even loses track of the sequential order of the different sections (i.e., the one-dimensional surrounding). In other words, he overlooks the relationship of "between" linking up each section of the knot according to its relative proximity. We find that where one part of the string passes beneath another, the child loses track of the real order of succession, the true proximity of neighboring parts, and passes over into another part of the knot which is not actually adjacent to the first. . . .

We do not have to look very far to see the reason for this shortcoming of perception and imagination. It is entirely because the child is unable to anticipate the result of tightening or slackening the knot he is studying that these momentary, static perceptual proximities tend to outweigh the real, permanent proximities which remain unaffected by such actions. . . . And in turn, the lack of a mental picture results in his being unable to trace the course of the intertwined string with one finger.

At bottom, it is because the underlying ideas are still far too perceptual in character and have not yet achieved a sufficient degree of flexibility. More precisely, the child's ideas are still tied to static configurations and are unable to grasp dynamic transformations, remaining centered on a particular shape rather than being decentrated, in the sense of being linked together in an imaginary reconstruction. . . .

Stage III. Operational Correspondence Between Simple Knots. Right- and Left-hand "Clover" Knots Distinguished.

Gel (7;10). Clover knot (3): *"It's the same as the earlier ones but it's not pulled tight yet*—(Shown left- and right-handed "clovers.") Are they alike?— *No, different; there it goes on top and there underneath*—How can you make them alike?—(Without saying a word, Gel turns one of them upside down, then passes the string on top and beneath)—If they're pulled will the knots be the same?—*No, one will be on top and the other will be underneath*— And these (true and false figures of eight)?—*There it'll come undone; there, you can't undo it, it'll stay put."*

. . . The child now begins to exploit simple perceptual notions as a basis for logical thought. The shape he perceives is sustained in thought by anticipation of the future outcome of tightening or slackening the knot, of spreading out the loops or bringing closer together parts that are widely separated, and so on. In a word, the perceived figure is located within a framework constituted by all its potential transformations, in terms of motor activity or its mental representation. . . .

In short, in the course of stage II, the actions originated at stage I become internalized as mental images and little by little are linked together as "articulated" ideas. Following this, as the action becomes entirely mental, a kind of picture of the three-dimensional surrounding which constitutes a knot appears in the form of the operation proper. Then and only then do the partial and incomplete notions which result from imagining the movements of contraction or expansion of the knotted string begin to play their full part in the attempt to establish correspondences between the various shapes. Whatever these imaginary contractions or expansions may be, from now on the child comprehends the fact that they leave the basic operation of "surrounding" unchanged. No matter what happens to the perceptual pattern, this fundamental relationship is preserved intact through all the seeming modifications which the knot undergoes, and it can be obliterated only by the reverse action of untying the knot. . . .

The adjacent parts of two knotted strings remain adjacent and the separated parts remain separated, the relative proximities of near and distant parts remain unaltered, the surroundings reapper unchanged in corresponding knots. Such is the principle which underlies the establishment of correspondences enabling children of this stage to judge two knots equivalent. A correspondence of this nature which embraces only topological relationships and does not involve metric relations, nor proportions (similarities), affinities or projections, is a purely qualitative homeomorphism based on operations which are concrete and not yet formal or abstract. . . .

The Idea of Points and the Idea of Continuity*

We saw how toward the age of 7, both linear and circular order become reversible and give rise to true operational correspondence. And we have just seen how this notion enables knots to be understood as simple homeomorphs. . . . To conclude this brief survey of the psychology of elementary topological relations, we intend to examine the development of the notion of continuity, from the form in which it first appears to that which it exhibits when formal thought emerges at the age of 11 or 12.

Considering the subtlety with which mathematicians have demonstrated the complexity of this notion, . . . it may seem somewhat absurd to embark on a problem of this kind by studying children. [But] the mind does not pass direct from perceptual notions of continuity to abstract schemata evolved for the purpose of formulating such a notion. On the contrary, to arrive at reciprocal schemata of the sort required in order to reduce a line or a surface to points and then reassemble the points to form a line or surface once more, necessitates the development of a complete mental structure.

Thus it will at once be seen that an examination of the ideas of point and continuity is an essential counterpart to the earlier studies, and one which can on no account be omitted from a study of [childish] topological conceptions. The relationships of proximity and separation really involve no more than extremely general notions of a type prerequisite to any operational concept of space, including topological relations themselves. In contrast to this, the relationships of order and surrounding result in true operations, such as those of "positioning" producing ordered series (logical addition) and the operations of establishing correspondences giving rise to simple qualitative homeomorphisms (logical multiplication).

Both these types of operation, however, only involve relationships which are extensions of proximity and are therefore merely the analogues of seriation in the field of logical relations. It still remains to discuss both the operation of subdivision which supersedes the original perceptual "separations," and the operation of reuniting the separated elements. In other words, the sublogical counterparts of the logical operations concerned with separating and reuniting classes.

Now the process of reducing what is regarded as continuous to a series of adjoining points and re-creating an operational continuity on the basis of these points, a process thereby identified as one of reversible combination, is the most advanced type of the operations involved in separating and reuniting enclosed parts. Hence the development of the notion of continuity is the necessary accompaniment to the development of operations concerned with order and surrounding, and it is therefore essential to the completion of a qualitative concept of topological space.

Now the growth of the idea of continuity does not depend upon what the child learns at school to anything like the degree that might be

---

*In collaboration with Mlle. U. Galusser. [The following section is from Chapter V.]

imagined. This is shown by the fact that it is possible to trace out, step by step, a more or less parallel process of development for the ideas of point and continuity, and those dealing with atoms and physical objects in the child's conception of the external world. Thus in watching a lump of sugar dissolve in a glass of water, he passes from the perception of visible though gradually diminishing particles to the idea of invisible grains, and finally to that of ultimately indivisible particles.* Similarly, with a line or a figure, the child proceeds from the notion of parts that are separable but still perceptible, to that of invisible parts, smaller than but similar in principle to the former, and finally to the idea of its being reduced to ultimate and indivisible points. The only difference between these two processes is that to the child's way of thinking, physical points or atoms still possess surface and volume, whereas mathematical points tend to lose all extension. . . .

Technique and General Results. The children were questioned on four main topics.

(1) To introduce the main problem of finding out how the child envisages the subdivision of a line or figure into its ultimate constituents, we began by asking a question which has already been used by Rey† . . . : a square is drawn on a sheet of paper and the child is asked, "here, right next to it, draw the smallest square that can possibly be drawn, one so small that nobody could make one smaller" (these instructions may be amplified, but all gestures indicative of size are avoided). The child is then asked to draw, "the biggest square that can be drawn on this sheet of paper" (a separate sheet). . . .

(2) The second problem examined is that of subdividing some figure (square, circle, triangle, etc.) or a straight line and seeing how far this process is carried. In this case, the method of bisection can be utilized. Shown a straight line, the child is asked to draw another half its length, then a half of the half, and so on. When he arrives at lines so short that he cannot draw them any shorter, the child is asked whether he cannot "continue in his mind": "You can do a lot of things in your mind, can't you? If one of your schoolmates is better than you at a game you can still beat him in your mind, even though you can't really? Well then, try and imagine you are going to go on cutting up this little bit without stopping. What is going to be left in the end?" If the child answers "A short line" he is told, "Very good. But go on cutting up this short line in your mind. What are you left with right at the end?"

To help the child understand the idea of indefinite subdivision one can ask him to cut a rubber band in half, following which, one of the cut halves is stretched and cut again. In this way one can show that however small the residual portion, it can always be thought of as expanded and therefore capable of being subdivided still further. . . .

(3) The third question concerns the shape of the end product of the subdivision. Basically it is a question of ascertaining whether or not this final term is a point, and whether or not this point will have a shape. Hence, if the child uses the word "point," one must ask him whether the

---

*See Piaget and Inhelder, *Le Développement des Quantités chez l'enfant,* Chapters IV–VI.

†André Rey, "Le problème des 'quantités limites' chez l'enfant," *Rev. suisse de Psychol.,* 2: 239–249.

point has a shape, and if so, what the shape is (for the younger children the residual point of a square remains a square, that of a triangle is triangular, and so on). In the case of a straight line he is asked whether it is still a length or whether it has no real shape at all. The child often asserts that at the end of the process of subdivision there will be "nothing left at all"; in this event he is asked what is left "just before nothing at all" which forces him to consider the shape of the point once more.

(4) The fourth question is concerned with the re-creation of the line or figure out of its ultimate elements. Can a line or a surface be conceived of as a collection of points? In dealing with this problem it is necessary to supplement the verbal questions by having the child draw a series of points and then insert extra points between them, or to insert as many points as possible in between two limiting points with the aim of finding out whether he thinks they will eventually form a line. . . .

The first period (stages I and II combined) lasts until about 7 or 8 years. With respect to the first question it is marked by the child's being unable to draw either the smallest or the largest possible square, since he lacks an operational schema of seriation. When trying to break up a line or a surface (question 2) he can only make a very limited number of subdivisions (many children cannot understand the meaning of "the half of a half"), and in question 3 they end up with so-called ultimate elements of a distinctly perceptible size which, curiously enough, are of the same shape as the original, the final terms of the square being square, those of the line being lines, and so on. Finally (question 4), subdivision and reassembly are both irreversible. The line is not regarded as a collection of points and if one has been rash enough to break up the short sections into points, these are fated to remain forever discontinuous.

Stage III covers the period from 7 or 8, up to 11–12 years. The first question, that of largest and smallest squares, is now solved as a result of the anticipatory schema formed by grouping the operations concerned with seriating items, so that one finds a greater flexibility in the treatment of subdivision (question 2). But though the child is now prepared to admit the possibility of a large number of subdivisions he does not regard them as being infinite. Moreover (question 3), these procedures never rise above the level of concrete operations, they are never generalized beyond the finite, beyond visible or tangible size. While the ultimate elements are no longer thought of as isomorphic with the original whole, as they were in stage II, their shape is regarded as dependent upon the particular mode of subdivision and they are never envisaged as an infinite number of points without surface area. Lastly (question 4), construction of the whole out of its constitutent elements is now seen as the reverse counterpart to subdivision, but this goes no further than a purely intuitive continuity, so that the child finds himself in a dilemma, since he cannot reconcile the discontinuous nature of the points which are to be reunited, with the continuity possessed by the structure which results from this reunion.

Last of all, at stage IV (beginning around 11–12 years) thought is liberated from the quasi-perceptual notions of the earlier stages, where the concrete operations were caged in under the restrictive conditions of actual drawing and handling. The operation of arranging items in series (question 1) no longer presents any difficulty and subdivision (question 2) is conceived of as unlimited. As for the structure of the ultimate elements (question 3), from now on this is seen to be entirely independent of the shape of the original figure or the mode of subdivision. The points or "spatial atoms" no longer possess either shape or surface and, most important of all, they are all homogeneous, whether they belong to a line or any sort of figure. The synthesis of the whole is now the reverse product of unlimited subdivision (question 4), although the children still seem to find a contradiction between the discontinuous points and the continuous whole formed from them. A number of children arrive independently at the idea of a term for term correspondence between the series of points forming a line and the series of numbers considered as infinite (though naturally, without having the least inkling of the concept of irrational numbers to fill intervening spaces). . . .

The Coordination of Perspectives*

We saw in Chapter VI† that perspective appears at a relatively late stage in the child's psychological development. In this respect our experiments merely confirm what had already been demonstrated through direct observation of children's drawing. According to Luquet "intellectual realism" is not superseded by "visual realism" until about the age of 8 or 9. Not until then does the child draw things "as he really sees them," according to his perspective as an actual observer. . . .

The question therefore arises as to why the child is so slow to master simple perspective relations and only does so when he is able to coordinate a number of possible points of view. The answer is that a perspective system entails his relating the object to his own viewpoint, as one of which he is fully conscious. Here as elsewhere, to become conscious of one's own viewpoint involves distinguishing it from other viewpoints, and by the same token, coordinating it with them. Thus it is evident that the development of perspectives requires a comprehensive, global construct, one which enables objects to be linked together in a coordinate system, and viewpoints to be linked by projective relations corresponding to various potential observers.

The experiments performed thus far have dealt only with perspective or projection for successive positions of a single object, whether seen by the child or by an imaginary observer. We must now proceed to examine the perspective of a group of objects as envisaged by an observer from different positions, or alternatively by a number of observers. The experiments which follow have two aims. Firstly, to study the construction of a global system linking together a number of perspectives. Secondly, to examine the relationships which the child establishes between his own viewpoint and those of other observers. These experi-

*In collaboration with Mlle. Edith Mayer. [The following section is from Chapter VIII.]
†[Chapter VI is not included in this volume.]

ments involve multiple perspectives of the sort which it is possible to imagine when standing before a mountain massif, or group of mountains which can be seen from various different positions.

The problem is therefore no longer one concerned simply with changes in apparent shape and size of objects, but mainly with the positions of objects relative to one another and to various observers (or the same observer in different positions). Hence we shall be concerned chiefly with the relations of before-behind, left-right, relations of within two of the three dimensions operative in imaginary perspectives.

. . . In a system of topological relations, the expressions "to the left" or "to the right" can only refer to alternative directions of travel along a linear series. They remain purely arbitrary so far as the viewpoint of an observer is concerned (this is well illustrated by the way in which some of the younger children reverse a series as if it were seen in a mirror). In a projective system, however, "left" and "right" are relative to the viewpoint of the observer, and the type of problem posed by the perspectives of a group of mountains involves several objects and several observers at the same time. It will be seen to depend, therefore, on a global projective system directly comparable to the type of coordinate system required in constructing maps or plans in the realm of Euclidean geometry.

Technique and General Results. A pasteboard model, one meter square and from twelve to thirty centimeters high, was made to represent three mountains (see Figure 17). From his initial position in front of the model (*A*) the child sees a green mountain occupying the foreground a little to his right. The summit of this mountain is topped by a little house. To his left he sees a brown mountain, higher than the green

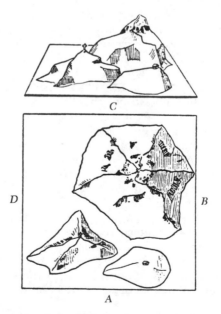

Figure 17

The three mountains.

one and slightly to its rear. This mountain is distinguished not only by its color but also by having a red cross at the summit. In the background stands the highest of the three mountains, a grey pyramid whose peak is covered in snow. From position C (opposite position A) a zigzag path can be seen running down the side of the green mountain, while from position B (to the right of the model, relative to position A) a little rivulet is seen to descend the brown mountain. Each mountain is painted in a single color, except for the snow cap of the grey mountain, and the only reference points are those described.

The children are also shown a collection of ten pictures, measuring 20 × 28 cm. These represent the mountains seen from different viewpoints and are painted in the same colors as the model. They are clearly distinguishable and are large enough for particular features such as the cross, the house and the snow-capped peak to be easily visible. The children are also given three pieces of cardboard, shaped and colored the same as each of the mountains, and these may be arranged to represent the mountains as seen in a given perspective.

Finally, the apparatus includes a wooden doll 2 or 3 cm. in height. The head of the doll is a plain wooden ball with no face painted on it so that the child can ignore the doll's line of sight and need only consider its position. This doll is put in a number of different places and the child's task is to discover what perspective the doll will "see" in each of the different positions. It is not the child who moves around the group of mountains—except to check his answers—but the doll which is supposed to be doing the traveling. The child has the problem of trying to imagine, and to reconstruct by a process of inference, the changes in perspective that will accompany the doll's movements, or the different positions which the doll must occupy to suit the various perspectives.

For this purpose we employed three separate but complementary methods of questioning the child. Firstly, the child is given the three pieces of shaped cardboard and asked to reconstruct the kind of "snapshot" which could be taken of the group of mountains from position A, laying the pieces in appropriate positions on the table. Next, the doll is put at position C and the child asked to make the kind of picture which the doll, or he himself, could take from that position. This procedure is repeated for positions B and D. After this the child is told to sit at B (or C or D) and asked to show with the pieces of cardboard, the picture he could take from there. He is also asked to reconstruct the picture he has already made from A or other positions he has occupied previously. With older children it is of course possible to arrange the doll in more complicated positions in order to differentiate the perspectives more clearly. Conversely, with the younger children, the emphasis is laid more on the child's own changes of position and on the coordination of his own changing perspectives. . . .

These experiments were carried out on a hundred children, 21 between 4 and 6;6 years, 30 between 6;7 and 8 years, 33 between 8 and 9;6 years, and 16 between 9;6 and 12 years. The results may be classified as follows, stages of development being the same as those of·previous chapters.*

*Children of stage I do not understand the meaning of such questions, so that it is pointless to attempt any consistent studies with them or report the sort of answers they give.

Throughout stage II the child distinguishes hardly or not at all between his own viewpoint and that of other observers (represented by the doll in different positions). At substage IIA for instance, each time the doll is moved the child makes a new picture with his bits of cardboard as if to reproduce the observer's point of view. Nevertheless, when examined, each of these pictures turns out to be the same. They all show the mountains from a single point of view, that of the child himself. During substage IIB the child shows some attempt at discrimination but usually relapses into the egocentric constructions of substage IIA. . . .

Stage III, on the other hand (7–8 to 11–12 years), shows a progressive discrimination and coordination of perspectives. At substage IIIA (averaging 7–8 to 9 years) certain relationships are varied with changes in the position of the observer, but there is still no comprehensive coordination of viewpoints. This is not achieved until substage IIIB (about 9–10 years), at which point the mastery of simple perspective is complete (as has already been seen) and perspective has begun to appear in drawing. . . .

Substage IIB. Transitional Reactions. Attempts to Distinguish Between Different Viewpoints. In order to understand the mechanism by which perspectives are coordinated and projective relationships transformed so that one perspective may be made to correspond with another, nothing is more instructive than to follow the child's progress step by step as he attempts to distinguish between different points of view. In this connection, substage IIB is especially interesting. The child senses that some of the relations are relative to others, that they vary according to the particular point of view, but he immediately stabilizes these nascent relations in the form of "false-absolutes" or "preconcepts" midway between the pseudo-constancy of substage IIA and the reciprocal constancy of stage III. Instead of reproducing their own viewpoint with their pieces of cardboard, like the children of substage IIA, the subjects belonging to this level attempt to break free of it. But their efforts remain unsuccessful and result only in the construction of one single pattern, though this occasionally comes near the doll's point of view. Sometimes the positions of individual mountains are reversed, though never that of the structure as a whole. Lastly, the child occasionally produces a picture which is an exact copy of what he himself sees, as at substage IIA, though turning each piece of card toward the doll before deciding on its eventual position.

Wan (8;3) is seated at A and tries to build the picture seen from C. He puts the grey card on the right, the green in the middle, and the brown on the left. After this he hesitates, picks up the green one again and puts it on the right of the grey, thus forming his own perspective A. He next tries to make perspective D (grey, green, brown) and remarks, *"the brown one will go first"* showing a clear grasp of the foreground of D. After this promising opening, however, he once more proceeds to build perspective A, but with all three cards pushed to the side of the board nearest D. Following this he is seated at D and asked to build the view seen from C. He turns the bases of the cards toward C, their apexes pointing toward D, but the actual arrangement of left-right, before-behind is that corresponding to position D where he himself is seated! The same thing happens when, still seated at D, Wan tries to construct the perspective of A. He again puts the grey on the left, the green to the right and higher up, the brown on the right and at the bottom (thus reproducing the view from D), but turning the cards to make the bases face A and the apexes face C.

This initial attempt to vary the relative positions of items is extremely interesting since it is transitional between the spatial egocentrism of substage IIA and the first signs of true relativity which appear at substage IIIA. Of course, the child does not alter the relations between the mountains in terms of the observer's point of view, but only the relations between the observer and the group of mountains as a whole, regarded as a fixed arrangement. The observer is imagined as seeing always the same picture. . . . In other words, the picture somehow or other turns itself round in the direction of the observer without changing its pattern or internal arrangement!

The fact that all the children without exception tend simply to reproduce their own point of view, no matter what the perspective, is a clear sign that they remain tied to a single "false-absolute" viewpoint. And, it should be noted, not only at the beginning of the experiment but right to the end, they are quite satisfied with their performance and fully believe they have reproduced the viewpoint of the observer. . . .

The relationships of left-right, before-behind are therefore not yet real to the child. That is to say, they are not yet subject to changes of sequence and reversals dependent upon the observer's position. They are still immutable, intrinsic properties of the group of mountains which define once and for all the pattern of the group as a whole.

The child has not yet begun to think in terms of "groupings" of projective relations and correspondences, to discern the invariance of the correspondences amid the endless transformations of the projective relationships. Instead, he fixes upon some kind of rigid, ideal picture. It is this picture alone, treated as a solid, immutable bloc, which he envisages as capable of being turned in various directions.

Conclusion

The main conclusion to be drawn from this discussion is, therefore, that global or comprehensive coordination of viewpoints is the basic prerequisite in constructing simple projective relations. For although it may be granted that such relations are invariably dependent upon a given viewpoint, nevertheless the last three chapters have made it abundantly clear that a single "point of view" cannot exist in an isolated fashion, but necessarily entails the construction of a complete system linking together all points of view, just as distances and metric relations are linked together within a coordinate system in Euclidean space. This is the prime and fundamental difference between projective space and topological relationships.

The second important difference derives from the way mental operations superimpose themselves on perceptions, or if one prefers to put it otherwise, the way they integrate the perceptual data. Topological space is wholly inherent to the object and consists of operations worked out step by step. It therefore corresponds to no more than a series of possible perceptions capable of being juxtaposed, and the main task of such operations is to assemble the data of this space into one coherent whole. The groupings involved in this process consist of additions and subdivisions of proximities and separations, the formation of ordered series, and enclosure by means of surrounding; the entire process raised to the level of operational continuity and of point-to-point and bicontinuous (homeomorphic) correspondence.

In contrast to this, a system of projective relations or perspective viewpoints consists essentially of operations which do not merely assemble perceptual data, but coordinate it in terms of reciprocal relationships. Hence the function of projective space is not to link up the various parts of the object, but to link together all the innumerable projections of it. Consequently, the perceptions to which these different projections or perspectives correspond are not like fragmentary pictures that have to be assembled, but each one of them complete views taken from different angles that have to be reconciled.

The problem raised by the experiment with three mountains is not one of topological proximities or enclosures, nor is it a Euclidean problem of measuring things by comparing adjoining elements or moving units from one part of the structure to another. It is a projective problem and for this very reason, no single perspective, no one visual picture corresponding to a particular point of view, can render the spatial character of the group of mountains as a whole. This can only be done by means of operations enabling one perspective to be linked with the rest. That is to say, by operations that link a particular perspective with the universe of possible perspectives.

The reason why no single perception can embrace every aspect of the entire group of mountains is not because it refers only to one small section of the whole (like one square of a chessboard in relation to the rest), but because it only relates to a single perspective. The sum total of all these various aspects can only be grasped through an act of intelligence which links together all the possible perceptions by means of operations. . . .

Thus the perspective system which the child builds up in the course of the four substages we have identified is not perceptual but conceptual in character. It is the psychological counterpart of a projective space which, unlike topological space, is based primarily on the group of transformations itself, a grouping initially qualitative, but becoming quantitative in course of development, and partaking of the nature of the mathematical group. . . .

In short, the sensorimotor coordination responsible for perception of perspective appears to develop, from the very outset, in a way that is functionally analogous to the operational coordination of viewpoints culminating in the concept of projective space. Operational coordination may thus be said to recapitulate in large measure all that has previously been achieved on the plane of perceptual activity, while completely surpassing it as regards the power of its deductive mechanisms.

The feature common to both processes of development is precisely the transition from egocentric realism to relational coordination. The fact that this process recurs in identical fashion after the lapse of several years demonstrates what a vital role it plays in forming the idea of projective space. Though there is, of course, the difference that at the perceptual or sensorimotor level it is only a matter of linking momentary perceptions or actions with earlier or later ones. At the conceptual level, however, the passage from actual centration to virtual decentration is brought about by the subject coordinating his own viewpoint with all possible viewpoints, replacing egocentrism by grouping. . . .

Systems of Reference and Horizontal-Vertical Coordinates*

As distinct from elementary topological relations which are concerned simply with the object as a thing in itself and with its various features taken in turn, we have shown that projective concepts imply a comprehensive linking together of figures in a single system, based on the coordination of a number of different viewpoints. But side by side with the development of this organized complex of viewpoints there also takes place a coordination of objects as such. This leads ultimately to the idea of Euclidean space, the concepts of parallels, angles and proportion providing the transition between the two systems. Such a coordination of objects naturally assumes the conservation of distance, together with the evolution of the notion of "displacement" or congruent transformation of spatial figures, culminating in the construction of systems of reference, or coordinates. . . .

At the outset, the coordinates of Euclidean space are no more than a vast network embracing all objects and merely consist of relations of order applied simultaneously to all three dimensions. . . .

It is due to the spontaneous construction of such a network that figures can be oriented and movements directed in space, and for lack of it that younger children are unable to make a straight line or a set of parallels, nor judge their inclinations or angles. The construction of these straight lines, parallels, and angles constitutes the preliminary phase of the general coordination formed by a network of coordinates.

[But] a reference frame is not simply a network composed of relations of order between the various objects themselves. It applies equally to positions within the network as to objects occupying any of these positions and enables the relations between them to be maintained invariant, independent of potential displacement of the objects. Thus the frame of reference constitutes a Euclidean space after the fashion of a *container*, relatively independent of the mobile objects *contained* within it, just as projective coordination of the totality of potential viewpoints includes each viewpoint actually envisaged. It is in this sense that projective and Euclidean space consist of comprehensive systems as contrasted with topological relationships which remain internal to each object regarded as an isolated thing in itself. . . .

Now if such a system gives rise to a homogeneous environment common to all objects, it is not merely because this so-called "container" consists of the entire assemblage of the relations of order and the intervals of "distances" between objects. It is also because the "container" differs from its "contents" in that these relations are not con-

*In collaboration with Mlle G. Ascoli, Mme M. Denis-Prinzhorn, Mlle M. Roth, and M. G. Lewinnik. [The following section is from Chapter XIII.]

fined to the objects at a particular moment, but include all their successive or potential positions, linking them all together and employing certain favored positions as reference points or "points of departure" for all subsequent positions. . . .

On the one hand, whenever objects or parts of figures are linked by relations of order, or by straight lines, parallels, and angles, and whenever these variously inclined lines are themselves oriented relative to each other, we have the preliminary outline of what invariably culminates in a complete frame of reference.

On the other hand, the grouping of displacements leads to the gradual replacement of positional relations between objects by relations of order and distance between the positions themselves. This "clarification" or "purging" of space (if the reader will forgive the metaphor), by progressively emptying it of objects in order to organize the space or "container" itself, leads to exactly the same result. Now this dual process does not take place all at once. The systems of reference are at first limited and circumscribed in character, only gradually becoming more extensive and being consolidated by including ever more items, while at the same time becoming more abstract. . . .

The first problem which arises is that concerning the choice of natural reference systems, such as the horizontals and verticals as part of the most stable, or least mobile, framework of everyday experience. . . . It is extremely important to find out whether or not the child can spontaneously utilize such a system of reference; and if so, under what conditions. This is the main problem which we have to examine in this chapter.

As adults we are so accustomed to using a system of reference and organizing our empirical space by means of coordinate axes which appear self-evident (like the vertical provided by the plumb line and the horizontal given by a water level), that it may seem absurd to ask at what age the child acquires these ideas. It will be said that as a result of lying flat on his back the child is aware of the horizontal right from the cradle, and he discovers the vertical as soon as he attempts to raise himself. The postural system would thus appear to provide a ready-made coordinate space, the organs of equilibrium with their only too well-known semicircular canals solving the entire problem. In which case it would appear odd to want to raise the problem all over again with the 4- to 10-year-old child!

Here we touch on one of the worst misconceptions which has plagued the theory of geometrical concepts. From the fact that the child breathes, digests, and possesses a heart that beats we do not conclude that he has any idea of alimentary metabolism or the circulatory system. At the very most he may have noticed his movements in breathing, or felt his pulse. Similarly, from the fact that he can stand up or lie flat, the child at first derives only a strictly empirical awareness of the two postures and nothing more. To superimpose upon this a more general schema he must at some point go outside the purely postural field and compare his own position with those of surrounding objects, and this is something beyond purely empirical knowledge.

. . . Everyone has seen the kind of drawings which children produce between the age of 4 and 8, showing chimneys perpendicular to sloping roofs and men at right angles to hills they are supposed to be climbing.

In such drawings we have at one and the same time an awareness of right angles inside the figure, together with a total disregard of the vertical axis. This suggests that the child has a long way to go in passing from a postural or sensorimotor space to a conceptual one. Nevertheless, the majority of authors cover this distance at a single leap by deriving a full-blown system of reference from these primitive notions. . . .

Horizontal and Vertical Axes. Technique and General Results. The simplest and most natural reference frame available to the child is most probably that provided by the physical world in the shape of vertical and horizontal axes (in the frontal-parallel or the line of regard). Such notions are, of course, purely relative to our own scale of empirical approximation, since on a slightly more accurate scale the level of a liquid is no longer flat and plumb lines are not parallel to each other! On the empirical level, the horizontal is given by the plane on which everyday objects rest, the earth itself (where flat), or the artificial planes of floors, terraces, and so on. Another important factor is the surface of a liquid, which for little children living in Geneva is illustrated daily by the surface of Lake Leman, to say nothing of the levels of drinks in cups and glasses. As for the vertical axis, this is provided by the walls of rooms and houses, by posts, chimney stacks, trees, and so on. . . .

On the one hand, the concepts of vertical and horizontal are by nature physical rather than mathematical, indicating as they do, simply the direction taken by a freely falling body or a line perpendicular to it. Yet on the other hand, the elaboration of these concepts introduces a question independent of, physics, or at any rate, a question whose independence is precisely the point at issue in the experiments about to be discussed; and this is the development of a coordinate system as a simple tool of geometrical orientation. . . .

The dual nature of these physical and geometrical problems raises a question of obvious importance from the point of view of psychology . . . : the physical and experimental nature of mathematics as opposed to its being of an a priori and purely intellectual character, together with all the intermediate possibilities available between these two extremes. Now this problem constantly recurs in an extremely crude, but all the more impressive, form in each of the experiments we are about to describe. From the very outset, starting with the arrangement and organization of the experimental session itself, one finds oneself at grips with the interdependence of the physical and intellectual functions involved.

In putting the problem of coordinates before the child one is compelled to make reference to the natural axes; namely, horizontal and vertical, since the child himself sooner or later introduces them of his own accord. To find out whether the child has any real understanding of these notions, however, it is necessary to study how he discovers real physical laws in drawing conclusions from his little experiments. That is to say, laws such as the constancy of the surface of a liquid whatever the angle of the container, or the constant direction of the plumb line, whatever the angle of nearby objects, etc. But in studying how the child learns to interpret these empirical facts for himself one is led to analyze afresh the schema by means of which he is able to [register] what he perceives, and this brings us back once more

to the question of a coordinate system. Thus from the outset, we seem
to be moving in a kind of circle between physics and geometry and the
first task is to devise a technique which recognizes this basic problem
without prejudicing the way in which it is to be, metaphorically speaking,
straightened out.

For the study of the horizontal the following method was found best.
The children are shown two narrow-necked bottles, one with straight,
parallel sides and the other with rounded sides. Each is about one-
quarter filled with colored water and the children are asked to guess
the position the water will assume when the bottle is tilted. Some empty
jars are placed before the child, the same shapes as the models, on which
he is asked to show with his finger the level of the water at various
degrees of tilt. In addition, the youngest children are asked to indicate
the surface of the water by a gesture so that one can be sure whether or
not they imagine it as horizontal or tilted. The experiment is then
performed directly in front of them and they are asked to draw what
they see. Children over 5 (on the average) are given outline drawings of
the jars at various angles and asked to draw the position of the water
corresponding to each position of the bottle, before having seen the
exepriment performed. The various inclinations are presented in random
order to avoid perseverative errors. Care is also taken to make the
children draw the edge of the table or the support holding the bottle,
in such a way that this horizontal, directly perceived, can assist in
judging the position of the liquid. As soon as he has made this drawing
the child compares it with the experiment which now takes place. He
is then asked to correct it or produce a new drawing and so passes onto
other predictions. Care [is] taken to have the level of the water at the
height of the child's eyes, or a little above, so that he can see the edge
of the surface clearly.

This basic method may be supplemented by others, such as giving
the child a set of cardboard cutouts representing the various bottles, with
the level of the liquid drawn on them. He is then asked to set them at
the angle appropriate to the water level. Alternatively, the child is given
a set of postcards bearing pictures of the jars in different positions.
Each card shows the water level, correct or incorrect, and the child has
to sort them out, rejecting the incorrect versions. Some children were
shown a large placard bearing pictures of the bottles in all positions,
here again the task being to distinguish drawings showing correct water
levels from others which are incorrect. Lastly, we made occasional
use of a paper cutout representing a cup, the contents being represented
by a second cutout. The child is then asked to fit the second to the
first, taking account of the slope of the vessel.

For studying verticals the following methods were employed. Firstly,
during the preceding experiment on the jars of water, we floated a
small cork on the surface of the water with a matchstick rising vertically from it. The child is asked to draw the position of the "mast" of
this "ship" at different inclinations of the jar and then correct his drawing after seeing the experiment. Secondly, we suspended a plumb line
inside the jars (now empty), the plumb bob being shaped to represent
a fish. The child has to predict the line of the string when the jar is
tilted at various angles. This done, the experiment of actually tilting the
jar is performed and the child is asked for further drawings. Thirdly, the

child is shown a mountain of sand, plasticine, etc., and asked to plant
posts "nice and straight" on the summit, on the ground nearby, or on the
slopes of the mountain. It is very important to get him to make clear
what he means by "straight" and "sloping" in referring to the posts (a
selection of drawings helps the experiment along). The child is also
asked to draw the mountain, showing the posts either "nice and
straight" or sloping. Finally, we sometimes combined the experiment
using the plumb line with that of the mountain, by getting the child to
predict the direction of the string when the bob was suspended from
hooks projecting from posts planted on the sides or the summit of the
mountain.

By means of these various methods we were able to demonstrate the
following stages of development. (See Figure 18.) During stage I (up to
4–5 years) the child is unable to represent either the water or the mountain as a plane surface. As far as the water is concerned, not only has

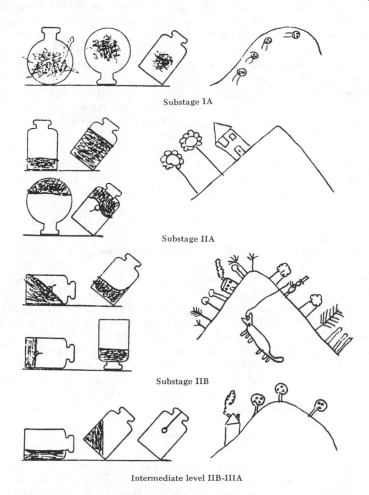

Substage IA

Substage IIA

Substage IIB

Intermediate level IIB-IIIA

Figure 18

Stages in development of horizontal and vertical axes.

the child not the faintest idea of a horizontal plane, but he does not even grasp the notion of planes at all. He either represents the water by means of scribbles going outside the jar itself or, when he overcomes the motor difficulties causing him to do this, draws the water as a round blot or a little ball inside the jar, without defining the straight line or the plane surface, or locating the water relative to the jar. At this level, trees and houses are either drawn lying flat on the sides of the mountain (the house appears to be parallel to the slope), or else placed in arbitrary fashion, using the mountain as a background.

In contrast to this, at stage II spatial orientation is determined by the particular configuration represented, rather than by an external system of reference. Horizontal and vertical axes are thus still undiscovered. At stage IIA the lines indicating the surface of liquids and solids are undefined, except that when the bottle is tilted the child imagines the movement of the water, not only without regard to any external reference system, but without regard to the sides of the jar itself. Thus the liquid is imagined as simply expanding or contracting, increasing or decreasing in volume. The child imagines it as approaching or receding from the neck of the bottle, because he thinks of the liquid moving toward the neck as the bottle is tilted and away from it as the bottle is replaced upright. The water level always stays parallel to the base of the jar, the mass of the liquid remaining in contact with it (though sometimes the opposite is shown, an empty space appearing between the base and the water which is then, as it were, suspended in mid-air, its underside remaining parallel to the base of the jar). It is interesting to note that the children of this stage, like those of stage I, are incapable of assessing the experiment at its true value, even when it is performed before their very eyes, because they do not know how to make use of reference systems external, or even internal, to the bottle. In the case of verticals, they draw the posts perpendicular to the mountain sides regardless of vertical axes and are unable to determine the direction of the plumb line relative to the mountain.

During stage IIB, however, we find that although the child cannot draw the water in the tilted jar as level (though he indicates its direction with his finger) he is nevertheless able to show it as no longer parallel with the base of the vessel. But he still fails to coordinate his predictions with any fixed reference system outside the jar (i.e., with the table or the stand) and merely connects the waterline with the corners of the jar, tilting it at an angle (and sometimes, accidentally, making it horizontal), though when the jar is inverted he makes the level horizontal. As for the verticals, children at this stage are usually able to stand the posts upright when planting them in the sides of the sand hill, though they continue to draw them perpendicular to the incline and often fail to predict the correct inclination of the plumb line in the tilted jars.

Next comes a transitional stage between IIB and IIIA. Here the child is able to predict the level of the liquid only when the rectangular jar is inverted or lying on one side; that is, when the level is parallel with the sides. Subsequent to this comes the discovery of horizontal and vertical axes. This is achieved at stage III, beginning around 7–8 years and divided into two substages. The first of these lasts from 7–8 until 9 years, during which the principle comes gradually to be applied to all cases, though at the beginning the level is often made oblique, ignoring the reference points external to the jar. Then, about the age of 9, sub-stage IIIB begins with the immediate prediction of horizontal and vertical as part of an overall system of coordinates. . . .

Stage III. The Discovery of the Vertical and Horizontal. Our hypotheses are strikingly confirmed by the results obtained in stage III. The children do not discover the vertical and horizontal at one stroke, as might well have been expected had they been unable to give correct answers merely for lack of skill in drawing. At stage I the child cannot isolate straight lines and planes, and at stage II he fails to make use of reference systems going outside the pattern he has in mind. At stage III, however, he begins, though only very gradually, to master more extended reference systems and to construct coordinate axes embracing the entire spatial field. . . .

First of all, the reactions which are midway between those of sub-stages IIB and IIIA merit particular attention. Though possessing but one novel feature distinguishing them from their forerunners, these reactions nevertheless mark an important step forward, since they indicate a widening of the rather limited system of reference with which the child has been satisfied so far. This new feature is the discovery of the horizontal when the bottle is lying on its side. The water is no longer drawn parallel with the base or joined to one corner (it will be recalled that at substage IIB the child drew the water horizontal with the jar inverted, though here it remained parallel with the base). Naturally, the horizontal is discovered as a result of parallelism between the water and the sides of the bottle. Nevertheless, such a form of parallelism, which is entirely different from that of the initial position (surface of water parallel with base of jar), suggests that the child is beginning to establish a connection of some sort with a reference system external to the jar, at any rate in this particular position. . . .

Web (7;9). With the spherical flask he begins by drawing the level as increasingly curved ellipses until they form a kind of ball at the neck (for the steep inclinations). We perform the experiment and he observes that "the water is straight." In the drawings that follow he shows levels which are all horizontal, indicating that he has taken note of what he has seen. But when we pass on to the straight-sided bottle he again predicts levels which are every one oblique, except when the bottle is lying flat. We then begin the demonstration and he checks the levels with a ruler. "Is the drawing you've just made correct?—No, it's wrong—And if I make it tilt more?—The water will tilt as well—Check it with the ruler—Sloping (he has great difficulty in judging whether the ruler is horizontal)—Are you sure?—No, it's straight—And the water?—It must be straight, because it's in the same position as the ruler—Arrange these cardboard models in the right order (cutouts representing the spherical flask with a variety of water levels)—(He arranges them with the waterline inclined, save for the one lying at 90°) —But you said it was always straight?—No, it's slanting—Place your ruler against the jar. How is it?—Slanting—Do you really think so?—Ah! no, it's straight! (with an air of astonishment)." The masts of the floats are drawn sometimes vertical, sometimes perpendicular to the surface of the water. . . .

These reactions reveal the first, nascent awareness of the concept of "horizontal," and for this reason they deserve the most careful attention. The position in which the water is shown when the jar lies on its side constitutes the first authentic expression of this concept—as distinct from the inverted position where the liquid is shown horizontal only because it lies parallel with the base of the jar. How then do the children of this level come to make such a discovery in this one particular case, and why are they unable to extend it to other cases?

There can be no doubt whatever that the experiment itself plays a vital part in enabling the child to make the purely physical discovery that the water level remains horizontal. But this experiment presents two aspects, both of which entail a geometrical framework extending beyond immediate physical data.

In the first place, the child has to observe that the surface of the water retains a constant shape, that it is not curved in the way Web draws it, or bent like Ros's trapezoid, but constitutes a flat plane. Now from the beginning of stage II, it is clearly the experiment which makes this apparent and thus enables Web and Ros to correct their errors—survivals of reactions found in stage I. Elementary though this may seem, the ability to note this fact undoubtedly presumes that the child can envisage a plane surface.

In the second place—and this is something far harder for him to grasp—the experiment is a physical proof that the liquid surface maintains a constant orientation. In other words, that a ruler held against the jar, level with the waterline, will remain parallel with it even though the jar be tilted. It is this second aspect of the experiment which amazes Web and so many other subjects. Indeed, they are as yet by no means able to appreciate it fully, though they begin to accept it in the form expressed by Web: the water "is straight because it is in the same position as the ruler."

But what does an experiment such as this really involve? Basically, certain specialized actions, such as checking up by eye or with a ruler, which bear upon specific features of the object (in this case its shape and orientation) and result in a particular abstraction. All of which amounts to abstracting from the object certain specific features which the subject can record and incorporate within his conceptual schemata.

[But] if the acquisition of such a concept required only a physical demonstration, one would be at a loss to understand why the process should be so difficult and protracted; consequently, other factors must be involved. Now an experiment is a practical possibility only if its result can, firstly, be observed (noting the experiment) and secondly, interpreted (drawing conclusions from it). This inevitably presumes a deductive system whereby the experiment may be rationally understood. That is to say, in order to gain accurate knowledge of a thing, it is not enough to perform certain specialized actions on particular aspects or features of it. It is also necessary to coordinate these actions (whether they be successive or simultaneous). But the process of coordinating actions is no part of the physical experiment, but a part of intelligence mechanisms, and is therefore basic to logical and mathematical operations, geometrical operations included.

Now to coordinate actions is, in effect, to link them together on the basis of their consequences, or else to enclose their schemata one within another. In either case, the net result is to coordinate or link together the objects affected by such actions, so that it is no longer a question of abstracting a particular feature from an object as with specialized, isolated actions. On the contrary, it involves adding new features to objects, features which are not abstracted from their physical nature, but exist in harmony with it. In this way, relationships like number, logical classes, or basic geometrical postulates are more closely linked with the actions whose coordination they express, than with the objects such actions bear upon (thus for example, it is enough to reverse the direction of an action to reverse the relationships). In the present instance, even the idea of a plane surface—which as we have just seen constitutes an abstraction from the object when it is simply a matter of observing that the surface of the water is flat—presupposes an abstraction based on this same coordination of actions.

As for the constant orientation of the liquid surface, that is to say, the horizontal axis itself, this is clearly one of those concepts that cannot be arrived at solely on the basis of physical experiments, because it entails the formation of a rich network of interconnections which will culminate in a coordinate system. Now it is precisely the inception of this process which enables the children just quoted to discover the horizontal axis in certain situations, whilst the obstacles they have to overcome in doing so explain why they are unable to apply their discovery to all situations. . . .

As distinct from this transitional level, stage III proper begins about the age of 7–8 on the average; that is, at the point where concrete operations first appear. The idea of the horizontal is now no longer a mere suggestion occurring in specially favorable positions of the jar, nor is the idea of the vertical any longer dependent upon the perceptual surround. On the contrary, stage III is distinguished by practical and effective application of these concepts to all positions and inclinations. In other words, as a result of concrete operations which replace the simple connected notions of stage II, the child can now interrelate the different parts of the patterns he is considering; the mobile reference systems within them, and the fixed systems outside them. But this ultimate goal, unlike the more elementary concepts (such as straight lines, parallels, etc.), which are completed about the age of 7 or 8, is not reached at a single stride. For the horizontal and vertical constitute a coordinate system, which entails an interrelation of the entire complex of objects lying within the field of action, and two stages are required for this to be achieved completely. . . .

Pau (9;10) draws an oblique waterline and a boat with mast perpendicular to it. He is shown the experiment. "I did it all wrong. The water was like that (gesture parallel with the table) and the mast was straight (vertical gesture)." But immediately following he again predicts an oblique level (experiment): "No, it's even more wrong—And if the jar is tilted even more? —(This time he makes a horizontal drawing, using a ruler which he places parallel to the edge of the table)." But oddly enough, when he comes to deal with another inclination he reverts to a tilted level, repeating the same error with the spherical flask. However, he finally succeeds in producing horizontals in all situations. . . .

Trip (11;4) hesitates up till the moment when, after watching the experiment, he says, "It will stay straight all the time. It must always be straight (he corrects his drawings)—How can you tell if it's right?—I draw it parallel to the table."

It is clear that by substage IIIA it is at last possible to speak of the horizontal being recognized and applied in all positions of the bottle; likewise the vertical, either in the same situation or in drawings of the mountain slope. Yet at the same time one is faced with an astonishing fact. These children, ranging between the ages of 6;4 and 11 years (with a few laggards of 12), only succeed in making this elementary comparison upon repeated attempts, after reproducing the same errors as were seen in stage II, and after having been made to note the result of the experiment with the jar. Pau is a particularly clearcut example of this, although he is nearly 10 years old. Hence the concepts of horizontal and vertical are not constructed at the beginning of stage III (that is, at the point where concrete operations first appear), save in exceptional cases, but during the actual course of this stage, at about the age of 9; in other words, not until these operations have been completely organized.

Having pointed this out, we must now inquire how the vertical and horizontal come to be discovered. . . . The most striking thing is, of course, the way in which the children infer the physical law from what they see, particularly as regards the horizontal in the case of the water level. Thus Wei [6;4] finds his predictions constantly contradicted by the experiment and is eventually compelled to admit that the water "is always straight." Wir [7;3] goes further and formulates the law empirically, "there's something I don't understand; the water stays still and the jar moves!" It is evident that without the experiments the child would not succeed in discovering that the liquid remains horizontal, for this is given empirically and not deduced a priori. But why is this experiment not effective until stage III? Why does it take so long to produce, first a simple observation (not possible at stage I), and then a general inference (not possible at stage II)? In other words, why are these children the first to conclude that the water will "always" be horizontal, on the basis of noting a few experimental facts?

It is at this point that one realizes the indispensable role of a frame of reference. In order to recognize that the water is permanently horizontal and the masts or plumb lines permanently vertical, regardless of the tilt of the jar, it is necessary—even without drawing, but only by holding a ruler in line with the water or the plumb line—to establish a relationship between the water or the thread, the ruler, and a set of objects external to the jar. For otherwise there is nothing to show whether the orientation of the water has or has not altered through being involved in the movement of the container (just as a relative movement cannot be understood without a system of reference). Now it is remarkable to observe that the children are, as a rule, more or less consciously aware of the need for an external anchorage. . . . True enough, one could very well ask them what they compare the level of the table with, and this would, in the last resort, refer them back to the level of the water. But it is quite evident, so far as the second aspect of the child's reactions is concerned, that it is no longer the physical problem which is important, but rather the geometrical problem of comparing different inclinations in terms of angles, parallelism, order, and distance. In short, by means of a comprehensive system, and this is precisely the beginning of a system of coordinate axes. . . .

Conclusions: The Construction of Frames of Reference. . . . When we view the familiar objects around us, they appear arranged within a grid of parallel straight lines, crossing each other perpendicularly in three dimensions. And if this view of things appears self-evident it is because physical experience itself seems to force upon us just such a structure, by virtue of all the verticals we perceive as parallel and appearing to cut the verticals at right angles. Indeed, any piece of squared paper, parquet flooring, street crossings, or groups of buildings suggest the same unbiquitous and ineluctable notion of coordinate axes. In short, a frame of reference may be likened to a double or treble entry table cross-referenced, with all the objects in space arranged in point-to-point correspondence by being entered in the appropriate columns, so that to coordinate such items would seem simplicity itself.

However, the findings of the present chapter show clearly enough that it would be a complete mistake to imagine that human beings have some innate or psychologically precocious knowledge of the spatial surround organized in a two- or three-dimensional reference frame. At the outset, the child has not even an awareness of physical or physiological notions of vertical and horizontal, and for a very simple reason, as these results show. The reason is that a perception covers only a very limited field, whereas a system of reference presumes operational coordination of several fields, one with another.

Far from constituting the starting point of spatial awareness, the frame of reference is in fact the culminating point of the entire psychological development of Euclidean space, just as the notions of succession and simultaneity, synchronous and isochronous, defining a homogeneous time, mark the culmination rather than the starting point for the concept of time.* A coordinate system or frame of reference presupposes, in the first instance, the topological notions of order and dimensionality. That is to say, a set of relationships enabling objects to be ranged in series along n dimensions.

. . . The topological concept of dimensionality was dependent initially on the simple notions of surroundings and enclosure. Such notions leave parallels and straight lines out of account, whereas the axes of the most elementary reference frames consist of straight lines cutting others at right angles, the former being either parallel (zero angle) or at specific inclinations. A frame of reference is thus the product of logical multiplication applied to topological series which have been modified by the introduction of the concepts of straight lines, parallels, distances, and angles, in n dimensions. It entails, apart from elementary topological relationships, the employment of the entire set of Euclidean concepts in order to link one object with another, thus constituting a global organization of Euclidean space, which is precisely the reason its development occurs so late.

It should now be equally apparent why perception alone is unequal to this task. True enough, perception provides a rough estimate of order, distance, parallels, and angles. And moreover, just as with intelligence, elementary systems of reference are always involved, so that every object is perceived in a "setting," in terms of which it is oriented and its size and shape estimated. Nevertheless, perceptual data always remain sketchy and inadequate, a circumstance which becomes obvious whenever the occasion arises to compare perception with intelligence. . . .

This naturally raises the question of whether perceptual development is the cause or the effect of intellectual progress. This question may be answered in the following way. Firstly, if the process of development

*Cf. Piaget, J., *Le Développement de la Notion de Temps chez l'Enfant.*

were purely perceptual in character it would be difficult to understand what its role was, and why its development should be so protracted. On the other hand, the role of intelligence is perfectly comprehensible. It consists of establishing permanent relations spanning ever greater spatio-temporal intervals, not merely within each successive perceptual field, but between each of these fields in turn. In this way, perceptual activity can be given a potential orientation by means of an operational mechanism, enabling virtual as well as actual orientations to be taken into account. Secondly, the reason for the slow development of thought is equally comprehensible since, as we have seen, it not only assumes the completion of operations concerned with order (as distinct from the mere notion of order)—because coordinates are logical multiplications between relations of order in two or three dimensions—but it also assumes that the concepts essential to Euclidean space (straight lines, distances and measurements, parallels and angles) are fused into a single operational whole.

To conclude this discussion, we may make these final observations. Topological relations are relations which remain purely internal to each object or pattern. As against this, Euclidean relations, completed by the construction of reference frames, are essentially relations established between numbers of objects or patterns (though still influencing their internal structure) and serve to locate them within an organized whole forming an all-embracing system. This is why horizontal-vertical axes are constructed at the same time as perspectives are coordinated, for these latter also constitute overall systems linking together objects or patterns. But projective space is in essence a coordination both of viewpoints—actual or virtual—and of the figures considered in relation to these viewpoints. Coordinates, on the other hand, which express the structure of Euclidean space, link together objects considered as such, in their objective positions and displacements, and at relative distances. The age of 9 or thereabouts, which lies midway through the period in which concrete operations first take shape, thus marks a decisive turning point in the development of spatial concepts; that of the completion of the framework appropriate to comprehensive Euclidean and projective systems. And it is interesting to observe that the other great comprehensive system—that of time, coordinating movements and speeds—is also completed at exactly the same age.

General Conclusions: The "Intuition" of Space*

What exactly is meant by geometrical intuition? Every mathematician will, of course, expect to find an answer to this question at the end of these experiments on the child's conception of space.

The ordinarily accepted view tends to treat geometrical intuition primarily as a "reading" or direct perceptual apprehension of the external world, supplemented by images recalling past or anticipating future

*[The following section is from Chapter XV.]

perceptions. "We have various kinds of intuitions," said Poincaré in a well-known passage, "firstly, those which are based directly on sensation and imagination, then those arrived at by the process of induction—on the pattern, as it were, of experimental scientific method —and finally, the intuition of pure number."* Geometrical intuition is usually considered as belonging to the first, or perhaps the first two, of these three categories; though this entails reducing induction to nothing more than anticipation of a possible perceptual experience. Yet, at the same time, it is perfectly true that the "intuition" of space does depend partly on sensation and imagination. The point which we cannot help "seeing" as a tiny round surface, or the line which we envisage as a fine thread, are hackneyed, yet nevertheless conclusive examples of this dependency of intuition on sense perception.

[But] to reduce spatial intuition to no more than an outcome of sensation and imagination would be to misunderstand its true character in exactly the same way as the associationists distorted that of thought, reducing it to a series of images and treating them as the ultimate, if not the sole elements of thought itself. On the contrary, one of the clearest results of our present experiments has been to show that images and sense data perform exactly the same function in geometrical intuition as in other thought processes. Namely, that of symbols or "signifiers" as opposed to the relationships they "signify."

It is perfectly true that when mathematicians describe intuition in terms of sensations and images, they generally do so with opposite intentions from those of the classical empiricists, since their aim is to condemn rather than to justify its demonstrative value. Intuition deceives us, they almost unanimously assert; thus after having distinguished three types of intuition in the passage given above, Poincaré adds, "the first two kinds of intuition cannot give us any certainty." Intuition, it is often said, is the instrument of invention, whereas demonstration or geometrical reasoning in the strict sense is a matter of logical analysis. And indeed, by developing axiomatic procedures, modern geometry has attempted to segregate the two processes as completely as possible.

Whether [the intent is to justify or condemn intuition] by reducing it to sensation and imagination, from the standpoint of psychology any such tendency is wholly misconceived, and indeed, has often had a deplorable effect on attempts to discuss the general problems of geometrical epistemology. The radical separation of intuition from logic or axiomatics has never been achieved in practice; and in fact, is unattainable in principle. It would be inappropriate, in the present context, to attempt an exhaustive analysis of all the different meanings, to say nothing of the various categories of intuition which numerous authors have promulgated with the aim of bridging—post factum—this gap between intuition and logic. Thus there is the kind of intuition which, according to Poincaré, governs the general direction of thought (as opposed to particular logical operations) and which Brunschvicg† regarded as indicating merely the "general groundwork of thought." There

---

*H. Poincaré, *La Valeur de la Science*, Paris, 1914, p. 22.

†L. Brunschvicg, *Les Étapes de la Philosophie Mathématique*, p. 451, 2nd edn., 1922.

is the "transintuitive intuition" of Winter,* and directly opposed to "naive intuition" there is Klein's "sophisticated" intuition, which according to this great mathematician, "was not, strictly speaking, an intuition at all."† Finally, there is Brouwer's idea of intuition as an operational construct.‡

In short, every possible shade of transition has been suggested to connect elementary intuition with logical operations; and what Brunschvicg has so subtly demonstrated is that in geometrical reasoning there always remains some link with intuitive experience. In converse fashion, from the outset of experience intelligence is operative in organizing intuition and giving it a definite structure. A similar view has recently been advanced by Gonseth** who suggests that the "schema" formed by formal logic always retains traces of intuition, while the primary intuition requires some degree of schematization in order to possess a structure.

All of which goes to show that even for mathematicians, intuition is far more than a system of perceptions or images. Rather is it the basic awareness of space, at a level not yet formalized. But this raises afresh the developmental problem. How can consciousness confront the external world so directly as to appear [to be] its perceptual or symbolic image, and then proceed to loosen all ties with externality so completely that it is able to replace it by concepts belonging entirely to the subject himself?

To this question, the experiments described in the course of the present work provide the simplest answer. The "intuition" of space is not a "reading" or apprehension of the properties of objects, but from the very beginning, an action performed on them. It is precisely because it enriches and develops physical reality instead of merely extracting from it a set of ready-made structures, that action is eventually able to transcend physical limitations and create operational schemata which can be formalized and made to function in a purely abstract, deductive fashion. From the rudimentary sensorimotor activity right up to abstract operations, the development of geometrical intuition is that of an activity, in the fullest sense; beginning with adaptive actions which link it with the object, and at the same time assimilate the object to its own functional structure, transforming it in the process as completely as geometry has transformed physics.

Action is first manifest in the form of sensorimotor activity regulating perception. Even at this stage the role of sense data is confined solely to that of "signifying" the relationships created by active, motor assimilation. . . .

It is at the stage of nascent mental imagery which immediately follows, that action begins to exercise its formative role. The image is at first no more than an internal imitation of previously performed actions, then later, of actions capable of being performed. Our experiments have shown how important such actions are in the mental

*Revue. de Métaph. et de Morale, p. 922, 1908. See also A. Reymond, ibid., p. 740, 1916.

†Quoted by Brunschvicg, Étapes, p. 450.

‡Rolin Wavre, "Mathématiques et philosophie," Arch. Soc. Belge de Philos., p. 9, 1933.

**F. Gonseth, Les Mathématiques et la Réalité.

construction of shapes, based on elementary topological relations such as proximity, order, and enclosure.

Finally, at the level, first of concrete, then of abstract operations, action is once more apparent, this time in the richer, yet purer form of the operations themselves. Richer, because in operational form actions are reversible and may be combined indefinitely; purer, because from now on they go beyond the physical objects with which they are concerned.

Now these operations on which the idea of space depends are important in three respects. Firstly, the order of their psychological development is in broad outline the same as that of formal geometrical construction. In both cases, topological relations precede projective and Euclidean ones, and in both cases the latter are equivalent as regards the complexity of the basic notions from which they stem.

The second important point about these operations, from the psychogenetic standpoint, is that they introduce a new element into the classical debate opposing intuition to logic. This is that to the extent that actions are internalized as operations, the initial perceptual and empirical intuitions become rational and coherent, even before having been formalized as propositions. Thus the rigor of the system of concrete operations exceeds that of elementary intuition without reaching that of abstract operations, the basis of hypothetico-deductive propositions. This makes it necessary to introduce new gradations between intuition and logic, the chief of which is the logic of concrete operations, superior to prelogical intuition and inferior to formal logic.

But the third and most important point is that concrete operations reveal another aspect of the relations between intuition and logic. Concrete operations of a logico-arithmetical character deal solely with similarities (classes and symmetrical relations) and differences (asymmetrical relations) or both together (numbers) between discrete objects in discontinuous wholes, independent of their spatio-temporal location. Exactly parallel with these operations there exist operations of a spatio-temporal or *sublogical* character, and it is precisely these which constitute the idea of space.

The term "sublogical" does not imply that these operations are in any way less rigorous than logico-arithmetical operations. It simply means that their function is to produce the concept of the object as such, in contrast to collections of objects (using the language of Russell's Theory of Types, they are beyond type O; which means precisely, that they are sublogical). Such operations deal not with class-inclusion, but with part-whole inclusions for single objects. They substitute the concept of proximity for that of resemblance, difference of order or position (especially the concept of displacement) for difference in general, and the concept of measurement for that of number. Once expressed in propositional form they are indistinguishable from logico-arithmetical operations, of which they constitute merely a particular species, that of continuity as opposed to discontinuity operations.

At the stage of concrete operations, however, they form just as complete a system as do logico-arithmetical operations, constituting "objects" of various kinds which it is the function of logico-arithmetical operations to arrange in sets or numerical collections. Since they constitute "objects," sublogical operations are accompanied by symbolic images (mental images or pictorial representations) which reflect them far more accurately (though not wholly adequately) than the images accompanying class or number concepts. This is why the persistence of a core of intuition is often admitted, even in the most abstract forms of axiomatic geometry, for this core is only the proof that the basic concepts of spatial proximity and succession are sublogical in origin.

In short, there is complete continuity in what mathematicians term geometrical intuition, between the motor element originally controlling perceptual activity and that which reappears at each successive stage of development, right up to the final operation. On the other hand, the sense data simply function as "signifiers" or pointers, right from the crude perceptual sign, up to the most abstract symbolic image. . . .

PART VIII

Figurative Aspects of Thought: Perception, Imagery, and Memory

INTRODUCTION

In this introduction we discuss Piaget's work on the figurative aspects of thought. His major publications on this subject are: *The Mechanisms of Perception* (1961), *Mental Imagery in the Child* (1966), and *Memory and Intelligence* (1968). Selection 33 is taken from *Mental Imagery*; Selection 34 is a useful summary from *The Psychology of the Child*.

The term *figurative* in Piaget's terminology refers to those aspects of thought that are related more directly to the states of objects than to their transformations. These terms, *states* and *objects*, should be opposed respectively to *transformations* and *subjects*. For Piaget, an object is "a polysensory complex which continues to exist beyond any perceptual contact."[*] Moreover, ". . . without conservation of objects there could not be any 'group,' since then everything would appear as a 'change of state.' The object and the group of displacements are thus indissociable, the one constituting the static aspect and the other the dynamic aspect of the same reality. But this is not all: a world with no objects is a universe with no systematic differentiation between subjective and external realities. . . . [s]uch a universe would be centered on one's own actions, the subject being all the more dominated by this egocentric point of view because he remains un-self-conscious. But the group implies just the opposite attitude: a complete decentralization, such that one's own body is located as one element among others in a system of displacements. . . ."[†]

Thus, the separation of subject and object, or self and world, and the emergence of the group structure have as one of their necessary conditions these figurative processes. The growth of the ego and the growth of the logical operations that permit the person to escape from the confines of the ego require a psychological world containing permanent objects.

But such objects are not given directly through perception. The object, for Piaget, is in its turn the invariant of the group of displacements. The world itself seems, in Piaget's work, to be conceived as something comprehensible only through its transformations. This is one way of interpreting his relativist constructivism. There is a strong relation with the ideas of Marx, and more especially with Marx's Eleventh Thesis on Feuerbach, as Marxist commentators on Piaget have observed.[‡]

On the one hand, then, the most consistent emphasis in Piaget's re-

---

[*] J. Piaget, *Les relations entre l'affectivité et l'intelligence dans le développement mental de l'enfant*, 1962.

[†] J. Piaget, *The Psychology of Intelligence*, 1947, pp. 113–114.

[‡] The similarity can be seen in the following quotation from a Marxist writer not explicitly discussing psychology at all: "By observing and interpreting changes as they occur, the philosophy of practice gains cognition which is never at a standstill; by the never-ending endeavor to affect the development of the changing world, it continually transcends pure observation and interpretation and becomes a motive force of practice. The celebrated Eleventh Thesis with which Marx's notes on Feuerbach end, is

search has been on the mental activity of the child, and in his theory on the growth of intellectual operations. On the other hand, however, in his general approach, the child does not merely act upon a yielding world, he interacts with it. It appears that Piaget realized this imbalance in his work, and set out to restore the balance, to which we owe the trilogy: *The Mechanisms of Perception, Mental Imagery in the Child,* and *Memory and Intelligence.* These three volumes deal with the resistance of the object to the assimilatory schemes of the subject, or put in more ceremoniously logical terms, the limits of deduction. If there were no such limits, there would be no external reality and knowledge would be either a pure, solipsistic exercise or an expression of philosophical idealism. In this matter, Piaget has maintained a position that is full of tension. On the one side, he recognizes the limit to the deductive powers of the knowing subject. But on the other side, he insists that this limit is always being pushed outward by the ingenuity of the subject, who goes on inventing new structures to overcome the resistances of the object. Such a position, it can be seen, is necessarily ambiguous. How does Piaget resolve this difficulty?

He begins by recognizing, in *The Mechanisms of Perception,* a distinction between deforming structures and conserving structures in which the whole is equal to the sum of its parts (the essence of additivity). Deforming structures are gestalten or configurations of the whole in which the whole is different from the sum of its parts; the very putting together of the parts or elements modifies them, ipso facto. According to Piaget, this contextual modifying effect is expressed in the common-sense phrase, "everything is relative." Notice that such a relationship introduces a kind of subjectivity into the getting of knowledge; at the other extreme, the sense in which additive structures do not modify the terms composing them is the source of objectivity.

Obviously perception offers the perfect domain for those interested in this distinction between conserving and deforming structures. Optical-geometrical illusions provide an easy demonstration of the distortions to which this form of knowledge can lead (if uncorrected by other forms of knowledge). This is why Piaget has devoted considerable effort to the study of such illusions, including some new variants suggested to him by his own discoveries and hypotheses. But he does not limit himself only to the study of illusions. He considers other aspects of perception that might seem to be straightforwardly regulated by cognitive invariants. His research on the perceptual constancies, for example, suggests that these are not very stable structures, but give rise to all sorts of phenomena of overconstancy and under-constancy, as a function of the age of the subject and the centration of visual regard or of attention.* The zone upon which the subject fixates or directs his

---

therefore not an either/or but a synthesis of philosophical interpretation and of the practical transforming of the world: 'The philosophers have only *interpreted* the world differently, the point is, to change it.' " Ernst Fischer, *Marx in His Own Words,* pp. 157–158.

* Perceptual constancy is a general term referring to the fact that, although the stimulus falling on a sensory surface such as the retina changes with every motion of the object or of the eye, the appearance of the object does not change. A person walking across the room away from you does not seem to shrink, although the image he casts on your retina shrinks with every step he takes. One way of explaining this is to say that the perceptual mechanism takes account of distance in computing size, thus an *invariant relationship* between image size and distance produces the constant size of the object. It is to the obvious imperfections in any such mechanism that Piaget addresses himself.

attention most often is enlarged in comparison wih neighboring regions that are less often looked at. This leads to a systematic error that Piaget calls "the error of the standard." Thus, the whole perceptual field is liable to various over- and underestimations. These distortions express the essential nonidentity or absence of conservation of the perceptual element, in spite of certain efforts on the part of the subject toward decentration. But it would be incorrect to think that deformations characteristic of perceptual relationships are distributed at random. They obey rather general statistical laws that in their turn depend on the actions of the subject. Piaget was able to reduce the known two-dimensional geometrical illusions to a single extremely simple law, *the law of relative centrations*, expressed in the following equation.

$$P = \frac{nL \ (L_1 - L_2) \times (L_1/L_{max})}{S}$$

where
$P =$ the magnitude of the illusion
$L_1 =$ the greater of the two lengths being compared
$L_2 =$ the smaller
$L_{max} =$ the maximum length of the figure
$nL =$ the number of comparisons to be made
$S =$ the total area of the figure.

A particularly striking example of such perceptual illusions is the Delboeuf illusion, in which two concentric circles exercise mutually distorting influences upon each other. In the well-known form of the illusion, the inner circle is objectively not much smaller than the outer; when compared with another, single circle, the inner circle of the illusion figure appears appreciably larger; to measure the magnitude of the illusion, one holds the outer circle constant and varies the diameter of the inner one.

After having analyzed the illusional deformation of the inner circle, Piaget studied the opposite effect. The outer circle is maximally overestimated when its diameter is 2 × the diameter of the inner circle, and the illusion reaches a minimum when the diameter of the outer circle is 1.5 × the diameter of the inner one. Piaget and his collaborators verified this result with children of different ages, and found that this maximum and minimum remains relatively constant.

One surprising aspect of these results is the following: the figure that corresponds to the minimum magnitude of the illusion when it is compared to a single circle appears larger than the figure corresponding to the maximum, when these pairs of concentric circles are directly compared with each other.

This example shows clearly the deforming character of perceptual knowledge as compared with conceptual knowledge. The evident contradiction in the above results can be explained by the law of relative centrations. Let $A =$ diameter of the inner circle, $A' =$ width of the ring between inner and outer circle, and $B =$ diameter of the outer circle. Then $B = A + 2A'$. In judging the sizes of the two circles there are various comparisons one can make, and he can do this by looking at the figure in various ways, centering his attention on one or another aspect of it. According to the law of relative centrations, the larger of two elements will always be overestimated because it is the one which will be centrated more often. Thus, if A is larger than $2A$ it will be overestimated, and if A is smaller than $2A$ it will be underestimated. The overestimation of A corresponds, of course, to the underestimation of B, and vice versa.

But a second factor also plays a role in determining whether B will be over- or underestimated, the comparison of the whole B (composed of $A + 2A$) with a separate circle (not so composed).

A detailed study of results of this kind is interesting for two reasons. First, it is a good illustration of the deforming relationships to be found in perception. Second, it shows that although these deformations violate logic, they are nevertheless explicable in terms of laws that include certain probabilistic considerations. For it should be noted that although the equation given above does not directly specify any probability function, the underlying idea is the hypothesis that the interplay of comparisons depends on the way in which the most probable number of centrations on any part of the figure is a function of the size of that part.

Finally, it should be noted that such deforming relations are not specific to perception, since they occur in full force in the entire preoperatory stage of development of intelligence, which is characterized by an almost complete absence of conservation.

The deforming relations of perception give rise to two different types of illusion: primary and secondary. *Primary illusions* are those that either remain constant or tend to decrease as the subject gets older because they are entirely dependent on the law of relative centrations, which governs field effects due to the immediate structuring of the perceptual field in figure-ground relationships.

But there is not only centration, there is *decentration*. By centering on different parts of the field successively, the subject creates a situation in which these parts affect each other reciprocally, thus reducing the errors caused by centering predominantly on the larger elements. The richness of exploratory activity increases with age and this would seem to promise more accurate perception, but there are some illusions, which Piaget calls *secondary illusions*, whose magnitude increases with age. One example (and there are not many) is the Oppel-Kundt illusion, in which a "filled space" is seen as larger than an "unfilled space." Figure 1 gives a typical form of the illusion. To simplify

Piaget's analysis somewhat, we can say that the basic illusion, which occurs at all ages tested, results from errors of centration: the cross-hatched line provokes more centrations and is therefore seen as larger. Older subjects, being more thoroughgoing than younger ones in their inspection of the figure, examine the differentiated parts (i.e., the segments produced by the cross-hatching) more completely, giving rise to an increase in the illusion.

Thus we see throughout Piaget's treatment of perception an emphasis on the action of the subject, which governs perception in the first place and is also the motor of perceptual development. The eye is not like a fixed camera directly measuring the geometrical properties of objects. Rather, it is an organ of action, inspecting the world according to its own laws of action, and it is the series of acts that comprise this inspection that furnish the materials of the subject's perceptual world.

This return to action is even more marked in the volumes devoted to the mental image and to memory, where the experiments invented by Piaget and his collaborators dealt directly with the images and memories of actions and even of mental operations.

For Piaget, representation in images is never a simple copy of the exterior world. He takes up some old arguments in French psychology, for example the conjecture that one cannot count the columns of the Parthenon in Athens as they are represented in a mental image at the same time as one walks up rue Soufflot toward the Panthéon in Paris. The mental image is a representational construction based on differentiated imitation and on interiorization of schemes of action by the subject. This is quite a different position from copy theories in which images derive from perceptions, which are in turn passive copies of external objects; such copy theories of the image are, of course, an integral part of empiricist theories of knowledge in which the external world is represented in mental life primarily in the medium of such copies, which result from the impression the world makes upon an essentially passive subject.

Since the construction of images is entirely internal, it belongs to the private life of each individual not directly observable by others. The experiments planned by Piaget and his collaborators have as their first aim to externalize these subjective events, so that some expression of them can be observed. The actions that must serve as the externally observable counterparts of mental images are gestures, drawings, verbal explanations, and reconstructions of the imagined situation with the help of a miscellany of material used freely by the child.

How is the mental image distinguished from the deferred imitation of a model as described by Piaget in *Play, Dreams and Imitation*? Deferred imitation takes place in the absence of the model because of internalization by the child of his own movements. It is a symbolic evocation, since it does not depend on the presence of the model. But it is not an image, since it is a representation-in-action with its shortcomings: lability, rigidity, and lack of differentiation. On the other hand, the image arises out of a coherent system of representation. This system is constructed during the semiotic or preoperatory period of cognitive development. It requires a clear distinction between the signifier and the signified, in which the signifier is the internal equivalent of an external object and the schemes of action attached to it. This distinction permits a growing flexibility in the cognitive life of the subject, since the child can from this point on freely project such images into the past or future. This expansion of the mental field permits memory on the one hand and intellectual anticipation on the other. Such anticipations are, for Piaget, nothing more than the prediction of the results of given actions.

As a result, the mental image develops in close relation with intellectual development. In the ensemble of cognitive development, the mental image occupies an intermediary position between intelligence and perception. From perception, the image takes its figurative character; from intelligence its mobility, without quite attaining that complete mobility, which Piaget calls reversibility, or the capacity for complete and conserving reciprocity and inversion that is characteristic of interiorized actions when they become operational.

Among the experimental results, the clearest is the finding that mental images do not display stages of development, strictly speaking. A second important result is the parallelism between the improving fit of mental images to reality, especially in the case of anticipatory images, and the operational level of intellectual development. This is not particularly surprising, since Piaget and his collaborators chose to study the genesis of mental images in situations of an operatory type.

For instance, they present the children with the customary tests for conservation of quantity but instead of questioning the subject about the transformations she has just observed, they ask her to anticipate what is going to happen by imagining the phases and results of the transformations. Most 5- to 7-year-old children anticipate, for instance, that the level of liquid in the three glasses used in the test for conservation of liquid will be the same regardless of the different sizes of these glasses *and* that the quantity of liquid will be the same in all three glasses. Others anticipate differences in level and infer nonconservation of quantity from that forecast.

In the third volume of this trilogy on figurative aspects of thought, *Memory and Intelligence*, the use of operatory experimental situations reaches a maximum, since all the experiments are of this kind: logical, causal, or spatial relationships. One finds in this work the principal warhorses of Piagetian psychology: seriation, classification, causality, placement, displacement, movement, and time.

The development of memory, like that of mental imagery, is characterized by progressive improvement in performance in general. There is nothing very surprising in this, since the child is in the full course of her mental development. What is astonishing, however, in the experimental results, is that memory depends more on the intellectual level achieved by the child at the moment of recall after 6 months than it does upon the level of development at the moment of the initial exposure to the material. In Piaget's thought, these results imply an active type of coding system, since it seems to undergo constant modification as a function of the subject's continuing cognitive growth. This is quite different from theories of memory according to which information is held in a kind of cold storage where it remains frozen until the moment it is used. For Piaget, memory is neither a warehouse of found objects nor a telephone switchboard. Rather than crude material images, memory appears to him as a veritable production that is elaborated in strict conjunction with the level of intellectual development of the moment. A long time ago, in a now classic work, Bartlett spoke of remembering as an active process of reconstruction.* Piaget's approach is similar, except for his emphasis on the repertoire of operations that the subject brings to bear on this process.

The fecundity of such an approach is evident for domains as diverse as cognitive psychology, psychoanalysis, the psychology of testimony, lying, myths, and legends. For it permits an explanation of the charm and the horror of remembering, the constant deformation without conservation, the occurrence of false memories such as the anecdote Piaget has told about himself to illustrate this point. He has an intense but completely false memory of an incident that occurred when he was a baby in his baby carriage: he was almost kidnapped, but saved thanks to the courage of his nurse. For a long time he "remembered" the epic struggle between the nurse and the kidnapper, the cape of the gendarme who eventually came to the rescue, and the very scene in Paris where the incident took place. But much later on the nurse, penitent, returned the gold Swiss watch the parents had given her as a reward, admitting that she had fabricated the whole story as an excuse for being late.

* F. C. Bartlett, *Remembering* (Cambridge: Cambridge University Press, 1931). There is a similar emphasis on active construction at the time of exposure and reconstruction at the time of recall in Luria's beautiful case study of "S," but again without any recourse to analysis of logical or operatory structures. See A. R. Luria, *The Mind of a Mnemonist* (New York: Basic Books, 1968).

It goes without saying, that by virtue of a kind of intellectual modesty that does him credit Piaget has not pursued all these possibilities in his research. He contents himself with demonstrating that his three essential theses on figurative aspects of thought apply not only to perception and imagery, but to memory as well. These three aspects are the following: First, figurative processes do lie just beyond the limits of deductive thought and, therefore, form nonreversible structures, or gestalten in which the whole is different from the sum of its elements. This irreducibility to additive composition excludes them from the domain of logical determinism, and they must be assigned to the domain of probabilist models. Second, all developmental changes appearing in figurative aspects of thought are attributable to the progress of operativity, of which figurative products are only a kind of sedimentation. Third, the figurative aspects of thought provide a support for intellectual operations without being their source, contrary to the claims of empiricism. Knowledge, a by-now familiar refrain runs, does not owe its origins to sensory experience, its roots are in action; but something has been added to the refrain here, for action gives rise to two sorts of thing, intellectual operations on the one hand and figurative sedimentations on the other.

Piaget, of course, is not the only psychologist to object to stimulus-bound approaches to perception, imagery, and memory. Among other such efforts, in the 1940s and 1950s a tendency known as the "New Look" flourished. Its emphasis, however, was on the influence of the subject's desires and expectations on these figurative processes.* This approach differs from Piaget's in two ways; first, its orientation toward specific objects or contents about which the subject has desires and expectations, as compared with Piaget's emphasis on much more general schemes of action; second, its complete neglect of the ontogenetic development of operatory mechanisms.

This figurative trilogy creates a problem for the reader. We seem to have here a transformation of the goal, or a doubling back on the trail. Having gone off in search of the figurative, Piaget comes home with the operatory. Certainly, the result that memories change with the development of operativity is very striking, but there are at least two theoretical alternatives. The subject might encode in memory a representation which remains unchanged, faithful to the original experience, i.e., in some sense a copy, and then transform it while decoding it at the time of recall, in a manner corresponding to his present level of operativity. This approach would give some independent status to figurative and operatory processes. Piaget has chosen a more radical approach, in which a changing operational structure continually governs and transforms what has been stored; this practically eliminates any independent status for figurative processes.

Further research is required to settle such issues. Meanwhile, the reason for Piaget's choice is fairly clear—his abiding distrust of copy theories in any form because they seem to permit an empiricist approach to the growth of knowledge coupled with his search for a description of all knowledge as permanently "under construction," with no end in sight.

---

* Two of the seminal papers in generating this movement were J. S. Bruner and C. C. Goodman, "Value and Need as Organizing Factors in Perception," *Journal of Abnormal and Social Psychology*, 42 (1947): 33–44; and J. S. Bruner and L. Postman, "On the Perception of Incongruity: A Paradigm," *Journal of Personality*, 18 (1949): 206–223.

33

Mental Images*

1963

The evolution of ideas concerning mental images is perhaps the clearest demonstration of the stages through which experimental psychology has passed. During the first stage at the height of associationism, images were considered both (1) as a direct product not only of perception but of sensation, of which they were allegedly the residual trace and (2) as one of the two fundamental elements of thought, conceived as a system of association between images. In 1897, it was still possible for Alfred Binet to write a whole work on *The Psychology of Reasoning*, in which he expressly defended the thesis that reasoning is based on a succession of associations linking images.

There followed a second stage, beginning around 1900, during which the same Alfred Binet† and also Marbe, Külpe, and the *Denkpsychologie* of the Würzburg school discovered the existence of "imageless thought" (affirmations and negations, relations, the act of judgment itself) and concluded that images cannot be considered as an element of thought but at the most as an auxiliary. Less emphasis was given to the analysis of images. Indeed it was relegated to the background without there having been any real experimental investigation, except in the field of memory and memory-images (or "eidetic" images, the nature of which is still a matter of controversy). The distinction between memory consisting in recognition, which appears earlier and is independent of images, and memory consisting in evocation, which implies images, suggests that there is little that is primitive in the genesis of images.

---

*From *Experimental Psychology: Its Scope and Method*, edited by Paul Fraisse and Jean Piaget, VII. Intelligence, by Pierre Oléron, Jean Piaget, Bärbel Inhelder, and Pierre Gréco, translated by Thérèse Surridge, © 1963 Presses Universitaires de France. English translation © 1969 Routledge and Kegan Paul Ltd., London, Basic Books, Inc., Publishers, New York. Reprinted with permission of the publishers. Originally published in French, 1963.

†A. Binet, *L'étude expérimentale de l'intelligence* (Paris: Schleicher, 1903).

In the third stage, which brings us to the present day, we have witnessed three kinds of progress which directly affect our knowledge of images. The first remains theoretical in nature: images are no longer interpreted as an extension of perception but tend (as Dilthey had foreseen) to acquire the status of a symbol* The second contribution comes from a set of psychophysiological studies and psychopathological observations that have helped to reveal some of the conditions governing the production of imaged representation. What they tend to stress particularly in the formation of images is the role of motor activity whereby an act is reproduced in outline. The third contribution comes from child psychology. It is twofold. First, it enables us to work out approximately the stage at which images are formed (beginnings of the symbolic function with language, symbolic play and deferred imitation). Second, it helps us to trace the development of imaged representation, especially in its multiple relations with the evolution of operations (independence, opposition, subordination, etc.).

Statement of Problems

We propose to describe some typical experiments concerning images and to point out the gaps that remain in our knowledge. . . . No good experiment is ever initiated except in answer to a question and a question cannot be properly asked unless it is correctly situated in relation to a number of other problems. We shall therefore begin by examining these problems, and we hope to present each experiment in its proper perspective in relation to them.

Images are an instrument of knowledge and therefore depend on cognitive functions. These present two distinct aspects according to a fundamental dichotomy which must be recognized if problems are to be correctly stated.

FIGURATIVE AND OPERATIVE ASPECTS OF COGNITIVE FUNCTIONS

The aspect to which mental images are referable is what we shall call the *figurative* aspect. It characterizes the forms of cognition which, from the subject's point of view, appear as "copies" of reality although, from the objective point of view, they offer only an approximate correspondence to objects or events. But this correspondence relates to the figural aspects of reality, that is, to configurations. It is possible to distinguish three fundamental varieties of figurative knowledge: perception, which functions exclusively in the presence of the object and through the medium of a sensory field; imitation in the broad sense (by means of gestures, sounds, or drawing, etc.), functioning in the presence or absence of the object but through actual or manifest motor

*I. Meyerson, "Les images," in G. Dumas, ed., *Nouveau traité de Psychologie*, Vol. 2 (Paris: Alcan, 1932).

reproduction; and mental images, functioning only in the absence of the object and by internalized reproduction.

The other aspect of cognitive functions, which does not directly concern images, but to which we shall sometimes be obliged to refer, is the *operative* aspect. This characterizes the forms of knowledge which consist in modifying an object or an event so as to grasp the actual transformations and their results, and not merely as before the static configurations corresponding to the "states" linked by these transformations. These forms of knowledge include (1) sensorimotor actions (except imitation), the only instruments of the sensorimotor intelligence which becomes organized before language; (2) internalized actions which are an extension of the above. They first appear at the pre-operational level (age 2 to 7); and (3) operations that are properly attributable to intelligence. These are actions which are internalized, reversible, and coordinated into integrated structures bearing on transformations.

We are speaking, for the moment, merely of two "aspects" of cognitive functions and not of two categories, for it is obvious that at a certain level of development one is capable of imagining some, if not all, transformations figuratively, as well as the states or configurations linked by these transformations. The two aspects of cognition, figurative and operative, thus become complementary. Whether this is so at all levels or whether mental images are at first too limited or too static to succeed in figuring transformations remains an open question.

MEANING AND SYMBOLIC FUNCTION

Another dimension of cognitive functions to which we must refer from the beginning in order that we may properly envisage the problems raised by images, is the dimension relating to the structure of meanings. All cognition implies meaning or signification and signification for its part supposes a significant and a significate. But there exist several categories of significants and of significates. [Here Piaget explains the terms *index*, *symbol*, and *sign*. It is helpful to remember that certain terms are used interchangeably: index = cue; signifier = significant = sign; signified = significate; symbolic function = semiotic function.]

Signs and symbols are thus considered to differ from what they signify because they require an *evocation* not just a perception of it. In view of this, we shall term *symbolic function* the ability to evoke objects or situations not actually perceived at the time, by the use of signs or symbols. As mental images are clearly a product of evocation and not of perception, two problems will arise, that of determining the links between images and the symbolic function and that of establishing whether images are significants or significates, or whether they partake of both functions.

. . . In perception there are both significants and significates but the latter consists only in undifferentiated "cues." Imitation itself includes several stages and the higher stages are probably orientated toward the constitution of symbolic significants (deferred imitation). . . .

CLASSIFICATION OF PROBLEMS

The main questions arising from what we have so far discussed are, broadly speaking: (1) to explain the formation of images within the series of figurative structures: are they a direct extension of perception or do they proceed from imitative behavior with its components of motor reproduction? (2) to establish whether the development of images constitutes an independent evolution, thus conferring a relative autonomy on imagery, or whether on the contrary it is subject to increasingly important contributions from outside (from operative mechanisms in particular). . . . In trying to formulate these questions in detail, one is led to the nine following problems:

[Here the authors list nine problems entailed in a systematic treatment of mental images. (1) "Are images motor or sensory or both?" (2) "the genetic level at which images are formed"; (3) "the relations between images and imitation"; (4) "the relations between images and drawing"; (5) the "classification of images" in a manner suitable to studying their development; (6) the process by which higher levels of imagery emerge from lower levels; (7) "the relations between images and thought," especially the operational aspects of thought; (8) the "relations between images and operations" in regard to spatial images; and (9) eidetic imagery and hallucination. The first eight problems are taken up below; the ninth is omitted by the authors because it is not sufficiently general—only a minority of subjects display eidetic imagery, and hallucinations are pathological.]

Psychophysiological Data and Problem of Whether Images Are Sensory or Motor

QUASI-SENSORY CHARACTER OF IMAGES

A visual image gives with varying approximations the shape, dimensions, and color of the object evoked. In individuals of a visual type the sensory qualities of images can sometimes attain a surprising degree of precision. However, as Lotze had already remarked, "images do not light up"; they lack the character of present and living reality found in perception. Similarly, a sound image can render a melody and in individuals of an auditory type it will reproduce it in some detail. Nevertheless the subject will not turn his head to see where the sound is coming from as in the case of perception. The first problem is therefore that of the physiological mechanism of quasi-sensory evocation and it is being solved experimentally by neurosurgical techniques (partial ablation and above all electrical stimulation) evolved by Foerster and remarkably developed by Penfield and his collaborators. When the cortical projections of the optic or auditory tracts are stimulated, one obtains sensory states which, according to Penfield, have nothing in common with hallucinations (therefore even less with images) and are purely sensations. On the other hand, temporal lobe stimulation leads to memory states which can be graduated according to the nature of the images involved and their vividness. Kubie* divides these experimental states into three groups: (1) states of which the content seems present and immediate, but where the subject nevertheless has the impression of being at once an actor and a spectator (as sometimes happens in dreams to which images in this group are closely related, according to Kubie); (2) states that are also quite vivid but evoked as past (according to Kubie these have a quality of imagery comparable to that of images occurring in dozing—hypnagogic reveries); (3) nonvivid memories, without sensation. . . .

Concerning the mechanism of evocations, Penfield† specifies that "the temporal cortex has some sort of selective connection with a detailed flashback record of the past, most of which has been forgotten as far as the individual's ability for voluntary recall is concerned." These flashbacks provoked by electrical stimulation unfold at the former rate of speed as long as the electrode is held in place. An example is hearing a musical theme to which the subject listened some years before. He sees at the same time the orchestra and the singer and is conscious once again of the emotion he felt during the actual performance.

But Lhermitte‡ specifies that it is not yet possible to locate the seat of the mechanisms enabling us "not only to imagine but to image." All that we know is that efferent impulses from the occipital region link up with the "centrencephalic system and also with the diencephalon." . . .

THE ROLE OF MOTOR ACTIVITY

A second problem arises in connection with the first: do images consist only in quasi-sensory evocation or are they in part an active reconstruction expressing itself through the necessary intervention of motor activity? It is this second question which has received most attention, for the following reason. In the days when images were conceived merely as a residual extension of perception (a tradition to which can be attributed the defective use of the word "image" in the expression "after-image"), their quasi-sensory character could encourage the illusion that there was no problem, since they were considered as a weakened form of perception. Yet, even then, authors who believed that movement played a part in perception, were trying to discover movement in the functioning of imaged representation. Thus, Jackson stressed that it contained a motor element in addition to the sensory element and Ribot laid stress on the presence of movements of the eyes and even of the limbs, in analogy with perception.

The problem of the role of motor activity in images takes on its full

---

*L. Kubie, "Discussion on Penfield Memory Mechanisms," *Arch. Neurol. Psychiat.*, 67 (1952): 191–194.

† W. Penfield, "Neurophysiological Basis of the Higher Functions of the Nervous System," in *Handbook of Physiology*, Sect. 1, Vol. 3 (Washington, 1960).

‡J. Lhermitte, "Les hallucinations leurs relations avec les lésions du lobe occipital," in *Les grandes activités du lobe occipital,* ed. T. Alajouanine (Paris: Masson, 1960).

meaning once images have been recognized as something other than residual perception. Thanks to modern techniques, it has been possible to deal with this problem by direct experimentation bearing in particular on the representation of a movement of one's own body. On this point, the alternative is quite plain: either the representative evocation of the movement is something other than the movement itself and consists in "imagining" it like a picture detached from the action, or else this process of imagining the movement rests on the motor adumbration of the movement itself. . . . Gastaut,* using electroencephalograms, observed the same beta waves during the mental representation of the act of flexing the hand and during actual flexing. Allers and Scheminsky,† followed by Jacobson,‡ detected, with electromyograms, the existence of a slight peripheral muscular activity during a representation of arm movements. This slight activity is parallel to that which occurs when the act in question is actually being performed. Conversely, one of Foerster's patients** could neither imagine nor perform the required movements after section of the sensitive posterior roots.

A. Rey†† showed the impossibility of imagining one's forefinger tracing a given figure while it is performing a simple rhythmical flexing movement. Either the real movement is well performed but there is no representation of the figure (e.g., a circle) or else representation is possible, but the rhythm is disturbed as seen from the instrument recording the flexion. A. Rey‡‡ also found that the time required for the internal representation of a movement is equal to or greater than the time required actually to perform it.

A. Rey also noted, in the case of visual representations of hand movements, that eye movements partly reproduced those of the hand. Complex oculo-manual coordinations are thus established. They serve to reinforce the precision of the image and, in our opinion, already show the character of imitative schemata found in images.

In short, imaged representation of a movement of one's own body does not rest on simple evocative pictures external to the movements, but implies an internalized imitation by which they are reproduced in outline, complete reproduction being held back by inhibition.

*H. Gastaut and I. Bert, "EEG Changes During Cinematographic Presentation," EEG Clin. Neurophysiol., 6 (1954): 433–444.

†R. Allers and F. Scheminsky, "Ueber Aktionsströme der Muskeln bei motorischen Vorstellungen und verwandten Vorgängen," Arch.f.d. ges. Physiol., 212 (1926): 169–182.

‡E. Jacobson, "Electrical Measurements of Neuromuscular States During Mental Activities. V. Variation of Specific Muscle Contracting During Imagination." Amer. J. Physiol., 96 (1931): 115–121; and "The Electrophysiology of Mental Activities," Amer. J. Physiol., 44 (1932): 677–694.

**O. Foerster and O. Bumke, Handbuch der Neurologie, Vol. 6 (Berlin, 1936).

††A. Rey, "L'évolution du comportement interne dans la représentation du mouvement (image motrice)," Arch. Psychol., 32 (1948): 209–234.

‡‡A. Rey, "Sur la durée de l'acte réel et de l'acte représenté mentalement," Arch. Sciences nat., Geneva, 64 (1947): 65–70.

EYE MOVEMENTS

The analysis of visual images led F. Morel* to similar conclusions. He began by observing a patient with protruding eyes which made it easier to observe his eye movements. When the patient was asked to shut his eyes and imagine a table, a round garden pond, etc., it was possible, by laying a finger on his eyeballs, to follow movements reproducing the shape of the objects he was imagining. Morel then constructed with Schifferli an apparatus to record eye movements by photographing projections of a light ray on the cornea. Schifferli† compared eye movements during perception and during imaged representation and was able to make the following observations. Regarding perception, his results corroborated the classical discovery that it consists of jerky explorations, with alternating fixations and movements. He was able to establish the existence of varied and relatively stable individual types of oculo-motor exploration. Regarding mental images, he again found the same types of movements in the same subjects as if the subjects followed in their imagination the contours of objects in a way comparable to that occurring in perceptual exploration. . . .

Several recent studies have also shown the existence of eye movements during dreams, thus confirming a hypothesis put forward as early as 1892 by G. Trumball Ladd. In 1955, Aserinsky and Kleitmann‡ distinguished two types of eye movements during sleep, the rapid type accompanied by a heightening of cardiac and respiratory activity and by a typically slow E.E.G. voltage in the frontal and occipital areas and sometimes by vocalizing on the part of the subject. These authors therefore assume that the rapid movements bear a relation to the visual imagery of dreams. In 1957, Dement and Kleitmann,** and in 1958, W. Dement and E. Wolpert†† measured differences in potential during eye movements, taking every precaution to avoid artifacts. They also woke the subjects [adults] during each eye-movement period and obtained accounts of dreams (including as a control some external stimuli, such as a doorbell). Dement and Wolpert concluded that the rapid eye movements thus recorded do not occur haphazardly during sleep or even dreams but that they are specific instruments of the dreamer's visual activity. These eye movements appear to be controlled by cortical centers different from those which control the majority of other movements, since these are not brought into play during sleep.

However, in connection both with the possible role of eye movements in dream images and with the observations of Morel and

*F. Morel, *Introduction à la psychiatrie neurologique* (Paris: Masson, 1947).

†P. Schifferli, "Étude par enregistrement photographique de la motricité oculaire dans l'exploration, dans la reconnaissance et dans la représentation visuelles," *Rev. mens. Psychiat. neurol.*, 126 (1953): 53–118.

‡E. Aserinsky and N. Kleitmann, "Two Types of Ocular Motility Occurring in Sleep," *J. Appl. Physiol.*, 8 (1955): 1–10.

**W. Dement and N. Kleitmann, "The Relation of Eye Movements During Sleep to Dream Activity," *J. Exp. Psychol.*, 53 (1957): 339–346.

††W. Dement and E. A. Wolpert, "The Relation of Eye Movements, Body Motility and External Stimuli to Dream Content," *J. Exp. Psychol.*, 55 (1958): 543–553.

Schifferli on the motor analogies between visual images and perception, there are a number of points that we wish to make. In doing so, we hope to show that what has been said is not simply a reversion to former ideas whereby images were conceived as mere extensions of perception. We should remember first of all that perception takes place on two or more distinct planes: there are those elements that result from the perceptual and are independent of motor activity (at least once they have been established) and there are perceptual activities such as exploration, transportation, etc., dependent on motor activity. If an analogy between images and perception exists, it must be between images and perceptual activities, in contrast to primary perception, which merely provides the prototype for the sensory substance of images. As to the analogy with movements of structuring exploration, it in no way implies that images merely "extend" perceptual activity in the way in which an automatized habit is an extension of the early phases of that habit. The analogy rests, on the contrary, on the two following circumstances: (1) Exploratory activity is already a kind of imitation, since exploratory perceptual activities follow the contours of the object and serve only to favor the "figurative" aspect of perception (and not to modify the object like "operative" actions); (2) the mental image which follows perception (in Schifferli's technique, etc.) is not a residual perception, but results from an active reproduction of perceptual movements and thus constitutes an imitation of them (to the second power), just as we saw that the representation of a movement of one's own body amounts to tracing the movement by internalized imitation.

AUDITORY IMAGES

Finally, we come to auditory images. These have been studied less and we shall confine ourselves to the following remarks. Taking verbal images first, we find that they consist in "hearing" a word belonging to internal language and therefore there is a trace of articulation proper:* there is proof of this in the fact that it is impossible to speed up an auditory evocation beyond a certain limit (especially in the case of a difficult word, such as "peripatetic" or "anacoluthon"). This limit coincides with the time required actually to say the word. Taking musical images next, we find that they are clear and distinct only insofar as one is capable of producing an approximate imitation. As to the orchestral background that accompanies the recollection of a melody after a concert, it is more in the nature of a sound continuum—sensible but not very structured—than of detailed evocation. Thirdly, if we take auditory images of odd noises (thunder, breaking china, tractors, airplanes, etc.) we find that they are remarkably vague and abstract, compared to images of sounds heard less frequently but which can be imitated (birdsong, for example).

---

*In deaf-mutes, who use sign language, Max observed that dreams are often accompanied by movements of the fingers.

Stage and Manner in Which Images Are Formed: Images and Imitation

Although psychophysiological data bring out the fact that images contain an element of active reconstruction, and consequently of motor activity, this in itself is not entirely sufficient to dissociate images from perception, for it is still possible to wonder to what extent similar factors enter into perceptual activities as opposed to sedimented and automatized field effects. The study of genetic data yields supplementary information which, added to the former, seems decisive.

LEVEL AT WHICH IMAGES APPEAR

It is indeed extremely instructive to note that although perception develops from the earliest months in forms that are already complex (perceptual constancies begin to emerge at least as early as 5 to 6 months), mental images do not appear to play any part in children's behavior until the middle of the second year. It is admittedly impossible to prove once and for all the nonexistence of a phenomenon, especially one as difficult to pin down as mental images. Nevertheless, a number of convergent reasons make it possible at least to affirm that all the behavior observed up to that level can be explained without recourse to "representation."

One set of facts concerns the evolution of behavior destined to play a part in the formation of the symbolic function: play and imitation. Symbolic or imaginative play (such as slowly moving a small white object while saying "miaow") leads to images or even already implies them. During the first year of life, however, games are merely practice games or functional games (repeating for the fun of it an action which is otherwise not playful) and symbolic play does not begin until the second year. . . . In the same way, "deferred" imitation (of the kind which starts only in the absence of the model) may lead to images or already suppose them. It also does not appear until the age of about 13 to 14 months. All earlier forms of imitation are learned in the presence of a model and through sensorimotor adjustments based on various signals or perceptual cues and there is no need to invoke imaged representation.

A second set of facts concerns behavior relating to objects that have disappeared from view. Here again, images play a part beyond a certain level, when the subject has to recall a series of successive displacements or reconstitute nonperceptible displacements. In this case too, such behavior appears late and it is not until approximately the age of 9 months that the infant even becomes capable of finding an object which has just been covered by a screen before his very eyes. . . . In short, the search for objects that have disappeared is subject to a particularly slow and complex development and one is obliged to conclude that if the child had from its first year the ability to form mental images, this evolution would be at once much shorter and simpler.

A third set of facts is concerned with the beginnings of representation in intelligent acts. One observes from the age of 14 to 18 months (but not before) the ability to solve problems through internalized coordinations of action; for example, in trying to open a box of matches that is nearly shut, the subject gropes for a while, then pauses, looks attentively at the aperture which has to be made bigger opening and shutting his mouth as he does so until finally he puts his finger in the slit and thus solves the problem. It is probable that there is in this a beginning of representation (and the presumably imitative movement of the mouth is perhaps a tentative evocation of the goal to be reached). The point is that such behavior is not encountered before the age of 12 to 14 months and all previous intelligent acts are the result of "step by step" adjustment and trial and error, with nothing to suggest representative evocation.

It is therefore not incautious to locate the formation of the first mental images at the level at which the symbolic function is constituted, that is, toward the middle of the second year. While the facts that have gone before lead us to dissociate the genesis of images from perception, the data that will now follow allow us to link it to a process that is at once general and clearly characterized, namely the internalization of imitation.

SYMBOLIC FUNCTION AND IMITATION*

Around the age of 14 to 18 months, one observes the first manifestations of the symbolic function in the form of differentiation between significants and significates. This fundamental transformation is shown in four activities which develop more or less simultaneously: (1) the acquisition of language; (2) the emergence of symbolic play following mere practice games; (3) the beginning of deferred imitation (once the different varieties of direct imitation have been systematically mastered); (4) the first manifestations of representation in intelligent acts (internalized coordinations in the sense indicated above). . . .

In a general way, sensorimotor imitation which develops very early (from the age of 3 to 4 months) already constitutes a kind of representation in action, allowing in particular a correspondence to be set up between the nonvisible parts of one's own body (face, etc.) and the visual spectacle of someone else's body, etc. Thereafter, imitation has only to acquire the faculty of extending itself in "deferred" forms to pass from the state of a direct sensorimotor copy to that of evocations which still consist of gestures but are already symbolic. Subsequently, in accordance with the general laws of internalization of behavior and in particular of social behavior (cf. internal language, etc.), we find that imitation, which can already be deferred (and thereby enriched) begins to extend also to internalized imitations. It is in the establishment of these that we can find the starting point of imaged representation and of images themselves in their capacity of motor reproductions.

In conclusion, there is no doubt that genetic data (by putting the

*From 1936 onward (English edition: The Origins of Intelligence in the Child, 1953, pp. 354–356), we have stressed the part played by imitation as a transition between the sensorimotor and the representative levels. H. Wallon developed the same idea in 1942 in a brilliant chapter in De l'acte à la pensée (Paris: Flammarion, 1942).

evolution of images so much later than that of perception and by relating images to symbolic processes proper, which govern representation in general) throw considerable light on psychophysiological facts. But these genetic hypotheses, of which certain consequences have yet to be verified by experiment, naturally explain only the beginnings of specifically reproductive images. There remains the whole problem of the subsequent development of images, particularly in their anticipatory form.

Experiments on Elementary Reproductive Images

Before attempting to classify the different varieties of images according to development, . . . we must justify the preceding hypothesis by analyzing what might almost be called copy-images. These are images of an object constructed in its presence. For instance, the object of the image may simply be displaced (without the displacement being in any way difficult to understand). In such cases, either the image merely prolongs perception, which would contradict our hypotheses, or else it differs from it and it will be necessary to examine to what extent it comes close if not to internal imitation (a reality which unfortunately it is difficult to penetrate) at least to external imitation, in the form of gesture or drawing.

REPRODUCTIVE IMAGE OF A ROD

We began by conducting with B. Matalon the following experiment on 110 children aged from 5 to 11 and 60 adults. A black and rigid rod A, made of wire and measuring 20 cm. in length and 1.8 mm. in diameter is presented to the subject and placed on a sheet of paper perpendicularly to the sagittal axis (henceforth referred to as the "horizontal" position), but on the left half of the sheet of paper. Then the subject is told that the rod is going to be rotated (showing him an actual rotation of 180°) until it reaches position A', a direct prolongation of the first position. He is then asked (question 1) to draw the rod A to the exact length that it will be in position A'. While he does so, the rod is left in its original position. Question 2 consists in picturing (again with a drawing) the length of rod A as it will be in A' after it has been displaced by a simple movement of translation, which is also physically performed before returning A to its original position so that the subject continues to have it before his eyes while drawing. Question 3 simply consists in drawing rod A in A' reproducing the exact length, A remaining where it is and no mention being made of displacement. One can see that in all three cases the task consists in drawing the same rod A, perceptually present, in the same position A', the only difference between the three questions being that the rod A is supposed to move by rotation or translation in questions 1 and 2 and to remain motionless in question 3. The results obtained were as shown in Table 1.

TABLE 1

Errors in drawings of the length of a 20 cm. rod when
subjects are first asked to imagine rotation and translation, or
simply to make a direct copy
(mean percentages)

	Rotation	Translation	Copy
Age 5			
(30 subjects)			
%	−20.5 (15.9 cm.)*	−19.0 (16.2 cm.)	−13.5 (17.3 cm.)
σ	2.8	2.2	1.7
Age 7			
(20 subjects)			
%	−20.5 (15.9 cm.)	−17.0 (16.6 cm.)	−10.5 (17.9 cm.)
σ	2.9	2.2	1.8
Age 11			
(60 subjects)			
%	−5.0 (19.0 cm.)	−4.5 (19.1 cm.)	−8.5 (18.3 cm.)
σ	1.7	1.2	1.0
Adults			
(60 subjects)			
%	+3.5 (20.7 cm.)	−2.5 (19.5 cm.)	+2.0 (20.4 cm.)
σ	1.5	1.2	1.1

* 15.9 = Mean of the actual length of the rods drawn.

It can be seen that (1) young children of 5 produce [significantly] shorter drawings after imagining a displacement (with no significant differences between rotation and translation) than when making a direct copy.* . . . (2) These underestimations diminish with age and are not found in adults. (3) The copy itself is subject to underestimation by young children and this too disappears with age.

Underestimation of length when copying proved very general in all the drawings of straight lines produced by children of 5 to 6. This is decidedly interesting from the point of view of images themselves, since it shows that the simple graphic reproduction of a line implies a previous schema which precedes the act of drawing. . . . This explains what happens in questions 1 and 2, when young subjects are asked to draw in the same position A' the same rod A, clearly visible in front of them. They make it even shorter simply because they first imagine a displacement on request. That they do this is a clear indication that there exists an imitative or quasi-imaged anticipatory motor schema before the process of drawing begins (since the difficulties in drawing are identical in all three cases, and reduced to the minimum); furthermore, it is proof that this imitative motor anticipation is partially inhibited as soon as the subject tries to imagine something further. What happens is not that subjects are distracted by their effort to imagine the rotation in detail, for we shall see that they are hardly capable of doing so. Nor is it simply that a curb is put upon the movement of the hand

*The three values all differ significantly from 20. Taking into account the fact that the three measures were recorded for the same subjects, we find for Student's t that t = 1.29 (not significant) between rotation and translation and t = 3.65 or 3.14 (highly significant) between rotation or translation and copy.

in drawing for although this factor probably plays a part . . . it does not explain the significant differences between the drawings following rotation or translation and direct copies. Finally, it cannot be ascribed either to nonconservation of the length of the rod in the case of rotation or of translation, such as occurred in the operational test based on the overlapping parallel sticks* since there is no overlap in this instance: 78 percent of the subjects examined affirmed conservation in these cases (against 25 percent of the same subjects in the case of the overlapping sticks). . . .

Classification of Images as a Function of Their Development

Images can be classified according to their content (visual, auditory, etc.) or according to their structure, and it is this second standpoint alone that will concern us here. A normal adult is capable of imagining static objects (a table), movements (the swing of a pendulum), known transformations (dividing a square into two equal rectangles). He can even imagine in anticipation a transformation that is new to him (thrice folding a square sheet in two, cutting off the point of intersection of the folds with scissors and imagining before unfolding the paper that he will see two holes and not just one, as when the paper is only twice folded in two). It is clear, however, that these various images are not all equally easy to build up and that there exist, therefore, hierarchic levels of images, possibly corresponding to stages in development. Unfortunately, research has not yet progressed far enough for us to be able to identify any such stages. [But] it is already possible to outline a structural classification of images and to base this classification on restricted studies showing that, in a given limited experimental situation, a particular category of images is formed before another particular category. We are now going to demonstrate this.

[To facilitate discussion], we shall begin by setting out the proposed framework, which we shall later show to be justified by the facts. We must first of all establish a dichotomy between *reproductive* images (R), consisting in the evocation of objects or events that are already known and *anticipatory* images (A) which represent in imagination an event not previously perceived. Reproductive images themselves fall into three categories. They are *static* (RS) if they evoke a motionless object or configuration and *kinetic* (RK) if they evoke a movement. Finally they may consist of images reproducing a *transformation* (RT), if they figure a transformation that is already known (such as the transformation of an arc into a straight line in the case of subjects who have already had experience of this with a piece of wire, etc.). Anticipatory images may also be *kinetic* (AK) or may refer to *transformations* (AT). This simple framework is not sufficient, however, and two further subdivisions must be introduced for the following reasons. In

*Test of conservation of length. Two equal rods measuring 15 or 20 cm. are presented to the subject and their equality is demonstrated by putting them together. Then, one of the rods is moved under the child's eyes until it overlaps the other by 5 to 7 cm. (allowing a gap of 3–5 cm. between the rods to facilitate comparison). Until about the age of 7 or 8, children consider one of the rods to be longer than the other because it overlaps it.

the first place, it may be of interest for genetic reasons to distinguish in the case of static reproductive images (*RS*) and kinetic reproductive images (*RK*) between images produced by immediate copy (*RSC* and *RKC*) and deferred images (*RSD* and *RKD*). Secondly, transformational images (*RT* and *AT*), to which this distinction cannot apply, nevertheless comprise two very different levels according to whether the subject imagines only the result or product *P* of the transformation (hence *RTP* and *ATP*) or forms clear images of (and could for instance draw) the stages of the transformation itself, with all its successive modifications *M* (hence *RTM* and *ATM*).

KINETIC REPRODUCTIVE IMAGES

We shall naturally not examine each of these classes of images but simply give a few typical examples. Taking *static or kinetic reproductive images* first, we find the need to distinguish between deferred images and the kind of image or preimage occurring in immediate copy. The following experiment is instructive from this point of view, but it concerns kinetic images only. Having observed with Lambercier the difficulty experienced by young subjects in reproducing the movements perceived in the configurations used by Michotte to study causality, we took up the problem with A. Etienne, in the following form. Two 1 cm. cubes (one red, one blue) are moved along a 75 cm. trajectory according to various patterns: *entraining* (the first cube starts from the beginning of the trajectory, joins the second, which is standing still in the middle, and carries it along by contact to the end of the trajectory;) *launching* (*id.* but the second moves alone after the impact); *crossing* (both cover the whole trajectory but in opposite directions to one another); *simultaneous displacements* (the first covers half the trajectory while the second covers the other half in the same direction); *symmetrical movements* (each starts from one end, touches the other at the halfway point and goes back in the opposite direction) and *partly symmetrical movements* (one makes the two half-journeys while the other starts from the middle and goes to the opposite end). The subject is given two similar cubes which he moves by hand on a table (but under a screen to avoid visual checks) and is then asked to reproduce the movements perceived, either during actual perception or immediately after the model has stopped moving. The results are as shown in [omitted table, which shows that 64 percent of the 4-year-old subjects readily succeed in simultaneous reproduction of the perceived movement patterns, whereas only 15 percent succeed in reproducing them immediately after they have stopped; by the age of 6, the respective figures are 100 percent and 80 percent.]

In considering failures in simultaneous reproduction, allowance must naturally be made for difficulties arising from the perceptual structurization of the model and for [difficulties] in motor coordination,* etc. But what interests us here is that there is a gap between simultaneous imitation and consecutive reproduction, which is very wide at the age of 3 to 4 and which narrows with age. [We have seen] that the simultaneous copy itself implies a preimaged motor sketch which becomes automatic with age. Taken together, these two facts show the complexity already present in ordinary static or kinetic reproductive

---

*In the case of asymmetrical models (these being the most difficult), subjects err particularly in the direction of "good motor forms," i.e., symmetrical movements.

images. We must therefore expect a much greater difficulty when we
come to transformational images. In particular we shall find that they
follow much clearer stages of development.

ANTICIPATION OF THE ROTATION OF A ROD

Between kinetic reproductive images and those that reproduce
transformations, we find all the intermediate forms, since a movement
may be considered as a transformation of positions. It is only in the
case of changes affecting at least orientation itself (coordinates) that
we shall speak of transformations, however. We shall now give a typical
example of the initial difficulty that subjects experience in reproducing
by means of images the simplest and most commonly encountered
transformations. It concerns merely the transition from the vertical to
the horizontal position of a rigid rod pivoting on its lower extremity
(research carried out with F. Paternotte).

The experimenter presents to the child a black vertical rod of which
the base is fixed and he shows with a quick gesture how it passes from
this original position to the final horizontal position. The subject is then
asked to represent these two extreme positions and some of the intermediate positions. There are four ways of reaching the mental images
of the child and although, naturally, none of them yields the internal
image itself, it is possible by comparing the results obtained with each
method to arrive at a relative approximation: (1) Subjects are required
to draw the vertical and horizontal positions (and are told that the
rods must be pivoted about the same point, if they begin by leaving a
space between the two lines). They must also show "how the rod will
fall" from one position to the other; (2) they are asked (but not immediately after making their drawings, which are not left on the table)
to choose the best of several ready-made drawings which include correct
drawings mixed with others reproducing the children's most frequent
errors; (3) they are asked to imitate by gestures, using the rod itself,
the actual movement that it describes: (4) finally, verbal commentaries
can be useful in cases, admittedly rare, where the child considers his
drawing an inadequate expression of his representation.

Results are so disconcerting before the age of 7 or 8 that one may
well wonder whether the question put before the children is not a matter

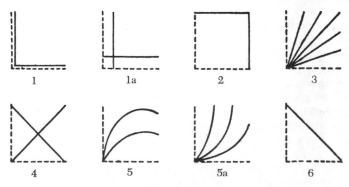

1   1a   2   3

4   5   5a   6

Figure 1

of comprehension and of geometrical operations rather than of images as such. Yet they are not asked to make a judgment but only to evoke an everyday situation, physically recalled at the beginning of the experiment. We shall distinguish two main classes of inadequate images, in addition to entirely negative reactions (no representation): I: Trajectories inscribed in a square, either parallel to the extreme positions (1 and 2, Figure 1) or correctly oblique but with the extremities inscribed in a square (3). II: Random trajectories (4), curved trajectories (5) or others that merge with the trajectory of the tip of the rod (6), which trajectory is represented by a straight line.

The results are as follows:

TABLE 2
Drawings, choice among figures or imitation by gesture,
of the trajectories of a rod falling from the vertical position
to the horizontal position
(in percentages)

		Drawings				
		Correct	Error I	Error II	Choice	Imitation
		%	%	%	% correct	% correct
Age	N					
4–5	18	23	54	18	21	7
6	17	47	29	24	46	43
7	17	65	6	29	81	87
8–9	11	82	9	9	82	82

It is clear that there is satisfactory concordance between the results of the three techniques, except that the imitation of trajectories in space is more difficult at the age of 4 to 5 than their graphic representation. Also, at the age of 7 drawing seems to be slightly behind choice and imitation. Choosing among ready-made drawings is no better than the drawings themselves. . . .

Mechanism of the Evolution of Images

INTRODUCTION

In studying the development of intellectual operations, one finds an evolution which can be described as autonomous in the sense that, despite the complexity of the factors involved (maturation, physical experience, social interactions, and equilibration), there occurs a progressive structurization which begins at the level of sensorimotor actions and ultimately extends to the higher operations. This structuring applies only to the operative aspect of the cognitive functions since this aspect progressively dominates the figurative aspect without being determined by it. On the contrary, the development of one of the main figurative mechanisms, that is, perception, appears progressively subordinated to the intervention of external factors, operative in origin: first the whole action and finally operations. We consequently feel that the main question concerning the evolution of images is to determine upon which of these two kinds of development it depends.

The method to be followed consists in analyzing anticipatory images, and in discovering to what extent they derive in direct line from an earlier level of reproductive images or at what point they begin to imply the intervention of new mechanisms which lie outside images. It goes without saying that we shall then again come across the question that was raised in connection with the trajectory of rods (Table 2): what makes an image appear? Is it simply the discovery of the objects which it evokes and is there therefore a progression whereby the first images to be formed are those of static objects, followed by those of movements, etc., and finally of operation (in the case of anticipatory images)? The image itself would not change in character but its content would simply grow richer. Could it be, on the contrary, that the process of internalized imitation, which constitutes the image, undergoes a transformation according to the type of behavior to be imitated (namely perceptual exploration in the case of static forms, but operations in the case of transformations to be imagined in anticipation)? Is the structure of the image thus modified according to what is to be represented?

TRANSFORMATION OF AN ARC INTO A STRAIGHT LINE

Starting with the study of images which anticipate a transformation, one of the simplest possible modifications—so simple that one could at first take it to be only a question of perceptual evaluation—is the transformation of an arc into a straight line or vice versa. The images required of the subjects may refer only to the result of the transformation (compared lengths of the straight line and of the arc) or to its stages (intermediate figures between the original and final configurations).

The child* is given three arcs measuring 10, 13, and 24 cm. (arcs of a circle with a circumference of 26 cm.), made of flexible wire, and he is asked (1) to copy these and also straight lines of the same length (this preliminary question is intended to assess the general underestimation inherent in the drawings of young children; it is given to a separate group of subjects, so as not to influence the remainder of the experiment); (2) to draw (reproducing their exact length) the straight lines that will result from drawing out the arcs (the transformation of an arc into a straight line is demonstrated with the aid of another piece of wire); (3) to indicate with his two forefingers (symbolism here takes the form of gesture and not of drawing) the length of these straight lines, while looking at the corresponding arcs; (4) to run his finger along an arc and to trace with his finger a straight line of equal length; (5) to choose straight lines equal in length to the arc among ready-made drawings or straight pieces of wire; (6) to draw the stages of the transformation by which the arc becomes a straight line (with a minimum of three drawings, two of which show the extreme positions and one— or more, if possible—shows an intermediate position); (7) to choose among ready-made drawings those which best represent these stages in the transformation.

All these questions are also asked about the transformation which results from bending a straight piece of wire into an arc. In addition, it is

*This research was carried out with Françoise Frank.

useful to have information about the level of understanding attained by the child concerning the conservation of length. He is therefore asked whether two straight lines of 11 cm., which are shown side by side, remain the same length if one is transformed into an arc. Finally he is shown an arc with a chord and asked (with the drawing still before him) whether the chord is equal to the arc, or longer, or shorter.

We shall report only three of the many findings which we obtained with this technique. The first is that the straight lines resulting from drawing out arcs are at first heavily underestimated (and this even in relation to the mean of the underestimations found in copies) and that this systematic error diminishes with age, while the arcs resulting from bending straight lines are greatly overestimated and this error likewise is corrected with age (see Table 3).

TABLE 3

Estimation of the results of the
transformation of an arc into a straight line
(mean of errors as percentages)

	Age 5 (10 subjects)	Age 6 (9 subjects)	Age 7 (10 subjects)	Age 8–9 (10 subjects)
Transformation of an arc into a straight line	−34	−22	−8	−11
Inverse transformation	+29	+8	+7	+7

The second finding was the discovery that children are not able, until about the age of 7, to picture, even by approximate images, the intermediate stages between the arc of a circle and the straight line that results from drawing it out, or vice versa. Rather than enter into statistical detail, we shall simply give the eight types of drawings that we obtained showing the transformation of an arc into a straight line, a transformation which was in fact suggested to the child by pulling symbolically the two ends of an arc made of wire. Yet, among the drawings obtained (Figure 2), series I (A–D) shows no increase in length (cf. Table 3) and drawing A even shows a decrease. Moreover, only drawings C and D show a flattening of the arc, but C does so in a

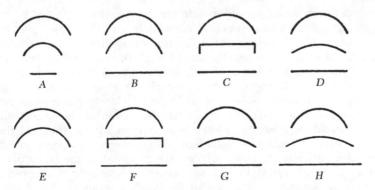

Figure 2

discontinuous fashion and *D* correctly but without increase in length. In series II, where the increase has been achieved (*E–H*), only *H* is correct, while *E–G* present discontinuities either in the curve or in its extension.

INTERPRETATION

What is striking about these drawings and about Table 3 is that the initial underestimation of the straight line derived from the arc or the overestimation of the arc derived from the straight line is brought about by the consideration of boundaries; thus, the straight line resulting from the arc does not extend beyond the boundaries of the arc and conversely the arc resulting from the straight line extends to the very boundaries of the line. This is a common reaction in representative (but not in perceptual) evaluations of length, at preoperational levels: through lack of differentiation between "long" and "far," two trajectories are judged to be of the same length if they have a common finishing point irrespective of their starting points.

One could perhaps object that, in these initial reactions, the child's mental image does no more than express his notion and presents nothing special or interesting as an image. But where does this notion come from? First of all from the initial primacy of ordinal over metrical considerations, and this initial primacy is indeed notional in character and unrelated to images. To this must be added, however, that (1) these relations of order apply in the first place only to the finishing points; (2) "far" does not replace "long" through mere semantic misunderstanding but through lack of differentiation between them; and (3) the consideration of boundaries that are not to be overstepped plays a general rather than a purely ordinal role, as we shall see in a later experiment. Our interpretation is therefore as follows: ordinal relations of a notional character are not the only factor responsible for initial reactions, indeed their excessive hold on the child comes precisely from the fact that they are linked to images. The characteristics peculiar to preoperational thought could therefore largely be explained by the fact that it rests on images. Thus, we are once more led back to images. It is therefore by comparing them to the operations that begin at the age of about 7 or 8 that we must try to find the reason for the preceding reactions.

The operation which is responsible for the transformation of an arc into a straight line, or vice versa, is essentially an "act" which has two characteristics: (1) it brings about the transformation in a continuous fashion, and (2) it conserves the fixed length throughout the transformation. However, conservation of length is accepted by only 15 percent at the age of 5 and it begins to be recognized only at the age of about 6 or 7; as to continuity, Table 3 and Figure 2 clearly show what conclusions we must draw. It is easy to see that, even at the operational level (and in adults even, no matter how mathematically inclined they may be) no mental image is sufficient to symbolize the operation adequately. No matter how adequately we try to visualize the transformation of an arc into a straight line or vice versa, our images proceed in jumps and do no more, according to Bergson's famous phrase (which was in fact a criticism of imaged representation and not of intelligence as revealed in operations!), than to take instantaneous "snapshots" amid the continuum, instead of attaining it as a transformation. What is more, none of our images, although in themselves static, give us the least assurance of conservation. Thus, images cannot exhaust the operation and there are gaps, which are particularly numerous at the pre-operational level. The results are: inability to anticipate in imagination, inadequate intermediate images, and (through failure to imagine the transitions symbolizing continuity) evaluation based only on the starting and finishing points and on the preferred character of boundaries. At the operational level, on the other hand, there appears a new type of image based on symbolic imitation of these operations which succeeds in multiplying "snapshots" to stimulate a continuum and in anticipating approximately the continuation of the sequence thus evoked.

IMAGES OF A SOMERSAULT

Another experiment shows equally clearly the link between anticipatory images and the constitution of operations. It consists in imagining the trajectory of a cardboard tube somersaulting in the air, with a rotation of 180°. Again drawings and gestures are used, but with the addition of verbal description. A 15 cm. cardboard tube is used. It projects over the edge of a springboard so that one has only to press the free end with a forefinger to produce a somersault and to make the tube drop on the table with its ends reversed. At the outset, the front half of the tube is red and the back blue. When it comes to rest the colors are therefore reversed, in a way that is clearly perceptible to the subject.

The tube is first placed on the springboard and the child is told to look carefully at what is going to happen as he will have to draw it. There follows the somersault and the tube is removed immediately after its fall. The child is then asked to draw the tube as it was on the "box" and as it comes to rest on the table. He is next asked to draw intermediate stages. ("Draw the tube as it was soon after leaving the box; a little after that;" etc.) Then the tube is given back to the child who is asked, while holding it in his hand, to reproduce the movement it described (as slowly as possible). It is therefore not a matter of reproducing the somersault, but of following its course in slow motion holding the tube from beginning to end. The subject is also asked for a verbal description if he has not given one as he went along. Finally he must draw the trajectory of the two ends of the tube, one in red and the other in blue.

Table 4 gives the results for drawing, gesture, and verbal description but does not take into account the degree of graphic success of the drawings. Eighty children were examined with E. Siotis, ranging in age from 4 to 7.

The verbal description was judged correct as soon as the idea of rotation was expressed in some way: "It fell over backwards," "It turned over," "This side (the back) came to the front," etc. We are thus concerned with global comprehension, which does not imply detailed determination of the trajectory in all its continuity, but which does include the notion of the final state seen as the outcome of the transformation. It is instructive to observe that this comprehension precedes imaged representation: it is better than reproduction by imitative gesture, which in its turn is better than drawing.

TABLE 4
Imagining the somersault performed by a tube
(rotation of 180°)
(successes as percentage of number of subjects)

	Drawings of intermediate positions	Imitation	Verbal description	Trajectory of the ends	
				One correct	Both correct
Age 4					
(4 subjects)	0	25	25	0	0
Age 5					
(18 subjects)	0	23	59	0	0
Age 6					
(19 subjects)	18	42	64	28	0
Age 7					
(20 subjects)	42	45	75	30	5
Age 8					
(19 subjects)	60	70	100	30	60

REVERSAL OF THE ENDS

As to the permutation of the colored ends following rotation, we tried to establish (1) whether it was noticed and (2) whether it can be imagined. In order to answer the second question, we gave other subjects a white tube and asked them, after drawing the starting and finishing positions, to assign a distinctive color to each of the ends in the starting position, and then to show how these are placed after the somersault. The results were as follows:

TABLE 5
Permutation of colors
(as percentage of successes)

	Age 5	Age 6	Age 7	Age 8
Colored tube	47	50	66	100
White tube	50	60	71	100

It is first of all apparent that what might be called copy-images are no better than anticipatory images, since they refer to the result of a transformation and in this sphere adequate observation calls for a measure of comprehension. Next, it is apparent that these results are better than those in Table 4, except where verbal description is concerned. This again shows that operational comprehension is ahead of representation or of images portraying the details of the transformation. But it shows, above all (and that is why we kept Tables 4 and 5 separate) that it is easier to imagine the result of a transformation (i.e., the new order of colors) than the transformation itself (i.e., the permutation as a reversal of order resulting from rotation). This is because the result of a transformation is only a state and a static image is all that is needed to represent it. This accounts for the simplicity of the images which we referred to as *RTP* and *ATP*. The transformation itself, however, is a dynamic continuum and imagining the successive stages (*RTM* or *ATM* in our notation) remains much more symbolic and subordinate to the operation. Yet, despite the greater simplicity of the image of the result (cf. the figure of 100 percent at age 8 as against 60 or 70 percent in Table 4), it is only at about the age of 7 or 8 that it rises to 75 percent because it is subordinate to operational comprehension. Thus, although the result of the transformation is only a state, it is a state that is imagined and even observed only insofar as it is produced by the transformation, and this presupposes that the latter is "understood" even if it cannot yet be represented by adequate images.

THE DISPLACEMENT OF A SQUARE

In view of the fact that anticipatory images relating to the change in shape or rotation of an object are so late in appearing, what of the anticipation of a transformation which is no more than the simple displacement (translation) of one of the elements of a figure in relation to another? We studied this with F. Frank and T. Bang.

Two 5 cm. square cards, one above the other and touching (Figure 3, *A*) are presented to the child and the experimenter checks first that the child can draw this configuration. Then the child is asked to make a drawing anticipating what the figure will look like after the top square has been slightly pushed from left to right while the lower square remains where it is (Figure 3, *H*). Once the child's drawing has been obtained, he is asked to choose the correct figure among ready-made drawings. It is necessary to take the usual precautions with the youngest subjects: showing only a few drawings at a time and, if several are said to be correct, asking which is the best. As the choices appeared to be affected by the perseveration of the anticipations [drawings] that had preceded them, we finally decided to study anticipations and choices with separate groups. As a final question, the children are asked to copy the correct figure (*H*) to make sure that such a drawing is possible. Several other controls were carried out: the same tests were administered but with noncontiguous squares separated by a space of

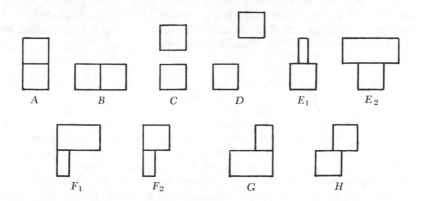

Figure 3

TABLE 6

Graphic anticipations of the displacement of a square
(in percentage of solutions) and choice
among ready-made drawings
(in brackets)

Figures drawn	A–D	E_1–E_2	F_1–F_2–G	H (Correct)
Age 4 (13 subjects)	55.5 (41.4)	11.1 (6.9)	5.6 (24.2)	27.8 (27.5)
Age 5 (21 subjects)	29.0 (33.3)	4.0 (9.8)	33.0 (23.5)	34.0 (33.3)
Age 6 (21 subjects)	7.0 (12.6)	7.0 (6.3)	40.0 (28.2)	53.0 (53.0)
Age 7 (10 subjects)	0.0 (0.0)	7.0 (7.0)	15.5 (15.5)	77.5 (77.5)

1 cm., or with contiguous squares of different colors, or varying the instructions by saying that both squares would move at once in opposite directions.

Choices among ready-made drawings, representing the possible solutions given in the anticipations, are except at the age of 4 remarkably in agreement with individual anticipations. This already provides an answer to the possible objection that the scarcity of correct solutions among young children is due to difficulty in drawing figure H and not to difficulty in visualizing it as an image. However, as we have already said, a control was carried out by asking the subjects to make a direct copy of figure H. Although an exact copy was made by only 32 percent of the 19 subjects at age 4 and by 48 percent of the 23 subjects at age 5 to 5;5, it was achieved by 79 percent of the 19 subjects at age 5;6 to 5;11. Let us also note that when a space is left between the squares, one still finds errors of the type A–C but mostly figures of type D. Using squares of two colors does not improve results. Imagining the simultaneous displacement of two squares in opposite directions complicates the solutions.

To conclude, it is interesting from the point of view of the theory of images to observe how static they remain until the age of 7 and 8, even in such a simple case as a straightforward relative displacement. The subject may very well show by gestures the displacement of the top square but this is a global image. As soon as it comes to visualizing detail, either the top square becomes detached from the bottom square (drawings B to D) or the child begins to imagine the spatial shift, but pictures it as symmetrical (E_1 and E_2) or else visualizes a projection to one side but a block at the other boundary (F, G).

KINETIC ANTICIPATORY IMAGES

We must now mention another type of experiment, relating to purely kinetic anticipatory images, that is, not to a transformation where a possible displacement is imagined but to the simple continuation of a movement of which the beginning is perceived. . . . In an experiment [with E. Siotis] where we used two moving objects traveling at unequal speeds, and where one was about to overtake the other before they both stopped, we had been struck by the fact that young subjects either did not anticipate the continuation of these movements or else took into account only the order of the finishing points with no regard to the movements themselves. Here, then, is a field to be explored from the point of view of anticipatory images.

The moving objects used as models follow two rectilinear and parallel courses 90 cm. long, the last third of which is through a tunnel. Before reaching the tunnel, the two cars. one red, one yellow, go through the following motions (with carefully regulated synchronism over 1½ seconds and with respectively constant speeds): (1) overtaking (just before entering the tunnel); (2) catching up (at the exact moment of entry); and (3) partial catching up. The points of departure are always staggered, one of the cars is always quicker than the other (but sometimes it is the one, sometimes the other) and both stop in the tunnel. The child is placed facing the halfway mark and looks down perpendicularly on the courses. He has a strip of paper 1.80 m. long, without a tunnel (but the part corresponding to the tunnel is colored blue like the tunnel); every 10 cm. there are little strokes dividing the strip into equal segments (so that the experimenter can see whether the subject varies the intervals between the cars). The only two questions that interest us here are: (1) reproducing the movements perceived (after the model cars have stopped inside the tunnel and so without a visible finishing point), and (2) anticipating (immediately after the reproduction called for in question 1 the continuation of the movements perceived, on the understanding that the respective speeds are maintained (that "they go on traveling as before"). These questions are then followed by a verbal question (3) on the speeds involved, to determine the operational level of the subject but this does not concern us here, except indirectly. Finally (4) the tunnel is removed and the subject is asked to reproduce the relative movements of the two cars (and not merely the starting and finishing positions).

It will be observed that the two questions (1 and 2) do in fact concern only mental images, reproductive in the case of 1 and anticipatory in 2. The subject is not asked to estimate speeds but exclusively to reproduce what he has seen, then to prolong it through anticipation. One could almost suspect, where success proves general, that such anticipation is no more than simple perseveration. The interest of the results obtained with 161 children aged 5 to 11 lay precisely in showing that, even where there is correct reproduction, anticipation does not result from it by way of a simple prolongation, but implies new and original contributions.

The reproduction of movements is far from being perfect and does indeed confirm what was said [above] about the difference between images and operations from the double standpoint of continuity and conservation: in young children, reproduction of movement proceeds in jerks, without conservation of speed, thus with noticeable acceleration before catching up and temporary increase in the interval between the moving objects after overtaking. It is only toward the age of 8 that subjects realize that in order to reproduce movements accurately it is necessary to see the objects move, that is, to take into account the kinetic continuum (with conservation) and not merely the finishing points, or starting and finishing points. . . .

Regarding anticipation, we shall distinguish three categories of reactions: (1) no anticipations, not even of the ordinal type; (2) purely ordinal anticipations, that is, taking into account only the order (before and after) of the cars and not the extent of the spatial intervals between them; (3) "hyperordinal" anticipation (taking the term in the same sense as Suppes), which foresees that the spatial interval between the

TABLE 7

Ordinal anticipations (O) and hyperordinal anticipations (Ho) in relation to the number of accurate reproductions *

	Overtaking		Catching up		Partial catching up	
	Ho	O	Ho	O	Ho	O
Age 5 (29 subjects)	10.6		0.0	50.0	0.0	15.3
Age 6 (30 subjects)	23.3		10.0	60.0	16.6	58.3
Age 7 (24 subjects)	40.0		22.2	53.3	25.0	25.0
Age 8 (25 subjects)	43.8		10.5	57.8	15.3	53.8
Age 9 (34 subjects)	50.0		27.2	45.4	38.8	55.5
Ages 10–11 (19 subjects)	76.5		72.2	16.6	77.0	23.0

* The O column refers to the anticipation of straightforward overtaking in cases where only catching up or partial catching up are visible. In the case of visible overtaking, relative ordinal anticipation has no meaning and merges with accurate reproductions.

cars increases progressively. The results computed in the absolute and also in relation to the number of subjects who gave a good reproduction are given [in] Table 7.

The conclusion to be drawn from this experiment is thus clear and confirms those of the three preceding experiments. In the first place, one observes that while hyperordinal consideration of increasing and decreasing intervals plays a fundamental part in the perception of speed,* it does not play a decisive part in anticipatory images (72–77 percent) until the age of about 10 or 11, when the ordinal operations of speed (overtaking) give way to metrical operations ($v = s/t$). Ordinal anticipations only gradually assert themselves (approximately between the ages of 6 and 8) linked this time with ordinal operations. Briefly, whereas reproductive images proceed in static and discontinuous "snapshots," images can only become anticipatory when directed by operations, by dint of multiplying "snapshots" and orientating them according to a new mode of comprehension, based on continuous transformation and no longer exclusively on the reproduction of configurations.

THE EVOLUTION OF IMAGES

. . . The anticipatory images which characterize the later stages do not simply derive from the reproductive images of earlier stages. Like perception, the activities of which are framed by the whole action and then by intelligence, images do not develop in an autonomous fashion and this appears to be a general characteristic of the figurative forms of cognitive activity; imitation also, in which images seem to be a product of internalization, cannot be achieved without the assistance of operative intelligence† since the child, like the chimpanzee, imitates only what it can at least partially understand. Images therefore begin at

*See Piaget, Feller, and McNear, 1957–1958.
†The reader is reminded that we use the term "operative" to refer to that aspect of intelligence which embraces actions (physical or internalized) and operations. This is by opposition to the term "operational," which refers to operations alone.

preoperational levels by being reproductive only and attached to configurations (including kinetic configurations) rather than to transformations. Proceeding as they do by discontinuous and static "snapshots,"
they long remain incapable of symbolizing transformations. But following the constitution of intellectual operations, whose role is precisely
that of grasping these transformations through acts of dynamic comprehension, there appears a new type of image based on the imitation of
these operations. Now, the imitation of an operation is not an operation, for it fails to capture the continuity of the operation as well as the
unique synthesis of invariances and transformations, but it imitates
these new characteristics by multiplying "snapshots" of the internal
movement of the operational act. In this it allows itself to be guided by
the movement itself and achieves the illusion of continuity by a diffuse
consciousness of the jumps leading from each snapshot to the next.

Images and Thought: The Role of Images in the Preparation and Functioning of Operations

INTRODUCTION

Binet and the Würzburg School showed the existence of "thought
without images," although it would be better described as thought distinct from images, since as I. Meyerson* stresses, it may be that all
thought, even when distinct from images, needs imaged symbolic support besides the system of linguistic signs. We now know that this
aspect of thought, distinct from images, is operational in nature. An
operation is, in fact, unrepresentable in itself, being an act which is
apt to become "pure" in the sense in which one speaks of "pure mathematics," that is, independent of any object. Thus, a number does not
carry with it any image, except in a symbolic capacity: if one tries to
imagine the number 4, one can "see" four apples, or the sign 4, etc.,
but the number as such is something quite different and is defined by
the bi-univocal correspondence between all sets of the same power. This
correspondence in turn may also be symbolized, for example by spatial
rows linked term for term, but in generalizing to "all" one no longer
imagines anything. That type of reasoning which, after verifying that a
property is true at O and that it is also true for $n + 1$ if it is true for n,
concludes that it is true of "all" numbers, may rest at the outset on
more or less distinct imaged "intuitions." These symbolize among other
things the succession of whole numbers, but these images provide an
evocation that is ridiculously restricted in relation to the infinite. If we
turn to the child, we find that he long denies all conservation. Eventually
he comes to admit that when the shape of an object is changed, the
quantity of substance remains invariant, because increase in one

*I. Meyerson, "Les images," in *Nouveau traité de Psychologie*, Vol. 2,
ed. G. Dumas (Paris: Alcan, 1932).

dimension is offset by decrease in another. The point here is that the child's image may well "symbolize" an approximate compensation but it cannot of itself represent exact conservation or compensation even though operational thought recognizes these to be necessary.

Nevertheless, it is unlikely that we ever carry out an operation without imaged symbolic support and the most abstract mathematicians recognize that even if "intuition" has no demonstrative value, it remains indispensable as a tool for further discovery. This presents a problem and it remains for us to try to establish how far reproductive or anticipatory images contribute to the formation or at least to the functioning of nascent or higher operations. But, here again, the answer cannot come from theoretical discussion. Experimentation alone is instructive.

The method consists in going back to a number of known operational tests and asking the subjects to anticipate by means of images some of the data and the products of particular transformations. This they must do prior to the manipulation and actual transformation of the objects concerned. . . .

ANTICIPATION OF THE SERIATION OF LENGTHS

An easily reproduceable experiment concerns the seriation of lengths.

The child is presented with ten little strips of wood ranging from 10 to 16.5 cm., placed in random order on a table, and he is asked to sort them into a "staircase," starting with the shortest and ending with the longest. Following the usual technique, which is not directed at the problem of images, the child is allowed to manipulate the elements from the beginning and one thus obtains three levels from the operational standpoint. There is first of all the failure level where the child proceeds in pairs or small series which bear no ordered relation to each other. Next there is a level of preoperational success where the child arrives at the correct series, but by trial and error and empirical corrections. Finally there is the operational level (age 7–8) where the child tries first to find, by paired comparisons, the smallest of all the elements, A, and having found it sets it down first; secondly the smallest of those that are left, B, which he puts in second place; thirdly the next smallest, C, etc. This level is called operational because the child uses a systematic and exhaustive method and because this method implies comprehension of the fact that a particular element, E, is at once bigger than those preceding it $(E > D, C, B, A)$ and smaller than those following $(E < F, G, . . .)$, which implies reversibility by reciprocity.* To analyze the possible role of images, one will then proceed as follows: (1) instead of allowing immediate manipulation of the strips of wood, the subject will be asked to imagine the result of seriation and, for instance, to draw in advance with a black crayon the "staircase" to be achieved. We shall call this "global anticipation" and it can also be symbolized by gestures; (2) strips of distinctive colors will be used and the child will be offered crayons of corresponding colors (with a few extra colors) and will be asked (before any manipulation) to make a colored drawing of the series to be constructed, observing the correspondence between colors and lengths: this we shall call "analytical anticipation."

The results obtained are very clear as to the distinction between global and analytical anticipations:

*This operational solution is achieved by 6 percent of the 5 year olds (the same children as will be mentioned in connection with images), 22 percent of 6 year olds, 80 percent of 7 year olds and 85 percent of 8 year olds.

TABLE 8

Percentage of graphic varieties of anticipation of seriation

	Age 4 (19 subjects)	Age 5 (33 subjects)	Age 6 (19 subjects)	Age 7 (10 subjects)	Ages 8–9 (7 subjects)
Failure in anticipation	89	42	5	0	0
Global anticipation only	11	55	73	20	0
Analytical anticipation	0	3	22	80	100

It is evident from this that global anticipation is found much earlier than operational seriation. This amounts to saying that a large number of subjects are perfectly capable of drawing the series in advance (in black or without taking the order of colors into account), but cannot for all this construct it by an operational method (they are content to make successive groping attempts until they arrive at a configuration that conforms to their internal model). Analytical anticipation, on the other hand, is at least as difficult as operational seriation.

INTERPRETATION

The reason for these facts seems clear. As global anticipation is not sufficient to give rise to the operation (there is a two years' time lag), it cannot be interpreted as a preparation for the operation, nor even as an anticipatory image, for a series of elements of uniform gradation is perceptually a "good form" and its evocation amounts to no more than a reproductive image copying this perceptible form. The fact of achieving a drawing without blurs does not imply operational reversibility, since this is a one-way action. It is much easier to produce pencil strokes of increasing length (since these are freely decided) than to find among disordered objects those which obey a law of regular increment. Analytical anticipation, on the other hand, supposes that the subject orders the objects themselves, since in this case he must assign to each pencil stroke a color corresponding to that of the object differentiated according to its size. Anticipation thus presupposes genuine seriation, by combination of percepts and images, but the overall image which is thus genuinely anticipatory rests ipso facto on the operation. In fact it merges with the "draft" or plan of the actual operation.

Another variety of anticipatory image was studied by A. Rey who showed that it was based on the operation of seriation. It enables us to confirm these two interpretations. Rey* had the ingenious idea of presenting to children a square sheet of paper with a square drawn in the middle and asking them to draw on the same sheet "the smallest possible square"† next to the square already drawn (or alternatively "the largest possible square" that can be drawn on the sheet). From the

*A. Rey, "Le problème psychologique des 'quantités limites' chez l'enfant," *Rev. suisse Psychol.*, 11 (1944): 238–249.

†The original square in the middle of the sheet was drawn by the child himself. He is then told: 'Now draw, next to it, the smallest square that can be drawn; draw a square so small that it couldn't be any smaller.' If the child fails, he is asked whether he can't make an even smaller square, etc.

age of 8, subjects succeed in drawing a square of 1–2 mm.[2] (or, in the opposite case, one closely following the edges of the paper), while the youngest subjects, despite their efforts at reducing or increasing the scale continue for a long time to produce squares scarcely smaller and scarcely larger than the original square. Rey correctly interprets this failure of small children as due to a lack of anticipation. They are not able to rely on operations of seriation but from the age of 7 or 8 the handling of this operational structure makes it possible to clear in one leap the series of intermediate squares between the one given and the one required. One then sees why it is that this anticipatory image, even if the question asked does not explicitly call for an operation, is of late development. It is because, like the analytical anticipation of drawings in color, it rests in fact on seriation as an operation, whereas global anticipation does no more then evoke in advance the required configuration, which could be the product of an operation but is not necessarily so (unlike Rey's largest and smallest possible squares), since it is also simply a good perceptual form.

ANTICIPATION OF CONSERVATION

A second experiment, itself the prototype of a series of others, has yielded similar results. It shows that images are partly ahead of operations and it also shows the use made of images in operations and the final subordination of states or configurations to transformations which cannot be represented figuratively in an adequate fashion.

Former observations had taught us that if one transfers a liquid from a glass A, to a glass B which is narrower and taller than A, or into a glass C which is wider and lower, a child of 5 to 6 does not believe in the conservation of the quantity of liquid transferred. . . . We therefore asked ourselves with S. Taponier: (1) whether children of 5 to 6 would imagine conservation or the reverse when the transfer was not physically performed (or else performed behind a screen so that only the outline of glasses B and C could be seen) but simply anticipated in thought; (2) what anticipatory image they would have of the levels reached by the liquid in the course of these imagined transfers; (3) how they would imagine the levels reached by two equal quantities (= the same amount "to drink") in glasses A and B.*

The results are very decisive. Out of 44 + 30 subjects (the latter with six glasses instead of three), 4 categories of responses were found. First, we should note that the levels were correctly anticipated (for 3 glasses: question 2) by 25 percent of the subjects at age 4 and 5, 38 percent at age 6, 63 percent at age 7, and 72 percent at age 8: . . .

1. 30 percent fail [both] to imagine levels and final conservation;
2. 23 percent succeed in imagining the levels but fail in the final conservation;
3. 42 percent succeed in imagining the levels and succeed with the final conservation;
4. 5 percent fail to imagine the levels but succeed with the final conservation.

It therefore seems that in cases where levels are accurately imagined prior to any notion of conservation (category 2), there is only a repro-

*Independently, therefore, of any transfer.

ductive image based on acquired experience. Every child may have occasion to pour liquid from a wider to a narrower container! It is also evident that the image of levels is not sufficient in itself to give rise to operations of compensation, which are the source of the notion of conservation. This is shown by the fact that subjects in this category (2) think that two identical quantities of liquid poured into two different glasses A and B will give the same levels (question 3) as if quantity was measured by level alone!

The conclusions to be drawn from this type of experiment, as from the [seriation of lengths] are therefore first that operations transcend images, while making use of them; and second that, once brought into play, operations direct images and even determine them almost entirely in some cases. That is why in order to imagine the inequality of levels in glasses A, B, and C, given equal quantities of liquid, it is necessary to introduce an operational system of compensation; since the image of the levels is here a function not of a transfer to be anticipated but of an equality to be achieved between two distinct quantities of liquid. In a general way, in fact, no image of compensation can acquire any true degree of approximation without relying on a system of operations, deductive or metrical.

Spatial Images and "Geometrical Intuition"

It is true in a general way that images constitute symbols which are relatively adequate when they represent static configurations but which become less and less adequate when they attempt to represent increasingly complex operational transformations. Nevertheless, there exists a whole category of images that have remarkable relative adequacy, even concerning transformations. We refer to spatial images, the source of what mathematicians call geometrical intuition. The psychological problem raised by these images consists in establishing whether their particular adequacy is due to an autonomous development of imagery itself, or whether it results from the progressive intervention of operations, indeed of specifically spatial operations. If it is to be attributed to these operations, there is no doubt that their specific character would account for the fact that they can be represented by adequate images.

DISTINCTIVE CHARACTER OF SPATIAL IMAGES

The particular position of spatial images is due to the relations between their form and content, and it is necessary to specify this point in order to understand the experiments that will follow. The "form" of an image is spatio-temporal in character, since images are an internalized imitation of objects and events as they appear in space (visual images, etc.) and in time (auditory images). When images have as their "content" (i.e., refer to) logical or arithmetical operations, these operations usually possess spatio-temporal points of reference. This makes it possible to have an image of their results. . . . On the other hand, these logico-arithmetical operations remain acts of transformation, which cannot be represented by images because they have nothing to do with spatial configurations. It is possible to imagine a sequence of numbers as a row of little strokes, etc., or to imagine classifying operations by means of circles (Euler circles) or of compartments that can be inserted or taken out. These images, however, provide only very approximate symbolism (except where there is isomorphism between certain algebraic and topological structures). What they do, in fact, is merely to translate non-spatio-temporal transformations into imaged, and therefore spatialized, forms. In the case of spatial images, on the other hand, the contents to be represented are spatial like the imaged forms which represent them and spatial operations (displacements, projections, etc.) are again figurative transformations and so, in a sense, figures in space. There is then more or less complete homogeneity between form and content and this is enough to account for the privileged character of spatial images.

From this particular homogeneity, there follow two fundamental consequences. The first is that spatial images are the only images in which the symbolizing form tends to complete isomorphism with the symbolized content. The image of a number or a class is not a number or a class but an image of numbered or classified objects, while the image of a square is approximately square and the image of a straight line, while having width, may be considered as a sheath of parallel straight lines. The second consequence is that the field of spatial images is the only one where images of transformations are situated on the same plane as static images and anticipatory images on the same plane as reproductive images. Given sufficient practice, geometrical intuition can thus enable one to "see in space" the transformations themselves, even at times the most complex and the furthest removed from common physical experience. This is because the image rests on a spatialized imitation of operations which are themselves spatial.

IMAGES OF DEVELOPMENT*

It is of vital interest to the theory of images to establish whether images of transformation, and in particular anticipatory images, derive simply from internal progress and the progressive flexibility of reproductive images or whether the development of geometrical "intuition" depends necessarily on that of operations. . . . Among the many examples available, we shall mention only one, which is particularly striking: that of so called "rotations" in children's drawings, so well described by Luquet, which we shall consider in conjunction with truly geometrical operations of development. The question lies in establishing whether or not imagery occurring in the former can lead to anticipatory images giving an adequate visual representation of the transformations involved in the corresponding operations.

Children's drawings are commonly characterized by a phenomenon which we shall call "pseudo-rotation" and which Luquet aptly described

*Translator's note: "Development" is used here in a technical sense: "Geom. The action of unrolling a cylindrical or conical surface, the unbending of any curved surface into a plane, or of any non-plane curve into a plane curve." (O.E.D.)

as a "mixture of viewpoints." In one of the examples which he quotes, a horse is drawn in profile pulling a cart which is not represented in the same perspective but shown in plain view from above. As for the wheels, they are all four on the same horizontal plane which supposes a rotation of 90° in relation to the floor of the cart.* In fact, therefore, three distinct viewpoints are mixed and juxtaposed. One can wonder whether subjects who are capable of thus dissociating viewpoints, will succeed in anticipating by images the result of the unfolding of cardboard cubes, cylinders, or cones, of which all the elements are developed on a single horizontal plane. The analysis of reactions, by age groups, gives two results contrary to this hypothesis: (1) imagining the result of true developments goes far beyond the level of spontaneous pseudo-rotations, since it supposes a *coordination* of viewpoints (and not simply a random mixture), hence an operational factor based on the action of unfolding itself; (2) correct images of these developments result from an internal imitation of the actions of unfolding and of their results and are not a mere extension of perceptions or of the spontaneous pseudo-rotations occurring in drawing. The latter merely express the diversity of possible perceptions (each imitated separately as a reproductive image), but the capacity for anticipation resulting from operational coordinations is lacking.

Three stages have been observed. During the first stage (until about the age of 6, that is, at the ages corresponding to pseudo-rotations in drawing) children are not yet capable of imagining any true development. They draw the whole object without transformation.

During the second stage, fruitless efforts are made to imagine development and the drawings express these attempts in a symbolic form. The side of a tube to be rotated is, for instance, drawn with a line indicating the direction of the rotation; or again, a slit is put in to symbolize the beginning of the action required to unfold the side, etc.

During the third stage (from the age of 7 or 8) development is at last imagined and drawn, but in progressive stages according to an order of hierarchy among objects; first cylinders and cones, then cubes—a little more difficult because of their six sides—and finally pyramids.

In short, this example like all the others so far observed seems to show that although geometrical intuition really is the preferred sphere of mobile and anticipatory images, there is no question of a capacity present at all ages nor of a product purely of mental imagery. Such "intuition" is in fact essentially operational and images play their essential part only when guided and informed by operations.

Conclusion

. . . Concerning the classification and evolution of images, our results seem to indicate that there is a fairly systematic difficulty in passing from reproductive to anticipatory images and that, in the course

*Two of the wheels are shown below the floor of the cart, as if they were situated in the same perspective as the horse, but the other two are drawn above, which therefore shows a general rotation of 90° for the four wheels, without relation to the position of the horse.

of this transition, it is necessary to introduce operational factors foreign to images. But these results refer only to averages irrespective of all typological considerations. The fact is that the diversity of imagery in adults has always been recognized. Some people are particularly visual, others mainly motor, auditory, etc. It would be very interesting to study the question from a genetic angle and where one finds early typological diversity, to select a few particularly visual or particularly nonvisual subjects in order to reexamine with both types problems relating both to the transition from reproductive images to anticipatory images and to the relations between images and operations.

With reference to the relations between images and thought, it is probable that the last word has yet to be said, for if one accepts the proposed distinction between the operative and the figurative aspects— and we shall need many more facts before we can decide whether such a distinction is fundamental or artificial—it follows that images are at once necessary to represent states but insufficient to understand trans- formations, and this somewhat modifies the terms of a classical prob- lem. It is probable that more detailed analysis of geometrical intuition in pure geometry and in the geometrical representation of phenomena will supply the key to these questions. Although we can nowadays study the beginnings of geometrical intuition, we are strangely at a loss regarding all that concerns both its functioning and the respective parts played by images and operations in the thought processes of scientists who make a daily and creative use of this "intuition." One of us (Piaget) was the pupil of a great tectonician who had founded "alpine embryology" and who was gifted with extraordinary vision in space, as shown for instance by his work on the overthrust of folds: "I can see them moving," he would say, looking at a chain of mountains of which he had made a particular study. What lessons could not be drawn from a close analysis of the play of images in the thought of such men? Yet no research of this kind is known to have been undertaken.

One day a connection will be established between genetic studies of the integration of functions and the psychopathological study of their disintegration. Had this already been done, it would probably have been impossible to write a chapter on images without recourse to the theories concerning hallucination. The fact that it has not been so clearly shows the extent of the field which remains to be explored before we can master in their most general forms the laws of images in their relations to the laws of thought.

34

Memory and the Structure of Image-Memories*

1966

Too little research has been done on the memory of the child, and what research there has been has centered primarily on the measuring of performance. For example, by reading fifteen words to the subject and finding out how many he retained after one minute, Claparède observed a gradual increase with age to an average of eight words in the adult.

The most important factor in the development of memory, however, is its gradual organization. There are two types of memory: the memory of *recognition*, which operates only in the presence of an object already encountered and which consists in recognizing it; and the memory of *evocation*, which consists in evoking the object in its absence by means of an image-memory. The memory of recognition is very precocious (it exists in the lower invertebrates) and is necessarily related to action-schemes or habits. In the newborn child, its roots are to be sought in the schemes of elementary sensorimotor assimilation: the baby recognizes the nipple during nursing and distinguishes it from the surrounding skin if it has slipped out of his mouth; the baby recognizes an object which he has been watching if it is lost from sight for an instant; and so on. Evocation memory, mental images, [and] the first beginnings of language (linked together by Janet when he speaks of the appearance of "recounting of events") start more or less simultaneously. This complex of new behavior patterns raises an essential problem: is it independent of or dependent on the general schematism of actions and operations?†

---

*From *The Psychology of the Child* by Jean Piaget and Bärbel Inhelder, translated by Helen Weaver, © 1969 by Basic Books, Inc., Publishers, New York. Reprinted by permission of Basic Books, Inc., and Routledge & Kegan Paul Ltd., London. Originally published in French, 1966.

†Bergson sought to introduce a radical opposition between the image-memory and the motor-memory of the *"mémoire habitude"* (habit-memory) (which is also related to recognition, for every habit presupposes the recognition of [indexes]. But this is the introspection of a philosopher, for if one studies the image-memory in its development one sees that it is also inseparable from action. For example, with F. Frank and J. Bliss we studied the memory, after several days, of an arrangement of cubes, tested under three different conditions: (1) the child had merely looked at them; (2) he had

In the light of these remarks, the problem of memory is primarily a problem of delimitation. Not all conservation of the past is memory; all schemes (from the sensorimotor schemes to the operatory schemes of classification, seriation, etc.) continue to function independently of "memory"; in other words, the memory of a scheme is the scheme itself. What is commonly called memory, then, once rid of the remnants of facultative psychology, is simply the figurative aspect of the systems of schemes as a whole, from the elementary sensorimotor schemes in which the figurative aspect is perceptual recognition to the highest schemes whose figurative and mnemonic aspect is the image-memory.

On this basis we have undertaken a series of studies which are far from complete but whose results are nevertheless instructive. For example, working with H. Sinclair, we presented ten sticks seriated according to their differences in length, and after a week asked the child to reproduce them by gesture or drawing. We worked with two groups of subjects: the first simply looked at the sticks, and the second described them verbally. Finally, we determined the operatory level of the subject with respect to seriation. The most important result obtained is that, with significant regularity, subjects produce a drawing that corresponds to their operatory level (pairs, uncoordinated short series, or   , etc.) rather than to the configuration presented. In other words, memory causes the schemes corresponding to the child's level to predominate: the image-memory relates to this scheme rather than to the perceptual model.*

Six months later, the same subjects provided a second drawing from memory (they had not seen the model again). In 80 percent of the cases [the second drawing] was slightly superior to the first (threes instead

---

actively copied the arrangement; and (3) he had watched an adult arrange the cubes. (The sequence of the conditions was varied.) Actively copying the arrangement gives better results than perception, and learning in the order action-perception succeeds better than in the order perception-action (with an interval of at least a week). The perception of adult activity adds almost nothing to the perception of the result alone. The memory-image is therefore itself related to schemes of action, and one finds at least ten intermediate stages between motor-memory with simple recognition and pure evocation in images independent of action.

*Another study (with J. Bliss) concerned the transitive nature of equalities. A long, narrow glass A contains the same quantity as an ordinary glass B, and B contains the same quantity as a short, wide glass C. These equalities are confirmed by transfer of the contents of A to B' (the equivalent of B) and back to A and from C to B" (the equivalent of B and B') and back to C. Subjects are tested to determine what is retained of these events after an hour and after a week. Here too the child retains what he has understood rather than what he has seen. This is not so obvious as one might think. Subjects at an elementary stage, in particular, draw the transfer from B to C and vice versa as if the two movements were simultaneous. "But didn't one happen before the other?" "No, both at the same time." "But then the liquids get all mixed up?" A goes into B' at the same time as it returns, etc.; the process has no transitive relation. The fact that the child has not understood and cannot memorize relationships that he has not understood goes without saying. Yet he might have retained the successive quality of the events perceived. On the contrary, however, he schematizes them in terms of intellectual rather than experienced schemes! The following stages are also in strict correlation with the operatory level of the subjects.

of twos, little series instead of threes, etc.). Intellectual progress in the scheme resulted in progress in memory.

As for the conservation of memories themselves, according to some authorities (Freud, Bergson), memories accumulate in the unconscious, where they are forgotten or remain ready to be evoked. According to others (Pierre Janet), remembering is a reconstruction comparable to that carried out by the historian (through testimony, inferences, etc.). W. G. Penfield's recent experiments on the reactivation of memories by electrical stimulation of the temporal lobes suggest a certain degree of conservation, but numerous observations (and the existence of false but vivid memories) also show that reconstruction plays a part. The connection between memories and schemes of action suggested by the preceding facts, along with the schematization of memories as such studied by F. Bartlett,* makes such a reconciliation conceivable by emphasizing the importance of motor or operatory elements at all levels of memory. Since, moreover, the image which occurs in image-memory constitutes an internalized imitation [and therefore] also includes a motor element, the conservation of particular memories can easily be reconciled with such an interpretation.

*F. C. Bartlett, *Remembering* (Cambridge: Cambridge University Press, 1932).

PART IX

Piaget on Education

INTRODUCTION

Why is there no Piagetian dogma about education? We suggest several reasons. To begin with, it is almost impossible to pin down any educational method and say that it is "the" or even "a" Piagetian method. Selection 33 explains this point. The actual psychological significance of any method changes in subtle ways depending on the teacher's *understanding* of children's thinking. Piaget has devoted his efforts to changing our understanding of the child; for some this is only a prelude to the development of new educational means, for others it is the new means.

Moreover, it is almost impossible to separate means from ends in applying Piaget's ideas to education. Activity is the means by which growth of cognitive structures comes about, and activity is the functioning of those structures. Activity nourishes the structures that guide the activity. Thus we cannot say simply that activity is the means and cultivation of the structures the end. They are inherently inseparable and, at least at this early stage, that makes orderly discussion difficult.

Finally, Piaget's contributions fall in three main areas, which leaves it up to educators looking for guidance to draw upon them in varying proportions: (1) He emphasizes the importance of *activity* in the growth of intelligence. (2) He explores in depth the growth of the child's thinking in relation to certain universals in the *contents* of human experience—such as the nature of objects, space, time, motion, chance, causality, moral responsibility, and social awareness. (3) He proposes that certain underlying, pervasive logico-mathematical *structures* are found repeatedly in these diverse content areas.

There are many contemporary developments in applications of Piagetian cognitive psychology to education, but this is not the place to review them. Instead, we offer a schematization of *possible* approaches, if two main issues are considered, the use of materials and exercises on the one hand, and the type of social relationships on the other. We have given each of four "models" a place name intended to bring out one of its strong points.

Taos: respect for the individual artisan. Emphasis is on carefully selected materials and exercises that will help each individual child to develop himself through his own activity which, while spontaneous in a sense, is molded by the nature of the materials and tasks. The educator's primary role is to design and supply these. At one extreme within this approach there can be a stockpile or library of tasks, from which the child draws freely. At the other extreme, decisive efforts can be made by the teacher to keep the child moving through sequences that correspond to certain norms. In any reasonable school modeled along these lines, some of the activities will have social-cognitive goals (e.g., imitation, decentration, moral judgment). But the

basic plan conceives of each child conducting his or her intellectual developments alone.

Paris: pleasures of discussion. Emphasis is on dialogue between equal
partners. Materials are unimportant except, perhaps, for the casual use of
limited resources at hand, such as the napkins and glasses in a bistro. If the
partners in discussion are thought of as children only, some of this happens
in most schools, but strong efforts are often made to suppress it. If the partners
are thought of as one adult and one child engaged in sharing ideas at an
intimate level, some teachers would admit that even a few minutes spent in
this way with each child can be valuable but most would consider this an unrealistic use of time. It is not easy, in a discussion, to maintain relations of
equality between child and adult. The adult dominates.

Athens: the Socratic method. Again, the basic format is the dialogue, but
there is no intention to create a relationship of equality.* The adult asks the
questions, poses the problems, and if there is any material involved, provides
it as he sees fit.

The adult brings her understanding of what is valuable knowledge and
of what the child knows to the situation, and conducts the questioning in
such a manner that the child will come to know more. This is the clinical
method of Piaget, transformed from a research instrument into a way of
teaching. As with "Paris," it takes up a lot of teaching time. Some educators
believe that a child can have dialogues with a computer. There are various
efforts under way to use computers to replace the human teacher, at least
partially, in this tutorial relationship.

Eldorado: The adult participates with the child in the processes of discovery and learning. The materials and situations used are important, for they
must be rich enough in possibilities to permit people at different levels of
development to entertain honest questions about them, to take an interest
in making them, playing with them, exploring them. A key point is that because the adult opens herself to the situation and develops herself in it, the
child has an opportunity to watch someone at another cognitive level, and in
his own fashion to imitate what he can.† Of course, the adults in the school
play a directive role along a spectrum of possibilities similar to that described
for "Taos." But the main idea is that the teacher shares her knowledge with
the child by living it.

Let us consider now the relation of three of these models to two avenues
of cognitive growth that form an important part of Piagetian theory, play, and
imitation (we are not yet ready to deal with dreams in this way, and we omit
the Paris model here because we do not know how to treat it). For cognitive
growth to occur through play and imitation, these processes must occur, and
a school that wishes to exploit their power must make them possible. The
following assertions seem plausible.

---

* Dialogue (non-Socratic) in Athens: Q. Which one is Socrates? A. The one wearing the tunic. Q. But they are both wearing tunics. A. Well, the one asking the questions.

† Various mixtures of Taos, Paris, and Athens occur in the Piaget-education literature. Eldorado is less familiar, but there is at least one example that seems to come
close to and, in fact, inspired this description: the Mountain View Center for Environmental Education at the University of Colorado. The origins of its approach are
described in *The Logic of Action: From a Teacher's Notebook* by Frances Pockman
Hawkins, Boulder, Colorado: published by Mountain View Center for Environmental
Education, 1969. The work of the Center is described and its approach discussed in
its publication, *Outlook*.

In a Taos school the child can and will certainly play with the materials *if* the teacher does not destroy the play atmosphere by being bossily directive, or preoccupied with fixed behavioral or even cognitive objectives. The child will be able to imitate other children doing similar things, *if* this is encouraged and matters are so arranged. In a Taos school the child will *not* be able to imitate a teacher having an intellectual growth experience, because that does not occur in relation to the materials the child works with; for example, a teacher using Cuisenaire rods is advised to master their rich possibilities before confronting the children, rather than together with them.

In an Athens school, play seems out of the question. A Socratic dialogue may be very absorbing, but it is not playful. Insofar as it is a one-to-one situation, the child imitating another child is not a possibility, but in certain variations this might occur. The child could only imitate the teacher by a reversal of roles and at a later time, since during the dialogue the roles are fixed.

In an Eldorado school, play, imitation of other children, and imitation of the teacher are all possible.

These points are summarized in Table 1.

TABLE 1.
Educational models favoring different cognitive functions

	Model		
Cognitive Function	Taos	Athens	Eldorado
Play	+	−	+
Imitating other children	+?	−	+
Imitating teacher	−	+?	+

Play and imitation are surely not the only cognitive processes that take place in schools, nor are the few considerations we have introduced the only important ones, nor are these four models even a small part of those conceivable. Nevertheless, this incomplete sketch may indicate the way in which Piagetian theory might be brought to bear in various educational settings.

Imitation has recently come into its own in American developmental and experimental psychology.* There have been some very fruitful results but thus far, beyond Piaget's work, there has been little recognition of the problems of the development of imitation itself. Perhaps it is thought that this function is completely developed by the age of 3–4 years, and if so, Piaget's work may have contributed to this impression. But if imitation is basically accommodative, the accommodations are accomplished by schemes already present. As these schemes develop, the very nature of imitation must change. A deeper study of this question might suggest avenues by which imitation at higher cognitive levels could be inserted into the process of education.

Play, for most psychologists, still lies in that part of the medieval map of the world marked out, "here be dragons." Nor does it fit in well with a school system interested in moving children ever more quickly through an increasingly well-defined curriculum, or set of behavioral objectives. The basic assimilative function of play means that it is a type of activity in which

* See Albert Bandura, "Behavior Theory and the Models of Man," *American Psychologist*, 29 (1974): 859–869, for some interesting reflections on the relation of this trend to education and other social issues.

established schemas are exercised rather than changed, things fit into schemas rather than schemas adjusting to things.* That is why play is fun.

In the short run, then, play does not seem like a very direct way of producing cognitive growth, if what is meant by growth is accommodation, or the change of schemas. In the longer run, however, as Piaget has insisted, the total process of growth requires an equilibration of accommodation and assimilation.

This leads us to an issue that Piaget has labeled "the American question." Can development through the Piagetian stages be accelerated by appropriate techniques of training? We have discussed the relation of this question to Piaget's general theory in the Introduction to this volume. Here we want to examine its relation to problems of education. If, as present research and theory suggest, such acceleration cannot be very great, it may be profitable to ask ourselves an almost unthinkable question, about a limiting case. Suppose no acceleration at all were possible, what would be the function of education? One answer would be that Piagetian concepts and stages would then have nothing to do with education, for that science must deal with what can be accomplished. An alternative answer, which we propose, would begin by saying that the importance of acceleration has been highly overrated.

If our aim is to help the person develop herself so that she will go through life with an active, inquiring, inventing mind, speed is not the only thing that counts, although there must be some lower limit on the rate of cognitive functions that remain adaptive. What else matters, then? To put it briefly, any cognitive structure can be widened, deepened, and linked more coherently with other structures. Greater conscious control of such structures can be attained. The affective range of a structure can also be modified, that is, it can be activated in the contexts of pleasure and pain as well as in the context of work. One of the central meanings of ego strength must certainly be that powerful cognitive structures do not become inactive in emotionally laden situations. Thus, even if no acceleration of movement through the celebrated stages were possible, there would still be lots to do.

Change the question!

We have said enough to support the statement that there is no Piagetian educational dogma. We can go further now: If there were a Piagetian educational dogma, it would be necessary to destroy it. Regardless of their many virtues, professional innovators know so much that they often have the effect of intimidating the people they are trying to help. This effect is especially harmful in education. We do not need intimidated teachers, even if they are coerced into doing the right thing. For the teacher, all dogma is bad, even good dogma. Probably the best thing that each group of teachers can do is to invent the approach that fits their situation. Piaget's remark, that only by reinventing a theory can the child understand it, applies equally well to all adults. If the teacher is to understand what he is doing, he must invent it; he can neither invent it well nor understand it if he does not understand the child. What Piaget has done can only be an aid to that understanding, without which teachers cannot invent and reinvent their practice.

---

* When a woman approached the English painter, Turner, and reproached him with the remark that real sunsets don't look like the ones he painted, he answered, "I know, madam, but don't you wish they did?"

35

Science of Education and the Psychology of the Child*

1935 and 1965

The New Methods: Their Psychological Foundations†

How is one to define the new methods of education, and from when should we date their first appearance? To educate is to adapt the child to an adult social environment, in other words, to change the individual's psychobiological constitution in terms of the totality of the collective realities to which the community consciously attributes a certain value. There are, therefore, two terms in the relation constituted by education: on the one hand the growing individual; on the other the social, intellectual, and moral values into which the educator is charged with initiating that individual. The adult, viewing the relationship between these terms from his own point of view, began by paying attention solely to the second, and thus by conceiving of education as a mere transmission of collective social values from generation to generation. And out of ignorance, or even on account of this opposition between the state of nature characteristic of each individual and the norms of socialization, the educator concerned himself at first with the ends of education rather than with its techniques, with the finished man rather than with the child and the laws of its development.

Because of this he was led, implicitly or explicitly, to look upon the child either as a little man to be instructed, given morals, and identified as rapidly as possible with its adult models, or as the prop of various original sins, that is, as recalcitrant raw material even more in need of reclamation than of instruction. It is from this point of view that the major part of our educational methods stem. It defines the "old" or "traditional" methods of education. The new methods are those that take account of the child's own peculiar nature and make their appeal to the laws of the individual's psychological constitution and those of his development. *Passivity as against activity.*

But let there be no misunderstandings. Memory, passive obedience,

*From *Science of Education and the Psychology of the Child* by Jean Piaget, translation by Derek Coltman. Translation Copyright © 1970 by Grossman Publishers. Reprinted by permission of Grossman Publishers, a division of the Viking Press, Inc., New York, and Longman Group Ltd., London.

†[The following section was written in 1935.]

imitation of the adult, and the receptive factors in general are all as natural to the child as spontaneous activity, Nor can it be said that the old methods, however antipsychological they may sometimes be, entirely neglected to observe the child in this respect. The criterion upon which a distinction between the two kinds of education is to be based should therefore be sought, not in the use made of any particular feature of the child's mentality, but in the general conception that the educator forms of the child in each case.

Is childhood a necessary evil, or have the characteristics of the childish mentality a functional significance that defines a genuine activity? According to the reply given to this fundamental question, the relation between adult society and the child to be educated will be conceived of as either unilateral or reciprocal. In the first case the child is called upon to receive from outside the already perfected products of adult knowledge and morality; the educational relationship consists of pressure on the one side and receptiveness on the other. From such a point of view even the most individual kinds of task performed by students (writing an essay, making a translation, solving a problem) partake less of the genuine activity of spontaneous and individual research than of the imposed exercise or the act of copying an external model; the student's inmost morality remains fundamentally directed toward obedience rather than autonomy. Whereas, on the other hand, to the degree in which childhood is thought of as endowed with its own genuine form of activity, and the development of mind as being included within that activity's dynamic, the relation between the subjects to be educated and society becomes reciprocal: the child no longer tends to approach the state of adulthood by receiving reason and the rules of right action ready-made, but by achieving them with his own effort and personal experience; in return, society expects more of its new generations than mere imitation: it expects enrichment.

Developments in Pedagogy*

There can be no question here of taking theoretical considerations as our starting point. The only way to begin is with the facts that sooner or later make such considerations necessary. Three sorts of data, at once disparate and selected from among many others, are instructive in this respect.

IGNORANCE OF RESULTS

The first observation—a surprising one—that comes to mind after the passage of thirty years is the ignorance in which we still remain with regard to the results achieved by our educational techniques. In 1965

*[The following and subsequent sections were written in 1965.]

we do not know any more than we did in 1935, what remains of the various kinds of knowledge acquired in primary and secondary schools, after five, ten, or twenty years, among representatives of the various strata of our population. Though we do, of course, possess indirect forms of information on this point, such as that provided by the post-school examinations given to conscripts into the Swiss army, the amazing story of which between the years 1875 and 1914 has been recorded for us by P. Bovet (and in particular the intensive revision courses organized in many localities in order to conceal the disastrous results these examinations produced when not prepared for by last-minute cramming). But we have no exact information, for example, as to what a 30-year-old peasant still remembers of the history and geography he was once taught, or as to how much a practicing lawyer may have retained of the chemistry, physics, or even geometry he acquired in his high school or lycée. We are told that Latin (and in certain countries Greek as well) is indispensable to the training of a doctor of medicine; but has anyone ever attempted to provide controls for such an affirmation, and to dissociate it from the factors of interested professional protection involved, by trying to evaluate what remains of such training in the mind of a practicing doctor (and also by drawing the relevant comparison between Japanese and Chinese doctors and European ones with regard to this relationship between medical value and classical studies)? . . .

It will be objected that our memory of what we have learned is unrelated to the culture acquired; but how is one to evaluate that culture other than by resorting to wildly generalized and subjective judgments? And is the culture that counts in any particular individual always that which results from the specifically scholastic part of his education (once the detailed knowledge acquired at final examination level has been forgotten), or is it the culture his school managed to develop in him through incentives or interests stimulated independently of what at that time appeared to be the essential part of his so-called basic education? . . .

Moreover, there are certain branches of instruction, quite obviously devoid of any formative value, that we continue to lay down as essential without knowing whether in fact they do or do not attain the utilitarian end that has been traditionally allotted to them. Everyone accepts, for example, the fact that in order to live a social existence it is necessary to know how to spell (leaving aside any discussion of the rational or purely traditionalist significance of such a necessity). But we continue to lack all decisive knowledge of whether specialized instruction in orthography increases our learning ability in this field, is wholly neutral in its effects, or can sometimes become an outright hindrance. . . .

In fact, all we have at our disposal as a basis for judging the productivity of our scholastic methods are the results of end-of-school examinations and, to some extent, certain competitive examinations. But the use of these data entails both a begging of the question and a vicious circle.

A begging of the question, to begin with, because we are postulating that success in those examinations constitutes a proof of durability of the knowledge acquired, whereas the real problem, still in no way resolved, consists precisely in attempting to establish what remains after a lapse of several years of the knowledge whose existence has been proved once by success in those examinations, as well as in trying to determine the exact composition of whatever still subsists independently of the detailed knowledge forgotten. On these two prime points, then, we still have almost no information.

A vicious circle, in the second place—and this is even more serious —because we are saying that it is possible to judge the value of scholastic instruction by success in final examinations when the fact is that a great deal of the work done in school is influenced by the prospect of those very examinations, and is even seriously distorted, according to some respected thinkers, as this preoccupation becomes increasingly dominant. It therefore goes without saying, if we are to achieve any scientific objectivity or even any honesty with regard to the parents and above all the students involved, that it must be a preliminary consideration of any pedagogical study of scholastic productivity to compare the results of schools without examinations, where the student's worth is evaluated by the teachers as a function of work done throughout the year, with those of ordinary schools where the prospect of final examinations may be falsifying not only the work of the students but even that of the teachers as well. . . .

The fact is that on all these fundamental questions, as on many others, too, experimental pedagogy—even though it does exist and has already accomplished much valuable work—still remains silent, thereby testifying to the terrifying disproportion that still subsists between the scope or importance of the problems facing it and the means being employed to resolve them. . . .

RESEARCH AND THE TEACHING BODY

In the period between 1935 and 1965, in almost all the branches of what we term the natural, social, or human sciences, one could quote the names of great writers, men of international reputation, who have revolutionized, more or less profoundly, the branches of learning to which they have devoted their labors. Yet, during that same period, no great pedagogue has appeared whom we can add to the list of eminent men whose names provide our milestones in the history of education. And this raises still another problem.

It is a problem, however, whose terms are not limited to the period in question. If we glance through the tables of contents in the various histories of education, the first observation inevitably thrust upon us is the very large proportion of innovators in the field of pedagogy who were not professional educators. Comenius created and ran schools, but he was by training a theologian and a philosopher. Rousseau never held classes, and though he may have had children we know that he did not occupy himself with them to any extent. Froebel, the creator of kindergartens and the champion of a sensory education (however inadequate it may have been) was a chemist and a philosopher. Herbart was a psychologist and a philosopher. Among our contemporaries, Dewey was a philosopher, Mme Montessori, Decroly, and Claparède were all doctors of medicine, and the latter two were psychologists as well. Pestalozzi, on the other hand, perhaps the most illustrious of the pedagogues who were purely and simply educators (though he was a very modern one), invented nothing in the way of new methods or approaches, unless we allow him the use of slates, and even that was simply for reasons of economy. . . .

There have doubtless been examples in other disciplines, too, of fundamental inspirations being contributed by men who were not "of the profession": everyone knows how much medicine, for example, is indebted to Pasteur, who was not a doctor. But medicine in its broad outline is nevertheless the work of doctors, the engineering sciences have been constructed by engineers, and so forth. So why is pedagogy so little the work of pedagogues? This is a serious and ever-present problem. The absence or scarcity of research on the results of scholastic instruction that we were emphasizing a moment ago is only one particular case. The general problem is to understand why the vast army of educators now laboring throughout the entire world with such devotion and, in general, with such competence, does not engender an elite of researchers capable of making pedagogy into a discipline, at once scientific and alive, that could take its rightful place among all those other applied disciplines that draw upon both art and science. . . .

The truth is that the profession of educator has not yet attained, in our societies, the normal status to which it has the right in the scale of intellectual values. A lawyer, even one of no exceptional talent, owes the consideration in which he is held to a respected and respectable discipline, that is, the law, whose prestige corresponds to clearly defined ranks among university teachers. A doctor, even one who does not always cure his patients, represents a hallowed science, the acquisition of which is a lengthy and arduous process. An engineer, like the doctor, represents a science and a technique. A university teacher represents the science he teaches and to whose progress he devotes his efforts. What the schoolteacher lacks, in contrast to all these, is a comparable intellectual prestige. And the reason for this lack is an extraordinary and rather disturbing combination of circumstances.

The general reason is, for the most part, that the schoolteacher is not thought of, either by others or, what is worse, by himself, as a specialist from the double point of view of techniques and scientific creativeness, but rather as the mere transmitter of a kind of knowledge that is within everyone's grasp. In other words, it is considered that a good teacher is providing what is expected of him when he is in possession of a general elementary education and has learned a few appropriate formulas that enable him to inculcate a similar education in the minds of his pupils. . . .

EXPERIMENTAL PEDAGOGY OR THE STUDY OF

PROGRAMS AND METHODS

Whether educational programs and teaching methods are imposed by the state or left to the initiative of teachers, it is still quite clear that we can make no justified statements about their practical productivity, or, above all, about the numerous unexpected effects they may have upon the general formation of individuals, without systematic study employing all the means so fertile in possibilities for cross-checking that have been developed by modern statistical science and the various fields of psychosociological research.

Several decades ago, as a result of this realization, a new discipline was constituted called "experimental pedagogy" whose task was the specialized study of such problems. Claparède, in a work bearing the double title *Psychologie de l'enfant et pédagogie experimentale* that went into numerous editions and was much translated at the beginning of this century, had already shown that this experimental pedagogy is not a branch of psychology (except in that it integrates all the activities of teachers themselves into the subject matter of the latter science). Experimental pedagogy is concerned, in practice, solely with the development and the results of pedagogic processes proper, which does not mean, as we shall see, that psychology does not constitute a necessary reference for it, but that the problems posed are different from those of psychology, and that they are concerned less with the general and spontaneous characteristics of the child and its intelligence than with their modification by the process in question.

It is, for example, a question for experimental pedagogy to decide whether the best way of learning to read consists in beginning with the letters, then graduating to words and finally to sentences, in accordance with the classical or "analytical" method, or whether it is better to work through these stages in reverse order, in accordance with Decroly's "total" method. Only a patient, methodical research program, using comparable groups of subjects for equally comparable periods of time, while taking care to neutralize as far as possible any adventitious factors (quality of the teachers and their preferences for one or other method, etc.) can permit a solution of the question; and there can be no question of seeking for a solution by means of deductive considerations based upon knowledge provided by psychology, however experimental in origin itself, about the role of "gestalts" in our perception, or about the syncretic or total character of perception in the child (even though it was such considerations that led Decroly to conceive and create his method, since that in itself does not constitute verification). . . .

This commonplace example demonstrates, in the first place, the complexity of the problems confronting experimental pedagogy if we wish to judge educational methods according to objective criteria and not merely according to the evaluations of them made by the teachers involved, by inspectors, or by the students' parents. It further shows that the problems are, in reality, of a pedagogical order and not purely psychological, since the measurement of scholastic productivity obeys criteria that are the concern of the educator alone, even if the methods employed do partly overlap with those of the psychologist. On the other hand, the question of the necessity for collaboration between experimental pedagogy and child psychology as against the desirability of a radical independence for the former has also been raised in recent years, particularly in French-speaking pedagogical circles.

This problem has not arisen, however, either in the Anglo-Saxon countries or in the peoples' republics, where it is tacitly accepted in all the research centers that are dependent upon universities and in the pedagogical academies that experimental pedagogy is bound to rely upon psychology in much the same way as medicine relies upon biology or physiology, while remaining distinct from them. . . .

Development of Some Branches of Teaching

Several branches of teaching in particular have given rise since 1935 to reexaminations of their programs and of their teaching methods stimulated by three sorts of causes, sometimes overlapping and sometimes quite independent of one another. The first of these causes is the internal development of the disciplines being taught: mathematics, for example, has undergone an extremely far-reaching reorganization during the past few years, to the point where its very language has been completely transformed, and it is therefore natural that there should be an attempt to adapt students, from the very earliest age, to a new world of concepts that would otherwise remain perpetually strange to them. The second cause is the appearance of new teaching methods: the first steps in arithmetical reckoning, for example, have provided a fruitful field for the use of new physical teaching aids. The third cause is the use being made, still on a modest scale but sometimes with marked effect, of the data provided by child and adolescent psychology. . . .

THE DIDACTICS OF MATHEMATICS

The teaching of mathematics has always presented a somewhat paradoxical problem. There exists, in fact, a certain category of students, otherwise quite intelligent and even capable of demonstrating above average intelligence in other fields, who always fail, more or less systematically, in mathematics. Yet mathematics constitutes a direct extension of logic itself, so much so that it is actually impossible to draw a firm line of demarcation between these two fields (and this remains true whatever interpretation we give to the relationship: identity, progressive construction, etc.). So that it is difficult to conceive how students who are well endowed when it comes to the elaboration and utilization of the spontaneous logico-mathematical structures of intelligence can find themselves handicapped in the comprehension of a branch of teaching that bears exclusively upon what is to be derived from such structures. Such students do exist, however, and with them the problem.

It is usually answered in a rather facile way by talk about mathematical "aptitude" (or "bump," in memory of Gall). But, if what we have just posited as to the relationship of this form of knowledge with the fundamental operational structures of thought is true, then either this "aptitude" or "bump" is indistinguishable from intelligence itself, which is not thought to be the case, or else it is related entirely, not to mathematics as such, but to the way in which mathematics is taught. In fact, the operational structures of the intelligence, although they are of a logico-mathematical nature, are not present in children's minds as conscious structures: they are structures of actions or operations, which certainly direct the child's reasoning but do not constitute an object of reflection on its part (just as one can sing in tune without being obliged to construct a theory of singing, and even without being able to read music). The teaching of mathematics, on the other hand, specifically requires the student to reflect consciously on these structures, though it does so by means of a technical language comprising a very particular form of symbolism, and demanding a greater or lesser degree of abstraction. So the so-called aptitude for mathematics may very well be a function of the student's comprehension of that language itself, as opposed to that of the structures it describes, or else of the speed of the abstraction process insofar as it is linked with such a symbolism rather than with reflection upon structures that are in other respects natural. Moreover, since everything is interconnected in an entirely deductive discipline, failure or lack of comprehension where any single link in the chain is concerned entails an increasing difficulty in following the succeeding links, so that the student who has failed to adapt at any point is unable to understand what follows and becomes increasingly doubtful of his ability: emotional complexes, often strengthened by those around him, then arise to complete the block that has been formed in an initiation that could have been quite different.

In a word, the central problem of mathematical teaching is that of the reciprocal adjustment between the spontaneous operational structures proper to the intelligence and the program or methods relating to the particular branches of mathematics being taught. This problem, in fact, has been profoundly modified during recent decades due to the transformations that have taken place in mathematics itself: by a process that is at first sight paradoxical, though in fact psychologically natural and clearly explicable, the most abstract and general structures of contemporary mathematics are much more closely linked to the natural operational structures of the intelligence and of thought than were the particular structures that provided the framework for classical mathematics and teaching methods.

We know, in effect, that since the research carried out by Bourbaki and his school (itself the extension of a long series of efforts in the same direction), mathematics today no longer appears as a collection of more or less separate chapters but as a vast hierarchy of interrelated structures all springing originally from a number of "mother structures" that can be combined together or differentiated in various ways. These elementary structures are three in number: the algebraic structures, characterized by a reversibility in the form of inversion $(T - T -^1 = O)$ and those whose prototype is the "group"; the ordering structures, whose reversibility is a reciprocity characteristic of systems of relationships, and whose prototype is the "network"; and the topological structures dealing with notions of continuity and proximity (bi-univocal and bicontinuous correspondences, etc.).

It so happens that these three "mother structures" correspond fairly closely with the fundamental operational structures of thought. As early as the "concrete operations" stage we have already discussed we find algebraic structures in the logical "groupings" of classes, ordering structures in the "groupings" of relationships, and topological structures in the child's spontaneous form of geometry (which is topological long before it reaches the projective forms or the metrics of Euclidean geometry, thus conforming to the theoretical order of the constitution of notions and running counter to the historical order). As soon as the stage of "propositional" operations begins we find operational structures of "groups" and "networks," etc.

Taking its inspiration from the trends initiated by Bourbaki, modern mathematics therefore emphasizes the theory of wholes and structural isomorphisms rather than traditional compartmentalizations, and an entirely new movement has become apparent, which aims at introducing such notions into our teaching at the earliest possible moment. And what is more, such a trend is fully justified, since the operations of putting together or intersecting wholes, the arrangements according to correspondences that are the sources of isomorphisms, etc., are precisely the operations constructed and utilized spontaneously by our intelligence from the age of 7 or 8 onward, and even more so from 11 or 12 onward (since at this stage the child can grasp the complex structure of "wholes of parts," which is the source of combinativity and "networks").

The intelligence, however, works out and employs these structures without becoming aware of them in any consciously reflective form, not in the sense that M. Jourdain spoke without knowing it, but rather in the sense that any adult who is not a logician nevertheless manipulates implications, disjunctions, etc., without having the slightest idea of the way in which symbolic or algebraic logic succeeds in expressing these operations in abstract and algebraic formulas. The pedagogic problem, therefore, despite the progress realized in principle by this return to the natural roots of the operational structures, still subsists in its entirety: that of finding the most adequate methods for bridging the transition between these natural but nonreflective structures to conscious reflection upon such structures and to a theoretical formulation of them.

And it is at this point, in fact, that we once more meet the conflict of which we spoke at the beginning of this section between the operational manipulation of structures and the symbolic language making it possible to express them. The most general structures of modern mathematics are at the same time the most abstract as well, whereas those same structures are never represented in the mind of the child except in the form of concrete manipulations, either physical or verbal. The mathematician who is unaccustomed to psychology, however, may suspect any physical exercise of being an obstacle to abstraction, whereas the psychologist is used to making a very careful distinction between abstraction based on objects (the source of experiment in the physical field and foreign to mathematics) and abstraction based on actions, the source of mathematical deduction and abstraction. We must avoid believing, in fact, that a sound training in abstraction and deduction presupposes a premature use of technical language and technical symbolism alone, since mathematical abstraction is of an operational nature and develops genetically through a series of unbroken stages that have their first origin in very concrete operations. Nor must we confuse the concrete either with physical experiment, which derives its knowledge from objects and not from the actions of the child itself, or with intuitive presentations (in the sense of figurative methods), since these operations are derived from actions, not from perceptual or visually recalled configurations.

These various possible misunderstandings demonstrate that, though the introduction of modern mathematics at the most elementary stages of education constitutes a great advance in principle from the psychopedagogic point of view, the results obtained may have been, in individual cases, either excellent or questionable according to the methods employed. This is why the International Conference on Public Education (International Bureau of Education and UNESCO), at its 1956 session, inserted the following articles in its Recommendation No. 43 (The Teaching of Mathematics in Secondary Schools):

20. It is important (a) to guide the student into forming his own ideas and discovering mathematical relations and properties himself, rather than imposing ready-made adult thought upon him; (b) to make sure that he acquires operational processes and ideas before introducing him to formalism; (c) not to entrust to automatism any operations that are not already assimilated.

21. It is indispensable (a) to make sure that the student first acquires experience of mathematical entities and relations and is only then initiated into deductive reasoning; (b) to extend the deductive construction of mathematics progressively; (c) to teach the student to pose problems, to establish data, to exploit them, and to weigh the results; (d) to give preference to the heuristic investigation of questions rather than to the doctrinal exposition of theorems.

22. It is necessary (a) to study the mistakes made by students and to see them as a means of understanding their mathematical thought; (b) to train students in the practice of personal checking and auto-correction; (c) to instill in students a sense of approximation; (d) to give priority to reflection and to reasoning, etc.

The importance of the student's personal research emphasized in these articles is valid at all levels. At the very first stages of initiation into arithmetical calculation, the Belgian teacher Cuisenaire introduced concrete teaching aids in the form of small sticks comprising groups of various units and known as "numbers in colors." The principle is exactly the same as that which was used by Mlles Audemars and Lafendel at the Maison des Petits in Geneva, but their innovation consisted in distinguishing between the sticks of various unit lengths, 1, 2, 3, etc., by their respective colors. Both the introduction of colors and the principle itself of the correspondence between spatial units and numbers can, however, give rise to extremely different interpretations and applications, despite the efforts made by C. Gattegno to introduce a kind of international supervision (of which we may all think what we like) of the "Cuisenaire method," since the Cuisenaire method does not in fact exist as a unified entity, but is rather a plurality of methods ranging from excellent to very bad (a remark that should not be taken as intended in any way to diminish the great merits of Cuisenaire himself). Though excellent when it gives rise to active manipulations and discoveries by the child itself, following the line of its spontaneous operational development, these aids may also tempt teachers to use them for demonstrations that are merely watched by the child, a process that does, of course, make comprehension easier than using more verbal or more static methods, but that runs the risk (and the risk is increased by the presence of the colors) of giving the configurations (and therefore the figurative aspects of thought: perception, imitation, and images) greater importance than the operations (and therefore than the operative aspects of thought: actions and operations). This risk becomes a reality, with all its attendant dangers, when the emphasis is placed definitively on the relationships of the colors (which is why the Maison des Petits decided to do without this ambivalent aid), and when the teacher, while under the impression that he is being faithful to the lines laid down by the active school, is in fact employing merely intuitive methods of teaching. . . .

FOSTERING THE SPIRIT OF EXPERIMENT AND INTRODUCING
CHILDREN TO THE PHYSICAL AND NATURAL SCIENCES

Contemporary society has been profoundly transformed (and it is for the future to say whether it has been for better or for worse) by the work of physicists, chemists, and biologists. It nevertheless remains true to say that the elite formed by such specialists and inventors constitutes no more than a minute and heterogeneous fraction of the social body, first because their research has been very poorly understood, not only in their technical details but also in their general spirit, and secondly because present-day intellectual training and public education have turned out to be singularly ill-adapted to our new needs in the way of training and recruiting, both in the technical and in the scientific fields.

The traditional education of certain great countries has placed all the emphasis, in fact, upon the humanities and upon mathematics, as though the two predominant qualities of rational man were to be at ease with history and with formal deduction. As for practical experimentation, that was seen as a minor activity, useful for civilizations with an empirical philosophy. . . . Consequently, a sufficient experimental training was believed to have been provided as long as the student had been introduced to the results of past experiments or had been allowed to watch demonstration experiments conducted by his teacher, as though it were possible to sit in rows on a wharf and learn to swim merely by watching grown-up swimmers in the water. It is true that this form of instruction by lecture and demonstration has often been supplemented by laboratory work by the students, but the repetition of past experiments is still a long way from being the best way of exciting the spirit of invention, and even of training students in the necessity for checking or verification.

In which case, if the aim of intellectual training is to form the intelligence rather than to stock the memory, and to produce intellectual explorers rather than mere erudition, then traditional education is manifestly guilty of a grave deficiency. . . . The child spontaneously acquires between the ages of 11 to 12 and 14 to 15 all the intellectual instruments necessary for experimentation properly so called. These instruments are of two sorts. First of all there are the tools of thought, in the form of a combinative and propositional operations, which enable the child to distinguish between implications and nonimplications, between nonexclusive disjunctions and exclusive disjunctions, between conjunctions and incompatibilities, and so forth. Secondly, there is a particular method of procedure, rendered possible by the operations just mentioned, that consists in dissociating factors according to previously stated hypotheses and in varying them experimentally, one by one, while neutralizing all the others, or in combining them in various ways. . . .

If, as he passes from the stage of concrete operations to that of propositional or hypothetico-deductive operations, the child becomes capable both of combining those hypotheses and of verifying them experimentally, then it goes without saying that our schools owe it to themselves to develop and to direct such capacities in order to use them in the development of the experimental attitude of mind and of methods of teaching the physical sciences that will emphasize the importance of research and discovery instead of relying on mere repetition.

This is something that has at last begun to be apparent to educators in several countries, and in this respect one example we might quote is the United States, where this movement is very interesting to follow since the large field in that nation that is left to private enterprise makes it easier to distinguish the influences involved and the various stages of success attained, however, partial those successes may be (or precisely because they are partial). . . .

The impulse thus provided has led to the constitution of many work groups in the field, groups that do not limit themselves, as might so easily happen on the Continent, to organizing meetings and lectures, but have gone resolutely to work in the schools themselves, undertaking field experiments in teaching methods. And moreover, a remarkable thing in itself, one often finds professional physicists in these research groups taking part in pedagogical investigations into the teaching of very young children in beginners' classes. . . .

It goes without saying that these field trials of "active" teaching methods in the sphere of physics are coordinated with the efforts being made to revolutionize the teaching of mathematics and even of logic in action. . . .

THE TEACHING OF PHILOSOPHY

The undeniable revival that characterizes the teaching of the sciences from the primary school up to baccalaureate or high-school graduation level, a revival from which we have quoted only one example for the experimental disciplines, although we could have analyzed many more (in the USSR, etc.), raises a general educational problem that has been discussed in several regions: the teaching of philosophy at the secondary level. Such teaching, considered important in certain countries, such as France (where its usefulness is nevertheless often questioned) and non-existent in others, where philosophy appears only in university curricula, is indubitably thought of in a variable way because it depends, even more than other branches of teaching, upon the aims assigned to it, and because those aims themselves, much more than with the other branches, reflect the ideology peculiar to the society in question.

If the principal aim of intellectual education is the training of the mind, then it follows automatically that philosophical reflection constitutes an essential objective both for those students one wishes to initiate particularly into mathematical deduction and experimental method and also for those who are orientated toward the humanities and the historical disciplines. But given that this is so, what form ought the introduction of these students to philosophy take in order to achieve such ends? . . .

Philosophy is, in the first place, and this is a constant common to all of its various systems, an attempt at coordinating values, in the widest sense, and at situating the values of knowledge within the totality of other human ends. From this point of view, the philosopher's aim is essentially to attain "wisdom," or a sort of reasoned faith, whether it be of a moral, social, or metaphysical nature. It therefore goes without saying that philosophical teaching, from this first point of view, will vary considerably from one country to another according to whether there exists a state philosophy (spiritual or materialistic, etc.), or whether, on the contrary, the state is a liberal one that desires to develop individuals with personal and varied opinions. . . .

For some, philosophy includes a form of knowledge proper of a para- or supra-scientific nature: from the fact that vital values go beyond the frontiers of science and correspond to irreducible intuitions of value, it is concluded that there exists likewise an epistemic intuition, which provides a specific mode of knowledge that should be considered as standing in contrast to scientific knowledge.

For others—for whom history provides arguments of steadily increasing strength—philosophical reflection does certainly lead to the constitution of knowledge, but a knowledge with the property of being unable to advance except by means of a delimitation of problems and a refinement of methods, both of which are characteristic of scientific procedure itself: in other words, as soon as any body of philosophical knowledge tends to attain a certain precision, it results in the constitution of a new and particular science, which then becomes detached from the common trunk.

Leaving aside mathematics, which was still living in symbiosis with philosophy in the work of Pythagoras or Plato, logic is a striking example of such a dissociation: an offspring of the thought of Aristotle and the Stoics, conceived of as capable of generalization by Leibnitz, by the nineteenth century it was already acquiring its autonomy and particular techniques, which continued to become ever richer and more complex . . . until the present, when logic is indissociable from mathematics, and the majority of philosophers are no longer able to teach it.

In the same way, psychology, too, was dissociated from philosophy during the early years of this century and, in many countries, is now taught in conjunction with biology under the aegis of the Faculty of Sciences.

. . . As for the theory of knowledge, or epistemology, which presupposes at one and the same time an advanced logical development, precise psychological data, and an increasingly technical analysis of the growth of the sciences, it gives rise to ever more specialized researches, the most important of which are today carried out by the scientists concerned rather than by professional philosophers (theories of the foundation of mathematics, of microphysical experiment, etc.).

The result of this complex situation is an undeniable crisis in philosophy, and consequently, in the teaching of it, as much at the university level as at the secondary-school level. In order to convince oneself of this, one need only observe the diversity that exists in the types of instruction offered in this branch of knowledge at the secondary-school level, and also the similar diversity in the types of training used to prepare those who are to be given the task of teaching philosophy.

The central problem is, of course, as is apparent from the preceding comments, the relationship between the philosophical and the scientific spirit: reconciliation, divorce, or various forms of compromise, such are the principal ideological or cultural tendencies that have resulted.

In the Eastern countries, the problem has been diminished in intensity by the fact that the official philosophy is that of dialectical Marxism, which claims to be scientific. Philosophy teaching at the secondary-school level is therefore quite simply an initiation into dialectical materialism, with various incursions into its scientific applications. In certain regions, such as Poland (whose school of logistics has for a long time been both flourishing and highly regarded), this is supplemented with a grounding in mathematical logic, which is sufficient to introduce the average student to problems of which, in our countries, students have no notion without special initiation courses. . . .

Another form of conciliation between the philosophical and the scientific spirit (though a more restrictive one, which entails undeniable dangers from the point of view of the sciences themselves, since their vitality is necessarily dependent upon their remaining indefinitely "open-ended"), is that of positivism or "logical empiricism," which first originated in the Vienna Circle and has since met with such great success in the Anglo-Saxon countries. But this movement, which has had such a strong influence on recent generations, is now beginning to decline, because of its inability (an inability common to all forms of empiricism) to maintain the essential role of the subject's activities.

In nonempiricist circles in the West, the crisis in philosophical instruction has been caused above all by the split between the scientific faculties and the faculties of letters at university level, and by the related split between the so-called literary and scientific departments in our secondary schools. It would be impossible to exaggerate the harm done by such compartmentalizations, the most evident result of which is the constitution of a sort of social caste of philosophers, who are called upon to deal directly with the total sum of reality without any personal initiation into what is meant by controlled scientific research. Whereas the great philosophers of the past all contributed in some way to the scientific movements of their time, or anticipated possible lines of research (as with the empiricists in the case of psychology, and Hegel in the case of sociology), today we are training specialists in transcendentalism who are then able to leap straight into the world of essences with an ease enormously increased by the fact that they are innocent of any form of scientific specialization, even in psychology. . . .

THE TEACHING OF "CLASSICS" AND THE PROBLEM OF THE HUMANITIES

The literary disciplines and the humanities, unlike the branches of knowledge dealt with in the preceding sections, have given rise to few modifications in their teaching methods. The reason for this is perhaps that they are branches of learning whose content itself has varied very little, even though linguistics has made considerable advances and history has perceptibly broadened its perspectives. But the principal reason is without doubt dependent upon quite different considerations: established positions and the traditions of vested professional interest. . . .

But the real problems raised by classical studies in secondary schools are those of the aims pursued and the adequacy of the means employed. It is on these two points that several interesting debates have taken place, albeit solely on the theoretical plane.

The aims are of two sorts, one of them essential and not subject to discussion, the other marginal and a source of all kinds of questions. The principal aim is the development of the historical attitude of mind and a knowledge of those past civilizations from which our own societies have evolved. It goes without saying, in effect, that just as a knowledge of the exact and natural sciences, together with philosophical reflection, [is] indispensable to our knowledge of man in the universe, so there is another aspect of humanity that necessitates an equally complex but different kind of information: man's cultures and their history. It is therefore perfectly legitimate, taking into account individual aptitudes and future specializations, to look forward to the formation of a humanism whose role will be no less indispensable to the life of society than that played by the sciences and rational knowledge.

The marginal aim, upon which more emphasis is often laid, in fact, than upon the preceding one, is the training of the mind in general terms. I refer particularly to the hypothesis that an initiation into the dead languages constitutes an intellectual exercise, the benefits of which may then be transferred to other activities. It is argued, for example, that the possession of a language from which the student's own tongue developed and the ability to manipulate its grammatical structures provide logical tools and develop a subtlety of mind from which the intelligence will benefit later on regardless of the use to which it is put. Supporters of this hypothesis, abusing a famous dictum on this subject, will even go so far as to imply an absolute contrast between this subtle or analytic type of mind (*esprit de finesse*) and the geometrical type of mind (*esprit de géométrie*), as though the latter were exclusive to the sciences and the former to the literary disciplines, whereas both, of course, are found everywhere. . . .

As for the acquisition of a humanist education and the formation of the historical mind, our classical studies do, broadly speaking, achieve these aims, though with one or two reservations that are being formulated with increasing frequency today. As early as the *Entretiens sur les Humanités* organized by the International Institute of Intellectual Cooperation in Budapest under the presidency of Paul Valéry, that writer expressed approval of the present author's insistence that we should provide a more effective link between the study of ancient civilizations and the history of ideas: why do we not put more emphasis on the fact that the Greeks, while discovering and clarifying an unsurpassable ideal of beauty in so many spheres, were also able to constitute a firmly based ideal of rationality, the wellspring of all our Western sciences and philosophy, whereas the Romans, though they produced great poets, were unable to crown their political and commercial activities with anything more than a juridical and military ideology? The Greek miracle is simply not intelligible, in effect, except upon condition that we have observed all its aspects, including the scientific ones, right up to its artistic and intellectual decadence in the Alexandrine period.

Where the teaching of the languages themselves is concerned, there exists a latent conflict between the grammarian's approach and that of the linguist, and there is some ground for concern over the obsolete character of certain traditional forms of "grammatical analysis" still being presented to the student as "logical," while modern linguistics, which represents such an incomparable fund of educational material, frequently remains almost totally absent from secondary-school programs. . . .

As for history, it is well known how much the introduction of economic considerations has done to enrich its subject matter in recent decades, and this, too, raises new problems. To justify spending years of school life on the study of ancient civilizations simply on the grounds of their importance for modern civilization is only acceptable today if we take a much more broadly sociological view of the subject than has been prevalent in the past.

Development of Teaching Methods

Up to this point I have limited myself to indicating a number of transformations that have occurred since 1935 in various fields, while maintaining the traditional and serene viewpoint of the observer concerned solely with the nature of the branches of knowledge to be taught, with the students' intellectual comprehension, and with the permanent values of society. In the sections that follow, on the other hand, we shall be confronting the three principal new developments that characterize the new situations of education or teaching, and that determine all sorts of choices in an ever accelerating and also a coercive way. In consequence, the accounts of the following matters will gradually abandon the calm tone of research and adopt the more immediate and concrete accents of narrative or debate.

These three developments are: the staggering increase in the number of students, due to a much more universal opportunity of admission to the various forms of education; the almost directly related difficulty in recruiting a sufficiently well-trained teaching body; and the totality of the new needs, above all the economic, technical, and scientific needs, of the societies for whose benefit public education is organized.

These three factors already wield a large and evident influence on the choice of educational methods in general, and lead to very understandable conflicts between the traditional verbal methods, which are easier to use when the teaching personnel has not been able to acquire a sufficiently advanced training; the active methods, which become more and more necessary with the increasing desire to train more technicians and scientists; the intuitive or audiovisual methods, which some think may produce the same results as the active methods while accomplishing the task more swiftly; and programmed teaching, whose growing success is in some danger of making us forget the questions that it raises.

THE RECEPTIVE METHODS, OR METHODS OF
TRANSMISSION BY THE TEACHER

It may appear somewhat nonsensical to discuss the traditional methods of oral teaching in a report whose purpose is to emphasize the new developments that have occurred since 1935. But it is a new fact that certain "progressive" countries such as the people's republics of the East claim justification for a teaching method essentially based on transmission by the teacher, or on the "lesson," now that they have perfected the method in detail by means of systematic and far-reaching psychopedagogic research. . . .

The latent conflict that I believe to be discernible springs from a duality of ideological inspirations that are perfectly compatible where the adult mind is concerned, but whose synthesis presents a problem in the educational field.

The first of these inspirations tends to present mental life as being the product of the combination of two essential factors: the biological factor and social life. The organic factor provides for the existence of the conditions for learning: the laws of primary "conditioning" (in the Pavlovian sense) and those of the second [signaling] system, or language. Social life, on the other hand, provides the totality of practical rules and bodies of knowledge arrived at collectively and passed on from one generation to the next. These biological and social factors are thus sufficient to account for mental life, and any appeal to the individual consciousness, given this point of view, is in danger of leading to a retrogressive individualism or idealism.

But then there is the second inspiration, from the same ideological source, that appears to fill what one might think looks suspiciously like a gap left by the first: this is the role of action in the transition between the biological and the social factors. This role played by action (or by *praxis*) has been abundantly emphasized by Marx, who quite rightly went so far as to consider perception itself as an "activity" of the sense organs. Moreover, this role has been invariably confirmed by Soviet psychologists, who have produced a great deal of very fine work on the subject.

From the point of view of the general methods of education, therefore, there subsists in effect a sort of duality of principles, or a dialectical conflict, according to whether one emphasizes the creative role of adult social life, which leads to a corresponding emphasis on the transmission of knowledge by the teacher, or whether one concentrates on the no less constructive role of action, which leads to placing an essential share of importance upon the activities of the student himself. In the majority of cases, in the people's republics, a synthesis is sought for in a system whereby the teacher directs the student but in a way that forces him into activity rather than merely giving "lessons" to the student. But it goes without saying, in these countries as everywhere else, that the lesson is always bound to conform to the natural tendencies of the teacher, since that is by far the easiest solution (and since everyone has not at his disposal either the necessary space or the wisdom of the Canadian school inspector who divided every class into two rooms, in order, he said, that the children should have time "to work," and that the teacher would not talk to all of them together the whole day long!). On the other hand, however, it also goes without saying that the share of importance accorded to action has led certain Soviet educators to develop it in the direction of the research activities of the child itself, as is the case, for example, with Suhomlinsky and the Lipetsk School. These free activities are even greater in number, naturally enough, in extra-scholastic institutions, such as the "Pioneer" centers and the clubs attached to them. I have also visited certain boarding schools, in Rumania for example, where the vocational training offered was such as to give rise to research activities on the part of the students themselves, as well as to happy combinations between individual work and team work. . . .

ACTIVE METHODS

It has finally been understood that an active school is not necessarily a school of manual labor. The child's activity at certain levels necessarily entails the manipulation of objects and even a certain amount of actual physical groping, insofar as elementary logico-mathematical notions, for example, are derived, not from the objects manipulated, but from the actions of the child and their coordination. At other levels the most authentic research activity may take place in the spheres of reflection, of the most advanced abstraction, and of verbal manipulations (provided they are spontaneous and not imposed on the child at the risk of remaining partially uncomprehended).

It has also been finally understood, at least on a theoretical level, that interest in no way excludes effort—quite the contrary in fact—and that an education providing a good preparation of life does not consist in replacing spontaneous efforts by dreary chores. It is recognized that although life does include a by no means negligible amount of imposed labor alongside other more freely accepted tasks, the necessary disciplines are still more efficacious when they are freely accepted than they are without such inner acceptance. So the active methods do not lead in any way to anarchic individualism, but rather, especially if they include a combination of individual work and team work, to a training in self-discipline and voluntary effort.

However, though these views are much more widely accepted today than heretofore, no great progress has been made in putting them into practice, simply because the active methods are much more difficult to employ than our current receptive methods. In the first place, they require a much more varied and much more concentrated kind of work from the teacher, whereas giving lessons is much less tiring and corresponds to a much more natural tendency in the adult, generally, and in the adult pedagogue, in particular. Secondly, and above all, an active pedagogy presupposes a much more advanced kind of training, and without an adequate knowledge of child psychology (and also, where mathematics and physics are concerned, without a fairly good knowledge of contemporary developments in those disciplines), the teacher cannot properly understand the students' spontaneous procedures, and therefore fails to take advantage of reactions that appear to him quite insignificant and a mere waste of time. The heartbreaking difficulty in pedagogy, as indeed in medicine and in many other branches of knowledge that partake at the same time of art and science, is in fact, that the best methods are also the most difficult ones: it would be impossible to employ a Socratic method without having first acquired some of Socrates' qualities, the first of which would have to be a certain respect for intelligence in the process of development.

Although there has been no tidal wave of active methods, and though this deficiency is only too easily explained by the difficulties that have been put in the way of even the best intentions by the recent increase in the numbers of students, by the lack of teachers, and by a considerable number of other material obstacles, we ought nevertheless to take note of certain individual and important efforts, such as that made by Freinet, and of a constant tendency to revive the major preoccupations that motivate the active methods as soon as social needs have required their reappearance. We have already noted, for example, the quite widespread movement in the United States that led to an entire rethinking of elementary instruction in mathematics and physics, and which has naturally resulted in a return to "active" methods. At its 1959 session, the International Conference on Public Education [recommended]: "In order to increase the interest shown by students in technical and scientific studies at the primary-school stage, it is advisable to employ active methods designed to develop a spirit of experiment."

As for the individual efforts of schoolteachers whose particular inventiveness or devotion to children has enabled them to find their way with their hearts to the best methods of training intelligence pure and simple (as was the case with Pestalozzi), I could quote a great number of them in the most various countries, some French-speaking, some German-speaking (considerable achievements have been made in both Germany and Austria since the defeat of Nazism), Italian-speaking, English-speaking, etc. But I shall limit myself, as an example of what can be done with modest means and without any particular encouragement from the appropriate governmental bodies, to recalling the remarkable work accomplished by Freinet, which has achieved a wide dissemination in many French-speaking areas, including French Canada. . . . Freinet attempted above all else to turn the school into a center for activities that are constantly in communion with those of the surrounding social collectivity. His famous idea of using printing in his school constitutes no more than one particular illustration among many in this respect, though it is an especially instructive one, since it is obvious that a child who is himself printing small fragments of text will succeed in learning to read, write, and spell in a very different manner from one who has no idea at all how the printed documents he has to use are made. Without explicitly aiming at an education of the intelligence and a method of acquiring knowledge in general through the medium of action, Freinet thus achieved these constant objectives of the active school by directing his thought above all to the development of the child's interest and his social training. And without priding himself on any theories, he thereby attained what are without doubt the two most central truths of the psychology of the cognitive functions: that the development of intellectual operations proceeds from effective action in the fullest sense (which is to say, including interests, though this in no way means that the latter are exclusively utilitarian), since logic is before all else the expression of the general coordination of actions; and secondly, that this general coordination of actions necessarily includes a social dimension, since the interindividual coordination of actions and their intraindividual coordination constitute a single and identical process, the individual's operations all being socialized, and cooperation in its strict sense consisting in a pooling of each individual's operations.

INTUITIVE METHODS

One of the causes of the slowness with which the active methods have been adopted, a cause that itself springs from the insufficient psychological training of the majority of educators, is the confusion that sometimes occurs between the active methods and the intuitive methods. A certain number of pedagogues—often in the best possible faith—imagine that the latter are an equivalent of the former, or at least that they produce all the essential benefits that can be derived from the active methods.

We are faced here, moreover, with two distinct confusions. The first, which has already been mentioned, is that which leads people to think that any "activity" on the part of the student or child is a matter of physical actions, something that is true at the elementary levels but is no longer so at later stages, when a student may be totally "active," in the sense of making a personal rediscovery of the truths to be acquired, even though this activity is being directed toward interior and abstract reflection.

The second confusion consists in believing that an activity dealing with concrete objects is no more than a figurative process, in other words nothing but a way of producing a sort of precise copy, in perceptions or mental images, of the objects in question. It is forgotten that knowledge is not at all the same thing as making a figurative copy of reality for oneself; it invariably consists in operative processes leading to a transformation of reality, either in actions or in thought, in order to grasp the mechanisms of those transformations and thus assimilate the events and the objects into systems of operations (or structures of transformations). It is also forgotten that the experience brought to bear on the objects may take two forms, one of which is logico-mathematical and consists in deriving knowledge, not from those objects themselves, but from the actions that modify the objects. And lastly, it is also forgotten that physical experiments in their turn, in which knowledge is abstracted from objects, consist in acting upon those objects in order to transform them, in order to dissociate and vary the factors they present, etc., and not in simply extracting a figurative copy of them.

Since all this has been forgotten, the intuitive methods come down, quite simply, to a process of providing students with [telling] visual representations, either of objects or events themselves, or of the result of possible operations, but without leading to any effective realization of those operations. These methods, which are, moreover, traditional, are continually being reborn from their own ashes and do certainly constitute an advance in relation to purely verbal or formal teaching techniques. But they are totally inadequate in developing the child's operative activity. . . .

Despite all this, however, the period between 1935 and 1965 has seen the reappearance of the intuitive methods in a great number of new guises, all of which, I must repeat, are all the more disturbing in that their champions usually believe in all good faith that they satisfy all the most modern requirements of child psychology. To begin with one example, I myself have received a Belgian textbook for beginners in mathematics, with a preface by a well-known educator, in which both the author and the writer of the preface refer to my own work and even do me the honor of considering it as one of the sources of their inspiration, even though in fact the manipulation of elementary logico-mathematical operations has been entirely banished from their method and its place given to figurational intuitions—often, indeed, essentially static ones.

There would be little point here in returning again to the subject of the Cuisenaire rods, since we have already seen that they are open to the most totally opposed methods of using them, some of them genuinely operative if the child is allowed to discover for himself the various operations made possible by spontaneous manipulations of the rods, but the others essentially intuitive or figurative when they are limited to external demonstrations and to explanations of the configurations laid out by the teacher.

One Swiss educator has had the notion of extracting the *maximum possible* dynamism and mobility from the intuitive methods by teaching mathematics, not with static images, but with films, whose visual continuity enables the child to watch the most striking decompositions and recompositions of figures in motion. For beginners in geometry, to give one outstanding example, this method provides the most remarkable illustrations of Pythagoras' theorem in which the relations involved acquire a visual clarity worthy of the highest praise. And yet, is this really training the child in geometrical reasoning and in operative construction in general? Bergson, who had a grudge against intelligence, compared its workings to the process of cinematography, and had he been correct in his comparison, this cinematic method of educational initiation would indeed be the last word in rational teaching methods. Unfortunately, however, Bergson missed the problem of operations and failed to understand in what way the operational transformation constitutes a genuine, continuous, and creative act: his critique of intelligence is, in fact, a critique, and a very profound one from this point of view, of visual representation, that is to say the figurative and not of the operative aspects of thought. By the same token, a pedagogy based on the image, even when enriched by the apparent dynamism of the film, remains inadequate for the training of operational constructivism, since intelligence cannot be reduced to images [on] a film: it might much more correctly be compared, in fact, to the projector that ensures the continuity of the film's images, or better still, to a series of cybernetic mechanisms ensuring such a continuous flow of images by dint of an internal logic and of autoregulatory and autocorrecting processes.

In short, the image, the film, and all the audiovisual methods with which any pedagogy anxious to persuade itself of its modernity is perpetually bombarding us at the moment, are precious aids as long as they are thought of as accessories or spiritual crutches, and it is obvious that they represent a clear advance on purely verbal methods of instruction. But there exists a verbalism of the image just as there is a verbalism of the word, and compared with the active methods, the intuitive methods—when they forget the irreducible primacy of spontaneous activity and of personal or autonomous investigation of truth— are merely substituting this more elegant and refined form of verbalism for the traditional kind of verbalism.

It should, however, be noted—and this is something that must be entered as a debit rather than an asset to psychology in its pedagogical applications—that the intuitive methods have been able to draw sustenance from an entire psychological movement that has shown great merit in other respects: the movement known as Gestalt psychology, which first arose in Germany before its subsequent proliferation elsewhere. It is therefore not a matter of chance that the intuitive methods have had their greatest development in German-speaking regions, where they are still looked upon with great esteem. The contribution of Gestalt psychology, after having revolutionized the problems of perception in an extremely profound and useful way, [has been] to seek in percepual structures, or "gestalts," the prototype of all other mental structures, including the rational or logico-mathematical ones. And needless to say, if this thesis were true it would constitute a definitive justification for the intuitive methods.

However, in the field of psychology itself the Gestalt theory has nowadays fallen from [favor], mainly because its neglect of the subject's activities in favor of elementary and overspecialized physical or neurological structurations has brought it into conflict with the triumphant functionalist movements in Britain, the United States, France, and the USSR. Moreover a Gestalt is a structural whole that is at once nonadditive and irreversible, whereas the operational structural wholes (classifications, seriations, numbers, correspondences, etc.) are both reversible and strictly additive (2 and 2 make exactly 4, and not a little more or a little less as in the perceptual sphere). This necessarily implies that operations are not reducible to perceptual or visual "forms," and that, as a direct consequence, the intuitive educational methods must remain very much inferior in status to the operative, or active, methods.

PROGRAMMED METHODS AND TEACHING MACHINES

In more or less close connection with the Pavlovian school of Soviet reflexology (the closeness varying according to individual cases), American psychology has evolved a certain number of theories of learning based on the stimulus-response view. First Hull then Tolman developed detailed theories depending upon the effects of habit formation, then of "hierarchies of habits," the use of indices of significance, etc. And although agreement has not been reached among such authors as to the exact importance of these factors in detail, they all recognize the importance of external "reinforcements" (success and failure or various forms of sanction) and the requirements of relatively constant laws of learning with regard to repetition and length of time employed.

The most recent of the great American learning theorists, Skinner, the author of some remarkable experiments with pigeons (the favorite animal for such experimentation had until then been the white rat, which is particularly teachable but unfortunately suspected of degeneracy in its domesticated behavior), adopted a more resolutely positive attitude. Convinced of the inaccessible nature of the intermediate variables and of the excessively rudimentary state of our neurological knowledge, he decided to confine his attention to stimuli, or *inputs*, that could be varied at will and to observable responses, or *outputs*, and then to take account only of the direct relationships between them, ignoring the internal connections. This "empty box" conception of the organism, as it has been called, thus deliberately thumbs its nose at all kinds of mental life, human or animal, and confines itself solely to behavior in its most material aspects, ignoring any possible search for explanations in order to concentrate exclusively on the broad laws revealed by scrupulously detailed experimentation.

This being so, Skinner, already in possession of the laws of learning he had either personally verified or evolved, and freed of any theoretical preoccupations that might have hampered his testing of their general or practical application, observed in the first place that his experiments always worked much better when the interventions of the human experimenter were replaced by efficient mechanical apparatus. In other words, the pigeons produced much more regular reactions when dealing with "teaching machines" capable of applying the stimuli with greater precision and fewer minute variations. Skinner, a teacher by profession as well as a learning theorist, then had the brilliant idea that this observation of his would be equally valid when applied to humans, and that teaching machines, provided they were sufficiently well-programmed, would produce better results than an oral method of teaching susceptible of great variation in its application. And since the empty-box conception of the organism renders so many preliminary considerations of the internal factors of human learning unnecessary, it was sufficient to be familiar with the general laws of learning and with the subject matter of the branches of knowledge to be taught, in order to construct programs at least equal in content to the body of knowledge commonly required.

The experiment was tried and proved a total success. And it goes without saying, if we confine ourselves to the usual methods of teaching by means of verbal transmission and receptive processes, that it could not fail to succeed. The sentimental and the natural worriers have been saddened by the fact that schoolmasters can be replaced by machines. In my view, on the other hand, these machines have performed at least one great service for us, which is to demonstrate beyond all possible doubt the mechanical character of the schoolmaster's function as it is conceived by traditional teaching methods: if the ideal of that method is merely to elicit correct repetition of what has been correctly transmitted, then it goes without saying that a machine can fulfill those conditions correctly.

It has also been objected that the machine eliminates all affective factors, but this is not true, and Skinner justly claims that it is often possible to achieve a greater intensity of "motivation" (needs and interests) with machines than is found in many traditional "lessons." The question is, in fact, to establish whether the teacher's affectivity always performs a desirable function. Claparède had already expressed the opinion, in his day, that a sufficient period in a teacher's training should always be given over to practice in animal training, since when that training fails the experimenter is bound to accept that it is his own fault, whereas in the education of children failures are always attributed to the pupil. And in this respect, it should be noted, Skinner's machines provided evidence of good psychology in that they make use exclusively of positive reinforcements and dispense totally with negative sanctions or punishments.

The principle of programming (which Skinner tried out in his own psychology lessons before generalizing it to cover all branches of teaching) is, in effect, the following: the preliminary definitions having been given, the student must begin by drawing the correct conclusions from them, which means, in practice, selecting one of the two or three solutions the machine offers him. If he selects the right one (by pressing a button), the work-sequence continues, whereas if he makes a mistake the exercise is repeated. Each new item of information provided by the machine therefore leads to choices that provide evidence of the comprehension attained, with as many repetitions as prove necessary and with uninterrupted progress in the event of constant successes. Any branch of learning can thus be programmed in accordance with this principle, whether it be a matter of pure reasoning or one of simple memorizing.

In practice, teaching machines conceived on these lines have had a considerable success and have already given rise to a prosperous industry. In a time of great increase in student population and scarcity of teachers they are able to render undeniable services, and, in general, save a great deal of time in comparison with traditional methods of teaching. They are used not only in schools but also in commercial concerns where, for one reason or another, a necessity exists for the rapid instruction of adults.

As for the intrinsic value of such a teaching method, that naturally depends upon the aims that are assigned to it in any particular field. In cases where it is a matter of acquiring a set body of learning, as in the teaching of languages, the machine does seem to be accepted as of undeniable service, especially as a means of saving time. In cases where the ideal is to reinvent a sequence of reasoning, however, as in mathematics, though the machine does not exclude either comprehension or reasoning itself on the student's part, it does channel them in an unfortunate way and excludes the possibility of initiative. It is interesting in this respect to note that at the Woods Hole conference at which mathematicians and physicists were seeking for means of recasting the teaching of the sciences, Skinner's propositions were received with no more than limited enthusiasm, since the particular problem facing the conference was less one of finding the means to achieve accurate comprehension than that of encouraging the development of inventive and inquisitive minds.

Generally speaking, since every discipline must include a certain body of acquired facts as well as the possibility of giving rise to numerous research activities and activities of rediscovery, it is possible to envisage a balance being struck, varying from subject to subject, between the different parts to be played by memorizing and free activity. In which case, it is possible that the use of teaching machines will save time that would have been needlessly wasted by more traditional methods and therefore augment the number of hours available for active work. Particularly if the periods of active work include team work, with all that such work entails in the way of mutual incentives and checks, while the machine presupposes an essentially individualized kind of work, then this balance would at the same time be realizing yet another necessary kind of balance: that between the collective and individual aspects of intellectual effort, both so essential to a harmonious school life.

But programmed teaching is still only in its beginnings, and it is a little too soon to make prophecies as to its future use. Like all teaching methods based on the study of one particular aspect of mental development, it may succeed from the point of view we have just examined while still proving inadequate when considered as a general teaching method. And this is a question, like all pedagogical questions, that cannot be resolved by any amount of abstract or notional discussion, but solely by accumulating the requisite amount of facts and controlled tests.

The curious fact, however, is that at the moment such tests are being made in the field of adult education rather than in the field of scholastic pedagogy proper, and there are at least two reasons for this. The first, which is saddening but also highly instructive, is that the effective results of a teaching method are much more closely tested and checked when it is destined for use on adults, who have no time to waste (and especially if that time is a financial consideration with a private commercial concern), than in the case of children, for whom time spent in study is just as precious in fact, but does not appear so in many people's eyes. . . .

The second reason is that the methods of programmed teaching are, in many cases, rendered valueless in advance by the fact that instead of constructing adequate programs based on the principle of progressive comprehension, those responsible for the programming often limit themselves to mere transposition into mechanically programmed terms of the contents of our current textbooks—and the worst textbooks at that! There seemed reason to hope that Skinner's method might at least have had the result of freeing us from the excessive tyranny of school textbooks, which are fairly widely recognized to be the source of many serious problems. . . . Quite often, in order to facilitate the task of programming, those involved simply make use of existing textbooks, naturally selecting those that lend themselves most easily to sequences of questions and answers cast in the most passive and automatic mold.

Training Teachers for Primary and Secondary Schools

. . . The most admirable of reforms cannot but fall short in practice if teachers of sufficient quality are not available in sufficient quantity. Child psychology can provide us with an ever-increasing fund of facts and knowledge concerning the mechanisms of development; but those facts and that knowledge will never reach the schools if the teachers have not absorbed them sufficiently to translate them into original applications. The demands of social justice and the economic needs of society may force an expansion in all sectors of education and increasing mobility for students within them; but it is still necessary that the teachers accept the very considerable responsibility of providing individual guidance, and that they acquire sufficient understanding of the complexity of these problems to provide the necessary collaboration. Generally speaking, the more we try to improve our schools, the heavier the teacher's task becomes; and the better our teaching methods, the more difficult they are to apply.

Yet, the tragic fact is that the widespread educational renaissance of recent years has coincided with an increasing dearth of teachers. There is nothing fortuitous about this coincidence: the same reasons that have rendered our school system inadequate have also led to the inadequacy of the social and (as an indirect consequence) of the economic position of the teacher.

Our school system, as much under left-wing as under right-wing regimes, has been constructed by conservatives (from the pedagogic point of view) who were thinking much more in terms of fitting our rising generations into the molds of traditional learning than in terms of training inventive and critical minds. From the point of view of society's present needs, it is apparent that those old molds are cracking in order to make way for broader, more flexible systems and more active methods. But from the point of view of the teachers and their social situation, those old educational conceptions, having made the teachers into mere transmitters of elementary or only slightly more than elementary general knowledge, without allowing them any opportunity for initiative and even less for research and discovery, have thereby imprisoned them in their present lowly status. And now, at the moment when we are witnessing an educational revolution of great historical importance, since it is centered on the child and the adolescent, and on precisely those qualities they possess that will be most useful to tomorrow's society, the teachers in our various schools can command neither a science of education sufficiently advanced to permit personal efforts on their part that would contribute to the further progress of that discipline, nor the solid [respect] that would be attached to such a scientific, practical, and socially essential form of activity. . . .

From every point of view then, the problem of teacher training constitutes the key problem upon whose solution those of all the other questions examined until now depend. So that the following examination of the solutions offered or proposed for this one problem, having been reserved for this final chapter, will serve as a conclusion to all the preceding analyses as a whole.

THE TRAINING OF PRIMARY-SCHOOL STAFF

Three sorts of systems are employed in various countries for the training of primary-school teachers: the *école normale*, or teacher training college (either residential or not), the colleges of education forming an intermediate group, and the university departments or faculties of education. The tendency over the past few years has quite clearly been toward a rise in the standard of this training. . . .

The disadvantages of the teachers' training colleges (*écoles normales*) are held to be of two kinds. The first is that they shut the primary teaching body in on itself, or in other words create a closed social entity, legitimately conscious of its merits but exposed to a sort of collective and endemic feeling of inferiority maintained by the causes given above. Everyone is aware of this phenomenon, which is a wholly artificial state of affairs created by social conditions and has become both one of the principal obstacles to recruitment (despite the improvement in salaries) and also a retarding factor in the expansion of the school system. The second disadvantage is that . . . the training college itself ultimately results in cultural limitations, whether one wishes it or not, simply because the students are deprived of the necessary exchanges with other students studying courses leading to different professions. In particular, the psychological training so indispensable to primary-school teachers is clearly more complex and difficult to impart than a secondary education, and cannot be carried out efficiently except in liaison with university research centers, where specialists can be closely observed at work. One cannot truly learn child psychology except by collaborating in new research projects and taking part in experiments, and it is useless to limit courses to exercises or practical work directed toward already known results. Such research work, however, is to be found solely in universities, and a university is the only place in which schoolteachers can learn to become researchers and to rise above the level of mere transmitters. And the same thing is equally true of experimental pedagogy itself, since its manifests destiny is to be the discipline par excellence of schoolteachers, whose individual activities would then attain a scientific status, if only they were sufficiently trained: but that training is inseparable from a high standard of psychological and sociological education.

The intermediate colleges or institutes of education attempt to remedy these defects by providing for a training in two stages: a course of general training at secondary level, acquired previously in the usual schools, and a specialized form of training given solely in these colleges or institutes. This obviously represents an advance, in that the entire emphasis can be laid, in these institutes, on psychopedagogical training. But there still remains the drawback of the future primary teachers' segregation as a social entity from secondary-school teachers, and above all from all those university students who are involved in branches of knowledge whose acquisition is inseparable from an initiation into research methods. The mere fact of having vocational training schools that are entirely divorced from the universities and solely concerned with training in the teaching of elementary subjects—whereas dentists, pharmacists, and many others, including above all the future secondary-school teachers, are required to attend a university in order to acquire their training—seems to indicate both that the vocational training of the primary-school teacher is different in status, and that it does in fact consist of nothing more than a somewhat closed-in professional training, as opposed to the initiation required for those disciplines providing opportunities for indefinite new developments and explorations.

. . . . By what criterion is elementary teaching judged to be easier than the teaching required in the upper classes of primary schools, and that in its turn less difficult than teaching in secondary schools? The only consideration that can justify this hierarchy is, of course, that of the subject matter to be taught, though solely when considered from the point of view of the standard of the knowledge itself and independently of the greater or lesser facility with which it can be assimilated by the students. . . . Is it factually true that it is easier to enable a young child of 7 to 9 to grasp an elementary structure, say in arithmetic or language, than to enable an adolescent to assimilate a more complicated structure? In fact, there is nothing to prove that the [latter], though from the point of view of science or the adult himself it is effectively more complex, is in any way more difficult to communicate, if only precisely because the adolescent is closer in mental development to the thought and speech habits of the adult. As far as the student's subsequent intellectual development is concerned, [is] satisfactory assimilation of the structure involved (as opposed to an approximate and more or less verbal assimilation) more important at the level of higher education or at the elementary level? . . .

From this twofold point of view of the difficulties of assimilation and of the objective importance of the ideas, it is in fact permissible to hold—if one takes the psychological and even the epistemological point of view rather than that of administrative common sense—that the younger the child the more difficult it is to teach him, and the more pregnant that teaching is with future consequences. That is why one of the most interesting experiments that has been attempted in the realm of teacher training is that directed over a period of years in Edinburgh by the great psychologist Godfrey Thomson, the head of Murray House, the university's department of education: the future teachers, once they had been educated (at secondary level and then at the university) in the subject they were intending to teach, then received at Murray House a psychological and didactic training proper, and it was not until this specialized pedagogic training was finished that they selected the educational level at which they hoped to work. In other words, the future primary- and secondary-school teachers were all trained together during these final years of educational training, and without deciding from the outset which of the two categories they intended to belong to. And this produced a twofold advantage: elimination of inferiority or superiority feelings, and a training centered on the needs of the pupil rather than on the advantages of either career (both becoming equal).

Without claiming that such an ideal situation must be made universal—since the budgetary requirements for it are only too clearly of a very high order—it does at least provide an introduction to the various attempts, either already made or projected, at training primary-school teachers in universities. Moreover, it is as well in this respect not to let ourselves be blinded with words but to make quite sure in each particular case exactly what level of university education is involved. Many American "Teachers' Colleges" are nothing more in fact, from this point of view, than "educational institutes" of the intermediary type discussed earlier; open, in other words, to undergraduates who will not be required to do very much in the way of research. In other cases, however, a genuine integration of the future teacher into university life has been attempted. . . .

Another experiment, carried out in Geneva during the past few years, is also instructive from the double point of view of its deficiencies and its successes. Its principle is that the future primary school teacher should begin by acquiring his baccalaureate and then go on to spend three years receiving his specialized training. During the first of these three years, the candidates take practical courses that enable them to become acquainted with the problems, and then, in the third year, they again return to practical work. The second year, on the other hand, is spent at the university, where the candidates take courses in psychology (science faculty), pedagogy (arts faculty), and special courses at the Institut des Sciences de l'Education (Institut J. J. Rousseau), after which they take examinations for their certificate (three written and four oral exams)....

. . . Everyone is in agreement (and this is true of all the systems, including the teacher training colleges—*écoles normales*) that the training of teachers necessitates a training in psychology. But the methods of the active school are still so far from being general practice in that which concerns the students themselves, that the psychological training is often reduced to no more than a set of lectures and examinations, the practical side consisting of no more than the application of a few tests. Yet it is even truer in the case of psychology than in other fields that the only way to understand the facts involved and their interpretation is to undertake some research project of one's own. This is naturally the part that is most difficult to organize, especially for beginners. In the particular example we are dealing with here the problem is solved in the following way: the institute has research programs that are planned in yearly stages by the professors and conducted by assistants, who go every afternoon to visit premises made available in each school and question the children involved. The student teachers are associated with these research projects and accompany the assistants—in groups of two or, at the maximum, three—on these visits, so that they learn how to record facts and how to question the children, and above all so that they can make periodic reports, thus involving them with the progress of the research in periods of both failure and success. This is the kind of collaboration to which the future teachers are increasingly being invited to contribute, and it is this kind of contact with the process of gradually isolating and then collating facts that constitutes their essential training: an intellectual training, since it forces them to understand the complexity of the questions involved (whereas the lectures are concerned solely with questions already solved, and therefore apparently much simpler than they are in reality), and a moral or social training, since it gives the educator a conviction that his subject embraces indefinite opportunities for theoretical exploration and technical improvements. In a word, it is by and through research that the teacher's profession ceases to be merely a trade and even goes beyond the level of the emotional vocation to acquire the dignity of all professions that draw upon both the arts and sciences, since the sciences concerned with children and their training constitute an inexhaustible field of endeavor, now more than ever.

THE TRAINING OF SECONDARY-SCHOOL TEACHING STAFF

In the majority of countries secondary-school teachers are trained in universities, where they acquire *at least* one degree. They are therefore accustomed to research, at least in the subjects they will be teaching, with the result, if they are sufficiently fired with enthusiasm for those subjects in themselves, that they will be able to pick out the future researchers from among their pupils and proceed to train them with a view to such activities as well as to the assimilation of established knowledge. It often happens, however, that the more enthusiastic a secondary-school teacher is about the subject he teaches, the less interested he is in educational science as such. Or rather, pedagogy being an art as much as a science where its application is concerned, the master with a gift for teaching and creating educational contact tends to suppose that such a gift is sufficient in itself, and that a detailed knowledge of mental mechanisms is something that only primary-school teachers working with young children need, whereas at the adolescent level such psychological analyses have nothing useful to add to the classroom experience of a good teacher with an individual knowledge of his students.

One small example will serve to show what the result of such thinking may be. Modern mathematics derives in part from the theory of [sets], and one new way of teaching this subject is based nowadays on an initiation into the elementary operations involving the joining and intersection of two [sets]: a reasonable enough project since the child already employs such operations spontaneously at the level of concrete operations. Yet a mathematics teacher at a secondary school was astonished at the difficulty his students displayed in manipulating such operations without errors, at the age of 12 to 13, when he had nevertheless furnished them with the appropriate formal definition in irreproachable terms. He was simply forgetting the fundamental psychological difference that exists between the capacity to employ an operation spontaneously and unconsciously, and the power to use reflection in order to derive an abstract formalization from it. A psychological analysis of the conditions governing the transition between these two stages of thought would have considerably simplified the problem of presentation; and simply because such an idea has not occurred to them one is constantly finding teachers today, excellent teachers otherwise, who are teaching the most advanced mathematics by means of the most antiquated educational methods.

It was therefore not without reason that the International Conference of Public Education, when dealing with the training of secondary-level teaching staff, at its 1954 session, emphasized the necessity for psychological instruction up to the same level as that bearing directly upon the subjects to be taught. However, such psychopedagogical training is much more difficult to obtain [for] teachers at this level than [for] those at the primary level. The difficulty resides above all in the fact that if one is to understand the psychology of the adolescent mental functions, it is first indispensable to have a thorough grasp of mental development in its entirety, from the earliest years up to adulthood, and that future secondary-school teachers, until they have understood how analysis of the formative processes as a whole can throw light on those peculiar to adolescence, consistently display a total lack of interest in the childhood years.

The two methods that have best succeeded up till now in persuading the trainee teachers themselves to accept such training—at least where future teachers in the sciences are concerned—are the following: the first naturally consists in associating them with psychopedagogic research bearing upon some particular logico-mathematical structure or some particular situation of physical causality; the often wholly unexpected character of the variously aged subjects is frequently sufficient to make it clear that there are problems involved of which a detailed knowledge would be of great benefit to any teacher. The second method concerns theoretical training. It often happens that future science teachers display an undisguised contempt for the psychology of development until one can succeed in making them grasp the epistemological bearing of the laws of that development. Whereas once the problems involved in the acquisition of knowledge have been posed for them in terms of relations between subject and object, or, in other words, in terms of empiricist, apriorist, or constructivist interpretations, etc., they become aware of a connection with some of the central problems of their special subject and perceive the interest of research whose mere pedagogic presentation had left them unmoved.

As for future liberal-arts teachers, the state of research permits less contacts of such a kind. But with the advances in linguistic analysis bearing on the individual evolution of language, they already look promising, not only from the point of view of linguistic structuralism itself but also from that of the relations between the semiotic function and thought. Here again, the field of possible research is immense and there is no doubt that a day will come when the sciences of education, benefiting from all these contributions, will perfect techniques of immeasurably greater refinement than anything we possess today, and will succeed, by that very fact, in achieving not only a much more thorough training of the teaching body but above all its active collaboration in the perpetually self-renewing development of such disciplines.

36

Comments on Mathematical Education*

1972

The orientation one would consider giving to mathematical education depends naturally on the interpretation adopted of psychological development or the acquiring of operations and logico-mathematical structures; this interpretation depends equally on the epistemological meaning given to those things, the two questions of their psychogenesis and their epistemological significance being very closely related. If Platonism is right and mathematical entities exist independently of the subject, or if logical positivism is correct in reducing them to a general syntax and semantic, in both cases it would be justifiable to put the emphasis on the simple transmission of the truth from teacher to pupil and to use, as soon as possible, the language of the teacher, that is, the axiomatic language, without worrying too much about the spontaneous ideas of the children.

We believe, on the contrary, that there exists, as a function of the development of intelligence as a whole, a spontaneous and gradual construction of elementary logico-mathematical structures and that these "natural" ("natural" in the way one speaks of the "natural" numbers) structures are much closer to those being used in "modern" mathematics than to those being used in traditional mathematics. There is, therefore, a body of facts which are, in general, little known to the teacher, but which, once he has a better psychological knowledge, would be of considerable use to him and would help him rather than make things more complicated. This would also favor the realization of creative vocations in pupils rather than treating them simply as conforming "receiving" instruments.

However, in order to arrive at this stage it is necessary to revise our ideas about the relation between language and action. It would seem, in fact, psychologically clear that logic does not arise out of language but from a deeper source and this is to be found in the general co-ordination of actions. In fact, before all language, and at a purely sensorimotor level, actions are susceptible to repetition and then to generalization thus building up what could be called assimilation schemes. These schemes organize themselves according to certain laws

*From J. Piaget, *Developments in Mathematical Education*, Proc. of the *Second International Congress on Mathematical Education*, ed. by A. G. Howson. Reprinted by permission of Cambridge University Press.

and it would seem impossible to deny the relationship between these and the laws of logic. Two schemes can be coordinated or dissociated (reunion), one can be partially nested in the other (inclusion), or only have a part in common with the other (intersection); the parts of a scheme or the coordination of two or more schemes can allow either an invariant order of succession or certain permutations (types of order), as well as one-to-one correspondences, one-to-many, or many-to-one (bijections, etc.), and once a scheme imposes a goal on an action it is contradictory for the subject to go in the opposite direction. Briefly, there is a whole logic of the action that leads to the construction of certain identities and these go beyond perception (for example, the permanence of the hidden object) and to the elaboration of certain structures (the practical group of displacements already described by Poincaré in his epistemological essays).

Therefore, it would be a great mistake, particularly in mathematical education, to neglect the role of actions and always to remain on the level of language. Particularly with young pupils, activity with objects is indispensable to the comprehension of arithmetical as well as geometrical relations (as was the case with the empirical mathematics of the Egyptians). The mathematics teacher's aversion to activities involving material experimentation is quite comprehensible. They probably see a sort of reference to the physical properties of objects and might fear that empirical verifications will harm the development of the deductive and purely rational mind which characterizes their discipline. But this is, in fact, a fundamental misunderstanding and psychological analysis allows us to dispel these fears and reassure mathematicians with regard to their essential demand that the deductive and formal aspect of the mind should be educated. There exist, in fact, two types of "experience," one very different from the other, which are related to the subject's actions. In the first instance, there is what is known as "physical experience" (in the broad sense) which consists in acting on objects in order to discover the properties of the objects themselves, for example, comparing weights or densities, etc. But there also exists, and this is generally not known, what could be called "logico-mathematical experience"; this type of experience gathers its information, not from the physical properties of particular objects, but from the actual actions (or more precisely their coordinations) carried out by the child on objects—these two types of experience are not equivalent. A friend of mine and a well-known mathematician says that the beginnings of his interest in mathematics were triggered off by an experience of the second type which happened to him when he was about 4 or 5 years old. Seated in his garden, he started to amuse himself by placing some pebbles in a straight line and counting them, for example, one to ten from left to right. After this he counted them from right to left and to his great surprise he still found ten. He put them in a circle and, with enthusiasm, counted them—again ten so he counted them in the opposite direction and he found there were ten in both directions. He went on arranging the pebbles in· all sorts of ways and finished by convincing himself that the sum, ten, was independent of the order of the pebbles. It is evident that neither the sum nor the order are physical properties of the pebbles until such time as the child has actually arranged them or put them all together. In this instance the child has discovered that the action of uniting the pebbles gives results and these results are independent of the action of ordering the pebbles. He could have observed this with any solid objects as, in this action, the physical properties of the pebbles played no particular role (apart from the fact that they "let themselves" be acted on; their nature, however, remains unaltered, that is, it is conserved, but conservation itself gives rise to logico-mathematical experience).

Thus this initial role of actions and logico-mathematical experience, far from hindering the later development of deductive thought, constitutes, on the contrary, a necessary preparation and this for two reasons. This first is that mental or intellectual operations, which intervene in the subsequent deductive reasoning processes, themselves stem from actions: they are interiorized actions and once this interiorization, with the coordinations it supposes, is sufficient, then logico-mathematical experience in the form of material actions is no longer necessary and interiorized deduction is sufficient. The second reason is that coordinations of actions and logico-mathematical experience, whilst interiorizing themselves, give rise to the creation of a particular variety of abstraction which corresponds precisely to logical and mathematical abstraction: contrary to ordinary or Aristotelian abstraction which derives its sources from the physical properties of objects and for this reason is called "empirical abstraction," logico-mathematical abstraction would be referred to as "reflective abstraction" and this for two related reasons. On the one hand, this abstraction "reflects" (in the same way as a reflector or projector) everything that was on a lower plane (for example, that of action) and projects it to a higher plane, that of thought or mental representation. On the other hand, it is a "reflective abstraction" in the sense of a reorganization of mental activity, as it reconstructs at a higher level everything that was drawn from the coordinations of actions.

However, between the age where material actions and logico-mathematical experience are necessary (before 7–8 years old) and the age where abstract thought begins to be possible (toward 11–12 years old and through successive levels until about 14–15 years), there is an important stage whose characteristics are interesting to the psychologist and useful to know for the teacher. In fact between the age of 7 and 11–12 years an important spontaneous development of deductive operations with their characteristics of conservation, reversibility, etc., can be observed. This allows the elaboration of elementary logic of classes and relations, the operational construction of the whole number series by the synthesis of the notions of inclusion and order,* the construction of the notion of measurement by the synthesis of the

*Several authors (Freudenthal, etc.) seems to have understood that I think the ordinal number is more primitive than the cardinal number, or the opposite. I have never made such a statement and have always considered these two aspects of finite numbers indissociable and psychologically reinforcing one another in a synthesis that goes beyond both the inclusion of classes and the order of asymmetrical transitive relations. If order is necessary it is because units which have become equivalent by the abstraction of their qualities can only be distinguished from one another by their ordered position. But the order of the elementary units is relative to the number (cardinal) of units which precede each of the units thus ordered.

subdivision of a continuum and the ordered displacement of a chosen part which serves as a unit, etc. Although there is considerable progress in the child's logical thinking it is nonetheless still fairly limited. At this level the child cannot as yet reason on pure hypotheses, expressed verbally, and, in order to arrive at a coherent deduction, he needs to apply his reasoning to manipulable objects (in the real world or in his imagination). For these reasons, at this level we refer to "concrete operations" as distinct from formal operations. These concrete operations are, in fact, intermediaries between the actions of the pre-operational stage and the stage of abstract thought which comes much later.

Thus, having established the continuity between the spontaneous actions of the child and his reflective thought, it can be seen from this that the essential notions which characterize modern mathematics are much closer to the structures of "natural" thought than are the concepts used in traditional mathematics. First, the importance should be pointed out of the spontaneous role of operations which allow the establishment of correspondences between sets and thus the construction of morphisms and in particular when these can be combined with recurring sequences. We have, for example, with B. Inhelder, asked children between 4–5 and 7–8 years old to put a bead from one hand into a transparent cylinder and simultaneously with the other hand put another bead into a second transparent cylinder which was, however, hidden behind a screen. The questions were designed to find out whether or not the child understood that the two sets, thus constituted, were equivalent and also to discover whether if this action were to be continued indefinitely, this equality would be conserved. All the children questioned admitted the equality of the two sets whilst the action was going on, however the youngest children refused to generalize to the case where the action was continued indefinitely. From about 5 or 6 years onward they admit this generalization and one small boy of 5½ found the following very amusing formula: "When one knows for one time, one knows for ever." However this same child, after having seen a set of ten red counters in a one-to-one correspondence with a second set of ten blue counters, refused to admit the conservation of this equivalence once the elements of one of the sets had been spaced out a little and the correspondence between the two was no longer visible. This example demonstrates the constructive role of the establishment of a correspondence combined with the idea of recurrence.

An extremely striking example of convergence between theory and the spontaneous development of the child is that of geometric intuitions. Historically these intuitions appeared in Euclidean geometry, the structures of projective geometry were not discovered until much later and topology only in the nineteenth century. Psychologically children of 3 and 4 years old, who do not yet know how to draw squares and tend to compare them to circles—shapes such as rectangles and triangles, etc., being assimilated to simple closed curves—are very careful, however, to make the distinction between closed and open figures, and they are able to draw with as much care a circle inside a figure, outside a figure, or on the frontier of a large figure. From these early topological intuitions arise, later and simultaneously, projective notions (with verification by "taking aim" or "sighting") and Euclidean notions according to a process which is nearer psychological theory than history.

From the level of concrete operations—at about 7–8 years—another interesting convergence can be found, that is the elementary equivalent of the three "mother structures" discovered by Bourbaki, and this itself shows the "natural" character of these structures. First of all there is the construction of structures of an algebraic nature, inasmuch as their laws of composition have an inverse and an identity element $+A - A = 0$. This can be observed particularly in the system of logical classes (classifications, etc. with quantification of the inclusion $A < B$ if $B = A + A'$—and neither are empty sets). Secondly, order structures can be found whose laws of composition are based on reciprocity and this characterizes the system of relations (ordering). Finally, topological structures based on ideas of continuity, neighborhood and separation can be observed. These elementary structures later combine with each other. In particular, inverses (or negations $(-A)$) and reciprocities, which do not combine with each other at the concrete operational level, can be composed with one another from the 11–12 formal level onward, in a four-group which renders possible such compositions: in this case the beginning of propositional logic with the combinatorial (set of all subsets) system, superposes itself on the elementary structures of logical classes and relations. The subject is then capable of handling systems that have four transformations. Let us take, for example, the propositional operation $p \supset q$ and define the four transformations:

(1) (I) the identity or "null" transformation I $(p \supset q) = p \supset q$,
(2) (N) the inverse transformation N $(p \supset q) = p \cap \smallfrown q$,
(3) (R) the reciprocal transformation R $(p \supset q) = q \supset p$,
(4) (C) the correlative transformation C $(p \supset q) = \smallfrown p \cap q$.

In this case RC = N, RN = C, NC = R, NRC = I which ensures finally the coordination in a unique system of inverses and reciprocities.

Many other examples, in particular the construction of elementary and "trivial" forms of categories, could be given. However, it is now the moment to describe how these convergences between the spontaneous thought of the child in his "natural" development and certain fundamental theoretical notions can be of use to the teacher. It can, of course, happen that certain people will try to teach young children "modern" mathematics with archaic teaching methods, based exclusively on verbal transmission from teacher to child with a premature use of formalisation. With such methods there are bound to be a certain number of failures and these help to explain the scepticism of certain great mathematicians such as J. Leray.[*] However, it is not the "modern" character of the mathematics programs that is at fault but the methodology and psychology used in such cases. In fact, it is often particularly difficult for the teacher of mathematics, who, because of his profession, has a very abstract type of thought, to place himself in the concrete perspective which is necessarily that of his young pupils. However, from the developmental point of view and in relation to the progressive assimilation of the structures already mentioned, there would seem to be no contradiction (as we have seen above) between the initial concrete phases of structures and the final stage when they

*See the very critical report presented by Leray for Académie des Sciences de Paris (Report No. 276, p. 95, Session of 13 March 1972).

become formal and abstract. The teacher can only be aware that there is no contradiction between these two levels of thought if he is fully acquainted with (and this is the difficulty for the teacher) the details and functioning of these successive spontaneous thought structures. Briefly, the practical problem that is difficult to solve is to graft these general types of notions which the teacher understands in his language onto particular cases of these same notions constructed and used spontaneously by the children, without these yet being for them objects of reflection or sources of generalization.

In order to make this necessary conjunction between the logico-mathematical structures of the teacher and those of the pupil at different levels of his development, certain very general psycho-pedagogical principles should perhaps be mentioned. The first is that *real comprehension of a notion or a theory implies the reinvention of this theory by the subject.** Once the child is capable of repeating certain notions and using some applications of these in learning situations he often gives the impression of understanding; however, this does not fulfill the condition of reinvention. True understanding manifests itself by new spontaneous applications, in other words an active generalization supposes a great deal more: it seems that the subject has been able to discover for himself the true reasons involved in the understanding of a situation and, therefore, has at least partially reinvented it for himself. Naturally, this does not mean that the teacher has no role any more, but that his role is less that of a person who gives "lessons" and is rather that of someone who organizes situations that will give rise to curiosity and solution-seeking in the child, and who will support such behavior by means of appropriate arrangements. Should the child have difficulties in his attempts to grasp a certain idea, the procedure with an active methodology would not be directly to correct him, but to suggest such counterexamples that the child's new exploration will lead him to correct himself.

A second consideration should constantly be present in the teacher's mind: that is, at all levels, including adolescence and in a systematic manner at the more elementary levels, *the pupil will be far more capable of "doing" and "understanding in actions" than of expressing himself verbally.*† In other words, a large part of the structures the child uses when he sets out actively to solve a problem remain unconscious. In fact, it is a very general psychological law that the child can do something in action long before he really becomes "aware" of what is involved—"awareness" occurs long after the action. In other words, the subject possesses far greater intellectual powers than he actually consciously uses.‡ Consequently, once the teacher has had the opportunity of becoming acquainted with the psychological research mentioned above, and knows the subjacent thought structures the child possesses, he can more easily help the child to become aware of these either by appropriate discussions between the child and himself, or by the organization of the work in groups where partners of the same age or similar ages (an older child acting as leader of a small

*[Our emphasis.]
†[Our emphasis.]
‡Euclid himself was not aware of all the operational structures he used in reality, for example, the group of isometries.

group) discuss between themselves, which in turn favorizes verbalization and "awareness."

A third remark would seem important: in traditional mathematics it was often necessary for children to solve quantities of problems, some of them quite absurd, and this would mean a huge number of numerical or metrical calculations. In this case, the only way to succeed with children who were not particularly talented in mathematics was to proceed in two stages (but this was often forgotten): the first stage was purely qualitative and dealt with the logical structure of the problem and only afterward in a second step were numerical or metrical facts introduced with the additional difficulties this type of calculation would create. With modern mathematics programs the problem is less acute as they are basically qualitative. However, in this case, the problem can be found at another level—the teacher is often tempted to present far too early notions and operations in a framework that is already very formal. In this case, the procedure that would seem indispensable would be to take as the starting point the qualitative concrete levels: in other words, the representations or models used should correspond to the natural logic of the levels of the pupils in question, and *formalization should be kept for a later moment as a type of systematization of the notions already acquired. This certainly means the use of intuition before axiomatization** and the scorn of logicians for all intuitive or "naïve" thought is well known. However, once it is remembered that mathematical intuition is essentially operational and the nature of operational structures is to dissociate "form" from "content," then the final formalization would seem to be prepared and becomes progressively necessary by the construction itself of these initial intuitive structures. We do not believe with Pasch that formalization goes in the opposite direction to that taken by "natural" thought, but so that there may be no conflict between the former and the latter, formalization should be allowed to constitute itself in its own time and not because it is forced to by premature constraints.

*[Our emphasis.]

PART X
Piaget's Philosophy

INTRODUCTION

Piaget's philosophy pervades all his work, be it labeled psychology, education, logic, biology, or prefaces to other authors' books. There is a very good reason for that. Unlike most scientists who generate problems from questions internal to their field of research, Piaget generates problems out of general philosophical questions so that his scientific specialized production appears, as he proudly quotes from the APA Distinguished Scientist Award, as a "byproduct" of his general philosophical preoccupations. Consequently, among his multiple contributions to knowledge, the one that pleases Piaget the most is undoubtedly his own brand of genetic epistemology, although contrary to a widespread idea, Piaget did not coin or invent the term *genetic epistemology*.

Besides epistemology almost every branch of philosophy has been touched on by Piaget's research. Probably the major exception is aesthetics, on which Piaget has been virtually silent. Important aspects of the domain of ethics and social philosophy are dealt with in his work on moral judgment. Although, as we have pointed out earlier, Piaget takes a dim view of actually trying to resolve ontological questions, at different points in his career he has dealt with the child's construction of reality and the child's conception of reality. Logic, of course, has received an important part of his attention. For each of these subjects we ask the reader to turn to other parts of this anthology.

In the present introduction, we circumscribe the discussion of Piaget's philosophy to a few dialectical tensions that, we think, underlie all his philosophical inquiries: (1) tension between philosophy and science; (2) tension between norms and facts; (3) tension between the unity of science and its differentiation into different disciplines; (4) tension between structuralism and geneticism in Piaget's genetic structuralism; (5) opposition between Piaget's emphasis on the role of action as prime mover of intellectual life and the absence in his work of the notion of struggle; and (6) tension between the empiricism of the philosophy of Enlightenment and the idealism of romantic thinkers.

The rest of the discussion to be found here is the result of these six basic oppositions. But sometimes it is a strange progeny, as the reader shall see for himself.

Psychology to Psychology versus
Philosophy to Psychology*

Many scientists function at an epistemological level of zero: they do not bother to question the hidden relations between their work and metaphysics, logic, or society. They inherit a certain existing *problématique*, a certain milieu of problems, and they seem very happy about spinning off some new research about the "field" as it has been defined for them by their predecessors. The French novelist, Louis-Ferdinand Céline, who was a microbiologist by training, once described this sort of normal science by saying that scientific conventions are the kind of place where somebody who has found a virus in the vagina of a 3-year-old girl that was previously described in the literature only in the penis of aged men is hailed as a brilliant contributor to the progress of knowledge. This one-dimensional accumulation of facts and the sort of reverence that it commands in some scientific spheres is far away from Piaget's approach to science. Piaget uses science as a means toward an end. To him science is a revelator of philosophical problems. For him, the greatest philosophical systems in the history of man were born out of reflection on science or out of projects to make new sciences possible. This means that science is fed by philosophical considerations and preoccupations; it also feeds back to philosophy answers that are considered by Piaget as valid because they are arrived at by means of true objectivity, methodological consensus (intersubjectivity), and the rest of the paraphernalia that science bestows on itself whenever confronted with other forms of knowledge such as religion, myth, and art. In the process, entire provinces of philosophy fall to science in a sort of domino theory. What was cosmology has become criticism of science. Physics has gone strictly scientific; biology, chemistry, geology, and all the rest of natural sciences have followed the same road. More recently, logic, psychology, and sociology have dissociated themselves from mother philosophy, who after having been the servant to theology seems to have become nowadays the servant to science.

This begetting of disciplines that Piaget envisions in *Insight and Illusions of Philosophy* reminds one of the genealogy of gods in Greek mythology. Like the Greek mythology and unlike the linear system of generation of sciences proposed by Comte, the various sciences that have differentiated themselves from philosophy entertain complex relationships with one another and with their common origin, philosophy. There is not only a mutual feedback between philosophical questions and scientific answers but there is also a sort of cross-fertilization of sciences among themselves: chemistry and biology beget biochemistry, astronomy and physics, astrophysics; geography and political sciences, geopolitics, psychology and physiology, psychophysiology. Sciences are always "baby-booming" and some wise men, once in a while, feel called upon either to bless this high fertility rate or to condemn it as overpopulation, waste, and a hazard to the intellectual environment of the planet of scientists.

Piaget's attitude, once again, is more middle of the road. He sees the cross among various sciences as a sign of progress and "mutual enrichment" but he considers certain intercourses among other sciences as bound to be sterile at

* J. Piaget, *Insights and Illusions of Philosophy*, 1965.

the second generation. He certainly feels that the movement from philosophy to science and back is the major way in which mankind has gained knowledge in the course of its history. This is the reason why he is so keen about the daily course of the various researches carried out in Geneva under his guidance. The results of these researches are supposed to provide him with the empirical materials for scientific solutions to philosophical questions that have puzzled humanity for centuries. In this sense, it would be as mistaken to reduce Piaget to one of his parts, be it the psychologist, epistemologist, biologist, or sociologist, as it would be to overlook that a good deal of the resignation, dignity, and self-control of the Indians of the Andes is sustained by their belief that they help the sun rise up above the sky every single day, for the sake of the rest of mankind. There is something of that Orphic quality in Piaget's work and devotion to work.

Some people have seen Piaget's constant reference to philosophy as a change in paradigm. This is not entirely true. In the beginnings of psychology an an independent science there was a strong current of ideas that never won complete acceptance but that was nevertheless powerful in some fields of psychology such as developmental psychology. That current was so vividly preoccupied with epistemological questions that it generated an opposition movement that was to become extremely popular in psychology: behaviorism. Behaviorism was an alternative to what its major exponents considered as undue and overwhelming concern for epistemological questions. In more than one way, Piaget continues that epistemological tradition. But what made the difference between the old kind of epistemological preoccupations to be found in scientific journals and the special brand of the developmental psychologists was the developmental perspective itself. It is one thing for a scientist to worry perpetually about the epistemological validity of concepts he uses in his own domain of research, and quite another to wonder about the criteria for truth that are successively used by growing children. In the first case, it might be rejected as navel contemplation. In the second it is the only possible bridge between the scientist and radically different people such as children, primitives, and psychopaths. The question of what is truth for others cannot be rejected simply on the basis that it is philosophical in nature. It is one that must be asked right away if one wants to gain an intimate understanding of these others. It has been the great merit of developmental psychologists in general and of Piaget especially to face this issue squarely.

Philosophy versus Science

There is a paradox in the fact that the same person, as an epistemologist, observes the constant spoliation of philosophy from its domain to the advantage of newly created sciences such as psychology, logic, and sociology (not to speak of epistemology itself) and at the same time has been very productive in all these fields.

The question arises then: is the differentiation among the different fields of science as drastic as Piaget tends to assert or is this diversification overdone, since one man, admittedly a very unusual one, can excel in them all? Perhaps the apparent diversity of scientific disciplines may conceal a profound unity? This viewpoint, usually held by empiricists, puts the unity of the sciences in a sort of synthesis of the complex from simples. All sciences share common assumptions at the methodological level; they speak the same language. As such, they form a unitary enterprise.

On the other hand, one can hold the view that an objective synthesis of the various sciences is impossible, since specific sciences require different local criteria to be understood. Therefore, internal unification becomes impossible. Unification can be accomplished only from an external vantage point. This vantage point is usually located in some remote entity such as a set of innate categories transcending the variety of experiences and the diversity of scientific enterprises. This position could be termed idealistic

As a young man, in his philosophical novel *Recherche*, Piaget seemed to favor the first horn of the alternative. His worldview was not very far from the one promised by A. Comte in his *Philosophie positiviste*: social salvation would come from the internally necessary obedience of mankind to the objective laws of nature as revealed in the synthesis of the various sciences. Later on, when his own psychological research was underway, Piaget insisted more on the active part taken by the subject in knowledge and he formulated the concept of an epistemic subject who is the aspect of the self that is common to all individual subjects at the same level of development. The epistemic subject is thus universal.

Such a universal creates a tension between the empiricistic viewpoint, according to which all the separate sciences speak the same language, and the idealistic one, according to which they are united by an external universal. In other words, the status of the epistemic subject is unclear. Is it an external agent transcending the variety of scientific experiences? Or is it simply the catalyst of the synthesis of simples expected by empiricism?

If the empiricist alternative is taken, then the triumph of science over philosophy is indubitable. Science is its own justification; it carries its philosophy in itself and an epistemology internal to the various sciences is not only possible but inescapable. Since science is the only valid form of knowledge, the one that cannot be superseded by any other, its increasing differentiation into multiple disciplines becomes a sign of fertility instead of a sign of impotence. Among the sundry human activities, only science speaks the truth and, moreover, truth is one.

If the idealist alternative is chosen, there are only two possibilities: either the necessary order of emergence of the various sciences rests upon a nativistic argument concerning a hierarchy of dispositions according to which putative later forms of knowledge cannot be manifested in the absence of earlier ones, or it rests upon a logical argument showing that putative later forms of knowledge presuppose "earlier" ones.

Piaget has clearly and emphatically rejected the first argument. He is against nativism as much as he is against empiricism. Consequently, there remains only one possibility: the logical argument. But in order to demonstrate this last point, one must admit that, right from the start, knowledge is transparent to itself, that, at any point in its development science is capable of a complete reflection upon itself, its goals and its methods. Along with the actual work goes a constant whispering of the child or the scientist to himself or herself not unlike the commands young children give themselves in the course of their daily activities as observed by Vygotsky. This sort of introspection presupposes at least a relative transcendence of the subject over his own activities that poses afresh the problem of the relationship between norms and facts as we shall see now.

Norms and Facts

Rules or norms are generally considered as dependent on structures in the subject. They do not depend on the structure of physical reality for their validation but are instead entirely determined by a principle of deduction that is not empirical in nature. Facts or reality, on the other hand, depend on the structure of the external world and are determined by observation or experimentation. Depending on their personal inclination, philosophers have either reduced facts to mere epiphenomena, sometimes even illusions, the lion's share going to subjective activity, or reduced norms to the mere perception of facts. In the first case, knowledge is reduced to the subject's knowledge of his own power. In the second case, knowledge is simply a spectator's art. Who is right?

To solve this difficult question, Piaget undertook the empirical study of the growth of knowledge in children. The result of his observations is that children start with a first period of adualism, i.e., the absence of the subject-object duality. The self and the world are fused together in one entity. The growth of knowledge consists in the gradual differentiation of this single entity into two separate entities and their subsequent integration. So, for Piaget, knowledge does not proceed from a subject aware of his difference from objects nor from objects imposing upon the subject their existence as entities separated from him or her. Knowledge comes from the differentiation of an initial chaos into an organized cosmos where waters are separated from earth, light from darkness, up from down, as in every true creation. This act of creation does not take seven days but the stages of cognitive development spelled out by Piaget and the Geneva School.

Such an approach presents the remarkable advantage of skipping the traditional philosophical question of *adequatio rei et intellectus* (the fit between mind and things, as Thomas of Aquinas used to put it). The question of the fit arises only because traditional philosophers have started with two distinct entities that have somehow to come to terms with each other. When one starts the other way around the question becomes superfluous. The two entities originating in the same primitive entity are forced to be akin and somewhat incestuous as evidenced by the various "partial isomorphisms" that Piaget discovers among different cognitive forms. But there is a price to pay for incest, as Oedipus knew. Incest blinds one to the distinction between norms and facts, self and not-self, reality and image or model. If these dichotomies originate in the same womb, what pushes them into differentiation? What force acts behind the screen? Why should the differentiation end up in the classical categories of traditional philosophy? This seems incomprehensible, unless these categories were put there right from the beginning. In his historical-epistemological studies of science as well as in his psycho-genetic investigations, Piaget does a wonderful job of showing the evolution of basic human categories of understanding such as time, space, and causality. These studies succeed in their strictly apologetical functions in the argumentation against apriorism, but they stop short of explaining the subject-object distinction.

If knowledge is the result of the interpenetration between subjects and objects instead of an exchange between forms distinct from the outset, whence comes the distinction between norms and facts? Piaget's answer to this question is, once again, different from what one would expect. Instead of approaching the question in this way, Piaget prefers to draw some analogies between the changes in rules and norms (if not values) both in the history of science and in the primitives among us, the children, and the changes occurring in facts. The two sorts of changes are shown to parallel each other in such a neat way that Piaget becomes able to change the focus from the opposition between norms and facts to the parallel development that they undergo.

Once the argument has changed structure, it becomes easy, for Piaget, to demonstrate how a deepening of the subjective powers corresponds to a deepening in the knowledge of the environment. This symmetrical movement of knowledge accounts for all the apparently prodigious fits between reality and the most abstract and "idealistic" domains of logic and mathematics. A familiar example, which Piaget uses, is Einstein's application of non-Euclidean geometries to the nature of the universe. Riemann's discovery, for a long time, looked like the perfect example of a purely mathematical game devoid of any possible application until Einstein used it as a means to account for some difficulties in the Newtonian view of the universe.

Such a solution hesitates between the more idealistic position that there is a mind to reign over the universe* and the more empiricistic postulate that such a manifestation of the spirit will occur through the constant groping of scientific theories considered as successive approximations of truth. In the latter view, the evolution of ideas is a hectic history and the end is nowhere near. No second coming is in sight.

Unity and Multiplicity of Science

Piaget is fully aware of the difficulties created by his position, which he considers as a *tertium*, that is, a third force between empiricism and idealism. It is, therefore, interesting to observe how he escapes the contradiction or the tension just mentioned above.

Piaget is convinced that a general synthesis of the different forms of science is possible today. This is the central idea of his genetic epistemology. Thus, genetic epistemology is the positive science, both empirical and theoretical, of the evolution of the positive sciences. For Piaget, science is a social institution, an ensemble of psychological attitudes and behavior and a system of signs; any systematic study of it therefore entails a triple approach: psychogenetic, sociogenetic, and logical. Any serious attempt at genetic epistemology requires the study of ordinary forms of knowledge, the study of the history of science, the developmental study of the child, and the study of the passage from natural logic to scientific logic considered as the grammar of knowledge.

The very fact that such an interdisciplinary approach is considered plausible shows how much Piaget believes in the fundamental unity of science. What then makes that unity possible as well as its diversity?

Here we reach a point where the way in which Piaget solves his own antitheses is truly marvelous. Genetic epistemology is the study of the suc-

* Notice that the invention of non-Euclidean geometries happens before its utilization by Einstein and that there is a constant progress of science toward truth.

cessive states of a science. Both words, *successive* and *states*, are important to understand Piaget's solution to this problem. Since states are recognized in the evolution of a science, these states must correspond to a certain moment of balance or equilibrium in the movement. The movement can then be broken down into meaningful unities or ensembles such as stages. Thus, these stages have a certain structure. But the structure of each stage must be such as to give way to the next one. In other words, the principle of globality or wholeness is completed by a principle of transformation. But some transformations are only local ones that serve to keep the system invariant against the aggressions of the environment whereas others bring along real transformational change, i.e., a new stage in the growth of knowledge. This balance between the old and the new cannot entirely be taken care of either by structuralism, which denies novelty, or by geneticism, which emphasizes change against invariance. So Piaget does not hesitate to manage a new tension between these two opposites under the form of his genetic structuralism where one recognizes both the classical features of structuralism: wholeness, transformation principles, and self-regulation for the maintenance of the existing equilibrium; and the classical features of geneticism: qualitative jumps, existence of a guiding final state or telos, and differentiations and integrations to reach the telos.

Structuralism versus Geneticism

By providing the possibility of a structure of all structures, a "mother" structure, so to speak, structuralism explains the unity. On the other hand, the multiplication and the differentiation of sciences is easily explained by the qualitative changes characteristic of geneticism.

But such a solution raises the hard question of the strife of systems. Structuralism is fundamentally a-genetic and geneticism is basically a-structural. The nongenetic dimension of structuralism stems from the closure principle that is inherent in the very notion of structure: the structure defines itself in such a way that all of its members and possible members are given in the definition; there is no freedom for anything new to emerge within a structure, because if it did it would not be a member of the structure. This principle of closure takes many forms. In mathematics, it is stated flatly as such. In social sciences, it takes the form of a new "unconscious" that Piaget calls a *cognitive* unconscious in contradistinction to the psychoanalytic unconscious that is made out of repressed material. This cognitive unconscious is composed of the implicit structures organizing human behaviors and productions into recognizable typical patterns of invariance.

Such a notion contrasts sharply with the idea of humanism in general and especially with the humanistic view that human beings are the measure of all things. If there are unconscious structures underlying all human activities, then man is no more the measure of all things; the structure is. Such an anti-humanism seems in opposition to a notion Piaget has insisted frequently is central to his work, the notion of activity of the subject as organizing reality (a very humanistic notion).

This tension between the existence of cognitive structures or competences behind the apparent performances of the subject and the active role attributed to this subject poses the question of the reality status of these concepts.

What is the subject? Is it a real, historical, and material subject struggling for survival in an antagonistic world? Obviously not. The concept of subject is strictly epistemic in Piaget's work. The idea of struggle is absent from such a constructed subject. The epistemic subject seems to be the anchorage of the successive cognitive structures that Piaget distinguishes in the development of the child.

On the other hand, even after close scrutiny, the reality of cognitive structures remains unclear. Sometimes Piaget gives the impression that he believes in the ontological reality of these structures. Sometimes they seem simply abstract models of behavior. This impression is particularly strong after reading his short essay, *Structuralism*. Discussing one of the most powerful contemporary movements in the social sciences, Piaget manages to overlook the monumental structuralistic approach to poetry, novel, literary criticism, semiology, and psychoanalysis in order to put the emphasis upon the mathematical variety of structuralism.

This shows a certain idea of what science should be all about. The import of logico-mathematical models is the key to success in social sciences. If models are simply a representation of reality, then Piaget's conception of science is not very far from the eighteenth-century conception of it; the task of the scientist is to give a plausible and elegant picture of reality. Science is no more than the mechanical mirror of reality. On the contrary, if modeling adds something to the previously existing reality, this should be specified clearly. Piaget constantly oscillates between the mechanical mirror and the romantic flame metaphors. For example, he criticizes Chomsky for not recognizing that linguistic structures are the product of speaking people since they invented these structures: Chomsky deprives them of the surplus value of their labor. But what does Piaget do himself? He insulates real, struggling, historical and material children and scientists into epistemic straitjackets. Their development takes place in the rarefied atmosphere of nonhistory. The romantic lamp of the laboring subject is put under the bushel or, at least, its flame burns behind the protective glass of epistemism, away from the winds of history.

So is there no development at all in Piaget's genetic epistemology? Not exactly: there is a sort of controlled development that requires some explanation. First of all, Piaget elaborated early in his life a system of sciences that he called the circle of sciences or better the spiral of sciences. This circle serves to protect the system against two difficulties, the excessive relativism of structuralism and the immanentism inherent in a system that does not go beyond itself for explanations.

Structuralism, by its very nature, considers totalities for their own sake. It fosters absolute relativism, since there are no interstructural norms, no universal criteria by which to evaluate the different structures. It sounds ideally objective. When Lévi-Strauss describes the elementary structure of kinship, he explains the invariant structure of coupling a coercive relationship with a permissive one. In Western societies, the father-son relation is coercive whereas the mother-son is permissive, hence the Oedipus complex. In other cultures, as anthropologists have shown, it is the relation between the son and the older brother of the mother (acting, in a society with short life expectancy, as the father of the mother) that is coercive, whereas father-son relations are permissive. The question of knowing which is better or worse for the growth of the child can be dispensed with. A cold, unemotional, clinical description of a universal structure is given as being the way things are (understood: forever and everywhere). In the structuralist position this is the idealized view that should be taken of matters. Value judgments are unnecessary. This is what is meant here by the relativism of structuralism. One knows that this concern for considering every organism or system of signs for its own sake led the Frankfurt school of sociology (Adorno, Horkheimer, and Marcuse) to suspend any judgment upon Nazism in spite of their own strong personal opposition to everything that National Socialism represented in Germany.

In Piaget's circle of sciences, such a relativism is impossible since each specific science leans back upon its neighbor for consolidation in full circle. In such a system, logic warrants psychology; psychology, biology; biology, chemistry; chemistry, physics; physics, mathematics; mathematics, logic. At the same time logic founds mathematics which founds physics, etc. The circle can be followed both ways. This mutual guarantee of sciences presents the advantages of not being dependent upon any external warrant that should be postulated either as innate or in God knows what sort of experience. The circle of sciences validates itself. Thus it is immanently fool-proofed. But it avoids the flaws of immanentism, since every specific science is validated by the one sitting at its frontier. In addition, it allows a certain open-endedness in the construction of new sciences, since borderline sciences would automatically be validated by the very existence of neighbors on its new frontiers. So the system is both formally closed and developmentally open. Think of what phenomenology and structuralism did when faced with the same problem. The first group decided to make the subject transcendental, the second to do away with the very notion of subject. Wasn't Piaget more creative?

We have been speaking here of Piaget's philosophy, not of his contribution to philosophy. What of that? Currents in philosophical thought move slowly, so it is probably far too early to say, and the present writers do not feel equipped for such a task. But we can make two points that may be useful. First, in spite of his denunciation of professional philosophy* and his claim that scientists can and must create their own philosophy as they go along, Piaget has spoken to philosophers, and many have reacted.† It is plausible to suppose that Piaget included among his ambitions a desire to change the course of philosophy. Second, his choice of an epistemological middle ground, the *tertium* around which he has organized so many of his discussions, gave him the standpoint from which he could explore a wide range of philosophically relevant questions with the tools of psychology. Philosophers have always been given to psychological presuppositions, often hidden. Piaget's work has done a great deal to bring these out in the open by exposing their genesis in childhood. Paradoxically, it may well be that his main contribution to philosophy will turn out to have been his massive infusion of psychological evidence into philosophical discussion. But the assimilation of such evidence, as Piaget would be the first to agree, will take a long time and in the long run, philosophers will have to create, as it were, a stable phenocopy of the phenotype, or better a *philocopy* of the *psychotype*.‡

---

* See his *Insights and Illusions of Philosophy* (1965).
† See, for example, J. Piaget, *Cognitive Development and Epistemology*.
‡ See Selection 41 for a treatment of the transformation of an ontogenetically produced phenotype into a genetically stable, or stabler, phenocopy.

37

The Myth of the Sensory Origin of Scientific Knowledge*

1957

The care devoted to verifying some opinions seems inversely proportional to their power of propagation because, considered as a whole, they appear to be self-evident, and especially because in the act of being transmitted they profit from the sanction of an increasing number of authors. In the wake of Aristotle and of empiricists of many kinds, it has become a commonplace in the majority of scientific circles to maintain that all knowledge has its origin in the senses and results from a process of abstraction which has sensory data as its starting point. One of the few physicists who cared to support this theory with facts, namely Mach, in his *Analyse des sensations*, even concluded that physical knowledge was pure perceptual phenomenism (a concept whose memory has lain heavily upon the whole history of the Circle of Vienna and of logical empiricism).

This myth (if we can thus describe such opinions, which have not had the benefit of precise verification because collective adherence to them has been too compelling) has even influenced some mathematicians in a sphere where sensation is little concerned. For example, the great d'Alembert attributed the development of arithmetical and algebraic concepts to the senses, and began by considering negative numbers to be less understandable than positive ones since they correspond to nothing which can be perceived through the senses. He subsequently conceded them to be equally understandable, insofar as they express an "absence"† but without, however, noticing the fact that the presence-absence duality refers to the action in its entirety and no longer to the simple process of sensation. Even today Enriquez still claims to explain the formation of the various branches of geometry (metric, projective,

---

*From *Psychology and Epistemology* by Jean Piaget, translated by Arnold Rosin. Translation copyright © 1971 by The Viking Press, Inc. Reprinted by permission of Grossman Publishers, a division of The Viking Press, Inc., New York, and Allen Lane, Penguin Books Ltd., London. This is a collection of essays. Selection 37 first appeared in French in 1957.

†For a discussion of d'Alembert's views, see M. Müller, *Essai sur la philosophie de J. d'Alembert* (Paris: Payot, 1926).

topological) by the predominance of this or that sensory modality (kinesthetic, visual, and so on).

The hypothesis of a sensory origin of knowledge nevertheless leads to paradoxes, the most significant of which has been set out by Planck in his *Initiations à la Physique*: our various forms of physical knowledge are drawn from sensation, but their progress consists precisely in liberating themselves from all anthropomorphism and consequently in removing themselves as far as possible from sensory data. Thus we may conclude that knowledge never derives from sensation alone, but from what action adds to this data. Nevertheless Planck remains loyal to the traditional view and thus does not succeed in resolving his own paradox.

However, at the beginning of the nineteenth century Ampère was already maintaining that sensation is simply a symbol and that those who allow it to be equated with objects are like the peasants (I would say like the children) who believe that there is a necessary correspondence between the names of things and the things which are named.

. . . The basic defect in an empiricist interpretation is that of neglecting the activity of the individual. The entire history of physics, the most advanced of the disciplines founded on experiment, is enough to show that experiment on its own is never sufficient, and that the progress of knowledge is the work of an inseparable union between experiment and deduction. This again suggests a necessary collaboration between the data afforded by the object and the actions or operations of the subject—these actions and operations themselves constituting the logico-mathematical framework outside which the individual never succeeds in intellectually assimilating the objects. Even in sciences as little evolved (in relation to physics) and as purely "empirical" in appearance as zoology and systematic botany, the classificatory (and consequently already logico-mathematical) activity of the individual remains indispensable in order to assure an objective reading of factual data.

If the systematician had been reduced to his sensory impressions alone, a work such as Linnaeus's *Systema naturae* would never have been constructed. In each of its manifestations, scientific knowledge thus reflects human intelligence which, by its operational nature, proceeds from the whole of action. To attempt to reduce knowledge to the passive role of mere recording, which is all the hypothesis of its sensory origin would allow, is to mutilate the characteristic of infinitely fertile construction presented by such knowledge, intelligence and action. . . .

38

The Multiplicity of Forms of Psychological Explanations*

1963

Unfortunately, there exists a great number of possible types of explanation in psychology, even more (and this is saying a lot) than in biology, and more than in the exact sciences such as physics or theoretical chemistry. This is not due to disagreements about the establishment of facts or laws; sooner or later agreement is reached on this level and, if there are still large areas where certain facts are recognized as such and considered to have general validity before being experimentally verified (in clinical psychology, for example), they always finish by becoming indispensable. The diversity of explanations stems mainly from the problem implicit in constructing a coordinated system of deductive principles, the deductive coordination of laws, not because the rules of deduction vary from one author to another, but because if some schools make a great effort at deductive coherence (for example, contemporary American learning theories), others are far less conscientious. But the main reason (by far) is the diversity of "models," which at least shows that the difference [does exist] between what we have called logical coordination and real coordination in the stages of causal explanation. We must stress the fact that if the possible "models" differ among themselves to the point where they are sometimes more of a hindrance than a help to the experimenter, this is essentially because of the difficulties arising from the need for a solution which is both theoretically acceptable and heuristically fertile (or at least suitable) for the problem of the relation between the structure of conscious reactions and organic structures. . . .

Having said this, let us try to classify, simply from the point of view of experimental psychology, the main types of explanation which the researcher can use. We shall not base this classification on the problem of psychophysiological parallelism, because the hypothesis

*From *Experimental Psychology: Its Scope and Method*, edited by Paul Fraisse and Jean Piaget, I. History and Method, by Jean Piaget, Paul Fraisse, and Maurice Reuchlin, translated by Judith Chambers, © 1963 Presses Universitaires de France, English translation © 1968 Routledge & Kegan Paul, Basic Books, Inc., Publishers, New York. Reprinted by permission of the publishers. Originally published in French, 1963.

which we have just developed on the part played by this question needs to be verified a posteriori and not to guide the analysis which follows a priori.

Nevertheless, the first point which arises in making such a classification is that there are two main types, or at least two extremes, in explanatory models, (1) where they aim at a reduction from the most complex to the most simple, or again from the psychological to the extra-psychological or (2) where they are directed toward a constructivism existing within the limits of "conduct." As the reductionist type of model may preserve a mainly psychological orientation or alternatively tend to reduce the mental to realities outside a certain framework, we finish up in fact with three main categories (A–C), the last two each comprising three varieties.

(A) First there is what we call a psychological reductionism which consists of seeking to explain a certain number of varied reactions or conduct by reducing them to the same causal principle which remains unchanged throughout the transformation. An example of this sort of explanation by identification can be found in the recent experimental work of Freudian psychoanalysts on the development of "object" relations.

(B) We shall distinguish the diverse forms of reductionism which tend to explain reactions or conduct by referring to realities extending beyond the frontiers of psychology. Hence, three varieties:

(B_1) Sociological explanations in psychology (psychosocial) which tend to interpret individual reactions as a function of the interaction between individuals or various levels of group structures.

(B_2) Physicalist explanations which, starting from an isomorphism between mental and organic structures as in field models, rest briefly, on physical considerations (for example the Köhlerian Gestalt psychologists).

(B_3) Organicist explanations in general, which insist on the reduction of the psychological to the physiological.

(C) Finally, one could consider as "constructivist" the types of explanation which, while giving a certain place to reduction (since it is one of the aspects of all explanation), mainly emphasize construction processes. This characteristic is quite distinct from type A and equally from type B, because insofar as one can give a constructive explanation of conduct or mental activity, a certain specifically psychological explanation is attained which is no longer reducible to social, physical, or organic properties. We shall distinguish, in this connection three main types of models:

(C_1) Models of the "behavior theory" type which, despite considerable differences existing between Hull and Tolman, for example, in fact have the common characteristic of coordinating diverse laws of learning in systems concerned principally with the acquisition of new conduct.

(C_2) Models of essentially a developmental type which look for constructive processes in development which would account for innovative behavior without simply building on experience which has already been acquired.

(C_3) Finally, "abstract" models, whose name does not imply a rejection of any real substrate . . . but rather because they refuse to choose between the diverse possible substrates, in order to define more clearly the way in which constructions themselves work in the most general form compatible with the demands of psychology.

Such a picture could not claim to be anything like complete without mentioning intermediate situations. It goes without saying that it is not a question of "preexplanatory" methods. For example, the so-called factor analysis method would be difficult to fit into any of the above categories, mainly because it does not in itself constitute an explanatory model. As a technique, it enables one to move from general to causal statements, but once the "factors" are determined, the problem of assigning an explanatory meaning of them remains, and we know well enough how far a particular author can use them in one direction or another. Only one or two explanatory concepts are to be found to be in common between, for example, R. Meili, who combined factor analysis with Gestalt schemata, authors who sought to coordinate the same analysis with schemata of "behavior" (C_1) and C. Spearman,* the creator of the factorial method and originator of "noögenesis."

It is appropriate, then, to examine each of these seven categories of explanatory models, in such a way as to extract, by means of comparison, the aspects which they have in common or which are complementary.

EXPLANATION BY REDUCTION TO A PSYCHOGENETIC PRINCIPLE

Let us briefly examine, as an example of this procedure, the method by which several present-day Freudian experimentalists (Hartmann, E. Kris, Spitz and K. Wolf, Glover, Th. Benedek, etc.) explain the formation of "object relations" during the first few months of development. We shall choose as our main reference an excellent study made by Th. Gouin-Décarié† on 90 subjects from 3 to 20 months, who were submitted simultaneously to a series of tests on the acquisition of the [notion] of a permanent object (through which the author arrived at the same succession of the stages of formation of the object as ours) and to parallel tests on the establishment of "object" relations in the affective and Freudian sense of the word.

We have hitherto maintained that Freudian explanation in this connection follows the Meyersonian model of identification. The same "psychic" energy ("libido") at first centered on certain organic activities (oral and then anal stages) shifts to one's own total activity (narcissism) and finally to outside persons (choice of the "object" and object relations), innovation thus resulting from a shift of affective charge or investment, and not from a change in its structure. It must be realized that the situation has become even more differentiated, since Hartmann took up his position on the independence of the "ego" system and since the direct observation and experimental research which have characterized the reexamination of these first stages of affective development.

Broadly speaking, the present schema rests on the following three stages. In the first stage, the newborn child will be centered on himself,

*C. Spearman, *The Nature of Intelligence* (London, 1923).

†Th. Gouin-Decarié, *Intelligence et affectivité chez le jeune enfant*, (Neuchâtel and Paris: Delachaux and Niestlé, 1962).

but as yet having no awareness of his own separateness. Physiological needs and the centers in interest which derive from them create "isles of consistency" (Escalona) to which the psychic energy is directed, but which are not dissociated from the actual activity of the subject. In the course of the second stage, the reactions of anticipation and certain favored perceptions (smiles) introduce the beginning of frontiers (albeit movable) between the actual activity and what one could call "intermediary objects" such as "the smiling human face" (Spitz). Lastly, the third stage will ensure a stable differentiation between subject and object with "the flowering of all the elements whose seeds were planted in the previous stages" (Gouin): hence the consciousness of self and a "cathexis which creates truly libidinous objects," and, similarly, the anguish allied to the loss of the loved object, etc.

It is evident from this that a structuring process takes place at the same time as the objects of affective energy are differentiated. Moreover, this structuring is necessarily accompanied by important cognitive modifications (anticipation, attention, understanding of the permanence of objects, etc.) which prudent authors may judge simply as parallel to the affective transformation, whilst others (Odier for example) would wish rather to treat as secondary. But the central question, from the point of view of this explanatory scheme, is to understand how such affective transformations occur. It appears that it is not yet possible to speak of a truly affective "construct," for the same source of affective strength exists whatever the time but it simply changes its objectives; the qualitative change will be assumed to result from these simple shifts or redistributions, by means of "flowering" and not by the inclusion of new elements.

Consequently, one has a choice: firstly to remain faithful to this scheme of identification, in which case the identity of the "libido" will not explain development. An explanation will then be sought in the structural transformations of the whole (differentiation of self, etc.). The second possibility is to attempt to coordinate the process of cognitive construction with a truly affective construct at the time of each particular transformation and this would enable one to dispense with models of identification. In short explanation by identification completes and corrects itself by itself, under the influence of the internal modifications of Freudianism,* in the direction of a constructivist principle (cf. the models of type C and especially C_1 and C_2).

*It is to show this internal evolution that we have quoted Freudians who have remained orthodox, rather than the English analysts (Bowlby, etc.) and Fromm, Alexander, Erikson, etc., and why we have not referred to the best explanatory theorist D. Rapaport. However, we must mention that psychoanalytical explanation is in Rapaport's view, oriented toward, if not abstract models, then at least a physicalism comprising theoretical extensions possible in all physicalism which has been elaborated on a little. Rapaport demonstrates, for example, that the constancy of cathexis (amount of psychic energy available) can indicate two distinct hypotheses: either this amount is theoretically constant with infinitesimal variations in the sense of d'Alembert's theorem, or replacements of a physiological nature intervene to compensate the losses of the cathexis invested in the structures which is therefore "tied." In both cases a new series of distinctions must be introduced, and Rapaport reproached Freud for having distinguished only a mobile and a "tied" cathexis: according to him one should differentiate between the structures which reduce the entropic discharge in order to

EXPLANATION BY REDUCTION TO PSYCHOSOCIOLOGICAL PRINCIPLES

If identification alone is insufficient, within the frontiers of psychology, it is because the logic of reductionism recognizes no limits to reduction. Thus, one could seek to reduce from the bottom: (organicism), or from the lateral point of view, regard the subject in relation to other subjects from his birth, hence explanatory models of a sociological type, which we will now examine.

Such an approach can be found today in the explanation of all areas of primary affective behavior (so-called cultural psychoanalysis: Fromm, etc.), from conduct in general (R. Benedict, M. Mead, etc.) to cognitive reaction (from J. M. Baldwin and P. Janet to the works of Vigotsky and Luria on the role of language and, incidentally in our own early works) and primarily social conduct (sociometry, etc.).

Its principle is as follows. When a new form of behavior occurs to enrich the previous ones in the course of development, it is due less to an internal change than to the effects of social interaction. . . . When P. Janet,* for example, explained the appearance of reflective thought (which was superimposed on direct or assertive thought) by reference to social conduct of deliberation and to its internalization in the form of a discussion with oneself, this was indeed a new behavioral development, but one on the interindividual or collective plane, and the newness of such behavior is reducible to an external mechanism, and need not be explained in terms of an earlier internal experience.

But two points must be made in connection with such a mode of explanation without, however, disputing its value. The first is that sooner or later it necessitates using a principle of internal development. For example, after believing that interindividual cooperation was enough to explain the formation of logical structures occurring in the child's development (logic of the relations based on reciprocity, etc.), we have been obliged later: (1) to admit that this formation also assumes, as an equally necessary condition, an internal constructive mechanism based on the coordination of the subjects' actions and their internalization in operations; (2) to recognize that cooperation itself derives from coordinating actions and the same laws of operation as coordination between individuals, so that a circular relation and not a one-way association between cooperation between individuals and their coordination.

---

neutralize the cathexis and the structural conditions which simply reduce the "displaceability" of the cathexis and transform it into a "tied" cathexis. Furthermore, if enough cathectic energy is invested in the formation of a structure, only one part of it becomes "tied" while the rest is released: this liberation corresponds to the mobilization of energy. Rapaport (finally) states (all this appears in a study on attention cathexis, ["The Theory of Attention Cathexis," mimeographed, 1960], where he attempts to bridge the gap between the affective processes and the basic cognitive structures, such as attention) that structures activated by cathexis are modified and later stabilized, while the "noncathectized" structures (for a long time) lose their stability and cohesion: thus, according to this author, there is a parallel with Piaget's conceptions of the "alimentation" of the sensorimotor schemata of assimilation, the "alimented" schemes providing, through their results, an "alimentation" for the others.

*P. Janet, De l'angoisse à l'extase, Vol. 2 (Paris: Alcan, 1926).

The second point is that, pushed to a certain degree of prediction sociological explanation (independently of reductions from the psychological to the social) falls back on abstract models, parallel with those used for psychological explanation (see C_3). All Claude Lévi-Strauss's work,* particularly his excellent works on kinship, apply certain algebraic techniques (lattices, etc.) to social relations so that sociological explanation coincides with a qualitative enumeration analogous to that found in the construction of logical arguments. Obviously, when concrete microsociology takes its pattern from such models (and dispenses with Moreno's naive, and not at all sociological, conceptualization), then psychosociological reductions will not only demand a certain principle of mental development (as in our first point) but will appear identical with modes of explanation using abstract models.

EXPLANATION BY REDUCTION TO PHYSICALIST PRINCIPLES

While it is natural that a reduction in a lateral direction, like that from the psychological to the social, will culminate in schemata of interaction and not of simple relationships (because this is naturally the point of the two remarks at the end of paragraph B_1), one might think that by contrast an explanation by reduction from higher to lower would mark a decisive victory for reductionism. A particularly daring and elegant model illustrating attempts of this kind is that of Gestalt theory, which tends not only to reduce mental phenomena (notably perception and intelligence) to physiological facts, but further to subordinate these to physical structures by using the concept of field. As a result, certain interpretations lead almost directly from the psychological to the physical, as in the case of "good perceptual form," which is explained in terms of structures of "physical Gestalts" and, like them, must submit to the principles of equilibrium and perfect immobility.

A celebrated example of this type of interpretation is that of after-effects, studied by Köhler and Wallach† and consisting of modifications which take place in estimating the size or shape of a figure, when one's perception follows immediately after perceiving another figure in the same region of the visual field. The explanatory hypothesis, once excitation is translated into potential differences and estimations of length into electrical resistance of the tissues, [refers] the observed effects to modifications in satiation. In permanent satiation (more frequent in the adult than in the child) the momentary and localized increase due to the inspection of figures, the restoration of equilibrium (more or less quickly according to the degree of satiation) by a homeostatic process and finally self-satiation depending on the point of fixation (less good in a child, and where there is a more extensive region capable of less satiation) should be differentiated. One arrives thus at an explanatory schema which takes account not only of the observed effects, but also of their evolution with age. It only remains to point out that owing to their orientation (Köhler was a physicist and

*C. Lévi-Strauss, *Les structures élémentaires de la parenté* (Paris: P.U.F., 1949).

†W. Köhler and H. Wallach, "Figural After-effects," *Proc. Amer. Philos. Soc.*, 88 (1944): 269–357.

Wallach a chemist before becoming psychologists), these authors tended to discount any effects arising from the functional behavior of the subject and, in this respect, did not use the possibilities these would open up in connection with their homeostatic view of satiation or the relations between self-satiation and the fixation point.

It is not our place to judge the value of the theories we have mentioned, but simply to analyze the explanatory models they set forth. We shall confine ourselves to the following three points.

The first is that although physical models undoubtedly represent an essentially important ideal, they will be used with more conviction when biology itself makes them necessary, and when the possible reduction of certain psychological structures to physical structures is mediated by a preliminary distinct reduction of the former to biological structures. In this respect, it is possible that the use of specific forms of field equilibrium often conceals certain types of balance achieved by active compensation on the part of the subjects; it is still to be established, for example, with what frequency perceptual constancies end in "overconstancy." One is often led to invoke overcompensation through precautions arising from the use of biological models rather than from any exact physical balance. But this does not necessarily lead us away from physicalism, as we shall see later.

In the second place, if the previous point seems to have a limited importance, one could set oneself to extend physicalism by quoting other models in addition to the Gestalt one. The physical characteristics which Gestalt psychology studies have been selected from among phenomena with nonadditive components which are thus irreversible. Planck has demonstrated that the most important dichotomy which occurs in physics is that of irreversible (for example, thermodynamics) and reversible phenomena (cinematics, mechanics). To use physical analogies most efficiently one would have to find an analogous division in psychology, which would then oppose reversible structures composed of additive elements (operational structures of intelligence) and simple structures, such as that in Gestalt psychology. This no longer conforms to the Gestalt theory, but is undoubtedly inspired by an extended physicalism.

This gives rise to our third point. The most interesting thing as far as psychology is concerned in relation to physics is not perhaps reduction of a mental structure (perception, for example) to a physical structure (for example, electromagnetic field), but the analogy between the manner of composition of the first and that used by the physicist to attain knowledge of the second. In this connection, the rift between irreversible and reversible phenomena is also a rift between the domain of explanations, particularly probabilistic ones, and that of simple deduction. Physicalist analogies suggest, thus, not only actual reduction, but also the use of abstract models. We know, in particular what a close relationship exists between explanatory schemata of thermodynamics and those used in the theory of chance or the theory of decision and information theory.* So it is in precisely this direction that several

---

*The calculation of this information is, in fact, copied from calculations of entropy in thermodynamics.

authors are now seeking their explanatory models in the domain of perception.* . . .

In brief, the two advantages of physicalist reduction are the precision which it can, in certain cases, add to organicist reduction and the opportunities it affords to [use] certain abstract models which are among the most fruitful available to us today.

EXPLANATION BY ORGANICIST REDUCTION

With the attempt to reduce mental phenomena to physiological reactions we join one of the main streams of experimental psychology. For many authors, since the area covered by psychology is that which divides biological from social methodology the best form of psychological explanation (on points where he is not subordinated to sociology) would be reduction from the higher to the lower, i.e., assimilation of physiological models.

The examples of such reductionist approaches are numerous, starting with the work of Helmholtz and Hering on perception. We have selected one which is perhaps the most classical and also the most instructive with regard to its central idea, which we defend in this chapter, that of the complementarity of reductionist and constructivist "abstract" models. Associationist psychology which, despite its "simplistic" mechanism, has had considerable influence on experimental psychology, sought to reduce mental structures to the supposedly elementary mechanism of association. But how does one account for this particularly in its most simple form of association by contiguity? At first the answer was by reduction to simple verbal physiological models, then Pavlov put forward his theory of conditioned reflexes, which he considered to be "completely identical" with associations as defined by psychologists and even as covering "what the genius Helmholtz described (in the field of perception) by the celebrated phrase 'unconscious [inference].' "

But the characteristic reduction is that it raises new problems by its indefinite regression and, while psychologists discovered the increasing complexity of association learning (the part played by anticipation, reinforcement, motivation, problems of stability, etc.), physiologists pursued their work by trying to answer the many questions left unanswered by Pavlov's hypothetical interpretation (the theories of irradiation, induction, etc.) were barely within the framework of general laws. Without listing all the new techniques (notably electrophysiological) which made it possible to progress, we should mention, following the excellent report by M.-A. Fessard and H. Gastaut,† the two main themes which the research touched on: the role of the main anatomo-functional structures (reticular formation, diencephalic integration, and the cortical association system), and the scale interpretation of the neurone organization.

*For example, W. P. Tanner and his team for the theory of thresholds (see above under C_3). W. P. Tanner, Jr., and J. A. Swets, "A Decision-making Theory of Human Detection," *Psychol. Rev.*, 61 (1954): 401–409.

†M.-A. Fessard and H. Gastaut, "Corrélations neuro-physiologiques de la formation des réflexes conditionnels," in *Le conditionnement et l'apprentissage* (Paris: P.U.F., 1958).

In connection with this last point, it is relevant to our present inquiry to examine how authors set about accounting for the fact that a signal s, usually associated with a response r, can be replaced by an unconditioned signal S to bring about a reaction R. On the one hand experimental evidence supplies a mass of important but limited information: for example that learning (at least in the adult) does not depend on the growth new nerve endings or on the formation of new synapses, but on a new function being established between already formed connections; that conditioning supposes a structure of the reticular type comprising numerous cells with starlike ramifications, etc. But, on the other hand, it is a question of making use of this information in an explanatory schema. Therefore, either the schema to be constructed must be devised in the form of an artificial model outlining (but with what ingenuity!) the conditions in which these results can be obtained: for example, Grey Walter's famous "machines," or one can construct a theoretical model of the reticular field of neurons, like Fessard's idea of the lattice all of whose elements have identical properties (where the choice of preferential routes is historically determined), but where the possibility of introducing a certain homeostatic stability can occur despite substitutions of routes. Obviously such models (the second, as much as the first) create a mass of logico-mathematical problems, some to do with structure and some with dynamics; their interdependence being stressed by Fessard.

From the dynamic point of view, first of all, it is a question of explaining the nature of the routes and one naturally resorts to a probabilistic schema. Fessard presented his lattice as a "dependent stochastic lattice"; stochastic, because each neuron in the system [has a] particular probability of discharge, which is a function of time, and dependent because it depends on the action of other similar neurons (A. Rapaport, Shimbel, and others have tried to go even further in treating analogous problems mathematically).

Looking at the problem of structure (all structures being conceived from a genetic point of view as alternatively the cause or effect of dynamic function) it is obvious that the choice of a "lattice" model leads to many fundamental implications, since it is one of the most representative structures of general (logical and mathematical) algebra and the basis of propositional logic. It is appropriate here to point out that W. McCulloch and Pitts* have shown precisely where the diverse combinations of neural connections are isomorphic with relations in propositional logic† (and in a general way with those in Boolean algebra), which is enough to demonstrate how lattice models sooner or later may be considered among the most daring of "abstract" models.

In brief, such an example indicates that organicist reduction does not conflict with the use of abstract models for the simple reason that, insofar as neurology tends to be precise (whether or not it duplicates mechano-physiological attempts) it overlaps with the treatment of probability and general algebra. This is why one of our colleagues, returning from a visit to McCulloch's team, described the workers as

---

*W. S. McCulloch and W. Pitts, "A Logical Calculus of the Ideas Immanent in Nervous Activity," *Bull. math. Biophys.*, 5 (1943): 45–133.
†Conjunction, disjunction, incompatibility, exclusion, implication, etc.

each sitting between two tables, on one of which he examines neurons through the microscope and on the other he carries out his logistic calculations.

BEHAVIORAL EXPLANATION

The three types of explanatory models remaining to be examined do not preclude any of the previous forms of reduction, but their specifically psychological form of construction, based on the laws of a single behavioral act (C_1), or of development which is both genetic and mental (C_2) or on abstract systems of mental activity (C_3) complement them.

At first one can only refer to the single behavioral act, which implies of course an underlying organicism, but also introduces the notion of new structures designed to operate at a higher level. For example, one of the central concepts of Hull's* theory of learning is that of habit-family hierarchies. This is a mechanism whose explanatory power is relatively independent of organicist reduction, which is not specifically demanded by this mode of explanation. In the same way Tolman's sign-Gestalt-expectations consist, at an equally molar level of behavior, of the organization of a number of relations between a sign, a signified object, and the anticipation of the fact that a particular type of behavior will lead from one particular aspect to another of the structured field.

What then does explanation consist of at this higher stage, in terms of neural connections? These, according to Hull, remain hypothetical and the subject of inference (at least those to which he himself referred); they are only intervening variables between the physical surroundings and observable reactions which make up behavior: what must be explained, therefore, is the causal connection between the environmental conditions and these observable reactions. But what is the nature of this causal connection?

On reading Hull, whose interpretative system is by far the most developed, one at first has the impression that nothing else exists but laws, without any reference to causality: these are the laws of association, of drive reduction, the types of reinforcement (success, etc.) which consolidate association, of goal-gradients (acceleration of response near the goal), of the formation and structuring of habit-family hierarchies. But here, as everywhere, it is the deductive connection between these laws which supplies the causal explanation and which is applied to a real state of affairs. It is the sum of ideas describing responses on a scale of behavior (what the behaviorists call "conceptualization," as opposed to general descriptions). What does this deduction consist of, which in Hull's system is the operative part of a truly causal explanation?

Hull and his followers gave three successive answers to this question. The first simply consisted of coordinating the laws obtained using only ordinary language, i.e., by using the deductive mode which logicians (with some arrogance) call "simple" deduction. This anticipated to some extent the second answer since Hull, in this first construction, indicated the frequencies involved to an often disconcerting number of decimal places though without constructing probabilistic schemata.

*C. L. Hull, *Principles of Behavior* (New York: Appleton Century Crofts, 1943).

The second solution was put forward by Bush and Mosteller* in a fundamental study in which they outlined a probabilistic theory of learning. In this case the deduction of laws was presented *more mathematico:* given a particular situation characterized by particular parameters, it could be deduced, if certain laws applied, that the probability of learning would conform to a particular mode of calculation.

The third reply was made by Hull himself. Following discussions arising from his contribution to the International Congress of Psychology in Paris in 1938, he visited England and met the logician, Woodger, a specialist in biological axiomatics. Under his influence Hull decided, with the help of Fitch another logician, to construct a formalization of his explanatory system. The result was a deductive theory *more logico* which this time described all the processes involved in the system in an entirely explicit way. It has since been shown that it is easy to formalize Tolman's system in the same way, and our colleague L. Apostel† has recently published in *Études d'épistemologie génétique* a comprehensive study supplying, among other things, the framework of a sort of algebra of learning and disentangling the formal laws used by those who are involved in interpretations of this kind.

Thus it is of interest to note that one of the most strictly experimental lines of thought in psychology came about through the use of abstract models, one of a probabilistic nature aimed at establishing statistical causality, the other logical revealing the deductive nature of the explanatory process. Moreover, this use of deductive schemata obviously does not in any way contradict the reductionist aspect of these systems since (as we saw under B_3) the eventual reduction to neural connections at this lower level raises questions of explanation for whose solution we must use analogous probabilistic or algebraic schemata.

GENETIC EXPLANATION

This method is assumed, by learning theorists, to account for mental development in all its aspects, except for the effects of maturation which may be regarded as combining with the learning patterns in various ways. For certain developmental theorists, on the other hand, maturation and learning as a function of the environment constitute only two of the factors involved, and do not exhaust all the possibilities. Not being afraid of a certain "mentalism" which the aforementioned theorists proscribe, they substitute for a single behavioral action the idea of "conduct" which they define, in common with Janet and many others, as behavior plus the internalized activity which accompanies various forms of "being conscious." Because of these nuances, one is confronted with modes of explanation distinct from the preceding one (C_1) and equally distinct from the diverse varieties of reductionism $(A$ to $B_2)$.

We must first quote E. von Holst, K. Lorenz, and N. Tinbergen, who represent a school of comparative psychology which is called "ethology" or "objectivism" and whose central idea is psychophysiological. It is the

*R. R. Bush and R. Mosteller, *Stochastic Models for Learning* (New York: Wiley and Sons, 1955).

†L. Apostel, "Logique et apprentissage," *Études d'Épistem. génét.*, Vol. 3 (*Logique, apprentissage et probabilité*), 1959, pp. 1–38.

notion of "spontaneous activity" of the organism, which is quite distinct from "response" and which can be seen in the rhythmical movements of worms (studied by von Holst) as well as in the movements of the new-born human child. But though these authors lay stress on the activities of the organism and the human subject, they do not, for all that, neglect the environmental situation, and their theory of "innate releasers" and instincts (hereditary or specific perceptual signals which release for example the following of the mother in chicks, ducklings, etc.) introduces a close form of interaction between the subject and the object whose subtle causal nature deserves detailed analysis.

However, to draw out the parallel with the theorists of human learning, perhaps we might be allowed to quote from our own work as an example of the C_2 type of explanation, because if we too have emphasized the activity of the subject (and essentially in the development of cognitive processes) we have done so to extract an explanation of intellectual development. We would like to outline briefly the particular form of causal explanation which we have used.

Given that people's actions are structured from birth (initially not very well but hereditarily determined) their reactions to situations will be on the one hand assimilatory, in which they tend to incorporate ... into their structures, and on the other hand accommodatory, in ... they tend to modify, i.e., to discriminate, these same structures ... the situation. It is therefore necessary to have at the outset a ... equilibration which will enable one to produce various com- ... assimilation and accommodation. The balancing mechanism ... compensating for external disturbances till they are ... the initial structures or into a transformation process the ... that the series of development arising from this interaction ... on increasingly complex rules governing the coordination of ... Since they are oriented toward an approximate reversibilty, these rules are transformed finally by systems of operations, or internalized actions coordinated in a reversible way, and it will be because of this operational process diverge levels of intelligence occur successively.

Because it is concerned with establishing operational structures, this kind of interpretation arrives at logico-mathematical constructs. It must be noted however that it is not a question of an already existing logical system being used by the psychologist, as in the formalization of Hull's system; nor is it a question of the processes and the logic of the subject itself, since the central problem has all along been to know how that is constructed.* Before resorting to abstract models, an attempt was made to work out a developmental type of explanation and the model employed traced the effects of learning and social factors, as well as maturation, to account for a system of equilibrium, so that the whole process could be treated as a probabilistic sequence. Taking, for example, a problem of the conservation of matter where an object is simultaneously modified in the directions $+a$ and $-b$, one would want

*There have been attempts since to integrate these results into Hull's system of explanation: D. Berlyne endeavored to do this by introducing "response-transformations" to account for "operations," and transforming one "copy-response" into another. D. E. Berlyne, "Les équivalences psychologiques et les notions quantitatives," *Théorie du comportement et opérations*, E.E.G., Vol. 12, 1960, pp. 1–103.

to know how the subject carries out the operation which describes the transformation of $+a$ and $-b$ in such a way that it will allow him to infer that the quantity remains the same despite the apparent modifications. The explanatory schema will consist firstly of determining why the initial reaction is not likely to be concerned with the transformation as such but only with one aspect of it (for example $+a$ but not $-b$); then it must determine why the most probable subsequent action (it is only the most probable after the first has been dealt with, not having been so all the time) will consist in noting the other aspect of the problem (previously neglected); then one must demonstrate how the oscillation between these two reactions renders it increasingly more likely that one will infer the relatedness of $+a$ and $-b$. This requires a shift from the initial emphasis placed on the single configuration to the whole transformation. Lastly one must determine why the reaction eventually becoming the most probable will consist of compensating one for the other, which means discovering the operation which mediates conservation.

It has been established, then, that this causal schema of equilibrium leads to an abstract probabilistic model and to models which are either algebraic or logical. But it remains for us to establish by what inner necessity it is always so. This we shall attempt now on a more general plane.

EXPLANATION BASED ON ABSTRACT MODELS

If causal explanation consists in deducing laws which link objects as functions of a certain substrate of reality, and if it supposes three conditions: (1) being in possession of laws, (2) choosing deductive schemata, and (3) choosing a substrate to which the deduction applies (society, nervous system, behavior, conduct, etc.), one can then define explanation based on abstract models in two distinct ways, one more general and the other particular:

(a) In a general way one would say that abstract models are used when, instead of being satisfied with "simple" deduction based on everyday language, one chooses a deductive scheme of a technical nature taken from probabilistic mathematics (the classical theory of probability, theory of chance, theory of decision, theory of information, etc.) or from general algebra comprising Boolean algebra and logic (theory of lattices, theory of groups, formalized propositional logic, etc.). According to general acceptance the use of abstract models completes one or other of the explanations so far envisaged when a higher degree of precision than that currently being used is required. This means first of all that an exact language is substituted for the ordinary language, but it later leads to new developments in the explanation, insofar as the chosen deductive schema requires consideration of specific relationships which would be helpful: the introduction of a "lattice" or "group" structure for example enables one to perceive a richer mass of well-determined relations [than] noticed before. But, according to this definition (a) the introduction of the abstract model changes nothing at the previously chosen substrate (3): it is still a question of the same neural systems, the same pattern of behavior, etc., seen in detail.

(b) More particularly one speaks of explanation by abstract model when a technical deductive schema (2) is employed for a collection of laws or general facts (1), without selecting an already defined substrate of reality (3) but trying instead to substitute what the possible different models may have in common for it. If this model is itself "abstract," the term "abstract" means simply "common to the different conceivable real models." Since the ideal in explanation consists of extracting the necessary and sufficient conditions for a collection of facts, the abstract model (3) aims at establishing these conditions and, even if it does not achieve this degree of generality, at least it succeeds in discovering a certain number of sufficient conditions. For example, to explain the perceptual effects of overestimation as a result of centering, we used a probability schema of "meets" (between the elementary segments of the perceived line and the elements of the subject's receptor organs) and "joins" (or correspondences between meets on different regions of the figure, these meets not having the same density in every region of the figure). Since we lacked certain data we refused to establish whether these meets were determined by the density of the retinal cells or the number of exploratory micromovements of the eyeball, etc. We even refused to establish whether the joins were due to neural links or whether they were to be found in abstractions which translate the connections which the subject makes consciously in perceiving. The model used suffices to account for the observed laws, not by choosing the real substrate (3), but by seeking what the various conceivable substrates have in common, and it is this which justifies its use, because, if it is correct it will sooner or later apply to one of the real substrates which are actually conceivable.

In these two forms (a) and (b) explanation by abstract models fulfills three uses. Firstly it makes precise otherwise imprecise deductions: it is this kind of service which Hull expected from the logical formalization of his theory, and he drew nothing else from it, but this in itself constituted an advance in explanation since it provides a deduction system of phenomena.

Secondly, the abstract schema enables us to discover new relations between general facts or laws which were not previously comparable. For example, in the development of a child's intellectual operations (see under C_2) a series of new thought processes is observed to occur between 11–12 years: the appearance of the idea of proportions, double reference systems, comprehension of physical relations between actions and reactions, etc. It seems that nothing can explain the simultaneous occurrence of these developments, whose relation to each other is imperceptible. But to account for the operational nature of propositional logic, we formed a "group" of four transformations (isomorphic with the Klein group) whose existence had eluded logicians: given [a] relation such as implication (p implies q) one can: (1) invert by negation, N (p and non-q); (2) transform it into its reciprocal R (q implies p); (3) transform it into its dual and correlative C (non-p and q); and (4) leave it unaltered, I. One then has $NR = C$, $CR = N$, $CN = R$ and $NRC = I$. This group is interesting from the psychological point of view in that it fuses in a single system the two previously separated forms of reversibility (between 7 and 11–12 years): the inversion N and reciprocity R. It can be said, then, that it simultaneously expresses the natural outcome of operations which develop earlier and the moment when propositional operations begin to occur between 11–12 and 14–15 years. So, it transpires that the new operational schemata which we have just discussed (proportions, etc.) is exactly reducible to such a group! The abstract schema enabled us therefore to discover a close relationship which was missed by the "simple" and nonalgebraic type of investigation.

Thirdly, the abstract schema can supply causal links which were previously overlooked. For example, von Neumann and Morgenstern constructed, for the use of economists, a probabilistic model called the theory of chance or decision, permitting one to calculate the "strategy" a gambler should adopt in various situations to obtain the *maximum* gain with the *minimum* loss (Bay's criterion) or to minimize to the *maximum* the losses due to the astuteness of his opponent (*minimax* criterion). This can also be applied to losses and gains of information. So, taking up the theory of thresholds of perception (which has not so far managed to be sufficiently precise in its mathematical calculations) W. P. Tanner (of Michigan) succeeded in applying the theory of chance to the discrimination of objective indices and of "noise" by adapting the computation tables. This success was enough to modify the causal interpretation: instead of explaining it in terms of very fine adjustments of perception one can use the concept of "decision" to suggest the mediation of unconscious inductive inference, which to a certain extent goes back to Helmholtz. . . .

Generally speaking, we maintain that the use of abstract schemata tends to set a certain standard of legitimacy and precision to constructive explanations by stressing the activity of the subject. Whereas reductionist hypotheses subordinate the higher to the lower, the abstract schema, while not denying that links with the organism are important, reveals the uniqueness and the novelty of developments occurring at the level of behavior and conduct. Moreover, as neurology (a factual science) cannot explain why $2 + 2 = 4$ or why $A = A$ (equivalences whose necessity rests not on facts but on deductive principles) the fact remains that the implications of consciousness, while reflecting organic connections, could not be understood in developmental terms without resorting to abstract models whose very force depends on their deductive necessity. But isn't this a series of vicious circles, since these models are the products of certain deliberate actions and since they are used in neurology, which is expected to explain psychological facts? These circles would, in fact, be vicious if the discussion of the problem of psychophysiological parallelism did not enable us to define their nature precisely.

Psychological Explanations and the Problem of Psychophysiological Parallelism

From what has gone before at least two conclusions can be drawn. It is essential that (1) psychological explanation allows a certain reduction to take place from the higher to the lower, since its organicism provides an irreplaceable model (capable of leading to physicalism); (2) in

order to interpret the higher forms of conduct (including their characteristic of "self awareness") one resorts to a certain form of construction, with all its technical demands (abstract models). There
cannot be any contradiction between these conclusions (1) and (2) and
the best proof of this is that when the neurologist studies the nervous
system he uses, as an active and intelligent subject, the higher forms of
conduct and deductive schemata whose logical necessity is not reducible
to material facts.

THE PROBLEM OF PARALLELISM

To overcome these difficulties it is necessary to foresee, in aiming
at a system of reduction, a method permitting one to respect the uniqueness of conscious necessity, while ensuring that it will continue to
reflect its factual origins to which it will be eventually reduced. For
example, if the truth of $2 + 2 = 4$ is inconceivable except in the consciousness of a mathematician (be he aged 7 years), a system of neural
connections must exist to enable him to recognize this. What, then, is
the nature of the link between the conscious judgment and the physiological connections which underlie them? Is it a causal relationship or
should we use other categories such as correspondence, parallelism, or
isomorphism? This is the eternal problem which forms of psychological
explanation have come up against and which we find again simply in
comparing these various forms.

First of all, let us note that this problem is not, as is sometimes
claimed, one of mind and body, but exclusively that of consciousness
and the underlying physiological structures. To speak of the mind is
either to reify consciousness, which amounts to prejudging the solution,
or to assign to the whole concept the global designation of "higher
nervous activity plus consciousness" and the problem then reappears
in the contents of that "mind." This is why to dispute the nomenclature
of a certain form of medicine which some call "psychosomatic" and
others "cortico-visceral" amounts to no more than a verbal argument: it
is generally agreed that psychological treatment can in certain cases act
on a somatic affective state, but this by no means settles the question of
knowing whether consciousness has acted causally or the subject has
"taken note" of the nervous activity.

Consequently, the various solutions which have been put forward to
account for the relations between the consciousness and its accompanying nervous mechanisms can be reduced to two (excluding idealism,
which is not concerned with psychological theories, since the same problem occurs in its own field): either there is interaction between consciousness and corresponding nervous processes, or it is a question of
two parallel series of phenomena whose basic differences prevent their
acting causally upon one another.

THE INTERACTIONIST SOLUTION

The interactionist solution seems confirmed by [everyday] observation: when a glass of wine makes us euphoric, we are tempted to see
this as a direct action of the organism on consciousness, and when one
moves one's arms to the side after having consciously decided to do so

there seems to be direct control of the organism by consciousness. But as soon as we seek to analyze these causal relations they become utterly incomprehensible, in both directions.

In the first place, to say that consciousness can direct a physiological process is either to endow it with force, in whatever form (strength, work, power, etc.) or to presuppose a sort of "psychic energy," which then poses the question of the relation existing between them. A force is a measurable quantity originating in the physical world, and to talk of energy in order to gloss over the difficulties merely increases them tenfold since it implies two consequences, the mutual transformation of the forces and the conservation of energy, neither of which [is] relevant to the eventual control of consciousness over the body. Actually, when one tries to envisage such an action, one imagines a sort of ethereal or material lining underlying consciousness which acts in its name when it releases an organic action. So it is obvious that it is not consciousness which "acts" in this instance, but rather the concomitant nervous activity, it being understood that nervous actions accompanied by consciousness are not identical with those unaccompanied by consciousness (cf. electrophysiological studies of awareness, etc.). But if these two functions are different does it not assume that interactionism depends on consciousness modifying the function? The problem of "how" reappears: either the nature of consciousness is simply to "be conscious" of reasons or causes (or a part of them) or it is a cause which must be given power energy, etc., with all the difficulties mentioned above.

Secondly, the direct causal action of an organic process on consciousness is no easier to understand. Such a process consists of material sequences involving mass, force, resistance, energy, etc. For these material sequences to modify consciousness they would have to find a point where contact could be made with consciousness whose nature was homogeneous with theirs, in the form of displacement of mass, speed of a moving body, diminution of resistance, etc., otherwise the modification would remain unintelligible. Therefore, if a glass of wine makes us gay, this is translated into an increase in the speed of association, by a lowering of inhibition, etc. But is this an action *on consciousness* or on a collection of neural connections, with consciousness confined to "being conscious" of them according to the role which even its name specifically evokes?

THE PARALLELIST SOLUTION

These insurmountable difficulties drive most authors to admit two distinct kinds of phenomena, one consisting of states of consciousness and the other of concomitant nervous processes (each state of consciousness corresponding to such a process, but without the reverse being true), and to consider that the relations between elements in one series and the other are never causally connected, but simply correspond or, as it is generally called, exist "parallel" to each other.

In this second solution several subvarieties can be distinguished. For example, the classic parallelism was atomistic and sought a correspondence between each element (in other words a physiological concomitant for each sensation, each "association," etc.). Gestalt theory (see 3, under B_2) on the other hand invokes an "isomorphic" principle by admitting a correspondence between structures. Another subdivision, independent of the former, divided authors with dualist tendencies (the body and "mind") from those favoring monism who saw the two as two sides of the same coin, which could be known internally (consciously) or externally (physiologically). Moreover, organicist monism put the accent on physiology and regarded consciousness merely as an "epiphenomenon," etc.

This second group of solutions effectively disposes of the difficulties involved in interactionism. But, in the form in which it is usually presented, other equally serious problems arise. In fact, if consciousness is nothing but the subjective aspect of certain nervous activities, it has no distinct function, since these activities can cope with everything. The fact that an external stimulus releases an adaptive reaction and that a problem of higher mathematics can be solved by the real brain in the same way as by an "electronic brain" suggest that these questions can all be explained without recourse to consciousness. One could, of course, maintain that the problem is badly formulated and that consciousness has no more functional significance than a neutral (or a fortiori lethal) mutation in the field of biogenetics. But it could be objected that consciousness obeys many laws and that, in psychogenesis as in sociogenesis, the construction of increasingly complex conduct is accompanied not only by an extension of the conscious area, but also by an evermore refined structuring of it. The history of science, to take but one example, is a history of the progress of conscious knowledge. This is true even of the history of behaviorist psychology (cf. C_1), which disregards consciousness by a curious usage of its own conscious thought.

All this then presents a problem and, [for] the parallelist solution [to] provide an adequate explanation [by] admitting two "parallel" or isomorphic series, it would be desirable for neither of the two types of phenomenon to cease to be functionally significant. It should be understood, at least how these heterogeneous phenomena can be complementary, without being causally interconnected.

Isomorphism Between Causality and "Implication"—Conclusions

Sciences more advanced than ours have realized long ago that progress, in moments of crisis, is generally associated with retroactive criticism of the ideas that have been used and so to epistemological criticism which is internal but independent of philosophy. This is appropriate when one is confronted by the problem of consciousness, and it makes it possible to do justice to the ideas of parallelism and isomorphism and, perhaps, to overcome the difficulties which they usually raise.

STATES OF CONSCIOUSNESS AND CAUSALITY

Thus we are immediately led to suppose that the principal difficulties arise from poor definition of specific ideas which apply to the unique consciousness and for which one has substituted current ideas which are more or less adapted to material causality (physical or physiological), but which are perhaps meaningless in the case of "states" of mind and even more so in that of the products of the mind (concepts, values, etc.).

In fact it is remarkable how carelessly so many great psychologists have used physical concepts to talk of consciousness. Janet used the terms "force of synthesis" and "psychological force." The expression "psychic energy" is frequently employed and "work" is commonplace. Therefore, either one refers implicitly to physiology and must therefore define and measure, or one talks of consciousness and immediately resorts to metaphors for lack of any clearly defined concepts comparable to those about physical laws and causality. These concepts all presuppose, directly or indirectly, the notion of mass or substance, which has no meaning as far as consciousness is concerned.

We can now define our previous points more accurately by saying that the idea of causality does not apply to consciousness. It does, however, apply to behavior, and even to conduct, giving rise to different types of causal explanation which we have already differentiated. But it is not "relevant" in the sphere of consciousness as such, because one state of consciousness does not "cause" another, but implies it according to other categories. Among the seven forms of explanation which we have recognized only abstract models (under C_3) apply to conscious processes precisely because they can disregard what we have called the real "substrate"; but, for causality to exist, deduction must apply to such a substrate, which is distinguished from the deductive process in that it is represented in material terms (even when it is a question of behavior or conduct). Furthermore (and this verifies our argument), the difficulties of interactionism arise from the fact that one is seeking to extend the sphere of causality to consciousness itself.

STATES OF CONSCIOUSNESS AND IMPLICATION

Consequently, if none of the constituent ideas of physical causality, except time, applies to facts of consciousness and particularly that of substance (the only one which experimental psychology refused to inherit when philosophical psychology bequeathed its burden), the only choice left is between the following alternatives: either consciousness is nothing, or it arises from original and specific categories which by their very nature ignore material facts. These categories do exist. Let us start with the facts of consciousness occurring in the higher forms of conduct (because here they are in their most characteristic form), the truth of $2 + 2 = 4$ is not the "cause" of the truth of $4 - 2 = 2$ in the same way that a cannon causes the movement of two billiard balls, or a stimulus is one of the causes of a reaction: the truth (we use the word "truth" since it refers explicitly to the consciousness of the author of the judgment) of $2 + 2 = 4$ "implies" that of $4 - 2 = 2$, which is quite a different matter. In the same way the value attributed to an aim or moral obligation is not the "cause" of the value of the means or of an action connected with the obligation: one of the values implies the other in a way similar to logical implication, and one can call this implication between values.

We claim then that however high one climbs toward simple states of consciousness one finds relations of this type. In fact, the most general characteristic of states of consciousness is undoubtedly that they consist of "meanings" of a cognitive nature (translated in terms of truth or falsehood) or an affective nature (values) or more probably, both at the same time. So, neither the connection between meanings nor the relation of the significant to the signified object arises from causality.

We will use "implication in the wide sense" therefore to characterize these two sorts of connections including the second (which can be distinguished by the term "designation") and we hypothesize that the mode of connection proper to phenomena of consciousness is implication in the wide sense, of which implication in the strict sense is a particular case.

Thus presented, the activity of the consciousness is no longer negligible and unimportant. For example, all the deductive sciences (logic and mathematics), the fine arts, ethics, and law arise from diverse forms of conscious implication, and if the nervous system is perfectly capable of rendering them possible, since it is responsible for the effective production of their material substrates, the fact remains that consciousness is essential in order to judge truth and value, i.e., to reach the implications which specifically characterize them.

ISOMORPHISM BETWEEN CAUSALITY AND IMPLICATION

This leads us to the problem of parallelism, the hypothesis being that the parallelism between states of consciousness and their concomitant physiological processes [is] in effect isomorphism between systems of implication in the wide sense and causal system. To justify this, recourse to mechanistic physiology supplies the clearest examples. An "artificial brain" is in effect capable, not only of conducting amazingly complex calculations, but even of working out new demonstrations.* Each operation which it uses is isomorphic with a logical or mathematical operation and there is a complete isomorphism between the conscious system of operations and the mechanical system. But there remains this difference: the mathematician judges the truth and falsehood of propositions and then evaluates their validity and that of their implications; the machine, on the other hand, is confined to producing results, which have an exact significance from the point of view of its constructor, but to which the machine itself remains indifferent because it is strictly determined and proceeds only by simple causality. True, it is capable of correction and regulation (feedback), but again without evaluation and as a function of single results determined causally by its programming. There is therefore only an objectively negligible difference: mathematics is a science because of the validity

---

*A machine has recently demonstrated a theory of Euclid in a way that one is ashamed to say is new. Given an isosceles triangle ABC whose apex is B and whose sides $AB = BC$. To be demonstrated that the angle BAC equals the angle ACB. Euclid drew a bisector, etc. The machine, when questioned, simply replied: the side AB equals the side CB beginning from the same point B; the side AC is common to the two angles, therefore $BAC = ACB$ because they can be placed symmetrically one upon the other.

of its implications, while the machine acts causally with the same detachment as a pebble takes on the form of a beautiful crystal if the conditions are right.

It can now be seen why neural connections, whose isomorphism with the propositional operations was demonstrated by McCulloch, can well culminate in causally producing a combination of the same kind as $2 + 2 = 4$, but without producing a necessary truth, because logical necessity does not arise from a question of fact but from conscious necessity inherent in implication. One could thus conceive of a completely isomorphic relationship between the causal system of neural connections or behavior, culminating by successive adjustments in the construction of "groups" of "lattices," etc., and the conscious system of implication and judgment using the same structures to validate and make deductions without losing the originality and functional specificity of the system.

CONCLUSION

What is equally evident, and this will be our conclusion, is the complex nature of explanation and of causality in general. We have seen that causality presupposes, (1) laws; (2) a deduction from these laws but (3) applied to a real substrate. Elements (1) and (3) of causality belong to the actual event to be explained (some of the conceptualization coming from the theoretician) while element (2) is introduced by the theoretician (as subject-author of the explanation). Briefly, causality is an assimilation of material actions between objects to the operations of the subject-theoretician. So, of the seven types of explanation which we have distinguished, the first six (A to C_2) are based on causality and are distinguished from each other essentially by the real substrate (3), which is invoked, whilst abstract models (C_3) are distinguished by the type of deduction (2) which is used and are based on deductive implication. Hence their possible application to the conscious structures (an application, moreover, which is not exclusive since this abstract deduction can also be applied to the real substrates (3) by virtue of the principle of isomorphism).

The essential results of our analysis are then: (1) that the favored and dominant directions of explanation in psychology are organicist reduction and interpretation by abstract models; and (2) that these two orientations, organicist and deductive, are in no way contradictory, but rather complementary. Until now we have justified this complementarity by stating how much each type of explanation refers, on the one hand to an explicit or implicit organicism while at the same time referring to abstract models; and added to this that the more exact neurology becomes the more it will need deductive models. We can now interpret this complementarity by basing it on deeper reasons: if parallelism between facts of consciousness and physiological processes is isomorphism between the implicative systems of meanings and the causal systems of the material world, it is then evident that this parallelism involves equally, not only a complementarity, but in the final analysis the hope of isomorphism between the organicist schemata and the logico-mathematical schemata used in abstract models.

39

Structuralism: Introduction and Location of Problems*

1968

Definitions

Structuralism is often said to be hard to define because it has taken too many different forms for a common denominator to be in evidence: the structures invoked by the several "structuralists" have acquired increasingly diverse significations. Nevertheless, upon examining and comparing the various meanings it has acquired in the sciences and, unfortunately, at cocktail parties, a synthesis seems feasible, though only on the condition of separating two problems which, while always conjoined in fact, are logically distinct. The first of these problems is to make out the nature of the affirmative ideal that goes with the very idea of structure, the ideal manifested in the conquests and hopes of every variety of structuralism. The second is to describe and analyze the critical intentions attendant on the birth and development of any particular variety of structuralism.

To dissociate the two problems is to admit in effect that there really is an ideal of intelligibility held in common, or at least aspired after, by all structuralists, even though their critical objectives vary enormously. For the mathematicians, structuralism is opposed to compartmentalization, which it counteracts by recovering unity through isomorphisms. For several generations of linguists, structuralism is chiefly a departure from the diachronic study of isolated linguistic phenomena which prevailed in the nineteenth century and a turn to the investigation of synchronously functioning unified language systems. In psychology, structuralism has long combatted the atomistic tendency to reduce wholes to their prior elements. And in current philosophical discussions we find structuralism tackling historicism, functionalism, sometimes even all theories that have recourse to the human subject.

*From Jean Piaget, *Structuralism*, Chaninah Maschler, editor and translator, © 1970 by Basic Books, Inc., Publishers, New York. Originally published in French as *Le Structuralisme* by Presses Universitaires de France, Paris, 1968, © 1968 by Presses Universitaires de France. Published in England by Routledge and Kegan Paul Ltd. Reprinted by permission of the publishers.

So, obviously, if we try to define structuralism negatively, in terms of its opposition to other positions, and refuse to consider it apart from these, we shall find nothing but diversity and all the contradictions that are linked with the vagaries in the history of the sciences and of ideas. On the other hand, once we focus on the positive content of the idea of structure, we come upon at least two aspects that are common to all varieties of structuralism: first, an ideal (perhaps a hope) of intrinsic intelligibility supported by the postulate that structures are self-sufficient and that, to grasp them, we do not have to make reference to all sorts of extraneous elements; second, certain insights—to the extent that one has succeeded in actually making out certain structures, their theoretical employment has shown that structures in general have, despite their diversity, certain common and perhaps necessary properties.

As a first approximation, we may say that a structure is a system of transformations. Inasmuch as it is a system and not a mere collection of elements and their properties, these transformations involve laws: the structure is preserved or enriched by the interplay of its transformation laws, which never yield results external to the system nor employ elements that are external to it. In short, the notion of structure is comprised of three key ideas: the idea of wholeness, the idea of transformation, and the idea of self-regulation.

The discovery of structure may, either immediately or at a much later stage, give rise to formalization. Such formalization is, however, always the creature of the theoretician, whereas structure itself exists apart from him. Formalization sometimes proceeds by direct translation into logical or mathematical equations, sometimes passes through the intermediate stage of constructing a cybernetic model, the level of formalization depending upon the choice of the theoretician. But, it is worth repeating, the mode of existence of the structure he earlier discovered must be determined separately for each particular area of investigation.

The notion of transformation allows us to delimit the problem of definition in a preliminary way; for if it were necessary to cover formalism in every sense of the word by the idea of structure, all philosophical positions that are not strictly empiricist would be let in again—those which invoke Platonic forms or Husserlian essences, not to forget Kant's brand of formalism, and even several varieties of empiricism (for example, the logical positivism of the Vienna Circle, who stress syntactic and semantic forms in their analysis of logic). Now in the narrower sense we are about to define, current logical theory only rarely takes account of "structures," for in many ways it has remained subservient to a rather stubborn atomistic tendency and is only beginning to open up to structuralism.

We shall, therefore, confine ourselves to the kinds of structuralism that are to be met in mathematics and the several empirical sciences, already a sufficiently venturesome undertaking. And in conclusion we shall take up some of the philosophical movements more or less inspired by the various kinds of structuralism that have sprung up in the social sciences. But first we must elaborate somewhat on the definition of structuralism in general that is here proposed, else it will be hard to understand why a notion as abstract as that of a "system closed under transformation" should raise such high hopes in all domains of inquiry.

Wholeness

That wholeness is a defining mark of structures almost goes without saying, since all structuralists—mathematicians, linguists, psychologists, or what have you—are at one in recognizing as fundamental the contrast between *structures* and *aggregates*, the former being wholes, the latter composites formed of elements that are independent of the complexes into which they enter. To insist on this distinction is not to deny that structures have elements, but the elements of a structure are subordinated to laws, and it is in terms of these laws that the structure *qua* whole or system is defined. Moreover, the laws governing a structure's composition are not reducible to cumulative one-by-one association of its elements: they confer on the whole as such overall properties distinct from the properties of its elements. Here is an example of what we have in mind: the integers do not exist in isolation from one another, nor were they discovered one by one in some accidental sequence and then, finally, united into a whole. They do not come upon the scene except as ordered, and this order of the integers is associated with *structural* properties (of groups, fields, rings, and the like), which are quite different from the properties of [individual numbers], each of which is even or odd, prime or nonprime, and so on.

The idea of wholeness does, however, raise a good many problems, of which we shall take up just the two principal ones, the first bearing on its *nature*, the other on its mode of *formation* (or preformation).

It would be a mistake to think that, in all domains, the epistemological alternatives reduce to just two options: either admit wholes defined in terms of their structural laws, or allow only for atomistic compounding of prior elements. No matter what area of science we subject to scrutiny, whether we consider the perceptual structures of the Gestalt psychologists or the social wholes (classes or entire societies) of sociologists and anthropologists, we find that not one but two alternatives to atomism have made their way in the history of ideas, only one of which appears to us in tune with the spirit of modern structuralism.

The first consists in simply reversing the sequence that appeared natural to those who wanted to proceed from the simple to the complex (from sense impressions to perceptual complexes, from individuals to social groups, and so forth). The whole which this sort of critic of atomism posits at the outset is viewed as the outcome of some sort of emergence, vaguely conceived as a law of nature and not further analyzed. Thus, when Comte proposed to explain men in terms of humanity, not humanity in terms of men, or when Durkheim thought of the social whole as emerging from the union of individuals in much the same way as molecules are formed by the union of atoms, or when the Gestalt psychologists believed they could discern immediate wholes in primary perception comparable to the field effects that figure in electromagnetism, they did indeed remind us that a whole is not the ·same as a simple juxtaposition of previously available elements, and for this they deserve our gratitude; but by viewing the whole as prior to its elements or contemporaneous with their "contact," they simplified the problem to such an extent as to risk bypassing all the central questions—questions about the nature of a whole's laws of composition.

Over and beyond the schemes of atomist association on the one hand and emergent totalities on the other, there is, however, a third, that of operational structuralism. It adopts from the start a relational perspective, according to which it is neither the elements nor a whole that comes about in a manner one knows not how, but the relations among elements that count. In other words, the logical procedures or natural processes by which the whole is formed are primary, not the whole, which is consequent on the system's laws of composition, or the elements.

But at this point a second, and much more serious, problem springs up, the really central problem of structuralism: Have these composite wholes always been composed? How can this be? Did not someone compound them? Or were they initially (and are they still) in *process* of composition? To put the question in a different way: Do structures call for *formation*, or is only some sort of eternal *preformation* compatible with them?

Structuralism, it seems, must choose between structureless genesis on the one hand and ungenerated wholes or forms on the other; the former would make it revert to that atomistic association to which empiricism has accustomed us; the latter constantly threaten to make it lapse into a theory of Husserlian essences, Platonic forms, or Kantian a priori forms of synthesis. Unless, of course, there is a way of passing between the horns of this dilemma.

As is to be expected, it is on this problem that opinion is most divided, some going so far as to contend that the problem of the genesis of structures cannot so much as be formulated because structure is of its very nature nontemporal (as if this were not in its own way a solution of the problem, namely, the choice of a preformational view of the origin of structures).

Actually, the problem we now are discussing arises with the notion of wholeness itself. It can be narrowed down once we take the second characteristic of structures, namely, their being systems of tranformations rather than of static forms, seriously.

Transformations

If the character of structured wholes depends on their laws of composition, these laws must of their very nature be *structuring*: it is the constant duality, or bipolarity, of always being simultaneously *structuring* and *structured* that accounts for the success of the notion of law or rule employed by structuralists. Like Cournot's "order"* (a special

*The reference is to Augustin Cournot's *Researches into the Mathematical Principles of Wealth* (1838; reprinted, New York: Kelley, 1927), the first systematic treatise on mathematical economics. See Oskar Morgenstern's article on mathematical economics in *Encyclopaedia of the Social Sciences*, V, 364ff.—trans.

case of the structures treated in modern algebra), a structure's laws of composition are defined "implicitly,"* i.e., as governing the transformations of the system which they structure.

When one considers the history of structuralism in linguistics and psychology, this last statement may seem somewhat surprising: In linguistics, structuralism started with the work of Saussure, which does not seem to bear out our claim; moreover, Saussure used the single word "system" to cover both laws of synchronic opposition and laws of synchronic equilibrium.† In Gestalt psychology, the perceptual forms that are said to have a Gestalt character are, generally speaking, static. But it is unwise to view an intellectual current exclusively in terms of its origin; it should be seen in its flow. Besides, even in their beginnings, linguistic and psychological structuralism were associated with the dawning of ideas of transformation. Synchronic language systems are not immobile; such systems exclude or allow for novelty (acceptance or exclusion being a function of requirements determined by the system's laws of opposition and connection). And it did not take long before Saussure's notion of some sort of dynamic equilibrium became elaborated into a theory of style by Bally.‡ Admittedly, we are not yet in the presence of Chomsky's "transformational grammar," but Bally's stylistic is headed toward the idea of transformation, at least in the weak sense of "individual variation." As for psychological gestalten, their inventors from the beginning spoke of laws of organization by which the sensory given is transformed, and the probabilistic interpretation we can today give of such laws accentuates this transformational aspect of perception.

Indeed, all known structures—from mathematical groups to kinship systems—are, without exception, systems of transformation. But transformation need not be a temporal process: $1 + 1$ "make" 2; 3 "follows hard on" 2; clearly, the "making" and "following" here meant are not temporal processes. On the other hand, transformation can be a temporal process: getting married "takes time." Were it not for the idea of transformation, structures would lose all explanatory import, since they would collapse into static forms.

The very centrality of the idea of transformation makes the question of origin, that is, of the relation between transformation and formation, inevitable. Certainly, the elements of a structure must be differentiated from the transformation laws which apply to them. Because it is the former which undergo transformation or change, it is easy to think of the latter as immutable. Even in varieties of structuralism which are not formalized in the strict sense, one finds outstanding workers who are so little concerned about psychological origins that they jump straight from the *stability* of transformation rules to their *innateness*. Noam Chomsky is a case in point: for him generative gram-

---

*For a brief account of the notion of "implicit definition" see, for example, Hermann Weyl, *Philosophy of Mathematics and Natural Science* (Princeton: Princeton University Press, 1949), pp. 24ff.—trans.

†See, for example, pp. 107, 117, 119–122 in Saussure's *Course in General Linguistics*, ed. C. Bally and A. Séchehaye, trans. W. Baskin (New York: Philosophical Library, 1959)—trans.

‡C. Bally, *Précis de stylistique* (Geneva, 1905) and *Traité de stylistique française* (Heidelberg, 1909)—trans.

mars appear to demand innate syntactic laws, as if stability could not be explained in terms of equilibrium mechanisms, and as if the appeal to biology implied by the hypothesis of innateness did not pose problems of formation just as complex as those involved in a psychological account.

Now the implicit hope of antihistorical or antigenetic structuralist theories is that structure might in the end be given a nontemporal mathematical or logical foundation (Chomsky has, in fact, reduced his grammars to a formal "monoid" structure).* But if what is wanted is a *general* theory of structure, such as must meet the requirements of an interdisciplinary epistemology, then one can hardly avoid asking, when presented with such nontemporal systems as a mathematical group or a set of subsets, how these systems were *obtained*—unless, of course, one is willing to stay put in the heavens of transcendentalism. One could proceed by postulate, as in axiomatic systems, but from the epistemological point of view this is an elegant way of cheating which takes advantage of the prior labor of those who constructed the intuitive system without which there would be nothing to axiomatize. Gödel's conception of a structure's relative "power" or "weakness" introduces a genealogical relation among structures which provides a method less open to epistemological objections. But once we take this tack the central problem, not as yet of the history or psychogenesis of structures but of their *construction*, and of the relation between *structuralism* and *constructivism*, is no longer avoidable. This will, then, be one among our several themes.

Self-regulation

The third basic property of structures is, as we said, that they are self-regulating, self-regulation entailing self-maintenance and closure. Let us start by considering the two derivative properties: what they add up to is that the transformations inherent in a structure never lead beyond the system but always engender elements that belong to it and preserve its laws. Again an example will help to clarify: In adding or subtracting any two whole numbers, another whole number is obtained, and one which satisfies the laws of the "additive group" of whole numbers. It is in this sense that a structure is "closed," a notion perfectly compatible with the structure's being considered a substructure of a larger one; but in being treated as a substructure, a structure does not lose its own boundaries; the larger structure does not

*The reference here may be to Chomsky's paper in the *Handbook of Mathematical Psychology*, ed. R. D. Luce, R. R. Bush, and E. Galanter (New York: John Wiley, 1963–1965), where he says (2.274): "A set that includes an identity and is closed under an associative law of composition is called a *monoid*. Because monoids satisfy three of the four postulates of a group, they are sometimes called *semigroups*. A *group* is a monoid, all of whose elements have inverses." *Syntactic Structures* makes no mention of "monoids."—trans.

"annex" the substructure; if anything, we have a confederation, so that the laws of the substructure are not altered but conserved and the intervening change is an enrichment rather than an impoverishment.

These properties of conservation along with stability of boundaries despite the construction of indefinitely many new elements presuppose that structures are self-regulating. There can be no doubt that it is this latter conception which makes the idea of structure so important and which accounts for the high hopes it raises in all domains of inquiry: Once an area of knowledge has been reduced to a self-regulating system or "structure," the feeling that one has at last come upon its innermost source of movement is hardly avoidable. Now self-regulation may be achieved by various procedures or processes, and these can be ranked in order of increasing complexity; we are thus brought back to our earlier question about a system's construction, i.e., in the last analysis, its formation.

At the highest level (though it should be remembered that what we call the top of the pyramid may be viewed as its base by others) self-regulation proceeds by the application of perfectly explicit rules, these rules being, of course, the very ones that define the structure under consideration. It might therefore be urged against us that talk about self-regulation is quite empty, since it refers either to the laws of the structure under consideration, and it goes without saying that they "regulate" it, or it refers to the mathematician or logician who "operates" on the elements of the system, and that he operates correctly under normal circumstances again goes without saying. Granted all this, there still remains the question: Just what *is* an operation structurally considered? From the cybernetic point of view, an operation is a "perfect" regulation. What this means is that an operational system is one which excludes errors before they are made, because every operation has its inverse in the system (e.g., subtraction is the inverse of addition, $+n - n = 0$) or, to put it differently, because every operation is reversible, an "erroneous result" is simply not an element of the system (if $+n - n \neq 0$, then $n \neq n$).

But there is, of course, an immense class of structures which are not strictly logical or mathematical, that is, whose transformations unfold in time: linguistic structures, sociological structures, psychological structures, and so on. Such transformations are governed by laws ("regulations" in the cybernetic sense of the word) which are not in the strict sense "operations," because they are not entirely reversible (in the sense in which multiplication is reversible by division or addition by subtraction). Transformation laws of this kind depend upon the interplay of anticipation and correction (feedback). As we shall see in Section 10, the range of application of feedback mechanisms is enormous.*

Finally, there are regularities in the nontechnical sense of the word which depend upon far simpler structural mechanisms, on rhythmic mechanisms such as pervade biology and human life at every level.†

*[Section 10 deals with organic structures. See Selections 39–43.]

†The study of such biological rhythms and periodicities (i.e., cycles of approximately 24 hours, which are remarkably general) has in recent years been turned into an entire new discipline with its own specialized mathematical and experimental techniques.

Rhythm too is self-regulating, by virtue of symmetries and repetitions. Though the self-regulation that is here involved is of a much more elementary sort, it would not do to exclude rhythmic systems from the domain of structure.

Rhythm, regulation, operation—these are the three basic mechanisms of self-regulation and self-maintenance. One may, if one so desires, view them as the "real" stages of a structure's "construction," or, reversing the sequence, one may use operational mechanisms of a quasi-Platonic and nontemporal sort as a "basis" from which the others are then in some manner "derived."

40

Structuralism and Dialectic*

1968

. . . To the extent that one opts for structure and devaluates genesis, history, and function or even the very activity of the *subject* itself, one cannot but come into conflict with the central tenets of dialectical modes of thought. It is therefore not surprising, and it is extremely instructive, to find Lévi-Strauss devoting almost the entire concluding chapter of *La Pensée sauvage* to a discussion of Sartre's *Critique de la raison dialectique*. An examination of this debate seems to us all the more in order because both of the antagonists appear to us to have forgotten the fundamental fact that in the domain of the sciences themselves structuralism has always been linked with a constructivism from which the epithet "dialectical" can hardly be withheld—the emphasis upon historical development, opposition between contraries, and *Aufhebungen* (*dépassements*) is surely just as characteristic of constructivism as of dialectic, and that the idea of wholeness figures centrally in structuralist as in dialectical modes of thought is obvious.

The principal components of dialectical thought as we find it in Sartre are constructivism and its corollary, historicism. We earlier touched on Lévi-Strauss's general critique of theories which assign a privileged status to history; Sartre is there singled out for special mention. The difficulties attaching to his view of the *I* and his notion of the *We* as no more than an *I* raised to the second power, hermetically sealed off from other *We*'s, are also pointed up. Though this last point is well taken, it should be mentioned that Sartre's subjectivist difficulties are the remains of his earlier existentialist phase; it is because his dialectic has not been schooled in the sciences but is merely doctrinal that it has not succeeded in erasing these vestiges of existentialism, for the dialectic of scientific thought implies, precisely, a reciprocity between perspectives. Sartre's constructivism we would defend, despite Lévi-Strauss's objections, except that we would deny what Sartre affirms,

*From J. Piaget, *Structuralism*, Chaninah Maschler, editor and translator. © 1970 by Basic Books, Inc., Publishers, New York. Originally published in French as *Le Structuralisme* by Presses Universitaires de France, Paris, 1968, © 1968 by Presses Universitaires de France. Published in England by Routledge and Kegan Paul Ltd. Reprinted by permission of the publishers.

namely, that constructivism is peculiarly philosophical and alien to science. Sartre's depiction of science is almost entirely derived from positivism and its "analytic" method. Now not only is positivism, a movement in *philosophy*, not the same as *science* (of which it gives a systematically distorted picture), but—as Meyerson often pointed out— even the most positivistic scientists do not act on the credo they expound in their prefaces; they do just about the opposite of what dogma requires as soon as they turn to the analysis and explanation of experience. It is one thing to accuse them of insufficient self-knowledge or epistemological sophistication, but quite another simply to assimilate their scientific work to positivism.

But this means that Lévi-Strauss's conception of the connection between dialectical reason and scientific thought, though more adequate than Sartre's, is also open to objection: it is alarmingly modest as to the requirements of science and obliges us to grant a much more important role to dialectical processes than Lévi-Strauss himself seems to want. Not that there is an inherent conflict between structuralism and dialectic; rather, Lévi-Strauss's version has been relatively static and ahistorical, and this is what has led him to underestimate the importance of dialectical processes.

What, for Lévi-Strauss, is dialectical reason? If we understand him aright, it is always "constitutive"* in the sense of being venturesome, building bridges and crossing them, whereas analytic reason separates because it wants not only to understand but to control. "Dialectical reason," Lévi-Strauss tells us, "is not . . . something *other than* analytic reason . . . it is *something additional in* analytic reason"†; it is analytic reason's own effort to transcend itself. But are we forcing the words if we say this comes down to a complementarity according to which synthetic reason's inventiveness and progressiveness make up for the lack of these in analytic reason while the job of verification remains reserved for the latter? The distinction is, of course, essential and, equally of course, there are not two reasons but two attitudes or two "methods" (in the Cartesian sense) which reason may adopt. Still, to describe the work of construction for which the dialectical attitude calls simply a matter of "throwing out bridges over the abyss of a human ignorance whose further shore is constantly receding"‡ is insufficient. It is often construction itself which begets the negations along with the affirmations, and the syntheses (*dépassements*) whereby they are rendered coherent as well.

This Hegelian or Kantian pattern is not a merely conceptual or abstract pattern such as would be of no interest to either the sciences or structuralism. It corresponds to a progression which is inevitable once thought turns away from false absolutes. In the realm of structure it matches a recurrent historical process well described by G. Bachelard in one of his best books, *La Philosophie du non*. Its principle is that, given a completed structure, one negates one of its seemingly essential or at least necessary attributes. Classical algebra, for example, was commutative, but since Hamilton we have a variety of noncommutative

---

*C. Lévi-Strauss, *The Savage Mind* (London, 1966), p. 246.
†Ibid.
‡Ibid.

algebras; Euclidean geometry has by "negation" (of the parallel postulate) engendered the non-Euclidean geometries; two-valued logic with its principle of excluded middle has, through Brouwer's denial of the unrestricted validity of this principle (in particular, its validity in reasoning about Cantorian sets), become supplemented by multivalued logics, and so on. In logic and mathematics, construction by negation has practically become a standard method; given a certain structure, one tries, by systematic negation of one after another attribute, to construct its complementary structures, in order later to subsume the original together with its complements in a more complex total structure. Griss's "negationless logic" goes so far as to "negate" negation. Furthermore, when what is in question is to determine whether it is system A which presupposes B or B which presupposes A (for example, whether ordinals or cardinals are prior, concepts or judgments, and so on) we can be quite sure that dialectical circles or interactions will always in the end replace linear orders of prior and posterior.

In physics and biology there is something analogous to what we called "construction by negation," though here it derives from what Kant called "real opposition."* Need we remind the reader of the oscillations back and forth between a corpuscular and a wave theory of light, or the reciprocities between electrical and magnetic processes of which we know since Maxwell? Here, as in the domain of abstract structures, the dialectical attitude seems essential to the full working out of structures; dialectic is both complementary to and inseparable from analytic, even formalizing, reason; so the "something more" which Lévi-Strauss grudgingly allows to it is not just the courage to "throw out bridges": dialectic over and over again substitutes "spirals" for the linear or "tree" models with which we start, and these famous spirals or nonvicious circles are very much like the genetic circles or interactions characteristic of growth.

This brings us back to the problem of history and Althusser's and Godelier's attempts to subject Marx's work, despite the essential role it assigns to historical development in its sociological interpretations, to structuralist analysis. That there is a structuralist strand in Marx, something just about halfway between what we called "global" and "analytic" structuralism, is obvious, since he distinguishes "real infrastructures" from "ideological superstructures" and describes the former in terms which, though remaining qualitative, are sufficiently precise to bring us close to directly observable relations. Althusser, who means to furnish Marxism with an epistemology, tries therefore, and with full justification, to differentiate the Marxist from the Hegelian dialectic and to reformulate the former in modern structuralist terms.

According to Althusser,† the "Hegelianism" of the young Marx is quite debatable; Marx took off rather from problems set by Kant and Fichte. Whether Althusser is right on this point we cannot judge. It is a corollary of two much more fundamental observations. The first is that for Marxism, in contrast to idealism, to *think* is to *produce*, thought being a kind of "theoretical practice" which is not so much the work of

---

*See L. Apostel's interesting chapter on logic and dialectic in *Logique et connaissance scientifique*, edited by Jean Piaget, 1967, where this Kantian notion of a contrast between real and logical opposition is discussed at length.

†Althusser, *Pour Marx* (Paris: Maspero, 1965)—trans.

an individual subject as the outcome of interactions between the subject
and his personal environment, into which social and historical factors
enter as well; it is in this light that Althusser interprets Marx's famous
passage where "the totality of the real" as a *Gedankenconcretum* is said
to be "in reality a product of thought and conception."*

We also accept Althusser's second observation, namely, that dialectical contradiction in Marx bears no resemblance to the Hegelian,
which is, in the final analysis, reducible to an identity of contraries,
whereas for Marx dialectical contradiction is the result of "overdetermination" (*surdétermination*), that is, if we understand him right, a
necessary consequence of the inseparability of interactions. Similarly,
Althusser rightly points up the difference between the Hegelian and the
Marxist notions of "totality."

It is this notion of "overdetermination"—the sociological counterpart to certain forms of causality in physics—which prompts Althusser
to insert the contradictions inherent in the relations of production or
the contradictions between these and the forces of production, in short,
all the apparatus of Marxist economics, into a transformational system
whose structure and principles of formalization he tries to articulate.
Althusser has been chided for his formalism, but this is the current
and unfounded criticism of all serious structuralist theories. The chief
objection urged against him is that—at least in the eyes of some critics
—he has too low an estimate of things human; but if the values of
the "person" (often regrettably confused with those of the ego) are
taken to be less important than the constructive activities of the epistemic subject, the characterization of knowledge as production is in
agreement with one of the best established traditions of classical
Marxism.

Godelier, in a footnote to his article "Système, structure, et contradiction dans le Capital,"† indicates, with great lucidity, how much
work remains to be done on the relations between historic structures
and their transformations. Social structures are comparable to mathematical "categories" (in the sense explained [earlier]—sets of objects
and their possible mutual "applications"). It is not at all difficult to
determine which functions are compatible and which incompatible with
a given social structure. The hard question is, given a systematic ensemble of such structures, how do the modalities of their mutual connections "induce a *dominant* function within one of the structures so
connected"? Not until contemporary structural analysis has perfected
its methods by studying historical and genetic transformations will it
be able to furnish the answer. Though Godelier (whose rounding off of
Althusser's analysis of contradiction in Marx is quite remarkable)
stresses the "priority of the study of structures to that of their genesis
or evolution," and notes that Marx followed this procedure himself in
opening *Das Kapital* with a theory of value, he can nevertheless be said
to approach the question from this perspective: Let us not forget that,
even in the domain of psychogenesis, genesis is never anything except
the transition from one structure to another, and while the second
structure is explained in terms of this transition, the transition itself

*Althusser uses the passage as an epigraph, ibid., p. 186—trans.
†*Les Temps modernes* (1966), p. 857, Note 55.

can only be understood in transformational terms if both of its termini are known. Godelier's final conclusion is worth citing in full, because it summarizes not only our objections to Lévi-Strauss but also the leading ideas of this work as a whole.

> Anthropology could no longer challenge history, nor history anthropology; the opposition between psychology and sociology, sociology and history, would become sterile. For the possibility of a "science" of man would, in the final analysis, depend upon the possibility of discovering the laws governing the operation, evolution, and internal relations of social structures . . . the method of structural analysis will, in other words, have to be generalized so as to become capable of explaining the conditions of variation and evolution of structures and their functions.*

For a structuralism of this sort, structure and function, genesis and history, individual subject and society are—once the instruments of analysis have been refined—inseparable, the more so the more it perfects its analytic tools.

*Ibid., p. 864.

PART XI

Factors of Development:
Biology and Knowledge

INTRODUCTION

In the selections grouped together in this section, Piaget expresses one of his most general aims, a synthesis that moves toward a deeper understanding of the way in which knowledge processes are integral with and yet an extension of life processes. He considers four "factors of development": maturation, experience with the physical environment, experience with the social environment, and equilibration. In addition, the stagewise nature of development resulting from the interplay of these factors is considered in a separate discussion. In dealing with maturation, heredity and environment are considered not as fixed entities but rather in their evolving interaction with each other.

Social experience, of course, can be thought of as a subheading under experience, and language is a further subdivision. At a certain level of discourse, if one wants to study the influence of society on development, one exploits natural experiments, for example, in cross-cultural studies, or one does laboratory studies in experimental social psychology; the central point is to explore systematically variables of social existence. Piaget himself has not done this kind of work, although his ideas have guided and stimulated a great deal of it. His own primary approach has been to argue that in every society the individual must go through certain intellectual developments in order to assimilate social experience and to accommodate to it. Naturally, this process takes place in a social medium, but Piaget has chosen to focus his attention on the development rather than on the medium. His main forays into these subjects are presented elsewhere in this volume (language and thought, imitation, moral judgment).

Among the four factors, equilibration is of a somewhat different logical order, since it pertains to the functioning of the system as a whole, and thus embraces the other three factors. It is Piaget's way of saying three things at once. First, endogenous restructuration is a continuous process. Second, the basic nature of this process is to seek out equilibrium states. Third, the movement toward equilibrium of interest in the study of biology and knowledge is not toward greater and greater passivity, like a clock running down; on the contrary, equilibration is an active process tending toward the growth of intelligence, more and more complex, flexible, and inclusive structures.

Piaget never entirely abandoned his early career as a biologist. In addition to carrying on, over long periods of time, one botanical and one zoological study, he has continuously striven for a synthesis of biological and psychological theory. The general theme, one he has long made familiar, is expressed in the title of one of his works: *Biology and Knowledge: An Essay on the Relations Between Organic Regulations and Cognitive Processes.*

The twin characteristics of living systems, organization and adaptation, are conceptually inseparable. An organized system could not survive if it did not adapt to its circumstances, but on the other hand, without such an organized system to be maintained we would need only speak of change, and the concept of adaptation would be superfluous. In general, what is maintained is a structure, or a set of relations, with constant change and renewal of contents; at the organic level this is accomplished by the continuous processes of metabolism, at the cognitive level by the continuous assimilation and transformation of information.

"Life is essentially autoregulation,"* Piaget states, echoing a theme that has been important at least since Claude Bernard introduced the concept of homeostasis. In some respects, there may be special regulatory organs, but in some cases we can only look to the totality of relationships among organs as providing this regulation. *"Cognitive processes seem, then, to be at one and the same time the outcome of organic autoregulation, reflecting its essential mechanisms, and the most highly differentiated organs of this regulation at the core of interactions with the environment,* so much so that, in the case of man, these processes are being extended to the universe itself."† Cognitive processes are "organs"? At first reading, this seems like a kind of objective idealism, giving material reality status to ideas. In another reading, what he seems to mean is simply that cognition cannot be said to occur in any one of the conventionally defined organ systems of the body, but draws upon them and reorganizes them in a new set of functional relations. Thus, "cognitive autoregulation makes use of the general systems of organic regulation such as are found at every genetic, morphogenetic, physiological, and nervous level, and forthwith adapts them to their new situation. . . . This situation constitutes the exchanges with environment that form the basis of behavior."‡

In good part this work is an exposition of some of the complex analogies between organic functioning in general and cognition in particular, justified by the point just made: since cognitive processes exploit the whole organism, such parallels are inevitable. But Piaget wants also to draw attention to crucial differences: the completeness, stability, and flexibility of the structures of intelligence. He compares organization at different levels.

Here, then, is the conclusion of this summary of our guiding hypotheses. The living organization is an equilibrated system (even if one avoids the term and substitutes Bertalanffy's "stable states in an open system"). But this organic equilibrium only represents a relative sort of stability in those very fields where it is best protected. The genome is isolated to the maximum degree from its environment, although it cannot be so completely; its equilibrium is nevertheless upset by mutations, etc., despite these ideal conditions. The epigenetic system is more open, but it finds its equilibrium by means of a number of processes, among them homeorhesis. Physiological systems are even more "open," and yet they react by homeostasis of the interior environment—an environment all the more remarkably stable as the various animal groups are evolved

---

* J. Piaget, *Biology and Knowledge*, p. 26.
† Ibid. Piaget's emphasis.
‡Ibid., p. 34.

and differentiated. The role of the nervous system is to be open to external stimuli and to react to them by means of its effectors; its increasing mobility does not prevent there being remarkably mobile equilibrium in the overall reactions. Finally, behavior is at the mercy of every possible disequilibrating factor, since it is always dependent on an environment which has no fixed limits and is constantly fluctuating. Thus, the autoregulatory function of the cognitive mechanisms produces the most highly stabilized equilibrium forms found in any living creature, namely, the structures of the intelligence, whose logico-mathematical operations have been of inescapable importance ever since human civilization reached the stage of being consciously aware of them*

One other crucial difference ought to be mentioned: ". . . the outstanding characteristic of cognitive organizations is the progressive dissociation of form and content."†

In at least four ways then, Piaget's formulations seem to have a ring of philosophical idealism: the teleological note of autoregulation, the assertion that cognitive processes are an organ, the claim of their universality and completeness, and the ultimate separation of form and content. On the one hand, this is an ontological issue of the kind that does not interest Piaget very much. On the other hand, he believes that modern developments in systems theory and cybernetics provide the conceptual tools for understanding the functioning of a growing, self-regulating, adaptive system without giving way to teleology.‡

Of the two poles of theoretical biology, organization and adaptation, the discussion up to this point has emphasized the first. *Biology and Knowledge* deals with both, but more recently Piaget has devoted a separate work to the second: "Biological adaptation and the psychology of intelligence: organic selection and phenocopy."** His aims here were to restate his critique of neo-Darwinism, to expound his own interactionist position, and to elaborate a broad hypothesis about the way in which changes in the gene complex can be viewed as an extension of the self-regulating activities of the organism. After developing the biological argument, he devotes a second part of the book to elaborating its analogues in cognition. Even the reader who remains sceptical of the seemingly neo-Lamarckian tone of the biological part may well find the psychological part challenging—especially if he is interested in the appearance of novelties, either in connection with psychological development or in the field of creativity. There are two key points in neo-Darwinism††

---

* Ibid., pp. 36–37. As this and other passages show, Piaget is particularly difficult to read in this area, for two reasons: first, his synthetic intentions lead him to refer rapidly, sketchily, and often parenthetically to a wide range of subjects; second, he oscillates between two moods, mainly elaborating the analogies but sometimes quite suddenly expanding upon the differences beween organic and cognitive processes.

† Ibid., p. 153.

‡ A similar note is struck in "The Integron," the concluding chapter of François Jacob's *The Logic of Life: A History of Heredity* (New York: Pantheon, 1974), first published in French in 1970. Hardly anyone would suspect Jacob of idealism.

** *Adaptation vitale et psychologie de l'intelligence: sélection organique et phénocopie* (Paris: Herman, 1974), as yet untranslated, except for the recapitulation presented in Selection 40 of this volume.

†† "Darwinism" because natural selection is the central concept, "neo" because it takes account of the genes that control the development of the phenotype upon which selection operates. It is agreed, even by some of its contemporary critics, that this synthesis of evolutionary and genetic theory was one of the great scientific achievements of the years 1925–1950, involving such figures as T. Dobzhansky, L. Fischer, J. B. S. Haldane, J. Huxley, G. Simpson, and S. Wright.

that provoke Piaget's criticism. First, mutation is considered to be a random process, in the sense that a given mutation, when it occurs, has no relation to the adaptive needs of the organism. Second, natural selection is a process in which the organism is essentially passive; it is the environment that responds to the mutation that has happened to the organism.

Piaget raises certain objections to this view. First, the sheer improbability of the evolution of complex organs or organisms on the basis of chance alone. He cites a calculation about the evolution of the human eye: "if the mutations necessary for the formation of this organ had been brought about simultaneously or conjointly, they would have had a probability of only 1 in 10^{42}, in other words practically none. On the other hand, if it had been a question of successive mutations, in which new ones were simply added to preceding mutations, so that a cumulative effect was achieved, then it would have taken as many generations as would correspond to the age of the world or even exceed it."*

Second, the gene complex is not sealed off from the rest of the body; we know that it controls the momentary functioning and the development of the organism. It is implausible to think that this relationship is entirely one-way, and that a system in such strong interaction with another system is not affected by it.

Third, each individual gene is not simply sitting there waiting for a mutation to happen to it, or not, as chance decrees. It is interacting with other genes, influencing their activity and being influenced by them.

Piaget rejects the neo-Darwinian model not only because of what he believes is an excessive reliance on chance, but because of the image of the organism it conveys as a passive recipient of events—first, whatever external event provokes the mutation and second, the external factors summed up in the term "natural selection," which decide the fate of the mutation after it has occurred. Piaget wants a model that presents the organism as perpetually active, choosing its environment, choosing (in some sense of the term) which mutations to try out, and presenting as small a target as possible to the vicissitudes of chance. Piaget wants a theory in which the initiative remains with the organism: the mutations that occur are in the first place part of the total process of organized self-regulation; and an internal process of "organic selection" plays a major role in determining which variants will be presented to the environment for further (natural) selection. This approach does not deny the role of chance, but minimizes it by insisting that fortuitous events are assimilated into strong structures. It is with these aims in mind that he advances the *phenocopy hypothesis.*

Piaget does not, of course, claim that these ideas are all original with him. Indeed, the history of this approach is quite complex. A brief account of it and an exposition of similar ideas may be found in a refreshing book, *Internal Factors in Evolution.*†

---

* *Biology and Knowledge,* p. 274.

† L. L. Whyte, *Internal Factors in Evolution* (New York: George Braziller, 1965). It should be mentioned that neither Piaget nor Whyte quite do justice to either Darwin or Lamarck. On the one hand, in the *Origin of Species,* especially in the section on "correlation of growth," Darwin shows his sensitivity to the issues under discussion. On the other hand, reducing Lamarck's theory of evolution to the idea of the inheritance of acquired characteristics is a gross oversimplification; it was probably obvious to Lamarck that the direct effects of the environment would be too easily reversible to produce progressive evolution, and he relied primarily on a principle

In Selection 38 Piaget first makes the general point that anticipation is a very general biological function in the sense that many structural changes occur in an organism that are not useful to it at the moment they occur, but will be useful later on. The development of anticipation, both phylogenetically and ontogenetically, must in some way depend on the past, i.e., on memory or something like it, stored information gleaned from previous exposure to the kind of situation being anticipated. His account of the series of feedbacks by which this might occur is very similar to Waddington's idea of genetic assimilation.* Thus, there is a continuum from memory to anticipation, and a stored scenario can be run either backward (memory) or forward (anticipation).

Over a period of years, while Piaget was collecting the material for his botanical monograph on *Sedum,* he took advantage of his many trips to collect varieties of the plant, which he therefore often had with him in his briefcase while lecturing to unsuspecting child psychologists or other nonbotanical audiences. The monograph is an attempt to illuminate the concept of anticipation through a study of such processes in plants. In the excerpt on anticipation from *Biology and Knowledge* (Selection 41), Piaget includes a resumé of this work.

For unbroken continuity in a scientific investigation by an individual, Piaget's work on the mollusc *Limnaea stagnalis* must set some kind of record. He described an albino form of it in 1912, and by 1913 he had written a paper that concludes with a discussion of the causes of variation in this and related forms. In 1928 he took eggs from one variant and placed them in a natural pool in which the species was absent, and on successive visits over many years studied morphological changes in the specimens to be found there.†

Selection 42 includes a brief resumé of this work. The main point is to advance the phenocopy hypothesis. In this paper, prepared especially for this volume, Piaget begins with an exposition of the idea in the cognitive realm and then elaborates it in the organic realm. In some ways, of course, the ideas presented are quite close to those he had developed earlier (see Introduction to this volume, discussion of interactionism), but there are some notable differences. The phenocopy hypothesis proposes that there are both exogenous and endogenous variations in phenotypes; once the exogenous form is established, the organism *reinvents* it, that is, changes itself in such a manner that the same phenotypic result is now produced by endogenous means; this endogenous or genotypic form is in some sense a copy of the phenotypic, hence *phenocopy*; the endogenous form is eventually substituted for the exogenous form.

How does this process come about? At each level, from gene complex to cognitive structures, the organism has a system for sensing that something is or is not working properly; if not, a process of variation (or mutation, or

---

inherent in living things of modification toward greater complexity and perfection. For a succinct account of Lamarck's views see the article, "Lamarck" by C. Bocquet in the *Encyclopaedia Universalis.* For a more general discussion see Howard E. Gruber and Paul H. Barrett, *Darwin on Man: A Psychological Study of Scientific Creativity* (New York: Dutton, 1974).

* C. H. Waddington, *The Nature of Life* (New York: Harper Torchbooks, 1966), first published 1961.

† J. Piaget, "Note sur des *Limnaea stagnalis* L. var. *lacustris* Stud. élevée dans une mare du Plateau vaudois."

"groping" as Piaget put it in his much earlier writings about infant development) begins, until a response occurs that solves the "problem." Thus, in clearly recognizing the role of exogenous knowledge, in the concepts of re-invention and substitution, and in specifying the role of chance,* Piaget's work on the phenocopy hypothesis represents a change from earlier positions.†

Selection 43 is the final chapter of *Biology and Knowledge*.

---

* From the simplest to the most complex biological processes, Piaget writes, "the role of chance is reduced to proportions which are not negligible but modest, since the essential characteristic of that cardinal function of life, assimilation, is precisely to struggle against chance in such a way as to make use of it." *Adaptation vitale*, p. 108, our translation.

†In the group of enterprises represented in this part of this volume, Piaget has been especially active in recent years, producing new works at a breathtaking pace: *Adaptation vitale et psychologie de l'intelligence: séléction organique at phénocopie* (Paris: Hermann, 1974) is not yet translated, but the essential ideas are summarized in Selection 42 in an article written especially for this volume; *L'Equilibration des structures cognitives: problème central du développement* (Paris: Presses Universitaires de France, 1975) is not yet translated, but the theme of equilibration is treated in Selections 44, 45, and 46; *Le Comportement, moteur de l'évolution* (Paris, Gallimard, 1976) is not yet translated, but the themes that it elaborates appear in Selections 9 and 47. Piaget's research group, the Centre International d'Epistémologie Génétique, devoted the year 1975–76 to studying the growth in the child of the idea of the possible, and the year 1976–77 to the idea of the necessary. Although no report is yet available of this work, Selection 44 gives a good idea of its roots in Piaget's earlier thinking.

41

Conservation of Information and Anticipation[*]

1967

[Here Piaget is comparing the relation between accommodation and assimilation in the organic and intellectual realms; there are two characteristics which give rise to the possibility of greater coherence in the intellectual realm than in the organic.]

The first of these characteristics is the existence of certain accommodation forms which are, so to speak, permanent. A theory in biology or physics is in no sense of the term permanently accommodated, since it only needs the intervention of [one new fact] to be checkmated. (It is well known that no experiment can ever be made that will exactly confirm any theory, but experiment can invalidate a theory.) On the other hand, not only will no experiment ever disprove logical or mathematical theorems, a fact which is self-evident because of their hypothetico-deductive nature, but also one can rest assured that any fact arrived at by means of experimentation will lend itself, not to an integral deduction (history cannot be deduced), but to a logico-mathematical treatment, carried out in greater or lesser depth, which the fact will not contradict. In this way, the isomorphic juggling, the order structures, and so on, which present-day mathematics are applying to anything and everything, are evidence of some kind of permanent accommodation within the most generalized thought structures. Now this fact is not unconnected with what is found in biology, for although no particular organic form undergoes a once-and-for-all accommodation, yet accommodation of the most generalized forms of living organization merges into life itself and thus lasts as long as life does. This will be one among several reasons put forward to justify the interpretation attempted [earlier], namely, that the reasons for the remarkable accord between logico-mathematical structures and reality are to be sought within the very laws governing the functioning of the living organization in its permanent continuity.

*Reprinted from *Biology and Knowledge* by Jean Piaget, translated by Beatrix Walsh, The University of Chicago Press, © 1971 by The University of Chicago and The University of Edinburgh. Reprinted by permission of the publishers. Originally published in French, 1967.

The second striking characteristic of intellectual accommodation is its capacity for anticipation. If adaptation in the intelligence were limited to the field of the immediate present and the reconstruction of the past, it would be found wanting, in the domain of experience, much more often than is the case. But there are a great many happenings that can be foreseen by the exercise of thought, and the mere fact that the object of mathematics is to discover the sum of all possible transformations, and not merely that part of them which can actually be realized, is sufficient proof of this deductive power of the human mind. Even in the sphere of chance, which is constantly interfering with what has already been determined, particularly where history is concerned, logico-mathematical operations allow for calculation of every kind of probability, which constitutes yet another instrument of anticipatory accommodation.

Here again, anticipation is not confined to cognitive mechanisms. But these anticipations as well as the permanent accommodations on which they are based are infinitely richer in the cognitive than in the organic domain. The conclusion to be drawn from the present section is, therefore, that cognitive adaptation is an extension of general biological adaptation but that its proper function is to attain such adaptive forms as are unattainable on the organic level owing to their infinite power of assimilation and accommodation and to the stability of equilibrium between these two subfunctions.

Conservation of Information Acquired Previously, and Anticipation

Anticipation, to which a general allusion has just been made, is something much greater than an extension of accommodation; it makes possible the formation of anticipatory accommodations, but, in its general form, it derives from a capacity for inference or transfer, based on information previously acquired—based, that is, on the conservation of their assimilation schemata. We thus find ourselves confronted by two new functions (possibly with generalized structural characteristics) which are common to life and to knowledge: a conservation-of-information function, or "memory," and an anticipation function.

MEMORY

The notion of "memory" as the conservation of information raises two important problems, one of them related to learning, or the acquisition of information, and the other to its conservation as such. These problems are interdependent, for it is impossible to speak of learning or acquiring information if what is learned is not conserved, and, on the contrary, one can only use the term "memory" where information from an external source is conserved (otherwise anything to do with heredity would be mixed up with memory); but these problems are, nevertheless, distinct, for learning and conservation correspond to two successive phases in a complete process.

The organism has often, and quite rightly, been regarded as a machine for learning, just as essential a capacity in the organism as those of assimilation and reproduction. Indeed, if a careful distinction must be made between learning and development—although all kinds of learning are partly dependent on environment, and, moreover, there is such a thing as development in all forms of knowledge, including learning—it is nonetheless true that various kinds of learning are to be found at every level of the evolutionary scale and at all the stages, at least the functional ones, of individual development. But what do these forms of learning consist of? The organism may be seen as a "black box" from which the "outputs" provide nothing more than the "inputs."* Or again, the organism may be seen as a center in which all the information supplied will be subjected to transformation, or, at least, to organization such that the output is rendered much richer than the input. Now it is obvious that the kind of conservation involved will not be the same in both cases, and that if every acquisition is responsible for an assimilation, the conservation of information is, in its turn, dependent on assimilation schemata.

This is why the notion of "memory" is, in fact, a rather equivocal one. In terms of human psychology, it covers a certain number of processes, of which the two extremes are as follows. The most elementary form is simple recognition in the presence of the object perceived but without evocation of it in its absence. Perceptual recognition is a function of a sensorimotor schema which can be set up only when a previously perceived object reappears (which marks the beginning of a habit) but which is, generally speaking, a habit schema in the proper sense of the word. In fact, every habit presupposes recognition of indices and situations, which is what gives it its close relationship to recognition and its partly mnemic character (again, motor memory or habit memory are terms which are used in this connection).

At the other extreme, there is the term "evocation" memory, used to designate the capacity for evoking objects or events that are not actually present by means of perception and in the form of picture memories. Evocation is something of a much higher order than recognition and presupposes a symbolic function (mental images or language, as in "storytelling behavior," which P. Janet sees as being the root of evocation memory) as well as the processes of inference and logical organization necessary for the mental reconstruction of the past. This does not, incidentally, exclude the possibility of unconscious registerings. Penfield produced some proof of such a possibility by exciting electrically the temporal lobes, but it is not yet known how far-reaching the unconscious registering is in relation to parts of it which have been decoded, nor how reliable it may be in relation to the reconstructions presupposed by such decoding.) It is therefore clear that evocation, too, presupposes certain schemata, but these are conceptual or operational, and necessary either for the organization or for the reconstruction or

---

*This is as much as to say that the only activities involved would be encoding and decoding, without any transformation, properly speaking, or any other mechanism, apart from translation or actualization.

merely for the decoding of memory or even for all these mechanisms at once.

Thus it can be seen how complex memory is, which takes us rather far from the concept formulated by Semon about what he called the "mneme." Instead of an automatic recording by "engrams" and a direct and exhaustive decoding by "ekphoria," we are confronted by encoding or decoding that is linked up with assimilation schemata, which is to say, action and operational schemata. This presupposes transformations between the two in the shape of organization, if no more. From that point, leaving on one side the question of how memory and learning are acquired, the problem of their conservation has two distinct aspects: the conservation of schemata *qua* schemata and the actualizing of memory (or decoding) by means of recognition or evocation.

The problem of the conservation of schemata is not, properly speaking, a problem of memory, unless the meaning of the term is extended in an unwarranted way, for the schema of an action, being the transferable or generalizable quality in the action, is self-conserving; the memory of a schema is thus nothing more or less than the schema itself, and so there is no need to talk of "memory" in connection with it except insofar as to show the schema to be an instrument of memory. On the other hand, memory in the strict sense of the term, which is to say recognition or evocation (including evocation touched off by experiments such as Penfield's), is simply the figurative aspect of this conservation of schemata—figurative in the sense of something perceived (recognition) or imagined (evocation by a memory-image).

In the following pages, therefore, it will be not so much memory in the strict sense that interests us but the conservation of previous information in the widest sense, that is, everything acquired or learned in terms of the external world. So we shall be talking mainly about conservation and transference of schemata insofar as such schemata are elaborated in conjunction with environment. (That is why we have used the term memory, until the beginning of the present section, only in quotation marks, for its usage in biology is much closer to notions of learning, of conditioning, of habit, etc., than to memory in the psychological sense of recognition and, more important, of evocation, the latter being incontrovertibly a human property or, at least, a property of the higher primates.)

The great difficulty, however, in dealing with schemata themselves is to draw the demarcation line between what is innate and what is acquired, since every transition takes place between two things, as, for example, between the reflex and the earliest habits (whether conditioned or simply instrumental). Between a hereditary system and some acquisition imposed on the subject by the environment and its regular sequences, there does, in fact, exist a *tertium quid*, which is exercise. Thus, it seems almost certain by now that maturation of such and such a sector of the nervous system is allied to some functional exercise, and, if one studies the manifestations of the sucking reflexes in a newborn human infant (as I have, indeed, done), one can observe increasing consolidation and adaptability during the earliest days (ability to find the nipple again after it has been moved slightly, etc.). But this exercise, though at first it teaches the subject nothing outside its hereditary programming, does, nevertheless, constitute a functional acquisition and presupposes some intervention by the environment. Now a functional acquisition may be extended into a structural organization. Thus, Hebb admits that part played by exercise even in the formation of perceptual "Gestalts"; Lehrmann similarly argues against the purely innate character of instinct, in favor of some early kind of exercise in the embryo. One might even go so far as to wonder whether the neurobiotaxia described by Kappers as existing in the embryonic organization of the nervous system from neuroblasts upward does not, even at that stage, show an effect of the same kind.

ELEMENTARY FORMS OF LEARNING

The object of the present [section] is simply to pick out the general isomorphisms between organic and cognitive functions or structures, not to define the epistemology of cognitive ones, that is, to find out their necessary and sufficient conditions *qua* knowledge. From the isomorphic angle, we need only point out that, with regard to conservation of previously acquired information, this essential function is common both to organic life and to knowledge, and that within these two fields the same initial difficulty of dissociating acquired from hereditary information recurs as well as the same necessity for taking account of an exercise factor between the actions of both.

These problems present themselves as early as the molecular stage in biology. For example, it has been possible to look at immunity as a kind of "memory." But, with the study of bacteria and the formation of antibodies set up specifically to combat antigens, two sorts of possibilities presented themselves, and the choice between them has not been determined. According to the first, the antigen constitutes a sort of matrix, which the antibody enters and takes shape in. This would constitute a piece of information acquired from the external world, implying that immunity was a memory, in the sense that it was conserved. According to the second possibility, which seems to be prevailing, the specific adaptation of the antibody to the antigen is supposed to be the result of selection within the genetic information already established, so that "memory" can no longer be spoken of. But such a selection cannot possibly be translated into terms of the survival or the elimination (death) of individuals, since it is essentially a matter of choice and regrouping on the basis of predetermined information that still has to be regrouped and adjusted. The kind of selection involved here is much more like learning by trial and error than an all-or-nothing process. We are dealing, then, with a "response" in Waddington's sense, and the conservation of this response can certainly be seen within the framework of the conservation of newly acquired structures, even if such acquisition presupposes a close interaction between external conditions and that which is endogenous and predetermined. Even if the term "morphopoietic genes" is used, it still remains true that, although morphopoiesis brings about a succession of choices, these choices are oriented by their successes or their failures, in other words, by the overall situation. The famous question of the Michigan planarians (whose information acquired by means of conditioning is supposed to be retained in cases of regeneration after artificial divisions of the creature or even after absorption by an unconditioned creature of the fragments of a trained individual) does seem, on the contrary, to be losing its effect. So long as sufficient precautions are not taken about genetic characteristics in the strains that are being used, the question arises whether the effects observed, which have not been corroborated by other experimenters in this field, are not due to an initial selection rather than to "memory."*

On the other hand, the problem that has been set remains intact: the localization of acquired information in the RNA or the necessity for a functionally intact RNA if such acquistions are to be conserved. This problem is of enormous theoretical interest, since RNA is closely dependent on DNA, which would seem to mean that acquired information is retained by virtue of activities requiring the action of a hereditary framework. Hyden, for example, has demonstrated, in his experiments on rats, that any further learning involves an increase in RNA, and the reply to this has been in the form of an alternative question: Is this the effect of learning as such, or of the activity expended? But if it is the activity, this may nonetheless be the result of the exercise itself, which is inherent in learning, independent of its content, and this, as we have seen, represents an intermediary factor between the innate and that which is acquired from outside.

Whatever may be the truth of the matter as regards such conservation of information at the macromolecular level, it does seem obvious that at the intervertebrate level there is already some acquiring of information from outside, even before there is any differentiated nervous system. In the Protozoa, for example, learning curves among paramecia have been established by making them turn about in a narrow tube in order to get out; the statistical improvement in the averages prevents any talk of instinct in this case. Positive results were obtained, even, by conditioning infusorians to associate light with food. Unfortunately, the possibility of the persistence of chemical traces left by the infusorians in the liquid does not altogether preclude the intervention of actual stimuli in what would generally seem to constitute the conservation of this association.

As soon as any sort of nervous system, even a noncentralized one, appears, it follows inevitably that acquisitions become current and capable of being conserved in terms both of the many factors analyzed by theories of learning and of the structures identified either by experimentation or by the intermediary of the learning "machines" constructed

---

*On the other hand, experiments which may prove decisive have recently been published by F. R. Babich, A. L. Jacobson, S. Bubash, and A. Jacobson. See *Science*, 149 (1965): 656 and *Proceedings Nat. Acad. of Science* 54 (1965): 1299. After submitting rats to a learning process in which they were guided toward food by means of a sound, the authors killed the animals they had trained, removed a piece of the brain, and injected RNA from it into a new group of rats; they then noticed that the latter did, in fact, show themselves capable of learning much more quickly. This experiment was repeated for control by E. F. Fjerdingstad, Th. Nissen, and H. H. Roigeerd Petersen (*Scand. J. Physiology*, 6; 1; [1965] with positive results, whereas Gh. G. Gross and F. M. Carey (*Science*, 150 [1965]: 3704, 1749) failed to discover any such facts. These latter authors are collaborating at the moment with the Babich team in order to try to discover why there should be this divergence.

by cyberneticians. In this way all the transitions between conservation of acquired information on the organic plane and on the plane of cognitive functions come into being, conditioned reactions occupying a specially privileged place in this respect because of their dual aspect of simply vegetative or visceral conditioning and conditioning relative to exteroceptive stimuli.

COGNITIVE ANTICIPATION

Conservation of information previously acquired does, moreover, cause anticipatory reactions at all the higher cognitive levels, to the extent that one of the essential functions of knowing is to bring about foresight. In the realm of scientific thought, the establishing of any law presupposes foresight, for in order to verify hypotheses relative to the law being investigated it is necessary to organize the experiment, that is, to orient it in terms of certain anticipations and not to allow events to run on in haphazard fashion. On the other hand, since the essential quality of a law is its generality, it applies to the future as much as to the present and the past, which is the same thing as saying that it not only permits foresight but actually makes it necessary. . . .

However, this anticipatory function is very far from being exclusive to scientific thought, and it is to be found over and over again at every level of the cognitive mechanisms and at the very heart of the most elementary habits, even of perception. Indeed, consideration of the future does not belong to thought alone, although thought, being theoretically unlimited in scope, naturally extends its foresight or its projects much farther into the future than sensorimotor action or perception can. Nevertheless, to distinguish between the immediate future and the distant future that is accessible to imagination or deduction, it remains true that any habit, by the very fact that it conserves acquired information, has some application to the immediate future. That is why Tolman, whose theory of learning is much more comprehensive than Hull's associationism, asserted that an essential factor is expectation, by virtue of which every sensorimotor organization is oriented, even when based on "sign Gestalts" or significant configurations, for these very significations are relative to expectations.

In the domain of perception, it is known, for example, that the weight illusion, according to which the larger of two boxes of equal weight will seem to be the lighter, presupposes the anticipation of an approximate proportionality between weight and volume. Mental defectives or very young children, who do not exercise this foresight, give evidence of no such illusion when they weigh the boxes in their hands, so that even if anticipation does not explain everything, it certainly does play a part as a necessary factor, though not a sufficient one. A Russian psychologist, Usnadze, has constructed a visual equivalent of this weight illusion in such a way as to eliminate the muscular factors involved when the box is actually weighed in the hand; two unequal circles of 20 and 28 mm. are shown to the subject several times in succession in the space of 1/10 second, and are then replaced in the same location by two equal circles, 24 mm. in diameter. What then happens is that circle A in the place of the 20 mm. circle is seen as

bigger than circle B, having the same diameter but being substituted
for the 28 mm. circle. To put it another way, the initial presentation
has brought about an effect of succession in time which has modified
the previous perception. Now, since this effect increases with age, and
the rapidity with which it is suppressed increases in the same way (so
that error in juvenile subjects is weaker but longer lasting), we clearly
have here a case of an anticipatory activity and not merely of after-
effects such as W. Köhler and Wallach talk about.*

Finally, the conditioned reflex itself is surely also anticipatory as
well as, and on account of, being an instrument for repetition and
generalization. The sound of a bell or a whistle releases the salivary
reflex only as long as it is the herald of food, and if this food is never
again forthcoming, the conditioning will fade away for lack of "confirmation" of this anticipation.

Thus, the function of anticipation is common to cognitive mechanisms at all levels. But the essential point to be noted in the comparisons
we are now going to make is that at each of these levels, even the
highest, anticipation presupposes no "final cause," deriving solely from
previous information, whether by inferential means (scientific deduction or representation of some kind or other), by motor transfer, or by
perceptual transposition.

The ambiguous character of the notion of final causes has, indeed,
already been stressed—an ambiguity which is the psychological outcome of a confusion between the physical or physiological relationship
of causality (cause a produces effect b) and logical, or consciousness-
connected, relationships of implication (the use of A implies the result
B) or of instrumentality (to reach B, A must be used).† But although
it does consist of a kind of bastard complex, finality as final cause embraces elementary notions, each one of which, if kept distinct, is both
clear and capable of causal or logical interpretation; of such a kind are
the notions of fundamental utility, adaptation, direction, and, most
important here, anticipation. In this connection, the latter characteristic
can be explained in full by processes of transfer or inference based on
previous information, in other words on the application or generalization of schemata which were originally nothing but simple causal series
and feedbacks, leading back from the result obtained to the initial
action, but without any help, at first, from the anticipations that become
possible later on, although any schema may become anticipatory once
it is constructed.

Let us try to set up the simplest kind of model of such a process.
A child of 11 or 12 months, accidentally pulling at a tablecloth or some
support (action A), sets off a slight movement in the object lying on it

---

*See J. Piaget, *Les mécanismes perceptifs*.

†J.-B. Grize, who has made a study of these three relationships from the
point of view of logistic calculation, demonstrates in the same way that the
relationship of "final cause" is an illogical concept because it mixes the real
relationships of language (instrumentality and causality) with isomorphic
relationships belonging to "mentalanguage" used in order to relate causality
$a \rightarrow b$ with instrumentality $B \rightarrow A$.

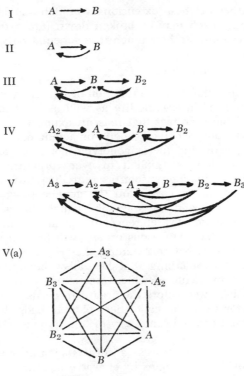

Figure 1

(result B): result B is immediately linked by feedback to action A, which then starts over again (passage from I to II in Figure 1); in other words, a chance act has become a schema. At this point two sorts of extensions are possible, one forward, which we shall call extrapolation, and the other backward, which we shall call recurrence.

Extrapolation consists of extending the previously obtained movement B into different positions, B_2 or B_3, each new result being fed back to the initial action A (III and IV in Figure 1). Recurrence, for its part, means that action A may be set off by indices which preceded those of the original situation in Figure 1; for example, the subject, not seeing at first that the object is placed on a solid support, discovers this when he notices the edges of the surface against which the object is perceived and realizes that, because of the difference in level of those edges, there must be some solid support which can be pulled, etc. In other words, action A will be set off by the recurrent indices $-A_2$ or $-A_3$, etc.

It is, then, the sum of the feedbacks linking B or B_2 or B_3, etc. to A or $-A_2$ or $-A_3$, etc., that makes anticipation possible, and anticipation is nothing other than a transfer or application of the schema (V or V[a]) to a new situation before it actually happens, the temporal order of terms A and B being immaterial since each can be linked to all the others (V[a]). To put it more precisely, schema AB, though not anticipatory at the outset, has become so by its double extension backward and forward. Either of these extensions would be sufficient in itself, but that is because each may be broken down into extrapolations and recurrences according to how much it is schematized.

ORGANIC ANTICIPATION

Looked at in this way, the function of anticipation is one of the most widely generalized in organic life as well as in cognitive mechanisms, by reason of the very fact that it is an extension of all forms of conserved information, whether genetic or acquired.

In the genetic and the epigenotypic domains, conservation, which we saw [earlier] to be implicit in every organization, is necessarily extended in anticipation as soon as reproduction is involved, since the subsequent generation carries on the genetic program transmitted by the preceding one, and the stages by which this is carried out must, then, be anticipatory by reference to the final adult state. So it goes without saying that the various organs will first appear in the form of a series of outlines before reaching their functional state. Cuénot deduced from this something that he calls "the law of anticipation in development," by virtue of which mechanisms are supposed to be set up in the embryo well before the organism needs them (preparation for the future, for example, callosities, plantar pads, hooves).* Guyénot, in his turn, talks in the same way of "the prophetic functioning of the organism."

To see anticipatory processes in facts such as these is perfectly permissible, provided one begins by characterizing anticipation causally as being the outcome of the transfer or generalization of information previously organized into schemata or cycles and preserved as such throughout the process. In this case the previous information is clear, and its organization with autoconservation is clear too, since the genetic program conserved by the organization of the genome is what is involved. The transfer and generalization are clear also, since hereditary transmission during the "reproduction," or multiplication, of the original model is involved. So there is no particular reason to introduce a finalist argument here, unless it is insisted on as part and parcel of any living mechanism.

If two scholars like Cuénot and Guyénot feel that there is something mysterious about elementary callosities and hooves in embryonic life, it is for a very different reason from the one applicable to anticipation, since there is no problem about anticipation as such. It is because, as they fiercely deny all environmental influence although callosities and hooves have clearly no meaning except to be made use of in an environment, they cannot possibly see anything in this embryonic preformation but some preestablished harmony, and it is from this standpoint and only from this standpoint, therefore, that they regard anticipation, as a kind of prophecy with an inescapable odor of finalism about it. But ever since Waddington exorcised the effect of environment and made it compatible with the endogenous reorganizations of the genome, and since cyberneticians did the same for finalism, making anticipation and even regulation independent, there has been no reason

*See *Invention et finalité en biologie.*

for confusing anticipation with prophecy or for attributing a psychoid to the genome, thus basing morphogenetic anticipations on some intelligent and conscious deduction; regulations and organic transfers are all that is necessary to this end.

Still to be reviewed is the vast collection of anticipatory processes which go to make up instinct, that is, in the field of anticipations that depend on the genetic program and not, or not exclusively, on acquired information. This subject was not dealt with above because, although behaviors are involved, they are not of the kind in which learning predominates. It is true that the younger generation of ethologists, who have given thought to the inseparable interactions between the genetic program and environmental influence demonstrated in every phenotypic process, are refusing to consider instinct as something entirely innate (they speak of "behavior such as used to be called innate"), and Lehrmann, in particular, underlines the part that exercise or acquisition can play at every level. This does not take away from the fact that the unleashing of an instinct does not follow the same laws as an act of learning based on information acquired from the external world. From that point, instinct is the model for behavior which is both preestablished, since it rests on genetic information to a large extent, and yet also remarkably anticipatory, since it adjusts itself to external environment as though it had both knowledge of the end in view and instrumental relationships subordinating to this end a series of successive and connected means in a soundly adapted manner.

In reality, the knowledge involved in instinct is merely reactions to "significant stimuli" to which the organism is sensitized by its hormones (appetitive behavior), leading to "consummatory actions" which succeed one another in a series of elementary reactions. It is nonetheless true that, from the point of view of the biological cycle that is maintained by means of this hierarchical behavior pattern, the instincts present a commonplace yet extremely impressive example of anticipations based on previous information that is largely genetic and, in varying proportion, also acquired.

AN EXAMPLE OF MORPHOGENETIC ANTICIPATION

IN THE PLANT KINGDOM

I have been planning for some years now to make a closer examination of one particular case of morphogenetic anticipation in the field of phenotypic reactions among organized entities lacking a nervous system, such as plants. The development of a flower or of the plant's essential organs provides, in a natural way, examples of anticipation as Cuénot understands it. These instances of anticipation, however, though closely dependent on external factors such as light and temperature, are too well programmed, genetically, to provide a field for easy analysis of how previous information is put to use. On the other hand, in plant reproduction there are enough variations between one species and the next and, sometimes, from one variety to the next, for more or less random comparisons to be made. For example, a species of lily, *Lilium bulbiferum* L., produces axillary bulblets, while the subspecies *L. croceum* produces none; in this case the formation of the bulblets surely has some anticipatory significance where reproduction is concerned, and this anticipation would seem to be due to the transfer to an above-ground level of processes which normally take place underground, such as the division of the bulb into bulblets.*

As a testing ground for my analysis, I therefore selected a case which is analogous but of wider application: that of the shedding of sterile secondary branches from the *Sedum*, a genus of thick-leaved plants (Crassulacae) whose branches often fail without dying (because of their fleshiness) and give birth to new plants by putting down adventitious roots that automatically take root. We raised, over a period of years, about 150 species of *Sedum*, the European, the Asiatic, the African, and the American kind, some indoors and some outdoors, and at varying altitudes. We also did a series of close studies of the same species or varieties in their natural conditions in varying environments.

The interesting fact with respect to anticipation, and that is what concerns us here, is that the shedding of these branches varies a great deal from one species to another (among those that have such branches) and even from one environment to another in the same species, and sometimes even in one particular plant. Now, in those cases where shedding is frequent or even systematic (as in the *Sedum nicaeene* All. in the Mediterranean basin and also in several American species), this shedding seems to have been prepared for by a fairly distinct morphological device, consisting of a circular groove (or channel) at the point where the branch is inserted (Figure 2B), or a groove which allows of some shrinkage so that abscission can be made (Figure 2C). The branches which are not going to be shed are usually of type A insertion. Moreover, it sometimes happens, not necessarily or even very frequently,

---

*In any attempt to describe the general characteristics of reactional processes, without limiting oneself to the cases in which these processes are subject to the activity of the nervous system, they will be seen to fall into two categories. The first kind of reaction (one higher form of which is the reflex action) has the two following characteristics: (1) the periodic triggering off of a hereditary apparatus, which then goes forward in *ne varietur* fashion; (2) this trigger action is provoked by external stimuli of a specific kind. Now the distinguishing factor about all plant growth, as compared with animal growth, is that there is a periodic recurrence of these triggered developments. Whereas an animal has one genital system, which always remains the same, and an invariable number of paws, etc., a plant loses its flowers every year only to see them bloom again, thanks to some specific stimulus (light, etc.) or never to bloom again, for lack of such stimulus. It also produces a number of stems, but this number may vary from one year to the next, and so on. The second class of reactions includes, on the contrary, processes which are variable in terms of exchanges with external surroundings. It is characteristic of this class to have transfer and generalization processes (generalization of the response, or of the stimulus or both). In the animal kingdom, the examples we can cite are the conditioning and formation of habits. In the plant kingdom, not much study has been made of transfer processes (except by Corner, Miège, and Agnès Aber), because they are only becoming acceptable again, no doubt, in an epigenetic context and have no meaning if looked at from the purely genotypic preformation point of view. The facts such as we shall describe them in the present section do seem to provide quite a clear example (for further details see J. Piaget, *Observations sur le mode d'insertion et la chute des rameaux secondaires chez les Sedum, Candollea,* 1966), but it is possible that these notions about functional generalization and transfer will throw some light on certain quite vital questions such as those of the flower's connection with the other parts of the plant (Goethe's theories, etc.).

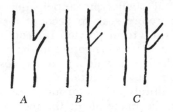

A   B   C

Figure 2

that adventitous roots sprout near the insertion even before the branch is shed. These characteristics taken together would seem to constitute a morphogenetic anticipation of the shedding, and, indeed, in the case of those species where the C type insertions predominate, it is difficult to touch one tuft of a plant or transplant it without abscission resulting from the slightest shake. In its natural state, all that is needed is a fall of rain or gust of air or a swarm of grasshoppers for fallen branches to be seen.

We must now point out that this anticipation is linked on to a definitely reactional process, which, in extreme cases, recalls the sort of autonomous reflex often found in crabs, lizards, dormice, and so on, although in this case the branch that has been shed engenders a completely new individual growth (which recalls a regeneration mechanism as in the shedding of leaves in the *Sedum stahlii Solms*) and does not break away in order to protect the parent plant. Of course, this reactional process is linked to genetic conditions, in the sense that not every species evinces it, at least not with the same frequency. There does exist one group of hardy species such as the *Sedum acre* L. in Europe or the *Sedum moranese* H.B. in Mexico, which only show infrequent shedding and have but few of the *B-C* insertions, and this is the case with nearly all the annual species whose reproduction is almost entirely sexual rather than vegetative. But in those species where shedding is frequent, its reactional character is typified by variations according to environment: the *Sedum album* L., for example, shows shedding and insertions of the *B-C* type, occurring much more frequently in the Alps at 2000 meters than at 1000 meters (in the case of the *Sedum montanum* the reverse is true). Some American species raised in Geneva alternately indoors and outdoors regularly changed the frequency of shedding and the modes of insertion as they went from one situation to the other.

It may be replied, at this point, that such shedding and insertion methods are constantly being subjected to a precise form of determinism: the part played by desiccation, aliment, light, and so on. This goes without saying, and I would expect such determinism to be recognized, although that is certainly not the case in this particular sector. However, the external factors do nothing to explain why there should be abscission, shedding, and vegetative reproduction rather than simple growth or necrosis; these factors must therefore be on a different plane from the overall process of separation—a process that remains anticipatory in nature (just as the flower is anticipated in the bud, and the stages of its development are not brought about simply by light or other factors that accelerate or inhibit its flowering).

This reactional and phenotypic anticipation calls for an explanation, and we shall therefore seek to account for it by starting off, in accordance with the rule, from previously acquired information.

In the first place it is possible to group the species in distinct categories according to whether they do, or do not, possess secondary sterile branches and whether they are attached to twigs or shoots growing along the ground or entirely off the ground. . . . Next, an exact statistical statement should be made about the methods of insertion (A, B, or C, with subdivisions that are of no interest in this context), by categories and species, and insertion methods in underground branches (roots, rhizomes, underground suckers) should be examined.

It will quickly be noticed that the separation processes begin in the parts underground and then extend throughout the ground shoots. Now, at these two levels there is nothing anticipatory about the process, which is simply a causal chain of events: (α) growth of the branch; (β) putting down of adventitous roots at its base but level with the top of the earth; (γ) gradual independence of the branch fed by its own roots as well as by the twig supporting it; (δ) beginning of separation (insertion A turns into form B or C); (ϵ) complete separation.

It will further be noticed that each of these links in the chain has caused a reaction in the one preceding it and has strengthened it, so that the lineal chain becomes a feedback system and, hence, a kind of schema whose parts become interdependent during the growth process.* Thus, all that is needed to account for the anticipatory nature of the process while the branches remain strictly aboveground level is to recognize a transfer of the schema, from underground to aboveground level, as in the case of the *Lilium* to which we referred earlier.

The best indication of the fact that transfer takes place is that the process is gradual. By comparing the statistics of insertion methods in two successive categories, a clear correlation will be found between the connections $(B + C)/A$ and C/B, which steadily increase in importance, and this shows a slow progression in the direction of insertion (form C) and abscission of branches.

In sum, we can confirm that in simple plant forms there are reactional processes which, acting as a schema, become anticipatory by the transfer of this schema from one level of the anatomo-physiological organization to another. The anticipatory function evident in every habit and every conditioning thus recurs both in phenotypic plant adaptations and in animal behavior. . . .

---

*Compare Figure 1 under V and V(2), the feedback system in this case being due to the fact that the causal actions are accompanied by return actions.

42

Phenocopy in Biology and the Psychological Development of Knowledge*

1975

In a work called *Biology and Knowledge* we sought to show the relationship and functional continuity that connect the process of the formation and development of knowledge to the biological mechanisms of autoregulation peculiar to the organism. In this brief article we should like to adduce a new example of these fundamental analogies. In order to facilitate this comparison, we will be using a terminology upon which it would be well to agree. In biology we can call "exogenous" a variation imposed by the environment, thus phenotypical and not hereditary, while we reserve the term "endogenous" for genotypical variations. The resulting phenotype is always dependent on the "norm of reactions" of the corresponding genotype but always with a momentary action by the environment as well. In psychology, in the same way, we will call "exogenous" the information drawn from experience and thus empirical, although it always presupposes an assimilative framework of endogenous origin. On the other hand, we will generalize the term "endogenous" when applying it to knowledge which, without being innate, is drawn from the internal and necessary coordinations of actions, since these coordinations are the product of interior structurations and not of exogenous experience.

The purpose of this essay is, first, to show that one of the most general processes in the development of cognitive structures consists in *replacing* exogenous knowledge by endogenous reconstructions that reconstitute the same forms but incorporate them into systems whose internal composition is a prerequisite. Second, we will seek to demonstrate the biological equivalent of this process in the mechanism of *phenocopy*: an exogenous phenotype is neither interiorized nor fixed, but followed by and entirely replaced by a genotype of the same form, now reconstructed by purely endogenous mechanisms. The convergence

*This selection was written and translated especially for this volume.

of these two processes, cognitive and biological, perhaps indicates a broader role for the phenocopy than has generally been granted—particularly in those widespread realms where modifications of organs and behavior are necessarily interdependent.

The Replacement of Exogenous Knowledge by Endogenous Reconstructions

(1) We will call "exogenous" knowledge originating in the *observables*, i.e., based on experience with external objects, or with material aspects and results of the actions of the subject; for example, to establish that one object is heavier than another or that one action is of longer duration than another. We will speak, on the other hand, of "endogenous" knowledge when it is derived from the internal coordination of the actions or operations of the subject: for example, in transitivity, we have $A < C$ if $A < B$ and $B < C$. The distinctive character of endogenous knowledge is thus its *necessity*, as opposed to the simple matters of fact that exogenous knowledge records.

But we must recall that all exogenous knowledge presupposes an endogenous framework, since it implies an "assimilation" and not simply associations among perceptions. Now assimilation requires assimilative instruments, such as setting into relation or into correspondence the attributions of predicates, etc.; these instruments apply endogenous frameworks or "forms," even if their "contents" are exogenous. Such endogenous inferences can be applied to any objects whatsoever and to functioning even without objects, as in "pure" mathematics.

Beginning with the cognitive development of the child and throughout the entire course of the history of scientific thought, we can observe a more or less continuous passage from exogenous to endogenous knowledge. This is the nature of the case, since the general tendency of the mind is to pass beyond empiricism in the direction of deductive models. But the fundamental problem is to establish what this passage consists of. There are two possible interpretations: either it can be reduced to a simple interiorization or else there is replacement with reconstruction on a new level. The hypothesis of interiorization would not reappear here merely for the purpose of admitting that all material experience can be interiorized as mental experience; this form of interiorization goes without saying and we admit it like everyone else.* But the hypothesis of pure interiorization would further imply that physical experiences thus interiorized in mental representations would then be able to acquire directly the status of logico-mathematical connections; logic and mathematics would thus constitute only a "well-made language" assuring exogenous knowledge a seemingly endogenous status but by a simple translation of physical properties into linguistically appropriate expressions. Now it is on this point that the difficulties arise.

---

*But let me recall that even in this case we have always insisted on the fact that all interiorization of action demands a reconstruction on the level of conceptualization.

The facts suggest that endogenous knowledge exhibits autonomous structuration without thereby being reduced to interiorization of exogenous contributions, but rather completing them by reconstructions that go far beyond them and tend to replace them more or less completely according to the areas involved.

Before turning to the examination of some of these facts, let us first remember that, according to all our earlier researches, it seemed clear that the formation of logico-mathematical structures starts well before language. It goes forward to general coordinations of actions that we see afterward developing from the constitution of sensorimotor intelligence itself: relations of order, elaboration of schemata and their inclusion in other schemata, making correspondences, etc. These "forms" of nature are already logico-mathematical, deriving from the coordination of actions and not from their material aspects or results, and preparing the way for the acquisition of language rather than deriving from it. There exist then some endogenous "forms" from the outset of mental life and they serve as frameworks or assimilative instruments in the recording of exogenous knowledge before acquiring their independence and functioning for themselves. Thus it is clear that endogenous knowledge does not result from an interiorization of exogenous acquired knowledge since it permits and conditions not only this interiorization but also the possession, that is to say, the understanding of all knowledge drawn from experience.

But the role of endogenous knowledge, logico-mathematical knowledge, is even more considerable, since after its elementary forms have allowed the registration of the exogenous facts, these forms develop to the point of engendering operatory structures (such as "groups" or "lattices") as prolongations of the coordination of actions. Such endogenous structures not only reinforce the experimental capacities of the subject—they tend to reconstruct the results of experience in the form of deductive models: by new objects of thought considerably more powerful and far-reaching than the observable objects still limited to the plane of phenomena.

(2) An observation made some time ago with B. Inhelder clearly showed the difference between exogenous and endogenous perceptions, as well as the difference between the simple interiorization of the former and its reconstruction when replaced by the latter. We asked a child to place with one hand a red bead in a container, at the same time as he placed, with the other hand, a blue bead in a second container—only the latter remained partly concealed. The two questions that arose then were to decide (a) if the two collections thus constructed were equal or not; and (b) if they would remain equal if there were an indefinite continuation of this setting into correspondence term for term. The principal interest in the observed reaction was that at an elementary level the child, even without being able to perceive the result of his action in the second container, accepts the equality of the two collections as self-evident, but refuses to predict the result of continuing the process, as if he were not certain that if $n = n$ one would always have $n + 1$ equaling $n + 1$, etc. At times, it is true, he supposes it as possible or even probable, but this would come under the heading of extensional or empirical generalization based on the results of preceding actions and not on the logical necessity of the coordination of actions $n + 1 = n + 1$. The proof

of this is that if one begins with a visible inequality (for example, 3 in the first jar and 0 in the second before screening it), the subject then thinks that in adding one bead to the container each time, one would end up by arriving at equality, $n = n$, as if the initial inequality $3 = 0$ could be canceled by the succeeding equal additions.

On a second level, however, the child no longer reasons simply on the result (observed or interiorized) of his already executed actions but on the coordinations themselves, from which certain generalizations are conceived as necessary (in this situation, to be sure, particularly simple); a 5½-year-old boy once told us, "When one knows once, one knows for always," in other words, the inequalities like the equalities are conserved even if one continues indefinitely the one-to-one correspondence.

(3) This example is representative of a number of others one could cite in the logico-mathematical realm. The general process is thus a *replacement* of exogenous knowledge by an endogenous reconstruction. At the outset, the subject acts on the objects and takes cognizance of only the result of these actions; thus the addition of a blue bead in one container for a red in the other without consciousness of either the internal mechanism of this correspondence as a system of connected actions or of the fact that the sums of the blues and the reds are the function of initial equalities or inequalities. The child's lack of awareness of the endogenous mechanism of the correspondence thus prevents him from foreseeing the result of actions not yet performed. As soon, however, as the setting into correspondence is understood as the endogenous coordination of the actions of the subject, the latter deduces that if $n = n$, then $n + 1 = n + 1$ and does so indefinitely. In this case the equalities are no longer simply based on empirical verification, material or interiorized, but on necessary combinations whose logical nature depends on their endogenous character. The result of actions is thereafter no longer seen as an aggregate of exterior observables, but as the intrinsic consequence of the coordination of actions themselves.

Thus we see that the relation between initial exogenous knowledge and final endogenous certitude is not a relation of simple prolongation or of interiorization but rather a replacement by deductive reconstruction— which is quite another matter—since there are then necessary inferences such as recurrences and grasping the "reasons" for the transition from $n = n$ to $n + n = n + 1$.

(4) Now it is essential to note that this tendency to replace exogenous knowledge by endogenous reconstructions is not confined to the logico-mathematical realm but is found throughout the development of physical causality. Let us examine, for example, one experiment on the "mediated" transmission of movement, that is across objects that do not change their positions. Let $ABCDE$ be a linear series of unmoving marbles that touch each other, P a moving ball that rolls down a slope and hits A; in this case balls A–D remain in their places and only ball E is propelled forward. To explain this phenomenon, children of 5 to 6 think that each ball displaces the following one by an "immediate" transmission, and they believe they have actually "seen" this happen. You cannot correct this error even by making a guiding mark that shows the immobility of one of the mediating balls or asking the child to put his finger on it. From 7 to 8, however, the deviant transmission is explained by a new notion: the "élan" that the active ball P gives to the

following ones and that "traverses" them up to the last one, E. Now, this notion of a "push that traverses" the intervening balls is endogenous from two points of view. In the first place, the passage "across" is no longer an observable but the product of a deduction. In the second, this inference does not arise without reason but is the result of transitivity ($A = C$ if $A = B$ and $B = C$), which at this age has been established in all situations, while before then it was not understood as necessary. This causal transitivity that characterizes mediate transmission of movement is interesting because in such a case, the transitivity is not simply utilized and "applied" by the subject; it is "attributed" to the objects themselves, then considered and conceived as "operators" of transitivity but on the models of endogenous operations of the subject. In a general way, any causal explanation (or deductive model of the phenomenon to be explained) consists in attributing operatory structures to objects and to external events that are mathematical and appropriate to the endogenous elaborations of the subject. Let us think, for example, of the immense importance that the structure of "group" has taken in explanatory theories of physical phenomena.

We see that causality itself consists in a deductive reconstruction and in this endogenous meaning knowledge is supplied by experience as much as by simple laws or repeatable relations among observables. From this point of view, there is once again replacement of the exogenous by the endogenous inasmuch as this leads to a reconstruction properly speaking and not to a purely extensional generalization of initial laws.

(5) Finally, to consider the various systems of regulations and equilibration that control the psychogenesis of knowledge, we observe a succession of three levels that are particularly instructive with regard to comparisons that must be drawn between cognitive processes and phenocopy.

On the first of these levels, when a perturbation occurs that alters goal-directed behavior, or an attempt to predict or to explain, this perturbation gives rise to an attempt at compensation or even of suppression. For example, when the child rolls ball A in the direction of the center of ball B, he knows that B will move away along the prolongation of the trajectory AB. If we now ask him to aim at a side of B, he believes that the effect will be the same, and when he sees B take off from the side opposite to B', he interprets this fact as merely an annoying perturbation; he begins again, for example, rolling A with greater force at B', as if this would cancel the perturbation. We shall call this attempt to cancel perturbations *alpha-behavior*.

In *beta-behavior*, the subject seeks to take the perturbation into account and to reconcile it with notions and predictions previously accepted. For example, before aiming at B' he predicts that B will take off to one side but without knowing which side. Then he changes his own position so as to be opposite B' and observes that B moves along the prolongation of AB'. He then comes back to his place and takes account of what he has just learned; it is this beginning of the integration of the perturbation that characterizes beta-behavior.

In *gamma-behavior*, finally, the subject no longer considers rolling the ball at the point B' as a perturbation but as one of the possible variations intrinsic to the system. This system is understood and generalized, the ball *B* taking off always on the side opposite to the point of impact reached by ball *A*, following a line that passes through the center of gravity of *B*. The integration of possible variations thus gives way to a deductive and explanatory system in which what was at first a perturbation has now become an integral part. Following the well-known formula of H. von Foerster, we have here an example of a process "from noise to order" and this is a new and indeed very general case of the replacement of exogenous knowledge by an endogenous reconstruction as a source of comprehension and explication.

Phenocopy Insofar as It Acts as Replacement of an Exogenous Phenotype by an Endogenous Genotype of the Same Form

(1) From the biological point of view, it seems clear that exogenous knowledge corresponds to phenotypical reactions, while endogenous knowledge is either related to a hereditary programming of structures, or to the regulations entailed in epigenesis that are in part controlled by the genome* and in part by adaptations to the milieu. That being so, if knowledge or endogenous reactions result only from the interiorization of exogenous events, we would be led to a Lamarckian interpretation of their formation. But the heredity of acquired characteristics has never been verified by biological or psychological experiments. If, however, endogenous knowledge has an origin entirely independent of all relation to exogenous events, that would mean that it is "innate," as the term is understood in contemporary genetics. This is the position of K. Lorenz, for example, who recognizes, however, that heredity varies from one animal species to another—which deprives innate knowledge of all its necessary generality and reduces it to a simple "innate working hypothesis." It is also the position of N. Chomsky with his innate deep strutures.†

Now the hypothesis of the purely "innate" character of endogenous knowledge raises the gravest problems. According to the dominant opinion in biology, hereditary characteristics are explained only by chance production and selection after the event that retains only those mutations that permit improved adaptation to the environment. But if notions of chance and exterior selection already appear insufficient to a good many authors on the level of organic variation, their meaning

---

*[*Genome*: The entire complex of hereditary material functioning as a whole and composed of interacting elements, i.e., genes. Piaget's choosing to speak of genomic rather genetic control of development is an extension of his particular type of interactionism, in which the main arena for the interaction of factors lies within the organism rather than between it and the environment.]

†But Chomsky's innate deep structures are more and more being abandoned by specialists in the problem; see the works of R. Brown, of E. Lenneberg and, more recently, of D. McNeill.

requires a serious reexamination in applying them to the formation of endogenous knowledge.

Can we say, for example, that logical and mathematical structures are born of hypotheses arising only by chance and that their correspondence with reality is due to a selection assuring a better survival or a better rate of sexual reproduction to the individuals capable of generalizing the operation $n + 1$ to infinity? It is clear that if chance can intervene at the time of mathematical discoveries, it is only in the course of trial and error and thus of gropings that are always directed, and that if selection intervenes in the choice among several models it is based on the power these models confer on the subject in his actions *upon* reality (and not a consequence of mechanical selection). If we want to connect the formation of endogenous knowledge to biological mechanisms, as is our intention, then we must find situations in which exogenous variations of phenotypes play a role from the start, but (a) without interiorization of the exogenous in the endogenous, which would be a return to Lamarckism; (b) with endogenous reconstruction corresponding to the initial exogenous characteristics. It would be essential to find in the biological terrain situations analogous to those we have analyzed in the first part of this article for the cognitive domain.

(2) Now these situations exist and are even more frequent than we think; these are cases of *phenocopies* but on condition that we interpret them as reconstructions by an *ulterior* genotype of the characteristics that an *anterior* phenotype presented. K. Lorenz, who cites the case of behavior at first phenotypical, then hereditarily, reconstituted, proposes the term *genocopy** but we prefer to retain the current term *phenocopy* since the majority of writers actually do interpret it in the way we have just suggested (without always saying so explicitly). It is true that other authors give a quite different meaning to the term phenocopy, such as that distinct genotypes can produce like phenotypes. In what follows, however, we will retain the indicated definition: replacement of an initial phenotype by a subsequent genotype presenting the same distinctive characteristics.

Given the interest of possible comparisons between phenocopy and cognitive processes, for many years we have studied by means of multiple breedings two clear cases of phenocopies, one concerned with a mollusc common in Swiss marshes and lakes, *Limnaea stagnalis*, and the other with several of the widely distributed species of juicy plants (*Crassulaceae*) known under the name of *Sedum*.

The case of *Limnaea stagnalis* is the more spectacular. In tranquil waters this species appears in elongated form while on pebbly shores that are agitated by the waves of large lakes, they assume a quite different, globular shape. In a great number of locations this is simply a matter of a nonhereditary phenotype (from the first generation born in an aquarium the descendants are elongated) the formation of which is easy to explain. At the time of each agitation by the waves the animal in the course of its growth attaches itself to its solid support, which dilates the opening. At the same time and even because of this, it draws on the muscle that attaches it to its shell and this tends to shorten the

*See K. Lorenz, *On Aggression* (New York: Harcourt, Brace and World, 1955).

spire (i.e., the upper part of the spiral shell). But if the forms exhibiting average contraction (thus globular) remain in the stage of phenotypes, we find on the shores most exposed to the wind (and only in these places) the most globular shapes, and these are hereditary. We have verified this for six generations in aquarium (in numerous lines), and for sixteen years in a small pond at quite a distance from the lake. This hereditary genotype, very similar in form to the phenotypes just mentioned (but more accentuated) thus constitutes a fine case of phenocopy.*

As to the *Sedum*, we are able to observe various forms of phenocopy. For example, *Sedum album*, very common in flat country, appears at a 2000 m. altitude, in the form of a phenotype of small size that, transplanted at 1000 m. or 1600 m., soon recovers its normal size. In Savoy, however, there are two summits where, at 1,900 and 2,000 m., the small-sized form constitutes a genotype (cf. var. *micranthum*) and retains its characteristics from one generation to the next, once it is transplanted at Geneva. We studied particularly a not-yet-known variety (that we have named var. *parvulum*) of the *Sedum sediforme*, very widespread around the Mediterranean. This type of species is of great size and its color is generally glaucous. The var. *parvulum* that one finds at heights or in places north of the usual habitat of the species are of very small size, with thicker leaves and generally of a dark green color, due (as one of our colleagues, a professional botanist, has confirmed) to an increase in chlorophyll and in photosynthetic power. In this case, as in preceding ones, we find numerous *parvulum* phenotypes but also we find in some places a genotype, the stability of which we have verified over thousands of descendants at 400 m., 1000 m., and 1600 m. altitudes. Here again the genotype, rarer than the phenotype, has replaced them under certain conditions, and this again constitutes a case of phenocopy.

(3) We must now seek to interpret this process of phenocopy, or the replacement of an exogenous variation by an endogenous variation of analogous morphology. The current explanation is one that Ehrlich and Holm have proposed,† drawing their inspiration from Lerner's two models of genetic and epigenetic homeostatis. In a constant environment, there is a production of a standard phenotype by the canalization of epigenesis. But in this case the same selective factors operated in the same way on the canalization of the mutations themselves, and a new genotype, actually imitating the preceding phenotype, will be genetically fixed, once having achieved a certain threshold or "selective plateau." This is due to the coadaptation of the genes and when it is achieved there are no longer any reversals, although these remain possible below this threshold.

But if all this is true, is it enough? What always amazes us in the interpretations of contemporary "orthodox" biology is the contrast be-

---

*If one were to raise the objection that the contracted genotype in the most agitated places is due only to an incidental mutation from natural selection, we would answer: (1) if it were due to chance, one would have to find a little of it everywhere (since we have verified that it survives in tranquil waters); this is not the case. (2) The selection of such a genotype would be useless since the contracted phenotype suffices for all needs.

†*The Process of Evolution* (New York: McGraw, 1963).

tween the active and "reactional" characteristics (in the sense of accommodative "responses") attributed to phenotypical variations, and the reliance on mere chance, without intrinsic directions with which the production of mutations must content itself. In the case of the phenotypes, the cause of the variations is exogenous since it is the environment, but the reaction emanates from an endogenous apparatus supplied with a system of highly differentiated and coordinated laws, the system of the epigenetic syntheses programmed by the genome and entering into interaction with the environment that selects the best responses. In the case of variations that are purely endogenous, thus entirely "innate" like mutations, their production is, however, supposed to remain purely accidental and there is no more than selection to expect, retaining what, by chance, will end up by resembling the phenotype, well adapted (over a long period).

In the case of our *Limnaea* and *Sedum* we thus see phenotypes exhibiting great reactivity. The globular *Limnaea* have chosen their environment (nothing prevents them living in tranquil surroundings and especially not from descending to several meters below the surface of the water) and they react by motor and muscular behavior that explains their shape. The *Sedum* also augment their powers by acting on the environment and are not simply under constraint; their reduced size achieves an optimal equilibrium between surfaces (nourishing) and volumes (to be nourished) and their increased chlorophyll is an active response to unfavorable environments and not a characteristic suffered merely as the effect of direct pressures.

Must it then be admitted that at the genotypical level the same properties must be rediscovered only after innumerable fortuitous variations not dictated by epigenetic demands of equilibration? At the genotypical level does the organism find only by chance selection, step by step, that which the phenotype meanwhile knows how to achieve so well?

(4) Let us then seek a model such that a relation exists between the phenotype and the genotype. In terms of dis- and re-equilibrations there are three relevant types of interaction: those among the regulations of the mutation, those of epigenetic syntheses (in particular the interlevel regulations that link the hierarchical stages of these synthesis), and those of the interior environment. New mutations would then come to be molded into the framework resulting from the formation of the anterior phenotype; this molding would thus be the result of organic selections (in Baldwin's sense) and not in a direct causal action of the phenotype on the genotype.

To make this hypothetical model more precise, let us call x, y, and z the characteristics of the exterior milieu that have evoked the formation of the initial phenotype, and call x', y', and z' the observable morphological characteristics that distinguish this phenotype; but let us specify that, beyond these new observable characteristics, there exist still others, not directly observable, that we will call x'', y'', and z'' that may modify the epigenetic syntheses and the interior milieu. There are then two possibilities. The first is that the characters x'', y'', and z'' do not disturb the equilibrium of the whole system; in this case the phenotype simply reconstitutes itself in each new generation and there is no production of phenocopy. The second is that, the characters x'', y'', and z'' modify the equilibrium at more and more profound levels; in this case, the disequilibrium gradually spreads until it sensitizes the regulatory genes controlling epigenetic syntheses and here is a "response" of the genome in the form of semiaccidental variations.*

But it must be emphatically specified that this gradually spreading disequilibrium contains nothing in the way of a coded or codable "message," and indicates in no way what is happening, nor what must be done, but only signifies that "something is not functioning," that there is some perturbation (but without indicating what it is). There is thus simply a series of blockages or disfunctions; now the feedbacks indicate only that this is not mysterious but that they are required by any relatively fine system of regulations: those of epigenesis are particularly rich in this regard.

As to the semiaccidental character of the responses of the genome, we understand by this that the mutations will not modify the regions of the system remaining in equilibrium and thus resistant, but will affect the disequilibrated zones, which implies a kind of regulation of mutation in the sense of L. L. Whyte or R. J. Britten and E. H. Davidson. Orienting these variations toward the unbalanced regions amounts to submitting them to organic selection imposed by the whole teleonomic system of epigenesis until the constitution of a new, stable equilibrium. These variations are thus adapted to the interior framework as modified by the phenotype. In this way there is a morphological continuity between the initial phenotype and the final genotype, but the latter is not an interiorization of the former, since it *replaces* and *reconstructs* it, without constituting a direct prolongation of it.

Conclusion

We can now see how much the process of phenocopy seems analogous, on the organic plane, to the replacement of the exogenous by the endogenous described earlier on the cognitive plane. In both cases the exogenous acquisition modifies the field of interior equilibrium of the organism or of the subject and in both cases there is a new and enriching reequilibration due to an endogenous reconstruction that replaces the exogenous contribution while reproducing its forms and integrating them in a restructuration of the whole. This is not explained by the pressures of the milieu but rather by the active and internal reactions (scanning, etc.) of the organism or of the subject acting on the milieu, which it modifies and utilizes without limiting itself to submission.

But does the process of phenocopy present some generalities? We believe that it must be supposed in all situations where the hereditary variations of an organ are from their beginning interdependent with a newly appearing behavior (the locomotion of tetrapod vertebrates, the

---

*See also the genetic assimilations of C. H. Waddington, but this noted author seems to us to go further than we do in the formative actions he attributes to the phenotype (see his "speculation" illustrated by Figure 36, p. 181, in his *The Strategy of the Genes* (London: Allen and Unwin).

flight of birds, etc.). Setting aside the problems of highly differentiated instincts, it is hard to see how a new behavior pattern could evolve without some phenotypical trials. It is thus in a collaboration between biology and psychology or ethology that we can expect certain kinds of progress in our knowledge.

We hope that we will be pardoned for the schematic and hypothetical character of this brief article. Right or wrong, we believe it is sometimes useful to formulate a general idea although it is not yet verified. Its role can then be precisely that of evoking new analyses the results of which may be positive or negative, but even the refutation of an adventurous hypothesis is an advance in knowledge.

43

The Stages of Intellectual Development in

Childhood and Adolescence*

1955

INTRODUCTORY NOTES

In the spring of 1955, a symposium was held in Geneva on the subject of stages of psychological development.* Piaget's paper, together with his remarks in the discussion, represent his fullest statement on this subject. In our translation of this eight-page paper, we have omitted two and a half pages that simply describe the three major periods of cognitive development, covered amply elsewhere in this volume. We have included some of Piaget's remarks made in discussion, in which he spoke trenchantly on the question of the unevenness of development, and gave a brief but subtle account of the relation between his more general metatheoretical views and his conception of stages. For the editors' commentary on Piaget on stages, see the Introduction to this volume.

The stages of intellectual operations constitute a privileged case from which we cannot generalize to other domains. If we consider, for example, the development of perception in the child, or the development of language, we observe a continuity quite different and much greater than can be observed on the terrain of logico-mathematical operations. In the domain of perception in particular, I would be unable to give you a table of stages like the one I can propose with regard to intellectual operations, because we rediscover that continuity of which Tanner was speaking from an organic point of view, a continuity which one can

* Le Problème des Stades en Psychologie de l'Enfant, Symposium de l'Association de langue française, by P. Osterrieth, J. Piaget, R. de Saussure, J. M. Tanner, H. Wallon, R. Zazzo, B. Inhelder, and A. Rey (Paris: Presses Universitaires de France, 1956). From J. Piaget, The Child in Reality. Copyright © 1973, The Viking Press, Inc. Adapted by permission of Grossman Publishers. Translated by H.E.G. and J.J.V. The conference was presided over by A. Michotte. The paper by B. Inhelder, "From Perceptual Configurations to Operatory Structures," was essentially a review of research then in progress, in which she and Piaget were collaborating.

divide up according to some agreed upon convention, but which presents no distinct and natural divisions.

In contrast, in the domain of intellectual operations, we can observe a double phenomenon: on the one hand, we see structures forming and we can follow them from the first lineaments, and on the other hand, we can observe their completion, that is, the constitution of stages of equilibrium. Take, for example, the organization of integers: we can follow this structuration beginning with the numbers 1, 2, 3, etc., until the moment when the child discovers the sequence of numbers and at the same time the first arithmetical operations. At a given moment, such a structure is therefore constituted and arrives at its level of equilibrium, and this equilibrium is so stable that the integers are not modified throughout the rest of life, even as they are integrated in more complex systems (fractional numbers, etc.). We are thus in the presence of a privileged domain, at the heart of which we can observe the formation of structures and their completion, and where different structures succeed each other, or are integrated with each other in various combinations.

In this special domain, and I repeat, without raising the problem of generalization, I will call *stages* those divisions that display the following characteristics:

(1) If we are to speak of stages, *the order of succession of acquisitions must be constant*. Not the timing, but the order of succession. One can characterize stages in a population by a chronology, but this chronology is extremely variable; it depends on the previous experience of the individuals, and not only on their maturation, and it depends especially on the social milieu that can accelerate or retard the appearance of a stage, or even prevent its appearance. We are confronted here with considerable complexity and I would not be able to pass judgment on the value of the mean ages of our stages with regard to any other population. I consider the ages only relative to the populations with which we have worked; they are therefore essentially relative. On the other hand, if we are speaking of stages, the order of succession of behaviors must be considered as constant, that is to say, a character will not appear before another in a certain number of subjects and after another in another group of subjects. Where we find such variations, the characters in question are not useable in establishing stages.

(2) The *integrative character of stages*: the structures constructed at a given age become an integral part of the structures of the following age. For example, the permanent object that is constructed at the sensorimotor level will be an integral element in notions of conservation formed later (when there will be conservation of an ensemble, or of a collection, or of an object undergoing deformation in its spatial appearance). In the same way, the operations that we call concrete will constitute an integral part of formal operations, in the sense that the latter will constitute a new structure but resting on the former, which are thus treated as their contents (formal operations thus constituting operations effectuated upon other operations).

(3) We have always sought, together with Inhelder, to characterize a stage, not by the juxtaposition of unrelated properties, but by a *structure of the whole* (*structure d'ensemble*) and this notion takes on a

precise meaning in the domain of intelligence, more precise than else-where. Such a structure would be, for example at the level of concrete operations, a grouping (*groupement*), with the logical characteristics of a grouping that one finds in classification or in seriation. Later on, the structure at the level of formal operations will be the group of four transformations of which I will speak in a moment, or the network. Thus one knows that a child who has achieved this or that structure is capable of a multiplicity of distinct operations, and sometimes without any obvious visible relationship among them. This is the advantage of the notion of structures: when they are complex, they permit us to reduce a collection of operatory schemes without any apparent relations among them to a higher unity; the structure of the whole as such is therefore characteristic of a stage.

(4) A stage includes a level of *preparation* on the one hand, and of *completion* on the other. For example, for formal operations the stage of preparation will be the whole period from 11 to 13–14 years and the completion will be the phase of equilibrium that then appears.

(5) But as the preparation of later acquisitions can bear on more than one stage (with varied overlappings among longer and shorter preparations), and as there exist different degrees of stability in these completions, it is necessary to distinguish, in every sequence of stages, the *processes of formation* or the genesis and the *forms of final equilib-rium* (in a relative sense): the latter alone constitute the structures of the whole referred to above while the formative processes appear in the successive differentiations of such structures (differentiation of the preceding structure and preparation of the following one).

I would like, finally, to emphasize the notion of *décalage*, to which we will return tomorrow since it might present an obstacle to the gen-eralization of stages, and to introduce certain cautions and limitations. *Décalages* characterize the repetition or the reproduction of the same formative process and different ages. We will distinguish *horizontal décalages* from *vertical décalages*.

We will speak of horizontal *décalages* when the same operation is applied to different contents. In the domain of concrete operations, for example, a child of about 7–8 years will know how to seriate quanti-tities of matter, lengths, etc.: he will know how to classify them, enumerate them, measure them, etc.: he will also arrive at notions of conservation relative to these same contents. But he will be incapable of any operations in the domain of weight, although two years later, on the average, he will be able to generalize them in applying them to this new content. From a formal point of view, the operations are the same in the two cases, but applied to different domains. In this case we will speak of horizontal *décalage* within a period.

A vertical *décalage*, on the other hand, is the reconstruction of a structure by means of other operations. The baby, toward the end of the sensorimotor period, attains what we may call, with H. Poincaré, a "group of displacements": he will be able to orient himself in his apart-ment with detours and returns, etc. But this "group" is solely practical and not at all representational. When, several years later, it is a matter of representing these same displacements, that is, imagining them or interiorizing them in operations, we find analogous developmental steps, but this time on another level, that of representation. It is then a matter of other operations, and in this case we will speak of vertical *décalage*. . . .

[At this point, in a few pages, Piaget describes the three major periods of intellectual development: sensorimotor, concrete operations, and formal operations.]

I will conclude by saying that these three major periods, with their particular stages, constitute processes of successive equilibration, steps toward equilibrium. As soon as equilibrium is attained in one matter, the structure is integrated into a new system being formed, until a new equilibrium is reached, always stabler and always over a wider field.

It should be recalled that equilibrium is defined by reversibility. To say that there is a movement toward equilibrium means that intellectual development is characterized by a growing reversibility. Reversibility is the most evident characteristic of the activity of intelligence, which is capable of detours and returns. This reversibility increases regularly, step by step, in the course of the stages that I have just briefly described.

In this privileged domain of intellectual operations, then, we arrive at a simple and regular system of stages, but this is perhaps specific to such a domain, and we cannot, for example, simply apply this system to perception, for example, where I would be incapable of describing such stages.

[In the discussion following the initial papers of the symposium, P. A. Osterrieth attempted to show that underlying the seeming diversity, sequences, and names assigned to stages of development by different authors, there were certain unifying tendencies and certain general stages that could be detected. Piaget objected strongly to this effort at conciliation. The gist of Piaget's remarks was: (a) the purpose of constructing stages is to provide an instrument of analysis and (b) the organism does not develop evenly: different subsystems are partially independent of each other and develop at different rates. This being the case, different authors, focusing on different aspects of development are bound to discover (or better, construct) different stages.]

Why does everyone speak of stages? One tries to construct stages because this is an *indispensable instrument for the analysis of formative processes*. Genetic psychology attempts to envisage the construction of mental functions, and stages are a necessary instrument for the analysis of these formative processes. But I must vigorously insist on the fact that stages do not constitute an aim in their own right. I would compare them to zoological or botanical classification in biology, which is an instrument that must precede analysis. . . .

We must consider different dimensions of growth: dental age, skeletal age, cerebral age, endocrinal age. These ages do not all exibit the same development. There are certain minor parallelisms, but there is a multiplicity of functions that develop in relative independence. This is a fundamental fact for psychology.

In *psychology*, who speaks of general stages invokes a postulate that seems to me unproven: the unity of the personality of the child. . . . In speaking of the unity of personality we can express two quite different things that it will be well to distinguish.

First, *functional unity*. Personality is the expression of a certain number of relatively independent functions, and, of course, at each moment the individual must arrive at some unity within himself among these tendencies, sometimes antagonistic, that lead him in diverging directions, and that he must reconcile. This functional unity is evident. Everyone admits it, but it is not sufficient for the construction of stages.

Second, *structural unity* of the person. I have nowhere seen structural unity, at any stage of development of the child. Neither do I see it in most adults. I am myself a multiple personality, divided and contradictory. In certain cases, I force myself to be a serious man, as in professional situations. But in other situations I am infantile or I behave like an adolescent. There are conflicts within me among these multiple tendencies. I do not achieve structural unity. The only structural unity I know of is the unity of the person as the social being that I represent, but which does not cover all. How then would you expect structural unity in the child if it does not exist in the adult? And if there is no structural unity, there are not general stages that permit fixed and verifiable correspondences in all domains, among all functions. . . .

[Piaget went on to point out that this lack of unity presents certain interesting research opportunities. For example, we can establish independently the sequence of stages pertaining to the object relationship in the psychoanalytic sense and the sequence of stages pertaining to the construction of the permanent object in the Piagetian sense; we can then examine the temporal relationship between these two sequences, and discover which precedes and might therefore cause the other. Later on in the discussion Piaget took up another aspect of the unevenness of development.]

Does the fact that stages are more clearly defined in the domain of logico-mathematical operations depend on the very nature of the reality to which these stages pertain? I was most attracted by the hypothesis presented by Fauville, but it seems to me that it conceals fundamental difficulties, revealed in the very language that he used. He spoke to the logical facts as if there existed logico-mathematical facts. What do abstract entities correspond to? That is the whole problem. Either one is a Platonist and one leaves psychology completely (which does not, however, eliminate the psychological problems, because we would still want to understand how such ideal beings are attained), or one remains within reality. In the latter case, the only way in which we can conceive of logico-mathematical realities existing by themselves, outside of the subject, is the well-known approach of linking them to a language. Logic would be a sort of general syntax, mathematics would itself be a language; this is the thesis of Anglo-Saxon logical empiricism. One can very well conceive of a theory of development that consists in saying that the child acquires logico-mathematical notions, all of the operations, from outside, by a sort of cultural transmission carried out by the family, the school, etc., but essentially by language. In this case, the child finds himself in the presence of an already organized system, and this would be why we find ourselves on this privileged terrain of integrations. But if all is given from outside and if there is only transmission, if this acquisition is the learning of an already existing reality, inscribed in the collective representations of the group, I do not understand the occurrence of regular stages of assimilation. This preexisting reality should penetrate the mind of the individual either as a *unit* or at *random*. What can be said to explain stages? We would have to admit that the simplest realities correspond to the elementary stages and that the more complex forms correspond to higher stages. This would be a hierarchy going from simplicity to complexity. But if you look more closely, and I have often tried, what do simplicity and complexity mean? These are not objective notions. These are notions that are only *meaningful to a subject*, and we arrive at the conclusion that the subject assimilates these external realities in a certain order, because *this order is the most natural from the point of view of the stages of intellectual development*. In this way, we do not resolve the problem at all: we fall back on the idea that, to assimilate an external reality, there must be instruments of assimilation, and the stages would simply be stages in the instruments of assimilation. . . .

In neither case, Platonism or the so-called linguistic solution, do we resolve the problem. I believe that the solution is as follows, and is oriented in a direction opposite to that proposed by Fauville. Rather than appealing to preexisting logico-mathematical realities, I conceive of operations as simply the most general form of the *coordination of actions*. For my part, I do not at all believe that logic relates only to language; it is profoundly involved in the coordination of actions and equally, I hope, in neural coordinations. And since it is a matter of the most general coordinations, we are naturally on a privileged terrain for establishing stages that are both distinct and integrative. . . .

44

Formal Thought from the Equilibrium Standpoint*

1955

Reality and Possibility in Formal Thought

We have just seen that concrete thought is the form of equilibrium toward which preoperational thought tends. When it appears, static situations and transformations are integrated into a single system such that the former are subordinated to the latter and such that the latter form an operations structure attaining reversibility by mutual compensation of the transformations. But we have also seen that the scope of this equilibrium is still limited, as much because of the form of the operations as because of the resistance of the content. Since the instruments of general coordination between the concrete operational groupings are lacking, the subject still regards what is possible as but a direct extension of empirical reality. With the more complex instruments of coordination found in formal thinking, a new form of equilibrium appears, encompassing all the partial fields covered by concrete thought and coordinating them into a general system. The links of this system are at once the second order operations and the combinatorial system by means of which propositional logic comes to assign reality a place within a structured set of possible transformations. But before we can understand the nature of this new equilibrating process, we must first spell out the meaning of *possibility* and *reality* in formal thought.

I. The possibilities entertained in formal thought are by no means arbitrary or equivalent to imagination freed of all control and objectivity. Quite to the contrary, the advent of possibilities must be viewed from the dual perspective of logic and physics; this is the indispensable condition for the attainment of a general form of equilibrium; and it is no less indispensable for the establishment of the requisite connections utilized in formal thought.

A. From the point of view of physics, we know that a state of equilibrium is characterized by compensation between all of the potential modifications compatible with the links of the system. Even in

*From *The Growth of Logical Thinking* by Bärbel Inhelder and Jean Piaget, Basic Books, Inc., © 1958. Reprinted by permission of Basic Books, Inc., New York, and Routledge & Kegan Paul Ltd., London.

experimental physics—i.e., in the science relating to reality in its most material aspect—the notion of possibility plays an essential positive role in the determination of the conditions of a state of equilibrium. To the extent that psychology feels the need to consider states of equilibrium as well, it is thus a fortiori indispensable to resort to the notion of *possibility* expanded into the notion of "potential" actions or mental transformations (in the sense that the physicist uses when he speaks of potential acceleration or potential energy). But, since the concept of equilibrium even plays a role of some importance in perceptual theory, as Gestalt psychology has shown us, it is even more useful in the analysis of intellectual operations; for once an operational system is established it may remain unchanged for the remainder of a person's life.

So we are not being vague in stating that at the formal level the subject subordinates *reality* to *possibility* and that this assertion can be related directly to the theory of equilibrium states. First, it means that when faced with a determinate situation the subject is not limited to noting the relations (between the given elements) that seem to thrust themselves on him. Rather, in order to avoid inconsistencies as new facts emerge, from the start he seeks to encompass what appear to be the actual relations in a set of relations which he regards as possible. In other words, to equilibrate his successive assertions (which is equivalent to avoiding contradiction by subsequent facts), the subject tends to insert links, which in the first instance he assumes as real, in the totality of those which he recognizes as possible; he does this in a way that allows him later to choose the true ones by the examination of certain transformations performed accurately within the set of the possible links. *Possibility* plays its role in this way from the moment of the first spontaneous attitude taken by the formal level subjects; and from their subjective point of view, it is the very condition of the equilibrium of their thought.

But the following point arises as soon as we shift from the subject's to the observer's point of view: if the subject is to conceive of the total set of possible links or transformations in a given situation, he has to deduce them by means of adequate logical operations. But this set of operations is still a system of potential transformations with respect to physical equilibrium. (Of course, only a part of the set is utilized in a particular situation or problem.) Only the operations actually at work in a given situation are for the moment "real"; the others are merely potential. There are two reasons why these potential operations (or logical transformations) are as necessary to functional equilibrium as the ongoing or "real" operations: (1) they insure reversibility, and (2) they can be developed as they are needed for the acquisition of possible new links.

Summarizing, in order to conceive of what is possible, formal thought must have a wide range of operations ready for any particular situation, operations in addition to those which are being made use of at any given moment. These *potential* operations are a necessary condition of equilibrium for two reasons: (1) they correspond to what equilibrium theory terms "potential transformations," and (2) equilibrium actually exists to the extent that these potential transformations compensate each other exactly. Or, in operational language, it exists to the extent that these possible operations form a system that is strictly reversible from the logical standpoint.

B. There is a second sense in which *possibility* plays a role in formal thinking, namely the logical sense. In a new perspective it will show us once more that the role of possibility is indispensable to hypothetico-deductive or formal thinking. Logically, formal possibility is the required correlate of the notion of deductive necessity. An assertion that refers to empirical reality only, such as an existential or predicative judgment, could not be considered deductively necessary; it is true or false insofar as it corresponds or does not correspond to a factual datum. But a deduction logically derived from a hypothesis (or from a factual datum assumed hypothetically) is necessarily true from the formal point of view independently of the value of the assumed hypothesis. The connection indicated by the words "if . . . then" (inferential implication) links a required logical consequence to an assertion whose truth is merely a possibility. This synthesis of deductive necessity and *possibility* characterizes the use of possibility in formal thought, as opposed to possibility-as-an-extension-of-the-actual-situation in concrete thought and to unregulated possibilities in imaginative fictions. But what is the nature of formal possibility? Anything which is not contradictory may be called possible. But the noncontradictory, strictly speaking, is the totality of reversible transformations performed in such a way that the composition of an operation and its inverse result in a product termed "identical" or null: $p \cdot \bar{p} = 0$. Thus, whereas from the standpoint of physics operational reversibility signifies the exact compensation of potential transformations (or operations), from the logical standpoint it refers to deductive necessity.

In the end, these two aspects of the concept of *possibility*, stemming from physics and logic, are psychologically equivalent. In feeding an actual set of conditions into a set of possible transformations, formal thought guarantees its own equilibrium by insuring that the structures it elaborates will be psychologically conserved. At the same time it assures its value as a necessary logical instrument in that it makes use of these structures as deductive instruments. The mental equilibrium being determined by a general operational structure, the notion of *possibility* acts in two capacities—as an equilibrium factor and as a logical factor. Which of these is brought into play depends on whether the observer deals with a problem from the standpoint of *explanation*, which is for the most part the point of view of the observing psychologist, or from the standpoint of *understanding*, which is above all the subject's own point of view. This is why the reversal of direction between *reality* and *possibility*, which marks the advent of formal thought, is a turning point in the development of intelligence, at least insofar as intelligence may be thought of as an organization tending toward a state of equilibrium that is both stable and mobile.

II. But we must go one step further, for psychological equilibrium cannot be reduced entirely to physical equilibrium. The comparison between physical and psychological explanation of the equilibrium state is as instructive for pointing up their differences as for pointing up their common aspects.

In physics a system such as a balance is said to be in equilibrium when all of the potential energies (elevations of the weights at one side or the other as expressed as angular displacements) completely compensate each other. From the standpoint of *possibility*, on the other hand, the balance could be displaced in a particular direction and consequently an opposing force would appear which would reestablish the equilibrium. But as long as these transformations do not actually take place, the "potential energy" which defines the intervention of possibility in equilibrium theory does not, strictly speaking, exist outside of the mind of the physicist. Certainly it is possible to maintain that it plays a role in reality, but it is an essentially negative role; it explains the fact that nothing changes if the system is not modified from without. Thus, in a state of physical equilibrium, one must distinguish a "reality" which is causal and temporal and a set of "possibilities" which are deductive, extemporaneous, and which reside in the brain of the physicist who constructs the theory about reality.

Psychologically, a system in equilibrium, such as the total number of relations understood by a subject who has succeeded in explaining the mechanism of the balance, has two aspects to it, one referring to *reality* and the other to *possibility*. On one hand the subject really performs certain mental operations and organizes certain relationships which really apply to the object which he has before his eyes at a given moment—for example, because he perceives and conceives it effectively, the subject asserts that the balance is horizontal and that a 2-kg. weight at a distance of 10 cm. from the axis compensates a weight of 1 kg. at 20 cm. from the axis suspended from the other arm. But these real operations and relations, real in the sense that they are used at a given moment, are not sufficient to account for the equilibrium attained in the act of understanding, since in the latter an entire set of possible or potential operations and relations intervenes. However, the line of demarcation between possibility and reality is much more difficult to trace in psychology than in physics. But it is just this difference between the two forms of equilibrium which is most instructive for the study of formal thought and which we may now analyze more closely.

First of all, we must distinguish carefully between two meanings of the word *possibility* as it is used here. First, one may speak of possible operations and relations in designating those which the subject himself regards as possible—i.e., those which he knows he is able to perform or construct, even without actually trying them out. We shall call this *instrumental possibility*. The reader will see immediately that this is identical with our earlier description of possibility from the subject's point of view. But one could also mean by *possibility* the operations and relations that the subject would be capable of performing or constructing without his thinking of doing so—i.e., without the subject's becoming aware of the contingency or even of his own capacity and regard to it. We shall call this *structural possibility*. Thus, it is possibility defined by the observer rather than the subject.

Let us return to our example concerning "instrumental possibility." In ascertaining the compensation between a 2-kg. weight at 10 cm. and a 1-kg. weight situated at 20 cm. from the axis, the subject, although not performing the physical actions, may assume that he might move the 2-kg. weight by 5 cm. away from the axis and likewise the 1-kg. weight outward by 10 cm. In so doing, he does not go beyond the realm of *potential* actions (actually, he does not move anything); still, the subject will deduce that these two hypothetical displacements will maintain the initial equilibrium because the inverse proportion of the weights and the distances will remain constant, etc. Returning to *reality* (the actual apparatus), he could verify his assertion. But, as he is deductively certain of the result, he could dispense with this verification. In both cases, these possible actions will help him and will even be indispensable to him if he is to understand the empirical data (horizontal position of the balance for 2 kg. at 10 cm. and 1 kg. at 20 cm.); thus, he will interpret the real relations as a function of a set of potential actions and explain them as necessary consequences of these possible operations or actions which are combined among themselves.

But one can see immediately that these "instrumentally possible" operations or relations are, from the psychological point of view, as real as the initial "real" operations or relations. It is only from the subject's point of view that they appear as possibilities. In other words, the subject distinguishes what is physically present from the transformations which it would be possible to introduce in the perceived system. But even when the subject's performance is based purely on potential actions, these possible transformations are thought over and thus, psychologically, may consist either in representations or in real operations. Hence, "the instrumentally possible" is but a particular modality of the real thinking of the subject. This modality gains a special importance at the level of formal thinking when, as a result, the modality of "reality" can be subordinated. Although this may contribute to the stabilization of operational equilibrium to the extent that the transformations effectively realized are further conditioned by the transformations which the subject conceives of as possible, on the psychological level this realm of the "instrumentally possible" is not wholly comparable with potential transformations in the theory of equilibrium in physics. To be more exact, it does not correspond to anything in the physical realm, since it is intermediate between pure reality (immediately present relations) and pure possibility (the "structurally possible") whereas in physics no *tertium* intervenes between the immediate and the potential.

It is an entirely different situation in the case of "structural possibility." For at the level of psychological equilibrium, "structural possibility" is wholly equivalent to the "potential transformations" of a physical system in equilibrium. Alongside the operations which he has actually performed (either as actions as such or as effective perceptions or as simple hypotheses "instrumentally possible"), the subject could have performed others, which he has not either in action or thought. Instead of imagining a displacement of 5 and 10 cm. for the 2- and 1-kg. weights respectively, he could have modified the weights themselves (in act or mentally), or he could have diminished a distance on one side and a proportional weight on the other, etc. It may even happen that, without explicitly referring to it, the subject acts as if he had utilized the operational schema of proportions; the same question which for another subject would not have provoked a conscious reaction for lack of an underlying structure would be for the subject in question a starting point for an immediate organization of new, well-formulated relationships. Thus, such observations, which are common, will furnish the proof—but only after the fact—that a determinate operation was "structurally possible" for one subject while it was not for the other. In short, in any act of intelligence one must always consider both real operations, in the sense of those actually made use of in the subject's conscious thought, and "structurally possible" operations, in the sense of those which the subject does not perform, but could perform. As we have seen above, it is this possibility, relative to the operational structures which are available to the subject, which constitutes *possibility* from the observer's point of view and which thus corresponds in the field of physics to the potential transformations not actually realized.

But if we are to construct a theory of the psychological mechanisms involved in operational equilibrium, we must give separate consideration to each one of these two distinct meanings of the notion of possibility even though, in this case, we are faced with three analytic levels (the real, the instrumentally possible, and the structurally possible) and not two (the real and the potential) as is the case in physics. Indeed, the instrumentally possible is closely related to the structurally possible of which it constitutes a first stage of realization—i.e., it is insofar as the subject has access to a large enough number of structurally possible operations that he is enabled to imagine the instrumentally possible transformations. Without a certain set of structural possibilities (and the consequences of this lack are clearly evident at the preoperational and even the concrete operational levels), he could not do more than ascertain the state of the facts he perceives in reality, whether static states or transformations in process, and would not succeed in representing to himself the hypothetical transformations which serve for devising new experiments. Thus instrumental possibility depends on structural possibility, but the first is more impoverished than the second. For this reason, even if the former derives from the latter at each instant, the two varieties must be carefully distinguished, for the second is both theoretically and practically of a much greater importance.

In these terms we can return to the comparison between the physical and psychological concepts of equilibrium. From the physical point of view, only reality is of a causal nature, for the potential or the possible plays a positive role only in the mind of the physicist; in other words, possibility is only an instrument of calculation or deduction, whereas reality alone is causal. But the situation is entirely different in the case of operational equilibrium. For, in this realm, reality and possibility are both of a psychological nature—i.e., both have their locus in the subject's mind and causally intersect only within the mechanisms which make up the subject's mental life. It is true that it could be maintained that only reality and the "instrumentally possible" (which in this case is still part of psychological reality) play a role in the subjects' minds, whereas the "structurally possible" is a concept that refers not to the subject himself but to the psychologist who attempts to analyze and explain the subject's behavior. In this case there would be complete parallelism between the physical and psychological points of view. However, to the extent that the "instrumentally possible" is conditioned by the "structurally possible"—and all of the research described in this work leads to this conclusion—we must exclude the notion of not attributing the structurally possible to the subject as such.

But then we are led to the paradoxical consequence that, in a state of psychological equilibrium, possibility (both structural and instrumental) plays as important a causal role as real operations. It could even be maintained that the whole of mental life is dominated by this sort of causality of the possible.

As for "instrumental possibility," this assertion does not contain anything that is especially surprising and it corresponds to the universally acknowledged fact that "hypothesis" plays a role in the functioning of thought. The causal function of instrumental possibility is actually hypothesis behavior, behavior which permits the subject to go beyond what he perceives or conceives while admitting the validity of the present situation and to involve himself in that which can be conceived without an immediate decision concerning its verification. From sensorimotor trial-and-error transfer to the most sophisticated experimental hypothesis, adaptation to present reality is complemented by a progressive adaptation to future reality. Thus possibility enters the adaptation process, in the field of adaptations indispensable to action, in the form of the potential future, since, when an internalized action becomes an operation, possibility intervenes at each bifurcation—i.e., in every case in which the subject, after having imagined where each of two or several possible courses of action leads, must make a choice. Finally, at the formal level, hypothesis intervenes from the moment of contact with reality insofar as immediate fact is thought to admit of giving rise to several interpretations.

But this causality of the "instrumentally possible" has nothing mysterious about it, since to think about a possible event by virtue of thinking itself is (and we repeat) to perform one or several real operations.

On the other hand, the potential causality related to the "structurally possible" raises a completely different problem but one which is much more important—how can the operations actually performed be causally affected by operations which are not accessible to the subject, at least not at the conscious level, and which sometimes remain latent to such a degree that they never belong in an explicit form to the subject's realm of available knowledge?

Let us first note that such a problem is by no means limited to the psychology of logical operations or even to psychology in general. In embryological theory for example, note is taken of partial or total "potentialities" whose appearance is linked with a determinate level of development and only a portion of which is actually realized. So it is difficult to accept the notion that these limited realizations are independent of the entire system of "potentialities" from which they carry a given segment of *possibility* over into *reality*. If, in psychology, we accept the view that the development of mental functions is linked to the maturation of the nervous system (a hypothesis which is a simple extension of the embryological point of view just mentioned) it follows as a matter of course that a coordination could appear in a potentially general form although it would first give rise to certain specific applications only. These latter, though the only ones realized, depend on the system of possible coordinations which appear as innate possibilities and which are more or less retarded in maturation.

Without committing ourselves to such hypotheses, we may note that the causality of possibility is resorted to in an implicit way more often than one would think by those studying mental processes and even general biology. But as regards our present problem, the frequency of certain synchronisms bears witness to the causal role of possibility; for these synchronisms would seem to be inexplicable if one or more integrated structures were not organized at a given moment as sources or reservoirs of possible operations. Only some of these come to be realized, but their realization is a function of the total system and consequently a function of the *potential* as much as the *actual*.

Beginning at the level of concrete operations, we have observed the striking fact that although they do not see the relationship between two objectively analogous problems and do not know that they are applying similar operations to them, on the average, the subjects react synchronously in the same manner to the two problems at a given level. For example, if the substage II-B subjects' responses to the balance scale problem are compared to their responses for the toy-dumping-wagon problem, it is clear that at 9–10 years the subjects begin to establish an inverse correspondence between weights and distances (from the axis) in the first case and begin to understand in the second that the more the rail is inclined, the more the wagon weights. But in the second case they bring in the concept of work while in the first case they have no conception of it; nevertheless, the operations of relating weights to distances from the center or to the height is the same in both cases. In either situation, the child understands that the force exerted by the weight changes as a function of the spatial relationships. Likewise, weight is related to volume at the same levels in the most varied problems without the subject's appealing explicitly to analogies. A great many examples of the same type could be furnished from the concrete level.

At the formal level, the synchronization of like reactions in the face of analogous problems is still more striking. For, in contrast with the preceding level, the operational form is entirely dissociated from thought content. Beyond the possibility of reasoning formally—i.e., by implications, exclusions, disjunctions, etc.—we see concepts of proportions and especially combinatory considerations* appearing at the same level in the most diverse areas. It is as if the system of possible operations were an internal network along which a given thought content, once it had engaged the network, spread out immediately in all directions at the same time. Thus the causal role of possibility is manifested as a kind of action of implicit schemata on explicit operations, the latter being determined not only by the cognitive acts actually performed just prior to the new operation but by the totality of the operational field constituted by the possible operations.

Certainly, nothing is more dangerous than recourse to the implicit—i.e., to the potential. But there are safeguards permitting the dissociation of the abusive usage of the concept (such as the passage from the potentiality to the act) and its legitimate usage. The true potential differs from the false in that it is calculable and is simply a response to the exigencies of the conservation of the total system (as the po-

---

*Not taught in class. The schema of proportions also appears in many cases before its scholastic introduction.

tential in physics). But in the case of "structurally possible" operations we are faced with a legitimate potential, since there are algebraic instruments which enable us to uncover the role of general structures and to calculate their extension as well as the elements. . . .

Meanwhile, let us limit ourselves to the following conclusion: in a state of *physical* equilibrium reality alone is causal and possibility relates only to the mind of the physicist who deduces this reality; in contrast, in a state of *mental* equilibrium the succession of mental acts is affected not only by the operations actually performed but also by the entire set of possible operations insofar as they orient the subject's searching toward deductive closure. For in this case it is the subject who deduces, and the possible operations are part of the same deductive system as the real operations he performs.*

The Problem of Structures

Despite this difference between physical and mental processes, it remains true that in both cases a system is in equilibrium when all of the potential transformations compatible with the system links compensate each other. This physical definition of equilibrium corresponds in the mental field to the following considerations: the state of fact—or reality—corresponds to the operations explicitly performed by the subject, whereas the potential transformations correspond to the possible operations that the subject could perform and that he may explicitly perform later on but which he has not or has not yet performed at the moment considered; the system links correspond to the givens of the problem posed—i.e., to the content on which his operations are exercised. Our problem is to find the point at which it can be said that equilibrium is attained for such a mental system.

In the first place, it is not attained as long as the problem is not solved—i.e., as long as it is still necessary to perform explicit operations. But here we must distinguish between two cases: (1) where the subject possesses all of the methods and all of the operations required for the solution; and (2) where he has not yet acquired them. Naturally, in the second case it would not be possible to speak of equilibrium, since a more or less considerable effort must still be provided before the question posed may be considered as resolved. In the first case, if there is still disequilibrium, it is only momentary and partial—i.e., relative to the single new problem whose solution is not immediately visible. For the rest—i.e., for the entire set of methods and operations which the subject utilizes in the solution of problems of this class—it can be said that even in a permanent sense equilibrium is attained, since the subject has become capable of solving all similar problems.

*From the standpoint of applied psychology, this is equivalent to saying that a subject should be evaluated not only by what he actually does but also by what he could do in other situations—i.e., by his "potential" or his aptitudes.

Thus, as in a physical equilibrium, equilibrium of this type is characterized by the compensation of the total number of potential transformations. This is equivalent to saying that once the data are given the subject can submit them to an indefinite number of operational transformations beyond those which he chooses in trying to answer the question posed but that these transformations are relative to a structure (the integrated structure of the operations available to the subject) and that this structure is reversible. There is then an equilibrium, because to each transformation that the subject could perform (as a function of the operational structure considered) there is a corresponding inverse possible transformation that could also be realized. Or, stated in simpler fashion, the system is in equilibrium when the operations which the subject is capable of constitute a structure such that these operations can be performed in either one of two directions (either by strict inversion or negation or reciprocity). Thus, it is because the total set of possible operations constitutes a system of potential transformations which compensate each other—and which compensate each other insofar as they conform to laws of reversibility—that the system is in equilibrium. The operational reversibility and the system equilibrium constitute, after all, a single unified property, and it is because the possible operations are reversible and mobile (i.e., can be combined in all ways, but with a complete liberty for a return to the initial starting point) that possibility acts in a continuous manner on the choice of new operations to be performed.

If such is the nature of operational equilibrium, the solution of the problem of formal thought is to be sought in an analysis of the structural integration which characterizes formal operations in contrast to concrete operations. On the one hand, the functioning of the equilibrium such as we have just attempted to describe implies the existence of an integrated structure, since only an integrated structure can explain the presence and the extent of the possible operations as well as their influence on the performed operations. On the other hand, as we have seen, formal thought is characterized by reversal of direction between reality and possibility in that the first is subordinated to the second and the second acquires an importance unknown up to this point. But here as well, if we are to determine the proportions between real operations and possible operations at the concrete and formal levels as well as the indefinite extension of the second to this latter level, we must compare the structural integrations of the operations involved in the two cases. . . .

But first, several further remarks are in order on the choice of the logico-mathematical instruments which we shall make use of in this analysis. When the problem is to determine the "factors" involved in a mental effort or simply the correlations between various returns, it seems obvious to psychologists that the mathematical methods of factorial analysis or probability calculation should be used, since they do not bias the results. But we must ask ourselves whether there are methods which are as precise as these in their calculational technique (and as objective as analytic instruments) which can resolve the question of the structural integration of operations.

The answer is *yes*. For several decades, mathematicians have striven to isolate the integrated structures which are found in the most varied areas but whose structural laws are independent of any application to a particular realm. Synthesizing the results already acquired in this field and adding the original contribution that their efforts at revising the principles of mathematics have made possible, the Bourbaki in their remarkable works have reached the conclusion that there are three kinds of basic structures of which the multiple combinations explain all of the others: (1) algebraic structures whose prototype is the "group"; (2) the order structures one of whose principal forms is the "lattice"; and (3) the topological structures relative to the continuum.

But, leaving aside the topological structures, since they are not relevant here* we see that group and lattice structures are common to both mathematical and logical operations. In other words, the general analytic instrument forged by mathematicians is as valuable in the qualitative study of the structures found in thinking as in any other structural research. It is easy to discern the *lattice* structure in the propositional calculus of symbolic logic, and we have shown elsewhere the multiple forms under which the *group* of four transformations (*Vierergruppe* or "Klein group")† reappears.

Thus it is not as logic (for logic has no more place in psychology than psychology does in logic), but as a calculus or an algebra that we are here using symbolic logic. Considered in this perspective, symbolic logic is badly needed at this point as an analytic tool for at least two reasons.

First, such an analytic instrument is generally the only possible one for determining the exact extent of possible operations. We know, for example, that with 1, 2, 3, 4, . . . propositions, it is possible to organize respectively 4, 16, 256, 65,536, etc., operations, and it is even easy to enumerate them one by one—an interesting exercise— up to the 256 ternary operations. Moreover, it makes it possible to demonstrate that these numbers, increasing by the square with disconcerting rapidity in proportion to the operations which will actually appear in the subjects' performance in an experimental situation, are not actually independent of each other; thus it is possible to reduce the 256 ternary operations to pairs or trios of binary operations or unitary-binary operations.

But especially, and this is most important for the problem at hand, using symbolic logic as a means of analysis makes it possible to show that these sets of operations do not consist of simple series of juxtaposed elements; on the contrary, these collections of elements have structure as wholes. These wholes are the integrated structures of formal propositional operations (equivalent to the concrete *groupings* of classes and relations) which it would be instructive to analyze in order to resolve the psychological problems posed in the present work. In this respect, symbolic logic allows for an analysis which goes more deeply into the heart of intelligence than arithmetical or statistical calculations. Whereas the latter bear either on the results of operations or on "factors" which do not directly furnish meaning, the qualitative analysis available to symbolic logic reaches the structures themselves—i.e., the

---

*But topological structures do correspond to what we call infralogical operations (see Chap. 17, p. 273, note 2).

†See Piaget, *Essai sur les transformations des opérations logiques.*

operational mechanism as such and not simply its results or its more or less general conditions.

Of course, such a use of structural analysis implies that experimental results and theoretical analysis will be continually compared with each other. From the experimental standpoint, intelligence is first a coordination of acts—then operations which orient themselves step by step toward certain forms of equilibrium. But these equilibrium forms, which are of vital importance in the explanation of development, can be analyzed from both perspectives, the genetic or experimental and the theoretical. In genetic logic, empirical research consists of determining, by tests appropriate to the various levels of evolution, which operations are involved in the subject's cognitive acts and how these operations are gradually organized into structures to the point where certain empirically verifiable forms of equilibrium are reached. On the other hand, theoretical analysis describes these same structures in their general or abstract aspects so as to show how the most complex can be derived from the simplest, and it determines the system of possible operations which would permit the utilization of this or that actually performed operation.

It is clear from the start that these two types of research can be mutually reinforcing in furthering our understanding of cognitive equilibrium states. We have tried to understand the transition from the concrete to the formal level in the thinking of childhood and adolescence by proceeding from this continual comparison of their results, after having sought in vain for the criteria of formal thought in verbal primacy, in second-degree operations, etc.

Moreover, it is clear that such recourse to the theoretical analysis of structures in no sense constitutes logical investigation. Throughout, the question is a psychological one; the calculus of symbolic logic is brought in as an analytical instrument insofar as it is a more general algebra than the elementary algebra founded on numerical operations. If we may compare those sciences in the process of growth with the sciences which have attained full control of their methods, experimental psychology can be seen as corresponding, on the mental level, to experimental physics in the study of matter, with pure symbolic (or axiomatic) logic corresponding to mathematics. As for the discipline which deals with constructing a theory of mental operations by means of symbolic calculus, its relationship to experimental psychology would be comparable to the present day relationship between laboratory and mathematical physics. It would remain a branch of psychology, as mathematical physics is a branch not of mathematics but of physics. But it would utilize the algebra of symbolic logic as an analytic instrument in the same way that mathematical physics now makes use of the techniques and notation of mathematics.

45

Equilibration Processes in the Psychobiological

Development of the Child*

1958

If it is granted (contrary to the impression my report may have given) that the organism is an open and essentially active system then development cannot be explained without having recourse to equilibration processes. In fact, although mental, like physical, life (and even more so) is a perpetual process of construction (and sometimes even of invention), it is by no means incoherent because of this, and what is required is to understand how the mechanism bringing about this continual construction may constitute at the same time a regulating mechanism ensuring coherence.

In the field of the cognitive functions in particular, the problem is to understand how new learning, discovery and creation may not only be reconciled with but take place at the same time as control and verification in such a way that the new remains in harmony with the acquired. This is once more a problem of equilibration. However, although everyone stresses the activity and renewal aspect of development, the equilibration aspect is only too often forgotten. Above all, it is often not sufficiently realized that these two aspects are inseparable and that the very same agencies which effect the new constructions are also those which simultaneously ensure their regulation.

An example of this is afforded by logical operations, under their

*From J. M. Tanner and B. Inhelder, eds., *Equilibration Processes in the Psychobiological Development of the Child*, Vol. 4. The proceedings of the World Health Organization study group on the psychobiological development of the child. Geneva, 1956. Reprinted by permission. In this conference, Piaget wrote a paper drawing upon the other participants' remarks and presenting his ideas about equilibration; this paper was then discussed, and the present selection represents Piaget's reply to that discussion. The specific individuals to whom Piaget's reply was addressed were: Konrad Lorenz, John Bowlby, Margaret Mead, Grey Walter, J. M. Tanner, René Zazzo, and Ludwig von Bertalanffy.

double aspect of agencies of indefinite construction and coherent reversibility. Although this example is almost unique, as we shall stress, from the viewpoint of degree of perfection in equilibrated adaptation, it constitutes no more than the final term of a long series of regulations of all kinds, which come into play with the most elementary learning and perception, and whose semi-equilibrated mechanisms of retroaction and anticipation provide the basis for the logical reversibility which characterizes logical operations. Furthermore, this example illustrates well what is doubtless true in general, namely, that analysis of regulation, in other words of equilibration, throws some light on the mechanism of construction itself (in the case of operations, in fact, every new construction, and consequently every invention, is reversible from the outset and therefore can be equilibrated).

1. The result of stabilization and, in particular, compensation processes, can be designated by the term equilibrium* or by that suggested by Bertalanffy, "stable state in an open system." Whatever the vocabulary employed, however, it must be stressed at the outset that such processes always exist in a living being, which amounts to saying that, for it, equilibrium does not represent an occasional or extrinsic characteristic but an intrinsic one, subsuming a certain number of specific functions. Thus, for a pebble, the fact of being in stable, unstable, or metastable equilibrium in no way affects its other properties: thus, its equilibrium is an occasional or added characteristic and the proof thereof is that in order to define a state of stable equilibrium the physicist calls in a system of "virtual work" [potential energy] which exists only in his mind and not in the pebble itself. On the other hand, a higher vertebrate which could not stand on its paws would be pathological; here a homeostatic disorder constitutes a disease. From the mental viewpoint, an adult whose thinking remains unstable as regards definitions, inferences or decisions is considered to be abnormal. In each of these latter cases, equilibrium under one form or another constitutes an intrinsic and not an extrinsic characteristic of the fields considered. (Naturally this does not signify that we have here a specific property of life, but only that wherever there is life there is also equilibrium.)

2. In the second place, it must be stressed that the equilibration process which thus constitutes an intrinsic characteristic corresponds, in living beings, to specific needs, tendencies, or functions and not merely to an automatic balance independent of the activities of the subject. Thus, in the case of the higher cognitive functions, there exists a tendency to equilibrium which manifests the need for coherence. In the case of the elementary cognitive functions (perception) the same holds true, although the forms of equilibrium attained are more fleeting and less stable. In other words, the force of the tendency is not entirely determined by its results, and this is why it is better to speak of *equilibration* as a process corresponding to a tendency rather than of equilibrium only.

*A translation of the original French word 'équilibre'. It should be noted that in French this word has a broader sense that the words 'equilibrium' or 'balance' in English.

3. To these needs, tendencies or functions correspond special mechanisms or agencies of equilibration whose activity is complementary to that of all behaviors aiming at the exploration or modification of the environment during the exchanges between it and the organism. Thus, all sensorimotor activity is accompanied by regulation of posture and tonus, etc. In the case of the cognitive functions, one may conceive of the elementary logical operations as constructing new forms or new assemblies within the environment (classifications, seriations, correspondences, etc.); but these activities are necessarily accompanied (necessarily, because this is a condition of their success) by a stabilization of their forms and elements (conservation, etc.). From this viewpoint, it may be said that the inverse and reciprocal operations taking place in this stabilization constitute the equilibrium agencies, it being understood, however, that these mechanisms or agencies are indissolubly linked with those affecting the new constructions.

4. In the sense in which we understand the term, then, equilibrium is therefore essentially bound up with the activities of the organism, not only because equilibration presupposes activities, but also because the stable states or equilibrium forms reached at the end of equilibration processes always represent the play of compensation between activities proper. Stable equilibrium may be defined locally by assuming that if a small perturbation ΔE_p is introduced in a state E by the observer or by nature, the subject reacts by a spontaneous movement of the same order, ΔE_s, which returns the system to the state E, or to a state close to this. It is then said that the reaction ΔE_s constitutes an activity.

5. If we prefer the term equilibrium (mobile or dynamic) to that of stable state, it is because the concept of equilibrium implies that of compensation and because the activities of the subject (see 4) are always compensatory at the same time as constructive. This concept is of general importance, since it doubtless concerns the fundamental mechanisms of assimiliation or learning. If these mechanisms are assumed to be on a simple process of association, the problem then remains of understanding why certain associations are unstable (for example, conditioning considered as merely association remains temporary or unstable) whereas others are stable. The problem can be solved only to the extent that a stabilization factor is introduced, in the form of the satisfaction of a need (which is thus a compensation in the sense that filling a gap is a compensation). In other words, in the event of a stable association between x and y, y is not only associated (externally) with x, but assimilated to x in the sense that y is merged into the x schema and fills a momentary gap (need) relating to this schema.

These considerations confirm what has been said (under 3) regarding the complementary and indissociable nature of equilibration and of assimilation; the concept of assimilation explains more than does that of association precisely insofar as it includes a stabilization factor.

6. The compensatory activities just discussed (5), which therefore constitute the specific agencies of equilibration (cf. 3), play a considerable part at all levels of behavior, in the form of retroactive proc-

esses necessary for the anticipations involved in construction. In this respect, it may be considered that the agencies of equilibration correspond in general to all regulatory systems in their dual retroactive and anticipatory aspect. However, these concepts recur continually in all theories explaining behavior, from the "feedback" common in the Anglo-Saxon countries to the reafferences and models of action of Soviet psychology. Even in a theory of learning as associationist as Hull's, retroactions play an essential part.

7. However, even if all this is commonplace, it is not often understood that the higher cognitive operations constitute, with their characteristics of combined retroaction and anticipation, structures similar to those of the regulations. However, there are two differences, namely, that they attain complete equilibrium and that, thanks to the complete reversibility which characterizes this equilibrium, the operational structures take an algebraic form simpler than the mathematical expression of "feedback."*

8. Thus, reversibility for an operation leading from state A to state B consists in the presence of an inverse operation leading back from state B to state A. Reversibility (in the form of inversion or reciprocity) is thus a special case of retroaction: that in which the retroaction brings about a complete return to state A and not only to a state A', close to A. It may therefore be said that, in the case of operations, operation BA is the same as operation AB, but reversed (an identity which is indicated by the consideration that when a subject understands an operation he also understands, by this very fact, the possibility of its inverse), whereas, in the case of a regulation, no matter of what kind, the two actions which lead from A to B and from B to A or A' respectively, are different. Apart from this distinctive characteristic, however, operational reversibility is nothing more than retroaction. It may therefore be said that operations represent a direct prolongation of regulations and it may even be considered that, from the viewpoint of equilibrium, the three great structures which dominate mental life and arise in hierarchic order during development are the basic rhythms, the regulations and the operations. These logical structures consequently do not represent an isolated sector of mental life (or a characteristic formed from outside by language, etc.) but the final stage of an edifice all of whose parts are interdependent.

9. The value of an equilibration theory is precisely in explaining this completion of the activo-cognitive structures (if they can be so termed). Indeed, it is this progressive equilibrium of the compensation (ΔE_s in relation to ΔE_p) which underlies operational reversibility, and not the reverse. If it were necessary to explain equilibrium by reversibility, it would be impossible to understand from whence the latter could arise, whereas one can understand (in outline) how coarse compensations become finer and how, with the aid of symbolic function and representation, these compensations may finally bring about, *in thought*, exact reversibility. To employ a comparison, which is more than a mere image, it might be said that when a physicist describes the èquilibrium

---

*These operational structures take simple forms such as groups, groupings, lattices, etc., while a "feedback" must be expressed as a complicated integral.

of a body, he calls into play systems of "virtual work" [potential energy] which exist in his mind and not in the said body, while in bringing about the equilibrium of his interiorized actions (which are his operations), a living and thinking subject establishes an interplay of compensations between the different components of virtual work, which then play an effective role in his actual thought.* This system of virtual work constitutes, in fact, a system of all possible operations for a given structure and it is precisely these possible operations which represent logic.

10. From such a viewpoint, logical structures are the only completely equilibrated structures in the organism (apart from a few similar structures which approach without attaining the same precision, i.e. the perceptual constancies and certain sensorimotor schemata relative to space and objects). As such, the operational structures constitute a very special case, whose properties cannot be generalized for the whole of mental life, even under its cognitive aspect. But as this special case also represents, at the same time, the final point of a very general process of equilibration and as this process concerns the regulations as a whole (and, beyond them, more basic rhythms), the study of logical structures is very important in order to determine the real significance of equilibrium mechanisms.

11. It should be noted further that, although equilibration thus constitutes a developmental factor to be added to the three classic factors of heredity, environment (external or internal), and social education, it is a factor which cannot be dissociated from them. To be more precise, equilibrium is a form (and equilibration a structuration), but this form has a content and this content can only be hereditary or acquired by physical or social learning. However, as none of these three factors acts alone, it would be useless to try to isolate the equilibration factor; it intervenes in every hereditary or acquired process, and intervenes in their interactions. It is in this sense that it is the most general of the four, but this in no way signifies that it is superimposed on the other three by an additive process.

12. In particular, the equilibrium factor is dominant in exchanges between the organism and the environment. These exchanges correspond to what is generally termed "adaptation" (Lorenz suggested that I replace the term "equilibrium" by "adaptive interaction"). All adaptation, both mental and physical, includes two poles: one corresponding to the assimilation of energy or matter from the environment by the structure of the organism (or mental assimilation of data perceived in the environment to the schemata of action followed by the subject); the other corresponding to the accommodation† of structures of schemata of the organism or subject to environmental situations or data. Adaptation is then nothing more than an equilibrium between this assimilation and organic or mental accommodation. This is why the most elementary exchanges between subject and object are already determined by the equilibrium factor.

---

*We might thus define virtual work without calling on concepts of force, etc., but considering merely $\triangle E_s$'s which are imaginable (in the true sense of the word) without being actually carried out.

†We use this term in the sense of phenotypes, i.e. variations undergone by the organism in relation to the environment.

Conclusion

This last remark (12) enables us to conclude by putting the equilibrium factor in its true perspective, which is a biological and not a logical one, although the special equilibrium of logical structures is one of the finest achievements of living morphogenesis.

We shall therefore conclude by saying that life, like thought (or thought, like life) is essentially active because it constructs forms. From this viewpoint, thought forms are a prolongation of living morphogenesis through the intermediary of nervous coordination, sensorimotor schemata of action, etc., without forgetting social structures, since the operation of reason is always dependent on cooperation. However these forms or structures, whether biological or mental, must constantly comply with the double requirement of assimilation of objects or external data to them and, in return, of accommodation to these objects or data. Without assimilation, the organism or subject would be like soft wax, as in the reproach leveled against empiricism, ceaselessly modified by chance encounters or changes in the environment. Without accommodation, the organism or the subject would be withdrawn within itself and beyond the reach of any external action. This equilibrium between assimilation and accommodation can only be limited and relatively unstable on the organic level, since the effects of one are attained at the expense of the other: equilibrium is only a compromise at the level of organic morphogenesis or variation of the species. With nervous organization and mental life, on the contrary, a twofold power of retroaction and anticipation, or reconstitution of the past and the foreseeing of the future, considerably enlarges the field of this equilibrium and replaces fleeting compromises by actual syntheses. Schemata of action already constitute such syntheses, with their power of general assimilation and multiple accommodation. Nevertheless equilibrium is only attained, from the operational and cognitive viewpoint, with logico-mathematical structures capable of assimilating the whole universe to thought, without being ever broken or even shaken by the innumerable accommodations called for by experience. We have studied the background of this cognitive equilibration in the modest sector represented by child development: but, even within this limited field, it is remarkably instructive and becomes much more so once properly situated in its general perspective.

46

Problems of Equilibration*

1975

The title "Equilibration" refers to one factor that I think is essential in cognitive development. In order to understand the role of this factor we must relate it to the classical factors that have always been understood to be pertinent in cognitive development. There are three such classical factors: (1) the influences of the physical environment, the external experience of objects; (2) innateness, the hereditary program; and, (3) social transmission, the effects of social influences. It is clear that all three are important in cognitive development. . . . Each one of them implies a fundamental factor of equilibration, upon which I shall place special emphasis. . . .

It seems to me there are two reasons for having to call in this fourth factor. The first is that since we already have three other factors, there must be some coordination between them. This coordination is a kind of equilibration. Secondly, in the construction of any operational or preoperational structure, a subject goes through much trial and error and many regulations which involve in a large part self-regulation. Self-regulations are the very nature of equilibration. These self-regulations come into play at all levels of cognition, including the very lowest level of perception.

I will begin with an example at the level of perception. We have studied a number of optical illusions, by asking subjects to make perceptual judgments of an optical illusion. For example, we have often used the Müller-Lyer illusion, an illusion of the diagonal of the lozenge, which is always underestimated. . . . The subject has to judge whether the variable is shorter, longer or equal to the standard. I have always admired the patience of children under seven years of age who will sit through 20 or 30 or 40 presentations at a time.

In children under seven years of age we find no notable transformations. That is, at the end of thirty or forty trials, they make the same errors they did in the beginning. With adults, on the contrary, the repetition of the judgment results in a very clear diminishing of the

*From an address by Jean Piaget to the Jean Piaget Society, Philadelphia, 1975 in *Topics in Cognitive Developments*, volume 1, M. Appal, ed., Plenum Press, 1977. Reprinted by permission. Translated by Eleanor Duckworth.

illusior. Some are able to eliminate the effect of the illusion altogether. Among children from seven years (the beginning of cognitive operations) to adulthood, one can observe a progressive diminishing of errors. It is important to note that the subject does not know the results of his judgments. There was no external reinforcement, yet the perceptual mechanism seems to have its own regulations, such that after 20 or 30 or 40 trials, an adult subject can eliminate the effect of the illusion altogether.

At the representational level, in both preoperational and operational structures, we can distinguish three kinds of equilibrium. The first one is the relationship between assimilation and accommodation. There is an equilibrium between the structures of the subject and the objects; [the subject's] structures accommodate to the new object being presented and the object is assimilated into the structures. . . .

The second kind of equilibrium is an equilibrium among the subsystems of the subject's schemes. In reality, the schemes of assimilation are coordinated into partial systems, referred to as subsystems in relation to the totality of the subject's knowledge. These subsystems can present conflicts themselves. For example, it is possible to have conflicts between a subsystem dealing with logico-mathematical operations (classifications, seriation, number construction, etc.) and another subsystem dealing with spatial operations (length, area, etc.). For example, when a child is judging the quantity of a number of sticks, there may be in one collection a small number of long sticks laid out. In another collection, a larger number of shorter sticks may be laid out. If he is basing his judgment on number, he would make one judgment of quantity. If he is basing his judgment on length, he would make a different judgment of quantity. These two systems can evolve at different speeds. Of course as they evolve there is a constant need for coordination of the two—an equilibration of subsystems.

The third kind of equilibrium in cognitive development appears to be fundamental. Little by little there has to be a constant equilibrium established between the parts of the subject's knowledge and the totality of his knowledge at any given moment. There is a constant differentiation of the totality of knowledge into the parts and an integration of the parts back into the whole. This equilibrium between differentiation and integration plays a fundamental biological role.

At the level of cognitive functions, this is a fundamental form of equilibrium because integration, as a function of differentiation, poses new problems. These new problems lead to the construction of new actions upon the previous actions, or new operations upon the previous operations. The construction of operations upon operations is probably the secret of development and of the transition from one stage to the next.

I would like to point out that the notion of operation itself involves self-regulatory mechanisms. They are, in the Ashby sense (in his cybernetic terms), the perfect regulations in that the outcome is anticipated before the act is actually carried out. The feedback, which at lower levels has incomplete reversibility, now becomes a feedback with perfect reversibility in the sense of inversion or reciprocity. This is an example of perfect compensation, otherwise said, attained equilibrium.

I would like to explain the reasons for the role of equilibrium. All operational subject structures, on the one hand, and all causal structures in the domain of physical experience, on the other hand, suppose a combination of production and conservation. There is always some production, that is, some kind of transformation taking place. Similarly there is always some conservation, something that remains unchanged throughout the transformation. These two are absolutely inseparable. Without any transformation we have only static identity. The world becomes rigid and unchanging in the sense that Parmenides (c. 539 B.C.) conceived it. Without any conservation we have only constant transformation. There is total change; the world is always new and it becomes unintelligible. It becomes like the world of Heraclitus with its river in which one was never able to bathe twice. In reality, there are always both conservation and production.

Conservation demands compensations, and consequenlty equilibration. If something is changed, something else must change to compensate for it, in order to result in a conservation. Even in physics all the transformations that take place involve compensations in order to lead to a conservation. These compensations are organized in group structures in the mathematical sense of the term. Furthermore, there is no conservation without production, and production with conservation results in a constant demand for new construction.

Where I speak of equilibrium, it is not at all in the sense of a definitive state that cognitive functioning would be able to attain. Attained equilibrium is limited and restrained, and there is a tendency to go beyond it to a better equilibrium. . . . Simply stated, there is a continual search for a better equilibrium. In other words, equilibration is the search for a better and better equilibrium in the sense of an extended field, in the sense of an increase in the number of possible compositions, and in the sense of a growth in coherence.

I would now like to point out the fundamental difference between biological or cognitive equilibrium and physical equilibrium. In physics, equilibrium is a question of a balance of forces. Take, for example, a balance with two weights—one on each side. Between the two are the lever and the fulcrum which are only organs of transmission. They are passive mediators permitting the action from one side to the other.

In another example, the Le Châtelier-Braun experiment, a piston presses down on a container that is full of gas. The gas is compressed while the force of the piston increases the pressure. The force of the piston heats the gas making it agitate. This makes the gas hit back with pressure on the sides of the container and eventually back on to the piston. It compensates for the initial force that was pressing down on the piston and presses the piston back up again. Le Châtelier referred to this as the moderation of the original cause. Here again the container plays the role of the transmitter, a passive mediator which receives and sends back the shocks.

In biological or cognitive equilibrium, on the other hand, we have a system in which all parts are interdependent. It is a system which could be represented in the form of a cycle. A has its influence on B, which has its influence on C, which has its influence on D, which again influences A. It is a cycle of interactions among the different elements. It also has a special feature of being open to influences from the outside. Each of the elements can interact with external objects. For instance, the cycle can take in A^1 and B^1.

In the case of biological or cognitive equilibrium the links are not passive; they are the very sources of action. The totality presents a cohesive force which is specific and which is precisely the source of the assimilation of new elements of which we have been speaking since the beginning of this talk. The system forms a totality in order to assimilate the outside elements. This equilibrium between the integration and the differentiation of the parts in the whole has no equivalent in physics. It is only found in biological and cognitive equilibrium.

In closing I would just like to make two references on the matter of the cohesive force of the totality, the source of equilibrium in biological and cognitive structures. The first is from Paul Weiss, the great biologist, who in his work on cells pointed out that the structure of the totality of the cell is more stable than the activity of its elements. Inside the cell the elements are in constant activity but the total structure of the cell itself has a much more continuing stability.

My second reference will be in the cognitive domain. I would like to speak of the works of Presburger, cited by Tarski, which point out the existence of systems which as totalities are closed on themselves— and are completely coherent. All aspects are decidable, in the logical sense of the term, within the total system, while the subsystems are not so closed and every aspect is not entirely decidable. This seems to me a very fine example of the kind of equilibrium about which I am talking: the totality has its own cohesion and equilibrium by integrating and differentiating the parts at the same time. . . .

47

The Various Forms of Knowledge Seen as Differentiated

Organs of the Regulation of Functional

Exchanges with the External World*

1967

Having reached the end of our analysis, we shall find it useful here to take another look at our main hypothesis. What it amounts to is, on one hand, the supposition that cognitive mechanisms are an extension of the organic regulations from which they are derived, and, on the other, the supposition that these mechanisms constitute specialized and differentiated organs of such regulations in their interactions with the external world.

. . . The reader may have had the impression that we were pushing our analogies too far at certain points, for example, as between the synchronic processes of equilibrium or general structuration, and the diachronic processes of historical construction, or, more especially, between the endogenous factors, which, at certain points, we have emphasized almost exclusively, and the exogenous factors, to which some may think we have occasionally accorded exaggerated importance.

To deal with the first of these basic questions, one might be tempted to draw a distinction between the problems of evolution and development and the problems of synchronic organization. . . . Now, it is essential to point out very clearly from the beginning that no synchronic biological system, however dependent on existing equilibrium conditions, can be independent of history, because it is itself a product of evolution. Reciprocally, no development, either phyletic or individual, can be independent of a progressive organization or, therefore, of equilibrations. There are certainly other spheres, such as linguistics or economics, in

*Reprinted from *Biology and Knowledge* by Jean Piaget, translated by Beatrix Walsh, The University of Chicago Press, © 1971 by The University of Chicago and The University of Edinburgh. Reprinted by permission of the publishers. Originally published in French, 1967.

which the opposition between the synchronic and the diachronic is much more clearcut because there one is dealing with "arbitrary" symbols or with values of temporary efficacy, whose significance or sum total depends far more upon present equilibrium than on their past history. But the closer the realities under consideration come to structures, whether normative (as with cognitive structures) or merely dominant and comprising an opposition between the "normal" and the aberrant or even the pathological (as in the case of living things), the slighter the opposition between the diachronic and synchronic factors becomes, just because such structures have a tendency to be conserved in time. To talk about conservation within a reality that is functioning, not static, is, ipso facto, to imply continuous reconstruction and construction of a kind in which even the functional invariants are constantly related to development.

Thus, the fundamental reality about living things is constituted neither by timeless structures, standing outside history or dominating it like equilibrated organization forms with permanent conditions, nor by a historical succession of chances or crises like a series of disequilibria without equilibrations. It consists, rather, of continuous processes of autoregulation implying both disequilibria and a constant equilibration dynamism. All that needs to be said here is that at all levels, whether historical stages or the echelons of some organizational hierarchy, we find the simultaneous intervention of exogenous factors, causing disequilibria but also setting off "responses," and endogenous factors, producing these responses and acting as equilibration agents.

This means that anyone who sees, in the present study, a belief in the systematic primacy of one or the other of these factors will have failed to understand me, my central idea being constantly that of interaction. If, however, one were to take some passage or other out of its context, one might have the opposite impression or else an impression of oscillation rather than of a continual quest for synthesis. In this connection, it will be helpful to note, before going any further in this summing up, that the main difficulty about what I have been trying to do is that I am addressing two kinds of reader. Psychologists, with their commonsensical approach, lay all the stress on learning factors and environmental influence, forgetting, when it comes to cognitive functions, the implications of modern biology and failing to see the contradiction between biological mutationism and epistemological Lamarckism (integral empiricism). Thus, when addressing myself to them, I had to emphasize the endogenous factors, especially in connection with progressive equilibration and the logico-mathematical structures which are largely dependent upon it. Biologists, in their turn, have their own kind of common sense, which takes no account of epistemology or thought processes and likes to treat the human brain as the mere product of selection, just like horses' hooves and fishes' fins; with them in mind, I had to remember that the harmony between mathematics and physical reality is not all that easy to conceive, so that perhaps we have to recast our models of interaction between environment and the organization itself. It is to be hoped that biologists and psychologists will collaborate in future, so that together they may uncover the secrets of the organizing organization, once they have discovered those of the already organized organization.

The Functions Proper to the Acquisition of Knowledge

During our study of the functional connections and partial structural isomorphisms between cognitive and organic functions, we noted the existence of a remarkable number of points of contact. We also saw, however, that there were a number of differences which demonstrated the fact that knowledge, too, fulfills functions proper to itself. Indeed, to deny this would be unthinkable, for if the organism were self-sufficient without the aid of instinct, learning, or intelligence, this would be an indication of some radical separation between life and knowledge, since cognitive mechanisms undoubtedly exist. It might be possible to recognize this separation from various metaphysical points of view, but it would raise insoluble difficulties for any epistemology which was aimed simply at explaining why science can come to grips with the real world.

BEHAVIOR, THE EXTENSION OF ENVIRONMENT, AND THE CLOSING UP OF THE "OPEN SYSTEM"

If one is to base one's conclusions on the elementary data of ethology, by far the greatest part of the knowledge that can be had from animals is of a "knowing how" type, utilitarian and practical. Instinct is always at the service of the three fundamental needs of food, protection against enemies, and reproduction. If, with migration or various modes of social organization, instinct seems to pursue secondary ends, they are only secondary as being interests grafted onto the three main ones and still dependent upon them, so that in the last resort they are subordinated to the survival of the species and, as far as possible, of the individual.

The elementary forms of perceptual or sensorimotor learning do not emerge from a functional framework of this kind, and the same is true of a great deal of practical or sensorimotor intelligence. However, in the latter field, one would probably have to admit that, in the case of mammals and particularly of anthropoids, there is a slight advance beyond this in the direction of a pleasure in understanding for understanding's sake, althoug this may be functional too. We do, in fact, know that the young mammal plays, and that this play is not, as K. Groos tried to prove, simply an instinctive exercise but a general one of all the kinds of behavior possible at any given level, without any utilitarian purpose or consummation at the time. Now play is only one pole of the functional exercises which take place during an individual's development, and the other pole is nonplayful exercise in which the young subject "learns how to learn" (Harlow),* not only in the context of play but in that of cognitive adaptation. One of my children, at about one year old, who had succeeded by chance in getting a toy he

---

*Cf. Butler's experiment, suggested by Harlow, in which the only external aid used in training well-fed young monkeys to discriminate between things, was to let them look, when they were successful, through the window of their shuttered cage and thus satisfy their curiosity (with no relation to the discrimination called for).

wanted through the bars of his playpen when the toy was too big to go through horizontally and so had to be turned vertically, was not at all satisfied by this chance success. He put the toy out again and began all over again until he "understood" what was being done. No doubt this kind of disinterested knowing is equally possible in monkeys.

But whether exclusively utilitarian or attaining advances beyond "knowing how" to "understanding," knowledge in animals is evidence of a definite and particular function, like survival or feeding or reproducing in their organic aspects, properly speaking; it is the function of the extension of the environment. To seek food, instead of drawing it out of the soil or the air as plants do, is in itself an extension of one's environment. To seek out a female and engage in furthering one's species is giving reproduction a greater spatio-temporal extension than the mere physiological function allows. To explore for exploration's sake, without any immediate need (as the rats did in Blodgett's experiment about "latent learning"), right up to "learning for the sake of learning," as can be foreseen at the level of sensorimotor intelligence—this too is a further extension of the available environment.

It is clear that, at later stages, the mere fact of having elaborated instruments of intelligent knowing, even if this knowing only began with a utilitarian purpose, sets up a new functional situation, since all organs tend to develop and feed themselves for their own ends, which accounts for the basic cognitive needs of understanding and inventing. These needs, however, lead to an ever-increasing extension of the environment—this time the sum total of the objects of knowledge.

We can, then, express in biological terms this slow—though, with man, more and more accelerated—extension of the environment accessible first to vital needs and then to truly cognitive needs, by relating it to the basic traits of the living organization. An organism, Bertalanffy tells us, is an "open system," by which he means precisely that the organism only succeeds in preserving its form through a continuous flow of exchanges with the environment. Now, an open system is a system that is perpetually threatened, and so it is not for nothing that the basic aspects of survival, feeding, and reproduction are extended into behavior whose result is the extension of the usable environment. This extension must, then, be translated into a language which expresses its effective functioning; it is essentially a search for the means to close the system simply because it is too "open." From the probabilistic point of view, which is the only valid one in this case, the risk adhering to the open system is the fact that its immediate environment or frontier does not supply the elements necessary for its survival. On the other hand, if the system constitutes a limit which is constantly sought for but never attained, this does not mean that the primary needs of food, protection, and reproduction are limitless; the truth is quite the other way. What it does mean is that, with the invention of the various behaviors used in the quest for means to satisfy these needs, thanks to a slight extension of the original environment, the cognitive regulations of these behaviors sooner or later produce a limitless extension of the system. There are two reasons for this.

The first concerns the probability of encounter with the desired elements (food or sex) or the dreaded ones (protection). So long as the living creature does not possess differentiated sensory organs, external events only become of concern at moments of immediate contact and cease to exist for it as soon as they are at a distance. Thus, its only needs are momentary ones, extinguished as soon as satisfied, recurring only later in the course of a periodic cycle of greater or lesser length. On the other hand, as soon as a perceptual regulation appears and olfactory or visual organs signal the distant approach of food or danger, needs are modified by this very extension; even if the appetite is satisfied for the time being, the absence of food that can be seen or smelt becomes worrying, as being a modification of the probabilities of occurrence. This will create a new need in the shape of a need for seeking food even though there is no compelling need for an immediate meal. In the same way, to catch sight of enemies, at even a relatively safe distance, arouses a new need for vigilance and alertness. In other words, the appearance of a perceptual control leads to its improvement as a functional consequence, and this improvement leads to an extension of the environment with no possibility of the closure of the "open system" at that elementary level. It should be noted, moreover, that a general extension process of this kind is built up already on the organic plane, before there is any sensory control. This is the case with the dissemination of seeds in vegetative sexual reproduction, a fine example of spontaneous extension without cognitive regulation. What would it be like if some perceptual control made it possible for the plant to get feedback information of the poor success rate of this kind of propagation?

BEHAVIOR AND COGNITIVE REGULATIONS

The second reason for the extension of environment in order to close the "open system"—which, however, constantly pushes the limits of this closure farther back—is the progress of the cognitive regulations in their internal mechanism itself. This brings us up against an essential point as to the nature and method of development of the processes by which knowlege is acquired.

Let there be a physiological cycle of some kind $(A \times A') \to (B \times B') \to \ldots (Z \times Z') \ldots (A \times A') \to$ (prop. 1), in which $A, B, \ldots Z$ represent the elements of the organism, and $A', B', \ldots Z'$ the elements of the environment with which they inevitably interact. One can then schematize the intervention of a cognitive mechanism at its inception in the form of a regulation which reveals the presence of some external element, informs the corresponding A organs of it, and thus intervenes in the $A \to B$ process by facilitating its unfolding.

Thus, from the outset, cognitive reactivity has a part to play in regulation and serves to facilitate, reinforce, moderate, compensate, or otherwise control the physiological process. It is, however, obvious that this elementary reactivity, which may be evidenced in the form of tropisms or faintly differentiated reflexes, contains, just because it is a regulatory mechanism, possibilities and even exigencies of unlimited development, because the very nature of a regulation enables it to bring about its autocorrection by dint of regulating its regulations. In the case of the elementary pattern given above, the feedback from A' to A, which includes some system of signs to A', and indeed to A (afference and effection), brings in its train two sorts of possible improvement of behavior regulations to the second power, while physiological or internal regulations can improve the $A \to B$ process. First, there can be refinements in the recording of A', such as various conditionings which assimilate new signals or indices into the original perceptual schemata and thus are constantly widening the perceptual scope by means of regulations differentiating the initial overall assimilation. Second, and more important, there are refinements in the reaction schemata intervening in A, and this is where new regulations prove possible in an uninterrupted series, a very striking example of which is the sensorimotor development of the human infant.

Here we see a whole succession of increasingly complex acts built up on the initial reflex schemata of sucking, grasping with the hand, and moving the eyes. Of these the two general principles are the accommodation of assimilation schemata, which leads to their differentiation, and, more especially, the reciprocal assimilation of the schemata (vision, prehension, etc.), which leads to their coordination. Now, to look at this from the point of view which concerns us here, the two basic lessons to be learned from this presensorimotor development of the intelligence are (1) that the progress observed is due to regulations of regulations entailing the exercise of cognitive functions for their own sake, quite apart from any utilitarian purpose or originally strictly biological one such as feeding, and (2) that this progress therefore postpones indefinitely the "closure" of the system that is open to the environment.

The fact that progress is made by regulations of regulations is immediately apparent in the case of differentiation by means of accommodation of assimilation schemata. In effect, this accommodation is carried out by gropings, and these are a prime example of feedbacks in which an action is corrected in terms of its results. On the other hand, this groping regulation does not take place as an absolutely new development but from within a previous framework, thus from acquired assimilation schemata or reflexes, and these initial schemata constitute the basic regulation whose differentiation is brought about by an additional regulation.

As for the coordination of schemata by reciprocal assimilation, here again there are regulations regulating previous regulations, and these second-power regulations are of particular importance, since they tend toward operations. A schema coordination is a process at once pro- and retroactive, because it leads to a new synthesis by modifying, in turn, the schemata thus coordinated.

This internal development in the mechanism of cognitive regulations therefore presupposes the exercise of them, that is to say, the formation of a series of new interests which are no longer confined to the initial interests which were aroused simply by the functioning of the system. These interests are the functional expression of the very mechanism of cognitive assimilation, but, as again we have just seen, they are so by direct extension of the original assimilations. The extension of environment brought about in this way, therefore, concerns the environment in the biological sense of the sum of the stimuli which are of interest to the physiological cycle of the organization, as well as the cognitive environment as the sum of the objects challenging knowledge.

Now this new extension of the environment is equally incapable of closing the "open system," since it is always at the mercy of whatever may happen, in other words, of the chances that may arise in the experience of the subject. It is only when it comes to representation or thought, which speeds up the multiplication of spatio-temporal distances characteristic of the subject's field of action and of his comprehension, that some possibility of closure comes in sight. But then closure assumes a collection of interindividual or social exchanges as well as the exchanges with the individual environment, and this problem will have to be faced later on.

ORGANIC AND COGNITIVE EQUILIBRIUM

If the first essential function of cognitive mechanisms is the progressive closure of the "open system" of the organism by means of an unlimited extension of the environment (even if—or especially if—it never actually achieves completion from a static point of view), then this function entails a whole series of others.

The second function to be borne in mind is of supreme importance because it appertains to the equilibration mechanisms of the system. The living organization is essentially an autoregulation. If what we have just observed is true, then the development of the cognitive functions does indeed seem, according to our main hypothesis, to be the setting up of specialized organs of regulation in the control of exchanges with the environment—exchanges that are initially physiological and have to do with matter and energy, and then exchanges of a purely functional kind, that is to say those involved with the functioning of actions or behavior. But if differentiated organs are formed, are their own regulations identical to those of the organism? In other words, are the equilibrium forms attained the same in both cases?

Everything said in this book leads to the answer yes and no. They are the same regulations or the same forms of equilibrium in the sense that the cognitive organization is an extension of the vital organization and so introduces some equilibration into those sectors where the organic equilibrium remains insufficient both in its scope (as has just been seen) and even in what it achieves. However, cognitive regulations and equilibrium differ from vital equilibrium in that they succeed where the latter fails.

To start with the evolution of knowledge itself, at first sight we might think ourselves confronted with a phenomenon of exactly comparable type. Leaving out of account the instincts and the elementary kinds of learning, in all their diversity, the evolution of human knowledge does not always give us the impression of a coherent development in which each new accommodation caused by experiment is written into some assimilating framework of a permanent kind, with no opposition, and then either widens or merely differentiates that framework. There is, however, an exception, and it is the one which has been most difficult to integrate into the usual biological systems: the major exception of logico-mathematical structures, extremely important in itself, and all the more so because such structures produce the chief assimilatory schemata utilized in experimental knowledge. Logico-mathematical structures do, in fact, present us with an example, to be found nowhere else in creation, of a development which evolves without a break in such a way that no new structuration brings about the elimination of those preceding it; the earlier ones may be said to be unadapted to such and such an unforeseen situation, but only in the sense that they proved insufficient to solve some new problem and not that they are contradicted by the very terms of this problem, as may be the case in physics.

Thus, as has already been emphasized, logico-mathematical structures involve a *sui generis* equilibrium situation with regard to the relationship between assimilation and accommodation. On one hand, they appear to be a continuous construction of new assimilation schemata: assimilation of a previous structure into a new one, which integrates it, and assimilation of the experimental datum into the structures thus set up. But, on the other hand, logico-mathematical structures give evidence of a permanent accommodation, insofar as they are modified neither by the newly constructed structures (except, of course, by being improved thereby) nor by the experimental data whose assimilation they make possible. It is true that new data from physical experiment may set mathematicians some unforeseen problems and thus lead to the invention of theories aimed at assimilating them; but in such a case the invention is not based on accommodation as a physical concept is, but, as we have seen, it is an integral derivation from previous structures or schemata, though at the same time accommodating itself to the realities of the new situation.

One might, then, put forward an interpretation of a rather daring kind, which does, nonetheless, appear to contain a profound biological truth if it is admitted that the primary source of the coordinations of actions on which mathematics are based is to be sought within the general laws of organization. We suggest that the equilibrium between assimilation and accommodation which is brought about by logico-mathematical structures constitutes a state—mobile and dynamic and, at the same time, stable—aspired to unsuccessfully by the succession of forms, at least where behavior forms are concerned, throughout the course of the evolution of organized creatures. Whereas this evolution is characterized by an uninterrupted succession of disequilibria and of re-equilibrations, logico-mathematical structures do, in fact, attain permanent equilibrium despite the constantly renewed constructions which characterize their own evolution.

This brings us back to the problem of "vection" or "progress." The chief characteristic of the vection which seems to be evinced by organic evolution is a remarkable alliance between two features that are antipathetic at first sight, although their working together is a necessary factor in the adaptations achieved at the higher levels. The first of these was brought out principally by Schmalhausen: ever-deepening integration making the development processes more and more autonomous in relation to the environment. The second, stressed by Rensch and Julian Huxley, is the increasing "opening" of possibilities of actions upon the environment and, consequently, insertion into wider and wider environments.

It is obvious, in the first place, that these two interdependent aspects are to be found yet again in the development of knowledge; insofar as human intelligence uses logico-mathematical structures as an instrument of integration that is more and more independent of experiment, it achieves an ever greater conquest of the environment on which it experiments. But in this connection again cognitive structures overtake organic ones by extending them, and this because of the very nature of the form taken by their equilibration—a common nature but, as has just been seen, carried on in the cognitive domain to forms which organic equilibrium can never achieve. Where vection is concerned, the difference is shown in the following way. Progress in integration, as Schmalhausen emphasized, is only concerned with the sort of integration that is, as it were, existing now, or synchronic, which means that it always has to be reconstituted in every new group without integrating the entire phyletic past as subsystems that are both conserved and overtaken. (To give a concrete example of this, mammals lost a part of their reptile characteristics in becoming mammals.) On the contrary, integration, as found in cognitive evolution, has the unique quality, as we have just seen, not only of existing now but of integrating the whole body of previous structures as subsystems into the integration now taking place. This integration, amazingly both diachronic and synchronic at the same time, is carried out in mathematics without disturbance of any kind, for, in mathematics, "crises" merely mean growth, and the only contradictions in it are temporary. In the field of experimental knowledge, however, a new theory may contradict those that have gone before, but it is noteworthy that a new theory always aims at the maximum integration of the past, so that the best theory is, once again, that which integrates all the preceding ones and simply adds on to this integration such retroactive corrections as may be necessary.

DISSOCIATION OF FORMS AND CONSERVATION

This victory, however, is due to another specific characteristic of the cognitive functions as compared to the forms of living organization: the possible dissociation of forms and contents. An organic form is inseparable from the matter organized within it and is only suited, in any particular case, to a limited and clearly determined body of matter whose eventual modification will entail a change of form. This sort of situation is again found (given the continuity linking the living to the cognitive organization) in the case of elementary forms of knowledge, such as sensorimotor and perceptual schemata, although these may be much more highly generalized than the countless forms of the living organization. But, as intelligence develops, operational schemata also become very generalized, although at the level of concrete operations they are still attached to their content as a structuration is to structured matter, when the former only acts approximately without sufficient deductive mobility. But with hypothetico-deductive operations, by a system of all possible combinations of propositions, a formal logic can emerge in the form of an organizing structure applicable to any content whatever. This is what makes possible the constitution of "pure" mathematics as a construction of forms of organization, ready to organize everything, but from time to time organizing nothing, insofar as it becomes dissociated from its application! Here again we are confronted with a biological situation which would be unthinkable in the organic domain, where microorganisms are seen to "transduce" a genetic message from one species to another, but in the form of content or matter, and where genetic "transduction" has yet to be seen affecting the organization alone as a form dissociated from all substance!

Now this purifying of form achieves, in the cognitive domain, successes that are constantly being sought after, so to speak, in the organic domain, but never fully attained. Emphasis was laid [above] on the analogies between the conservation of biological forms, which is so evident in the regulating autoconservation of the genome, and the exigencies of conservation found in the various forms of intelligence, starting from the sensorimotor type (for example, the schema of the permanence of objects) and on up to operational conservations. The reader may get the impression often in reading this book that I am making an artificial comparison between quasi-physical systems on one hand and normative or ideal ones on the other. But since the time that a clearer view emerged of the essential nature of the regulation pertaining to elementary cognitive functions and the way in which the regulations become operations, my comparison has become more easily acceptable, since organic conservation is, in fact, brought about by regulatory mechanisms. However, these analogies we have been talking about lead to one important difference, and this is precisely what interests us here: organic conservations are never anything more than approximate. This is the case, too, with preoperational cognitive forms (perceptual constancies, etc.), whereas only the operational conservations of the intelligence are binding and "necessary," on account of the dissociation of forms and contents that has just been noted.

Conservation is closely linked to operational reversibility, which is its source and evinces, moreover, the particular form of equilibration attained by logico-mathematical structures. Here we have certainly reached the crux of the differences which, at the heart of their analogies, distinguish the constructive work of intellectual operations from organic transformations. The profound analogy is, we have seen, that both of them have constantly to struggle against the irreversibility of events and the decay of energy and information systems. Again, both of them succeed in their struggle by means of elaborating their organized and equilibrated systems, the principle of which is compensation for deviations and errors. Thus, as soon as there are regulations of any homeostasis, genetic or physiological, there is a fundamental tendency to reversibility, the outcome of which is the approximate conservation of the system. Whatever solutions, as yet undecisive, may eventually be found to the problem of the antichance function which is necessary both to organization and to evolution, it does, in fact, remain true that an autoregulatory system includes actions directed in two opposite ways, and that the progress of this approximate reversibility can be followed during the development of cognitive regulations. But, as was pointed out above—and is generally the outcome of the interplay between reflective abstractions and convergent reconstructions with overtakings—the overtakings that mark the progress of each stage in relation to the preceding one are more dependent on regulations of regulations—which means on a reflexive fining down of the system or of the controls superimposed—than on a simple horizontal extension. It is thus that the "operations" mechanism of thought is something more than a mere extension of regulations at a lower stage and marks a kind of transition up to the point at which strict reversibility is constituted when the retroactive feedback action becomes an "inverse operation" and thus guarantees an exact functional equivalence between the two possible directions of construction.

The most remarkable aspect of the way in which human knowledge is built up, as compared with the evolutionary transformations of the organism and such forms of knowledge as are accessible to animals, is that it has a collective as well as an individual nature. One can, of course, see this characteristic faintly sketched out in a few animal species, notably the chimpanzee. But the novel aspect of it where man is concerned is that external or educative transmission, as opposed to the hereditary of internal transmission of instincts, has culminated in the sort of organization that has been able to engender civilizations.

Two sorts of development have to be recognized—one organic (belonging to a single organism) and the other genealogical (including filiation trees, either social or genetic). Yet the history of human knowledge unites these two developments in one whole; ideas, theories, schools of thought are engendered in genealogical order, and trees can be constructed which represent their structural filiations. But these structures are integrated into a single intellectual organism to such a point that the succession of seekers is comparable, as Pascal said, to one man continuously learning throughout time.

Human societies have been viewed in turn as the result of individual initiative perpetuated by imitation, like totalities shaping individuals from outside or as complex systems of interaction, whose products are individual action—always part and parcel of some more or less important sector of the group—as well as the whole group constituting the system of these interactions. In the realm of knowledge, it seems obvious that individual operations of intelligence and operations making for exchanges in cognitive cooperation are one and the same thing. The "general coordination of actions" to which we have continually referred [is] an interindividual as well as an intraindividual coordination because such "actions" can be collective as well as executed by individuals. The question whether logic and mathematics are essentially individual or social attainments loses all meaning; the epistemological subject constructing them is both an individual, though decentered in relation to his private ego, and the sector of the social group decentered in relation to the constraining idols of the tribe. This is because these two kinds of decentering both manifest the same intellectual interactions or general coordinations of action of which knowledge is constituted.

The result of this, then, is the last fundamental difference we shall have to point out between biological and cognitive organizations: the most generalized forms of thought, those that can be dissociated from their content, are, by that very fact, forms of cognitive exchange or of interindividual regulation, as well as being produced by the common functioning which is a necessary part of every living organization. Of course, from the psychogenetic point of view, these interindividual or social (and nonhereditary) regulations constitute a new fact in relation to the thought processes of the individual—which, without them, would be subject to all the egocentric distortions—and a necessary condition for the formation of a decentered epistemological subject. However, from the logical point of view, such higher regulations are nonetheless dependent upon the conditions of any general coordination of actions and thus become part, once more, of the common biological foundation.

Organic Regulations and Cognitive Regulations

This collective overtaking of forms constructed originally on the basis of the living organization presents the right framework for the conclusions that must now be drawn from our discussion. The hypothesis still to be justified is that cognitive functions constitute a specialized organ for regulating exchanges with the external world, although the instruments by which they do so are drawn from the general forms of the living organization.

LIFE AND TRUTH

It may be said that to talk of the necessity of a differentiated organ falls short of the meaning we are trying to convey, since the property of knowledge is the attainment of truth, whereas the property of life is simply the quest for survival. While we may not know exactly what life is, we know still less about the meaning of cognitive "truth." There is a sort of general agreement that it is something more than a faithful copy of the world of reality for the very good reason that such a copy could not possibly be made, since only the copy could supply us with the knowledge of the model being copied, and, moreover, such knowledge is necessary for the copy to be made. Attempts to make this copy theory acceptable have only resulted in simple phenomenalism, in which the subjectivity of the ego is perpetually interfering with the perceptual datum—a theory which itself betrays the inextricable mixture of subject and object.

If the true is not a copy, then it must be an organization of the real world. But an organization due to what subject? If this subject is merely a human one, then we shall be in danger of extending egocentrism into a sort of anthropo- or even socio-centrism, with minimal gain. As a result, all philosophers in search of an absolute have had recourse to some transcendental subject, something on a higher plane than man and much higher than "nature," so that truth, for them, is to be found way beyond any spatio-temporal and physical contingencies, and nature becomes intelligible in an intemporal or eternal perspective. But then the question is whether one can possibly jump over one's own shadow and thus reach the "Subject" in oneself, without its remaining "human, too human," as Nietzsche put it. Indeed, the whole trouble has been, from Plato to Husserl, that this transcendental subject has been changing its appearance all the time but with no improvements other than those due to the progress of science—the progress of the real model rather than the transcendental one.

Thus, what we must try to do here is not to get away from nature, for no one can escape nature, but to penetrate it gradually with the aid of science, because, despite all that philosophers say, nature is still very far from having yielded up all her secrets, and before we locate the absolute up in the clouds, it may well be helpful to take a look inside things. Once we do that, if the true is an organization of the real, then we first need to know how such an organization is organized, which is a biological question. To put it another way, as the epistemological problem is to know how science is possible, then what we must do, before having recourse to a transcendental organization, is to fathom all the resources of the immanent organization.

Just because the true is not egocentric and must not remain anthropocentric, do we have to reduce it to a biocentric organization? Just because truth is greater than man, do we have to look for it back among the Protozoa, the termites, and the chimpanzees? If we defined truth as being that which there is in common between all the different views that all creatures, including man, have held about the world, we would get a rather poor result. But the very nature of life is constantly to overtake itself, and if we seek the explanation of rational organization within the living organization *including its overtakings*, we are attempting to interpret knowledge in terms of its own construction, which is no longer an absurd method since knowledge is *essentially construction*.

THE SHORTCOMINGS OF THE ORGANISM

These overtakings, as essential a part of the organization as its original data are, seem to us, from the cognitive point of view, to be inherent in the living organization. Such an organization is a system of exchanges with the environment; it therefore tries to extend as far as the environment as a whole does, but it does not succeed. This is where knowledge comes in, for knowledge functionally assimilates the whole universe and does not remain within the limits of material physiological assimilations. This living organization is capable of creating forms, and its tendency is to conserve them in a stable state, but it does not succeed, and this is why knowledge is necessary—to extend these material forms of actions or operation so that it becomes possible to conserve them through applying them to the various contents from which they have been dissociated. This living organization is the source of homeostases at every rung of the evolutionary ladder. These proceed by means of regulations, which guarantee the equilibrium of quasi-reversible mechanisms. This equilibrium, however, is tenuous and can resist environmental reversibility only at momentary periods of stability, so that evolution appears to be a series of disequilibria and re-equilibrations, which then—without attaining it themselves—give place to a mode of construction with integrations and reversible mobility that only cognitive mechanisms will be able to realize by integrating regulation into construction itself in the form of "operations."

To put it briefly, the necessity for differentiated organs for regulating exchanges with the external world is caused by the living organization's inability to achieve its own program as written into the laws which govern it. On one hand, the organization does contain genetic mechanisms which are not only transmitters but are also formative. But the modes of formation known of at present by recombinations of genes are only one limited sector of construction, confined by the exigencies of a hereditary program which is itself always limited because it cannot reconcile construction and conservation in one coherent dynamic whole, as knowledge can, and because its information about the environment is not sufficiently fluid. On the other hand, phenotypes, which achieve quite a detailed interaction with the environment, are distributed in a "reaction norm," which is itself limited, but, above all, whose every achievement remains both limited and of no influence upon the whole—since phenotypes lack the social or external interactions that man will have in his cognitive exchanges—other than by means of genetic recombinations, the limitations of which have been pointed out.

This dual incapacity of organisms in their material exchanges with the environment is partly compensated for by the way behavior is constituted—invented by the organization as an extension of its internal program. In fact, behavior is simply the organization of life itself, applied or generalized to a wider range of exchanges with the environment. Such exchanges become functional, since material and energy exchanges are guaranteed from the outset by physiological organization. Here "functional" means that actions or action forms or schemata are involved, extending the scope of the organic forms. Nevertheless, these new exchanges, like all the others, consist of accommodations to the environment, taking account of the events in that environment and their consequences; but above all they consist of assimilations which exploit the environment and often even impose forms upon it, using constructions or arrangements of objects in terms of the organism's requirements.

Behavior, as with all kinds of organization, includes regulations, whose function is to control constructive accommodations and assimilations on the basis of the results obtained as the action goes on, or by means of anticipation, which allows it to foresee what events may prove favorable or unfavorable and to make sure the necessary compensations are provided. It is these regulations, differentiated from the internal controls of the organism (since now we are dealing with behavior), that constitute cognitive functions. The problem, then, is to understand how they can surpass organic regulations to the point where they can carry out the internal program of the organization in general without being limited by the shortcomings just referred to.

INSTINCT, LEARNING, AND LOGICO-MATHEMATICAL STRUCTURES

The fundamental facts to be borne in mind here are, first, that cognitive regulations begin by using the only instruments used by organic adaptation in general, that is to say heredity, with its limited variations, and phenotypic accommodation; hereditary modes of learning, instincts in particular, follow this pattern. But then the same shortcomings as those seen in the original organization and for which the new echelon of behavior is only a mild corrective are found in innate knowledge, hence, though only at the higher stages of evolution, the final bursting of the instinct, leading to dissociation between its two component parts —internal organization and the phenotypic accommodation. The result, as we have seen—not because of this dissociation but by means of complementary reconstructions in two opposite directions—is the dual formation of logico-mathematical structures and experimental knowledge, remaining undifferentiated in the practical intelligence of anthropoids (which are geometers as well as technicians) and in the technical intelligence of the beginnings of humanity.

The three basic types of knowledge being innate knowledge, whose prototype is instinct, knowledge of the physical world, by which learning is extended in terms of the environment, and logico-mathematical knowledge, the relationship between the first and the two last appears to be essential if we are to understand how it is that the higher forms do in fact constitute an organ for regulating exchanges.

Instinct certainly includes cognitive regulations, as witnessed, for example, by the feedback system set up by Grassé's "stigmergia." But such regulations are only of a limited and inflexible kind, because they take place within the framework of a hereditary program, and a programmed regulation is incapable of inventing anything. Of course, it may happen that an animal succeeds in coping with some unforeseen circumstance by means of readjustments which herald the dawn of intelligence. We have seen that the schema coordinations produced on such an occasion are comparable to the innate coordinations of the transindividual instinctive cycle. [This is] a valuable indication of the possible similarity of function between instinct and intelligence, despite the difference in epigenetic and phenotypic levels which separates them. However, such phenotypic extensions of the instinct are very limited and their incapacities are thus chronic. [This] shows that a form of knowledge still subject only to the instruments of organic adaptation, although it may have the beginnings of a cognitive regulation, cannot go very far toward achieving what intelligence can in relation to life.

The sphere of learning proper, which is beyond the innate, begins even at the protozoic level but develops very slowly up to cerebralization in the higher vertebrates, and however remarkable the exceptions may be in the case of certain insects, there is no sign of any systematic spurt until the primate stage.

THE BURSTING OF INSTINCT

The basic phenomenon of the bursting—in other words, the almost total disappearance, in the case of anthropoids and man—of a cognitive organization which has remained dominant throughout the entire evolution of animal behavior, is thus of the very greatest significance. It is significant, not, as is usually said, because a new mode of acquiring knowledge—namely, intelligence considered as a unit—suddenly replaces a wornout mode. There is much more to it than this. It has the much deeper significance that a still virtually organic form of knowledge is extended into new forms of regulation, which, though substituted for the preceding form, do not really replace it but inherit it, dividing it and using its component parts in two complementary directions.

What does disappear, with the bursting of instinct, is hereditary programming, and this is in favor of two new kinds of cognitive autoregulations, mutable and constructive. It will be said that this is surely a replacement and a total one at that. But to say so is to ignore two essential factors. Instinct does not consist exclusively of hereditary apparatus; Viaud wisely calls this a limit-concept. Instinct derives its programming and its "logic" from an organized functioning typical of the most highly generalized forms of the living organization. It extends this programming into individual or phenotypic actions, which include a considerable margin of accommodation and even of assimilation, partly learned and, in certain cases, quasi-intelligent.

What vanishes with the bursting of instinct is exclusively the central or median part, that is, the programmed regulation, whereas the other two realities persist: the sources of organization and the resultants of individual or phenotypic adjustment. Thus, intelligence does inherit something from instinct although it rejects its method of programmed regulation in favor of constructive autoregulation. The part of instinct that is retained allows the intelligence to embark on two different but complementary courses: interiorization, in the direction of its sources, and exteriorization, in the direction of learned or even experimental adjustments.

The condition which must exist before this dual advance can take place is, of course, the construction of a new method of regulation. Such regulations, which now become mobile instead of being set in a program, consist, first of all, of the usual correction processes expressed in terms of the results achieved by actions or anticipations. But being an integral part of assimilation schemata and their coordinations, these regulations develop into operations, thanks to a combination of proactive and retroactive effects. Such operations are no longer corrections but pre-correction regulations, and the inverse operation guarantees complete rather than approximate reversibility.

With the aid of this new type of regulation constituting a differentiated organ of deductive verification and of construction, intelligence now embarks simultaneously in the directions of reflective interiorization and experimental exteriorization just referred to. It will be clearly understood that this dual orientation does not by any means imply a mere dividing up of what is left of instinct. On the contrary, all that is left of instinct is the source of its organization and its resultants of individual exploration and research. In order to get back to its source and to extend the resultants, intelligence must therefore undertake new constructions—some by means of reflective abstractions, by identifying the necessary conditions for the general coordinations of action, others by means of assimilation of the experimental datum into the operational schemata thus constructed. It remains true, nevertheless, that these two directions are extensions of two former components of the instinct.

With the bursting of instinct, a new cognitive evolution thus begins, and it begins all over again from zero, since the inner apparatus of instinct has gone, and, however hereditary the cerebralized nervous system and the learning and inventive powers of intelligence may be, the work to be done thereafter is phenotypic. It is, moreover, just because intellectual evolution begins all over again from zero that its relations with the living organization are so rarely perceived, still less its relations with the constructions of the instinct, striking as these are. Here we have a fine example of what I called "convergent reconstructions with overtaking." In human knowledge, in fact, the reconstruction is so complete that almost no theorist of logico-mathematical knowledge has thought of explaining that knowledge by going back to the obviously necessary frameworks of the living organization. This was true, at least, until work done in the field of mechano-physiology showed the affiliation between logic, cybernetic models, and the workings of the brain, and until McCulloch began talking about the logic of neurons.

KNOWLEDGE AND SOCIETY

If such a complete reconstruction is possible, it is because, when abandoning the support of hereditary apparatus and developing constructed and phenotypic regulations, intelligence gives up the transindividual cycles of the instinct only to adopt interindividual or social interactions. Nor does there seem to be any discontinuity in this, since even chimpanzees work only in groups.

It has already been pointed out that the social group—in this connection and in cognition—plays the same role that the "population" does in genetics and consequently in instinct. In this sense, society is the supreme unit, and the individual can only achieve his inventions and intellectual constructions insofar as he is the seat of collective interactions that are naturally dependent, in level and value, on society as a whole. The great man who at any time seems to be launching some new line of thought is simply the point of intersection or synthesis of ideas which have been elaborated by a continuous process of cooperation, and, even if he is opposed to current opinions, he represents a response to underlying needs which arise outside himself. This is why the social environment is able to do so effectively for intelligence what genetic recombinations of the population did for evolutionary variation or the transindividual cycle of the instincts.

But however externalized and educative its modes of transmission and interaction may be as opposed to hereditary transmissions or groupings, society is nevertheless a product of life. Its "collective representations," as Durkheim calls them, still presuppose the existence of a nervous system in each member of the group. So the important question is not how to assess the respective merits of individual and group (which is a problem just like that of deciding which comes first, the chicken or the egg), but to see the logic in solitary reflection as in cooperation, and to see the errors and follies both in collective opinion and in individual conscience. Whatever Tarde may say, there are not two kinds of logic, one for the group and the other for the individual; there is only one way of coordinating actions A and B according to relationships of inclusion or order whether such actions be those of different individuals A and B or of the same individual (who did not invent them single-handed, because he is a part of society as a whole). Thus, cognitive regulations cooperations are the same in a single brain or in a system of cooperations.

CONCLUSION

On the whole, I think that I have justified the two hypotheses which were linked together in my main thesis: that cognitive functions are an extension of organic regulations and constitute a differentiated organ for regulating exchanges with the external world. The organ in question is only partially differentiated at the level of innate knowledge, but it becomes increasingly differentiated with logico-mathematical structures and social exchanges or exchanges inherent in any kind of experiment.

There is nothing unusual about these hypotheses, I know, and I am sorry that it should be so. Nevertheless, they are hypotheses which must be constantly and more extensively explored, because, strangely, specialists in epistemology, particularly mathematical epistemology, are too much inclined to leave biology out of account, while biologists, as a rule, completely forget to ask why mathematics is adapted to physical reality.

This book has many shortcomings, the principal one being that it proves nothing and that I put forward nothing except possible interpretations based on facts, although constantly going beyond them. Nevertheless, this essay seemed worth writing, for to provide proofs would necessitate the sort of collaboration between biologists, psychologists, and epistemologists that hardly exists at the present time but is devoutly to be wished. It is only by interdisciplinary effort that a scientific epistemology is possible, and such cooperation is still much too rare to respond to the outstanding problems. It is in the hope of furthering this cooperation that I have attempted to project the ideas contained in this volume.

BIBLIOGRAPHY

1907—Un moineau albinos. *Le rameau de sapin*, Organe du Club jurassien, Neuchâtel, *41*:36. (The albino sparrow. This volume, p. 6, editors' translation.)

1909—La Xerophila obvia au canton de Vaud. *Le rameau de sapin*, Organe du Club jurassien, Neuchâtel, *43*:13;44 (1910):4. (Xerophila in the canton of Vaud. This volume, p. 7 editors' translation.)

1912—Les récents dragages malacologiques de M. le Prof. Émile Yung dans le lac Léman. *Journal de conchyliologie*, Paris, 60:205–232. (Recent malacological draggings in the lake of Geneva by professor Emile Yung. This volume, pp. 10–12, editors' translation.)

1913—Les mollusques sublittoraux du léman recueillis par m. le. Prof. Yung *Zoologischer Anzeiger*, Leipzig, 42:615–624.

1913—Nouveaux dragages malacologiques de m. le Prof. Yung dans la faune profonde du Léman. *Zoologischer Anzeiger*, Leipzig, 42: 216–223.

1914—Bergson et Sabatier. *Revue chrétienne*, Paris, 61:192–200.

1914—L'espèce mendelienne a-t-elle une valeur absolue? *Zoologischer Anzeiger*, Leipzig, 44:328–331. (Has the Mendelian Species an Absolute Value? (This volume, pp. 19–22, editors' translation.)

1914—Notes sur la biologie des limnées abyssales. *Internationale Revue der gesamten Hydrographie*, Leipzig, *Biologisches Supplement*, 6:15 pp. (Notes on the biology of deep-water limnaea. This volume, pp. 13–18, editors' translation.)

1915—*La mission de l'idée.* Lausanne, Édition La Concorde, (couverture:1916): 68 pp. The mission of the idea. (This volume, pp. 26–37, editors' translation.)

1917–1918—La biologie et la guerre. *Feuille centrale de la Société suisse de Zofingue* (Zentralblatt des schweizerischen Zofinger-Vereins), 58:374–380. Biology and war. (This volume, pp. 39–41, editors' translation.)

1918—*Recherche.* Lausanne, Edition La Concorde, 210 pp. Editors' summary, this volume, pp. 42–50.

1919–1920—La psychanalyse dans ses rapports avec la psychologie de l'enfant. *Bulletin mensuel de la Société Alfred Binet*, Psychologie de l'enfant et pédagogie expérimentale, Paris, 20:18–34, 41–58. Psychoanalysis in its relations with child psychology. (This volume, pp. 55–59, editors' translation.)

1921—Essai sur quelques aspects du développement de la notion de partie chez l'enfant. *Journal de psychologie normale et pathologique.* Paris, *18*:449–480. The child's idea of part. (This volume, p. 60, editors' translation.)

1921–1923—La pensée symbolique et la pensée de l'enfant. *Archives de psychologie*, Genève, *18*:273–304.

1921–1923—Une forme verbale de la comparaison chez l'enfant. Un cas de transition entre le jugement prédicatif et le judgement de relation. Thèse présentée à la Faculté des Sciences de l'Université de Genève pour obtenir le droit d'ensigner en qualité de pri-

vatdocent. Extrait des *Archives de psychologie*, Genève, Kundig,
18:141–172.

1922—Essai sur la multiplication logique et les débuts de la pensée
formelle chez l'enfant. *Journal de psychologie normale et pathologique*, Paris, *19*:222–261.

1922—Pour l'étude des explications d'enfants. *L'éducateur*, Lausanne
& Genève, *58*:33–39.

1923—Le langage et la pensée chez l'enfant. Édouard Claparède,
preface. Neuchâtel & Paris, Delachaux & Niestlé, XIV, 318 pp.;
1926—The language and thought of the child. London, Kegan
Paul, Trench, Trubner, XXIII, 246 pp. (This volume, pp. 65–88.)
Collaborators: Alice Deslex, Germaine Guex, A. Leuzinger-
Schuler, Hilda de Meyenburg, Valentine Jean Piaget, Liliane
Veihl.

1924—Le jugement et le raisonnement chez l'enfant. Neuchâtel &
Paris, Delachaux & Niestlé, 343 pp. (Judgment and reasoning
in the child. This volume, pp. 89–117.) Collaborators: Emmy
Cartalis, Sophie Escher, Ulrike Hanhart, L. Hahnloser, Olga
Matthes, Suzanne Perret, Marcelle Roud.

1924–1925—La notion de l'ordre des événements et le test des images en
désordre chez l'enfant de 6 à 10 ans. With Hélène Krafft.
Archives de psychologie, Genève, *19*:306–349.

1925—De quelques formes primitives de causalité chez l'enfant.
Phénoménisme et efficace. With Hélène Krafft. *L'année psychologique*. *26*:31–71.

1926—*La représentation du monde chez l'enfant.* Paris, Alcan, XLIII,
424 pp.; 1929—*The child's conception of the world.* Joan and
Andrew Tomlinson, translators. London, Kegan Paul, Trench,
Trubner, IX, 397 pp. Collaborators: A. Bodourian, Germaine
Guex, R. Hepner, Hélène Krafft, Émilie Margairaz, S. Perret,
Valentine Jean Piaget, M. Rodrigo, M. Roud, N. Swetlova,
Versteeg.

1927—*La causalité physique chez l'enfant.* Paris, Alcan, 347 pp.;
1930—*The child's conception of physical causality.* London,
Kegan Paul, Trench, Trubner, VIII, 309 pp. (This volume, pp.
119–153.) Collaborators: G. Bieler, A. Bodourian, Daiber, Germaine Guex, L. Hahnloser, R. Hepner, Herzog, Hélène Krafft, J.
Lebherz, Émilie Margairaz, Valentine Jean Piaget, H. Rehfous,
M. Rodrigo, M. Roud, N. Swetlova, Versteeg, Zwickhardt.

1927–1928—La causalité chez l'enfant. *The British journal of psychology, General section, 18*: 276–301. Address given in Cambridge, England, March 4, 1927 to the Cambridge Education
Society.

1927–1928—La première année de l'enfant. *The British journal of psychology, General section, 18*:97–120. Paper read before the British
Psychological Society March 7, 1927. (The first year of life
of the child. This volume, pp. 198–214, editors' translation.)

1928—"Immanence et transcendance." In Jean Piaget and Jean de
La Harpe. *Deux types d'attitudes religieuses: immanence et
transcendance.* Lausanne & Genève, Éditions de l'Association
chrétienne d'étudiants de Suisse romande; Genève, Labor, pp.
7–40.

1932—*Le jugement moral chez l'enfant.* Paris, Alcan, XI, 478 pp.;
1932—*The moral judgment of the child.* Marjorie Gabain,
translator. London, Kegan Paul, Trench, Trubner, IX, 418 pp.
(This volume, pp. 159–193.) Collaborators: N. Baechler, A. M.
Feldweg, Marc Lambercier, L. Martinez-Mont, N. Maso, Valentine Jean Piaget, M. Rambert.

1941—*La genése du nombre chez l'enfant.* With Alina Szeminska.
Neuchâtel & Paris, Delachaux & Niestlè, IV, 308 pp.; 1952—
The child's conception of number. Caleb Gattegno and Frances
Mary Hodgson, translators. London, Routledge & Kegan Paul,
IX, 248 pp. (This volume, pp. 298–341.) Collaborators. Zahara

Glikin, Juan Jaen, Taitana Katzaroff-Eynard, Refia Mehmed-Semin, Zoe, Trampidis, Edith Vauthier Florintine Zakon.

1946—*Le devéloppement de la notion de temps chez l'enfant.* Paris, Presses Universitaires de France, VII, 298 pp.; 1969—*The child's conception of time.* A. J. Pomerans, translator. London, Routledge & Kegan Paul, XI, 285 pp. (This volume, pp. 547–575.) Collaborators: Esther Bussmann, Edith Meyer, Vroni Richli, Myriam van Remoortel.

1946—*Les notions de mouvement et de vitesse chez l'enfant.* Paris, Presses universitaires des France, VII, 284 pp.; 1970—*The child's conception of movement and speed.* G.E.T. Holloway and M. J. Mackenzie, translators. London, Routledge & Kegan Paul, XI, 306 pp. (This volume, pp. 520–546.) Collaborators: Barbara von Albertini, Madeleine Blanchet, Esther Bussmann, M. et Mme. Claude Ferrière, Olga Frank, J. Frei, Monique Lagier, Madeleine Martin, A. Mauris, Madeleine Reymond.

1948—*La représentation de l'espace chez l'enfant.* With Bärbel Inhelder. Paris, Presses universitaires de France, 581 pp.; 1956—*The child's conception of space.* F. J. Langdon and J. L. Lundzer, translators. London, Routledge & Kegan Paul, XII, 490 pp. (This volume, pp. 576–642.) Collaborators: Hans Aebli, G. Ascoli, E. Bussmann, B. Demetriadès, Marianne Denis-Prinzhorn, U. Galusser, M. Gantenbein, J. Halpérin-Goetschel, E. De Jongh, T. Kiss, G. Lewinnew, Édith Méyer, Albert Morf, J. Nicolas, E. de Planta, ch. Renard, M. Roth, E. Sontag.

1949—*Traité de logique. Essai de logistique opératoire.* Paris, Colin, VIII, 423 pp.

1950—*Introduction à l'épistémologie génétique.* Vols. 1–3. Paris, Presses universitaires de France. Vol I: *La pensée mathématique,* 361 pp.; Vol. II: *La pensée physique,* 355 pp.; Vol. III: *La pensée biologique, La pensée psychologique et la pensée sociologique,* 334 pp.

1950—*The psychology of intelligence.* Malcolm Piercy and Daniel Ellis Berlyne, translators. London, Routledge & Kegan Paul, VIII, 182 pp.; Originally published in French in 1947 (*La psychologie de l'intelligence.*)

1951—*Le developpement chez l'enfant, de l'idee de patrie et des relations avec l'etranger.* With d'Anne-Marie Weil. From Nouvelles méthodes pour l'étude des stéréotypes *Bulletin international des sciences sociales,* Paris (Unesco), 3:539–630; 605–621.

1951—*Play, dreams and imitation in childhood.* With author's preface to English trans. Caleb Gattegno and Frances Mary Hodgson, translators. Melbourne, London, Toronto, Heinemann, X, 296 pp.; Originally published in French in 1945 (*La formation du symbole chez l'enfant.*)

1952—*Essai sur les transformations des opérations logiques. Les 256 opérations ternaires de la logique bivalente des propositions.* Paris, Presses universitaires de France, XI, 239 pp.

1952—Jean Piaget autobiography.) Donald MacQueen, translator. In *A history of psychology in autobiography,* Vol. 4. Edwin G. Boring, Herbert S. Langfeld, Heinz Werner, and Robert M. Yerkes, eds. Worcester, Massachusetts, Clark University Press, pp. 237–256.; 1966—Autobiographie, In: Jean Piaget et les sciences sociales. A Monsieur Jean Piaget à l'occasion de son 70e anniversaire (*Cahiers Vilfredo Pareto,* Genève, 4:129–149.

1952—La logistique axiomatique ou "pure," la logistique opératoire ou psychologique et les réalités auxquelles elles correspondent. *Methodos,* Milan, 4:7284, avec discussion de Vittorio Somenzi, p. 85.

1952—*The origins of intelligence in children.* Margaret Cook, translator. New York, International Universities Press, XI, 419 pp.; Originally published in French in 1936 (*La naissance de l'intelligence chez l'enfant.*) (This volume, pp. 215–249.)

1953—*Logic and psychology.* Wolfe Mays and Frederick Whitehead, translators. With an introduction on Piaget's logic by Wolfe Mays. Based on three lectures delivered at the University of Manchester in October 1952. Manchester, Manchester University Press, XIX, 48 pp. (This volume, pp. 445–477.)

1954—La résistance des bonnes formes à l'illusion de Müller-Lyer. With F. Maire, and F. Privat, *Archives de Psychologie,* no. 135.

1954—*The construction of reality in the child.* Margaret Cook, translator. New York, Basic Books, XIII, 386 pp. Originally published in French in 1937 (*La construction du réel chez l'enfant.*) (This volume, pp. 250–294.)

1954—"The problem of conciousness in child psychology: developmental changes in awareness." Edith Meyer, translator. In *Problems of consciousness. Transactions of the 4th Conference on problems of consciousness,* Harold A. Abramson, ed. New York, Josiah Macy Jr. Foundation.

1956—"Les stades du developpement intellectuel de l'enfant et de l'adolescent." In *Le problème des stades en psychologie de l'enfant.* 3rd Symposium de l'Association de psychologie scientifique de langue française, Genève, 2–4 Avril 1955 (Paris, Presses Universitaires de France, pp. 33–42.

1957—"Logique et équilibre dans le comportement du sujet." In *Études d'épistémologie génétique,* vol. 2, *Logique et Equilibre.* Paris, Presses Universitaires de France, pp. 27–118.

1957—*The Strategy of the Genes,* Waddington, C.H. London, Allen and Unwin.

1957–1958—Essais sur la perception des vitesses chez l'enfant et chez l'adulte. With Yvonne Feller and Elizabeth McNear. *Archives de psychologie,* Genève, 36:253–325.

1958—"Les isomorphismes partiels entre les structures logiques at les structures perceptives." In *Logique et Perception, Études d'Epistémologie Génétique,* Vol. 6, Paris, Presses Universitaires de France. Collaborators: Jerome S. Bruner, François Bresson.

1958—"Les préinférences perceptives et leurs relations avec les schèmes sensiore-moteurs et opératoires." In *Études d'Epistémologie Génétique.* Vol. 6, Paris, Presses Universitaires de France. Collaborators: Jerome S. Bruner, François Bresson.

1958—*Logique et perception.* With Jérôme Seymour Bruner, François Bresson, Albert Morf. Paris, Presses Universitaires de France, V, 204 pp.

1958—*The growth of logical thinking from childhood to adolescence. An essay on the construction of formal operational structures.* With Bärbel Inhelder. Anne Parsons and Stanley Milgram, translators. New York, Basic Books, XXVI, 356 pp. Originally published in French in 1955 (*De la logique de l'enfant a la logique de l'adolescent.*) (This volume, pp. 405–444.)

1960—"La portée psychologique et épistémologique des essais néohulliens de D. Berlyne." In D. Berlyne and J. Piaget *Theorie du comportement et opérations, Études d' Épistémologie Génétique,* Paris, Presses Universitaires de France, pp. 105–123.

1960—*The child's conception of geometry.* With Bärbel Inhelder and Alina Szeminska. Eric A. Lunzer, translator. London, Routledge & Kegan Paul, VII, 411 pp. Originally published in French in 1948. (*La géométrie spontanée de l'enfant.*)

1962—"Les relations entre l'affectivité et l'intelligence dans le développement mental de l'enfant." Paris, Centre de Documentation Universitaire.

1963–1966—*Traité de psychologie expérimentale.* Paul Fraisse and Jean Piaget, eds. Vols. 1–9, Paris, Presses universitaires de France. 1968—*Experimental psychology: its scope and method.* London, Routledge & Kegan Paul, New York, Basic Books.

1964—*The early growth of logic in the child. Classification and seriation.* With Bärbel Inhelder. Eric A. Lunzer, introduction. Eric

A. Lunzer and D. Papert, translation. London, Routledge & Kegan Paul, XXV, 302 pp. (This vol. pp. 359–393.)

1965—Note sur des Limnaea stagnalis L. var. lacustris Stud. élevées dans une mare du plateau vaudois. *Revue suisse de zoologie*, 72: 769–787.

1966—Observations sur le mode d'insertion et la chute des rameaux secondaires chez les Sedum. Essai sur un cas d'anticipation morphogénétique explicable par des processus de transfert. *Candollea*, Genève, 21: 137–239.

1966—*L'image mentale chez l'enfant. Etude sur le développement des représentations imagées.* With Bärbel Inhelder. Paris, Presses universitaires de France, VIII, 461 pp.; 1971—*Mental imagery in the child. A study of the development of imaginal representation.* P. A. Chilton, translator. London, Routledge & Kegan Paul and New York, Basic Books, XIX, 396 pp. Collaborators: Maurice Aboudaram, Monique Anthonioz, Paulette Antonini, Joan Bliss, Magali Bovet, Marianne Boehme, Rémy Droz, Claire Emery-Menthonnex, Ariane Étienne, Catherine Fot, Françoise Franc-Pfaelzer, Monique Levret-Chollet, Benjamin Matalon, Pierre Mounoud, Daniel Nicollier, Hanna Niedorf, Androula Papert-Christofides, Juan Pascual-Leone, Françoise Paternotte-Agoston, Laszlo Pecsi, Louis-Paul Poirier, Albert Politi, Adina Sella, Hermine Sinclair-De Zwart, Elsa Schmid-Kitskis, Suzanne Taponier, Tuât Vinh-Bang. Kazimiera Tyborowska, Gilbert Voyat.

1967—"Logique et connaissance scientifique," J. Piaget, ed. *Encyclopédie de la Pléide*, Vol. 22. Paris, Gallimard. Collaborators: Léo Apostel, Louis de Broglie, Oliver Costa de Beauregard, Jean T. Desanti, Dominique Dubarle, Lucien Goldman, Gilles-Gaston Granger, Pierre Gréco, Jean-Blaise Grize, Benoit Mandelbrot, Benjamin Matalon, Françoise Meyer, Czeslaw Nowinski, Seymour Papert, Jean Ullmo.

1968—*Mémoire et intelligence.* With Bärbel Inhelder. Paris, Presses universitaires de France, VII, 487 pp. Collaborators: André Bauer, Joan Bliss, Christiane Challande, Jean et Marie-José Delcourt, Muriel Depotex, Catherine Fot, Monique Levret-Chollet, Laszlo Luka, Robert Maier, Olga Maratos, Pierre Mounoud, Sylvia Opper, Andrula Papert-Christophides, Paul Petrogalli, Elso Schmid-Kitzikis, Hermine Sinclair-De Zwart, Tuât Vinh-Bang, Gilbert Voyat, Christiane Widmer.

1969—*The mechanisms of perception.* Preface by the author for the English translation. Gavin Nott Seagrim, translator. New York, Basic Books, XXIX, 384 pp. Originally published in French in 1961. (*Les méchanismes perceptifs.*)

1969—*The psychology of the child.* With Bärbel Inhelder. Helen Weaver, translator. London, Routledge & Kegan Paul and New York, Basic Books, XIV, 173 pp. Originally published in French in 1966 (*La psychologie de l'enfant.*)

1970—*Science of education and the psychology of the child.* Derek Coltman, translator. New York, Orion Press, 186 pp. Originally published in French in 1935 (*Psychologie et pédagogie.*) (This volume, pp. 695–725.)

1970—*Structuralism.* Chaninah Maschler, notes and translation. New York, Basic Books, VI, 153 pp. Originally published in French in 1968 (*Le structuralisme.*) (This volume, pp. 775–779.)

1971—*Biology and knowledge. An essay on the relations between organic regulations and cognitive processes.* Beatrix Walsh, translator. Chicago, University of Chicago Press, XII, 384 pp. Originally published in French in 1967 (*Biologie et connaissance.*)

1971—*How the Mouse Was Hit on the Head and So Discovered the World,* Étienne De Lessart. Foreword by J. Piaget. New York, Doubleday.

1971—*Insights and illusions of philosophy.* Wolfe Mays, introduction and translation. New York and Cleveland, The World Publishing Co., XVII, 232 pp. Originally published in French in 1965 (*Sagesse et illusions de la philosophie.*)

1971—*Psychology and epistemology.* Arnold Rosin, translator. New York, Grossman (Orion Press), 166 pp. Originally published in French in 1957 (*Psychologie et épistémologie.*)

1973—"Comments on mathematical education." In *Developments in Mathematical Education, Proc. of the Second International Congress on Mathematical Education,* ed. by A. G. Howson. Cambridge, Cambridge University Press.

1974—*Adaptation vitale et psychologie de l'intelligence: selection organique et phénocopie.* Paris, Hermann.

1974—"Conservation des longeurs et illusions perceptives." With Christiane Gilliéron. *Recherches sur la contradiction.* Études d'Epistémologie Génétique, 32, Paris, Presses Universitaires de France, pp. 73–75.

1974—*La Prise de Conscience.* Paris, Presses Universitaires de France. Collaborators: A. Blanchet, J.-P. Bronckart, N. Burdet, A. Cattin, C. Dami, M. Fluckiger, C. Gilliéron, A. Henriques, D. Liambey, O. de Marcellus, A. Munari, M. Robert, A. M. Zutter.

1974—*Understanding Causality.* With R. Garcia. New York, Norton, 208 pp.

1975—"Phenocopy in Biology and the Psychological Development of Knowledge." Essay written especially for this volume (pp. 803–813) by J. Piaget. Translated by H.E.G. and J.J.V. [It appeared, with our permission, in *The Urban Review,* Vol. 8, 1975, pp. 209–218].

1975—*The Origin of the Idea of Chance in Children.* With Bärbel Inhelder. Lowell Leake, Jr., Paul Burrell, and Harold D. Fishbein, translators. New York, Norton, Originally published in French in 1951 (La genèse de l'idée de hasard chez l'enfant.) Collaborators: Myriam van Remoortel, Marianne Denis-Prinzhorn, Gaby Ascoli, A. Morf, M. Laurent.

NAME INDEX

Note: Page numbers in italics refer to introductory material

SUBJECT INDEX

Note: Page numbers in italics refer to introductory material

Abstract models, see Psychological explanation, abstract models of
Abstraction
  of geometrical shapes, 588–592
  teaching of mathematics and, 703
Accommodation, *xxviiin, xxxvi, 63, 216, 279, 485, 789*
  anticipation and, 790
  assimilation and, relationship between: logico-mathematical structures and equilibrium, 848–849
    sensorimotor period, 273–277
    transition from sensorimotor intelligence to conceptual thought, 280–281, 291–294
  of babies, 202–205, 213, 214
  equilibration and, 836, 837, 839
  logico-mathematical structures, 848–849
  invention of new means and, 241–246, 248, 272
  motor, 200–203, 205, 213, 214
  object concept and, 253–257, 270
  of reflexes, 226–228, 233
  visual, to rapid movements, 253
Acquired adaptations, see Habits
Acquired associations, 227
Acquired traits, 40
  See also Hereditary factors
Action(s), *xxxvii*
  abnegation of, 47
  behaviorist view of, *xxxii–xxxiii*
  faith and, 43
  general coordination of, cognitive functions, 852–853
  operations as regulations of, 352, 353
  perception and, relationship between: knowledge and, *xviii–xxiii*
  seriation, 371, 393
  receptive teaching methods and, 711
  as servant of the Idea, 28
  thought and, *155*,297
  transition to verbal plane, see Conceptual thought, transition from sensorimotor intelligence to
  words and, 72–74
Active teaching methods, 712–713
Activity
  education and, 691, 695, 696
  See also Action(s); Motor activity; Play
Adaptation(s)
  acquired, see Habits
  consciousness and, 95, 97
  evolutionary, 40
  See also Accommodation; Assimilation; Evolution
Adaptation vitale et psychologie de l'intelligence, 788n
Adapted information, in language of child, 69–71, 75–78, 82, 83
Addition, logical, 287
Additive composition of relations, see Relations, additive and multiplicative composition of

Adherences, 131–134, 137, 138
Adolescence
  affective transformations of, 403–404, 442–444
  social bias of studies on, 404
Adolescent thinking, 434–444
  adult roles and, 435–439
  affective changes and, 442–444
  decentering and, 439–441
  theories and, 435, 437–440
Adualism, *486,* 739
Adult roles, adolescent assumption of, 435–439, 443
Adults and children, intercourse between, 92–93
Affective transformations of adolescence, 403–404, 442–444
Affectivity
  of teachers, teaching machines and, 717
  See also Feelings; *and entries starting with "Emotional"*
Age, concept of, 563–569
"Albinism in *Limnaea stagnalis*," *3, 9*
"Albino Sparrow, An," *3, 6*
Algebra
  Boolean, 447, 450, 451–453
  of logic, 447
    See also Operational structures, of algebra of logic
All and some, relations between, 360–361, 365, 367
Alpha-behavior, 807
Altruism, 38, 41, 49, 189
Analytic weakness, syncretism and, 104, 105, 109
Animals, classification of, 381–383
Animism (animistic causality or dynamism), *118,* 133, 137, 140–142, 147, 214, 290, *488,* 521
Answers, children's, 71, 79, 82, 83
Anticipation
  accommodation and, 790
  cognitive, conservation of information and, 795–798
  morphogenetic, in the plant kingdom, 799–802
  objective phenomena as permitting, 270
  organic, 798–799
  of seriation, 370
    serial configurations with elements perceived visually, 385–393
Anticipatory images, 499, 664, 666–668
  conservation and, 680–681
  displacement of a square and, 673–674
  evolution of, 676–677
  geometrical intuition and, 681–683
  global vs. analytical, 678–679
  kinetic, 674–676
  ordinal and hyperordinal, 675–676
  reversal of the ends and, 672–673
  rotation of a rod, anticipation of, 666–667
  seriation of lengths and, 678–680

somersault, images of, 671–672
  transformation of an arc into a straight lines, 668–671
  transition from reproductive images to, 683–684
A priori norms, 189
Apriorism, *xviii, xxxv–xxxvii,* 138, 146
Argument(s), 75–78
  verification and, 92
Arithmetical reasoning, 95–96
Artificialism, *118,* 119, 133, 134, 138, 140, 145, 147, 290, *488*
Assimilation, *xxviiin, xxxvi,* 40, 41, 48, 63, 117, *216,* 279, 485, 789–791
  accommodation and, see Accommodation, assimilation and
  in babies (autistic assimilation), 202–205, 208, 213, 214
  causality and, 146, 213, 214
  cognitive regulations and, 846
  dynamic realism and, 278
  equilibration and, 834, 836, 837, 839
  "functional," 39, 41
  invention of new means and, 241–247
  mutual, of schemata, 487
  object concept and, 256, 270–272
  reciprocal, *217,* 244, 246, 270–274
  reflexes and, *216*–217, 228–231, 233–234, 251
  reproductive, *216,* 228–229, 231, 233–234, 251, 256
  symbolic play and, 492–495
Associationism, 97, 246, *488,* 345, 347, 348, 350, 351, *652,* 753
  mental images and, 498
Associations
  acquired, 227
  emotional, in babies, 202, 204
  empirical, and precausal explanations, 413–414
  See also Correlations
Athens school, *692, 693*
Atomism, 344
Atomistic composition, causal explanation by, 143, 145
Attention, field of
  logical forms and, 60
  narrowness of, 99–101, 113
Audiovisual teaching methods, 715
Auditory images, 659
Authority, justice and, *187,* 189–192
Autism (autistic thought), 48–50, 56–59, 85–87, 92, 95, 111, 151
  in babies (autistic assimilation), 200–205, 213, 214
  children's thought and, 93, 94
Autonomy, 158, 200
  justice and, 188–192
  moral, 404, 443–444
  rules and, 176, 178–180, 184, 185
Autoregulation, see Equilibration; Self-regulation
Axiomatic logic, 464–465

Babies, see Infants
Balance scale experiment, see Equi-